THE LAW AND ECONOMICS OF ARTICLE 82 EC

The Law and Economics of Article 82 EC is a comprehensive, integrated treatment of the legal and economic principles that underpin the application of Article 82 EC to the behaviour of dominant firms. Traditional concerns of monopoly behaviour, such as predatory pricing, refusals to deal, excessive pricing, tying and bundling, discount practices, and unlawful discrimination are treated in detail through a review of the applicable economic principles, the case law and decisional practice, and more recent economic and legal writings. In addition, the major constituent elements of Article 82, such as market definition, dominance, effect on trade, and applicable remedies are considered at length. Jointly authored by a lawyer and an economist, *The Law and Economics of Article 82 EC* contains an integrated approach to the legal and economic principles that frame policy in this major area of competition law. It is essential reading for anyone with an interest in competition-law enforcement against monopoly behaviour.

The Law and Economics of Article 82 EC

Robert O'Donoghue and A Jorge Padilla

•HART•
PUBLISHING
OXFORD AND PORTLAND, OREGON
2006

Published in North America (US and Canada) by
Hart Publishing
c/o International Specialized Book Services
920 NE 58th Avenue, Suite 300
Portland, OR 97213–3786
USA
Tel: +1 503-287-3093 or toll-free: (1) 800-944-6190
Fax: +1 503 280 8832
Email: orders@isbs.com
Website: www.isbs.com

First published 2006, Reprinted 2006 (twice), 2007 (twice), 2008, 2010 and 2011

Hart Publishing, 16C Worcester Place, Oxford, OX1 2JW
Telephone: +44 (0)1865 517 530 Fax: +44 (0)1865 510 710
Email: mail@hartpub.co.uk
Website: www.hartpub.co.uk

British Library Cataloguing in Publication Data
Data Available

ISBN–13: 978–1–84113–502–1 (hardback)
ISBN–10: 1–84113–502-X (hardback)

Typeset by Hope Services, Abingdon
Printed and bound in Great Britain by
TJI Digital, Padstow, Cornwall

To my loving parents, Geoffrey and Mary, for instilling the confidence to do great things, and the belief to always try to do good things.

Robert O'Donoghue

To Araceli, Aitana, and Claudia for their unconditional support and infinite patience

A Jorge Padilla

FOREWORD

Article 82 has always been a subject of considerable intellectual and practical difficulty. The first question (can it apply to a merger?) was answered only in 1973. The next question (does it require different kinds of analysis for exploitative and anticompetitive abuses?) was answered affirmatively later, but raised further questions. What is the test of "unfair" prices or contract terms under Article 82(a)? What tests distinguish legitimate competition from anticompetitive conduct under Article 82(b)? Is harm to consumers necessary for an abuse under Article 82(c)? Can conduct be unlawful as a reprisal abuse if it would not be illegal anyway? Is there an "unexpressed" category of abuses which do not fall under one of the four clauses of Article 82, but which result from the "special responsibility" of dominant companies, and if there is, what could it be? Can lawyers and economists agree on the answers to these questions, and until they do so, what advice (if any) can usefully be given to companies?

It is perhaps surprising that these, undoubtedly difficult, questions have not been more thoroughly analysed. Every company which is, or may be, dominant has to have a pricing policy. A too-broad concept of anticompetitive abuses would discourage legitimate competition. *Per se* rules would be unjustifiable, but some economists seem to believe that no useful general tests or guidelines are possible either. In particular in recent years, lawyers and economists have criticised what the Commission and the Community Courts said in particular cases, but usually without offering constructive suggestions. National competition authorities in EC Member States have always had power to apply Article 82, but most of them did not try to develop principles on which they could do so.

Questions that are so important and have caused so much difficulty for so long need to be dealt with by combining legal and economic knowledge and experience. This Robert O'Donoghue and Jorge Padilla have done. They have identified and analysed all of the fundamental questions concerning the interpretation and implications of Article 82. They have offered carefully considered answers, making it clear where their conclusions suggest that the Commission and the Community Courts have expressed themselves, in individual cases, in ways that obscure rather than clarifying the general principles which underlie the case law. They have formulated general principles which seem to me to be sound and reasonable, both as law and as economics. They have written a new kind of competition law book, deliberately avoided merely compiling case summaries, but providing an intellectual framework.

Above all, they have dealt with one of the most important and difficult issues, the test of anticompetitive abuses, by returning to the language of Article 82. As long ago as 1975 the Court of Justice, in the *Sugar Cartel* judgment mostly concerned with what is now Article 81, decided that Article 82(b) prohibits conduct by a dominant company which limits the production, marketing or technical development *of its competitors*, that is anticompetitive abuses. That little-noticed finding (since confirmed in other judgments) was in fact more important than the description of an anticompetitive abuse given later in the *Hoffmann-La Roche* judgment. "Methods different from those which condition normal competition", the phrase in the judgment, does not provide a useful test of anticompetitive conduct. "Limiting" possibilities of production, marketing or technical development which would, but for the supposedly unlawful conduct, be available to competitors provides a test, and may well provide the only possible or necessary definition, of anticompetitive conduct.

By regarding Article 82(b) as the legal basis for all cases of foreclosure, exclusionary or anticompetitive abuses, the authors clarify the whole law on abuse of dominance. There are, in essence, three kinds of abuses: exploitative abuses (Article 82(a)), exclusionary abuses (Article 82(b)), and discrimination between companies *not* associated with the dominant enterprise (Article 82(c)). Discrimination in favour of the dominant company's own operations comes under Article 82(b). Tying and bundling (Article 82(d)) can be either exclusionary or exploitative, or both. Reprisal abuses are exclusionary, since they discourage aggressive competition. The test for exclusionary conduct is that set out in the Treaty, which is both theoretically sound and suitable for use by dominant enterprises.

The most important consequence, in practice, is to make possible a rational and operational approach to pricing by dominant companies. Price reductions which are conditional on the buyer buying exclusively from the dominant company are illegal, except in very special circumstances. Other price reductions, such as quantity rebates, benefit consumers and do not "limit" marketing possibilities otherwise open to competitors. This solves the greatest single problem facing dominant companies under the Commission's practice up to now, and does so in a way which, because it is based on the words of the Treaty and the case law of the Court of Justice, will be difficult for any competition authority to reject. It provides much more legal certainty than any economic test which has been suggested, and avoids the ambiguity of the Commission's "exclusivity inducing" test. Exclusivity, in the sense of buying only from one source, can also result from the dominant company offering the lowest price or the best value. By analysing the case law, the authors have brought out the underlying principles, and clarified both the principles and the issues unresolved by the case law, or indeed created by apparent inconsistencies in it.

By establishing basic principles and identifying and discussing the questions which arise from them, the authors have provided an intellectual framework into which all the case law can be fitted and analysed, and from which conclusions can be drawn about important questions which the accidents of litigation have not so far raised. They have offered tests and conclusions more, it seems to me, than most other authors who have summarised the cases and made general comments, which were true but which have not always provided much practical guidance except in clear situations.

This book will make it necessary in future for anyone writing seriously about Article 82 to take into account the fundamental legal principles to which the authors have called to our attention, to propose rules and make comments which reconcile both legal and economic analysis, and to suggest tests which can be used in practice and which give answers which would be generally accepted as correct. In short, they have greatly raised the intellectual level of the discussion of Article 82, and provided practical and acceptable answers to many of the questions which have concerned lawyers, economists and companies for many years.

This book also creates another precedent, which others should follow. Books on substantive competition law are better if they are written jointly with economists and books on competition economics are better if they are written jointly with lawyers. One of the strengths of this book is that it combines so well the legal framework and the economic analysis. That combination is particularly important in Article 82 cases, but it is also essential in cases involving State measures restricting competition, which are subject to Article 86 EC.

The Commission has published a Discussion Paper on the interpretation of Article 82. Whatever the final version of this may be, it is clear that it will not answer all the important questions about Article 82 which will inevitably arise. All of the issues discussed in this book are likely to come before the Community Courts (and increasingly also national courts). It may be some time before the Courts have given their answers to all these questions. But judgments, even in leading cases, cannot reasonably be expected to provide an intellectual framework for an entire area of law: judges are not legislators, and their role is to decide individual cases. The framework which the authors have provided will be of great value to everyone concerned with Article 82 in the future, and will enable courts and national authorities to decide Article 82 cases correctly with greater confidence than has been possible up to now.

In an area of law such as this, no book can be expected to be both seminal and definitive in all respects at the same time. But a book can create a new paradigm which provides a basis for subsequent analysis, and be definitive on some issues, in the sense that some of the conclusions reached are so clearly convincing and correct that nobody questions them again. It seems to me that this book has achieved both.

John Temple Lang[1]

[1] Cleary Gottlieb Steen and Hamilton LLP, Brussels and London; Professor of Law, Trinity College Dublin; Visiting Senior Research Fellow, Oxford University.

AUTHORS' PREFACE

This idea of this book was conceived in 2003 at the European University Institute's roundtable entitled "*What is an abuse of dominance?*" Perhaps unusually for a lawyer and an economist, the authors found themselves in agreement on a number of issues. In particular, we were dissatisfied with traditional competition law textbooks that ignored the influence of economics and equally unhappy with competition economics textbooks that ignored the need for administrable rules and legal certainty. Fortified with this initial consensus, we set out to produce a textbook that would be useful to both lawyers and economists.

The subject of the book—abuse of dominance under Article 82 EC—is topical. In addition to the European University Institute roundtable mentioned above, Article 82 EC has received detailed comment from the Global Competition Law Centre's *Research Papers on Article 82 EC* (2005), the Organisation for Economic Cooperation and Development's *Competition on the Merits* study (2005), the Economic Advisory Group on Competition Policy's *An Economic Approach to Article 82* (2005), and, most notably, DG Competition's Staff Discussion Paper on Article 82 EC (2005). Similar initiatives are underway in the United States in the context of their on-going antitrust modernisation review.

Significant interest in Article 82 EC has been prompted by a series of factors. First, distinguishing abusive unilateral conduct from legitimate competition is inherently difficult, since they often look similar (e.g., low prices). Unless competition law is to have the perverse effect of chilling competition, clear rules are needed.

Second, Article 82 EC has been the "poor relation" of EC competition law in that it has not benefited from modernisation to bring it into line with economic thinking in the same way as have Article 81 EC and the merger control rules.

Third, with the advent of modernisation, national authorities and courts will apply Article 82 EC and equivalent national laws much more frequently than they have done in the past. Indeed, this is already a reality with significant fines for abusive conduct increasingly becoming the norm at national level. It is vital for firms operating in multiple jurisdictions that similar principles are applied and that levels of expertise are relatively uniform.

Finally, and perhaps most importantly, our practical experience in counselling firms is that the application of Article 82 EC is unclear in material respects. Firms with 40% market shares often unnecessarily worry that they are, or may be, dominant, with the significant consequences that this entails for their commercial practices. The welfare cost of this lack of clarity and excessive caution must be enormous to the EU economy as a whole—something the EU can ill-afford given its lack of competitiveness relative to other international blocs and the stated objectives of the Lisbon Agenda in this regard.

This book does not, as such, seek to develop new principles for the application of Article 82 EC. Our primary objective is to inform readers of the current law, both as to the constituent elements of Article 82 EC and in more detail for the main categories of exclusionary and exploitative abuses. Although we have been involved in a number of the cases discussed in the book—sometimes on opposing sides—we hope that the law is stated clearly and neutrally (or at least that our respective biases have cancelled each other out).

But the book is also hopefully more ambitious in certain respects. In the first place, each chapter on the main categories of abuse includes a detailed section on the applicable economic principles. We have endeavoured to present these principles in a non-technical manner to the fullest extent possible, bearing in mind the advice of Professor Stephen Hawking ("*Someone told me that each equation I included in the book would halve the sales.*").

Second, we have tried to put forward a more coherent framework for the consistent analysis of particular types of conduct. A simple but important example concerns exclusionary abuses. Commentators are struggling to verbalise tests for exclusionary conduct and various alternatives have been proposed. But it seems to us that Article 82(b) already contains a good basic test: conduct is exclusionary when it "limits" rivals' production and causes "prejudice to consumers." This captures the two key features of abusive conduct: that it materially harms rivals and causes consumer harm. Similarly, a lot of confusion has arisen under Article 82 EC concerning discrimination. We make a modest, but important, suggestion: that all discrimination aimed at rivals should be analysed as exclusionary conduct, and not as discrimination *per se*. Discrimination may be necessary in this regard, but is not generally sufficient to prove an exclusionary abuse. This would mean that the residual importance of discrimination under Article 82 EC would be limited—essentially to situations of secondary-line injury (for which we see no convincing basis for competition law intervention)—which is consistent with economic thinking and would aid clarity considerably.

Finally, we consider a number of issues or practices that have not received detailed treatment under Article 82 EC, setting out the arguments for and against particular conclusions, and tentatively suggesting the way we think the issues should be analysed.

We are reluctant to attach a label to the overall approach adopted in the book. Our hope is that it is more or less the right one. But we consider that the choice sometimes posited between an approach based on legal form and one based on economic effects is false. Relying only on legal form almost certainly leads to incorrect conclusions by ignoring the mixed economic effects of many unilateral practices. Proponents of an economic effects analysis, however, also need to recognise that the law would be *much* less clear than it is already if each case depended on an assessment of the economic benefits and harm of conduct, most of which can only be assessed *ex post* (if at all). Economists sometimes underestimate the importance of legal certainty to businesses.

An intermediate approach—which we support—is to use simple error-cost analysis based on economic evidence to structure administrable legal rules ("structured rule-of-reason"). Take above-cost unconditional price cuts. There is a case in economic theory that such price cuts can harm consumer welfare in certain circumstances. But no clear legal rule has been devised to say when harm to consumer welfare occurs. Absent a clear rule, restricting unconditional above-cost price cuts is likely to greatly chill price competition. The optimal solution is therefore to do nothing, even if in so doing certain anticompetitive practices thereby escape censure.

This book is a first edition, but comes at an important juncture. The Commission may well publish guidelines on Article 82 EC in the next 12–18 months. Important cases are also pending before the Community Courts, including *Microsoft* (tying and refusal to deal), *British Airways/Virgin* (rebates), *Wanadoo* (predatory pricing), *Deutsche Telekom* (margin squeeze), and *AstraZeneca* (use and abuse of patent approval system). A second edition therefore seems likely sooner rather than later.

As with any endeavour of this kind, we have benefited from the input and assistance of numerous people, without whom the book would never have been completed. These include: Paul Bury, Alexandra Deege, Alfonso Donato Giuliani, Tanya Dunne, Rupert Elderkin, Simon Genevaz, Thomas Graf, Rogier Groen, Urs Hagler, Hertta Hyrkas, Joachim Keller, Philip Kienapfel, Paul Marquardt, Joanna O'Sullivan, and Brendan Reddy.

A number of other individuals deserve special mention. Nicholas Levy (Cleary Gottlieb) and David Evans (LECG) were very supportive of the idea of the book and helped obtain the support of our respective firms for this project (including, in one case, a leave of absence). Caroline Brennan (Arthur Cox), Christopher Cook (Cleary Gottlieb), Cynthia Ngwe (McDermott Will & Emery), Ian Reynolds (BP Collins), and David Spector (Paris Science Economiques) each helped on various chapters, which we gratefully acknowledge. We also benefited from discussions with a number of people that greatly improved our understanding and presentation of certain issues, including Christian Ahlborn (Linklaters), Maurits Dolmans (Cleary Gottlieb), Inmaculada Gutierrez (LECG), Alison Oldale (LECG), and Romano Subiotto (Cleary Gottlieb). We also had first-rate paralegal, secretarial, and library assistance from Axelle Arbonnier, Kevin Copeland, Henk Dekeyzer, Satu-Anneli Kauranen, Barbara Martinez, Anneliese Rosengarten, and Karl Willemijns (all Cleary Gottlieb). Our publishers, Hart Publishing, have been excellent and Richard Hart in particular has always been flexible and responsive. Finally, John Temple Lang has been a constant source of encouragement from the inception of this book until its conclusion. He also kindly agreed to write a foreword, which is fitting since he has, for many years, been the leading thinker on Article 82 EC issues.

In the time-honoured tradition, none of the above is responsible for any blunders that follow. Equally, each co-author blames the other for anything said in this book that might later prove inconvenient or embarrassing before a court, competition authority, or other tribunal. Finally, we should make clear that any opinions expressed in this book are personal only and do not represent those of our respective firms or clients.

The law is stated as of March 31, 2006.

ROBERT O'DONOGHUE
A. JORGE PADILLA

TABLE OF CONTENTS

TABLE OF CASES

I. TABLE OF COMMISSION COMPETITION DECISIONS

II. TABLE OF COMMISSION MERGER DECISIONS

III. OTHER COMMUNITY DECISIONS

ECSC Treaty

Council of Ministers

IV. TABLE OF COURT OF FIRST INSTANCE CASES

TABLE OF CFI CASES (numerical)

V. TABLE OF EUROPEAN COURT OF JUSTICE CASES

TABLE OF EUROPEAN COURT OF JUSTICE CASES (numerical)

VI. EUROPEAN COURT OF HUMAN RIGHTS

VII. TABLE OF NATIONAL CASES

Belgium

Denmark

France

Germany

Ireland

Italy

Netherlands

Spain

Sweden

United Kingdom

VIII. TABLE OF FOREIGN CASES

Australia

Canada

New Zealand

United States

World Trade Organisation

TABLE OF LEGISLATION

EU Treaties

EU Secondary Legislation

National Legislation

Canada

France

Germany

Netherlands

United Kingdom

United States

Chapter 1

INTRODUCTION, SCOPE OF APPLICATION, AND BASIC FRAMEWORK

1.1 INTRODUCTION

Article 82 EC in the context of the EC Treaty. Ensuring a system of free competition is a central objective of the EC Treaty. Article 4 EC states that the activities of the Community and its Member States should be "conducted in accordance with the principle of an open market economy with free competition." Similar principles are repeated in Article 98 EC—a provision concerning economic policy—which requires Member States and the Community to "act in accordance with the principle of an open market economy with free competition, favouring an efficient allocation of resources." These broad policy objectives are reflected in detail in Title VI, Chapter I of the EC Treaty, which contains the competition provisions.

A basic distinction can be made under EC competition law between contractual relations involving two or more firms and the unilateral conduct of a single firm. Article 81 EC and Council Regulation 139/2004 on the control of concentrations between undertakings[1] are the basic Community legal instruments governing agreements. The latter concerns agreements that bring about a lasting change in the control of an undertaking—mergers, acquisitions, and fully-functional joint ventures—whereas the former deals with other types of horizontal and vertical agreements that have a non-trivial impact on competition.

Article 82 EC complements the provisions of EC competition law dealing with agreements by placing certain restrictions on the *unilateral conduct* of firms. It provides that "any abuse by one or more undertakings of a dominant position within the common market or in a substantial part of it shall be prohibited as incompatible with the common market insofar as it may affect trade between Member States." The text goes on to offer the following examples of an "abuse:"

> "(a) directly or indirectly imposing unfair purchase or selling prices or other unfair trading conditions; (b) limiting production, markets or technical development to the prejudice of consumers; (c) applying dissimilar conditions to equivalent transactions with other trading parties, thereby placing them at a competitive disadvantage; (d) making the conclusion of contracts subject to acceptance by the other parties of supplementary obligations which, by their nature or according to commercial usage, have no connection with the subject of such contracts."

---

[1] Council Regulation (EC) No 139/2004 of January 20, 2004, on the control of concentrations between undertakings (hereinafter, the "EC Merger Regulation"), OJ 2004 L 24/1.

The Community Courts have insisted on the broad unity of the purpose that exists between the competition provisions of the EC Treaty.[2] One reason is that the laws on agreements and unilateral conduct share a common concern: to curb the adverse welfare effects of monopoly power. It is well-documented in industrial organisation literature that a firm, or group of firms, with a dominant position (or its synonym market power) have the possibility to reduce output and raise prices, thereby harming consumer welfare.[3] In the case of mergers and acquisitions and other agreements, market power can be acquired, maintained, or increased through contractual arrangements. Such agreements may be subject to review under Article 81 EC and merger control laws. In the case of anticompetitive unilateral conduct, a firm typically relies on its market power to engage in *strategic actions* that unlawfully exclude rival firms, to the detriment of consumers (or it may also *directly* exploit consumers by charging excessive prices). Article 82 EC, and analogous provisions of national laws, therefore seek to place restrictions on unilateral conduct that harms consumer welfare.

The general scheme of Article 82 EC. The basic aim of Article 82 EC is to set standards for the conduct of firms with a position of such economic strength that they have a degree of immunity from the normal disciplining effects of a competitive market. In markets characterised by the presence of one or more firms with economic power of this kind, Article 82 EC seeks to bring about some of the results that would occur if competition did exist. Thus, Article 82 EC has been used, for example, to force prices down towards a level that would exist in a competitive market,[4] to increase prices where low prices are part of a deliberate plan to exclude rivals and raise prices following exit,[5] or to require a dominant firm to share key non-replicable assets with rivals.[6] But Article 82 EC also goes further and requires dominant firms to refrain from certain acts that would be perfectly lawful if carried out by a non-dominant firm.

The wording of Article 82 EC requires a number of cumulative conditions to be satisfied before a violation can be established: (1) there must be an undertaking; (2) that undertaking must hold a dominant position on a properly defined relevant market; (3) the dominant position must be held in a substantial part of the common market; (4) there must be an abuse; and (5) that abuse must affect trade between Member States. A basic overview of these minimum requirements for the application of Article 82 EC is provided below:

1. *Undertaking.* In common with Article 81 EC, Article 82 EC only applies to "undertakings." The EC Treaty does not define this term, but it has been extensively developed in the decisional practice and case law. In basic terms, an undertaking is any person engaged in an "economic activity." Most of the controversy surrounding this issue concerns State undertakings and private firms

[2] See Case 6/72, *Europemballage Corporation and Continental Can Company Inc v Commission* [1973] ECR 215.

[3] For a detailed treatment of the welfare effects of monopoly conditions and behaviour, see D Carlton & J Perloff, *Modern Industrial Organisation* (4th edn., Boston, Pearson Addison Wesley, 2005) Ch. 4.

[4] See Ch. 12 (Excessive Prices) below.

[5] See Ch. 5 (Predatory Pricing) below.

[6] See Ch. 8 (Refusal to Deal) below.

that are not for profit and whether such entities can be regarded as "undertakings" for purposes of EC competition law. Section 1.3 below discusses the main areas of difficulty in detail.

2. *Dominant position.* The concept of dominance contained in Article 82 EC relates to a position of economic strength on a properly-defined relevant market. The relevant market therefore provides a framework for analysing whether an undertaking holds a dominant position. The techniques used in this regard are similar to those used under Article 81 EC and EC merger control: a detailed analysis of the category of products that consumers regard as effective substitutes based on characteristics, use, or price. However, once such a market is defined, the assessment of dominance further requires the calculation of market shares, an analysis of barriers to entry, and other factors that might affect the nature and scope of dominance. Consistent with economic theory and the EC Merger Regulation, dominance can be that of a single firm or a number of collectively dominant firms. Market definition and dominance are treated in detail in Chapters Two and Three, respectively.

3. *Substantial part of the common market.* The requirement that dominance should arise in a substantial part of the common market reflects the consideration that EC competition law should not be concerned with trivial or localised matters. In practice, this condition is nearly always satisfied. For example, a single port within a Member State has been regarded as a substantial part of the common market in several cases. This requirement is analysed in more detail in Chapter Three (Dominance).

4. *Abuse.* The key element of Article 82 EC is to identify conduct that amounts to an "abuse." A basic distinction can be made between: (a) exclusionary abuses, i.e., unlawful attempts to exclude rival firms; (b) exploitative abuses, i.e., direct exploitation of consumers through, e.g., excessive prices; and (c) reprisal abuses, i.e., when a dominant company injures or damages another company to punish it for having, e.g., dealt with a rival.[7] Even if these basic categories are reasonably clear, the operational definition of an abuse under Article 82 EC has generated a great deal of controversy. Some of the controversy is inevitable given that legitimate, harsh competition and unlawful exclusion look very similar. Charging a low price for example, if it is low enough, will put a rival out of business and is generally the essence of competition. In some cases, however, the price may be so low as to be predatory and therefore potentially harmful to consumers in the long-run. The challenge under Article 82 EC is therefore to develop clear standards that allow legitimate and harmful behaviour to be distinguished. The majority of this book deals with the principal types of behaviour that raise abuse concerns.

---

[7] This classification was initially proposed in C Bellamy and G Child, *European Community Law of Competition* (2nd edn., London, Sweet & Maxwell, 1978), and developed further in J Temple Lang, "Abuse of Dominant Positions in European Community Law" in BE Hawk (ed.), *Fifth Fordham Corporate Law Institute* (New York, Law & Business, 1979) pp. 25–83.

5. *Effect on trade.* The final criterion for the application of Article 82 EC is that the abuse should affect trade between Member States. This condition delineates the jurisdictional divide between Community and Member State competencies. The concept of effect on trade is discussed in Chapter Fourteen.

The basic objectives of Article 82 EC. The precise objectives of Article 82 EC have never been articulated in any formal Community document or decision. DG Competition's discussion paper on the application of Article 82 EC now sets out, for the first time, the core objectives of Article 82 EC, at least in respect of exclusionary abuses:[8]

> "With regard to exclusionary abuses the objective of Article 82 is the protection of competition on the market as a means of enhancing consumer welfare and of ensuring an efficient allocation of resources. Effective competition brings benefits to consumers, such as low prices, high quality products, a wide selection of goods and services, and innovation."

In addition to economic efficiency and consumer welfare, other objectives have undoubtedly played a role under Article 82 EC. These include promoting fairness, ensuring that small and medium-sized firms are not unduly hampered by firms with market power; and furthering other EC Treaty objectives, most notably market integration. These latter objectives are obscure in certain respects and controversial in others, but they undeniably play some role in the application of Article 82 EC.

a. Promoting economic efficiency and welfare. The first objective under Article 82 EC—which is the basic legitimacy for all competition law enforcement—is to prevent practices that would harm society and consumers through the exercise of market power; in other words, to promote efficiency and welfare. There is a complicated debate among economists on whether the welfare concerns under competition law should refer to: (1) *consumer welfare*— the difference between what a person is willing to pay for a commodity and the amount he/she actually is required to pay; (2) *producer welfare*—the difference between what producers are willing and able to supply a product for and the price they actually receive; or (3) *total welfare*—the sum of (1) and (2).[9] As noted, consumer welfare is the preferred standard under EC competition law.[10]

The potential adverse effects of the exercise of significant market power are well-documented in the industrial organisation literature.[11] The measurement of optimally competitive markets is perfect competition—a largely theoretical benchmark of a market in which there are homogenous products, many suppliers, consumers with full information, and no transaction costs. Price and output are optimal under this theorem. Against this benchmark, degrees of market power can be measured. All profit-

[8] See DG Competition discussion paper on the application of Article 82 of the Treaty to exclusionary abuses, Brussels, December 2005, (hereinafter the "Discussion Paper"), para. 4.

[9] See M Motta, *Competition Policy: Theory and Practice* (Cambridge, Cambridge University Press, 2004), section 1.3.1 (Objectives of competition policy) for a review of the competing arguments.

[10] Discussion Paper, above. See also S Bishop and M Walker, *The Economics of EC Competition Law—Concepts, Application and Measurement* (2nd edn., London, Sweet & Maxwell, 2002) p. 24.

[11] See, e.g., D Carlton & J Perloff, *Modern Industrial Organisation* (4th edn., Boston, Pearson Addison Wesley, 2005) Ch. 4.

maximising firms have, in the short-term at least, a degree of market power as compared to conditions of perfect competition due, *inter alia*, to sunk investments and other factors that may prevent immediate and costless switching to other suppliers. Such "power" is of no concern under competition law. Instead, competition law is concerned with the exercise of a significant degree of market power, that is where a firm, or group of firms acting together, have the power, for a meaningful period, to profitably sustain prices above the level that would prevail in a competitive market and/or to reduce output, innovation, or quality. The key concern under competition law is *significant* power over price for a *persistent* period. Market power is always a matter of degree and a function of the performance of a particular market: even a monopoly or oligopoly can function in a manner consistent with effective competition.

Increases in prices above the competitive level as a result of the exercise of market power have two negative effects on consumer welfare: first, they transfer wealth, or rents, from consumers to firms, as every consumer who purchases the goods and services on offer pays more for them than in a competitive market; second, they destroy rents by forcing out of the market some consumers with relatively modest valuations. These effects are illustrated in Figure 1 below. The first effect is given by area *A*, while the second effect is given by area *B*. The sum of areas *A* and *B* measures the reduction in consumer welfare resulting from supra-competitive prices. In economic theory, area *B* is known as the "deadweight loss of monopoly," since it measures the loss in overall welfare (consumer welfare plus firms' profits) resulting from a market price above the competitive benchmark.[12] In economic terminology, at perfectly competitive prices, the allocation of resources is allocatively efficient and all gains from trade are exhausted: there is no deadweight loss.

Figure 1: The deadweight loss of monopoly

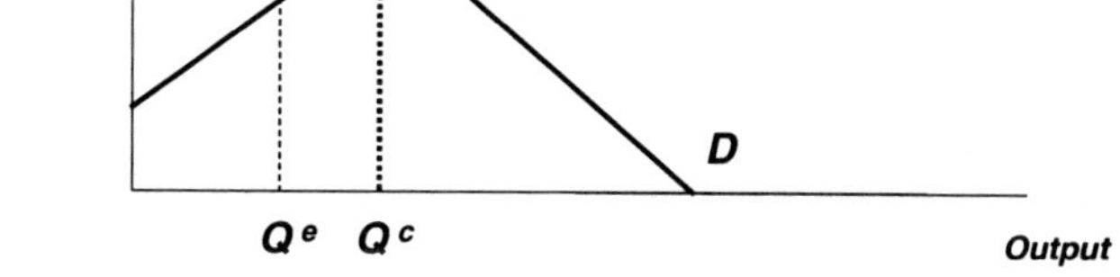

Article 82 EC does not, however, condemn the mere possession of dominance. Instead, it is directed at strategic actions carried out by a firm in a dominant position that

[12] The "deadweight loss of monopoly" does not include area *A*, because this area corresponds to the increase in profits associated to the above-competitive price. Hence, area *A* captures a pure transfer of rents from consumers to firms.

unlawfully exclude competition and therefore risk maintaining or strengthening the dominant position. Firms without a dominant position may lawfully engage in such actions: the general implication is that, without market power, such actions are either irrational or would not have sufficient adverse long-term effects on consumer welfare to justify policy intervention. The identification of a dominant position is therefore of enormous potential significance and not without controversy given the difficulties of unambiguously identifying a position in the continuum of market power in which a firm acquires such a position.

b. Promoting the EC Treaty's wider objectives. Uniquely among legal instruments that seek to control abuses of dominance, Article 82 EC is not a stand-alone piece of competition legislation: it forms part of the EC Treaty. The EC Treaty includes a wide range of different objectives that may affect the scope and meaning of the competition provisions, including Article 82 EC.[13] Indeed, the Commission has stated that "it is inconceivable that competition policy could be applied without reference to the priorities fixed by the Community."[14] The Commission has also spoken of the "federating" role of EC competition law,[15] which explains why the integration of national markets has featured prominently in competition policy.[16]

These views have also spilled over to a certain extent into leading cases. For example, in *British Leyland*, the Community institutions objected to an excessive fee imposed by a dominant firm for a document that was necessary to import a car from mainland Europe to the United Kingdom.[17] In *United Brands*,[18] the Court of Justice objected to a series of measures designed to impede intra-Community trade in bananas, including export restrictions, price discrimination, and threats to de-list distributors who dealt in competing products. And several cases involving tariffs set by national rail and airport operators were pursued by the Community institutions on the grounds that they discriminated against foreign undertakings.[19]

The application of Article 82 EC to further the market integration objectives of the EC Treaty is controversial in certain respects. One problem is that the meaning of the competition provisions is likely to be much less clear if they also include the broad, and poorly-defined, remit of furthering market integration. Firms can take a range of unilateral measures that reduce trade between Member States, without implying that they are also abusive. There is, however, growing evidence that the Community Courts

[13] For example, environmental protection, a core EC Treaty objective, has played a role in EC competition analysis. See JH Jans, *European Environmental Law* (2nd edn., Groningen, Europa Law Publishing, 2000) Ch. 7 (Competition Policy and Environmental Protection) and in particular p. 285; H Vedder, *Competition Law and Environmental Protection in Europe: Towards Sustainability?* (Groningen, Europa Law Publishing, 2003).

[14] XXIIIrd Report on Competition Policy (1993), p. 1.

[15] XXVIIth Report on Competition Policy (1997), foreword by the then Commissioner responsible for competition policy, Karel Van Miert.

[16] See CD Ehlermann, "The Contribution of EC Competition Policy to the Single Market" (1992) 29 *Common Market Law Review* 257.

[17] Case 226/84, *British Leyland plc v Commission* [1986] ECR 3263 (hereinafter "*British Leyland*").

[18] *Chiquita*, OJ 1976 L 95/1, confirmed by the Court in Case 27/76, *United Brands Company and United Brands Continentaal BV v Commission* [1978] ECR 207.

[19] See Ch. 11 (Abusive Discrimination).

are conscious of these difficulties and that there is a greater reluctance than in the past to use competition tools to promote wider and ill-defined policy objectives, however legitimate. A recent example is the *SYFAIT* case, which concerned the reduction by a pharmaceutical manufacturer of quantities supplied for parallel trade to Greek wholesalers engaged in export activity to other, higher-priced Member States. The wholesalers, backed by the Commission, argued that it was abusive for the dominant manufacturer to refuse to supply wholesalers engaged in parallel trade with the quantities of products that they requested. This was essentially on the grounds that unilateral conduct that reduced intra-Community trade was contrary to the fundamental market integration objectives of the EC Treaty. The case was ultimately declared inadmissible by the Court of Justice, but the Advocate General's opinion was unsympathetic to the argument that Article 82 EC could be relied upon in these circumstances.[20] Instead, he concluded that the pharmaceutical industry's specific characteristics justified the refusal to supply products for parallel trade. But he was careful to limit these findings to the pharmaceutical sector, noting that it was "highly unlikely" that the same features would be present in any other industry, thereby leaving open the possibility that market integration concerns could still be relevant in other circumstances.

c. ***Fairness and protection of small and medium-sized firms.*** Basic notions of "fairness" and the idea that large, well-resourced firms should not unduly hamper the activities of small and medium-sized undertakings feature more prominently under Article 82 EC than, say, the equivalent provision in Section 2 of the United States Sherman Act 1890. "Unfair" prices and contractual terms are specifically mentioned in Article 82(a), although enforcement of this provision has been limited in practice. The Court of Justice has also sought to justify the rules on predatory pricing on the basis that below-cost prices "can drive from the market undertakings which are perhaps as efficient as the dominant undertaking but which, because of their smaller financial resources, are incapable of withstanding the competition waged against them."[21] The origins of "fairness" concerns under Article 82 EC are not entirely clear, but they most likely reflect the impact of German ordoliberal thinking—which attached importance to the notion that large firms should not unfairly limit their rivals' production and access to markets—on the initial drafting of Article 82 EC, as well certain populist notions that sometimes underpin competition law enforcement. This issue is discussed in detail in Section 1.2 below.

1.2 HISTORY, DEVELOPMENT, AND MODERNISATION OF ARTICLE 82 EC

Overview. Article 82 EC forms part of the Treaty of Rome (or the EC Treaty), signed in 1957 between the six founding Member States. The EC Treaty does not merely create legal rights and obligations: the Court of Justice confirmed from the outset that it

[20] See Opinion of Advocate General Jacobs in Case C-53/03, *Synetairismos Farmakopoion Aitolias & Akarnanias (Syfait) and Others v GlaxoSmithKline plc and GlaxoSmithKline AEVE* [2004] ECR I-4609 (hereinafter "*SYFAIT*"), para. 53.

[21] See Case C-62/86, *AKZO Chemie BV v Commission* [1991] ECR I-3359, para. 72.

also created a "new legal order of international law."[22] Article 82 EC therefore reflects a number of the underlying political, economic, and social objectives of the EC Treaty. The historical and political context of Article 82 EC had, and continues to have, an important impact on its interpretation and development. The principal influences in this regard are described below. The application of Article 82 EC has also evolved over time. In the early years, there was virtually no enforcement. Indeed, the general policy at the time was precisely the opposite: to strengthen European industry in the post-war environment rather than to attack firms with market power. Later, in the 1970s, a series of judgments of the Court of Justice established the main principles that the Community institutions apply in defining the various elements of Article 82 EC. Armed with these tools, the Commission pursued a vigorous enforcement policy in the 1980s and 1990s. Recently, there appears to be an important shift in Commission thinking and practice. In particular, there is acceptance that the limits of Article 82 EC have not always been clearly defined and that there is a greater need to align them with modern economic thinking. The adoption of a set of guidelines is therefore currently under consideration.

1.2.1 The Historical Context Of Article 82 EC

The various influences on the wording of Article 82 EC. Perhaps surprisingly, the origins of the wording of Article 82 EC, and what its author(s) intended it to mean, are not that well documented. In particular, records of the 1955 Messina Conference—which laid the foundations for the Treaty of Rome—and the other background documents to the EC Treaty are limited. But there is a good deal of consensus that at least three different sources had a significant impact on the drafting and intended meaning of the competition provisions. The first was the so-called "ordoliberal" school of thought that gained prominence in post-war thinking in Germany, as well as under German competition law. A second influence was the European Coal and Steel Community (ECSC) Treaty, which pre-dated the EC Treaty and contained a number of competition provisions that were transplanted, with modifications, to the EC Treaty. A final, and underestimated, influence was United States antitrust law, which reflected the involvement of several US lawyers, including antitrust lawyers, in the establishment of the Community and the drafting of the competition provisions.

Ordoliberal thinking. Establishing themselves in the 1930s, a small group of German economists and lawyers belonging to the so-called "Freiburg School" espoused a new form of liberal thought which concluded that the lack of an effective, dependable legal framework had led to the economic and political disintegration of Germany, particularly evident from the collaboration between the Nazi government and private cartels as vehicles of totalitarian control.[23] They considered that a competitive economic system

[22] See Case 26/62, *NV Algemene Transport en Expeditie Onderneming van Gend & Loos v Netherlands Inland Revenue Administration* [1963] ECR 95.

[23] For a discussion of Frieburg and Ordoliberal thinking and its effects on European and German competition law see DJ Gerber, *Law and Competition in Twentieth Century Europe: Protecting Prometheus* (Oxford, Clarendon Press, 1998). See also W Möschel, "Competition Policy from an Ordo Point of View" in A Peacock and H Willgerodt (eds.), *German Neo-Liberals and the Social Market Economy* (London, Macmillan, 1989) p. 145; G Amato, *Antitrust and the Bounds of Power* (Oxford, Hart Publishing, 1997) p. 41; and W Eucken, *Grundsätze der Wirtschaftspolitik* (Tübingen, Mohr Siebeck, 1990) p. 254. For a short synthesis, see J Kallaugher and B Sher, "Rebates Revisited:

was necessary for a prosperous, free, and equitable society. Central to this was the establishment of a legal system to prevent the creation and misuse of private economic power. Post-war, several intellectual groups developed out of the Freiburg School such as ordoliberals, who believed, in particular, that social welfare was achievable only through an economic order based on competition, where law would have the specific role of creating and maintaining the conditions under which competition could function properly.

Ordoliberal thinking on the goal of competition law was based on notions of "fairness" and that firms with market power should behave "as if" there was effective competition.[24] This reflected a view that small and medium sized enterprises were important to consumer welfare and that they should receive some protection from the excesses of market power. Ordoliberal thought therefore considered that certain restrictions on dominant firm behaviour were necessary and appropriate. The basic notion was that firms with economic power should not engage in conduct that unfairly limited rivals' access to markets or production. Of course, dominant firms had to be allowed the commercial freedom to compete on the merits. In this regard, ordoliberal thinking developed a notion of "performance-based competition" (*Leistungswettbewerb*). For example, non-predatory lower prices, better quality products, or better service were all considered as legitimate ways of excluding rival firms and should be permitted, whereas conduct that was not performance-based competition (e.g., below-cost prices) should be prohibited.

Many of the key figures involved in the foundation of the European Community were associated with the ordoliberal school of thought.[25] Some commentators have therefore argued that the abuse concept contained in Article 82 EC originates from a distinctly German doctrine of economic philosophy that had developed separately from the American notion of economic efficiency that underpinned the Sherman Act 1890.[26]

Experience with the ECSC Treaty. The ECSC Treaty, created by the Treaty of Paris in 1951, was one of the principal developments that led to the Treaty of Rome in 1957.[27] The idea was to pool the coal and steel industries of the signatories in an effort to place the essential factors of production under the control of a supranational organisation, which, it was thought, would reduce the prospects of another war in Europe. The ECSC was the institutional model for the European Community established by the Treaty of

---

Anticompetitive Effects and Exclusionary Abuse Under Article 82" (2004) 25(5) *European Competition Law Review* 263.

[24] DJ Gerber, *Law and Competition in Twentieth Century Europe: Protecting Prometheus* (Oxford, Clarendon Press, 1998) p. 241.

[25] These included Walter Hallstein, who became the first president of the European Commission, and Hans von der Goreben, one of the two principal drafters of the Spaak Report—the document on which the EC Treaty was fashioned. See W Hallstein, *Europe in the Making* (London, George Allen and Unwin, 1972); and Hans-Jürgen Küsters, *Die Gründung der Europäischen Wirtschaftsgemeinschaft* (Baden-Baden, Nomos-Verlagsgesellschaft, 1982) pp. 135–60.

[26] DJ Gerber, "Law and the Abuse of Economic Power in Europe" (1987) 62 *Tulane Law Review* 85.

[27] The ECSC Treaty was signed by the governments of France, the West German Federal Republic, Italy, Belgium, the Netherlands and Luxemburg on 18 April 1951 in Paris, entered into force on 23 July 1952 and expired on 23 July 2002. For discussion of the ECSC Treaty see G Bebr, "The European Coal and Steel Community: A Political and Legal Innovation" (1953) 63 *Yale Law Review* 1.

Rome, and included a Council of Ministers (representing national governments), a High Authority (equivalent to the Commission), an Assembly of national parliamentarians, and a Court of Justice. The drafting of the ECSC Treaty was charged to Jean Monnet, the leading architect of the various EC treaties.

Various objectives were set under the ECSC Treaty: to ensure that all comparably placed consumers in the market have equal access to sources of production; to ensure the establishment of the lowest prices without this resulting in higher prices being charged by the same undertakings in other transactions or in a higher general price level at another time; to promote expansion and modernisation of production; and to promote the growth of international trade.[28] Monnet also called for a strong competition law on the grounds that this was necessary to achieve the broader integrative Community goals. Two competition law provisions, one prohibiting cartels and anticompetitive agreements and another dealing with concentrations and misuses of economic power, provided legislative support for these objectives.

At the time of the founding Community treaties, no European country—with the possible exception of Germany—had any significant competition laws. Because there was no other relevant comparator, the competition provisions of the ECSC Treaty had a significant impact on those contained in the EC Treaty. Article 82 EC therefore contains similar wording to Article 66(7) ECSC.[29] The general political and economic concerns that underpinned the ECSC Treaty also led to the addition of specific clauses to Article 82 EC.[30]

Influence of US thinking and lawyers. An underestimated influence on the wording and meaning of Article 82 EC was the prominent role played by several US lawyers, including antitrust lawyers, in the establishment of the various Community treaties and the drafting of the competition provisions in particular. The reasons for this were both political and intellectual. Politically, at the time the ECSC Treaty was being negotiated, the United States was an occupying power in West Germany. It was also a major influence in other European countries through the Marshall Plan, which was conditional, *inter alia*, on European countries dismantling trade barriers and creating conditions under which their own recovery could take place. The various Community

[28] Article 3 ECSC.

[29] Article 66(7) ECSC provides that, "if the High Authority finds that public or private undertakings which, in law or in fact, hold or acquire in the market for one of the products within its jurisdiction a dominant position shielding them against effective competition in a substantial part of the common market are using that position for purposes contrary to the objectives of this Treaty, it shall make to them such recommendations as may be appropriate to prevent the position from being so used."

[30] For example, given the preponderance, at the time, of undertakings that had received exclusive or special rights from their national governments, there was widespread fear that discrimination against foreign undertakings would be rife. This was most likely one of the reasons why Article 82(c) included a specific non-discrimination clause. The ECSC Treaty also obliged steel and coal companies to publish and stick to their price lists, precisely to prevent discrimination. The result was of course very anticompetitive, but made some sense in the 1950s. See J Temple Lang, "Anticompetitive Non-Pricing Abuses Under European and National Antitrust Law" in BE Hawk (ed.), *2003 Fordham Corporate Law Institute* (Huntington, Juris Publishing, Inc., 2004), ch. 14. Indeed, in practice, most cases arising under Article 82(c) have concerned direct and indirect nationality discrimination: see Ch. 11 (Abusive Discrimination).

treaties were a central part of this recovery. US influence on the background and drafting of the Community treaties was therefore significant.[31]

At the same time, it is important to appreciate that there were and are differences between Article 82 EC and its analogue under US antitrust law, Section 2 of the Sherman Act.[32] Some of the reasons are historical and may therefore be less important today. US antitrust law was borne of the desire to dismantle a number of cartels and conglomerates, or "trusts" as they were known, that had come to dominate late nineteenth century economic life in the United States, with adverse effects for consumers. The genesis of competition law in Europe was very different and reflected a desire to break down trade barriers and promote economic integration, in the hope that this would lead to a period of stability and peace in the post-war European environment. A second set of differences could broadly be described as philosophical. Section 2

[31] See DL McLachlan and D Swann, *Competition Policy in the European Community* (London, Oxford University Press, 1967) p. 196. In terms of intellectual inspiration, it so happened that Robert Bowie, a professor of antitrust law at Harvard University, who then worked in the office of the US High Commissioner for Germany, was given the task of drafting the competition provisions of the ECSC Treaty, which in turn had a significant impact on Articles 81 and 82 EC. According to Jean Monnet, these provisions, "drafted with great care by Robert Bowie, represented a fundamental innovation in Europe." See J Monnet, *Mémoires* (Fayard, Paris, 1976) p. 413. In formulating the wording of these provisions, Bowie was "building unmistakably on American antitrust tradition." See ML Djelic, "Exporting The American Model–Historical Roots Of Globalisation" in JR Hollingsworth, KH Mueller, and EJ Hollingsworth (eds.), *Advancing Socio-Economics: An Institutional Perspective* (Lanham, Rowman & Littlefield, 2002). See also W Diebold, *The Schuman Plan* (New York, Praiger, 1959) p.352, cited in DJ Gerber, *Law and Competition in Twentieth Century Europe: Protecting Prometheus* (Oxford, Clarendon Press, 1998) p. 339. According to Diebold, Bowie's draft was rewritten in an European idiom, emerging as a "blend [of] several European approaches to cartel questions with elements drawn from American practice and experience" before being adopted. Other US lawyers were equally prominent at the time in elaborating the founding European treaties. A number deserve specific mention. George Ball, an American lawyer and diplomat, was asked by the French government to help Jean Monnet think through the general direction and approach of the French recovery plan. Together with another lawyer, Eugen Rostow, he played a significant role in helping Monnet identify the key features of the American economic model for incorporation in the French plan. Ball and Rostow remained involved with Monnet and the strategic thinking that took place around the ECSC Treaty and Treaty of Rome. Robert Bowie acted as General Counsel to the American High Commissioner in Germany, John McCloy. As a personal friend of Monnet, McCloy agreed to lend Bowie to Monnet for a few months in 1950, during which time Bowie drafted the competition provisions of the ECSC Treaty. It is also notable that works describing and analysing US antitrust became increasingly common around this period, while groups of practising lawyers, bureaucrats and academics visiting the United States were impressed by how the antitrust laws operated. These broadly positive experiences provided a strong basis for the inclusion of analogous competition law provisions in the ECSC and EC treaties.

[32] For more discussion of the differences between Article 82 EC and Section 2, see R Joliet, *Monopolisation and Abuse of Dominant Position: A Comparative Study of the American and European Approaches to the Control of Economic Power* (The Hague, Nijhoff, 1970); BE Hawk, "Antitrust in the EEC—The First Decade" (1972–1973) 41 *Fordham Law Review* 282; SM James, "The Concept of Abuse in EEC Competition Law: An American View" (1976) 92 *The Law Quarterly Review* 242; and RE Bloch, HG Kamann, JS Brown, and JP Schmidt, "A Comparative Analysis Of Article 82 And Section 2 Of The Sherman Act," paper submitted to the International Bar Association 9th Annual Competition Conference, October 21–22, 2005. For an economic perspective, see FM Fisher, "Monopolisation versus Abuse of Dominant Position: An Economist's View" in BE Hawk (ed.), *2003 Fordham Corporate Law Institute*, chapter 9 (Huntington, Juris Publishing, Inc., 2004), ch. 9.

adopts a more minimalist, or less interventionist, approach to enforcement than Article 82 EC.[33]

Finally, the substantive conditions of Article 82 EC and Section 2 of the Sherman Act also differ in certain respects. In particular, the difference in the language of the provisions show that the laws were conceived to allow government intervention in somewhat different circumstances. Article 82 EC aims to prevent powerful firms from using their power abusively, but the mere existence of dominance is not unlawful. Section 2, on the other hand, does not require a prior formal finding of a dominant position, but seeks to identify anticompetitive conduct that creates or threatens to create a monopoly. Another important difference is that Section 2 contained no corresponding provision to Article 82(a) on excessive pricing. Article 82 EC is also thought to diverge from Section 2 in the areas of predatory pricing (unlike Section 2, there is no need to show an ability to recoup losses under Article 82 EC), loyalty rebates (these are generally treated as lawful under Section 2, whereas under Article 82 EC these have in some cases been subject to a presumption of illegality), and refusals to deal (the "essential facility" doctrine is more vibrant in Europe than in the United States).

1.2.2 Development Of Article 82 EC

Overview of the various stages of development of Article 82 EC. Any synthesis of the development of Article 82 EC that seeks to identify distinct stages runs the risk of being arbitrary. Nonetheless, it is possible to make a meaningful distinction between several different stages in the development of Article 82 EC. The first stage, lasting from the period of the adoption of EC Treaty in 1957 throughout most of the 1960s, was characterised by non-enforcement. The second phase, lasting from the late 1960s until the late 1970s, saw a more active enforcement policy and, significantly, a series of judgments that elaborated on the basic elements of abuse that still form the cornerstone of policy and practice today. A final phase lasting from the 1980s throughout most of the 1990s was characterised by a more interventionist approach by the Commission in which it developed several operational rules for specific abuses.

---

[33] This is based perhaps on a greater faith in the United States that market forces are better at correcting inefficiencies than government intervention and a corresponding fear that excessive intervention could chill desirable activity. See, e.g., *Brooke Group Ltd v Brown & Williamson Tobacco Corp*, 509 US 209, (1993), where the US Supreme Court's reluctance to treat price cuts as predatory was based, *inter alia*, on the concern that a strict rule could chill legitimate price competition. A more practical, and often overlooked, reason for a less interventionist approach under Section 2 is that the financial consequences of competition-law violations for defendants are generally much more serious than in Europe. Civil damages for Section 2 violations are three times the actual damage—so-called treble damages—whereas, in Europe, only single damages are, for now, the norm. Private antitrust litigation is also much more pervasive in the United States, which, again, helps explain a certain reluctance on the part of the government agencies to enunciate some of the broad principles established under Article 82 EC. It may also be that the more interventionist approach to competition law in Europe is justified by a greater incidence of State monopolies and other exclusive rights. Europe remains unique among global economic and political concentrations in that it is not composed of a single nation state, but several sovereign Member States. Sovereign nation states had, and continue to have, reasons of national interest that help explain a relatively high incidence of State measures that distort competition. Indeed, eliminating national restrictions of competition continues to be very important in Europe given the residual effects of communist control on the economies of several recently-acceded States.

The early years of non-enforcement. The Commission's enforcement of Article 82 EC was practically non-existent in the years following the adoption of the EC Treaty. This is generally thought to have reflected two considerations. First, the practical application of Article 82 EC was unclear: the concept of abuse of a dominant position was not defined in the text of the EC Treaty; nor did any national competition law system explain how the concept should be interpreted or applied. While several European countries, such as France, Belgium, and Germany, had established national legislation based on the abuse principle, enforcement was extremely limited. Likewise, at the time Article 82 EC was enacted, Article 66(7) ECSC had never been applied either. The absence of defined criteria led some commentators to fear that Article 82 EC would ultimately become a dead letter.[34]

A second obstacle to Article 82 EC enforcement was politically motivated. During the early period of European unification, many saw economic integration as the only means of dealing with the combined economic and political strength of the United States. European policy was focused on creating an integrated market in which European businesses, often "national champions," could grow to a sufficient size to compete with US corporations. Accordingly, there was, in the early years, a lack of willingness to enforce Article 82 EC. Strict application meant that dominant European firms who were well-placed to compete against their US rivals could have been hampered in their ability to grow or compete internationally.[35]

Developing the framework for the application of Article 82 EC. Beginning in the late 1960s, the Commission sought to develop a basic framework for the application of Article 82 EC. The Commission's first statement concerning the interpretation of the concept of an abuse—the 1966 Memorandum on Concentration—signalled that its reticence to apply Article 82 EC was on the wane.[36] Not long after the Memorandum on Concentration was published, the Commission and the Court of Justice sought to develop the concept of an abuse in several decisions and cases.[37] In a series of cases

[34] See I Samkalden and IE Druker, "Legal Problems relating to Article 86 of the Rome Treaty" (1966) 3 *Common Market Law Review* 158 183.

[35] This policy can also be seen in the Commission's earlier permissive stance toward many horizontal agreements involving small and medium-sized companies. See BE Hawk, "Antitrust in the EEC—The First Decade" (1972–1973) 41 *Fordham Law Review* 234 and 268.

[36] The Memorandum on Concentration contained two basic principles aimed at answering the question: what constituted an abuse? According to the Memorandum, an abuse could only occur where there is a direct causal link between the firm's market power and its effect on the market, meaning that a dominant firm could use its position of dominance to obtain benefits that it could not obtain if it were exposed to effective competition. The second principle of interpretation is even broader—and less helpful—than the first, claiming that an abuse occurred when a dominant firm's conduct is incompatible with the objectives of the EC Treaty (para. 676). See Mémorandum sur le Problème de la Concentration dans le Marché Commun (December 1, 1965), reprinted in (1966) *Revue Trimestrielle de Droit Européen* 651–77, p. 670 (reprinted in (1966) 26 *Common Market Law Review* 1–30).

[37] See also First Report on Competition Policy (1971), p. 74 ("In 1971 the European Commission's competition policy which, during the first decade had concentrated on the application of rules concerning agreements, entered the phase of application of Article 82. As a result of considerable efforts made to define the interpretation and application of this important provision, and following a constant supervision of the market with a view to finding out whether there were threats of abuse of dominant positions, the Commission took its first two decisions in the *Gema* and *Continental Can* cases.").

relating to purported misuse of intellectual property rights the Court of Justice had its first opportunity to interpret Article 82 EC.[38] The Court stated that, although the existence of these rights was not affected by the EC Treaty, their exercise may nevertheless fall under the prohibitions laid down in Articles 81 and 82 EC.

The 1970s saw a number of important judgments in which the principal elements of Article 82 EC were elaborated. In *Continental Can*,[39] the Court of Justice held, somewhat controversially, that mergers and acquisitions could, in certain circumstances fall under the prohibition in Article 82 EC. This ruling is generally regarded as a striking example of judicial legislation intended to compensate for the fact that there were no Community rules on merger control at the time. But the Court also established two other important general principles: first, that the examples of abuses in Article 82 EC were not necessarily exhaustive and, second, that the concept of an abuse covers not only direct harm to competition, but also indirect harm in the form of conduct that adversely affects the structure of competition.[40] The following year, in *Commercial Solvents*,[41] the Court held that a dominant supplier of an essential raw material may have a duty to deal with a downstream customer that depends on it and that the dominant firm's self-interest in dealing only with its downstream subsidiary is not necessarily a defence. This case forms the basis of the current principles on refusal to deal under Article 82 EC.

Three subsequent cases in the 1970s laid the foundation for most of the basic principles under Article 82 EC. In *Suiker Unie*, the Court of Justice dealt with a wide range of abusive practices, including exclusive contracts, payments in return for not dealing with rival firms, discrimination under Article 82(c), and "limiting production" under Article 82(b).[42] The latter concept in particular has significant implications for the definition of exclusionary abuses. In *United Brands*,[43] the Court dealt with its first major case of abuse that affected market integration. United Brands was found guilty of a series of measures aimed at limiting competition between its distributors and retailers, including export bans, price discrimination, and threats to de-list distributors who dealt with rival firms. The case is also notable for its treatment of excessive pricing because the Court struck down the Commission's finding due to inadequate proof. The final

---

[38] See Case 24/67, *Parke, Davis and Co v Probel, Reese, Beintema-Interpharm and Centrafarm* [1968] ECR 55; Case 40/70, *Sirena Srl v Eda Srl and others* [1971] ECR 69; and Case 78/70, *Deutsche Grammophon Gesellschaft mbH v Metro-SB-Großmärkte GmbH & Co KG* [1971] ECR 487.

[39] See Case 6/72, *Europemballage Corporation and Continental Can Company Inc v Commission* [1973] ECR 215.

[40] *Ibid.*, para. 26.

[41] Joined Cases 6-7/73, *Istituto Chemioterapico Italiano SpA and Commercial Solvents Corporation v Commission* [1974] ECR 223.

[42] Joined Cases 40 to 48, 50, 54 to 56, 111, 113 and 114-73, *Coöperatieve Vereniging "Suiker Unie" UA and others v Commission* [1975] ECR 1663 (hereinafter "*Suiker Unie*"), paras. 399, 482–83, and in particular paras. 523–27.

[43] Case 27/76, *United Brands Company and United Brands Continentaal BV v Commission* [1978] ECR 207.

case, *Hoffmann-La Roche*, is among the more important cases under Article 82 EC, since it laid out the Court's basic definition of an exclusionary abuse:[44]

> "The concept of abuse is an objective concept relating to the behaviour of an undertaking in a dominant position which is such as to influence the structure of a market where, as a result of the very presence of the undertaking in question, the degree of competition is weakened and which, through recourse to methods different from those which condition normal competition in products or services on the basis of the transactions of commercial operators, has the effect of hindering the maintenance of the degree of competition still existing in the market or the growth of that competition."

Elaboration of the general principles laid down by the Court of Justice. Although the basic concept of an abuse had been articulated by the Court of Justice in a series of cases in the 1970s, very few operational rules had been laid down by the Commission as a result. Throughout the 1980s and 1990s, the Commission, backed by the Community Courts, developed a number of rules for specific examples of abusive conduct. An important early case was *Michelin I*,[45] where the Court of Justice laid down the conditions for abusive loyalty discounts. The case is also notable for the Court's formulation that, while "a finding that an undertaking has a dominant position is not in itself a recrimination but simply means that, irrespective of the reasons for which it has such a position, the undertaking concerned has a special responsibility not to allow its conduct to impair genuine undistorted competition on the common market."[46]

In *AKZO*,[47] the Commission first laid down the conditions for predatory pricing. It concluded that prices below a firm's average variable costs—costs that vary with output—were presumptively abusive and that prices above average variable cost, but below average total cost—the sum of average variable and average fixed costs—could also be regarded as abusive if they were part of a plan to eliminate a competitor. A related rule concerning price squeeze abuses was laid down in *Napier Brown/British Sugar*.[48] There, the Commission ruled that the vertically-integrated dominant firm would be guilty of a price squeeze abuse against a downstream rival to whom it supplied an important input if the dominant firm's own business could not make a profit on the basis of the price charged by the dominant firm to the rival.

One of the most significant innovations by the Commission during this period was the adoption of an interventionist approach to the circumstances in which a dominant firm can be compelled to deal with rival firms. This doctrine was first developed in a series of cases concerning access to essential port infrastructure, airport facilities, and essential assets owned by a consortium of competing firms.[49] In *Bronner*, the Court of Justice sought to place clearer limits on the doctrine by insisting on proof that the input was

[44] Case 85/76, *Hoffmann-La Roche & Co AG v Commission* [1979] ECR 461, para. 6 (hereinafter "*Hoffmann-La Roche*").

[45] Case 322/81, *NV Nederlandsche Banden Industrie Michelin v Commission* [1983] ECR 3461 (hereinafter "*Michelin I*").

[46] *Ibid.*, para. 10.

[47] *ECS/AKZO*, OJ 1985 L 374/1 (hereinafter "*AKZO*"), upheld on appeal in Case C-62/86, *AKZO Chemie BV v Commission* [1991] ECR I-3359, paras. 72 and 73.

[48] *Napier Brown/British Sugar*, OJ 1988 L 284/41 (hereinafter "*Napier Brown/British Sugar*").

[49] See Ch. 8 (Refusal to Deal).

non-replicable and truly essential for effective competition.[50] A controversial application of this doctrine concerned the case of intellectual property rights. Although the Court of Justice had confirmed in 1988 in *Volvo*[51] that the exercise of an intellectual property right might involve abusive conduct, the extension of that principle in *Magill*[52] to require dominant broadcasters to licence their televisions listings information to a publisher that wished to produce a new composite television guide generated enormous controversy. The outcome in that particular case was probably correct, but there was also widespread concern that valuable property rights could also be subject to mandatory sharing. Similar concerns were expressed following the *IMS Health* interim decision where the Commission, on admittedly usual facts, concluded that an intellectual property right could be subject to a duty to share where the refusal to do so risked the elimination of competition.[53] The case was seen, with some justification, as running the risk of conflicting with the well-established principles of intellectual property laws.[54]

1.2.3 The Modernisation Of Article 82 EC

The need for modernisation. The Commission's expansion of the concept of an abuse has become more controversial in recent years. Some of that controversy stems from the inherent difficulty of distinguishing the type of exclusion that competition law encourages—legitimate competition—and unlawful exclusion. An abuse has been variously defined under Article 82 EC as conduct that does not amount to "competition on the merits"—that is by lower prices and better products,[55] the "special responsibility" of a dominant firm not to restrain any remaining competition,[56] or conduct that is not "normal competition."[57] Unfortunately, as discussed in Chapter Four (The General Concept of an Abuse), these definitions are largely conclusory and lack a clear normative content that would allow a firm to determine *a priori* when its conduct might run afoul of the law. This lack of clarity surrounding the definition of an abuse has stimulated a lively current debate on what the standard for assessing exclusionary behaviour is or should be. In particular, the debate has moved towards the search for a

---

[50] Case C-7/97, *Oscar Bronner GmbH & Co KG v Mediaprint Zeitungs- und Zeitschriftenverlag GmbH & Co KG, Mediaprint Zeitungsvertriebsgesellschaft mbH & Co KG and Mediaprint Anzeigengesellschaft mbH & Co KG* [1998] ECR I-7791 (hereinafter "*Bronner*").

[51] Case 238/87, *AB Volvo v Erik Veng (UK) Ltd* [1988] ECR 6211 (hereinafter "*Volvo*").

[52] *Magill TV Guide/ITP, BBC and RTE*, OJ 1989 L 78/43 (hereinafter "*Magill*"), confirmed on appeal in Case T-69/89, *Radio Telefis Eireann (RTE) v Commission* [1991] ECR II-485, Case T-70/89, *British Broadcasting Corporation and BBC Enterprises Ltd (BBC) v Commission* [1991] ECR II-535, and Case T-76/89, *Independent Television Publications Ltd (ITP) v Commission* [1991] ECR II-575, and further confirmed in Joined Cases C-241/91 P and C-242/91 P, *Radio Telefis Eireann and Independent Television Publications Ltd (RTE & ITP) v Commission* [1995] ECR I-743.

[53] *NDC Health/IMS Health—Interim Measures*, OJ 2002 L 59/18 (hereinafter "*IMS Health*").

[54] See Ch. 8 (Refusal to Deal).

[55] See, e.g., Comments by Mario Monti on the speech given by Hew Pate, Assistant Attorney General, US Department of Justice, at the Conference "Antitrust in a Transatlantic Context," Brussels, June 7, 2004 ("I think we can both agree that in competition the best should win on the merits, but only on the merits. Whenever dominant companies can use their market power to win in a market for reasons that are not related to the price or quality of their products, then we should consider intervening.").

[56] Case 322/81, *NV Nederlandsche Banden Industrie Michelin v Commission* [1983] ECR 3461, para. 87.

[57] Case 85/76, *Hoffmann-La Roche & Co AG v Commission* [1979] ECR 461, para. 91.

single, unified standard that would define abusive conduct. Several different tests have been proposed.[58] The detailed application of the various tests is discussed in Chapter Four, but it is sufficient to note here that a great deal of uncertainty continues to exist regarding the relative merits of each test and how they would work in practice.

The current controversy surrounding the application of Article 82 EC is not only confined to the inherent difficulty of verbalising a unified test that would define abusive conduct. Indeed, most of it concerns the Commission's application of Article 82 EC in practice. Several criticisms have been levelled. First, the law is unclear in important respects and certain ill-considered statements by the Commission, particularly on pricing abuses, suggest a broad definition of abusive conduct without clear limiting principles. Another reason for the lack of clarity is that there have been relatively few reported Article 82 EC decisions and cases at Community level—less than 60 in almost fifty years of enforcement. The case-law and practice has also arisen pragmatically, and largely in response to complaints to the Commission and appeals to the Community Courts against Commission decisions adopted on the basis of such complaints. With the exception of specialised Notices and guidance in the telecommunications and postal sectors,[59] the Commission has not attempted to develop any kind of general or comprehensive statement on abusive behaviour. Instead, the Commission and the Community Courts have dealt with individual cases that were said to raise questions of abuse by reference to the facts of the specific case, seemingly without having any clear general analytical or intellectual framework for doing so. As a result, a number of basic questions were not answered or even discussed because due to the accidents of litigation, or otherwise, they did not arise in any of the cases that have been decided.

A second criticism of Commission practice is that it sometimes runs the risk of protecting competitors at the expense of competition.[60] One of the areas most criticised concerns above-cost conditional discounts, such as loyalty rebates and similar schemes.[61] Although there is some economic consensus that such schemes can, in certain circumstances, raise competition concerns, the position under Article 82 EC is that, following *British Airways/Virgin*,[62] such schemes are effectively treated as *per se* illegal. In this circumstance, the concern has been expressed that a strict rule on conditional above-cost discounts denies consumers the benefit of lower prices on the grounds that they would harm competitors.

A final criticism is that the influence of economics has not been felt as strongly under Article 82 EC as it has been under Article 81 EC and EC merger control law.[63] Under Article 81 EC, the Commission has published block exemptions and detailed guidelines that deal with the treatment of vertical restraints,[64] horizontal cooperation agreements,[65] and technology licensing.[66] In the area of merger control, the Commission has also published guidelines outlining the principles applied in its analysis of the most common type of merger cases—mergers between direct competitors.[67] All of these documents

[58] For a good overview of the main competing theories, see J Vickers, speech to the 31st conference of the European Association for Research in Industrial Economics, Berlin, September 3, 2004.

[59] See Notice on the application of the competition rules to access agreements in the telecommunications sector—framework, relevant markets, and principles, OJ 1998 C 265/2; Notice from the Commission on the application of the competition rules to the postal sector and on the assessment of certain State measures relating to postal services, 1998 OJ C 39/2.

were prepared with extensive consultation, including with leading economists, and they reflect a clear willingness on the part of the Commission to embrace current economic thinking in the areas of agreements and mergers. No comparable documents exist under Article 82 EC, apart from a couple of specialised Notices in the telecommunications and postal sectors.

Another difficulty is that there is a disconnect between some of the economic thinking that underpins the Commission's public documents under Article 81 EC and EC merger control and its practice under Article 82 EC. For example, in the area of vertical restraints, the Commission's guidelines under Article 81 EC recognise that exclusive dealing and analogous arrangements can have important procompetitive features. In essence, they encourage distributors to focus their promotional efforts on a single manufacturer and prevent other firms from "free-riding" on that manufacturer's success. Exclusive dealing may also have anticompetitive effects, but the guidelines recognise that it is necessary in each case to evaluate the net effects of the agreement. In contrast, under Article 82 EC, a strict presumption of illegality has been applied to exclusive dealing arrangements and analogous schemes such as loyalty discounts.[68] Although this presumption has been relaxed somewhat in recent decisions,[69] the Commission has routinely rejected under Article 82 EC several procompetitive features of distribution arrangements that it accepts under Article 81 EC.[70] While the presence of dominance under Article 82 EC clearly affects the analysis, there is no reason *a priori* to conclude that the procompetitive features of vertical restraints recognised under Article 81 EC cannot also exist under Article 82 EC.

---

[60] See, e.g., EM Fox, "We Protect Competition, You Protect Competitors" (2003) 26(2) *World Competition* 149–65.

[61] See Ch. 7 (Exclusive Dealing, Loyalty Discounts, and Related Practices).

[62] Case T-219/99, *British Airways Plc v Commission* [2003] ECR II-5917.

[63] See J Vickers, speech to the 31st conference of the European Association for Research in Industrial Economics, Berlin, September 3, 2004; A Fletcher, "Towards a More Economics-Based Approach to Article 82," initial comments on an initial paper by the Competition Law Forum Review Group: *The Reform of Article 82: Recommendations on Key Policy Objectives*, March 15, 2004.

[64] Commission Regulation (EC) No 2790/1999 of December 22, 1999, on the application of Article 81(3) of the Treaty to categories of vertical agreements and concerted practices, OJ 1999 L 336/21; Commission Notice—Guidelines on Vertical Restraints, OJ 2000 C 291/1.

[65] Commission Regulation (EC) No 2658/2000 of November 29, 2000 on the application of Article 81(3) of the Treaty to categories of specialisation agreements, OJ 2000 L 304/3; Commission Regulation (EC) No 2659/2000 of November 29, 2000 on the application of Article 81(3) of the Treaty to categories of research and development agreements, OJ 2000 L 304/7; Commission Notice—Guidelines on the applicability of Article 81 to horizontal cooperation agreements, OJ 2001 C 3/2.

[66] Commission Regulation (EC) No 772/2004 of April 27, 2004 on the application of Article 81(3) of the Treaty to categories of technology transfer agreements, OJ 2004 L 123/11; Commission Notice—Guidelines on the application of Article 81 of the EC Treaty to technology transfer agreements, OJ 2004 C 101/2.

[67] Guidelines on the assessment of horizontal mergers under the Council Regulation on the control of concentrations between undertakings, OJ 2004 C 31/5.

[68] In *Hoffmann-La Roche*, for example, the Court of Justice stated that the concept of abuse "in principle includes *any* obligation to obtain exclusively from an undertaking in a dominant position, which benefits that undertaking." See Case 85/76, *Hoffmann-La Roche & Co AG v Commission* [1979] ECR 461, para. 121 (emphasis added).

[69] Case T-65/98, *Van den Bergh Foods Ltd v Commission* [2003] ECR II-4653.

[70] See Ch. 7 (Exclusive Dealing, Loyalty Discounts, and Related Practices).

Scope of the Commission's Article 82 EC review. The Commission announced in 2003 that it would undertake a review of policy under Article 82 EC. The review was said to be prompted by several considerations that reflect many of the criticisms outlined above.[71] First, the Commission accepts that Article 82 EC has lagged behind Article 81 EC and merger control laws in that there had been no reassessment and modernisation of policy and practice. In particular, the Commission accepts that, unlike Article 81 EC and merger policy, it has "never had a comprehensive reassessment of policy under Article 82 in the light of economic thinking."[72] Second, Article 82 EC is an area in which predictable rules are important and, at present, remains an area where there is little policy guidance. Certain commentators argued that the Commission should adopt guidelines on the most important practices, in particular pricing.[73] Third, in an environment where national authorities and courts are increasingly responsible for applying Article 82 EC, a common set of core principles is important to ensure consistent enforcement. Finally, the Commission recognises that many companies operate on a global scale and that greater convergence with the competition policies of other major jurisdictions—in particular the United States—is desirable where possible.

In July 2005 by a report by the Economic Advisory Group on Competition Policy—group of around fifteen leading academic economists that advises the Commission's Competition Directorate on competition policy issues—set out the case for "an economic approach to Article 82."[74] Following extensive consultation with the national competition authorities (NCAs), a discussion paper setting out the Competition Directorate's thinking on exclusionary abuses was published in December 2005. This will be followed by public consultation and possible amendment in 2006, with final publication intended for late 2006. The Commission has also indicated that it intends to produce similar documents on exploitative abuses and discrimination in due course. Detailed reference is made to the Discussion Paper in subsequent chapters.

The role of economics under Article 82 EC. The principal idea behind the modernisation of Article 82 EC is to bring it more in line with the type of economic analysis routinely applied under Article 81 EC and EC merger control; in other words, to apply "sound economic assessment."[75] The basic tools for formulating a proper economic approach are in place with the recent creation of the position and office of Chief Economist within DG Competition. The Chief Economist reports directly to the competition Director General with: (1) guidance on economics and econometrics in the

---

[71] See P Lowe, speech at the Thirtieth Annual Conference on International Antitrust Law and Policy, Fordham Corporate Law Institute, October 23, 2003.

[72] *Ibid.*

[73] See J Temple Lang and R O'Donoghue, "Defining Legitimate Competition: How to Clarify Pricing Abuses under Article 82" (2002) 26 *Fordham International Law Journal* 83, 85 ("It is on pricing issues that a clear and comprehensive statement of the legal and economic principles is most urgently needed, not only to guide the thinking of the Commission, companies, and their lawyers, but also for the guidance of national competition authorities which are intended, under the Commission's proposals for decentralisation of Community competition law, to apply Article 82 more than they have in the past.").

[74] Report by the Economic Advisory Group on Competition Policy (EAGCP), "An Economic Approach to Article 82" (July 2005).

[75] See N Kroes, "Preliminary Thoughts on Policy Review of Article 82", speech at the Fordham Corporate Law Institute, New York, September 23, 2005.

application of competition rules; (2) general guidance in individual competition cases from the early stages; and (3) detailed guidance in the most important competition cases involving complex economic issues, in particular those requiring sophisticated quantitative analysis. Opinions, guidance, or final advice from the Chief Economist are not, however, made public. In order to develop and disseminate economic expertise and knowledge, the Chief Economist also interacts with the antitrust community in various ways.[76] A recent example of this is a report commissioned by the Chief Economist from leading academic industrial organisation economists setting out an economic approach to Article 82 EC.[77]

Although the influence of economics on Article 82 EC has historically been much less marked than in the case of Article 81 EC and the EC Merger Regulation— sometimes with adverse consequences for a sensible interpretation of Article 82 EC—there are already signs in recent years of the growing use of economics under Article 82 EC. Examples include *Microsoft*[78] and *Wanadoo.*[79] In Microsoft, the Commission accepted much of the modern economic thinking on tying arrangements that underpins US antitrust law by moving towards an effect-based analysis (although the Commission's application of that thinking to the facts of the case is strongly disputed by the defendant on appeal). The Commission's decision in Wanadoo marks an important advance on Article 82 EC policy on predatory pricing. There, the Commission moved away from a mechanical application of tests based on pricing below an appropriate measure of cost and towards a more coherent test based on the need to identify a plausible theory of predation, backed by appropriate evidence. Thus, the Commission made allowances for: (1) the treatment of start-up losses under Article 82 EC; (2) the application of the *AKZO* predatory pricing test to industries with large up-front fixed costs investments and low variable costs; (3) strategic-based theories of exclusion other than market exit; (4) recoupment; (5) the need for analysis of foreclosure effects; and (6) business justification for below-cost selling, including network externalities, learning-by-doing, and other dynamic efficiencies.

---

[76] These include: (1) by establishing the Economic Advisory Group on Competition Policy (EAGCP)—a group of academic economists that advises the Commission on selected important policy issues; (2) an annual internal one day event where DG COMP discuss past cases with EAGCP, in particular with regard to the appropriate usage of economic analysis; (3) a monthly public seminar, where external academic speakers present their latest work in the field of competition policy; (4) an internal luncheon, where DG COMP case handlers discuss economic analysis of cases in an informal setting; and (5) bilateral meetings between economists from Commission and the US antitrust agencies to discuss case work, in particular economic methodology. See LH Röller, "Using Economic Analysis to Strengthen Competition Policy Enforcement" in P Bergeijk and E van Kloosterhuis (eds.), *Modelling European Mergers: Theory, Competition Policy and Case Studies* (London, Edward Elgar, 2005).

[77] Report by the Economic Advisory Group on Competition Policy (EAGCP), "An economic approach to Article 82" (July 2005).

[78] See Case COMP/C-3/37.792, *Microsoft*, Commission Decision of March 24, 2004, not yet published, (hereinafter "*Microsoft*").

[79] See Case COMP/38.233, *Wanadoo Interactive,* Commission Decision of July 16, 2003, not yet published, (hereinafter "*Wanadoo*").

1.3 ENTITIES AND ACTIVITIES BOUND BY ARTICLE 82 EC

Overview. Article 82 EC, in common with Article 81 EC, applies only to the conduct of an "undertaking."[80] The definition of an undertaking is obviously of central importance under Article 82 EC, since an entity that does not constitute an undertaking is not bound by the prohibition on abuse of dominance contained in that article. The EC Treaty does not define the term "undertaking." The definition has instead been extensively developed by the case law of the Community Courts in a manner sufficiently broad to capture any meaningful form of economic activity. Some difficult questions arise concerning the activities of the State and when they can be considered sufficiently economic in nature to justify the characterisation of the State as an undertaking. The general principles concerning the definition of an undertaking in the case of public bodies and the principal difficulties it raises are discussed below.

A second set of issues concerns entities that qualify as undertakings, but whose conduct is shielded from action under EC competition law because it results from State action that compels the conduct in question. Where the conduct is genuinely compelled by national law, responsibility for the infringement lies properly with the State, not the undertakings subject to the law in question. Of course, EC competition law on State action is not limited to the State action doctrine, but includes a number of affirmative obligations on the State in respect of the conduct of public undertakings and other State action. These obligations are discussed in Section 1.4. below: the current section discusses the circumstances in which an entity can *avoid* the application of Article 82 EC on the grounds that the conduct in question results from State action.

Finally, the circumstances in which a parent company can be liable for conduct carried out by its subsidiary in violation of Article 82 EC should also be considered. Although a parent and a subsidiary under its control will generally be considered as one and the same entity for purposes of Article 82 EC, it is important to identify the circumstances in which the parent's liability for an infringement committed by its subsidiary can be automatically imputed and when evidence of the parent's involvement in the infringement or the actual exercise of its control rights in respect of the infringing conduct is also required.

1.3.1 The Definition Of An Undertaking

1.3.1.1 Generally

All "economic activities" covered. The Community Courts have taken a broad view of the concept of an undertaking, focusing on the type of activity performed rather than on the formal characteristics of the entity in question. An entity will thus qualify as an

[80] EC competition law also applies with modifications in certain sectors. For example, in the agriculture sector, Council Regulation 26 lists certain products that are exempt from the application of Article 81 EC. However, these exceptions do not extend to Article 82 EC. See Council Regulation 26 applying certain rules of competition to production of and trade in agricultural products, OJ 1962 30/993. Certain exemptions also exist for transport services, but these are mainly procedural rather than substantive in nature. See generally J Faull and A Nikpay, *The EC Law of Competition* (2nd edition, Oxford University Press (2006)), chapter 14 (transport).

undertaking regardless of whether it possesses legal personality.[81] Case law has held that the "the concept of an undertaking encompasses every entity engaged in an economic activity, regardless of the legal status of the entity and the way in which it is financed."[82] For example, in *Höfner & Elser* an issue arose whether a public employment agency could be characterised as an undertaking.[83] The Court of Justice reasoned that employment procurement is inherently an "economic activity" and that the fact that employment procurement activities are normally entrusted to public agencies does not affect the economic nature of such activities. Employment procurement has not always been, and is not necessarily, carried out by public entities, in particular for executive recruitment. Applying this broad definition, many different kinds of entities have been found to carry on an economic activity including limited companies,[84] partnerships,[85] trade associations,[86] sporting bodies,[87] agricultural co-operatives,[88] not-for-profit firms,[89] self-employed professionals,[90] and professional bodies regulating entry into a profession.[91]

1.3.1.2 Public bodies as undertakings

Generally. The fact that a particular activity is carried out under the auspices of the State is not a barrier to the entity in question being regarded as an undertaking for purposes of Article 82 EC. An entity may be an undertaking even if it engages in ostensibly social activities. The essential test in each case is whether the specific activity at issue involves offering goods or services on the market or, if this is not the case, is something that could in principle be carried out by a private entity for profit.[92] Different kinds of public bodies have been found to carry on an economic activity, such as the German Federal Employment Office's handling of employment procurement,[93] or

---

[81] See *Polypropelene,* OJ 1986 L 230/1, para. 99 ("The subjects of EEC competition rules are undertakings, a concept which is not identical with the question of legal personality for the purposes of company law or fiscal law. The term 'undertaking' is not defined in the Treaty. It may, however, refer to any entity engaged in commercial activities and in the case of corporate bodies may refer to a parent or to a subsidiary or to the unit formed by the parent and subsidiaries together.").

[82] Case C-41/90, *Klaus Höfner and Fritz Elser v Macrotron GmbH* [1991] ECR I-1979, para. 21 (hereinafter "*Höfner and Elser*").

[83] *Ibid.*, paras. 20–23.

[84] Case 258/78, *L.C. Nungesser KG and Kurt Eisele v Commission* [1982] ECR 2015.

[85] See, e.g., *Breeders' Rights: Roses*, OJ 1985 L 369/9.

[86] See, e.g., Case 71/74, *Nederlandse Vereniging voor de fruit- en groentenimporthandel, Nederlandse Bond van grossiers in zuidvruchten en ander geimporteerd fruit "Frubo" v Commission* [1975] ECR 563.

[87] Case T-193/02, *Laurent Piau v Commission* [2005] ECR II-nyr.

[88] Case 61/80, *Coöperatieve Stremsel-en Kleurselfabriek v Commission* [1981] ECR 851.

[89] *Distribution of Package Tours During the 1990 World Cup*, OJ 1992 L 326/31.

[90] Case T-513/93, *Consiglio Nazionale degli Spedizionieri Doganali v Commission* [2000] ECR II-1807.

[91] Case C-309/99, *JCJ Wouters, JW Savelbergh and Price Waterhouse Belastingadviseurs BV v Algemene Raad van de Nederlandse Orde van Advocaten, intervener: Raad van de Balies van de Europese Gemeenschap* [2002] ECR I-1577.

[92] Case C-67/96, *Albany International BV v Stichting Bedrijfspensioenfonds Textielindustrie* [1999] ECR I-5751, para. 311.

[93] *Ibid.*

the Italian autonomous administration of State monopolies offering goods and services on the market for manufactured tobacco.[94]

The regulation of professions. Activities that involve the exclusive exercise of the functions of public authority, without an accompanying economic activity, fall outside the scope of EC competition law. For example, in *Royal Pharmaceutical Society of Great Britain*, the Court of Justice held that measures adopted by a professional body, which laid down ethical rules applicable to all members of the profession and had a committee to which national legislation had conferred disciplinary powers, did not constitute measures adopted by undertakings within the meaning of EC competition law.[95]

In contrast, in a case involving rules in the Netherlands prohibiting multi-disciplinary practices between lawyers and other professionals, the Court of Justice found that the relevant bar association was, in that specific capacity, acting as an undertaking.[96] The Court reasoned that, when it adopted a regulation concerning partnerships between members of the bar and members of other professions, the bar of a Member State is neither fulfilling a social function based on the principle of solidarity, nor exercising powers typical of those of a public authority. Instead, it acts as the regulatory body of a profession, the practice of which constitutes an economic activity. The fact that governing bodies of the bar are composed exclusively of members of the bar who are elected solely by members of the profession, and that in adopting acts such as that regulation, the bar is not required to do so by reference to specified public-interest criteria, supported the conclusion that such a professional organisation with regulatory powers could not escape the application of EC competition law.

The essential difference between the two cases is that, in the former, the action criticised did not seek to regulate the economic activity of the profession, but only concerned its ethical and disciplinary rules, whereas, in the latter case, the agreement at issue specifically prevented partnerships with other professions and, therefore, directly affected the scope for economic activity. The cases also confirm another important point: that an entity may be acting as an undertaking in one area of its activity but not another.

Activities carried out in the interests of public safety or the environment. The *Eurocontrol* case concerned whether or not the international organisation responsible for air traffic control over much of Europe constituted an undertaking for the purposes of Articles 81 and 82 EC.[97] The Court explained that while the concept of undertaking encompasses any entity engaged in an economic activity, regardless of its legal status and the way it is financed, a task undertaken in the public interest, namely the safety of air passengers, could not be described as an economic activity. The collection of route

[94] Case C-387/93, *Giorgio Domingo Banchero* [1995] ECR I-4663.

[95] Joined Cases 266/87 and 267/87, *The Queen v Royal Pharmaceutical Society of Great Britain, ex parte Association of Pharmaceutical Importers and others* [1989] ECR 1295, para. 16.

[96] Case C-309/99, *JCJ Wouters, JW Savelbergh and Price Waterhouse Belastingadviseurs BV v Algemene Raad van de Nederlandse Orde van Advocaten, intervener: Raad van de Balies van de Europese Gemeenschap* [2002] ECR I-1577.

[97] Case C-364/92, *SAT Fluggesellschaft mbH v Eurocontrol* [1994] ECR I-43.

charges could not be separated from the organisation's other activities, which taken as a whole, resembled the exercise of public authority more than economic activities. Consequently, the organisation could not be considered an undertaking to which Articles 81 and 82 EC could apply.

Similarly, a company established to perform services to prevent and remove pollution in the Port of Genoa which acted on behalf of the port operator was held not to be an undertaking in *Diego Cali*.[98] Despite the fact that the company charged for its services, the Court held that its anti-pollution and cleaning up facilities involved the performance of a task in the public interest which formed part of marine environment protection, a central function of the State.

However, in contrast to these two rulings, an ambulance service which provided both emergency transport and also routine patient transport for which payment was made was considered an undertaking in *Ambulanz Glöckner*.[99] The Court of Justice held that the provision of emergency services was an economic activity since the services provided by Ambulanz Glöckner did not necessarily need to be carried out by public authorities, but could be offered on the market. The fact that payments were received from the public authority and from insurers was immaterial.

Insurance and social security funds. The area that has given rise to most litigation concerning the definition of an undertaking is when the State can be said to be acting in accordance with principles of "solidarity" rather than engaged in an economic activity, i.e., not-for-profit mutual insurance funds. Solidarity entails, for example, the redistribution of income between those who are better off and those who, in view of their resources and state of health, would be deprived of the necessary social cover. In other words, higher contributors to the fund receive the same basic entitlement as lower contributors. In principle, activities based on the principle of solidarity are excluded from the definition of an undertaking under EC competition law.[100] In practice, however, identifying exempt activities is not straightforward.

a. Situations in which healthcare and insurance activities are not "economic." In *AOK Bundesverband*,[101] the Court of Justice confirmed its consistent line of case law to the effect that organisations involved in public social security systems are not public undertakings where they are engaged in an economic activity governed by the principle

---

[98] Case C-343/95, *Diego Calí & Figli Srl v Servizi ecologici porto di Genova SpA (SEPG)* [1997] ECR I-1547.

[99] Case C-475/99, *Firma Ambulanz Glöckner v Landkreis Südwestpfalz* [2001] ECR I-8089 (hereinafter "*Ambulanz Glöckner*").

[100] See Case 238/82, *Duphar BV and others v The Netherlands* [1984] ECR 523, para. 16 ("[I]t is not possible...to equate the competent authority of a Member State which, within the framework of a health care insurance scheme financed by contributions from the insured persons and by financing from the public authorities, draws up rules governing and limiting reimbursement of the costs of health care, with an economic operator who in each case freely chooses the goods which he acquires on the market.").

[101] Joined Cases C-264/01, C-306/01, C-354/01 and C-355/01, *AOK Bundesverband and others v Ichthyol-Gesellschaft Cordes and others* [2004] ECR I-2493 (hereinafter "*AOK Bundesverband*").

of solidarity.[102] It held that the regional associations of German sickness funds were not undertakings engaged in an economic activity. Several pharmaceutical companies challenged the maximum prices for certain products under EC competition law. The Court held that "sickness funds in the German statutory health insurance scheme...are involved in the management of the social security system and fulfil an exclusively social function which is founded on the principle of national solidarity and is entirely non-profit making."[103] Their management was therefore not subject to Article 82 EC.

Likewise, in *FENIN*, the Court of First Instance upheld the Commission's decision that the public body responsible for the management of the Spanish national health system (SNS) was not an undertaking for the purposes of Article 82 EC as it was governed by the principle of solidarity: [104]

> "[A]n organisation which purchases goods—even in great quantity—not for the purpose of offering goods and services as part of an economic activity, but in order to use them in the

[102] In *Poucet*, the Court of Justice pointed to the principle of solidarity to hold that the French organisations involved in the public social security system were not public undertakings engaged in an economic activity: "Sickness funds, and the organisations involved in the management of the public social security system, fulfill an exclusively social function. That activity is based on the principle of national solidarity and is entirely non-profit making. The benefits paid are statutory benefits bearing no relation to the amount of the contributions." See Joined Cases C-159/91 and C-160/91, *Christian Poucet v Assurances Générales de France and Caisse Mutuelle Régionale du Languedoc-Roussillon* [1993] ECR I-637, para. 18. The Court noted that the principle of solidarity was reflected by the fact that the scheme was financed by contributions proportional to the income, or pensions, of the contributor, whereas the benefits were identical for all those who received them. In contrast, in *Fédération Française des Sociétés d'Assurance* the benefits were based on the financial results of the fund's investments and were proportionate to the contributions paid. The manager of the scheme was thus carrying on an economic activity in competition with the life insurance companies. See Case C-244/94, *Fédération Française des Sociétés d'Assurance, Société Paternelle-Vie, Union des Assurances de Paris-Vie and Caisse d'Assurance et de Prévoyance Mutuelle des Agriculteurs v Ministère de l'Agriculture et de la Pêche* [1995] ECR I-4013. Likewise, in *Cisal* the fact that the amount of benefits and contributions was, in the last resort, fixed by the State led the Court of Justice to hold that a body entrusted by law with a scheme providing insurance against accidents at work and occupational diseases (such as the Italian National Institute for Insurance against Accidents at Work) was not an undertaking for the purpose of EC competition law. See Case C-218/00, *Cisal di Battistello Venanzio & C. Sas v Istituto nazionale per l'assicurazione contro gli infortuni sul lavoro (INAIL)* [2002] ECR I-691, para. 22.

[103] *Ibid.*, para. 51. The Court also noted that the sickness funds must by law offer each member essentially identical obligatory benefits regardless of each member's contributions. Concerning the element of competition between sickness funds relating to the amount of the required contributions, the Court held that this was introduced to encourage the sickness funds to operate in accordance with the principles of sound management in the most effective and least costly manner possible, in the interest of the proper functioning of the German social security system. Further, only the precise level of the fixed maximum amounts was not dictated by legislation, but decided by fund associations having regard to the criteria laid down by the legislature. The Court concluded that the latitude available to the sickness funds when setting the contribution rate and their freedom to engage in some competition with one another in order to attract members was insufficient to classify the activity as economic. Finally, the Court held that the equalisation mechanism—which included financial compensation between the funds whose health expenditure was lowest and those whose expenditure was highest—negated any notional competition that existed between the funds.

[104] Case T-319/99, *Federación Nacional de Empresas de Instrumentación Científica, Médica, Técnica y Dental (FENIN) v Commission* [2003] ECR II-357, para. 37 (hereinafter "*FENIN*").

> context of a different activity, such as one of a purely social nature, does not act as an undertaking simply because it is a purchaser in a given market. Whilst an entity may wield very considerable economic power, even giving rise to a monopoly, it nevertheless remains the case that, if the activity for which that entity purchases goods is not an economic activity, it is not acting as an undertaking for the purposes of Community competition law and is therefore not subject to the prohibitions laid down in Articles 81(1) EC and 82 EC."[105]

In light of the Community Courts' precedents, it seems that EC competition rules are unlikely to apply where: (1) the entities are engaged in an activity which forms part of a social security scheme, such as a pension or sickness insurance scheme; (2) the benefits conferred on individuals by the entities are compelled by law; (3) the level of benefits granted is not proportionate to or dependent upon the amount of the contribution paid; (4) the principle of solidarity is ensured by a mechanism under which there is an equalisation of costs between those entities with a higher expenditure and those with a lower expenditure; and (5) an economic activity is a prerequisite for another activity that is not economic in nature, for example where a purchasing activity does not lead to the purchased goods being used for an economic activity downstream.

b. Situations in which healthcare and insurance activities may be considered "economic." It may be possible in certain cases that the activities of a public undertaking, while primarily based on the principle of solidarity, also include elements of economic activity. For example, in a number of Member States, public hospitals offer medical services to private individuals for commercial payment. If these activities fall outside the scope of their public service obligation and were non-trivial in nature, it may be possible to argue that the public authority acts as an undertaking for purposes of competition law. The Community institutions will therefore weigh the solidarity principle against other factors to determine whether the entity is an undertaking carrying on an economic activity.

The *Albany* case involved a supplementary pension fund based on a system of compulsory affiliation that applied a solidarity mechanism to determine the amount of contributions due and benefits received. The Court of Justice concluded that the fund was engaged in an economic activity in competition with insurance companies, noting that the fund itself determined the amount of the contributions and benefits and operated in accordance with the principle of capitalisation, i.e., the amount of benefits was calculated on the basis of the amount of contribution.[106] Moreover, the amount of the

---

[105] *FENIN, ibid.*, is on appeal to the Court of Justice on the basis that each activity carried out by the organisation must be considered separately in order to determine whether it should be classified as an economic activity. Accordingly, it is claimed that the Court of First Instance should have considered SNS's provision of health care separately from its members' requirement to have insurance. While the compulsory insurance requirement may be governed by the principle of solidarity, the provision of health services is not subject to the solidarity exemption if competition exists amongst different health service providers and those insured remain free to choose who will treat them. The Court of Justice is yet to deliver its judgment on the issue. However, Advocate General Maduro concluded that the applicant is correct in its claim that the provision of health care by SNS must be considered separately from the compulsory requirement of membership. Whether the Court will follow the Advocate General's advice remains to be seen. Even if the relevant activities are to be considered separately, it is still possible that both would be governed by the principle of solidarity.

[106] Case C-67/96, *Albany International BV v Stichting Bedrijfspensioenfonds Textielindustrie* [1999] ECR I-5751 (hereinafter "*Albany*").

benefits provided by the fund depended on the financial results of its investments, in respect of which it was subject to supervision by the Insurance Board. Thus, the Court held that neither the fact that the fund was non-profit-making nor the fact that it pursued a social objective was sufficient to deprive it of the status of an undertaking within the meaning of EC competition law.

1.3.1.3 Sporting and cultural activities

Each activity to be looked at on its merits. Activities of general public interest are not limited to public authority, public safety, and health services. Sporting and cultural activities may also fall outside the ambit of economic activities and, therefore, escape the application of EC competition law. Although there have not been any cases directly related to cultural activities to date, the treatment of professional sport as an economic activity for the purposes of establishing an undertaking subject to EC competition law has been specifically addressed by the Community Courts.

Meca-Medina concerned two long-distance swimmers who had been disqualified by the Court of Arbitration for Sports after having tested positive for a banned substance.[107] The Court of First Instance made clear that sport is subject to competition law only to the extent that it constitutes an economic activity. Rules which relate to the nature and context of a sporting event, particularly rules which regulate the proper conduct of sports competitions, are not subject to competition law unless such rules have economic repercussions for the individuals subject to them. The anti-doping rules in question were considered sporting rules with purely social rather than economic objectives, and were not therefore subject to competition law.

In contrast, in *Laurent Piau*, FIFA, the international football association, was considered an undertaking for the purposes of Article 82 EC.[108] Since FIFA is an emanation of various football associations, of which the football clubs are undertakings, FIFA was considered an undertaking for the purposes of EC competition law. Moreover, football players' agents who initiate and manage player transfer contracts in exchange for a fee were also considered to be involved in an economic activity for purposes of EC competition law.

Increased professionalism in a number of different sports is bound to bring more sporting issues within the ambit of EC competition law. Though the rules are not fully developed, it is clear that the activities in which a body or organisation is involved will be considered individually and not merely on the basis that they generally concern activities that are typically non-economic in character. The fact that an entity may be involved in other non-economic activities, whether sporting, cultural or otherwise in the public interest, does not preclude the economic activities in which it is involved from the application of EC competition law. Each case will turn on whether the particular activity is economic or non-economic.

107 Case T-313/02, *David Meca-Medina and Igor Majcen v Commission* [2004] ECR II-30.
108 Case T-193/02, *Laurent Piau v Commission* [2005] ECR II-nyr.

1.3.2 State Action Defence

Basic definition. Anticompetitive State measures may occur by two principal methods: (1) direct restrictions of competition through legislative or regulatory measures; or (2) situations in which the State indirectly restricts competition by requiring that private undertakings act in an anticompetitive manner. EC competition law places a number of restrictions on State action falling into the former category. These are discussed in Section 1.4. However, the second category is also important, since an undertaking that can demonstrate the requisite degree of State involvement in its actions can avoid the application of Article 82 EC.[109] This is based on the notion that the State may not only restrict competition directly, but may also leave the actual restriction of competition to the economic operators in the market. In this situation, the undertaking escapes liability under EC competition law (but the State does not).

Examples of the State action defence. According to the case law of the Community Courts, undertakings cannot be found to infringe Article 82 EC if: (a) the persons engaging in the restrictive conduct are acting in the public interest; or (b) the undertakings concerned were compelled to participate by a State measure; or (c) State regulation eliminated the possibility of competitive activity. Undertakings participating in a State-implemented scheme that restricts competition can raise any of these points as a *defence* for their participation. These defences are available irrespective of whether or not the prior State measure appears to be legal, i.e., the defendant is *not* required, as a condition of this defence, to challenge the validity of the measure in question.[110] However, once the measure has been declared contrary to EC competition and/or national law, any immunity ceases with immediate effect.[111]

a. State nominated bodies. Anticompetitive conduct may be carried out pursuant to decisions by a State nominated body, such as a committee of experts. It may be the case that the undertakings who benefit from the anticompetitive conduct were also responsible for the appointment of the members of the body. These undertakings will only escape liability under Article 82 EC if the members of the body can establish that they are representatives of the public interest, and not of the undertakings who benefited

---

[109] See Case 311/85, *ASBL Vereniging van Vlaamse Reisbureaus v ASBL Sociale Dienst van de Plaatselijke en Gewestelijke Overheidsdiensten* [1987] ECR 3801, para. 10; Case 267/86, *Pascal Van Eycke v ASPA NV* [1988] ECR 4769, para. 16; Case C-18/88, *Régie des télégraphes et des téléphones v GB-Inno-BM SA* [1991] ECR I-5941, para. 20; Case C-2/91, *Wolf W. Meng* [1993] ECR I-5751, para. 14; Case C-185/91, *Bundesanstalt für den Güterfernverkehr v Gebrüder Reiff GmbH & Co KG* [1993] ECR I-5801, para. 14; Case C-320/91, *Paul Corbeau* [1993] ECR I-2533, para. 10; Case C-153/93, *Bundesrepublik Deutschland (Germany) v Delta Schiffahrts- und Speditionsgesellschaft mbH* [1994] ECR I-2517, para. 14; Case C-96/94, *Centro Servizi Spediporto Srl v Spedizioni Marittima del Golfo Srl* [1995] ECR I-2883, para.20; Joined Cases C-140/94, C-141/94, and C-142/94, *DIP SpA v Comune di Bassano del Grappa, LIDL Italia Srl v Comune di Chioggia and Lingral Srl v Comune di Chiogga* [1995] ECR I-3257, para. 14.

[110] Joined Cases C-359/95 P and C-379/97 P, *Commission v Ladbroke Racing Ltd* [1997] ECR I-6265, paras. 31–33. See also Case T-228/97, *Irish Sugar plc v Commission* [1999] ECR II-2969, para. 130; and Case T-513/93, *Consiglio Nazionale degli Spedizionieri Doganali v Commission* [2000] ECR II-1807, para. 58.

[111] Case C-198/01, *Consorzio Industrie Fiammiferi (CIF) v Autorità Garante della Concorrenza e del Mercato* [2003] ECR I-8055.

from the abusive conduct complained of (even though the undertakings were responsible for their appointment to the body).

To avail of this defence, it must thus be established that: (1) the members are not bound by orders or instructions from the undertakings concerned; (2) the members are required by national legislation to take into account the general public interest and are thus prevented from acting in the exclusive interests of individual undertakings or a particular industry sector; and (3) public authorities verify that the decisions taken by the body in question correspond to the public interest and if necessary, substitute their decision for that of the organisation. If these conditions are satisfied, the members of the organisation in question are considered as independent experts and decisions taken by them are treated as public acts that do not fall under Article 82 EC.[112] If the above conditions are not met, the undertakings responsible for the members' appointment will be held liable for their actions under Article 82 EC (assuming abusive conduct is made out).[113] The legal nature of the organisation or its classification under national law does not influence such a finding.[114]

b. ***State compulsion.*** Article 82 EC applies only to conduct that undertakings adopt autonomously. Undertakings cannot be held responsible for anticompetitive conduct that is required by the State.[115] State compulsion may result either from State legislation or from "the exercise of irresistible pressure"[116] by State authorities, such as the threat to adopt State measures that would cause substantial losses for the undertakings concerned. On the other hand, the mere encouragement, approval or authorisation of anticompetitive conduct by State authorities is not sufficient to exempt undertakings from liability under Article 82 EC.[117]

---

[112] Case C-185/91, *Bundesanstalt für den Güterfernverkehr v Gebrüder Reiff GmbH & Co KG.* [1993] ECR I-5801, paras. 19 and 24; Case C-153/93, *Bundesrepublik Deutschland (Germany) v Delta Schiffahrts- und Speditionsgesellschaft mbH* [1994] ECR I-2517, paras. 17–18; and Joined Cases C-140/94, C-141/94, and C-142/94, *DIP SpA v Comune di Bassano del Grappa, LIDL Italia Srl v Comune di Chioggia and Lingral Srl v Comune di Chiogga* [1995] ECR I-3257, para. 18.

[113] Case T-513/93, *Consiglio Nazionale degli Spedizionieri Doganali v Commission* [2000] ECR II-1807, paras. 54–56; Case C-35/96, *Commission v Italy (Customs agents)* [1998] ECR I-3851, paras. 41–45.

[114] Case 123/83, *Bureau national interprofessionnel du cognac v Guy Clair* [1985] ECR 391, para. 17; *Commission v Italy (Customs agents)*, *ibid.*, para. 40.

[115] Case T-513/93, *Consiglio Nazionale degli Spedizionieri Doganali v Commission* [2000] ECR II-1807, para. 58; Case T-387/94, *Asia Motor France SA and others v Commission* [1996] ECR II-961, para. 61; Joined Cases C-359/95 P and C-379/97 P, *Commission v Ladbroke Racing Ltd* [1997] ECR I-6265, para. 33; Case T-228/97, *Irish Sugar plc v Commission* [1999] ECR II-2969, para. 130. This applies also where compulsion is exercised by a non-Member State. See *Franco-Japanese Ballbearings,* IIIrd Report on Competition Policy (1974), para. 20.

[116] Case T-387/94, *Asia Motor France SA and others v Commission* [1996] ECR II-961, para. 65.

[117] Case 13/77, *SA GB-Inno-BM v Association des détaillants en tabac (ATAB)* [1977] ECR 2115, para. 34; Joined Cases 43/82 and 63/82, *Vereniging ter Bevordering van het Vlaamse Boekwezen, VBVB, and Vereniging ter Bevordering van de Belangen des Boekhandels, VBBB, v Commission* [1984] ECR 19, para. 40; Case T-151/89, *Société de Treillis et Panneaux Soudés v Commission* [1995] ECR II-1191, para. 99; Case T-37/92, *Bureau Européen des Unions des Consommateurs and National Consumer Council v Commission* [1994] ECR II-285, para. 69; Case T-387/94, *Asia Motor France SA and others v Commission* [1996] ECR II-961, para. 71; *Franco-Japanese Ballbearings*, IIIrd Report on Competition Policy (1974); *Aluminium imports from eastern Europe*, OJ 1985 L 92/1, para. 10;

The possibility to invoke State compulsion as a defence for anticompetitive conduct is construed narrowly. An undertaking relying on this defence has to demonstrate on the facts that it "was deprived of all independent choice in its commercial policy."[118] It must show that the State eliminated "any margin of autonomy" on the part of the undertaking.[119] Even if undertakings are forced by the State to coordinate their conduct, Article 82 EC may apply if the undertakings enjoy a margin of discretion with regard to their conduct. In such a case the undertakings must adopt the solution that restricts competition in the least possible way in order to comply with Article 82 EC.[120]

c. ***Regulatory elimination of competition.*** Where State regulation eliminates any possibility of competitive activity, Article 82 EC does not apply since the conduct of undertakings cannot affect the competitive structure of the market.[121] Whether State regulation eliminates the possibility of competitive activity depends on a detailed analysis of the facts of the case and will only be assumed under exceptional circumstances. State regulation must reduce competition to such an extent that the remaining scope for competition loses all significance.[122] The fact that State regulation limits the scope of competition or renders competition more difficult is not sufficient to exclude an application of Article 82 EC. In such circumstances Article 82 EC requires undertakings to respect the scope of competition left by State regulation.[123] The Commission considers it all the more important where State measures limit the scope of competition to avoid any added restrictive effects by private action.[124]

Question left open in Case 260/82, *Nederlandse Sigarenwinkeliers Organisatie v Commission* [1985] ECR 3801, para. 30.

[118] Case T-228/97, *Irish Sugar plc v Commission* [1999] ECR II-2969, para. 129.

[119] Case T-387/94, *Asia Motor France SA and others v Commission* [1996] ECR II-961, para. 63.

[120] See Case T-513/93, *Consiglio Nazionale degli Spedizionieri Doganali v Commission* [2000] ECR II-1807, paras. 71–73. The Italian association of custom agents was required by national legislation to adopt a tariff for the services of custom agents. However, the legislation did not impose certain price levels. Because the association enjoyed a margin of discretion in this regard the Court of Justice held that the association infringed EC competition law by adopting a minimum price that exceeded the prices then in force by 400%.

[121] Joined Cases 40 to 48, 50, 54 to 56, 111, 113 and 114-73, *Coöperatieve Vereniging "Suiker Unie" UA and others v Commission* [1975] ECR 1663, paras. 67–72; Case T-513/93, *Consiglio Nazionale degli Spedizionieri Doganali v Commission* [2000] ECR II-1807, para. 58; *Asia Motor*, above, para. 61; Joined Cases C-359/95 P and C-379/97 P, *Commission v Ladbroke Racing Ltd* [1997] ECR I-6265, para. 33; *Irish Sugar*, above, para. 130.

[122] The only case where the defence has been successful so far is *Suiker Unie*, *ibid.* The Court of Justice held in this case that the regulation of the Italian sugar market had fundamentally restricted competition such that the conduct of undertakings could not appreciably affect competition (paras. 67–72). The Court also observed that without the Italian regulation the conduct of the undertakings would have been different from that which effectively took place (para. 65). However, it does not appear that this can be invoked as an independent defence without showing that State regulation eliminated the possibility of competitive activity.

[123] Joined Cases 209 to 215 and 218/78, *Heintz van Landewyck SARL and others v Commission* [1980] ECR 3125, paras. 131–32; Joined Cases 240, 241, 242, 261, 262, 268 and 269/82, *Stichting Sigarettenindustrie and others v Commission* [1985] ECR 3831, para. 29; Case T-513/93, *Consiglio Nazionale degli Spedizionieri Doganali v Commission* [2000] ECR II-1807, para.72.

[124] See Joined Cases 209/78 et al., *Heintz van Landewyck SARL and others v Commission* [1980] ECR 3125, para.124; *Stichting Certificatie Kraanverhuurbedrijf and the Federatie van Nederlandse Kraanverhuurbedrijven*, OJ 1994 L 117/30, para. 239.

The scope of the State regulatory action defence under Article 82 EC has been raised squarely in the *Deutsche Telekom* case.[125] The case concerned the prices Deutsche Telekom (DT) charged its competitors for unbundled access to local loops in Germany. The Commission received complaints from competitors of DT, who claimed that these prices were incompatible with Article 82 EC. In its defence, DT argued that its local access tariffs had been approved by the national regulatory authority (NRA), the RegTP. DT contended that if there was any infringement of Community law, the Commission should not be acting against an undertaking whose charges were regulated, but against Germany under Article 226 EC.[126] The Commission, however, rejected that argument on the ground that "competition rules may apply where the sector-specific legislation does not preclude the undertakings it governs from engaging in autonomous conduct that prevents, restricts or distorts competition."[127] The Commission considered that, despite the intervention of the RegTP, DT retained a commercial discretion, which would have allowed it to restructure its tariffs further so as to reduce or put an end to the margin squeeze.[128] The Commission therefore considered the margin squeeze constituted the imposition of unfair selling prices within the meaning of Article 82(a) and imposed a fine of €12.6 million on DT.

The Commission's decision—which is strongly disputed on appeal on this issue—suggests that, even when a NRA has adopted a decision on the basis of sector-specific regulation, the Commission (or a NCA) remains entitled to intervene when the outcome of this decision fails to prevent competition-law violations from occurring. This approach has very significant consequences for dominant operators since it implies that, when a NRA adopts rules that fail to sufficiently protect the conditions of competition, a dominant operator could also itself be held responsible for violating competition rules if it nonetheless had the commercial freedom to adapt its tariff structure in such a way as to prevent a violation from occurring. Thus, incumbents would have to ensure that, to the extent possible, their pricing schemes are compatible with competition rules even in circumstances where they have been expressly approved by the competent regulator.

Whether regulatory action will be a defence will obviously vary from case to case, but a number of general remarks can be made. First, the scope for residual application of competition law in circumstances where there is also regulation of course depends on the level of detail of the regulatory regime. The more prescriptive and detailed the regulatory framework, the less likely that competition law has any residual role. One useful contrast is between *Deutsche Telekom*—where the Commission applied Article 82 EC notwithstanding the existence of regulation—and *Trinko*—where the United States Supreme Court refused to apply Section 2 of the Sherman Act in circumstances where a regulatory framework also existed.[129] An important factor in this regard was that the US regulatory regime applicable to telecommunications—the 1996

[125] *Deutsche Telekom AG*, OJ 2003 L 263/9 (hereinafter "*Deutsche Telekom*"), currently on appeal in Case T-271/03, *Deutsch Telekom AG v Commission*, OJ 2003 C 264/29. See also *France Télécom/SFR Cegetel/Bouygues Télécom*, Conseil de la Concurrence, Décision No. 04-D48 of October 14, 2004, where the same principles were applied in rejecting the defence.

[126] *Deutsche Telekom, ibid.*, para. 53.

[127] *Ibid.*, para. 54.

[128] *Ibid.*, para. 57.

[129] See *Verizon Communications Inc v Law Offices of Curtis V. Trinko LLP*, 540 US 398 (2004).

Telecommunications Act and its numerous implementing orders—is more extensive than the EC regulatory framework on electronic communications. The 1996 Act is a 600-page piece of legislation, which regulates in enormous detail the various aspects of the US telecommunications industry. By contrast, the new EC regulatory framework on electronic communications is composed of a small number of directives imposing a limited number of obligations on operators holding significant market power.[130]

Second, when there is a sector-specific remedy that protects a competitive market structure in a given industry, and which has been correctly enforced by a national regulator and that does not violate EC competition rules (i.e., there is an "effective" regulatory remedy), a competition authority should not intervene. Sector-specific regulators will be generally better placed than the Commission to address the relevant issues, such as the pricing of wholesale inputs or retail products, etc. These issues require technical expertise, as well as a range of information, that the Commission does not generally possess.[131] Moreover, pricing decisions require constant monitoring (e.g., as costs evolve), which is not compatible with competition authorities' publicly-stated reluctance to act as price control agencies.[132] Further, having two sets of rules and two distinct authorities determining a similar issue raises the risk of contradictory decisions or the imposition of inconsistent remedies.[133]

Finally, when there is a sector-specific regime designed to protect a competitive market structure, but that regime has not been applied by the regulator (i.e., the presence of a "lazy" and/or "captured" regulator), competition authorities should be free to launch proceedings on the basis of Article 82 EC. The Commission should also be entitled to act when the decision adopted by the NRA is not compatible with EC competition law.[134] In this scenario, however, as the Commission has done in the majority of cases in the telecommunications sector to date, the case should be transferred to the NRA to allow it to take a decision on the basis of the sector-specific legislation.[135] But such a transfer should only take place when the Commission is confident that the matter will be sufficiently addressed by the NRA(s) on the basis of sector-specific rules. This was, apparently, not the case in *Deutsche Telekom*.

[130] See A de Streel, "The Integration of Competition Law Principles in the New European Regulatory Framework for Electronic Communications" (2003) 26 *World Competition* 489; D Geradin and JG Sidak, "European and American Approaches to Antitrust Remedies and the Institutional Design of Regulation in Telecommunications" in M Cave, S Majumdar, and I Vogelsang (eds.), *Handbook of Telecommunications Economics, Vol. 2* (Amsterdam, Elsevier, 2005).

[131] See Organisation for Economic Co-operation and Development, "Relationship Between Regulators and Competition Authorities" DAFFE/CLP(99)8, Ch. 8.

[132] See, e.g., Xth Report on Competition Policy (1975) point 76.

[133] See N Petit, "The Proliferation of National Regulatory Authorities Alongside Competition Authorities: A Source of Jurisdictional Confusion" 02/04 *Global Competition Law Centre Working Paper Series* (Bruges, College of Europe).

[134] In such case, the Commission could not only start proceedings against the incumbent as it did in *Deutsche Telekom*, but it could also launch proceedings against the NRAs themselves on the basis of Article 10 EC. See section 1.4 below.

[135] See, e.g., the approach taken by the Commission with regard to the pricing of leased lines and mobile termination charges. See Commission Press Release IP/02/1852 of December 11, 2002. See also Commission Press Release IP/98/707 of July 27, 1998.

1.3.3 Parent Liability For A Subsidiary's Actions Under Article 82 EC

The single economic unit doctrine. Entities that form part of a "single economic unit" cannot be found liable for violating Article 81 EC, e.g., restrictive agreements between a parent and a wholly-owned subsidiary.[136] The rationale is that there is no meaningful scope for competition between a parent and a wholly-owned subsidiary, since the parent could always achieve the same result as the agreement by exercising its prerogatives as shareholder. By the same token, however, companies that belong to the same economic entity constitute a single "undertaking" for purposes of application of Article 82 EC.[137] This is presumably based on the fact that an undertaking should not be able to circumvent the obligations arising from Article 82 EC by means of internal re-structuring, e.g., by splitting its business between different subsidiaries in order to reduce the market share held by each separate legal entity. If not, an undertaking could in theory arrange for several of its subsidiaries to carry out aspects of the infringing conduct, and, once all rivals had been foreclosed, recombine the businesses of its separate subsidiaries, without intervention under Article 82 EC.

Two entities are likely to form part of a single economic unit if one or more of the following conditions are met: (1) the subsidiary is wholly owned by the parent;[138] (2) the parent has a majority of voting rights, the right to appoint a majority of board members, and/or the right to appoint or otherwise control management;[139] (3) the parent issues very precise directions to the subsidiary;[140] (4) the parent has the right to approve all decisions within an area essential to the subsidiary's operations;[141] (5) the parent and subsidiary share a common marketing strategy[142] or sales team;[143] (6) the two companies cooperate on a relatively permanent basis in other ways, such as the exchange of information, innovation, patents, and know-how;[144] (7) the parent and the subsidiary themselves consider that the subsidiary is not an autonomous entity;[145] and/or (8) the parent actually exercises its rights to control the subsidiary.[146]

Circumstances in which a parent may be responsible for subsidiary conduct. Perhaps surprisingly, the legal position on parent-subsidiary liability under EC competition law is unclear, and the case law somewhat confused. Broadly speaking,

---

[136] See, e.g., Case C-73/95 P, *Viho Europe BV v Commission* [1996] ECR I-5457.

[137] See, e.g., *Chiquita,* OJ 1976 L 95/1, para. 1, confirmed by the Court in Case 27/76, *United Brands Company and United Brands Continentaal BV v Commission* [1978] ECR 207, ("United Brands Company...and its other subsidiary companies, which are under its control and do not possess any real autonomy, form a single economic unit and therefore constitute an undertaking within the meaning of Article 8[2]."). See also *ECS/AKZO*, OJ 1985 L 374/1, para. 90.

[138] See Case 107/82, *Allgemeine Elektrizitäts-Gesellschaft AEG-Telefunken AG v Commission* [1983] ECR 3151, para. 50.

[139] See *Gosme/Martell-DMP*, OJ 1991 L 185/23; *Eirpage*, OJ 1991 L 306/22, para. 9.

[140] See *Kodak,* OJ 1970 L 147/24. See also Case 48/69, *Imperial Chemical Industries Ltd v Commission (Dyestuffs)* [1972] ECR 619, para. 133.

[141] See *Distribution of Package Tours During the 1990 World Cup*, OJ 1992 L 326/31.

[142] See Case 30/87, *Corinne Bodson v SA Pompes Funèbres des regions libérées* [1988] ECR 2479, para. 20.

[143] See Case C-73/95 P, *Viho Europe BV v Commission* [1996] ECR I-5457, para. 17.

[144] See *Christiani & Nielsen,* OJ 1969 L 165/12.

[145] See *Gosme/Martell-DMP*, OJ 1991 L 185/23, para. 30.

[146] See Case 48/69, *Imperial Chemical Industries Ltd v Commission* [1972] ECR 619, paras. 130–35.

two strands of thought seem to permeate the case law and legal doctrine. The first and, at least within the Commission, preponderant view insists that sole control over a subsidiary confers strict liability for the conduct of that subsidiary.[147] The basis for this view is the notion that Articles 81 and 82 EC are addressed to "undertakings" (an economic concept that transcends legal entities) and that the overall structure and consistency of EC competition law dictates that the concept of an "undertaking" must coincide with the notion of "sole control" under the EC Merger Regulation (which focuses on the "ability" to exercise decisive influence, rather than the actual exercise of such influence). Accordingly, whenever a single parent company has the ability to exercise decisive influence over the strategic commercial behaviour of another legal entity, they form a single undertaking (or "single economic unit").

The second view is that the mere ability to exercise decisive influence over a subsidiary is not, in itself, sufficient to impute liability for competition law infringements to the parent. According to this view, 100% ownership of a subsidiary should at most give rise to a rebuttable presumption that the parent could and/or did in fact exercise decisive influence over its subsidiary's conduct, as a basis for establishing the parent's own liability. This view seems rooted in more traditional civil/corporate law notions that require some form of "culpability" on the part of the parent company before it can be held liable for its subsidiary's conduct. In its purest form, this view would hold that a parent should escape liability for its 100% owned subsidiary's conduct if it demonstrates either that: (1) it does not have the ability to exercise decisive influence over the subsidiary; or (2) while it has the ability to exercise decisive influence, it did not (a) actively direct the subsidiary's infringing conduct, (b) know of the subsidiary's infringing conduct, and (c) act negligently in its oversight duties, i.e., it could not have been expected to have known and prevented the conduct.

The Community Courts have adopted a case-by-case—and at times apparently inconsistent—approach. From the most recent pronouncement of the Court of Justice on this issue—the *Stora* judgment—it would seem that it has adopted somewhat of a "middle ground" between the two views outlined above. The Court's starting position in *Stora* is that "the fact that a subsidiary has separate legal personality is not sufficient to exclude the possibility of its conduct being imputed to the parent company, especially where the subsidiary does not independently decide its own conduct on the market, but carries out, in all material respects, the instructions given to it by the parent company."[148]

---

[147] According to this view, 100% ownership of a subsidiary creates a presumption that the parent has sole control, in the sense that full ownership normally allows it to exercise decisive influence over the strategic commercial behaviour of the subsidiary. This presumption can be rebutted only by showing that, despite 100% ownership, the parent company does not have sole control—for example, where the parent had temporarily assigned or otherwise ceded certain key rights over the subsidiary to a third party (e.g., under a management contract). It is irrelevant, under this view, whether the parent effectively exercised decisive influence over the subsidiary's commercial behaviour and/or the infringing conduct. All that is relevant is that it had the ability to do so. See generally W Wils, "The Undertaking as Subject of EC Competition Law and the Imputation of Infringements to Natural or Legal Persons" (2000) 25(2) *European Law Review* 99.

[148] See C-286/98 P, *Stora Kopparbergs Bergslags AB v Commission* [2000] ECR I-9925.

The Court of Justice's current position appears to be that the Commission must prove that the parent company not only has the ability to exercise decisive influence, but also in fact exercised decisive influence over its subsidiary's conduct. In the case of a wholly-owned subsidiary, that burden will be easily met if the Commission can point to additional *indicia*, such as the fact that the parent company presented itself during the administrative procedure as the Commission's sole interlocutor concerning the infringement.[149] It would then be for the defendant to reverse the presumption on the basis that it did not in fact exercise decisive influence.

What is not clear from the Court's case law is whether, in order to rebut the presumption, the defendant must establish that it did not, as a general matter, exercise decisive influence over the subsidiary's (strategic) commercial conduct (in the sense of approving budgets, business plans, and major investments, or steering pricing policies) and that the subsidiary in fact enjoyed complete autonomy or whether it suffices to establish that the parent company did not exercise decisive influence over the *infringing conduct*. The first interpretation would approach the "strict liability" view outlined above, and would make it exceedingly difficult for a parent to avoid liability for a wholly-owned subsidiary. The second interpretation would approach the "own culpability" view outlined above, and allow the parent company to argue that it did not direct, know of, or need to know of the infringing conduct. On balance, the better view is probably that the Community Courts would require a parent company to show that it did not have the ability to or, at least, did not in fact exercise decisive influence over the general commercial behaviour of the subsidiary over the reference period.

One matter to which the Community institutions attach importance in practice is whether the parent and subsidiary present themselves as sole, joint, or separate interlocutors at the administrative stage. If both the parent and subsidiary present themselves as separate interlocutors, leading to each of them receiving a separate statement of objections from the Commission and making separate responses, the conduct complained generally lacks the requisite unity of action to find the parent liable for the subsidiary's infringement.[150] For example, in *TKS/Thyssen*, the Commission sent separate statements of objections to the parent company (TKS) and the subsidiary (Thyssen) and both undertakings replied separately concerning the acts imputed to each of them. In these circumstances, the Community Courts confirmed that it was incumbent on the Commission to question and hear the views of TKS concerning Thyssen's actions before deeming it responsible for the latter and fining TKS for an

[149] The Advocate-General stated that "a mere 100% shareholding does not in itself suffice as a ground for the parent company's liability" (*ibid.*, para. 40) and that, as a second stage, it should be assessed whether the parent actually exercised decisive influence (*ibid.*, para. 41). However, he suggested that, in the case of a wholly-owned subsidiary, the Commission's burden is "eased" in that it must show "something more than the extent of the shareholding" but this "may be in the form of indicia" (*ibid.*, para. 48). The Court noted that the defendant had not disputed its ability to exercise control, had not put forward any evidence pointing to a lack of decisive control, and had not identified any autonomous behavior by its subsidiary (*ibid.*, para. 27). In that circumstance, "as that subsidiary was wholly owned, the Court of First Instance could legitimately assume…that the parent company in fact exercised decisive influence over its subsidiary's conduct," particularly since it had presented itself during the administrative procedure as the sole interlocutor on the infringement (*ibid.*, para. 29).

[150] See Joined Cases C-65/02 P and C-73/02 P, *Thyssen Krupp Stainless GmbH and Thyssen Krupp Acciai speciali Terni SpA v Commission* [2005] ECR I-nyr.

infringement attributed to Thyssen.[151] The Commission argued that these separate representations were merely formal in nature.[152] Nevertheless, the Court of Justice held that the exception to the principle that a natural or legal person can only be penalised for acts imputed to them individually must be interpreted strictly. TKS was not the economic successor of Thyssen; nor was there sufficient unity of action between them.[153] Accordingly, liability for Thyssen's conduct could not automatically be attributed to TKS.

1.4 RELATIONSHIP BETWEEN ARTICLE 82 EC AND OTHER LEGAL INSTRUMENTS

Overview. As part of the competition chapter of the EC Treaty, Article 82 EC raises a number of issues concerning its interaction with other provisions of EC competition law, as well as other legal instruments. A basic and preliminary point is that Article 82 EC must be interpreted in light of the general principles of EC law such as proportionality, equality, and the rule of law. The first main issue concerns the relationship between Articles 81 and 82 EC. It is well-established that both provisions can apply in parallel and that decisions under each provision should not seek to undermine their common aims. But it is not entirely clear where the boundary between Articles 81 and 82 lies. A second major area of interface between Article 82 EC and merger control laws and in particular whether there is continued scope for applying Article 82 EC to mergers and acquisitions. A third issue concerns the relationship between Article 82 EC and the other Treaty provisions that affect State measures which restrict competition. As noted above, EC competition law on State action is not limited to the State action defence: it also imposes a number of affirmative obligations not to restrict competition directly on the State. The final area of interaction between Article 82 EC and other instruments of EC competition law concerns the interface between principles of competition law and the objectives of regulation.

Article 82 EC also interacts with legal instruments other than those contained in EC competition law. Most notably, Member States remain competent under the Commission's modernisation reforms to apply their national abuse of dominance laws in parallel and to adopt stricter principles than would apply under Article 82 EC. Similarly, they remain competent to apply national laws that pursue predominantly different objectives to Article 82 EC, such as unfair competition laws. Finally, Article 82 EC is often applied in the context of arbitration and the interaction between this system of law and Article 82 EC raises a number of important practical issues.

1.4.1 Article 82 EC And General Principles of Community Law

General principles of Community law. Article 82 EC must be interpreted in light of the general principles of Community law. These principles have been developed through the case law of the Community Courts and include for example the guarantee of

[151] *Ibid.*, para. 86.
[152] *Ibid.*, para. 78.
[153] *Ibid.*, para. 88.

proportionality, subsidiarity, equality, legal certainty, and rights of defence in the application of EC competition law.[154] These principles have been applied in numerous EC competition cases. For example, in *France v Commission*, the Court of Justice held that even if the EC Merger Regulation contained no express power for third parties to be heard in the event that they would be considered as being in a collectively dominant position with the merging parties,[155] "observance of the right to be heard was nonetheless, in all proceedings liable to culminate in a measure adversely affecting a particular person, a fundamental principle of Community law which must be guaranteed even in the absence of any rules governing the procedure." Thus, general principles of law can imply superior substantive and procedural rules even where none are provided in primary or secondary Community legislation or case law.

Fundamental rights and EC competition law. By virtue of a series of judgments,[156] it is also "well settled that fundamental rights form an integral part of the general principles of law whose observance the Court ensures."[157] To this end, the Community Courts rely on the constitutions of Member States and the international treaties to which Member States are party, with specific reference to the European Convention of Human Rights (ECHR), as sources of interpretation. It is thus accepted that the protection of human rights is guaranteed in EC competition law. In *Huls* the applicant contested a Commission decision that it had infringed Article 81 EC on the basis that the Commission had breached its fundamental right to the presumption of innocence as guaranteed by Article 6(2) of the ECHR. Although the Court held that the presumption

---

[154] See generally T Tridimas, *The General Principles of EC Law* (Oxford, Oxford University Press, 2000); and K Lenaerts and P Van Nuffel, R Bray (eds.), *Constitutional Law of the European Union* (London, Sweet & Maxwell, 2005).

[155] Joined Cases C-68/94 and C-30/95, *France and Société commerciale des potasses et de l'azote (SCPA) and Entreprise minière et chimique (EMC) v Commission* [1998] ECR I-1375, para. 174.

[156] In the *Internationale Handelsgesellschaft* ruling in 1970 the Court of Justice held that fundamental rights formed part of the general principles of Community law that it was obliged to uphold, and that it should be guided by the constitutional traditions of the Member States in safeguarding those rights. See Case 11/70, *Internationale Handelsgesellschaft mbH v Einfuhr- und Vorratsstelle für Getreide und Futtermittel* [1970] ECR 1125. The *Nold* ruling reinforced *Internationale Handelsgesellschaft* and also referred specifically to international treaties (though not to the ECHR itself) which Member States had ratified as guidelines to be followed within the framework of Community law. No measure could have the force of law unless it was compatible with the fundamental rights recognised and protected by the Member States' constitutions. See Case 4/73, *J. Nold, Kohlen- und Baustoffgroßhandlung v Commission* [1974] ECR 491. In *Rutili*, the Court of Justice referred explicitly to the ECHR. See Case 36/75, *Roland Rutili v Ministre de l'intérieur* [1975] ECR 1219. In *Wachauf*, the Court of Justice ruled that its review powers extended to the acts of Member States, to the extent that they fell within areas of Community law. See Case 5/88, *Hubert Wachauf v Bundesamt für Ernährung und Forstwirtschaft* [1989] ECR 2609. The liability of Member States to apply fundamental rights was made clear in the *ERT* case, in which the Court of Justice ruled that States were obliged by Community law to respect fundamental rights when they implement it or when they rely on derogations from fundamental Treaty rules. See Case 22/70, *Commission v Council (European Agreement on Road Transport)* [1971] ECR 263.

[157] Opinion of the Court 2/94, *Accession by the Community to the European Convention for the Protection of Human Rights and Fundamental Freedoms* [1996] ECR I-1759.

of innocence had not been infringed, it stated that the principle is one of the fundamental rights that is protected under Community law.[158]

More recently, the application of Council Regulation 1/2003 on the implementation of the competition rules laid down in Articles 81 and 82 EC introduces two significant human rights issues.[159] The first concerns the strengthened powers of the Commission to investigate suspected competition law violations. The second relates to the enforcement of competition law by national competition authorities. These issues are touched upon in Section 1.5 in the context of the procedural reforms introduced under Regulation 1/2003.

1.4.2 The Relationship Between Article 82 EC And Article 81 EC

Basic principles. From the outset, the Court of Justice made clear that Articles 81 and 82 EC seek to achieve the same paramount aim: the maintenance of effective competition in the common market,[160] albeit by different means. The common objective of the two provisions also requires that there should be consistency between them. Several principles have therefore been confirmed by the Community institutions in order to ensure consistency between the two provisions and to preserve the integrity of each.[161] First, Articles 81 and 82 EC can apply in parallel to the same matter.[162] Second, while Article 81 EC is the main provision governing agreements, Article 82 EC can also apply to agreements, since many examples of abuse arising under that provision originate in contractual relations.[163] Third, the fact that conduct complies

[158] Case C-199/92 P, *Hüls AG v Commission* [1999] ECR I-4287, para 149. This principle "applies to the procedures relating to infringements of the competition rules applicable to undertakings that may result in the imposition of fines or periodic penalty payments." (para 150). *Huls* was confirmed in the *Sumitomo* case. See Joined Cases T-22/02 and T-23/02, *Sumitomo Chemical Co Ltd and Sumika Fine Chemicals Co Ltd v Commission* [2005] ECR II-nyr, para 105. See also Opinion of Advocate General Kokott in Case C-105/04 P, *Nederlandse Federatieve Vereniging voor de Groothandel of Elektrotechnisch Gebied and Technische Unie (FEG) v Commission* [2005] ECR-nyr; and Opinion of Advocate General Kokott of December 8, 2005 in Case C-113/04 P, *Technische Union v Commission*, [2005] ECR I-nyr. The severity of potential penalties imposed by competition law is therefore sufficient to guarantee that the fundamental rights of the parties concerned will be upheld. The fact that an undertaking constitutes a legal as opposed to a natural person does not preclude it from asserting its fundamental rights. However, the rights of a legal entity will be subject to stricter limitations than those of a human person. See Case C-136/79, *National Panasonic (UK) Ltd v Commission* [1980] ECR 2033.

[159] Council Regulation 1/2003 on the implementation of the rules on competition laid down in Articles 81 and 82 of the Treaty, OJ 2003 L 1/1 (hereinafter the "Regulation 1/2003").

[160] See Case 6/72, *Europemballage Corporation and Continental Can Company Inc v Commission* [1973] ECR 215; and Case T-51/89, *Tetra Pak Rausing SA v Commission* [1990] ECR II-309.

[161] See also Discussion Paper, para. 8.

[162] See Case 85/76, *Hoffmann-La Roche & Co AG v Commission* [1979] ECR 461, para 116. See also Case 66/86, *Ahmed Saeed Flugreisen and Silver Line Reisebüro GmbH v Zentrale zur Bekämpfung unlauteren Wettbewerbs* eV [1989] ECR 803.

[163] *Ibid.* The Commission had historically adopted a broad definition of the notion of an "agreement" under Article 81 EC that, on several occasions, included conduct that *prima facie* seemed unilateral in nature. See, e.g., Case C-277/87, *Sandoz prodotti farmaceutici SpA v Commission* [1990] ECR I-45. In the *Bayer* litigation, the Community Courts rejected this wide interpretation of Article 81 EC (and the correspondingly narrow interpretation of unilateral conduct). It is now clear the concept of an agreement under Article 81 EC "centers around the existence of a concurrence of wills between at least two parties, the form in which it is manifested being unimportant so long as it constitutes a faithful

with Article 81 EC does not necessarily immunise it from review under Article 82 EC, assuming the provisions for the application of the latter provision are met. Thus, the mere fact that an agreement benefits from a Community block exemption does not preclude a challenge to aspects of that agreement under Article 82 EC.[164] And there is no need for the benefit of the relevant block exemption to have been formally withdrawn by a court or competition authority for Article 82 EC to apply.

A fourth principle is that a competition authority or court should not allow an undertaking to benefit from Article 81(3) if, in so doing, the agreement would lead to an abuse of a dominant position. This was in essence the outcome in *Tetra Pak Rausing*,[165] although the case concerned a block exemption, not an individual exemption. Finally, the mere fact that an agreement would create a dominant position does not mean that no exemption under Article 81(3) is possible. In its Notice on the application of Article 81(3), the Commission has stated that the condition under Article 81(3) that the agreement should not allow the parties "the possibility of eliminating competition in respect of a substantial part of the products in question" has an autonomous meaning,[166] and, citing *Atlantic Container Line*, one that is narrower than dominance.[167] In practice, however, the greater the degree of dominance that is created by an agreement, the less likely it is that an exemption would apply (absent compelling efficiencies).

1.4.3 Article 82 EC And Merger Control Laws

The residual scope for applying Article 82 EC to mergers and acquisitions. The adoption of the EC Merger Regulation is a relatively recent innovation, having entered into force in September 1989. Prior to this, the Commission had, in exceptional cases,

expression of the parties' intention." The threshold has therefore been raised for the Commission to prove to the requisite legal standard the express or implied adherence of wholesalers to a manufacturer's unilateral policy of preventing parallel imports. See Case T-41/96, *Bayer AG v Commission* [2000] ECR II-3383, para. 69, confirmed on appeal in Joined Cases C-2/01 P and C-3/01 P, *Bundesverband der Arzneimittel-Importeure eV and Commission v Bayer AG* [2004] ECR I-23. The Court of Justice's judgment in the pending *Volkswagen II* appeal will hopefully clarify matters further. See Case T-208/01, *Volkswagen AG v Commission* [2003] ECR II-5141, currently on appeal to the Court of Justice. See Opinion of Advocate General Tizzano of November 17, 2005, in Case C-74/04 P, *Volkswagen AG v Commission,* [2005] ECR I-nyr.

[164] See Case T-51/89, *Tetra Pak Rausing SA v Commission* [1990] ECR II-309, paras. 25–30. See also Joined Cases C–395/96 P and C-396/96P, *Compagnie Maritime Belge Transports SA, Compagnie maritime belge SA and Dafra-Lines A/S v Commission* [2000] ECR I-1365, para. 133 ("the fact that operators subject to effective competition have a practice which is authorised does not mean that adoption of the same practice by an undertaking in a dominant position can never constitute an abuse of that position."). See, too, Joined Cases T-191/98 and T-212/98 to T-214/98, *Atlantic Container Line AB and Others v Commission* [2003] ECR II-3275.

[165] *Tetra Pak Rausing SA v Commission, ibid.*

[166] See Commission Notice—Guidelines on the application of Article 81(3) of the Treaty, OJ 2004 C 101/97, para. 106.

[167] Joined Cases T-191/98 and T-212/98 to T-214/98, *Atlantic Container Line AB and Others v Commission* [2003] ECR II-3275 (hereinafter "*Atlantic Container Line*"), para. 939 ("As the concept of eliminating competition is narrower than that of the existence or acquisition of a dominant position, an undertaking holding such a position is capable of benefiting from an exemption"). See also Case 27/76, *United Brands Company and United Brands Continentaal BV v Commission* [1978] ECR 207, para. 113; Case 85/76, *Hoffmann-La Roche & Co AG v Commission* [1979] ECR 461, paras. 39 and 90; and Case T-51/89, *Tetra Pak Rausing SA v Commission* [1990] ECR II-309, para. 28.

sought to apply Articles 81 and 82 EC to mergers and acquisitions. As early as *Continental Can*, the Court of Justice held that Article 82 EC was in principle applicable to concentrations in circumstances where that acquisition would strengthen the existing dominant position of the acquiring party.[168] But, prior to the adoption of the EC Merger Regulation, only one prohibition decision had been upheld on the basis of this theory.[169]

Notwithstanding the adoption of the EC Merger Regulation, the question of whether Article 82 EC can apply to mergers and acquisitions remains relevant. Two situations should be contrasted. The first is whether Article 82 EC can be applied to transactions that are subject to notification under the EC Merger Regulation. The EC Merger Regulation requires mandatory changes in control over an undertaking that meet certain worldwide and EU-wide turnover thresholds and, as a general rule, precludes the parallel application of national merger control rules to the same transaction. A second situation concerns the possible application of Article 82 EC to transactions that do not fall under the jurisdiction of the EC Merger Regulation or national merger control laws.

Application of Article 82 EC to transactions that fall under the EC Merger Regulation. As a piece of secondary legislation, the EC Merger Regulation cannot preclude the application of primary legislation such as Article 82 EC. And because Article 82 EC is directly effective in application, there is no reason in theory why it could not continue to be applied to transactions falling under the mandatory prior approval regime established by the EC Merger Regulation. At the time of the adoption of the EC Merger Regulation, however, the Commission confirmed that it would not seek to apply Article 82 EC to transactions that required notification under the EC Merger Regulation.[170] The same clear statement was made by the Commissioner responsible for competition policy at the time.[171] Taken together, these statements probably create a legitimate expectation on the part of companies that Article 82 EC will not be applied by the Commission to transactions falling under the EC Merger Regulation.

Procedural considerations also explain the Commission's policy in this regard. None of the Commission's powers and procedures under Regulation 1/2003, or the sector-specific rules, apply to mergers and acquisitions that fall under the EC Merger Regulation. The only option open to the Commission would be to apply its powers under Article 85 EC, which permits the Commission to investigate possible infringements of Articles 81 and 82 EC upon application by a Member State or on its

[168] Case 6/72, *Europemballage and Continental Can v Commission* [1973] ECR 215, para. 24 ("[B]ut if Article 3(f) [now 3(g) EC] provides for the institution of a system ensuring that competition in the common market is not distorted, then it requires *a fortiori* that competition must not be eliminated. This requirement is so essential that without it numerous provisions of the Treaty would be pointless.").

[169] See *Warner-Lambert/Gillette and Others*, OJ 1993 L 116/21. In Joined Cases 142/84 and 156/84, *British American Tobacco Company Ltd and RJ Reynolds Industries Inc v Commission* [1987] ECR 4487, the Commission's decision was overturned due to lack of evidence.

[170] See Notes entered in the Minutes of the Council, December 21, 1989.

[171] See L Brittan, "The Law and Policy of Merger Control in the EEC" (1990) 15(5) *European Law Review* 351 ("I do not intend to seek the application of the EEC Treaty rules in Articles [81] and [82] by any means.").

own initiative. But these powers are limited, since any remedial action remains in the hands of the Member States, acting on a recommendation by the Commission, and not under the direct control of the Commission itself.

At national level, competition authorities cannot apply Article 82 EC to transactions falling under the EC Merger Regulation, since the provisional regime contained in Article 84 EC has been brought to an end for cases under the EC Merger Regulation. National courts can, in theory, apply Article 82 EC to transactions falling under the EC Merger Regulation, even in the absence of specific implementing rules. There are a handful of examples of complainants seeking to avail of this opportunity before national courts.[172] But these cases concerned the period before the entry into force of the EC Merger Regulation. A national court today would almost certainly defer to the Commission's jurisdiction, in particular because of the automatic prohibition on the implementation of transactions subject to the EC Merger Regulation.

Application of Article 82 EC to transactions falling outside merger control laws. Article 82 EC can in principle apply to transactions that fall outside the EC Merger Regulation and national merger control laws. At the time of the adoption of the EC Merger Regulation, however, the Commission indicated that it would not seek to apply Article 82 EC to transactions falling outside the scope of the EC Merger Regulation that were *de minimis* in nature.[173] Admittedly, the Commission on one occasion sought to apply Article 82 EC to acquisitions of a minority interest in a competitor.[174] But this transaction took place before the entry into force of the EC Merger Regulation and it is very unlikely that the Commission would take similar action today.

Practical reasons also explain why the Commission is highly unlikely to apply Article 82 EC to transactions falling outside the EC Merger Regulation. First, most meaningful transactions falling outside the EC Merger Regulation will be subject to review under national merger control laws, which exist in all but one Member State (i.e., Luxembourg). Second, Article 82 EC is not a particularly effective tool for reviewing mergers and acquisitions falling outside the EC Merger Regulation. It can only be applied in situations where the purchaser is *already* dominant on the relevant market(s) at the date of the acquisition and cannot therefore challenge the most common concern in merger control—transactions that create dominance. Third, the introduction of the EC Merger Regulation has also allowed the Commission to remove or reduce interlocking shareholdings or minority interests as a remedy in problematic transactions. Finally, the legal basis for intervention—the *Continental Can* judgment—is regarded as

---

[172] See, e.g., *Carnaud/Sofreb*, XVIIth Report on Competition Policy (1987), para. 70 (contested bid suspended by national court until after a Commission ruling under Article 82 EC); and *GEC-Siemens/Plessey*, OJ 1990 C 239/2 (target of hostile takeover sought interim relief on grounds that takeover would infringe, *inter alia*, Article 82 EC).

[173] The Commission defined *de minimis* as transactions involving less than €2 billion of worldwide turnover and €100 million of Community-wide turnover. See Notes entered in the Minutes of the Council, December 21, 1989.

[174] In *Gillette*, the Commission considered that a leveraged buyout of the Wilkinson Sword wet-shaving business by Eemland, a company in which Gillette held a 22% equity stake, was contrary to Article 81 EC and/or Article 82 EC as it would have restricted competition between Wilkinson Sword and Gillette in the Community wet-shaving market. See *Warner-Lambert/Gillette and Others*, OJ 1993 L 116/21.

a striking piece of judicial activism based on a clear gap, at the time, in EC competition law. Now that the Community and its Member States have detailed merger control regimes, there are strong policy reasons why the basis for earlier interventions is much less compelling. There may also be arguments based on legal certainty, as well as the *lex specialis* created by the EC Merger Regulation, why reliance on Article 82 EC in these circumstances would now be unattractive. Taken together, these considerations help explain why, in the period following the introduction of the EC Merger Regulation, the Commission has not made use of its prerogatives under Article 82 EC to investigate a transaction that escaped its mandatory jurisdiction.

National authorities and courts also remain competent in principle to apply Article 82 EC to transactions falling outside the EC Merger Regulation. But, as indicated, for the overwhelming majority of transactions, this need does not arise, since all Member States but one have merger control laws.[175] Nonetheless, it is not true to say that the *Continental Can* doctrine is a dead letter.[176] On rare occasions, Member States have sought, largely unsuccessfully, to challenge non-notifiable transactions on this basis.[177] However, the risk that the Commission, a national authority, or court would seek to apply Article 82 EC to non-notifiable mergers today remains a remote possibility.

1.4.4 Article 82 EC And The Rules On State Action

General principles on State action. EC competition law on State action is not limited to the State action defence whereby abusive conduct by private undertakings that is required by national measures cannot be imputed to the undertakings concerned. In addition, a number of affirmative obligations apply to the State that, in essence, seek to prevent State measures that directly restrict competition. A number of basic principles

---

[175] Some of these laws also operate very low thresholds for intervention, e.g., Ireland, where a combined Irish turnover of €15 million is sufficient, if total worldwide turnover exceeds €40 million. And of course each Member State remains competent to lower the thresholds under national merger control laws if they wish. Moreover, some Member States are considering amendments to national law that would allow non-notifiable mergers to be reviewed for certain period following closing (e.g., France). All of these developments have considerably reduced the need to apply Article 82 EC to non-notifiable mergers at national level.

[176] See, most recently, Case T-210/01, *General Electric Company v Commission* [2005] ECR II-nyr, para. 83 ("The strengthening of a dominant position [e.g., through an acquisition] may in itself significantly impede competition and do so to such an extent that it amounts, on its own, to an abuse of that position.").

[177] In *E.ON/Ruhrgas*, the German Federal Cartel Office prohibited the merger of energy companies E.ON and Ruhrgas. The parties then applied for clearance of the merger by the German Minister of the Economy, based on public interest considerations (a possibility that exists under German law). The German Monopoly Commission, an advisory body for competition issues, delivered an opinion advising the Minister not to clear the merger since, *inter alia*, clearance would violate Article 82 EC under the *Continental Can* doctrine. The Minster did not follow this advice and cleared the merger. See the German Monopoly Commission's opinion in *EON/Gelsenberg AG and EON Bergmann GmbH*, *Sondergutachten der Monopolkommission*, No. 34, May 21, 2002. In France, a similar attempt was made by the *Conseil de la concurrence* when it asked the French Minister of the Economy to prohibit, *ex post*, a merger between Compagnie Générale des Eaux and Lyonnaise des eaux. See Decision n° 02-D-44, *Conseil de la concurrence*, July 11, 2002. There are also one or two pending, non-public cases in which other national authorities are also seeking to apply Article 82 EC in this way.

are clear, although their precise ambit in individual cases may be complex. The overriding principle is that national authorities, which includes State organs other than competition authorities, should not take action that would render EC competition law ineffective.[178] This broad principle has been repeated in a number of cases, but might be summarised as saying that Member States are required to ensure that EC competition law, and the Community institutions' application of it, are not rendered ineffective.[179] The basis for this principle is Article 10 EC—which requires Member States not to frustrate Community objectives—and Article 3(g) EC—which requires a system of effective competition.[180]

The broad principle that Member States should not take action that would render EC competition law ineffective has given rise to a number of more specific principles.[181] These principles do not concern the application of Article 82 EC as such and are mainly mentioned here for sake of completeness. First, Member State should not order companies to infringe EC competition law or approve infringements through administrative action or other decisions. The most obvious cases concerns price-fixing or prices that are contrary to Article 82 EC for some other reason, such as excessive prices, discriminatory tariffs, predatory prices, or a margin squeeze. Second, national authorities should disregard rules of national law, including non-competition laws, that lessen the effective enforcement of EC competition law.[182] A final, related principle is that the power to disregard national law that is contrary to EC competition law also implies that national authorities, including non-judicial authorities, have the power and the duty to declare that national legislation is contrary to EC competition law.[183]

A second broad set of principles concern the rules on the grant of special or exclusive rights by Member States. This mainly involves the application of Article 86 EC, which

---

[178] See generally R Wainwright and A Bouquet, "State Intervention and Action in EC Competition Law" in BE Hawk (ed.), *2003 Fordham Corporate Law*, chapter 23 (Huntington, Juris Publications, Inc., 2004), ch. 23.

[179] See, e.g., Joined Cases 46/87 and 227/88, *Hoechst AG v Commission* [1989] ECR 2859, para. 33.

[180] See, e.g., Case 311/85, *ASBL Vereniging van Vlaamse Reisbureaus v ASBL Sociale Dienst van de Plaatselijke en Gewestelijke Overheidsdiensten* [1987] ECR 3801 (Belgian law granting a permanent and general effect to an agreement concluded between certain private undertakings in violation of Article 81(1) struck down). See also Case 267/86, *Pascal Van Eycke v ASPA NV* [1988] ECR 4769, para. 16; Case C-185/91, *Bundesanstalt für den Güterfernverkehr v Gebrüder Reiff GmbH & Co KG* [1993] ECR I-5801, para. 14; Case C-153/93, *Bundesrepublik Deutschland (Germany) v Delta Schiffahrts- und Speditionsgesellschaft mbH* [1994] ECR I-2517, para. 14; Case C-96/94, *Centro Servizi Spediporto Srl v Spedizioni Marittima del Golfo Srl* [1995] ECR I-2883, para. 20; Case C-35/99, *Manuele Arduino* [2002] ECR I-1529, para. 34; and Case C-198/01, *Consorzio Industrie Fiammiferi (CIF) v Autorità Garante della Concorrenza e del Mercato* [2003] ECR I-8055, para. 45.

[181] See generally J Temple Lang, "General Report, the Duties of Cooperation of National Authorities and Courts and the Community Institutions Under Article 10 EC," in *XIX FIDE Congress* (Helsinki, 2000) Vol. I, pp. 373–426 and Vol. IV, pp. 65–72; J Temple Lang, "The Duties of Cooperation of National Authorities and Courts Under Article 10 EC: Two More Reflections" (2001) 26(1) *European Law Review* 84–93.

[182] See Case C-453/99, *Courage Ltd v Bernard Crehan and Bernard Crehan v Courage Ltd and Others* [2001] ECR I-6297 (Member States required to dis-apply a rule of national law that prevented a party to an anticompetitive agreement from recovering damages against the other party).

[183] See Case C-198/01, *Consorzio Industrie Fiammiferi (CIF) v Autorità Garante della Concorrenza e del Mercato* [2003] ECR I-8055.

limits the extent to which Member States may intervene in the market through public undertakings. Three basic rules apply. First, Article 86(1) provides that in the case of public undertakings or undertakings to which Member States grant special or exclusive rights, Member States should not enact or maintain in force any measure contrary to the rules contained in the Treaty, including, but not limited to the competition provisions. Second, under Article 86(2) EC, Member State may, exceptionally, entrust an enterprise with the operation of services of general economic interest, in which case it may be relieved from the rules contained in the EC Treaty, and in particular the rules on competition, insofar as the application of these rules would obstruct the performance of the particular tasks given to them. This exception is far-reaching—it would allow for example a Member State to grant State aid to fund the public service obligations,[184] which would otherwise be unlawful—and has therefore been interpreted restrictively. Thus, it has been applied only to natural monopolies and/or universal service obligations.[185] Finally, under Article 86(3), the Commission has special supervisory powers to ensure compliance with the provisions of Article 86 EC. Under this provision, the Commission has sole authority to adopt decisions declaring that a Member State has infringed Article 86(1) and obliging the Member State to terminate the infringement. The Commission also may adopt directives in order to specify the obligations contained in Article 86(1). This provision has mainly been used as a tool for eliminating unjustified monopolies in utility markets through the adoption of legislation and individual decisions.

State action that creates or extends monopolies or leads to abuses. Two principles concerning State action are, however, more directly relevant to the application of Article 82 EC. The first—which is relatively clear—is that Member States should not take action that would facilitate abuses of dominance contrary to Article 82 EC. This rule is not limited to the situation outlined in the previous section, i.e., when the State orders an undertaking to commit an abuse, or approves such action by a decision. It also includes Member State action that encourages, facilitates, or makes it very likely that violations of Article 82 EC will occur. The case law has adopted a range of different formulations, including that the State should not take actions that: (1) are "liable to create a situation in which that undertaking is led to infringe" Article 82 EC;[186] (2) "induce" firms to commit an infringement of Article 82 EC;[187]

---

[184] See Case C-280/00, *Altmark Trans GmbH and Regierungspräsidium Magdeburg v Nahverkehrsgesellschaft Altmark GmbH, and Oberbundesanwalt beim Bundesverwaltungsgericht* [2003] ECR I-7747. Strict conditions were laid down in the judgment to ensure that any State funding is purely limited to the relevant public service obligation and does not spill over into competitive areas.

[185] See, e.g., Case 10/71, *Ministère public luxembourgeois v Madeleine Muller, Veuve J.P. Hein and others* [1971] ECR 723; Case C-266/96, *Corsica Ferries France SA v Gruppo Antichi Ormeggiatori del porto di Genova Coop arl, and others* [1998] ECR I-3949; Case 41/83, *Italian Republic v Commission* [1985] ECR 873; Case C-18/88, *Régie des télégraphes et des téléphones v GB-Inno-BM SA* [1991] ECR I-5941. Case 155/73, *Giuseppe Sacchi* [1974] ECR 409; Case C-260/89, *Elliniki Radiophonia Tiléorassi AE and Panellinia Omospondia Syllogon Prossopikou v Dimotiki Etairia Pliroforissis and others* [1991] ECR I-2925; *Commission Decision On The Exclusive Right To Broadcast Television Advertising In Flanders*, OJ 1997 L 244/18, on appeal Case T-266/97, *Vlaamse Televisie Maatschapij NV v Commission* [1999] ECR II-2329 (advertising monopoly struck down).

[186] See Case C-260/89, *Elliniki Radiophonia Tiléorassi AE and Panellinia Omospondia Syllogon Prossopikou v Dimotiki Etairia Pliroforissis and others* [1991] ECR I-2925, para. 38; Case C-462/99,

(3) create situations in which a dominant firm "cannot avoid infringing" Article 82 EC;[188] or (4) create situations in which "the provision of a service is limited" contrary to Article 82 EC, i.e., that the dominant firm cannot meet demand.[189] But these formulations amount to essentially the same thing: the State should not adopt laws or practices that create situations in which abuses of dominance are very likely to occur.

The second principle—which is less clear—concerns the circumstances in which the State is acting unlawfully when it creates or extends a dominant position without justification. This concerns the scope of Article 86(1) and the justification for derogations from the prohibition contained therein under Article 86(2) EC. The main source of confusion is whether: (1) the creation or strengthening of a dominant position automatically makes it possible that an abuse of dominance will occur, and so is unlawful;[190] or (2) the enterprise merely by exercising the exclusive rights granted to it, is led to abuse its dominant position.[191] The first interpretation assumes that distortions of competition inevitably follow from exclusive or special rights that lack a proper justification. The second is narrower in that it also requires some proof that abuses of dominance are likely to follow from the grant of an exclusive or special right.

Which interpretation is preferred is unclear from the case law and the various precedents are not easily reconciled. The Court of Justice's most recent judgment, in *Ambulanz Glöckner*,[192] makes clear that extending a monopoly without justification can be illegal without, however, expressly clarifying which of the two interpretations outlined above it prefers. Nor does the judgment clarify the underlying question of how far it is unlawful to create a monopoly in the first place. The better view is probably that: (1) measures which are likely to lead to a dominant firm committing an abuse, contrary to Article 82 EC, are unlawful; and (2) measures that extend an existing dominant position, or which create a monopoly or a privileged position, are unlawful absent objective justification.

1.4.5 Article 82 EC And Regulation

Scope for parallel application of competition law and regulatory principles. Governments sometimes regulate markets in order to deal with structural or other

Connect Austria Gesellschaft für Telekommunikation GmbH v Telekom-Control-Kommission, and Mobilkom Austria AG [2003] ECR I-5197, para. 80.

[187] Case C-179/90, *Merci convenzionali porto di Genova SpA v Siderurgica Gabrielli SpA* [1991] ECR I-5889, paras. 17–19.

[188] See Case C-41/90, *Klaus Höfner and Fritz Elser v Macrotron GmbH* [1991] ECR I-1979, para. 27; Case C-55/96, *Job Centre coop. arl* [1997] ECR I-7119, at paras. 29, 31, 35, 38; Case C-179/90, *Merci convenzionali porto di Genova SpA v Siderurgica Gabrielli SpA* [1991] ECR I-5889, para. 17; Case C-323/93, *Société Civile Agricole du Centre d'Insémination de la Crespelle v Coopérative d'Elevage et d'Insémination Artificielle du Département de la Mayenne* [1994] ECR I-5077.

[189] *Höfner and Elser, ibid*; Case C-258/98, *Giovanni Carra and Others* [2000] ECR I-4217; and *Job Centre, ibid.*, paras. 31–36.

[190] See, e.g., Case C-18/88, *Régie des télégraphes et des téléphones v GB-Inno-BM SA* [1991] ECR I-5941, para. 24.

[191] See, e.g., Case C-323/93, *Société Civile Agricole du Centre d'Insémination de la Crespelle v Coopérative d'Elevage et d'Insémination Artificielle du Département de la Mayenne* [1994] ECR I-5077, paras. 21 et seq.

[192] Case C-475/99, *Firma Ambulanz Glöckner v Landkreis Südwestpfalz* [2001] ECR I-8089.

features that limit effective competition. The expectation is that regulating aspects of former monopolies—such as price caps, rate-of-return, and cost-based access to key inputs—will smooth out market imperfections and allow a transition towards full competition over time.[193] There is some debate among commentators whether regulation is, on the whole, a good thing,[194] and whether *ex post* control under competition law is preferable.[195] Issues such as inadequate information, reduced incentives for incumbents to invest, regulatory capture (where regulators are lobbied or pressurised into adopting industry-friendly rules), and regulatory lag (where changes in the incumbent's actual costs are not quickly reflected in regulatory decisions) may limit the effectiveness of regulation. But there is also a good deal of evidence in Europe and elsewhere that regulation in the telecommunications sector has produced enormous benefits for consumers.

As noted, competition law and regulatory principles may apply in parallel unless regulation is so detailed and prescriptive as to eliminate the scope for independent competitive action.[196] In the area of telecommunications for example, the Commission and NCAs may apply EC competition law in an environment where regulation also exists. NRAs too will often apply regulatory principles in areas in which competition law applies. And some NRAs even have parallel powers to apply competition law and regulation to the same industry (e.g., Ofcom in the United Kingdom). Parallel application is most likely to occur in the case of Article 82 EC and regulation, since the addressees of the principal obligations are essentially the same, i.e., firms with significant market power. It is clearly important therefore to clarify the main differences between the two regimes.

Community law contains certain rules providing for cooperation between regulatory agencies and competition authorities, but these are mainly procedural in nature.[197] The substantive differences have not yet been clarified. Below, the principal differences between the two sets of rules are noted in the context of the telecommunications sector, since this is the most advanced form of regulation under Community law. But much the same analysis would apply to other regulated sectors, such as post and energy.

---

[193] See D Geradin, "The Opening of State Monopolies to Competition: Main Issues of the Liberalization Process" in D Geradin (ed.), *The Liberalisation of State Monopolies in the European Union and Beyond* (The Hague, Kluwer Law International, 1999).

[194] See, e.g., D Carlton & J Perloff, *Modern Industrial Organisation*, (4th edn., Boston, Pearson Addison Wesley, 2005), p. 682 ("Government regulation of firms may increase welfare in markets that are not perfectly competitive. Unfortunately, actual regulation often deviates considerably from optimal regulation and exacerbates market efficiencies...Optimal regulation can force a monopoly to set the competitive price. However, if the monopoly is badly regulated, shortages occur or the monopoly is encouraged to produce inefficiently. Even where regulations are properly applied, the cost of administering them may exceed the benefits.") and p. 706 ("[T]here is considerable doubt that regulatory bodies do lower prices.").

[195] See D Geradin and M Kerf, *Controlling Market Power in Telecommunications: Antitrust vs. Sector-specific Regulation* (Oxford, Oxford University Press, 2000).

[196] See section 1.3.2. above.

[197] See, e.g., Commission guidelines on market analysis and the assessment of significant market power under the Community regulatory framework for electronic communications networks and services, OJ 2002 C 165/6.

The basic differences between competition law and regulation. At first sight, the objectives of regulation and competition law would seem to converge: both in essence seek to identify conditions in which effective downstream competition can function.[198] On closer inspection, however, the objectives of regulation and competition law may not only diverge, but may in fact be flatly at odds with each other. A first basic difference is that competition law applies *ex post*, a largely backward-looking assessment of conduct that has already taken place. A specific feature of most sector-specific regimes is that they apply "asymmetrically" in that the most demanding obligations will be imposed *ex ante* on one or a limited number of firms.[199] While Article 82 EC imposes a "special responsibility" on dominant firms, specific remedies will only be imposed when an abusive conduct has been established.[200]

Second, regulatory obligations are generally much more extensive and can specify more precise obligations. Under regulation, the incumbent firm may have affirmative duties that could not be imposed under competition law. For example, the new regulatory framework on electronic communications seems to allow a NRA to mandate the incumbent to grant access to its network infrastructure in circumstances that would not be covered under the so-called "essential facilities" doctrine under Article 82 EC.[201] Nothing under Article 82 EC would authorise an enforcement authority to mandate a firm to give access to essential inputs at a rate that does not cover its own costs, whereas this possibility can arise when a NRA mandate access prices based on long-term product specific costs methodology.

Third, competition law is a set of principles which protects competition from anticompetitive conduct. It does not give a competition authority power to impose any *new* obligations (except as part of a remedy, based on existing competition law rules, for a breach of existing rules). Nor does it give a competition authority power to pursue any policy objectives, however legitimate, other than the protection of competition. In particular it does not empower a competition authority to offset or compensate rivals for any lawfully acquired competitive advantages of a dominant company. This is particularly important in margin squeeze and duty-to-contract cases in which the authority may need to fix the terms of contracts. If the authority is acting under competition law, it may fix the price or the terms of the contract only on the basis of competition law considerations.

In contrast, regulatory powers may impose new types of obligations on the addressees of the particular regulatory framework. For instance, sector-specific regimes contain universal service obligations that impose operators to serve certain categories of

---

[198] See in this regard Opinion No. 04/A-17, of the Conseil de la Concurrence, October 14, 2004 (extensive discussion of the relationship between antitrust and sectoral regulations).

[199] For instance, pursuant to the new EC regulatory framework on electronic communications, obligations of access, non-discrimination, etc., will only be imposed on operators that hold significant market power. See A de Streel, "The Integration of Competition Law Principles in the New European Regulatory Framework for Electronic Communications" (2003) 26 *World Competition* 489.

[200] R Subiotto, "The Confines of the Special Responsibility of Dominant Undertakings Not to Impair Genuine Undistorted Competition" (1995) 18 *World Competition* 5.

[201] See D Geradin and JG Sidak, "European and American Approaches to Antitrust Remedies and the Institutional Design of Regulation in Telecommunications" in M Cave, S Majumdar, and I Vogelsang (eds.), *Handbook of Telecommunications Economics, Vol. 2* (Amsterdam, Elsevier, 2005).

customers, which a normal profit-making firm would not necessarily serve.[202] Moreover, retail price controls will not only seek to prevent exploitative abuses on the part of the incumbent, but also be based on social considerations. This may in some cases force incumbents to price below costs on some market segments, a situation which could never occur through the application of competition rules. Finally, sector-specific regimes can in some cases take pro-active measures to effectively create competition on downstream markets. Incumbents may be, for instance, forced to divest their upstream operations even in the absence of any proven abuse of dominance. In the case of margin squeeze, an NRA may also be tempted to adopt wholesale rates that are favourable to the incumbent's competitors to stimulate entry.

The final comment is that specific competition law duties should be imposed only if, on balance, more competition is promoted than discouraged. In considering access obligations or pricing terms to rivals under Article 82 EC, for example, a competition authority, or regulatory authority relying on competition law powers, should consider if the downstream market is easy to enter and so relatively unprofitable for objective and unavoidable reasons. If so, to impose an access requirement could dampen competition than increase it because that it might discourage investment in the only, or most, profitable level in the industry.

In contrast, regulatory authorities are empowered to take action under regulatory powers even if it reduces the ability and incentives of the incumbent to compete. For instance, a regulator can, if authorised by legislation to do so, impose a duty on a dominant incumbent to give access on more favourable terms to competitors which are investing in their own networks (e.g., if the regulatory framework favours network competition over service competition in the long-run). This may affect the ability and incentives of the incumbent to invest in its own infrastructure.

1.4.6 Article 82 EC And National Abuse Of Dominance Laws

The scope for Member States applying stricter national abuse of dominance laws. Prior to the adoption of the Commission's modernisation reforms in 2004, national authorities and courts were competent to apply their national abuse of dominance laws in parallel with Article 82 EC. Rules intended to avoid the conflicts that might result from the parallel application of national law and Article 82 EC were limited. The principal limitations were that: (1) a national court ruling on a practice, the compatibility of which with Article 82 EC is already the subject of a Commission decision, could not take a decision running counter to that of the Commission;[203] (2) a national court should stay its proceedings if the prior Commission decision was subject to an action for annulment, or, alternatively, seek a preliminary ruling;[204] and (3) national law could not impose sanctions on undertakings for behaviour that had already been subject of action at the Community level.[205] Two Notices dealing with

[202] See P Larouche, "Telecommunications" in D Geradin (ed.), *The Liberalisation of State Monopolies in the European Union and Beyond* (The Hague, Kluwer Law International, 2000), pp. 42–44.

[203] Case C-344/98, *Masterfoods Ltd v HB Ice Cream Ltd* [2000] ECR I-11369.

[204] *Ibid.*

[205] Case 14-68, *Walt Wilhelm and others v Bundeskartellamt* [1969] ECR 1.

cooperation between the Commission and NCAs and courts also tried to ensure consistency of approach, but these were rarely applied in practice and were non-binding in any event.

The modernisation reforms have not changed much in this regard. Article 3(1) of Regulation 1/2003 requires that where the competition authorities of the Member States or national courts apply national competition law to any abuse prohibited by Article 82 EC, they shall also apply Article 82 EC. However, Article 3(2) goes on to provide that, in so doing, Member States are not precluded from adopting and applying on their territory stricter national laws which prohibit or sanction unilateral conduct engaged in by undertakings. (Member States cannot, however, approve measures under national law that would be contrary to Article 82 EC.) This represents an important change in the Commission's position. Under the draft proposal, the application of national abuse of dominance laws could not lead to the prohibition of practices that would be permitted under Article 82 EC. In the final version, this obligation was retained only for Article 81 EC. The exception under Article 3 is also potentially broad, since it did not require Member States to state from the outset whether they intended to apply stricter laws. Further, Member States remain entitled under this provision to adopt new laws on unilateral conduct.

The change from the draft proposal reflects certain Member States' desire to continue to apply national abuse of dominance laws aimed at protecting small and medium-sized enterprises, i.e., situations of so-called "economic dependence."[206] The scope for Member States applying stricter national abuse of dominance laws is clearly regrettable from the perspective of legal certainty and consistency. Indeed, the obligation contained in the draft proposal—that Member States could not apply stricter standards than those applicable under Article 82 EC—was widely trumpeted at the time as a key component to preserve the overall integrity of the modernisation reforms. The then

[206] The main examples are Germany and France. Under Article 20 (1) of the German Act against Restraints of Competition, dominant firms are required not to "directly hinder in an unfair manner other undertakings engaged in business activities open to similar undertakings, nor directly or indirectly treat them differently from similar undertakings, nor...grant them preferential terms without any objective justification" (translation from original). This obligation is not limited to dominant firms, but also applies to undertakings with a so-called "superior" market position. Where small or medium-sized enterprises depend on undertakings in a "superior" market position—in the sense that insufficient alternative sources of supply do not exist—German law has imposed wide-ranging obligations *vis-à-vis* distributors and retailers, including obligations to deal. See, e.g., *Lotterievertrieb*, Bundesgerichtshof , judgment of March 7, 1989, WuW/E BGH 2535; *Bahnhofsbuchhandel*, Bundesgerichtshof, judgment of March 17, 1998, WuW/E DE-R 134; *Depotkosmetik*, Bundesgerichtshof, judgment of May 12, 1998, WUW/E DE-R 206 (RIW 1998, 962). In France, small and medium-sized enterprises are also protected from arbitrary conduct by suppliers upon whom they are dependent, in addition to the normal protection offered by the national abuse of dominance laws. Article L 420-2 of the Commercial Code provides *inter alia* that "the abusive exploitation of a state of economic dependency of a client or a supplier by an undertaking or a group of undertakings, where such abuse may affect competition or the structure of competition is [...] prohibited" (translation from original). This provision has been applied for example to absolute and qualified refusals to deal. See, e.g., Paris Court of Appeals, *La Cinq*, February 10, 1992, confirmed in Cour de cassation, March 1, 1994.

Director-General of DG Competition, Dr. Alexander Schaub, explained the importance of ensuring that a single set of common rules applied in the following terms:[207]

> "When all authorities apply the same law it will be possible to develop a truly common competition policy drawing on the experiences of each authority. This is essential from the point of view of the internal market. In an integrated market it is inefficient to have multiple barriers. Multiple barriers create distortions of competition and increase companies' costs. Each time companies engage in intra-Community trade they must examine the position not only under Community law but also under each of the laws of the Member States affected by the agreement. And worse: they will have to comply with the strictest national law, which can reduce the benefits created by the agreement in other Member States. In the case of agreements affecting cross-border trade, the interest of the Community and other Member States will necessarily be affected. A common market therefore requires a common competition policy that takes due account of the Community interest."

While the decision to reject the draft proposal for Article 3 in favour of the current text is to be regretted, the actual scope for divergence should be seen in perspective. A first point to note is that more or less the same situation existed prior to modernisation for over forty years. Member States were free to apply less strict laws on unilateral conduct and had no general obligation to take the position under Article 82 EC into account unless it would directly conflict with a prior Commission decision on the same matter or result in the approval of a practice that would be prohibited under Article 82 EC.

Second, there is a good argument that, even allowing for Article 3 of Regulation 1/2003, Member States cannot adopt any decision that would run contrary to the objectives of the EC Treaty (assuming there is an effect on trade). As a general rule, the combined application of Articles 82, 3 and 10 EC prevents Member States, which includes their NCAs and courts, from adopting any measure that would deprive the competition rules of their effectiveness. Under Article 10 EC, Member States must take all appropriate measures to ensure the fulfilment of the obligations arising out of the EC Treaty. One of these obligations, which is codified in Article 3(g) of the EC Treaty, is the maintenance of "open and free competition." One could, for example, envisage situations in which national laws on "economic dependence" prevent an undertaking in a dominant position from offering lower prices to one customer. Where the effect of applying a non-discrimination obligation in this scenario would be to prevent the dominant firm from offering a lower price to another customer, national law would be applied in a manner contrary to EC competition law. Other scenarios could doubtless also be imagined.

---

[207] See A Schaub, "Efficient Protection of Competition in an Enlarged Community Through Full Association of National Competition Authorities and National Courts," *Reform of European Competition Law*, conference held at Freiburg, November 9, 2000. See also *White paper on modernisation of the rules implementing Articles 85 and 86 [now 81 and 82] of the EC Treaty*, April 28, 1999. ("[The draft] Article 3 ensures that agreements and practices capable of affecting cross-border trade are scrutinised under a single set of rules, thereby promoting a level playing field throughout the Community, and removing the costs attached to the parallel application of Community law and national laws for both competition authorities and business."). See too G Marenco, "Consistent Application Of EC Competition Law In A System Of Parallel Competencies," *Reform of European Competition Law*, conference held at Freiburg, November 10, 2000 ("The adoption of this provision would boost consistency to a marked degree.").

Third, even if Member States were obliged to interpret national law consistently with Article 82 EC—as they must do in the case of Article 81 EC—some divergence in approach would have been inevitable in practice. Procedural and substantive rules can only go so far in ensuring that Member States interpret and apply the law in the same way. There will always be some differences in approach, differing interpretations on subtle points, and variations in expertise and sophistication between authorities and courts. In other words, in a system of parallel competence shared between twenty five Member States and the Community, divergence will, to a greater or lesser extent, always be a feature. Finally, it is also worth noting that a number of Member States in any event have express provisions in national competition laws that require national law to be interpreted in a manner consistent with EC competition law (e.g., the United Kingdom and Ireland).

Applying national laws that are predominantly different to Article 82 EC. The second principal exception to the obligation to apply national law in a manner consistent with EC competition law concerns Member States' ability to apply national laws that "predominantly pursue an objective different from that pursued by Articles 81 and 82 of the Treaty."[208] This provision is intended to allow Member States to continue to apply laws that are concerned with tortious acts committed against rival firms and consumer protection laws. For example, the German Act Against Unfair Practices (*Gesetz gegen den unlauteren Wettbewerb* (UWG)) sets forth a number of "ethical" standards for the conduct of a trade or business. Firms are obliged for example to advertise their products and services truthfully to consumers and to refrain from certain forms of comparative advertising or terms (e.g., "the best" or "the largest") that cannot be clearly verified. Measures also exist to protect competitors, such as unfairly disparaging rivals' offerings. Similar laws exist in several other Member States (e.g., France).

1.4.7 Article 82 EC And Arbitration

The application of Article 82 EC by arbitral bodies. Issues under Article 82 EC sometimes arise in the context of contractual and other disputes before arbitral bodies. Comprehensive up-to-date information on how frequently they arise is not available,[209] which probably reflects the fact that many arbitral awards are not made public and that possible competition law violations are likely to be a good reason for non-publication. But it is reasonable to assume that the application of Article 82 EC in the context of arbitration proceedings is of some importance. And it is also likely that this will grow in future given the widespread increase in competition law enforcement generally and its greater use in contractual and other disputes between private parties.

A number of principles apply to arbitral awards in which issues of Article 82 EC are, or may be, relevant.[210] First, where a national court is asked to annul an arbitral award, it

[208] See Article 3(3), Regulation 1/2003.

[209] The principal research dates from the 1990s and obviously excludes non-public awards. See H Verbist, "The Application of European Community Law in ICC Arbitrations, a Presentation of Arbitral Awards" (December 1994) *ICC International Court of Arbitration Bulletin, Special Supplement* 33.

[210] See M Dolmans and J Grierson, "Arbitration And The Modernisation Of Antitrust Laws: New Opportunities And New Responsibilities" (2003) 14(2) *ICC International Court of Arbitration Bulletin* 37.

must refuse to uphold the award if to do so would contravene EC competition law.[211] This is based on the notion that EC competition law is a mandatory rule of public policy.[212] Second, although a national court hearing an appeal from an arbitral award can refer questions concerning EC competition law to the Court of Justice under Article 234 EC, an arbitral body cannot, since it is not a "court or tribunal" for purposes of this provision.[213] In practice, this means that preliminary references are only possible where there is an appeal to a national court or enforcement requires the use of exequatur proceedings before a court or tribunal. Third, although it is not entirely clear whether arbitrators should raise issues of EC competition law of their own motion, the consensus is that they must,[214] unless the particular arbitration rules prevent them from doing so. This is based on the fact that, under Article 1(3) of Regulation 1/2003, which can be relied upon between private parties, "the abuse of a dominant position referred to in Article 82 of the Treaty shall be prohibited, no prior decision to that effect being required," as well as arbitrators' overriding obligation to ensure that their award is enforceable at law.[215] A final, more difficult, issue is whether non-EEA arbitrators must also apply Article 82 EC, assuming that the basic conditions for the application of this provision are satisfied. It seems reasonably clear, however, that they must do so where the award: (1) concerns EEA-based parties; (2) is to be implemented in whole or in part in the EEA; or (3) though less clear, is likely to have foreseeable effects on competition within the EEA for some other reason.[216]

1.5 THE BASIC PROCEDURAL FRAMEWORK

Overview of the key components of the modernisation reforms. With effect from May 1, 2004, the procedural framework for the application of Articles 81 and 82 EC underwent significant change. Regulation 1/2003 provided for changes in three

[211] See Case C-126/97, *Eco Swiss China Time Ltd v Benetton International NV* [1999] ECR I-3055.

[212] *Ibid.* See also Case C-381/98, *Ingmar GB Ltd v Eaton Leonard Technologies Inc* [2000] ECR I-9305, where the Court of Justice held that provisions of secondary Community legislation protecting commercial agents are mandatory in nature where the situation is closely connected with the Community and cannot be derogated from by choice of law clauses.

[213] See Case 102/81, *Nordsee Deutsche Hochseefischerei GmbH v Reederei Mond Hochseefischerei Nordstern AG & Co KG and Reederei Friedrich Busse Hochseefischerei Nordstern AG & Co KG* [1982] ECR 1095. Arbitral bodies are not courts or competition authorities for purposes of Regulation 1/2003 either, which means that none of the obligations contained in that regulation apply to them. This does not mean, however, that the Commission would not be receptive to requests for assistance from arbitral bodies on competition matters in individual cases, as has occurred in the past. See in this regard C Nisser and G Blanke, "Draft Best Practice Note On The European Commission Acting As Amicus Curiae In International Arbitration Proceedings," *ICC Task Force for Arbitrating Competition Law Issues*, October 2005.

[214] See M Dolmans and J Grierson, "Arbitration And The Modernisation Of Antitrust Laws: New Opportunities And New Responsibilities" (2003) 14(2) *ICC International Court of Arbitration Bulletin* 44.

[215] See, e.g., Article 35 International Chamber of Commerce Arbitration Rules (arbitral bodies to make "every effort" to ensure that the award is "enforceable at law").

[216] See M Dolmans and J Grierson, "Arbitration And The Modernisation Of Antitrust Laws: New Opportunities And New Responsibilities" (2003) 14(2) *ICC International Court of Arbitration Bulletin* 45–46.

principal areas of EC competition law enforcement: (1) it abolished the system created by Council Regulation 17/62 of notifying agreements, decisions and concerted practices to the Commission to obtain an exemption under Article 81(3) EC; (2) it created a system of parallel competences whereby NCAs and courts have the power to apply Article 81(3) EC and are required to apply Articles 81 and 82 EC to activity with cross-border effects; and (3) it reinforced the Commission's powers of investigation. A joint statement was also issued by the Commission and the Council of Ministers upon the adoption of Regulation 1/2003 provides for the creation of a "Network" for cooperation comprised of the Commission and NCAs. In addition, Commission Regulation 773/2004, details the Commission's procedures in cases involving Articles 81 and 82 EC.[217]

These basic texts raised many questions about how the system of parallel competences would work in practice. Most of these questions have been answered in a series of Notices aimed at clarifying the implementation of the new procedural framework established by Regulation 1/2003. The Notices deal with: (1) cooperation within the Network of competition authorities;[218] (2) cooperation between the Commission and national courts;[219] (3) informal guidance by the Commission in individual cases through guidance letters;[220] (4) guidelines on the application of Article 81(3) EC;[221] (5) complaints under Articles 81 and 82 EC;[222] and (6) the concept of effect on trade between Member States.[223] The Notices were developed in consultation with the Member States and each Member State has signed a declaration agreeing to be bound by the principles set out in the Notices.

The following sections outline the principal aspects of the modernisation reforms in so far as they are relevant to the enforcement of Article 82 EC. This outline is not intended to be exhaustive, but simply to alert the reader to the basic procedural framework in which Article 82 EC is now applied. None of the new procedural framework is unique to Article 82 EC, but concerns the enforcement of EC competition law more generally. Moreover, the most significant change effected by the reforms—the direct application of Article 81(3) EC—changed nothing in regard to Article 82 EC. For further

[217] Commission Regulation (EC) No 773/2004 of 7 April 2004 relating to the conduct of proceedings by the Commission pursuant to Articles 81 and 82 of the EC Treaty, OJ 2004 L 123/18.

[218] Commission Notice on cooperation within the Network of Competition Authorities, OJ 2004 C 101/43 (hereinafter "Cooperation Notice").

[219] Commission Notice on the co–operation between the Commission and the courts of the EU Member States in the application of Articles 81 and 82 EC, OJ 2004 C 101/54 (hereinafter "National Courts Notice").

[220] Commission Notice on informal guidance relating to novel questions concerning Articles 81 and 82 of the EC Treaty that arise in individual cases (guidance letters), OJ 2004 C 101/78 (hereinafter "Informal Guidance Notice").

[221] Commission Notice—Guidelines on the application of Article 81(3) of the Treaty, OJ 2004 C 101/97.

[222] Commission Notice on the handling of complaints by the Commission under Articles 81 and 82 of the EC Treaty, OJ 2004 C 101/65 (hereinafter "Complaints Notice").

[223] Commission Notice—Guidelines on the effect on trade concept contained in Articles 81 and 82 of the Treaty, OJ 2004 C 101/81 (hereinafter "Effect on Trade Notice"). Ch. 14 deals with the Notice and the concept of effect on trade in detail.

information, the reader is referred to specialist textbooks dealing with procedure,[224] as well as to a wealth of material from practitioners and other commentators explaining experience with the modernisation reforms to date.[225]

1.5.1 Cooperation Within The Network Of Competition Authorities

Case allocation within the network of competition authorities. Regulation 1/2003 is based on a system of parallel competences in which all competition authorities have the power to apply Articles 81 and 82 EC. Under this system, cases may be dealt with by: (1) a single NCA, possibly with the assistance of other NCAs; (2) several NCAs acting in parallel; or (3) the Commission. Authorities will investigate a matter triggered by a complaint or start proceedings on their own initiative. In most instances, the authority that receives a complaint or starts an *ex officio* proceeding will remain in charge of the case. Cases will be re-allocated normally only at the outset of a proceeding, either where the seised authority considers that it is not well placed to act or where other authorities consider themselves also well-placed. In such instances, cases will be re-allocated to a single well-placed authority as often as possible. [226]

Reallocation of cases to another authority. If an issue of re-allocation arises, it should be resolved promptly, normally within two months starting from the date of the first information sent to the Network, avoiding further re-allocation. An authority may suspend or close its proceedings if another authority is dealing with the same case, but it may decide to continue or re-open an investigation even if another authority has issued a decision. The Commission can take over a case, thereby relieving the NCAs of their jurisdiction. During the initial allocation phase, the Commission can do this after consulting with the NCA concerned. If, after the initial allocation period, the case has

[224] See C Kerse and N Khan, *EC Antitrust Procedure* (5th edn., London, Sweet & Maxwell, 2004). See also L Ortiz Blanco, *EC Competition Procedure* (Oxford, Oxford University Press, 2006).

[225] See, in particular, the conference papers for the IBA Conference, "Antitrust Reform in Europe: A Year in Practice", Brussels, March 9–11, 2005. A practical view of how the reforms have worked is provided in the joint paper by F Montag and S Cameron, "Effective Enforcement: The Practitioner's View Of Recent Experiences Under Regulation 1/2003."

[226] The Cooperation Notice sets out three cumulative conditions for an authority to be well-placed to pursue a case: (1) there is a material link between the infringement and the Member State, i.e., the infringement has substantial direct actual or foreseeable effects of the potential infringement on competition in its territory or is implemented within or originates from its territory; (2) the authority is able to bring the entire infringement effectively to an end, i.e., it can adopt cease and desist order and sanctions sufficient to terminate the entire infringement, if appropriate; and (3) the authority can collect the necessary evidence, if necessary with other authorities' assistance. Accordingly, if competition is mainly affected in one NCA's territory, that NCA would usually be considered well-placed. Even if more than one NCA were well-placed, action by one NCA might be appropriate if it is sufficient to terminate the entire infringement. Parallel action by two or three NCAs may be appropriate where the infringement has substantial effects mainly on competition in their respective territories and no single NCA would be able to bring it to an end or sanction it adequately. In such situation, the NCAs may designate a lead authority which would coordinate the investigation. The Commission is well-placed: (1) if the infringement consists of one or several agreements or practices, including networks of agreements, that effect competition in more than three Member States (cross-border markets covering more than three Member States or several national markets); (2) if the Community interest requires a Commission Decision to develop Community competition policy or to ensure effective enforcement; or (3) if a case is closely linked to other Community provisions which are more effectively applied by the Commission or are within the Commission's exclusive competence.

been investigated at NCA level, the Commission will, following a further consultation proceeding, in principle only intervene if either there: (1) is a risk for the consistent application of EC competition law; (2) NCAs are unduly drawing out proceedings; (3) there is a need for a Commission decision to develop EC competition policy; or (4) the NCAs do not object.

Information exchange. Regulation 1/2003 provides for the Network members' obligation to exchange information within the Network for the purpose of the application of Articles 82 EC, including confidential information. Network members need to give notice on the investigation of new matters in order to detect multiple proceedings and to ensure that cases are dealt with by a well-placed authority. If they contemplate adopting a decision in a proceeding applying Article 82 EC, they need to provide information about the envisaged decision. They may transmit information they obtained in their initial investigation if they suspend or close their proceedings because another authority is dealing with the same case.

Regulation 1/2003 contains certain safeguards for the protection of undertakings' and individual's rights in this respect. Information exchanged within the Network can only be used as evidence for the application of Article 82 EC and for the subject matter for which it was collected, or for applying national competition law in parallel in the same case, but only if the application of national law does not lead to a different outcome. Since individuals normally enjoy more extensive rights of defence than companies, information collected from companies cannot be used in a way that would circumvent this higher level of protection. Sanctions may only be imposed on individuals based on information exchanged within the Network if the transmitting and receiving authorities provide for sanctions of a similar kind, or the transmitting authority has respected the rights of the individual concerned to the same standard as they are guaranteed by the receiving authority.[227]

Challenging case allocation decisions. The Cooperation Notice confirms the Commission's view that the allocation of cases within the Network, including the Commission's decision to initiate proceedings, does not amount to a decision that is subject to separate appeal by the parties under investigation, because, according to the Cooperation Notice, allocation does not create a right for cases to be handled by particular authorities. As far as complainants are concerned, they can request a formal rejection decision from the Commission if the Commission rejects the complaint, including the case that the complaint is rejected because another authority is dealing with the case, and this decision is subject to appeal with the Court of First Instance.

---

[227] Regulation 1/2003 presumes that, if both jurisdictions provide for similar kinds of sanctions for individuals, the standard of procedural safeguards in collecting of evidence is equivalent. Accordingly, the evidence transmitted can then be used without examining whether the individual's rights have actually been sufficiently protected in the particular case. The Cooperation Notice states that the notion of "similar kind of sanctions" is independent from the sanction's classification under national law as criminal or administrative. Rather, the notion should relate to different types of sanction distinguishing between custody on one hand, and fines on individuals or other personal sanctions on the other hand. Custodial sanctions may thus only be imposed where both the transmitting and the receiving authority have the power to impose such sanctions. Since the Commission cannot impose custodial sanctions, a referral from the Commission cannot lead to custodial sanctions before a NCA or court.

Challenges concerning decisions to reject or re-allocate a complaint at NCA level are subject to national law, i.e., possible to the extent that national law provides such possibility. The Cooperation Notice does not deal with the questions whether NCAs can challenge a Commission decision to take over a case. The Cooperation Notice, of course, only expresses a non-binding view which may be tested if companies or NCAs decide to appeal allocation decisions in court. For companies, this may be relevant concerning the transfer of cases to another authority under which jurisdiction the standard of procedural rights or rights to challenge a NCA decision are different.

1.5.2 Cooperation Between The Commission And National Courts

The basic rules. The National Courts Notice addresses cooperation between the Commission and the national courts when these courts apply, *inter alia*, Article 82 EC. In terms of substance, it notes that national courts are bound by the case law of the Community Courts insofar as they apply Article 82 EC, Commission block exemption regulations, and Commission decisions in the same case (subject to the national court's power to request for a preliminary ruling from the Court of Justice under Article 234 EC).[228] Procedurally, the National Courts Notice observes that the procedure for application of Article 82 EC is largely set out in national law, but refers to Community law principles applicable to national courts, including the principle of effectiveness (i.e., enforcement of Community law must not be rendered excessively difficult or practically impossible) and the principle of equivalence (i.e., the rules applied must not be less favourable than the rules applicable to equivalent national law).

Measures designed to avoid conflict. If national courts apply EC competition rules to agreements or concerted practices at the same time or subsequent to the Commission, Regulation 1/2003 provides that the national court must avoid taking a decision

[228] An interesting issue regarding the protection of fundamental rights in competition law proceedings could arise at national court level. Conflicting rulings from the Community Courts and the European Court of Human Rights regarding human rights protection in the application of competition law could potentially result in national courts diverging from the Court of Justice's case law. For example, in the *Orkem* case, which concerned the powers of the Commission to demand information in the course of its investigation into possible infringements of competition law, the Court of Justice held that neither Member State national laws, nor Article 6 ECHR gave a legal person the right not to give evidence against itself in the case of infringements in the economic sphere, in particular in matters of competition law. See Case 374/87, *Orkem v Commission* [1989] ECR 3283. However, in *John Murray v the United Kingdom*, the European Court of Human Rights affirmed that the privilege against self-incrimination should be recognised as a standard "which lies at the heart of the notion of fair procedure under Article 6.1 ECHR." See *John Murray v the United Kingdom* [1996] *European Court of Human Rights Cases* 18731/91. Such differences between the two courts on the interpretation of fundamental rights may mean that national courts have to choose between different interpretations of the ECHR. Within the sphere of Community law, national courts are bound to apply Community law which includes the Community Courts' interpretation of human rights. However, under Article 1 of the ECHR, Contracting States are bound to secure the rights and freedoms set out in the Convention as interpreted by the European Court of Human Rights. A national court could find itself obliged to take a position either contrary to the Convention or Community law. An appropriate mechanism of reconciling potentially diverging judgments is therefore necessary. Accession by the EU to the ECHR, as provided for in the Charter of Fundamental Rights, could also overcome the problem by placing the Community Courts subject to the external control of the European Court of Human Rights in appropriate cases.

conflicting with a decision contemplated by the Commission. National courts may consider whether to stay their proceedings. The Notice states that the Commission will give priority to cases in which it has initiated proceedings and that are subject to stayed national proceedings. If a national court wants to adopt a decision running counter to that of the Commission, it must refer a question to the Court of Justice under Article 234 EC. If the Commission's decision is appealed by the parties, the national court should stay its proceedings. When staying proceedings, the national courts must consider whether interim measures are required to safeguard the parties' interests.

The Commission may also seek to play the role of *amicus curiae* in national cases. In this role, it will transmit information and opinions at the request of the national court, and may also submit observations upon its own initiative in writing, or, if admitted by the national court, in some case orally. The Commission will only provide national courts with business secrets and other confidential information where the court guarantees the protection of such information, and may in any case refuse to transmit information to safeguard Community interests or to avoid interference with its functioning and independence. The National Courts Notice explains that, since it acts in the public interest, the Commission will remain neutral and not hear the parties involved in a case before a national court. Member States are required by Regulation 1/2003 to send the Commission copies of judgments of national court applying Article 82 EC. This will enable the Commission to submit observations in case of an appeal of the judgment (though there is no such mechanism to ensure that the Commission can submit observations in the first instance).

Supervisory role of national courts in inspections. The National Courts Notice briefly reviews the role played by national courts in Commission inspections under Regulation 1/2003. If the Commission requests authorisation to seek assistance from national authorities, either because it is required to do so under national law or as a precautionary measure, the court may control that the Commission's decision is authentic and that the measures envisaged are not arbitrary or excessive, in light of the subject matter of the inspection (and in the case of inspections of private residences, the seriousness of the suspect infringement, the importance of the evidence sought, the involvement of the undertaking concerned and the reasonable likelihood that relevant documents are kept there). The court may not question the lawfulness of the Commission's decision or the necessity for the inspection, nor may it demand information in the Commission's file.

1.5.3 Guidance Letters

Conditions for seeking guidance letters. The Commission has the power to issue informal guidance in individual cases arising under Article 82 EC. The Informal Guidance Notice gives details on the situations in which the Commission intends to use its discretion to issue guidance letters, indications on how to request guidance, the processing of such requests, and the content and effect of guidance letters. The Commission will consider issuing guidance letters under three cumulative conditions: (1) the agreement, decision or practice in question poses a novel question on the application of Article 82 EC; (2) a *prima facie* evaluation of the case suggests that the clarification of the novel question is useful (taking into account the economic importance of the issue from the consumer's point of view; the extent to which the case represents a widely spread practice; the scope of the investment related to the transaction in relation to the size of the undertakings concerned; and the extent to which the transaction affects a structural operation, such as the creation of a non-full function joint venture); and (3) the guidance letter can be issued on the basis of the information provided, i.e. without further fact-finding. These conditions are relatively restrictive, but it is hoped that the Commission will be more open to applying them in the case of Article 82 EC, since it raises some of the most difficult questions in EC competition law.

Procedure. If the Commission issues a guidance letter, it will contain a summary description of the facts and the principal legal reasoning underlying the Commission's understanding of the novel question on Article 82 EC raised by the request. All guidance letters will be published on the Commission's website, subject to the rules on business secrets. Guidance letters will not bind the Community Courts, NCAs, or national courts, or even the Commission itself. However, the Informal Guidance Notice indicates that the Commission would, in the absence of any new facts or any development of the case law of the European Courts, normally take the previous guidance letter into account. The Commission's view expressed in a guidance letter can also be taken into account by courts.

Legal effect of a guidance letter. Guidance letters are similar in effect to comfort letters, i.e., administrative letters that the Commission has used under Regulation 17 to close files without adopting formal decisions. The Informal Guidance Notice leaves open whether guidance letters can be subject to appeal, which seems unlikely given that they are not legally binding. Given the extremely limited legal effect of guidance letters, and their limitation to situations raising novel questions of EC competition law, it is not clear that their practical impact will be significant.

1.5.4 Methods Of Bringing Article 82 EC Claims

The choice between administrative action and private enforcement. The Complaints Notice provides guidance on the advantages and disadvantages of different procedures to pursue an alleged infringement of Article 82 EC: lodging a complaint with the Commission or with a NCA or bringing an action before a national court. The Notice covers the role of complaints in the new enforcement system; the complementary role of private and public enforcement; work-sharing between the competition authorities and courts; the conditions for the Commission handling a complaint, including the complaint form and content required and the requirement that complainants have a legitimate interest; principles of the assessment of a complaint, including Community interest and Article 82 EC; and the Commission's procedures when dealing with a complaint, including the complainant's procedural rights.

If the purpose of bringing action is to safeguard individual rights, the Complaints Notice suggests that litigation before national courts may be preferable. In contrast to the Commission and NCAs, national courts have the power to award damages, to rule on other contractual obligations based on an agreement to be examined under Article 82 EC, to determine the full legal effects of a violation of Article 82 EC, to decide upon a combination of claims under Community competition law and other claims, and to award legal costs to the successful applicant. They are usually also better placed to order interim measures. In addition, with the abolition of the notification system of Council Regulation 17/62, national court proceedings can no longer be delayed by undertakings notifying agreements to the Commission.

Procedure for making an administrative complaint. If the choice is between NCAs and the Commission, the Complaints Notice refers to the principles of case allocation as explained in the Cooperation Notice (see above), which complainants should consider when making the choice of which competition authority to approach. It also recalls the rationale of the new system: the Commission intends to concentrate on the most serious infringements and on cases involving the definition of Community competition policy and/or ensuring consistent application thereof.

Regulation 773/2004 explains in more detail the information expected from complainants. To this end, it annexes "Form C" which identifies the minimum information that is generally required by the Commission. This includes information on the complainant and the undertakings subject to the complaint, details of the infringement alleged and supporting evidence, proof that the complainant has a legitimate interest in making the complaint, an explanation of why action at the Community level is necessary, and details of any prior or pending proceedings at national level. Three paper copies and, if possible, an electronic copy of the complaint should be submitted to the Commission. The complainant must also submit a non-confidential version of the complaint, if confidentiality is claimed for any part of the complaint. Only complaints submitted in one of the official languages of the Community will be accepted.

1.5.5 The Conduct Of Commission Proceedings

Basic procedure. Regulation 773/2004 contains procedural rules governing Commission proceedings under Regulation 1/2003, including the initiation of Commission proceedings; investigations by the Commission (including taking statements and asking oral questions during inspections); the treatment of complaints; the exercise of the right to be heard; access to the Commission's file; and treatment of confidential information. Most of the regulation consolidates the Commission's previous practice, but some points of interest are noted below.

New power to take statements. Article 19 of Regulation 1/2003 confers on the Commission a new power to take statements, and Regulation 773/2004 provides details on the recording of such statements. The process is voluntary, i.e., the Commission cannot compel a statement or sanction a refusal to give one. Where consent to an interview is granted, the Commission must make the recorded statement available for correction by the interviewed person or, if the statements are taken during inspections, allow the undertaking concerned to comment thereon if the representative or staff member questioned was not authorised by the company to make any statement.

Access to file. Both complainants and parties subject to an investigation may request access to the file under certain conditions. Complainants may inspect the Commission's file only if the Commission intends to reject the complaint, while parties subject to an investigation may do so only after they receive a statement of objections. Regulation

773/2004 clarifies that documents in the file may only be used for the application of Articles 82 EC. This seems to indicate that information received through the Commission's investigation cannot be used in subsequent litigation unrelated to Article 82 EC, for instance litigation under national competition laws. This provision, however, does not seem to prevent the use of documents for damage claims based on violation of EC competition rules.

Confidentiality. The Commission may request companies to identify confidential information and other companies *vis-à-vis* which this information should be considered confidential. The Commission may set a time limit for the undertakings to: (1) substantiate their claim for confidentiality with regard to each individual item; (2) provide the Commission with a non-confidential version; and (3) provide a concise description of each piece of deleted information. If the relevant company fails to comply with these obligations, the material shall be deemed not to contain confidential information. The Commission can only disclose a piece of information identified as confidential after having informed the relevant company in writing, including giving reasons, and if the undertaking does not object. If the Commission wishes to disclose the information against the undertaking's will, it needs to issue a formal decision, which can be appealed to the Court of Justice.[229] If the Court decides that the information is considered confidential, the Commission cannot disclose it. However, this does not prejudice the Commission's right to disclose and use information necessary to prove an infringement of Article 82 EC. The term "necessary" clearly leaves scope for interpretation and is not explained further in Regulation 773/2004.

1.5.6 Sector Inquiries

Legal basis. Sector inquiries are investigations into a particular sector of the economy or into a particular type of agreement across various sectors. Article 17 of Regulation 1/2003 empowers the Commission to launch a sector inquiry where the trend of trade between Member States, the rigidity of process or other circumstances suggest a restriction or distortion of competition. The Commission considers that, in the framework of Regulation 1/2003, sector inquiries are particularly appropriate for

[229] In *AKZO*, it was claimed that documents taken by officials of the Office of Fair Trading and the Commission during a dawn raid were legally privileged and should not be made available to the Commission for the purposes of its investigation. The documents included: (1) memoranda drafted for the purpose of a telephone conversation with a lawyer concerning a potential procedure; and (2) communications with Akzo's in-house counsel. Although the President of the Court of First Instance was sympathetic to the companies' arguments on legal privilege, the Court of Justice overturned the order on the basis that, in the event that the documents were ultimately held to be covered by legal privilege, the Commission would be unable to rely upon them as evidence for the purposes of any later Decision. Article 6(1) of the ECHR and Article 47 of the legally persuasive EU Charter of Fundamental Rights guarantee the right to a fair trial, but there are no specific provisions on legal privilege. *AKZO* is under appeal and the Court of Justice's judgment is much anticipated. See Joined Cases T-125/03 R and T-253/03 R, *Akzo Nobel Chemicals Ltd and Akcros Chemicals Ltd v Commission* [2003] ECR II-4771, on appeal Case C-7/04 P(R), *Commission v Akzo Nobel Chemicals Ltd and Akcros Chemicals Ltd*, [2004] ECR I-8739. The precise ambit of legal privilege was left open in Case 155/79, *AM&S Europe Limited v Commission* [1982] ECR 1575.

investigating cross-border market concerns and examining sector-wide practices that do not normally fall within the scope of an individual case.[230]

Process and practical experience to date. Sector inquiries typically comprise the following phases: (1) decision to open an inquiry; (2) investigation; (3) assessment of evidence and publication of preliminary conclusions; and (4) finalisation of inquiry report and follow-up actions:[231]

1. *Deciding to open an inquiry.* While the power to undertake sector inquiries is not new—Council Regulation 17/62 contained a similar power—sector inquiries are in practice becoming a much more important part of the Commission's work as the need for pro-active enforcement of competition rules has substantially increased post-modernisation. So far, the Commission has launched sector inquiries into the markets for energy, financial services, telecommunications, and new media. Defining candidate sectors is not entirely scientific and there may also be certain political motivations. The general approach to choosing sectors has been to rely on day-to-day case management and market monitoring to identify gaps in markets, i.e., to find out which markets are not functioning well. If a potential "gap" is spotted, the Commission will consider a number of factors in order to evaluate whether or not an inquiry would be appropriate. First, whether the formality of a sector inquiry, with the possibility of sanctions and inspections, is necessary. Second, would specialist technical advice be sufficient to explain the dynamics of the market in question? Third, what type of competition problems have been identified?

2. *Investigation.* The investigation will focus on the gaps in the market that have been identified where no information is available. The Commission will then collect statistical and analytical data in order to evaluate: (a) the general functioning of the market in question, i.e., the barriers within the market, the regulatory framework; and (b) the facts that raise specific infringement issues, e.g. prevalence of long-term agreements. Sources of information might include publicly-available information, information requests, Commission surveys, and technical reports. On-premises inspections or site visits might also be used. Information collected in the course of the inquiry can be used in subsequent proceedings—the questionnaires themselves state that information can be used for individual enforcement. But conclusions reached in a sector inquiry cannot simply be transposed into a statement of objections or decision: each case must be developed in its own right.

3. *Preliminary conclusions.* The preliminary report will be placed on the Commission's website for 6–8 weeks and there will be a public hearing. This gives stakeholders an opportunity to put forward further submissions and

[230] See Communication from the Commission—a pro-active Competition Policy for a Competitive Europe (COM (2004) 293 final).

[231] See J Stragier, AMCHAM EU: Competition Policy Committee Meeting, *Sector Inquiries*, Brussels, January 27, 2006.

suggest possible remedies. It will also give an opportunity for any mistakes made by the Commission to be corrected.

4. *Final Report.* Article 17 of Regulation 1/2003 does not oblige the Commission to publish this report: it simply says that the Commission "may publish" such a report. The Commission would not publish a report if the whole inquiry was confidential or if there were significant competition issues and publication would jeopardise further investigations. The report will typically contain some or all of the following elements: (a) specific enforcement action (either by the Commission or NCAs) relating to infringements of Articles 81, 82, or 86 EC by specific companies; (b) recommendations of other less specific measures, e.g., regulations; and/or (c) sector guidelines.

Chapter 2

MARKET DEFINITION

2.1 INTRODUCTION

The role of market definition under Article 82 EC. Article 82 EC only applies to the conduct of firms that are dominant at the time the alleged abuse is committed, i.e., firms that can act with a degree of independence from their competitors, customers, and consumers.[1] Assessing dominance requires an assessment of whether the firm under investigation faces significant competitive constraints. The first step in that assessment is the definition of the relevant market, which comprises all those products (and their geographic locations) that impose an effective competitive constraint on the product(s) of the firm whose unilateral practices are under scrutiny.[2] The second step involves an assessment of the competitive position of the allegedly dominant firm on the relevant market, i.e., its ability to raise prices or reduce output in relation to their competitive levels for a sustained period of time. Both steps are vital in an Article 82 EC investigation.

Market definition therefore constitutes a critical step in the assessment of dominance:[3] the Community Courts have consistently held that the definition of a relevant market is an essential prerequisite for the assessment of dominance.[4] For example, the two most common indicators of the existence of a dominant position are market shares and the ease of entry. Market shares can only be calculated once the boundaries of the relevant market have been correctly established. The importance attached to market shares is based on the (often incorrect) presumption that market structure—i.e., market shares and concentration indices—influences the behaviour of firms, and, ultimately, market

---

[1] See Case 85/76, *Hoffmann-La Roche & Co AG v Commission* [1979] ECR 461(hereinafter "*Hoffmann-La Roche*"), para. 38. See Ch. 3 (Dominance) below.

[2] The same reasoning has been endorsed by the Office of Fair Trading in its national guidelines on market definition. See Office of Fair Trading, *Market Definition*, OFT 403, December 2004, (hereinafter "OFT Market Definition Guideline"), paras. 2.1 and 2.2.

[3] See DG Competition discussion paper on the application of Article 82 of the Treaty to exclusionary abuses, Brussels, December 2005 (hereinafter the "Discussion Paper"), para. 11.

[4] See Case 6/72, *Europemballage Corporation and Continental Can v Commission* [1973] ECR 215 (hereinafter "*Continental Can*"), para. 32 ("the definition of the relevant market is of essential significance"). See also Case 27/76, *United Brands Company and United Brands Continentaal BV v Commission* [1978] ECR 207 (hereinafter "*United Brands*"), para. 10; Case 31/80, *L'Oreal v De Nieuwe AMCK* [1980] ECR 3775 (hereinafter "*L'Oreal*"), para. 25; and Case 62/86, *AKZO Chemie BV v Commission* [1991] ECR I-3359 (hereinafter "*AKZO*"), para. 51. The Community Courts have reaffirmed the importance of market definition in recent cases. See, e.g., Case T-65/96, *Kish Glass & Co Ltd v Commission* [2000] ECR II-1885, para. 62, confirmed on appeal in Case C-241/00 P, *Kish Glass & Co Ltd v Commission* [2001] ECR I-7759; and Case T-219/99, *British Airways plc v Commission* [2003] ECR II-5917, para. 91.

outcomes.[5] Market definition also makes it possible to identify the constraints on exercise of market power that stem from potential entry.[6]

Whether a firm actually enjoys a dominant position is materially influenced by the scope of the relevant market defined. An overly narrow definition will be under-inclusive and lead to the imposition of obligations on a firm that are unjustified. An excessively broad definition will be over-inclusive and allow unilateral conduct that threatens effective competition to escape scrutiny. Both errors are costly.

Market definition also plays a key role in the identification and assessment of the actual or likely effects of the alleged abusive conduct. Market definition helps delineate the markets that are affected by an alleged abuse of dominance, i.e. the markets where competition is affected by the behaviour of a dominant firm. The abuse of a dominant position may have an effect either on the market where the firm under investigation holds a dominant position, or on a different market that is adjacent to the market where the firm is dominant. To conclude that a given commercial practice in market A has an exclusionary effect on market B, both markets A and B must have been properly defined. Again, an overly narrow definition for market B may lead to the conclusion that exclusion is likely when it is not, and *vice versa*.

Relevant product and geographic markets. The relevant market is typically defined along a *product dimension* and a *geographic dimension*. In its product dimension, the relevant market includes those products that compete with each other to satisfy customers' needs. The Commission's Notice on the definition of the relevant markets defines the relevant product market as comprising "all those products and/or services which are regarded as interchangeable or substitutable by the consumer, by reason of the products' characteristics, their prices and their intended use."[7] Substitution is most accurately measured by the extent to which consumers of Firm A's product would be minded to switch to other firms' products in response to a price rise by Firm A, i.e., the effect on demand of non-trivial price increases. Where such a price rise would be unprofitable for Firm A—in the sense that the value of the sales lost to rival firms

---

[5] See S Bishop and S Baker, "The Role of Market Definition in Monopoly and Dominance Inquiries" *Economic Discussion Paper 2*, OFT 342, July 2001, para. 2.6. This presumption dates back to the structure-conduct-performance paradigm developed by Bain. According to this view, it is the structure of the market that determines its performance, via the conduct of its participants. Performance is measured by the ability to charge prices above the competitive level, thereby earning a positive mark-up, for a sustained period of time, while structure is given by concentration. See JS Bain, *Barriers to New Competition: Their Character and Consequences in Manufacturing Industries* (Cambridge, Harvard University Press, 1956); and JS Bain, "Relation of Profit Rates to Industry Concentration: American Manufacturing, 1936–1940" (1951) 65 *Quarterly Journal of Economics* 293–324. The structure-conduct-performance paradigm was shown to lead to incorrect predictions by modern developments in industrial organisation based on the application of game theory. See A Jacquemin, *The New Industrial Organisation* (Oxford, Oxford University Press, 1987).

[6] M Motta, *Competition Policy: Theory and Practice* (Cambridge, Cambridge University Press, 2004), p. 117. See also AJ Padilla, *The Role of Supply-Side Substitution in the Definition of the Relevant Market in Merger Control*, NERA, A Report for DG Enterprise, European Commission, June 2001, pp. 65–78.

[7] Commission Notice on the definition of the relevant market for the purpose of Community competition law, OJ 1997 C 372/5, para. 7 (hereinafter the "Market Definition Notice").

exceeds Firm A's profits from the price rise—Firm A's product and its rivals' products are likely to be in the same relevant product market. Where quantitative analysis of this kind cannot be performed, the relevant product market may be defined according to qualitative criteria, such as product characteristics. This is, however, a second-best solution, as explained below.

The relevant geographic market encompasses a geographic area in which the conditions of competition are sufficiently homogeneous. The Market Definition Notice states that "the relevant geographic market comprises the area in which the undertakings concerned are involved in the supply and demand of products or services, in which the conditions of competition are sufficiently homogeneous and which can be distinguished from neighbouring areas because the conditions of competition are appreciably different in those areas."[8] Depending on the degree of homogeneity of the conditions of competition between different areas, the relevant geographic market may be global, regional, trans-national, national, sub-national, or, in rare cases, confined to a facility in a single geographic location (e.g., a port).

Relationship between market definition under Article 82 EC and other legal instruments. The approach to market definition under Article 82 EC is broadly consistent with the principles applied in merger cases and Article 81 EC. This is hardly surprising, since the Market Definition Notice is intended to provide an overview of the general principles that the Commission employs in assessing market definition in the three main areas of EC competition law (i.e., Articles 81, 82, and the EC Merger Regulation). In each case, the purpose of the delineation of the relevant market is to identify the competitive constraints that the firm(s) under investigation face. For example, as the Commission's horizontal merger guidelines state, the purpose of defining a relevant market is "to identify in a systematic way the immediate competitive constraints facing the merged entity."[9] It is also notable that the definition of the relevant market in Form CO (Section 6) adopts almost verbatim the formulation used by the Community Courts for the definition of the relevant market.[10]

Despite the doctrinal equivalence of the definition of market power under both Article 82 EC and the EC Merger Regulation, a number of differences should be noted. First, and most importantly, the competitive constraints that are the focus of market definition under Article 82 EC and the EC Merger Regulation are not the same. In merger control, the objective of market definition is to identify the competitive constraints faced by the merging parties *at pre-merger prices,* without questioning the

[8] *Ibid.*, para. 8.

[9] Guidelines on the assessment of horizontal mergers under the Council Regulation on the control of concentrations between undertakings, OJ 2004 C 31/5, para. 10. See also Case COMP/M.3108, *Office Depot/Guilber*, para. 22 ("[T]he precise boundaries of the relevant market are difficult to determine, but this should not distract from the main purpose of defining a market, namely to identify those competitors of the undertakings involved that are capable of constraining their behaviour.").

[10] See, e.g., Case 27/76, *United Brands Company and United Brands Continentaal BV v Commission* [1978] ECR 207, paras. 12–35. See also Case 31/80, *L'Oreal v De Nieuwe AMCK* [1980] ECR 3775, para. 25 ("[T]he possibilities of competition must be judged in the context of the market comprising the totality of the products which, with respect to their characteristics, are particularly suitable for satisfying constant needs and are only to a limited extent interchangeable with other products.").

legitimacy of those prices. Instead, under Article 82 EC, market definition is used to assess whether the firm whose practices are deemed abusive enjoys market power, and that involves investigating the existence of competitive constraints *at competitive prices*. This makes market definition under Article 82 EC inherently more difficult than in merger control: while pre-merger prices are readily observable, defining whether a price is competitive or not is a daunting task.[11]

A second, difference between market definition under Article 82 EC and the EC Merger Regulation is that the latter makes greater use of quantitative techniques to test the degree of substitution among products. Recent decisional practice under the EC Merger Regulation shows increasing use of econometric techniques, such as co-integration analysis and regression studies, in order to determine the relevant correlations and price elasticities for purposes of defining the relevant market.[12] This willingness to use sophisticated, data-intensive techniques under the EC Merger Regulation contrasts with the largely qualitative approach to market definition historically adopted by the Commission and the Community Courts under Article 82 EC.

There is no obvious reason, however, why quantitative techniques should be used more widely in the EC Merger Regulation than under Article 82 EC. Lack of specialism or resources is not an explanation, since the Chief Economist's Unit may be involved in any matter subject falling within DG Competition's jurisdiction. Time constraints are also not a factor. Indeed, if anything, the strict time-limits imposed for merger review are much less conducive to data-intensive econometric studies than investigations under Article 82 EC (which have no formal time limits).

One possible explanation is that the Community Courts' use of economics in the context of its judicial review function has been more widespread to date in appeals from decisions adopted under the EC Merger Regulation than Article 82 EC, which may have led the Commission to make greater use of quantitative techniques in order to bolster its assessments. In *Schneider Electric*,[13] for example, the Commission's prohibition of a proposed merger was overturned due to "several obvious errors, omissions, and contradictions in the Commission's economic reasoning."[14] Market definition was critical in this regard, since the Commission based its market definition (and, therefore, its views on dominance) on the existence of several national markets, but then assessed the transaction's competitive impact on the basis of unsubstantiated trans-national concerns. In other words, the Commission's market definition and substantive analyses did not marry.[15] Errors in economic assessment were also central to the Community

[11] See Ch. 12 (Excessive Prices) for a detailed explanation of the practical difficulties involved in the definition and calculation of competitive prices.

[12] Some of these techniques are briefly described in section 2.3 below.

[13] Cases T-310/01, *Schneider Electric SA v Commission* [2002] ECR II-4071, and Case T-77/02, *Schneider Electric SA v Commission* [2002] ECR II-4201.

[14] See Court of First Instance Press Release No. 84/02, of October 22, 2002.

[15] The Court of First Instance found that "the Commission incorporated, not only in its presentation, but also in its analysis, of the facts, the unmatched geographic coverage of the merged entity throughout the whole of the EEA, in order to show that a dominant position would be created or strengthened on the national sectoral markets for switchboard components and for ultraterminal equipment." See Case T-310/01, *Schneider Electric SA v Commission* [2002] ECR II-4071, para. 176.

Courts' decision to annul the merger prohibition decisions in *Airtours*[16] and *Tetra Laval/Sidel*.[17]

Another, more pragmatic, explanation for the greater use of econometric techniques under the EC Merger Regulation than Article 82 EC is that the output data required to perform econometric studies will only be available in a small number of cases. Because the number of decisions under the EC Merger Regulation greatly exceeds those adopted under Article 82 EC, suitable candidate cases for detailed econometric study are more likely to arise in the merger area. Moreover, if econometric data are supportive of their case, the notifying parties will often have an incentive to create a data set and volunteer it as part of the analysis.

The paramount role of economics in market definition. The largely qualitative approach to market definition for purposes of Article 82 EC historically adopted by the Community institutions does not correspond with economists' current understanding of how markets should be defined. This is hardly surprising, since many of the leading cases under Article 82 EC pre-date the major advancements in economic thinking on market definition—most notably the introduction of the hypothetical monopolist test in the 1982 United States Horizontal Merger Guidelines.[18] Market definition in leading Article 82 EC cases in the 1970s and 1980s might well be decided differently today, or at least would require more rigorous analysis.

For example, in *United Brands*, the Commission and Court of Justice essentially used qualitative evidence in concluding that bananas were a separate relevant market to other fruits,[19] relying in particular on the seedlessness and softness of bananas as important defining characteristics for the young and the elderly. They declined to investigate cross-price elasticities, relying instead on a largely subjective assessment, which arguably overstated United Brands' market power.[20] The existence of modern supermarket scanner data would enable the relative own-price and cross-price elasticities to be easily calculated today. This would allow an empirical evaluation of whether qualitative differences between bananas and other fruits also led to distinct demands for individual products, or whether a range of ready-to-eat fruits competed in a broader market. The important point to note is that economic thinking almost certainly provides a more reliable indicator of current and future policy on market definition than older cases under Article 82 EC.

---

[16] Case T-342/99, *Airtours plc v Commission* [2002] ECR II-2585.

[17] Case T-5/02, *Tetra Laval BV v Commission* [2002] ECR II-4381, confirmed on appeal in Case C-12/03 P, *Commission v Tetra Laval BV* [2005] ECR I-987.

[18] See G Werden, "The 1982 Merger Guidelines and the Ascent of the Hypothetical Monopolist Paradigm," speech at the *20th Anniversary of the 1982 Merger Guidelines: The Contribution of the Merger Guidelines to the Evolution of Antitrust Doctrine*, June 4, 2002 ("The hypothetical monopolist paradigm was the lens through which all evidence was to be viewed.").

[19] Case 27/76, *United Brands Company and United Brands Continentaal BV v Commission* [1978] ECR 207, paras. 12–35.

[20] See V Korah, *An Introductory Guide to EEC Competition Law and Practice* (4th edn., Oxford, ESC Publishing Ltd., 1990), p. 59 ("The interests of the toothless are sufficiently protected by the inability of the dominant firm to discriminate against them. It would lose so much market share from the rest of the population that it would not be worth raising prices to exploit the weak.").

A related point, and a further reason why economics should play the paramount role in market definition under Article 82 EC, is that many earlier market definition decisions under Article 82 EC have been criticised as being result-oriented. In other words, there may have been a temptation to define markets narrowly in order to support a finding of dominance and the pursuit of particular policy goals. The result-oriented tendency in older Article 82 EC cases has been summarised as follows:[21]

> "It has been said from time to time that the Commission and Court of Justice have tailored market definitions to reach particular outcomes that reflect substantive policies other than those based on conventional antitrust concerns over market power. There is some truth in this observation, at least with respect to Article 8[2] cases dealing with essential facilities, refusals to deal and some other vertical restraints. Markets in these decisions do seem to have been drawn more narrowly than a purely economic concern about adverse price and output effects would warrant. But this is a very limited number of relatively discrete cases."

One example is *Hilti*,[22] where the Commission concluded that power-actuated fastening systems (nail guns) were a distinct market from other fastening systems (e.g., welding, screws, rivets, bolts, and nuts). Again, the Commission focused largely on the differences in characteristics between the products in concluding that there was insufficient demand-side substitution.[23] The Commission did not consider whether the pricing of one product constrains the pricing of the other products. No consideration was give to whether the number of marginal customers who would switch in response to a price rise for nail guns was sufficiently large to act as a constraint. The Commission's subsequent decision in *Pelican/Kyocera*[24] illustrates a more nuanced approach, in particular in markets in which primary equipment and consumables are involved.

Need for caution in respect of market definition. Excessive importance should not, however, be attached to the outcomes of a market definition exercise: it is, at best, a proxy for identifying a range of products over which a monopolist could in theory exercise market power. As noted by the previous Commissioner for Competition, Mario Monti, the Commission uses "market definition and market shares as an easily available proxy for the measurement of the market power enjoyed by firms."[25] Thus, market definition is "a cornerstone of competition policy, but not the entire building." It is a "a tool for the competitive assessment, not a substitute for it. What is ultimately important is to understand the nature of the competitive situation facing the firms involved in a certain practice."[26] In short, "markets cannot be defined in a vacuum; market definitions make sense only in the context in which the questions are posed."[27]

---

[21] See T Kauper, "The Problem of Market Definition Under EC Competition Law" in B Hawk (ed.), *International Antitrust Law and Policy: Fordham Corporate Law Institute* (London, Sweet and Maxwell, 1997), p. 303.

[22] *Eurofix-Bauco/Hilti*, OJ 1988 L 65/19.

[23] *Ibid.*, para. 61.

[24] *Pelican/Kyocera,* XXVth Report on Competition Policy (1997), para. 86–87.

[25] M Monti, "Policy Market Definition As A Cornerstone Of EU Competition policy" *Workshop on Market Definition*, Helsinki, October 5, 2001.

[26] *Ibid.*

[27] See WE Schrank and N Roy, "Market Delineation in the Analysis of the United States Groundfish Market" (1991) 36(1) *Antitrust Bulletin* 91–154, at 107.

2.2 PRODUCT MARKET DEFINITION: BASIC CONCEPTS

Overview. A relevant product market under Article 82 EC comprises all those products and/or services that impose a competitive constraint on the product(s) of the company whose behaviour is being analysed. The most important constraint is exerted by those consumers who can switch their consumption to products that they regard as interchangeable (*demand-side substitution*). A second, but less important, constraint is created by those competing firms who can quickly produce and commercialise products that are demand-side substitutes to those of the firm in question (*supply-side substitution*).

Supply-side substitution is different from *potential competition*. Potential competition concerns the ability of firms outside the relevant product market to enter in the long term; supply-side substitution concerns the ability of firms to switch production in the short term and without incurring large sunk costs. Only when the competitive constraint imposed by entry is equivalent in its effect to that of demand-side substitution—i.e., when the entrants offer products or services that can be regarded as supply-side substitutes to those in the market—entry is considered at the market definition stage. Potential competition is therefore only assessed at the stage of analysing dominance. Finally, it may be that two directly competing products are indirectly constrained by competition from a third product, where the products are linked by so-called "*chains of substitution*." The basic features of each of these sources of competitive constraint are explained below.

2.2.1 Demand-Side Substitution

Definition. The most important competitive constraint faced by a firm comes from consumers who are prepared to switch to substitute products in the event of a price increase. When a firm's customers have demand-side substitutes available, the firm cannot profitably raise the price of its products because that would trigger substitution and, therefore, a loss of business. An increase in price leads to a higher margin per unit sold, but causes a fall in output. In the presence of demand-side substitutes, however, the loss of sales outweighs the higher unit margin. The dominant role played by demand-side substitution in the process of defining a relevant product market is therefore due to the immediate character of the competitive constraint it gives rise to.[28] As the Market Definition Notice states, "demand substitution constitutes the most immediate and effective disciplinary force on the suppliers of a given product, in particular in relationship to their pricing decisions."[29]

The scope and scale of demand-side substitution depends entirely on consumer preferences: what matters for demand-side substitution are the products that consumers view as substitutes. Whether the products have similar physical characteristics is generally unimportant: consumers might view products with distinct physical characteristics as close substitutes; and they might regard products that are physically similar as not being interchangeable. All products that consumers regard as close

[28] See *Tetra Laval/Sidel*, OJ 2004 L 43/13, para. 163.

[29] Commission Notice on the definition of the relevant market for the purpose of Community competition law, OJ 1997 C 372/5, para. 13.

substitutes to the product or products of the firm whose behaviour is analysed should be part of the same relevant market, since they impose a competitive constraint on the firm concerned.

Testing for demand-side substitution. Demand-side substitution can be examined either directly or indirectly. Direct evidence of substitution is provided by evidence of consumers' past behaviour. This is what economists term as "revealed preference." If consumers reacted to past changes in the prices of the firm in question by switching their consumption to other products, then there is clear evidence of demand-side substitution. In some instances, such evidence is not readily available, either because the firm did not change its prices, because the prices of all products that are potential substitutes changed at the same time (and thus there was no change in relative prices that could have triggered substitution), or because of the presence of other factors that masked the volume impact of the price change. In these circumstances, indirect evidence of demand-side preference is required: counterfactual estimation of the influence of price on demand (i.e., the price elasticity of demand) using multiple regression analysis or, if that is not possible, inspection of product characteristics and intended use. Both qualitative and, ideally, quantitative evidence are relevant in this connection:[30]

> "In its analysis of demand-substitutability, the Commission may make use of both qualitative and quantitative methods. Qualitative methods could, for example, include an examination of product characteristics and the intended use of a product by consumers, whereas quantitative methods could involve the examination of price trends and the estimation of cross-elasticities using econometric methods."

The Commission's basic analytical approach to demand-side substitution. An interesting, recent example of the Commission's analytical approach to demand-side substitution is *Wanadoo*,[31] where Wanadoo, a subsidiary of France Télécom, was fined for predatory pricing in the high-speed internet access market in France. A central issue was whether ADSL (or broadband) internet access was a separate product from narrowband (or dial-up) and cable-based access, and whether the market should be further segmented between residential and business users. The Commission ultimately concluded that there was a single market for high-speed internet access for residential users, which included cable and ADSL services, but excluded narrowband access.

Factors cited by the Commission in support of this conclusion included: (1) high speed internet access is "always on;" narrowband required dial-up each time and, unless the user has a second line, does not permit simultaneous use of the telephone; (2) for certain multimedia applications (e.g., music downloading), narrowband was not an effective option due to excessive download times; (3) there was considerable asymmetry in consumer substitution between the high-speed internet access and narrowband, i.e., consumers would less often switch back to a phone connection when the price of the

[30] See XXIVth Report on Competition Policy (1994), para. 280. See also Commission Notice on the definition of the relevant market for the purpose of Community competition law, OJ 1997 C 372/5, para. 39.

[31] Case COMP/38.233, *Wanadoo Interactive*, Commission Decision of July 16, 2003, not yet published (hereinafter "*Wanadoo*").

high-speed internet was raised, whereas when the high-speed internet access price was lowered France Telecom would see a large increase in new customers;[32] and (4) prices for high-speed internet access differed as between business and residential users.

2.2.2 Supply-Side Substitution

Definition. Supply-side substitution occurs when suppliers of products that are not demand-side substitutes to the products in the relevant product market can—quickly and without incurring significant costs—switch their production plans to offer products that compete with those in the relevant market. When two products are supply-side substitutes, they are taken to be part of the same relevant product market. That is, the possibility of supply-side substitution broadens the scope of the relevant product market. Supply-side substitutability is likely to be of relevance in situations where firms produce a wide range of different qualities, or different grades of a product, that are not seen as substitutable by consumers, but which are produced on similar equipment.

A trivial, but intuitive, example of supply-side substitution is shoes. An individual using shoes of size X is not willing to switch to shoes of size Y size if the price of shoes of the size he uses is raised. Shoe manufacturers, however, can easily switch production from shows of size X to shoes of size Y, and *vice versa*, and are able to supply shoes of both sizes immediately and without incurring any additional costs. In this example, shoes of sizes X and Y are supply-side substitutes and form part of the same relevant product market. Another example is the production of paper. Paper plants usually produce paper in a range of different qualities, for products as diverse as art books, writing paper, etc. While consumers do not regard the different paper product as substitutes, manufacturers can easily and at negligible costs adjust production at short notice. Such an instance of supply-side substitution would lead to a wide relevant market definition that includes all qualities of paper.[33]

Testing for supply-side substitution. The disciplinary effect exerted by supply-side substitution is subject to strict conditions. Of particular importance is the need for supply-side substitution to be sufficiently proximate or immediate so as to be considered equivalent to demand-side substitution:[34]

> "Supply-side substitutability may also be taken into account when defining markets in those situations in which its effects are equivalent to those of demand substitution in terms of effectiveness and immediacy. This means that suppliers are able to switch production to the relevant products and market them in the short term without incurring significant additional costs or risks in response to small and permanent changes in relative prices."

From an economic point of view, effective supply-side substitution requires consideration of a number of conditions: (1) the assets needed to produce, distribute and

---

[32] *Ibid.*, paras. 193–202.

[33] See Commission Notice on the definition of the relevant market for the purpose of Community competition law, OJ 1997 C 372/5, para. 22.

[34] *Ibid.*, para. 20. See also Office of Fair Trading, *Market Definition*, OFT 403, December 2004, paras. 3.15–3.18.

commercialise the relevant products are readily available;[35] (2) the firm can purchase or lease additional necessary assets without incurring sunk costs; (3) suppliers of supply-side substitutes have the economic incentive to engage in production of the relevant goods/services; (4) other suppliers are able to divert production from supply-side substitutes to the relevant products because, for example, they possess unused plant capacity that can be brought into production at a reasonable cost; and (5) consumers regard their products as valid substitutes for the existing set of products.[36]

Conditions (1) to (5) are necessary but not sufficient. Supply-side substitution also requires that *a large number* of suppliers can switch production to the relevant product in response to a modest price increase.[37] Consideration of supply-side substitutability translates into market aggregation and will therefore lead to wider markets than those that would obtain by considering demand substitution factors only. Yet, aggregating markets for products that are not seen as substitutes by consumers goes against the established principles of economic analysis and may incorrectly enlarge the actual boundaries of the relevant market. It is perhaps for this reason that the Market Definition Notice requires that "most of the suppliers" or "most if not all manufacturers,"[38] must be able to produce and market demand-side substitutes in order to enlarge the relevant product market. This is the condition required under the US Horizontal Merger Guidelines to aggregate markets as a result of supply substitution: two products A and B which are not demand-side substitutes belong to the same relevant product market if supply-side substitution between them is "nearly universal."[39]

Distinction between supply-side substitution and potential competition. Potential competition represents a competitive constraint that is different from supply-side substitution. While supply side substitution takes places immediately, potential competition represents a threat of entry either in the long term or one that involves significant sunk costs. The Market Definition Notice therefore states that "potential competition, is not taken into account when defining markets, since the conditions under which potential competition will actually represent an effective competitive constraint depend on the analysis of specific factors and circumstances related to the conditions of entry."[40] There is no doubt that the threat of entry, even when costly and long term,

[35] This includes access to the required technology, know-how, machinery, and facilities. It also requires access to the appropriate transport infrastructure and distribution channels. Moreover, a supplier must also be able to commercialise the products immediately—i.e., no investment in marketing and brand building is necessary.

[36] Commission Notice on the definition of the relevant market for the purpose of Community competition law, OJ 1997 C 372/5, paras. 22–23.

[37] *Ibid.*, paras. 23–24.

[38] *Ibid.*, para. 34.

[39] US Department of Justice Antitrust Division and Federal Trade Commission 1992 Horizontal Merger Guidelines 57 Fed. Reg. 41522 (1992), (hereinafter "US Horizontal Merger Guidelines"), fn 14.

[40] Commission Notice on the definition of the relevant market for the purpose of Community competition law, OJ 1997 C 372/5, para. 24. Thus, in *Clearstream*, the Commission has analysed the threat of potential competition in the section on the assessment of dominance. See Case COMP/38/096, *Clearstream (Clearing and settlement)*, Commission Decision of June 4, 2004, not yet published, paras. 209–15. This view is consistent with the US approach which considers potential entry as factor that reduces market power rather than as an element of market definition. US Department of Justice

constrains the extent to which a firm can exert market power. However, the threat of long-term entry imposes a different competitive constraint than supply-side substitution. To the extent that it involves irreversible investments, the former entails a strong "commitment." Potential entrants do not respond to modest price increases and do not commit resources to markets where post-entry prices are expected to be low. In contrast, supply-side substitution represents a form of "uncommitted" or "hit-and-run" entry. It responds to modest increases in current prices sufficiently fast to render any retaliatory strategy pointless.[41]

More precisely, potential entry and supply-side substitution can be distinguished in at least three respects. First, by the length of time that goes from the price rise to the commencement of supply by the new entrant. Supply-side substitution responds promptly to price increases, while potential entrants may take longer than a year or so to commence supplying the market with their products. Second, supply-side substitution involves "uncommitted entry," i.e., entry at a low cost and without incurring irreversible investment. Potential entry or "committed entry" refers to entry at a substantial sunk cost.[42] Finally, the competitive constraint imposed by supply-side substitutes has a clear-cut significant impact on both pre-entry and post-entry prices. Meanwhile, potential entry is felt via lower post-entry prices only. When entry involves incurring in sizeable sunk costs, entrants do not decide whether to join the market on the basis of current prices but, instead, they focus on the price level that would prevail in the market once entry occurs, which obviously depends on the credibility of retaliation by incumbents and, thus, ultimately hinges on whether the fundamental characteristics of the market are likely to support high post-entry prices or not.

The Commission's basic analytical approach to supply-side substitution. Analysis of supply-side substitution has featured prominently in the decisional practice of the Community institutions. In *Continental Can*, the Commission's decision was annulled by the Court of Justice on the grounds, *inter alia*, that it had not considered supply-side substitution when defining the relevant product market.[43] The Commission distinguished several markets: (1) light containers for canned meat products; (2) light containers for canned seafood; and (3) metal closures for the food packing industry (other than crown corks).

On appeal, the Court of Justice criticised the Commission for not considering how these three markets differed from each other, how they differed from the general market for light metal containers, namely the market for metal containers for fruit and vegetables, condensed milk, olive oil, fruit juices, etc., and whether particular characteristics of production made them specifically suitable for their specific purpose. The defendant's

Antitrust Division and Federal Trade Commission 1992 Horizontal Merger Guidelines 57 Fed. Reg. 41522 (1992), para. 3.

[41] See AJ Padilla, *The Role of Supply-Side Substitution in the Definition of the Relevant Market in Merger Control*, NERA, A Report for DG Enterprise, European Commission, June 2001, p. 21.

[42] The concept of "uncommitted" and "committed" entry was first defined in the US Department of Justice Antitrust Division and Federal Trade Commission 1992 Horizontal Merger Guidelines 57 Fed. Reg. 41522 (1992), para. 1.32.

[43] Case 6/72, *Europemballage Corporation and Continental Can v Commission* [1973] ECR 215, para. 33. See also Case No IV/M.32, *Granari/Ültje/Intersnack/May Holding*, paras. 20–23.

high share on the "market" for light metal containers for meat and fish was irrelevant in the absence of evidence that competitors from other sectors of the market for light metal containers were not in a position to enter this market, by a simple adaptation, with sufficient strength to create a serious counterweight.

In contrast, in *Michelin I*, the Court of Justice upheld the Commission's definition of separate markets for heavy vehicle car tyres. It held that these two categories of tyre were produced using different production techniques, so that time and considerable investment was required to switch production from one type of tyre to the other. Consequently, the Court considered that they could not be regarded as supply-side substitutes, and given that they were not demand-side substitutes either, the Court defined separate relevant markets for heavy vehicle and car tyres.[44]

The Commission now routinely considers supply-side substitution, even if, in practice, this circumstance rarely broadens the boundaries of the relevant market.[45] In *Microsoft*, for example, the Commission spent considerable effort on analysing supply-side substitution, but ultimately concluded that it did not broaden the market identified from a demand-side perspective.[46] For each of the three relevant markets (i.e., client operating systems, work group server operating systems, and streaming media players), the Commission checked systematically for demand-side substitutes and then supply-side substitutes before concluding on the relevant market. The Commission found that supply-side substitution was not relevant in the three markets concerned.[47] Similarly, in *Clearstream*, while the Commission ultimately concluded that demand-side substitution was the principal determinant,[48] supply-side substitution was cited as a relevant factor in various security clearing services markets.[49]

[44] See Case 322/81, *NV Nederlandsche Banden Industrie Michelin v Commission* [1983] ECR 3461 (hereinafter *"Michelin I"*), para. 41.

[45] See *Eurofix-Bauco/Hilti*, OJ 1988 L 65/19, para. 55, upheld on appeal in Case T-30/89, *Hilti AG v Commission* [1991] ECR II-1439, and on further appeal Case C-53/92 P, *Hilti AG v Commission* [1994] ECR I-667; Case COMP/C-3/37.792, *Microsoft*, Commission Decision of March 24, 2004, (hereinafter *"Microsoft")*, not yet published, para. 322; Case COMP/38/096, *Clearstream (Clearing and settlement)*, Commission Decision of June 4, 2004, not yet published, para. 200; *DSD*, OJ 2001 L 166/1, paras. 65–86; *Virgin/British Airways*, OJ 2000 L 30/1, upheld on appeal Case T-219/99, *British Airways plc v Commission* [2003] ECR II-5917, para. 74; *Van den Bergh Foods Ltd*, OJ 1998 L 246/1, para. 135; *Trans-Atlantic Conference Agreement*, OJ 1999 L 95/1, para. 75. See also AJ Padilla, "The Role of Supply-Side Substitution in the Definition of the Relevant Market in Merger Control," NERA, A Report for DG Enterprise, European Commission, June 2001, pp. 38–56, for a discussion of the case law on supply-side substitutability in merger control.

[46] Case COMP/C-3/37.792, *Microsoft*, Commission Decision of March 24, 2004, not yet published, paras. 321–425. See similarly *DSD*, OJ 2001 L 166/1, paras. 65–86; *P&I Clubs/Pooling Agreement*, OJ 1999 L 125/12, paras. 52–64; and *De Post–La Poste*, OJ 2002 L 61/32, paras. 36–50.

[47] Case COMP/C-3/37.792, *Microsoft*, Commission Decision of March 24, 2004, not yet published, paras. 342, 401, and 425.

[48] Case COMP/38/096, *Clearstream (Clearing and settlement)*, Commission Decision of June 4, 2004, not yet published, paras. 135–37.

[49] *Ibid.*, para. 200.

2.2.3 Chains of Substitution

Definition. Within a relevant market, it is not necessary that all products or services (or regions) are substitutes for each other: it might be sufficient for some products to be indirect substitutes to other products to be included in the same market. Products can be indirectly substitutable if they are linked through so-called "chains of substitution." The Commission has endorsed this concept and indicated in the Market Definition Notice that:[50]

> "In certain cases, the existence of chains of substitution might lead to the definition of a relevant market where products or areas at the extreme of the market are not directly substitutable....product B is a demand substitute for products A and C. Even if products A and C are not direct demand substitutes, they might be found to be in the same relevant product market since their respective pricing might be constrained by substitution to B."

Economic theory provides support for a market definition that takes into consideration chains of substitution. A number of contributions have examined the effect of so-called "straddling firms" on the behaviour of companies who do not compete directly.[51] One model analyses situations in which there are three differentiated products. Company A offers one of the product varieties and company B offers a different product variety. The product varieties offered by companies A and B are distant substitutes. There is a "straddling" company, company C, which sells a variety that competes with the varieties of both A and B. The model shows how the presence of the "straddling" firm creates indirect competition between the products of companies A and B. The ability of company A to raise its price profitably is constrained directly by the presence of Firm C, and indirectly by the existence of firm B.

Suppose that company A considers increasing the price of its product. It will obviously take into account the possibility that some of its sales are diverted to company C, who offers a direct substitute. The loss of business will be smaller if company C responds to the price increase of A by raising the price it charges for its own product. However, the response of company C depends on the reaction of company B. If company C expects company B to keep its prices constant, then it likely will not raise its own prices by as much in response to the price increase of company A, which may then decide not to increase its price. In other words, competition from B deters the company C from responding to the price increase of company A, making the price rise less profitable, and thereby imposing an indirect competitive constraint on company A.

Examples of chains of substitution. The Commission has applied the concept of substitution chains in several market definition exercises, primarily in the merger control area.[52] In *AstraZeneca/Novartis*, for example, the Commission identified two

---

[50] *Ibid.*, para. 57. See also Office of Fair Trading, *Market Definition*, OFT 403, December 2004, para. 3.11.

[51] See T Cooper, "Indirect Competition with Spatial Product Differentiation" (1989) 37(3) *The Journal of Industrial Economics* 241–57. See also PJ DeGraba, "The Effects of Price Restrictions on Competition Between National and Local Firms" (1987) 18(3) *RAND Journal of Economics* 333–47.

[52] Case COMP/M.1806, *AstraZeneca/Novartis*, paras. 57, 58, and 60. See also Case COMP/M.2333, *De Beers/LVMH*, paras. 25–27; Case No IV/M.1780, *LVMH/PRADA/FENDI*, para. 11; and Case COMP/M.1882, *Pirelli/BICC*, para. 17.

specific herbicides for two different kinds of weed that were not direct substitutes and a broad-spectrum herbicide that could be used for both kinds of weed. The Commission concluded that a chain of substitution operating through the broad-spectrum herbicide linked the two specific herbicides, preventing a hypothetical monopolist for one of the herbicides from raising profitably its price. Its reasoning was as follows:[53]

> "In this case, a natural question to ask would be whether a hypothetical sole supplier of all herbicides capable of controlling grasses (i.e. graminicides and, to a lesser extent, broad spectrum herbicides) would find it profitable to increase prices for these products in the way described above. This is not necessarily the case. After all, given that broad spectrum herbicides are competing with broadleaf weed herbicides, an increase in the price of the first would not only lead to a drop in sales stemming from farmers no longer using the broad spectrum product for grass control, but also stemming from farmers that used to buy the product for broadleaf weed control switching to "pure" broadleaf herbicides. To the extent that many buyers of broad spectrum herbicides buy the product to control both types of weeds and the value of broad spectrum products is substantial in comparison with grass weed herbicides, broadleaf weed herbicides do exercise a competitive pressure on the prices of broad spectrum herbicides and, hence, on the prices of graminicides. This is the so-called chain of substitution effect."

2.3 RELEVANT PRODUCT MARKETS: FROM THEORY TO PRACTICE

2.3.1 Hypothetical Monopolist Test: Overview

Basic elements of the hypothetical monopolist test. Definition of the relevant product market requires a determination of which products, if any, are reasonably close substitutes for the products under examination, and so are in competition with them. Such a determination cannot be based on anecdote or intuition. Rather, it must be based on a rigorous assessment of economic substitutability. The search for an analytical means of identifying such products has led to the development of an economically sound methodology—the "hypothetical monopolist test" ("HMT"). Under this test, a market is defined as a product or a group of products that a hypothetical firm, seeking to maximise its profits not subject to price regulations and constituting the unique present and future seller of these goods, could impose a significant and lasting price increase. In short, the hypothetical monopolist test seeks to determine the narrowest market on which a hypothetical monopolist could exercise market power.

The HMT test was first developed by the US enforcement agencies in their Horizontal Merger Guidelines, amended most recently in 1997.[54] The HMT has subsequently gained widespread acceptance among competition authorities and courts worldwide, authorities including the Commission,[55] the Community Courts, and national courts.

---

[53] Case COMP/M.1806, *AstraZeneca/Novartis*, para. 60.

[54] US Department of Justice and Federal Trade Commission Merger Guidelines issued April 2, 1992, revised April 8, 1997, para. 4, reprinted in 4 Trade Reg. Rep. (CCH).

[55] See Commission Notice on the definition of the relevant market for the purpose of Community competition law, OJ 1997 C 372/5, s. III. The Commission also followed the principles of the hypothetical monopolist test in several cases. See, e.g., *Tetra Pak I (BTG licence)*, OJ 1988 L 272/27, para. 30; *Eurofix-Bauco/Hilti*, OJ 1988 L 65/19, para. 60; and *1998 Football World Cup*, OJ 2000

The HMT has made a valuable contribution in providing a more rigorous basis for market definition in EC competition law. This test is a "thought experiment"[56] that can be applied in practice relying on both quantitative and qualitative evidence. The translation of the theory of the HMT into a practical tool applied to the facts of a particular case may not always be easy, however. While the theory behind the HMT is reasonably clear, implementing it in practice is much less so. Crisp equations and clean demand curves often become blurred and imprecise when the HMT theory is applied to a given set of facts. The actual definition of the relevant market necessarily involves the exercise of judgment and discretion in practice.

Iteration of the HMT test. The HMT test iterates through three steps. The first step is to define a candidate set of products for the hypothetical monopolist to control. This defines the so-called *candidate market*,[57] which in an Article 82 EC investigation is given by the products or services of the allegedly dominant firm that are the subject of commercial practices under investigation.[58] For example, in a predation case, the candidate market will be given by the product(s) of the allegedly dominant firm which are allegedly priced below cost.

The second step is to consider the effect of demand-side substitution on the profitability of a price rise by the hypothetical monopolist. The test asks whether this would be rendered unprofitable by defections of customers who choose to buy products outside the candidate market rather than paying the higher price.

The final step in the process is to consider the effect of supply-side substitution. The test asks whether suppliers of products outside the candidate market could and would respond to an increase in price by the hypothetical monopolist by quickly entering the candidate market and offering a substitutable product. If the hypothetical monopolist is not able to raise prices profitably over the initial set of products for a sustained period of time, it means that consumers would switch to products outside the candidate market. The candidate market would have to be redefined to include those substitutable products. This process would continue iteratively until a putative market is found for which the hypothetical monopolist is able to raise prices profitably.

L 5/55, para. 66. See also Case IV/M.214, *Du Pont/ICI*, para. 23 ("For two products to be regarded as substitutable, the direct customer must consider it a realistic and rational possibility to react to, for example, a significant increase in the price of one product by switching to the other product in a relatively short period of time."). The United Kingdom competition authorities have also confirmed that the HMT is the central plank of their analysis. See Office of Fair Trading, *Mergers: Substantive Assessment Guidance*, OFT 516, May 2003; and Competition Commission, *Merger References: Competition Commission Guidelines*, CC 2, June 2003.

[56] See J Gual, "Market Definition in the Telecoms Industry," *CEPR Discussion Paper* No. 3988 (2003).

[57] The term "candidate market" originates from Werden. See GJ Werden, "Market Delineation and the Justice Department's Merger Guidelines" (1983) *Duke Law Journal* 514; and GJ Werden, "The 1982 Merger Guidelines and the Ascent of the Hypothetical Monopolist Paradigm" (2003) 71 *Antitrust Law Journal* 253–75.

[58] The candidate market should not be disagregated further. See GJ Werden, "Market Definition Algorithms Based on the Hypothetical Monopolist Paradigm" July 2002, *US DOJ Antitrust Division Economic Analysis Group Discussion Paper No. 02-8.*

2.3.2 Assessing Demand-Side Substitution Under The HMT

Overview. Several *quantitative techniques* can be used to undertake a HMT. The most satisfactory of all—because it attempts to directly implement the HMT test—is the small but significant non-transitory increase in price (SSNIP) test. This test uses data on prices and sales volumes to assess whether a hypothetical monopolist could profitably increase the prices of the products in the candidate market by 5%–10% during a sustained period of time.[59] An alternative quantitative approach is to investigate how the prices of the products in the candidate market react to changes in the prices of some products outside the candidate market, but which are in principle related to them. Price correlation studies and co-integration analysis are the main techniques used in this connection. If a reduction in the price of a product outside the candidate market triggers a price cut within the candidate market, then there are reasons to argue that the market should be enlarged. The SSNIP test and price correlation and co-integration techniques are described in detail below, as well as their respective limitations.

A second-best approach to the HMT test is the use of *qualitative evidence* based on an analysis of product characteristics and customer preferences and needs. This information is used to identify substitutable products that may undermine the attempt to raise the prices of the products in the putative market. Qualitative evidence is less reliable than quantitative techniques, since it does not measure the hypothetical monopolist's ability to raise prices, either accurately or at all. As noted earlier, qualitative evidence has historically played an important role in Article 82 EC cases, although quantitative techniques are increasingly being used, with qualitative evidence providing a useful cross-check. The role of qualitative evidence under Article 82 EC is also discussed below. Finally, other evidence—such as consumer surveys and natural experiments—may be used in some cases to support market definition.

2.3.2.1 Quantitative techniques

Basic operation of the SSNIP test. The SSNIP test operates as follows. Starting with the candidate market, the analyst considers whether a hypothetical monopolist with control over this (initial) set of products is able permanently and profitably to raise the price of these products by 5–10%, assuming that the prices of all other products remain constant. If the answer is affirmative, then the relevant product market contains that (initial) set of products—i.e., coincides with the candidate market. Otherwise, new products should be added to the market and the exercise repeated. The relevant market is then defined as the smallest set of products that meets the "hypothetical monopolist" test. According to the Market Definition Notice:[60]

> "The question to be answered is whether the parties' customers would switch to readily available substitutes…in response to an hypothetical small (in the range 5%–10%), but permanent relative price increase in the products and areas being considered. If substitution

[59] As noted by Baker, "this figure is not a tolerance level for anticompetitive price increases; it is merely a conceptual benchmark for assessing buyer substitution," See J Baker, "Market Definition" in WD Collins (ed.), *Directions in Antitrust* (ABA Publishing, 2006, forthcoming).

[60] Commission Notice on the definition of the relevant market for the purpose of Community competition law, OJ 1997 C 372/5, para. 17.

were enough to make the price increase unprofitable because of the resulting loss of sales, additional substitutes and areas are included in the relevant market. This would be done until the set of products...is such that small, permanent increases in relative prices would be profitable."

A price increase has two opposing effects on profits: a higher price leads to a higher unit margin and greater profits, but reduces demand. Only if the first effect outweighs the second is the price increase profitable. This trade off is resolved by means of the *critical loss analysis*. This analysis compares the actual losses that are likely to result from a price increase with a threshold—the critical loss—which is equal to the level of sale losses for which a given price increase is just profitable.[61] Thus, the critical loss is the point where the two opposing effects of a price increase offset each other so that the net effect in profits is nil. If the actual losses of a price increase exceed this threshold, then the price increase is not profitable.

Formal steps in a critical loss analysis. A critical loss analysis involves three steps: (1) the calculation of the critical loss; (2) an estimate of the sales likely to be lost to competitors in the event of a price increase; and (3) a comparison of two figures in order to see if a price increase would be profitable or not.

1. *Assessing the critical loss.* Consider a hypothetical monopolist with control over the products and services included in the relevant product market. Suppose that it considers increasing its prices by X per cent (where X is equal to 5 or 10 in the typical experiment). Suppose in addition that prior to that price increase the gross margin (the difference between revenues and the cost of sales) achieved by the monopoly supplier was m per cent.[62] The profits earned by the hypothetical monopolist prior to the price increase were equal to m p Q, where Q denotes the monopolist's output and p its price. After the price increase, the monopolist's profits equal (m + X) p Q (1-z), where z captures the reduction in output that results from the price increase. The critical loss is then given by the value of z that makes the profits before and after the price increase equal:

$$z^* = \frac{X}{X+m}$$

A greater loss (i.e., a value of z greater than z^*) would render the price increase unprofitable. Note that the critical loss is lower when the gross margin m is higher. When m is high, the negative impact on profits of a reduction in volume is large.

61 The critical loss analysis was formally developed by BC Harris and JJ Simon, "Focusing Market Definition: How Much Substitution is Necessary?" (1989) 12 *Research in Law and Economics* 207–26. See also J Langefeld and W Li, "Critical Loss Analysis in Evaluating Mergers" (2001) *Antitrust Bulletin* 299–337 (reprinted in D Evans and J Padilla (eds.), *Global Competition Policy, Economic Issues and Impacts,* LECG, 2004); and DP O'Brien and AL Wickelgren, "A Critical Analysis of Critical Loss Analysis" (2003) 71(1) *Antitrust Law Journal* 161–84.

62 Formally, $m = (p - c)/p$, where c denotes the unit variable cost of the monopolist. This is also known as the Lerner index.

2. *Assessing actual losses*. The loss in sales that results from an *X* per cent price increase is given by the price elasticity of demand of the product or products in the candidate market. The elasticity of demand measures the response of consumers to a change in price and, therefore, provides information on the amount of sales lost as a result of a small though significant and non-transitory increase in price of X per cent. A high elasticity indicates that consumers are very responsive to price changes and, consequently, that the loss in sales resulting from the price increase is large. Let *e* denote the elasticity of demand of the products in the candidate market, then the actual loss in sales associated with a price increase is greater when *e* is large.

3. *Comparison*. If the price increase leads to a loss in sales lower than the critical loss, the overall effect on profits is positive and the price increase is profitable. If that is the case, the candidate market constitutes a properly defined relevant product market. If, instead, the price increase leads to a loss in sales that exceeds the critical loss z^*, then the candidate market does not constitute a relevant market and, therefore, needs to be enlarged to encompass those products which attracted consumers from the products in the candidate market following the price increase. The actual loss associated to an X per cent price increase likely will exceed the critical loss, and hence the market will be broader than the candidate market, when the elasticity of demand *e* is large and the gross margin *m* is high. A high elasticity of demand implies a significant loss in volume, while a high gross margin indicates than the opportunity cost of losing volume is high.

A practical example. Sauces like mustard, ketchup, brown sauce and other condiments are "cold sauces," to use the language of the Commission in its merger decision in *Unilever/Best Foods*.[63] Suppose two makers of a variety of condiments wish to merge in a national market and wish to ascertain whether the approving agency is likely to conclude that different product categories (e.g., mayonnaise, barbecue sauce, brown sauce, ketchup etc.) constitute separate or combined markets. In order to apply the SSNIP test to each of these product categories, the merging firms would need to provide data on the gross margins for each product. With these data, the critical loss for each product could be calculated.

A complete analysis would require the econometric estimation of a full demand model in order to compute the loss that would result from a modest but non-trivial price increase. The simplest technique would be to regress sales volumes against the price of each product (controlling for product characteristics as well as for time-specific and company-specific fixed effects). Supermarket scanner data from firms such as ACNielsen, GfK, or IRI would allow the sales volume and prices of each product category, and for each firm selling that product, to be calculated over multiple periods. The coefficient of the price variable in such a regression would provide a direct estimate of the elasticity of demand for each product, which could then be used to calculate the actual loss associated to a price increase, which would then be compared with the

[63] Case No IV/M.1990, *Unilever/Bestfoods*.

critical loss value calculated previously to see if its is larger (narrow market) or smaller (broad market).

Criticisms of the SSNIP test. The SSNIP test has been subject to two principal criticisms. The first criticism relates to false conclusions that may result from the measurement of the elasticity of demand in Article 82 EC cases—known as the "cellophane fallacy." A fallacy arises when Firm A's products are *already* priced supra-competitively. In this circumstance, the elasticity of demand of Firm A's products may be very large simply because at those prices some products which consumers would not regard as substitutes at competitive prices become credible alternatives. So, the SSNIP test may show switching to other products at prevailing prices, whereas, had Firm A priced its product at a competitive level, switching would either not have occurred at all or at a level insufficient to constitute demand-side substitution. This defect in the SSNIP test is discussed below, together with the principal solutions proposed.

A second criticism also concerns the practical application of the SSNIP test and, in particular, the relationship between the estimated values of the elasticity of demand and the gross margin. Normally, when gross margins are high, one would expect a low value of the critical loss, so that it would be unprofitable for a firm to risk a price increase. However, a high margin is typically associated to a low elasticity of demand.[64] And, as we saw above, a low elasticity of demand constitutes evidence in favour of a narrow market. Therefore, it is not possible to rely exclusively on the size of the gross margin in the delineation of the relevant product market. Each of these criticisms is developed in more detail below.

a. The cellophane fallacy. The cellophane fallacy highlights a practical flaw of the SSNIP test and the critical loss analysis when applied to Article 82 EC cases.[65] The SSNIP test requires examining whether a hypothetical monopolist could profitably and permanently raise prices above their "competitive level." However, if a firm is dominant, its prices are already likely be at supra-competitive levels. The implication of this is that the estimated elasticity of demand and gross margin will be greater than if prices corresponded to a competitive market. The elasticity of demand will therefore be overestimated because, at high prices, consumers regard even inferior substitutes as attractive, whereas, if prices were at the lower, competitive level, they would not. As a result, the application of the SSNIP test in abuse of dominance cases may lead to excessively broad market definitions that will tend to mask the existence of dominant positions. As noted in the Discussion Paper:[66]

> "The existence of the cellophane fallacy implies that market definition in Article 82 cases needs to be particularly carefully considered and that any single method of market definition, including in particular the SSNIP-test, is likely to be inadequate."

---

[64] Economic theory shows that a monopolist maximising short-term profits would set prices (quantities) so that its gross margin is inversely related to its own elasticity of demand: $m = 1/e$. This is known as the Lerner equation.

[65] The cellophane fallacy received its name from *United States v E.I. Du Pont De Nemours & Co*, 351 US 377 (1956). DuPont (wrongly) claimed that cellophane was not a separate market, since there was a high cross-price elasticity of demand with other flexible packaging material.

[66] See Discussion Paper, para. 13.

A number of solutions have been proposed to address the problem of the cellophane fallacy. Ultimately, however, there is no single, best solution. Much will depend on what evidence is available to estimate the extent to which prices already exceed the competitive level, including by reference to qualitative criteria and experience in comparable markets:

1. *Estimate the competitive price before undertaking a critical loss analysis.* One obvious solution in order to avoid drawing a wrong inference from the existence of supra-competitive prices is to estimate the competitive price level prior to engaging in a critical loss analysis.[67] But, in practice, this is not a very realistic alternative, given the enormous difficulties of estimating a competitive price in most industries.[68] These problems have plagued the analysis of excessive pricing under Article 82 EC and, as discussed in Chapter Twelve (Excessive Prices), no effective solution has emerged. A second difficulty is that estimating the competitive price level would transform the SSNIP test into a direct test of dominance. If, somehow, the competitive price level could be identified, then there would be no need to go through the whole process of defining relevant markets and assessing dominance on the basis of structural and behavioural proxies.[69]

2. *Use a combination of qualitative and quantitative evidence.* Another proposed solution is to adopt a qualitative approach based on the analysis of product characteristics and intended use, *but* taking into account the logic and principles of the SSNIP test and the critical loss analysis.[70] The SSNIP test forces analysts to take a structured view of the process of market definition and takes into account only those products that are potentially demand or supply-side substitutes of those forming part of the relevant market. A purely *ad hoc* market definition, which ignores these basic principles, is likely to produce overly narrow markets. What is important is not the difference in physical characteristics *per se*, but the manner in which these differences influence demand. Relying on the sound principles of the SSNIP test ensures that: (a) two physically similar products which, however, are not regarded as substitutes by consumers, are not included in the same market; and (b) two products with relatively dissimilar functionality, but which consumers regard

[67] S Bishop and S Baker, "The Role of Market Definition in Monopoly and Dominance Inquiries" *Economic Discussion Paper 2*, OFT 342 July 2001, para. 3.4. Both the Commission and the OFT acknowledge the distinction between the prevailing and the competitive price level in their respective guidelines. See Commission Notice on the definition of the relevant market for the purpose of Community competition law, OJ 1997 C 372/5, para. 19; and Office of Fair Trading, *Market Definition*, OFT 403, December 2004, para. 2.10.

[68] Rejecting the prevailing price level in favour of some notional "competitive" price also renders correlation analysis irrelevant and complicates consumer surveys. See Wik Consult and Squire Sanders, *Methodologies for Market Definition and Market Analysis*, Study for ICP-ANACOM, 2003, p. 23.

[69] S Bishop and S Baker, "The Role of Market Definition in Monopoly and Dominance Inquiries" *Economic Discussion Paper 2*, OFT 342, July 2001, para. 3.7.

[70] *Ibid.*, paras. 3.35–3.40.

as substitutes, are included in the same relevant product market. The Discussion Paper notes that:[71]

> "The SSNIP test at prevailing prices remains useful in the sense that it is indicative of substitution patterns at those prices. Products and areas that can be excluded from the relevant market at prevailing prices would also be excluded at any lower competitive price."

The application of the SSNIP test results in a putative relevant market, that may be defined too widely. The characteristics and intended use of the products included comprised in that putative market needs to be carefully examined to assess whether they are indeed substitutes.

3. *Use other comparable markets as a crosscheck.* A third alternative complements the critical loss analysis approach to market definition with: (a) the qualitative analysis of product characteristics and customer needs; and (b) the study of competition in "comparable" markets, i.e., markets with similar structural and non-structural characteristics. Direct application of the critical loss analysis provides an upper bound to the scope of the relevant product market: all products that are found to be outside the relevant product market using a critical loss analysis at prevailing (high) prices can be safely excluded.[72] The additional analysis of physical product characteristics could help to limit the size of the possibly overly wide market emerging from the critical loss analysis. Another possible way to refine the market definition resulting from the quantitative analysis is to investigate market conditions in similar markets that are more competitive than the one under investigation. If the price level in these markets is not significantly lower than in the market defined using a standard critical loss analysis, then it is unlikely that the cellophane fallacy plays a major role.[73]

4. *Examine the competitive reactions of the allegedly dominant firm.* Another possibility is to investigate whether the allegedly dominant firm monitors and reacts to the price changes and new products introductions of its competitors. If it does, then those products are likely to be close substitutes for its own products. And the locations where those rivals operate are likely to be part of the same geographic market than the firm in question.[74]

5. *The small but significant non-transitory decrease in prices (SSNDP) test.* An alternative way to delineate the boundaries of the relevant market is to consider the impact on the volume sold by a hypothetical monopolist of a 5–10%

---

[71] See Discussion Paper, para. 16.

[72] S Bishop and S Baker, "The Role of Market Definition in Monopoly and Dominance Inquiries" *Economic Discussion Paper 2*, OFT 342, July 2001, para. 3.34.

[73] *Ibid.*, para. 3.46.

[74] See J Baker, "Market Definition" in WD Collins (ed.), *Directions in Antitrust,* ABA Publishing, 2006 (forthcoming).

reduction in the prevailing price (unlike an *increase* in the case of SSNIP).[75] If the prevailing price was supra-competitive, the price reduction would lead to a relatively small increase in sales (otherwise, the price would not have been increased to its prevailing level in the first place). On the contrary, if the prevailing price was competitive, the output response to the price reduction would be large or small depending on the degree of substitution between the products in the candidate market and those outside it. Therefore, evidence that the response to a price reduction would trigger a significant output response suggests a broad market and a high degree of competition. On the other hand, if a small price reduction does not cause a significant increase in output, then the candidate market is likely to be a proper antitrust market where market power can be, or already is, exercised.

b. Consistency between elasticity and margin estimates. As explained above, a higher gross margin is typically associated with a lower value of the critical loss threshold. This fact has been used by defendants to argue that a firm enjoying high gross margins is unlikely to find a price increase profitable and, hence, to support a finding of a wide product margin. This argument is conceptually flawed and may lead to incorrect delineations of the relevant product market. Economic theory shows that in markets where firms maximise short-term profits, the gross margin is inversely related to the own price elasticity of demand. A high gross margin is therefore associated to a low elasticity of demand and *vice versa.* But since a low elasticity of demand implies that the actual volume loss resulting from a price increase is small and hence points to a narrow market finding, it is not possible to establish an unambiguous relationship between the size of the gross margin and the dimension of the relevant product market. In sum, it is not possible to conclude that the relevant product market is likely to be broad based on an analysis of gross margin only. And, furthermore, unless there are good reasons to sustain otherwise,[76] a rigorous critical loss analysis must take into account the inverse relationship between the gross margin and the own price elasticity of demand.[77]

Other quantitative techniques for assessing demand-side substitution. The SSNIP test is not the only quantitative approach to market definition. An alternative is to analyse the behaviour of the prices of the products in the candidate market in response to changes in the prices of products with characteristics that place them *outside* the candidate market. Two common methodologies for this sort of analysis are price correlations and co-integration analysis.

---

[75] See Baker, *ibid.* See also PB Nelson and LJ White, *Market Definition and the Identification of Market Power in Monopolisation Cases: A Critique and a Proposal,* Working Paper #EC-03-06 of Stern School of Business, (November 2003).

[76] This may be the case, for example, because firms do not maximise short-term profits but rather engage in dynamic pricing to penetrate a market or because they operate in two-sided markets.

[77] See ML Katz and C Shapiro, "Critical Loss: Let's Tell the Whole Story" *Antitrust,* Spring 2003, 49-56. For a response, see DT Scheffman and JJ Simons, "The State of Critical Loss Analysis: Let's Make Sure We Understand the Whole Story" *Antitrust Source,* November 2003. For a counter-response, see ML Katz and C Shapiro, "Further Thoughts on Critical Loss" *Antitrust Source,* March 2004.

a. Price correlations. Price correlation analysis measures the extent to which the prices of two or more different products are interrelated.[78] A strong positive correlation between the prices of two different products suggests, but does not prove, that the two products belong to the same market. If two products A and B are in the same relevant market, their relative price (the ratio of the price of A with respect to the price of B) cannot change significantly: a change in their relative prices would trigger a process of demand-side or supply-side substitution that would bring the relative price back to its starting point.[79]

The Commission has used correlation analysis in several cases, most notably in the *Nestle/Perrier* merger decision. The Commission found that the prices of all water brands were highly correlated, regardless of whether the water was still or sparkling. In contrast, the prices of the water brands were poorly correlated with those of soft drink brands. In these circumstances, the Commission concluded that there was a separate market for all bottled waters, distinct from the soft drink market.[80]

This methodology presents two problems. First, there is no threshold coefficient above which the two products can be considered conclusively part of the same relevant market. In other words, the test specifies a methodology, but no operative rules or conclusion. Second, the correlation may be *spurious*, i.e., due to factors other than demand-side or supply-side substitution. For example, the prices of two products may move together over time in response to common external factors, such as cost shocks, exchange rate shocks, etc. They may be correlated simply as a result of having a common trend. In short, a positive correlation need not necessarily indicate that two products are close substitutes.[81]

b. Co-integration analysis. The goal of a co-integration analysis is to estimate possible relationships between economic data series, such as price series, that are non-stationary. Broadly speaking, a non-stationary time series varies widely over time without exhibiting a long-run stable trend. Two price series (the price series of, say, products A and B) are co-integrated if a combination of two price series (for example, the difference between two prices) is stationary and exhibits a long-run trend.[82] If the

[78] Instead, *price level* comparisons are not useful for market definition. Two products A and B may have very different prices and still be part of the same relevant product market. This is because consumers may be willing to substitute the high price (but high quality) product A for the low price (but low quality) product B. The OFT *Market Definition Guidelines* are explicit on this point: "Athough a one is of a lower quality, customers might still switch to this product if the price of the more expensive product rose and if they no longer felt that the higher quality justified the price differential." See Office of Fair Trading, Market Definition, OFT 403, December 2004, para. 3.5.

[79] This relationship is given mathematically by the "correlation coefficient." Two prices are perfectly positively correlated prices if their correlation coefficient is + 1, while they are perfectly negatively correlated if they have a correlation coefficient of – 1. A coefficient of 0 means that two prices are uncorrelated.

[80] *Nestlé/Perrier*, OJ 1992 L 356/1.

[81] See LECG, *Quantitative Techniques In Competition Analysis*, OFT Research paper 17, October 1999, pp. 53–55.

[82] For a formal treatment of co-integration, see RF Engle and CWJ Granger, "Co-integration and Error Correction: Representation, Estimation and Testing" (1987) 55 *Econometrica* 251–76. For a discussion of how to apply co-integration analysis to market definition, see S Gürcan Gülen,

price series of two products are co-integrated, this means that there is a strong relationship between the two, which indicates that both products may be interchangeable.

This method is superior to price correlation analysis. Because the analysis focuses on relative price changes between two series, common influences are cancelled out and do not contaminate the results. Co-integration analysis is capable of identifying delayed price responses, something that is impossible with contemporaneous price correlations.[83]

The Commission has employed co-integration analyses in several merger cases.[84] In *Gencor/Lonrho*, for example, the Commission had to consider whether platinum, gold, silver, rhodium, and palladium were part of separate markets. The Commission found high correlation coefficients between those products, but noted that "a high correlation does not in itself imply a causal relationship...indeed economic price-series data are often non-stationary (i.e., trended) and therefore automatically correlated."[85] Accordingly, the Commission undertook a co-integration analysis that led to the conclusion that the products were separate markets.[86]

2.3.2.2 Qualitative evidence

Comparing prices, product characteristics, and functions. The Market Definition Notice does not limit demand-side substitution to consumers' willingness to switch in response to increases in price, but also includes non-quantitative factors such as the product characteristics and intended use. Indeed, if anything, this qualitative approach to market definition characterises most of the major decisions and judgments under Article 82 EC.[87] One of the seminal cases under Article 82 EC—*United Brands*—

"Rationalisation in the World Crude Oil Market" (1997) *The Energy Journal* 109–26; I Horowitz, "Market Definition in Antitrust Analysis: A Regression-based Approach" (1981) 48 *Southern Economic Journal* 1–16; M Forni, "Using Stationarity Tests in Antitrust Market Definition" (2004) 6(2) *American Law and Economics Review* 441–64; AE Rodriguez and MD Williams, "Is the World Oil Market 'One Great Pool'? A Test" (1993) *Energy Studies Journal* 121–30; ME Slade, "Exogeneity Tests of Market Boundaries Applied to Petroleum Products" (1986) 34(3) *Journal of Industrial Economics* 291–303; JG Werden and LM Froeb, "Correlation, Causality, and All that Jazz: the Inherent Shortcomings of Price Tests for Antitrust Market Definition" (1993) 8 *Review of Industrial Organisation* 329–53, 344; and H Wills, "Market Definition: How Stationarity Tests Can Improve Accuracy" (2002) 23(1) *European Competition Law Review* 4–6. For a recent defence of these methods, see M Forni, "Using Stationarity Tests in Antitrust Market Definition" (2004) 6(2) *American Law and Economics Review* 441–64.

[83] Lexecon, *An Introduction to Quantitative Techniques in Competition Analysis*, 2004, p. 10.

[84] See Case IV/M.619, *Gencor/Lonrho*, upheld on appeal in Case T-102/96, *Gencor Ltd v Commission* [1999] ECR II-753. See also Case COMP/M.2187, *CVC/Lenzing*; and Case IV/M.315, *Mannesmann/Vallourec/Ilva*.

[85] *Gencor*, *ibid.*, para. 52.

[86] *Ibid.*, para. 53.

[87] Case 27/76, *United Brands Company and United Brands Continentaal BV v Commission* [1978] ECR 207, paras. 12–35. See also *Decca Navigator System*, OJ 1989 L 43/27, paras. 83–85; *ECS/AKZO—Interim Measures*, OJ 1983 L 252/13; *Warner-Lambert/Gillette and Others*, OJ 1993 L 116/21, para. 6; *GVL*, OJ 1981 L 370/49, paras. 18, 19, and 45; *Eurofix-Banco v Hilti*, OJ 1988 L 65/19, paras. 55–56; *Magill TV Guide/ITP, BBC and RTE*, OJ 1989 L 78/43, para. 20; *Bandengroothandel Frieschebrug BV/NV Nederlandsche Banden-Industrie Michelin*, OJ 1981

decided the relevant market on the basis of a subjective evaluation of the product's characteristics. The Commission and Court of Justice concluded that bananas were in a separate relevant market to other fruits because of their seedlessness, softness, and ease of handling (which were said to be important for the very young, the sick, and the elderly).[88] No quantitative evidence of United Brands' ability to successfully raise prices was put forward: indeed, the Court of Justice declined to undertake such an analysis. This largely subjective approach to market definition has characterised much of the main precedents under Article 82 EC:[89]

> "Demand substitutability was measured in large part on physical and technical characteristics, with price differences, cross elasticity of demand and distribution differences also playing a role, primarily to confirm what the physical characteristics analysis seemed to indicate...The Commission also defined markets in terms of end uses, even when products were physically identical, without inquiry into the ability of the seller to segregate particular end users with regard to price."

More recent decisions under Article 82 EC have also relied in part on qualitative evidence. For example, in *Microsoft*, the Commission defined a product market for "streaming" media players distinct from the market for media players not including streaming functionality by pointing to their different functionality.[90] The Commission also undertook a detailed analysis in *Clearstream* to assess demand-side substitutes and identified a number of characteristics of specific securities clearing services that distinguished them from other services in consumers' eyes.[91] Finally, in *Wanadoo*,[92] the Commission relied not only on quantitative data showing asymmetries in switching between high-speed internet access and dial-up, but also relied on qualitative factors, such as the unavailability of many streaming media and global games products to users without high-speed internet. But reliance on qualitative evidence is almost certainly on the wane and the more systematic use of econometric techniques in second-phase merger review is likely to accelerate this trend further under Article 82 EC. In these circumstances, qualitative data are most likely to be used in future as a cross-check on

L 353/33, paras. 31–34; *London European/Sabena*, OJ 1988 L 317/47, paras. 13–15; Case C-333/94 P, *Tetra Pak International SA v Commission* [1996] ECR I-5951, paras. 7–20; *Vitamins*, OJ 1976 L 223/27, para. 20; Case COMP/38/096, *Clearstream (Clearing and settlement)*, Commission Decision of June 4, 2004, not yet published, paras. 199–200; and *Van den Bergh Foods Ltd*, OJ 1998 L 246/1, paras. 129–33. See also Case 31/80, *L'Oreal v De Nieuwe AMCK* [1980] ECR 3775, para. 25 ("The possibilities of competition must be judged in the context of the market comprising the totality of the products which, with respect to their characteristics, are particularly suitable for satisfying constant needs and are only to a limited extent interchangeable with other products."). See also Case T-7/93, *Langnese-Iglo GmbH v Commission* [1995] ECR II-1533, para. 61.

[88] Case 27/76, *United Brands Company and United Brands Continentaal BV v Commission* [1978] ECR 207, para. 31

[89] See T Kauper, "The Problem of Market Definition Under EC Competition Law" in B Hawk (ed.), *International Antitrust Law and Policy: Fordham Corporate Law Institute* (London, Sweet and Maxwell, 1997) (1996), p. 251.

[90] Case COMP/C-3/37.792, *Microsoft*, Commission Decision of March 24, 2004, not yet published, paras. 411–25.

[91] Case COMP/38/096, *Clearstream (Clearing and settlement)*, Commission Decision of June 4, 2004, not yet published, para. 199.

[92] Case COMP/38.233, *Wanadoo Interactive*, Commission Decision of July 16, 2003, not yet published.

quantitative data, which would be preferable to reliance on qualitative data only. That said, in some cases, good data may not be available, in which case competition authorities have no choice but to use qualitative techniques.

2.3.2.3 Other sources of evidence

Consumer surveys. Market studies and consumer survey data may reveal information on consumer preferences and, therefore, may be useful to identify those products that consumers regard as interchangeable with those in the candidate market.[93] The Market Definition Notice states that:[94]

> "Marketing studies that companies have commissioned in the past and that are used by companies in their own decision making as to pricing of their products and/or marketing actions may provide useful information for the Commission's delineation of the relevant market. Consumer surveys on usage patterns and attitudes, data from consumer's purchasing patterns, the views expressed by retailers and more generally, market research studies...are taken into account to establish whether an economically significant proportion of consumers consider two products as substitutable."

Of course, the reliability and validity of such studies must be carefully considered. The Commission is aware of the risk that studies prepared *ad hoc* for the case at hand may not be objective since "[u]nlike pre-existing studies, they have not been prepared in the normal course of business for the adoption of business decisions."[95]

Natural experiments. Unexpected events may provide valuable information on substitution patterns between different products. Such events include strikes, promotions and advertising campaigns, unexpected plant outages, supply shortages, regulatory intervention, and market entry.[96] For example, consumers may react to a disruption in supply due to a strike by switching consumption to other products which they regard as substitutes, thereby revealing information on demand-side substitution.

Internal business documents. Internal documents may also reveal which products a firm regards as close substitutes to its own. Business and strategic plans, internal pricing studies, and analyses of promotions, may provide information on competitors and the degree of substitutability between their products and those in the candidate market. Again, however, it should be appreciated that such documents are usually prepared for purposes other than market definition under competition law. The approach taken in such documents is also likely to offer a narrower appreciation of a firm's competitive constraints than would result from a properly-defined relevant market.

---

[93] See, e.g., Case COMP/38/096, *Clearstream (Clearing and settlement)*, Commission Decision of June 4, 2004, not yet published, paras. 146 and 166.

[94] Commission Notice on the definition of the relevant market for the purpose of Community competition law, OJ 1997 C 372/5, para. 41.

[95] *Ibid.*

[96] Lexecon, *An Introduction to Quantitative Techniques in Competition Analysis, 2004*, p. 34.

2.3.3 Assessing Supply-Side Substitution Under The HMT

Conditions for supply-side substitution. To determine whether two products A and B are regarded as supply-side substitutes, a number of cumulative conditions must be satisfied. Only if all of these questions are answered positively can products A and B be considered as supply-sides substitutes. Then, and only then, does supply-side substitution have a similar effect as demand-side substitution "in terms of effectiveness and immediacy," as required by the Market Definition Notice.[97] The conditions are as follows:

1. *Ability of other suppliers to switch production without major additional investment.* For supply-side substitution to be effective, other suppliers must be able to switch production quickly and relatively costlessly. This involves consideration of the assets needed to produce the relevant products and in particular whether manufacturers of supply-side substitutes: (a) possess the required technology, know-how, machinery and facilities; (b) have access to the appropriate transport infrastructure and distribution channels; and (c) possess the relevant marketing assets, such as brand name, and/or the ability to develop those assets within a reasonable period of time.[98] If any relevant assets are missing, it is relevant to ask whether they can be acquired without the need for significant, irreversible new investments by buying assets that involve no sunk costs or contracting with third parties.

2. *Economic incentives of manufacturers to divert production.* Even if manufacturers of potential supply-side substitutes could divert production, it must still be shown that they have the economic incentives to do so. It would thus be relevant to ask whether: (a) suppliers are contractually tied to continue production of existing products; and (b) spare capacity is available or whether additional capacity that can be brought into production at a reasonable cost.[99] Unless manufacturers can economically adapt production—in other words they do not face opportunity costs sufficiently large to make switching production

[97] Commission Notice on the definition of the relevant market for the purpose of Community competition law, OJ 1997 C 372/5, para. 20.

[98] The Commission seems to have endorsed this condition. In several cases, the Commission rejected the presence of supply-side substitution because of costly switching or because of the long time horizon needed. For example, in *Industri Kapital (Nordkem)/DYNO*, the Commission did not include supply-side substitutes into the relevant market, because it considered that switching production capability was "time-consuming and costly." See Case COMP/M.1813, *Industri Kapital (Nordkem)/DYNO*, paras. 26–27. See also Case COMP/M.1879, *Boeing/Hughes*, para. 22 (Commission rejected supply-side substitutability between satellites with different orbits because it took three to five years for a producer to develop the technical capacity to develop a new satellite); and Case COMP/M.2314, *BASF/Eurodiol/Pantochim*, para. 35.

[99] A lack of commercial incentives was one of the arguments by the Commission not to include supply-side substitutes in the relevant market in Case IV/M.774, *Saint-Gobain/Wacker-Chemie/NOM*, para. 36. See also Case COMP/M.2420, *Mitsui/CVRD/Caemi* (Commission's market investigation indicated that the low degree of supply-side substitution was due to lack of economic incentives). See too Case COMP/M.1381, *Imetal/English China Clays*, para. 16 (supply-side substitution between kaolin, a form of china clay, and certain other pigments was considered "technically possible" but unlikely in practice given that the "economics of the additional processing would make the product non-competitive").

unprofitable (even without sunk costs)—supply-side substitution is not effective.[100]

3. *Consumer reaction.* The final, and decisive, condition is that consumers must regard potential supply-side substitute products as valid substitutes for the existing set of products. That is, the existence of supply-side substitutes must influence the market behaviour of the alleged dominant firm by allowing supply-side substitutes to steal sales from incumbents charging excessively high prices. In this regard, it is important to assess whether consumers are really willing to change consumption. For example, in the presence of switching costs, consumer might not be willing to change to a substitute product, rendering supply-side substitution ineffective. Therefore, it may be useful to distinguish between situations in which firms compete with products that are currently available from others and where they compete by producing to order or on the basis of blue prints. In the last set of cases supply-side substitutability is much more likely to be of importance since switching costs do not play a major role.

These cumulative conditions are not enough, however. The Commission requires that "that most of the suppliers are able to offer and sell the various qualities under the conditions of immediacy and absence of significant increase in costs described above."[101] Thus, before including supply-side substitutes in a single separate market, the Commission must assess the universal character of supply-side substitution. That is, a sufficiently large number of suppliers of supply-side substitutes must be ready to respond and move production before their products would be included in the relevant market.

Examples of effective supply-side substitution in the decisional practice and case law. Supply-side substitution is most likely to be effective where a market contains a number of different grades, varieties, or sizes of the essentially the same underlying of product. For example, no shoemaker manufacturer only one shoe size; no car manufacturer produces only white cars. In some cases, supply-side substitution may not require adjustments in production, but a repositioning of an existing brand or product through, for example, a successful marketing strategy, design changes or revised marketing. In this circumstance, supply-side substitution occurs only if the repositioning involves no sunk costs.

The strict conditions for supply-side substitution have resulted in the expansion of the market to include supply-side substitutes in only a small number of cases. For example, in *Electrolux/AEG*, the Commission found that all models and sizes of each type of major domestic appliance constituted a single relevant market because "high degree of supply side substitutability" permitted producers to use the same production line to

[100] See Case IV/M.1313, *Danish Crown/Vestjyske Slagterier*, paras. 62–64. The Commission defined a narrow relevant geographical market due to contractual obligations.

[101] Commission Notice on the definition of the relevant market for the purpose of Community competition law, OJ 1997 C 372/5, para. 21.

manufacture a broad range of different models and sizes.[102] Likewise, in *Volvo/Scania*, the Commission determined that, notwithstanding some differences in functional characteristics, rigid trucks and tractor trucks comprised part of a single market for all heavy-duty trucks, *inter alia*, because the costs related to switching from the production of one type of heavy truck to another were not substantial.[103] Finally, in *Kish Glass*, the Court of First Instance upheld the Commission's finding that the production of 4mm glass is technological identical to the production of glass of other thicknesses and that manufacturers could easily switch production "without excessive costs."[104]

2.4 GEOGRAPHIC MARKET DEFINITION

2.4.1 Key Concepts

Definition. Geographic market definition is the second essential step in the definition of the relevant market: a product market is essentially meaningless without a corresponding definition of its geographic scope. As early as *United Brands*, the Court of Justice stated that the opportunities for competition must be considered "with reference to a clearly defined geographic area in which the product is marketed and where conditions of competition are sufficiently homogenous for the effect of the economic power of the undertaking concerned to be able to be evaluated."[105] More recently, the Market Definition Notice defines the relevant geographic market as the area where: (1) the company or companies whose behaviour is in question are involved in the supply and demand of products or services, (2) the conditions of competition are sufficiently homogeneous, and (3) those conditions are appreciably different from the conditions of competition in neighbouring areas.[106]

The principles of product market definition apply with equal force to the definition of the relevant geographic market.[107] The relevant geographic market therefore includes all those regions where consumers can find demand-side substitutes for the products of the firm under scrutiny (*demand-side substitution*) and there are suppliers who can readily shift production to the markets where the firms whose commercial practices are investigated operate (*supply-side substitution*). The *chain of substitution* logic is also relevant to delineate the scope of the relevant geographic market.

[102] Case IV/M.458, *Electrolux/AEG*, para. 9. See also Case IV/M.2498, *UPM/Kymmene/Haindl*, para. 13; and Case IV/M.2499, *Norske Skog/Parenco/Walsum*, para. 13 (single market for newsprint).

[103] Case IV/M.1672, *Volvo/Scania*, paras. 24–30.

[104] Case T-65/96, *Kish Glass & Co Ltd v Commission* [2000] ECR II-1885, para. 68, confirmed on appeal in Case C-241/00 P, *Kish Glass & Co Ltd v Commission* [2001] ECR I-7759.

[105] Case 27/76, *United Brands Company and United Brands Continentaal BV v Commission* [1978] ECR 207, paras. 11. See also Case 247/86, *Société alsacienne et lorraine de télécommunications et d'électronique (Alsatel) v SA Novasam* [1988] ECR 5987 (Commission's finding of dominance was rejected on the basis of an incorrect geographic definition).

[106] Commission Notice on the definition of the relevant market for the purpose of Community competition law, OJ 1997 C 372/5, para. 8.

[107] M Motta, *Competition Policy: Theory and Practice* (Cambridge, Cambridge University Press, 2004), p. 113.

Consider, for example, broadband internet access. In many countries, this service is offered by local cable companies and national telecommunications providers offering ADSL services. Typically, a country is subdivided into non-overlapping regions, each of which is served by one or more local cable providers. Although consumers cannot switch between local cable providers active in distinct regions, the presence of the national supplier ensures that there is nevertheless (indirect) competition between those local firms. Decisions taken by local cable companies are likely to influence the policy adopted by the national telecommunications provider, which in turn may affect the actions chosen by cable companies in other regions.[108]

Basic analytical process. According to the Market Definition Notice, the analytical approach used when defining relevant geographic markets involves three steps:

1. *Identifying the putative market from the demand-side.* A preliminary view on the scope of the relevant geographic market must first be taken. This defines a putative geographic market. Market shares and prices in and out of the putative market must then be compared to ascertain whether the conditions of competition are homogenous or heterogeneous across regions. None of this is conclusive, however. For example, market shares may be evenly distributed across regions and yet the relevant market may be regional. Also, prices may differ widely from region to region and yet the market may cover all the regions. This is why the Commission considers the characteristics of the products and services offered at different locations to determine whether producers that are available in locations outside the putative market can be regarded as *demand-side substitutes* by consumers in the putative market.[109]

2. *Supply-side factors.* Supply-side substitution factors must then be considered. The goal is to investigate whether suppliers located outside the putative market would be able to enter the market in response to a price increase. For example, the Commission investigates whether that reaction is feasible or there are impediments to entry, such as limited access to distribution channels, regulatory barriers and substantial set-up costs.[110]

3. *Scope for widening the market based on future integration.* Finally, it is relevant to ask whether there is a continuing process of market integration. As a result, it may identify a wider geographic market when there is a rational

[108] See, e.g., Case IV/36.539, *British Interactive Broadcasting/Open*; Commission Notification Case COMP/M.2845, *Sogecable/Canalsatélite Digital Vía Digital*. Note, however, that the validity of the chain-of-substitution argument hinges crucially on the inability of the "straddling" firm to price-discriminate across local markets. In the broadband example, the scope for price discrimination of this type seems to be limited, which is due in particular to either regulatory constraints or reputation considerations. The same logic can be applied to Pay-TV and telecommunications markets, but also to markets such as food retailing where frequently large supermarket chains compete with local retailers. In many of these instances, a large national supplier faces competition only in some regions, but is unable to exert market power because of the inability to price-discriminate between regions.

[109] Commission Notice on the definition of the relevant market for the purpose of Community competition law, OJ 1997 C 372/5, paras. 28 and 29.

[110] *Ibid.*, para. 30.

expectation that legislative or technical barriers are likely to fall in the near future.[111]

2.4.2 Defining Geographic Markets In Practice

Sources of evidence. The Community institutions and national authorities and courts have relied on various sources of evidence to assess the extent of demand-side and supply-side substitution across different geographic areas. They have also gathered and analysed information on transport costs, trade barriers, or contractual obligations to assess the extent to which suppliers located outside the candidate market effectively constrained the behaviour of those located inside. The principal types of evidence are discussed below.

a. ***Price evidence.*** The scope of the relevant geographic market can be investigated by means of price correlation and co-integration studies, with the same caveats described in Section 2.3 above. The prices of a product sold in the region that forms a candidate market cannot be constantly higher than the prices for the same product in region outside the candidate market *unless* there are substantial obstacles to trade. Thus, a strong positive correlation between the prices of products sold in regions within and outside the candidate market indicates that: (1) consumers located in the candidate market can easily purchase the product in regions outside it; or (2) suppliers outside the candidate market do not face obstacles to shipping their products into the boundaries of the candidate market.

b. ***Trade flows (quantity evidence).*** Although not conclusive, information on trade flows and the pattern of shipments can be used to obtain an understanding of geographic purchasing patterns, and hence, to delineate the boundaries of the relevant geographic market.[112] Some commentators have suggested defining geographic markets on the basis of data on product flows, arguing that "the only data required to estimate market areas—at least in most cases—are shipments data in physical terms."[113] Their "shipment test" measures quantify the export and import flows taking place between two regions: if both levels were high, the relevant geographic should comprise both regions.[114]

This proposal has been severely criticised, since high levels of imports and exports are neither a necessary nor sufficient condition for a broad geographic market.[115] Products

[111] *Ibid.*, para. 32. See also R Whish, *Competition Law* (London, LexisNexis Butterworths, 2003) p. 41.

[112] *Ibid.*, para. 49.

[113] KG Elzinga and TF Hogarty, "The Problem of Geographic Market Definition in Antimerger Suits" (1973) 18 *Antitrust Bulletin* 45–81, at 73; and KG Elzinga and TF Hogarty, "The Problem of Geographic Market Delineation Revisited" (1978) 23 *Antitrust Bulletin* 1–18.

[114] See M Motta, *Competition Policy: Theory and Practice* (Cambridge, Cambridge University Press, 2004), p. 114 ("Suppose for instance that a considerable proportion of trade was observed between one region and another. This would be a clear indication that the regions' producers are exercising a competitive constraint on each other.").

[115] See DL Kaserman and H Zeisel, "Market Definition: Implementing the Department of Justice Merger Guidelines" (1996) 41(3) *Antitrust Bulletin* 665–90; See also G Stigler and R Sherwin, "The Extent of the Market" (1985) 28 *Journal of Law and Economics* 555–86.

may move between two regions and yet the to regions may belong to separate product markets: if there are differences in demand between the two regions, and producers are able to price discriminate, trade may occur in great quantities and yet the products sold in one of the regions are not constrained by the products sold in the other. On the contrary, there may be few imports and exports between two regions and yet they may belong to a single market: if transportation costs are small, each region exerts a competitive constraint on the other but there may be no trade between the two because prices are the same in the two regions. The threat of imports may be enough to discipline prices in both regions. If the threat of imports is credible and substantial, it should lead to broader geographic markets. The Commission appeared to have ignored this in *Italian Flat Glass*.[116] It argued that market definition ought to be based on actual product shipments, not those that were "theoretically possible." Since Italian producers supplied 80% of Italian flat glass, there could be no doubt that the geographic market was Italy, the Commission concluded.[117]

c. ***Barriers to trade.*** The existence of barriers to trade gives rise to separate relevant product markets. The following barriers have been identified in the economic literature and the case law:

1. *Transport costs*. Transport costs are the most important factor in the definition of the relevant geographic market. The impact of transport costs is likely to be high for bulky, low value products. Import tariffs are also direct costs that increase the price of transportation. In *British Plasterboard*, for instance, the Commission based the definition of the relevant geographic market on the existence of significant transport costs and identified Great Britain and Ireland as separate relevant markets. The Commission relied on estimates of transport costs and information of competing firms about entry plans to conclude that imports between Europe, Great Britain and Ireland represented no competitive threat.[118]

2. *Consumer preferences*. An important factor in the definition of the relevant geographic market is to assess whether consumers have a marked preference for local products. Local preferences are not uncommon and may stem from cultural differences, differences in lifestyle or differences in language. The Market Definition Notice states that differences in consumer preferences must

[116] *Italian Flat Glass*, OJ 1988 133/34. The Court of First Instance seemed troubled by geographic market definition because certain documents indicated that Italian producers took account of competition from producers in other member states and in Turkey and Eastern Europe. See Joined Cases T-68 and 77-78/89, *Società Italiana Vetro SpA, Fabbrica Pisana SpA and PPG Vernante Pennitalia SpA v Commission* (*re Italian Flat Glass*) [1992] ECR II 1403.

[117] *Italian Flat Glass*, OJ 1981 L 326/12, para. 77.

[118] *BPB Industries plc*, OJ 1989 L 10/50, paras. 21–24. Other case where transport costs were considered in the definition of the relevant market include *Napier Brown/British Sugar*, OJ 1988 L 284/41; Case 27/76, *United Brands Company and United Brands Continentaal BV v Commission* [1978] ECR 207; *ECS/AKZO—Interim Measures, OJ 1983 L 252/13*; *Italian Flat Glass*, OJ 1981 L 326/12; *Eurofix-Banco v Hilti*, OJ 1988 L 65/19; and *Tetra Pak I (BTG licence)*, OJ 1988 L 272/27; *Tetra Pak II*, OJ 1992 L 72/1.

be taken into account in the definition of the relevant geographic market.[119] If differences in local preferences are strong, as in the case of media markets, the geographic market is likely to be defined narrowly.[120] In *Magill*, for example, the Commission emphasised the importance of Ireland's cultural identity in the definition of a region-wide geographic market (Ireland and Northern Ireland).[121]

3. *Capacity constraints*. If firms in remote regions could offer their products in the regions forming part of the candidate market without incurring any significant additional costs, those regions should be included in the relevant product market. However, the existence of capacity constraints may lead to separate geographic markets.

4. *Long-term contracts*. Similarly to capacity constraints, firms in different regions might be committed by long-term contracts and, therefore, be unable to divert sales from their regions to regions in the candidate market even after a price increase. Thus, those regions would not form a single geographic market.[122]

5. *Regulatory barriers*. There is a wide range of regulatory barriers that may limit the size of the relevant geographic market. Examples of regulatory barriers are legal monopolies, price regulation, or technical standards.[123] The Commission has defined nationwide relevant geographical markets in the case of fiscal monopolies and exclusive rights.[124]

---

[119] Commission Notice on the definition of the relevant market for the purpose of Community competition law, OJ 1997 C 372/5, para. 29.

[120] See *Bass*, OJ 1999 L 186/1, paras. 115–16; *Scottish and Newcastle*, OJ 1999 L 186/28, paras. 85–86; and *Tetra Pak I (BTG licence)*, OJ 1988 L 272/27, para. 37. See also Case T-69/89, *Radio Telefis Éireann (RTE) v Commission* [1991] ECR II-485, Case T-70/89, *British Broadcasting Corporation and BBC Enterprises Ltd (BBC) v Commission* [1991] ECR II-535, and Case T-76/89, *Independent Television Publications Ltd (ITP) v Commission* [1991] ECR II-575, confirmed in Joined Cases C-241/91 P and C-242/91 P, *Radio Telefis Éireann and Independent Television Publications Ltd (RTE & ITP) v Commission* [1995] ECR I-743.

[121] See Case T-69/89, *Radio Telefis Éireann (RTE) v Commission* [1991] ECR II-485. The Commission did not, however, mention national/regional preferences when defining the geographical market. See *Magill TV Guide/ITP, BBC and RTE*, OJ 1989 L 78/43, para. 21.

[122] See Case IV/M.1313, *Danish Crown/Vestjyske Slagterier*, paras. 62–64. The Commission defined Denmark as the relevant geographical market despite the fact of price correlation of 0.93–0.98 between the Danish market and other northern European markets, because Danish farmers had to supply locally due to contractual obligations.

[123] M Monti, "Policy Market Definition as a Cornerstone of EU Competition Policy" *Workshop on Market Definition*, Helsinki, October 5, 2001.

[124] *Amministrazione Autonoma dei Monopoli di Stato*, OJ 1998 L 252/47, upheld on appeal in Case T-139/98, *Amministrazione Autonoma dei Monopoli di Stato (AAMS) v Commission* [2001] ECR II-3413; *Deutsche Post AG*, OJ 2001 L 125/27; and *Deutsche Post AG—Interception of cross-border mail*, OJ 2001 L 331/40. See also *British Sugar plc*, OJ 1999 L 76/1; *Soda-Ash/Solvay*, OJ 1991 L 152/21.

6. *Local presence.* When it is important to have a local distribution or an after-sales network, foreign competitors might be at a competitive disadvantage and not able to exert a competitive constraint on domestic suppliers.[125]

Examples of geographic market definitions in the decisional practice and case law. Depending the degree of homogeneity of the conditions of competition between different areas, the relevant geographic market may be global, regional, trans-national, national, sub-national, or, even, confined to a facility in a single geographic location (e.g., a port):

1. *Worldwide markets.* Worldwide markets are most likely for globally-traded commodities such as minerals, metals, and oil.[126] Technology, such as software and hardware, may also give rise to global markets given standardisation and ease of distribution. In *Microsoft* for example the Commission concluded that a worldwide market existed with respect to work group server operating system software and media player software. It noted that multinational computer manufacturers enter into worldwide licensing agreement for the software, and then sell computers globally. An important element of the Commission's determination was the lack of significant import restrictions and transport costs associated with Microsoft's software.[127]

2. *EU-wide markets.* When products are sold on a similar price and scale across the EU, EU-wide market definitions are likely. In *Chiquita* for example the Commission found that the relevant geographical market for the company's bananas consisted of a substantial portion of the EU, including Denmark, Germany, the Netherlands, Ireland, Switzerland, and Austria. Despite sometimes-lengthy transport routes, the Commission found that transport costs were not so high as to constitute a significant barrier to entry within these nations. The Commission did not provide a detailed explanation of its exclusion of France, Italy, and the United Kingdom from the relevant market, but noted generally the unfavourable "import arrangements and trading conditions in these countries and the fact that bananas of various types and origin are sold there."[128] In *Hilti*, the Court of First Instance provided greater guidance in its determination that the relevant geographic market for nail guns and consumables was EU-wide. Specifically, the Court found that the transport cost of nails was low, and that price differences between the Member States were sufficient to encourage parallel trade.[129]

---

[125] See *Tetra Pak I (BTG licence),* OJ 1988 L 272/27, para. 41 (Commission considered the need to establish a local distribution network and concluded that the costs of doing so were not high enough to narrow the definition of the relevant geographic market). See too *PO–Michelin,* OJ 2002 L 143/1.

[126] See, e.g., Case IV/M.1161, *Alcoa/Alumax* (aluminium); Case IV/M.1383, *Exxon/Mobil* (crude oil); Case COMP/M.2413, *BHP/Billiton* (copper); and Case IV/M.619, *Gencor/Lonrho* (platinum).

[127] Case COMP/C-3/37.792, *Microsoft,* Commission Decision of March 24, 2004, not yet published, para. 427.

[128] *Chiquita,* OJ 1976 L 95/1, Art. 1.

[129] Case T-30/89, *Hilti AG v Commission* [1991] ECR II-1439, para. 79–81. See also *Tetra Pak I (BTG licence),* OJ 1988 L 272/27, para. 41 ("Even if there exist the differing demand conditions between Member States [for milk cartons], the EEC is the relevant geographical market for the cartons

3. *National markets.* National markets have featured most prominently in the decisional practice under Article 82 EC.[130] For example, in *Irish Sugar*, the Commission concluded that the relevant geographic market for sugar was Ireland. Although sugar prices were higher than in other areas of the EU as to encourage imports to Ireland, the Commission noted that sugar importing was in fact minimal. Barriers to entry, in the form of transport costs, helped explain this trend. The Commission also observed that, "[d]uring the price war in the United Kingdom, Irish Sugar was able to continue to maintain a substantial price difference for, in particular, retail sugar in Ireland. As regards industrial sugar, Irish Sugar [also maintained] significantly higher prices for those customers operating only on the home market."[131] In contrast, in *DSD* the Commission relied almost exclusively on differences between technical regulatory schemes among Member States in determining that the waste-management sector was divided into national markets.[132]

4. *Local markets.* The relevant geographic market has been found to be limited to a local facility in cases where the nearest alternative facility was in practical terms unsuitable or where the product or service by definition must be provided within the local facility. In *Stena Sealink*, the Commission deemed the port of Holyhead to be the entire relevant market because the nearest alternative port, Liverpool, was nearly twice the distance from Dublin to Holyhead. Because there was no practical substitute for the port, the Commission limited the relevant geographic market to the local facility.[133] Similarly, the Court of Justice found in *Aéroports de Paris* that, because ground handling services must be supplied within the airport only, the relevant geographic market was limited to the local facilities at the airport.[134]

---

and machines under discussion....all types of carton and machine are found to a significant extent in all Member States. Secondly transport costs for both machines and cartons are not significant."). See also *Tetra Pak II*, OJ 1992 L 72/1, para. 98 (noting that the market consisted of the entire EU).

[130] Case 127/73, *Belgische Radio en Televisie v SV SABAM and NV Fonior* [1974] ECR 313; *HOV SVZ/MCN*, OJ 1994 L 104/34; Case 322/81, *NV Nederlandsche Banden Industrie Michelin v Commission* [1983] ECR 3461; Case T-69/89, *Radio Telefis Éireann (RTE) v Commission* [1991] ECR II-485; Case C-333/94 P, *Tetra Pak International SA v* Commission [1996] ECR I-5951; and *Virgin/British Airways*, OJ 2000 L 30/1, upheld on appeal Case T-219/99, *British Airways plc v Commission* [2003] ECR II-5917.

[131] *Irish Sugar plc*, OJ 1997 L 258/1, para. 92–97. See also *Napier Brown/British Sugar*, OJ 1988 L 284/41, para. 43–49 (noting transport costs and trade flow statistics in concluding that the United Kingdom was the relevant geographic market).

[132] *DSD*, OJ 2001 L 166/1, para. 87–91 (noting that "the laws and regulations governing the disposal of packaging, including their implementing rules, differ widely from one country to another....One result of this is that the take-back and exemption system operated by DSD is restricted to Germany.").

[133] *Sea Containers v Stena Sealink—Interim measures*, OJ 1994 L 15/8, para. 62–65. See too *FAG—Flughafen Frankfurt/Main AG*, OJ 1998 L 173/32, paras. 55–56; *Ilmailulaitos/Luftfartsverket (Finnish Airports)*, OJ 1999 L 69/24, paras. 24–33.

[134] Case C-82/01 P, *Aéroports de Paris v Commission* [2002] ECR I-9297, at para. 95–96. See also Case T-128/98, *Aéroports de Paris v Commission* [2000] ECR II-3929, para. 141–42 (noting that "land and buildings in the Paris region cannot be taken into consideration, since they do not in themselves enable those services to be provided" and that "for most passengers leaving or arriving in the Paris

2.5 SELECTED ISSUES ON MARKET DEFINITION

Overview. Market definition can raise more complex issues in certain settings. First, the impact of price discrimination on market definition is considered. When firms can effectively price discriminate between customers, this may impact on the relevant market definition. Second, market definition in cases of tying and bundling presents issues, in particular whether separate markets exist for: (a) the bundled products alone; (b) each of the bundled products on a stand-alone products; or (c) markets comprising the bundled products and each of the stand-alone products. Third, market definition in aftermarkets—where consumers of a primary market need to purchase compatible consumables—require consideration. At the extreme, a firm's own consumables may be a relevant market. Finally, market definition in so-called two-sided markets—where firms compete simultaneously for two groups of customers A and B whose demands are interrelated—is considered.

2.5.1 Impact Of Price Discrimination On Market Definition

Issue stated. Very often firms can and do price discriminate, often in astoundingly multifarious ways.[135] For example, airlines generally operate complex yield-management systems whereby they try to differentiate ticket prices between customers based on time of purchase, ticket flexibility etc. Price discrimination is an ubiquitous business practice,[136] which, on its own, does not evidence market power,[137] and which, even where there is market power, is a type of behaviour that almost invariably enhances market efficiency (although not necessarily consumer welfare).[138]

Price discrimination can sometimes be relevant for market definition. The Commission's Notice on market definition states that "[a] distinct group of customers for the relevant product may constitute a narrower, distinct market."[139] This may be appropriate "when such group could be subject to price discrimination."[140] As the Commission's Notice clarifies, the first condition needed for a group of customers to form a separate relevant market is that "it is possible to identify clearly which group an individual customer belongs to."[141] If it is not clear to which group a customer belongs,

region or other French regions, the air transport services...are not interchangeable with the services offered in other airports").

[135] See for example the amount of price discrimination on display in just one Broadway theatre (in what is a highly competitive industry) in P Leslie, "Price Discrimination in Broadway Theatre" (2004) 35(3) *RAND Journal of Economics* 520–41.

[136] See for example the extensive, unanimous discussion (involving a round-table discussion of six US academic economists) in the *Empirical Industrial Organisation Roundtable*, Federal Trade Commission, 2001, at p. 104ff.

[137] S Carbonneau, P McAfee, H Mialon and S Mialon, *Price Discrimination and Market Power*, Emory Economics 0413, 2004, mimeo.

[138] See R Schmalensee, "Output and Welfare Implications of Monopolistic Third-Degree Price Discrimination" (1981) *American Economic Review* 239–4. See also AS Edlin, M Epelbaum and WP Heller, "Is Perfect Price Discrimination Really Efficient: Welfare and Existence in General Equilibrium" (1998) 66 *Econometrica* 897–922.

[139] Commission Notice on the definition of the relevant market for the purpose of Community competition law, OJ 1997 C 372/5, para. 43.

[140] *Ibid.*

[141] *Ibid* (emphasis added).

the particular price intended for the group will also be charged to many customers outside the group. If a hypothetical monopolist attempts to offer the same product at different prices to two different groups, customers will (all else equal) all attempt to buy at the lower price. The profitability of the price offered to the "high-price" group will be constrained by demand substitution if the members of that group can buy at the lower price, and, consequently, demand substitutes will need to be included in the market.

Similarly, if the hypothetical monopolist charges a price based on some observable feature that is only partially associated with the target group, the result will be that many customers outside the target group will be charged the target price, and the demand substitutes of these other customers must be included in the relevant market. However, price discrimination not only requires the existence of clearly identifiable sets of consumers, but also requires that trade among customers belonging to different groups or arbitrage by third parties is nor feasible. Otherwise, the hypothetical monopolist would not be able to price discriminate among different customer groups.

Effect of price discrimination on demand-side substitution. To better understand the impact of price discrimination on market definition, it is useful to distinguish between *third-degree price discrimination* (where consumers are grouped according to observable characteristics and each group is charged a different price for the same good) and *second-degree price discrimination* (where consumers are offered a menu of price/quality combinations and each consumer selects his most preferred combination, i.e., groups are formed by self-selection).

Third-degree price discrimination is only feasible when consumers of one group are clearly identifiable and there is no arbitrage. Each group of consumers constitutes a separate product market. This is the case we explained above and the one that has been explicitly covered in the Commission's Notice on market definition.

Market definition is not as straightforward, however, in the case of second-degree price discrimination. Consider a market scenario where firms offer different versions of the same product at different prices. In this way, they induce consumers to reveal their preferences by selecting their most desired version.[142] Some consumers will choose a low quality version because of its low price, while others will be willing to pay extra to have access to a higher quality version. For each version, a separate group of consumers can be identified. However, unlike in the case of third-degree price discrimination, those self-selected groups need not constitute separate relevant product markets: unless the price differential between the various versions is sufficiently high, consumers will regard them as substitutes and may be ready to switch between them in response to changes in their relative prices. The Commission has in many occasions recognised the possibility of substitution between different price/quality combinations in its market definition decisions.[143]

[142] This strategy is known as "versioning". See C Shapiro and HR Varian, *Information Rules* (Cambridge, Harvard Business School Press, 1998) ch. 3.

[143] Case COMP/38.233, *Wanadoo Interactive*, Commission Decision of July 16, 2003, not yet published, fn 182; Case T-342/99, *Airtours plc v Commission* [2002] ECR II-2585, para. 34. In *Carnival/P&O Princess*, whilst not taking a definitive decision, the Commission considered the

Substitution may be asymmetric, however. For example, it may happen that at prevailing prices the high quality version may exert a considerable competitive constraint on the pricing of a low quality version—i.e., a price increase for the low quality version would trigger substitution towards the high quality variant—whereas the opposite is not true. In this example, there are two separate product markets: one including the low and high quality versions, and another one including the high quality version only.[144]

Effect of price discrimination on supply-side substitution. Price discrimination does not represent an obstacle to supply-side substitution. On the contrary, "challenges based on such price discrimination markets have to overcome formidable supply-side obstacles that reduce the likelihood of anticompetitive effects."[145] In the case of third-degree price discrimination, the products sold to different groups of consumers are functionally identical, which makes supply-side substitution a credible constraint and could lead to broad market definitions. When firms engage in versioning strategies (second-degree price discrimination), supply-side substitution is also relevant. A producer of a high-quality version can often downgrade his product at no significant cost and almost instantaneously. If that were the case, supply-side substitution would represent an effective competition constraint that would have to be taken into account when delineating the market. Price discrimination may even facilitate supply-side substitution. This is because, when price discrimination is feasible, the entrant into the candidate market can compete aggressively in it by setting low prices for a downgraded version of its product while charging high prices in its "home" market with the high-quality version of its product.

2.5.2 Market Definition In Tying And Bundling Cases

Issue stated. Consider two components, A and B, which could be supplied separately or together. If there was sufficient demand, competing businesses could provide AB, A, and B. Sometimes businesses do just that: one can buy headache medicine, sinus medicine, and combined headache and sinus medicine. Other times there is not sufficient demand for A and businesses provide AB and B: cars come with tyres and one can buy tyres separately, but not cars without tyres. And sometimes there is sufficient demand only for the combined product AB, which is the case for most

possibility that cruises of different quality were in the same market. See Case COMP/M.2706, *Carnival Corporation /P&O Princess*. In *Nestle/Ralston Purina*, the Commission, even though stating that to some extent makers of pet food segment their products into "economy," "mainstream" or "premium" categories, decided to not define separate product markets on quality levels. See Case COMP/M.2337, *Nestle/ Ralston Purina*.

144 In Case COMP/38.233, *Wanadoo Interactive*, Commission Decision of July 16, 2003, not yet published, the Commission followed this logic to conclude the existence of a separate high-speed Internet access market. It commissioned a survey of high-speed users to determine whether they would switch back to low speed access if the price of high-speed access increased. It found that the rate of switching from high speed to low speed was much less than from low speed to high speed, an asymmetry that suggested the existence of a separate market for high-speed access

145 JA Hausman, GK Leonard and CA Vellturo, "Market Definition Under Price Discrimination" (1996) 64(2) *Antitrust Law Journal* 367, at 383.

books—generally one cannot buy chapters separately, even if they cover distinctly different subjects that are themselves the subjects of other books.[146]

Tying and bundling occurs when a firm offers two products A and B jointly. Tying refers to a situation where product A (the tying good) can only be purchased with product B (the tied good); so only AB and B are sold in the market. In contrast, mixed bundling occurs when products A and B are sold in a bundle but are also available separately, albeit at a greater total cost. Finally, pure bundling occurs when the two products can only be purchased as part of a bundle, i.e., only AB is commercialised.

Effect on market definition: tying and pure bundling. The effect of tying and bundling practices on market definition varies according to the type of bundling at issue. Consider first tying and bundling. The first key question in cases involving allegations of illegal tying and bundling is to establish whether A and B are "separate products" from the viewpoint of consumer demand or whether instead they should be treated as components of a single product.[147] Two products can only be tied if they are genuinely distinct products. That is, when an independent product market exists for each of them; or, in other words, when there are separate product markets for both A and B.

As noted by Professors Areeda, Elhauge, and Hovenkamp:[148]

> "However, under the competitive market practices test, a distinct market for the tied item does not imply separate products absent widespread sales of the tying item in unbundled form. For example, an independent market for carburettors does not make a car with carburettor installed two products because no significant independent market exists for cars stripped of their carburettors. Nor does an independent market for television tubes prove that a television and its installed tube are separate products because we have no significant independent market for televisions lacking tubes. Two items constitute one product under the market practices test unless *each* could efficiently be sold without the other."

That is, one cannot determine whether the bundle AB is a single product or the combination of two separate products by looking solely at the demand for product B. In fact, once it is established that B is a separate product, the relevant question is whether there is demand for A as a stand alone product. Are there are consumers prepared to pay a price to acquire product A without product B attached? If so, than A and B are separate products; otherwise, there are two products AB and B, and A is just a component of the first of the two products.

A recent case that considered this issue is *BT Analyst*.[149] In that case, the Office of Fair Trading (OFT) was concerned about a product (BT Analyst) which British Telecom

[146] M Salinger, "A Graphical Analysis of Bundling" (1995) 68(1) *Journal of Business* 85–98; DS Evans and M Salinger, "Why Do Firms Bundle and Tie? Evidence from Competitive Markets and Implications for Tying Law" (2005) 22(1) *Yale Journal on Regulation* 37; S Stremersch and GJ Tellis, "Strategic Bundling of Products and Prices: A New Synthesis for Marketing" (2002) 66(1) *Journal of Marketing* 55–72; and DS Evans and M Salinger, "An Empirical Analysis of Bundling and Tying: Over-the-Counter Pain Relief and Cold Medicines," CESifo Working Paper No. 1297, 2004.

[147] See Ch. 9 (Tying and Bundling) below.

[148] P Areeda, E Elhauge and H Hovenkamp, *Antitrust Law* (2nd edn., New York, Aspen Publishers, 2004) vol. X, p. 183, ¶ 1745d2.

[149] *Pricing of BT Analyst*, OFT Decision of October 26, 2004.

(BT) was giving to multi-line customers free of charge. BT Analyst provides a retail telephony electronic bill provision service. A rival company, Magictelecom, complained alleging that BT was attempting to foreclose the market. The OFT decided that BT Analyst did not constitute a separate product. Instead, it concluded that there was a single market for retail telephony services, which should be considered as a "cluster" and which included *inter alia* an electronic bill provision service:[150]

> "In a cluster market, consumers choose suppliers on the basis of the most competitively priced cluster of products offered. Once a supplier is chosen on this basis, the consumer will purchase all products/services within the cluster from the chosen supplier. This means that purchasing decisions are not made on the basis of the individual prices of products. Consequently, the practice of 'bundling' these services together is not in itself anti-competitive."

Effect on market definition: mixed bundling. There are several candidates for the relevant market when companies compete by offering mixed bundles. First, the bundle and the single products may all be part of the same relevant market. Second, there may be different relevant markets for the bundle and for the separate products. The first option is the correct one if at current prices consumers are practically indifferent between buying the bundle and the two product separately—that is, if a small increase in the price of the bundle induces consumers to acquire the two products separately. Alternatively, separate markets for the bundle and its constituent products may be found when consumers derive a large benefit from buying the products jointly, so that at current prices no substitution is likely in response to a small increase in the price of the bundle.[151]

2.5.3 Aftermarkets

Issue stated. In some instances, the consumer of a product, typically a durable good (e.g., a jet engine), must subsequently purchase a complementary follow-on product (e.g., spare parts or maintenance and repair services). The market for the durable good is denoted as the "primary market" or the foremarket, while the markets for the follow-on products are known as "secondary markets" or "aftermarkets." Examples of foremarkets and aftermarkets include inkjet printers and replacement cartridges, game consoles and game cartridges, electric toothbrushes and replacement heads, and photo cameras and their repair parts.[152]

The application of the hypothetical monopolist test to situations where competition occurs both in primary and secondary markets requires great care. As noted by the Commission's Market Definition Notice, the "method to define markets in these cases is the same, i.e., assessing the responses of customers based on their purchasing decisions

---

[150] *Ibid.*, para. 43. See also the Office of Fair Trading, Market Definition, OFT 403, December 2004, para. 5.11.

[151] Europe Economics, "Market Definition in the Media Sector—Economic Issues" Report for the European Commission, DG Competition, 2002, pages. 24–26.

[152] See C Shapiro, "Aftermarkets and Consumer Welfare: Making Sense of *Kodak*" (1995) 63(2) *Antitrust Law Journal* 483–512.

to relative price changes."[153] The difference lies in that attention needs to be paid to the "constraints on substitution imposed by conditions in the connected markets,"[154] and in particular to the extent to which competition in the foremarket prevent exploitation of consumers in the aftermarket(s).

Effect on market definition. Consider the example of jet engines and the maintenance, repair, and overhaul (MRO) services for jet engines.[155] There are in principle three conceivable market configurations: (1) *two dual markets*—one for all jet engines and one for the spare parts and MRO services for all engine brands; (2) a *single system market* for jet engines including their spare parts and MRO services; or (3) a *primary market* for jet engines and *separate secondary* MRO *markets* for each engine brand.

Which of these market configurations is appropriate depends on the particular facts of the case.[156] If the spare parts and the MRO services for each engine brand are compatible with the spare parts and the MRO services for other brands (and are perceived as such by customers), then market configuration (1) is likely to be most appropriate. In this scenario, the purchase of a particular jet engine brand does not "lock-in" customers, who remain free to use the maintenance service providers and the spare parts of competing engine brands.[157]

If, instead, the spare parts and the MRO services of one brand are incompatible with those of other brands (or are perceived as such by customers), then the right configuration is either (2) or (3). Customers of a given engine brand are "forced" to make use of the spare parts for that engine, i.e., they are locked in. Which of the two is correct depends on the extent to which a rise in the price of spare parts and MRO services affects the sales of jet engines. That is, it depends on the extent to which current and future customers of jet engines react to a price increase in spare parts and MRO services, which *inter alia* depends on whether customers take into account the whole-life cost of the jet engine, including its maintenance and repair, when choosing the primary product.[158]

---

[153] Commission Notice on the definition of the relevant market for the purpose of Community competition law, OJ 1997 C 372/5, p. 56. See also Office of Fair Trading, *Market Definition*, OFT 403, December 2004, paras. 6.1–6.7.

[154] *Ibid.*

[155] This example is taken from the Commission's Decision in Case COMP/M.2220—*General Electric/Honeywell*, and the judgment in Case T-210/01, *General Electric Company v Commission* [2005] ECR-nyr.

[156] XXVth Report on Competition Policy (1995), para. 86. See also C McSorley, AJ Padilla and M Williams, "Switching Costs" OFT-DTI Discussion Paper, April 2003, para. 7.16

[157] See Discussion Paper, para. 248.

[158] *Ibid.* at para. 249. The approach adopted in the Discussion Paper is somewhat different, however. The Discussion Paper (para. 247) considers "whether the secondary products in a given aftermarket can be considered to form a relevant product market without taking into account effects on sales of the primary product given rise to this particular aftermarket." This approach is inconsistent with the logic of the hypothetical monopolist test. A hypothetical monopolist may not find it profitable to raise prices in the market for its secondary products because of the loss of profits in the primary market, and not only due to the loss of business in the aftermarket.

If they do take into account the cost of spare parts and MRO services when acquiring an engine, and the "characteristics of the primary good market make quick and direct consumer responses to relative price increases of the secondary products feasible,"[159] then a price increase in the aftermarket (spare parts and MRO services) would not be profitable due to a fall in sales of the primary product (jet engines) and the aftermarket. In such circumstances, the aftermarket does not constitute a separate product market, and so market definition (2) is likely to be appropriate.[160]

However, in many cases customers either do not consider whole-life costs or underestimate them. This may make a unilateral rise in the price of spare parts and MRO services profitable, as it will not lead to an offsetting fall in sales of the jet engines. In other cases, even if aircraft buyers correctly estimate the whole-life costs of an engine, a unilateral price rise for the aftermarket product will be profitable if: (1) the installed base of jet engine customers is locked in because it is extremely onerous to replace the existing jet engines with new ones in response to a price increase in spare parts and MRO services; and (2) the new customers of jet engines are a small proportion in relation to the size of the aftermarket (i.e., a small number in comparison with the installed base of locked-in customers). Under such circumstances, a strict application of the hypothetical monopolist test will find that there is a separate market for the aftermarket product for each brand.

Conclusion. The following basic conclusions apply in the case of primary markets and aftermarkets:

1. If the secondary products are compatible, then there are separate product markets for the primary good and the secondary good.

2. If the secondary products are incompatible and an increase in aftermarket prices affects consumers' choices in the foremarket, then there is a single system market. The increase in aftermarket price will impact foremarket competition when: (a) consumers take into account the prices for the secondary product when purchasing the primary good; and (b) there are no, or limited, switching costs in the primary market.

3. If secondary products are incompatible and an increase in aftermarket prices does not affect consumers' choices in the foremarket, then there is a single market for the primary good and a series of brand-specific aftermarkets.

---

[159] Commission Notice on the definition of the relevant market for the purpose of Community competition law, OJ 1997 C 372/5, para. 56.

[160] See, for example, the European Commission approach in its investigation of *Kyocera/Pelikan*. Kyocera was accused of dominating the aftermarket for the supply of spare parts to its printers. The Commission found that Kyocera was not dominant in the market for spare parts as it was constrained by competition in the market for printers, since customers took into account the price of the consumables when considering which printer to buy. See *Pelikan/Kyocera*, XXVth Report on Competition Policy (1995), para. 87.

Table 1 summarises the above conclusions.

Table 1: Market definition in aftermarkets

	Secondary products are compatible	Secondary products are brand specific	
		Increase in aftermarket prices impacts on foremarket choices	Increase in aftermarket prices does not impact on foremarket choices
Dual markets	✓		
Single system market		✓	
Foremarket plus aftermarkets			✓

2.5.4. Market Definition In Two-Sided Industries

Issue stated. In many industries firms compete simultaneously for two groups of customers A and B whose demands are interrelated. As two leading economists note, "many if not most markets with network externalities are two-sided."[161] This is certainly the case of the software industry at large. The video game market constitutes a neat example of a two-sided market. No game platform, such as Sony's PlayStation 2 or Microsoft's Xbox, can sell consoles without games to play on. But no game platform will ever convince game developers to write for its console without the prospect of an installed base of consumers.

The key feature of two-sided markets is therefore that, to succeed, competitors must get both sides of the market on board. This requires solving a typical "chicken-and-egg problem." Competitors in two-sided industries have to decide which side of the market will be subsidised and which one will be charged to make money. This explains why prices below cost, sometime zero or even negative prices, are typically observed in multi-sided industries. For example, videogame manufacturers treat the console side as a loss leader and make money on game developers by charging per-unit royalties on games and fixed fees for development kits. Manufacturers of PC operating systems use the opposite price structure. They aim to make money on end users and do not make or lose money on application developers. The choice of an appropriate business model seems to be the key to commercial success and is, therefore, the subject of significant corporate attention.

Effect on market definition. In two-sided industries, if a firm (a two-sided platform in the jargon of those businesses) raises the price it charges to one group of customers

[161] C Rochet and J Tirole, "Platform Competition in Two-Sided Markets," (2003) 1(4) *Journal of the European Economic Association* 990–1029.

(group A), it will not only lose sales made to those customers, but also will experience a reduction in the volume of sales to the other group of customers (group B), since the members of group B value the product offered by the firm more when it attracts more group A customers. That is, when a two-sided platform raises the price charged to the A side of the platform, it negatively impacts the B side of the market, which then causes an additional negative impact on the A side and so on.

A recent paper has shown that the standard techniques used to test for a relevant antitrust market are incorrect when the firms under scrutiny operate two-sided platforms.[162] In particular, they have shown that applying standard (one-sided) critical loss analysis to a two-sided business would lead to excessively narrow market definitions. This is because the one-sided formulation when applied to a price increase for group A consumers fails to take into account the loss in volume (and hence on profits) on the B side of the platform, as well as the subsequent reduction of activity on both sides of the business. The authors have extended the standard (one-way) critical loss analysis formulas to the case of two-sided platforms, showing that the bias from the misuse of one-sided formulas in a two-sided setting can be very large.

[162] DS Evans and MD Noel, "Analysing Market Definition and Power in Multi-Sided Markets," (2005) *Social Science Research Network*, electronic paper, available at www.ssrn.com.

Chapter 3

DOMINANCE

3.1 INTRODUCTION

The central importance of dominance under Article 82 EC. Once the relevant market on which the allegedly dominant undertaking operates is defined, its potential dominance falls to be assessed. Establishing dominance is an essential pre-requisite under Article 82 EC: if dominance is not proven, no abuse can be made out, regardless of the anticompetitive effects of the conduct in question. Dominance itself is not, however, contrary to Article 82 EC.[1] This is an important point of distinction from other legal regimes that sanction unilateral conduct. For example, under Section 2 of the United States Sherman Act 1890, a firm that is not yet dominant may commit a violation if its conduct would lead to monopolisation or, in the case of attempted monopolisation, there is a dangerous probability that it would succeed in doing so. Thus, at least in theory, a firm with a small market share could violate Section 2 so long as there was a dangerous probability that its attempt to monopolise would eventually succeed. In contrast, it is essential under Article 82 EC to establish dominance at the time of the alleged abuse. The fact that a non-dominant firm's conduct might, if unchecked, lead to dominance in future is irrelevant.

The basic legal concept of dominance. Dominance in law implies that a firm has a high degree of immunity from the normal disciplining forces of rivals' competitive reactions and consumer behaviour. The working definition established in *United Brands* is that dominance "relates to a position of economic strength enjoyed by an undertaking which enables it to prevent effective competition being maintained on the relevant market by giving it the power to behave to an appreciable extent independently of its competitors, customers and ultimately of its consumers."[2] This test was cited with approval in *Hoffmann-La Roche*, although the Court of Justice added the caveat that "such a position does not preclude some competition...but enables the undertaking...if not to determine, at least to have an appreciable influence on the conditions under which that competition will develop, and in any case to act largely in disregard of it so long as such conduct does not operate to its detriment."[3]

The basic economic concept of dominance. The economic concept of dominance does not fully correspond with the above legal definition. In economics, the notion of dominance is broadly associated with the concept of market power. A firm enjoys a

---

[1] Case 322/81, *NV Nederlandsche Baden-Industrie Michelin v Commission* [1983] ECR 3461, para. 10 ("[A] finding that an undertaking has a dominant position is not in itself a recrimination.").

[2] *Chiquita*, OJ 1976 L 95/1, confirmed on appeal in Case 27/76, *United Brands Company and United Brands Continentaal BV v Commission* [1978] ECR 207 (hereinafter "*United Brands*"), para. 65.

[3] See *Vitamins*, OJ 1976 L 223/27, confirmed on appeal in Case 85/76, *Hoffmann-La Roche & Co AG v Commission* [1979] ECR 461 (hereinafter "*Hoffmann-La Roche*"), para. 39. See also *United Brands*, *ibid.*, para. 113.

dominant position if it has significant market power, i.e., if it is able to charge prices significantly above competitive levels or restrict output significantly below competitive levels for a sustained period of time. However, a firm may enjoy significant market power (i.e., setting supra-competitive prices), even if it cannot behave to an appreciable extent independently of its competitors, customers, and ultimately consumers. That is, for example, the case of all firms operating in oligopolistic markets. Their pricing policies are constrained both by the prices set by actual and potential competitors and the behaviour of their customers, who in most cases will cut down their consumption in response to a price increase. Strictly speaking, only a monopolist operating in a market protected by insurmountable barriers to entry and facing a completely inelastic demand would be able to behave independently of its competitors, customers, and consumers.

The term "dominance" is also sometimes used in the economic literature to describe a situation in which a firm with market power (the "dominant" firm) competes with a number of smaller, price-taking firms (which comprise the so-called "competitive fringe").[4] The dominant firm has the ability to set the market price, which is accepted by all members of the competitive fringe. But it cannot be said to be capable of behaving independently of rivals and consumers, because it must take into account the aggregate capacity of the competitive fringe. The dominant firm enjoys market power because the competitive fringe cannot produce enough output to clear the market. However, its power to raise prices is restricted to its residual demand, i.e., the portion of market demand that cannot be satisfied by the fringe.

The different types of dominance. Different types of dominance are considered in this chapter. The first, and simplest, situation is when a single firm is dominant as a seller. Section 3.2 treats this concept in detail. A second concept is "collective dominance"—a situation that arises in oligopolistic markets when firms are interdependent and realise that competing with each other would ultimately be self-defeating and, hence, behave "as if" they had coordinated their behaviour in the marketplace. Coordination of this kind can give rise to dominance and is discussed in Section 3.3. A degree of market power may also exist on the buying side. Indeed, as discussed in Section 3.4, buyer power may itself rise to the level of dominance. Finally, some decisions and cases under Article 82 EC have mentioned a concept of "superdominance"—a situation in which a firm is a near-monopolist. The relevance of this concept is discussed in Section 3.5.

3.2 SINGLE FIRM DOMINANCE

3.2.1 Basic Approach

Need for comprehensive assessment in the specific market context. Dominance cannot be assessed on the basis of a single factor or checklist of factors. Market power is not an absolute term but a matter of degree, and the degree of market power will depend on the circumstances of each case. For this reason, Community Court judgments and Commission decisions emphasise that a firm's ability to behave

[4] See GJ Stigler, "The Dominant Firm and the Inverted Price Umbrella" (1965) 8 *Journal of Law and Economics* 167.

independently of competitive constraints must be assessed in light of all relevant market circumstances:[5]

> "In general a dominant position derives from a combination of several factors which, taken separately, are not necessarily determinative. In order to find out whether...an undertaking [holds] a dominant position on the relevant market it is necessary first of all to examine its structure and then the situation on the said market as far as competition is concerned."

Such an examination requires a "comprehensive survey" of the competitive conditions on the relevant market before making any determination as to dominance.[6] This comprehensive survey aims to assess the firm's degree of market power and determine whether that amounts to a dominant position. This means taking fully into account all of the influences that strengthen or weaken its market position, its advantages and disadvantages, and constraints on its competitive behaviour in the relevant market.

Although the measurement of dominance cannot be approached in a mechanical fashion, the decisional practice and case law have established a reasonably well-defined series of steps to assess dominance. Several steps are involved. The first is to measure the relative strength of the firms on the relevant market based on their market shares. The second broad step is to assess whether entry or expansion by rival firms is sufficiently easy for them to contest the market share of the leading firm. The ability of buyers to off-set seller power should also be analysed. Finally, all of these elements should be cross-checked against the evidence of actual competition on the market.

3.2.2 The Starting Point: Market Shares

Generally. Market share data are the first and most important element in the assessment of dominance. According to the former Commissioner responsible for competition policy, Mario Monti, the Commission uses "market definition and market shares as an easily available proxy for the measurement of the market power enjoyed by firms."[7] Both the market share of the firm under investigation and the market shares of its rivals on the same market must be examined.

The calculation of the market shares of particular undertakings is only possible once the relevant market on which the undertakings operate is identified. Market share is calculated on the basis of sales generated by the undertaking on the relevant product and geographic market.[8] The importance of a correct market definition is therefore obvious. If the market is correctly defined, a market share calculation will prove very useful and may even allow a presumption of dominance if market shares are sufficiently high. In

[5] Case 27/76, *United Brands Company and United Brands Continentaal BV v Commission* [1978] ECR 207, paras. 66–67.

[6] See Opinion of Advocate General Roemer in Case 6/72, *Europemballage Corporation and Continental Can Company Inc v Commission* [1973] ECR 251, para. 262.

[7] M Monti, "Policy Market Definition as a Cornerstone of EU Competition Policy," Workshop on Market Definition, Helsinki, October 5, 2001.

[8] Commission Notice on the definition of the relevant market for the purposes of Community competition law, OJ 1997 C 372/5, para. 53 ("The definition of the relevant market in both its product and geographic dimensions allows the identification of suppliers and the customers/consumers active on that market. On that basis, a total market size and market shares for each supplier can be calculated on the basis of their sales of the relevant products in the relevant area.").

contrast, an ill-founded market definition will make market share calculations meaningless. And, as discussed in Chapter Two (Market Definition), there is good reason to believe that a number of prior market definitions adopted by the Community institutions were not correct, or at least required further empirical investigation.

Assigning market shares. There is no single correct approach to assigning market shares. In most cases, volume or value data will suffice. The Notice on market definition sets forth a number of basic points.[9] First, the total market size and market shares should be calculated on the basis of the most readily-available information (e.g., companies' estimates, studies commissioned to industry consultants and/or trade associations). Volume data will often be available and may constitute a first point of reference. In *Clearstream*, the market share in the market for primary clearing and settlement services under German law was based on the number of securities deposited at Clearstream facilities.[10] In *Wanadoo,* market shares were based on the number of broadband internet subscribers signed up to the company.[11] In *TACA*, shares of the market for maritime transport services between North America and Europe were based on the volume of transported container cargo. [12] Volume of the mail order trade, calculated in terms of the number of parcels delivered, was the basis of the market share findings in *Deutsche Post.*[13]

Second, in cases of differentiated products, sales in value and their associated market share will usually better reflect the relative position and strength of each supplier. A similar principle applies in respect of services, where volumes do not generally convey meaningful information.

Finally, for certain industries and products, volume and/or value data may not be meaningful indicators of competitive strength. Other relevant indicators might therefore include capacity, the number of players in bidding markets, units of fleet (e.g., as in aerospace), the reserves held (e.g., as in mining), or the total number of the company's products currently in use (customer base). An extensive decisional practice has arisen under the EC Merger Regulation in respect of using data other than volume or value for assessing market shares.[14] For example, in *Mitsui/CVRD/Caemi*, the Commission used publicly-available capacity data of the iron ore suppliers active on the market to calculate market shares.[15] When considering the merger of a number of banks the

[9] *Ibid*., Part IV (calculation of market shares).

[10] Case COMP/38/096, *Clearstream (Clearing and settlement)*, Decision of June 4, 2004, not yet published (hereinafter "*Clearstream*").

[11] Case COMP/38.233, *Wanadoo Interactive*, Commission Decision of July 16, 2003, not yet published (hereinafter "*Wanadoo*").

[12] *Trans-Atlantic Conference Agreement* OJ 1999 L 95/1 (hereinafter "*TACA*"), on appeal Joined Cases T-191/98 and T-212/98 to T-214/98, *Atlantic Container Line AB and Others v Commission* [2003] ECR II-3275.

[13] *Deutsche Post AG*, OJ 2001 L 125/37, para. 32.

[14] See N Levy, *European Merger Control Law: A Guide To The Merger Regulation* (Matthew Bender/Lexis Nexis, 2005) Ch. 9 (Market Share Calculation and Assessment).

[15] See Case COMP/M.2420, *Mitsui/CVRD/Caemi.*

Commission used league tables to establish the market positions of the investment banks in question because market shares were too difficult to determine.[16]

In bidding markets, the Commission has sometimes looked at the market share data of previous years to help determine market positions. In *Price Waterhouse/Coopers & Lybrand*, the Commission considered it relevant to look at tender offers and bidding data over several years "in order to appraise more fully the nature and extent of the competitive process in the Big Six [accountancy] market for large companies."[17] Finally, determining market shares in markets subject to constant technological innovation is often difficult. For example, the Commission has pointed out that "there is no reliable publicly available estimate of the size of either the Internet sector as a whole or of any relevant sub-sector."[18]

Final problematic aspects of calculating market shares include the treatment of captive production and private label sales. Captive production (i.e., output that is consumed by the supplier internally) is generally excluded by the Commission when calculating market shares on the basis that "these quantities are not available [for sale to non-integrated competitors] in the market."[19] Private label sales—which constitute sales to retailers under whose own brands the products will be sold—are not often included with sales of the suppliers' own branded products when considering market shares.[20] However, both sets of data may be relevant when establishing market position as discounting private label sales may underestimate a manufacturer's market strength if it is the main or only source of supply for private label products.

Need for caution with market shares. The Commission has recognised that market shares are not conclusive evidence of dominance and therefore not a proper substitute for a comprehensive examination of market conditions. The Court of Justice expressed a similar opinion in *Hoffmann-La Roche*, acknowledging the importance of market shares in the assessment of dominance, but also their limitations:[21]

> "The existence of a dominant position may derive from several factors which, taken separately, are not necessarily determinative but among these factors a highly important one is the existence of very large market shares. [Nevertheless,] a substantial market share as evidence of the existence of a dominant position is not a constant factor and its importance varies from market to market according to the structure of these markets, especially as far as production, supply and demand are concerned. [In addition,] the relationship between the market shares of the undertakings involved in the concentration and of its competitors, especially those of the next largest...[is] significant evidence of the existence of a dominant position."

---

[16] Case COMP/M.2158, *Credit Suisse Group/Donaldson, Lufkin & Jenrette*.

[17] Case IV/M.1016, *Price Waterhouse/Coopers & Lybrand*, paras. 85–94.

[18] Case IV/M.1069, *WorldCom/MCI*, para. 95.

[19] Case IV/M.214, *Du Pont/ICI*, para. 30.

[20] Case T-290/94, *Kaysersberg v Commission* [1997] ECR II-2137, para. 174.

[21] Case 85/76, *Hoffmann-La Roche & Co AG v Commission* [1979] ECR 461, paras. 38–40, 48. See also Case 27/76, *United Brands Company and United Brands Continentaal BV v Commission* [1978] ECR 207, paras. 66–67.

These statements make sense.[22] First, market definition and market shares are simply a proxy for measuring market power: they cannot be decisive in themselves. Second, experience with market definition under Article 82 EC has shown that it is more art than science, in particular given the Community institutions' reluctance to embrace the use of quantitative techniques and the corresponding over-reliance on qualitative evidence. Identifying even high shares in markets defined in this way should not be enough to show dominance. Third, high market shares may not confer much market power where rival firms offer products that are differentiated in characteristics or branding. Market dynamics also matter. Market shares will be more important in mature or declining markets than markets characterised by rapid growth and technological change. Finally, the most important point is not the existence of high market shares, but whether such shares are likely to confer *lasting* market power. This involves a proper assessment of entry barriers. If barriers to entry are low, firms with very high market shares may have no market power. If they are high (e.g., due to the existence of exclusive or special rights), firms with even modest shares may have market power.

The Commission is therefore required to, and generally does, carry out a "comprehensive survey" of the competitive conditions on the relevant market before making any determination as to dominance, even in cases involving high market shares. Accordingly, in assessing dominance, elements such as market entry, exclusive rights, capacity utilisation, maturity of the market, and technical and financial resources may factor in the assessment. For instance, an undertaking with a high market share may be effectively constrained by another firm without a large market share or by actual or potential competitors.[23] Moreover, countervailing buying power may negate a dominant position. In cases where competition is dynamic, such as bid markets or industries with high innovation, market shares are subject to frequent fluctuation and may be unreliable as indicators of dominance.

General market share indicators. Although market shares cannot be mechanically assessed, the Community institutions' practice allows some generalisations to be made about the relative importance of certain market share levels. In general, very high

---

[22] See N Kroes, "Preliminary Thoughts on Policy Review of Article 82", speech at the Fordham Corporate Law Institute, New York, September 23, 2005, ("[H]igh market shares are not—on their own —sufficient to conclude that a dominant position exists. Market share presumptions can result in an excessive focus on establishing the exact market shares of the various market participants. A pure market share focus risks failing to take proper account of the degree to which competitors can constrain the behaviour of the allegedly dominant company. That is not to say that market shares have no significance. They may provide an indication of dominance—and sometimes a very strong indication—but in the end a full economic analysis of the overall situation is necessary."). See also D Geradin, P Hofer, F Louis, N Petit, N Walker, "The Concept of Dominance," *Global Competition Law Centre Research Papers on Article 82 EC*, College of Europe, July 2005, p. 15.

[23] See Case 85/76, *Hoffmann-La Roche & Co AG v Commission* [1979] ECR 461, para. 41 ("An undertaking which has *a very large market share and holds it for some time*, by means of the volume of production and the scale of the supply which it stands for—without those having much smaller market shares being able to meet rapidly the demand from those who would like to break away from the undertaking which has the largest market share—is by virtue of that share in a position of strength which makes it an unavoidable trading partner and which, already because of this secures for it, *at the very least during relatively long periods*, that freedom of action which is the special feature of a dominant position.") (emphasis added).

shares (i.e., in excess of 70%) raise a strong presumption of dominance. Large market shares (i.e., between 50% and 70%) raise a weaker presumption of dominance. Shares between 40% and 50% require particularly close examination of the facts and do not raise presumptions as to the presence or absence of dominance. Finally, shares below 40% have, in all but exceptional cases, been regarded as incapable of supporting a dominance finding. But it bears emphasis that all of these statements are, at most, presumptions, and not a proper substitute for a detailed fact-based assessment of the market and the practices at issue. The Community institutions' practice in this regard differs materially from the treatment of monopolisation conduct under US law, where monopolisation concerns have usually only been found when market shares exceed 70%.[24] Many commentators therefore argue that a significant problem with Article 82 EC is that the threshold for intervention is *too low*.[25]

a. ***Market shares exceeding 70%.*** The Community institutions have held that very high market shares are, "in themselves," save in exceptional circumstances, evidence of the existence of a dominant position.[26] In *AAMS*, the Court of First Instance found, unsurprisingly, that a trader with 100% share of the market for wholesale distribution of cigarettes held a *de facto* monopoly and thus held a dominant position.[27] A share of over 70% is generally considered as strong evidence of a dominant position. Indeed, as a practical matter, most Article 82 EC cases have involved undertakings with very high market shares. *Hoffmann-La Roche* concerned a firm with markets shares of 70–90% in several vitamins, which was deemed "so large that they prove the existence of a dominant position" [28] In *Hilti* the Court of Justice upheld the Commission's view that market shares of between 70% and 80% were so high as not to require further evidence

---

[24] See RE Bloch, HG Kamann, JS Brown, and JP Schmidt, "A Comparative Analysis Of Article 82 And Section 2 Of The Sherman Act," paper presented to the *International Bar Association 9th Annual Competition Conference*, October 21–22, 2005, European University Institute, Fiesole, p. 12 ("In contrast, U.S. courts tend to require higher levels of market share in order to find monopoly power. A 70 percent market share generally is the dividing line above which a firm may be found to have monopoly power; below this, courts typically do not find monopoly power to exist absent particular market structures that are likely to confer the ability to raise prices or exclude competitors. Historically, U.S. courts considered a predominant share of the market to give rise to an inference of monopoly power. This approach more recently has been discarded in favour of an analysis that considers other market conditions in conjunction with market share, the most important of which is the existence or lack of barriers to entry. Thus, U.S. courts have held that a market share of 100 per cent does not necessarily establish monopoly power absent a showing that the respective market is protected by entry barriers. In this respect, U.S. law under Section 2 seems less restrictive than Article 82 abuse of dominance standards.").

[25] *Ibid.* ("Thus, one of the shortcomings of the current interpretation of Article 82 is that the threshold of what constitutes market dominance is set too low, i.e., 50 percent market share, and meeting this threshold, without more, immediately suggests dominance. This has significant ramifications from a policy standpoint in terms of discouraging efficiency-enhancing conduct that is not unlawful.").

[26] See Case IV/M.68, *Tetra Pak/Alfa-Laval.*

[27] See Case T-139/98, *Amministrazione Autonoma dei Monopoli di Stato (AAMS) v Commission* [2001] ECR II-3413, para. 52.

[28] See Case 85/76, *Hoffmann-La Roche & Co AG v Commission* [1979] ECR 461, para. 59.

to establish dominance.[29] The same situation arose in *Tetra-Pak*, where the undertaking concerned held a market share of around 90%.[30]

b. Market shares between 50% and 70%. Large market shares are also likely to raise a presumption of dominance. For example, in *Michelin I*, market shares of 57% and 65% were considered, in the absence of any countervailing indications, sufficient evidence of dominance.[31] In *AKZO*, the Court of Justice went as far as to establish a rebuttable presumption of dominance based on market shares in excess of 50%.[32] At the same time, however, the Court also referred to the relevance of all other economic evidence on the market when establishing market power.[33] Likewise, the Commission carried out comprehensive examinations of competitive conditions in the affected markets before reaching a conclusion as to dominance, emphasising that:[34]

> "Market share, while important, is only one of the indicators from which the existence of a dominant position may be inferred. Its significance in a particular case may vary from market to market according to the structure and characteristics of the market in question. To assess market power for the purposes of the present case, the Commission must consider also the relevant economic evidence [in addition to market share data]."

c. Market shares between 40% and 50%. A share between 40% and 50% is not conclusive evidence of the presence or absence of dominance, but requires the assessment of additional factors for confirmation. In *Hoffmann-La Roche*, the Court of Justice overturned the Commission's finding of dominance on the vitamin B3 market because its market share of 43% did not by itself "constitute a factor sufficient to establish the existence of a dominant position" since there was insufficient corroborative support from other factors.[35]

---

[29] Case T-30/89, *Hilti AG v Commission* [1991] ECR II-1439, para. 92, on appeal Case C-53/92P, *Hilti AG v Commission* [1994] ECR I-667.

[30] See *Tetra Pak II*, OJ 1992 L 72/1, on appeal Case T-83/91, *Tetra Pak International SA v Commission* [1994] ECR II-755, para. 109, and confirmed in Case C-333/94 P, *Tetra Pak International SA v Commission* [1996] ECR I-5951. See also Joined Cases C-395/96 P and C-396/96P, *Compagnie Maritime Belge Transports SA, Compagnie maritime belge SA and Dafra-Lines A/S v Commission* [2000] ECR I-13655.

[31] Case 322/81, *NV Nederlandsche Baden-Industrie Michelin v Commission* [1983] ECR 3461.

[32] See *ECS/AKZO*, OJ 1985 L 374/1, upheld on appeal in Case C-62/86, *AKZO Chemie BV v Commission* [1991] ECR I-3359, para. 60.

[33] *Ibid.*, paras. 59–61.

[34] See *ECS/AKZO*, OJ 1985 L 374/1, paras. 68–69. See also *Napier Brown/British Sugar*, OJ 1988 L 284/41; and Case T-36/91, *Imperial Chemical Industries plc v Commission* [1995] ECR II-1847. Likewise, the Commission has in several cases approved mergers that involved very high market shares. See, e.g., Case IV/M.42 *Alcatel/Telettra* (81% share of transmission equipment and 84% share of microwave equipment in Spain); Case IV/M.9, *Fiat Geotech/Ford New Holland* (58% share in the Italian combine harvester market); Case IV/M.72, *Sanofi/Sterling Drug* (74% share of the cold preparations market in the Netherlands); Case IV/M.323, *Procordia/Erbamont* (85% share of Irish sales of urological preparations and 78% share of Italian sales of local anaesthetic); and Case IV/M.458 *Electrolux/AEG* (70% of sales of certain major domestic appliances in Scandinavia).

[35] See Case 85/76, *Hoffmann-La Roche & Co AG v Commission* [1979] ECR 461, para. 58. See also, in the context of merger control, Case IV/M.784 *Kesko/Tuko*, confirmed on appeal in Case T-22/97, *Kesko Oy v Commission* [1999] ECR II-3775.

d. ***Market shares below 40%.*** Shares between 30% and 40% have, in general, not supported a finding of dominance, barring other supporting factors.[36] Special circumstances would generally be required to substantiate a finding of dominance in these circumstances. For example, in *Magill*, the Commission found that three broadcasters had a factual and legal monopoly over the supply of their respective copyright-protected television listings information, notwithstanding the fact that no single undertaking accounted for more than 33% of the total televisions listings information.[37] Market shares below 30% are, however, extremely unlikely to create dominance, but there is no presumption that a market share below 30% offers a "safe harbour." Significant barriers to entry would be required to substantiate dominance at such low market share levels. Very low market shares are considered definitive indicators of the absence of dominance. Thus, in *SABA II*, a market share of 10% was considered to be conclusive evidence of the absence of dominance.[38]

Rivals' market shares. A finding of dominance requires evidence that a firm's competitors are unable to constrain its market behaviour by acting as a viable alternative source of supply to customers. The competitive constraint exerted by rivals is therefore a critical part of the assessment of dominance and market shares are highly relevant in this connection.[39] In general, where the Commission has found the market share difference between the "dominant" firm and its next largest competitor to exceed 20%, it has considered there to be a greater likelihood of dominance. This consideration has been given greater weight when the gap between the leading firm and its nearest competitor has remained stable over a significant period of time.[40]

---

[36] See *Virgin/British Airways*, OJ 2000 L 30/1, paras. 91–94, where the Commission found that British Airways was dominant with a share of 39.7% of the relevant market (which had dropped from around 45% during the period under investigation). On appeal in Case T-219/99, *British Airways plc v Commission* [2003] ECR II-5917, the Court of First Instance confirmed that in the circumstances of the case, a share of 39.7% is "to be regarded as large"—in particular where that share "constitutes a multiple of the market shares of [the] main competitors" (para. 211). The following factors were also considered as indicative of British Airways' dominance: (1) its world-ranking in number of passenger-kilometres flown and the range of its transport services and hub network (para. 212); (2) the fact that the services operated by British Airways to and from the United Kingdom airports had the "cumulative effect of generating the purchase by travellers of a preponderant number of British Airways tickets through travel agents in the United Kingdom, and, correspondingly, as many transactions between British Airways and the those agents" (para. 215); and (3) the fact that British Airways is an obligatory business partner of travel agents (para. 217).

[37] *Magill TV Guide/ITP, BBC and RTE*, OJ 1989 L 78/43, confirmed on appeal in Case T-69/89, *Radio Telefis Eireann (RTE) v Commission* [1991] ECR II-485, Case T-70/89, *British Broadcasting Corporation and BBC Enterprises Ltd (BBC) v Commission* [1991] ECR II-535, and Case T-76/89, *Independent Television Publications Ltd (ITP) v Commission* [1991] ECR II-575, and further confirmed in Joined Cases C-241/91 P and C-242/91 P, *Radio Telefis Eireann and Independent Television Publications Ltd (RTE & ITP) v Commission* [1995] ECR I-743.

[38] *SABA's EEC distribution system*, OJ 1983 L 376/41.

[39] See Case T-102/96, *Gencor Ltd v Commission* [1999] ECR II-753, para. 202 (quoting Case 85/76, *Hoffmann-La Roche & Co AG v Commission* [1979] ECR 461, para. 48).

[40] See, e.g., Case IV/M.214, *Du Pont/ICI*, para. 4; Case IV/M.53, *Aérospatiale-Alenia/de Havilland*, para. 28; Case IV/M.269, *Shell/Montecatini*, paras. 61–62; and Case COMP/M.1741, *MCIWorldCom/Sprint*.

The Commission will not only consider the individual market shares of the allegedly dominant firm's rivals, but will also look at their cumulative share value to determine whether or not they collectively generate sufficient competition on the market which prevents the undertaking under investigation from acting independently of them. In *British Airways/Virgin*, the Court of First Instance held that there was a substantial gap between the market share of British Airways (BA) and both the market share of its closest rival and the cumulative shares of its five main competitors in the period between 1992 and 1998.[41] In 1992, the difference in market shares between BA and its nearest competitor, British Midland, was 42.4%. Its closest competitor over the entire period was American Airlines in 1996 when it held 7.6% of the market, i.e., BA's market share was still 32.9% greater. The difference between BA and the cumulative share value of its five closest competitors varied between 21.8% and 34.4%. These differences were seen as sufficiently substantial to support a finding of dominance.

The relative weight to be attached to rivals' market shares relative to the firm under investigation should not, however, be overstated. The point is not so much their market share, but whether they can quickly expand production to meet demand. In *Hoffmann-La Roche* the Court of Justice explained that even a "very large market share" does not confer dominance if "competitors with much smaller shares" are "able to meet rapidly the demand from those [customers] who would like to break away from the undertaking which has the largest market share."[42] Particularly in markets characterised by excess capacity, even competitors with small shares may be able to constrain any efforts by the leading firm to reduce output or raise prices, indicating that, notwithstanding a high share, the leading firm is not dominant.

3.2.3 Barriers To Entry And Expansion

Overview. The Community institutions have long-recognised that the prospect of new entry or expansion by existing rivals may constrain the commercial behaviour of the leading firm and therefore preclude dominance. A firm with a high market share is much less likely to be able to behave independently of competitors, customers, and consumers in a market where entry or expansion barriers are low. When the likelihood of new entry or expansion by existing firms in the market is high, incumbent firms will be constrained by the fear that increased prices would lead to actual or potential rivals expanding output in response to price rises. On the other hand, significant entry/expansion barriers make it easier for a leading firm to increase prices or adopt strategic exclusionary actions.[43] Assessing barriers to entry and expansion is thus an essential second step in identifying a dominant position.[44]

[41] Case T-219/99, *British Airways plc v Commission* [2003] ECR II-5917.

[42] Case 85/76, *Hoffmann-La Roche & Co AG v Commission* [1979] ECR 461, para. 41.

[43] See XXIst Report on Competition Policy (1991), pp. 85–86.

[44] See, e.g., Case 6/72, *Europemballage Corporation and Continental Can Company Inc v Commission* [1973] ECR 215, paras. 29–37 (Court of Justice annulled the Commission's finding of dominance due to the Commission's failure to examine supply-side substitution); and Case COMP/M.2097, *SCA/Metsä Tissue*, para. 93.

3.2.3.1 Definition of barriers to entry

Basic definition. Barriers to entry have been defined as "factors which prevent or hinder companies from entering a specific market."[45] Entry barriers may result for instance from a particular market structure (e.g. industry with high sunk costs, brand loyalty of consumers to existing products) or the behaviour of incumbent firms. Governments can also in practice be a source of entry barriers, for example through licensing requirements and other regulations.

There is some disagreement among economists about what should be considered as a barrier to entry. A number of different positions can be identified:

1. *Bain.* The seminal work of Joe Bain, published in 1956, defined barriers to entry as factors that allow established firms to "elevate their selling prices above the minimal average costs of production and distribution...without inducing potential entrants to enter the industry."[46] These factors include, among many others, economies of scale and scope, capital requirements and product differentiation. According to Bain, those entry barriers determine the number of firms in the industry, the prices that obtain in equilibrium and the welfare enjoyed by consumers. This view has been criticised on several levels.[47] First, the number of firms in the industry is determined by more than just those factors. In many industries, for example, high concentration is not the consequence of entry barriers but of vigorous competition. Second, many of the factors that Bain treats as determinants of industry structure and performance, such as the economies of scale or scope or the degree of product differentiation, are not exogenous but can be altered by investment. In industries where competition requires investment and the creation of new products, concentration is typically high and prices are often above marginal cost, and yet consumer's welfare is maximised. In sum, the factors listed by Bain as barriers to entry do not tell us much about: (a) the actual market power of the industry players; or (b) the satisfaction of consumers given market outcomes.

2. *Stigler.* In 1968, George Stigler defined a barrier to entry in narrower terms: a barrier to entry is a cost advantage that an incumbent firm enjoys compared to entrants. That is "a cost of producing...which must be borne by a firm which seeks to enter the industry but which is not borne by firms already in the industry."[48] In the absence of such differential cost advantage the incumbent would be unable to earn supra-competitive returns: any attempt to raise prices above costs would be beaten by entry. The key, therefore, lies in the existence of asymmetries between established competitors and potential entrants: a barrier to entry exists only if the potential entrant's long run costs after entry

[45] See European Communities, *Glossary of Competition Terms* (2003).

[46] JS Bain, *Industrial Organisation* (New York, John Wiley, 1968), p.2. See also JS Bain, *Barriers to New Competition* (Cambridge, Harvard University Press, 1956), p. 3.

[47] See DW Carlton, "Why Barriers to Entry are Barriers to Understanding," *American Economic Review Papers and Proceedings,* (2004) 466–470.

[48] GJ Stigler, "Barriers to Entry, Economies of Scale and Firm Size," in GJ Stigler, *The Organisation of Industry* (Homewood, Irwin, 1968), p. 67.

are greater than those of the incumbent.[49] It follows that economies of scale cannot give rise to barriers to entry *unless* the cost functions of entrants and incumbents are dissimilar. Likewise, according to Stigler's definition, and unlike Bain's, capital requirements are not a barrier to entry *unless* the incumbent never paid for them. The problem with Stigler's definition is that in some cases an incumbent may be able to earn supra-competitive rents even if it enjoys no cost advantage over entrants. Suppose that the incumbent invests in a new plant and commits itself to producing so much output that no other firm is able to enter at a profit. Then entry is blocked even if both the entrant and the incumbent incur the same sunk investment costs.

3. *Bork.* A few years later, Robert Bork proposed an even narrower definition than Stigler's. He argued that defining barriers to entry as including anything that makes it difficult for a new firm to enter the market is too broad. In his opinion, economic and technical barriers merely represent the realities of doing business (e.g., sunk costs of entry) or the superior efficiency of the incumbent firm relative to rivals (e.g., due to economies of scale or scope or network effects). The only obstacles to entry that should be of interest from an antitrust perspective are what he denotes as "artificial" barriers to entry such as, for example, price predation.[50]

4. *More recent definitions.* More recently, other economists have proposed alternative definitions. For example, Franklin Fisher defined as a barrier to entry any factor that prevent entry when is socially beneficial.[51] Christian Von Weizsacker defined as an entry barrier any differential cost advantage that prevented an efficient allocation of resources. Both Fisher and Von Weiszacker had in mind a total welfare standard (i.e., a standard which aggregates both consumer welfare and industry profits).[52] The number of firms in an industry may often exceed the socially optimal under a total welfare standard: this is because the increase in consumer welfare that results from greater rivalry is not enough to offset the inefficient duplication of fixed costs.[53] In such an industry, some of the entry barriers identified by Bain and Stigler could prove to be welfare increasing.

Which of these definitions, if any, should be adopted in the assessment of dominance under Article 82 EC? The Community institutions' practice is to look at all the relevant factors that might limit entry or expansion and so delay, deter, or prevent actual and potential rivals from effectively competing with the incumbent firm and hence may

[49] RP McAfee, HM Mialon and MA Williams, "What is a Barrier to Entry?" *American Economic Review Papers and Proceedings* (2004), 461-465.

[50] See, e.g., R Bork, *The Antitrust Paradox: A Policy at War with Itself* (New York, Basic Books, 1978), 310.

[51] FM Fisher, "Diagnosing Monopoly," 19 *Quarterly Review of Economics and Business* (1979) 7-33.

[52] C Von Weizsacker, "A Welfare Analysis of Barriers to Entry," 11 *Bell Journal of Economics*, (1980) 399-420.

[53] NG Mankiw and MD Whinston, "Free Entry and Social Inefficiency," 17 *RAND Journal of Economics* (1986) 48-58.

result in a loss of consumer welfare. Since dominance can be regarded as the ability of the incumbent to maintain supracompetitive prices for a sustained period of time without being disciplined by existing rivals or new entrants to the market, any circumstances that bar entry or prevent expansion, and hence leave supra-competitive prices unchecked, are considered relevant to the assessment of dominance.[54] It follows immediately that Bork's narrow focus on "artificial" barriers to entry is unjustified, as well as Fisher's and Von Weiszacker's interesting definitions based on a total welfare standard.

Stigler's definition is also problematic from the viewpoint of Article 82 EC. Consider the following example.[55] An entrant faces a sunk cost of entry F, which is smaller than the sunk cost of entry borne by the incumbent a few years ago. If F is sufficiently high, the entrant may not find it privately profitable to enter the market even when the incumbent charges supra-competitive prices. Since there is no cost advantage for the incumbent, there is no barrier to entry according to Stigler's definition. And yet entry is delayed and consumer welfare is diminished. Therefore, it appears that the economic definition of a barrier to entry that best suits Article 82 EC is Bain's: any factor that protects the market power of the incumbents and allows them to charge inefficiently high prices. However, as discussed above, this does not mean that all the factors identified by Bain are proper barriers to entry. For example, scale economies do not constitute a barrier to entry unless the incumbent can pre-commit to maintain its pre-entry output level, which is possible if, for example, the incumbent possesses a locked-in customer base. In sum, the right mix appears to be Bain's definition with Stigler's theoretical rigour.

Practice under Article 82 EC. Although, the Community institutions do not limit themselves to any particular framework in assessing barriers to entry or expansion when considering potential competition, it is useful in light of the existing case law to distinguish different types of potential barriers to entry and expansion: (1) characteristics inherent in the relevant market; (2) characteristics of the allegedly dominant firm; and (3) conduct of the allegedly dominant firm. The Community institutions will consider the entirety of the applicable circumstances and conclude whether, on balance, effective entry and/or expansion is possible. If not, a finding of dominance is very likely (absent countervailing buyer power (see below)).

3.2.3.2 Characteristics inherent in the relevant market

Legal or administrative barriers to entry. Legislation and other state measures are often a source of barriers to entry. Market regulation can constitute an insurmountable entry barrier if the number of participants in the market is limited by licensing or exclusive rights, since new players cannot enter, either at all or without an incumbent

[54] This expansive approach to defining barriers to entry has been criticised. See S Turnbull, "Barriers to Entry, Article 86 and the Abuse of a Dominant Position: An Economic Critique of European Community Competition Law" 96 *European Competition Law Review* (1996); and D Harbord and T Hoehn, "Barriers to Entry and Exit in European Competition Policy," 14 *International Review of Law and Economics* (1994) 422.

[55] R Schmalensee, "Sunk Costs and Antitrust Barriers to Entry" *American Economic Review Papers and Proceedings* (2004), 471-477.

firm exiting the market. Examples include State monopolies, authorisation or licensing requirements, and intellectual property.

a. ***State monopolies.*** Assuming they are acting as an "undertaking" for purposes of EC competition law,[56] public monopolies or undertakings vested with special or exclusive rights to operate in a particular market will usually be considered dominant under Article 82 EC. In practice, State monopolies have been an important source of entry barriers in the EU, since Member States have historically entrusted services such as telecommunications, energy and transport in the hands of State-owned entities. Certain barriers to entry have been reduced through liberalisation and accompanying regulation designed to promote a move towards full competition, but statutory monopolies holding dominant positions have been found, *inter alia*, in the markets for telecom services,[57] the provision, maintenance and repair of telecom equipment,[58] the operation of railway infrastructure,[59] postal delivery,[60] recruitment services,[61] and a State tobacco distribution monopoly.[62]

b. Authorisation or licensing requirements. The requirement to obtain authorisation or a licence to enter a particular market can constitute an absolute or significant barrier to entry. In *Clearstream*, the Commission found that the defendant bank had infringed Article 82 EC by refusing to supply cross-border securities clearing and settlement services and by applying discriminatory prices.[63] Clearstream's dominant position in the market of the provision of primary clearing and settlement services for securities issued according to German law was guaranteed by legislative provisions which only allowed recognised central securities depositories provide clearing and settlement services, rendering it a *de facto* monopoly. German law required new entrants to the market to obtain authorisation from the Frankfurt Stock exchange. The Commission concluded that the Frankfurt Stock Exchange would not support any new entry because clearing and settlement were subject to significant economies of scale and scope and network effects.

c. ***Intellectual property rights.*** Intellectual property rights may also prevent expansion and entry, or at least make it more difficult. Indeed, intellectual property legislation is in practice probably the most pervasive form of entry regulation elaborated by governments. It is important to appreciate, however, that intellectual property rights do not constitute automatic entry barriers and do not necessarily imply dominance, since firms may be able to invent around them. As the Court of Justice held in *Magill*, "so far as dominant position is concerned…mere ownership of an intellectual property right

---

[56] See Ch. 1 (Introduction, Scope of Application, and Basic Framework), Section 1.3 above.

[57] Case 41/83, *Italy v Commission (British Telecommunications)* [1985] ECR 873.

[58] Case C-202/88, *France v Commission (Telecommunication terminals)* [1991] ECR I-1223; and Case C-18/88, *Régie des télégraphes et des telephones (RTT) v GB-Inno-BM SA* [1991] ECR I-5941.

[59] See *GVG/FS*, OJ 2004 L 11/17, paras. 82-85.

[60] Case C-320/91, *Paul Corbeau* [1993] ECR I-2533.

[61] Case C-41/90, *Klaus Höfner and Fritz Elser v Macrotron GmbH* [1991] ECR I-1979.

[62] *Amministrazione Autonoma dei Monopoli di Stato*, OJ 1998 L 252/47, upheld on appeal in Case T-139/98 *Amministrazione Autonoma dei Monopoli di Stato v Commission*, [2001] ECR II-3413.

[63] Case COMP/38/096, *Clearstream (Clearing and settlement)*, Commission Decision of June 4, 2004, not yet published.

cannot confer such a position."[64] More precisely, the Court held that an intellectual property right would not confer a dominant position as long as competitors were able to provide close substitutes.[65] In *IMS/NDC*, the Commission found that rivals could not effectively invent around IMS's copyright and, therefore, concluded that IMS held a dominant position.[66] However, the decision was later withdrawn because rivals could lawfully invent around the copyright.[67]

d. ***Other regulatory barriers.*** Planning and licensing laws that impose limits on the number of retail outlets restrict the expansion possibilities of existing competitors and entry prospects for new retailers. Furthermore, tariff and non-tariff barriers can give advantages to incumbent firms.[68] Regulation may also impose objective standards on all competitors. If such standards do not apply equally and/or are more costly to meet for entrants than for incumbent firms, then they may constitute a barrier to entry.

Economic barriers to entry. In many cases the source of restrictions on entry and expansion is not legal or administrative, but is inherent in the economic characteristics of the relevant market. Examples include sunk costs of entry, economies of scale or scope, and network effects.

a. ***Sunk costs of entry.*** Sunk costs are costs that a firm must incur to enter a market but that are not recoverable upon exit of the market. A high level of sunk costs will constitute a barrier to entry and will therefore stifle potential competition. Sunk costs may be either exogenous or endogenous. Examples of exogenous sunk costs are investments in facilities and machines that are needed to enter a specific market and that cannot be used for other purposes. For example, in *United Brands*, the Court of Justice noted that "the particular barriers to competitors entering the market are the exceptionally large capital investments required for the creation and running of banana plantations."[69] In *Clearstream*, the Commission identified sunk costs, such as investment in information technology development and human resources, at an estimated cost of €156 million.[70] As a new entrant would be required to set up complex and costly systems—without the assurance that it could provide orderly or economically viable services—sunk costs contributed to high entry barriers. Endogenous sunk costs include expenditures for research and development, quality improvements, and advertising that are necessary to compete against existing firms in the relevant market. The level of such costs will be determined by the particular strategy of the incumbent firms. Markets with endogenous sunk costs typically exhibit high degrees of concentration. Furthermore, concentration does not necessarily increase as the industry

---

[64] Joined Cases C-241/91 P and C-242/91 P *Radio Telefis Eireann and Independent Television Publications Limited (RTE & ITP) v. Commission* [1995] ECR I-743, para. 46.

[65] Case 40/70 *Sirena S.r.l. v. Eda S.r.l,* [1971] ECR 69, para. 16; Case 78/70 *Deutsche Grammophon v. Metro* [1971] ECR 487, para. 16.

[66] *IMS Health/NDC*, OJ 2002 L 59/18 (interim measures).

[67] See *NDC Health/IMS Health: Interim measures*, OJ 2003 L 268/69.

[68] See DG Competition discussion paper on the application of Article 82 of the Treaty to exclusionary abuses, Brussels, December 2005 (hereinafter, "Discussion Paper"), para 40.

[69] Case 27/76 *United Brands v. Commission* [1978] ECR 207, para. 122.

[70] Case COMP/38.096 *Clearstream*, Commission Decision of June 2, 2004, not yet published, para. 214.

grows (i.e., they constitute "natural oligopolies"); instead product quality, R&D investment and/or advertising increase.[71]

b. Economies of scale/scope. A firm enjoys *economies of scale* in the production (and/or distribution) of a product when its average costs fall as output increases. Where a firm produces two or more products, it may also be cheaper to produce the two products than it would be to make each of them separately. In this case, the firm enjoys *economies of scope*. When a market exhibits significant positive returns to scale, the largest firm will have a significant advantage over firms who have not yet reached the same level of production (or distribution). That will be the case if the incumbent firm enjoys significant cost advantages due to learning-by-doing, or if its position in the market is entrenched by brand loyalty or any other switching costs. In those circumstances, economies of scale or scope may give rise to barriers to entry.

In *United Brands*, the Court of Justice held that, among other factors, "the particular barriers to competitors entering the market are...economies of scale from which newcomers to the market cannot derive any immediate benefit."[72] Commission decisions such as *BPB Industries plc* also expressly refer to the large economies of scale from which the companies benefited as a factor relevant for a finding of dominance.[73] BPB produced plasterboard for the plasterboard market in Great Britain and Ireland. It enjoyed substantial economies by producing on a large scale in integrated industrial complexes. It had extensive technical and financial resources. And as the sole producer in the relevant geographical markets, it alone benefited from the economies that flowed from the placing of plasterboard production close to its markets. These factors supported the ruling that BPB held a dominant position on the market for plasterboard in Great Britain and Ireland.

c. Network effects. Network effects arise where the benefit of a good or service increases with the addition of other users. An obvious example is the telecommunications sector where the value of, say, a telephone to a user will depend, *inter alia*, on how many other users each user is able to speak to. Products such as a telephone or a fax machine are characterised by the existence of *direct* network effects: they are not only valued because of their inherent characteristics, but also due to the additional value derived from being able to interact with other users of the product. Other products, such as electronic game consoles, exhibit *indirect* network effects. No game platform, such as Sony's PlayStation 2 or Microsoft's Xbox, can sell consoles without games to play on. But no game platform will ever convince game developers to write for its console without the prospect of an installed base of consumers. The key feature of these markets is therefore that, to succeed, competitors must get both sides of the market (consumers and software developers) on board.

In *Microsoft*, the Commission relied heavily on network effects as evidence of high entry barriers into the client personal computer operating system market and, to a lesser

---

[71] See J Sutton, *Sunk Costs and Market Structure* (Cambridge, MIT Press, 1991).

[72] Case 27/76, *United Brands Company and United Brands Continentaal BV v Commission* [1978] ECR 207, para. 122.

[73] *BPB Industries plc*, OJ 1989 L 10/50, para. 116.

extent, the server software market.[74] The regular daily use of a personal computer involves running applications on it. The overall utility that a customer derives from the operating system of a computer depends therefore on the applications he or she can use on it or expect to use on it in the future. Yet software vendors write applications to the operating systems that are most popular among users. Therefore, the more popular an operating system is, the more applications will be written to it and the more applications are written to an operation system, the more popular it will be among users. The Commission concluded that, among other things, these (indirect) network effects guaranteed the dominant position of Microsoft, as they constituted a significant entry barrier to potential competitors.

Switching costs for consumers. A barrier to entry may also exist if customers face high enough costs when switching suppliers. In some cases, these switching costs are exogenous, such as the costs of information, learning, or transaction costs. In others, they are the result of the technological or commercial choices of the incumbents. In *IMS/NDC*, for example, the Commission concluded that German pharmaceutical companies were economically dependent on the so-called "1860 brick structure" used by IMS to classify the sales data they used in their marketing and remuneration decisions, and that it would not be viable for them to switch to data provided in another structure.[75] In *Microsoft*, the Commission referred to the fact that Microsoft was fully aware that it could behave independently of its end-customers due to the high costs of switching to alternative operating systems.[76] And in some other cases, incumbent firms rely on long-term contracts with customers to make it difficult for rivals to find a sufficient number of customers able to switch supplier to render expansion or entry profitable.[77]

The effect of switching costs on the likelihood of entry is, however, ambiguous. Academic literature has shown that switching costs can, under certain circumstances, actually be conducive to entry, even though the conventional wisdom points in the opposite direction.[78] As explained by McSorley et al., switching costs deter entry when most consumers are captive and their switching costs are high. Entry may also be difficult when switching costs are low, because in this case the incumbents are likely to fight entrants in order to retain their clients and avoid losing market share. However, switching costs can actually facilitate entry into the market, albeit on a limited scale, when switching costs are neither too high nor too low and firms cannot price discriminate between locked-in and uncommitted consumers.[79] In those cases, incumbents may find it optimal to focus on exploiting their locked-in customer base, leaving to entrants those consumers with low (or no) switching costs. And entrants may

[74] Case COMP C-3/37.792 *Microsoft*, Commission decision of March 24, 2004, not yet published, paras. 448 and 515-517.

[75] *IMS Health/NDC*, OJ 2002 L 59/18 (interim measures).

[76] Case COMP C-3/37.792 *Microsoft*, Commission decision of March 24, 2004, not yet published, para. 463.

[77] See Discussion Paper, para. 40.

[78] See C McSorley, AJ Padilla and M Williams, *Switching Costs*, DTI-OFT Discussion Paper No 5, (2003) and references therein.

[79] See PD Klemperer, "Entry Deterrence in Markets with Consumer Switching Costs," 97 *Economic Journal*, (1987) 99 117.

prefer to operate at a low scale, leaving incumbents to exploit their bases of captive consumers, rather than invest in the development of a large customer base, which may trigger a price war with the incumbents and force them to exit the market.[80]

3.2.3.3 Characteristics specific to the allegedly dominant firm

Overview. Entry or expansion by competitors may also be difficult when the allegedly dominant firm possesses one or more competitive advantages over its actual and potential rivals. Examples include access to key inputs or special knowledge, vertical integration, brand recognition or other forms of product differentiation, and financial strength and performance.

Access to key inputs or special knowledge. In every market, firms need certain inputs in order to compete. Significant entry barriers exist if incumbents have privileged access to such inputs. Exclusive or preferential access to such inputs may give a firm an absolute, or at least a significant, advantage over rival firms. Numerous examples of this type of entry barrier exist in the decisional practice and case law. An early example was *Commercial Solvents*,[81] where the dominant company controlled the supplies of aminobutanol and nitropropane—the essential raw materials for the production of ethambutol—in Europe. Other examples include the various port cases where the incumbent firm's control over the port infrastructure made it an essential trading party in that port.[82] Thus, in *Sea Containers/Stena Sealink*,[83] the port of Holyhead was considered to have unique advantages over Liverpool for ferry travel between Ireland and Great Britain.

A firm's significant advantage over rivals may also result from superior technology or knowledge. In cases such as *Hilti*[84] and *Michelin II*,[85] account was taken of the "indisputable technological lead" of the dominant firms over rivals. Similarly, in *United Brands*, the Court of Justice considered that potential competitors could not expect to reach the level of the incumbent's advanced research and development in drainage systems, improving soil deficiencies, and combating plant disease and that this constituted an effective barrier to entry.[86]

Spare capacity. If the allegedly dominant firm is able to increase its output at short notice because it is has spare production capacity it may be in a position to deter any potential competition. Thus, in *Hoffman-La Roche,* the Court of Justice accepted that the company's over-capacity was a relevant factor to the issue of dominance.[87] An incumbent's threat of a price war or expansion of output in response to a new entry on

[80] See PD Klemperer, "Price Wars Caused by Switching Costs," 56 *Review of Economic Studies*, (1989) 405.

[81] Joined Cases 6/73 and 7/73, *Istituto Chemioterapico Italiano S.p.A. and Commercial Solvents Corporation v Commission* [1974] ECR 223.

[82] See, e.g., *Port of Rødby*, OJ 1994 L 55/52; *ACI—Channel Tunnel*, OJ 1994 L 224/28; *European Night Services*, OJ 1994 L 259/20; *Eurotunnel*, OJ 1994 L 354/66; *Ijsselcentrale*, OJ 1991 L 28/32; and *Irish Continental Group CCI Morlaix-Port of Roscoff*, XXVth Competition Policy Report (1996), para. 43.

[83] *Sea Containers v Stena Sealink (Interim measures)*, OJ 1994 L 15/8.

[84] *Hilti*, OJ 1988 L 65/19, para. 69.

[85] Case T-203/01 *Michelin v Commission* [2003] ECR II-4071, paras. 183-184.

[86] Case 27/76 *United Brands v Commission* [1978] ECR 207.

[87] Case 85/76, *Hoffmann-La Roche & Co AG v Commission* [1979] ECR 461.

the market may therefore amount to a sufficient barrier to entry to support a finding of dominance. Dominance also usually implies that actual and potential rivals lack sufficient capacity to meet total market demand. But even when rivals have spare capacity, it may be so expensive to employ that these costs constitute a barrier to expansion. For instance, the costs of introducing another shift in a factory may constitute a barrier to expansion.[88]

Vertical integration. Vertical integration may give a firm significant advantages over non-integrated firms.[89] Benefits of vertical integration include lower transaction costs (e.g., no/less need to write and enforce contracts with outsiders), secure supply of inputs, correcting market failure (e.g., ensuring uniform quality), and avoiding government rules (many government rules, e.g., antitrust, do not apply to a single entity but only to bilateral or multilateral relations between independent firms). But it is not axiomatic that vertical integration is advantageous and much less that it constitutes a barrier to entry. Vertical integration may actually increase costs when the market is more efficient than the vertically-integrated firm's own operations. Costs may also arise because of the difficulty of managing a larger firm.

Because of the possible mixed effects of vertical integration, the decisional practice and case law have mainly relied on vertical integration only when it was clear that the fact of integration conferred a material advantage on one firm over non-integrated rivals. Typically, this concerned exclusive or privileged access to raw materials or other inputs, particularly in relation to scarce resources. In *Commercial Solvents*,[90] Commercial Solvents' control over the European production of aminobutanol and nitropropane made it an essential trading party for non-integrated rivals interested in the production of ethambutol. The same general point can be made about several cases in which a duty to deal has been considered under Article 82 EC.[91]

On the output side, a highly developed distribution and sales network which may include a dense outlet network, established distribution logistics or wide geographical coverage may also impede potential competition. In *United Brands*, the dominant firm's activities in the various stages in bringing bananas to the market supported the finding that it held a dominant position, particularly in light of the fact that its rivals did not share the same levels of integration.[92] The Court of Justice noted that United Brands' integration was evident at each of the stages from the plantation to the loading on wagons or lorries in the ports of delivery and after those stages, as far as ripening and sale prices were concerned.[93] United Brands even extended its control to ripener/distributors and wholesalers by setting up a complete network of agents. At the production stage, it owned large plantations in Central and South America. At the

---

[88] See Discussion Paper, para. 40.

[89] For an overview of the costs and benefits of vertical integration, see DW Carlton and JM Perloff, *Modern Industrial Organisation*, 4th ed, (Boston, Pearson Addison Wesley, 2005), pp.396-400.

[90] Joined Cases 6/73 and 7/73, *Istituto Chemioterapico Italiano S.p.A. and Commercial Solvents Corporation v Commission* [1974] ECR 223.

[91] See Ch. 8 (Refusal to Deal).

[92] Case 27/76, *United Brands Company and United Brands Continentaal BV v Commission* [1978] ECR 207, para. 113.

[93] *Ibid.*, paras. 70–81.

carriage by sea stage, United Brands was the only undertaking that was capable of carrying two thirds of its exports by means of its own banana fleet. For packaging and presentation, United Brands had at its disposal factories, manpower, plant and material which enabled it to handle the goods independently. All of these factors were found to guarantee United Brands' commercial stability and well being.

Brand recognition. The incumbent's ownership of well-known brands may constitute a barrier to entry in fast-moving consumer goods markets. This may be because brand loyalty makes it difficult for new entrants to compete on the market.[94] Or it may, simply be difficult to enter a market where experience or reputation is necessary to compete effectively with, as yet, unknown brands.[95] Note, in particular, that the advertising and marketing required to compete with established brands are often sunk costs, which cannot be recovered in the case of exit from the market.

Financial and economic strength as an indicator of dominance. The Community institutions' position on the relevance of the financial and economic power of the incumbent firm as indicators of dominance is so far ambiguous. In *Hoffmann-La Roche*, the Court of Justice held that the fact that Hoffmann-La Roche was the world's largest vitamin manufacturer, that it was at the head of the largest pharmaceuticals group in the world, and that it had the largest turnover, had no bearing on the finding of dominance.[96] This makes sense, since overall size is not strong evidence of dominance in a particular market.

However, economic and financial power—the so-called "deep pockets" argument—has occasionally been a factor used to corroborate a finding of dominance under Article 82 EC. In *Continental Can*, the Commission took into account in finding dominance that the undertaking's parent company, Continental, was the world's largest producer of metal cans, enjoyed large turnover and profits, and employed 62,000 staff.[97] Moreover, the German subsidiary under investigation was the largest producer of metal cans in Europe and employed 13,000 people. Its nearest competitor in Germany only employed 1,600 people.[98] And, finally, its economic and financial strength facilitated easier access to finance than its competitors could expect.[99] Similarly, in *BPB Industries*, the Commission stated that it was necessary to consider "not only the position of BPB in the market but also its technological and financial resources" when deciding whether or not the undertaking dominated the market.[100] Finally, in *Solvay*,

[94] See, e.g., Case IV/M.623 *Kimberly-Clark/Scott*, para. 87; and Case IV/M.833 *The Coca-Cola Company/Carlsberg A/S*, para. 72. See also Case IV/M.794 *Coca-Cola/Amalgamated Beverages GB*, para. 137; and Case IV/M.938 *Guinness/Grand Metropolitan*, para. 52.

[95] See Discussion Paper, para. 40.

[96] Case 85/76 *Hoffmann-La Roche v Commission* [1979] ECR 461, para. 47.

[97] See *Continental Can Company*, OJ 1972 L 7/25, para. 12.

[98] *Ibid.*

[99] For example, under the EC Merger Regulation, the Commission has noted that an existing firm with strong financial backing would have greater market power because it would be better able to endure a protracted price war than new competitors. See Case COMP/JV.55 *Hutchison/RCPM/ECT*, para. 95.

[100] *BPB Industries* OJ 1989 L 10/50, para. 115.

the Commission took into account the undertaking's manufacturing strength and the fact that it had plants in six different Member States in its assessment of dominance.[101]

There is some basis for the view that access to finance may be relevant in considering dominance. This is the case when: (1) access to finance is relevant to the competitive process in the industry under review; (2) there are significant asymmetries between competitors in terms of their internal financing capabilities; and (3) particular features of the industry make it difficult for firms to attract external funds. If capital markets were perfect, new entrants with profitable investment projects would be able to finance their entry and expansion in a market at no disadvantage. The financial strength of the incumbent firm should not be relevant. However, capital markets do not work efficiently as a result of, among other factors, asymmetries of information.[102] And in any event, even if potential competitors can obtain finance to facilitate their entrance or expansion on the market, they must still bear the costs of obtaining the capital necessary to do so. Practical realities mean that an undertaking that possesses considerable economic and financial strength will find it easier to fund its risky projects, by means of both internal and external resources, than a company that does not. The financial strength of the incumbent may therefore represent a barrier to entry.[103]

Profitability. Whether and to what extent profitability and dominance have a positive correlation has been the subject to enormous debate among economists.[104] The most that can be said is that the empirical relationship between performance and market structure is not clear. Serious measurement problems have affected the reliability of most studies. And accounting profits do not reflect economic profits except under the most unrealistic assumptions.[105] As two critics note "there is no way in which one can look at accounting rates of return and infer anything about relative economic profitability or, *a fortiori*, about the presence or absence of monopoly profits."[106]

Notwithstanding the lack of clarity on the precise relationship between profits and market structure, profits have been relied upon as a factor contributing to dominance in certain Article 82 EC decisions and cases. In *Microsoft,* for example, the Commission considered that the financial performance of the undertaking was consistent with its near monopoly position. Its profit margin was approximately 81%, which was considered high by any measure and reinforced the conclusion that Microsoft held a dominant position.[107]

It is clear, however, that *lack of profitability* is not a contra-indication of dominance. A dominant firm that faces a sudden decline in demand may continue to operate even if it makes losses. Indeed, losses may be necessary for certain abusive conduct, such as

---

[101] *Soda-ash* OJ 1991 L 151/21.

[102] See JS Bain, *Barriers to New Competition*, (Cambridge, Harvard University, 1956).

[103] Discussion Paper, para. 40.

[104] For a summary of the main contributions, see DW Carlton and JM Perloff, *Modern Industrial Organisation*, 4th ed, (Boston, Pearson Addison Wesley, 2005), Ch. 8.

[105] See FM Fisher and JJ McGowan, "On the Misuse of Accounting Rates of Return to Infer Monopoly Profits" 73 *American Economic Review* (1983) 82.

[106] *Ibid.*, 90.

[107] Case COMP/C-3/37.792, *Microsoft*, Commission Decision of March 24, 2004, not yet published, para. 464.

predatory pricing. Thus, in *Michelin I*, the Court of Justice rejected the argument that since Michelin was running losses, it was not dominant. The Court pointed to the overall economic strength of the undertaking and its ability to engage in research and investment.[108] It referred to "the advantages which [Michelin] may derive from belonging to groups of undertakings operating throughout Europe or even the world... Amongst those advantages was the lead which the Michelin group has over its competitors in the matters of investment and research and the special extent of its range of products." The Court correctly decided that a lack of profits may be temporary and says little about the overall firm's ability to exert market power.

The undertaking's own assessment of its position. The undertaking's own assessment of its position as evidenced by internal documentation may be taken into account when considering dominance. In *BBI/Boosey & Hawkes* the Commission relied upon internal documents in which the supplier stated that its musical instruments were the "automatic first choice" of all top brass bands.[109] However, it does not follow that internal documentation which claims that the undertaking is not dominant will be given the same attention.

3.2.3.4 Conduct of the allegedly dominant firm

Abusive behaviour as evidence of dominance. Conventionally, the Commission must first prove that an undertaking holds a dominant position on the relevant market and then prove abuse of that dominance. The conduct of a firm in the market normally relates to the issue of abuse, and not to the assessment of dominance. However, the Community institutions have sometimes taken behavioural facts into account when assessing dominance. In *United Brands*, the Court of Justice held that, in assessing dominance, "it may be advisable to take account if need be of the facts put forward as acts amounting to abuses without necessarily having to acknowledge that they are abuses."[110] In both *Michelin* cases, the Commission relied on Michelin's allegedly abusive practices as indicators of market power, noting that "as is often the case in situations such as that being examined here, the finding of a dominant position is supported inter alia by the evidence relating to the abuse of that position."[111] Finally, in *Hilti*, the Commission referred to the commercial behaviour of the undertaking as being "witness to its ability to act independently of, and without due regard to, either competitors or customers."[112] The firm was found to hold a dominant position as its behaviour, and the economic consequences which followed, would not normally be present if a company faced real competitive pressure.

---

[108] Case 322/81, *NV Nederlandsche Baden-Industrie Michelin v Commission* [1983] ECR 3461, paras. 54–55. See also *Hilti*, OJ 1988 L 65/19, para. 69.

[109] *BBI/Boosey & Hawkes* OJ 1987 L 286/36.

[110] See Case 27/76, *United Brands Company and United Brands Continentaal BV v Commission* [1978] ECR 207, paras. 82–84.

[111] *Bandengroothandel Frieschebrug BV/NV Nederlandsche Banden-Industrie Michelin*, OJ 1981 L 353/33, para. 35; *PO–Michelin*, OJ 2002 L 143/1, paras. 198–99.

[112] *Eurofix-Banco v Hilti*, OJ 1988 L 65/19, para. 71, upheld on appeal in Case T-30/89, *Hilti AG v Commission* [1991] ECR II-1439, and on further appeal in Case 3/92 P, *Hilti AG v Commission* [1994] ECR I-667.

Relying on abusive conduct as evidence of dominance is problematic in certain respects. First, this approach runs the risk of being circular. A company may be found dominant due to its conduct; and dominance and the "special responsibility" can in turn lead to conduct itself being catalogued as anticompetitive without any evidence on actual abusive character. If used at all, this approach should therefore be a complement rather than a substitute for the careful analysis of market conditions in the assessment of dominance. Second, this approach is mainly useful for exploitative abuses. For instance, if it can be shown that excessive prices persist for long periods and the market resists change, dominance is a likely explanation. Most firms, dominant or not, can engage in practices that may be regarded as exclusionary abuses, such as exclusive dealing, predatory pricing, and loyalty discounts. They are probably less likely to be successful if they are not dominant, but the point is that simply observing such practices proves nothing about dominance. For example, relying on conduct such as price reductions as evidence of dominance could have the paradoxical effect of discouraging firms, fearful of being held to be dominant, from competing on the merits.[113] Third, relying on possible abuses as evidence of dominance could lead to a false inference in the case of collective dominance where the conduct of one firm might amount to cheating and dismantling the collusive oligopoly rather than evidence of abuse. Perhaps for all these reasons, the Discussion Paper does not list the market behaviour of the undertaking under investigation as an indicator of dominance.

3.2.4 Countervailing Buyer Power

Overview. The negotiating positions and commercial practices of key buyers in the relevant market inevitably affect the state of competition therein and consequently will have an influence on whether or not a supplier can be deemed dominant. Indeed, the notion of buyer power is provided for in the seminal case-law definition of dominance: a dominant firm must be able "to behave to an appreciable extent independently of its competitors *and customers* and ultimately of consumers."[114] In other words, if a supplier's competitive behaviour is significantly constrained by its customers, it cannot be dominant.

Definition of buyer power. The OECD has defined buyer power as "the ability of a buyer to influence the terms and conditions on which it purchases goods."[115] Thus, if buyers are able to influence the terms and conditions on which they acquire goods, then suppliers in that market are *ipso facto* not able to act independently of their customers. Buyer power is a matter of degree, and it may be that only one of several buyers in a given market is able to exert significant buyer power. It may also be that even a monopoly seller facing a monopsony purchaser lacks dominance.[116] Thus, the relevant

---

[113] See R Whish, *Competition Law* (3rd edn., London, Butterworths, 1993) p. 368.

[114] Case 322/81, *NV Nederlandsche Baden-Industrie Michelin v Commission* [1983] ECR 3461, para. 30 (emphasis added).

[115] OECD Roundtable on Buying Power of Multiproduct Retailers (2000) 1 *OECD Journal of Competition Law and Policy*. For a similar definition, see M Bloom, "Retailer Buyer Power" in B Hawk (ed.), *2000 Fordham Corporate Law Institute* (New York, Juris Publishing Inc., 2001) p. 399.

[116] See K Binmore and D Harbord, "Bargaining Over Fixed-To-Mobile Termination Rates: Countervailing Buyer Power as a Constraint on Monopoly Power," *Journal of Competition Law and Economics* (2005) 1(3), 449-472.

test for buyer power in relation to the dominance assessment is whether one or more customers in the relevant market are able to appreciably influence the prices or other terms on which they acquire goods and, in so doing, to materially constrain the commercial independence of the allegedly dominant supplier. If they are so able, then under the Community Courts' definition of dominance, that market cannot have any dominant suppliers.

Both in the merger context and under Articles 81 and 82 EC, the Commission has increasingly recognised the role of buyer power as a countervailing force limiting the market power of suppliers and shifting the balance of negotiating leverage in many markets from suppliers towards customers. Buyer power can result in a "neutralisation"[117] or offsetting of the effects of supplier dominance or concentration, i.e., "removing the possibility of suppliers exercising market power."[118] In *Italian Flat Glass* the Court of First Instance reproached the Commission for not having "even attempted to gather the information necessary to weigh up the economic power of the three [allegedly collectively dominant] producers against that of Fiat, which could cancel each other out."[119] Strong buyer power constrains suppliers' ability to raise prices,[120] and in many cases obliges suppliers to lower prices.

Assessment of buyer power. To assess buyer power, the Commission will examine a number of factors to assess whether customers' influence over the commercial negotiating process constrains their suppliers from exercising market power. In the first place, the relevant procurement market must be defined. The procurement market comprises those demand sources to which suppliers may realistically sell their products.[121]

Second, the concentration of customers in the relevant procurement market will be examined. This is the most important factor in assessing the extent to which a market is likely to be influenced by buyer power.[122] Customer concentration is significant both in absolute terms (i.e., the percentage of demand accounted for by the largest buyer or buyers) and relative to concentration on the supply side.[123] In assessing demand-side concentration in procurement markets, the Commission has typically looked at the

---

[117] Case COMP/M.2498, *UPM-Kymmene/Haindl*.

[118] Case COMP/M.1225, *Enso/Stora*, para. 97.

[119] Joined Cases T-68/89, T-77/89 and T-78/89, *Società Italiana Vetro SpA, Fabbrica Pisana SpA and PPG Vernante Pennitalia SpA v Commission* [1992] ECR II-1403 (hereinafter "*Italian Flat Glass*"), para. 366.

[120] M Bloom, "Retailer Buyer Power" in B Hawk (ed.), *2000 Fordham Corporate Law Institute* (New York, Juris Publishing Inc., 2001) p. 409.

[121] J Lücking, "Retailer Power in EC Competition Law" in B Hawk (ed.), *2000 Fordham Corporate Law Institute* (New York, Juris Publishing Inc., 2001) p. 473.

[122] See *Buyer Power and Its Impact in the Food Retail Distribution Sector of the European Union*, report prepared for the European Commission by Dobson Consulting, October 13, 1999, p.32.

[123] In recent years, and in a wide variety of markets, the Commission has found that buyer power played a significant role in constraining suppliers' behaviour and made unlikely the possibility of supplier dominance in cases where demand-side concentration was equal to or greater than supply-side concentration. See, e.g., Case COMP/M.2072 *Philip Morris/Nabisco*, para. 25 (demand-side concentration ratio 50–60%; supply-side 40–50%); Case COMP/M.1225, *Enso/Stora*, para. 84 (demand-side and supply-side concentration equal on the liquid packaging board market, with top three accounting for close to 100% of the market).

percentage of purchases of the relevant products accounted for by the largest customers in the market. It should be noted, however, that even where individual demand-side market shares are relatively small, buyer concentration could also be generated by the presence of centralised "buying groups."[124]

Third, retailer practices will be considered. Evidence of buyer power includes delisting or threatening to delist branded suppliers' products or demanding payments or other conditions that do not benefit the supplier correspondingly. Other issues such as the retailers' share of the supplier's turnover and whether or not retailers have a private or "own brand" label are also considered relevant in assessing buyer power. In addition, the Commission may compare the switching costs for the supplier if it had to switch retailers with the costs for the retailer if it had to switch suppliers.

Fourth, and most importantly from the viewpoint of economic analysis, the Commission may compare the switching costs for the supplier if it had to switch retailers with the costs for the retailer if it had to switch suppliers. That is, it may compare the *outside options* open to suppliers and customers, respectively. The economics of bargaining is a well-established field in modern economic theory. It deals with the question of what determines the bargaining outcome and the relative bargaining power of the involved parties. A basic insight of bargaining theory is that the bargaining power of a party is fundamentally determined by its outside options, i.e., by the set of alternatives available to that party in case the negotiations break down.[125] Large customers will have significant buyer power when they have multiple outside options while their suppliers have few. The outside options of buyer are given by, but not restricted to, the firms established in the market. Large buyers may be able to sponsor entry, either alone or in cooperation with other buyers.[126]

If the analysis of these factors reveals that sufficient buyer power exists so that the supplier cannot act independently of its customers, the supplier will not be found dominant for the purposes of Article 82 EC. The key overall point is that buyers' response to price increases by the allegedly dominant firm paves the way for effective new entry or leads existing suppliers in the market to significantly expand their output so as to defeat the price increase. In other words, the strong buyers should not only protect themselves, but effectively protect the market.[127]

Examples of buyer power. Examples of buyer power have commonly arisen in two sectors: grocery retailing and pharmaceuticals. In both sectors, sellers typically face powerful buyers using sophisticated procurement techniques. In the retailing sector, increased concentration on the buyer side has led to a handful of major large-scale purchasers of food and groceries in most Member States. Indeed, concerns in respect of

[124] See *National Sulphuric Acid Association*, OJ 1989 L 190/22.

[125] See, e.g., J Sutton, "Non-cooperative Bargaining Theory: An Introduction," 53 *Review of Economic Studies* (1982) 709-728; K Binmore, A I Rubinstein, and A Wolinsky, "The Nash Bargaining Solution in Economic Modelling," 17 *RAND Journal of Economics* (1986), 176-88; A Muthoo, *Bargaining Theory with Applications*, (Cambridge University Press, 1999); and MJ Osborne and A Rubinstein, *Bargaining and Markets*, (Academic Press, 1990).

[126] See UK Competition Commission, *Deutsche Börse AG, Euronext NV and London Stock Exchange plc.*, November 2005, paras. 5.115 to 5.124.

[127] See Discussion Paper, para. 41.

supermarket buyer power have been expressed within the EU and elsewhere.[128] The pharmaceutical sector is perhaps even more conducive to buyer power, since manufacturers typically face a single purchasing entity—the State—which often has express price regulation or profit cap powers. The relevance of buyer power in these two sectors is discussed in detail below, although it should be noted that these sectors are by no means unique. Other examples which are claimed to have focused on the issue of buyer power range from the timber industry and the meat-packing industry,[129] to the very sophisticated cash trading and derivatives trading exchanges. Buyer power thus needs to be examined in its specific market context.

a. Grocery retailing. A good example of buyer power is the grocery industry. As the Commission explains:[130]

> "Manufacturers are more and more dependent on distributors and grocery retail for getting their products to the consumers. Since the shelf space for new products is limited, conflicts arise between the increasing number of new product launches and the retailers' objective [of] profit optimisation. This conflict has resulted in retailers asking for listing fees (key money) or for discount schemes which sometimes go beyond possible cost savings of the manufacturers. Given the pressure on shelf space, products which are not in a number one or two position increasingly run the risk of being delisted and replaced by large retailers' own brands."

The effect of this strong buyer power is to "[prevent] manufacturers from exploiting their position as fully as they could do if they were faced with a less concentrated retail sector...[and] force manufacturers to reduce investment in new products or product improvements, advertising and brand building, eliminate secondary brands and weaken primary brands while strengthening the position of private-label (store) brands, and in the process cause wholesale prices to small retailers to rise, further weakening them as competitors."[131] Moreover, "buyer power also gives a trader considerable influence over the choice of products which come to market and hence are obtainable by consumers. Products which are not bought by a dominant buyer have practically no chance of reaching the final consumers as the supplier lacks alternative outlets. Lastly, the dominant buyer determines the success or otherwise of product innovations."[132]

Even large suppliers may be constrained by buyer power. For example, in *Enso/Stora*, the Commission found that buyer power on the liquid packaging board market removed the possibility of suppliers exercising market power (despite these suppliers having up to 70% share of the relevant market).[133] This is particularly true with respect to manufacturers' "non-core" brands: "a large supplier's bargaining hand is weakened

---

[128] AA Foer, "Introduction to Symposium on Buyer Power and Antitrust" (2005) 72(2) *Antitrust Law Journal* 505.

[129] See SC Salop, "Anticompetitive Overbuying by Power Buyers" (2005) 72 *Antitrust Law Journal* 669 for a discussion of these examples.

[130] Commission's Green Paper on Vertical Restraints, para. 233, available at http://www.europa.eu.int/comm/competition/antitrust/96721en_en.pdf.

[131] *Buyer Power and Its Impact in the Food Retail Distribution Sector of the European Union,* report prepared for the European Commission by Dobson Consulting, October 13, 1999.

[132] Case COMP/M.1221 *Rewe/Meinl*, paras. 72–74.

[133] Case COMP/M.1225, *Enso/Stora*, para. 74.

since even though they own powerful brands, they also rely on the retailer for sales of their secondary brands (e.g. those that compete with own label brands)."[134]

b. Pharmaceuticals. Buyer power is of particular relevance to the pharmaceutical sector because there is frequently a highly concentrated demand side, whether in the form of a single buyer, such as a national health authority, or of a few powerful purchasers, such as clinics or hospitals, that often have sufficient leverage against the suppliers to affect price. Under the EC Merger Regulation, the Commission has examined buyer power of various actors in the vertical supply chain for pharmaceuticals. For example, in *Behringwerke/Armour Pharmaceutical*,[135] the Commission confirmed the relevance of buyer power in the Factor VIII plasma products market. There, the highly concentrated nature of the demand side would render access to the market easier for new entrants. The Commission stated that, "the structure of the demand side in plasma-derived products, in particular in factor VIII, in Germany, nonetheless allows smaller or new entrants to achieve a position in the market."[136] Accordingly, the Commission held that the demand side in Factor VIII exercised buyer power that would constrain the behaviour of the joint venture.[137]

National law precedents also widely recognise the existence of buyer power among State purchasing entities. In *Difar*, the Spanish Competition Service concluded that certain manufacturers did not have a dominant position, based, *inter alia*, on the facts that the "national health system had an enormous purchasing power;" and that the overall regulatory framework precluded the independent behaviour of manufacturers.[138] The Competition Service thus concluded that there was no effective way for manufacturers to develop a truly independent commercial policy without taking account of competitors or consumers. Similarly, in *Cofares/Organon*,[139] the Spanish Tribunal for the Defence of Competition stated that, when assessing dominance, regard must be given to the powerful bargaining positions on the demand side. In particular, "the monopoly position of the national health system must be underlined, due to the fact that its purchases from laboratories, accounting only for the sales through pharmacies, form approximately three quarters of the volume of sales of these laboratories (73.8% in 2000) having regard to all the prescribed medicines."[140] The strength of the bargaining power of the Spanish national health system was also referred to in *Laboratorios Farmaceuticos*,[141] where the Tribunal for the Defence of Competition emphasised that the administrative fixing of prices eliminates an essential characteristic of market dominance which is the possibility to determine the price.

[134] M Bloom, "Retailer Buyer Power" in B Hawk (ed.), *2000 Fordham Corporate Law Institute* (New York, Juris Publishing Inc., 2001) p. 399.

[135] Case No.IV/M.495, *Behringwerke/Armour Pharmaceutical.*

[136] *Ibid.*, para. 34.

[137] *Ibid.*, para. 36.

[138] Case R 388/01, *Difar*, rejected by the Spanish Competition Service on April 27, 2001, upheld on appeal by the Tribunal for the Defence of Competition on December 5, 2001 (translation from original).

[139] Resolution of the Tribunal for the Defence of Competition File R.547/02, *Cofares/Organon* of September 22, 2003, p. 9.

[140] *Ibid.*

[141] Resolution of the Tribunal for the Defence of Competition File R.488/01, *Laboratorios Farmacéuticos* of December 5, 2001, p. 2.

Buyer power arguments have also been rejected by the Commission and national authorities. In *Genzyme*[142] the Competition Appeal Tribunal undertook a comprehensive analysis of the effects of the countervailing buyer power of the National Health Service. Genzyme argued that the buyer power of the NHS, the fixing of prices under the PPRS[143] and the Department of Health's price fixing powers all exert a measure of control over the supplier that prevents any alleged abuse.[144] The Tribunal held that the NHS exerted insufficient buyer power due to the fact that there was only one drug, Cerezyme, available to treat Gaucher's disease. Further, the conduct of Genzyme, which in the past had been able to ignore NHS requests to supply Cerezyme separately from homecare services and to maintain its prices, was evidence of the lack of buyer power and "the hallmark of dominance."[145] With regard to prescribing Cerezyme, the Tribunal noted that the actual decision to do so is taken locally by clinicians on medical grounds. Thus, in practice, once the clinician takes the decision, the NHS has little option but to fund the product. Therefore, the Tribunal concluded, "even though the NHS is the only purchaser of Cerezyme, its bargaining position is relatively weak in the face of Genzyme's monopoly in the supply of the drug."[146]

3.2.5 Evidence of Actual Competition on the Relevant Market

Need to examine actual competition on the market. Analysis of market shares, barriers to entry and expansion, and the effects, if any, of countervailing buyer power are obviously essential steps in the analysis of dominance. But they are ultimately only proxies for identifying the existence of dominance. It is also critical that these elements are corroborated by an analysis of *actual* competition on the relevant market. Evidence of actual competition on the market may prove that a particular undertaking cannot exercise dominance. As the Court of Justice noted in *Hoffmann-La Roche*, the "fact that an undertaking is compelled by the pressure of its competitors' price reductions to lower its own prices is in general incompatible with that independent conduct which is the hallmark of a dominant position."[147] At the same time, the Community Courts have consistently held that a finding of dominance does not preclude the existence of some competition.[148]

How much competition is needed to preclude a finding of dominance is not clear. The Court of Justice has held that a dominant firm must be able to disregard, or at least, materially disregard, competitive pressure that exists.[149] But this is imprecise, since, in the short-term at least, even firms with a small market share will, unless switching costs are zero, be able to act with a degree of independence from customers and rivals. The key element of dominance is that the dominant firm acts successfully as a price setter

[142] *Genzyme Ltd v The Office of Fair Trading* [2004] CAT 4, judgment of March 11, 2004.

[143] The PPRS system is one of an overall control on profits, based on a permitted rate of return from a company's NHS business as a whole, across its range of licensed medicinal products.

[144] *Genzyme*, above, para. 178.

[145] *Ibid.*, para. 255.

[146] *Ibid.*, para. 250.

[147] *Ibid.*, para. 71.

[148] Case 85/76, *Hoffmann-La Roche & Co AG v Commission* [1979] ECR 461, para. 39. See also Case 27/76, *United Brands Company and United Brands Continentaal BV v Commission* [1978] ECR 207, para. 113.

[149] *Ibid.*, para. 39.

and its rivals as price takers.[150] The allegedly dominant firm must therefore be shown to have appreciably more influence over pricing than rivals, such that rivals are effectively forced to follow its prices. If a firm has been able to consistently behave as a price leader, and to impose significant price increases or alter its strategy with impunity or success, this will be regarded as a strong indication of dominance. For example, in *Soda-Ash/ICI*, the Commission cited the firm's "traditional role as price leader" and its ability to maintain higher prices in a national market where it had a 93% share than in neighbouring Member States where its share was lower as factors indicating dominance.[151]

Markets that are characterised by frequent new product introductions, entry by new competitors, unstable market shares or declining shares of leading suppliers, anticipated demand growth, and shifting consumer behaviour or preferences are likely to be less conducive to dominance on the part of a single firm or group of firms than mature, stagnant markets in which sales or market shares can only be gained at the expense of existing competitors.[152] Indeed, demand growth and a continuous influx of new products is also strong evidence of a market that is competitive.[153]

The fact that rivals might win sales at certain accounts, or that the dominant firm is forced to cut its price to win some marginal sales, is not conclusive evidence of the absence of dominance. Rivals' ability to set prices, and the allegedly dominant firm's ability to act with a degree of independence from rivals' pricing, must also be more than merely marginal or transitory. Evidence that the allegedly dominant firm has been forced to make successive price cuts in response to rivals and still has not gained market share should, however, offer a good *prima facie* indication of a lack of dominance. In contrast, if the firm with the highest market share has been unable to impose significant price increases, or if it realises low margins, over an extended period, this suggests strongly that the firm is not dominant. Beyond these generalisations, however, there is no precise benchmark which determines the amount of competition necessary to rule out a finding of dominance. Each case requires a thorough analysis of market dynamics.

---

[150] See DW Carlton & JM Perloff, *Modern Industrial Organisation* (4th edn., Boston, Pearson Addison Wesley, 2005) p. 110.

[151] *Soda-Ash–Solvay, ICI*, OJ 1991 L 152/1, paras. 6, 45, and 48. See also *ECS/AKZO*, OJ 1985 L 374/1, para. 69 (Commission considered relevant the fact that AKZO had been able even during periods of economic downturn to maintain its overall margin by regular price increases and/or increases in sales volume).

[152] See, e.g., *Tetra Pak I (BTG licence)*, OJ 1988 L 272/27, para. 44 (Commission found that the milk market was mature with little or no room for overall expansion and the technical life for the related equipment in the relevant market was in excess of 10 years, making it difficult for newcomers to enter since, in order to sell their products, they had to either compete in the limited market for renewing old equipment or persuade dairies to replace existing equipment); and *Eurofix-Bauco v Hilti*, OJ 1988 L 65/19, para. 69.

[153] See Case COMP/M.2276, *The Coca-Cola Company/Nestlé/JV*, OJ 2001 C 308/13. para. 38 (Commission concluded that even though the joint venture would account for 85–95% of iced tea sales in Spain, competitive concerns did not arise because the iced tea segment was nascent, and over the coming years was expected to grow and the number of choices and competitors to increase).

3.2.6 Conclusion

The need for a more nuanced approach to single-firm dominance. Dominance does not result from any single factor: in any given case it will be necessary to consider the totality of evidence. Essential issues to consider include the market shares of the allegedly dominant firm relative to its competitors, barriers to entry (e.g., economies of scale/scope, technological advantages, product differentiation, vertical integration etc.), barriers to expansion, customer switching costs, the ability of the allegedly dominant firm to act independently of its competitors, and countervailing buyer power. Only if all factors point to consistent conclusions can any reasonable inference of dominance be made.

Historically, however, dominance under Article 82 EC has often been analysed in a cursory fashion by courts and competition authorities. This is not to say that any of the conclusions reached in particular cases were necessarily wrong; simply that further analysis was needed. A specific problem concerns over-reliance on market share presumptions, either to treat relatively low market share levels (e.g., 40–50%) as raising *prima facie* dominance concerns or to conclusively presume that high shares always imply dominance. The practical result is that firms with market shares in excess of 40% often have to consider the possibility that they may be found dominant, with the significant consequences that this entails for their commercial practices.

There are indications that the rather formalistic approach to dominance under Article 82 EC is changing. The Discussion Paper for example cites statements from case law suggesting that high market shares are not necessarily decisive, while also giving prominence to other factors such as barriers to entry and buyer power. But this arguably does not go far enough, since it simply summarises past cases. A more fundamental question is whether the threshold for intervention is *too low*, which is arguably the case. At a minimum, a strong case can be made for saying that the analysis should adopt on a wider-ranging inquiry based on the economic realities of the relevant market, as occurs under US law. This is evidence that a more rigorous, economic-based approach to dominance is being applied by certain national authorities,[154] which, it is hoped, will be followed by other authorities and courts.

[154] See, e.g., Case COM/05/03, *Drogheda Independent Company Limited*, December 7, 2004 (Irish Competition Authority). The Irish Competition Authority did not consider that a publisher with a 75% market share was dominant. This was based, *inter alia*, on the following considerations: (1) the publisher's market share had fallen from a previous monopoly level; (2) the publisher did not face a small competitive fringe, but a single, large, well-resourced, and innovative rival; (3) the publisher was actually unable to increase advertising rates due to the existence of its rival; (4) the absence of capacity constraints; (5) low barriers to entry due to the ability to outsource printing operations at relatively low cost; (6) low barriers to expansion due to growing demand; (7) the ability of customers to play the two firms off each other to obtain lower advertising rates; and (8) evidence of switching by advertisers between rival newspapers. See also Case COM/107/02 *TicketMaster Ireland*, September 26, 2005 (firm with 100% market share not found dominant). See too Resolution of the Tribunal for the Defence of Competition, *Bacardí y Cía*, September 30, 1999; Case R 388/01, *Difar*, rejected by the Spanish Competition Service on April 27, 2001, upheld on appeal by the Tribunal for the Defence of Competition on December 5, 2001; Resolution of the Tribunal for the Defence of Competition File R.547/02, *Cofares/Organon* of September 22, 2003; and Resolution of the Tribunal for the Defence of

3.3 COLLECTIVE DOMINANCE

3.3.1 Introduction

Collusion and EC competition law generally. Express agreements between horizontal competitors that fix prices and output or allocate markets constitute the most serious violation of EC competition law. Such agreements are unlawful under Article 81(1) and cannot benefit from exemption under Article 81(3). Article 81 EC also prohibits "concerted practices" between undertakings or associations of undertakings which have as their object or effect the prevention, restriction or distortion of competition. Concerted practices do not have all the elements of an express agreement, but "arise out of coordination which becomes apparent from the behaviour of the participants."[155]

It is well-established in economics, however, that rival sellers may be able to coordinate their activities without entering into agreements or other forms of communication that amount to a concerted practice. In oligopolistic markets, they may be able to coordinate their activities where each oligopoly member realises that competing other members would ultimately be self-defeating. The absence of effective competition within an oligopoly, and between the oligopoly and other firms on the relevant market, is sometimes referred to as "collective dominance," "joint dominance," "coordinated effects," or "tacit collusion." Many economists prefer the term "tacit collusion," on the basis that it more accurately captures the economic insight that a tight oligopoly can behave in a similar way to a cartel. But this phrase is somewhat confusing to lawyers, who tend to view "collusion" as requiring either an actual agreement or a concerted practice.

The application of Article 82 EC to tacit coordination. Article 82 EC states that the prohibition on abuse of dominance applies to "one or more undertakings," thus in principle allowing for the possibility that collective dominance could fall under the prohibition on abuse of dominance. Recognising the potential for economic harm as a result of the failure to tackle tacit coordination, and the limitations of merger control laws in this regard,[156] the Community institutions have for some time accepted that

Competition File R.488/01, *Laboratorios Farmacéuticos* of December 5, 2001 (all rejecting dominance findings based, *inter alia*, on buyer power and absence of barriers to entry).

[155] See Case 48/69, *Imperial Chemical Industries Ltd v Commission (Dyestuffs)* [1972] ECR 619, para. 65. The terms "agreement" and "concerted practice" have strong similarities: they are "intended to catch forms of collusion having the same nature and are only distinguishable from each other by their intensity and the forms in which they manifest themselves." See Case C-49/92 P, *Commission v Anic Partecipazioni SpA* [1999] ECR I-4125, paras. 131 and 115–18. For example, in the case of concerted practices, independent firms can remove market uncertainty by making advance price announcements or complaining about rivals' pricing activities. If the rival firm responds with similar price rises of its own, or accepts the rivals' complaints and adjusts its prices accordingly, then, in the absence of any other legitimate explanation for parallel conduct, a concerted practice may be found. In contrast, in the case of agreements, the same ends are achieved through express contacts.

[156] Mergers and acquisitions that create or strengthen situations of collective dominance are of course subject to mandatory merger control laws in the EU and elsewhere. But merger control laws can only tackle the problem of collective dominance as and when transactions *happen* to arise: many anticompetitive oligopolies never lead to merger activity, not least because the merging firms know that a favourable outcome is unlikely. The absence of an effective enforcement tool for dealing with tacit collusion represents a potential major lacuna in the treatment of collusion. Indeed, many respected

firms may be collectively dominant for purposes of Article 82 EC.[157] This possibility was first mentioned in 1988 in the context of firms that were structurally linked,[158] which led to an erroneous view that such links were necessary in collective dominance cases. This misconception was clarified in subsequent cases, but doubt remained as to the precise legal conditions for collective dominance under Article 82 EC, and in particular how they related to an extensive decisional practice and case law developed under the EC Merger Regulation. Recent case law and guidance have for practical purposes assimilated the treatment of collective dominance under both areas of law, with the result that, certain inevitable differences aside, the basic principles are the same.[159]

3.3.2 The Economics Of Collective Dominance

Overview. Collusion allows firms to exert market power and artificially restrict competition. It may arise when firms act through an organised (explicit) cartel or when firms act in a non-cooperative way to maintain supra-competitive prices; that is, when

---

commentators argue that the economic harm from tacit collusion is at least as serious as express collusion, and possibly more given the fact that companies know that explicit cartels are *per se* illegal. See R Posner, *Antitrust Law* (2nd edn., Chicago, Chicago Press, 2001).

[157] This represents a major difference with Section 2 of the US Sherman Act, where situations of jointly-held monopolies are not caught. See, e.g., P Areeda & H Hovenkamp, *Antitrust Law* (Boston, Little, Brown and Company, 1996) para. 810.

[158] Case 247/86, *Société alsacienne et lorraine de télécommunications et d'électronique (Alsatel) v SA Novasam* [1988] ECR 5987, paras. 21–22. The Court of Justice did not respond to this invitation from the Commission, since the issue was not raised by the referring court.

[159] The policy objectives of EC merger control and Article 82 EC also differ in certain respects. Merger control seeks to prevent structural changes from occurring on markets that would lead to substantially less competition, in particular by creating dominance (whether single firm or collective). In other words, it seeks to prevent long-term changes in market structure. Article 82 EC is neutral on the issue of dominance and also has a narrower focus in terms of dealing with market activity. It does not concern structural changes to a market, but strategic conduct within a market that limits production to the prejudice of consumers (as well as exploitative acts that take advantage of existing dominance). This raises the question of whether the standard for intervention is, or should be, different under the EC Merger Regulation and Article 82 EC. There are good arguments that the standard should be higher under the EC Merger Regulation than under Article 82 EC. One obvious reason is that merger control is by nature predictive whereas Article 82 EC concerns know past or present market conditions. Authorities are almost certainly more likely to get more merger decisions wrong than abuse of dominance cases. Although there are no comparative data, one study puts the rate of error in merger decisions as high as one in four. See T Duso, D Neven, & LH Röller, "The Political Economy of European Merger Control: Evidence Using Stock Market Data," CEPR Discussion Paper 3880 (April 2003). A more compelling reason perhaps is that the cost of wrongly-prohibiting a merger is, in general, likely to be higher than wrongly finding an abuse where there is none, since it has a lasting structural effect on the market. These differences should not, however, be overemphasised, since any assessment of collective dominance under both sets of rules involves complex economic assessment and judgment rather than purely factual analysis. And *Airtours* makes clear that the Community Courts will apply a high standard for intervention in merger cases too, requiring "convincing evidence" of collective dominance. See Case T-342/99, *Airtours plc v Commission* [2002] ECR II-2585, para. 63. On the policy issues, see generally J Temple Lang, "Oligopolies and Joint dominance in Community Antitrust Law" in B Hawk (ed.), *2001 Fordham Corporate Law Institute* (New York, Juris Publications Inc., 2002) pp. 269–359; and D Geradin, P Hofer, F Louis, N Petit, N Walker, "The Concept of Dominance," *Global Competition Law Centre Research Papers on Article 82 EC*, College of Europe, July 2005, p. 35.

collusion emerges tacitly through repeated market interactions.[160] For many years, economists believed that tacit collusion was not merely a possibility in concentrated industries, but rather an inevitable outcome.[161] The consensus at the time was that the line between "tacit collusion" and "interdependent action without collusion" was blurred.[162] This led one economist to conclude that "to legislate against oligopoly and against quasi-agreements [i.e., tacit coordination] is less promising than some optimists may have believed…not much is gained by trying to group oligopolists as if they were not aware of their individual influence on each other's policies."[163]

This *laissez faire* attitude to oligopoly behaviour changed after the publication of Stigler's model of oligopoly in the 1960s. He understood that, although all members of an oligopoly would benefit if they could coordinate their conduct to maximise joint profits, "if any member of an oligopoly can secretly violate it, he will gain larger profits than by conforming to it."[164] Spontaneous coordination will emerge only in oligopolistic industries where the incentives to deviate are low or where deviations are easy to detect and punishments are sufficiently strong. It thus became clear that that oligopolistic interaction does not necessarily equate to coordination, thus re-establishing the dividing line between unilateral oligopolistic interaction and tacit collusion. In other words, not all oligopolies are uncompetitive. Following this insight, economic theory focused attention on the identifying the set of circumstances where the members of an oligopoly would be able to coordinate their strategies so as to maximise joint profits.

Using the tools of game theory,[165] modern oligopoly theory has shown that tacit collusion between firms is likely when two basic cumulative conditions are satisfied:[166] (1) firms have the *incentive* to avoid competing, i.e., to raise their profitability; and (2) they have the ability to do so, i.e., tacit agreement is *feasible*. These basic conditions in turn give rise to a number of more specific criteria, including: (a) the need for firms have common interests in reaching tacit agreement; (b) the need for low transaction costs in reaching a tacit agreement; (c) the ability of the participating firms to effectively impose their agreement on their customers; and (d) difficulties of defecting from the (tacitly) agreed course of action.

3.3.2.1 Firms have the incentive to avoid competing

The need for firms to have common interests. Firms' interests must be aligned to reach tacit agreement. For example, an incumbent firm with a large customer base and

---

[160] See J Friedman, "A Non-Cooperative Equilibrium for Supergames" (1979) 20(1) *International Economic Review* 147–56. For an up-to-date, non-technical summary of modern oligopoly theory and its implications for antitrust law, see GJ Werden, "Economic Evidence on the Existence of Collusion: Reconciling Antitrust Law with Oligopoly Theory" (2004) 71 *Antitrust Law Journal* 719.

[161] See EH Chamberlain, *The Theory of Monopolistic Competition* (Cambridge, Harvard University, 1933).

[162] JS Bain, *Industrial Organisation* (Cambridge, Harvard University Press, 1968) p. 315.

[163] See W Fellner, *Competition Among the Few* (New York, AA Knopff, 1949), p. 309-310.

[164] See G Stigler, "A Theory of Oligopoly" (1964) 72 *Journal of Political Economy* 46.

[165] For a basic introduction, see DG. Baird, RH Gertner and RC Picker, *Game Theory and the Law* (Cambridge, Harvard University Press, 1994).

[166] See M Ivaldi, B Jullien, P Rey, P Seabright and J Tirole, "The Economics of Tacit Collusion," IDEI, Toulouse, Final Report to DG COMP. March 2003. See also KN Hylton, *Antitrust Law: Economic Theory and Common Law Evolution* (Cambridge, Cambridge University Press, 2003).

significant goodwill would have very little incentive to enter into tacit coordination with a competitor who entered the market much later and with no reputation in the market. The incumbent may want the entrant to agree to high prices, but this makes little sense for the entrant, because it effectively makes it impossible for the entrant to grow its share for the duration of the agreement. The entrant may want to agree to split the market, but such an agreement will likely be turned down by the incumbent as it may see no reason to concede market share given its vast competitive advantage.

The parties will have common interests if their *strategic goals* are sufficiently aligned. This can arise in a variety of factual settings, but most commonly occurs where: (1) some members of the oligopoly have financial interests in competitors, whether or not they involve control (cross-ownership); (2) absent those structural links, they are sufficiently alike (symmetry); and (3) no firm acts as a "maverick." Only if firms have common incentives to maintain or raise prices (and by a similar amount) will tacit collusion be possible.

a. ***Cross-ownership.*** When company A has a financial interest in company B, its strategic decisions take into account not just their impact on the profits of company A, but also the impact on the profits of company B. In other words, the effect of cross-ownership is to align the incentives of companies, which otherwise are rivals in the market place.[167]

b. ***Symmetry.*** If firms (or their products) are substantially different, there may be no common price that is acceptable to all parties. That is, collusion is less likely if there are important *asymmetries* amongst competitors.[168] Factors that may give rise to asymmetries include the following:

1. *Different cost structures.* Tacit collusion is less likely when cost asymmetries among undertakings are high, given that industry profit maximisation results in different output and profit levels for the members of the cartel and may require the exit of some of its participants.[169]

2. *Differences in market shares.* Tacit collusion is less likely in markets where there remain significant differences in the market shares (or customer bases) of the different competitors.[170] This applies *a fortiori* when there are some economies of scale or indivisibilities in production, given that those firms with lower market shares will seek efficiency improvements. And it is also a more

[167] See D O'Brien and S Salop, "Competitive Effects of Passive Minority Equity Interest: The Reply,"(2001) 69 *Antitrust Law Journal* 611 and references therein.

[168] Kühn shows that if a firm is large enough relative to the rest of the market it cannot credibly participate in a collusive scheme. Furthermore he shows that firms have no incentive to induce slight asymmetries through mergers since this is profit reducing. See KU Kühn, "The Coordinated Effects of Mergers in Differentiated Products Markets," CEPR Discussion Papers 4796 (2004).

[169] See A Jacquemin and ME Slade, "Cartels, Collusion and Horizontal Merger" in R Schmalensee and RD Willig (eds.), *Handbook of Industrial Organisation* (Amsterdam, North Holland, 1989) p. 418. See also J Harrington, "The Determination of Price and Output Quotas in a Heterogeneous Cartel" (1991) 32(4) *International Economic Review* 767–92; R Rothschild, "Cartel Stability when Costs are Heterogeneous" (1999) 17(5) *International Journal of Industrial Organisation* 717–34.

[170] See Case IV/M.355, *Rhône Poulenc/SNIA II*; and Case IV/M.358, *Pilkington Techint/SIV*.

important factor when firms have excess capacity that they seek to put into productive use.

3. *Heterogeneous products and asymmetric product lines.* Tacit collusion is less likely when firms compete with differentiated products,[171] or when their products lines differ in size and scope. For example, a high quality producer is less likely to seek an agreement with a less competitive, low quality producer than with a competitor offering the same quality as the latter represents a bigger competitive threat.

4. *Asymmetric growth prospects.* A growing firm will usually have little or no incentive to cooperate with a declining firm, and may prefer the latter to exit the market as quickly as possible.[172]

c. ***Absence of "maverick" player(s).*** Coordination is much less likely in the presence of a "maverick," i.e., a firm that declines to follow the industry consensus and thereby constrains effective coordination. A maverick can be identified by certain characteristics, such as excess capacity and aggressive pricing and non-pricing conduct (e.g., advertising), etc.[173] A firm with these characteristics is likely to deviate from any consensus or tacit agreement among firms, thus hindering coordination in the marketplace. A maverick would grow its market share at the expense of its competitors, thus disrupting any attempts to stabilise the market into tacitly agreed quotas. Sales growth—in an otherwise stable market—is thus a good indicator of maverick behaviour.

3.3.2.2 Reaching and maintaining a tacit agreement is feasible

Negotiating an agreement involves low (transaction) costs. The cost of reaching tacit coordination must be relatively small. Several factors determine the costs of negotiating an agreement. In the first place, the market must be relatively concentrated: the costs of negotiating an agreement rise rapidly with the number of parties involving the negotiation. Collusion (whether explicit or tacit) is therefore more likely in highly

[171] However, note that a collusive agreement may be difficult to sustain in a market with differentiated products. See in this regard, TW Ross, "Cartel Stability and Product Differentiation" (1992) 9 *International Journal of Industrial Organization* 453–69; and S Martin, "Endogenous Firm Efficiency in a Cournot Principal-Agent Model" (1993) 59(2) *Journal of Economic Theory* 445–50.

[172] A difference in growth prospects also affects the sustainability of the collusive agreement, as the firm with declining demand has a large incentive to deviate today (when its demand is high) and has no fear of future punishments (when its demand is low). See JE Harrington, "Collusion Among Asymmetric Firms: The Case of Different Discount Factors" (1989) 7 *International Journal of Industrial Organisation* 289–307.

[173] See Guidelines on the assessment of horizontal mergers under the Council Regulation on the control of concentrations between undertakings, OJ 2004 C 31/5, para. 42 (defining a "maverick" as a firm "that has a history of preventing or disrupting coordination, for example by failing to follow price increases by its competitors, or has characteristics that gives it an incentive to favour different strategic choices than its coordinating competitors would prefer."). See also JB Baker, "Mavericks, Mergers and Exclusion: Proving Coordinated Effects Under the Antitrust Laws" (2002) 77 *New York University Law Review* 166 ("But when firms differ, any firm that is nearly indifferent between coordination and cheating will constrain efforts by its rivals to make coordination more effective. Such a firm is the industry's maverick.").

concentrated markets.[174] Second, a stable market is necessary for the proper functioning of a collusive agreement. If the market conditions change frequently over time, it becomes very difficult, if not impossible, for suppliers to co-ordinate their behaviour.[175] Dynamic and innovative markets are therefore less susceptible to collusion.

Finally, it must be possible for the firms to tacitly agree on the collusive price with relative ease. Collusive mechanisms may work for different prices that result in firms getting very different levels of profits.[176] This means that firms that are tacitly colluding may be able to sustain any price level, from the competitive price to the monopoly (or fully collusive) price. This raises questions about the likelihood of the alternative outcomes, and about how firms can manage to achieve their preferred outcome. There might be different situations that explain why a particular price is selected in a tacitly collusive equilibrium. The first reason might be habit or history: if firms have coordinated in the past on a certain collusive price, it may be risky for them to experiment and change it.[177] This is one of the reasons why past coordination is an indicator of the likelihood of future coordination in an oligopolistic market. Alternatively, firms may be able to overcome coordination problems through exchanges of information about future prices or production.[178]

Firms can effectively impose their agreement on their customers. In addition to being able to reach tacit agreement between themselves, the oligopolists must be able to impose the terms of that agreement on customers. Consider two competing firms that find it in their mutual interest to set their prices at a very high level. This agreement makes sense only if their customers have no other option but to purchase the goods at that price, that is if they cannot find other suppliers selling at lower prices and, in addition, if their demands are relatively inelastic so that they cannot simply cut their consumption in response to the price increase rendering it privately unprofitable. If the parties cannot effectively impose their agreement on their customers, then the agreement is not feasible.

Collusion is therefore less likely in markets where: (1) elasticity of demand is high (an increase in prices will lead consumers to switch their demand to other producers or to

---

[174] See O Compte & P Jehiel, "Multi-party Negotiations," mimeo, CERAS, 2002; and M Ivaldi, B Jullien, P Rey, P Seabright and J Tirole, "The Economics of Tacit Collusion," IDEI, Toulouse, Final Report to DG COMP, March 2003, pp. 12 and 13.

[175] See Case T-342/99, *Airtours plc v Commission* [2002] ECR II-2585, recitals 9 and 10 and paras. 111 and 139. See also J Rotemberg and G Saloner, "A Supergame-Theoretic Model of Business Cycles and Price Wars during Booms" (1986) 76 *American Economic Review* 38; J Haltiwanger and J Harrington, "The Impact of Cyclical Demand Movements on Collusive Behaviour" (1991) 26 *RAND Journal of Economics* 86–106.

[176] D Abreu, "Extremal Equilibria of Oligopolistic Supergames" (1984) 50(2) *Journal of Economic Theory* 285–99; D Abreu, D Pearce and E Stachetti, "Optimal Cartel Equilibria with Imperfect Monitoring" (1986) 39 *Journal of Economic Theory* 251–69; and D Fudenberg and E Maskin, "The Folk Theorem in Repeated Games with Discounting or with Incomplete Information" (1986) 54(3) *Econometrica* 533–54.

[177] See W Bentley MacLeod, "A Theory of Conscious Parallelism" (1985) 27 *European Economic Review* 25–44; and J Rotemberg and G Saloner, "Collusive Price Leadership" (1990) 34 *Journal of Industrial Economics* 93–111.

[178] KU Kühn "Fighting Collusion by Regulating Communication Between Firms" (2001) 32 *Economic Policy* 167–97, and references therein.

reduce their consumption of the relevant products);[179] (2) there are sufficient actual or potential competitors that fall outside the coordinated behaviour (non-members can counteract the pricing policies of collusive undertakings, in particular where they are large, efficient, and have excess capacity);[180] and (3) customers exert buyer power (where buyers enjoy significant bargaining power, colluding firms will not be able to impose abusive pricing policies).[181]

Defection from the tacitly-agreed course of action is difficult. Even if firms find it in their mutual interest to agree to set very high prices, and can effectively impose that agreement on customers, it must also be clear that any attempt to cut prices will be rapidly acted upon by the non-deviating oligopoly members with price reductions of their own. If price competition that might undermine the tacitly-agreed course of action can be rapidly detected, and retaliatory price cuts implemented, then the only effect of a price cut will be to lower margins for all suppliers and to leave market shares broadly unaltered. In this scenario, the logical course of action will be to refrain from competing vigorously. Absent the ability to detect and punish deviations, collusion is unlikely. More specifically, tacit collusion is feasible only if it is sustainable, which in turn requires that: (1) the parties have no incentive to deviate; and (2) defection is easy to detect and punish. If defection is easy and/or punishment threats are not credible, then the agreement is not feasible.

a. Incentives to deviate. Firms' incentives to deviate from the tacitly-agreed course of action are typically large in three situations. First, when demand elasticity is high, collusion is more difficult to enforce. This is because each firm has a strong incentive to deviate from the agreed price. If customers are very price sensitive, each firm knows that it can "steal" high volumes from its rivals simply by slightly undercutting them.[182] On the other hand, a more elastic demand makes any punishment on the deviant more severe, so the effect of demand elasticity on the likelihood of coordination is ambiguous overall. Second, collusion is less likely in those markets characterised by rapid product innovation, given that innovation constitutes another competitive tool to win market share thus making collusive agreements unstable. This applies *a fortiori* when the introduction of new products is not easily predictable, and existing market positions can be eroded very quickly.[183] Finally, when firms' capacities are asymmetric, increasing the capacity of one of the firms in the dominant oligopoly increases the incentives of that firm to deviate and reduces the ability of its competitors to punish it, which makes collusion less likely.[184]

---

[179] See and M Ivaldi, B Jullien, P Rey, P Seabright and J Tirole, "The Economics of Tacit Collusion," IDEI, Toulouse, Final Report to DG COMP, March 2003, pp. 50–52.

[180] The Commission took into account such considerations in Case IV/M.446, *ABB/Daimler Benz*.

[181] The Commission examined buyer power as a relevant factor in assessing the likelihood of tacit collusion in Case IV/M-368 *Snecma/TI*. See generally section 3.2.4 above.

[182] The Commission has pointed out the inelasticity of demand as a factor facilitating collusion. See, e.g., Case IV/M.190, *Nestlé/Perrier*; and Case IV/M.315, *Mannesmann/Valourec/Ilva*.

[183] See M Ivaldi, B Jullien, P Rey, P Seabright and J Tirole, "The Economics of Tacit Collusion," IDEI, Toulouse, Final Report to DG COMP, March 2003, pp. 32–35.

[184] See C Davidson and RJ Deneckere, "Horizontal Mergers and Collusive Behaviour" (1984) 2 *International Journal of Industrial Organisation* 117–32; VE Lambson, "Some Results on Optimal Penal Codes in Asymmetric Bertrand Supergames" (1994) 62(2) *Journal of Economic Theory* 444–68;

In contrast, a firm's incentives to deviate will be less when there are practices that facilitate adherence to a common course. For example, a firm may offer customers most favoured company (or "nation") clauses. Such clauses can increase the cost of a deviation because they force the deviant company to apply to all of its customer base the same terms and conditions offered to the customers of rival companies (i.e., the marginal customers). Much the same disincentive can arise when a firm has a financial interest (whether active or passive) in a competitor. In that case, a deviation has two profit effects: the standard increase in the profits of the deviant company, and the reduction on the profits of the company or companies where the deviant has a financial interest. Depending on which of the two is larger, the incentives to deviate may be more or less.

b. Credibility of punishment. Credible punishment threats require a number of cumulative conditions to be satisfied. First, the market must be transparent, so that deviations can be detected with immediacy. Markets in which firms' behaviour in respect of their realised prices is transparent are more likely to be subject to collusive outcomes because it is easier for firms to monitor each other and respond rapidly to any attempt to compete aggressively.[185] Market transparency is a function of several factors: (1) concentration (concentrated markets are more likely to suffer cooperative outcomes than unconcentrated ones, as cheating is more easily spotted);[186] (2) price transparency (markets where prices are posted are more transparent than markets where prices are formed through bargaining or informal bidding processes, e.g., in auction markets, transparency is greater when the auction is organised as an open auction than as a sealed-bid auction);[187] (3) price complexity (e.g., a market where firms employ many different discount schemes, varying from customer to customer, over time and from product to product is unlikely is one where each competitor is unlikely to understand whether its competitors are complying with the tacit agreement or not); (4) stability of demand (markets with unstable demand are less prone to collusive outcomes because observed changes in the market are less likely to be the result of actions by rivals than external shocks to the market);[188] and (5) the extent of information

O Compte, F Jenny and P Rey, "Capacity Constraints, Mergers and Collusion" (2002) 46(1) *European Economic Review* 1–29; and H Vasconcelos, "Tacit Collusion, Cost Asymmetries and Mergers" (2005) 36(1) *RAND Journal of Economics* 39–62.

[185] See G Stigler, "A Theory of Oligopoly" (1964) 72 *Journal of Political Economy* 44–61; and E Green and R Porter, "Non-Cooperative Collusion under Imperfect Price Information" (1984) 52(1) *Econometrica* 87–100. See also R Porter, "Optimal Cartel Trigger-Price Strategies" (1983) 29 *Journal of Economic Theory* 313–38; M Kandori, "The Use of Information in Repeated Games with Imperfect Monitoring" (1992) 59 *Review of Economic Studies* 561–79; O Compte, "Communication in Repeated Games with Imperfect Private Monitoring" (1998) 66 *Econometrica* 597–626; M Kandori and H Matsushima, "Private Observation, Communication and Collusion" (1998) 66(3) *Econometrica* 627–52; and S Athey and K Bagwell, "Optimal Collusion with Private Information" (2001) 32(2) *RAND Journal of Economics* 428–65.

[186] See M Ivaldi, B Jullien, P Rey, P Seabright and J Tirole, "The Economics of Tacit Collusion," IDEI, Toulouse, Final Report to DG COMP, March 2003, pp. 12–13.

[187] See PD Klemperer, "Bidding Markets," UK Competition Commission, Occasional Paper, June 2005, and references therein.

[188] See N Fabra, "Collusion with Capacity Constraints over the Business Cycle" (2005) 9 *International Journal of Industrial Organisation* 497–511.

exchange among competitors (firms can facilitate the detection of deviants by exchanging information on market outcomes, especially prices).[189]

Second, the punishment must be *credible*, which means that it must be more in the interest of firms to engage in the punishment action (i.e., retaliate) than to do nothing.[190] Firms complying with the agreement may need to coordinate their behaviour to impose a punishment on the deviator. This may be very difficult when the number of firms in the collusive group is large.

Finally, the punishment must be *sufficiently strong*. The profit loss imposed on a deviant firm through punishment must be sufficiently large to deter deviations.[191] Relevant factors include: (1) demand growth (higher demand growth increases the strength of the punishment as it makes the future profit loss from retaliation larger);[192] (2) excess capacity (retaliation may be stronger in situations of excess capacity; alternatively, it could be argued that excess capacity gives firms large incentives to cut prices, increase sales and lower costs);[193] and (3) multi-market contacts (where firms interact on two or more markets, they may punish deviations in one market by retaliating in others).[194] It is not clear, however, how the presence of switching costs affects the ability and incentive of firms to successfully sustain co-ordination. Switching costs can have effects that simultaneously pull in opposite directions.[195]

---

[189] See, e.g., KU Kühn and X Vives, "Information Exchanges Among Firms and their Impact on Competition," mimeo, IAE Barcelona (1994), prepared at request of the Directorate General for Competition of the European Commission. See also, CA Holt and D David, "The Effects of Non-Binding Price Announcements in Posted-Offer Markets" (1990) 39(1) *Economic Letters* 307–10. Hence, formal and informal exchanges of commercially sensitive information among competitors, whether bilateral, multilateral or mediated through trade associations, must be viewed with suspicion. Information on individual prices and quantities is more helpful for firms to sustain collusion than aggregate information about demand from market studies. High frequency data and data disaggregated across markets helps detect deviations and draw inferences about demand and thus sustain collusion. See DS Evans, "Trade Associations and the Exchange of Price and Non-Price Information" in BE Hawk (ed.), *1992 and EEC-US Competition and Trade Law* (The Hague, Kluwer Law International, 1998).

[190] See M Ivaldi, B Jullien, P Rey, P Seabright and J Tirole, "The Economics of Tacit Collusion," IDEI, Toulouse, Final Report to DG COMP, March 2003, p. 6.

[191] *Ibid*,. p. 7.

[192] *Ibid*., pp. 26–28.

[193] See C Davidson and RJ Deneckere, "Excess Capacity and Collusion" (1990) 31 *International Economic Review* 521–41.

[194] See D Bernheim and M Whinston, "Multimarket Contact and Collusive Behaviour" (1990) 21(1) *Rand Journal of Economics* 1–26; WN Evans and IN Kessides, "Living by the 'Golden Rule': Multimarket Contact in the US Airline Industry" (1994) 109(2) *Quarterly Journal of Economics* 341–66, P Martin and N Fernandez, "Market Power and Multi-Market Contact: Some Evidence from the Spanish Hotel Industry" (1998) 46(3) *Journal of Industrial Economics* 301–15.

[195] The presence of switching costs can increase transparency in a mature market with switching costs as, if most customers are already locked-in to a supplier, a larger price cut may be required for customers to switch. Such price reductions are more likely to be observed by rivals and so monitoring any agreement is likely to be easier. See PD Klemperer, "Markets with Consumer Switching Costs" (1987) 102(2) *Quarterly Journal of Economics* 375–94. Switching costs also reduce the incentives to deviate. However, they also reduce the severity of punishments, as it is harder to punish the deviator by reducing price. Padilla finds that when switching costs are large, this latter effect dominates so that the presence of switching costs reduces the likelihood of tacit collusion. His model assumes complete

3.3.2.3 Conclusion

The contribution of economics to understanding tacit collusion. Modern oligopoly theory has identified a series of factors that facilitate tacit coordination, and others which make it more difficult. Some of these factors relate to the structural features of the market; others to the way oligopolists interact between themselves and with their customers. Economic theory has shown that tacit collusion is more likely when markets have certain minimum structural or behavioural aspects.

Structural characteristics conducive to situations of tacit collusion include: (1) a small number of firms; (2) firms are symmetric—they have similar costs, capacities, products, growth prospects, and financial strength; (3) stable demand and cost conditions; (4) limited or no innovation activity; (5) high barriers to entry and no buyer power; (6) firms interact in multiple markets; (7) firms have financial interests in their competitors; and (8) prices are transparent or known. Behavioural factors might include facilitating practices such as the offering of most favoured company (or "nation") clauses to customers. Many other factors are ambiguous. For example, a more elastic demand makes collusion more profitable and increases the strength of the punishment imposed on deviants, but at the same time it increases the incentives to deviate. Other ambiguous factors include switching costs, excess capacity, and demand growth.

In sum, economic theory identifies the structural and behavioural factors that make tacit coordination likely. But it cannot determine with precision when tacit collusion exists. Hence, economic theory can be used to construct "negative" or "safe harbour" tests,[196] but cannot be expected to provide the tools needed to establish the existence of a collective dominant position. To meet the evidentiary hurdles laid by the Community institutions in respect of collective dominance, it is necessary to investigate the conduct of the allegedly dominant oligopolists, as well as the degree of competition in the relevant market. As discussed in the next section, this is far from a straightforward task.

3.3.3 Legal Principles Governing Collective Dominance

3.3.3.1 Evolution

Overview. Although the principle of collective dominance is now relatively well-established under Article 82 EC, the applicable legal conditions have evolved significantly over the years. Earlier case law concerned firms that were united by structural links such as cross-shareholdings or other agreements. This led to a misapprehension that structural links were necessary for collective dominance and raised the possibility that "mere" oligopolistic interdependence was not covered. Subsequent case law clarified that structural links were not essential: the key point was

---

information but the impact of switching costs on punishment mechanisms should hold whichever information set is assumed. It is not however clear that this effect would be sufficient to outweigh other pro-collusive effects under situations of imperfect information. See AJ Padilla, "Revisiting Dynamic Duopoly with Consumer Switching Costs" (1995) 67 *Journal of Economic Theory* 520–30. On switching costs more generally, see C McSorley, AJ Padilla and M Williams, *Switching Costs*, Economic Discussion Paper 5, Part one: Economic models and policy implications, OFT, April 2003.

[196] See KU Kühn, "Closing Pandora's Box? Joint Dominance After the Airtours Judgment" in M Bergman (ed.), *The Pros and Cons of Merger Control* (Stockholm, Swedish Competition Authority, 2002).

the absence of effective competition between the oligopolists, whether due to structural or other economic links, which led the firms concerned to behave in a coordinated fashion. The interpretation of collective dominance under EC merger control was then clarified in *Airtours*.[197] But it remained unclear following *Airtours* whether the same basic principles would also apply under Article 82 EC. Any doubt in this regard has now been removed following the judgment in *Laurent Piau*,[198] as further reflected in the Discussion Paper. Thus, apart from certain inevitable differences between the two regimes, the basic principles for defining collective dominance are essentially the same under both Article 82 EC and EC merger control.

Early case law on collective dominance under Article 82 EC. Early case law concerning collective dominance under Article 82 EC was vague and ambiguous in many respects. Though it was generally accepted that capturing situations of collective dominance was useful, there was uncertainty as to how and when it would actually apply. The first case to address collective dominance in detail under Article 82 EC was *Italian Flat Glass* in 1992.[199] The Commission found that three Italian producers of flat glass had infringed Article 82 EC by virtue of holding a collective dominant position as they operated in a "tight oligopoly" that enabled them to impede the maintenance of effective competition by not having to take account of the behaviour of other market participants. Though the Court of First Instance held that the Commission did not meet the requisite standard of proof—essentially because it recycled the elements of an Article 81 EC violation as also constituting proof of collective dominance under Article 82 EC—it made some broad statements on the concept of collective dominance:[200]

> "There is nothing, in principle, to prevent two or more independent economic entities from being, on a specific market, united by such economic links that, by virtue of that fact, together they hold a dominant position vis-à-vis the other operators on the same market. This could be the case, for example, where two or more independent undertakings jointly have, through agreements or licences, a technological lead affording them the power to behave to an appreciable extent independently of their competitors, their customers and ultimately of their consumers."

However, the precise scope of collective dominance under Article 82 EC remained unclear. The confusion was two-fold. First, it was not clear whether the presence of structural links between the alleged collectively dominant oligopoly members in *Italian Flat Glass* was necessary or sufficient. Although the Court spoke more generally about "economic links," this led to a degree of confusion as to whether cases exhibiting tacit coordination, but not involving structural links between the coordinating firms, were covered by the notion of collective dominance under Article 82 EC.

[197] Case T-342/99, *Airtours plc v Commission* [2002] ECR II-2585 (hereinafter "*Airtours*"). For commentary, see R O'Donoghue and C Feddersen, "*Commentary on the Airtours Judgment*" (2002) *Common Market Law Review* 1171.

[198] Case T-193/02, *Laurent Piau v Commission* [2005] ECR II-nyr (hereinafter "*Laurent Piau*").

[199] Joined Cases T-68/89, T-77/89 and T-78/89, *Società Italiana Vetro SpA, Fabbrica Pisana SpA and PPG Vernante Pennitalia SpA v Commission* [1992] ECR II-1403.

[200] *Ibid.*, para. 358.

A second problem was the suggestion in certain case law that undertakings dominant on related, but separate, markets could be collectively dominant under Article 82 EC. Following *Italian Flat Glass*, it had been understood that collective dominance implied the absence of effective competition between two or more firms on the same relevant market. However, in *Almelo*, the issue was whether a series of regional electricity distributors in the Netherlands occupied a collective dominant position on the market for the public supply of electricity to local distributors.[201] Although the Court of Justice cited the correct basic principle for collective dominance—that the undertakings must be linked in such a way that they adopt the same conduct on the market[202]—the case appeared to concern undertakings that were dominant on a series of different sub-national markets rather than a group of firms active on the same relevant market. Similarly, in *La Crespelle*, the Court of Justice appeared to consider that the establishment of local monopoly artificial insemination centres that were territorially limited but together covered the entire territory of France might create collective dominance.[203] Both cases caused confusion as to whether Article 82 EC recognised a broader concept of collective dominance than had generally been understood in economics and merger control rules.

Towards clearer reliance on "economic links" leading to tacit collusion. Developments in the application of collective dominance under the EC merger regulation during the 1990s had significant consequences for clarifying the interpretation of collective dominance under Article 82 EC. *Gencor* concerned the legality of a decision adopted by the Commission under the EC Merger Regulation which prohibited a particular merger in the platinum industry on the grounds that it would lead to the creation of a duopoly market conducive to a situation of oligopolistic dominance.[204] On appeal, it was argued that the Commission had failed to prove the existence of "links" between the members of the alleged duopoly within the meaning of *Italian Flat Glass*, i.e., structural links. The Court of First Instance responded by stating, *inter alia,* that there was no support for the notion that "economic links" were restricted to structural links between the undertakings concerned:[205]

> "[T]here is no reason whatsoever in legal or economic terms to exclude from the notion of economic links the relationship of interdependence existing between the parties to a tight oligopoly within which, in a market with the appropriate characteristics, in particular in terms

[201] Case C-393/92, *Gemeente Almelo and others v NV Energiebedrijf Ijsselmij* [1994] ECR I-1477.

[202] *Ibid.*, paras. 42 and 43. See also Case C-96/94, *Centro Servizi Spediporto Srl v Spedizioni Marittima del Golfo Srl* [1995] ECR I-2883; and Case C-140/94, *DIP SpA v Comune di Bassano del Grappa, LIDL Italia Srl v Comune di Chioggia and Lingral Srl v Comune di Chiogga* [1995] ECR I-3257.

[203] Case C-323/93, *Société Civile Agricole du Centre d'Insémination de la Crespelle v Coopérative d'Elevage et d'Insémination Artificielle du Département de la Mayenne* [1994] ECR I-5077.

[204] Case No. IV/M 619, *Gencor/Lonhro*.

[205] Case T-102/96, *Gencor Ltd v Commission* [1999] ECR II-753, paras. 276–77 (emphasis added). See also Joined Cases C-68/94 and C-30/95, *France and Société commerciale des potasses et de l'azote (SCPA) and Entreprise minière et chimique (EMC) v Commission* [1998] ECR I-1375, para. 221. The Court of Justice described a collective entity for the purpose of joint dominance as "one or more other undertakings which together, in particular because of the factors giving rise to a connection between them, are able to adopt a common policy on the market and act to a considerable extent independently of their competitors, their customers and also of consumers."

of market concentrations, transparency and product homogeneity, those parties are in a position to anticipate one another's behaviour and are therefore strongly encouraged to align their conduct in the market, in particular in such a way as to maximise their joint profits by restricting production with a view to increasing prices. In such a context, each trader is aware that highly competitive action on its part designed to increase its market share (for example a price cut) would provoke identical action by the others, so that it would derive no benefit from its initiative. All the traders would thus be affected by the reduction in price levels...[E]ach undertaking may become aware of common interests and, in particular, cause prices to increase without having an agreement or resort concerted practice."

In other words, "mere" oligopolistic interdependence without structural links was covered by EC merger control rules. This corrected a misapprehension that had arisen following *Italian Flat Glass* that collective dominance necessarily required structural links. *Gencor* clarified that market structure *alone* could give rise to collective dominance. The same point was essentially confirmed under Article 82 EC in *Compagnie Maritime Belge*,[206] where a collectively dominant liner-shipping conference was party to anticompetitive exclusionary agreements and carried out exclusionary pricing known as "fighting ships," and various related practices. Although *Compagnie Maritime Belge* was typical of other collective dominance cases under Article 82 EC, in that the undertakings' coordinated interaction was made possible by agreements and structural links, and not merely by facilitating market conditions, the Court of Justice took the opportunity to make a number of more general statements on the scope of collective dominance under Article 82 EC. In particular, the Court clarified that structural links are not a pre-requisite under Article 82 EC for collective dominance: the key point is that the undertakings constitute a collective entity *vis-à-vis* their rivals and together hold a dominant position on the relevant market.[207] The precise reasons for those links are not important provided they are sufficient to enable the undertakings behave in a coordinated manner and dominate the relevant market.

Further clarification of the legal conditions in *Airtours*. An appeal in 2002 from the Commission's merger prohibition decision in *Airtours/First Choice* gave the Court of First Instance the opportunity to clarify a number of principles concerning the interpretation of collective dominance under the EC merger regulation and, indirectly, Article 82 EC.[208] The Commission prohibited the merger of two U.K. tour operators, Airtours and First Choice. Together, Airtours/First Choice and the two other leading vertically-integrated tour operators, Thomas Cook and Thomson, would have accounted for approximately 85% of the U.K. short-haul package holiday market. The Commission's case was that "the resulting structure [of the market for the supply of short-haul package holidays in the United Kingdom would] create an incentive for and

[206] *Cewal, Cowac and Ukwal*, OJ 1993 L 34/20, upheld on appeal in Joined Cases T-24/93, T-25/93, T-26/93, and T-28/93, *Compagnie Maritime Belge Transports SA and Others v Commission* [1996] ECR II-1201, and in Joined Cases C-395/96 P and C-396/96 P, *Compagnie Maritime Belge Transports SA and Others v Commission* [2000] ECR I-1365.

[207] Joined Cases C-395/96 P and C-396/96 P, *Compagnie Maritime Belge Transports SA and Others v Commission* [2000] ECR I-1365, para. 45 ("The existence of an agreement or of other links in law is not indispensable to a finding of a collective dominant position; such a finding may be based on other connecting factors and would depend on an economic assessment and, in particular, on an assessment of the structure of the market in question.").

[208] Case IV/M.1524, *Airtours/First Choice*.

make it rational" for the remaining three suppliers to restrict overall capacity put onto the market and thereby ultimately increase the prices for holiday packages to above a competitive level.[209] Following an appeal by Airtours, the Court concluded that the Commission prohibited the transaction without having proved to the requisite legal standard that the concentration would give rise to a collective dominant position.[210]

The Court held that three cumulative conditions must be satisfied for a finding of collective dominance:[211]

> "[F]irst, each member of the dominant oligopoly must have the ability to know how the other members are behaving in order to monitor whether or not they are adopting the common policy...[S]econd, the situation of tacit co-ordination must be sustainable over time, that is to say, there must be an incentive not to depart from the common policy on the market...The notion of retaliation in respect of conduct deviating from the common policy is thus inherent in this condition...Third...the Commission must also establish that the foreseeable reaction of current and future competitors, as well as of consumers, would not jeopardise the results expected from the common policy."

Thus, for collective dominance to be successful, the market characteristics must allow the members of the oligopoly to reach profitable terms of coordination and to detect and punish deviations from those terms. The Court also made it clear that new entry and the ability of non-members (or "fringe" players) to undermine successful coordination excludes successful coordination. The test laid down by the Court has since become the cornerstone of Commission decisional practice in the area of merger control, which is hardly surprising given that Commission had given its prior agreement on the conditions for collective dominance as set out in the *Airtours* judgment.[212] The pronouncement of specific conditions that are each necessary to establish collective dominance marked a welcome development in the law as it provided a more structured analytical framework rather than a haphazard, non-exhaustive list of "economic links."

Assimilation of Article 82 EC with the *Airtours* conditions. It remained unclear for a period following *Airtours* whether the conditions for collective dominance as set out in the Court of First Instance's judgment equally applied under Article 82 EC. There were and are certain inevitable differences between the two sets of rules, most notably the fact that merger control applies *ex ante* and Article 82 EC *ex post*. But it quickly became clear that the Community institutions regarded the basic conditions for establishing collective dominance as essentially the same under both Article 82 EC and merger control rules. For example, in *TACA*, the Court of First Instance cited *Airtours* with approval, even though, as in *Compagnie Maritime Belge*, the case concerned

[209] Case IV/M.1524, *Airtours/First Choice*, para. 147.

[210] Case T-342/99, *Airtours plc v Commission* [2002] ECR II-2585.

[211] *Ibid.*, para. 62.

[212] See H Haupt, "Collective Dominance Under Article 82 EC and EC Merger Control in the Light of the *Airtours* Judgment" (2002) 23(9) *European Competition Law Review* 434. See also M Clough, "Collective Dominance—the Contribution of the Community Courts" in *Essays for Judge David Edwards* (Oxford, Hart Publishing, 2003).

structural links between the firms concerned.[213] More recently, in *Laurent Piau*, the Court of First Instance also cited the *Airtours* conditions with full approval.[214]

Essentially the same conditions are now outlined in the Discussion Paper, which states as follows:[215]

> "Firstly, each undertaking must be able to monitor whether or not the other undertakings are adhering to the common policy. It is not sufficient for each undertaking to be aware that interdependent market conduct is profitable for all of them, because each undertaking will be tempted to increase his share of the market by deviating from the common strategy. There must, therefore, be sufficient market transparency for all undertakings concerned to be aware, sufficiently precisely and quickly, of the market conduct of the others."
>
> Secondly, the implementation of the common policy must be sustainable over time, which presupposes the existence of sufficient deterrent mechanisms, which are sufficiently severe to convince all the undertakings concerned that it is in their best interest to adhere to the common policy.
>
> Finally, it must be established that competitive constraints do not jeopardise the implementation of the common strategy. As in the case of single dominance, it must be analysed what is the market position and strength of rivals that do not form part of the collective entity, what is the market position and strength of buyers and what is the potential for new entry as indicated by the height of entry barriers."

3.3.3.2 Establishing collective dominance under Article 82 EC

Preliminary remarks. The assessment of collective dominance under Article 82 EC has undergone significant recent development, in particular the adoption of the *Airtours* conditions under Article 82 EC and recognition in the Discussion Paper that Article 82 EC can also apply to tacit collusion based only on market interactions. These developments build significantly on past case law. Indeed, all Article 82 EC decisions and judgments to date have found collective dominance only in situations in which agreements between the firms led them to behave as a collective entity.[216] Article 82 EC has thus not yet been applied to mere tacit collusion, which has meant that a number of issues have not been considered, either sufficiently or at all. The Discussion Paper answers certain questions, but also raises others.

A first issue is whether a finding of structural links is relevant only to the extent it has a bearing on the *Airtours* conditions or whether it can independently support a collective dominance finding. The Discussion Paper distinguishes collective dominance based on

---

[213] Joined Cases T-191/98 and T-212/98 to T-214/98, *Atlantic Container Line AB and Others v Commission* [2003] ECR II-3275, paras. 652, 654.

[214] Case T-193/02, *Laurent Piau v Commission* [2005] ECR II-nyr, para. 111.

[215] Discussion Paper, paras. 48–50.

[216] These cases are unlikely to be repeated in future, since they are the direct result of legislation in the liner shipping sector that, exceptionally, permits collective rate setting. The Commission has now proposed a regulation repealing this legislation. The proposal would bring liner shipping and maritime tramp and cabotage services under the scope of the general procedural rules on competition law, giving the Commission jurisdiction to apply competition rules to this sector. After adoption of the proposal the Commission will publish guidelines on the application of the competition rules to this sector. See Proposed Council regulation: COM 2005/651 of December 14, 2005; and Commission Press Release IP/05/1586 of December 14, 2005 (Questions and Answers).

agreements and collective dominance as a result of market interactions, i.e., mere tacit collusion.[217] But it is not clear from its elaboration of the conditions for collective dominance under Article 82 EC whether they apply only to tacit collusion based on market interactions or also to collective dominance resulting from agreements between the firms concerned. The better view must be that the conditions are the same in both cases, even if, in practice, it will usually be much easier to show tacit collusion where agreements lead the firms to behave in a coordinated fashion. Indeed, structural links are primarily relevant because they *facilitate* the adoption of a common strategy that allows the undertakings in question to present themselves or to act together as a collective entity. It would not help consistency if two different tests were applied. Much of the confusion in this regard would be resolved if the Community institutions only applied Article 82 EC to collective dominance in situations in which Article 81 EC did not apply.

Second, the first condition outlined in the Discussion Paper—that there is sufficient market transparency for each undertaking to monitor whether or not the other undertakings are adhering to the common policy—is incomplete. Transparency is necessary but not sufficient. Instead, the key overall condition, as outlined in section 3.3.2, is that the firms have *the incentive and ability not to compete*. They must first have the common incentives to tacitly collude. But this is insufficient unless they also have the ability to effectively reach coordinated terms and impose them on their customers. Transparency is simply one element of this condition.

Finally, the Discussion Paper is silent on a very important issue: the standard of proof. It assumes that Article 82 EC applies to mere tacit collusion without offering an indication of what standard of proof applies. The Community Courts have laid down strict standards for proving collective dominance under the EC Merger Regulation, requiring the Commission to produce "convincing evidence" of collective dominance.[218] But because Article 82 EC involves an assessment of past or present market facts the standard of proof for collective dominance should arguably be higher than under EC merger control. The conditions in the Discussion Paper are simply *indicators* of tacit collusion, but, without more, there is still no real proof that tacit collusion is taking place. This problem does not arise in the context of merger review, since this involves a forward-looking assessment of whether the change in market structure potentially effected by a merger would create conditions in which tacit collusion is likely to occur. In contrast, under Article 82 EC, there should arguably be a convincing basis for saying that tacit collusion *has* occurred, i.e., evidence of actual effective coordination on whatever the focal point of collective dominance is alleged to be. However, the Discussion Paper appears to assume that proof that tacit collusion is both possible and sustainable is sufficient to establish collective dominance.

Condition #1: the incentives to arrive at tacit collusion. The key first condition for collective dominance is that the firms concerned have stronger *incentives* to reach a common understanding on a focal point of coordination than to. The parties will have common interests if their *strategic goals* are sufficiently aligned. This may be due to

[217] Contrast Discussion Paper, para. 45 with para. 47.

[218] Case T-342/99, *Airtours plc v Commission* [2002] ECR II-2585.

cross-ownership arrangements or symmetry between the firms concerned. In addition, the firms must be able to reach an effective agreement on the focal point of coordination. This requires the presence of certain market characteristics such as a high degree of concentration, a stable environment, and transparency.

The recent decision by the Irish Commission for Communications Regulation (ComReg) in *O_2/Vodafone* is illustrative in this regard.[219] ComReg found that O_2 and Vodafone held a collectively dominant position based on a 94% combined market share. The analysis revealed that the retail mobile market is highly concentrated. There are only four licensed vertically integrated mobile operators in Ireland and Vodafone and O_2 held a 94% share of subscribers at the time of the decision. Furthermore, O_2 and Vodafone were relatively symmetric: there was a high level of interaction between the two firms, and they share similar levels of innovation. The market was relatively stable due to constant demand for mobile telephony services. For these and other reasons, ComReg felt that there would be sufficient incentive on the part of O_2 and Vodafone to coordinate behaviour.

Condition #2: the ability to sustain tacit collusion. The implementation of the common policy must be sustainable over time. This presupposes the existence of deterrent mechanisms, which are sufficiently severe to convince all the undertakings concerned that it is in their best interest to adhere to the common policy.[220] In other words, the oligopolists must be able to detect deviations and retaliate in the event of deviant conduct. But an essential precondition for an effective is that the market is sufficiently transparent to allow firms to detect the *need* for retaliation.

a. Market transparency. A deviation from the common policy can only be deterred if it is detected, which in turn is only possible if the market is sufficiently transparent so that the members of the oligopoly can observe the behaviour of their competitors or infer it from market outcomes with a high degree of certainty. Tacit collusion is not sustainable in markets which are not transparent.

In *Airtours,* the Court of First Instance concluded that capacity coordination could not take place on the United Kingdom package holidays market, since decisions on capacity expansion were not sufficiently transparent by virtue of a complex range of variables such as destination, departure date, airport location, aircraft model, type and quality of accommodation, duration of stay and price. Transparency was not sufficient to allow each of the major tour operators to be aware of the conduct of the others, to detect any deviations from the common policy, and to confirm retaliatory measures.[221] The Court observed that, due to the large number of short-haul package holiday destinations served from various U.K. airports, thousands of different permutations would have to be

[219] O_2 and Vodafone had a 94% share of subscribers in the retail market for mobile communications in September 2004. "Market Analysis—Wholesale Mobile Access and Call Origination," Commission for Communications Regulation, Document No: 04/118, para. 4.33 (hereinafter "*O_2/Vodafone*"). The decision has recently been annulled, mainly on procedural grounds: see Decision No: 08/05 of the Electronic Communications Appeals Panel in respect of Appeal Numbers ECAP6/2005/03, 04, 05, 06, 07, 08. However, the legal principles of collective dominance and the application of the *Airtours* criteria were not challenged.

[220] Discussion Paper, para. 51.

[221] Case T-342/99, *Airtours plc v Commission* [2002] ECR II-2585, para. 283.

monitored by the three large operators to have up-to-date information on each other's activities. Further, it was apparent that the capacity planning process did not, as the Commission found, involve simply renewing capacity budgeted or sold in the past, but was a complex attempt to predict how demand will evolve on both a macroeconomic and microeconomic level in the future. The Court also found that the Commission had failed to prove that each member of the oligopoly would have detailed knowledge regarding the overall level of capacity (i.e., number of holidays) offered by the other members.[222]

The most recent major decision on collective dominance—*Sony/BMG*[223]—continues to show the significant practical difficulties of proving collective dominance. The Commission examined the record music industry to determine whether or not coordination took place between the major players on the market, and if it did, whether it would be accentuated by the merger of Sony and BMG. However the Commission could not demonstrate, to the requisite standard, that the five major players in the music record industry were involved in coordinated behaviour in any of the markets affected by the planned merger. To test this, the Commission undertook a thorough analysis of their pricing strategies, focusing on whether or not prices were parallel, whether there was price coordination, and whether or not discounts offered were aligned and sufficiently transparent to indicate coordination. It concluded that although some elements of coordinated behaviour were evident, the evidence as a whole was not sufficient to establish collective dominance. The following factors were relevant:

1. To assess whether the majors' wholesale prices had been coordinated, the Commission first analysed the development of *average net prices* on a quarterly basis for the top 100 albums of each major in the five largest Member States. The Commission then analysed transaction data in real (inflation-corrected) prices (provided by the merging parties and the other majors). To ensure comparability, the Commission relied on price data for a consistent product, namely single sleeve album CDs (thereby excluding singles, maxi-singles, double albums, boxes, and enhanced albums). The Commission analysed the development of: average net prices, published prices to dealers (PPDs), gross and net price ratios, invoice discounts, and retrospective discounts.

2. With these basic data, the Commission analysed price coordination in three steps. First, it analysed the majors' pricing behaviour on the basis of their average wholesale net prices. As a second step, the Commission examined whether any price coordination, on the basis of a parallelism in average prices, could have been reached in using PPDs (or list prices) as focal points. Finally, the Commission analysed whether the different majors' discounts were aligned and sufficiently transparent to allow efficient monitoring of any price coordination also on the level of net prices.

3. The Commission then undertook these basic steps for each of the five largest countries. (Only the example of Germany is relied upon here, although the

[222] *Ibid.*
[223] Case COMP/M.3333, *Sony/BMG*.

results for the other countries were substantially the same.) The different majors' net average real prices developed within a range of approximately € 1.50 to € 2.00. The average difference between the bottom and the top of the range was € 1.81, and the maximum difference was more than € 3.00 at times. On the basis of net average real prices, the Commission thus found some parallelism and a relatively similar price development of the majors. However, these observations were as such not conclusive enough to show coordinated pricing behaviour in the past.

4. The Commission therefore further investigated whether additional elements, namely list prices and discounts, were aligned and sufficiently transparent to provide evidence of coordination. The Commission's analysis showed that transaction net prices were closely linked to gross list prices (PPDs) as, for both Sony and BMG, their average gross real prices and average net real prices had moved closely in parallel over the last six years, as also reflected by very stable net to gross price ratios across albums and time. However, the Commission found that the level of the different majors' various discounts varied to some extent. On a customer-by-customer basis, the Commission found a certain degree of fluctuation and differences of 2–5% between Sony's and BMG's invoice discounts for most of their common top 10 customers, and of more than 5% for some customers in several years. The merging parties also submitted data showing that invoice discounts for a given customer varied over time and from album to album, and discounts for a given album varied from customer to customer. Finally, although the merging parties systematically monitored competitors' prices on a weekly basis, promotional pricing was a strong feature of the market and reduced transparency. On the basis of these observations, the Commission felt unable to prove that invoice discounts were sufficiently aligned.

5. Finally, the Commission looked at other factors to confirm the lack of price alignment. First, it noted that recorded music was homogenous in format, but not in terms of content. This reduced transparency in the market and makes tacit collusion more difficult since it requires some monitoring on the level of individual albums. The Commission further noted that devices in the market that could increase transparency and facilitate the monitoring of an agreement were insufficient. Although the weekly album charts and the merging parties' own monitoring did increase transparency to a certain extent, the Commission did not find sufficient evidence that, by monitoring retail prices or by contacts with retailers, the majors have overcome in the past the deficits as regards the transparency of discounts already identified by the Commission.

In sum, the Commission could not show that the merger between Sony and BMG would have resulted in the strengthening or the creation of a collectively dominant position because it was unable to establish that the affected market was sufficiently transparent: (1) there was evidence that the merging parties and their rivals offer secret discounts to their clients; (2) the product was heterogeneous; and (3) the various market institutions that could increase market transparency (PPDs, album charts, etc.) had not led to the degree of price and discount alignment that could be expected in a transparent market.

b. ***Situations where structural links or other agreements facilitate retaliation.*** Retaliation mechanisms may be explicitly provided for if a written agreement exists between the parties (which would almost certainly also violate Article 81 EC). For example, the enforcement provisions for common tariffs in the *TACA* agreement were sufficient to prevent deviation.[224] Similarly, in *Laurent Piau*, sanctions such as warnings, fines and the withdrawal of an agent's licence against deviating agents as set down by the FIFA Players' Agents Regulation also amount to sufficient deterrent mechanisms to ensure that members adhere to the common policy.[225]

c. ***Retaliation in the absence of express mechanisms.*** Absent express disincentives to depart from common strategy, firms may still have incentives to maintain coordinated behaviour. Indeed, the Court of First Instance noted in *Airtours* that the Commission did not have to bring evidence of the existence of a specific retaliatory mechanism. Rather it just had to show that a potential retaliatory mechanism might give incentives to firms not to deviate.[226] A robust and effective coordinating mechanism, where "each member of the dominant oligopoly is aware that highly competitive action on its part designed to increase its market share would provoke identical action by the others, so that it would derive no benefit from its initiative," will also be sufficient deterrence to maintain the common policy over time.[227]

The Court concluded, however, that the Commission had not met even this low threshold. It held that the Commission was wrong in its decision that the tour operator oligopoly enjoyed sufficient means to counteract a capacity expansion deviation by one member since the market features were such as to render effective retaliation difficult. Any capacity expansions by other members in response to a deviation by one particular member could only take effect in the next holiday season and "late added" packages tended to be of lower quality.[228] Therefore, the retaliatory mechanisms were not sufficient to prevent firms from deviating from the common policy. Similarly, in *Sony/BMG*, retaliation was found to be ineffective as a discipline. The possible retaliatory mechanism against deviant action was the exclusion from, or termination of, other joint ventures between the major record companies such as the release of compilation CDs. However, since there was no evidence of exclusion or termination having occurred, the Commission found that it was not a sufficient retaliatory mechanism.

d. ***Problems with retaliation based on threatened capacity expansion.*** Practical difficulties may prevent effective retaliation where the alleged mechanism is threatened capacity expansion. One difficulty concerns the ability to withdraw capacity once it has been expanded to punish deviations. Not only would the oligopolists have to collude on capacity expansion to discipline the cheating oligopolist, but they would also need to collude on the retrenchment or freezing of added capacity to keep output tight in the

---

[224] *Trans-Atlantic Conference Agreement,* OJ 1999 L 95/1, para. 527.

[225] Case T-193/02, *Laurent Piau v Commission* [2005] ECR II-nyr.

[226] For criticism of this view, see A Nikpay and F Houwen "Tour de Force or a Little Local Turbulence? A Heretical View on the *Airtours* Judgment" (2003) 24(5) *European Competition Law Review* 199.

[227] Case T-342/99, *Airtours plc v Commission* [2002] ECR II-2585, para. 62.

[228] *Ibid.*, para. 204.

expectation of being able to charge above-competitive prices in the future. The oligopolists' ability to engage in two separate instances of collusion in this way independently of normal market forces seems questionable. Again, collusion over prices will usually be easier in these circumstances, since prices can usually be decreased and increased without the need to consider any longer-term issues of retrenchment.

Recent Commission decisions on collective dominance confirm some of these practical difficulties. In *Mitsui/CVRD/Caemi*, the Commission did not maintain its initial collective dominance concerns on capacity, but suggested that retaliation based on capacity expansion designed to punish the "cheating" oligopolist might be successful where: (1) the "punishment period" (i.e., the period of excess capacity) was relatively short-lived; (2) excess capacity can be absorbed by growing demand during the punishment period; and (3) the oligopolists are not committed to using the extra installed capacity in the long-term.[229] The logic of this reasoning seems questionable. As a general matter, it will be difficult to tailor capacity in the manner envisaged by the Commission, particularly where capacity expansion can only be done on a large scale leading to lumpy quantities and in markets where future demand is uncertain. This suggests that it will in practice be relatively difficult for the oligopolists to retaliate effectively relying only on the threat of capacity expansion.[230]

e. The advantages of targeted retaliation. One issue that has not received detailed treatment in the decisional practice and case law is whether retaliation needs to be capable of being targeted at the "cheating" oligopolist. The point is that retaliation mechanisms which inflict more damage on the deviating oligopolist than on the firms adhering to the tacit agreement compliant members are easier to sustain and, therefore, more credible. Economic theory has shown that a punishment mechanism may be credible even if it is not targeted to the deviant. However, a retaliatory mechanism which involves a long punishment period and which imposes significant damage on those undertakings that did not deviate from the tacit agreement is less credible than one in which the deviant is punished more severely and the punishment period is short. The Commission's Horizontal Merger Guidelines do not deal with the issue specifically.[231] They state that the "credibility of the deterrence mechanism depends on whether the other coordinating firms have an incentive to retaliate." Although this does not preclude some short-term losses (e.g., through price-cutting), the Guidelines make clear that "the

[229] See Case COMP/M.2420, *Mitsui/CVRD/Caemi*, paras. 236–37.

[230] In two linked transactions, *UPM-Kymmene/Haindl* and *Norske Skorg/Parenco/Walsum*, the Commission's case was that, post-transaction, the oligopolists would coordinate downtimes during demand slowdowns and limiting capacity through coordination of investment in new capacity. The Commission added that the "retaliation mechanism would lie in the very threat that other oligopolists would engage in an investment race, which would result in over-capacity, in prices collapsing and ultimately in low profitability for the whole industry." See Case COMP/M.2498, *UPM-Kymmene/Haindl* and Case COMP/M.2499, *Norske Skorg/Parenco/Walsum*, para. 131. The Commission subsequently abandoned these concerns because the oligopolists could and would only learn about an investment project after they had been committed and made irreversible by the cheating member. In other words, any retaliatory threat based on capacity would lack credibility and effectiveness and would be too costly to pursue.

[231] Guidelines on the assessment of horizontal mergers under the Council Regulation on the control of concentrations between undertakings, OJ 2004 C 31/5.

short-term loss [must] be smaller than the long-term benefit of retaliating resulting from the return to the regime of coordination."[232]

There are undoubtedly mechanisms that in practice can effectively target the deviating firm. One obvious method is selective price cuts,[233] which may be possible where the deviating firm has, for historical or geographic reasons, had its "own" customers. Another mechanism capable of being used for targeting concerns the exclusion from the deviating firm from joint ventures, which was mentioned in *Sony/BMG*, but ultimately found not to be credible. Targeting would also be possible where the punishment takes place on another product market where the deviating firm is active. If the punishing firms are not generally active in this market, it may be possible for one or more of them to enter and take a targeted action. Finally, it seems implicit in the notion of credible targeting that the method concerned should be legal. If it concerned unlawful measures such as a collective boycott, the mechanism could hardly be said to be "credible."

f. A higher burden of proof on retaliation under Article 82 EC than EC merger control? It is sometimes argued that a higher burden of proof on the issue of retaliation should be required in Article 82 EC proceedings.[234] The argument is that the *ex post* nature of Article 82 EC requires proof of the existence of a specific retaliatory mechanism which had a deterrent effect and led the oligopolists to maintain a common line of action. In contrast, the *ex ante* nature of merger control means that the Commission need only identify a credible and timely mechanism and not its actual use. But it would be wrong to conclude that the absence of evidence of actual use of a retaliatory mechanism implies that no effective punishment mechanism exists: the most effective mechanism is one where the mere *prospect* of retaliation is so effective that no deviation actually occurs.

In *O_2/Vodafone*, the Irish telecommunications regulator concluded that a major factor deterring the use of price as an instrument of deviation was the threat of retaliation.[235] Price structures made it possible for O_2 and Vodafone to distinguish between price changes that represented deviations and price changes that were compatible with tacit collusion. If one firm sought to acquire a significant increase in customers by lowering price, this would result in the other firm reacting with an identical response. The regulator considered that the most likely retaliatory response to a deviation along the price dimension, which would be immediately transparent, was via a reduction in price, as this can be effected swiftly.[236] The fact that retaliation was possible if either firm diverged from common policy was seen as a sufficient deterrent to prevent deviation from occurring. No evidence of actual use was required.

---

[232] *Ibid.*, para. 54.

[233] See, e.g., Case COMP/M.3314, *Air Liquide/Messer Targets* (selective price-cutting possible in a duopoly where contracts were relatively large).

[234] See D Geradin, P Hofer, F Louis, N Petit, and N Walker, "The Concept of Dominance," *Global Competition Law Centre Research Papers on Article 82 EC*, College of Europe, July 2005, p. 35.

[235] See "Market Analysis—Wholesale Mobile Access and Call Origination," Commission for Communications Regulation, Document No: 04/118, para. 4.92.

[236] *Ibid.*, para. 4.94

In sum, it does not seem correct under Article 82 EC to require evidence of the actual exercise of a retaliatory mechanism: the key point is that the specific mechanism, whatever it happens to be, is sufficiently credible to constitute an effective deterrent. However, evidence that a retaliatory mechanism was used, but failed, will ordinarily be fatal to a collective dominance claim.

Condition #3: inability of non-participating rivals and consumers to destabilise the tacit agreement. Tacit coordination is only sustainable if the undertakings that coordinate their behaviour do not face competitive constraints that can jeopardise the implementation of the common strategy. As in the case of single dominance, it must be analysed what is the market position and strength of rivals that do not form part of the collective entity, what is the market position and strength of buyers, and what is the potential for new entry (i.e., entry barriers). Collective dominance will not arise if such competitive constraints are able to counterbalance tacit collusion on the part of the oligopolists. Market concentration is again relevant in this connection. If the undertakings behaving as a collective entity do not have sufficient market power to behave independently of rivals and customers, it will not be possible to maintain the agreed course.

In *Airtours*, the oligopolists would together have accounted for approximately 85% of the U.K. short-haul package holiday market. Notwithstanding this very high degree of concentration, the Court of First Instance held that smaller tour operators could exert countervailing competitive pressure on the major players in the market. It found that smaller tour operators could increase (and had increased) capacity in times of shortages of supply and were particularly interested in attractive accommodations and/or destinations that the major suppliers declined to offer. Furthermore, smaller tour operators could obtain airline seats offered by independent third parties such as overseas and low-cost carriers, scheduled and charter airlines, and did not depend on the major suppliers' offerings in this regard.

In *O_2/Vodafone*, actual and potential market constraints were found to be insufficient to prevent O_2 and Vodafone acting independently. Meteor, the only fringe competitor, had little impact on the behaviour of both firms. High market entry barriers, particularly in terms of infrastructure, prevented potential competitors, such as "3", from affecting the market.[237] For these reasons, COMREG found that both participating and non-participating rivals, as well as consumers, were unable to destabilise the tacit agreement between Vodafone and O_2.

In *TACA*, the defendants claimed that the conference was not in a dominant position by virtue of external competition. They argued that it had a significant number of competitors whose market share increased during the relevant period, that the market share of those competitors increased more than the liner conference's did and that the capacity offered by independent shipping lines increased following the entry on to the market of a number of different companies.[238] In deciding whether or not external

[237] See "Market Analysis—Wholesale Mobile Access and Call Origination," Commission for Communications Regulation, Document No: 04/118.

[238] Joined Cases T-191/98 and T-212/98 to T-214/98, *Atlantic Container Line AB and Others v Commission* [2003] ECR II-3275, para. 953.

competition was effective the Court considered the following factors: (1) the number of competitors of the TACA parties and the increase in their market share (competitors held a cumulative market share of no more than 20–25% and any increase was very small);[239] (2) the rate of increase in the volume of freight carried by the TACA's competitors (the increase was not sufficient to threaten TACA's 70–75% market share);[240] (3) insufficient competition from competing shipping lines, Evergreen and Lykes (no evidence to suggest that the two companies were capable of bringing significant external competition to bear on the TACA parties);[241] (4) TACA's leadership in pricing matters and the role of follower played by independent competitors;[242] and (5) insufficient competition from the Canadian gateway.[243] The Court concluded after analysing these factors that actual competition was not effective.[244]

It then went on to determine whether potential competition was possible on the basis of: (1) the cost of market entry (the cost of market entry was very high due to the difficulty in deploying vessels from other routes to operate on the routes in question);[245] (2) recent entry on the relevant market (though new shipping operators had entered the market, it was not likely that they would constitute a source of significant potential competition for the TACA parties);[246] and (3) whether service contracts constituted a barrier to entry (service contracts constituted a barrier to significant entry by potential competitors).[247] The Court therefore held that potential competition was also ineffective due to the high barriers to entry. New entrants would be forced to either join TACA or align their prices with the liner conference.

One issue that remains unclear is *how much* competition between the oligopolists must be eliminated to render competition ineffective for the purposes of collective dominance. In *TACA* the Commission concluded that the extent of competition between the parties to the agreement was insufficient to preclude a finding of collective dominance. The fact that the conference members were obliged under US law to file their tariffs publicly, and adhere to those fixed rates, reduced competition amongst the members as it prevented them from offering special discount rates to particular shippers.[248] Moreover, enforcement measures—which included the payment of substantial guarantees and fines for deviation from the agreement—ensured members complied with the fixed rates and thereby reduced competition.[249] Separate non-TACA vessel sharing and slot exchange agreements, to which many of the TACA members were party, further decreased opportunities for competition.[250] There was accordingly no evidence of effective competition between the parties.

[239] *Ibid.*, paras. 957–63.
[240] *Ibid.*, paras. 964–68.
[241] *Ibid.*, paras. 969–78.
[242] *Ibid.*, paras. 979–81.
[243] *Ibid.*, paras. 982–87.
[244] *Ibid.*, para. 998.
[245] *Ibid.*, paras. 1013–21.
[246] *Ibid.*, paras. 1022–30.
[247] *Ibid.*, paras. 1031–36.
[248] *Trans-Atlantic Conference Agreement,* OJ 1999 L 95/1, para. 175.
[249] *Ibid.*, para. 177.
[250] *Ibid.*, para. 197.

On appeal, the TACA members disputed the Commission's decision and argued that it had failed to take into account evidence of competition between them, particularly in relation to price. However the Court held that a certain level of competition between the parties would not negate the possibility of a finding of collective dominance, adding that "there can be no requirement, for the purpose of establishing the existence of such a dominant position, that the elimination of effective competition must result in the elimination of all competition between the undertakings concerned."[251] The Court did not, however, articulate a test for the level of competition that would preclude a finding of collective dominance. It simply asked whether or not competition between the parties was significant or not. In this connection, it looked at price competition between the members and concluded that common prices were essentially in place, i.e., no evidence of significant competition.[252] For non-price competition, it focused on whether or not conference members had different individual strategies regarding service contracts and again found that competition levels were not significant.[253] Since there was no evidence of internal price and non-price competition of an degree and intensity to constitute effective competition between the parties, collective dominance was made out.[254]

3.3.3 Selected Issues On Collective Dominance

Abuses of collective dominance. Being collectively dominant is not illegal in itself, any more than being single firm dominant is.[255] However if collective dominance is proved, each undertaking is in principle subject to duties under Article 82 EC. If they abuse their collective dominance, their conduct will be deemed illegal. But considerable uncertainty surrounds what *abuses* of collective dominance Article 82 EC attempts to capture. A number of comments can be made.

First, while the case law suggests, correctly, that one collectively dominant company can commit an abuse even if the others do not act in a similar fashion,[256] the key point is that the conduct is the *manifestation* of the collective dominant position. The conduct

---

[251] Joined Cases T-191/98 and T-212/98 to T-214/98, *Atlantic Container Line AB and Others v Commission* [2003] ECR II-3275, para. 654.

[252] *Ibid.*, paras. 696–711.

[253] *Ibid.*, para. 712.

[254] *Ibid.*, para. 718.

[255] See Case 322/81, *NV Nederlandsche Baden-Industrie Michelin v Commission* [1983] ECR 3461, para. 10 ("[A] finding that an undertaking has a dominant position is not in itself a recrimination."). In the context of collective dominance specifically, see Decision N° 06-D-02 of February 20, 2006, *Bitumen Manufacturers*.

[256] See Case T-228/97, *Irish Sugar plc v Commission* [1999] ECR II-2969, para. 66 (The abuse "does not necessarily have to be the action of all the undertakings in question. It only has to be capable of being identified as one of the manifestations of such a joint dominant position being held. Therefore, undertakings occupying a joint dominant position may engage in joint or individual abusive conduct. It is enough for that abusive conduct to relate to the exploitation of the joint dominant position which the undertakings hold in the market."). See also Case C-393/92, *Gemeente Almelo and others v NV Energiebedrijf Ijsselmij* [1994] ECR I-1477. See too J Temple Lang, "Oligopolies and Joint Dominance in Community Antitrust Law" in B Hawk (ed.), *2001 Fordham Corporate Law Institute* (New York, Juris Publications Inc., 2002) 269-359 ("[I]t would not make sense to say that behaviour by one oligopolist with anticompetitive effects was lawful as long as the others did not do the same thing, but became unlawful as soon as they did.").

must therefore be part of a tacitly agreed course of action and not simply any (unrelated) conduct that an individual firm happens to carry out in an oligopolistic market. In practice, it is very unlikely that an exploitative abuse (e.g., excessive pricing) could be committed by one collectively dominant firm acting alone. In theory, exclusionary abuses and reprisal abuses (e.g., punishing or warning another company to discourage it from bringing an antitrust complaint or from competing aggressively) could be carried out by one firm even if the other members do not behave similarly. But there must be evidence that the conduct of one firm is part of a tacitly agreed course of action in order for it to be linked to an abuse of collective dominance.

Second, it makes no sense to treat as abusive conduct that is *inherent* in the nature of collective dominance. For example, collective dominance usually implies that the firms concerned can interact to raise prices above a competitive level. But this, in itself, cannot be abusive, in the same way as the power over price that single firm dominance potentially implies is not abusive. Of course, the definition of single firm and collective dominance pre-supposes that firms can raise (or already have raised) prices above competitive levels. This is not *ipso facto* an abuse: there would need to be additional proof of excessive pricing (or some other abuse). Otherwise, dominant firms would be condemned for their mere existence, which would be impractical, to say the least.[257]

Third, the most sensible rationale for abuses of collective dominance is that the firms concerned tacitly collude on a course of action to unlawfully exclude firms that do not form part of the oligopoly, thereby maintaining or strengthening their overall dominance. An example was *Compagnie Maritime Belge* where the firms concerned adopted collectively low freight rates to exclude a new entrant. Collective refusals to deal falling short of an agreed boycott are also a possible example. Of course, it may be that the collectively dominant firms collude over a certain course of action, but each carry out different aspects of it. For example, they may each defend a certain area or group of customers in case of entry, with the allegedly abusive conduct only being observed on the part of one of the dominant undertakings as entry had only occurred in the area or customer group that it was supposed to defend.[258] Predatory pricing in these circumstance may be an example of an abuse of collective dominance. But corroborating evidence of an exclusionary strategy should be required, since discounting within an oligopoly is often a sign of more competition, not less (i.e., destablisation of the oligopoly).[259]

---

[257] Whether mere participation in tacit collusion should in itself be considered anticompetitive gave rise to an interesting debate between two leading antitrust commentators. See R Posner, *Antitrust Law* (2nd edn., Chicago, Chicago Press, 2001) (arguing in favour of prohibiting mere tacit collusion) and D Turner, "The Definition Of An Agreement Under The Sherman Act: Conscious Parallelism And Refusals To Deal" (1962) 75(4) *Harvard Law Review* 655 (arguing that this would be impractical as it would condemn mere participation in tight oligopolies and force firms to behave irrationally). The latter view is more persuasive for practical reasons.

[258] See Discussion Paper, para. 75.

[259] *Ibid.*, para. 98 ("Companies that are collectively dominant are less likely to be able to predate because it may be difficult for the dominant companies to distinguish predation against an outside competitor from price competition between the collective dominant companies and because they usually lack a (legal) mechanism to share the financial burden of the predatory action.").

Finally, Article 82 EC should not deal at all with collusive conduct that falls under Article 81 EC (e.g., concerted practices and agreements). To hold otherwise risks blurring the important distinction between unilateral conduct and collusion and the corresponding provisions of the EC Treaty dealing with these two types of anticompetitive conduct.

"Vertical" collective dominance. From an economic viewpoint, collective dominance assumes that firms are active in the same relevant market and can, under certain conditions, behave in a coordinated fashion to act in a similar way to a cartel. In other words, it concerns interactions between horizontal competitors. For this reason, undertakings operating in different markets should not be considered collectively dominant. However, some confusion has been created in this regard by *Irish Sugar*.[260]

Irish Sugar was the only processor of sugar beet in Ireland, as well as the main supplier of sugar. It also held a 51% stake in Sugar Distributors Ltd (SDL), a distributor and seller of sugar, and acquired the remaining shares in that company in 1990. While it held a 51% stake, Irish Sugar appointed half of SDL's board, which included a number of senior Irish Sugar executives. SDL was also responsible for sales and pricing decisions and Irish Sugar and SDL had joint discussions on the problems that each faced as a result of imports and the defensive measures to be taken. Details of prices for individual customers were also discussed in meetings between representatives of SDL and Irish Sugar. There were direct also economic ties between the companies. SDL was committed to buying all its sugar from Irish Sugar. Irish Sugar paid for all consumer promotions and rebates offered by SDL to individual customers.

Despite the apparently vertical nature of the relationship between Irish Sugar and SDL, the Commission concluded that the economic links between the parties "created a clear parallelism of interest of the two companies vis-à-vis third parties," and that, under the principles set out in *Italian Flat Glass*, a position of joint dominance existed.[261] On appeal, the Court of First Instance upheld the Commission's joint dominance finding. Somewhat elliptically, the Court held that the case law does not "contain anything to support the conclusion that the concept of a joint dominant position is inapplicable to two or more undertakings in a vertical commercial relationship."[262] It added that, to hold otherwise, would create a lacuna in Article 82 EC in respect of the abusive exploitation of a joint dominant position.

The findings in *Irish Sugar* merit a number of comments. First, the entire premise of collective dominance is that firms are active on the *same market* and can behave in a coordinated fashion. This possibility does not apply to vertical relationships where the firms concerned are typically active on separate markets. Second, the relationship between Irish Sugar and SDL was not really vertical during the relevant period. The Court noted that the two companies were "active on the same market" during the period

---

[260] *Irish Sugar plc*, OJ 1997 L 258/1, affirmed on appeal in Case T-228/97, *Irish Sugar plc v Commission* [1999] ECR II-2969 and Order of the Court of Justice in Case C-497/99 P, *Irish Sugar plc v Commission* [2001] ECR I-5333.

[261] *Irish Sugar*, OJ 1997 L 258/1, para. 112.

[262] Case T-228/97, *Irish Sugar plc v Commission* [1999] ECR II-2969, para. 63.

in which Irish Sugar held 51% of SDL's shares.[263] In this circumstance, it was unnecessary for the Commission to rely on a new concept of "vertical" joint dominance: there was horizontal coordination. Finally, the correct interpretation of the relations between Irish Sugar and SDL during the period in question was probably that they constituted a single economic entity, which would have resulted in the imputation of any conduct carried out by SDL to Irish Sugar. A majority interest—which Irish Sugar had in SDL—normally raises a presumption of a single entity. It is not clear why the Commission did not proceed on this basis. Even if the Commission did not feel it could go this far, Article 81 EC would still have applied to most (though not all) of the conduct carried out by Irish Sugar and SDL. In other words, it is not clear why the Commission needed to rely on "vertical" collective dominance.

Vertical relationships may of course be relevant to aspects of collective dominance and abusive conduct. For example, where firms interact on multiple markets, a firm active on an upstream market may use the possibility of retaliation in another market as a means of enforcing the tacit agreement. But this is simply a factor that may affect the scope for collective dominance between firms active on the *same* market: it is not vertical collective dominance. In terms of abuse, it would presumably be unlawful for a dominant firm to instruct another independent firm to carry out abusive acts on its behalf. But this is not vertical collective dominance either. The firm is simply seeking to avoid the application of Article 82 EC by getting another firm to carry out abusive acts intended to benefit the dominant firm. Collective dominance could also presumably arise where horizontal competitors agree to allow an entity not active on the relevant market to organise or supervise aspects of their economic activities. But this too concerns horizontal coordination: the entity in question simply acts on behalf of the collectively dominant firms.[264] Nor does the fact that an undertaking active on a different level of trade derives some benefit from abusive conduct, and has an interest in seeing it carried out, amount to vertical collective dominance. Some abuses simply

[263] *Ibid.*, para. 62.

[264] This appears to have been the reasoning applied in Case T-193/02, *Laurent Piau v Commission* [2005] ECR II-nyr. The case concerned rules enacted by FIFA, football's governing authority, on dealings between agents, players, and football clubs. The rules in question were binding on FIFA members, including clubs. Mr. Piau complained that aspects of the rules were anticompetitive under Article 81 EC, as well as abusive under Article 82 EC due to the collective dominant position of FIFA and the football clubs. The Commission found that an exemption under Article 81(3) was appropriate and that FIFA was not in a collective dominant position. On appeal, the Court of First Instance upheld the exemption decision, but concluded that FIFA was collectively dominant together with the football clubs. However, no abuse was made out. Again, the relationship between FIFA and the clubs looked vertical in nature. This was true, in a sense, but was not the relevant legal point for purposes of collective dominance. The key point was that FIFA acted *on behalf of* the clubs and the clubs agreed to be bound by its decisions. The Court considered that FIFA was an "emanation" of the clubs as a second-level association of undertakings formed by the clubs (para. 112). The clubs and FIFA therefore presented them "as a collective entity vis-à-vis their competitors, their trading partners and consumers" (para. 113). But the coordination in question was horizontal in nature. The outcome in the case would presumably have been no different if the clubs had not agreed to act through FIFA as supervisory authority, but instead had a series of multi-lateral arrangements among themselves. The clubs, via FIFA, collectively laid down the conditions under which agents services were to be provided. The fact that FIFA was not itself active on the market for football agents' services was irrelevant in circumstances in which it had assumed the power to exercise in respect of such services. FIFA effectively operated on this market through its member clubs.

have the incidental effect of also benefiting undertakings in other markets. Finally, whilst it is true to say that vertical mergers and certain conduct that arises in the context of vertical integration can in rare cases facilitate collusion, the key point is that the collusion still occurs between *horizontal* competitors: the vertical element simply affords greater possibilities for collusion (e.g., if activity on another market level allows a firm to gain access to sensitive information on rivals).[265]

3.4 DOMINANT BUYERS

Dominance on the buying side of the market. Though most of Article 82 EC case law concerns the dominant position of suppliers, it equally applies to dominant buyers. If buyer power rises to the level of a dominant position (e.g., as a result of a supermarket merger leading to a high share of retail grocery sales[266]), the buyer could be subject to Article 82 EC proceedings if it is suspected of abusing its dominant position.

Seller power and buyer power essentially the same in economics. Buyer power is simply market power on the buyer side of a market. As monopoly is to the seller context so "monopsony" is to the buyer context. In the real world (as with monopoly) such a pure case is rare, but an example might be (at least in the short-run) a small town with few other employment opportunities whose inhabitants sell their labour to a local coal mine. The coal mine is a local monopsonist of the town's labour. The economic principles of monopsony are ultimately the same as for monopoly,[267] except that whereas a monopolist directly reduces supply for the purpose of raising price (which reduces consumer welfare), a monopsonist indirectly achieves the same effect simply by refusing to buy more inputs. If a firm is simultaneously a monopsonist (towards input suppliers) *and* monopolist (towards final customers), then the situation is one of a double retraction in final supply: the welfare effect is (unsurprisingly) worse than if only one of either monopoly or monopsony existed.

Examples of dominant buyers. The only reported case under Article 82 EC where buyer dominance was found is *British Airways/Virgin*.[268] The Commission found that British Airways (BA) was dominant on the United Kingdom market for the purchase of airline travel agency services, despite having a market share of less than 40%. BA appealed this finding to the Court of First Instance which confirmed the Commission's finding. The Court relied mainly on: (1) BA's market share as a purchaser of travel agency services in the United Kingdom; (2) the fact that that share was multiple times larger than rivals' shares; (3) the fact that sales of air tickets handled by travel agents established in the United Kingdom represent 85% of all air tickets sold; (4) evidence that BA had unilaterally reduced agency commissions; (5) BA's world rank in terms of international scheduled passenger-kilometres flown and the extent of the range of its

[265] See, e.g., Case IV/M.1327, *NC/Canal+/CDPQ/BankAmerica*; and Case COMP/M.2510, *Cendant/Galileo*.

[266] See, e.g., Case IV/M.784, *Kesko/Tuko,* affirmed on appeal in Case T-22/97, *Kesko Oy v Commission* [1999] ECR II-3775. See also Case COMP/M.1684, *Carrefour/Promodes*.

[267] See RG Noll, "Buyer Power and Economic Policy" (2005) 72 *Antitrust Law Journal* 591 ("Asymmetric treatment of monopoly and monopsony has no basis in economic analysis.").

[268] Case T-219/99, *British Airways plc v Commission* [2003] ECR II-5917.

transport services and its hub network; and (6) agents' substantial dependence on BA for revenue. Taken together, the Court found that these circumstances made BA an "obligatory business partner of travel agents established in the United Kingdom."[269]

A controversial aspect of these conclusions was the fact that they included no real analysis of BA's position on the downstream airline markets. Instead, the Commission simply aggregated all BA tickets sold through travel agents established in the United Kingdom over all routes to and from United Kingdom airports. The Court of First Instance agreed with this assessment, finding that "there is no need to assess its economic strength on that market by reference to the competition between airlines providing services on each of the routes served by BA and its competitors to and from United Kingdom airports."[270] But this conclusion seems questionable. Demand for travel agents services was largely determined by conditions of competition on the downstream travel markets, since agents perform a marketing function on airlines' behalf. Simply aggregating BA's total ticket sales without any analysis of whether it was subject to effective constraints on individual route pairs therefore ignored the most important parameter of competition between airlines. BA's success or otherwise on a market for the purchase of travel agency services was overwhelmingly a function of its position on the downstream travel markets. And yet no analysis was made of the relevant downstream markets.

3.5 "SUPERDOMINANCE"

Definition. Because market power exists essentially along a continuum, concerns regarding dominance are at their most acute where a firm's strength approaches a position of near-monopoly. Recognising this concern, a small number of decisions and judgments under Article 82 EC and/or equivalent provisions of national law have expressly referred to a concept of "superdominance." The concept was first mentioned by Advocate General Fennelly in his opinion in *Compagnie Maritime Belge*.[271] Compagnie Maritime Belge (CMB) concerned a liner shipping conference agreement. By virtue of that agreement and other factors, the members of the conference were found to be in a collective dominant position. Advocate General Fennelly did not content himself with finding that the liner conference members were dominant in the relevant market. In view of their 90% market share, he also labelled the group "superdominant" and found, that, in this circumstance, they owed had a particularly onerous duty not to preclude the emergence of new competition:[272]

> "To my mind, Article 8[2] cannot be interpreted as permitting monopolists or quasi-monopolists to exploit the very significant market power which their superdominance confers so as to preclude the emergence either of a new or additional competitor. Where an undertaking, or group of undertakings whose conduct must be assessed collectively, enjoys a position of such overwhelming dominance verging on monopoly...it would not be consonant

[269] *Ibid.*, para. 217.

[270] *Ibid.*, para. 197.

[271] Opinion of Advocate General Fennelly in Joined Cases C-395/96 P and C-396/96P, *Compagnie Maritime Belge Transports SA, Compagnie maritime belge SA and Dafra-Lines A/S v Commission* [2000] ECR I-1365.

[272] *Ibid.*, para. 137.

> with the particularly onerous special obligation affecting such a dominant undertaking not to impair further the structure of the feeble existing competition for them to react, even to aggressive price competition from a new entrant, with a policy of targeted, selective, price cuts designed to eliminate that competitor."

The Court of Justice did not refer to the concept of "superdominance," but did note the quasi-monopolistic position enjoyed by the liner conference. *Compagnie Maritime Belge* is also notable because the Court of Justice was prepared to conclude that even prices above average total cost could be abusive where, *inter alia*, a position approaching a near monopoly existed. A similar fact pattern was noted by the Court of Justice in *Tetra Pak II* where the fact that Tetra Pak held a "quasi-monopolistic position" on the market in question was among the "special circumstances" considered by the Court when holding that the undertaking had infringed Article 82 EC.[273] In *Irish Sugar*, reference was made to the "extensive dominant position" of the undertaking when reaching the conclusion that its conduct amounted to an abuse.[274] Finally, the Commission explicitly referred to the link between an undertaking's degree of dominance and whether or not its conduct constitutes an abuse in *Football World Cup* when it stated that "the scope of the parties' responsibility must therefore be considered in relation to the degree of dominance held by the parties."[275]

National case law has also embraced the concept of "superdominance." Extensive reference was made to this concept in *Napp Pharmaceutical*, a judgment of Competition Appeal Tribunal in the United Kingdom:[276]

> "We for our part accept and follow the opinion of Mr. Advocate General Fennelly in Compagnie Maritime Belge...that the special responsibility of a dominant undertaking is particularly onerous where it is a case of a quasi-monopolist enjoying 'dominance approaching monopoly', 'superdominance' or 'overwhelming dominance approaching monopoly'...Napp's high and persistent market shares put Napp into the category of 'dominance approaching monopoly'—i.e., superdominance—and the issue of abuse in this case has to be addressed in that specific context."

It went on to state that, since Napp held well over 90% of the market share and had only one significant competitor during the period of infringement, "Napp is a superdominant undertaking in both the hospital and community segments with, in consequence, a particularly onerous responsibility not to impair further the structure of the feeble existing competition."[277]

Problems with "superdominance." The concept of superdominance is problematic in several respects. First, Article 82 EC makes no reference to varying degrees of

---

[273] Case C-333/94 P, *Tetra Pak International SA v Commission* [1996] ECR I-5951, paras. 28–31.

[274] Case T-228/97, *Irish Sugar plc v Commission* [1999] ECR II-2969, para. 185.

[275] See also *1998 Football World Cup*, OJ 2000 L 5/55, para. 86 ("[T]he scope of the parties' responsibility must therefore be considered in relation to the degree of dominance held by the parties.").

[276] *Napp Pharmaceutical Holdings Limited Subsidiaries v the Director General of Fair Trading*, judgment of January 15, 2002, para. 219. Although this judgment applied UK law, the relevant section of the UK Competition Act is virtually identical to the wording of Article 82 EC, and the Act requires that it is to be interpreted and applied in a manner consistent with EC competition law.

[277] Joined Cases C-395/96 P and C-396/96P, *Compagnie Maritime Belge Transports SA, Compagnie Maritime Belge SA and Dafra-Lines A/S v Commission* [2000] ECR I-1365, para. 338.

dominance and corresponding levels of responsibility. The rule is clear: all dominant companies should be free to compete by legitimate means, and none should be allowed to compete by exclusionary means. There is no obvious or identifiable reason why companies with especially high market shares should have additional duties not applicable to other dominant companies.

Second, there is no basis in economics for specifying a point in a spectrum of market power in which a firm could be said to acquire "superdominance." Economics recognises two broad concepts: the concept of a monopoly, that is where only one seller exists; and the concept of a dominant price-setting firm that faces a competitive fringe who act as price takers.[278] There is no objective economic test for determining when, outside the situation of pure monopoly, a firm could be said to possess a position of "superdominance." Thus, not only is there no legal basis for "superdominance" in text of Article 82 EC, economics provides no clear basis for saying when it might arise.

Third, to the extent the term "superdominance" implies that the responsibility of a dominant firm not to abuse its position is higher, significant uncertainty would be added to the law. Abuses which are considered contrary to Article 82 EC fall under three headings—exploitation, discrimination and exclusionary conduct. If "superdominance" was to impose a higher degree of responsibility on incumbent firms, the notions of abuse under each of these categories would be require re-definition. A test to establish when "superdominance" exists would also be needed.

Finally, the concept of superdominance in so far as it refers to very high levels of market share, seems beside the point. As discussed in Section 3.2, the main issue is not so much a firm's market share, but whether that share is likely to persist due to barriers to entry. Firms with very high shares may have very little market power if barriers to entry are low; firms with modest shares may enjoy a high degree of market power if protected by entry barriers. The concept of "superdominance" might therefore lead to unnecessary and protectionist intervention.

Conclusion. There would be several practical, legal, and economic problems if the duties imposed on dominant firms were higher when a position of "superdominance" is identified. There is significant doubt that such a position can be accurately identified in economics. Accordingly, the best way to understand "superdominance" is that it merely encapsulates an obvious practical point: undertakings with a high degree of market power usually have greater incentive and ability to abuse their dominance. This should not mean, however, that different legal principles apply (although it may be easier to show anticompetitive effects where a firm with a very high degree of dominance excludes actual or potential rivals).

[278] See DW Carlton & JM Perloff, *Modern Industrial Organisation* (4th edn., Boston, Pearson Addison Wesley, 2005) pp. 105–10.

3.6 COMPARING DOMINANCE UNDER ARTICLE 82 EC AND OTHER COMMUNITY LEGISLATION

Relationship between dominance under Article 82 EC and the EC Merger Regulation. There has been long-standing debate over whether the concept of dominance under Article 82 EC differs from the substantive standard for merger review under the EC Merger Regulation. This debate is partly academic now, since the amended EC Merger Regulation replaced the old substantive test based on whether the merger "creates or strengthens a dominant position as a result of which effective competition...would be significantly impeded" with a test based on "significantly impeding effective competition, in particular as a result of the creation or strengthening of a dominant position" (i.e., "significant lessening of competition" or SLC). Indeed, one of the reasons for adopting the SLC test was that it would have the "additional advantage of not linking the definition of dominance under the [EC] Merger Regulation to any future interpretations given by the [Community Courts] to the concept of dominance under Article 82."[279] The definition of market power under the two regimes has thus been uncoupled. But both Article 82 EC and the EC Merger Regulation are concerned with market power and it is therefore appropriate to note the main differences between the two legal instruments.

The first and most important difference between dominance under Article 82 EC and the SLC test under the EC Merger Regulation is that the former looks at dominance *ex post* whereas the latter involves an *ex ante* assessment. In short, one looks at present, existing dominance; the other assesses whether a notifiable transaction would lead to SLC if approved. A finding of SLC (or in the past dominance) under the EC Merger Regulation therefore has no necessary implications for the presence or absence of dominance under Article 82 EC.[280] This is not merely a matter of perspective, since the prospective nature of the SLC test entails a degree of speculative assessment of future conditions of competition as a result of the notified transaction that is generally irrelevant under Article 82 EC.

For example, in a merger case, a competition authority will need to look at existing evidence of dominance, to see whether it will still exist in future, changed, circumstances. In particular, it will need to see if sufficiently probable future developments, including all companies' reactions to other developments, will increase or lessen or offset dominance-inducing effects which have been identified. The duties of competition authorities to make prospective assessments under merger control raise particularly difficult issues in the area of technology and research-based industries where the effect of future technologies or products may, if sufficiently proximate, require detailed assessment (e.g., pipeline pharmaceutical products). In contrast, under Article 82 EC, if dominance already exists, there is usually no need to see whether it might be eroded in future.

The distinction between *ex post* review under Article 82 EC and *ex ante* control under merger rules, and the consequences for the standard of proof, was a central issue in the

---

[279] See Explanatory Memorandum to the Draft Merger Regulation, OJ 2003 C 20/4, para. 57.

[280] See Joined Cases T-125/97 and T-127/97, *The Coca-Cola Company and Coca-Cola Enterprises Inc v Commission* [2000] ECR II-1733.

Tetra Laval litigation.[281] The Community Courts made two important findings. First, the inherently predictive nature of merger control requires great care in making assessments as to future events, in contrast to the assessment of present or past known facts, as occurs under Article 82 EC:[282]

> "A prospective analysis of the kind necessary for merger control must be carried out with great care since it does not entail the examination of past events—for which often many items of evidence are available which make it possible to understand the causes—or of current events, but rather a prediction of events which are more or less likely to occur in future if a decision prohibiting the planned concentration or laying down the conditions for it is not adopted."

A second finding specific to conglomerate type mergers—where the merging parties' products do not directly overlap, but the combination of a portfolio of products may create scope for exclusionary conduct that would harm rivals—is that the Commission is not obliged to assess under merger control rules whether such conduct would, if carried out, constitute a violation of Article 82 EC.[283] The Court of Justice reasoned that such a finding would be too speculative, although it held that the Commission should take into account the effect of commitments by the merging parties not to engage in certain types of exclusionary acts.

Second, some commentators argue that the threshold for intervention under merger control should be lower than the dominance standard under Article 82 EC.[284] This is based on the argument that public policy should be more hostile to the acquisition of market power by contract or stock purchase than to the unilateral actions of successful firms—most of whom will have built that success by serving customers well. Certainly, there is some evidence that intervention under the EC Merger Regulation has occurred at market share levels that would not be capable of supporting a dominance finding under Article 82 EC.[285] An equivalent application of the concept to Article 82 EC cases would put many firms with relatively low market shares under special responsibility, leading to an excessively interventionist practice.[286] Thus, the main reason for initially

---

[281] Case C-12/03P, *Commission v Tetra Laval BV* [2005] ECR I-987.

[282] *Ibid.*, para. 42.

[283] *Ibid.*, para. 77 ("It follows that, at the stage of assessing a proposed merger, an assessment intended to establish whether an infringement of Article 82 EC is likely and to ascertain that it will be penalised in several legal orders would be too speculative and would not allow the Commission to base its assessment on all of the relevant facts with a view to establishing whether they support an economic scenario in which a development such as leveraging will occur.").

[284] See, e.g., J Vickers, "How Does the Prohibition of Abuse of Dominance Fit with the Rest of Competition Policy?" in *2003 European Competition Law Annual: What Is an Abuse of Dominant Position?* (Oxford, Hart Publishing, 2006 (forthcoming)) ("The threshold of market power that triggers intervention to maintain competitive incentives by preventing anti-competitive structural changes in markets ought to be lower than that which triggers liability for the breach of competition law prohibitions on firms that have become dominant.").

[285] See, e.g., Case COMP/M.1684, *Carrefour/Promodes* (share of 20–30% on procurement market found to raise concerns); Case COMP/M.2337, *Nestlé/Ralston Purina* (35% market share in pet food required remedies); and Case COMP/M.1712, *Generali/INA* (35% share in insurance markets found to create dominance).

[286] The Review of the EC Merger Regulation, 32nd Report of the House of Lords Select Committee on the European Union, HL Paper 165, Session 2001–02, para. 153.

adopting a dominance standard under the EC Merger Regulation—that it contained familiar terminology—is now considered subsidiary to the risk of a potentially misguided application of dominance standards under Article 82 EC as a result of cross-contamination.[287]

A final (and in practice probably the most important) difference between dominance under Article 82 EC and the substantive standard under EC merger control rules is the degree of sophistication of the Commission's assessment under the latter. Article 82 EC has historically been characterised by a lack of economic rigour and the definition of the relevant market and the assessment of dominance have not been immune from this criticism. In contrast, under the EC Merger Regulation, the Commission has routinely made use of quantitative techniques to measure the likely effects of a merger and has also undertaken a qualitative assessment of other factors that is superior to that applied under Article 82 EC.[288] The Commission's on-going review of Article 82 EC will almost certainly mean that the quality of analysis will improve, in particular by applying greater economic rigour.

Relationship to "significant market power" under EC Telecommunications Directives. Under the new regulatory framework (NRF) for telecommunications, one or more undertakings may be designated as having "significant market power" (SMP) and thus subject to *ex ante* regulation under the applicable legislation. Because EC competition law applies in parallel with regulation, the implications of SMP for dominance need to be made clear. The NRF is not entirely clear or consistent in dealing with the relationship between dominance and SMP. According to Article 14(2) of the Framework Directive, "an undertaking shall be deemed to have significant market power if, either individually or jointly with others, it enjoys a position of economic strength affording it the power to behave to an appreciable extent independently of competitors, customers and ultimately consumers."[289] This is the same as the Community Courts' definition of dominance under Article 82 EC.

But the accompanying guidelines on market definition and SMP also make clear that SMP under the NRF does not automatically imply dominance.[290] They state in this regard that the policy objectives behind the designation of SMP are different to Article 82 EC: SMP designates undertakings who, in the short to medium term, would be able to distort competition; dominance under Article 82 EC is only relevant when potentially abusive conduct occurs. A number of other differences between SMP and

[287] *Ibid.*, para. 152 ("When the ECMR was first established, one of the reasons the Committee was in favour of the dominance test was on account of its 'familiar terminology'.").

[288] See N Levy, *European Merger Control Law: A Guide To The Merger Regulation* (Matthew Bender/Lexis Nexis, 2005) Ch. 24 (The Role Of Economics In European Merger Control).

[289] Directive 2002/21 of the European Parliament and of the Council on a common regulatory framework for electronic communications networks and services, OJ 2002 L 108/33, para. 2. See also Commission Guidelines on market analysis and the assessment of significant market power under the Community regulatory framework for electronic communications networks and services, OJ 2002 C 165/6, Part 3, which cite the Community Courts' case law on Article 82 EC in defining SMP.

[290] Commission Guidelines on market analysis and the assessment of significant market power under the Community regulatory framework for electronic communications networks and services, OJ 2002 C 165/6, para. 30.

dominance under Article 82 EC should also be noted. These differences should not be overstated, however: in general, SMP and dominance are similar in approach.

First, SMP applies *ex ante*; Article 82 EC investigations are *ex post*. Thus, the assessment under SMP is more akin to that under the EC Merger Regulation than Article 82 EC. The Commission's guidelines on market analysis and the assessment of significant market power state that "SMP will be assessed using the same methodologies as under competition law" but on the basis of an "appreciation of the future development of the market."[291] National regulatory authorities (NRAs) thus rely on slightly different sets of assumptions and expectations to those relied upon by competition authorities when applying Article 82 EC *ex post*.

Second, the definition of collective dominance under the NRF is less precise than the definition of collective dominance now applied under Article 82 EC. The guidelines on marker definition and SMP put forward a more general checklist of factors that are relevant to the assessment of collective dominance under SMP, without precisely indicating the relative weight and importance of these factors. But this difference is largely a function of the fact that, until recently, the concept of collective dominance under Article 82 EC and the EC Merger Regulation was also vague and included an unhelpful checklist of factors. The NRF has not been updated in the period following clarification of the conditions for collective dominance under EC competition law. As a practical matter, however, collective dominance is probably less important under the NRF since most markets are either competitive or characterised by the presence of a single dominant firm.[292]

A final difference—which is likely to be important in practice—is that NRAs are not "competition authorities" subject to the coordination mechanisms under the Modernisation Regulation. The NRAs are therefore less obliged to apply SMP in a manner consistent with Article 82 EC. It is also unclear to what extent NRAs are required to act consistently with a Commission decision under EC competition law. Regulation and competition law are different Community regimes with different objectives. The general duty on national authorities to act consistently with Community law is clearly less strong where they are expressly mandated to apply regulation in preference to competition law. NRAs thus have greater scope for grounding decisions on a concept of SMP that is not equivalent to that accepted by the Commission, Community Courts, and national competition authorities and courts. The NRF contains a number of mechanisms for consultation between NRA and the Commission and for NRAs *inter se*, but these are primarily intended to ensure the consistent application of the NRF and not to ensure consistency between regulation and competition law.

Decisions of regulatory authorities are of course subject to judicial review, and the courts involved may refer questions of interpretation to the Court of Justice under

---

[291] *Ibid.*, paras. 24, 27, 30, 70, 98, 135.

[292] See M Cave, "Economic Aspects of the New Regulatory Regime" in PA Buiges and P Rey (eds.), *The Economics Of Antitrust Regulation And Regulation In Telecommunications* (Northampton, Edward Elgar, 2004), p. 31.

Article 234 EC (and may do so even if formally national law is being applied).[293] In the long term this should contribute to a greater uniformity of interpretation. However, questions of dominance depend primarily on facts, and not on the type of legal questions that can be asked under Article 234 EC, which means that unsatisfactory or unclear decisions may go unchallenged.

3.7 SUBSTANTIAL PART OF THE COMMON MARKET

Broad concept of "substantial part." The application of Article 82 EC requires a firm to hold a dominant position in a substantial part of the common market. This is a jurisdictional question rather than an economic one. It is also different from the geographic delineation of the relevant market. The latter is part of the definition of the relevant market, while the former requirement is similar to the *de minimis* doctrine under Article 81 EC, i.e., to ensure that cases of minor importance are not caught.

Global or EU-wide markets are clearly "substantial." It is also likely that a market corresponding to the entire territory of a Member State is "substantial," in particular where the firm under scrutiny holds a statutory monopoly.[294] Issues only really arise where the volume of trade affected is very small or the conduct in question concerns a single facility in a Member State. But, even then, the Community institutions have applied an expansive interpretation to the concept of a "substantial part of the common market." The Court of Justice has held that it is not the geographical dimension that matters but the relevance in terms of volume and economic opportunities.[295] For example, the Community institutions have found the test to be satisfied for single facilities such as maritime ports or airports.[296] Even small volumes of trade can be considered "substantial." In *BP* for instance, the Dutch market for petrol was found to be a substantial part of the common market, despite only accounting for 4.6% of the overall EU market.[297]

[293] See Case C-28/95, *A. Leur-Bloem v Inspecteur der Belastingdienst/Ondernemingen Amsterdam 2* [1997] ECR I-4161.

[294] Case 127/73, *Belgische Radio en Televisie v SV SABAM and NV Fonior* [1974] ECR 313, para. 5; Case T-229/94, *Deutsche Bahn AG v Commission* [1997] ECR II 1689; and Case T-228/97, *Irish Sugar plc v Commission* [1999] ECR II 2969, para. 99. The test of substantiality is also satisfied where a Member State grants a contingent series of local legal monopolies that together cover the entire Member State. See Case C-323/93, *Société Civile Agricole du Centre d'Insémination de la Crespelle v Coopérative d'Elevage et d'Insémination Artificielle du Département de la Mayenne* [1994] ECR I-5077, para. 17. See also *Portuguese Airports,* 1999 OJ L 69/31, paras. 21–22.

[295] See Joined Cases 40 to 48, 50, 54 to 56, 111, 113 and 114-73, *Coöperatieve Vereniging "Suiker Unie" UA and others v Commission* [1975] ECR 1663, para. 371.

[296] Case C-179/90, *Merci convenzionali porto di Genova SpA v Siderurgica Gabrielli SpA* [1991] ECR I-5889, para. 15; *Sea Containers v Stena Sealink—Interim measures*, OJ 1994 L 15/8, para. 40; *Flughafen Frankfurt/Main AG*, OJ 1998 L 72/30; Case C-18/93, *Corsica Ferries Italia Srl v Corpo dei Piloti del Porto di Genova* [1994] ECR I-1783; *Portuguese Airports*, 1999 OJ L 69/31, upheld on appeal Case C-163/99, *Portugal v Commission* [2001] ECR I-2613; *Finnish Airports*, OJ 1999 L 69/24; and *Spanish Airports*, OJ 2000 L 208/36.

[297] Case 77/77, *Benzine en Petroleum Handelsmaatschappij BV and others v Commission* [1978] ECR 1513.

Chapter 4

THE GENERAL CONCEPT OF AN ABUSE

4.1 INTRODUCTION

The basic types of abuses under Article 82 EC. Article 82 EC is the major provision of EC competition law that seeks to control anticompetitive unilateral conduct, i.e., conduct that does not require the express or implied cooperation of another party.[1] It prohibits "any abuse by one or more undertakings of a dominant position within the common market…in so far as it may affect trade between Member States." Only "abuse" is banned: creating or having a dominant position is not prohibited. The term "abuse" broadly covers exclusionary or other strategic acts that are designed to extend or maintain the dominant firm's market power, to the detriment of consumers. Exclusionary unilateral acts are "bad" in the sense that they either have no redeeming features from the perspective of consumer welfare—the welfare standard that applies under Article 82 EC—or possess little consumer benefit when compared to the harm that they simultaneously cause.

Broadly speaking, three types of abuses under Article 82 EC have been distinguished: (1) exploitative abuses; (2) exclusionary abuses; and (3) reprisal abuses.[2] Exploitative abuses are pricing and other practices that result in a direct loss of consumer welfare. In economic terms, the dominant firm takes advantage of its market power to extract "rents" from consumers that could not have been obtained by a non-dominant firm or to take advantage of consumers in some other way. Excessive pricing, discussed in Chapter Twelve, is an obvious example, but a number of abusive contractual clauses and other practices carried out by a dominant firm fall into the same category.[3]

Exclusionary abuses—the most common and important category of abuse—concern strategic acts directed against rivals that *indirectly* cause a loss to consumer welfare

---

[1] This definition is only party correct. A number of potential abuses (e.g., exclusive dealing) are expressly based on contractual arrangements. The basic distinction between cooperative arrangements and unilateral conduct is nonetheless correct and useful. In general, competition law is more hostile to collusive arrangements, be they mergers or other agreements, between firms than unilateral conduct. This is mainly on the assumption that competitive harm is generally more likely to occur from two or more firms agreeing to limit their output than unilateral action by one firm. Put differently, it is one thing for a firm to acquire market power through superior products or skill, but another for two or more firms to restrict competition between them in favour of cooperative arrangements that confer market power. This distinction is not necessarily hard and fast—many dominant firms may acquire a monopoly position by means other than skill and foresight (e.g., special rights from the government)—but it is correct, as a general matter, to treat the contractual acquisition of market power differently from unilateral action that resides in market power.

[2] Initially in C Bellamy & GD Child, *European Community Law of Competition* (2nd edn, London, Sweet & Maxwell, 1978). See also J Temple Lang, "Abuse of Dominant Positions in European Community Law, Present and Future: Some Aspects" in Hawk (ed.), *Fifth Fordham Corporate Law Institute* (New York, Law & Business, 1979), pp. 25–83.

[3] See Ch. 13 (Other Exploitative Abuses).

where they unlawfully limit rivals' ability to compete. The key element is the loss to consumer welfare, since legitimate competition that excludes rivals is an essential component of consumer welfare maximisation. Predatory pricing—selling below some measure of cost for exclusionary reasons—is a commonly-cited example of an exclusionary abuse, although actual cases are rare (or undetected). But, as with the means of competing, the range of potential exclusionary acts is myriad and includes matters as diverse as refusal to deal, tying and bundling, price squeezes, discrimination against downstream rivals, discount practices, exclusive dealing, vexatious litigation, the use and abuse of government approval procedures to exclude rivals, and abuses in connection with the adoption of standards or other specifications.

The final broad category of abusive conduct under Article 82 EC concerns reprisal abuses.[4] This involves situations in which a dominant firm punishes or disciplines a rival firm to prevent it from competing aggressively or indirectly seeks to achieve the same end, e.g., by punishing a customer for dealing with a rival firm. For example, in *United Brands*,[5] the Court of Justice held that it was abusive for a dominant supplier to terminate supplies to a distributor on the grounds that the distributor had participated in an advertising campaign for a competitor of the supplier. Similarly, in *Boosey & Hawkes*,[6] Boosey & Hawkes refused all further supplies to a customer who had transferred its central activity to the promotion of a competing brand of musical instruments. An important evidentiary point was that Boosey & Hawkes had embarked on a plan to exclude the competitive threat from that rival and that the refusal to supply the customer was part of that plan.[7] Both cases stand for a general principle that, while a dominant firm can lawfully protect its interests (e.g., by terminating relations with other trading parties), it must act proportionately in doing so and not overreact.

The Community institutions' basic definition of abuse. Building on the basic categorisation of abuses, the Community Courts have articulated a number of different general formulations intended to elaborate on the meaning of the term "abuse." The seminal definition of exclusionary abuses was provided in *Hoffmann-La Roche*, where the Court of Justice defined an abuse as conduct "which, through recourse to *methods different from those governing normal competition* in products or services on the basis of transactions of commercial operators, has the *effect of hindering the maintenance of the degree of competition* still existing in the market or the growth of that competition."[8] Under this definition, the concept of an abuse is anything that cannot be regarded as normal competition based on quality and price *and* which has the effect of restricting competition.

---

[4] See generally J Temple Lang, "Anticompetitive Non-Pricing Abuses Under European and National Antitrust Law" in Hawk (ed.), 2003 *Fordham Corporate Law Institute* (New York, Juris Publication Inc., 2004), pp. 235–340.

[5] *Chiquita*, OJ 1976 L 95/1, confirmed by the Court in Case 27/76, *United Brands Company and United Brands Continentaal BV v Commission* [1978] ECR 207 (hereinafter "*United Brands*").

[6] *BBI/Boosey & Hawkes—Interim Measures*, OJ 1987 L 286/36 (hereinafter "*Boosey & Hawkes*").

[7] *Ibid.*, para. 19.

[8] Case 85/76, *Hoffmann-La Roche & Co AG v Commission* [1979] ECR 461 (hereinafter "*Hoffmann-La Roche*"), para. 6 (emphasis added).

An alternative formulation is to say that abuse is anything that is not legitimate competition or "competition on the merits." Thus, in *AKZO*, the Commission made clear that a dominant firm is entitled to compete on the merits."[9] The Commission added that aggressive, legitimate competition was to be encouraged and that it did not suggest that "large producers should be under an obligation to refrain from competing vigorously with smaller competitors or new entrants."[10] A similar formulation was put forward in *Michelin II*, where the Court of First Instance defined exclusionary conduct as conduct that lacks "objective economic justification."[11]

Other definitions of abuse put forward by the Community institutions suggest that dominant firms have certain responsibilities towards the competitive process. For example, in *Michelin I*, the Court of Justice first used the phrase "special responsibility" in connection with a dominant firm's duty not to abuse its position. According to the Court of Justice, while the finding of dominance is not a recrimination in itself, it means "that, irrespective of the reasons for which it has such a position, the undertaking concerned has a special responsibility not to allow its conduct to impair genuine undistorted competition on the common market."[12]

Uncertainty surrounding the definition of exclusionary conduct. There is currently a great deal of debate among practitioners and antitrust commentators as to what the definition of an exclusionary abuse is or should be. This debate has been prompted by a series of difficulties. First, distinguishing legitimate competition and exclusionary conduct is inherently difficult, since they are very similar in appearance. For example, low prices are the essence of competition but they can sometimes be too low and exclusionary. Put differently, both legitimate competition and exclusionary conduct harm rivals, but, in the former case, such "harm" is an essential part of a properly-functioning competitive process. Second, the ways in which a firm can exclude competitors are myriad: a single, overarching definition of exclusionary conduct therefore might risk being either under-inclusive or over-inclusive.

A third problem is that the Community institutions' definition of an abuse under Article 82 EC is imprecise, and does not encapsulate a normative concept capable of satisfying the basic requirements of the rule of law and legal certainty. "Normal competition," as per *Hoffmann-La Roche*, is a vague phrase, since it begs the question of what is "normal." Conduct carried out by a dominant undertaking that is also routinely carried out by non-dominant firms should be presumed "normal" and efficiency-enhancing. And, yet, the Commission has rejected the notion that a common practice within an industry would necessarily constitute "normal competition."[13]

---

[9] *ECS/AKZO*, OJ 1985 L 374/1 (hereinafter "*AKZO*"), para. 81 (emphasis added), upheld on appeal in Case C-62/86, *AKZO Chemie BV v Commission* [1991] ECR I-3359.

[10] *Ibid.*

[11] Case T-203/01, *Manufacture française des pneumatiques Michelin v Commission* [2003] ECR II-4071 (hereinafter "*Michelin II*"), paras. 107, 110.

[12] Case 322/81, *NV Nederlandsche Banden Industrie Michelin v Commission* [1983] ECR 3461 (hereinafter "*Michelin I*"), para. 10. But see Joined Cases T-191/98, T-212/98 to T-214/98, *Atlantic Container Lines AB and Others v Commission* [2003] ECR II-3275, para. 1460.

[13] See Case COMP/C-3/37.792, *Microsoft*, Decision of March 24, 2004 (hereinafter "*Microsoft*"), not yet published, footnote 877 (citing Case 322/81, *NV Nederlandsche Banden Industrie Michelin v*

"Competition on the merits," and "genuine undistorted competition" are similarly vague. These terms have been defined as competition on the basis of "price, quality and functionality" of the product.[14] But this is unclear and does not provide sufficient limiting principles. For example, all predatory pricing and loyalty discounts are competition based on "price," but they are not always allowed. Tying is competition by adding functionality, but is not always allowed. Finally, the term "special responsibility" fares no better. The Court of First Instance has recently clarified that the term "special responsibility means only that a dominant undertaking may be prohibited from conduct which is legitimate where it is carried out by non-dominant undertakings."[15] In other words, it simply encapsulates a general, obvious statement that conduct carried out by firms that are not dominant may be abusive when carried out by a dominant firm rather that constituting a normative definition in itself.

A fourth problem is that a practice may be regarded as not constituting "normal competition," "competition on the merits," and "genuine undistorted competition" in one situation, but not in others. A good example is unconditional price reductions. The rules established under the *AKZO* line of case law state that, first, prices below average variable cost are presumed abusive, and, second, that prices above average variable cost but below average total cost may be regarded as abusive when they are part of a plan to eliminate a rival firm.[16] From this, one might reasonably assume that an unconditional price cut above average total cost is not abusive. And yet, in *Compagnie Maritime Belge*,[17] the Community Courts found that such prices could, in exceptional cases, constitute an abuse. They indicated that the *AKZO* case law was not exhaustive, i.e., that unconditional price cuts could be unlawful in other circumstances. In other words, the terms "normal competition," "competition on the merits," and "genuine undistorted competition" are not merely vague, but also conclusory. That is, they are defined according to what the Community institutions or national authorities happen to conclude is an abuse in each case. This is highly unsatisfactory.[18]

Fifth, the practical application of Article 82 EC by the Community institutions and national authorities has been criticised as lacking clarity, consistency, and economic

Commission [1983] ECR 3461, para. 57; and Case T-111/96, *ITT Promedia NV v Commission* [1998] ECR II-2937, para. 139).

[14] See, e.g., Comments by M Monti, European Commissioner for Competition, to the speech given by Hewitt Pate, Assistant Attorney General, US Department of Justice, at the Conference "Antitrust in a Transatlantic Context," Brussels, June 7, 2004 ("I think we can both agree that in competition the best should win on the merits, but only on the merits. Whenever dominant companies can use their market power to win in a market for reasons that are not related to the price or quality of their products, then we should consider intervening.").

[15] See Joined Cases T-191/98, T-212/98 to T-214/98, *Atlantic Container Lines AB and Others v Commission* [2003] ECR II-3275, para. 1460.

[16] See *ECS/AKZO*, 1985 OJ L 374/1, upheld on appeal in Case C-62/86, *AKZO Chemie BV v Commission* [1991] ECR I-3359.

[17] *Cewal, Cowac and Ukwal*, OJ 1993 L 34/20, upheld on appeal in Joined Cases T-24/93, T-25/93, T-26/93, and T-28/93, *Compagnie Maritime Belge Transports SA and Others v Commission* [1996] ECR II-1201 and in Joined Cases C-395/96 P and C-396/96 P, *Compagnie Maritime Belge Transports SA and Others v Commission* [2000] ECR I-1365 (hereinafter "*Compagnie Maritime Belge*").

[18] Similar criticisms have been made of Section 2 of the United States Sherman Act. See E Elhauge, "Defining Better Monopolisation Standards" (2003) 56 *Stanford Law Review* 253.

rigour.[19] Among the reasons suggested for this are as follows:[20] (1) the Commission has underestimated the risk of causing harm through inadequately considered statements and actions, in particular about pricing abuses;[21] (2) the only general statements about the application of Article 82 EC have been made by the Commission in specialised contexts, notably the telecommunications industry;[22] (3) the Community Courts analysing antitrust cases in detail only in appeals from the Commission has led to judicial statements very closely tied to the facts of particular cases, rather than general principles; and (4) there are few cases—European companies are less litigious than US companies, and may be less willing to sue dominant enterprises.

Finally, economists have, until recently, largely ignored the assessment of unilateral practices, focusing instead on mergers and other forms of agreements. This has been particularly true in Europe. Moreover, much of the limited economic work on unilateral practices is theoretical rather than empirical.

4.2 THE ECONOMICS OF ABUSIVE UNILATERAL CONDUCT

4.2.1 Evolution Of Economic Thinking On Unilateral Conduct

Overview. As with other areas of antitrust, economic thinking on unilateral conduct has evolved considerably over time. Earlier decisions on unilateral conduct tended to focus on formalistic rules or intuitions that lacked a clear economic foundation. Many of these assumptions were questioned by lawyers and economists associated with the so-called "Chicago School" of antitrust thinking, which explained why practices that had hitherto been regarded as anticompetitive were either legitimate or required further elements before unlawful conduct could be made out. This school of thought had a significant influence on the approach to unilateral conduct under US antitrust law and, though clearly less marked, has also impacted on EC competition law. More recently, a number of commentators have questioned some of the general assumptions made by the Chicago School and identified situations in which conduct that the Chicago School considered to be legitimate might be harmful to consumer welfare. These basic phases

---

[19] See, e.g., B Sher, "The Last of the Steam-Powered Trains: Modernising Article 82" (2004) 25 *European Competition Law Review* 243 ("There is no internal consistency of application. There is no consistency between the application of Art. 82 and the application of other competition provisions of the Treaty. More fundamentally, there is no longer any coherent policy basis for applying Art. 82."); SB Völcker, "Developments in EC Competition Law in 2003: An Overview" (2004) 41(4) *Common Market Law Review* 1048.

[20] See J Temple Lang, "Anticompetitive Non-Pricing Abuses Under European and National Antitrust Law" in BE Hawk (ed.), *2003 Fordham Corporate Law Institute* (New York, Juris Publication Inc., 2004), pp. 235–340.

[21] See J Temple Lang and R O'Donoghue, "Defining Legitimate Competition: How to Clarify Pricing Abuses Under Article 82 EC" (2002) 26 *Fordham International Law Journal* 83–162. See Ch. 7 (Exclusive Dealing, Loyalty Rebates, and Related Practices) for more detail.

[22] See Notice on the application of the competition rules to access agreements in the telecommunications sector—framework, relevant markets and principles, OJ 1998 C 265/2.

of thinking on unilateral conduct are outlined below.[23] More detailed reference is made in subsequent chapters to the evolution of economic thinking where appropriate.

Pre-Chicago thinking. The "pre-Chicago approach" refers to judgments concerning business practices that are not based on an economic analysis of whether firms with market power have the incentive or ability to engage in such practices for anticompetitive reasons. These judgments typically failed to consider whether, and to what extent, those business practices result from pro-competitive efforts to achieve efficiencies. The pre-Chicago approach, instead, is based on what might best be described as "intuitions" about whether practices are objectionable or not. The US Supreme Court used this intuitive approach in many cases that examined unilateral practices in the first three quarters of the twentieth century—a period that is sometimes called the pre-Chicago era in antitrust.

One of the major pre-Chicago contributions is the so-called "leverage doctrine," where a dominant firm seeks to extend its market power in one market into adjacent markets. The belief was that a firm with a monopoly in one market has always an incentive to extend that monopoly to a market for a complementary product, and thereby get two monopoly profits instead of one.[24] Following this reasoning, several types of unilateral practices were considered to be illegal *per se*. One concern was that a monopolist would tie the purchase of its monopoly product to other competitive products in order to extend its monopoly power to previously competitive markets. Tying was therefore illegal *per se*.[25] Another significant pre-Chicago view was that firms could use predatory actions to drive rivals out of the market, thereby creating a monopoly position for the predator.[26] For example, a large firm could set low, predatory prices so that its competitors would lose money and exit. Predatory pricing was considered under the rule of reason, but courts were free to apply reason as they thought best, and many defendants lost.[27]

Chicago School thinking. The Chicago School made a significant contribution to antitrust by applying basic price theory to a variety of practices that were viewed suspiciously by competition authorities and courts. Much has been written on the influence of the Chicago School on modern antitrust.[28] For example, the Chicago

[23] This section draws heavily on AJ Padilla, "Designing Antitrust Rules for Assessing Unilateral Practices: A Neo-Chicago Approach," (2005) 72(1) *University of Chicago Law Review*, 73-98.

[24] See *United States v Terminal Railroad Association*, 224 US 383 (1912).

[25] See *International Salt Co v United States*, 332 US 392, 396 (1947).

[26] See *Standard Oil Co v United States*, 221 US 1 (1911).

[27] See JS McGee, "Predatory Price Cutting: The *Standard Oil* (N.J.) Case" (1958) 1 *Journal of Law and Economics* 137.

[28] See, e.g., R Posner, "The Chicago School of Antitrust Analysis" (1979) 127 *University of Pennsylvania Law Review* 925–26; H Hovenkamp, "Antitrust Policy After Chicago" (1985) 84 *Michigan Law Review* 213; A Cucinotta et al. (eds.), *Post-Chicago Developments in Antitrust Law* (Northampton, Edward Elgar Publishing Company, 2002); ILO Schmidt and JB Rittaler, *A Critical Evaluation of the Chicago School of Antitrust Analysis* (New York, Springer-Verlag, 1989); EW Kitch, "The Fire of Truth: Remembrance of Law and Economics at Chicago, 1932–1970" (1983) *Journal of Law and Economics* 163; MS Jacobs, "An Essay on the Normative Foundations of Antitrust Economics" (1995) 74 *North Carolina Law Review* 219; MW Reder, "Chicago Economics: Permanence and Change" (1982) 20 *Journal of Economic Literature* 1–28; AJ Meese, "Tying Meets the

School's arguments have made significant inroads in the treatment of vertical restraints. One of the earliest Chicago-influenced decisions overruled precedent and analysed territorial restraints imposed by manufacturers on distributors under the rule of reason, rather than finding them illegal *per se*.[29] Some, though by no means all, of this thinking has found its way into Article 81 EC—the major provision of EC competition law dealing with agreements.[30]

In terms of unilateral conduct, two specific insights of the Chicago School should be mentioned. The first, and most famous, is the "single monopoly profit theorem." This holds that in a vertical chain of production there is a single monopoly profit to be had. A firm that has a monopoly at one level of the vertical chain can secure that profit if it charges a monopoly price for its product and everyone else charges a competitive price for their products. It would then prefer to have as much competition as possible at every other level of the chain because that will reduce the price of the final product, increase sales, and thereby maximise the total profit that it receives. This theorem is fatal, or so it appeared, to the leverage doctrine. The monopoly has no incentive to monopolise competitive levels of the chain because it can never get more profit than it currently obtains from having a monopoly at one level.[31] Variants of the single monopoly profit theorem have been applied to tying, essential facilities, and, more broadly, to the analysis of vertical integration and restraints. Another significant Chicago contribution concerns the treatment of predatory pricing claims, which reasoned that predatory pricing was generally irrational unless the predator could reasonably expect to recoup its losses. This view has strongly influenced US Supreme Court decisions, with the result that predatory pricing claims are very difficult to pursue in US courts.[32]

Post-Chicago thinking. Beginning in the 1980s, certain economists began to question the broad assumptions underlying Chicago School thinking. In particular, they found that it was possible to develop models in which leveraging behaviour could be shown to harm consumer welfare.[33] These models show for example that, under certain assumptions, a monopoly has incentives to tie its monopoly product to a secondary

New Institutional Economics: Farewell to the Chimera of Forcing" (1997) 146 *University of Pennsylvania Law Review* 1; WH Page, "The Chicago School and the Evolution of Antitrust: Characterization, Antitrust Injury, and Evidentiary Sufficiency" (1989) 75 *Virginia Law Review* 1221; H Hovenkamp, "Post-Chicago Antitrust: A Review and Critique" (2001) *Columbia Business Law Review* 257; and CS Yoo, "Vertical Integration and Media Regulation in the New Economy" (2002) 19 *Yale Journal on Regulation* 187–205.

[29] See *Continental TV v GTE Sylvania*, 433 US 36 (1977).

[30] See Commission Regulation (EC) No 2790/1999 of December 22, 1999, on the application of Article 81(3) of the Treaty to categories of vertical agreements and concerted practices, OJ 1999 L 336/21; Commission Notice—Guidelines on Vertical Restraints, OJ 2000 C 291/1.

[31] In fact the monopolist even has legitimate incentives to destroy market power at other levels of the chain. A second monopoly for example would result in a higher price for the final product and reduce its sales. This result, known unhelpfully as double marginalisation, dates back to Cournot in 1838. See AA Cournot, *Researches into the Mathematical Principles of Theory of Wealth* (Homewood, RD Irwin, 1986) (1838).

[32] See, e.g., *Brooke Group Ltd v Brown & Williamson Tobacco Corp*, 509 US 209 (1993).

[33] The seminal article is probably MD Whinston, "Tying, Foreclosure, and Exclusion" (1990) 80 *American Economic Review* 837.

product to eliminate competition in the secondary market. More precisely, they show that leveraging a monopoly position in the tying market onto an adjacent tied market may be profitable when the tied market is subject to economies of scale and, therefore, is imperfectly competitive, and when leveraging successfully induces the exit, or deters the entry, of competitors in the tied market. Subsequent articles have identified other sets of assumptions under which a dominant firm has both the incentive and ability to foreclose competition in a secondary market, either to attain an additional monopoly profit there or to protect their monopoly profit in the primary market.[34] Likewise, another strand of modern economics literature undercuts the proposition that firms lack the incentive or ability to engage in predatory pricing.[35]

The post-Chicago approach has had a significant impact on US thinking on unilateral conduct. In *Kodak* the Supreme Court essentially rejected the *per se* legal approach to tying in aftermarkets that would follow from the Chicago School in favour of a rule-of-reason approach that would consider the possibility of anticompetitive behaviour in the particular factual circumstances of the case.[36] The US Department of Justice also relied on post-Chicago approaches in two well-known cases initiated in the late 1990s. In *Microsoft*, it argued that Microsoft had promoted its own browsing software for the purpose of deterring a challenge to its operating system monopoly, i.e., the monopoly maintenance exception to the Chicago leveraging critique.[37] The economic subtext for this case can be found in an article associated with the post-Chicago tradition.[38] In *American Airlines*, the Justice Department also pressed a post-Chicago predatory pricing theory,[39] which was rejected by two courts.[40]

There are also indications that recent Commission decisions attach weight to post-Chicago theories, mainly as support for findings of abuse. For example, in *Microsoft*, the decision found, *inter alia*, that Microsoft's tying its media player to its operating system had spillover effects not only on competition in related products such as media encoding and management software, but also in client PC operating systems for which media players compatible with quality content are an important application.[41] This

[34] See JP Choi and C Stefanadis, "Tying, Investment, and the Dynamic Leverage Theory" (2001) 32 *RAND Journal of Economics* 52; DW Carlton and M Waldman, "The Strategic Use of Tying to Preserve and Create Market Power in Evolving Industries" (2002) 33 *RAND Journal of Economics* 194. For a non-technical summary, see Report by the Economic Advisory Group on Competition Policy, "*An Economic Approach to Article 82*," July 2005, (hereinafter "EAGCP Report").

[35] See P Bolton, JF Brodley and MH Riordan, "Predatory Pricing: Strategic Theory and Legal Policy" (2000) 88 *Georgetown Law Review* 2239. Post-Chicago thinking on predatory pricing is discussed in detail in Ch. 5 (Predatory Pricing).

[36] *Eastman Kodak Co v Image Technical Serv. Inc*, 504 US 451 (1992).

[37] These claims were more or less upheld on appeal. See *United States v Microsoft*, 253 F.3d 34 (D.C. Cir. 2001).

[38] DW Carlton and M Waldman, "The Strategic Use of Tying to Preserve and Create Market Power in Evolving Industries" (2002) 33 *RAND Journal of Economics* 194.

[39] As academic support the Justice Department cited, for example, the post-Chicago theories discussed in P Bolton, JF Brodley, and MH Riordan, "Predatory Pricing: Strategic Theory and Legal Policy" (2000) 88 *Georgetown Law Review* 2239.

[40] *United States v AMR Corp*, 140 F. Supp. 2d 1141 (D. Kan. 2001), *aff'd*, 335 F.3d 1109 (10th Cir. 2003).

[41] See Case COMP/C-3/37.792, *Microsoft*, Commission Decision of March 24, 2004, not yet published, para. 842.

argument echoes economic literature showing that under some assumptions markets can tip and that firms can engage in anticompetitive actions to make markets tip to themselves and thereby establish a monopoly.[42] Similarly, on the refusal to deal abuse, the Commission countered Microsoft's argument that any leveraging was efficient under the "single monopoly profit" theory by pointing to economic thinking to the effect that this theory only applied where the products on the two markets are perfect complements with fixed ratios, which it said did not hold good in the case of the linkages between the Windows PC operating system and server-side products.[43] Finally, in *Wanadoo*, the Commission referred in several places to a recent post-Chicago article on predatory pricing as support for the view that the defendant's actions were a rational and exclusionary strategy of predatory pricing.[44]

4.2.2 Designing Economically Optimal Rules For Unilateral Conduct

Balancing error costs. Lawyers and economists have long advocated that legal rules, including competition law rules, should be designed in a way that makes their practical enforcement efficient.[45] This is premised on the notion that perfect information allowing competition authorities and courts to weigh the procompetitive and anticompetitive effects of a practice in every case will almost never be available. A related point is that, for unilateral conduct, it is not reasonable to expect firms to subject everyday business decisions to detailed balancing analysis to scrutinise their compatibility with competition law. Antitrust commentators therefore propose that legal rules should be guided by several considerations that make their enforcement optimal. The overriding concern is that a legal rule should not allow anticompetitive practices to go unpunished (so-called "false positives" in statistical parlance) and should not result in practices that are procompetitive being wrongly found to be anticompetitive (so-called "false negatives"). Which of the two errors is likely to be more costly depends on whether a particular practice is, on balance, more likely to lead to harm or good.

A good example concerns unconditional price cuts by a dominant firm. Price competition is of course to be encouraged. At some point, however, price competition may cause harm to consumers, where for example a dominant firm charges low prices to cause rivals' exit, and later recoups its investment through increased prices in future. While the precise measurements differ, economists have long argued that firms should be presumed to be acting lawfully when prices are above production costs, usually marginal cost or some analogous measure. This insight is captured by the first rule on predatory pricing in the *AKZO* case, that prices below average variable cost (a proxy for

[42] See, e.g., WB Arthur, "Competing Technologies and Lock-In by Historical Events: The Dynamics of Allocation Under Increasing Returns" (1989) 99 *Economic Journal* 116.

[43] Case COMP/C-3/37.792, *Microsoft*, Commission Decision of March 24, 2004, not yet published, para. 767.

[44] See Case COMP/38.233, *Wanadoo Interactive*, Commission Decision of July 16, 2003, not yet published (hereinafter "*Wanadoo*"), paras. 266, 307, and 334.

[45] See, e.g., R Posner, "An Economic Approach To Legal Procedure And Judicial Administration" (1973) 2 *Journal Of Legal Studies* 399–458. For a recent application more specific to unilateral conduct, see D Evans, "How Economists Can Help Courts Design Competition Rules: An EU And US Perspective" (2005) 28(1) *World Competition* 93–99.

marginal cost) are presumed to be exclusionary.[46] (However, even that presumption has been relaxed in recent years given the legitimate reasons why a dominant firm might price below cost for a period (e.g., introducing new products, building a network).)

Some economists have also devised theoretical models showing that even prices above cost can sometimes harm consumer welfare.[47] The basic idea is that less efficient rivals can bring about reductions in price that are sufficient to compensate for their relative inefficiency, as well as the notion that many firms will become as or more efficient over time. But this insight has not led to general restrictions on above-cost prices cuts under Article 82 EC, precisely because of the very high risk of wrongly condemning aggressive, but legitimate, price competition. Instead, such price cuts have been condemned in only exceptional cases, usually where the firm in question is a virtual monopolist and/or the pricing strategy is part of a series of abusive acts with the same aim.[48] Many commentators would argue that even this exception goes too far and risks false negatives. Nonetheless there is a strong consensus that above-cost unconditional price cuts should be presumed lawful in all but extreme cases.

Form versus effect. An evaluation of the risks of false negatives and positives, and prior beliefs about the degree of benefit and harm of particular practices, has led to the application of different types of tests for antitrust rules. At one extreme are practices that subject to *per se* legality or illegality rules, i.e., the practice is deemed lawful or unlawful without the need for a detailed inquiry into its actual or likely effects on competition. A *per se* rule may be absolute in the sense that no exceptions are permitted or modified in the sense that a rebuttable presumption of legality or illegality applies. *Per se* rules are only appropriate where: (1) experience and logic suggests that the benefit/harm resulting from a practice is so clear and unambiguous that there is no point in wasting court or regulatory resources in investigating its effects; and (2) the risk of false positives or false negatives is small.

At the other extreme lie rule of reason inquiries where the benefits and harm caused by a practice are evaluated. This inquiry may be structured, in the sense that conduct is evaluated through a series of screens to distinguish lawful and unlawful conduct, or unstructured in that harm and benefit are simply assessed and compared. Economists overwhelmingly agree that a rule of reason (or effects) based approach is correct when dealing with unilateral conduct and have criticised past policy under Article 82 EC for its excessive reliance on form over effects. A recent report by the Economic Advisory Group on Competition Policy on Article 82 EC—which was commissioned by the Chief Economist of DG Competition—proposes an effects-based approach for the following reasons:[49]

---

[46] See Case C-62/86, *AKZO Chemie BV v Commission* [1991] ECR I-3359, paras. 70–71. See generally Ch. 5 (Predatory Pricing).

[47] See M Armstrong and J Vickers, "Price Discrimination, Competition, and Regulation" (1993) 41(4) *Journal of Industrial Economics* 335. See generally Ch. 5 (Predatory Pricing).

[48] See, e.g., Joined Cases C–395/96 P and C-396/96P, *Compagnie Maritime Belge Transports SA, Compagnie maritime belge SA and Dafra-Lines A/S v Commission* [2000] ECR I-1365. See generally Ch. 5 (Predatory Pricing).

[49] See Report by the Economic Advisory Group on Competition Policy, "*An Economic Approach to Article 82*," July 2005, p. 6.

> "A more consistent approach would start out from the effects of anticompetitive conduct…and consider the competitive harm that is inflicted on consumers. Adopting such an effects-based approach would ensure that these various practices are treated consistently when they are adopted for the same purpose. In contrast, a form-based approach creates the risk that they will be treated inconsistently, with some practices possibly enjoying a relatively more lenient attitude (e.g., because of different standards). Arbitraging among these different treatments may facilitate exclusion, or induce the dominant firm to adopt alternative exclusionary methods, which may well inflict a higher cost on consumers."

Another way of looking at these types of rules is to consider whether unilateral practices should be assessed on the basis of their form or actual or likely effect. Historically, a number of practices under Article 82 EC could have been considered as subject to modified *per se* legality rules. Exclusive dealing was subject to a strong presumption of illegality in earlier cases such as *Suiker Unie* and *Hoffmann-La Roche*.[50] This presumption has been relaxed in recent cases, most notably in *Van den Bergh*,[51] with the result that exclusive dealing under Article 82 EC is now more aptly characterised as based on the rule of reason, in much the same way as applies under Article 81 EC.

Similarly, regarding predatory pricing, the *AKZO* case suggested that pricing below average variable cost is subject to a *per se* rule. This finding has also been relaxed in recent cases, in line with economic thinking indicating that pricing below average variable cost may have a non-exclusionary explanation. For example, in *Wanadoo*, the Commission did not conclude that the dominant firm's prices were unlawful from the mere fact that they were below average variable cost for a significant period, but in addition looked at their strategic rationale and effects on competition. The current rules might therefore best be described as modified *per se* illegality.

Finally, individualised retroactive loyalty rebates that apply over a relatively long reference period were also effectively subject to a *per se* illegality rule (absent objective justification).[52] Again, however, this rule has been substantially relaxed and has shifted towards a rule of reason-type inquiry, with some structural screens to eliminate unproblematic cases. In sum, there are now virtually no practices that could be described as *per se* unlawful under Article 82 EC.

4.2.3 Recent Advances In Defining Exclusionary Conduct

Overview. Given the uncertain and vague nature of current definitions of exclusionary behaviour, lawyers and economists have made a number of recent proposals that seek to offer a unified definition of exclusionary conduct.[53] A first test is based on the notion of

[50] See Joined Cases 40 to 48, 50, 54 to 56, 111, 113 and 114-73, *Coöperatieve Vereniging "Suiker Unie" UA and others v Commission* [1975] ECR 1663 (hereinafter "*Suiker Unie*"); and Case 85/76, *Hoffmann-La Roche & Co AG v Commission* [1979] ECR 461.

[51] See Case T-65/98, *Van den Bergh Foods Ltd v Commission* [2003] ECR II-4653.

[52] See D Waelbroeck, "*Michelin II*: A *Per Se* Rule Against Rebates by Dominant Companies?" (2005) 1 *Journal of Competition Law & Economics* 149–71. See generally Ch. 7 (Exclusive Dealing, Loyalty Rebates, and Related Practices).

[53] For an overview of the main tests, see J Vickers, "*Abuse of Market Power*," Speech to the 31st conference of the European Association of Research in Industrial Economics, Berlin, September 3, 2004. See also Organisation for Economic Co-operation and Development, "Competition on the Merits," Background Note, May 9, 2005.

profit sacrifice, meaning that exclusionary conduct requires a firm to deliberately forego a more profitable course of action.[54] A closely-related test is the "no economic sense" test, which would treat as exclusionary conduct that would make no economic sense but for its tendency to exclude rivals.[55] A second test is the equally efficient competitor test.[56] This holds that the only conduct that is exclusionary is that which would exclude an equally or more efficient rival. Conduct that excludes less efficient rivals is deemed competition on the merits on the grounds that the competitive process would result in the elimination of such undertakings in any event. The final test suggested is a test based on consumer welfare. Under this test, only conduct that harms consumer welfare, or harms consumer welfare more than it enhances efficiency, is considered exclusionary.[57] This test is expressly rooted in the consumer welfare maximisation objectives of competition law. The main elements of these tests, and the principal criticisms, are outlined below. But the differences between these tests should not be overstated. They all in essence seek to identify situations in which conduct is inefficient and so is anti-consumer and, conversely, to promote efficient conduct that yields consumer benefits over time.

4.2.3.1 The profit sacrifice test and its close relations

Elements of the profit sacrifice test. The profit sacrifice test assumes that a firm would not rationally engage in exclusionary conduct unless it considers that any short-term sacrifice of profits would be less than any expected gains as a result of the exclusion or discouraging of rival firms if the conduct is successful. The most obvious example concerns predatory pricing. The theory is that a firm would not knowingly sell below cost unless it had a reasonable expectation that short-term losses will be less than additional profits that come in the medium- to long-term from the exclusion of rivals. The issue of recoupment—which arguably plays a role under Article 82 EC—in effect seeks to measure whether profit sacrifice would be rational by assessing whether the longer term gains of below-cost pricing are likely to outweigh its short-term costs.

---

[54] The profit sacrifice test was originally proposed by industrial economists in the early 1980s. See J Ordover and R Willig, "An Economic Definition of Predation: Pricing and Product Innovation" (1981) 91 *Yale Law Journal* 8. The test was intended to provide a objective, transparent, and economically based framework for assessing exclusionary unilateral behaviour. The economists defined exclusionary behaviour as a "response to a rival that sacrifices part of the profit that could be earned under competitive circumstances were a rival to remain viable, in order to induce exit and gain consequent additional monopoly profits." *Ibid*., pp. 9–10.

[55] See G Werden, "*The 'No Economic Sense' Test for Exclusionary Conduct*," paper submitted to the British Institute of International and Comparative Law, 5th Annual Antitrust dialogue, London, May 9–10, 2005.

[56] R Posner, *Antitrust Law* (2nd edn., Chicago, University of Chicago Press, 2001) pp. 194–95.

[57] See AI Gavil, "Exclusionary Distribution Strategies by Dominant Firms: Striking a Better Balance" (2004) 72 *Antitrust Law Journal* 3; S Salop, "Section 2 Paradigms and the Flawed Profit-Sacrifice Standard" (forthcoming, 2006) *Antitrust Law Journal*; and M Dolmans, "Efficiency Defences Under Article 82 EC Seeking Profits Or Proportionality? The EC *2004 Microsoft* Case in Context of *Trinko*," 24th Annual Antitrust And Trade Regulation Seminar, NERA, Santa Fe, New Mexico July 8, 2004 (on file with authors).

Recent antitrust case law in the United States has endorsed a profit sacrifice test to some extent, but judicial acceptance of the test has been mixed. In *American Airlines*,[58] the Justice Department (as plaintiff) argued that the appropriate inquiry in a predatory pricing case was whether incrementally-added capacity was money losing, even if the service provided by the incumbent airline as a whole remained profitable on the city pair as a whole. The 10th Circuit held that, even under the standard advanced by the Justice Department, they had failed to demonstrate that the additions of capacity at issue were unprofitable.[59]

In *Trinko*,[60] the Justice Department advocated (as *amicus curiae*) essentially the same sacrifice test for assessing unilateral refusals to deal. Although the Supreme Court majority opinion did not expressly refer to the sacrifice test, it justified past cases in which a duty to deal was imposed on the basis that the defendant was foregoing a more profitable course of conduct in refusing to deal. For example, in its discussion of *Aspen Skiing*, the Court attached importance to the fact that the defendant had refused to deal even when the requesting party offered a price equal to the retail price charged by the defendant downstream. It pointed to the defendant's willingness to forego short-term benefits through "[t]he unilateral termination of a voluntary (and thus presumably profitable) course of dealing," and its "unwillingness to renew the ticket *even if compensated at retail price*," as facts that suggested its "distinctly anticompetitive bent." As a result, the Justice Department has indicated that it plans to assert the sacrifice standard with renewed confidence following *Trinko*.[61]

Criticisms of the profit sacrifice test. The profit sacrifice test has been criticised in important respects. The first set of criticisms is fundamental in nature. Certain commentators have argued that the test is flawed in two critical respects.[62] First, they argue that a number of types of conduct do not involve profit sacrifice, but have been recognised as exclusionary. For example, filing a false or overbroad patent application may be cheaper than filing a correct and properly-defined one. The same point can be made about other forms of non-price predation (e.g., falsely disparaging a rival), reprisal abuses, and anticompetitive forms of raising rivals' costs. A profit sacrifice test would therefore seem to wrongly exclude such abuses.[63]

A second criticism is that a profit sacrifice test could capture a number of forms of highly desirable market activity. For example, in the area of intellectual property or

---

[58] *United States v AMR Corp*, 140 F. Supp. 2d 1141 (D. Kan. 2001), *aff'd*, 335 F.3d 1109 (10th Cir. 2003).

[59] See R Hewitt Pate, "*The Common Law Approach and Improving Standards for Analysing Single Firm Conduct*," Fordham International Antitrust Conference, October 23, 2003.

[60] *Verizon Communications Inc v Law Offices of Curtis V. Trinko LLP*, 540 US 398 (2004) (hereinafter "*Trinko*").

[61] See "*The Struggle For Standards*," remarks by JB McDonald, Deputy Assistant Attorney General, Antitrust Division, US Department of Justice, presented at American Bar Association Section of Antitrust Law, Spring Meeting, quoting *Verizon Communications, Inc v Law Offices of Curtis V. Trinko LLP*, 124 S.Ct. 872 (2004) (emphasis in original).

[62] See E Elhauge, "Defining Better Monopolisation Standards" (2003) 56 *Stanford Law Review* 253.

[63] See Brief for the United States and Federal Trade Commission as *Amici Curiae* Supporting Petitioner, *Verizon Communications, Inc v Law Office of Curtis V. Trinko LLP*, No. 02-682 (docketed US Sup. Ct. Dec. 13, 2002).

major investments in tangible property, the initial investments would typically be unprofitable but for the prospect of later monopoly returns reaped by (lawfully) excluding competitors. A literal application of the sacrifice test might treat such investments as predatory despite the fact that, in general, they clearly benefit consumer welfare by offering a better market option. Of course, it might be argued that good sense would prevail in such circumstances and that the conduct in question would be seen as creating dynamic benefits. But a rule that contains exceptions based on the notion that "we will know them when we see them" is precarious.

Another set of criticisms concerns the ease of application and predictability of the profit sacrifice test in practice. A number of difficulties are said to arise.[64] First, there is the problem of determining the sacrifice: a sacrifice relative to what? It is not clear, for example, whether the profit sacrifice requires a firm to opt for the *most* profitable course of action to avoid a finding of exclusionary conduct or whether it should be required to have passed on a *more* profitable alternative. It is also not clear what degree of sacrifice would be sufficient to establish exclusionary conduct or whether the rule is a strict one, i.e., is any profit sacrifice automatically abusive?

Second, many abuse of dominance cases do not involve extending a monopoly and increasing profits, but actions designed to *maintain* a monopoly. For example, a reprisal abuse may be carried out simply to make clear to rivals and customers that aggressive competition, or actions by customers to support rival firms, or complaints to competition authorities will meet with an immediate response by the dominant firm. In such cases there may be no additional profits resulting from the dominant firm's conduct, but it may serve to insulate an existing dominant position from future erosion. This also exposes a related problem: that the dominant firm's current prices may *already* be above the competitive level, with the result that the absence of higher prices as a result of the exclusionary conduct could falsely show an absence of exclusionary effect on the grounds that no sacrifice occurred, i.e., a variant of the "cellophane fallacy," discussed in Chapter Two (Market Definition).

Finally, although one of the main benefits of the profit sacrifice standard is said to be its objectivity,[65] it is argued that the test would in practice be highly subjective and speculative. In its most basic form, the profit sacrifice test asks a court to assess the dominant firm's likely conduct in the hypothetical absence of an ability to raise prices. This is hypothetical, speculative, and uncertain. Different outcomes could be imagined on the basis of the same set of facts.

The no economic sense test as a variant of profit sacrifice. Criticism of the profit sacrifice test has led the US Department of Justice to argue for a variant of the test: the "no economic sense" test. The Justice Department has argued in recent antitrust cases that it is relevant to ask whether the conduct would make economic sense for the defendant but for its tendency to eliminate or lessen competition. It argues that conduct is not exclusionary or predatory if it would not make economic sense for the defendant

[64] See S Salop, "Section 2 Paradigms and the Flawed Profit-Sacrifice Standard" (forthcoming, 2006) *Antitrust Law Journal*.

[65] See, e.g., M Patterson, "The Sacrifice of Profits in Non-Price Predation" (2003) 18 *Antitrust* 37.

but for its tendency to eliminate or lessen competition.[66] The Justice Department contends that this type of "sacrifice" is more accurate for exclusionary abuses than profit sacrifice, since it entails a choice between a business strategy that would make no business sense but for the probability that the conduct would create or maintain monopoly power.[67]

The no economic sense test addresses some of the criticisms of the profit sacrifice test. In particular, it does not characterise as unlawful every departure from short-run profit maximisation. This would permit investments that confer long-term benefit by allowing a firm to retain exclusive control over its inventions, something which could in theory be regarded as suspect under the profit sacrifice standard. But it is clear in some instances, particularly those involving network effects, that the elimination of competition, and the survival of a single competitor, is beneficial. Investments in network effects of this kind would only make economic sense if rivals are eliminated. It is not clear how such cases would be treated under the no economic sense test, but they could in theory result in a finding of exclusionary conduct.

A further problem is that the no economic sense test involves an assessment of the range of options that were open to the company at the time it embarked on a particular course of conduct. In most cases, the best evidence of a company's options will be its business plans. Assessing whether a course of conduct made sense only if competitors were eliminated on the basis of such plans is extremely difficult in practice. For example, assume that a firm enters a new market in which initial capital costs are very high and it needs to acquire scale and scope economies and learning experience to reduce costs and enter into profitability, i.e., the firm needs to acquire volume. There is no effective way in this scenario of distinguishing between volume growth that is justified in itself and volume growth that is predicated, in whole or in part, on the elimination of a rival. It may be that, in this instance, the firm would pass the no economic sense test on the basis that there was a reasonably-anticipated non-exclusionary reason for its strategy (even if that turned out to be wrong). But this is not obvious and, even if it were, runs the risk of being under-inclusive by allowing exclusionary conduct in the vital early stages of a new market to go unchecked. Of course, these types of cases are difficult under any test, but the point is that the no economic sense test does not appear to have any unique advantages over the profit sacrifice test, or other tests, in this regard.

Conclusion. Both the profit sacrifice and no economic sense tests are useful in that they seek to move the debate on abusive conduct away from a subjective assessment of what is competition on the merits towards a more objective measure of whether conduct is profit maximising or economically rational. But the criticisms of both tests are compelling. In particular, it is not even clear whether the sacrifice test is a single unified substantive standard for assessing all exclusionary conduct or simply a more objective measure of the defendant's intent, or the likely effects of a practice. As one commentator notes, "while the sacrifice test might be useful in assessing wilfulness or intent, it does not naturally yield a substantive standard of what behaviour is

[66] Brief for the United States and Federal Trade Commission as *Amici Curiae* Supporting Petitioner, *Verizon Communications, Inc v Law Office of Curtis V. Trinko LLP*, No. 02-682 (docketed US Sup. Ct. Dec. 13, 2002).

[67] *Ibid.*

exclusionary. There is no escape from the fundamental question of what is [exclusionary]."[68] In other words, the sacrifice test may, at best, constitute a useful characterisation of certain types of abuses—in particular pricing abuses—it is not, in itself, capable of identifying exclusionary conduct and clearly distinguishing it from legitimate conduct.

4.2.3.2 Equally efficient competitor test

Elements of the equally efficient competitor test. Exclusionary conduct has also been defined as conduct that would exclude an equally efficient rival firm. This definition was originally proposed by Judge Posner in his seminal book, *Antitrust Law.* The latest edition offers the following definition of exclusionary conduct:[69]

> "[T]he plaintiff must first prove that the defendant has monopoly power and second that the challenged practice is likely in the circumstances to exclude from the defendant's market an equally or more efficient competitor. The defendant can rebut by proving that although it is a monopolist and the challenged practice exclusionary, the practice is, on balance, efficient...[P]ractices that will only exclude less efficient firms, such as a monopolist's dropping his price nearer to (but not below) its costs, are not actionable, because we want to encourage efficiency. Only when monopoly power is used to discourage equally or more efficient firms and thus perpetuate a monopoly not supported by superior efficiency should the law step in. Even then, it should be alert to the possibility that the exclusionary effect of the monopolist's practice is offset by efficiency gains."

The equally efficient test certainly has some basis under Article 82 EC. For example, the *AKZO* predatory pricing rules are grounded in the economic insight that a profit-maximising dominant firm should be allowed to price down to the level of its average variable costs. This applies even if the dominant firm's costs are lower than those of rivals. Similarly, the test usually applied in margin squeeze cases—whether the dominant firm's own downstream arm could trade profitably if it had to pay the same input prices as third parties—relies on an equally efficient competitor test. Indeed, in *Bronner*, Advocate General Jacobs made clear that "the primary purpose of Article 8[2] is to prevent distortion of competition—and in particular to safeguard the interests of consumers—rather than to protect the position of particular competitors."[70] Consumers are generally best served by the most efficient firms, i.e., those with the lowest costs.

Criticisms of the equally efficient competitor test. A number of criticisms can be made of the equally efficient competitor test. First, less efficient competitors can, in theory, enhance consumer welfare when the increased competition they bring in the market benefits consumers more than the cost of their relative inefficiency.[71] For this

[68] See J Vickers, "*Abuse of Market Power*," Speech to the 31st conference of the European Association of Research in Industrial Economics, Berlin, September 3, 2004.

[69] R Posner, *Antitrust Law* (2nd edn., Chicago, University of Chicago Press, 2001) pp. 194–96.

[70] See Opinion of Advocate General Jacobs in Case C-7/97, *Oscar Bronner GmbH & Co KG v Mediaprint Zeitungs- und Zeitschriftenverlag GmbH & Co KG, Mediaprint Zeitungsvertriebsgesellschaft mbH & Co KG and Mediaprint Anzeigengesellschaft mbH & Co KG* [1998] ECR I-7791, para. 58.

[71] See, e.g., M Armstrong and J Vickers, "Price Discrimination, Competition and Regulation" (1993) 41(4) *Journal of Industrial Economics* 334. See also A Edlin, "Stopping Above-Cost Predatory Pricing" (2002) 111 *Yale Law Journal* 941.

reason, the duties imposed on dominant firms under Article 82 EC are not limited to equally efficient competitors, but, exceptionally, may include duties towards less efficient firms. Under the *CEWAL* line of case law, unconditional price cuts that remain above the dominant firm's average total costs may be abusive in certain circumstances. Chapter Five (Predatory Pricing) criticises rules seeking to place restrictions on unconditional above-cost price cuts, mainly on the grounds that they are in practice likely to chill desirable competition, but it is undeniable that a number of existing rules under Article 82 EC assume that less efficient firms can confer a net benefit on consumer welfare. This suggests that the "equally efficient rival" test could not be unreservedly accepted under Article 82 EC.

A second problem concerns the definition of equal efficiency where the dominant firm has a first mover or some other cost advantage over new entrants or rivals have not yet reached their minimum efficient scale. For example, in the area of conditional above-cost pricing schemes (e.g., loyalty rebates), discussed in Chapter Seven, much of current uncertainty in the law stems from how to treat economies of scale for purposes of defining an "equally efficient firm." The objection in such cases is usually that the dominant firm's large volume of past sales gives it a scale or scope advantage over rivals and that, by extending this advantage to marginal units and customers, the dominant firm can, in certain instances, offer prices at the margin that a rival only competing for the marginal units cannot match. While there is some merit in the view that only the most efficient firm should serve a customer, the Commission has taken the opposite approach in several cases. Whether this is correct or not is discussed elsewhere in this work.

Third, for certain types of abuses, the concept of equal efficiency is of limited use when assessing the legality of conduct. For example, in the case of false declarations by a dominant firm to regulatory approval agencies, or concealment of essential patents within the context of standard setting organisations, rivals' relative efficiency will be of little relevance if the action in question materially limits their access to the market. Of course, a less efficient firm is, all things equal, likely to be more adversely affected by conduct of this kind by a dominant firm than an equally efficient one, but this issue goes more to the effects of the practice rather than the definition of operational rules as to when certain conduct is abusive or not.

Finally, the equally efficient competitor test may require complex balancing exercises in some cases where the conduct would harm an equally efficient firm, but generates efficiencies sufficient to offset this harm. Of course, efficiencies, if asserted, would also need to be assessed under any other test for exclusionary abuses, but the point is that the outcome of the equally efficient competitor test may not always be predictable by a firm at the time when it embarks on a particular course of action.[72]

[72] Another efficiency-based test, proposed by Professor Elhauge, focuses on whether the alleged exclusionary conduct increases the firm's dominance because it enhances its own efficiency or only because it limits rivals' production. He states as follows: "The proper monopolisation standard should instead focus on whether the alleged exclusionary conduct succeeds in furthering monopoly power (1) only if the monopolist has improved its own efficiency or (2) by impairing rival efficiency whether or not it enhances monopolist efficiency...which would permit the former conduct and prohibit the

Conclusion. The equally efficient competitor certainly captures an important insight under competition law: that less efficient firms should not, in general, receive any protection from aggressive competition, since consumers are best served by more efficient firms. To hold otherwise risks protecting competitors, not competition. But a number of valid criticisms can be made of this general statement. First, at least on a theoretical level, consumers can benefit from the presence of less efficient firms on the market (though the practical effect of rules protecting less efficient firms may lead to net harm). Second, a definitional issue arises as to define equal efficiency where the dominant firm has a first mover advantage or significant scale of scope advantages over rivals. And finally, equal efficiency is of limited relevance where the activity in question concerns non-market conduct, such as abusing regulatory approval processes. However, a good case can be made for saying that conduct harming an equally efficient firm should be presumed abusive, absent compelling efficiencies. The equally efficient competitor test therefore offers perhaps the most promising basic economic test for exclusionary conduct.

4.2.3.3 Consumer welfare test

Elements of the consumer welfare test. The final test seeks to shift the focus away from the economic motivation for the alleged exclusionary conduct, and the relative efficiency of competitors, towards an assessment of whether the dominant firm's practices had, or are likely to have, a material adverse effect on consumer welfare.[73] Under this test, exclusionary conduct violates Article 82 EC if "it reduces competition without creating a sufficient improvement in performance to fully offset these potential adverse effects on prices and thereby prevent consumer harm."[74] In other words, only conduct that produces anticompetitive effects overall would be regarded as exclusionary. An analysis of whether the conduct causes net harm to consumer welfare would take account of all available information relevant to the likely effects of conduct on consumers. The most relevant evidence is output and prices, but quality and

latter." This test certainly has certain advantages over some of the other tests. In particular, it avoids complex *ex post* balancing acts where conduct is both exclusionary and efficient. It also treats efficiency-enhancing conduct by a dominant firm as presumptively lawful, whereas in certain situations under the profit sacrifice test it might not be (e.g., long-term investments in intellectual property or tangible assets). Use of vague phrases such as "competition on the merits" and "normal competition" is also avoided under this test. But use of this test as an operational rule remains untested in practice. It would still need to be decided whether conduct is efficiency-enhancing or efficiency-reducing, which is often complex. Moreover, the articulation of the test by Elhauge focuses mainly on refusals to deal where the trade off between short-term static efficiency and long-term dynamic efficiency is clearer. It is not clear how it would apply in other situations where the trade offs to be made are less capable of measurement. See E Elhauge, "Defining Better Monopolisation Standards" (2003) 56 *Stanford Law Review* 253. The test has received endorsement from the OECD: see Organisation for Economic Cooperation and Development, "Competition on the Merits," Background Note, May 9, 2005, para. 65.

[73] See AI Gavil, "Exclusionary Distribution Strategies by Dominant Firms: Striking a Better Balance" (2004) 72 *Antitrust Law Journal* 3; S Salop, "Section 2 Paradigms and the Flawed Profit-Sacrifice Standard" (forthcoming, 2006) *Antitrust Law Journal*; and M Dolmans, "Efficiency Defences Under Article 82 EC Seeking Profits Or Proportionality? The EC *2004 Microsoft* Case in Context of *Trinko*," 24th Annual Antitrust And Trade Regulation Seminar, NERA, Santa Fe, New Mexico July 8, 2004 (on file with authors).

[74] See S Salop, "Section 2 Paradigms and the Flawed Profit-Sacrifice Standard" (forthcoming, 2006) *Antitrust Law Journal*.

innovation may also play a role. There is some divergence among proponents of the consumer welfare test regarding whether efficiencies should be assessed on the basis of whether they simply outweigh any inefficiencies,[75] or subject to a more detailed proportionality inquiry.[76] The latter has two elements. First, it would need to be shown that any harm caused by the dominant firm's conduct is necessary to achieve the overall efficiencies. Second, it would need to be assessed whether the harm caused to competition is disproportionate when compared to any benefits that it brings.

The consumer welfare test certainly has some pedigree in the case law in Europe and elsewhere, as well as in the wording of Article 82(b) which uses the phrase "prejudice to consumers." In the various Microsoft proceedings, the United States Court of Appeals and the Commission essentially applied a consumer harm standard to the various practices alleged.[77] The United States Court of Appeals elaborated a multi-stage analysis of the various alleged exclusionary practices. First, the plaintiff has to show that consumers would be harmed. Second, if such harm is shown, the defendant may offer a procompetitive justification for its conduct. Third, the procompetitive justification can be rebutted by the plaintiff or its positive impact on consumers shown to be outweighed by its negative effects on consumers.[78] On the facts, the Court performed little actual balancing, since it was clear, on the evidence, that most of Microsoft's conduct was overwhelmingly anticompetitive or procompetitive. For example, regarding the claim that Microsoft had deceived Java developers about the Windows-specific nature of the tools, the Court noted that no efficiency justification had been advanced by Microsoft.

A more explicit balancing exercise was undertaken by the Commission in Microsoft. The Commission found that, in relation to the tying of Windows Media Player (WMP) with Windows operating system (OS), Microsoft had "not submitted adequate evidence to the effect that tying WMP is objectively justified by procompetitive effects which would outweigh the distortion of competition caused by it...what Microsoft presents as the benefits of tying could be achieved in the absence of Microsoft tying WMP with Windows."[79] In particular, the Commission found that: (1) ease of use could be achieved without tying (OEMs could do the bundling at no cost to Microsoft);[80] (2) distribution efficiencies were minor and did not outweigh distortion of competition;[81] (3) there was no evidence of technically superior performance due to

---

[75] See AI Gavil, "Exclusionary Distribution Strategies by Dominant Firms: Striking a Better Balance" (2004) 72 *Antitrust Law Journal* 3.

[76] See PE Areeda & H Hovenkamp, *Antitrust Law* (2nd edn., New York, Aspen Publishers, 2002) para. 651a.

[77] See *United States v Microsoft*, 253 F.3d 34, 59 (D.C. Cir. 2001); and Case COMP/C-3/37.792, *Microsoft*, Commission Decision of March 24, 2004, not yet published.

[78] *Ibid.*

[79] Case COMP/C-3/37.792, *Microsoft*, Commission Decision of March 24, 2004, not yet published, para. 970.

[80] *Ibid.*, para. 970.

[81] *Ibid.*, para. 956ff.

code integration of WMP with the OS;[82] and (4) platform efficiency (i.e., desire to keep applications focused on Microsoft interfaces) was not a recognised efficiency.[83]

More generally, the consumer welfare test, if accepted, would unify the principles concerning mergers and other agreements with those under Article 82 EC. Cooperative agreements between firms that restrict competition are subject to an express balancing act under Article 81(3), including an assessment whether the anticompetitive effects are necessary and proportionate to achieve the alleged efficiencies. The Commission's Guidelines on Article 81 EC provide that "for an agreement to be restrictive by effect it must affect actual or potential competition to such an extent that on the relevant market negative effects on prices, output, innovation or the variety or quality of goods and services can be expected within a reasonable degree of probability."[84] Similarly, efficiencies under EC merger control are subject to the conditions that they: (1) benefit consumers; (2) result from the merger; and (3) are verifiable. A sliding scale is also applied, i.e., mergers with the greatest scope for causing consumer harm also require the most compelling evidence of counterbalancing efficiencies.[85]

Criticism of the consumer welfare test. The consumer welfare test presents a number of difficulties. While balancing procompetitive and anticompetitive effects may be appropriate when firms choose to make an agreement—in particular when, as under merger control rules, that agreement is subject to mandatory prior approval—judging unilateral conduct in the same way is precarious and might lead to haphazard outcomes. In particular, a firm embarking on a course of conduct *ex ante* may be unsure as to where the balance between procompetitive and anticompetitive aspects lies and when such effects will materialise. Much would depend on the effect of a practice on the dominant firm's rivals, which the dominant firm cannot generally be expected to know. Moreover, what a firm expects *ex ante* may turn out to be different to what occurs *ex post*. These problems are most likely to be acute in markets in which technology evolves rapidly and new entry is a strong feature, since actual market outcomes may differ materially from many firms' expectations.

Proponents of the consumer harm test have responded to these criticisms with several clarifications. First, they argue that any balancing would not turn courts and competition authorities into central planners in that it would require them to apply a total welfare standard, i.e., comparing the harm to consumer welfare with the benefits to producer welfare. Second, they say that courts and competition authorities would not be required to apply sophisticated quantitative techniques to measure the probability and weight of certain effects. Instead, they would apply a preponderance of evidence approach to determine whether the benefits and harm are each proven by the evidence and, if so, to compare which is greater. Third, proponents argue that firms would not be judged *ex post*, but based on the types of effects that were reasonably foreseeable *ex ante*, even if they turned out to be wrong. Finally, issues of uncertainty are said to be exaggerated. Most cases, they say, can be resolved at an early stage without the need

[82] *Ibid*., para. 958.

[83] *Ibid*., para. 962.

[84] See Guidelines on the application of Article 81(3) of the Treaty, OJ 2004 C 101/97, para. 24.

[85] See Guidelines on the assessment of horizontal mergers under the Council Regulation on the control of concentrations between undertakings, OJ 2004 C 31/5, paras. 80–86.

for complex balancing exercises, either because there is no material harm to consumers or because it is clear that the conduct in question is overwhelmingly harmful or beneficial. But, even with these clarifications, it is clear that the consumer harm test could present significant complexities in many cases and that it will not be easy for a dominant firm to apply such a test *ex ante*.

Conclusion. The consumer harm test undoubtedly asks the correct theoretical question for assessing unilateral conduct: does it cause net harm to consumers? This test has a clear basis under Article 82(b), which mentions conduct that "limits production" to the prejudice of consumers. It also has some pedigree in the decisional practice and case law under Article 82 EC—most recently *Microsoft*—and is consistent with the overall assessment of anticompetitive effects under Article 81 EC and the substantive analysis under EC merger control. But whether all unilateral conduct should be subject to such an overarching inquiry is questionable. What unilateral conduct a firm can engage in without violating the law should be subject to clear rules in all but exceptional cases, without the need to balance exclusionary effects against procompetitive aspects.

Although proponents of the consumer harm test have made its operational features as useful as possible, complex and precarious balancing acts are still likely to be necessary in marginal cases where the cost of error is likely to be high. Moreover, if issues of proportionality come into play, economics contributes very little by way of predictability and the outcomes will represent matters of policy rather than precision. Of course it might be argued that much the same exercise is sometimes conduct under Article 81 EC and EC merger control. But cases involving agreements are different in the sense that the firms can always choose not to make an agreement, or to make a different agreement, or amend some aspect of it to comply with objections under competition law. The firms are also much more likely to have detailed knowledge of the effect of an agreement on their output and to be able to quantify the synergies created by cooperation. The same cannot generally be said of most unilateral conduct.

4.3 THE CATEGORIES OF ABUSE UNDER ARTICLE 82 EC

Overview. There is no statutory definition of "abuse" in Article 82 EC. Instead, it merely lists four categories of abusive conduct, which the Community institutions and national authorities have elaborated upon in several cases. The four clauses of Article 82 EC can, generally, be classified as exploitative, exclusionary, or reprisal abuses. But some abuses, such as discrimination or tying, can be exploitative or exclusionary, or both at the same time. Indeed, some commentators argue that, ultimately, the only conduct that is truly abusive is that which has a material adverse effect on consumer welfare in the form of exploitation of market power. In other words, it has been suggested that there is only one type of anticompetitive unilateral action—that which is exploitative.[86] This view is perhaps a valid overall comment, but it is nonetheless important, for analytical reasons, to be clear about which clause of Article 82 EC applies, when, and what the scope of that clause is. In each case, the

[86] This distinction was first mentioned in various works by Professor Eleanor Fox. See, e.g., E Fox, "We Protect Competition, You Protect Competitors" (2003) 26(2) *World Competition* 149.

legal and economic principles are somewhat different, even if, at the same time, it is important that the overall concept of an abuse should have a unified meaning.

4.3.1 Exploitative Abuses (Article 82(a))

Excessive prices. Article 82(a) covers exploitative conduct, that is "directly or indirectly imposing unfair purchase or selling prices or other unfair trading conditions." This covers taking undue advantage of consumers by using market power to charge grossly excessive prices or impose unjustifiably onerous or unfair terms. The Community institutions have generally applied a two-stage test to assess whether a price is excessive. This test requires, first, comparing actual costs and prices (the price-cost limb of the test), and, second, determining whether a price is excessive in itself or by comparison to competitors' products (the price comparison limb of the test).[87] The second limb of the test is in practice crucial, since there are a variety of legitimate reasons why prices may significantly exceed cost.

Pursuing excessive pricing arguably only makes sense in cases where there are significant barriers to entry that cannot be overcome by new entry investments. Absent these conditions, competition is usually a better way to remedy excessive prices given the enormous difficulties of identifying a "competitive" price. As noted in Chapter Twelve (Excessive Prices), however, excessive pricing decisions are rarely taken by the Commission due to its reluctance to regulate prices using general competition law powers. National cases are more common though.

Unfair contractual terms and conditions. A second category of exploitative abuse, discussed in Chapter Thirteen (Other Exploitative Abuses), concerns unfair terms and conditions. There is no clear definition of these abuses, but they essentially concern contractual clauses that are unfair in that the dominant firm takes advantage of its market power to impose terms that could not be imposed by a firm that did not have market power. As the Commission's 1965 Memorandum on the Concentration notes, "an improper exploitation of a dominant position must be assumed when the dominant firm utilises the opportunities resulting from its dominance to gain advantages it could not gain in the face of practicable and sufficiently effective competition."[88] In other words, abuse consists of taking advantage of dominance.[89]

Examples of unfair contract terms and conditions include:[90] (1) contractual clauses preventing a customer from adding accessory parts to a machine purchased from a dominant supplier (or adding or removing parts); (2) the need to obtain prior permission from the dominant supplier for the resale or transfer of the equipment; (3) exclusive rights to repair and maintain a machine for the lifetime of that machine; (4) equipment leases of excessive duration; (5) a clause requiring members of a copyright-collection society to

---

[87] See Case 27/76, *United Brands Company and United Brands Continentaal BV v Commission* [1978] ECR 207.

[88] Mémorandum sur le Problème de la Concentration dans le Marché Commun (December 1, 1965), reprinted in Revue Trimestrielle de Droit Européen 651–77 (1966), at 670 (reprinted in (1966) 26 *Common Market Law Review* 1–30), para. 24.

[89] See R Joliet, "Monopolisation and Abuse of Dominant Position" (1970) 31 *Collection Scientifique de la Faculté de Droit de l'Université de Liége*.

[90] See Ch. 13 (Other Exploitative Abuses) for more detail.

assign all of their present and future rights to the society, including for a period of five years following their withdrawal from the society; and (6) long-term maintenance contracts allowing a dominant firm to unilaterally set the price of maintenance. Some of these clauses are also objectionable because they have the added effect of excluding rival firms, but it is nonetheless clear that unfair trading conditions and terms constitute an independent ground of violation under Article 82(a).

4.3.2 Exclusionary Abuses (Article 82(b))

The need for a unified basis for exclusionary abuses. A legitimate question is whether it is useful or necessary to have an overall definition of exclusionary abuses or whether it is sufficient to simply define operational rules depending on the categorisation of the specific practice at issue. The latter approach would be highly problematic. Significant difficulties would arise if the notion of an abuse depended on the formal categorisation of a practice, since a number of practices fit into multiple categories, which could lead to different outcomes depending on how they happened to be categorised. Take for example the abuse of margin squeeze, discussed in Chapter Six, where a vertically-integrated dominant firm charges a price, or combination of prices, that renders downstream rivals' activities uneconomic. This practice might be categorised as an "excessive" upstream price (or, more precisely, one that is excessive in relation to the downstream price). Alternatively, it might be categorised as predatory pricing by a vertically-integrated dominant firm. Margin squeezes also involve discrimination, since the dominant firm in effect discriminates in favour of its own downstream business. Finally, another characterisation of margin squeezes is that they are simply a constructive refusal to deal: the dominant firm will only deal on terms that render rivals uneconomic. Similar comments can be made in relation to other abuses.[91] Accordingly, it would not be helpful or consistent to simply analyse practices according to their formal categorisation.

None of this is to say, however, that it is not meaningful to analyse specific practices and the operational rules that have been put forward for assessing such practices, which is essentially the approach adopted in the remainder of this work. The point is that there must be an overall coherent framework for the assessment of exclusionary abuses and, within that framework, the operational rules that most accurately capture prior beliefs about the type of harm caused by a specific practice should be developed. The types of rules may vary from practice to practice but there should be no overall difference in treatment between practices that broadly raise the same economic issues.

---

[91] See Report by the Economic Advisory Group on Competition Policy, "*An Economic Approach to Article 82*," July 2005, p. 5 ("For example, predatory pricing can take the form of selective rebates, targeted at the rival's prospective customers. Alternatively, the predator can engage in explicit discrimination and charge more attractive prices or, more generally, offer better conditions to these customers. Other instruments in the predator's toolbox include implicit discrimination (e.g. in the form of fidelity or quantitative rebates that are formally available to all, but in fact tailored to the specific needs of the targeted customers) and mixed bundling or tying, when these customers are particularly interested in the bundle in question. To take another example, a firm that controls a key input may distort competition in a downstream market by refusing to deal with independent downstream firms; alternatively, it can engage in exclusive dealing arrangements or engage in explicit or implicit price discrimination such as mentioned above; yet other instruments include specific (in-)compatibility choices, physical or commercial tying, and so forth.").

Article 82(b): the legal basis for defining exclusionary conduct. Article 82(b) states that "limiting production, markets or technical development to the prejudice of consumers" is illegal. Unlawful foreclosure or handicapping of competitors, by which competition is reduced still further, are examples of "limiting production." Limiting production is the most frequent and important category of abuse in practice, since it broadly covers any type of exclusionary conduct that limits rivals' possibilities and causes harm to consumers. And in the same way as firms can compete in a myriad of ways, so too they can seek to exclude rivals through a multiplicity of strategies. The vast majority of infringement decisions under Article 82 EC have concerned exclusionary abuses and, therefore, Article 82(b).

Article 82(b) has unique advantages as the legal basis for defining exclusionary conduct. It is expressly based, as it should be, on the words of the EC Treaty. Most importantly, it captures the two fundamental insights of any sensible definition of exclusionary conduct. The first is that it ensures that only conduct that results in output limitation (or "limiting production") is considered exclusionary. All exclusionary conduct results in the limitation of either the dominant firm's production, or, more likely, that of competitors (either because rivals are forced to exit the market or remain in the market but face marginalisation due to increases in their costs caused by the dominant firm's strategic actions). Although the Community Courts do not always refer to specific clauses of Article 82 EC in their judgments, multiple judgments have confirmed that Article 82(b) captures both types of limitation, i.e., it prohibits a dominant enterprise from limiting the production, marketing or development of its competitors, as well as its own.[92] The Commission has also applied Article 82(b) in its seminal decision in *Microsoft*,[93] where Microsoft's conduct was characterised as

---

[92] See, e.g., Joined Cases 40 to 48, 50, 54 to 56, 111, 113 and 114-73, *Coöperatieve Vereniging "Suiker Unie" UA and others v Commission* [1975] ECR 1663, paras. 399, 482–83, and in particular paras. 523–27; Case 41/83, *Italy v Commission* (*British Telecommunications*) [1985] ECR 873; Case 311/84, *Centre belge d'études de marché - Télémarketing (CBEM) v SA Compagnie luxembourgeoise de télédiffusion (CLT) and Information publicité Benelux (IPB)* [1985] ECR 3261, para. 26; Case 53/87, *Consorzio italiano della componentistica di ricambio per autoveicoli and Maxicar v Régie nationale des usines Renault* [1988] ECR 6039; Case 238/87, AB *Volvo v Erik Veng (UK) Ltd* [1988] ECR 6211; Joined Cases C-241/91P, *Radio Telefís Éireann (RTE) and Independent Television Publications Ltd (ITP) v Commission* (*Magill*) [1995] ECR I-743, para. 54; Case C-41/90, *Klaus Höfner and Fritz Elsner v Macrotron GmbH* [1991] ECR I-1979, para. 30; Case C-55/96, *Job Centre coop arl* [1997] ECR I-7119, paras. 31–36; and Case C-258/98, *Giovanni Carra and Others* [2000] ECR I-4217. For commentary, see J Temple Lang, "Abuse of Dominant Positions in European Community Law, Present and Future: Some Aspects" in BE Hawk (ed.), *Fifth Fordham Corporate Law Institute* (New York, Law & Business, 1979) pp. 52, 60; J Temple Lang, "Anticompetitive Non-Pricing Abuses Under European and National Antitrust Law" in BE Hawk (ed.), 2003 *Fordham Corporate Law Institute* (New York, Juris Publication Inc., 2004), pp. 235–340; C Bellamy & GD Child, *European Community Law of Competition* (2nd edn, London, Sweet & Maxwell, 1978) pp. 754–55; L Ritter, DW Braun and F Rawlinson, *EC Competition Law–A Practitioner's Guide* (2nd edn., The Hague, Kluwer Law Institute, 2000) pp. 362–63; M Waelbroeck & A Frignani, *European Competition Law* (New York, Transational Publishers Inc, 1999) p. 551; and P Mercier, O Mach, H Gilliéron & S Affotten, *Grands Principes du Droit de la Concurrence: Droit Communautaire: Droit Suisse*, *Dossiers de Droit Europeen No. 7* (Geneve, Helbing et Lichtenhahn, 1999) pp. 260–65.

[93] See Case COMP/C-3/37.792, *Microsoft*, Commission Decision of March 24, 2004, not yet published, Section 5.3.1.3.1 ("Microsoft's refusal to supply limits technical development to the prejudice of consumers") and paras. 693 et seq.

limiting innovation to the prejudice of consumers. The second key insight captured in Article 82(b) for defining exclusionary conduct is that the only output limitation of interest under Article 82 EC is that causing prejudice to consumers. Article 82(b) makes it clear that a dominant company may limit its rivals' possibilities if no prejudice to consumers results, such as by offering better products or lower prices.

No other clause of Article 82 EC captures these two key insights of exclusionary conduct—that it limits production and causes prejudice to consumers—explicitly, even if implicitly consumer welfare concerns necessarily underpin the other clauses of Article 82 EC too. Article 82(a) deals mainly with exploitative abuses: "fairness" is not an objective or useful criterion for defining exclusionary conduct, even if, in some sense, a dominant firm's duty not to engage in exclusionary acts broadly involves elements of fairness. Article 82(c) is also very limited as a basis for defining exclusionary conduct, since it only views conduct through the lens of discrimination. Many exclusionary acts do not involve discrimination. Moreover, the interpretation applied by the Community institutions to Article 82(c) has been largely jurisdictional, without a meaningful inquiry into competitive effects. Finally, Article 82(d) only captures a very specific practice—tying.

Article 82(b) also has a clearer normative content for defining exclusionary conduct than any of broad definitions used by the Community institutions. "Normal competition," as per *Hoffmann-La Roche*, is a vague phrase, not least because the Commission has rejected the notion that a common practice within an industry would necessarily constitute "normal competition" if carried out by a dominant firm.[94] "Competition on the merits," and "genuine undistorted competition" are also vague, since not all competition on the basis of price, quality, and functionality is allowed under Article 82 EC. And, as noted above, the term "special responsibility" is simply an overall label for conduct that is abusive if carried out by a dominant firm. Article 82(b) is also more precise and certain than saying that each practice should be judged according to its positive and negative effects on consumer welfare. Economists sometimes underestimate the importance of legal certainty. This general principle of Community law requires that firms should, to the extent possible, be able to judge whether their conduct is legal or not when they decide to embark on a particular course of conduct.[95]

Finally, Article 82(b) is sufficiently flexible to incorporate the economic tests outlined in Section 4.2.3 above as a basis for verifying exclusionary conduct. Although these tests have no clear legal basis, they may be useful to verify the "limiting production"

[94] *Ibid.*, footnote 877 (citing Case 322/81, *NV Nederlandsche Banden Industrie Michelin v Commission* [1983] ECR 3461, para. 57; and Case T-111/96, *ITT Promedia NV v Commission* [1998] ECR II-2937, para. 139).

[95] See T Tridimas, *The General Principles of EC Law* (Oxford, Oxford University Press, 1999) pp. 165–66; J Temple Lang, "Legal Certainty and Legitimate Expectations as General Principles of Law" in U Bernitz and J Nergelius (eds.), *General Principles of European Community Law* (Boston, Kluwer Law International, 2000) pp. 163–84. For non-competition cases, see Case C-313/99, *Gerard Mulligan and others v Minister of Agriculture and Food, Ireland and Attorney General* [2002] ECR I-5719; Case C-63/93, *Fintan Duff, Liam Finlay, Thomas Julian, James Lyons, Catherine Moloney, Michael McCarthy, Patrick McCarthy, James O'Regan, Patrick O'Donovan v Minister for Agriculture and Food and Attorney General* [1996] ECR I-569, paras. 19–20.

test. In particular, Article 82(b) does not prevent the use of the profit sacrifice, equally efficient competitor, and consumer welfare tests where valid and useful. Moreover, in circumstances where each test is said to exclude the application of the other tests, and all tests remain essentially untested under Article 82 EC, it is important that Article 82(b) should be relied upon as the basic test for defining exclusionary conduct. This applies not least because economists can and do change their views or evolve them over time. To the extent relevant, the limiting production test is also similar to the test proposed by the leading treatise on US antitrust law for defining exclusionary conduct.[96]

Explanation of the "limiting production" test. Article 82(b) captures the key feature of exclusionary conduct, that it makes competitors' products or services less attractive or less available, rather than simply making the dominant company's product better or more available. Offering better or cheaper products must generally be legal, however great the difficulties it causes to rivals. In contrast, creating difficulties for competitors in other ways is not. In basic terms, the application of these principles to the most common pricing and non-pricing abuses is relatively straightforward. The bare wording of Article 82(b) does not of course solve every problem or question, but it at least provides some satisfactory underlying principles, as well as consistency.

For example, in the area of predatory pricing, pricing below average variable cost (or some analogous measure of marginal cost) will usually harm rivals who are at least as efficient as the dominant firm and so limit their production. Of course, reducing prices will ordinarily increase the dominant firm's output. But if the effect of its pricing below cost is to cause rivals to exit or marginalise them, the dominant firm can subsequently limit its own production and increase prices, which causes consumer prejudice. It would also be open to the dominant firm to argue that no consumer prejudice would occur if it would be unable to recoup past losses. Similarly, for unlawful exclusive dealing, requirements contracts, or loyalty rebates, the basic objection is not so much that the dominant firm offers an unbeatable price, but that that price is only available on condition that customers do not deal with rival firms.

The same basic analysis can be applied to non-pricing abuses. Refusal to deal issues raise some of most intractable issues under Article 82 EC. But the basic rubric is consistent with a limiting production test. In general, a dominant firm can invest in capital assets, patents, or other intellectual property rights. Successful investments may of course limit the possibilities open to its competitors, in particular when backed by legal monopolies such as intellectual property laws, but they normally benefit consumers by expanding production and creating new or better market options. In exceptional circumstances, however, the limitation of rivals' production causes such prejudice to consumers that a duty to share may be appropriate. Strict conditions apply: the refusal must substantially eliminate all existing competition, prevent new kinds of products from coming on the market for which there is a clear and unsatisfied demand, or suppress an existing product that consumers wish to go on using.

---

[96] See PE Areeda & H Hovenkamp, *Antitrust Law* (2nd edn., New York, Aspen Publishers, 2002) para. 651a (defining exclusionary conduct as acts that "(1) are reasonably capable of creating, enlarging, or prolonging monopoly power *by impairing the opportunities of rivals*; and (2) that either (2a) do no benefit consumers at all, or (2b) are unnecessary for the particular consumer benefits that the acts produce, or (2c) produce harms disproportionate to the resulting benefits.") (emphasis added).

Finally, the emphasis on prejudice to consumers in Article 82(b) would expressly allow for efficiency defences for conduct that limits rivals' production. Such defences would appear to be precluded under the profit sacrifice and equally efficient competitor tests. For example, an exclusive dealing obligation by a dominant firm will usually limit rivals' production or access to market, but it may have a valid defence if the dominant firm is making a substantial customer-specific investment and needs some assurance that the customer will buy from it to justify the investment. Pricing below cost may also have a consumer benefit in limited circumstances. Promotional pricing is legitimate where a new product requires consumer familiarity before customers can appreciate its enhanced qualities. Customer familiarity with product in question during the promotional pricing phase may render them loyal and therefore willing to pay a higher price in future because of the product's added qualities. In such circumstances, the low price is intended to allow customers to try the product. Higher future prices do not depend on competitors' exclusion, but on the product's enhanced characteristics over existing products.

The Discussion Paper's comments on exclusionary abuses. The Discussion Paper makes some useful contributions to clarifying the approach to exclusionary abuses under Article 82(b). First, it confirms that exclusionary abuses are concerned with preventing harm to consumer welfare, or "prejudice to consumers" in the language of Article 82(b).[97] Competition, and not competitors, is to be protected. In assessing exclusionary conduct, the Commission intends to apply a test based on actual or likely anticompetitive effects in the market and which can harm consumers in a direct or indirect manner.

Second, the Discussion Paper outlines the basic framework for assessing exclusionary abuses. Relying on the definition of abuse in *Hoffmann-La Roche*,[98] the Discussion Paper states that exclusionary conduct has two basic components. The first is that the conduct in question is inherently *capable* of foreclosing competitors from the market.[99] To establish such capability it is in general sufficient to investigate the form and nature of the conduct in question. The second component is to establish *market distorting foreclosure*, that is conduct which hinders the maintenance of the degree of competition still existing in the market or the growth of that competition and thus have as a likely effect that prices will increase or remain at a supra-competitive level. In this connection, the incidence of conduct on the market (i.e., how widespread the dominant firm applies a particular practice) is said to be important. The degree of dominance is also a relevant factor: firms with near-monopoly positions have much greater ability and incentive to foreclose than firms on the cusp of what might be regarded as dominance.[100] Finally, certain conduct has no efficiency explanation (e.g., knowingly making false patent declarations), in which case a rebuttable presumption of abuse applies.[101]

A significant problem, however, with the above definition of exclusionary conduct is that it does not distinguish efficient conduct that harms rivals from unlawful conduct. Dominant

[97] DG Competition discussion paper on the application of Article 82 of the Treaty to exclusionary abuses, Brussels, December 2005 (hereinafter, the "Discussion Paper"), para. 54.
[98] Case 85/76, *Hoffmann-La Roche & Co AG v Commission* [1979] ECR 461, para. 91.
[99] Discussion Paper, para. 58.
[100] *Ibid.*, para. 59.
[101] *Ibid.*, para. 60.

firms can take a number of actions that cause great harm to rivals, but are obviously pro-competitive (e.g., introducing better products or offering lower prices). Such conduct is not "foreclosure" in any relevant antitrust sense. The Discussion Paper thus needs to make clear that legitimate competition is immune from criticism regardless of its adverse effects on rivals. In this regard, the wording of Article 82(b)—that the conduct "limits" the possibilities otherwise open to rivals and causes "prejudice to consumers"—is much more accurate. Admittedly, the Discussion Paper includes an express "efficiency defence," but the burden of raising an affirmative defence should not fall on the dominant firm if the conduct in question does not give rise to unlawful foreclosure to begin with. Moreover, as discussed below (see Section 4.5), the conditions set out in the Discussion Paper for asserting an efficiency defence are strict and would likely have the consequence that such defences are unlikely to succeed in practice.

Third, the Discussion Paper draws some useful distinctions between different types of exclusionary conduct. The first concerns price and non-price exclusionary conduct. Price-based abuses include predatory pricing, loyalty discounts, and margin squeezes. Non-price exclusionary abuses include tying, refusal to deal, and exclusive dealing. For pricing abuses, the Discussion Paper confirms that, in general, Article 82 EC is only concerned with conduct that would exclude firms that are *as efficient* as the dominant firm, i.e., with the same or lower costs.[102] Consumer welfare is not generally well-served by allowing firms that are less efficient than the dominant firm to seek protection from price competition under Article 82 EC. If an equally efficient competitor cannot survive because of the dominant firm's pricing practices, the Commission would assume that conduct has the capability to foreclose and therefore examine the effects on the market.[103]

The Discussion Paper acknowledges that using the equally efficient competitor test may require certain modifications in practice.[104] In some cases reliable data on the dominant firm's costs may not be available, in which case it may be necessary to apply the as efficient competitor test using cost data of apparently efficient competitors. It may also be that no reliable information on cost data is available, but the Commission can build a credible case of abuse on the basis of other (non-price) information. In this circumstance, the dominant company can still rebut an inference of abuse by showing that it is not pricing below the appropriate cost benchmark. Finally, the Discussion Paper states that, in exceptional circumstances, it may be necessary to protect firms that are less efficient in the short-term but would become equally efficient over time (e.g., where the market exhibits significant economies of scale and scope, learning curve effects, or first mover advantages).

The second broad distinction made in the Discussion Paper is between horizontal and vertical exclusion.[105] The former concerns the exclusion of direct rivals on a horizontal level; the latter the exclusion by a dominant upstream supplier of an input of downstream rivals. Examples of horizontal exclusion are predatory pricing and tying. Vertical exclusion issues are raised by refusal to deal and margin squeezes. This distinction is useful in that the dominant firm's ability and incentive to exclude rivals may differ in the case of horizontal and vertical exclusion. All things equal, a dominant firm will always be

---

102 Discussion Paper, para. 64.
103 *Ibid.*, para. 66.
104 *Ibid.*, para. 67.
105 *Ibid.*, paras. 69–73.

better off if a horizontal rival exits the market. In contrast, when its downstream rivals are also actual or potential users of an input supplied by the dominant firm, the dominant firm's incentives to exclude are much less clear. Indeed, depending on the relative profitability of the upstream and downstream market, and the respective downstream efficiency and capacity of the dominant firm and its rivals, the dominant firm may have no incentive to exclude at all.

4.3.3 Discriminatory Abuses (Article 82(c))

The need to distinguish different categories of discrimination. Article 82(c) prohibits a dominant firm from "applying dissimilar conditions to equivalent transactions with other trading partners, thereby placing them at a competitive disadvantage." This provision is not as strict as anti-discrimination laws in other jurisdictions, such as the United States Robinson-Patman Act 1936, since Article 82(c) requires dominance as a pre-condition. But Article 82(c) remains potentially very broad and gives rise to perhaps the greatest scope for potential confusion of any clause under Article 82 EC. Several difficulties arise.

A first general problem is that discrimination, and in particular price discrimination, is, in some sense, implicated in most abuses, which makes it difficult, if not impossible, to have a single unified definition of abusive discrimination. Loyalty discounts and other forms of volume reductions may involve commitments by a seller to price discriminate in favour of large volume buyers or buyers meeting other conditions. Predatory pricing also usually involves discrimination by a dominant firm between its existing customers and actual or potential customers of rival firms. Price squeeze cases also involve hidden price discrimination by a vertically-integrated dominant firm in favour of its own downstream business, to the detriment of rivals. Essential facility cases could be analysed as involving an extreme situation of discrimination in the sense that the dominant firm discriminates in favour of its vertically-integrated business by denying downstream rivals access to essential inputs or dealing with some rivals but not others. Finally, one explanation for tying and bundling practices is the dominant firm's desire to extract more of the consumer surplus from undertakings that value the tied/bundled products more than they value each separately, i.e., price discrimination. Thus, in broad terms, the analysis of the effects of discrimination, and in particular price discrimination, can arise in many cases under Article 82 EC.

Second, the decisional practice and case law have created confusion by not clearly distinguishing between different types of abuses that may involve some element of discrimination. Many Article 82 EC cases have concerned the cumulative or combined anticompetitive effects of several practices committed simultaneously by the dominant firm.[106] These cases have given rise to decisions and judgments which, even though

[106] See, e.g., Case 27/76, *United Brands Company and United Brands Continentaal BV v Commission* [1978] ECR 207; Case 53/87, *Consorzio italiano della componentistica di ricambio per autoveicoli and Maxicar v Régie nationale des usines Renault* [1988] ECR 6039; Case T-30/89, *Hilti AG v Commission* [1991] ECR II-1439, on appeal Case C-53/92P, *Hilti AG v Commission* [1994] ECR I-667; Case T-83/91, *Tetra Pak International SA v Commission* [1994] ECR II-755; T-65/89, *BPB Industries plc and British Gypsum Ltd v Commission* [1993] ECR II-389; Case T-228/97, *Irish Sugar plc v Commission* [1999] ECR II-2969; Joined Cases C–395/96 P and C-396/96P, *Compagnie Maritime*

they are probably correct in outcome, are not clear in their analysis of issues of discrimination or in their implications.

A recurrent theme concerns the application of Article 82(c) to situations involving foreclosure of competitors of the dominant firm (e.g., price reductions given on condition of exclusivity, a selective lower price which is predatory, and discrimination by a vertically integrated dominant enterprise in favour of its own downstream operations). In a number of cases, the Community institutions have analysed exclusionary conduct that had *elements* of discrimination as being unlawful simply because it was discriminatory.[107] The reason for this is probably expediency: it is invariably easier to show that something is unlawful merely because there is a difference in treatment than to go further and show that that difference in treatment is also exclusionary. This applies not least because the historical interpretation of the various conditions of Article 82(c) has been generous to competition authorities and plaintiffs.

A final problem is that most cases in which Article 82(c) has been applied have involved direct or indirect discrimination on the grounds of nationality or residence,[108] which is subject to a very strict rule. Indeed, in the *1998 Football World Cup* case, the Commission held that discrimination on the basis of nationality by a dominant firm fell within Article 82(c) "notwithstanding the absence of *any* effect on the structure of competition."[109] The fact that a very strict rule applies to nationality discrimination under Article 82(c) may also have (wrongly) led the Community institutions to apply equally strict rules to other examples of discrimination, even if they raise very different economic and legal issues.

Clarifying the treatment of discrimination under Article 82 EC. Article 82 EC would be clearer and more rational if a more explicit distinction was made in the decisional practice and case law between: (1) discrimination by a dominant firm against its rivals (whether on horizontally- or vertically-related markets); and (2) discrimination by a dominant firm between companies to whom it sells on a level of trade in which it is

Belge Transports SA, Compagnie maritime belge SA and Dafra-Lines A/S v Commission [2000] ECR I-1365.

[107] For example, in *Irish Sugar*, the Court of First Instance seemed to confuse discrimination that forecloses competitors of the dominant firm (i.e., an exclusionary abuse) with discrimination that distorted competition between customers of the dominant firm (i.e., pure discrimination). In condemning Irish Sugar's rebates offered to customers at border areas exposed to competition as exclusionary, the Court of First Instance suggested that the rebates were objectionable because customers located in non-border areas would have paid higher prices—in effect, subsidising the low prices in the border area. The Court's approach in *Irish Sugar* creates unnecessary confusion between cases of "pure" discrimination (i.e., discrimination that produces effects at a vertical level against companies that do not compete with the dominant firm) and discrimination against competitors (i.e., discrimination that products effects against firms that compete on a horizontal level with the dominant firm). See Case T-228/97, *Irish Sugar plc v Commission* [1999] ECR II-2969.

[108] See, e.g., Case 226/84, *British Leyland plc v Commission* [1986] ECR 3263; Case T-229/94, *Deutsche Bahn AG v Commission* [1997] ECR II-1689; Case T-128/98, *Aéroports de Paris v Commission* [2000] ECR II-3929, confirmed on appeal in Case C-82/01 P, *Aéroports de Paris v Commission* [2002] ECR I-9297; Case C-163/99, *Portugal v Commission* [2001] ECR I-2613; *Brussels Airport*, OJ 1995 L 216/8; and *Ilmailulaitos/Luftfartsverket*, OJ 1999 L 69/24.

[109] *1998 Football World Cup*, OJ 2000 L 5/55, para. 100 (emphasis added).

not itself active, i.e., customers. In simple terms, the former involves the exclusion of rivals—which is sometimes referred to as primary-line injury in antitrust economics—whereas the latter concerns differences in treatment between customers with whom the dominant firm does not compete—or secondary-line injury. In each of these situations, the dominant firm's ability and incentives to distort competition differ and, as a result, so do the applicable legal and economic principles. The same basic distinction underpins US antitrust law.[110] In essence, this would mean that: (1) Article 82(b) would apply to exclusionary abuses; and (2) the prohibition under Article 82(c) would deal mainly with issues of secondary-line injury, that is discrimination between customers with which the dominant firm is not otherwise associated. The two provisions would not then apply simultaneously.[111]

a. The analysis of exclusionary abuses that involve elements of discrimination. There are various examples of exclusionary conduct that, in some sense, involve elements of discrimination. But these cases still concern the foreclosure of competitors. In such cases, the issue is not discrimination *per se*, but merely that discrimination is a *vehicle* for exclusionary conduct. The determinative issue is whether the conduct is truly exclusionary, and not merely whether it has discriminatory effects. Discrimination may simply make the exclusionary conduct possible, reinforce its anticompetitive or exploitative effects, or allow the dominant firm to take advantage of that conduct.

An obvious example of an exclusionary abuse that involves some element of discrimination concerns selective price cuts by a dominant firm, discussed in Chapter Five (Predatory Pricing). Such price cuts generally discriminate between the dominant firm's own customers and rivals' actual or potential customers, by offering more favourable prices to the latter. Again, in this scenario, it is not really informative (though it is usually relevant) to observe that the dominant firm is discriminating. The real issue is whether the lower prices are predatory, in the sense that they would make no economic sense but for their tendency to eliminate competition. This involves consideration of a range of issues, including whether the dominant firm's prices are below the relevant measure of its costs and the strategic reasons for the price cuts. Discrimination may mean that any losses suffered by the dominant firm are less extensive than in the case of an across-the-board price cut, but no clear conclusions can be drawn from the presence or absence of discrimination in itself.

Margin squeeze abuses, discussed in Chapter Six, also involve actual or implied discrimination by a vertically-integrated incumbent in favour of its own downstream business. But the test for a price squeeze abuse—whether the dominant firm's business

[110] In *Brooke Group*, the Supreme Court held that discriminatory pricing directed at rivals should be analysed under Section 2 of the Sherman Act and not the non-discrimination provisions of the Robinson-Patman Act. See *Brooke Group v Brown & Williamson Tobacco*, 509 US 209 (1993). Thus, all cases involving primary-line injury fall under Section 2, even if an element of the alleged exclusionary conduct is discrimination. Cases involving secondary-line discrimination only fall to be assessed under the Robinson-Patman Act (although, significantly, there is no public enforcement of this Act).

[111] Both types of discrimination can obviously result from the same conduct. For example, a discriminatory rebate scheme could foreclose competitors of the dominant firm, as well as distort competition between customers of the dominant firm downstream. But this does not call into question the soundness, or need for, the basic distinction.

would make a profit if had to pay the same price as rivals do for the input—is essentially a test based on whether an equally efficient entrant would be excluded. A related example concerns refusal to deal, discussed in Chapter Eight. In many refusal to deal cases, the dominant firm may not refuse to deal outright but may apply discriminatory conditions between its own downstream business and rivals, or may decide to deal with one rival, but not another. In this scenario, it is again not meaningful to say that the dominant firm is discriminating: the relevant issue is whether it is unlawfully excluding rivals in refusing to deal, which requires consideration of the exceptional circumstances in which such a refusal is exclusionary. Discrimination is simply one way in which the exclusionary conduct may be manifested. It says very little about whether the refusal to deal is exclusionary.

Although it can be criticised in terms of its substantive analysis, the *British Airways/Virgin* case at least makes a correct basic distinction between the principles of foreclosure and discrimination.[112] British Airways granted bonus commissions to travel agents that increased their sales of British Airways tickets as compared to a previous reference period. The bonus commission was not calculated on the basis of absolute increases in sales applicable to all travel agents. Instead, it depended on the extent to which an agent had increased its individual sales over a period as compared to its sales in the same period in the past. One possible effect of this scheme therefore was that agents selling the same number of tickets would receive different commissions depending on whether they had increased their sales relative to sales in the past.

In analysing the effects of the bonus commission scheme, the Commission and the Court of First Instance distinguished between the exclusionary effects of the scheme *vis-à-vis* British Airways' competitors on the one hand and the discriminatory effects of the scheme on travel agents on the other.[113] In regard to exclusionary effects of British Airway's conduct, the Commission applied the principles on exclusionary loyalty rebates. Concerning the discriminatory effects of the bonus commissions on competition between travel agents, however, the Commission only relied on Article 82(c). The same distinction has been confirmed in several cases, including *Michelin I*[114] and *Soda-Ash.*[115]

b. The analysis of discrimination by a dominant firm between non-associated customers. Pure discrimination—that is discrimination by a dominant seller or buyer against trading parties with whom it does not compete—raises fundamentally different legal and economic issues from exclusionary abuses directed against rivals that may have elements of discrimination. Exclusionary abuses essentially concern whether the conduct in question unlawfully limits rivals' production and, if so, whether it also causes harm to consumers. In contrast, discrimination that leads to secondary-line

[112] *Virgin/British Airways*, OJ 2000 L 30/1 (hereinafter "*BA/Virgin decision*"); Case T-219/99, *British Airways plc v Commission* [2003] ECR II-5917 (hereinafter "*BA/Virgin judgment*").

[113] See *BA/Virgin decision, ibid.*, paras. 97 et seq (exclusionary rebate schemes) and paras. 108 et seq. (discrimination); *BA/Virgin judgment, ibid.*, paras. 233 et seq. (discrimination) and paras. 241 et seq.

[114] Case 322/81, *NV Nederlandsche Banden Industrie Michelin v Commission* [1983] ECR 3461, paras. 87 et seq.

[115] *Soda-Ash/Solvay*, OJ 1991 L 152/1, para. 62.

injury involves an analysis of whether two similarly-situated customers are treated differently, with the result that the party paying the higher price or receiving worse terms is placed at a "competitive disadvantage" *vis-a-vis* the other party, and whether there is any legitimate justification for the difference in treatment. Such an analysis has *no* necessary connection with the analysis of exclusionary abuses (even if such abuses have elements of discrimination): indeed, the consumer welfare basis for interfering with pricing and non-pricing conduct where the only issue is that a dominant seller or buyer treats two non-associated companies differently is not at all obvious. The consumer welfare rationale for prohibiting exclusionary unilateral practices is much stronger.

The treatment of discrimination in subsequent chapters. Because no separate legal rule is required for exclusionary abuses that may involve elements of discrimination against rivals, the remainder of this work simply analyses the principal categories of exclusionary conduct, commenting, where appropriate, on the relevance, if any, of discriminatory conduct within each category of abuse. The same comment applies to discrimination by a dominant firm in favour of its own downstream business (i.e., vertical discrimination). The issue in such cases remains whether the conduct is exclusionary, although it is correct to say that actual discrimination by a dominant firm in favour of its own downstream business, to the detriment of rivals, is subject to a strict rule under Article 82 EC. Various exclusionary abuses are treated in detail in Chapters Five–Ten, including, if applicable, the relevance of issues of discrimination that may arise in the context of such abuses. In contrast, the treatment of secondary-line discrimination—Article 82(c)—is discussed separately in Chapter Eleven (Abusive Discrimination).

4.3.4 Tying Abuses (Article 82(d))

A narrow but potentially complex abuse. The final abuse defined in Article 82 EC concerns tying or "making the conclusion of contracts subject to the acceptance by the other party of supplementary obligations which, by their nature or according to commercial usage, have no connection with the subject of such contracts." Tying may be contractual (i.e., where customers cannot purchase the second product separately), economic (i.e., where the price for two products is sufficiently low relative to their stand-alone price to coerce customers into buying the products as a package), or technical (i.e., where two separate products are technically integrated as one). The distinctions between these forms of tying are not always hard and fast. For example, at a certain point, the stand-alone price for a second product may be so high as to lead consumers to only purchase it as part of a package with another product where the price of the package is low enough.

Cases on tying have thus far been very rare under Article 82 EC, the most notable and controversial example being the Commission's findings in *Microsoft*. This concerned the bundling of Windows Media Player with the Windows operating system software, which, according to the Commission, operated to the detriment of stand-alone vendors of media players and, ultimately, consumers.[116] Tying cases raise some of the most

[116] See Case COMP/C-3/37.792, *Microsoft*, Commission Decision of March 24, 2004, not yet published.

complex issues under Article 82 EC. For example, economists disagree about: (1) how to define a tie (i.e., when products should be regarded as separate); (2) whether the ubiquity of tying shows that it is generally efficient; and (3) when anticompetitive effects are likely to arise from tying. These difficulties are most acute in the area of technological tying which frequently arises in the information technology and software sectors. Tying and bundling are discussed in Chapter Nine.

4.3.5 Leveraging Abuses

Definition of "leveraging." The enforcement of Article 82 EC is not limited to situations in which a firm exercises market power in one market and uses that power to engage in abusive conduct in that market. In certain circumstances, it may also be an abuse for a dominant firm to use its position in one market to commit an abuse on a separate, but closely related, market. Such conduct is sometimes referred to as "leveraging." This is, however, an imprecise and potentially misleading term, since it encompasses a wide range of conduct that may be either procompetitive or anticompetitive, or a mixture of the two. The most that can probably be said therefore is that leveraging is simply a label for various types of conduct that have in common the feature that they involve a firm that is active in two or more related markets. Without more, the term says nothing about whether the conduct in question is lawful or not.

A leveraging abuse could occur under any one of the four clauses of Article 82 EC. In practice, however, most leveraging abuses concern the foreclosure of competitors (Article 82(b)) or tying (Article 82(d)). In terms of effects, leveraging abuses may be carried out in either horizontal or vertical adjacent markets. An example of horizontal leveraging might include a firm that is dominant in one market and carries out a campaign of predatory pricing not only in the dominant market, but also in adjacent markets in order to signal to potential entrants in other markets that it will react aggressively to potential threats. Another recent example is the recent *Microsoft* case where the Commission found that Microsoft sought to leverage its near-monopoly in computer operating systems to gain an (unfair) advantage in related markets for server operating system software and streaming media players.

Examples of vertical leveraging include situations in which a dominant firm controls an input (e.g., a raw material) that acts a "bottleneck" for entry into downstream markets. The most commonly-cited example concerns the local loop in telecommunications, or essential transport infrastructure such as railway lines, which may allow a firm owning or controlling such inputs to distort competition on downstream product or service markets that depend on the input in question to compete, i.e., refusal to deal cases.[117] But essentially the same issue arises in other situations involving vertical foreclosure, including excessive access charges (margin squeezes), incompatibility between the dominant firm's own products and downstream rivals' products,[118] tying,[119] and discriminatory pricing and licensing.

[117] See Ch. 8 (Refusal to Deal).
[118] See Ch. 10 (Exclusionary Non-Price Abuses).
[119] See Ch. 9 (Tying and Bundling).

The need to distinguish procompetitive and anticompetitive leveraging. Many forms of leveraging conduct are inherently procompetitive, even for dominant firms. Indeed, any firm with activities in two or more markets will engage in leveraging conduct all the time. For example, economies of scope—where it is cheaper to produce the two products together than to make each separately—are an example of leveraging, but are a legitimate advantage. The same principle applies to any other synergy that can be achieved across markets: it is, in general, legitimate for a firm, including a dominant firm, to take full advantage of cost, knowledge, or any other synergy between two markets where that creates efficiencies in the markets concerned. And the rule is no different even if this gives the firm significant cost or non-cost advantages over rival firms.

It is also important to appreciate that behaviour in markets in which a firm directly exercises market power is different from the actions of a firm in an adjacent market in which it does not.[120] A firm's ability and incentives to distort competition in an adjacent market in which it is not dominant are, all things equal, much less than in the case of behaviour in a market in which it exercises market power. In terms of ability, a firm's power to exclude competition in a market in which it does not exercise market power is obviously less than in situations in which does. Its incentives may also differ. Where the dominant firm's rivals in the second, competitive market are also its customers, the dominant firm may lower its overall profits by taking actions that would raise rivals costs. For example, it would make little sense for a dominant supplier of an input to attempt to exclude rival firms in downstream markets in which that input is used to produce a final product or service if the rivals offer differentiated products.

The reasons why leveraging has, incorrectly, acquired something of a pejorative meaning under Article 82 EC are not entirely clear. One possible reason is that the critique by the Chicago School of antitrust thinking of vertical leveraging, as refined by recent economic advances, has not been fully recognised under Article 82 EC. The Chicago School of antitrust thinking questioned the conventional wisdom that a dominant firm's efforts to extend its monopoly from the dominated market to a vertically-related non-dominant market are anticompetitive. In essence, their argument was that, in a single chain of production, there is only one monopoly profit. If dominant firm can reap that profit at one market level, it would prefer that the related markets at other levels are as competitive as possible. As discussed in detail in Section 4.2.1 above, some exceptions to this rule have been identified. But the basic point of the critique is sound—at least in cases involving vertical foreclosure—and has not been fully reflected in decisions under Article 82 EC.

Another possible explanation is a spillover to Article 82 EC of the analysis in leveraging cases under EC merger control rules. The Commission has prohibited a number of high-profile mergers and acquisitions on the grounds that, post-merger, the firms would be able to extend advantages in a dominant market into a related, but non-dominant

[120] For a good summary, see P Rey, J Tirole, and P Seabright, "*The Activities Of A Monopoly Firm In Adjacent Competitive Markets: Economic Consequences And Implications For Competition Policy*," Institut d'Economie Industrielle, Université de Toulouse, unpublished manuscript dated September 21, 2001 (on file with authors), pp. 24–26. See also Report by the Economic Advisory Group on Competition Policy, "*An Economic Approach to Article 82*," July 2005, pp. 23–29.

market, even *without* engaging in conduct that would, if carried out, be abusive under Article 82 EC. These cases have been strongly criticised as ignoring many of the efficiencies that result from synergies between two markets and protecting (less efficient) competitors at the expense of consumers.[121] But it is undoubtedly fair to say that the Commission has historically applied an expansive interpretation to anticompetitive leveraging under EC merger control rules, which may have also affected the analysis under Article 82 EC. A number of recent judgments, however, signal a return to a more orthodox position.[122]

Circumstances in which leveraging conduct amounts to an abuse. The decisional practice and case law have identified a number of situations in which leveraging conduct may amount to an abuse. Examples include denying an essential raw material to downstream rivals,[123] trying to extend a monopoly in primary equipment into competitive aftermarkets,[124] exclusionary discounting in a non-dominant market that is closely related to the dominant market,[125] and extending legitimate State monopolies or special rights into unjustified ancillary markets.[126] The essential point in each case is

[121] See e.g., D Patterson and C Shapiro, *Trans-Atlantic Divergence in GE/Honeywell: Causes and Lessons, Antitrust Magazine*, November 12, 2001; and W Kolasky, "Mario Monti's Legacy: A US Perspective" (2005) 1(1) *Competition Policy International* 155.

[122] In two recent judgments, the Community Courts clarified the principles regarding the assessment of leveraging theories under merger control. In essence, the judgments held that: (1) a high standard of proof applies where the objection to a merger is that the merged entity would engage in leveraging conduct: there must be "convincing" evidence to support a conclusion that the relevant anticompetitive effects will occur in the future; and (2) the Commission does not need to examine whether the leveraging conduct would also constitute an abuse of dominance under Article 82 EC, although behavioural commitments not to engage in certain types of abusive leveraging conduct should be taken into account in assessing the need for a prohibition decision. See Case T-310/01, *Schneider Electric SA v Commission* [2002] ECR II-4071; Case T-5/02, *Tetra Laval BV v Commission* [2002] ECR II-4381, and Case T-80/02, *Tetra Laval BV v Commission* [2002] ECR II-4519, confirmed on appeal in Case C-12/03, *Commission v Tetra Laval BV* [2005] ECR I-987. See also Case T-210/01, *General Electric Company v Commission* [2005] ECR II-nyr where, contrary to the Court of Justice's judgment in *Tetra Laval*, the Court of First Instance appeared to impose a stricter burden on the Commission. The Court of First Instance held that the Commission must, in principle, take into account the potentially unlawful, and thus sanctionable, nature of certain conduct as a factor which might diminish, or even eliminate, incentives for an undertaking to engage in particular leveraging conduct. However, its appraisal should not require an exhaustive and detailed examination of the rules of the various legal orders responsible for applying Article 82 EC. Thus, where the Commission, without undertaking a specific and detailed investigation into the matter, can identify the unlawful nature of the conduct in question under Community law, it must take account of it in its assessment of the likelihood that the merged entity will engage in such conduct (paras. 73-75). As noted, this standard appears stricter on the Commission than the Court of Justice's findings in *Tetra Laval*.

[123] Joined Cases 6-7/73, *Istituto Chemioterapico Italiano SpA and Commercial Solvents Corporation v Commission* [1974] ECR 223. See also Case 311/84, *Centre belge d'études de marché—Télémarketing (CBEM) v SA Compagnie luxembourgeoise de télédiffusion (CLT) and Information publicité Benelux (IPB)* [1985] ECR 3261; and Joined Cases C-241/91 P and C-242/91 P, *Radio Telefís Éireann and Independent Television Publications Ltd (RTE & ITP) v Commission* [1995] ECR I-743.

[124] Case 238/87, *AB Volvo v Erik Veng (UK) Ltd* [1988] ECR 6211.

[125] Case T-65/89, *BPB Industries plc and British Gypsum Ltd v Commission* [1993] ECR II-389. Case C-310/93P, *BPB Industries plc and British Gypsum Ltd v Commission* [1995] ECR I-865; and Case C-62/86, *AKZO Chemie BV v Commission* [1991] ECR I-3359.

[126] Case C-260/89, *Elliniki Radiophonia Tiléorassi AE and Panellinia Omospondia Syllogon Prossopikou v Dimotiki Etairia Pliroforissis and Sotirios Kouvelas and Nicolaos Avdellas and others*

the same: that a company which is dominant in one market may not use its dominance to restrict competition or otherwise commit an abuse in a second, related market. Within the apparently straightforward definition of abusive leveraging, however, a number of important points should be borne in mind.

a. No independent abuse of leveraging. Leveraging is not an independent ground of abuse. It is simply a convenient (and sometimes misleading) label to identify cases that have in common the feature that a dominant firm uses its power on one market to commit an abuse that has effects in an adjacent horizontal or vertical market. Crucially, the dominant firm's conduct must *itself* be capable of being regarded as abusive, even if it has effects on a non-dominant market. This point is often overlooked and has created unnecessary confusion about the scope of abusive leveraging. Abusive leveraging therefore stands for a relatively simple proposition: that in certain circumstances, a dominant firm can use its dominance on one market to unlawfully exclude rivals on a horizontally- or vertically-related market in which it is not dominant. There must still be abusive conduct, however, and not merely the use of dominance in one market to gain an advantage in another market.[127]

b. The need for a causal connection between the dominance and the abusive conduct. A related point is that there must be some causal connection between the firm's dominance and the conduct on the adjacent market. In other words, an abusive leveraging case "presupposes a link between the dominant position and the alleged abusive conduct," even if the conduct is carried out on the non-dominant market.[128] Such links are not normally present where conduct on a market distinct from the dominated market produces effects on that distinct market. However, in the case of distinct, but associated markets the application of Article 82 to conduct found on the associated, non-dominant, market and having effects on that associated market can be justified by "special circumstances."[129]

One example of "special circumstances" was *Tetra Pak II*, where the Court of Justice found that there were sufficient "associative links" between the dominant aseptic carton market and the non-dominant non-aseptic carton market to treat predatory pricing on the latter market as abusive. This was based on the following circumstances: (1) a substantial proportion (35%) of Tetra Pak's customers had purchased both aseptic and non-aseptic packaging systems; (2) the fact that Tetra Pak held nearly 90% of the market in the aseptic sector meant that, for customers, it was not only an inevitable supplier of aseptic systems, but also a favoured supplier of non-aseptic systems; (3) the main producers operated on both markets, thereby confirming the links between the

(Greek television) [1991] ECR 2925, paras. 22–26 and 38. See also Case C-18/88, *Régie des télégraphes et des téléphones v GB-Inno-BM SA* [1991] ECR I-5941, para. 19–28; and Case C-202/88, *France v Commission* (*Telecommunication terminals*) [1991] ECR I-1223, para. 51.

[127] This point has recently been confirmed by a number of senior US courts. See *Verizon Communications Inc v Law Offices of Curtis V. Trinko LLP*, 540 US 398, 410 (2004) ("leveraging presupposes anticompetitive conduct"). See also *Covad Communications Company v Bell Atlantic Corporation*, 398 F.3d 666, 365 U.S.App.D.C. 78, (2005).

[128] See Case C-333/94 P, *Tetra Pak International SA v Commission* [1996] ECR I-5951 (hereinafter "*Tetra Pak II*"), para. 27. See also Case T-83/91, *Tetra Pak International SA v Commission* [1994] ECR II-755.

[129] *Ibid.*

markets; and (4) Tetra Pak, by virtue of its quasi-monopoly in the aseptic sector, was able to focus its competitive efforts on the non-aseptic markets without fear of retaliation in the aseptic sector.[130] Taken together, these factors were found to give Tetra Pak a position "comparable to that of holding a dominant position on the markets in question as a whole."[131]

A similar conclusion was reached in connection with personal computer (PC) operating systems and work group servers in *Microsoft* concerning Microsoft's abusive refusal to supply interoperability information to rival firms. The Commission concluded that a comparison of the relevant operating system markets and an evaluation of Microsoft's position on both reveals a degree of inter-relation which is similar to that which prevailed in *Tetra Pak II*. The relevant factors were as follows:[132] (1) typical organisations that purchase work group servers also need to purchase client PCs; (2) Microsoft is active in both the client PC operating system market and the work group server operating system market and enjoys a quasi-monopoly on the client PC operating system market and has a leading position on the market for work group server operating systems; (3) almost all customers purchasing work group servers run Microsoft's Windows on their client PCs; (4) a vast majority of OEMs selling servers also supply client PCs, and are therefore dependent on Microsoft; and (5) various technological links exist between the products in question (e.g., physical linking in computer network, other network effects).

c. ***The relevance of "associative links."*** The Community Courts' formulation that there should be "associative links" between the two markets in abusive leveraging cases is not particularly helpful and may obscure the central point. Associative links are neither necessary nor sufficient in abusive leveraging cases.[133] Instead, a distinction should be made between a number of different situations involving conduct in two markets: one dominant; the other non-dominant. The first two do not require "associative links"—though they may in practice be present—whereas the latter requires a very close connection between the market in which the dominance exists and the non-dominant market on which the abuse is carried out:

1. The first situation is where the abuse takes place on the dominant market but its effects are felt on another market in which the firm is not dominant. The classic situation is a refusal to deal, which was already recognised as an abuse prior to the Community Courts' findings in *Tetra Pak II*. The important point in this situation is not whether "associative links" exist between the two markets, but whether the refusal to supply an essential input on the upstream dominant market has a sufficiently serious effect on competition in the second, downstream market. It may be that the dominant firm's ownership or control over an essential input creates as "associative link" with the downstream

[130] *Ibid.*, paras. 28–30.
[131] *Ibid.*, para. 31.
[132] Case COMP/C-3/37.792, *Microsoft*, Commission Decision of March 24, 2004, not yet published, paras. 530–34.
[133] See N Levy, "Tetra Pak II: Stretching the Limits of Article 86?" (1995) 2 *European Competition Law Review* 105.

market, but this adds nothing of substance to the analysis. (It is of course also possible that the firm concerned is already dominant on the second market.)

2. A second situation is where the abuse is committed on a non-dominant market, but the effect is to maintain or strengthen the firm's position on the dominant market. In *GVG*, the Commission applied Article 82 EC to a situation in which the dominant firm sought to maintain its dominant position on a market where it held an effective monopoly. Ferroviere delle Stato (FS) was found to occupy dominant positions on the markets for certain train services (traction) as well as on the downstream market for rail passenger services. A competitor, GVG, asked FS to supply it with train services so that GVG could provide a train service between Basle and Milan but was denied. FS was already offering a Basle-Milan service and its refusal on the traction market insulated FS's dominant position from competition on the market for train services. The Commission held that FS infringed Article 82 EC, finding that by refusing to provide traction to GVG, FS was "preserving its monopoly position" on the market for rail passenger services.[134] Again, in this situation, the presence or absence of "associative links" is not the central point: the main issue is whether the conduct could be said to strengthen the dominant firm's position on the relevant market on which it is already dominant. Such links may in practice be present in many cases involving the strengthening of dominance, but they are not essential.

3. The third situation—which was raised in *Tetra Pak II*—is where the abuse takes place on a market that is separate from, but related to and connected with, the market dominated by the firm concerned. In this scenario, it is essential to show that the firm's position on the dominant market allows it to exploit horizontal or vertical links between the two markets to such an extent that it uses its dominance to commit an abuse on a second, non-dominant market. Or, looked at differently, there would clearly be *no* basis for finding abusive conduct in circumstances where the dominant position and the abuse are in different and unrelated markets. The exact nature of the links between the two markets will vary from case to case, but they must be very close if Article 82 EC is to maintain any sensible or predictable meaning. Factors to consider would include: the structure of supply and demand on the two markets, use by the dominant firm of its power on the dominant market to penetrate the non-dominant market (e.g., tying practices), and market shares on the dominant and non-dominant markets. As a practical matter, it bears emphasis that the Commission has only found such "links" in two cases—

---

[134] See *GVG/FS*, OJ 2004 L 11/17. Although the judgment is not particularly clear on this point, the Court of Justice suggested in *AKZO* that AKZO's below-cost pricing might have infringed Article 82 EC even if carried out in a non-dominant market. This was based on the notion that AKZO's below-cost pricing on the flour additives segment was intended to strengthen its position on the plastics segment, where AKZO was dominant. See Case C-62/86, *AKZO Chemie BV v Commission* [1991] ECR I-3359, para. 45 ("The Commission was in those circumstances justified in regarding the organic peroxides market as the relevant market, even though the abusive behaviour alleged was intended to damage ECS's main business activity in a different market.").

Tetra Pak II and *Microsoft*.[135] Both cases concerned firms with a long-standing virtual monopoly on the dominant market and a market share on the second market that was at or above the level at which dominance is traditionally presumed under Article 82 EC.[136] Further, in each case, various cumulative factors were cited by the Community institutions as a basis for close commercial and technical links between the two markets. Taken together, these factors suggest that the Community institutions will only find an abuse on a non-dominant market in very rare cases.

4.3.6 The List Of Abuses In Article 82 EC: Illustrative Or Exhaustive?

The ambiguity in the decisional practice and case law. The Community Courts have sometimes stated that Article 82 EC should not be understood to list exhaustively the kinds of conduct which it prohibits, most notably in *Continental Can* where the Court of Justice held that Article 82 EC could be applied to mergers and acquisitions even in the absence of any specific clause dealing with changes in control.[137] In other words, the Court of Justice suggested that the examples of abuse given in the four clauses of Article 82 EC are merely illustrative. The precise meaning and scope of this statement has not, however, been clearly articulated in any judgment. In particular, it is not clear whether the Community Courts intended to say that: (1) the principal *categories* of abusive conduct are listed exhaustively in Article 82 EC (but all the possible *examples* of abuses *within those categories* are not); or (2) the *categories* of abuse under Article 82 EC extend beyond the four clauses mentioned therein.

Arguments in favour of an exhaustive definition of abuses under Article 82 EC. A number of compelling arguments suggest that the principal categories of abusive conduct are listed exhaustively under Article 82 EC, even if all possible examples of abuse within those categories are not (and could not be). First, the Court of Justice's statements in *Continental Can* regarding the non-exhaustive nature of the abuses listed in Article 82 EC were made in the context of a teleological interpretation of the EC Treaty intended to fill an important lacuna in the law—the absence at the time of rules governing mergers and acquisitions. That need no longer arises, since concentrations with a Community dimension are now dealt with under the EC Merger Regulation. When the EC Merger Regulation was adopted, the Commission made clear that it did not intend to apply Articles 81 or 82 EC to concentrations that had a Community dimension. With respect to concentrations that did *not* have a Community dimension, the Commission expressly reserved the right to use its powers under Article 81 EC (but

[135] Some national cases have also found "special circumstances" justifying a finding of abuse on a non-dominant market. See, e.g., Case No. CA98/05/2004, *First Edinburgh/Lothian*, April 29, 2004, (Case CP/0361-01) (predatory pricing allegation in a non-dominant market based, *inter alia*, on associative links between Edinburgh bus market and routes in the surrounding area).

[136] In *Tetra Pak II*, Tetra Pak accounted for approximately 48% of non-aseptic carton sales and for 52% of non-aseptic machine sales. In *Microsoft*, Microsoft had over 95% of the PC operating system market and a 50-60% share of the work group server market.

[137] See, e.g., Case 6/72, *Europemballage Corporation and Continental Can Company Inc v Commission* [1973] ECR 215, para. 26.

not Article 82 EC), at least in regard to concentrations that exceeded *de minimis* turnover thresholds.[138]

Second, the Court of Justice arguably did not need to develop a new type of abuse in *Continental Can*, since it would be reasonable to argue that Article 82(b) applies to a concentration that ends all scope for independent marketing, production and technical development of the company acquired. This is analogous to cutting off supply of an essential raw material or making exclusive contracts with customers, both of which may be abusive. Indeed, shortly after *Continental Can*, the Court of Justice confirmed that Article 82(b) can be applied to conduct limiting the possibilities available to competitors of the dominant firm where there is prejudice of consumers.[139] An anticompetitive merger or acquisition that causes consumer prejudice is an example of unlawfully "limiting production." Thus, *Continental Can* may not, after all, be an example of an abuse which does not fall under any of the four clauses of Article 82 EC.

Third, it is very difficult to think of any kind of unilateral conduct that falls outside these categories, and which should be subject to competition law. Article 82(a) is ample to cover exploitative abuses and other unfair trading conditions. All exclusionary abuse cases fall within Article 82(b) since they can all be characterised as limiting either rivals' production or that of the dominant firm, to the prejudice of consumers. Article 82(c) contains a discrimination principle that is sufficiently broad to capture discrimination by a dominant firm against non-associated companies. Finally, as evidenced by *Microsoft*, Article 82(d) is more than capable of treating sophisticated tying and bundling cases. Even the miscellaneous abuses that could be broadly characterised as "raising rivals' costs" (e.g., vexatious litigation, use and abuse of patent system) fit within the notion of "limiting production" under Article 82(b): conduct without a legitimate business rationale which limits rivals' product and causes consumer harm is abusive. Given the broad scope of the existing clauses of Article 82 EC, the Community Courts' statement that the examples in Article 82 EC are not exhaustive should probably be regarded as no more than a confirmation that there are kinds of conduct (e.g., refusal to contract and bundling) which are not *explicitly* described and prohibited by Article 82 EC, but clearly fall *within* the clauses listed therein. This is hardly surprising, since the ways in which firms may commit an abuse are myriad. No legislation could therefore exhaustively list all possible examples of abuse.

Finally, the notion that there may some unexpressed underlying principles in Article 82 EC that prohibit other kinds of abuses would be contrary to legal certainty. Legal certainty requires that a dominant company should be able to know what its legal duties are under Article 82 EC. It cannot be right that defendants should find themselves exposed to the risk that courts and competition authorities could apply words and principles not mentioned in Article 82 EC. It would be highly unsatisfactory

[138] The Commission identified as €2 billion of worldwide turnover and €100 million of Community-wide turnover as the relevant thresholds. See Notes entered in the Minutes of the Council, December 21, 1989.

[139] See Joined Cases 40 to 48, 50, 54 to 56, 111, 113 and 114-73, *Coöperatieve Vereniging "Suiker Unie" UA and others v Commission* [1975] ECR 1663, paras. 399, 482–83, and in particular paras. 523–27.

to rely on an implied underlying principle unless a case arose which clearly fell outside the four clauses of Article 82 EC.

4.4 ANTICOMPETITIVE EFFECTS UNDER ARTICLE 82 EC

Overview. As early as *Hoffmann-La Roche*, the Court of Justice made clear that the concept of abuse covered conduct that has "*the effect* of hindering the maintenance of the degree of competition still existing in the market or the growth of that competition."[140] The scope of this basic principle has given rise to some of the most contentious issues under Article 82 EC; in particular whether it is necessary to examine anticompetitive effects in all cases, what the standard for anticompetitive effects is or should be, and how the presence or absence of such effects should be measured. The following sections consider a number of central issues on the meaning of anticompetitive effects under Article 82 EC.

A first basic point is to what extent there is a requirement that a firm's dominance causes the abusive effect(s). Second, the standard for anticompetitive effects under Article 82 EC has been subject to conflicting statements. Some judgments suggest that possible or potential anticompetitive effects suffice; others say that the standard is actual or likely anticompetitive effects. Third, it is surprisingly unclear what type of anticompetitive effects are relevant under Article 82 EC and how they might be shown. Most agree that harm to consumer welfare is the ultimate test but there is disagreement over what this means and how it should be demonstrated. Fourth, it is not clear whether harm to consumer welfare is necessary under all four clauses of Article 82 EC, since only Article 82(b) mentions "consumers." Finally, the role of documentary or other evidence of exclusionary intent requires consideration, and in particular whether it sheds light on the likely effects of conduct.

4.4.1 The Need For Causation Between Dominance And The Abuse

Causation and Article 82 EC. A number of statements in the decisional practice and case law suggest that there is no requirement to show a causal connection between dominance and abusive effects. For example, in *Continental Can*, the Court of Justice held that "the question of the link of causality raised by the applicants which in their opinion has to exist between the dominant position and its abuse, is of no consequence, for the strengthening of the position of an undertaking may be an abuse and prohibited under Article 8[2] of the Treaty, regardless of the means and procedure by which it is achieved, if it has the effect [of substantially fettering competition]."[141] Later, in *Hoffmann-La Roche*, the Court of Justice stated that "the interpretation suggested by the applicant that an abuse implies that the use of the economic power bestowed by a dominant position is the means whereby the abuse has been brought about cannot be

[140] Case 85/76, *Hoffmann-La Roche & Co AG v Commission* [1979] ECR 461, para. 91 (emphasis added).

[141] See Case 6/72, *Europemballage Corporation and Continental Can Company Inc v Commission* [1973] ECR 215, para. 27.

accepted."[142] These statements have led a number of commentators to argue that there is no need for a causal link between the dominance and the abuse.[143]

Saying that causation is generally irrelevant under Article 82 EC, however, goes too far.[144] While there are undoubtedly some statements by the Community Courts which might suggest that causation is not a central issue in abuse cases, many more clearly suggest that it is. In *Tetra Pak II*, the Court of Justice held that Article 82 EC "presupposes a link between the dominant position and the alleged abusive conduct,"[145] although the Court was, exceptionally, prepared to accept that an abuse could be carried out in a non-dominant market that was very closely related to the dominant market. Similarly, in *Continental Can*, Advocate General Roemer stated that the wording of Article 82 EC "with its expression 'abuse...of a dominant position within the Common Market,' appears to hint that its application can be considered only if the position on the market is used as an *instrument* and is used in an objectionable manner; these criteria are therefore essential prerequisites of application of the law."[146]

The main categories of abuse under Article 82 EC also expressly or implicitly depend on a connection between dominance and abuse.[147] Abuses such as excessive pricing can only be successfully carried out by a firm with dominance: in a fully competitive market, attempts to charge excessive prices would be unsuccessful. Such abuses have a clear causal connection with dominance. A second category is abuses that would not occur if the firm in question is not dominant. A good example is predatory pricing. Below-cost prices confer a net benefit on consumers unless a firm can expect to recover any short-term losses in the longer term (i.e., recoupment), which assumes that dominance would exist. Or, put differently, no harmful effect would occur unless there is dominance. In this situation, dominance is also related to the scope for abusive effects. Finally, there are situations in which a harmful effect could occur if the conduct in question was carried out by a non-dominant firm, but the effect is exacerbated by the existence of dominance. For example, filing a false patent declaration could be done by any firm, but the effects are more likely to give rise to harm to competition—as opposed to harm to a particular firm—if the firm in question is dominant and eliminates competition from already weak competitors. In sum, some link between dominance, abuse, and anticompetitive effects is necessary under Article 82 EC.

---

[142] Case 85/76, *Hoffmann-La Roche & Co AG v Commission* [1979] ECR 461, para. 91.

[143] See, e.g., B Sufrin and A Jones, *EC Competition Law: Text, Cases, And Materials* (2nd edn., Oxford, Oxford University Press, 2004) p. 278.

[144] See T Eilmansberger, "How To Distinguish Good From Bad Competition Under Article 82 EC: In Search Of Clearer And More Coherent Standards For Anticompetitive Abuses" (2005) 42 *Common Market Law Review* 129, 140–42.

[145] See Case C-333/94 P, *Tetra Pak International SA v Commission* [1996] ECR I-5951, para. 27.

[146] See Opinion of Advocate General Roemer in Case 6/72, *Europemballage Corporation and Continental Can Company Inc v Commission* [1973] ECR 215, at 254. See also Case 27/76, *United Brands Company and United Brands Continentaal BV v Commission* [1978] ECR 207, para. 249 ("[I]t is advisable therefore to ascertain whether the dominant undertaking has made use of the opportunities arising out of its dominant position in such a way as to reap trading benefits which it would not have reaped if there had been normal and sufficiently effective competition.").

[147] See P Vogelenzang, "Abuse of a dominant position in Article 86: The problem of causality and some applications" (1976) 13 *Common Market Law Review* 62.

It would also be absurd to blame a dominant firm for adverse effects on a rival firm or competition that are not caused by anything done by the dominant firm. As a practical matter, most national procedural and substantive rules on causation would simply not allow an action to proceed without the particulars showing how the dominant firm's abusive conduct caused loss and damage to the defendant. The Community institutions have also accepted that a lack of causation disposes of a claim. In *National Carbonising*[148] for example the Commission finally concluded that there was no margin squeeze on the market for industrial coke. Instead, the source of National Carbonising's problem was that it had few long-term contracts for industrial coke. When demand for industrial coke fell, National Carbonising became too dependent on its domestic coke sales, where the retail price was limited by the prices of other kinds of domestic energy. National Carbonising's difficulties had not been caused or increased by the dominant Coal Board's actions, and the Board's long-term contracts (which of course reduced the demand for National Carbonising's product) were legitimate, even though National Carbonising was not so well placed to make such contracts.

Finally, the Court of Justice's comments in *Continental Can* should be seen in context. The case is generally regarded as a striking piece of judicial activism intended to cover a gap that existed at the time due to the lack of a merger control system at EU level. The Court's comments on causality cannot therefore be transposed, without qualification, to other abuses, and, arguably, at all given that the gap in question has now been corrected with the introduction of the EC Merger Regulation. Moreover, the abusive act in *Continental Can* was unusual in that it involved the strengthening of dominance, which meant that the link between the *initial* dominance and the abusive act of strengthening it was not in point. It is also questionable whether the Court's comments actually have the meaning ascribed to them by certain commentators. The Court's comments on causation were in response to an argument by the acquiring party that, for an abuse to be made out, it would be necessary to show that a firm *used* its dominant position *to purchase* the acquired firm's stock.[149] The Court quite rightly rejected this argument: the relevant point was not the source of the funds, but whether the acquisition would strengthen existing dominance and thereby amount to an abuse.[150]

4.4.2 The Standard For Anticompetitive Effects Under Article 82 EC

Conflicting statements in the decisional practice and case law. The decisional practice and case law are inconsistent on the standard for anticompetitive effects under Article 82 EC. On the one hand, several cases indicate that there must be a concrete assessment of a practice's effect on the market before a finding of material adverse

[148] Case 109/75R, *National Carbonising Company Ltd v Commission* [1975] ECR 1193 and *National Coal Board, National Smokeless Fuels Limited and the National Carbonising Company Limited,* OJ 1976 L 35/6.

[149] See Case 6/72, *Europemballage Corporation and Continental Can Company Inc v Commission* [1973] ECR 215, 225.

[150] It might be abusive for an undertaking vested with exclusive rights in a reserved area to acquire a rival in a non-reserved area using funds that result from an *abuse* of dominance in the reserved area (e.g., excessive pricing). See Case T-175/99, *UPS Europe SA v Commission* [2002] ECR II-1915. But this did not arise in *Continental Can*, since the acquiring firm had no exclusive State rights.

effect can be made.[151] This is consistent with the fact that there are no *per* se Article 82 EC violations. It is also consistent with the notion that the hallmark of abusive conduct is that it has the effect of foreclosing competitors to the detriment of consumers (i.e., of restricting competition), which means that it is necessary to examine the effects of the challenged practices.

On the other hand, in *Michelin II*, the Court of First Instance indicated that anticompetitive object or potential restrictive effects are sufficient to prove an abuse.[152] The Court rejected Michelin's argument that, as its market share and general price levels had fallen during the period of the practices in question, the Commission had failed to prove that the alleged abuses had in fact reinforced its dominant position or restricted competition. According to the Court, in order to fall under Article 82 EC, it is sufficient that a dominant undertaking's behaviour is liable to restrict competition or by its very nature did so.[153] Thus, where it is established that a dominant undertaking's behaviour has the object of restricting competition, such behaviour potentially has a restrictive effect: it is unnecessary to prove that there was an actual or concrete effect.[154] In support of this proposition, the Court cited the principles established in the *AKZO* case, where prices below average variable cost were presumed unlawful without the need to examine their market effect.[155] Similar comments have been made in margin

[151] For example, in *BPB Industries*, the Court of First Instance held that promotional payments made by a dominant supplier to a customer in return for an exclusive purchasing commitment are "a standard practice forming part of commercial cooperation between a supplier and its distributors" that "cannot, as a matter of principle, be prohibited," but rather must be assessed in the light of their effects on the market in the specific circumstances. See Case T-65/89, *BPB Industries plc and British Gypsum Ltd v Commission* [1993] ECR II-389, paras. 65 and 66. More recently, in *Van den Bergh Foods Ltd*, the Court of First Instance examined the effects of exclusive contracts on the market in detail before concluding that they gave rise to material foreclosure under Article 82 EC. The Court held that contracts by which a dominant ice-cream firm insists that the refrigerators it provides to customers should be used exclusively for the dominant firm's products were abusive. This conclusion was based on a detailed examination of several facts as evidence that the exclusivity clauses had a foreclosure effect. See Case T-65/98, *Van den Bergh Foods Ltd v Commission* [2003] ECR II-4653. The Commission has also routinely examined actual market effects in other abuse cases. See *ECS/AKZO,* OJ 1985 L 374/1, para. 86 (concluding after an analysis of the potential reaction from other competitors "that the elimination of ECS from the organic peroxides market would have had a substantial effect upon competition notwithstanding its still minor market share and the existence of other suppliers"); *Deutsche Post AG,* OJ 2001 L 125/27 at paras. 36–37 (finding that below cost pricing where there is no prospect of price rise inhibited growth of more efficient rivals (para. 36) with identifiable welfare loss (para. 37)). See also Case T-83/91, *Tetra Pak International SA v Commission* [1994] ECR II-755, para. 151, where the Court of First Instance noted that the Commission's analysis that Tetra Pak's prices were below cost was "corroborated by the eliminatory effect of the competition engendered by Tetra Pak's pricing policy," including "the increase of sales of Tetra Rex cartons in Italy and the corresponding reduction in the growth of sales of Elopak cartons, during a period of market expansion, followed by their decline as from 1981.").

[152] Case T-203/01, *Manufacture française des pneumatiques Michelin v Commission* [2003] ECR II-4071.

[153] *Ibid.*, para. 239.

[154] *Ibid.*, para. 241.

[155] *ECS/AKZO,* OJ 1985 L 374/1; Case C-62/86, *AKZO Chemie BV v Commission* [1991] ECR I-3359. See also Case T-219/99, *British Airways plc v Commission* [2003] ECR II-5917, para. 293, where the Court of First Instance adopted essentially the same reasoning as in *Michelin II*. The Court held that that it is sufficient for an abuse that the conduct "tends to restrict competition" or "in other words... is

squeeze cases under Article 82 EC and national law.[156] At the same time, a number of national decisions have rejected margin squeeze allegations based, *inter alia*, on the lack of actual or probable anticompetitive effects.[157]

Resolving the conflict in the decisional practice and case law. The standard for judging anticompetitive effects under Article 82 EC is (or should be) evidence of actual or likely consumer harm. Ignoring such effects in favour of a legal presumption of effect—which was advocated in *Michelin II*—is plainly inconsistent with the Commission's current emphasis on an economics-based approach and, indeed, the entire basis for the on-going review of policy under Article 82 EC. Moreover, evidence of actual or likely anticompetitive effects was already recognised in major Commission decisions on abuse of dominance prior to the on-going review of Article 82 EC. Most notably, in *Wanadoo*, the Commission undertook an extremely detailed recoupment and effects analysis,[158] despite the fact that Wanadoo's prices were found to be below average variable cost—which is considered as presumptively unlawful under the *AKZO* case law—and there was a range of evidence of an express exclusionary plan. The Commission relied on the fact that: (1) Wanadoo's market share rose by nearly 30% during the period of the infringement; (2) Wanadoo's main competitor saw its market share tumble; and (3) one competitor even went out of business. If such an analysis is undertaken for the practice under Article 82 EC that is generally considered to be

capable of having, or likely to have, such an effect." At para. 295, the Court added, "where an undertaking in a dominant position actually puts into operation a practice generating the effect of ousting its competitors, the fact that the hoped-for result is not achieved is not sufficient to prevent a finding of abuse." As in *Michelin II*, the Court disregarded the decline in BA's share of sales and a corresponding increase in competitors' sales in favour of an assumption that competitors would have done better in the absence of BA's unlawful practices. The Advocate General's opinion in *British Airways/Virgin* does not clarify matters, and arguably confuses them further. She found the distinction between conduct that is "capable of having" and "likely to have" an anticompetitive effect to be "semantic." But "likely" at least implies more probable than not, whereas "capable of having" does not imply any specific degree of likelihood. Moreover, in the end, she said that it was enough, at least in the case of loyalty discounts, that conduct would "tend" to have anticompetitive effect, which seems a lower and more open-ended standard again. See Opinion of Advocate General Kokott in Case T-219/99 *British Airways plc v Commission* [2006] ECR I-nyr, paras. 76-77.

156 *Deutsche Telekom AG*, OJ 2003 L 263/9, paras. 179–80 (once a margin squeeze was shown, it was not necessary to assess any effects on competition: such effects were presumed from the mere existence of a margin squeeze). However, the Commission nonetheless undertook a detailed analysis of likely exclusionary effects, noting Deutsche Telekom's 90% share of the affected market and competitors' falling share of analogue connections. For national law, see *France Télécom/SFR Cegetel/Bouygues Télécom,* Conseil de la Concurrence, Décision No. 04-D48 of October 14, 2004, para. 242, (finding that, under *Deutsche Telekom*, once margin squeeze is established, it is not necessary to evaluate its actual impact on competition).

157 See e.g., Case CW/00615/05/03, *Suspected margin squeeze by Vodafone, O2, Orange and T-Mobile*, Ofcom decision of May 21, 2004; and *Investigation by the Director General of Telecommunications into alleged anticompetitive practices by British Telecommunications plc in relation to BTOpenworld's consumer broadband products*, Oftel Decision of November 20, 2003.

158 See Case COMP/38.233, *Wanadoo Interactive,* Commission Decision of July 16, 2003, not yet published, paras. 332 et seq. (recoupment) and paras. 369 et seq. (effects on competition).

closest to a *per se* abuse (pricing below average variable cost), the same *a fortiori* applies for other (less clear) abuses.[159]

Another practical point to bear in mind is that, in contrast to merger control decisions, abuse of dominance cases involve situations in which the defendant is *already* in a dominant position. In other words, abuse of dominance usually concerns known present facts and established conduct. In these circumstances, it should normally be possible to consider whether the market is consistent with potential exclusion or exhibits characteristics more consistent with a competitive environment. In most cases, there should be relevant information regarding actual effects or, failing that, information on which reasonable assumptions as to future likely effects can be made. Whichever information is more readily-available should dictate whether the analysis concerns actual or likely effects. There is no case, however, for insisting on proof of actual consumer harm in all cases. Otherwise, competition authorities and courts would have to wait for obvious anticompetitive effects to arise before they could act, which would in many cases be ineffective and too late. Moreover, in cases that involve actions intended to *maintain* a dominant position, there would be no perceptible additional effects.[160]

There would also be severe problems if statements by the Commission and Court of First Instance in *British Airways/Virgin* and *Michelin II* that *prima facie* evidence of *lack of adverse effect* can be ignored in favour of a presumption of effects were widely accepted. There is no effective counter thesis to this assumption: it can *always* be assumed that practices had an adverse effect on competitors if evidence of lack of effect is disregarded in favour of such an assumption. This reasoning is also circular and inconclusive. It is circular because the conduct is said to be unlawful *only* because it ousts competitors, but if that is the reason, it cannot then be said that one does not need to look to see if it had that effect. It is inconclusive because legitimate competition can also result in competitors' exit (i.e., the problem of observational equivalence). If a practice would be illegal because it caused foreclosure and so had anticompetitive effects, it cannot be shown to have those effects by merely stating that it is illegal. Even in a case where the practices in question had no effect on competition, an abuse could be found by relying on a presumption of law. In sum, there are good reasons why the analysis of anticompetitive effects under Article 82 EC should be based on actual or likely anticompetitive effects, and not on merely potential, possible, or presumed effects.

---

[159] See also Case COMP/C-3/37.792, *Microsoft*, Commission Decision of March 24, 2004, not yet published, paras. 693 et seq. (effect of Microsoft's refusal to deal on technical development and consumers analysed in detail) and paras. 879 et seq. (detailed analysis of likely adverse effects of Microsoft's conduct on content providers and software developers).

[160] Whether proof of actual anticompetitive effects should be required has led to a lively debate among US antitrust commentators. Most of the debate, however, seemed to concern the *type* of effects that need to be shown rather than disagreement about the underlying legal standard. See T Muris, "The FTC and the Law of Monopolisation" (2000) 67 *Antitrust Law Journal* 693; D Balto and E Nagata, "Proof of Competitive Effects in Monopolisation Cases: A Response to Professor Muris" (2000) 68 *Antitrust Law Journal* 309; T Muris, "Anticompetitive Effects in Monopolisation Cases: Reply" (2000) 68 *Antitrust Law Journal* 325.

That actual or likely anticompetitive effects is the relevant test for exclusionary conduct under Article 82 EC is now confirmed by the Discussion Paper. It states that Article 82 EC prohibits "exclusionary conduct which produces actual or likely anticompetitive effects in the market and which can harm consumers in a direct or indirect way."[161] It adds that, the longer the conduct has already been going on, the more weight will in general be given to actual effects. Not only short-term harm, but also medium- and long-term harm arising from foreclosure will be taken into account.

4.4.3 Identifying Actual Or Likely Anticompetitive Effects

The relevant criterion: consumer harm. There is more or less universal agreement that harm to consumers (i.e., consumer surplus) is the relevant test for anticompetitive unilateral conduct. As the Commissioner responsible for competition policy, Neelie Kroes, made clear, "consumer welfare is now well established as the standard the Commission applies when assessing...infringements of the Treaty rules on cartels and monopolies."[162] A number of elementary principles follow from this. First, harm to a competitor does not mean harm to competition or, equivalently, consumers. Competition can and should harm competitors. Moreover, the fact that one or more competitors exit a market does not mean that competition has been reduced if enough effective players remain on the market.

Second, although harm to an "effective competition structure" has sometimes been mentioned as a possible alternative to direct consumer harm,[163] the two concepts should amount to the same thing: unless there is consumer harm, there is no relevant harm to the "structure of competition."[164] Put differently, there can be no case for intervention

---

[161] Discussion Paper, para. 55.

[162] See N Kroes, *European Competition Policy—Delivering Better Markets and Better Choices*, speech during the European Consumer and Competition Day, London, September 15, 2005.

[163] See, e.g., Case 6/72, *Europemballage Corporation and Continental Can Company Inc v Commission* [1973] ECR 215, para. 26 ("As may further be seen from letters (c) and (d) of Article 86(2), the provision is not only aimed at practices which may cause damage to consumers directly, but also at those which are detrimental to them through their impact on an effective competition structure, such as is mentioned in Article 3(f) of the Treaty. Abuse may therefore occur if an undertaking in a dominant position strengthens such position in such a way that the degree of dominance reached substantially fetters competition, [i.e.] [t]hat only undertakings remain in the market whose behaviour depends on the dominant one.").

[164] See J Vickers, "*Abuse of Market Power*," Speech to the 31st conference of the European Association of Research in Industrial Economics, Berlin, September 3, 2004 ("In the limit, the idea that there could be harms to the competitive process, justifying competition policy intervention, that are not even capable of harming consumers is unattractive. Competition to serve the needs of the general public of consumers—not some abstract notion of competition for its own sake—is the point of competition policy."). See also D Evans, H Chang, and R Schmalensee, "Has The Consumer Harm Standard Lost Its Teeth?" in RW Hahn (ed.), *High-Stakes Antitrust: The Last Hurrah?* (Washington DC, Brookings Institution, 2003) pp. 72 et seq. But see Opinion of Advocate General Kokott in Case T-219/99 *British Airways plc v Commission* [2006] ECR I-nyr, para. 68 ("Article 82 EC...is not designed only or primarily to protect the immediate interests of individual competitors or consumers, but to protect the *structure of the market* and thus *competition as such (as an institution)*, which has already been weakened by the presence of the dominant undertaking on the market. In this way, consumers are also indirectly protected.") (emphasis in original). This comment is not understood if, by this, the Advocate General considers that there could be harm to the "structure" or "institution" of competition, thereby justifying intervention, in circumstances where there was no direct or indirect harm to consumers.

under competition law where there is harm to the competitive process, but none to consumers. Of course, at some point, the absence of a sufficient number of effective competitors, or other distortions to the competitive structure, can lead to consumer harm, but this observation is trite: the real issue remains whether adverse effects on competitors and market structure lead to actual or probable harm to consumers, which is discussed below.

Third, the burden of showing consumer harm rests with the party asserting such harm. It is not enough to identify a theory of possible harm: some effort must be made to validate it on the facts. The burden then shifts to the defendant to rebut a *prima facie* case of anticompetitive effects.[165]

Finally, evidence of consumer harm is not necessarily the end of the inquiry. In some cases, it may be possible to show that, notwithstanding such harm, a practice generates efficiencies that are large enough to off-set any harm to consumers. This defence is for the dominant firm to raise in the first instance and is discussed in detail in Section 4.5.

Proving consumer harm. Although proof of actual or likely consumer harm is generally accepted as the relevant standard for assessing unlawful unilateral conduct, there is surprisingly little agreement on how such harm should be measured, or, indeed, whether it can be measured with any degree of accuracy or consistency. Many economists doubt that the effects of unilateral practices on output and price can be measured accurately by a firm *ex ante* or by courts and competition authorities *ex post*. Thus, they would prefer to truncate the analysis and focus instead on designing rules for specific practices that capture, as accurately as possible, the scope for competitive harm based on economic evidence, as well as considerations of whether over-deterrence or under-deterrence is more important.[166] And, as noted in Section 4.2.3, other economists favour apparently simple rules such as profit sacrifice that would not require firms to predict the consumer welfare effects of their actions.

These approaches have not, however, gained widespread acceptance under Article 82 EC, even if many of the operational rules make some attempt to incorporate evidence of prior belief on the incidence and type of consumer harm likely to follow from certain practices. It is still necessary therefore to decide under Article 82 EC what harm to consumers is and how it might be shown. The following principles are suggested by way of guidance:

1. The best evidence of harm to consumers is evidence that a practice has had a material effect on output and prices, i.e., reducing the former or increasing the latter. Output in this context does not only mean quantity, but should also

[165] See Report by the Economic Advisory Group on Competition Policy, "*An Economic Approach to Article 82*," July 2005, p. 13 ("In the first place, in deciding to bring a case, the competition authority should therefore focus on identifying the competitive harm of concern. To do so, the authority must analyze the practice in question to see whether there is a consistent and verifiable economic account of significant competitive harm. The account should be both based on sound economic analysis and grounded on facts. In particular, since many practices can have pro- as well as anticompetitive effects, *merely alluding to the possibility of a story is not sufficient. The required ingredients of the story must therefore be properly spelled out and shown to be present.*") (emphasis added).

[166] See Section 4.2.3 above for a detailed discussion.

include reductions in quality or innovation (where these can be measured). Such inquiries are often fact-intensive, but they are routinely carried out in the context of merger review and Article 81 EC. Difficulties may arise with issues such as observational equivalence (i.e., the effects of exclusionary conduct and legitimate competition may look similar) and comparing counterfactual situations (i.e., the but-for world). But it seems reasonable to leave such difficulties for the defendant to raise and prove.

2. In many cases it will of course not be possible to examine the direct impact of a practice on consumers by reference to effects on output or prices. These effects may not yet have materialised (e.g., where intervention occurs at an early stage) or may never materialise (e.g., where an important nascent competitor has been excluded). In such cases it should still be possible to *infer* consumer harm based on an examination of the reasonably likely consequences for consumers of the dominant firm's actions. Difficult cases arise where a dominant firm's practices do not cause competitors' market exit, but raise their costs or distort competition in some other indirect way. But it should still be possible in this instance to evaluate whether harm to rivals is likely to also lead to harm to consumers. Such harm is present at least where: (a) the harm to competitors is sufficient to have a material impact on their effectiveness; (b) the competitors affected are important enough so that their effectiveness matters to consumers in the long run; and (c) any short-term injury to competitors cannot be overcome by existing competitors or new entrants over time.[167] The Commission has applied a similar analysis in evaluating competitive harm in recent merger cases.[168]

3. Economics can usefully contribute to measuring such effects. Quantitative economic techniques can be used to test for effects, for example where information is available that allows prices and output to be compared in the period before and after the alleged infringement (e.g., natural experiments).

4. Where such techniques cannot be applied, "second-best" solutions can still be used. For example, evidence of new entry, lack of market exit, stable or

[167] See also D Evans, H Chang, and R Schmalensee, "Has The Consumer Harm Standard Lost Its Teeth?" in RW Hahn (ed.), *High-Stakes Antitrust: The Last Hurrah?* (Washington DC, Brookings Institution, 2003) p.81.

[168] For example, in Case COMP/M.3304, *GE/Amersham*, the Commission applied the following analysis of foreclosure. First, it established its theory of possible competitive harm—namely that the merged entity would engage in various types of anticompetitive bundling. Second, having identified a relevant theory of possible harm, the Commission assessed whether, in the case at hand, the merged entity would be able to engage in it, in particular through its ability to "leverage its pre-merger dominance in one product to another complementary product." Third, the Commission assessed whether, even if such a strategy was possible, there was a "reasonable expectation that rivals will not be able to propose a competitive response." Fourth, if rivals were not able to respond, the Commission assessed whether "their resulting marginalisation will force them to exit the market." Finally, even if rivals would exit the market, the Commission assessed whether the merged firm could "implement unilateral price increases and such increases need to be sustainable in the long term, without being challenged by the likelihood of new rivals entering the market or previously marginalised ones re-entering the market."

growing market shares among rivals, and falling prices during the period of the alleged abusive conduct should point towards a lack of material adverse effect.[169] In contrast, evidence of market exit, no new entry, increases in the dominant firm's market share at the expense of rivals, and price increases by the dominant firm normally merit the opposite inference. Care should be taken, however, with inferring too much from changes in relative market shares. The fact that the dominant firm's share has decreased or remained stable does not mean that there has been no harm to competition, in particular in a monopoly maintenance case. Similarly, the fact that rivals' shares have not diminished does not show an absence of harm to competition, especially if demand has grown. The converse may also be true.

4.4.4 Harm To Consumers Under The Four Clauses Of Article 82 EC

An essential requirement of all four clauses of Article 82 EC. A surprising feature of Article 82 EC is that the only clause that expressly mentions harm to consumers is Article 82(b), which uses the phrase "prejudice to consumers." None of the other clauses contains a comparable phrase. Notwithstanding this, it would be extremely surprising if the other clauses of Article 82 EC involve a notion of abuse that does not necessarily include harm to consumers. Competition cannot be protected for competition's sake: conduct only adversely affects competition where it operates to the detriment of consumer welfare. As made clear by Advocate General Jacobs in *Bronner*, "the primary purpose of Article [82] is to prevent distortion of competition and in particular to safeguard the interests of consumers—rather than to protect the position of particular competitors."[170] The Commission has also clarified that "consumer welfare is now well established as the standard [for] assessing...infringements of the Treaty rules on...monopolies."[171]

Moreover, the clauses of Article 82 EC that do not expressly mention consumer welfare do take this into account, both implicitly and in practice. Exploitative abuses covered

[169] One interesting contrast in this regard was the different conclusions reached by the US courts and EU authorities in respect of Virgin's complaint against British Airways' incentive schemes. The Commission assumed that competitors were harmed by BA's loyalty rebates despite evidence that their market share had *increased* during the relevant period and BA's had decreased by 10% during the period of the infringement ("Despite the exclusionary commission schemes, competitors of BA have been able to gain market share from BA since the liberalisation of the United Kingdom air transport markets. This cannot indicate that these schemes have had no effect. *It can only be assumed that competitors would have had more success in the absence of these abusive commission schemes.*" See *Virgin/British Airways*, OJ 2000 L 30/1, paras. 105–06 (Emphasis added)). Similar (although clearly not identical) facts were presented to the US courts in Virgin's lawsuit against BA and the Second Circuit concluded that no adverse competitive effect was made out. The Second Circuit held that business practices presumptively should not be viewed as anticompetitive when "the practices have been on-going for several years and rivals have managed to profit, new entry has occurred, and their aggregate market shares are stable." See *Virgin Atlantic Airways v British Airways*, 257 F.3d 256 (2d Cir. 2001), citing PE Areeda & H Hovenkamp, *Antitrust Law* (2nd edn., New York, Aspen Publishers, 2002) para. 807f.

[170] Opinion of Advocate General Jacobs in Case C-7/97, *Oscar Bronner GmbH & Co KG v Mediaprint Zeitungs- und Zeitschriftenverlag GmbH & Co KG* [1998] ECR I-7791, para. 58.

[171] See N Kroes, *European Competition Policy—Delivering Better Markets and Better Choices*, speech during the European Consumer and Competition Day, London, September 15, 2005.

by Article 82(a) incorporate some element of loss of consumer welfare through excessive pricing. The Commission's recent practice in tying cases under Article 82(d) has also clearly included detailed analysis of effects on consumers, as evidenced by *Microsoft*. There are also good arguments that consumer welfare is also, or should be, part of the analysis under Article 82(c). Many forms of discrimination can enhance consumer welfare, for example by allowing buyers who can only afford to pay less for a product to receive more favourable terms.[172] It would be anomalous, and contrary to the underlying objectives of Article 3(g) of the EC Treaty,[173] if Article 82(c) did not allow such contracts.[174] If, as is certainly the case, efficiency defences are available under the other provisions of Article 82 EC, it would be unreasonable if it was not a defence under Article 82(c) to show that there had been no prejudice to consumers, and that they would benefit from the different treatment. (It would be reasonable to presume harm to consumers conclusively, however, in cases of discrimination on the basis of nationality.[175]) If not, the criticism that Article 82 EC protects competitors and not competition would be true.

Internally inconsistent treatment of consumer harm within Article 82 EC would also lead to haphazard outcomes. As noted, many practices could fall under more than one clause of Article 82 EC or, depending on the context, could fall under different clauses. It would make no sense if the outcome of a case depended on which clause under Article 82 EC conduct happened to be classified under. Plaintiffs, competition authorities, and defendants could then engage in "category shopping" depending on their objectives. Inconsistency would also arise with Article 81 EC, which the Court of Justice has held should be interpreted consistently with Article 82 EC.[176] Since Article 81(3) incorporates an analysis of consumer interests, so too should Article 82 EC. It would also make no sense to have consistency between Articles 81 and 82 and at the same time to have internal inconsistency within the four clauses of Article 82 EC.

4.4.5 The Role Of Intent Evidence

Reliance on intent evidence in pricing abuse cases under Article 82 EC. The Community institutions have long held that abuse is "an objective concept," implying that exclusionary intent is not relevant to the determination of whether conduct is

[172] See generally Ch. 11 (Abusive Discrimination).

[173] Article 3 is relevant to the interpretation of Article 82 EC. See Case 6/72, *Europemballage Corporation and Continental Can Company Inc v Commission* [1973] ECR 215, para. 24; Joined Cases 6-7/73, *Istituto Chemioterapico Italiano SpA and Commercial Solvents Corporation v Commission* [1974] ECR 223, para. 32; Case 27/76, *United Brands Company and United Brands Continentaal BV v Commission* [1978] ECR 207; Case 85/76, *Hoffmann-La Roche & Co AG v Commission* [1979] ECR 461; and Case T-83/91, *Tetra Pak International SA v Commission* [1994] ECR II-755.

[174] As the US Department of Justice explained in a long report on the Robinson Patman Act 1936, a wide ban on discrimination is anticompetitive and damaging to consumers. See *Journal of Reprints for Antitrust Law and Economics* (2000 Reprint), US Department of Justice Report on the Robinson-Patman Act, Vol. XXIX number 1, 259.

[175] Case C-18/93, *Corsica Ferries Italia Srl v Corpo dei Piloti del Porto di Genova* [1994] ECR I-1783 and the performing rights societies cases; Case C-281/98, *Roman Angonese v Cassa di Risparmio di Bolzano SpA* [2000] ECR I-4139.

[176] Case 6/72, *Europemballage Corporation and Continental Can Company Inc v Commission* [1973] ECR 215.

abusive.[177] Nonetheless, it is clear, at least in pricing abuse cases, that weight can sometimes be attached to evidence of exclusionary intent. The second *AKZO* rule on predatory pricing states that prices below average total cost but above average variable cost are abusive if they are "part of a plan for eliminating a competitor."[178] Applying this test the Community institutions have relied on documentary and other evidence in several pricing abuse cases as a factor supporting a violation. Moreover, reliance on intent evidence has not been limited to the rule identified in *AKZO*, but has also been applied to prices above average total cost where, *inter alia*, there was documentary evidence that a near-monopoly liner shipping conference wished to eliminate a rival.[179]

The treatment of intent evidence in predatory pricing cases is discussed in detail in Chapter Five, but the salient points are as follows: (1) the Commission distinguishes between formal presentations to management and informal remarks made to or by sales staff, attaching a higher value to the former; (2) the documents must show such intent on the part of senior staff capable of having a material influence on company policy; and (3) the Commission does not focus on isolated documents, but on the totality of evidence pointing to a unity of purpose in the company's actions. While these statements impose some necessary and useful limits, it remains extremely difficult to distinguish between the language that characterises aggressive, but legitimate, price cuts and predatory pricing. They look the same and their motive forces are also very similar. For these reasons, Chapter Five advocates a more objective approach to issues of intent in predatory pricing cases based on whether the dominant firm's strategy was incrementally profitable irrespective of its ability to exclude. Subjective intent would then be irrelevant.

Intent evidence in other abuse cases. The Community institutions' statement that abuse is an objective concept, and the problems with relying on (subjective) intent evidence in predatory pricing cases might suggest that reliance on intent evidence in other contexts is misplaced. This is not the case, however, and common sense dictates that it should not be either.[180] The fundamental problem with relying on subjective evidence of intent to eliminate a rival is where legitimate competition and exclusionary conduct look almost identical, such as in the area of price cutting. This objection has much less force where conduct has little or no plausible efficiency justification. For example, a dominant firm's knowingly filing a false patent declaration has no efficiency justification. It would be curious if clear documentary evidence of intent to knowingly file a false patent was ignored by courts or competition authorities. Intent evidence may also be useful as a cross-check for conduct that, objectively, looks without merit. For example, in *ITT/Promedia*,[181] the Court of First Instance held that the test for predatory litigation is whether the action: (1) cannot reasonably be considered as an attempt to

[177] See, e.g., Case 85/76, *Hoffmann-La Roche & Co AG v Commission* [1979] ECR 461, para. 91.

[178] See Case C-62/86, *AKZO Chemie BV v Commission* [1991] ECR I-3359, para. 71.

[179] See Joined Cases C–395/96 P and C-396/96P, *Compagnie Maritime Belge Transports SA, Compagnie maritime belge SA and Dafra-Lines A/S v Commission* [2000] ECR I-1365.

[180] The same approach has recently been advocated under US antitrust law. See M Lao, "Reclaiming a Role for Intent Evidence in Monopolisation Analysis" (2004) 54 *American University Law Review* 151.

[181] Case T-111/96, *ITT Promedia NV v Commission* [1998] ECR II-2937, discussed in detail in Ch. 10 (Exclusionary Non-Price Abuses).

establish the rights of the undertaking concerned and can therefore only serve to harass the opposite party; and (2) is conceived in the framework of a plan whose goal is to eliminate competition.

Even if common sense dictates that intent evidence may be relevant in certain instances, it is important that courts and competition authorities should distinguish as clearly as possible between statements that may be consistent with legitimate competition and statements that are only or mainly consistent with exclusionary conduct. The latter might be described as specific intent, which courts and triers of fact often deal with in other areas of law. A good example of this distinction is the *Decca Navigator* case,[182] which concerned the circumstances in which design changes to a dominant firm's product can be considered exclusionary. There is of course no *general* principle of law that a firm, even a dominant firm, has a duty to make its products compatible with rivals' products. But in *Decca Navigator*, the dominant firm deliberately changed its equipment transmission signals for the sole purpose of rendering rivals' compatible equipment unusable, while allowing its own products to continue to work effectively. There was no plausible explanation for the frequency changes other than exclusion. Internal documents from the company left no doubt as to the intention behind these changes. They noted that "it was decided that alterations to the transmissions would be by far the best method of preventing [rivals'] sales."[183] Again, it would be extremely surprising if specific and unambiguous evidence of this kind was ignored. The most useful purpose of intent evidence therefore is that it helps a court or competition authority to understand the *likely effects* of the dominant firm's conduct and thus to interpret facts and to predict consequences.

4.5 OBJECTIVE JUSTIFICATION

Objective justification generally. Although Article 82 EC does not contain an exemption clause similar to Article 81(3), it is well-established that "objective justification" can immunise conduct that would otherwise be an abuse under Article 82 EC from liability.[184] The defence of objective justification is in some ways a tautology. As Advocate General Jacobs stated in *SYFAIT*, "the very fact that conduct is characterised as an 'abuse' suggests that a negative conclusion has already been

[182] *Decca Navigator System*, OJ 1989 L 43/27, discussed in detail in Ch. 13 (Other Exploitative Abuses).

[183] *Ibid.*, para. 25.

[184] See, e.g., Case 40/70, *Sirena Srl v Eda Srl and others* [1971] ECR 69, para. 17; Case 24/67, *Parke, Davis and Co v Probel, Reese, Beintema-Interpharm and Centrafarm* [1968] ECR 55; Case 78/70, *Deutsche Grammophon Gesellschaft mbH v Metro-SB-Großmärkte GmbH & Co KG* [1971] ECR 487; Case 395/87, *Ministère public v Jean-Louis Tournier* [1989] ECR 2521; Case 27/76, *United Brands Company and United Brands Continentaal BV v Commission* [1978] ECR 207; Case 77/77, *Benzine en Petroleum Handelsmaatschappij BV and others v Commission* [1978] ECR 1513, paras. 33–34; Case 311/84, *Centre belge d'études de marché—Télémarketing (CBEM) v SA Compagnie luxembourgeoise de télédiffusion (CLT) and Information publicité Benelux (IPB)* [1985] ECR 3261; *Magill TV Guide/ITP, BBC and RTE*, OJ 1989 L 78/43; *Eurofix-Bauco v Hilti*, OJ 1988 L 65/19; Case T-83/91, *Tetra Pak International SA v Commission* [1994] ECR II-755; Case T-228/97, *Irish Sugar plc v Commission* [1999] ECR II-2969; and Case C-163/99, *Portugal v Commission* [2001] ECR I-2613.

reached."[185] It seems odd, then, that abusive conduct can be justified. A more accurate view is that objective justification means that "certain types of conduct on the part of a dominant undertaking do not fall within the category of abuse at all."[186]

Objective justification has a number of different facets under Article 82 EC: (1) situations in which the dominant firm's conduct is objectively necessary because of factors external to the dominant firm's conduct; (2) situations in which the dominant firm takes defensive measures to protect its commercial interests; and (3) situations in which the dominant firm's conduct is justified by market-expanding or other efficiencies. The practical application of these defences is discussed in detail in subsequent chapters: only the basic elements of each defence are outlined below.

a. Defences of objective necessity. A dominant firm's conduct may be justified by objective necessity. For example, in refusal to deal cases, capacity limitations or concerns about quality, security, or safety at a facility may justify a refusal to deal. Such defences will, however, be scrutinised carefully. In *Frankfurt Airport*,[187] the airport operator argued that its refusal to allow self-handling or additional ramp handling suppliers was justified by a lack of capacity and concerns over safety and quality degradation concerns. An experts report was also submitted by the airport operator to bolster these concerns. The Commission did not accept this report at face value, but set up a group of technical experts consisting of representatives of the airport operator and the complainant and chaired by an independent expert. When the technical group could not reach an unanimous conclusion, the Commission appointed a leading industry expert to compile a detailed independent report. The Commission evaluated the various reports in reaching its conclusion that the airport operator's defences were, for the most part, unjustified.[188]

b. Reasonable steps by a dominant firm to protect its commercial interest. A dominant firm may be justified in taking reasonable defensive measures to protect its commercial interests. This defence most commonly arises in connection with price cuts—the so-called "meeting competition" defence—and is discussed in detail in Chapter Five (Predatory Pricing). A similar principle has been elaborated in connection

[185] See Opinion of Advocate General Jacobs in Case C-53/03, *Synetairismos Farmakopoion Aitolias & Akarnanias (Syfait) and Others v GlaxoSmithKline plc and GlaxoSmithKline AEVE* [2005] ECR I-4609, para. 53.

[186] *Ibid.* There is some confusion in the case law on the availability and scope of the defence of objective justification. In *Atlantic Container Lines*, the Court of First Instance suggested that objective justification has a narrow scope and is solely intended to "enable a dominant undertaking to show not that the practices in question should be permitted because they confer certain advantages, but only that the purpose of those practices is reasonably to protect its commercial interests in the face of action taken by certain third parties and that they do not therefore in fact constitute an abuse." See Joined cases T-191/98, T-212/98 to T-214/98, *Atlantic Container Line AB and Others v Commission* [2003] ECR II-3275, para. 1114. In other words, the Court suggested that objective justification is limited to reasonable and proportionate defensive measures by a dominant firm. This statement was, however, more attuned to the particular circumstances of the case rather than suggesting that objective justification only concerns the defensive strategies that a dominant firm can adopt.

[187] See *FAG-Flughafen Frankfurt/Main AG*, OJ 1998 L 72/30.

[188] See also *Eurofix-Bauco v Hilti,* OJ 1988 L 65/19, paras. 88–89 (defence based on safety concerns rejected).

with acts that might be construed as reprisals by a dominant firm against customers/distributors that deal with competing firms. In *United Brands*, the Court of Justice held that it was abusive for a dominant supplier to terminate supplies to a distributor on the grounds that the distributor had participated in an advertising campaign for a competitor of the supplier. The Court accepted that a dominant firm can take "reasonable steps" to protect its own commercial interests if they are attacked, but that any countermeasures must still be proportionate to the threat "taking into account the economic strength of the undertakings confronting each other."[189]

Later, in *Boosey & Hawkes*, the Commission clarified that, in situations where a customer transfers its central activity to the promotion of a competing brand, a dominant producer is entitled to review its commercial relations with that customer and on giving adequate notice terminate any special relationship.[190] Although the notion of a proportionate response is somewhat vague, it seems to imply that the dominant firm should not terminate relations without warning but should give notice that is reasonable when the totality of the circumstances of the distributor are considered (e.g., whether the distributor relies exclusively on the dominant firm). But in most cases a distributor will have equivalent contractual or other rights anyway.

c. ***Efficiency defences.*** A final broad category of objective justification is where a dominant firm claims that its conduct is justified by the fact that it enhances its efficiency. Numerous examples are discussed in detail in subsequent chapters: only the principal examples are summarised here. In the area of predatory pricing, price cuts may be introduced to increase demand for the dominant firm's products. For example, short-term promotional offers are intended to allow consumers to become familiar with a product in the hope that, when they do, they will pay a higher price once the promotional phase ends. Loss-leading has a similar rationale in that price cuts on certain products are offered in order to increase demand for other (complementary) products. Price cuts may also be intended to expand the market or increase efficiency in other ways, such as by acquiring learning experience to reduce costs over time or creating network effects. A slightly different defence is that, in situations of excess capacity, the maximum market price may not exceed any firm's relevant costs, in which case the least inefficient option is to sell below cost for a period until the market corrects itself. The availability and scope of these defences are discussed in detail in Chapter Five.

Objective justification is also a central issue in the case of exclusive dealing, loyalty, rebates, and other vertical restraints. Such restraints may be motivated by the need to recover fixed costs more efficiently, the need to provide optimal incentives to retailers, and the need to ensure that customer-specific investments by the dominant firm are adequately protected.[191] Many of the same justifications underpin price discrimination by a dominant firm, which should generally be presumed to be efficient where it expands output more than in situations in which uniform prices apply.[192] The same

[189] Case 27/76, *United Brands Company and United Brands Continentaal BV v Commission* [1978] ECR 207, paras. 189–91.

[190] *BBI/Boosey & Hawkes—Interim measures,* OJ 1987 L 286/36.

[191] See Ch. 7 (Exclusive Dealing, Loyalty Discounts, and Related Practices) for more detail.

[192] See Ch. 11 (Abusive Discrimination) for more detail.

comment can be made in respect of tying and bundling, discussed in Chapter Nine. In essence, all of these defences seek to put forward explanations of why the conduct in question is efficient or justified by some legitimate consideration other than the dominant firm's interest in excluding competitors.

The burden and standard of proof for efficiencies. Proof of efficiencies requires a number of different steps, now outlined in detail in the Discussion Paper.[193] It states that four cumulative conditions apply, which essentially mirror those applicable under Article 81(3).[194] First, the dominant firm must show that the conduct was undertaken to improve the production or distribution of products or to promote technical or economic progress (e.g., by improving the quality of its product or by obtaining specific cost reductions), or to generate another efficiency. Such claims must be substantiated, though the evidence may be less demanding in the case of qualitative efficiencies such as improvements in distribution.

Second, the dominant firm must show that the conduct is indispensable to achieve the alleged efficiencies. It is for the dominant company to demonstrate that there are no other economically practicable and less anticompetitive alternatives to achieve the claimed efficiencies, taking into account the market conditions and business realities facing the dominant company. The dominant company is not required to consider hypothetical or theoretical alternatives. The Commission will only contest the claim where it is reasonably clear that there are realistic and attainable alternatives, when viewed in the overall context of the dominant firm's conduct and the market realities faced by the dominant firm at the time it made the relevant decision.[195] The dominant company must explain and demonstrate why seemingly realistic and less restrictive alternatives would be significantly less efficient.

Third, the dominant company needs to show that efficiencies brought about by the conduct concerned outweigh the likely negative effects on competition and in particular

[193] See Discussion Paper, para. 84. See also Joined Cases C-204/00P et al., *Aalborg Portland A/S and Others v Commission* [2004] ECR I-123, paras. 78–79 ("[I]t should be for the party or the authority alleging an infringement of the competition rules to prove the existence thereof and it should be for the undertaking or the association of undertakings invoking the benefit of a defence against a finding of an infringement to demonstrate that the conditions for applying such defence are satisfied, so that the authority will then have to resort to other evidence. Although according to those principles the legal burden of proof is borne either by the Commission or by the undertaking or association concerned the factual evidence on which a party relies may be of such a kind as to require the other party to provide an explanation or justification, failing which it is permissible to conclude that the burden of proof has been discharged.").

[194] *Ibid.*, para. 84.

[195] For example, in *Hilti*, Hilti attempted to block the sale of independents' nails by making it known that guarantees on its nail guns would not be honoured if non-Hilti nails were used. The ostensible reason for this was safety concerns with rivals' nails. The Commission found that, whilst it may be legitimate not to honour a guarantee if a faulty or sub-standard non-Hilti nail causes malfunctioning, premature wear, or breakdown in a particular case, Hilti's policy was disproportionate. In particular, there was no evidence that Hilti sought to: (1) generally inform customers in writing of these concerns; (2) communicate these concerns to the suppliers in question; or (3) report the matter to the relevant national authorities dealing with safety issues. All of these alternatives were considered by the Commission to be less restrictive than refusing to honour all guarantees outright. See *Eurofix-Bauco v Hilti,* OJ 1988 L 65/19, paras. 87 et seq.

the likely harm to consumers that the conduct might otherwise have. This will be the case when the Commission, on the basis of sufficient evidence, is in a position to conclude that the efficiencies generated by the conduct are likely to enhance the ability and incentive of the dominant company to act procompetitively for the benefit of consumers.

The fourth condition is that the efficiencies not only outweigh the negative effects on competition, but also that, on balance, consumers benefit from the conduct concerned. This reflects the consideration that Article 82 EC protects competition on the market as a means of enhancing consumer welfare and of ensuring an efficient allocation of resources. This requires that the pass-on of benefits must at least compensate consumers for any actual or likely negative impact caused to them by the conduct concerned. If consumers in an affected relevant market are worse off following the *prima facie* abusive conduct, the conduct cannot be justified on efficiency grounds.

In making this assessment, the Commission states that it must be take into account that the value of a gain for consumers in the future is not the same as a present gain for consumers. In general, the later the efficiencies are expected to materialise in the future, the less weight the Commission or national authorities can assign to them. This implies that, to be considered as a countervailing factor, the efficiencies must arise in the short-term.

The incentive on the part of the dominant company to pass efficiency gains on to consumers is often related to the existence of competitive pressure from the remaining firms in the market and from potential entry. This incentive may often be already small as a result of the dominant position. The greater the actual or likely negative effects on competition, the more the Commission or national authorities have to be sure that the claimed efficiencies are substantial, likely to be realised, and to be passed on, to a sufficient degree, to the consumer. It is therefore highly unlikely that *prima facie* abusive conduct of a dominant company with a market position approaching that of a monopoly, or with a similar level of market power, can be justified on the ground that efficiency gains would be sufficient to outweigh its actual or likely anticompetitive effects and would benefit consumers. Similarly, in a market where demand is very inelastic it is highly unlikely that abusive conduct of a dominant company strengthening its dominant position can be justified on the ground that efficiency gains would be sufficient to counteract the actual or likely anticompetitive effects and would benefit consumers.

The final condition is that competition in respect of a substantial part of the products concerned is not eliminated. The Discussion Paper states that when competition is eliminated the competitive process is brought to an end and short-term efficiency gains are outweighed by longer-term losses stemming *inter alia* from expenditures incurred by the dominant company to maintain its position (rent seeking), misallocation of resources, reduced innovation, and higher prices.[196] This is a recognition of the fact that rivalry between undertakings is an essential driver of economic efficiency, including dynamic efficiencies in the shape of innovation.

[196] Discussion Paper, para. 91.

Ultimately, according to the Commission, the protection of rivalry and the competitive process is given priority over possible procompetitive efficiency gains. Thus, it is highly unlikely that abusive conduct of a dominant company with a market position approaching that of a monopoly could be justified on the ground that efficiency gains would be sufficient to counteract its actual or likely anticompetitive effects. This accords with the sliding scale applied to efficiencies under EC merger control rules.[197] By way of guidance, the Discussion Paper suggests that a 75% market share would substantially eliminate competition in circumstances where there is no effective competition from other actual competitors in the market (e.g., because they have higher costs or capacity constraints).[198]

Evaluating the approach to efficiency defences under Article 82 EC. The explicit recognition of potential efficiencies under Article 82 EC is clearly welcome, since a good deal of unilateral conduct will have a mixture of positive and negative effects on consumers. But significant difficulties remain. A first point is that, despite general recognition of objective justification in the case law, there are very few cases under Article 82 EC in which objective justification has actually been accepted by courts and competition authorities. This may reflect the fact that the basis for the defence put forward in several cases was not strong enough, but more likely suggests that there is something of a disconnect between theory and practice on objective justification. Efficiency defences have typically been rejected with cursory analysis by the Community institutions and without any indication of the analytical framework in mind. This deficiency should be addressed, since a defence that is recognised in theory, but not in practice, is the same as no defence.

A second point is that, although the theory of balancing procompetitive and anticompetitive effects sounds straightforward, it is often anything but. In theory, the exercise is easy: the amount of the benefits (increased consumer welfare) is compared with welfare loss caused by the exclusion of rivals (e.g., reduced consumer surplus or deadweight monopoly loss). Whichever is larger determines the outcome. But in practice it may not be easy, or indeed possible, for a dominant firm to make such detailed assessments at the time it decides on its commercial strategy, in particular if this involves detailed knowledge of the effects of a particular practice on rivals and more generally on consumer welfare. One commentator summarises these practical concerns as follows:[199]

> "The problem, however, is that neither economic actors nor law enforcement entities are omniscient. Given real world limitations, market-wide balancing tests that seek to assess the benefits and competitive harms of exclusionary conduct are intractable for courts and antitrust agencies, and even more so for firms trying to decide in real time what conduct is permitted and what is prohibited. Prospective defendants cannot be expected to know in real time, *ex ante*, whether their efficiency-generating conduct will cause disproportionate harm to their rivals or consumers because, in order to know that, the defendants would have to know more

[197] See Guidelines on the assessment of horizontal mergers under the Council Regulation on the control of concentrations between undertakings, OJ 2004 C 31/5, paras. 80–86.

[198] Discussion Paper, above, para. 92.

[199] See AD Melamed, "Exclusionary Conduct Under the Antitrust Laws: Balancing, Sacrifice, and Refusals to Deal" (2005) 20 *Berkeley Technology Law Journal* 1249.

than they can be expected to know about consumer demand, their rivals' costs and prospects for innovation and for mitigation of harm, future entry conditions, and the like. From the perspective of the defendants, therefore, a balancing test would likely either be ignored, impose excessive transaction costs (a kind of tax on entrepreneurship), or result in excessive caution. There is little reason to expect that a balancing test would create optimal *ex ante* incentives for marketplace behaviour."

Third, it is questionable whether it is correct in law to require the dominant firm to show that the efficiencies outweigh the anticompetitive effects. Article 2 of Regulation 1/2003 provides that "the burden of proving an infringement of...Article 82...shall rest on the party or the authority alleging the infringement."[200] In *SYFAIT*, Advocate General Jacobs made clear that proof of objective justification means that "certain types of conduct on the part of a dominant undertaking do not fall within the category of abuse at all."[201] It is true that Article 2 of Regulation 1/2003 places the burden of proving the benefit of the conditions of Article 81(3) on the defendant, but it clearly does not apply the same principle to Article 82 EC and objective justification. In these circumstances, it should be for a plaintiff or competition authority to show that the anticompetitive effects outweigh the efficiencies, since, otherwise, no abuse has been proven. The dominant firm should simply bear the initial burden of producing colourable evidence to substantiate the efficiencies claimed. The legal burden should then shift to the plaintiff or competition authority.

Fourth, a particular problem arises because the last condition of the efficiency defence under Article 82 EC—that the conduct does not "substantially eliminate competition"—is in practice likely to preclude the availability of the defence. Under Article 82 EC, an efficiency defence would be raised in circumstances where, first, a firm is already dominant and, second, its conduct has been found to have an actual or likely exclusionary effect on competition. Although the Community institutions have made clear that dominance does not necessarily mean that competition is "substantially eliminated,"[202] a finding of dominance *and* material foreclosure effect under Article 82 EC may, for practical purposes, mean that competition is substantially eliminated. But, even then, the conduct in question may still enhance consumer welfare overall. In other words, there appears to be a logical contradiction between the substantive test for abuse and the availability of an efficiency defence: because of the addition of the "substantial elimination of competition" condition, the former seems to preclude the latter.[203] It is also worth noting that, as a practical matter, the Commission

[200] Council Regulation 1/2003 on the implementation of the rules on competition laid down in Articles 81 and 82 of the Treaty, OJ 2003 L 1/1.

[201] See Opinion of Advocate General Jacobs in Case C-53/03, *Synetairismos Farmakopoion Aitolias & Akarnanias (Syfait) and Others v GlaxoSmithKline plc and GlaxoSmithKline AEVE* [2005] ECR I-4609, para. 53.

[202] See Commission Notice—Guidelines on the application of Article 81(3) of the Treaty, OJ 2004 C 101/97, para. 106; Joined Cases T-191/98 and T-212/98 to T-214/98, *Atlantic Container Line AB and Others v Commission* [2003] ECR II-3275, para. 939 ("As the concept of eliminating competition is narrower than that of the existence or acquisition of a dominant position, an undertaking holding such a position is capable of benefiting from an exemption.").

[203] It is not clear why the Discussion Paper proposes to transpose the conditions for exemption under Article 81(3) to the efficiency defence under Article 82 EC. The most likely reason is consistency, but

has rarely exempted under Article 81 EC arrangements that created dominance (except, perhaps, in the case of beneficial new technologies and markets).

Fifth, many economists question whether balancing anticompetitive effects is meaningful where those effects are a function of a restriction that is indispensable to achieve the stated efficiency.[204] For example, if exclusive dealing is indispensable to achieve an efficiency (e.g., to justify a customer-specific investment), the source of the anticompetitive concern is the same as the source of the efficiency. And, yet, under the fourth condition for an efficiency defence—no elimination of competition—an efficient clause would probably be condemned in this instance. A related problem is the suggestion in the Discussion Paper that an efficiency defence will generally be unavailable at market shares in excess of 75%.[205] It is not clear why this statement was added: either conduct is efficient or it is not.

A final important point is that the scope and availability of an efficiency defence cannot be looked at in isolation from the substantive rules that apply for specific practices. For example, the non-discrimination clause in Article 82(c) has sometimes been applied in a mechanical fashion, with little regard for the many legitimate reasons why firms charge different prices or offer different terms.[206] The effect of this rule may be to require dominant firms to put forward efficiency justifications for everyday business decisions. But most differences in prices or terms result from the relative skills and bargaining power of customers and do not have (or need) a formal efficiency justification beyond this. It makes no sense to require a dominant firm to provide an elaborate explanation for something as innocuous as other firms' negotiation skills or bargaining power. The same could be said of conditional discount schemes. The broad (and arguably vague) rules historically applied by the Commission in respect of such practices—whether the discounts have a "fidelity-building" effect—require dominant firms to offer efficiency justifications for many practices that have a simple, obvious, and procompetitive logic.[207] Applying a detailed efficiency justification test in every instance to such practices is unnecessary and wrong.

there is certainly nothing in the wording of Article 82 EC that requires the use of the same conditions as Article 81(3).

[204] See *Selective Price Cuts And Fidelity Rebates*, Economic Discussion paper prepared by RBB for the Office of Fair Trading, July 2005, para. 4.146 et seq.

[205] Discussion Paper, para. 92.

[206] See Ch. 11 (Abusive Discrimination).

[207] See Ch. 7 (Exclusive Dealing, Loyalty Rebates, and Related Practices).

Chapter 5

PREDATORY PRICING

5.1 INTRODUCTION

The importance of price competition. Encouraging firms to compete on price is a basic tenet of competition law and policy. The fundamental goal of competition is that rivalry and price competition should force firms to maximise their output thereby selling their products as close as possible to the minimum profitable price—in theory their marginal cost of production (i.e., pricing at the level of the extra cost of producing the last unit of production). The notion that firms should price as close as possible to their lowest profitable price applies with equal force in the case of firms with a dominant position, since the existence of market power gives rise to the possibility that a dominant firm will seek to increase prices above the level that a competitive market would bring about. It is therefore desirable that firms, including dominant firms, are strongly encouraged to offer lower prices.

The above principles are widely reflected in case law under Article 82 EC. In *Eurofix-Bauco/Hilti,* for example, the Commission emphasised that "aggressive price rivalry is an essential competitive instrument."[1] Likewise, in *AKZO*, the Commission stated that "a dominant firm is entitled to compete on the merits" and that the Commission does not suggest that "larger producers should be under an obligation to refrain from competing vigorously with smaller competitors or new entrants."[2] More recently, in *Compagnie Maritime Belge*, Advocate General Fennelly made clear that EC competition law's fundamental goal of encouraging price competition applies equally to dominant firms:[3]

> "Price competition is the essence of the free and open competition which it is the objective of the Community policy to establish on the internal market. It favours more efficient firms and it is for the benefit of consumers both in the short and the long run. Dominant firms not only have the right but should be encouraged to compete on price...Community competition law...should not offer less efficient undertakings a safe haven against vigorous competition even from dominant undertakings."

Price competition that can harm consumers. Not all forms of price competition are legitimate under Article 82 EC. The most obvious example concerns predatory pricing, discussed in this chapter. Although there is no universal definition of predation, it

---

[1] *Eurofix-Bauco v Hilti*, OJ 1988 L 65/19, para. 81.

[2] *ECS/AKZO*, OJ 1985 L 374/1, para. 81 (hereinafter "*AKZO*"), upheld on appeal in Case C-62/86, *AKZO Chemie BV v Commission* [1991] ECR I-3359.

[3] See Opinion of Advocate General Fennelly in Joined Cases C–395/96 P and C-396/96P, *Compagnie Maritime Belge Transports SA, Compagnie maritime belge SA and Dafra-Lines A/S v Commission* [2000] ECR I-1365 (hereinafter "*Compagnie Maritime Belge*"), paras. 117, 132. See also *Cewal, Cowac and Ukwal*, OJ 1993 L 34/20, upheld on appeal in Joined Cases T-24/93, T-25/93, T-26/93, and T-28/93, *Compagnie Maritime Belge Transports SA and Others v Commission* [1996] ECR II-1201.

generally refers to strategies whereby a firm offers low prices in the short-term in order to induce competitors' market exit, followed by higher prices in the medium- to long-term. It may be rational and profitable for a dominant firm to invest in loss-making activities for a certain period if the elimination of a rival allows it to increase prices following market exit to a level that compensates for the losses suffered during the predation phase. Predation thus involves reduced short-term profits, or even losses, that exclude actual or potential rivals, followed by higher prices in the medium- to long-term as a result of the additional market power that rivals' exit confers. The challenge faced by a court or competition authority in predatory pricing cases is therefore to identify those limited situations in which the very conduct that competition law is intended to encourage—low prices output—operates to consumer detriment.

Rules that deal with predatory pricing must decide, first, which economic model should determine whether price-cutting is rational and, second, what legal rules should govern the application of the underlying economic model to determine when price-cutting should be unlawful. The overriding objectives are to ensure that the chosen approach does not allow predatory behaviour to go undetected, and to allow firms to compete on price to the widest possible extent. Consumers benefit from low prices, including, in the short-term at least, low predatory prices. Objections to low prices should be looked at critically to ensure that the rules are clear and no more than necessary in the circumstances. If the rules are not clear or unnecessarily restrictive, there is a significant risk that companies will be cautious about lowering prices. This in turn could lead to a chilling of desirable price competition, with potentially significant welfare implications. In addition, enforcement of whatever approach is chosen must not be too complicated, since a rule that is difficult to enforce creates enforcement and welfare costs of its own. It should also be borne in mind that perfect information will almost never be available in the context of litigation or administrative action. In other words, the optimal framework may not be possible to apply in practice, which has important implications for the choice of economic and legal rules.

5.2 THE ECONOMICS OF PREDATORY PRICING

Overview. Predatory pricing has given rise to a vast economic literature. The literature discloses a wide measure of disagreement as to the appropriate rules, with theories ranging from the proposition that predatory pricing is so irrational that it never occurs to the view that any reactive price cut by a dominant firm in response to new entry should be subject to restrictions.[4] Notwithstanding the diversity of views, a good deal of consensus exists on two core principles. The first is that cost benchmarks are useful in deciding whether a firm's prices are predatory or not. This principle rests on a basic premise of industrial organisation: that firms act for profit, which in turn depends on total revenues exceeding total costs. Unfortunately, the consensus ends there, since a wide range of differing views exist as to which measure of costs is appropriate in predatory pricing cases.

[4] For a good overview of the main competing theories, see Organisation for Economic Cooperation and Development, *Predatory Pricing*, May 31, 1989, Section IV.

A second core principle is that predatory pricing should not be mechanically assessed on the basis of price/cost tests, but requires an appreciation of the strategic context in which the pricing behaviour takes place. This principle has two different, and opposing, facets. The first is that predatory pricing is indeed a rational strategy in certain factual settings. This view rejects an earlier view that predatory pricing was so irrational as to be non-existent.[5] A second facet is that there may also be legitimate reasons why a firm would price below cost for a limited period, in particular where short-term losses are necessary to stimulate demand and reduce costs over time.

5.2.1 Basic Cost Definitions

Types of costs. Economists have devised a number of standard measurements of firms' costs. It is important to appreciate that these are economic, not accounting, costs and may include for example a return on capital. The basic idea is simple: that a profit-maximising firm will act to ensure that marginal revenue exceeds marginal costs, since, otherwise, it will go out of business. But a number of different cost measurements, and types of costs, should be distinguished within this basic axiom of industrial organisation:

1. *Variable, fixed, and total costs.* A firm's costs can be divided into those that vary with output and those that do not. Costs that do not vary with output are termed *fixed costs*, since they must be incurred regardless of the amount produced during the relevant period (e.g., rent). All other costs are *variable* in that they vary in proportion to output (e.g., raw materials). The sum of fixed and variable costs is *total cost*. Costs can be averaged over output to give *average cost*. For example, *average total cost* (ATC) is the sum of average fixed costs and average variable cost (AVC).

2. *Marginal and incremental costs.* A concept that is closely related to variable cost is *marginal cost* (MC), which is the cost of producing one additional unit of output. MC is a function of variable costs only, since fixed costs, by definition, do not vary according to output. The MC of a unit of output and the average cost of all units of output can differ. For example, suppose it costs €100 to produce 100 units and €102 to produce 101 units. The average cost of the first 100 units is €1; the MC of the 101st unit is €2. The usefulness of MC is limited in practice, since a firm will rarely be interested in the cost of producing only one additional unit. A firm is more likely to be interested in the additional cost incurred by a larger increment in output, which is sometimes referred to as *incremental cost*. The difference between MC and incremental cost is partly definitional and many economists therefore treat them as equivalent. Formally, however, MC assumes a continuous cost function, whereas incremental cost is a more generic concept that allows for increments that are larger than a single additional unit of output. Thus, MC

[5] See, e.g., J McGee, "Predatory Price Cutting: The Standard Oil (N.J.) Case" (1958) 1 *Journal of Law and Economics* 1376; RH Bork, *The Antitrust Paradox: A Policy at War with Itself* (New York, Basic Books, 1978); FH Easterbrook, "Predatory Strategies and Counter Strategies" (1981) 48 *University of Chicago Law Review* 263; and H Demsetz, "Barriers to Entry" (1982) 72 *American Economic Review* 52.

and incremental cost are likely to be the same when the increment in output is very small, but may differ substantially when it is large. MC may thus be either above or below average cost.

3. *Avoidable and sunk costs.* Fixed costs should also be divided into recoverable, or *avoidable*, costs and non-recoverable, or *sunk*, costs. For example, a lease on an office building may be either a sunk or an avoidable cost. The lease would be a sunk cost where there was no possibility for the firm to sublet the office for the remainder of the lease, whereas it would be avoidable if the firm could sublet to another firm for the rest of the contract period.

4. *Common and joint costs.* A final cost measure is unique to multi-product firms: where a firm produces two or more products, it will usually have *common costs* that are incurred in common for a number of products. Common costs may be fixed or variable, but most are fixed. A firm may also have *joint costs* where the production of one product simultaneously involves the production of another, inseparable product (e.g., a by-product).

The reason why costs may increase, fall, or remain unchanged depends on the nature of the economies generated at certain levels of production. In the case of a single product, a firm may have *economies of scale*, which means that average costs fall as output increases. Average costs may actually increase as output increases, leading to *diseconomies of scale*. Or average costs may remain unchanged as output increases, in which case the activity is said to generate *constant returns to scale*. Where a firm produces two or more products, it may also be cheaper to produce the two products than it would to make each separately. In this case, the firm has *economies of scope*. For example, it may be that one production process generates a by-product that can be used in the production of another product.

The distinction between the short-run and the long-run. The relevant time period over which costs are assessed also has an important bearing on the classification of the relevant costs. A basic distinction should be made between the short-term—the period in which the factors of production cannot be varied without incurring additional cost—and the long-run—the period in which all factors of production are variable. In the example of the lease given above, the short-term would be the period in which the lease cannot be broken without incurring additional cost. The long-term would be the period after the lease expires, where the company has the choice to renew it or not, or to purchase an office rather than rent one. Thus, in the long-term, no cost is by nature fixed, variable, sunk, or avoidable. Or, looked at differently, virtually all costs are fixed in the very short-term, whereas all are variable in the long-run.

Certain commentators argue that, while selling below short-run costs is generally irrational, selling below long-run costs is a better measure of whether a price is profit-maximising or not.[6] Long-run costs include not only the short-run costs that influence a

[6] See PL Joskow and AK Klevorick, "A Framework for Analysing Predatory Pricing Policy" (1979) 89 *Yale Law Journal* 213-270; P Bolton, JF Brodley, and MH Riordan, "Predatory Pricing: Strategic Theory and Legal Policy" (2000) 88(8) *Georgetown Law Journal* 2239; and RA Posner, *Antitrust Law* (2nd edn., Chicago, University of Chicago Press, 2001).

firm's immediate production decisions, but all other product-specific costs incurred in entering a market. Long-run costs would therefore include research, development, and marketing costs, even if they were sunk before the period of predatory pricing. In the case of a retail outlet, long-run expenses would include rent, insurance, and other overhead costs, as well as inventory costs.[7] Long-run costs are also thought to be preferable because "they measure the present worth of the productive assets by replacement costs, and not by historic costs, which may give little indication of their current value."[8]

The time period to be taken into account in calculating the relevant costs. The time period taken into account can have a decisive impact on the classification of costs, since all costs are variable in the long-run and few are variable in the very short-term. The time period over which predation is assessed can therefore have a significant bearing on whether a price is treated as predatory or not. Most commentators agree that the correct period for assessing which costs are variable is the period of the alleged predatory pricing, that is the period in which the allegedly predatory prices prevailed or could be reasonably be expected to prevail.[9] (The latter qualification is important: it would make no sense to limit the assessment of costs to the period when regulatory or court intervention occurs if the campaign was scheduled to last for longer.) The basic logic is simple: if a low price is in force for, say, three months, it will be capable of driving an equally efficient rival out of business only if the price is less than the average per unit cost that a rival would incur in that period.[10] Until the alleged predatory price lasts long enough to be exceeded by those costs that were variable for that period, "an equally efficient entrant cannot have suffered any loss it could have avoided by exit, and thus cannot have had any incentive to exit."[11] In other words, prices in excess of the variable

[7] RA Posner, *Antitrust Law* (2nd edn., Chicago, University of Chicago Press, 2001) p. 215.

[8] P Bolton, JF Brodley, and MH Riordan, "Predatory Pricing: Strategic Theory and Legal Policy" (2000) 88(8) *Georgetown Law Journal* 2239, 2272.

[9] See, e.g., PE Areeda, *Antitrust Analysis: Problems, Text, Cases* (3rd edn., Boston, Little, Brown, and Company, 1981) p. 199; PE Areeda and H Hovenkamp, *Antitrust Law* (2nd edn., New York, Aspen Law & Business, 2000) para. 740d; and WJ Baumol, "Predation and the Logic of the Average Variable Cost Test" (1996) 39 *Journal of Law & Economics* 49, 50. See also Assessment of Conduct: Draft Competition Law Guideline for Consultation, OFT 414a, para. 4.4 ("The relevant time period is usually that over which the alleged predatory price(s) prevailed or could reasonably be expected to prevail.").

[10] Baumol, *ibid.* But see *Aberdeen Journals Limited v Office of Fair Trading* [2003] CAT 11 (United Kingdom). The Office of Fair Trading (OFT), the UK Competition Authority, found that, although predation prevailed from 1996–2001, variable costs could have been assessed on the basis of periods limited to a single month, as the predator produced management accounts monthly and it was a period over which short term planning for the predatory product was determined. This was despite the fact that the OFT held that Aberdeen's revenues had been less than the costs that would have been avoided if the predatory product had not been published over the period 1996–2001. On appeal, the Competition Appeal Tribunal doubted the correctness of this approach (para. 385), but did not overturn the OFT's findings, since it had adopted the approach most favourable to Aberdeen, which still indicated below-cost selling (para. 386).

[11] See E Elhauge, "Why Above-Cost Price Cuts To Drive Out Entrants Are Not Predatory and the Implications for Defining Costs and Market Power" (2003) 112 *Yale Law Journal* 681-795, 708. Elhauge elaborates as follows: "Alleged predatory prices that last only one month cannot cause an equally efficient rival to lose any money by not exiting unless those prices are lower than the very short-run costs the rival incurred by operating that month. In contrast, pricing that lasts for ten years will cause an equally efficient rival to lose money (relative to exit) if the price does not suffice to cover

cost for the relevant period cannot, by definition, cause an equally-efficient rival to exit: it would be cheaper to stay in the market.

The principal cost tests for predatory pricing. Predatory pricing has given rise to a vast literature that involves widely-differing approaches to the applicable tests. Early thinking associated with the Chicago school of antitrust considered that predatory pricing was generally irrational and in any event impossible to accurately detect without also wrongly condemning legitimate prices. At the other extreme lie complex rule-of-reason inquiries that require in-depth examination of the circumstances and effects of particular business conduct within the specific market context.[12] The approaches that have gained mainstream acceptance in the decisional practice and case law, however, are limited in number. Essentially, there are three: the Areeda and Turner AVC test; the avoidable cost test; and the long-run incremental cost test.

a. The Areeda and Turner AVC test. The first quantitative rule for detecting predatory prices was based on a simple piece of economics by Areeda and Turner.[13] This test is based on the profit-maximising (or loss-minimising) condition for firms in competitive markets, by which a firm sets price at least equal to MC—the increase in total expenditure resulting from a small rise in the output of the relevant product. As setting a price below MC entails a sacrifice of profits, such behaviour is deemed to be an indicator of predation. Accordingly, the rule classifies as unlawful any price below reasonably-anticipated MC. The relevant time period proposed by Areeda and Turner for assessing costs was the short-run—a period during which a firm does not change production assets, such as plant.

Because of the difficulties of measuring MC—it does not generally appear on firm's accounts—Areeda and Turner suggested using AVC as a surrogate. They argued that a price below AVC was irrational for a profit-maximising firm and could therefore be presumed predatory, whereas a price above AVC was, in the short-run at least, sustainable and therefore a reasonable benchmark for a legitimate price. Implicit in this test was the notion that competition law should only protect firms who are at least as efficient as the dominant firm. A test based on MC, and its surrogate AVC, allowed firms with the same or greater efficiency to compete on the merits with the dominant firm, while not offering unnecessary protection to firms with higher cost structures. The Areeda and Turner test has had a major influence on predatory pricing laws in developed countries, including the EU and its Member States.

b. The avoidable cost test. Problems with the classification of fixed and variable costs, the allocation of common fixed and variable costs between two or more products,

---

the fixed costs of producing anything next year (like overhead) or the future capital costs of rebuilding facilities that seemed like sunken costs in the short run but are variable over a time horizon of ten years. Thus, we need not pick one time period or cost measure in the abstract; the choice is dictated by the time period of the alleged predation."

[12] FM Scherer, "Predatory Pricing and the Sherman Act: A Comment" (1976) 86 *Harvard Law Review* 869. Although Scherer's approach was considered unworkable, a paper by L Phlips, *Predatory Pricing* (Commission of the European Communities, 1987) suggested a wide inquiry in the same spirit as Scherer.

[13] PE Areeda and DF Turner, "Predatory Pricing and Related Practices Under Section 2 of the Sherman Act" (1975) 88 *Harvard Law Review* 697-733.

and developments in economic thinking have led commentators to propose certain modifications to the AVC standard proposed by Areeda and Turner. One approach that has gained prominence is the use of average avoidable cost (AAC).[14] AAC involves comparing the incremental cost of remaining in the market with the decremental, or avoidable, cost of exiting it. If the former exceeds the latter, it would make more sense to discontinue the line of business than to remain. Accordingly, a rational business would not sell below its AAC, since it would be cheaper to exit than to remain in the market at current prices.

In simple terms, the AAC test examines whether a firm would save more money by exiting the market entirely than it would gain by remaining in the market at current prices. AAC therefore includes all variable costs of staying in the market, as well as "all fixed costs that are not sunk, so that they can be escaped if the firm exits from the market;"[15] in other words, the sum of the reduction in current operating expenses (i.e., variable costs) plus any monies recoverable from the salvage of fixed assets. Common costs and sunk costs are therefore excluded from AAC.

The AAC test has the advantage of not requiring a segregation of fixed and variable costs, as well as the fact that, unlike AVC, it includes any additional fixed costs entailed by the alleged predatory pricing campaign. In theory, if all relevant information is available, the AAC can accurately measure if the firm would lose more by embarking on the alleged predatory pricing campaign than it would in exiting the product line. The AAC test assumes that enterprises will rationally continue to produce a given product only if the revenue from the sale of that product exceeds the costs that could be saved by ceasing production (i.e., the product's avoidable costs). Pricing below AAC is assumed to be irrational and, therefore, predatory.

c. ***Long-run incremental cost tests.*** As indicated, a number of commentators favour the use of long-run product-specific cost measures as a standard for predatory pricing.[16] Several reasons are advanced. First, they argue that the decision to enter and remain in a market depends not only on the short-run costs that influence immediate production decisions, but also includes the long-term total costs of entering and remaining on the market, including capital costs. Second, the AVC test may be under-inclusive where fixed costs are high and variable costs are very low or near-zero. This is true of many network industries and most intellectual property. Third, long-run costs do not require classification of costs as fixed or variable, which is often complex and arbitrary. Finally, long-run product-specific cost measures avoid the great difficulties of allocating common costs between two or more operations.

---

[14] See WJ Baumol, "Predation and the Logic of the Average Variable Cost Test" (1996) 39 *Journal of Law & Economics* 49; and Organisation for Economic Cooperation and Development, *Predatory Foreclosure* (2005) DAF/COMP 14 (hereinafter "OECD Report"), p. 23. See also P Bolton, JF Brodley, and MH Riordan, "Predatory Pricing: Strategic Theory and Legal Policy" (2000) 88(8) *Georgetown Law Journal* 2239, which advocates use of the average avoidable cost test in place of the AVC test.

[15] *Ibid.*, p. 56.

[16] *Ibid.*

The measure of long-run average total costs is sometimes referred to as long-run average incremental cost (LRAIC), that is "the firm's total production cost (including the product), less what the firm's total cost would have been had it not produced the product, divided by the quantity of the product produced."[17] In simple terms, LRAIC is the total value of costs that are needed to enter and start supplying a specific product, as an average over output. Thus, unlike the average avoidable cost test, it includes *all* product-specific sunk costs. Observing a price below LRAIC may not, however, be sufficient to prove predation. Companies will sometimes charge prices below LRAIC once they have entered a market, even though they have no intention of excluding rivals. This is because LRAIC includes sunk costs, which should not affect production decisions going forward. Even if a company regrets the high costs of entering the market, it may be more profitable to ignore past sunk costs—precisely because they are sunk—and to remain in the market. For this reason, proponents of the long-run cost tests argue that a price below LRAIC should not be considered predatory unless accompanied by intent to exclude an equally or more efficient competitor.[18]

d. Evaluating the different price/cost tests. There is no single price/cost test that has unambiguous advantages over others. Each test has a clear rationale in economic theory, but they can all raise significant complexities in practice. The AVC test has gained the most acceptance, probably because it is the most easily understood by lawyers. But the AVC has also been criticised in important respects. First, the task of classifying a cost as variable or fixed may be complex in certain cases. Second, as noted above, commentators have argued that short-run variable costs are not the only determinant of a firm's prices and that regard should also be had to long-run costs, including sunk costs. Third, the AVC rule may allow "gaming" by a dominant firm where it over-invests in fixed assets in order to have spare capacity to engage in predatory pricing, without, however, pricing below its AVC. Finally, in many industries involving intellectual property and networks, a firm's variable cost of adding a customer may be negligible.

The AAC test seeks to correct certain problems with the AVC test by measuring not only the variable costs that would be saved if the firm decided to exit rather than embark on the allegedly predatory campaign, but also any product-specific fixed costs that could be avoided. In theory, it offers a precise measure of whether it would be more profitable for the firm to shut down the particular product line than to embark on the allegedly predatory campaign. Although theoretically perhaps the optimal test,[19] the AAC test can raise significant practical problems.

---

[17] P Bolton, JF Brodley, and MH Riordan, "Predatory Pricing: Strategic Theory and Legal Policy" (2000) 88(8) *Georgetown Law Journal* 2239, 2272.

[18] RA Posner, *Antitrust Law* (2nd edn., Chicago, University of Chicago Press, 2001) p. 215.

[19] A number of jurisdictions favour the AAC test for this reason. See *Commissioner of Competition v Air Canada* (CT-2000/004) Competition Tribunal, Decision of July 22, 2003 (Air Canada found to have operated/increased capacity at fares below its AAC on certain routes contested by WestJet Airlines Ltd. and CanJet Airlines); and *Regulations Respecting Anticompetitive Acts of Persons Operating a Domestic Service* (SOW2000-324) paras. 1(a) and 1(b) and *Draft Enforcement Guidelines on the Abuse of Dominance in the Airline Industry*, Competition Bureau (Canada) (both prescribing an AAC test); and *US v AMR Corp, et al*, 335 F.3d 1109 (10th Cir. 2003) (Predatory pricing claims by

A first problem is that the AAC test does not avoid the difficulty under the AVC test of defining the appropriate time period over which costs should be assessed. Very few costs are avoidable in the very short-run; most will be avoidable in the long-run. Second, significant problems arise in connection with transferable assets—assets that can be redeployed between markets. Assets that can be redeployed across different geographic locations or products create much larger avoidable costs that those which cannot. Which assets can be deployed and to what extent can raise complex issues. Third, there may be a need to adjust the AAC benchmark for revenue spill over in cases where the sale of one product increases the sale of another, i.e., demand complementarity. Prices that are below AAC may be recovered if the loss-leading sales generate follow-on revenues in other higher margin products. Fourth, the test may need adjustment for situations in which a dominant firm could minimise losses by reducing sales and charging a higher price than by exiting. Finally, considerable accounting problems may arise in measuring something that never took place (i.e., market exit).[20] Although many of these problems also arise in connection with other cost benchmarks, ease of implementation is not a compelling argument in favour of the adoption of the AAC test.

Proponents of LRAIC argue that rules based on short-term costs such as AVC and AAC ignore important aspects of predatory pricing behaviour. In particular, firm's production decisions are governed not only be short-run costs, but also by the long-term cost of entering and remaining on a market. Sunk costs, for example, will usually be an important cost of market entry, such as in the case of network industries. For these reasons, LRAIC has been widely used by the Commission, national competition authorities, and national regulatory authorities with powers to apply competition law in the case of telecommunications, gas, and water. LRAIC calculations are fact-intensive, but they are routinely carried out by the Commission and national authorities. As with the AAC test, one advantage of LRAIC is that it does not require classification of costs as fixed or variable. One drawback, however, is that LRAIC generally excludes common and joint costs between two or more products, which may create a significant bias against rivals who are only active in one product and have to support all the stand-alone costs of that product.

5.2.2 Strategic Considerations

Strategic settings in which predatory pricing may be rational. Modern economic thinking identifies a number of settings in which predatory pricing may be profitable and therefore a rational strategy for a dominant firm.[21] A first theory is so-called financial market predation. The traditional "deep pockets" theory—whereby firms with large capital reserves could exclude a smaller, poorly-resourced rival—has generally been discredited in competition policy. This is essentially because capital markets should fund an efficient entrant, which assumes, probably correctly, that new entrants

American Airlines rejected on the facts, but court accepted in principle that the market-wide AVC test can "obscure a predatory scheme," and that a test based, *inter alia*, on AAC may be appropriate).

[20] See R Craswell and MR Fratrik, "Predatory Pricing Theory Applied: The Case Of Supermarkets v Warehouse Stores" (1985/1986) 36 *Case Western Reserve Law Review* 29–35.

[21] See P Bolton, JF Brodley, and MH Riordan, "Predatory Pricing: Strategic Theory and Legal Policy" (2000) 88(8) *Georgetown Law Journal* 2239, 2285 et seq.

have more or less the same access to capital markets as established firms. The financial predation theory suggests, however, that more subtle strategies are available than deep pockets. Because capital markets are imperfect, a dominant firm can undermine the on-going availability of such funding by charging predatory prices. Low prices and revenues for a non-trivial period may make investors nervous about profitability and therefore affect future lending. The issue is thus not so much that new entrants cannot obtain initial capital funding, but that investors' willingness to continue to make funds available can be jeopardised by incorrect signals on profitability caused by predatory pricing.

A second theory that has gained prominence concerns signalling strategies and reputation effects. Under this theory, the dominant firm is said to be able to limit entry by engaging in predatory pricing in an effort to signal to would-be entrants that market conditions are unfavourable. This dissuasive effect can be increased if the dominant firm has activities in multiple markets: predatory prices in one market may lead entrants in other markets to believe that predation is also likely to occur if they enter. Related theories include so-called "test market predation" whereby a dominant firm cuts prices in a market in which an entrant is trying to gauge demand and learn about market conditions, in an attempt to signal to the entrant that the market is less profitable than it actually is.

The above theories have been criticised in certain respects.[22] The main criticism is that, while strategic theory helps explain why predatory pricing might occur, it does not follow that the strategic conduct underpinning it should itself be unlawful under competition law. Rather, strategic theory merely shows how and why predatory pricing may be a viable strategy for a dominant firm. It is still necessary therefore to show that the prices violate the relevant legal benchmark for predatory prices. Critics have also faulted the conditions proposed by strategic theorists on the grounds that they are unworkable as useful legal tests for predatory pricing, a concern that is probably well-founded.

Legitimate reasons for below-cost prices. A second facet of modern economic thinking on predatory pricing is that there may be legitimate, non-exclusionary reasons why a firm would, for a limited period, price below the relevant measure of its costs. This applies in particular in the context of markets in which dynamic efficiencies can be achieved over time. Markets with these characteristics usually require large, up-front risky investments and involve start-up losses in order to increase consumer uptake and thereby acquire the scale, experience, or other efficiencies needed to reduce costs over time.[23] Low prices can lead to recovery of initial losses by creating cost savings over time as a company achieves a more efficient scale, greater learning experience, or another efficiency capable of reducing costs. The scope and availability of this justification for below-cost prices is discussed in detail in Section 5.6 below.

---

[22] See, e.g., KG Elzinga and DE Mills, "Predatory Pricing and Strategic Theory" (2001) 89 *Georgetown Law Journal* 2475. For a response, see P Bolton, JF Brodley, and MH Riordan, "Predatory Pricing: Response to Critique and Further Elaboration" (2001) 89 *Georgetown Law Journal* 2495.

[23] See P Bolton, JF Brodley, and MH Riordan, "Predatory Pricing: Strategic Theory and Legal Policy" (2000) 88(8) *Georgetown Law Journal* 2239, 2274 et seq.

5.3 THE BASIC RULES ON BELOW-COST PRICE CUTTING UNDER ARTICLE 82 EC

Overview. The legal test for predatory below-cost pricing has been consistently laid down by the Community institutions in several cases.[24] Two principal rules apply. The first rule is that a price below AVC—costs that vary depending on the quantities produced—is generally regarded as abusive. The second rule is that prices below ATC—average fixed costs plus average variable costs—but above AVC must be regarded as abusive if they are "part of a plan for eliminating a competitor." The Discussion Paper proposes certain minor modifications to these basic rules. First, it says that the AAC test is a more appropriate measure of marginal cost than AVC.[25] Second, it concedes that appropriate documentary evidence of intent may not be available in all cases and that it may be necessary to refer to other objective factors capable of indirectly supporting a "plan" to eliminate a competitor.[26] These basic rules are explained in more detail below.

The legal test for below-cost predatory pricing under Article 82 EC represents something of a hybrid of the various rules discussed in Section 5.2 for determining unlawfully low prices. In the first place, the requirement of dominance under Article 82 EC incorporates an analysis of the barriers to entry that are generally thought to be necessary for predatory pricing to be a credible strategy.[27] Second, reliance on

---

[24] See Case C-62/86, *AKZO Chemie BV v Commission* [1991] ECR I-3359, paras. 70 et seq; Case T-83/91, *Tetra Pak International SA v. Commission* [1994] ECR II-755, para. 150, on appeal Case C-333/94 P, *Tetra Pak International SA v Commission* [1996] ECR I-5951; Joined Cases T-24/93, T-25/93, T-26/93, and T-28/93, *Compagnie Maritime Belge Transports SA and Others v Commission* [1996] ECR II-1201, paras. 139–41, on appeal Joined Cases C–395/96 P and C-396/96P, *Compagnie Maritime Belge Transports SA, Compagnie Maritime Belge SA and Dafra-Lines A/S v Commission* [2000] ECR I-1365; and Case COMP/38.233, *Wanadoo Interactive*, Commission Decision of July 16, 2003, not yet reported.

[25] See DG Competition discussion paper on the application of Article 82 of the Treaty to exclusionary abuses, Brussels, December 2005 (hereinafter "Discussion Paper"), para. 106.

[26] *Ibid.*, paras. 113, 115.

[27] This is not necessarily the case in other jurisdictions. In an important Australian case, the High Court grappled with the issue of whether a firm could be guilty of predatory pricing without being dominant. See *Boral Besser Masonry Limited v Australian Competition and Consumer Commission* [2003] HCA 5. The rationale of the case is not entirely clear, but the High Court seemed to conclude that, under the language of the relevant statutory provision, a predatory pricing case against a non-dominant firm is not precluded, so long as it can be said that the firm would have the ability to engage in predation to eliminate, reduce, or discipline competition and thereby achieve the ability profitably to charge supra-competitive prices. On the facts, the court found that the defendant did not have such power. See generally GA Hay, "Boral–Free at Last" (2003) 10 *Competition & Consumer Law Journal* 323. A case of this kind would generally be precluded under Article 82 EC, which requires dominance on a relevant market. However, it might be possible for a case under Article 82 EC to involve dominance on one market and predatory pricing on another closely related market, as per the *Tetra Pak II* "leveraging" doctrine. See, e.g., Case No. CA98/05/2004, *First Edinburgh/Lothian*, April 29, 2004, (Case CP/0361-01) (predatory pricing found on non-dominant market based, *inter alia*, on associative links between Edinburgh bus market and routes in the surrounding area). *AKZO* is sometimes considered as a case involving dominance on one market and predatory pricing on a different, but related, market. This reading of the case is, however, incorrect. The Court found that AKZO had engaged in predatory pricing on the organic peroxides market, on which AKZO had been found to be dominant, i.e., the abusive conduct was implemented on the market of dominance.

AVC as the lower benchmark for legality reflects the Areeda and Turner insight that prices below this level are in most cases irrational, a view that has been widely, although not universally, recognised by courts in the United States.[28] Third, the fact that prices above AVC, but below ATC, may be unlawful recognises that prices at such levels can also exclude equally-efficient firms in the long-run. Finally, prices above ATC have in limited circumstances been treated as unlawful under Article 82 EC, which reflects a view among certain commentators that strategic pricing can have anticompetitive results even if the prices concerned remain above total cost.[29] This view is controversial and is discussed in detail in Section 5.5.

5.3.1 Pricing Below AVC

Basic rationale for the first *AKZO* rule. The first *AKZO* rule captures a basic principle of industrial organisation: a firm's revenues should at least exceed the costs that vary with output. While selling above AVC permits a return on capital where the market will not bear a higher price, selling below AVC over an extended period should normally cause a company to shut down its operations.[30] The Community Courts have therefore reasoned that a dominant undertaking has no interest in applying such prices except that of eliminating competitors so as to enable it subsequently to raise its prices by taking advantage of its monopolistic position. This rule has been relaxed somewhat in recent years and, as discussed in Section 5.6, legitimate explanations for prices below AVC may exist. The rule might thus be restated as saying that pricing below AVC is presumptively predatory, but that presumption can be rebutted in certain cases.

Definition of fixed and variable costs. Variable and fixed costs are economic concepts that differ from the accounting costs that typically appear in company accounts. The basic definition of variable and fixed costs is simple. A firm that produces a certain output *quantity* over a period of *time* incurs various costs for the inputs in the production process. Costs the firm would have incurred regardless of the amount produced during the relevant period are *fixed*; the rest are *variable*. Fixed costs generally include management overheads, depreciation, interest and property taxes. Variable costs generally include materials, energy, direct labour, supervision, repair and maintenance, and royalties.[31] Total cost is the sum of fixed and variable costs and average cost is total cost divided by output.

Admittedly, two distinct market segments were identified: the plastics and flour segments. But the dominant and abusing market were one and the same, i.e., the organic peroxides market. See Case C-62/86, *AKZO Chemie BV v Commission* [1991] ECR I-3359. The Discussion Paper also envisages that predatory pricing might occur in a non-dominant market on the basis of cross subsidisation by a legal monopoly into a non-reserved area. See Section 5.4.3 below.

[28] In *Brooke Group Ltd v Brown & Williamson Tobacco Corp*, 509 US 209 (1993), the Supreme Court refused to endorse any particular cost benchmark for determining whether a price is predatory, preferring to leave the matter open based on an "appropriate measure of cost." A large number of lower courts have, however, endorsed the Areeda and Turner standard. See PE Areeda and H Hovenkamp, *Antitrust Law* (Revised edn., Boston, Little Brown, 1996) for an overview of the judicial decisions.

[29] See Section 5.4 below for a detailed discussion of the circumstances in which above-cost price cuts may be unlawful under Article 82 EC.

[30] See Opinion of the Advocate General Fennelly in Joined Cases C-395/96 P and C-396/96 P, *Compagnie Maritime Belge Transports SA and Others v Commission* [2000] ECR I-1365, para. 127.

[31] See *ECS/AKZO*, OJ 1985 L 374/1, para. 58.

Certain costs do not depend on actual output produced during the period in question for two reasons. The first is that the firm is already committed to a particular level of cost for a period. For example, once a large factory has been built the firm is committed to paying the financing charges needed to fund its construction, regardless of whether the factory operates at full capacity or not. Similarly, once a firm has signed a long-term contract to lease an office, it must pay the rent even if it does not in fact use all the space. Once a decision is taken to incur these costs, they are generally irrecoverable or sunk, and would be incurred even if the company had no output at all. (Certain fixed costs are avoidable, however, and therefore not sunk. Put differently, all sunk costs are fixed, but not all fixed costs are sunk.) The second reason why costs may not depend on actual output is that certain costs are highly divisible, in the sense that they will vary in proportion to output, while others are not. For example, the cost of raw materials and fuel will usually vary with output. In contrast, other costs will not: companies usually have just one CEO; restaurants have just one licence; all nuclear reactors are above a minimum size etc.

Classifying costs as fixed or variable may be a complex exercise. Furthermore, the determination of whether a cost is fixed or variable is not always susceptible to *a priori* analysis: costs that are fixed in one scenario may be variable in others. For example, in *Wanadoo*, a dispute arose as to whether advertising expenditure for residential broadband services was a fixed or variable cost. Wanadoo argued that it was a fixed sunk cost, since it was an investment in long-term product awareness and not intended to have an absolutely immediate impact on sales. The Commission rejected this on the facts of the case, reasoning that advertising in an expanding market characterised by information campaigns, such as broadband, was directed at ensuring an immediate impact on sales in the form of new subscriptions. This was confirmed, according to the Commission, by a strong correlation between advertising and new subscription rates. The Commission accepted, however, that the situation might be different in other contexts, such as general communication expenditure designed to promote the company and its trademark.[32]

The use of the AAC test. Another proxy for marginal cost mentioned in the Discussion Paper is the AAC test. This standard measures whether it would be more profitable for a firm to cease production of a particular product line than continue to sell at the alleged predatory prices. AAC covers not only all of the AVC, but also any part of the fixed cost (and therefore ATC) that could be avoided if the firm ceased production. It will be immediately obvious that AVC and AAC are the same when all fixed costs are sunk. Many economists favour the use of the AAC test, since it more accurately captures the relevant costs that govern the decision to stay in business or not, i.e., variable costs plus any fixed costs that can be avoided by exit. Another benefit is that the AAC allows an

[32] Case COMP/38.233, *Wanadoo Interactive*, Commission Decision of July 16, 2003, not yet published. See also Case C-62/86, *AKZO Chemie BV v Commission* [1991] ECR I-3359. AKZO argued that only raw materials, energy, packaging and transport were variable, whereas the Commission considered that labour, maintenance, warehousing, and dispatching should also be included on the basis that they were more commonly treated as variable rather than fixed. The Court of Justice confirmed AKZO's view on the treatment of labour costs as fixed. The Court cited evidence from AKZO on annual changes in output and employment, which showed that, in some years, output rose while employment fell, and *vice versa*.

assessment of any additional costs incurred by a dominant firm in adding capacity, a fact pattern that is common in most predatory pricing cases.

The AAC is not, however, without its problems. In theory, a rational firm should know not only its AVC, but also its AAC. In practice, significant problems can arise because the AAC measures something that never took place, i.e., exit. Complex issues can also arise where assets can be transferred or redeployed from one operation to another and whether this circumstance renders those costs avoidable or not. This issue was raised in *Air Canada* where the airline was found to have operated at fares below AAC on certain routes.[33] An issue arose over whether the redeployment of resources such as planes and staff, following the cancellation of a scheduled flight, rendered the associated cost on that flight avoidable (in whole or in part). (Redeployment might be achieved by shifting the resources of the cancelled flight, such as the aircraft, pilots, and cabin crew, among others, to other flights (including newly scheduled flights) or to third party contracts.)

Air Canada insisted that it lacked these extensive opportunities for redeployment and that evidence of specific opportunities must be shown,[34] absent which the general presumption must be that Air Canada could not avoid costs through redeployment.[35] It relied on an economist's opinion who claimed that avoidability should not be defined in relation to an assumption of redeployment based on "second guessing."[36] Rather, a specific analysis of "real-world opportunities" is required. Moreover, he disputed the assumption that redeployment categorically saves costs. For example, staff hiring and terminations require time for training, notice and severance. Furthermore, the moving of employees such as baggage handlers to other flights would not save costs because of scheduling problems.

The Competition Commissioner's expert argued that Air Canada's use of part-time workers to cover peak periods; its ability to redeploy ramp workers and sales and gate agents; and the changes made by Air Canada to the flight schedule, without "rebuilding the entire schedule," would allow costs to fall "proportionately."[37] Another expert—who in fact was the original proponent of the AAC test for predatory pricing—argued that redeployment is generally profitable.[38] Considering the balance of evidence, the Competition Tribunal concluded that the Commissioner had shown that redeployment is a means by which costs can be avoided, i.e., Air Canada did have profitable

---

[33] *Commissioner of Competition v Air Canada*, (CT-2000/004) Competition Tribunal, Decision of July 22, 2003.
[34] *Ibid.*, para. 124.
[35] *Ibid.*, para. 165.
[36] *Ibid.*, para. 125.
[37] *Ibid.*, para. 131.
[38] *Ibid.*, para. 136 ("For example, one cannot operate an airline between, say, New York and Milwaukee without investing in at least one airplane, an outlay whose amount does not vary with number of passengers until capacity is reached. Thus, this cost is fixed, and does not become variable even in the long run, because one cannot run an airline on the route with zero airplanes. In contrast, this cost is not sunk because, if traffic between New York and Milwaukee declines drastically, the plane can be shifted to serve another route.").

opportunities to redeploy resources during the periods at issue in the application.[39] But this example shows the complexities that can be raised by the AAC rule in practice.

5.3.2 Pricing Above AVC/AAC But Below ATC

Basic rationale for the second *AKZO* rule. Under the second *AKZO* rule, prices above AVC but below ATC are only abusive where the low prices form "part of a plan for eliminating a competitor."[40] While a company may have no reason to price below AVC/AAC, there are many reasons, at least in the short term, why a firm might price below ATC (e.g., a temporary shortfall in demand). Such sales do not cover ATC, but they will cover all of the AVC and a portion of the fixed costs. For these reasons, additional elements are needed to show that pricing above AVC/AAC, but below ATC, is abusive. The Community institutions have generally relied on two principal types of evidence to show a "plan" to eliminate a rival. The first is direct evidence of intent from the dominant firm's documents. The second, and more satisfactory, source of a "plan" concerns indirect factors that, taken together, show an anticompetitive purpose behind the price-cutting. Both types of evidence may also be looked at in individual cases.

Direct evidence of intent. The Community institutions' practice in predatory pricing cases has focused heavily on direct evidence of intent. Indeed, all cases in which predatory pricing has been found expressly rely on direct documentary evidence. In *AKZO*, the dominant firm was active in the production of a wide range of organic peroxides. A small segment of this overall market concerned the use of organic peroxide as a flour additive to bleach flour. ECS was active in this sector, which accounted for the majority of its turnover. The Commission found that AKZO engaged in a series of below-cost pricing practices in the flour additives sector, including prices below ATC but above AVC. The factors relied upon by the Commission to identify anticompetitive intent on AKZO's part included documentary evidence of a detailed plan made by AKZO to eliminate ECS as a competitor in the plastics sector, as well as threats in two meetings that ECS would face retaliation in other markets if it did not withdraw from the additives sector.[41] Relying on this cumulative evidence, the Court of Justice held that "AKZO's intention was not to pursue a general policy of favourable prices, but to adopt a strategy that could damage ECS."[42] Similarly, in *Tetra Pak II*,[43] the Community Courts relied, *inter alia*, on a report by the board of directors referring to the need to make major financial sacrifices (resulting in pricing below ATC) in the area of prices and supply terms in order to fight competition.

Wanadoo represents the first comprehensive attempt by the Commission to corroborate the exclusionary nature of losses by strong reliance on intent evidence. Although much

---

[39] *Ibid.*, para. 143.

[40] Case C-62/86, *AKZO Chemie BV v Commission* [1991] ECR I-3359, para. 7; Case C-333/94 P, *Tetra Pak International SA v Commission* [1996] ECR I-5951, para. 41; Case COMP/38.233, *Wanadoo Interactive*, Commission Decision of July 16, 2003, not yet published, para. 256.

[41] *ECS/AKZO*, OJ 1985 L 374/1, para. 81.

[42] Case C-62/86, *AKZO Chemie BV v Commission* [1991] ECR I-3359, para. 72.

[43] *Tetra Pak II*, OJ 1992 L 72/1, on appeal Case T-83/91, *Tetra Pak International SA v Commission* [1994] ECR II-755, confirmed in Case C-333/94 P, *Tetra Pak International SA v Commission* [1996] ECR I-5951.

of the information concerning intent is treated as confidential in the decision, the Commission's case appears to have been that Wanadoo did not restrict itself to incurring the start-up losses necessary to enter the market, but had pursued a broader policy of incurring whatever losses were necessary to exclude rivals and maintain future dominance; in other words a "plan to pre-empt the market by stealing the march on competitors."[44] Thus, the Commission found that Wanadoo was "knowingly weighing short-term profitability against an objective of vigorous penetration of the market."[45] The Commission also attached importance to the apparent awareness within the company of the legal dangers of its conduct.[46]

Wanadoo challenged the Commission's characterisation of internal company documents. It argued that the documents were not evidence of an anticompetitive plan, but the "dialectic of the decision-making progress in a large organisation" that "reflected the views of their authors and not the company as a legal person."[47] Wanadoo also argued that many of the remarks were "informal," "impromptu," "off-the-cuff," or represented "aimless conversations."[48] The Commission rejected these arguments on the grounds that the remarks were principally made in the context of formal presentations at management meetings, rather than informal discussions with sales staff on the ground.[49] Further, even if certain documents could be classified as informal, the Commission discounted this fact on the grounds that, first, several documents from different sources had the same "unity of purpose,"[50] and, second, the exclusionary statements emanated from senior managers.[51]

Although there were disputes between Wanadoo and the Commission as to the characterisation of statements in company documents, the case does illustrate a more nuanced approach by the Commission to intent evidence. First, the Commission draws a distinction between formal presentations to management and informal remarks made to or by sales staff, attaching a higher value to the former. Second, for anticompetitive intent to arise, the documents must show such intent on the part of senior staff capable of having a material influence on company policy. Finally, the Commission does not focus on isolated documents, but on the totality of evidence pointing to a unity of purpose in the company's actions.

Problems with direct intent evidence. Identifying anticompetitive intent is difficult in practice, if intent is taken to mean subjective evidence of intent to exclude on the part of the dominant firm. All profit-maximising companies "intend" to eliminate their rivals and one obvious way of doing this is through price competition. It is extremely difficult to distinguish between the "intent" that Article 82 EC prohibits and the legitimate price-

[44] Case COMP/38.233, *Wanadoo Interactive*, Commission Decision of July 16, 2003, not yet published, para. 111.

[45] *Ibid.*, para 126. See also para. 135 ("regardless of the short-term financial disadvantage") and para. 139 (serious internal doubts about future economic viability of losses).

[46] *Ibid.*, paras. 142 et seq.

[47] *Ibid.*, para. 119.

[48] *Ibid.*, paras. 119, 121.

[49] *Ibid.*, para. 121.

[50] *Ibid.*, para. 122.

[51] *Ibid.*, para. 123.

cutting "intent" that it encourages. Sales hyperbole could become easily confused with anticompetitive strategies, since, "there is no good way to determine what the management of a firm really had in mind...and economists have no particular professional qualifications for delving into anyone's mental state."[52] The Commission seems to have recognised these inherent dangers when it stated that "it does not consider an intention even by a dominant firm to prevail over its rivals as unlawful."[53]

Wanadoo continues to illustrate the problems with subjective intent evidence in predation cases based on internal documents or statements. Most documents are capable of more than one interpretation and each side will advance the explanation most favourable to them. Although the intent evidence in *Wanadoo* may have been convincing overall—this will be determined in the pending appeal—a fine line nonetheless exists between an internal company policy designed to gain as much share as possible in order to recover initial costs and one that invests in market share for the purpose of excluding rivals. At some point the two necessarily coincide and there is usually no clear way of distinguishing between them. There is also a danger that undue emphasis on internal documents would result in well-counselled firms escaping liability for predation, while firms who are less well-counselled, but engaged in legitimate pricing, would run afoul of the law due to careless language. Competition law enforcement should not depend on whether business managers and sales personnel use "commercially-correct" language. This danger was less apparent in *Wanadoo* given that the Commission also relied on recoupment, effects on competition, and objective justification to assess the legitimacy of Wanadoo's prices, but the problem is nonetheless real.

Towards a more objective definition of intent. The Discussion Paper acknowledges a number of the problems with evidence of direct intent and also proposes that reliance can be placed on indirect evidence of intent.[54] Indirect evidence of intent refers to factors that tend to show that the explanation for the price-cutting is predatory. This definition of intent fits well with the current economic approach to predatory pricing. As discussed in Section 5.2, economists view predatory pricing as not only requiring proof of pricing below cost, but also evidence of a plausible predatory strategy in the particular market setting. Indeed, the Discussion Paper expressly refers to the economic theories of "reputation effects" and "financial market predation" discussed in Section 5.2. Other evidence of indirect intent mentioned in the Discussion Paper includes the actual or likely exclusion of the prey, whether certain customers are selectively targeted,

---

[52] See WJ Baumol, "Principles Relevant To Predatory Pricing" in E Hope (ed.), *The Pros And Cons Of Low Prices* (Konkurrensverket/Swedish Competition Authority, 2003) p.15.

[53] *ECS/AKZO,* OJ 1985 L 374/1, para. 81. One US Circuit Court vividly described the problems with penalising intent as follows: "[F]irms "intend" to do all the business they can, to crush their rivals if they can....Rivalry is harsh, and consumers gain the most when firms slash costs to the bone and pare price down to cost, all in pursuit of more business. Few firms cut price unaware of what they are doing; price reductions are carried out in pursuit of sales, at others' expense. Entrepreneurs who work hardest to cut their prices will do the most damage to their rivals, and they will see good in it. You cannot be a sensible business executive without understanding the link among prices, your firm's success, and other firms' distress. If courts use the vigorous, nasty pursuit of sales as evidence of a forbidden 'intent,' they run the risk of penalising the motive forces of competition." See *A.A. Poultry Farms, Inc v Rose Acre Farms, Inc*, 881 F.2d 1396 at 1402 (7th Cir. 1989).

[54] See Discussion Paper, paras. 113, 115.

whether the dominant company actually incurred specific costs in order for instance to expand capacity, the scale, duration and continuity of the low pricing, the concurrent application of other exclusionary practices, the possibility of the dominant company to off-set its losses with profits earned on other sales, and its possibility to recoup the losses in the future through (a return to) high prices.

But even prior to the Discussion Paper, the Community institutions generally looked at indirect evidence of intent. In *AKZO*, the Commission and Court of Justice looked not only at direct evidence of intent, but also at evidence of selective price cuts to the rival's customers and AKZO's subsidising of price cuts in the flour additives sector by below-cost transfer prices from the plastics and elastomers division. In *Tetra Pak II*, the Community Courts looked at a "whole series of important and convergent factors" to prove that prices below ATC but above AVC were abusive. These included: (1) duration, that is the continuity and the scale of the loss-making over a six-year period; (2) evidence that Tetra Pak—which did not manufacture Tetra Rex cartons in Italy—imported them in order to resell them in that country at up to 35% lower than their purchase price; (3) prices of cartons sold in Italy were lower by 20–50% than the prices applied in other Member States; (4) evidence that Tetra Pak's prices continued to fall in response to competitors' offers even though this entailed even greater losses; and (5) an increase of sales of Tetra Rex cartons in Italy and the corresponding reduction in the growth of sales of Elopak cartons, during a period of market expansion, followed by the reverse situation when the abusive practices stopped.

The overriding point in cases involving indirect evidence of intent is that there must be a strong evidential basis for saying that the price-cutting has no legitimate explanation other than predation. If the pricing behaviour only makes commercial sense as part of a predatory strategy and there are no other reasonable explanations, this will normally suffice to show a strategy to predate. The notion of a "reasonable explanation" is directly linked to what types of objective justification can explain prices that are temporarily below cost. Objective justification is discussed in detail in Section 5.6 below. Where no such justification is present, the Discussion Paper states that it will not be necessary to show that a foreclosure effect is likely.[55] But in all other cases, evidence that a foreclosure effect is likely, in view of the scale, duration, and continuity of the low pricing, is necessary.[56]

5.4 SPECIFIC ISSUES WITH BELOW-COST PRICING UNDER ARTICLE 82 EC

Overview. Although the basic test for predatory pricing under Article 82 EC is clear, a number of subtleties and additional complexities arise in practice. A first issue arises whether recoupment—the need to show that the supposed predator would recover the initial losses through increased prices in future—should be a formal condition in predatory pricing cases. A second issue concerns multi-product firms that have joint or common costs in two or more operations. There is no reliable way of measuring the average cost of either product in this scenario and complicated issues of cost allocation

[55] *Ibid.*, para. 116.
[56] *Ibid.*, para. 117.

may therefore arise. A third, related issue for multi-product firms is whether a cross-subsidy—the use of profits from a monopoly area to fund losses in a competitive area—should be regarded as unlawful and if so under what circumstances. A fourth issue concerns products with high fixed costs and low variable costs, such as network industries and intellectual property. In this situation, the AVC test may be under-inclusive. Finally, many products incur start-up losses in the early phase as firms try to achieve economies of scale and scope over time. How such initial losses should be assessed in the context of a predatory pricing claim needs to be resolved. Most of these issues are well-documented in the economics literature, but the legal position under Article 82 EC is not entirely clear.

5.4.1 Recoupment

Recoupment: definition and measurement. Many economists and commentators argue that recoupment should be an essential element of the legal test for predatory pricing,[57] as it is under US law.[58] Recoupment requires proof that the loss-making prices would increase the predator's market power and allow it to recover the initial losses through supra-competitive prices in future. In other words, "there must be a reasonable prospect of recoupment of at least whatever initial costs to the firm were entailed in the firm's adoption of the price in question, that recoupment taking the form of monopoly profits (i.e., super-competitive profits) made possible by reduction (as a result of the suspect price) in the number of competitors facing the alleged predator."[59] Unless a firm can recoup its initial loss-making investment in a predatory scheme, proponents of the recoupment test argue that there is no harm to consumers. Indeed, in the short-term, they argue that consumers may even benefit if there is no prospect of recoupment, since they receive the benefit of lower (loss-making) prices.

Recoupment is therefore a *defence* that can be put forward by the alleged predator to show that, even if its prices were below the relevant measure of cost, no harm occurred to consumer welfare because the loss-making prices could not be recovered by increased prices in future. This is different from the argument that initial losses will be recovered in future based on legitimate considerations (see Section 5.6 below). The former is a negative argument to show that there is no anticompetitive effect; the latter a positive argument to show that the initial losses did not have an exclusionary purpose, but were based on legitimate initial losses designed to stimulate demand over time or to further another efficiency.

Recoupment in the negative, or anticompetitive, sense is generally tested by analysing market structure and/or conduct in order to see whether the market is conducive to the recovery of past losses.[60] Structural elements include market share, capacity

---

[57] See, e.g., WJ Baumol, "Principles Relevant To Predatory Pricing" in E Hope (ed.), *The Pros And Cons Of Low Prices* (Stockholm, Swedish Competition Authority, 2003), pp. 19–20; P Bolton, JF Brodley, and MH Riordan, "Predatory Pricing: Strategic Theory and Legal Policy" (2000) 88(8) *Georgetown Law Journal* 2239, 2267–70.

[58] See *Brooke Group Ltd v Brown & Williamson Tobacco Corp*, 509 US 209 (1993).

[59] See WJ Baumol, "Principles Relevant To Predatory Pricing" in E Hope (ed.), *The Pros And Cons Of Low Prices* (Stockholm, Swedish Competition Authority, 2003), p. 25.

[60] See S Hemphill, "The Role Of Recoupment In Predatory Pricing Analyses" (2001) 53 *Stanford Law Review* 1581.

constraints, and barriers to entry.[61] Market share offers an indication of the range of products over which a firm might enjoy power, while capacity constraints and entry barriers measure the ability of the would-be predator to raise prices without an adequate response from competitors. Conduct involves an assessment of whether "the predatory scheme alleged would cause a rise in prices above a competitive level that would be sufficient to compensate for the amounts expended on the predation."[62] This determination may also depend on structural factors, including a "close analysis of both the scheme alleged by the plaintiff and the structure and conditions of the relevant market."[63]

Arguments in favour of the adoption of a recoupment condition. Recoupment certainly has much to commend it in the context of predatory pricing claims. First, it is central to the definition of predatory pricing. Predatory pricing entails short-term profit sacrifice in order to eliminate a rival firm and, following the market exit of the rival, a price rise that compensates the predator for the losses incurred during the period of non-remunerative selling. Implicit in the notion of recoupment is that firms act rationally and will not incur certain losses unless there is a reasonable probability of recovering them at a later stage. If the price-cutting does not lead to a recovery phase, this means that rivals have been able to offset the effects of the below-cost selling or re-enter at a later stage, or that new entry is possible and will keep prices at competitive levels. In either case, there is no harm to competition, since consumers benefited from low prices during the predation phase and, once it has finished, from prices that were no higher, or maybe lower, than in the pre-predation phase.

Second, requiring proof of a reasonable prospect of recoupment may be a useful way to minimise the cost of errors in predation cases. Competition policy seeks to promote low prices and the costs of falsely condemning low prices are seen by certain commentators as higher than the costs of allowing certain instances of predatory pricing to go unpunished.[64] Further, practical experience with cost-based rules is that they are often complex to apply in practice, in particular for multi-product firms. Predation should not be inferred from the mere failure to pass a price/cost test, since this may simply be the result of the assumptions applied in the classification of costs or the time period taken into account. A recoupment analysis helps provide a cross-check, based on market structure or conduct, on whether the inference of predation is credible. Recoupment therefore provides an additional screen to ensure that low prices benefit from a strong presumption of legality.

Finally, a recoupment analysis is a useful way to distinguish between harm to competitors—which competition law should not concern itself with—and actual or likely harm to consumers—which competition law should be concerned with. Loss-making prices directed at competitors may well be tortious or contrary to unfair trading

[61] *Ibid.*, at 1587.

[62] See *Brooke Group Ltd v Brown & Williamson Tobacco Corp*, 509 US 209, 225 (1993).

[63] *Ibid.*, 226.

[64] See, e.g., WJ Baumol, "Principles Relevant To Predatory Pricing" in E Hope (ed.), *The Pros And Cons Of Low Prices* (Stockholm, Swedish Competition Authority, 2003), pp. 19–20; P Bolton, JF Brodley, and MH Riordan, "Predatory Pricing: Strategic Theory and Legal Policy" (2000) 88(8) *Georgetown Law Journal* 2239, 2267–70.

laws, but they should not justify intervention under competition law unless the harm directed at competitors will also lead to harm to consumers.

Arguments against the adoption of a recoupment condition. There are several reasons to be cautious about a recoupment condition in predatory pricing cases. First, it could lead to perverse results. Cost-based tests, such as those applied under Article 82 EC, assume that firms act rationally and that the further a price is below the appropriate measure of cost, the more suspiciously it should be regarded. However, the deeper the price cut, the more difficult it would be to show recoupment, since the higher the degree of future price rises that would be needed to compensate for it. A recoupment condition could therefore have the paradoxical result that those price cuts that are most suspicious and irrational are treated most leniently.

Second, there are substantial measurement problems in practice, since it is often difficult to prove what the dominant company could do successfully in the future. Unless the post-predation price rises have already occurred, recoupment involves a high degree of guesswork as to the future. It would be necessary to show that there will be no entry by more competitive or more determined rivals, and that when the dominant company increases its price, it will not attract new entry. It would also be necessary to show that the price elasticity of the product was such that, although buyers were accustomed to low prices, they would be willing to pay significantly more in the future. This suggests that the burden of proof is crucial. If the burden of proof was on the party alleging illegal low prices, it would make it difficult to bring a successful case.[65] If the burden of proof was on the dominant company, it would be obliged to prove a negative, that is, to prove that it would be unable to recoup its losses if it tried to do so.

Third, predatory pricing by a dominant company may have anticompetitive effects even if the dominant company does not or could not recoup its losses. Economic thinking suggests that an effective form of predatory pricing is one where a company discourages market entry, or causes exit, by signalling to actual or potential competitors that their profitability in the market in question will be low as long as the dominant company is price leader in that market.[66] This signalling would be more effective, and the effects of it would last longer, if the dominant company did not have to recover its losses, but held its prices only a little above competitive levels. This discouraging or signalling effect is particularly likely to be important if the dominant company is active on several markets, because predatory pricing on one market may discourage market entry on the others.[67]

[65] In the United States, the recoupment requirement is widely seen as having sounded the "death knell" of predatory pricing claims: See S Hemphill, "The Role Of Recoupment In Predatory Pricing Analyses" (2001) 53 *Stanford Law Review* 1581, 1586 (and sources cited therein).

[66] Discussion Paper, para. 122.

[67] See P Bolton, JF Brodley, and MH Riordan, "Predatory Pricing: Strategic Theory and Legal Policy" (2000) 88(8) *Georgetown Law Journal* 2239, 2241–62. Scherer refers to it as: "the demonstration effect that sharp price cutting in one market can have on the behaviour of actual or would be rivals in other markets. If rivals come to fear from a multimarket seller's actions in Market A that entry or expansion in Markets B and C will be met by sharp price cuts or other rapacious responses, they may be deterred from taking aggressive actions there. Then the conglomerate's expected benefit from predation in Market A will be supplemented by the discounted present value of the competition-inhibiting effects its example has in Markets B and C." See FM Scherer, *Industrial Market Structure and Economic Performance* (2nd edn., Chicago, Rand McNally, 1980) p. 338.

It may even be possible to make effective signals based on false information if rivals have imperfect information on costs or market conditions.[68]

Fourth, predatory pricing may have anticompetitive effects even if the rival is not forced out of the market, but instead decides to raise its prices to approximately the prices of the dominant company. In particular, in a concentrated market predatory pricing may demonstrate the dominant company's ability and willingness to retaliate against aggressive pricing by a competitor, and so may give rise to oligopolistic pricing. In such circumstances it would be extremely difficult to prove that recoupment had occurred, even if it had.

Finally, it is reasonable as a matter of law to punish conduct that, if firms always acted rationally, would be self-deterring. Similarly, it seems reasonable to punish conduct even if the benefits of that conduct have not fully materialised to the actor in question, or as quickly as that actor had anticipated. Indeed, this was precisely what the Court of First Instance held in *BA/Virgin* when it stated that "where an undertaking in a dominant position actually puts into operation a practice generating the effect of ousting its competitors, the fact that the hoped-for result is not achieved is not sufficient to prevent a finding of abuse."[69] An inference of predation may well be credible even if the precise losses caused by the low prices are less than the monies recovered through increased prices.[70]

The approach to recoupment under Article 82 EC. Reaction to a recoupment condition under Article 82 EC has been mixed. In *Tetra Pak II*, the Court of Justice found that it would not be appropriate, in the circumstances of the case, "to require in addition proof that Tetra Pak had a realistic chance of recouping its losses." Although this statement might be interpreted as specific to the case at hand—leaving open the possibility of requiring proof of probable recoupment in others cases—the Court of Justice added "it must be possible to penalise predatory pricing whenever there is a risk that competitors will be eliminated" and that this "rules out waiting until such a strategy leads to the actual elimination of competitors."[71]

---

[68] See J Roberts, "A Signalling Model of Predatory Pricing" (1986) 38 *Oxford Economic Papers (Supplement: Strategic Behaviour and Industrial Competition)* 75.

[69] *Virgin/British Airways*, OJ 2000 L 30/1, and Case T-219/99, *British Airways plc v Commission* [2003] ECR II-5917 (hereinafter "*BA/Virgin*"), para. 295. As noted in Ch. 7, however, this finding can be criticised in important other respects.

[70] This was, in effect, the basis for the dissent by Justice Stevens in *Brooke Group Ltd v Brown & Williamson Tobacco Corp*, when he held that "when a predator deliberately engages in below-cost pricing targeted at a particular competitor over a sustained period of time, then price-cutting raises a credible inference that harm to competition is likely to ensue." See *Brooke Group Ltd v Brown & Williamson Tobacco Corp* , 509 US 209, 256–57 (1993).

[71] Case C-333/94 P, *Tetra Pak International SA v Commission* [1996] ECR I-5951, para 44. National competition laws are also generally hostile to the need for recoupment. The UK Competition Authority, the Office of Fair Trading (OFT), takes the position that dominance raises a reasonable inference of probable recoupment, while adding that recoupment may be relevant if a dominant firm uses revenues from a dominated market in order to engage in predatory conduct in a non-dominated market, i.e., in cases of cross-subsidisation. According to the OFT, if pricing below cost occurs in a dominated market, it can be assumed that the dominant firm can recoup losses afterwards: see Assessment of Conduct: Draft Competition Law Guideline for Consultation, OFT 414a, para. 4.25. See

Recent cases have been more supportive of the need for recoupment as a condition for predatory pricing. In *Compagnie Maritime Belge*, Advocate General Fennelly stated that recoupment was implicit in the Court of Justice's statements in *AKZO* and *Hoffmann-La Roche* and that recoupment "should be part of the test for abusively low pricing by dominant undertakings." Indeed, in that case, the Advocate General stated that the sharing of revenue shortfalls resulting from the price-cutting among the CEWAL members was in essence a form of recoupment.[72] This was not strictly correct, since recoupment refers to the recovery of losses, not their sharing. More recently, in *Wanadoo*, the Commission rejected a formal recoupment requirement under Article 82 EC,[73] but went on to find that the recovery of losses was plausible due to market structure.

The Commission's recoupment analysis in *Wanadoo* was whether "the obstacles to entry guarantee the dominant undertaking the maintenance in the long-term of a large degree of market concentration in its favour."[74] Obstacles to entry might include insurmountable barriers such as regulatory, technical or legal barriers, as well as obstacles that slow down new entrants' progress, including the dominant firm's economies of scale, brand image, and entry-deterring behaviour.[75] The higher these barriers are, the more the market is conducive to successful recoupment. On the facts, the Commission identified a number of strategic barriers: (1) various disincentives to switching subscribers on the part of existing customers; (2) high costs of entering and acquiring critical size in the broadband market (e.g., fixed costs, advertising costs);

also Case No. 2000:2, *Statens Järnvägar v Konkurrenverket & BK Täg AB* (Decision of the Swedish Market court rendered on February 1, 2000), where the Swedish Market Court held that it was inherent in setting prices below AVC that a dominant company expects to recoup them. However, the Court also held that, in fact, the dominant railway company concerned would face little or no competition in future procurement, thereby allowing it to recover its losses. In other words, the Court did not insist on recoupment as an express requirement, but found on the facts that it was likely. Some national authorities do consider recoupment, but mainly when rejecting predatory pricing claims, i.e., inability to recoup. See, e.g., Case COM/05/03, *Drogheda Independent Company Limited*, December 7, 2004 (Irish Competition Authority) and *AOL France SNC and AOL Europe SA*, Conseil de la Concurrence, Decision No. 04-D-17 of May 11, 2004.

[72] This conclusion seems questionable. In the first place, recoupment was unnecessary in *Compagnie Maritime Belge*, since the dominant liner conference was not selling below cost. Further, while collective sharing of reduced profits from the price-cutting may make it easier to share the cost of eliminating a competitor (the first limb of the recoupment test under US law), it does not directly affect the possibility for supra-competitive prices to be maintained thereinafter (the second limb under US law), which requires a separate analysis. See Opinion of Advocate General Fennelly in Joined Cases C–395/96 P and C-396/96P, *Compagnie Maritime Belge Transports SA, Compagnie maritime belge SA and Dafra-Lines A/S v Commission* [2000] ECR I-1365; and Joined Cases T-24/93, T-25/93, T-26/93, and T-28/93, *Compagnie Maritime Belge Transports SA and Others v Commission* [1996] ECR II-1201.

[73] Case COMP/38.233, *Wanadoo Interactive*, Commission Decision of July 16, 2003, not yet published, paras. 334, 338. The Commission noted the argument outlined above—that recoupment may not always be the objective of predation. For example, it argued that multi-product undertakings may pursue predation strategies if they are active in other highly profitable markets where losses can be offset, in particular where they are State-owned undertakings with reserved monopolies. The Commission also suggested that predation may not seek recoupment but rather the expansion of the customer base and an increase in the potential value of future goodwill.

[74] *Ibid.*, para. 337.

[75] *Ibid.*

(3) self-building of the upstream infrastructure needed for a broadband network was not viable; and (4) Wanadoo was well on its way to restoring profitable margins, whereas new entrants were not.

The upshot of the above cases is that recoupment is not a formal condition in predatory pricing cases under Article 82 EC.[76] The Commission may, however, analyse whether recoupment is likely, at least in cases in which it proposes to find an infringement. Thus, it is open to the defendant to rebut an inference of predation by showing that future market conditions would not be conducive to lower output and higher prices.[77] Presumably, even if the defendant could do this, it would still be open to the Commission to assess whether it accepted the defendant's version of future events.

Evaluating the approach to recoupment under Article 82 EC. The absence of a formal recoupment requirement under Article 82 EC is not an obvious weakness in the law. The current practice of treating existing dominance as raising a *prima facie* inference of dominance and then allowing the defendant to rebut that inference by showing an absence of recoupment is a reasonable and pragmatic compromise. In the first place, the prohibition on predatory pricing under Article 82 EC only applies to companies that are already dominant. In jurisdictions where recoupment is a requirement (e.g., United States), a pre-existing dominant position is not a formal condition. Instead, the law requires that the conduct should create or threaten to create a monopoly. Insisting on a recoupment conditions therefore serves as a screen to exclude cases in which predation is unlikely to be rational. In contrast, requiring dominance *a priori* involves an assessment of market structure, which includes factors such as market share, capacity, and barriers to entry that characterise the structural approach to a recoupment analysis. Thus, the prevailing market conditions that contribute to dominance may also offer a good indication that rivals' exclusion will lead to higher prices in future, and that recoupment is therefore probable.

At the same time, however, it should be appreciated that proof of dominance does not *necessarily* imply that the dominant firm will also be able to recoup its losses. While proof of recoupment means that the dominant firm's monopoly would persist in future, it is important to appreciate that the loss-making and recoupment phases do not coincide in predatory pricing cases. The fact that a firm was dominant at the time it engaged in below-cost selling does not mean that it will in future be able to recover past losses by raising prices: conditions of competition may well be different in future. Much will depend therefore on the stage at which a plaintiff or competition authority intervenes in a predatory pricing case: if intervention follows shortly after conclusion of the predation phase and there is evidence of price increases due to additional market power, recoupment might be made out. In contrast, if intervention takes place during the predation phase, proof of dominance at that stage may not imply much, or indeed anything, about the ability to recoup in future.

Second, predatory pricing claims have in practice only succeeded under Article 82 EC where recoupment was either actually established or probable on the facts. In

[76] See Discussion Paper, para. 122.
[77] *Ibid.*, para. 123.

Wanadoo, the Commission undertook a detailed assessment of whether recoupment was probable and concluded that it was. But, even in cases where no express analysis was made, recoupment seemed probable. In *AKZO* and *Tetra Pak II*, the companies concerned were dominant in a wide range of products but only engaged in selective price-cutting for one product that a competitor offered. Given their dominance in a wide portfolio of products, it was probable that the threat of retaliation against a rival supplying only one of those products was a credible deterrent that would have allowed recoupment. Moreover, Tetra Pak was the overwhelming market leader and maintained a stable market share for several years. Likewise, in *Compagnie Maritime Belge*, the dominant firm's insistence on exclusive contracts, its 100% loyalty rebates, its reputation for taking significant retaliatory measures against the only competitor, and the high fixed costs that would have be incurred by a new entrant raised an inference of probable recoupment.

Finally, even if the Commission institutions do not formally apply a recoupment condition, they generally perform an assessment of the effects on competition in predatory pricing cases.[78] This approach is similar in substance to a recoupment analysis. For example, in *Tetra Pak II*, the Court of First Instance noted that the Commission's cost analysis was "corroborated by the eliminatory effect of the competition engendered by Tetra Pak's pricing policy," including "the increase of sales of Tetra Rex cartons in Italy and the corresponding reduction in the growth of sales of Elopak cartons, during a period of market expansion, followed by their decline as from 1981."[79]

But a number of cautionary points should be noted in connection with inferring recoupment from dominance. First, the Discussion Paper states that a firm with a state monopoly or exclusive right may commit predatory pricing by cross-subsidy to a non-dominant market, even where the effects of the abuse only materialise on the non-dominant market.[80] An analysis of recoupment seems essential in such cases, since the dominant firm has no market power on the non-dominant market. This issue is discussed in more detail in Section 5.4.3 below. Second, recoupment also seems essential in the case of price cutting by collectively dominant firms, since, otherwise, there is no effective way of distinguishing such cuts from destablisation of the oligopoly. Finally, in addition to the scenarios outlined above, competition authorities and courts should be open to the possibility that dominance and recoupment may have no strong correlation in other situations (e.g., if the excluded firm's assets are sold to existing firms or new entrants).

---

[78] See *ECS/AKZO*, OJ 1985 L 374/1, para. 86 (concluding after analysis of potential reaction from other competitors "that the elimination of ECS from the organic peroxides market would have had a substantial effect upon competition notwithstanding its still minor market share and the existence of other suppliers."): See also *Deutsche Post AG*, OJ 2001 L 125/27, paras. 36–37 (finding that below cost pricing where there is no prospect of a price rise inhibited growth of more efficient rivals, para. 36, with identifiable welfare loss, para. 37); and Case COMP/38.233, *Wanadoo Interactive*, Commission Decision of July 16, 2003, not yet published (Commission relied on the fact that: (1) Wanadoo's market share rose by nearly 30% during the period of the infringement; (2) Wanadoo's main competitor at the time had seen its market share tumble; and (3) one competitor (Mangoosta) went out of business).

[79] Case T-83/91, *Tetra Pak International SA v Commission* [1994] ECR II-755, para. 151.

[80] Discussion Paper, para. 101.

5.4.2 Dealing With Joint And Common Costs

Problem stated. Calculating variable and fixed costs is reasonably straightforward when a company only supplies a single product. Where, however, a company supplies two or more products, additional and unique complexities arise. Most notably, a firm may have fixed and variable costs that are incurred in common or jointly with two or more products. Determining average cost when two or more products have common or joint costs raises significant problems. The main one is there is no unambiguous way of calculating the average cost of either product, since there is no unique output over which that average can be measured. Instead, there are two or more relevant output levels and shared costs between each. Total output could be defined as the sum of the quantities of Product A and Product B, but there is no reason why this would give a meaningful average cost any more than any other two numbers.[81] This problem is important in practice, since most firms will have common/joint costs between two or more operations.

The possible solutions. There is no one solution to calculating costs in the case of a multi-product firm. All methods have advantages and disadvantages and many of them involve arbitrary judgments on cost allocation. The first solution—which many economists would endorse—is essentially to do nothing and ignore the presence of common costs. Instead, the focus is only on the costs that are purely incremental to the business at issue, i.e., causally related to the production of the specific product. This solution is based on the consideration that common costs would be incurred in any event because of the firm's other operations.[82] Or, put differently, the business decision is whether additional revenues will exceed the specific cost incurred in adding a product line, and not whether the product would not only cover its own specific costs, but also contribute something towards common costs. For this reason, the leading treatise on US antitrust law politely describes common cost allocation efforts as "nonsense."[83] And this is not merely because allocating common costs is difficult and arbitrary (though it is that too), but mainly due to the fact that only incremental fixed and variable costs guide the business decision to add a particular product line or not.

One problem of this approach is that it could create a significant disadvantage for a rival firm that is only active in one market and therefore has to incur all the stand-alone costs of serving that market. Even if that firm was as efficient as the dominant firm in that single market, the dominant firm could put it out of business by exploiting the fact that certain costs can be spread over two or more activities. The rival, in contrast, can only

[81] See PA Grout, "Recent Developments in the Definition of Abusive Pricing in European Competition Policy" (2000) CMPO Working Paper Series No. 00/23, p. 12 ("[I]f a firm produces both bicycles and cars and has common costs then, while it is possible to identify total cost or variable cost, it is not possible to add together bicycles and cars and divide to get an average cost.").

[82] *Deutsche Post AG*, OJ 2001 L 125/27, para 6 ("[W]hen establishing whether the incremental costs incurred in providing [a specific product] are covered, the additional costs of producing that service, incurred solely as a result of providing the service, must be distinguished from the common fixed costs, which are not incurred solely as a result of this service.").

[83] See PE Areeda and H Hovenkamp, *Antitrust Law* (Revised edn., Boston, Little Brown, 1996) para. 741f.

spread them over one. The extent of the disadvantage will depend on the dominant firm's economies of scope between the two operations, but may be very significant.

An alternative solution is thus to require the dominant firm to allocate its common costs between the two operations on some reasonable basis, which is sometimes called fully-allocated cost. The advantage of this approach is that the dominant firm can continue to benefit from any economies of scope, as long as there is a reasonable allocation of common costs between its various operations. It seeks to correct a basic objection to a pure incremental costs test: that no allocation is made for fixed costs incurred in common between two products. This may be questionable in circumstances where a large proportion of the dominant company's costs are common costs and its revenues in one product are above its costs only if the common costs incurred in producing that product are exclusively allocated to another product. A significant problem with the fully-allocated cost approach is that it can be highly arbitrary, since there are no standardised techniques for allocating common costs.[84] The practical solutions to this difficulty are discussed in detail below.

Treatment of multi-product firms under Article 82 EC. Whether common cost allocation is required under Article 82 EC is not clear from case law. In *Deutsche Post*, the Commission applied a pure incremental costs approach (LRAIC) to the allocation of costs between a reserved State monopoly and a competitive business that used common infrastructure.[85] This means that, when establishing whether the incremental costs incurred in providing a service in the competitive sector are covered, the Commission distinguished the additional costs of producing that service, incurred solely as a result of providing the service, from the common fixed costs, which were not incurred solely as a result of this service. In other words, Deutsche Post was allowed to allocate all its common costs to its monopoly operations, even if they also benefited its competitive activities. In this circumstance, its costs in the competitive market were only incremental costs, and these will be less than the stand-alone costs of its competitors (all other things being equal). The dominant firm's precise cost advantage will depend on the extent of the economies of scope or synergies between its two sets of operations.

The pure incremental costs approach in *Deutsche Post* was strongly motivated by the specific features of the case. Deutsche Post had a statutory monopoly, and also a legal duty to provide a universal postal service throughout Germany at standard postal rates. For this purpose it was obliged to maintain infrastructure that it was able to use for both its monopoly and competitive services, but no part of which involved an incremental cost of providing the competitive service. Further, some of the incremental costs of its competitive service were fixed costs. Some of the infrastructure used in this service was distinct from the infrastructure that Deutsche Post needed and used for its universal

[84] For example, the salaries of research and development personnel will in most companies be attributable across the range of a company's output. Identifying which products benefit most, and in what proportions, is more a matter of policy than precision. Similarly, there is no reliable way of allocating the costs of the salaries of senior management with responsibility for several distinct product lines to individual products. Common cost allocation to individual products on a *pro rata* basis will therefore inevitably involve some policy judgments rather than precise calculations.

[85] *Deutsche Post AG*, OJ 2001 L 125/27.

service.[86] But Deutsche Post had a legal obligation to offer minimum universal service levels in Germany and would have incurred the costs that were common to the reserved and non-reserved areas in any event. In other words, it had an on-going obligation to maintain a level of network capacity that a firm operating in a competitive market would not have had. In this circumstance, the Commission considered that applying a pure incremental cost test to the non-reserved activity made sense.

It is not clear whether, absent Deutsche Post's public service obligation, a purely incremental cost approach would have been applied by the Commission. For example, if Deutsche Post had used every post office for rent-free banking, insurance, and travel agency activities, the pure incremental costs approach may have been difficult to justify. In the absence of a universal service obligation, commentators have argued that the pure incremental costs approach would be too favourable to the dominant firm because it would create or legitimise a barrier to entry into the competitive market.[87] Unless there was an objective criterion, such as the universal service obligation, the dominant company could have too much freedom to decide which of its costs in the competitive market were incremental and which were not.[88]

Recognising the above concerns, the Community institutions have indicated that an allocation of common costs between operations may be appropriate.[89] In *Ahmed Saeed*, for example, the Court relied on Article 3 of Directive 87/601/EEC to use long-term fully allocated costs to construct an appropriate cost measure to determine whether prices were excessive in the airline sector.[90] The directive laid down the criteria to be followed by the aeronautical authorities for approving tariffs, including the need for tariffs to be reasonably related to the long-term fully allocated costs of the air carrier,

---

[86] *Ibid.*, para. 10 ("Emphasising the coverage of costs attributable to a particular service also makes it possible to take account of the additional burden incurred by [Deutsche Post] as a result of fulfilling its statutory obligation of maintaining network reserve capacity. As this emphasis is expressly intended to take account of network capacity costs as an additional burden, [Deutsche Post] is required only to cover the costs attributable to the provision of mail-order parcel services. This means that these operations are not burdened with the common fixed cost of providing network capacity that [Deutsche Post] incurs as a result of its statutory universal service obligation.").

[87] See J Temple Lang and R O'Donoghue, "Defining Legitimate Competition: How to Clarify Pricing Abuses Under Article 82" (2002) 26 *Fordham International Law Journal* 83, 155.

[88] *Ibid.* The authors accept, however, that the pure incremental costs approach might be correct where the competitive market is not really an independent market, but is always and necessarily a by-product of the market in which the dominant company is dominant (that is, the competitive market is uneconomic except in combination with the other market). If this is the situation as a result of the inherent economics of the two markets, then the incremental-costs-only approach might be right, because the barrier to entry into the competitive market is due to the competitor's underlying need to enter the main market and not to the dominant company's cost allocation. But in this situation it would be necessary to prove objectively that independent activities in the competitive market were inherently uneconomic, and were not uneconomic for competitors only because of predatory pricing by the dominant company.

[89] Discussion Paper, para. 122 ("Where necessary to apply a cost benchmark based on ATC, the Commission will allocate common costs in proportion to the turnover achieved by the different products unless other cost allocation methods are for good reasons standard in the sector in question or in case the abuse biases the allocation based on turnover.").

[90] Case 66/86, *Ahmed Saeed Flugreisen and Silver Line Reisebüro GmbH v Zentrale zur Bekämpfung unlauteren Wettbewerbs eV* [1989] ECR 803, para. 43.

while taking into account the needs of consumers, the need for a satisfactory return on capital, the competitive market situation, including the fares of the other air carriers operating on the route, and the need to prevent dumping. Similarly, in a Notice on the postal sector, the Commission has indicated that allocation of common costs may be appropriate.[91] The Commission stated that the price of a product/service should thus include not only directly-attributable (or pure incremental) costs, but also an appropriate proportion of the common and overhead costs.[92] More recently, in *Claymore Dairies*,[93] the United Kingdom Competition Appeal Tribunal also suggested that common cost allocation may be necessary in predatory pricing cases.

Methods of allocating common/joint costs. On the assumption—which many question—that common cost allocation would be required under Article 82 EC, a number of possibilities might be envisaged. In general, allocating common costs raises significant practical problems and it is worth recalling that there is *no* unambiguous solution.[94] In theory, the solution is that costs should be allocated in inverse proportion to each product's price elasticity, with the product with the lowest elasticity bearing the higher share.[95] This allows costs to be allocated in accordance with demand. In practice, however, this is very difficult to evaluate, even for specialist regulators, due to the amount of information required.[96] Competition authorities and courts are *a fortiori* even less well-equipped to perform this exercise given that they will invariably have much less information about the industry concerned.

Alternative methods have therefore been applied. The following techniques have gained widespread usage in practice, in particular by specialist regulators.[97] A first method is to allocate common costs in proportion to the costs of the two products. For example, if the incremental costs of two products are €2 and €3, respectively, and common costs are €2.5, each product would bear an equal proportionate mark-up (i.e., 50% each), leading to a common cost allocation of €1 and €1.5 to each product. A problem with this approach is that it focuses purely on supply-side considerations, whereas the demand-side is generally a better indicator of the relative importance of common costs.

---

[91] See Notice from the Commission on the application of the competition rules to the postal sector and on the assessment of certain State measures relating to postal services, OJ 1998 C 39/2, para. 3.4.

[92] *Ibid.*

[93] See *Claymore Dairies Limited and Arla Foods UK PLC v Office of Fair Trading* [2005] CAT 30.

[94] *Ibid.*

[95] This is referred to as "Ramsey pricing" in the economics literature. See, generally, JJ Laffont and J Tirole, *Competition in Telecommunications* (Cambridge, MIT Press, 2001) s. 2.2.

[96] *Ibid.*, s. 3.4. See also *Vodaphone, O2, Orange and T-Mobile: Reports on references under Section 13 of the Telecommunications Act 1984 on the charges made by Vodafone, O2, Orange and T-Mobile for terminating calls from fixed and mobile networks*, United Kingdom Competition Commission (2003) (use of Ramsey pricing rejected, *inter alia*, due to informational issues).

[97] See generally M Canoy, P de Bijl, and R Kemp, "Access To Telecommunications Networks" in PA Buigues & P Rey (eds.), *The Economics of Antitrust and Regulation in Telecommunications: Perspectives for the New European Regulatory Framework* (Cheltenham, Elgar, 2004) s. 4.3; and Oxford Economic Research Associates (OXERA), "Cost Allocation in Competition Policy" (May, 2003) *Competing Ideas*.

A second approach is to allocate costs on a *pro rata* basis (e.g., turnover).[98] This is essentially the method outlined by the Commission in the Notice on the postal sector, where it indicates that objective criteria, such as volumes, time (labour), or intensity of usage can be used to determine the appropriate proportion to be allocated between the two operations.[99] A third approach is to subtract the purely incremental cost of the operation from its stand-alone cost. This gives the total common costs, which would then permit allocation between the two operations. This method is similar to the second outlined above, but perhaps more arbitrary since it does not contain a method for deciding how the allocation should be made between two products. A final method is to set prices in line with what they would be in a commercial negotiation context, i.e., at arm's length. This approach is not useful under competition law, since it does not yield a benchmark that can be used *a priori*.

In *Claymore Dairies*, the United Kingdom Competition Appeal Tribunal set out general guidance on how common cost allocation exercises should be undertaken:[100] (1) there are conventional accounting methods for making such allocations (e.g., by volume, value, time, etc.), but the most appropriate yardstick to use may be debateable; (2) one approach is to seek to identify "the cost drivers," i.e., to determine the factors that cause the costs to be incurred and then make allocations appropriately; (3) so far as possible, cost allocations should reflect the underlying business reality, i.e., a reasonably detailed understanding of the nature of the business and how costs arise; (4) how the business itself treats the costs in its internal management accounts will normally be an invaluable source of information; and (5) however the allocations are ultimately to be made, it is important in our view that the investigation is grounded on a firm and reliable assessment of total costs, cross-checked as far as possible against the dominant undertaking's statutory and management accounts.

Ultimately, if cost allocation is necessary (which is questionable), there is no easy solution to the choice of method. A useful starting point is to see what the overall scale of the common costs is. If they are relatively small, there is little risk to accuracy to ignore them and include only the total product-specific costs—whether based on LRAIC, average avoidable cost, or depreciated AVC/ATC over time—as the relevant measure. If common costs are relatively high, it should be assessed which of the above allocation methods is most reasonable, based on the information available.[101] While common cost allocation raises considerable practical problems, and inevitably involves some value and policy judgments, it does not follow that allocation, on some consistent and reasonable basis, cannot be made, or that no common costs need to be attributed to the other products for which they are incurred. What particular method is used to allocate common costs will vary from case to case and there is some merit in applying a

[98] See Discussion Paper, para. 65.

[99] *Ibid.*

[100] See *Claymore Dairies Limited and Arla Foods UK PLC v Office of Fair Trading* [2005] CAT 30, paras. 210 et seq.

[101] See C Ritter, "Does The Law of Predatory Pricing and Cross-Subsidisation Need a Radical Rethink?" (2004) 27 (4) *World Competition* 613-649 ("I propose that the issue of common cost allocation be subject to a 'reasonableness' test on a case-by-case basis. Thus, the defendant would have the opportunity to justify the way it allocates common costs and the courts or agencies would have a margin of appreciation in deciding on the matter.").

series of different approaches given the scope for error. Finally, when there is doubt or ambiguity, the cost of falsely finding a predatory price where there is none requires that the benefit of any doubt should be given to the defendant.

5.4.3 Cross-Subsidies

Definition of a cross-subsidy. Another issue that arises in the context of multi-product firms is the scope for a cross-subsidy, that is when a company uses funds generated from one area of activity to fund activities in another area of its activity. Cross-subsidies raise a number of regulatory issues, particularly in the context of utilities and regulated markets (e.g., the need for structural and accounting separation between reserved monopoly and competitive businesses).[102] Secondary Community legislation in the area of utilities for example requires incumbents to keep separate accounts between wholesale and retail businesses.[103] Similar issues arise for State undertakings with a mixture of reserved and non-reserved activities.[104] Such undertakings may have the ability and incentive to use funds from a reserved activity to distort competition on a neighbouring market.

---

[102] For a discussion of cross-subsidies under Community law, see L Hancher and JL Buendia Sierra, "Cross-Subsidisation and EC Law" (1998) 35 *Common Market Law Review* 901.

[103] See, e.g., Directive 2002/21/EC of the European Parliament and the Council of 7 March 2002 on a common regulatory framework for electronic communications networks and services, OJ 2002 L 108/33, Art. 13 (accounting separation and financial reports) and Directive 2002/19/EC of the European Parliament and the Council of 7 March 2002 on access to, and interconnection of, electronic communications networks and associated facilities, OJ 2002 L 108/7, Art. 11 (obligation of accounting separation).

[104] A number of important constraints under EC competition law significantly limit the scope for cross-subsidies. First, in order to avoid classification as unlawful State aid, government subsidies for public service obligations must satisfy several cumulative conditions: (1) the public service obligation must be clearly defined; (2) the subsidy recipient must actually be required to discharge public service obligations; (3) the parameters on the basis of which the compensation is calculated must be established beforehand in an objective and transparent manner; and (4) the compensation must not exceed what is necessary to cover all or part of the costs incurred in discharging the public service obligations, taking into account the relevant receipts and a reasonable profit for discharging those obligations. See Case C-280/00, *Altmark Trans GmbH and Regierungspräsidium Magdeburg v Nahverkehrsgesellschaft Altmark GmbH, and Oberbundesanwalt beim Bundesverwaltungsgericht* [2003] ECR I-7747. In *Chronopost*, the Court of Justice clarified this rule and held that "there is no question of State aid... if, first, it is established that the price charged properly covers all the additional, variable costs incurred in providing the logistical and commercial assistance, an appropriate contribution to the fixed costs arising from the use of the postal network and an adequate return on the capital investment in so far as it is used for [the] competitive activity and if, second, there is nothing to suggest that those elements have been underestimated or fixed in an arbitrary fashion." See Joined Cases C-83/01 P, C-93/01 P and C-94/01 P, *Chronopost SA, La Poste and French Republic v Union française de l'express (Ufex), DHL International, Federal express international (France) and CRIE* [2003] ECR I-6993, para. 40. Second, a State monopoly cannot use funds derived from abusive behaviour in connection with the reserved monopoly to fund the acquisition of an undertaking active in a neighbouring market open to competition. See Case T-175/99, *UPS Europe SA v Commission* [2002] ECR II-1915, para. 55. Finally, the scope of a State monopoly may be open to challenge under Article 86 EC, although, in practice, much of this area of law has been superseded by legislation under liberalisation reforms: See, e.g., Case C-320/91, *Paul Corbeau* [1993] ECR I-2533 and, generally, Ch. 1 (Introduction, Scope of Application, and Basic Framework).

Questions of how businesses finance particular activities are generally irrelevant, however, under competition law: the effects of an abusive practice are likely to be the same whether the resulting losses are sustained by cash flow from other activities within the same company—which may lie in completely unrelated markets—or from another source such as capital markets or financial reserves.[105] There is, however, one potential exception: predatory pricing. Where it can be shown that there is a *causal link* between losses on one market and profits on another, it may be appropriate to find an abuse of predatory pricing. The abuse remains predatory pricing, but the source of funding for the losses is the cross-subsidy from the profitable market. Thus, in the context of Article 82 EC, cross-subsidy cases are in essence cases in which the abuse, if there is one, is predatory pricing. Multi-product companies cross-subsidise all the time, whether or not they realise that they are doing so. There is no abuse of cross-subsidy in the absence of predatory prices, since an above-cost price does not, by definition, need any subsidy: it is incrementally profitable.[106]

Conditions for an unlawful cross-subsidy. Predatory pricing by cross-subsidy gives rise to issues under Article 82 EC only if two minimum conditions are satisfied. First, there must be a link between the subsidising and subsidised markets. A cross-subsidy arises if a firm has a dominant position in one market, and uses funds from that market to subsidise losses in another *related* market where it is in competition with competitors that sell only in the second market. Unless there is a clear link between the two markets, establishing the existence of cross-subsidy would be nigh on impossible (and is difficult in any event). The only clear case of a cross-subsidy is where losses in activity X are financed from profits arising from activity Y, which requires a demonstration that, but for the profits from Y, the losses in activity X could not be sustained. In other words, there must be a *causal* connection between activities X and Y: it is not sufficient

[105] This appears to have been the conclusion reached in *Tetra Pak II*, OJ 1992 L 72/1, on appeal Case T-83/91, *Tetra Pak International SA v Commission* [1994] ECR II-755, confirmed in Case C-333/94 P, *Tetra Pak International SA v Commission* [1996] ECR I-5951. Tetra Pak was found to have committed a range of pricing and other abuses in two different but related markets; aseptic and non-aseptic machinery and cartons. Tetra Pak's market shares in the aseptic and non-aseptic markets were approximately 90% and 50%, respectively. There were also important associative links between these two markets. The Commission's case was that Tetra Pak had engaged in predatory pricing in relation to its Tetra Rex non-aseptic carton by pricing below average total cost. The Commission argued that Tetra Pak was able to incur losses in the non-aseptic sector by substantial profits made in the monopoly aseptic sector. Tetra Pak argued before the Community Courts that it had not engaged in cross-financing from the aseptic to the non-aseptic sector. The Court of First Instance did not rule on this point, but simply noted that the "application of Article 8[2] of the Treaty does not depend on proof that there was cross-financing between the two sectors" (para 186). In other words, the source of the funding for the losses was not relevant if the conditions for predatory pricing under Article 82 EC were satisfied.

[106] See Guidelines on the Application of the EEC Competition Rules in the Telecommunications Sector, OJ 1991 C 233/2, para. 86 (predatory behaviour as a result of cross-subsidisation). See also Notice from the Commission on the application of the competition rules to the postal sector and on the assessment of certain State measures relating to postal services, OJ 1998 C 39/2. Although the Notice (para. 3.3) states that a cross-subsidy may be unlawful where it "distorts competition," it goes on to clarify that "dominant companies too many compete on price, or improve their cash flow and obtain only partial contribution to their fixed (overhead) costs, unless the prices are predatory or go against relevant national or Community regulations." This was confirmed in Case T-175/99, *UPS Europe SA v Commission*, [2002] ECR II-1915, para. 62.

that there simply are profits in one area of activity and losses in another. A contrary rule would impose enormous, and questionable, constraints on the internal decision-making of a dominant firm.

For example, in *Deutsche Post* there was a clear link between the reserved letter mail market and the parcel delivery market that was open to competition. It will be recalled that Deutsche Post was accused of using profits from its reserved monopoly in the reserved letter mail sector to cross-subsidise a loss-making business in the competitive parcel sector. Deutsche Post had a statutory monopoly, and also a legal duty to provide a universal postal service throughout Germany at standard postal rates. For this purpose, it was obliged to maintain infrastructure that it was able to use both for its monopoly and its competitive services. But much of the infrastructure used to collect, transport, store, and deliver letter mail could be simultaneously used to transport parcels. The letter mail business was found to be very profitable and to exceed the stand-alone cost of running this business. In contrast, the parcel business had consistently failed to cover its product-specific costs for a period lasting over five years. The Commission reasoned that, without the cross-subsidies from the reserved area, Deutsche Post would not have been able to finance below-cost selling in the competitive parcel area. This was because the profitable reserved monopoly "is a likely and permanent source of funding."[107] The Commission therefore prohibited Deutsche Post's below-cost sales in the parcel area and, in order to remove the scope for cross-financing between the profitable reserved market and the related loss-making competitive market, required the structural separation of the two businesses.

The second condition is to test for the presence of a cross-subsidy. In this regard, the Commission has relied on the so-called "combinatorial test."[108] Under this test, the price of each product in a group should cover its own purely incremental costs and the total revenues from the two products should cover their combined total cost. The latter includes any joint/common costs shared between the two, but, unlike the cost allocation rules outlined in the previous section, does *not* allocate them to any particular product. Instead, the test is whether the products cover their own incremental costs and their combined total cost.[109] The Commission summarised the combinatorial test as follows in *Deutsche Post*:[110]

> "From an economic point of view cross-subsidisation occurs where the earnings from a given service do not suffice to cover the incremental costs of providing that service and where there is another service or bundle of services the earnings from which exceed the stand-alone costs. The service for which revenue exceeds stand-alone cost is the source of the cross-subsidy and the service in which revenue does not cover the incremental costs is its destination."

[107] *Ibid.*, para. 6.

[108] See GR Faulhaber, "Cross-subsidisation: Pricing in Public Enterprises" (1975) 65 *American Economic Review* 966. See also EE Bailey and AF Friedlaender, "Market Structure and Multiproduct Industries" (1982) 20 *Journal of Economic Literature* 1024; and TJ Brennan, "Cross-Subsidisation and Cost Misallocation by Regulated Monopolists" (1990) 2(1) *Journal of Regulatory Economics* 3751.

[109] The more products, the greater the number of tests that need to be applied. See PA Grout, "Recent Developments in the Definition of Abusive Pricing in European Competition Policy," (2000) *CMPO Working Paper Series No. 00/23*, p. 19, for an overview of the combinatorial test.

[110] *Deutsche Post AG*, OJ 2001 L 125/27, para. 6.

On the facts, Deutsche Post's non-reserved parcel business did not even cover its own incremental costs for a period of five years and, therefore, made no contribution to the common fixed costs either. It was not therefore necessary to perform the other limbs of the combinatorial test.

Need for separate cross-subsidy abuse under Article 82 EC is unclear. It is not clear what a cross-subsidy analysis adds to the analysis of predatory pricing issues in the case of multi-product firms. Deutsche Post's pricing below LRAIC in the non-reserved parcel delivery market could have been regarded as predatory in itself without proof that the source of the funding was a reserved monopoly with revenues that exceeded its stand-alone cost. The combinatorial test applied by the Commission simply helps identify the likely *source* of the funding for the losses. But it is not obvious why this matters: the conduct could be predatory regardless of the source.

A number of explanations for the reference to a separate abuse of predatory pricing by cross-subsidy might be offered. First, a cross-subsidy analysis helps to identify an anticompetitive element in the case of State undertakings with a reserved monopoly in the sense that a reserved monopoly with revenues that exceed the stand-alone costs is likely to be a permanent source of funding for losses in other markets. The same considerations do not apply to undertakings without a reserved monopoly. This suggests that cross-subsidy as an abuse is not relevant outside the area of State undertakings (except perhaps under State aid rules) or entities with State-sponsored legal monopolies or other special rights. This point is now expressly confirmed in the Discussion Paper, which states that a cross-subsidy analysis is mainly relevant where the source of the subsidy is a legal monopoly and that monopoly is used to fund predatory pricing on a non-reserved market.[111]

Second, a combinatorial test is useful perhaps in that it avoids the need to allocate common costs between operations, which is difficult, arbitrary, and, some would argue, wrong. The combinatorial test simply asks whether one product covers its own specific (or incremental) costs and the revenues from another product exceeds its stand-alone costs. If the answer to the former is no and the latter yes, a possible source of funding for losses in a competitive market may be identified without the need to allocate costs between multiple products. But this seems a weak explanation for the Commission's practice, since the Commission also appears to favour cost allocation between multiple products in certain situations. Opponents of common cost allocation between multiple products would also presumably dispute the relevance of an analysis of stand-alone costs in cases where a firm has common costs.

[111] See Discussion Paper, para. 125. More controversially, the Discussion Paper states that this rule is an exception to the rule that predatory pricing is only an abuse where the firm is dominant on the relevant market or uses predatory pricing on a non-dominant market to strengthen its position on the dominant market. The Discussion Paper states that there is no requirement to show dominance where a legal monopoly is used to fund predatory pricing on a non-dominant market, and the adverse effects on competition only arise on the non-dominant market. Presumably, such a finding would require proof of "associative links" between the two markets under the conditions for abusive "leveraging," as well as a detailed effects analysis of the scope for actual or likely exclusion on the non-dominant market. On the conditions for leveraging abuses, see Ch. 4 (The General Concept Of An Abuse) above.

A final possible reason is that the most obvious basis for cost allocation in the case of multi-product firms—in proportion to turnover in the two sectors involved—is defective if the lower price is only predatory because it results from an unlawful cross-subsidy. In this situation, the cost allocation might have to be recalculated using a corrected turnover in the lower price sector. It might be important in certain cases to calculate the extent of the predation accurately, e.g., for the rights of injured competitors to claim compensation.

5.4.4 Situations Involving High Fixed And Low Variable Costs

Problem stated. A common feature of certain industries is a very high overall ratio of fixed costs to variable costs, and low variable costs. For example, once an airplane is scheduled to fly, the incremental cost of adding a passenger is likely to be very small. The same applies to other network industries characterised by scale and/or scope economies, such as telecommunications, post, and energy. Similarly, the cost of downloading software from the internet is likely to be very low relative to the fixed costs incurred in its development and would involve a near-zero AVC. The same is true of many forms of intellectual property where the cost of dissemination is low relative to the costs of production. In such cases, the dominant firm's prices may never be below AVC even if they are at near-zero levels. The AVC test may therefore provide limited guidance on the legitimacy of pricing practices in industries with these features.

The proposed solution: LRAIC. Recognising the above concerns, certain commentators argue that the AVC standard is an unsuitable cost measure where the principal costs incurred by a firm are not operating (or variable) costs, but high levels of fixed (or capital) costs.[112] They argue that the concept of LRAIC, discussed in Section 5.2 above, should instead be used to offer a more realistic assessment of the long-term costs of entering the market and remaining on it. The LRAIC of a product is defined as "the firm's total production cost (including the product), less what the firm's total cost would have been had it not produced the product, divided by the quantity of the product produced."[113] In simple terms, LRAIC measures the total costs, both capital and operational, of supplying a *specific* product or service rather than a larger category of sales, i.e., all costs that are causally related to a specific product.

LRAIC relies on a similar economic insight to short-run marginal cost rules such as AVC: that a firm will act to maximise profits. A profit-maximising firm will not only maximise profit in the short run by equating marginal revenue with short-run marginal cost, but will also maximise profit in the long run by ensuring that revenue exceeds long-run marginal cost. LRAIC is thought by certain commentators to be superior to short-run cost measures, since it: (1) includes all product-specific costs incurred in the research, development, and marketing of the allegedly predatory output, even if they were sunk; (2) avoids the need to classify costs as fixed or variable, which is sometimes complex and arbitrary; (3) does not require courts to allocate joint and common costs, which is a significant problem in practice; (4) includes any costs incurred to effectuate the predatory scheme following formation of the predatory strategy; and (5) measures

[112] P Bolton, JF Brodley, and MH Riordan, "Predatory Pricing: Strategic Theory and Legal Policy" (2000) 88(8) *Georgetown Law Journal* 2239, 2271–73.

[113] *Ibid.*, 2272.

the present worth of the productive assets by replacement costs, and not by historic costs, which may not correspond with current value.[114]

Use of LRAIC under Article 82 EC. The use of LRAIC has been endorsed in a number of instances under Article 82 EC, as well as national law.[115] The Commission's Access Notice on telecommunications indicates that it may be appropriate to depart from the *AKZO* tests and use a LRAIC benchmark in the case of telecommunications network pricing.[116] This is justified on the basis that "cost structures in network industries tend to be quite different to most other industries since the former have much larger common and joint costs." The Notice goes on to cite the rationale for departing from the *AKZO* test in certain industries: a price which equates to the variable cost of a service may be substantially lower than the price the operator needs in order to cover the cost of providing the service. Thus, the Notice states the costs that are relevant to the operator's decision to invest are "the total costs which are incremental to the provision of the service." In terms of the relevant time period to be taken into account in assessing LRAIC, the Notice indicates that neither the very short nor very long-run are appropriate and accordingly favours a middle-run period "over a longer period than one year."[117] Essentially the same point is now made in the Discussion Paper: that LRAIC is the appropriate benchmark for industries with high fixed costs and low variable costs (e.g., network industries).[118]

In *Deutsche Post*, the Commission applied a LRAIC benchmark to test for predatory pricing in the postal sector.[119] The case concerned predatory pricing in the context of a State postal letter monopoly and a mail order parcel delivery service that was open to competition. The allegation was that Deutsche Post was engaged in predatory pricing in the mail order business and that it funded those losses by a cross-subsidy from its profitable State monopoly letter business. In testing for losses in the parcel delivery sector, the Commission relied on a LRAIC benchmark to calculate the product-specific costs of providing this service. This excluded common costs that would have been incurred in any event due to the reserved monopoly business and included only the costs of collection, sorting, transport, and local delivery that were truly incremental to the parcel business. Adding the various product-specific costs, the Commission found that, in the period 1990–1995, Deutsche Post's revenue from the parcel business was below the incremental costs of providing this specific service; in other words, every sale in the parcel business during this period represented a loss.

Other solutions. A similar outcome to the LRAIC test can be reached by depreciating the value of assets over their useful lifetime rather than treating them as costs or revenue

---

[114] *Ibid.*

[115] See, e.g., Competition Act 1998: The Application in the Telecommunications Sector, OFT 417. See also Assessment of Conduct: Draft Competition Law Guideline for Consultation, OFT 414a, para. 4.10 ("In certain sectors (for example telecommunications), long run incremental cost (LRIC) may be a preferable cost benchmark to variable cost.").

[116] See Notice On The Application Of The Competition Rules To Access Agreements In The Telecommunications Sector, OJ 1998 C 265/2, paras. 113–14.

[117] *Ibid.*

[118] See Discussion Paper, para. 126.

[119] See *Deutsche Post AG*, OJ 2001 L 125/27.

as entered in the company's accounts. In this scenario, plants, assets, and other expenses are treated as variable costs that should be depreciated over time. The reason is that plant and equipment are not necessarily a fixed expense: they wear out over time or through intensity of use. This approach was applied in *Wanadoo*, which concerned the recurrent and non-recurrent variable costs of recruiting a broadband Internet customer. A major initial expense for firms in this market is customer acquisition costs, such as trial offers and free equipment (e.g., modems). These costs are a one-off expense for the company, which may or may not yield a lasting benefit in terms of a long-term subscription. The Commission did not treat customer acquisition costs as an immediate expense for the defendant, but instead spread them over a period of four years, i.e., as if the costs were a commercial investment to be written off over a customer's realistic lifetime. This was "based on the consideration that it is not the firm's objective to produce an instantaneous profit" and that, instead the firm will seek to achieve a "return on its investment within a reasonable time."[120] In this context, "it may be that prices will not cover its costs in the first few years of business, without driving off the market competitors with less financial stamina who are likewise investing with a view to reasonable profitability."[121]

The appropriate depreciation period will depend on the "economic equilibrium" of the product in question; in other words, the period in which it is usual in the industry in question to recover non-recurrent entry costs. In *Wanadoo* the Commission used a period of four years over which to spread the costs of acquiring broadband internet customers, despite the fact that customer subscriptions tied the customer to the service for a period of only one year. In adopting this period, the Commission considered that it had applied the approach most favourable to the defendant, since both competitors and the French telecommunications regulator relied on shorter amortisation periods.[122] Following this adjustment, the Commission calculated Wanadoo's AVC and ATC over time and found that they were higher than its revenues for significant periods.

The above approach more or less corresponds with the argument by certain commentators that the AVC test does not need modification in the case of products with very low AVC if the proper time period is taken into account.[123] If the period of near-zero pricing is short, there can be no anticompetitive effect, since an equally efficient rival will also have near-zero marginal costs during that period and thus be able to also post a profit. In contrast, if the near-zero pricing lasts several years, the pricing could be predatory if it does not allow an equally efficient competitor to recover the costs of updating or replacing the relevant output in order to stay in the market. The costs of updating or replacing plant, software, or equipment would all be variable if the period of predatory pricing is long, but not if it was brief.[124] In other words, the relevant consideration is not whether a product has low variable costs or not, but to determine

[120] Case COMP/38.233, *Wanadoo Interactive*, Commission Decision of July 16, 2003, not yet published, para. 76.

[121] *Ibid.*

[122] *Ibid.*, para. 79.

[123] See E Elhauge, "Why Above-Cost Price Cuts To Drive Out Entrants Are Not Predatory – and the Implications for Defining Costs and Market Power" (2003) 112 *Yale Law Journal* 681-795, 708–10.

[124] *Ibid.*, 710.

which costs are in fact variable during the period of alleged predation.[125] Again, this approach is likely to be similar in outcome to the use of the LRAIC benchmark, since it seeks to measure the firm's total variable costs during the alleged period of predation, even if some of them would be fixed costs when looked at over a shorter period.

5.4.5 Situations In Which A Product Incurs Inevitable Start-Up Losses

Problem stated. Start-up losses are inevitable in many industries given large up-front investments and the need to stimulate demand over time. Calculating variable and total costs in the above circumstances requires certain adjustments for cost amortisation over time, and asset and use depreciation. If costs were only assessed at the initial stage, they could suggest the product was loss-making whereas, over time, the product may in fact be profitable, or less loss-making than originally thought. How such losses should be treated under Article 82 EC is therefore important in practice. This exercise is essentially concerned with correcting potential accounting distortions where products involve inevitable start-up losses. It has no implications on whether any losses incurred by the dominant firm could legitimately be recovered in future, which falls to be assessed at a second stage under objective justification.[126]

Suggested solutions. A number of different approaches to the issue of start-up losses are possible and, given the scope for error, it may be necessary to use the various approaches in parallel. First, it may be possible to exclude all or part of the start-up period from the calculation of costs. In *Wanadoo*, the Commission excluded from the assessment of losses a period of fourteen months in which residential broadband internet services had been made available by the dominant firm in France on the basis that "the high-speed internet market ha[d] not developed sufficiently for a test of predation to be significant."[127] This suggests that such adjustments will be made principally in the case of emerging markets. At the same time, however, the Commission has stressed that this does not mean that emerging markets are necessarily immune from review under competition law.[128] It simply means that part of the start-up phase in such markets may not be fully taken into account in the analysis.

A second approach is that outlined in the previous section: to depreciate initial losses over time on the basis, for example, that they are a long-term investment in customer

---

[125] A variant of this test was first proposed by J Temple Lang, "European Community Antitrust Law: Innovation Markets And High Technology Industries" in BE Hawk (ed.), *Fordham Corporate Law Institute* (London, Sweet & Maxwell, 1997) 519, 575 ("In industries where the marginal cost of additional production is near to zero, it is suggested that the test to be applied is whether a company charges a price for good or services which, although above the average variable cost of the providing the specific goods or services for which the price in question is paid, is so low that its overall revenues for all the goods or services in question would be less than its average variable cost of providing them if it sold the same proportion of its output at the same price on a continuing basis, even where no intent to exclude a competitor is proved.").

[126] See Section 5.6 below.

[127] Case COMP/38.233, *Wanadoo Interactive*, Commission Decision of July 16, 2003, not yet published, para. 71.

[128] *Ibid.*, para. 301.

acquisition. In *Wanadoo*, this was the Commission's preferred approach and, on the facts, it opted for a depreciation period of four years.

A third approach is to apply standard techniques used to measure cash flow over time in the context of investment-making decisions. This involves evaluating the cost/benefit of tying up capital in a project—the opportunity cost of capital. The most commonly-used method is discounted cash flow (DCF), which may be forward-looking or historical. DCF analysis proceeds in two steps. First, future cash flows (i.e., revenues and costs) are forecast. Second, future net cash flows are discounted at the appropriately adjusted discount rate and added up to yield a single net present value (NPV) figure. The appropriate adjustment (i.e., the risk premium added to the pure time-value-of-money component incorporated in the discount rate) becomes necessary whenever future cash flows are subject to uncertainty. This reflects the fact that most investors are averse to risk and therefore need to be compensated for taking on this risk in the first place.

If the NPV of a project is positive, it denotes that it is better to do the project than not to do it. If it is negative, then it is better to do nothing than to undertake the project and stick with it to the end. NPV analysis can also be used to decide whether to abandon a project. So if the NPV of the project going forwards is positive then it is better to stick with the project to the end than to abandon it. If it is negative, it is better to abandon the project than to continue to the end. Finally, NPV analysis can be used to decide which of two courses of action to take—if the choice must be made once and for all, making projects mutually exclusive, then it is better to choose the project with the higher NPV.[129]

A DCF approach was considered in *Wanadoo*, but rejected for several reasons. First, the DCF has a flaw when applied in predation cases. A DCF analysis may show positive returns over time, but it does not distinguish between situations in which positive margins are due to legitimate pricing and situations in which the only reason for the profits is the exclusion of competitors.[130] In other words, it could have the effect of showing positive returns where the only reason for them was exclusionary conduct.[131] Second, the Commission argued that the DCF analysis only included customers from a specific period and did not take into account the benefit beyond that period of the prospects of growth in later periods.[132] Finally, there are often accounting problems in

---

[129] Another DCF measure is the internal rate of return (IRR), which relates to the size of the original investment. IRR measures the rate of return on an investment; NPV measures the size of the return. DCF is explained in more detail in Competition Act 1998: The Application in the Telecommunications Sector, OFT 417.

[130] Case COMP/38.233, *Wanadoo Interactive*, Commission Decision of July 16, 2003, not yet published, para. 91.

[131] See CA98/20/2002, *BSkyB*, OFT Decision of December 17, 2002, para. 384 ("A positive net present value could therefore be interpreted not as evidence of anticompetitive [abuse] but partly as evidence that the exercise of a[n] [abuse] is a viable strategy, as... losses incurred... are subsequently recovered.").

[132] Case COMP/38.233, *Wanadoo Interactive*, Commission Decision of July 16, 2003, not yet published, para. 92.

that the information available may not allow a proper *ex post* reconstruction of anticipated revenue flows.[133]

A final approach is to assess whether profitability was foreseeable *ex ante* on the basis of reasonable and plausible assumptions applied to the information available to the company. If not, this may offer further evidence of loss-making. This test is based on the original Areeda and Turner formulation and whether the costs concerned were "reasonably anticipated" by the dominant firm. In *Wanadoo*, the Commission relied on this method as a cross-check for its conclusion that Wanadoo's prices did not cover AVC or ATC, even when spread over a period in line with asset depreciation and use.[134] In conducting this exercise, the Commission attached importance to the need for a link between the dominant firm's assumptions and the information available to it at the time when those assumptions were made. For example, the Commission partially discounted the assumption made by Wanadoo at the end of 2001 that upstream access and routing charges were scheduled to reduce in 2002, thereby reducing its costs. This was because the reductions would not take place at once in 2002: the year would be divided into the periods before and after the reduction in charges. Wanadoo assumed the same level of cost reduction for the entire year, which was not reasonable, according to the Commission, at the time when the assumption was made.

5.5 EXCLUSIONARY ABOVE-COST PRICE CUTS UNDER ARTICLE 82 EC

Overview. Predatory pricing under Article 82 EC is not limited to situations in which the dominant firm adopts non-remunerative prices below the relevant measure of cost, but may also include exclusionary prices that remain above ATC. In *Compagnie Maritime Belge*, the Court of Justice explained this expansive view of predatory pricing on the basis that: (1) Article 82 EC does not exhaustively enumerate potential abuses; (2) an abuse may occur if an undertaking in a dominant position strengthens that position in such a way that the degree of dominance reached substantially fetters competition; (3) costs may not be a reliable guide to the legitimacy of a firm's conduct where variable costs are very low or near-zero; (4) the actual scope of the "special responsibility" imposed on a dominant firm must be considered in the light of the specific circumstances of each case that show that competition has been weakened.[135]

Less clear, however, are the theoretical underpinnings of the objection under Article 82 EC to above cost price-cutting. Neither the Commission nor the Community Courts have explained in any satisfactory way how the rules for above-cost predatory pricing differ from those concerning below-cost predatory pricing. Instead, they have decided cases according to the particular facts without a clear underlying legal framework. Many of the cases rely on circumstantial evidence of intent to eliminate a rival by the dominant firm. However, as explained above, the second *AKZO* rule

[133] *Ibid.*, para. 96.
[134] *Ibid.*, paras. 97–106.
[135] See Joined Cases C-395/96 P and C-396/96 P, *Compagnie Maritime Belge Transports SA and Others v Commission* [2000] ECR I-1365, paras. 111–14, as well as the Opinion of the Advocate General Fennelly, para. 133.

provides that pricing above AVC but below ATC is unlawful if there is proof of a plan to eliminate a competitor. The strong implication therefore is that pricing above ATC is lawful and that anticompetitive intent cannot, in itself, also lead to such pricing being regarded as unlawful.

Economic arguments in favour of treating above-cost price cuts as unlawful. Certain economists agree that above-cost price cuts by a dominant firm can in theory lead to undesirable exclusion of rival firms in circumstances where the continued presence of that rival would have constrained the dominant firm's pricing over time.[136] The paradigm case concerns well-documented situations in the air transport sector where, in response to new entry, an incumbent hub monopolist adds capacity and reduces prices to levels that remained above-cost only to increase prices back to pre-entry (monopoly) levels when the entrant had been successfully eliminated.[137] Restrictions on reactive above-cost price cuts by the dominant firm have been suggested in order to ensure that new entrants remain in the market.[138]

In quantitative terms, it is also possible to explain how above-cost pricing might lead to socially undesirable exclusion. Suppose a new entrant has costs labelled MC_e that are below price P_m charged by the dominant company but greater than the dominant firm's costs MC_m. Upon entry, the dominant firm lowers its price to P_c, the entrant's break even point. Under the Areeda and Turner model, the dominant company can still lower its price further below P_c as long as it does not go below its own costs. The entrant is therefore making a loss and exits the market. The price returns to the pre-entry monopoly level, P_m:

[136] That above-cost prices could in theory have anticompetitive effects was first recognised in R Schmalensee, "On the Use of Economic Models in Antitrust: The Realemon Case" (1978–79) 127 *University of Pennsylvania Law Review* 994. For a more recent exposition, see M Armstrong and J Vickers, "Price Discrimination, Competition and Regulation," (1993) 41(4) *Journal of Industrial Economics* 335.

[137] This was in essence the basis of the unsuccessful predatory pricing claim pursued by the US Department of Justice in *United States of America v AMR Corporation, American Airlines, Inc, and AMR Eagle Holding Corporation*, 140 F. Supp. 2d 1141 (D. Kansas 2001). See also CV Oster and JS Strong, *Predatory Practices in the US Airline Industry* (Washington, US Department of Transportation, 2001) p.7 ("In recent years, some of the incumbent network carriers' responses to entry by low-fare carriers have given rise to concerns about the use of what might be termed predatory practices or unfair methods of competition...The second example, involving the Detroit-Philadelphia market, raises questions about the ability of incumbents to 'dump' large quantities of low-fare seat capacity in response to entry, even though the network carrier did not make major changes in the number of flights or in total seats available. Together, they raise potential issues for competition policy.").

[138] These considerations appear to have motivated the Commission in 2001 to impose an unusual commitment in return for clearing a partnership between Austrian Airlines and Lufthansa. The Commission required, *inter alia*, that, each time the airlines reduced a published fare on a route where they face the presence of a new entrant, they should apply the same fare reduction, in percentage terms, on three other routes on which they did not face competition: see Commission announces intention to clear partnership between Austrian Airlines and Lufthansa, Commission Press Release IP/01/1832 of December 14, 2001. It is doubtful, however, whether such a remedy could be lawfully imposed in a final decision.

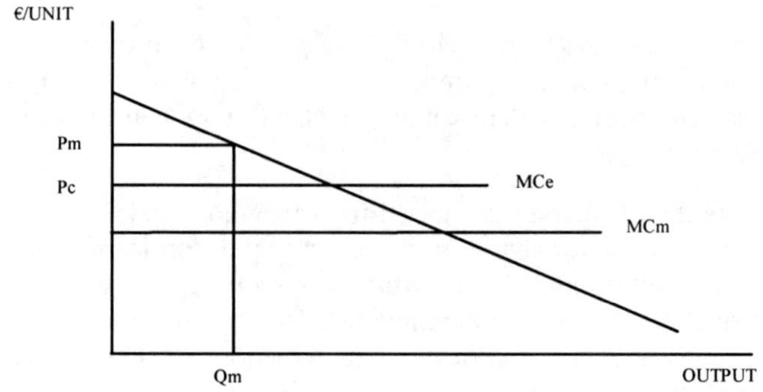

Exit in these circumstances might seem undesirable but the key question is whether there is a net deadweight loss. Conceivably, yes. Assuming the new entrant captures a certain market share on the basis of price P_c, consumers will benefit from lower prices than in the pre-entry situation where the price was P_m. This should offset any deadweight loss caused by the lesser efficiency achieved by the new entrant. It should also be remembered that the new entrant should, over time, progress along the learning curve in the market and achieve greater efficiency. Thus, economic theory provides a basis for saying that above-cost price cuts are capable of harming consumer welfare.

Relying on this basic economic insight, a number of commentators have proposed certain restrictions on a dominant firm's ability to offer above-cost price cuts. An early contribution argued that cost-based rules were inappropriate to assess predation, since firms can adapt their conduct, including their investment in plant and capacity, to the relevant legal rule. For example, using the Areeda and Turner AVC benchmark, it was argued that firms could invest in additional capacity so that it could produce at sufficiently high output levels in response to entry without violating a prohibition on pricing below AVC: until entry occurred the firm would, consistent with monopoly behaviour, restrict output and raise price, while maximising profits at that level of capacity. To avoid these effects, the commentator proposed restrictions on output expansion by the dominant firm following entry for a period of 12–18 months. This period was thought sufficient to allow the entrant to establish itself in the market and move down the cost curve.[139]

Shortly thereafter, a variant of the above rule was proposed. Instead of preventing output expansion, it was proposed that the dominant firm should be prevented from making price increases after the new entrant had been forced to cease operations. If the dominant firm wished to decrease prices in response to entry, it would have to maintain those low prices in the medium- to long-term. The would-be predator would therefore have to take the long-term cost of a price reduction into account, thereby precluding the period of recoupment that is generally thought to characterise predatory pricing. This

[139] See OE Williamson, "Predatory Pricing: A Strategic And Welfare Analysis" (1977–78) 87 *Yale Law Journal* 284, 290–92.

proposal also avoided one of the criticisms of the output restriction rule—that the dominant firm would be prevented from making any price cut following entry.[140]

Economic arguments against treating above-cost price cuts as unlawful. A number of leading antitrust commentators, including advocates of the need for legal rules to prevent predatory pricing, argue that all pricing above the relevant measure of cost should be presumed lawful. In essence, this conclusion assumes that firms who are equally or more efficient than the dominant firm can compete on the merits on the basis of pricing above cost and that there is no reason why competition law should offer them a safe haven against price competition. There is no net welfare loss if less-efficient companies are eliminated, since any properly-functioning competitive process would have the same effect. As one commentator noted, "a seller may want to weaken or destroy a competitor, but if the only method used is underselling him by virtue of having lower costs there is no rational antitrust objection to the seller's conduct."[141] The original proponents of the AVC test, Areeda and Turner, make a similar point, namely that "the low price at or above average cost is competition on the merits and excludes only less efficient rivals."[142]

The above arguments are, however, largely conclusory. The real question is whether it is socially desirable to keep less efficient firms in the market because of their ability to constrain the dominant firm's prices in the medium- to long-term and enhance consumer welfare. Put differently, would a rule against above-cost price cuts encourage more entry and lead to lower prices than would occur in the absence of such a rule? In this regard, several situations have been distinguished:[143]

1. A restriction on above-cost price cuts is unnecessary for less efficient firms who would have entered anyway in the absence of such a restriction. In such circumstances, the effect of a restriction on above-cost price cuts by the dominant firm is entirely negative. It would raise post-entry prices unnecessarily by creating a price floor, reducing output and thus harming consumer welfare.

[140] See WJ Baumol, "Quasi-Permanence Of Price Reductions: A Policy For Prevention Of Predatory Pricing" (1979) 89 *Yale Law Journal* 1, 2–3. A recent variant on both of the above theories is that a dominant firm should be prevented from responding with substantial price cuts or significant product enhancements until the entrant has had a reasonable time to recover its entry costs and become viable, or until the incumbent firm loses its dominance. For practical purposes, this restriction would be limited to situations in which the new entry qualifies as "substantial," which would be satisfied where the entrant's prices are 20% below those of the dominant firm. In other cases, different rules would define meaningful entry. For example, where a new entrant begins construction of the relevant infrastructure needed to enter a market (e.g., laying cable), this event would qualify as "substantial" for entry purposes. In either case, the proposed restriction is that the dominant firm's prices would be frozen for twelve to eighteen months after the moment of "substantial entry." See AS Edlin, "Stopping Above Cost Predatory Pricing" (2001–02) 111 *Yale Law Journal* 941. See also BS Yamey, "Predatory Price Cutting: Notes And Comments" (1972) 15 *Journal of Law and Economics* 129.

[141] RA Posner, *Antitrust Law* (2nd edn., Chicago, University of Chicago Press, 2001) p. 214.

[142] PE Areeda and DF Turner, "Predatory Pricing and Related Practices Under Section 2 of the Sherman Act" (1975) 88 *Harvard Law Review* 697-733, 706.

[143] See E Elhauge, "Why Above-Cost Price Cuts To Drive Out Entrants Are Not Predatory–and the Implications for Defining Costs and Market Power" (2003) 112 *Yale Law Journal* 681-795, 701–02.

2. The effects of a restriction on above-cost price cuts on firms that are less efficient than the dominant firm, but would be mildly encouraged to enter due to the existence of such a restriction, are also largely negative. Where capital costs are high, a restriction of this type will usually be insufficient to encourage such a new entrant from staying in the market since it would be excluded once the restriction expired whether because of passage of time or because the incumbent loses its dominant position. Where capital costs are low, the entrant probably would have entered anyway. Thus, at most, the restriction will probably offer only weak encouragement for those entrants who have intermediate entry costs where the prolongation of the short-run period allows it to cover entry costs. Thus, the effect on consumer welfare is at best mixed, but more likely negative, where the entrant receives some (weak) encouragement from a restriction on post-entry price cuts by the dominant firm.

3. For entrants who are just as efficient as the dominant firm, or more efficient, the consumer welfare effects of restrictions on above-cost price cuts by the dominant firm are wholly negative. They raise post-entry prices for consumers, lower output and so harm consumer welfare. They may also make the overall mix of entrants less efficient by artificially increasing the returns for inefficient entry.

4. For entrants who are less efficient than the dominant firm, but would become more efficient over time, the effect of a restriction on above-cost price cuts by the dominant firm is also largely negative. If the entrant would become more efficient over time, capital markets should find it attractive to fund such entry, in which case concerns similar to those outlined in (3) would arise. In addition, allowing the entrant to become more efficient over time by placing restrictions on the dominant firm's ability to engage in price cuts post-entry will necessitate a decline in the dominant firm's overall efficiency.

Article 82 EC precedent on exclusionary above-cost price cuts. The Commission and Community Courts have objected to above-cost price cuts by a dominant firm in several cases. *Hilti* concerned a series of cumulative measures by a manufacturer of nail guns designed to deter customers who purchased its nail guns to also purchase nails from competing nail manufacturers.[144] These measures included tied sales, inducing independent distributors not to fulfil export orders, refusal to honour guarantees for customers who purchased competing nails, and various selective and discriminatory pricing policies. Hilti was found to have offered more favourable discounts to customers who purchased both its nails and guns than those that purchased Hilti's guns and a competitor's nails, including in certain cases giving away products for free. The discounts were not based on any efficiencies but the fact that the customer would be dissuaded from purchasing competing nails. The Commission's conclusion that these discounts were abusive did not depend on a showing that they were below-cost, but on the targeting of discounts at competitors' customers:[145]

[144] *Eurofix-Bauco v Hilti*, OJ 1988 L 65/19.
[145] *Ibid.*, para. 81 (emphasis added).

> "[A] selectively discriminatory pricing policy by a dominant firm designed purely to damage the business of, or deter market entry by, its competitors, whilst maintaining higher prices for the bulk of its other customers, is both exploitive of these other customers and destructive of competition. As such it constitutes abusive conduct by which a dominant firm can reinforce its already preponderant market position. *The abuse in this case does not hinge on whether the prices were below costs* (however defined—and in any case certain products were given away free). *Rather it depends on the fact that, because of its dominance, Hilti was able to offer special discriminatory prices to its competitors' customers with a view to damaging their business, whilst maintaining higher prices to its own equivalent customers.*"

On appeal, the Court of First Instance did not specify the antitrust objection to Hilti's pricing practices. It held that the strategy employed by Hilti was "not a legitimate mode of competition," since a selective and discriminatory policy is liable to deter other undertakings from establishing themselves in the market and that, consequently, the Commission "had good reason to hold that such behaviour on Hilti's part was improper."[146] The Community Courts did not explain how Hilti's prices—which were not found to be below cost—would exclude rivals or deter their entry.

Above-cost exclusionary pricing was also addressed in detail in *Compagnie Maritime Belge*.[147] The case concerned various practices carried out by the CEWAL liner shipping conference operating between Zaire and certain European ports, including adherence to an agreement with the government of Zaire that led to *de facto* exclusivity on certain routes for CEWAL, the imposition of 100% loyalty contracts, and the practice of "fighting ships." "Fighting ships" is a practice in maritime transport whereby sailing times are fixed as closely as possible to those of a competing liner and special discounted freight rates applied for those sailings only. CEWAL, which enjoyed a *de facto* monopoly on the relevant routes, carried out "fighting ship" practices for the avowed purpose of "getting rid" of its only competitor, G&C.

Both Community Courts held that this practice was abusive. In reaching this finding, they expressly rejected the appellants' argument that selectively low prices could not be abusive unless they were below cost within the meaning of *AKZO*. The following features of CEWAL's conduct were found to have rendered the selectively low prices abusive: (1) the practice was carried out for the express purpose of eliminating G&C; (2) CEWAL apportioned the loss of revenue incurred by the price-cutting among the liner conference members; and (3) price competition was already weakened in the maritime transport sector because the applicable Community legislation allowed

---

[146] Case T-30/89, *Hilti AG v Commission* [1991] ECR II-1439, para. 100. Contrast *BPB Industries plc*, OJ 1989 L 10/50, para. 113, where the Commission allowed BPB to maintain discounts for retailers in certain areas of England that were exposed to foreign competition, since there was no suggestion that these (above-cost) discounts "were in themselves predatory, nor that they were part of any scheme of systematic alignment."

[147] *Cewal, Cowac and Ukwal*, OJ 1993 L 34/20, upheld on appeal in Joined Cases T-24/93, T-25/93, T-26/93, and T-28/93, *Compagnie Maritime Belge Transports SA and Others v Commission* [1996] ECR II-1201 and in Joined Cases C-395/96 P and C-396/96 P, *Compagnie Maritime Belge Transports SA and Others v Commission* [2000] ECR I-1365. See also *Irish Sugar plc*, OJ 1997 L 258/1, affirmed on appeal in Case T-228/97, *Irish Sugar plc v Commission* [1999] ECR II-2969 and Order of the Court of Justice in Case C-497/99 P, *Irish Sugar plc v Commission* [2001] ECR I-5333 (selective rebates above ATC found abusive based on, *inter alia*, geographic price discrimination and market-partitioning effect).

collective tariff-setting. At the same time, the Community Courts were very careful to limit their findings to the unusual circumstances of the case: their judgments did not address in what circumstances a dominant company may be allowed to respond to competitive offers with selectively low prices. The Court of Justice limited its findings to the specific case at hand and the virtual monopoly possessed by the defendant on the relevant market.[148]

Framework for analysing exclusionary above-cost price cuts under Article 82 EC. Article 82 EC envisages situations in which prices above ATC may be abusive. The case law does not, however, provide a clear basis for distinguishing between legitimate and unlawful above-cost price cuts. This is regrettable, since a lack of clarity on the circumstances in which a dominant firm can price above ATC without violating Article 82 EC runs a much higher risk of chilling legitimate price competition than restrictions on below-cost pricing. A suggested framework for analysis is set forth below. Whether Article 82 EC should prohibit unconditional above-cost pricing at all, however, first deserves serious consideration.

a. Should Article 82 EC prohibit above-cost price cuts? Economic thinking to the effect that prices above the dominant firm's costs can be anticompetitive in certain circumstances provides a theoretical explanation of why such pricing practices have been condemned in several cases under Article 82 EC. However, there are compelling arguments that, in practice, restrictions on above-cost price cuts do not lead to higher entry levels or lower prices than would have occurred in the absence of such a rule.[149] These practical implications deserve serious consideration, since, if they are correct, they suggest that the net effect of such rules is unnecessarily high prices for consumers in the short-term and reductions in allocative efficiency, without any countervailing increase in effective entry levels or a reduction in the dominant firm's prices in the medium to long-term.

These practical effects are quite separate from the considerable implementation difficulties of framing clear legal rules on above-cost price cuts that capture only or mainly anticompetitive pricing, but allow legitimate pricing to take place. Condemning above-cost pricing should be approached with considerable reserve, since price competition is almost always desirable and it is very difficult, if not impossible, to formulate a legal rule to distinguish between an above-cost low price that will eliminate a competitor and one which will not. Speculative future gains through legal restrictions

---

[148] Judgment of the Court of Justice, *ibid.*, paras. 118 and 119 ("It is not necessary, in the present case, to rule generally on the circumstances in which a liner conference may legitimately, on a case by case basis, adopt lower prices than those of its advertised tariff in order to compete with a competitor who quotes lower prices... It is sufficient to recall that the conduct at issue here is that of a conference having a share of over 90% of the market in question and only one competitor. The appellants have moreover... admitted at the hearing, that the purpose of the conduct complained of was to eliminate G&C from the market.").

[149] See E Elhauge, "Why Above-Cost Price Cuts To Drive Out Entrants Are Not Predatory—and the Implications for Defining Costs and Market Power" (2003) 112 *Yale Law Journal* 681-795.

on above-cost price cuts should not be favoured over the present certainty of lower prices and, in the short-term at least, higher output.[150]

Although implementation difficulties are to some extent inherent in any rule that prohibits certain forms of pricing, the predatory pricing rules under the *AKZO* case law are at least based on an economic insight on which there is a wide measure of agreement: that pricing below AVC/ATC (or other measures of cost) is generally irrational. There is no similar consensus in relation to above-cost price cuts and, indeed, a very strong consensus that above-cost price cuts are not harmful to consumers at all. Thus, the risk of condemning a price that is in fact legitimate is much higher in the context of above-cost pricing restrictions than below-cost pricing, and almost certainly greater than the cost of allowing certain forms of exclusionary above-cost pricing to go unpunished.

b. Explaining the case law on exclusionary above-cost price cuts. If, consistent with the precedent outlined above, an exceptional rule against reactive above-cost price cuts should exist under Article 82 EC, an explanation of when it should apply is necessary. The most convincing explanation is that pricing above ATC is only unlawful when it is coupled with a range of other exclusionary measures, i.e., there is cumulative evidence of abuse as part of a plan to eliminate a rival. The pricing is not unlawful in itself but can be viewed as unlawful where linked with other exclusionary practices. The pricing is a key part of an overall exclusionary policy and there is no other explanation for it. It could not be regarded as procompetitive conduct that happened to coincide in time with an exclusionary policy: it made sense only as part of that policy and was clearly linked to that policy.

Irish Sugar,[151] *AKZO*, *Hilti*, and *Tetra Pak* could all be explained on this basis. In those cases there were not only selectively low prices, but also a series of other abuses with similar objectives, including fidelity rebates, tying, exclusive contracts, and target rebates. This was also the approach effectively taken by the Advocate General and the judgment of the Court of First Instance in *Compagnie Maritime Belge*. The Advocate

---

[150] Another (often ignored) implementation difficulty is that any rule restricting price cuts or output changes in response to new entry must by necessity define when it would apply and when it expires. If entry is defined as the moment the new entrant first makes actual sales or any other specified period after entry is foreseeable, the dominant firm could easily circumvent the rule by lowering prices just before then. Rules based on foreseeable entry fare no better because they risk raising prices to consumers for a period in which there is no new entrant to offset them with lower prices. A moment of entry defined too far in advance also runs the risk that the relevant restriction on price cuts will have expired before entry actually occurs. Any defined period thus runs the risk of circumvention. *Ad hoc* rules are likely to introduce greater uncertainty and administrative costs into the law. For example, one commentator would limit the restriction on above-cost price cuts to situations in which the new entry qualifies as "substantial," which would be satisfied where the entrant's prices are 20% below those of the dominant firm. However, in other cases, different rules would make entry "substantial;" for example, where a new entrant begins construction of the relevant infrastructure needed to enter a market (e.g., laying cable). See AS Edlin, "Stopping Above Cost Predatory Pricing" (2001–02) 111 *Yale Law Journal* 941, 945, 988. These rules raise too many exceptions, and would require further definition in so many different contexts, that they are not useful as legal norms.

[151] See *Irish Sugar plc*, OJ 1997 L 258/1, affirmed on appeal in Case T-228/97, *Irish Sugar plc v Commission* [1999] ECR II-2969 and Order of the Court of Justice in Case C-497/99 P, *Irish Sugar plc v Commission* [2001] ECR I-5333.

General said that the various practices were designed to drive the competitor from the market at minimal cost to the dominant companies, so as to restore their virtual monopoly and raise their prices thereafter. Finally, in the context of loyalty rebates, the Court of First Instance has confirmed that it is appropriate to have regard to the cumulative effect of a series of practices with similar objectives when assessing their legality.[152] While this does not absolve a plaintiff or competition authority from proving that certain abuses did occur, it may allow a practice that would otherwise be lawful to be regarded as unlawful in circumstances where it is a part of an overall strategy of abusive behaviour.

Two other explanations are put forward in the Discussion Paper. First, the Discussion Paper suggests that *Compagnie Maritime Belge* should be confined to its own special facts.[153] In other words, where companies in a collective dominant situation with a near-monopoly position apply a clear strategy to collectively exclude or discipline a competitor by selectively undercutting the competitor, while collectively sharing the loss of revenues, prices above ATC may, exceptionally, be considered abusive. In practice, this situation is extremely unlikely to arise outside the shipping sector, since any express or implied agreement between two or more firms to share losses resulting from an exclusionary pricing strategy would constitute a violation under Article 81 EC. (In *Compagnie Maritime Belge* the applicable maritime legislation at the time allowed certain forms of collective rate setting. The Commission has now proposed the repeal of this legislation.)

The second example presented in the Discussion Paper is more controversial. It states that price cuts above ATC may be predatory where a single dominant company operates in a market where it has certain non-replicable advantages or where economies of scale are very important and entrants necessarily will have to operate for an initial period at a significant cost disadvantage because entry can practically only take place below the minimum efficient scale.[154] By pricing above its own ATC, but below that of an entrant, the Discussion Paper states that a dominant firm may commit an abuse. It adds that, for such price cut to be assessed as predatory, it has to be shown that the dominant firm has a clear strategy to exclude, that the entrant will only be less efficient because of these non-replicable or scale advantages, and that entry is being prevented because of the disincentive to enter resulting from specific price cuts.

This example has some theoretical attraction, but its implementation in practice raises significant concern. The basic point suggested is that a dominant firm should refrain from price cuts above ATC where rivals have not yet reached the minimum efficient scale and price cuts above ATC by the dominant firm would prevent them from doing so. Several problems arise. First, it is not clear how a dominant firm can be expected to

[152] Case T-203/01, *Manufacture française des pneumatiques Michelin v Commission* [2003] ECR II-4071, para. 111 ("Furthermore, *the quantity rebates formed part of a complex system of discounts*, some of which on the applicant's own admission constituted an abuse....") (emphasis added). See also *ECS/AKZO,* OJ 1985 L 374/1, para. 82 ("The behaviour of AKZO has to be considered as a whole."). See too *Napier Brown/British Sugar*, OJ 1988 L 284/41, para. 66 ("taken in the context of the other abuses as outlined above").

[153] See Discussion Paper, para. 128.

[154] *Ibid.*, para. 129.

know that its rivals have not yet reached the minimum efficient scale, or at what point they will in future. Second, it will usually be very difficult, if not impossible, for the dominant firm to know whether it is pricing below the entrant's ATC and at what point price cuts above the dominant firm's ATC, but below that of rivals, would deny the entrant sufficient scale. (It may also be illegal for the dominant firm to seek such information.) Third, if the entrant can achieve scale over time, capital markets, though imperfect, should find it rational to fund entrants that will become as efficient as the dominant firm. Entrants that are, and will remain, less efficient confer no benefit on consumers and there is harm to consumer welfare in the short and long term in protecting them. Finally, and most importantly, the rule proposed in the Discussion Paper is not sufficiently precise and runs a very significant risk of deterring legitimate price competition.

5.6 OBJECTIVE JUSTIFICATION

5.6.1 Introduction

Legitimate reasons for below-cost prices. There is widespread acceptance under Article 82 EC and analogous provisions of national competition laws that even prices below AVC (and *a fortiori* those above AVC/AAC but below ATC) may in certain circumstances have a legitimate justification. This is reflected in the leading textbooks on EC competition law,[155] the decisional practice and case law of the Community institutions,[156] national competition authorities' guidelines on abuse of dominance,[157] and national case law.[158] As the Discussion Paper states, "in a case where a presumption of predatory pricing is established, the dominant company may rebut that finding by justifying its pricing behaviour even if the price is below the relevant cost benchmark."[159]

Recognition that temporary losses may be rational for a dominant firm even if no rival is excluded reflects a number of different considerations. First, practical experience with the AVC benchmark in the thirty years since it was originally proposed has shown that cost calculations are complex, often arbitrary, and therefore prone to a material

[155] See, e.g., R Whish, *Competition Law* (5th edn., London, LexisNexis UK, 2003) p. 706; V Korah, *An Introductory Guide To EC Competition Law And Practice* (7th edn., Oxford, Hart, 2000) p. 127.

[156] See, e.g., Case T-83/91, *Tetra Pak International SA v Commission* [1994] ECR II-755, para. 147 ("[I]t may be acceptable for an undertaking in a dominant position to sell at a loss in certain circumstances."). See also Case COMP/38.233, *Wanadoo Interactive*, Commission Decision of July 16, 2003, not yet published, paras. 305 et seq.

[157] See Assessment of Conduct: Draft Competition Law Guideline for Consultation, OFT 414a, para. 4.8. See also Competition Act 1998: The Application in the Telecommunications Sector, OFT 417, paras. 7.17–7.18.

[158] See, e.g., *Yeheskel Arkin v Borchard Lines Limited & Ors* [2003] EWHC 687 (Comm), para. 298 ("Whereas one of the effects of a dominant undertaking selling at below average variable cost may well be to diminish the continuing ability of competitors to offer the same level of competition, nonetheless the dominant undertaking's primary purpose in so doing may be objectively justifiable, such as in the case of short run promotions and where in a service industry, such as telecommunications, charging below average variable cost will bring in more customers thereby increasing the value of the service to existing customers.").

[159] See Discussion Paper, para. 130.

degree of error. The ATC standard is perhaps even more problematic in this regard, since it lacks a clear definition in the case of multi-product firms. Distinguishing legitimate low prices from exclusionary low prices is extremely difficult in practice, thereby making courts and competition authorities reluctant to find an abuse solely on the basis of a failure to pass a price/cost test.

A second related reason is that modern economic thinking on predation has moved away from a mechanical adherence to cost-based tests towards a more strategic appreciation of the need for a coherent predatory strategy *ex ante* and probable exclusion *ex post*. This strategy-based approach, discussed in Section 5.2 above, suggests not only that predation strategies may be more credible than once thought,[160] but also that strategies that might, at first sight, fit traditional definitions of predatory pricing may, on fuller examination, have a non-exclusionary explanation.[161]

Finally, the emergence of so-called "new economy" markets has affected the premise upon which traditional definitions of predatory pricing are based. High technology markets often require large, up-front risky investments and involve start-up losses in order to increase consumer uptake, acquire scale, or to gain the learning experience needed to reduce costs over time. In certain cases, it may also be that monopoly or near-monopoly conditions are necessary if a firm is to achieve optimal scale (e.g., network effects). In such cases, exclusion may be a necessary and pro-competitive feature of market development. While these features certainly do not immunise such markets from the application of Article 82 EC, they at least indicate that a more nuanced approach may be necessary in certain circumstances.

Categories of objective justification. Categorising the range of possible justifications for below-cost pricing is not straightforward, since there may be a high degree of overlap between different defences in any given instance. A basic distinction can be made, however, between justifications that are defensive in nature, in the sense that they are intended to respond to rivals' behaviour (e.g., meeting competition), and justifications based on offensive or market-expanding efficiencies (e.g., network externalities, learning-by-doing etc.) That said, the following individual categories of objective justification have acquired a reasonably clear meaning: (1) meeting competition; (2) short-term promotional offers; (3) market-expanding efficiencies, such as scale economies, learning-by-doing, and forward-pricing; (4) loss-leading; (5) loss-minimising; and (6) miscellaneous defences such as mistake and obsolescence. A number of defences may also apply in parallel.

5.6.2 Meeting Competition

Basic definition and rationale. Even markets characterised by the presence of a dominant firm may become more competitive for a period or experience a change in

[160] See, e.g., P Bolton, JF Brodley, and MH Riordan, "Predatory Pricing: Strategic Theory and Legal Policy" (2000) 88(8) *Georgetown Law Journal* 2239, 2246–49.

[161] *Ibid.*, 2274 ("A business justification or efficiencies defence serves as a means of eliminating cases where below-cost pricing by a firm with market power is likely to be welfare-enhancing, rather than predatory. In these cases, the sacrifice of present profits through low pricing is justified for reasons other than exclusion or disciplining of rivals. The defence therefore serves as a necessary shield against an overly inclusive legal rule.").

market conditions that forces firms to cut prices in order to retain or expand business. In such situations it may be profit-maximising, in the short term at least, for a dominant firm to match or undercut rivals' prices. The temporary price cut is short-run profit-maximising in the sense that it "maximises the incumbent's immediate or short-run profit even though its rival remains in the market" and, therefore, is "simply an independently justified, profit-maximising response to the prevailing market conditions."[162] On a more pragmatic level, the ability of a dominant firm to respond to competitors' prices may reflect the notion that no firm should have to sit idly by and watch its market position erode.

The meeting competition defence in the case-law. The decisional practice and case law under Article 82 EC recognise that a dominant undertaking is entitled to take reasonable, proportionate measures to protect its own commercial interests, including responding to competitive offers on the market in order to maintain its customers.[163] The Commission has followed this reasoning in several cases and has recognised, at least in principle, a defence of meeting competition. Relevant cases include *AKZO,*[164] *Hilti,*[165] *Tetra Pak II,*[166] *BPB Industries,*[167] *British Sugar/Napier Brown,*[168] *Irish Sugar,*[169] *Digital,*[170] and *Wanadoo.*[171]

---

[162] See P Bolton, JF Brodley, and MH Riordan, "Predatory Pricing: Strategic Theory and Legal Policy" (2000) 88(8) *Georgetown Law Journal* 2239, 2275.

[163] See Case 27/76, *United Brands Company and United Brands Continentaal BV* [1978] ECR 207, para. 189 ("[T]he fact that an undertaking is in a dominant position cannot deprive it of its entitlement to protect its own commercial interests when they are attacked, and...such an undertaking must be allowed the right to take such reasonable steps as it deems appropriate to protect those interests... ."). Although *United Brands* was not a predatory pricing case, the Community Courts have repeated and affirmed this statement in several pricing abuse cases. See, e.g., *BPB Industries*, OJ 1989 L 10/50, para. 69; *Tetra Pak II*, OJ 1992 L 72/1, para. 147; and Joined Cases C-395/96 P and C-396/96 P, *Compagnie Maritime Belge Transports SA and Others v Commission* [2000] ECR I-1365, para. 189.

[164] *ECS/AKZO*, OJ 1985 L 374/1, Art. 4, providing for interim measures against AKZO, but allowing AKZO "to offer or supply below the minimum prices determined as above ... if it is necessary to do so in good faith to meet (but not to undercut) a lower price shown to be offered by a supplier ready and able to supply to that customer." See also Case C-62/86, *AKZO Chemie BV v Commission* [1991] ECR I-3359, para. 156. AKZO had threatened ECS that it would exclude it from the market unless it withdrew from competing in certain end-uses. AKZO then circumvented the interim measures ordered by the Commission and sold below average variable cost with predatory intent. Prices charged by AKZO were "well below" those of its competitors, showing that AKZO's intention "was not solely to win the order, which would have induced it to reduce its prices only to the extent necessary for this purpose" (*ibid.*, para. 102).

[165] *Eurofix-Bauco v Hilti*, OJ 1988 L 65/19. Hilti was obliged to cease all price discrimination by ensuring that any differences in its prices were justified by differences in costs, except where it was necessary to meet a competitive offer, in making promotions, or where to do so would generate sales that Hilti would not otherwise make.

[166] *Tetra Pak II*, OJ 1992 L 72/1, para. 148 (argument that Tetra Pak was merely meeting competition recognised but rejected on factual grounds).

[167] See *BPB Industries plc*, OJ 1989 L 10/50, para. 133, where the Commission accepted BPB's "Super Schedule A" prices because they were neither predatory nor part of any scheme of systematic alignment.

[168] See *Napier Brown/British Sugar*, OJ 1988 L 284/41, para. 31, where the Commission suggested that while undercutting a competitor's prices would be abusive, matching them would not.

[169] See *Irish Sugar plc*, OJ 1997 L 258/1, para 134 ("[T]here is no doubt that a firm in a dominant position is entitled to defend that position by competing with other firms on its market.").

Despite widespread general reference to the defence of meeting competition in the decisional practice and case law, the precise circumstances in which it will be admitted remain unclear. A basic distinction should be made between defensive price cuts that are below AVC/AAC and those that are above AVC/AAC but below ATC. The latter should in principle be treated more leniently, since they cover short-run variable costs, contribute something to fixed costs, and are therefore profit-maximising, or loss-minimising, for a period. In contrast, prices below AVC/AAC mean that each sale is loss-making in both the short- and long-run. The defence of meeting competition should therefore only be admissible where there is evidence that prices below AVC/AAC will lead to long-term profits even if no rival is excluded, i.e., where necessary to achieve an internal efficiency that does not depend on any rival exiting.

a. Prices below AVC/AAC. Whether a defence of meeting competition is, or should be, permitted under Article 82 EC where the dominant firm's prices are below AVC/AAC raises difficult issues. On the one hand, allowing such a defence would seem fundamentally at odds with the rationale for the rule against predatory pricing under Article 82 EC: that a price below AVC/AAC in not profit-maximising for the dominant firm and is therefore presumed to be based on an exclusionary motive. A meeting competition defence for prices below AVC/AAC could therefore produce anomalous results in that the defence would be permitted precisely in those circumstances where the rules on predatory pricing suggest that it should not be, i.e., where the dominant firm cuts prices below AVC/AAC in order to respond to rivals' entry. A number of commentators have therefore rejected the application of a defence of meeting competition where prices are below AVC/AAC.[172] The same view is put forward in the Discussion Paper.[173] Were this view to be accepted under Article 82 EC, it is important to emphasise that it should only apply to the defence of meeting competition and does not imply that prices below AVC/AAC would lack justification where other defences are raised.

On the other hand, dominant firms should arguably still be allowed to compete where there is a genuine price war with rivals. National case law has therefore permitted

[170] 1997 Digital Undertaking, (1998) 19(2) *European Competition Law Review* 108–15, para. 3.1. The Commission recognised that dominant companies must be allowed to offer prices reductions (called "Allowances") in individual cases "to meet comparable service offerings of a competitor. No Allowance shall be offered until Digital has completed an internal review process designed to verify that the proposed Allowance is offered in good faith as a proportional response to real or (based upon information from the customer or other reliable sources) reasonably anticipated competitive offerings and will not result in a foreclosure or distortion of competition for the servicing of Digital Systems in any Member State."

[171] See Case COMP/38.233, *Wanadoo Interactive*, Commission Decision of July 16, 2003, not yet published, para. 316.

[172] See PE Areeda and DF Turner, "Predatory Pricing and Related Practices Under Section 2 of the Sherman Act" (1975) 88 *Harvard Law Review* 697-733, 713 ("A monopolist may attempt to justify prices below marginal cost by claiming... that he is simply meeting an equally low price of a rival. We conclude, however, that these justifications are either so rarely applicable or of such dubious merit for a monopolist that the presumption of illegality for prices below both marginal costs and average [variable] cost should be conclusive."); P Bolton, JF Brodley, and MH Riordan, "Predatory Pricing: Strategic Theory and Legal Policy" (2000) 88(8) *Georgetown Law Journal* 2239, 2275.

[173] See Discussion Paper, para. 83.

dominant firms to meet, but not to undercut, a rival's price where the price is below AVC/AAC. In *Berlingske Gratisaviser*,[174] the Danish *Konkurrencestyrelsens* (Competition Council) determined that a newspaper publisher had abused its dominant position by selling advertising space at below its AVC/AAC. The Council held, however, that as its rival (i.e., the complainant) was also selling its advertising space at below AVC/AAC, Berlingske Gratisaviser was entitled to meet the competitive price in order to defend its customer base and compete on the market. The Council simply prohibited Berlingske Gratisaviser from undercutting its competitors' prices if this resulted in pricing below its AVC/AAC. The result in this case has a pragmatic appeal, since it aims to strike a balance between allowing a dominant firm to defend its interests, without at the same time allowing it to systematically exclude competitors by relying on a meeting competition defence to undercut them. Moreover, such a rule should not lead to price collusion between the dominant firm and its rivals: the dominant firm will have no interest in agreeing on prices below AVC/AAC.

Another important reason why selling below AVC/AAC should be accepted, at least for a certain period, concerns so-called "option values" or "real options." When a firm is losing money, the logical step is to exit the market in question. However, in many cases there may be a value of retaining the option of staying in the market if there is a reasonable prospect that, in the near future, revenues will exceed costs. For example, in markets such as broadband internet and third-generation mobile telephony, many suppliers are losing money, but see a strong option value in remaining in the market in order to take advantage of future revenue streams from multimedia and other applications. The size and timing of these revenues may not be precise, but they are nonetheless real in terms of sources of value in a commercial venture. Projects often comprise a multitude of possible actions that can give rise to valuable real options. Real options often found in capital investment projects include the following:[175] (1) abandon the project; (2) wait and learn before investing; (3) make a follow-on investment; or (4) to vary output or productions method. Each type of option has the potential to overturn an investment decision that would be regarded as wrong under standard investment-making decision techniques.[176] Much the same analysis can be applied to price cuts that would otherwise seem irrational.

The Commission's decision in *Wanadoo* is ambiguous on the status of the meeting competition defence where prices are below AVC/AAC. The Commission found that Wanadoo had priced below AVC/AAC for the period January 2001–October 2002. In considering possible objective justification for Wanadoo's prices, the Commission seemed to indicate that, as a matter of principle, a dominant firm cannot align its prices to those of a competitor if they are below AVC/AAC.[177] At the same time, however, the Commission proceeded to evaluate the merits of Wanadoo's meeting competition

[174] *Berlingske Gratisaviser*, Decision of the *Konkurrencestyrelsens*, discussed in the Danish Competition Council's Annual Report (2002), Section 2.5.

[175] See RA Brealey and SC Myers, *Principles of Corporate Finance* (6th edn., Sydney, McGraw Hill, 2000).

[176] See TA Luehrman, "Strategy as a Portfolio of Real Options" (1998) 76 *Harvard Business Review* 89–99.

[177] Case COMP/38.233, *Wanadoo Interactive*, Commission Decision of July 16, 2003, not yet published, para. 316.

defence, suggesting that the defence of meeting competition was applicable. The Commission attached importance a number of considerations in rejecting Wanadoo's defence.

First, certain of Wanadoo's prices were set before rivals entered the market and did not change following their entry.[178] Indeed, it was rivals who had aligned their prices to Wanadoo, not the reverse. Second, a number of rivals' prices were appreciably higher than Wanadoo's comparable prices.[179] In other words, Wanadoo's prices did not meet, but undercut, rivals' prices. Third, the Commission attached importance to the fact that certain Wanadoo budgetary decisions on future prices were set well in advance of rivals' announcements of their market prices,[180] again suggesting that Wanadoo was not actually responding to competitive offers but pre-empting them. Finally, the Commission's overriding objection to Wanadoo's defence seems to have been that it was not part of a defensive strategy of responding in a proportionate manner to actual competitive threats, but an offensive strategy to pre-empt the market and maintain such losses as were necessary to deter rivals' entry and future continuation in the market.[181]

b. Prices below ATC but above AVC/AAC. The defence of meeting competition should in principle be more likely to apply where prices are above AVC/AAC but below ATC, since prices at this level at least cover the dominant firm's short-run costs and make some contribution to fixed costs. Whether the defence applies depends on whether the second *AKZO* rule—that there is a "plan" to eliminate a rival—is satisfied or not. This condition is discussed in detail above.[182] Briefly, however, the decisional practice and case law seem to have set a reasonably high evidentiary threshold to distinguish "mere" meeting competition from an exclusionary plan. Evidence of a plan to eliminate a rival typically requires all or some of the following conditions: (1) detailed documentary evidence of an exclusionary plan; (2) reductions of a long duration and not merely temporary prices cuts; (3) evidence of a strategy of present profit sacrifice and future recovery of losses by price increases; (4) evidence of specific retaliatory threats to competitors; (5) evidence of ever-increasing losses over time; and (6) material growth in the dominant firm's share and corresponding reductions in competitors' shares.

Section 5.3 above discussed the problems with relying on subjective intent evidence in predatory pricing cases. Briefly, because legitimate prices and unlawful prices look very similar, the motive forces and language of harsh competition and unfair competition are very difficult to distinguish in practice. An enforcement policy that relies exclusively on subjective intent evidence could therefore lead to incorrect conclusions that predatory pricing has taken place. Section 5.3 suggested that a better approach to intent would be to assess whether there was a legitimate explanation for the losses on the basis of more *objective* considerations. This requires proof of a plausible predatory strategy in the specific market setting, or, put differently, evidence that the

[178] *Ibid.*, para. 321.
[179] *Ibid.*, paras. 323–25.
[180] *Ibid.*, para. 326.
[181] *Ibid.*, para. 331 ("while the argument based on alignment of competitors' prices would have been admissible in principle").
[182] See Section 5.3.2 above.

pricing had a legitimate explanation other than competitor exclusion. The relevance of objective evidence (or indirect intent) in predatory pricing cases is now expressly recognised in the Discussion Paper.[183]

Another important factor in assessing the legitimacy of price cuts above AVC/AAC but below ATC is the proportionality of the dominant firm's actions. The meeting competition defence will generally only apply if it is shown that the dominant firm's response is suitable, indispensable, and proportionate.[184] The Discussion Paper states that this requires that there are no other less anticompetitive means to minimise the losses and that the conduct is limited in time to the absolute minimum and does not significantly delay or hamper entry or expansion by competitors.[185] It adds that objective justification is not possible if, for example, it is established that the conduct involves extra investments in capacity and is not minimising losses directly resulting from the action taken by certain competitors. The burden of proof is said to rest with the dominant firm in this regard.[186]

c. ***The relevance of price discrimination where prices are above AVC/AAC but below ATC.*** Whether the selective nature of the dominant firm's price cuts makes a difference when prices are above AVC/AAC but below ATC is not clear. Offering rivals' actual or potential customers a lower price, while maintaining higher prices for the dominant firm's own customers, certainly makes it cheaper to engage in price-cutting: offering an across-the-board price cut would be more expensive. Evidence of selective price cuts in the context of other convergent factors pointing towards a "plan" to eliminate a competitor is therefore treated as an exacerbating factor under the case law.[187] The Discussion Paper endorses many of these points and states that selective pricing may be "important evidence" of a predatory strategy and that such evidence might be stronger in the context of other exclusionary practices.[188]

But this view of the law seems to go too far. The mere fact of price discrimination should not be enough, in itself, to conclude that price-cutting is predatory. In the first place, it should be recalled that prices above AVC/AAC are rational at least in the short-term and this is true whether they are selective or not. Second, it cannot be assumed that merely because the dominant firm *attempts* to price discriminate that it will be able to do so. As noted in Chapter Eleven (Abusive Discrimination), price discrimination is only possible under certain conditions, in particular the ability of the dominant firm to prevent arbitrage between customers receiving the lower price and those receiving the higher price. If arbitrage is possible, it should generally be irrelevant that the dominant firm attempted to sort customers in this way. Third, a selective price that defends the dominant firm's customers from attack by a rival is likely to have the same impact on a rival as a general price cut: in either case, the effective price faced by the rival is the same. Fourth, it certainly makes no sense to infer anticompetitive intent where a dominant firm engages in selective price cuts in one geographic market, but not another.

[183] See Discussion Paper, paras. 113, 115. For a detailed discussion, see Section 5.3 above.
[184] *Ibid.*, para. 132.
[185] *Ibid.*
[186] *Ibid.*, para. 82.
[187] *Ibid.*, para. 118.
[188] See, e.g., Case C-62/86, *AKZO Chemie BV v Commission* [1991] ECR I-3359, para. 72.

If the markets are truly separate relevant markets, they can, and often will, have different returns. Fifth, it seems curious to say that the dominant firm could perhaps avoid a finding of abuse by engaging in a more widespread loss-making strategy by reducing the price generally to levels below ATC but above AVC/AAC.

A final, important reason why there should be no *general* ban on selective price cuts for prices above AVC/AAC but below ATC is that rivals would then benefit from a "price umbrella," most likely leading to higher price overall.[189] In this instance, the rival would know (if prices were transparent or the customer was reliable) that the dominant firm could not undercut its price without extending the same reduction to all its other similarly-situated customers. The rival would therefore know that it need not undercut the dominant company's standard price by very much or at all. The customer will also have an interest in claiming that a rival is offering a lower price, with the result that the perceived lawfulness of a dominant company's price would largely depend on the customer's truthfulness. A dominant company will often find itself competing against two rivals whose prices are unlikely to be identical. In these circumstances it may match the lower price, but this means that it undercuts the higher of the two rivals' prices. It would be odd (and perverse) to say that it was acting lawfully if the buyer was planning to take the lower price offer, but acting unlawfully if it planned to take the higher of the two offers. In other words, a rule that limited a dominant firm to meeting competitive offers could itself lead to anticompetitive and perverse results. It could also lead to companies' verifying each other's prices, which could give rise to serious issues under Article 81 EC.

The real issue thus remains whether price cuts to meet competition can truly be said to be predatory. Such an inference cannot be made from the mere fact of price discrimination, although it may of course be relevant. Instead, it would be necessary to consider all of the factors that are, or should be, relevant in a predatory pricing case. Thus, it should be asked whether the market has the structural characteristics necessary for predation to succeed, whether rivals are sufficiently well-resourced to withstand selective price-cutting, what the rivals themselves have done in response, how long the selective price cuts lasted (the longer they last, they harder they are to justify), whether the dominant firm could realistically expect to recoup any losses incurred as a result of the price-cutting (e.g., did prices to the low-priced customers increase following rivals' exit?), and any clear documentary or other evidence which shows that the selective price cuts were not merely a rational, profit-maximising response to competition from a rival, but a strategic attempt to actively damage rivals by offering targeted prices to their actual or potential customers.

5.6.3 Short-Term Promotional Offers

Basic rationale. Short-term price reductions given by the dominant enterprise when it launches a new product or enters a new market have in certain instances been permitted under Article 82 EC.[190] These cases do not make clear, however, whether the situation

[189] See PE Areeda and H Hovenkamp, *Antitrust Law* (Revised edn., Boston, Little Brown, 1996) para. 745b.

[190] See, for instance, the 1997 Digital Undertaking, (1998) 19(2) *European Competition Law Review* 108–15), allowing Digital to grant price reductions for "short-term promotional programs" provided

is different if the prices are below AVC/AAC or between AVC/AAC and ATC. A defence along these lines ought to be permitted, subject to certain limitations. The obvious example of where this defence should apply is where a new product requires consumer familiarity before customers can appreciate its enhanced qualities. Customer familiarity with the product in question during the promotional pricing phase may render them loyal and therefore willing to pay a higher price in future because of the product's added qualities. In such circumstances, the low price is intended to allow customers to try the product and the higher future prices do not depend on competitors' exclusion, but on the product's enhanced characteristics over existing products. In other words, promotional offers in this situation are not designed to exclude competitors, but constitute normal competition "on the merits." If these conditions are met, it seems unimportant whether prices are below AVC/AAC or ATC: the point is that a genuine introductory or short-term offer can have no material effect on competition.[191]

New products and new customers. Whether a promotional pricing defence should be available in the case of only new products, or also in the case of new customers, is not clear. On the one hand, the rationale for allowing promotional prices for new products and new customers is essentially the same: to allow a customer who is not familiar with the product in question to sample it for a limited period at a favourable price in the expectation that, if they like it enough, they would be willing to pay a higher price in future. On the other hand, the need for a firm which is already dominant on a market to promote its existing products has been questioned.[192] Provided, however, that the limitations on promotional pricing set forth below are respected, there seems to be no compelling reason under Article 82 EC to object to a genuine, temporary promotional offer for either new products or new customers.

Limitations on promotional offers. Several limitations should apply if below-cost promotional prices are permitted under Article 82 EC. First, the promotional price should be strictly temporary in scope and not amount to systematic below-cost selling. The period in question will obviously vary from industry to industry: in certain industries, consumers will need a very short period to familiarise themselves with a product; in others, a meaningful trial period may be much longer. For example, most consumer goods can be evaluated reasonably quickly by customers. In contrast, there are industries where customers will need to measure the effectiveness of a product over a long period, in particular where a change of supplier would entail significant internal disruption and other switching costs. Second, it seems inherent in a promotional offer that it is limited in scope: repeat promotional offers may be tantamount to a predatory

that these are published, available on a non-discriminatory basis, and do not result in below-cost pricing.

[191] See Discussion Paper, para. 110 ("The dominant company may also wish to show that, although the price is below the relevant cost benchmark, for clear-cut reasons the dominant company's pricing behaviour should not be considered predatory pricing because there is no possibility that it could have an exclusionary effect on rivals. This may for instance be the case where the low price is part of a one-off temporary promotion campaign to introduce a new product and where the duration and extent of the campaign are such that exclusionary effects are excluded.").

[192] See PE Areeda and DF Turner, "Predatory Pricing and Related Practices Under Section 2 of the Sherman Act" (1975) 88 *Harvard Law Review* 697-733, 713.

pricing campaign.[193] Finally, the available evidence should be consistent with the promotional purpose of the price reduction. Evidence that the low prices were expressly intended to eliminate a rival, or force it to sell its business to the dominant firm, would render the defence of promotional pricing inapplicable.[194]

5.6.4 Market-Expanding Efficiencies

Basic definition and rationale. Recognition of a non-exclusionary justification for prices that are temporarily below AVC/AAC (or above AVC/AAC but below ATC) may be important in the context of markets in which efficiencies can only be achieved over time. Markets with these characteristics usually require large, up-front risky investments and involve start-up losses in order to increase consumer uptake and thereby acquire the scale or experience needed to reduce costs over time. These markets are not only more likely than other markets to exhibit below-cost pricing for a period, but are also more likely to have a non-exclusionary reason for doing so.[195] Efficiencies can lead to recovery of initial losses by creating cost savings over time as a company achieves greater scale or scope, more learning experience, or another efficiency capable of reducing costs. Low prices in markets with these types of efficiencies are therefore a form of promotional pricing. But they differ in character to one-off, short-term promotional pricing, discussed above. Most obviously, recovery of losses in the case of short-term promotions stems from consumers' increased willingness to pay in future. Loss recovery in the case of industries where dynamic linkages can be achieved are primarily a function of the ability to reduce costs over time, not of price increases.

Legitimate reasons for below-cost prices in new and emerging markets and network industries. Efficiencies in the sense outlined above can lead to reductions in cost in several well-established ways. Many of these efficiencies may be simultaneously present in a given situation:

1. *Scale/scope economies*. Economies of scale exist when average cost declines as output increases. The reason is usually that average cost declines as fixed costs are spread over increasing output. Another reason is specialisation, which allows a product or service to be provided more efficiently at a certain level of output. For example, if a law firm expands, it may be more efficient to train a lawyer to specialise in competition law than to have the lawyer do a range of general commercial work. Formally, scale economies arise if the

[193] See Assessment of Conduct: Draft Competition Law Guideline for Consultation, OFT 414a, para. 4.8 ("A dominant undertaking which adopts a one-off short-term promotion [below AVC for a limited period] is unlikely to be found in contravention of the Chapter II prohibition [abuse of a dominant position]. However, a series of short term promotions could, taken together, amount to a predatory strategy.").

[194] See *Aberdeen Journals Limited v Office of Fair Trading* [2003] CAT 11 (United Kingdom), paras. 423–32 (pricing below AVC for one month found unlawful in circumstances where the dominant firm intended to either put the prey out of business or force it to sell its business).

[195] See Case COMP/38.233, *Wanadoo Interactive*, Commission Decision of July 16, 2003, not yet published, paras. 260–61 (Commission made allowance for features of launching a new product) and para. 264 (recognition that a more "nuanced" approach to prices below AVC was appropriate in growing markets).

marginal cost of adding one unit of output is less than ATC. Similar considerations apply to economies of scope, where total costs decline if two or more products are made simultaneously.

2. *Market education.* Economies of scale are not limited to manufacturing, but can arise in marketing and other functions. When offering a new product, a company often has a difficult task convincing potential customers to buy it and must achieve awareness, in particular for technology products with new uses. Once the product has achieved a certain level of awareness, marketing expenditure can be reduced because it eventually benefits from "cost-free" advertising due to the impact of "word of mouth." Early adopters play a critical role in enhancing the awareness for a product, which is why companies are particularly keen on attracting this type of subscriber through promotional efforts.[196] Winning early adopters is often costly, since a company has to spend heavily on marketing in order to learn about customers' characteristics. For these reasons, the business might not be profitable in the early phase of the adoption process.

3. *Learning by doing.* It is well-established that suppliers become better and more cost-efficient as the installed base increases. At the heart of the learning-by-doing theory lies the observation that individuals' performance of a task improves with experience.[197] At the beginning, the optimal processes have yet to be found and the tasks to be carried out need to be learned. But effectiveness increases as output increases. At an early stage of the product life cycle, the supplier may not be able to effectively compete on the product market or serve the whole market at a price that covers costs. It might therefore be profitable and efficient for a firm to set low prices and forego profits in the short run in order to move faster along the learning curve, ultimately being able to offer cheaper and/or better products than at an earlier point in time.

4. *Network effects.* Network effects arise where the benefit of a good or service increases with the addition of other users. An obvious example is the telecommunications sector where the value of, say, a telephone to a user will depend, *inter alia*, on whether the user can access other users that he/she wishes to speak to. Products with the potential for network effects are therefore not only valued because of their inherent characteristics, but also due to the additional value derived from being able to interact with other users of the product. Below-cost pricing in the presence of such effects may therefore have nothing to do with exclusion, but reflect a legitimate desire to increase network size and attractiveness.[198]

---

196 See EM Rogers, *Diffusion Of Innovations* (5th edn., New York, The Free Press, 2003).

197 See, e.g., T Wright, "Factors Affecting the Cost of Airplanes" (1936) 3(4) *Journal of Aeronautical Science* 122–28; KJ Arrow, "The Economic Implications Of Learning By Doing" (1962) 29(3) *Review of Economic Studies* 155–173.

198 See Assessment of Conduct: Draft Competition Law Guideline for Consultation, OFT 414a, para. 4.12 ("In these circumstances it can be beneficial for the undertaking to sell part of the service to

The Commission's approach to such defences is not entirely consistent. On the one hand, the Discussion Paper states that "an efficiency defence can in general not be applied to predatory pricing."[199] But it says elsewhere that pricing below AVC/AAC may be justified by "strong learning effects."[200] Moreover, the Commission's actual practice in at least one recent case has been to pay significant attention to scale and scope economies and network effects. In a case involving discounts offered by Euronext in response to new entry by the London Stock Exchange in Amsterdam, the Commission took a favourable view of Euronext's discounts based, *inter alia*, on the fact that a high rate of stock exchange liquidity was essential to the competitiveness of a stock exchange. The Commission stated that there are good reasons to believe that a digressive fee schedule is welfare enhancing because it stimulates marginal trading, making markets more liquid (with macroeconomic externalities on cost of capital and enhanced return on risk-equivalent investments). It also noted that this form of pricing existed prior to new entry, and is also used by most other exchanges.[201]

Distinguishing lawful from unlawful start-up losses under Article 82 EC. Recognition that there may be a legitimate (i.e., non-exclusionary) justification for initial low prices, including by a dominant firm, requires competition authorities and courts to devise rules that distinguish situations of legitimate pricing from those involving unlawful pricing. In practice, this problem is apt to be acute in the case of new or emerging markets. In the first place, there is an evidential problem in that, often, the only evidence of the rationale for start-up losses is the company's business plan. Unless the business plan contains express evidence of anticompetitive purpose, there would be severe practical problems in inferring such purpose from an assessment of the reasonableness or plausibility of the plan. In growing dynamic markets, it is very difficult to say with confidence whether assumptions about future levels of competition reflect exclusionary behaviour or are simply reasonable assumptions about the future evolution of the market.[202]

Another problem is that theories of anticompetitive harm (or lack thereof) based on future market conditions are by nature speculative. There is significant scope for

customers at below AVC. This will encourage expansion of the network, which benefits all network customers who then have access to a larger number of subscribers. The undertaking may then recoup the loss by charging higher prices for other, related services."). For a detailed treatment, see A ten Kate and G Niels, "Below Cost Pricing in the Presence of Network Externalities" in E Hope (ed.), *The Pros And Cons Of Low Prices* (Stockholm, Swedish Competition Authority, 2003) p. 97. This defence was accepted in No. CA98/05/2004 *First Edinburgh/Lothian*, April 29, 2004, (Case CP/0361-01), based, *inter alia*, on the need to grow a bus route network, even where prices were below AVC for several months.

[199] See Discussion Paper, para. 133.

[200] *Ibid.*, para. 131.

[201] No public decision is yet available. For a discussion, see S Greenaway, "Competition Between Stock Exchanges: Findings From See DG Competition's Investigation Into Trading in Dutch Equities" (2005) 3 *Competition Policy Newsletter* 69–71.

[202] As Professor Baumol notes, there is "no generally effective way" of determining whether a pricing decision is a legitimate business practice or an unlawful one. This is effectively impossible if the issue is said to turn on the probabilities of forecasts of future profits in a developing market. See WJ Baumol, "Principles Relevant To Predatory Pricing" in E Hope (ed.), *The Pros And Cons Of Low Prices* (Stockholm, Swedish Competition Authority, 2003) p. 25.

divergence between business plans and actual market outcomes. Businesses may fail, apply overly-conservative or optimistic assessments, or simply get it wrong. The more risky the investment, the greater the scope for failure and, therefore, for assumptions in business plans that, *ex post*, turn out to be wrong. The decision to enter a particular market or to introduce a new pricing strategy is itself based on *ex ante* forecasts and takes place in a world of uncertainty. A business plan therefore represents, at best, a reasonable assessment by the company concerned of its options at a given time based on the information available to it. In any given scenario, companies may choose a range of different options *ex ante*, without any one option being unreasonable or implausible. Companies would often have chosen a different option *ex post*.

Allied to the above problems is the fact that there are no clear economic or financial tests to distinguish cases of legitimate start-up losses from those of illegality. In developing a useful legal principle for assessing start-up losses in new or emerging markets, one cardinal principle should be borne in mind: start-up losses should only be condemned where there is convincing evidence of an exclusionary strategy. This results from two considerations. In the first place, there is a high social cost of (wrongly) hampering or preventing product launches that involve legitimate start-up losses. A second consideration is that assumptions as to future recovery of start-up losses are by definition matters of forward-looking assessment rather than fact. A firm should therefore be afforded a margin of error in making such assessments, in much the same way as competition authorities have discretion in making complex future economic assessments in mergers and other cases.

Suggested solutions. Only two types of evidence arguably constitute an appropriate legal test in the case of start-up losses in dynamic markets. In the first place, there may be evidence of express exclusionary intent on the part of the dominant firm. This was the interpretation applied by the Commission in *Wanadoo*, where there were not merely start-up losses necessary to enter the market, but an express plan of incurring whatever losses were necessary as part of a richly-documented "plan to pre-empt the market."[203] The Commission's strong reliance in *Wanadoo* on extensive documentary evidence of exclusionary intent, probable recoupment, and actual or likely exclusionary effects suggests that a high evidentiary threshold applies before start-up losses can be found to be predatory.

In the absence of express evidence of intent, evidence of an anticompetitive object could be inferred from a number of "convergent factors" that, taken together, clearly demonstrate anticompetitive purpose rather than legitimate start-up losses.[204] Thus, there must be convincing evidence that no reasonable company in possession of the

---

[203] See Case COMP/38.233, *Wanadoo Interactive*, Commission Decision of July 16, 2003, not yet published, heading preceding para. 256. See also *Deutsche Telekom AG*, OJ 2003 L 263/9, where the Commission interpreted the application of the *AKZO* rules to a margin squeeze test in a new market (broadband internet access) as requiring both below-cost selling and evidence that prices "are set as part of a plan aimed at eliminating a competitor" (para 179).

[204] See *ECS/AKZO*, OJ 1985 L 374/1, para. 80; Case COMP/38.233, *Wanadoo Interactive*, Commission Decision of July 16, 2003, not yet published, para. 271. See also P Lowe, "EU Competition Practice On Predatory Pricing," at the Konkurrensverket/Swedish Competition Authority seminar "Pros and Cons of Low Prices", Stockholm, December 5, 2003.

information available to the dominant firm at the time it formulated its business plan would have adopted the same course of action. This evidence would need to be similar in quality to express evidence of anticompetitive intent, since, otherwise, the latter would be treated comparatively more leniently than the former, which would not make sense. In other words, there must be evidence that the business plan or projections are "unjustified or implausible;"[205] in effect, a sham. In this circumstance, any future recovery of losses envisaged in such business plans is premised on the additional market power that the low exclusionary prices would confer rather than on legitimate efficiencies.

5.6.5 Loss-Leading And "Follow On" Revenues

Basic definition and rationale. Loss-leading is practised by companies selling a number of products, and is designed to attract buyers to the seller in the expectation that, once the buyer is on the seller's premises or committed to certain purchases anyway, the buyer will buy enough of other products to provide a profit greater than the loss on the product used as the loss leader. The most common form of loss-leading is probably groceries sold in a supermarket, where a staple item or well-known brand is priced low in order to attract customers who will then obtain their full shopping needs in the one-stop premises. But the same kind of issues are raised by a company that sells capital equipment at a loss with a view to recovering the loss on subsequent sales of spare parts, consumables, or maintenance or repair services. Similarly, new technology markets may be more susceptible to revenues from follow-on services; for example, by establishing a technology platform on which multiple different services can be accessed.

A wide range of different explanations have been offered to explain why loss-leading is practiced and what the effects on competition are likely to be. One important preliminary issue concerns empirical evidence to the effect that the profits of firms who practice loss-leading are not higher than comparable firms who do not.[206] This either suggests that the traditional justification advanced for loss-leading is weak or that loss-leading is not of great concern under competition law. Certain commentators view loss-leading as a situation of demand complementarity between the loss-leading and follow-on products.[207] Losses on the leading products are therefore said to be justified by the following products. This is sometimes referred to as a "net revenue" defence.[208]

---

[205] See Competition Act 1998: The Application in the Telecommunications Sector, OFT 417, para. 7.23 ("It will not always be possible for an undertaking to meet all the targets set out in its business plan. Evidence of an abuse of dominance may be provided, however, where a business case is based on unjustified and implausible assumptions or where there has been a failure by the undertaking to take remedial action once it became apparent that it would not meet the targets.").

[206] See RG Walters and SB MacKenzie, "A Structural Equations Analysis of the Impact of Price Promotions on Store Performance" (1988) 25(1) *Journal of Marketing Research* 51–63.

[207] J Hess and E Gerstner, "Loss Leader Pricing and Rain Check Policy" (1987) 6(4) *Marketing Science* 358–74. Customers may also believe that low advertised prices on loss-leaders means prices on unadvertised items are also low. See R Lal and C Matutes, "Consumer Expectations And Loss-Leader Pricing in Retail Stores" (1991) *Stanford University Graduate School of Business Research Paper No. 1142*.

[208] See Assessment of Conduct: Draft Competition Law Guideline for Consultation, OFT 414a, para. 4.16 ("A shop cutting its price of one product to below its average variable cost of supplying that product, for example, might still be incrementally profitable if the price cut led to a significant increase

Other commentators suggest a different rationale: price discrimination.[209] Loss leaders are said to be a means of competing for higher profit customers by offering them discounts that are not available to less profitable customers. Loss leader pricing can be a way of price discriminating among groups of customers. Thus, "a product could be priced as a loss leader if, in a market in which certain customers purchase bundles of products that are more profitable than bundles purchased by others, the product is purchased primarily by customers that purchase more profitable bundles."[210] The reason is that, for more profitable customers, "sellers have an incentive to compete more vigorously to keep them from purchasing from another seller."[211]

The various approaches to loss-leading. While the approach to predatory pricing by a multi-product firm has been raised under Article 82 EC, the issue of demand complementarities raised by loss-leading and follow-on products has not. The issue has been partly addressed under national laws and non-EU laws, revealing a wide divergence in approach. One approach is sector-specific guidance. For example, in Canada, guidelines on grocery retailing suggest that pricing below cost on less than fifty items is not likely to raise competition concerns.[212] No explanation is given, however, for the chosen benchmark of fifty products or below and it clearly has limited or no relevance where customers do not typically purchase many products simultaneously.

The United Kingdom competition authorities and courts have dealt with the issue of loss-leading and follow-on revenues more often than other jurisdictions, without, however, arriving at a single clear legal test. A 1997 OFT report into competition in retailing suggests that a simple price/cost test may not be a useful guide to predatory behaviour in retailing.[213] This is based on the observation that manufacturers provide

in sales of complementary products. Assessing whether a price cut is incrementally profitable is sometimes referred to as a **net-revenue test**"(emphasis in original)).

[209] See P DeGraba, *Volume Discounts, Loss Leaders, and Competition for More Profitable Customers*, Federal Trade Commission, Draft Working Paper (April, 2003).

[210] *Ibid.*, page 1.

[211] *Ibid.*

[212] Canadian Competition Bureau (2001b), *Enforcement Guidelines: The Abuse of Dominance Provisions (Sections 78 and 79 of the Competition Act) as Applied to the Retail Grocery Industry*, Canadian Competition Bureau (Draft, December 17, 2001). See also *Commissioner v Air Canada*, CT-2001/002, [2003] Competition Tribunal 13, para. 301 ("[T]he beyond contribution could be considered as a legitimate business reason for operating a scheduled flight below avoidable cost"). On the facts, the Competition Tribunal did not, however, undertake an assessment of the follow-on revenues.

[213] *Competition in Retailing*, Report prepared for the Office of Fair Trading by London Economics, September 1997, Research Paper 13, p. 96. See also Competition Commission Report, *Supermarkets: A Report On The Supply Of Groceries From Multiple Stores In The United Kingdom*, UK Competition Commission Report (Cm 4842, October 10, 2000) ("We found that all the main parties... engaged in the practice of persistently selling some frequently purchased products below cost, and that this contributed to the situation in which the majority of their products were not fully exposed to competitive pressure and distorted competition in the supply of groceries. We took account of the fact that some consumers could benefit from being able to buy goods below cost, particularly low-income consumers, but at the same time that the practice damaged smaller reference stores and non-reference grocery outlets. This would in turn impact adversely on consumers, in particular the elderly and less mobile who tend to rely more on such stores. We conclude that the practice of persistent below-cost selling... operates against the public interest."). A subsequent report attached less importance to the issue of below-cost selling through loss-leading and focused instead on the ability of certain UK supermarkets to exercise collective or unilateral market power following the acquisition of a leading competitor: See Report by

differential discounts to retailers, which means that, if they want to, larger retailers may be able to drive smaller retailers out of the retail market without even making losses. The report goes on to identify a two-stage test for predation in the retailing sector—whether the retailer is deviating from short-run profit maximising behaviour and whether predation would be a rational strategy. Unfortunately, the report provides little guidance on how these questions should be resolved. The report later addresses the issue of loss-leading separately, but its findings are equally inconclusive. It simply notes that the only justification for loss-leading on one product would be the recovery of those losses on other products, but that unlawful loss-leading is very hard to distinguish from normal pricing of high-elasticity, strong-branded, fast-selling products.[214]

Subsequent OFT guidelines on abusive practices accept that "assessing whether [loss-leading] has resulted in higher or lower profits is not straightforward."[215] The OFT suggests that the best comparison is between the undertaking's profits before and after the price cut. However, it also recognises the limitations of this approach where the price cut occurred at the same time as a new entrant entered the market, since the dominant firm's profitability would have been reduced by the new entrant in any event. Similarly, there is a problem in relying on profit comparisons if the price cut occurred during a period of volatile demand or costs because the dominant firm's profits would also have changed irrespective of the price cut. Indeed, the loss-leading may simply have failed in creating additional demand.

A net revenue defence was also considered by the UK Competition Appeal Tribunal (CAT) in *Napp*.[216] Napp was found to be dominant in the supply of certain morphine-based pain-relief products dispensed in hospitals, on the one hand, and prescribed to outpatients (or the community segment) on the other. There were strong links between the hospital and community markets: the brand of morphine prescribed at the hospital would in many cases continue to be prescribed in the community market. The hospital market was therefore an important "gateway" to sales in the follow-on community market. Napp was found to have priced persistently below cost in the hospital market and to have charged unlawful excessive prices in the community market.

One of Napp's defences was that losses in the hospital segment were compensated by profits from follow-on sales in the community segment. This defence was rejected by

the Competition Commission in *Safeway plc and Asda Group Limited (owned by Wal-Mart Stores Inc); Wm Morrison Supermarkets PLC; J Sainsbury plc; and Tesco plc*, UK Competition Commission Report (Cm 5950, September 26, 2003).

[214] *Ibid*., p. 101.

[215] See Assessment of Conduct: Draft Competition Law Guideline for Consultation, OFT 414a, para. 4.17. See also Competition Act 1998: The Application in the Telecommunications Sector, OFT 417, para. 7.19. ("An additional factor that will need to be taken into account is the extent to which there is strong complementarity between two or more services in respect of which there are different supply and demand conditions. Where there is strong complementarity, in applying the relevant tests it may be more appropriate to take into account the costs and revenues of all the complementary services rather than require each individual service to cover its costs."). The guidelines do not explain, however, how complementary revenues can be measured or whether the same approach would be applied outside the telecommunications sector.

[216] *Napp Pharmaceutical Holdings Limited and Subsidiaries v Director General of Fair Trading* [2002] CompAR 13.

the CAT on the grounds, *inter alia*, that it was "little more than a circular argument to the effect that it is, in a general sense, 'profitable' for Napp to sell at low prices in hospitals in order to deny to competitors a toehold in the hospital segment and the "hospital influence" which might flow from that."[217] The CAT also attached importance to Napp's exclusionary intent,[218] and was no doubt influenced by the fact that prices in the community segment were up to fourteen times higher than in the hospital segment. In other words, Napp was not merely recovering its losses through follow-on prices, but unlawfully exploiting consumers through excessive prices in the community segment.

A final approach involves a complex two-stage test and detailed analysis of statistical information across multiple retailing outlets.[219] As a first stage, it would need to be analysed whether the multiproduct retailer is pricing below cost on a product or certain combination of products. If so, further analysis would be required as a second stage to assess whether below-cost pricing was necessary to take full advantage of the alleged demand complementarities justifying the loss-leading products. This assessment would be based not only on the dominant firm's revenues and costs in a single store, but also on prices and sales of other stores operated by the predator in the same and different markets, or estimates of cross-price elasticities. The authors recognise that this approach is both complex and time-consuming and might therefore be best reserved for large-scale loss-leading by nationwide retailers.

Reconciling the different approaches to loss-leading. The preceding examination shows that, while there is a basic recognition of the possible procompetitive and anticompetitive aspects of loss-leading, no legal test has been devised to clearly distinguish between the two. The two-stage economic test set out above is not practical as an *ex ante* legal rule in most cases. In these circumstances, the following suggestions are offered by way of guidance:

1. An analysis of loss-leading cannot be divorced from the overall scale of the alleged problem. For example, if there was evidence that a retailer practised loss-leading for a large proportion of its product range on a nationwide basis, this would require a more convincing justification than loss-leading on a small number of items on a local scale.

2. The dominant firm must have a reasonable basis for expecting that, as a result of the sale below cost, revenue will be obtained from other sales which would not otherwise have been made, and that the expected or average additional revenue will exceed the amount of the loss. One important factor therefore is that the follow-on revenue defence should have been planned *ex ante* by the dominant firm and not merely put forward *ex post* for purposes of defending an alleged infringement, as occurred in *Napp*.[220] Although any such assessment

[217] *Ibid.*, para. 336.

[218] *Ibid.*, para. 334.

[219] See A Eckert and DS West, "Testing for Predation by a Multiproduct Retailer" in E Hope (ed.), *The Pros And Cons Of Low Prices* (Stockholm, Swedish Competition Authority, 2003) pp. 39–69.

[220] *Napp Pharmaceutical Holdings Limited and Subsidiaries v Director General of Fair Trading* [2002] CompAR 13, para. 235.

necessarily involves future speculation, the dominant firm's follow-on revenue should be based on more than mere assertion. At a minimum, there must be evidence of a likely follow-on revenue effect and that the dominant firm took this effect into account *ex ante* when setting its prices for the loss-making and profitable products.

3. In the absence of any clear legal or economic test to distinguish legitimate loss-leading from the exclusionary kind, an error-cost approach requires that a finding of illegality should be based on convincing evidence of an anticompetitive strategy. Thus, there may be evidence of specific anticompetitive intent in the dominant firm's documents. Alternatively, the dominant firm's *ex ante* assumptions and calculations regarding future follow-on revenues may be "unjustified or implausible" and, therefore, likely to be based on an exclusionary object.[221] Forward-looking projections are by nature matters of (often complex) judgment rather than fact and a margin of error should be afforded to the dominant firm. Provided the dominant firm's assumptions were reasonable at the time they were made, a competition authority or court should not later interfere with them if they do not turn out to have been fully correct. In this connection, it may be useful to show that the dominant firm's competitors adopted the same strategy, even if the competitors are not subject to the obligations of dominant firms.

4. There must be an element of proportionality in that the dominant firm must show that initial losses were necessary to achieve the follow-on revenues. Thus, if above-cost prices, or below-cost prices , could have achieved the same result within a shorter period, the loss-leading strategy may be disproportionate. A loss-leader sale should be lawful if the information available to the company showed that, on average, it was probable that the loss incurred would be recovered from sales of other products or services which would not have been made without the below-cost sale.

5.6.6 Excess Capacity And Loss-Minimising

Basic rationale. The original proponents of the AVC test, Areeda and Turner, recognised that it contained a potential anomaly: in situations of excess capacity, the maximum market price may not exceed any firm's AVC (and *a fortiori* ATC). In this situation, the *AKZO* rule would imply that it would be unlawful for firms to continue production, even in order to minimise losses. And, yet, absent an upswing in demand, situations of excess capacity would persist unless some capacity is eliminated from the market. Thus, it should arguably be a defence to say that the losses are being made during a period of reduced demand in which no supplier of the product or service is able to sell at a price sufficient to cover its AVC.[222] A dominant company in such circumstances must be free to sell what it can at whatever prices it can obtain, for cash-flow reasons.

[221] See Competition Act 1998: The Application in the Telecommunications Sector, OFT 417, para. 7.23.

[222] See Discussion Paper, para. 131.

The various approaches to excess capacity. Areeda and Turner recognised the excess capacity anomaly, but simply proposed that intervention under competition law would not be warranted in such situations.[223] Their rationale is that the elimination of capacity though the exit of a competitor restores the market closer to the optimal scale, which is procompetitive. The OFT recommends a similar approach, at least where the dominant firm only matches competitors' prices:[224]

> "[S]ome markets are able to support only one or two undertakings because, for example, there are significant economies of scale. If a new entrant mistakenly believes there is a profitable entry opportunity, its entry may force all undertakings in the market to sell below average variable costs. The incumbent undertakings would then have the choice of remaining in the market, and incurring losses, or exiting the market, perhaps leaving the market to be supplied by a less efficient new entrant. In such circumstances the incumbent's decision to remain in the market, and match the entrant's prices, would not necessarily be considered to be predatory."

Another suggested solution involves an assessment not of whether the predator's *entire* output is profitable, but whether the predator could profitably displace the *competitor's output*.[225] While both companies' costs are below AVC in a situation of excess capacity, the predator may be able to produce the rival's output more cheaply by increasing its own output, which would justify allowing the more efficient firm to price down to the level of AVC of *the increase in* its output (even when this is less than its overall AVC).

5.6.7 Miscellaneous Defences

Mistake. There may also be a defence if the dominant company genuinely did not know the facts which showed that its price was unlawful and corrected the price as soon as it found out. This occurred in *General Motors*, although it was not a predatory pricing case.[226] The case concerned allegedly excessive prices charged by General Motors for conformity certificates required for the export of motor vehicles from Belgium. These certificates had previously been provided by State testing stations, but were then assumed by the car manufacturers. In carrying out its first five inspections, General Motors charged a fee considerably in excess of the cost of conducting the relevant conformity tests. However, the Court of Justice refused to find that this amounted to unlawful excessive pricing, since this was a new activity for General

---

[223] PE Areeda and H Hovenkamp, *Antitrust Law* (2nd ed, New York, Aspen Law & Business, 2000) para. 740b3.

[224] See Assessment of Conduct: Draft Competition Law Guideline for Consultation, OFT 414a, para. 4.8. See also *Predatory Pricing Enforcement Guidelines*, Canadian Competition Bureau, Section 2.2.2. ("[A] price in [between AVC and ATC] may be reasonable in circumstances of declining demand or substantial excess capacity in the market, even if it is associated with the exit of other firms.").

[225] E Elhauge, "Why Above-Cost Price Cuts To Drive Out Entrants Are Not Predatory and the Implications for Defining Costs and Market Power" (2003) 112 *Yale Law Journal* 681-795, 708 ("A firm pricing at marginal costs that are below its overall average variable costs necessarily lowers those average variable costs by expanding output. Thus, the fact that its prices are below its overall average variable costs does *not* mean they would be below the additional variable costs it would incur by adding output equal to what the rival used to produce. In such a case, the declining demand that created the excess capacity simply means that the minimum efficient scale can sustain fewer firms than before.").

[226] Case 26/75, *General Motors Continental NV v Commission* [1975] ECR 1367, paras. 20–21.

Motors and it had voluntarily refunded the excess charge before any intervention on the part of the Commission and thereafter set its rates in line with actual costs. In *Tetra Pak II*, the Commission appeared to suggest a similar defence, when it noted that management error was not the reason for Tetra Pak's below-cost selling.[227] Allowing this defence may or may not be consistent with the notion that an abuse is an objective concept, and that inadequacies in cost accounting should not be a defence to an abuse. Provided, however, that the error is genuine, short-lived, and corrected at the earliest opportunity, the harm in allowing this defence seems limited.

Obsolescent goods. Loss-minimising is also the basis for the defence when goods are sold below AVC/ATC because they are obsolescent, deteriorating, or would cost so much to store until they could be sold at a higher price that losses would be minimised by their immediate sale.[228]

[227] See *Tetra Pak II*, OJ 1992 L 72/1, para. 148.
[228] See Discussion Paper, para. 131.

Chapter 6

MARGIN SQUEEZE

6.1 INTRODUCTION

Foreclosure by a vertically integrated dominant firm. It is well-recognised under Article 82 EC that a vertically integrated dominant firm can take various actions to unlawfully foreclose downstream rivals to whom it supplies essential inputs. A classic example is a refusal to deal, discussed in Chapter Eight. But vertical foreclosure abuses are not limited to refusals to deal. They may also concern analogous price or non-price strategies intended to raise rivals' costs and exclude them from the relevant downstream market. A commonly-cited example of vertical foreclosure is the abuse of margin (or price) squeeze. This is a strategy whereby a vertically integrated dominant firm can use its control of the input price and the retail price to "squeeze" the profit margins of downstream rivals to whom it also supplies the input. The dominant firm can use the fact of its vertical integration and control over the input and retail prices to effectively discriminate against non-integrated downstream rivals.

Definition of a margin squeeze. Margin squeeze abuses have been recognised as a distinct violation under Article 82 EC. In basic terms, a margin squeeze involves situations in which a vertically integrated dominant firm not only engages in self-supply of an input used on a downstream market, but also supplies independent third parties active on the downstream market, which are in competition with its own business. In these circumstances, various strategies may be open to the vertically integrated dominant firm to render downstream rivals' activities unprofitable. The dominant firm could raise the input price to levels at which rivals could no longer sustain a profit downstream. Alternatively, it could engage in below-cost selling in the downstream market, while remaining profitable overall through the sale of the upstream input. Finally, the dominant firm could raise the price of the upstream input and lower the price of the downstream retail product to reduce the margin between them to a level at which rivals would be unprofitable. These strategies in fact amount the same thing: a price, or combination of prices, that would render non-integrated downstream rivals' activities uneconomic. The key point is that the dominant firm uses its position as an essential supplier to rivals and a downstream seller to *cause* a reduction in rivals' profit margins.

Importance of margin squeeze in practice. Margin squeeze cases were a rarity under Article 82 EC between 1960–2000. The decisional practice and case law was limited to an interim measures decision (*National Carbonising*[1]) and a final decision in which a margin squeeze was only one of several abuses found (*Napier Brown/British Sugar*[2]).

---

[1] Case 109/75R, *National Carbonising Company Ltd v Commission* [1975] ECR 1193 and *National Coal Board, National Smokeless Fuels Limited and the National Carbonising Company Limited*, OJ 1976 L 35/6 (hereinafter "*National Carbonising*").

[2] *Napier Brown/British Sugar*, OJ 1988 L 284/41 (hereinafter "*Napier Brown/British Sugar*").

Recent years have, however, seen an increase in the number of margin squeeze decisions, at both EC (*Industrie des Poudres Sphériques*,[3] *Deutsche Telekom*[4]) and national level (e.g., Denmark, Finland, France, Italy, Netherlands, Sweden, and United Kingdom), leading to a lively debate among lawyers and economists.[5] Recent precedents have primarily arisen in liberalised utility sectors (e.g., telecommunications, electricity, gas, and water) where downstream rivals remain wholly or partially reliant upon a former monopolist for essential inputs or raw materials. Margin squeeze complaints represent an important tool in the commercial strategies of new entrants that seek to compete with incumbent operators. While new entrants have made significant inroads in several liberalised markets, many claim that further growth is constrained by exclusionary practices carried out by incumbents. Margin squeeze allegations feature prominently in this regard.

6.2 THE ECONOMICS OF MARGIN SQUEEZE

6.2.1 Types Of Margin Squeeze

Predatory and refusal to deal margin squeezes. Margin squeeze describes a situation in which a vertically integrated firm with a dominant position in an upstream market prevents its (non-vertically-integrated) downstream rivals from achieving an economically viable price-cost margin. In broad terms, two principal strategies are open to a vertically integrated firm in this connection: (1) charging a price for its input that is too high given the downstream product price; or (2) setting a downstream product price that is too low relative to the input price. In either case, the result of a successful margin squeeze is that some or all downstream rivals are driven out of the market, or remain marginalised with significantly weaker competitive positions.

The first way a downstream rival's margin can be "squeezed" is direct and involves an increase in the input price. This practice is equivalent to a refusal to deal, as well as

---

[3] Case T-5/97, *Industrie des Poudres Sphériques SA v Commission* [2000] ECR II-3755 (hereinafter "*Industrie des Poudres Sphériques*").

[4] *Deutsche Telekom AG*, OJ 2003 L 263/9 (hereinafter "*Deutsche Telekom*"), currently on appeal in Case T-271/03, *Deutsche Telekom AG v Commission*, OJ 2003 C 264/29.

[5] See, e.g., D Geradin and R O'Donoghue, "The Concurrent Application Of Competition Law And Regulation: The Case Of Margin Squeeze Abuses In The Telecommunications Sector" (2005) 1 *Journal of Competition Law and Economics* 355–425; P Crocioni and C Veljanovski, "Vertical Markets, Foreclosure and Price Squeezes Principles and Guidelines" *Case Associates Case Research Paper No. 1* (2002); Case Associates, "Testing For A Price Squeeze: A Critical Review Of Recent Competition Law Decisions" (May 2004); P Grout, "Defining a Price Squeeze in Competition Law" in *The Pros and Cons of Low Prices* (Stockholm, Swedish Competition Authority, 2003), p.71; W Taylor and T Tardiff, "Anticompetitive Price Squeezes in the Telecommunications Industry: A Common Complaint About Common Facilities" in *NERA Antitrust Insights* (December 2004); J Kallaugher, *The "Margin Squeeze" under Article 82: Searching for Limiting Principles*, paper presented to the BT/Global Competition Law Centre Conference on Margin Squeeze, December 10, 2004; A Whelan, *Margin Squeeze—A View From Within The Commission*, paper presented to the BT/Global Competition Law Centre Conference on Margin Squeeze, December 10, 2004; P Palmigiano, *Abuse of Margin Squeeze Under Article 82 of the EC Treaty and its Application to New and Emerging Markets*, IBA 16th Annual Communications and Competition Law Conference, May 23–24, 2005; and G Brunekreeft, E van Damme, P Larouche, and V Sorana, *The Law And Economics Of Price Squeeze In Telecommunications Markets: A Project For KPN*, TILEC, Tilburg University, February 14, 2005.

"raising rivals' costs"[6] or vertical foreclosure. The simple formula is: retail price < downstream costs + wholesale price = margin squeeze. This type of margin squeeze is illustrated below:

Figure 1: Margin squeeze by raising input price

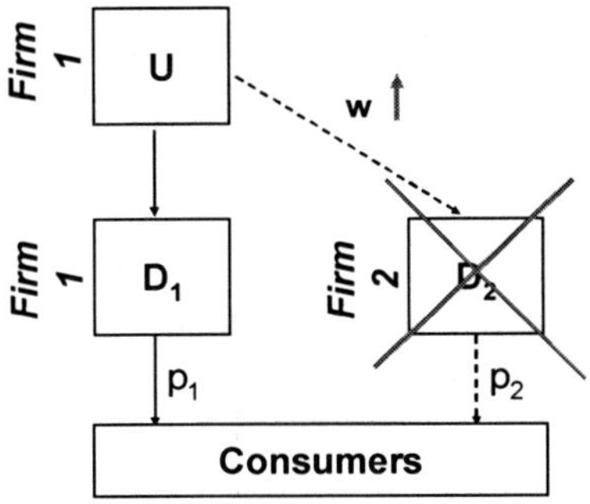

The second method of margin squeeze is indirect and involves a reduction in the downstream retail price. When the vertically integrated firm lowers its own retail price, rivals usually follow suit to avoid losing a large number of customers. This practice is very similar to price predation. The simple formula is: retail price – downstream costs < wholesale price = margin squeeze. This type of margin squeeze is illustrated below:

Figure 2: Margin squeeze by lowering retail price

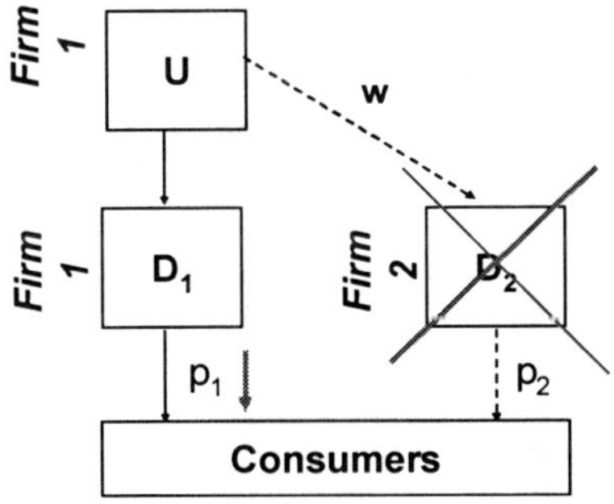

6.2.2 Basic Economic Conditions For A Margin Squeeze

Structural and other pre-requisites. The purpose of a margin squeeze is foreclosure of one or more downstream rivals. Foreclosure may either be complete, leading to their actual exclusion of downstream rivals, or partial, in which case the vertically integrated firm is content with restricting their output and possibly obtaining a larger market share

[6] See generally SC Salop, D Scheffman and W Schwartz, "A Bidding Analysis of Special interest Regulation: Raising Rivals' Costs in a Rent Seeking Society" in B Yandle and R Rogowsky (eds.), *The Political Economy of Regulation: Private Interests in the Regulatory Process*, (1984) Federal Trade Commission; and SC Salop and D Scheffman, "Cost-Raising Strategies" (1987) 36(1) *Journal of Industrial Economics* 19–34.

for itself. Foreclosure is motivated by the vertically integrated firm's desire to extract as much profits as possible from its activities on the upstream and downstream markets.[7] Economic theory helps identify certain conditions that make margin squeeze feasible and profitable, respectively. The minimum conditions are as follows:

1. *Significant upstream market power.* A vertically integrated firm must have significant market power in the upstream market to carry out a margin squeeze. Typically, the vertically integrated firm would need to enjoy a dominant position in the upstream market which is derived from the fact that it supplies an "essential" input, or "bottleneck" good.[8] Such a good does not have effective substitutes in production (or only inferior ones); nor can it be replicated at low cost and in a short period of time.[9] Absent market power of this kind, downstream firms could simply source at the same quality from competing upstream firms.

2. *A degree of market power downstream.* In addition to a very high degree of upstream market power, a vertically integrated firm requires a degree of market power on the relevant downstream market in order to carry out a margin squeeze successfully. There is some disagreement, however, as to how much market power is required in the downstream market in a margin squeeze case. Economists tend to think that downstream dominance is also required, since the vertically integrated firm would need to have a strong expectation of capturing most sales from the displaced rivals. If the vertically integrated firm is not dominant downstream, rivals may in fact profit more from an attempted margin squeeze by capturing the exiting or marginalised firm's sales to a greater extent than the vertically integrated firm. Another related reason is that the vertically integrated firm must be able to control the margin between the wholesale and retail prices. A high input price will be ineffective as a margin squeeze tool if downstream rivals can pass the cost on to consumers. In order to make sure that rivals make a loss, the company must prevent this pass-on using its own retail price, i.e., the vertically integrated firm must control the retail price (or more precisely the margin) too.

3. *Barriers to entry and re-entry.* There must be barriers to entry and re-entry in both upstream and downstream markets. Such barriers ensure that firms will not enter the downstream market in the event of a price increase. This is especially true for instances of predatory margin squeeze where a successful strategy requires a recoupment period of high retail prices. But it is also true for cases of "excessive" wholesale prices where higher input prices (often, but not always) lead to higher retail prices. Entry barriers prevent the entry of a downstream firm that may source inputs from an inferior upstream competitor.

[7] There is an upper bound of profits that a dominant firm or a monopolist can extract from its market activities (see discussion of Chicago school critique below).

[8] The same notion can also be applied to situations where the bottleneck good is not an input but is bundled with another, potentially competitive, good and thus sold directly to end consumers. See P Rey and J Tirole, "A Primer on Foreclosure," in M Armstrong and R Porter (eds.), *Handbook of Industrial Organisation,* vol. III (North Holland, 2005).

[9] *Ibid.*

Entry barriers in the upstream market are necessary for the vertically integrated firm to reap the additional profits accruing from the margin squeeze without being confronted with entrants.

4. *Asymmetries between predator and prey.* Most exclusionary pricing requires a degree of asymmetry between the predator and prey for predation to be rational. The same can be said, to some extent, for a margin squeeze. If firms were symmetric or had the same knowledge, it would be more difficult for the vertically integrated firm to convince downstream rivals that staying in the market is unprofitable in the long-term. Those asymmetries may be of informational character (e.g., signalling),[10] reputation,[11] or concern different levels of access to financial resources.[12] These are discussed in more detail in Chapter Five (Predatory Pricing). This point should not, however, be overstated in the context of margin squeeze, since, unlike a predatory pricing case, the dominant firm may still earn a profit overall on sales of the product. This is possible because the effect of its conduct on rivals is governed by whether retail prices are high enough to cover the price those rivals must pay for the input, together with their downstream costs. The profitability of the vertically integrated company is governed by whether retail prices cover end-to-end costs. There is, however, an *opportunity cost* to the dominant firm in a margin squeeze case (e.g., raising the input price may reduce its sales), so the extent of the opportunity cost may be an informational asymmetry between the dominant firm and rivals.

6.2.3 Anticompetitive Motivation For A Margin Squeeze

The issue of incentives: Chicago and post-Chicago thinking. Although margin squeeze seems an obvious strategy for a vertically integrated dominant firm, there are many reasons why it may not be in practice. Under certain circumstances, the vertically integrated firm may prefer downstream rivals to be present in the market. An important consideration in practice is the degree of product differentiation on the downstream market. The higher the degree of product differentiation in the downstream market, the lower the incentives for foreclosure. The reason is that differentiated products facilitate the appropriation of monopolistic rents, as downstream rivals' products pose less of a competitive threat to the vertically integrated firm's own output. The vertically integrated firm has less incentive to foreclose products that are differentiated to an extent that they do not exercise a significant competitive constraint in the downstream market. Another reason that might significantly reduce the incentives to commit a margin squeeze is where the dominant firm does not have enough downstream capacity to expand sales and has no wish to acquire additional capacity.

---

[10] P Bolton, JF Brodley, and MH Riordan, "Predatory Pricing: Strategic Theory and Legal Policy" (2000) 88(8) *Georgetown Law Journal* 2239–2330.

[11] P Milgrom and J Roberts, "Predation, Reputation and Entry Deterrence" (1982) 27 *Journal of Economic Theory* 280–312.

[12] See, e.g., P Milgrom and J Roberts, "New Theories of Predatory Pricing" in G Bonanno and D Brandolini (eds.), *Industrial Structure in the New Industrial Economics* (Oxford, Oxford University Press, 1990) pp. 112–37; and P Bolton and D Scharfstein, "A Theory of Predation Based on Agency Problems in Financial Contracting" (1990) 80 *American Economic Review* 93–106.

A more fundamental critique of vertical foreclosure is the Chicago school "single monopoly profit" theorem, discussed in detail in Chapter Four. This posits that a firm—vertically integrated or not—with an upstream monopoly has no incentive to foreclose downstream rivals, as there is only a single monopoly rent to be earned in the industry.[13] In other words, it is not possible for the firm to "leverage" its upstream-market power into the downstream segment: the total profit obtainable is the same whether the firm tries to extract it upstream, downstream, or using a combination of both.

Post-Chicago thinking has questioned the single monopoly rent theory by identifying a number of situations in which vertical foreclosure is a rational anticompetitive strategy.[14] More recent thinking has rationalised margin squeeze as a viable anticompetitive strategy used: (1) to restore market power upstream; (2) as defensive leveraging to deter entry in the long run; and (3) to monopolise or relax competition downstream:

1. *Restoring market power upstream.* What threatens the ability of an upstream monopolist to reap the benefits from its position in the first place is that it cannot always commit to restrict output at the monopoly level.[15] Several contributions have demonstrated that vertical foreclosure may be an effective means to restore the monopolist's ability to reap full profits.[16]

2. *Defensive leveraging.* In many markets with rapid technological change, an upstream monopolist might reasonably worry that successful downstream firms will try to integrate backwards into the upstream market, thereby threatening the monopoly of the vertically integrated dominant firm. The monopolist might want to foreclose downstream rivals to secure its position in the long run.[17]

3. *Monopolisation or relaxation of competition of downstream market.* A vertically integrated firm might also exploit its dominant position in the upstream and downstream markets by extracting more profits from the latter. In some circumstances, the vertically integrated firm may want to purchase a

[13] See, e.g., R Bork, *The Antitrust Paradox: A Policy at War with Itself* (New York, Basic Books, 1978).

[14] See, e.g., SC Salop and D Scheffman, "Cost-Raising Strategies" (1987) 36(1) *Journal of Industrial Economics* 19–34; MA Salinger, "Vertical Mergers and Market Foreclosure" (1988) 103(2) *Quarterly Journal of Economics* 345–56; and MD Whinston, "Tying, Foreclosure and Exclusion" (1990) 80(4) *American Economic Review* 837–59.

[15] Suppose that the monopolist has already sold output to a downstream firm at terms that reflect monopoly output level and price. The monopolist might still be tempted to sell additional output to another firm, but that additional output will lower the profits of all downstream firms. Any downstream firm can anticipate such a behaviour and will not accept the initial terms based on monopoly output.

[16] P Rey and J Tirole, "A Primer on Foreclosure" in M Armstrong and R Porter (eds.), *Handbook of Industrial Organisation,* vol. III (North Holland, 2005). See also O Hart and J Tirole, "Vertical Integration and Market Foreclosure" (1990) *Brookings Papers on Economic Activity: Microeconomics* 205–76; and P Baake, U Kamecke and H Normann, "Vertical Foreclosure versus Downstream Competition with Capital Precommitment" (2004) 22(2) *International Journal of Industrial Organisation* 185–92.

[17] DW Carlton and M Waldman, "The Strategic Use of Tying to Preserve and Create Market Power in Evolving Industries" (2002) 33(2) *RAND Journal of Economics* 194–220.

proportion of inputs for the downstream product from external sources although it supplies them itself in an efficient way. In this way, it effectively increases input costs for the rival downstream firms. Although the vertically integrated firm incurs costs too, it can shift the competitive outcome on the downstream market in its favour.[18]

Procompetitive explanations for a margin squeeze. Although negative margins of a vertically integrated dominant firm (or its rivals) may be an indication of anticompetitive conduct, there are a number of reasons why this cannot be assumed automatically. For example, it is very difficult to distinguish between an instance of anticompetitive margin squeeze and a growing market where prices may be temporarily below costs for, e.g., promotional reasons (see Section 6.5 below). Emerging markets are characterised by high entry and exit rates of firms; and the total number of firms often falls sharply after an initial rise.[19] It is sometimes difficult therefore to distinguish margin squeeze behaviour from the natural shake-down that occurs in many emerging markets.

Second, a margin squeeze may have plausible efficiency gains, such as allowing output to expand and achieve economies of scale (e.g., network effects).[20] Third, as in any duty to deal case, regulating the price at which a dominant firm may sell an input—which a rule prohibiting a margin squeeze does—will reduce the incentives of firms to make risky investments in socially-valuable assets.

Finally, the notion that a vertically integrated dominant firm may have to charge a price or combination of prices that allow all equally efficient firms to enter the market can lead to excessive and socially-undesirable entry.[21] Entry may also be excessive in markets where firms produce different varieties that each require sunk costs.[22]

6.3 BASIC LEGAL CONDITIONS FOR A MARGIN SQUEEZE

The basic legal conditions. The only official statement by the Commission on margin squeeze abuses is contained in the Notice on the application of the competition rules to

[18] See SC Salop and D Scheffman, "Cost-Raising Strategies" (1987) 36(1) *Journal of Industrial Economics* 19–34.

[19] These patterns are well documented by empirical research. See, e.g., S Klepper and KL Simons, "Industry Shakeouts and Technological Change" (2005) 23 *International Journal of Industrial Organisation* 23–43; and B Jovanovic and GM MacDonald, "The Lifecycle of a Competitive Industry" (1994) 102(2) *Journal of Political Economy* 322–47.

[20] WJ Baumol, "Quasi-Permanence of Price Reductions: A Policy for Prevention of Predatory Pricing" (1979) 89 *Yale Law Journal* 1.

[21] NG Mankiw and MD Whinston, "Free Entry and Social Inefficiency" (1986) 17(1) *RAND Journal of Economics* 48–58.

[22] AK Dixit and JE Stiglitz, "Monopolistic Competition and Optimum Product Diversity" (1977) 67(3) *American Economic Review* 297–308; and JJ Gabszewicz and JF Thisse, "On the Nature of Competition with Differentiated Products" (1986) 96(381) *Economic Journal* 160–72.

access agreements in the telecommunications sector,[23] which defines the abuse as follows:[24]

> "A price squeeze could be demonstrated by showing that the dominant company's own downstream operations could not trade profitably on the basis of the upstream price charged to its competitors by the upstream operating arm of the dominant company...In appropriate circumstances, a price squeeze could also be demonstrated by showing that the margin between the price charged to competitors on the downstream market (including the dominant company's own downstream operations, if any) for access and the price which the network operator charges in the downstream market is insufficient to allow a reasonably efficient service provider in the downstream market to obtain a normal profit (unless the dominant company can show that its downstream operation is exceptionally efficient)."

Building on this basic definition, a number of minimum conditions are required to substantiate a margin squeeze abuse:[25] (1) the supplier of the input is vertically-integrated; (2) the input in question is in some sense essential for downstream competition; (3) the vertically integrated dominant firm's prices would render the activities of an efficient rival uneconomic; and (4) there is no objective justification for the vertically integrated dominant firm's pricing arrangements.

Condition #1: vertical integration. All margin squeeze cases concern situations of vertical integration, that is where a firm dominant on a market for an upstream input supplies that input to rivals operating on a downstream market where the dominant firm is also active, i.e., cases involve two markets and downstream rivals which are both customers and competitors of the dominant firm.[26] Where a firm is not vertically-

[23] Notice on the application of the competition rules to access agreements in the telecommunications sector framework, relevant markets and principles, OJ 1998 C 265/2.

[24] *Ibid.*, paras. 117–18. See also Guidelines on the application of the Competition Act 1998 in the telecommunications sector, OFT 417, para. 7.26 ("Where a vertically integrated undertaking is dominant in an upstream market and supplies a key input to undertakings that compete with it in a downstream market, there is scope for it to abuse its dominance in the upstream market. The vertically integrated undertaking could subject its competitors to a price or price squeeze by raising the cost of the key input ... and/or by lowering its prices in the downstream market. The integrated undertaking's *total* revenue may remain unchanged. The effect would be to reduce the gross margin available to its competitors, which might well make them unprofitable."). The same definition appears in the OFT's Guideline Assessment of Individual Agreements and Conduct, OFT 414. See also Joint Guidelines issued by the Dutch Competition Authority and the Dutch Postal and Telecommunications Authority for the appraisal of unfairly low end user prices charged by telecommunications companies that have significant power within the meaning of the Dutch Telecommunications Act or that have a dominant position within the meaning of the Dutch Competition Act (2001).

[25] See also Office of Telecommunications (now Ofcom), *Analytical Framework for New Freeserve Case*, August 14, 2003, para. 22 ("A margin squeeze occurs where a firm: [(1)] is vertically integrated, i.e., operates in both upstream and downstream markets; [(2)] is dominant in the upstream market, so that downstream competitors have a degree of reliance upon the firms upstream input; [(3)] sets a margin between its downstream retail price and upstream wholesale charge (paid by downstream competitors) that is insufficient to cover its downstream costs; [(4)] on an "end-to-end" basis, i.e. aggregating across the firm's upstream and downstream activities, the firm may be profitable; [(5)] but an equally (or more) efficient downstream competitor could be unable to compete, because, in effect, it is being charged a higher price for the upstream input than its competitor, the vertically integrated firm's own downstream arm.").

[26] See, e.g., *National Coal Board, National Smokeless Fuels Limited and the National Carbonising Company Limited,* OJ 1976 L 35/6 (markets for coal production and coke); *Napier Brown/British*

integrated, or is not active on the market in which a margin squeeze is alleged, a margin squeeze abuse cannot arise. For example, rising raw material costs may impact on the ability of undertakings engaged in the transformation of those raw materials into a final product to make a profit. This is not, however, a concern under the abuse of margin squeeze, unless the supplier of the input in question is also vertically integrated in the downstream market for the final product. The only remedy open to downstream operators in this situation would be to show that the raw material price is excessive and exploitative within the meaning of Article 82(a).

Vertical integration is essential to the definition of a margin squeeze for one obvious reason: it offers the dominant firm scope for taking the profit either upstream or downstream and, therefore, the ability to conceal what is, in effect, a form of discrimination against non-integrated rivals. Unless the dominant firm is actually discriminating in the prices charged to downstream rivals and its own integrated business—which may in itself be contrary to the non-discrimination clause in Article 82(c)—the transfer charge that its downstream business pays to its upstream business *appears* to be the same as the input charge paid by downstream competitors. This is only superficially true, however, since vertical integration makes the dominant firm's charge to its downstream business a paper transfer price and not an actual cost faced by the downstream business (even if the firm sets an internal transfer price or produces separate upstream and downstream accounts). The objection therefore in a margin squeeze case is that the *implicit* transfer charge imposed on downstream rivals is higher than the input charge that the dominant firm's own downstream business faces. Using the language of the Commission in *Deutsche Telekom*, a "price squeeze imposes on competitors additional efficiency constraints which the incumbent does not have to support in providing its own retail services."[27]

Condition #2: a dominant position in the supply of an essential upstream input. The input supplied by the dominant upstream firm to downstream rivals must in some sense be "essential" for competition on the downstream market.[28] Where downstream rivals can and do rely on alternative technologies or inputs, they will be much less at risk from an attempted margin squeeze.[29] For example, in *National Carbonising*, the

Sugar, OJ 1988 L 284/41 (markets for industrial sugar and retail sugar); Case T-5/97, *Industrie des Poudres Sphériques SA v Commission* [2000] ECR II-3755 (markets for primary calcium metal and broken calcium metal); and *Deutsche Telekom AG*, OJ 2003 L 263/9 (markets in access to local fixed networks (wholesale and retail) and narrowband and broadband retail Internet access). In *Genzyme Limited v Office of Fair Trading* [2005] CAT 32, the Competition Appeal Tribunal (CAT) imposed a margin squeeze remedy even after the dominant firm had ceased to be active in the relevant downstream market (the business was subject to a management buyout). But the abuse was committed when the dominant firm was active downstream, i.e., the remedy corrected for past abusive effects. The remedy was also intended to as offer guidance for the future in case the two operations were again merged, which reflected the CAT's implicit concern that the spin off was intended to avoid the consequences of the infringement decision.

[27] *Deutsche Telekom AG, ibid.*, para. 141.

[28] See, e.g., J Bouckaert and F Verboven, "Margin Squeezes In A Regulatory Environment," *Centre For Economic Policy Research, Discussion Paper Series*, p. 27 ("[A margin squeeze] assumes that the incumbent has an upstream monopoly over an essential input.").

[29] *Ibid.* ("In practice, the incumbent's upstream market power may not be that strong. While the incumbent operator typically owns the copper line, substitute networks in the form of cable, wireless

National Coal Board had a virtual monopoly—backed by legislation—on the supply of coal, the principal raw material in the production of the downstream product, industrial and domestic hard coke. By contrast, in *Industrie des Poudres Sphériques*, one of the reasons mentioned by the Court of First Instance in upholding the Commission's decision to reject the margin squeeze allegation was that alternative sources of the raw material in question were available from China and Russia.[30] In *Deutsche Telekom*, there was no effective alternative to Deutsche Telekom's telecommunications network, in particular for local loop access. An unresolved issued, discussed in the next section, is whether the "essential" nature of the input also requires that it should be an "essential facility" for purposes of Article 82 EC.

A margin squeeze also assumes that the input supplied by the dominant firm constitutes a relatively high, fixed proportion of downstream operators' overall costs. If it represents a small proportion, or is used in variable proportions by downstream competitors, there would be practical problems in inferring that downstream rivals' apparent lack of profitability was caused by the dominant firm's input pricing. For this reason, margin squeeze complaints have generally been upheld in situations in which there was a clear linear pass through of inputs from the upstream market to the downstream market. For example, in *National Carbonising*, coal was, in essence, the only important raw material used in the downstream production of coke. Moreover, the proportion of coal used to make coke did not vary materially according to use, but had a simple linear relationship. Likewise, in *British Sugar/Napier Brown*, industrial sugar was essentially repackaged to product sugar for retail use, again showing that the raw material was used in high, fixed, and constant proportions in order to produce the final product.

Condition #3: the vertically integrated dominant firm's prices would render the activities of an efficient rival uneconomic. The most important element of a margin squeeze concerns the methodology to be applied to identify (or impute) an abuse. This raises several issues. First, what legal test should be applied to determine whether the dominant firm's upstream price, downstream price, or the combination of both prices, causes the activities of a downstream rival to be uneconomic, i.e., either loss-making or insufficient to provide a "reasonable profit." The most commonly-applied test is whether the dominant firm's own downstream operations would make a profit if they had to pay the same input price as rivals. A second, related issue is whether a different test based on the costs of a "reasonably efficient entrant" can also be applied. Third, the relevant cost standard to be applied to the dominant firm's downstream operations needs to be identified. Finally, it needs to be ensured that the compared inputs, costs, and downstream revenues are truly comparable.

---

etc...are available. In other words, the incumbent's essential facility is not absolute. The downstream competitors may therefore bypass the incumbent's network and consider purchasing access from alternative providers, or investing in an own network.").

[30] Case T-5/97, *Industrie des Poudres Sphériques SA v Commission* [2000] ECR II-3755, para. 139. See also *Investigation by the Director General of Telecommunications into the BT Surf Together and BT Talk & Surf Together Pricing Packages*, Oftel Decision of May 4, 2001 (margin squeeze rejected since alternative technologies competed on the retail market).

a. ***The basic legal test.*** A number of alternative tests could be envisaged in order to ascertain whether the dominant firm's prices would unlawfully exclude downstream rivals: (1) whether the dominant firm's own downstream operations could trade profitably on the basis of the wholesale price charged to third parties for the relevant input; (2) whether the dominant firm's downstream rivals could trade profitably on the basis of the wholesale price charged by the dominant firm; (3) whether some notional or hypothetical "reasonably efficient operator" could trade profitably on the basis of the dominant firm's input prices; or (4) a combination of some or all of the preceding tests.

In practice, the first test—the dominant firm's own costs—has been applied in virtually all instances under Article 82 EC and equivalent national laws. In *National Carbonising*, the Commission appeared to suggest a "reasonably efficient operator" test,[31] but in fact only applied a margin squeeze test based on the costs of the vertically integrated firm, National Carbonising Company (and its subsidiary, National Smokeless Fuels Limited). Later, in *British Sugar/Napier Brown,* the Commission was more explicit that the relevant costs were those of the dominant firm, i.e., a firm at least as efficient as the dominant firm. British Sugar plc (BS) was found dominant in the UK markets for the supply of raw and granulated sugar to retail and industrial clients. Its pricing policy towards Napier Brown—which acted as a buyer and re-seller of sugar in competition with BS—was found to result in "insufficient margin for a packager and seller of retail sugar, *as efficient as BS* itself in its packaging and selling operations, to survive in the long-term."[32]

The same test was applied most recently in *Deutsche Telekom*. The Commission stated that a margin squeeze would occur where the competing services were comparable and "the spread between DT's retail and wholesale prices is either negative or at least insufficient to cover DT's own downstream costs."[33] This would mean that DT would have been unable to offer its own retail services without incurring a loss if it had had to pay the wholesale access price as an internal transfer price for its own retail operations. As a consequence, competitors' profit margins would be squeezed, even if they were just as efficient as DT.[34]

---

[31] *National Coal Board, National Smokeless Fuels Limited and the National Carbonising Company Limited,* OJ 1976 L 35/6, para. 14 ("[A]n undertaking which is in a dominant position as regards the production of a raw material (in this case coking coal) and therefore able to control its price to independent manufacturers of derivatives (in this case, coke) and which is itself producing the same derivatives in competition with those manufacturers, may abuse a dominant position if it acts in such a way as to eliminate competition from these manufacturers in the market for derivatives. From this general principle the services of the Commission deduced that the enterprise in a dominant position may have an obligation to arrange its prices so as to allow a reasonably efficient manufacturer of the derivatives a margin sufficient to enable it to survive in the long term.").

[32] *Napier Brown/British Sugar*, OJ 1988 L 284/41, para. 65 (emphasis added). See also para. 66 ("[M]aintaining...a margin between the price which it charges for a raw material to the companies which compete with the dominant company in the production of the derived product and the price which it charges for the derived product, which is insufficient to reflect that dominant company's *own costs of transformation* (in this case the margin maintained by BS between its industrial and retail sugar prices compared to its own repackaging costs) with the result that competition in the derived product is restricted, is an abuse of dominant position.") (emphasis added).

[33] *Deutsche Telekom AG*, OJ 2003 L 263/9, para. 140.

[34] *Ibid.*, para. 102.

Use of the dominant firm's own costs as the test for a margin squeeze abuse was also confirmed indirectly by the Court of First Instance in *Industrie des Poudres Sphériques*. Industries des Poudres Sphériques (IPS) applied for the annulment of a Commission decision rejecting its request for a finding that an infringement of Article 82 EC had been committed by Pechiney Electrometallugie (PEM). PEM was the sole Community producer of primary calcium metal and also marketed broken calcium metal, a derivative of primary calcium metal. IPS competed with PEM in the derivative market for broken calcium metal. IPS alleged that PEM set the price of primary calcium metal abnormally high, which in combination with the very low price for broken calcium metal, forced its competitors to sell at a loss if they were to remain in the market. IPS claimed that that PEM's primary calcium metal offer gave rise to a margin squeeze. The Court rejected its appeal.

The Court of First Instance defined a margin squeeze as arising where a vertically integrated dominant firm supplies input to rivals at prices "at such a level that those who purchase it do not have a sufficient profit margin on the processing to remain competitive on the market for the processed product."[35] The Court suggested that this might occur in two ways: (1) where the prices for the upstream product were abusive; or (2) the prices for the derived product were predatory.[36] However, in practice, the Court applied a single test for abuse, since it held that the upstream price would be abusive or the downstream price predatory if "an efficient competitor" could not compete on the basis of the dominant firm's pricing.[37] The Court expressly excluded from this definition a company with higher processing costs than the dominant firm,[38] thereby suggesting, implicitly, but clearly, that the relevant benchmark is the costs of firms at least as efficient as the dominant firm, i.e., a test based on the dominant firm's own costs.

Finally, the Discussion Paper confirms that, in general, Article 82 EC is only concerned with conduct that would exclude firms that are *as efficient* as the dominant firm, i.e., with the same or lower costs.[39] Consumer welfare is not generally well-served by allowing firms that are less efficient than the dominant firm to seek protection from price competition under Article 82 EC. If an equally-efficient competitor cannot survive because of the dominant firm's pricing practices, the Commission would assume that conduct has the capability to foreclose and therefore examine the effects on the market.[40]

b. General inappropriateness of a "reasonably efficient operator" as sole margin squeeze test under competition law. Reliance on tests other than the dominant firm's own costs has been suggested in certain limited instances under Article 82 EC and equivalent national laws. For example, the Commission's Access Notice in the telecommunications sector puts forward a second test, in addition to the dominant firm's own costs: where the margin is "insufficient to allow a reasonably efficient service

[35] Case T-5/97, *Industrie des Poudres Sphériques SA v Commission* [2000] ECR II-3755, para. 178.
[36] *Ibid.*, para. 179.
[37] *Ibid.*, para. 180.
[38] *Ibid.*, para. 179.
[39] DG Competition discussion paper on the application of Article 82 of the Treaty to exclusionary abuses, Brussels, December 2005 (hereinafter, the "Discussion Paper"), para. 64.
[40] *Ibid.*, para. 66.

provider to obtain a normal profit."[41] In a later Open Network Provision document,[42] however, the Commission confirmed that it uses the dominant firm's costs as the benchmark for a "reasonably efficient service provider:"[43]

> "The suspicion of a "price squeeze" arises when the spread between access and retail prices of the incumbent's corresponding access services is not wide enough to reflect *the incumbent's own downstream costs.* In such a situation, alternative carriers normally complain that their margins are being squeezed because this spread is too narrow for them to compete with the incumbent. [...] Provided access and retail services are strictly comparable, *a situation of a price squeeze occurs where the incumbent's price of access combined with its downstream costs are higher than its corresponding retail price.*"

Decisions by national competition authorities (NCAs) or national regulatory authorities (NRAs) applying competition law have, however, focused to some extent on whether the margin between the dominant firm's wholesale and retail prices would be insufficient based on downstream rivals' costs or those of a "reasonably efficient operator." For example, in rejecting a margin squeeze allegation under competition law, Ofcom partly relied on the fact that the margin was positive overall taking into account a cost disadvantage faced by downstream rivals that the incumbent did not suffer from.[44] Whether this should be read as a general endorsement of a "reasonably efficient operator" test for margin squeeze under competition law, however, seems doubtful. In the first place, Ofcom only relied on downstream rivals' costs as one of a series of tests to show that, on any view, there was no abuse. It does not seem therefore that Ofcom was proposing that an abuse would be found where the *only* test suggesting a margin squeeze is one based on rivals' costs or those of a hypothetical "reasonably efficient operator." Indeed, in all other cases in the United Kingdom, only the dominant firm's costs have been used as the relevant test for a margin squeeze.[45]

---

[41] Notice on the application of the competition rules to access agreements in the telecommunications sector framework, relevant markets and principles, OJ 1998 C 265/2, para. 118.

[42] See European Commission, "Pricing Issues in Relation to Unbundled Access to the Local Loop" (2001) *ONPCOM*, p. 1–17.

[43] *Ibid.*, p. 5 (emphasis added).

[44] Case CW/00760/03/04, *Investigation against BT about potential anticompetitive exclusionary behaviour*, Ofcom Decision of July 12, 2004.

[45] See, e.g., CA98/20/2002, *BSkyB*, OFT Decision of December 17, 2002 (hereinafter "*BSkyB*"), para. 356 ("The Director considers that the correct test...should determine whether an undertaking as efficient in distributing as BSkyB can earn a normal profit when paying the wholesale prices charged by BSkyB to its distributors, and that this should be tested by reference to BSkyB's own costs of transformation."); Case CW/00760/03/04, *Investigation against BT about potential anticompetitive exclusionary behaviour*, Ofcom Decision of July 12, 2004; *Investigation by the Director General of Telecommunications into alleged anticompetitive practices by British Telecommunications plc in relation to BTOpenworld's consumer broadband products*, Ofcom Decision of November 20, 2003; and Case CW/00615/05/03, *Suspected margin squeeze by Vodafone, O2, Orange and T-Mobile*, Ofcom Decision of May 21, 2004. Margin squeeze allegations have also been rejected in several decisions by the UK competition authorities. See, e.g., CA98/19/2002, *The Association of British Travel Agents and British Airways plc* (2002) (reduction in travel agents' booking payments found not to give rise to a margin squeeze *vis-à-vis* British Airways' own on-line booking services); Case CP/1139-01, *Companies House* (2002) (no evidence of Companies House cross-subsidising its competing activities so as to allow it to engage in predatory pricing, or impose a margin squeeze on its competitors); *British Telecom/UK-SPN*, Oftel Decision of May 23, 2003 (margin squeeze rejected for loss-making new

The Discussion Paper also envisages certain exceptions to the general principle that exclusionary abuses can only be committed against firms that are at least as efficient as the dominant firm, i.e., the equally-efficient competitor test.[46] It states that, in some cases, reliable data on the dominant firm's costs may not be available, in which case it may be necessary to apply the as efficient competitor test using cost data of apparently efficient competitors (which presumably means the complainant or other firms active in the market). But it confirms that the dominant company can still rebut an inference of abuse by showing that it is not pricing below the appropriate cost benchmark. Finally, and more controversially, the Discussion Paper states that, in exceptional circumstances, it may be necessary to protect firms that *are* less efficient in the short-term but would become equally efficient over time (e.g., where the market exhibits significant economies of scale and scope, learning curve effects, or first mover advantages).

Notwithstanding the comments in the Discussion Paper, there are compelling reasons why reliance on a "reasonably efficient operator" test (or the "apparently efficient competitor" test) as the sole test for a margin squeeze would be wrong under competition law.[47] In the first place, the only margin squeeze test endorsed by the Community Courts is the dominant firm's costs. As the Court of First Instance held in *Industrie Poudres Sphériques*, if the dominant firm's downstream business could trade profitably based on the wholesale prices charged to rivals, "the fact that the [rival] cannot, seemingly because of its higher processing costs, remain competitive in the sale of the derived product cannot justify characterising [the dominant firm's] pricing policy as abusive."[48] Thus, under competition law, the important question is whether the rival is as efficient as the dominant company's downstream operations. If it is, and if the dominant company's operations are profitable, the rival should be able to be so. The fact, if it is a fact, that they are both unusually efficient, or that neither is efficient, is irrelevant for this purpose.

Second, a "reasonably efficient service provider" test is not capable of *ex ante* application by a dominant firm, i.e., at the time when it formulates its pricing policy.

telecommunications service on grounds, *inter alia*, that BT's predictions of future profits were not implausible); Case CA98/01/2004, *Albion Water/Dwr Cymru*, Ofwat Decision of May 26, 2004 (Dwr Cymru prices for water access found not to give rise to a margin squeeze); and Case CA 98/07/2004, *TM Property Services Limited/Transaction Online*, OFT Decision of August 18, 2004 (allegation of margin squeeze by Transaction Online in the market for property searches rejected).

46 Discussion Paper, para. 67.

47 A "reasonably efficient service provider" test might be valid in a regulatory context. Regulators might find it justified to promote the entry of relatively inefficient operators in the short term, in the expectation that they will become more efficient in the long run. However, this test makes little sense, on its own, from a competition policy perspective. Under competition law, a dominant firm is not required to price its products to maximize social welfare in the long run. Nor is it required to price artificially high in order to encourage (inefficient) entry into its market so as to increase the competitiveness of that market in the long run. The responsibility of the dominant firm is limited to competing on the merits. Competition on the merits is consistent with the exclusion of less efficient competitors, but is not compatible with the unlawful exclusion of equally efficient rivals. Using the dominant firm's costs as the basis for a margin squeeze test, while imperfect in some respects, is a test of competition on the merits and, therefore, the most relevant test from a competition policy perspective.

48 Case T-5/97, *Industrie des Poudres Sphériques SA v Commission* [2000] ECR II-3755, para. 179.

The lawfulness of its prices should not depend on its rivals' costs, which it cannot know, or on those of a hypothetical entrant. This would be contrary to the general principles of legal certainty and the rule of law: the law must provide a precise test or tests which a dominant company can use without the need for confidential information about its downstream competitors' costs, and before it adopts the pricing policy the lawfulness of which is under consideration.

Third, a test based on the dominant firm's costs takes into account any relevant advantages or disadvantages arising from its vertical integration. Using the dominant company's downstream profits automatically takes into account its competitive advantages, including any advantages due to vertical integration, and any disadvantages which its rivals may be under. Any other advantages or disadvantages suffered by either the dominant firm or its rivals are irrelevant under competition law.

Finally, a reasonably efficient competitor test might encourage dominant firms to try to obtain information on their rivals' costs or profits—which could be illegal and undesirable.

c. ***The relevant costs in a margin squeeze case.*** The correct imputation test in a margin squeeze case—a test based on the dominant firm's own costs and firms who are at least as efficient as the dominant firm—requires the identification of all product-specific costs that the dominant firm faces in the relevant downstream market, treating the cost of the input supplied by the dominant firm to rivals as given (and whether or not the dominant firm's own internal transfer price is actually lower or higher). This imputation test broadly assesses whether, given the dominant firm's total product-specific costs in the downstream market, it would remain profitable on the basis of the input price that it charges to rivals. If it would, a margin squeeze can be dismissed. If not, there is a suspicion of a margin squeeze and the emphasis then shifts to seeing whether there are non-exclusionary reasons for the notional (or actual) negative margins shown by the dominant firm's downstream business.

The definition and relevance of the different cost measures is discussed in detail in Chapter Five (Predatory Pricing) and will not be repeated here. But, as noted, the notion of average total cost is not well-defined under Article 82 EC. In particular, it is not clear how costs shared between two products (common costs) should be treated, i.e., whether they should be allocated in some manner. This problem has in practice largely been avoided under the margin squeeze decisional practice and case law, since it has, almost without exception, used incremental, or product-specific, cost measures.

The most commonly-applied cost benchmark is long-run incremental cost (LRIC), which includes all the product specific variable and fixed costs of the relevant activity, excluding any common or joint costs. The widespread use of LRIC is almost certainly a function of the fact that virtually all margin squeeze findings have been made in the context of the telecommunications sector in which the applicable legislation either stipulates the use of LRIC or regulators have routinely applied LRIC to take account of the low variable network costs.[49] This was essentially the approach applied by the

[49] See Discussion Paper, para. 126 (confirming that LRIC is the correct cost measure for recently-liberalised sectors and network industries).

Commission in *Deutsche Telekom.* But there is no reason in principle why other incremental cost measures, such as avoidable costs (variable costs plus any fixed costs that are not sunk (i.e., that could be avoided if the firm shut down the business)), could not also be used. All of these correspond to a concept of average total cost first used in *AKZO*,[50] though modified in the context of identifying the product-specific costs required in a margin squeeze case.

The Commission and national authorities have, however, used different accounting methodologies when assessing profitability. In *BSkyB*[51] and *Wanadoo*, the Office of Fair Trading and the Commission both relied on modified versions of *historic accounting costs* to examine the profitability of BSkyB and Wanadoo's consumer pay television and broadband services, respectively, i.e., a backward-looking assessment. In contrast, in *Freeserve*,[52] Oftel applied a dynamic, forward-looking assessment based on *discounted cash flow* (DCF). DCF analysis proceeds in two steps. First, future cash flows (i.e., revenues and costs) are forecast. Second, future net cash flows are discounted at the appropriately adjusted discount rate and added up to yield a single net present value (NPV) figure: if the NPV of a project is positive, then it is better to do the project than not to do it; if it is negative then it is better to do nothing than to undertake the project and stick with it to the end.

Neither the DCF nor the historical accounting approach is unambiguously right or wrong: each has benefits and drawbacks. Problems with the DCF approach include:[53] (1) it may show positive returns over time, but it does not distinguish between situations in which positive margins are due to legitimate pricing and situations in which the only reason for the profits is the exclusion of competitors;[54] (2) it only includes customers from a specific period and does not take into account the benefit beyond that period of the prospects of a growth in later periods; and (3) there are often accounting problems in that the information available may not allow a proper *ex post* reconstruction of anticipated revenue flows.[55] The main problem with the historical accounting approach is that there is significant scope for accounting distortions if each sub-period in a product's lifetime is expected to show a positive return. Distortions can result from the use of depreciation and amortisation techniques, which can vary significantly. The DCF approach does not look at individual periods in which there are losses, but looks at the overall profitability over the expected business lifetime. For this reason, the DCF approach is probably more suitable in new and emerging markets where profitability

---

[50] See *ECS/AKZO*, OJ 1985 L 374/1, upheld on appeal in Case C-62/86, *AKZO Chemie BV v Commission* [1991] ECR I-3359.

[51] See CA98/20/2002, *BSkyB*, OFT Decision of December 17, 2002.

[52] *Investigation by the Director General of Telecommunications into alleged anticompetitive practices by British Telecommunications plc in relation to BTOpenworld's consumer broadband products*, Ofcom Decision of November 20, 2003.

[53] See Case COMP/38.233, *Wanadoo Interactive*, Commission Decision of July 16, 2003, not yet published (hereinafter "*Wanadoo*"), paras. 91, 92, 96.

[54] See *BSkyB*, above, para. 384 ("A positive net present value could therefore be interpreted not as evidence of anticompetitive [abuse] but partly as evidence that the exercise of a[n] [abuse] is a viable strategy, as... losses incurred... are subsequently recovered.").

[55] *Wanadoo*, above, para. 96.

only occurs after time. The historic accounts approach is better suited to stable and mature markets.

d. ***The need to ensure that wholesale and retail services are comparable.*** It is inherent in a margin squeeze test that the dominant firm's wholesale and retail services are comparable. Otherwise, comparing wholesale prices with retail costs would be meaningless. An obvious example is where the dominant firm uses one type of network infrastructure, but its rivals uses a different input also supplied by the dominant firm. For example, in the telecommunications sector, if a dominant firm supplies both wholesale cable and copper wire access to rivals, it would make no sense in a margin squeeze analysis to look at whether the dominant firm's downstream cable-based business would make a profit if it had to pay the copper wire wholesale access charge paid by rivals. This does not compare like with like.

More complicated issues arose in *Deutsche Telekom.* The basic finding was that Deutsche Telekom's local loop wholesale access charges gave rise to a margin squeeze. To prove this, the Commission showed that Deutsche Telekom charged competitors more for unbundled broadband access at the wholesale level than it charged its subscribers for access at the retail level. The relevant wholesale and retail costs and revenues comprised: (1) the wholesale price for local loop access (which was regulated); (2) end-user prices charged by Deutsche Telekom; and (3) the incremental (or product specific) costs incurred by Deutsche Telekom in providing the service.

Issues (2) and (3) presented greater difficulties in comparing upstream costs and downstream revenues. Deutsche Telekom argued that the relevant end-user revenues should include both access revenues and revenue from telecommunications services, in particular telephone calls, and not merely access revenues from Internet access. This was based on the consideration that "the wholesale costs for the local loop are overheads both for the provision of retail access and for telephone calls, so that any attempt to allocate costs to individual services in order to investigate the possibility of below cost selling makes no sense and is consequently arbitrary."[56]

The Commission rejected this argument for essentially two reasons. First, the Commission stated that separate consideration of access charges and call charges is in fact required by secondary Community legislation on telecommunications regulation. For purposes of cost-oriented pricing, access to local network lines and the offer of different categories of call are considered separate services.[57] Second, the Commission asserted that, on "economic grounds," it was also reasonable and legitimate to apply the margin squeeze test by looking at Deutsche Telekom's revenue from access charges in isolation, and to exclude revenue from call traffic.[58] This was based on the consideration that the margin squeeze test seeks to compare charges for two particular services at different commercial levels and that comparison would be distorted if revenue from call traffic were to be included, because call services, which are additional to access services, cannot also be included in the calculation on the wholesale side.

---

[56] *Deutsche Telekom AG,* 2003 OJ L 263/9, para. 117.
[57] *Ibid.*, para. 120.
[58] *Ibid.*, para. 126.

The Commission's reasoning raises a number of important questions that form a large part of Deutsche Telekom's appeal. It is not obvious why the decision to treat access charges and call charges separately for purposes of regulation necessarily implies that the same treatment is merited under competition law. Separation of accounts or activities under regulation is based on very different considerations to the duties that apply to dominant firms under Article 82 EC. It could also be argued that it would in fact be more justified on "economic grounds" to treat total revenues from wholesale access—access revenue and calls—together, since this more accurately captures the economic reality of how competitors use access to the local loop, i.e., their full incremental revenue opportunities. Telecommunication service providers generally compete on bundles of access and individual call services, which is why other jurisdictions also include other revenue in a local loop margin squeeze analysis.[59]

Indeed, the Commission's underlying argument seems more bound up in policy than law. It stated that a margin squeeze analysis presumes that competitors can "at least replicate the established operator's customer pattern" and that the "primary consideration…is the effect on market entry by competitors, and not the question whether the end-user regards access services and calls as a single bundle of products."[60] The decision thus seemed more rooted in creating favourable entry conditions for rivals than whether Deutsche Telekom's pricing arrangements harmed equally-efficient competitors. The Commission did not consider for example: (1) whether Deutsche Telekom's competitors could duplicate Deutsche Telekom's mixture of access and call revenues; (2) the effects of Deutsche Telekom's pricing on those who had in fact done so; or (3) why, under Article 82 EC, ability to duplicate is even a relevant test.[61]

Condition #4: absence of legitimate business justification for the dominant firm's prices. The final basic condition for an illegal margin squeeze is that there is no objective justification or explanation for the dominant company making a loss downstream. There are many legitimate reasons why a company may set prices below its own costs for a period of time. These are discussed in detail in Chapter Five (Predatory Pricing), but, briefly, could include any of the following considerations: (1) market conditions may be temporarily bad but expected to improve; (2) the company may be setting low prices as a temporary marketing device; (3) it may have introduced a new product and currently have low volumes, but expects volumes to increase; (4) a competitor may be charging unsustainable prices but will probably leave the market or revise its policies; (5) the market may be in decline but some market participants are expected to exit; (6) the company may have made a mistake and entered the market on

[59] See e.g., *Verizon New Hampshire & Delaware Order 2002*, 17 FCC Rcd 18660 Rz 148.

[60] *Deutsche Telekom AG*, OJ 2003 L 263/9, para. 127.

[61] The underlying policy issue in the case seemed to be the Commission's desire to use Article 82 EC to correct the adverse effects of the failure by the German regulator to rebalance tariffs fully. Local loop access is required to be cost-oriented under secondary Community legislation on telecommunications. But former State monopoly telecoms providers have historically made losses on certain classes of calls and services and subsidised those losses with profits from other categories of services. If retail services are in some cases below cost, even wholesale prices that are cost-oriented will not allow rival firms to compete. This lack of tariff rebalancing has led the Commission to bring a number of infringement actions against Member States. In *Deutsche Telekom AG*, Germany had made some rebalancing, but the Commission's action suggests that this was insufficient and not fast enough.

too large a scale; (7) it may be inefficient but believes it may be able to improve its performance or its products, etc. An important question in practice concerns the treatment of margin squeezes in the case of new products and emerging markets. This is discussed in detail in Section 6.5 below.

6.4 THE RELATIONSHIP BETWEEN MARGIN SQUEEZE AND OTHER ABUSES

Overview. In broad terms, a margin squeeze could be said to arise where the dominant firm sets an "excessive" upstream price, a "predatory" downstream price, or cross subsidises downstream losses through upstream profits. Margin squeeze also involves what is, in effect, a refusal to deal. By dealing on terms that would render a downstream rival unprofitable, or by discriminating in the terms offered to associated and non-associated downstream companies, the dominant firm engages in a constructive refusal to deal. Excessive pricing, predatory pricing, cross-subsidies, and refusal to deal may constitute distinct violations of Article 82 EC. In these circumstances, it is important to consider to what extent margin squeeze is truly an independent ground of abuse and whether principles applied in the context of other abuses can usefully aid the analysis of a margin squeeze.

6.4.1 Margin Squeeze And Excessive Pricing

Definition of excessive pricing. Prices which are set significantly and persistently above the competitive level may be regarded as "excessive" and abusive under Article 82(a) and equivalent national laws.[62] Excessive pricing has in practice proved a notoriously difficult abuse to prosecute due to the problems in calculating a "fair" price and the Commission's publicly-stated reluctance to act as a price control authority.[63] The Community institutions have endorsed no single test to assess when a price is excessive.[64] A variety of different tests have been suggested, including: (1) a price/cost comparison; (2) a comparison of the dominant firm's price with prices in competitive markets; (3) the "economic value" of the product service; and (4) a price comparison in different geographic areas.

Comparison with margin squeeze. At first sight, margin squeeze cases involve upstream prices that are "excessive" for downstream operators. Indeed, in *Deutsche Telekom*, the Commission went as far as to suggest that margin squeeze abuses are an example of "imposing unfair selling prices" contrary to Article 82(a). The Commission stated as follows:[65]

> "The Commission concludes that DT is abusing its dominant position on the relevant markets for direct access to its fixed telephone network. Such abuse consists in charging unfair prices

---

[62] See Ch. 12 (Excessive Prices).

[63] See Vth Report on Competition Policy (1975), para. 76.

[64] EC Treaty Art. 82(a). See, e.g., Case 27/76, *United Brands Company and United Brands Continentaal BV v Commission* [1978] ECR 207; Case 26/75, *General Motors Continental NV v Commission*, [1975] ECR 1367. See also *Deutsche Post AG—Interception of cross-border mail*, OJ 2001 L 331/40.

[65] *Deutsche Telekom AG*, OJ 2003 L 263/9, para. 199.

for wholesale access services to competitors and retail access services in the local network, and is thus caught by Article 82(a) of the EC Treaty."

No specific reasons were advanced by the Commission for this conclusion. Moreover, it is not necessarily consistent with the Commission's earlier conclusion that margin squeeze is an independent ground of abuse.[66] The Commission's conclusion also overlooks a number of important differences between excessive pricing and margin squeeze. In the first place, their legal basis and normative content are different. An excessive price is an "exploitative" abuse within the meaning of Article 82(a), whereas a margin squeeze is an "exclusionary" abuse contrary to Article 82(b). Calling an upstream price that gives rise to a margin squeeze abuse "excessive" is likely to cause unnecessary confusion between exploitative and exclusionary abuses.

Second, the principal legal tests for identifying an excessive price under Article 82 EC are different to those for identifying a margin squeeze abuse. In assessing an exploitative excessive price, a commonly-applied benchmark is the firm's own costs of supplying the relevant product or service compared to similar products in the same market or other related markets. In a margin squeeze case, a price is not excessive in relation to the dominant firm's costs, but in relation to the relevant price and profit margin on a downstream market. An exploitative excessive price is abusive because of its relation to the relevant costs of supplying a single product, whereas an exclusionary margin squeeze is concerned with the excess of the price relative to prices on another related market. Put differently, excessive prices concern the *maximum legal price*, whereas a margin squeeze concerns the *minimum (non-exclusionary) profit.*

Finally, it is possible that an upstream price that is not excessive within the meaning of Article 82(a) could nonetheless give rise to a margin squeeze abuse under Article 82(b). The converse is also true: an upstream price that is excessive within the meaning of Article 82(a) may not give rise to a margin squeeze abuse under Article 82(b). Thus, if an upstream price is regarded as "unfair" and excessive, and so contrary to Article 82(a), merely because of its exclusionary effect in the downstream market, including Article 82(a) in the analysis does not appear to add anything useful. In sum, the legal basis for a margin squeeze abuse cannot be exploitative excessive pricing under Article 82(a).

6.4.2 Margin Squeeze And "Pure" Predatory Pricing

Similarities. The basic conditions for a margin squeeze bear the closest resemblance to a "pure" predation case, i.e., predatory pricing in the context of a single market against horizontal competitors.[67] Although margin squeeze has been recognised as a distinct abuse under Article 82 EC, many of the principles relevant to the analysis of "pure" predation can inform the analysis of margin squeeze abuses. These include the need for

[66] *Ibid.*, para. 105 ("Contrary to DT's view, however, the margin squeeze is a form of abuse that is relevant to this case. On related markets on which competitors buy wholesale services from the established operator, and depend on the established operator in order to compete on a downstream product or service market, there can very well be a margin squeeze between regulated wholesale and retail prices.").

[67] See Ch. 5 (Predatory Pricing).

a credible strategy of predation, evidence of exclusionary intent, issues of recoupment, and adverse effects on consumers.

The first and most obvious similarity between a margin squeeze and a pure predation case concerns the applicable legal test. Margin squeezes could be said to arise in three different ways: (1) where the downstream price is unduly low relative to the upstream price; (2) where the upstream price is too high relative to the downstream price; and (3) where the combination of upstream and downstream prices leaves insufficient margin for rivals. In fact, these amount to the same thing and have therefore been subsumed under a single legal test: whether the dominant firm's own downstream business would be profitable if it had to pay the same actual input prices as third parties. This test is, in effect, a test of downstream predatory pricing in the context of vertical integration.

A second similarity is that both a margin squeeze and "pure" predatory pricing require that a firm has market power sufficient to engage in successful exclusion. A third is that both abuses require consideration of whether the conduct at issue is commercially rational or is only rational because of its ability to exclude rivals. Finally, both abuses require that the conduct in question is likely to have an exclusionary effect on competitors; in particular whether the exit of rivals would allow profitable exploitation of market power in future.

Differences. At the same time, there are a number of differences between a margin squeeze and a "pure" predatory pricing case. First, in a predation case the competition authority looks at all the relevant costs of the dominant company. In a margin squeeze case, it looks only at the costs in the downstream market, including the upstream price (taking it as a given on the downstream market (unless there is actual discrimination against rivals)).

Second, in a margin squeeze case the dominant company is not necessarily losing money overall (though it may be). It might be merely taking its profit upstream rather than downstream: the business engaged in a margin squeeze can be profitable on an "end-to-end" (i.e., integrated) basis throughout the period of abuse. It follows that in a margin squeeze case the question of future recoupment does not necessarily arise as it often does in predation cases. Or, more precisely, the fact that, in a margin squeeze case, the dominant firm remains profitable upstream can make recoupment more or less simultaneous. In a pure predation case, the loss-making and recoupment phases necessarily involve two different time periods.

But it is wrong to claim that predation is different to margin squeeze because the former involves necessarily a profit sacrifice while the latter does not. It is true that a margin squeeze does not imply a direct loss on each unit sold as in the case of predation. However, there is an *opportunity cost* on each unit not sold to the downstream competitor. The level of this cost may be very large when the wholesale price is above upstream marginal costs, the downstream competitor sells differentiated products, and/or downstream firms are more efficient producers than the dominant firm. By raising the input price, the dominant firm effectively reduces the size of the downstream market and therefore sell less upstream output.

Third, the incentives to engage in exclusionary behaviour differ as between margin squeeze and predation cases. In predation cases there is usually no need to consider whether or not the alleged predator would benefit from successfully excluding rivals—it always will, to some extent. In contrast, in a margin squeeze case, a vertically integrated company may have reduced incentives to exclude rivals from a downstream market, since the competitor will also be an upstream customer. A vertically integrated dominant company might lose more by losing upstream customers than it could gain as a result of their withdrawal from the downstream market. The analytical tests for a margin squeeze should therefore include an analysis of whether market conditions are such that a company has any incentive to exclude. Without such incentives, any failure to pass a price-cost test is more likely to be the result of a reasonable and temporary business strategy than a deliberate attempt to exclude.

Fourth, a margin squeeze does not necessarily benefit consumers, whereas a predatory price does, at least in the short-term. In a pure predation case the dominant company is deliberately sacrificing short-term profits, for long-term exclusionary reasons. In a margin squeeze it is not necessarily sacrificing short-term profits, although, in practice, the prices which are most effective at excluding rivals will be downstream prices which do not maximise short run profits (in which case consumers also benefit in the short-term).

Finally, the scope of the available remedies may differ as between a margin squeeze and pure predation case. In a pure predation case, the remedy is usually to increase the (loss-making) price. In a margin squeeze case, the dominant firm could be required to lower the input price, increase the retail price, or slightly adjust, either upwards or downwards, the upstream and retail prices.

6.4.3 Margin Squeeze And Cross Subsidies

Cross-subsidy analysis adds nothing to margin squeeze. Margin squeeze abuses may also involve elements of cross-subsidy, i.e., the use of funds generated from one area of activity to fund activities in another area of its activity. Specifically, vertical integration may allow a firm to subsidise losses in a downstream market by taking the profit at the level of the sale of the upstream input. In these circumstances, the issue arises whether a margin squeeze should more accurately be characterised as an abusive cross-subsidy.[68]

It is difficult to see, however, what a cross-subsidy analysis would add to the substantive inquiry for a margin squeeze abuse. Clearly, there are situations in which the source of funding for downstream losses is a profitable upstream (dominant) market, but the competition law effects of conduct are likely to be the same whether the funds concerned come from the upstream market, another totally unrelated market, or from capital market sources. Applying a cross-subsidy analysis would therefore simply have the effect of requiring a competition authority or plaintiff to show that the source of the funds to support the downstream losses is the profitable upstream market (i.e., a causal connection), in addition to having to satisfy all the other conditions for a margin squeeze. This condition would, however, have the benefit of requiring precision in the

[68] See *Deutsche Post AG*, OJ 2001 L 125/27. Cross-subsidies are treated in detail in Ch. 5 (Predatory Pricing).

identification of the method by which a margin squeeze could be carried out, which would be desirable.

6.4.4 Margin Squeeze And Refusal To Deal Under Article 82 EC

No duty to deal implies no duty to deal at a minimum price? A fundamental question concerning a margin squeeze abuse is what relationship, if any, it has with the principle that there is no general duty to deal under Article 82 EC.[69] The principles underlying a margin squeeze abuse require a dominant firm to deal on certain minimum terms with downstream rivals. But a preliminary question arises whether a margin squeeze can be illegal only if exclusionary behaviour monopolising the downstream activities would be contrary to Article 82 EC (or equivalent provisions of national law). Thus, it is argued that, if there is no general duty to deal under competition law, a dominant firm cannot be criticised for dealing on exclusionary terms, i.e., terms that would render non-integrated rivals unprofitable on a downstream market.[70] Saying that a firm has refused to deal or will only deal on unattractive terms are undistinguishable.

The relationship between essential facilities principles and margin squeeze abuses raises complex issues that go to the heart of the efficiency objectives of competition law and policy. The issue is rendered more difficult by the fact that the status of the essential facilities doctrine is not clear, either under U.S. antitrust law[71]—where the doctrine was first developed—or under Article 82 EC.[72] Case law that has considered the issue is unsatisfactory. In *BSkyB* the OFT appeared to suggest that there could be a margin squeeze even if there was no duty to contract,[73] but still concluded that there were insufficient grounds for a finding of abuse. The OFT's conclusion appears to have been based on a distinction made in the case law between the duties to deal with new customers (i.e., essential facilities) and existing customers (i.e., voluntary dealing).

Article 82 EC case law could be read as suggesting that a dominant firm's duties in respect of third parties with whom it is already dealing are stricter than those in

---

[69] See Ch. 8 (Refusal to Deal).

[70] See, e.g., PE Areeda & H Hovenkamp, *Antitrust Law*, IIIA (2nd edn., New York, Aspen Publishers, 2002) para. 767c5 ("It makes no sense to prohibit a predatory price squeeze in circumstances where the integrated monopolist is free to refuse to deal."). This quote was cited with approval in *Covad Communications Company v Bell Atlantic Corporation,* 398 F.3d 666, 365 U.S.App.D.C. 78, 2005.

[71] In *Trinko*, the U.S. Supreme Court cast serious doubt on future reliance on the "essential facilities" doctrine by stating that it had only been applied by lower courts and had never been recognised by the Supreme Court itself. The Court also cited, with approval, a seminal article strongly criticising the general application of the doctrine. See P Areeda, "Essential Facilities: An Epithet in Need of Limiting Principles" (1989) 58 *Antitrust Law Journal* 841, cited in *Verizon Communications Inc v Law Offices of Curtis V. Trinko LLP,* 540 U.S., 2, 682, (2004).

[72] The recent Court of Justice judgment in Case C-418/01, *IMS Health GmbH & Co OHG v NDC Health GmbH & Co KG* [2004] ECR I-5039, while recognising the existence of an exceptional duty to deal, left open a number of important interpretative issues regarding its application (e.g., the degree to which the requesting party's product needs to be new in order to justify such a duty, the nature of vertical integration in essential facilities cases, and whether customer preferences are relevant in assessing the "indispensability" of an input).

[73] See CA98/20/2002, *BSkyB*, OFT Decision of December 17, 2002, paras. 352–53.

situations in which it has never previously supplied a third party. Even if such a distinction were valid—which is doubtful[74]—it offers an unsatisfactory explanation of why there can be a duty to deal on certain terms under margin squeeze principles absent a general duty to supply. A prior course of dealings may offer a useful indication that an obligation to deal is reasonable and workable, assuming that the other strict conditions for a duty to deal are satisfied. But this does not answer the fundamental question of why there can be a duty, under a margin squeeze abuse, to deal on specific terms unless there is also a basic obligation to deal in the first place. The fact that the dominant firm is already dealing with a third party is more likely to reflect happenstance and does not provide a satisfactory basis for saying that stricter legal duties apply. In these circumstances, there are strong reasons to suggest that a margin squeeze can only be illegal if there is a duty to supply the input in question.[75]

Need to consider potential adverse effects of a duty to deal in margin squeeze analysis. Whatever the merits of the above arguments, margin squeeze abuses under Article 82 EC should at least take account of the well-known potential pitfalls of applying a duty to deal. The key considerations are that: (1) adding more competitors does not necessarily improve competition, in particular if two or more firms simply share the previous monopoly profits;[76] (2) there must be scope for meaningful added-value competition on the downstream market before a duty to deal (or to deal on

[74] See Ch. 8 (Refusal to Deal).

[75] This does not, however, necessarily mean that a vertically integrated dominant firm's prices cannot be abusive unless the input in question is an essential facility. The upstream price may be "excessive" under Article 82(a). As noted above, there is no necessary connection between margin squeeze abuses and excessive pricing. An excessive price under Article 82(a) may not lead to a margin squeeze abuse under Article 82(b). Likewise, a margin squeeze may also be made out even in circumstances where the upstream price would not be excessive within the meaning of Article 82(a). In these circumstances, there is some merit to limiting the principles under Article 82(a) to situations in which the dominant firm is not in competition with downstream customers and only applies the principles of margin squeeze abuses to pricing arrangements where the dominant firm competes with non-associated companies downstream. In the former case, the issue is exploitation; in the latter case, it is exclusion. The dominant firm may also be discriminating between rivals and its own downstream business, in contrast to the implied (or hidden) discrimination in a margin squeeze. This issue is discussed in detail in Section 6.5 below.

[76] See J Temple Lang, "The Principle of Essential Facilities in European Community Competition Law—The Position Since *Bronner*" (2000) 1 *Journal of Network Industries* 375, 379–80. See also P Areeda, "Essential Facilities: An Epithet in Need of Limiting Principles" (1989) 58 *Antitrust Law Journal* 852 ("No one should be forced to deal unless doing so is likely substantially to improve competition in the marketplace by reducing price or by increasing output or innovation. Such an improvement is unlikely…when the plaintiff merely substitutes itself for the monopolist or shares the monopolist's gains."). The need to balance *ex ante* effects on investment incentives and *ex post* benefits to competition of forced sharing was made clear recently in Case COMP/C-3/37.792, *Microsoft*, Decision of March 21, 2004), not yet published, para. 783 ("[A] detailed examination of the scope of the disclosure at stake leads to the conclusion that, on balance, the possible negative impact of an order to supply on Microsoft's incentives to innovate its outweighed by its positive impact on the level of innovation of the whole industry (including Microsoft). As such the need to protect Microsoft's incentives to innovate cannot constitute an objective justification that would offset the exceptional circumstances identified."). It seems unlikely in practice, however, that such trade-offs can be accurately made.

specific terms) can be imposed;[77] and (3) any duty to deal should encourage more competition than it discourages, i.e., the *ex post* benefits of a duty to deal to consumers must outweigh any harm to firms' *ex ante* incentives to develop products.[78] In view of the complexity of margin squeeze cases, there is also some pragmatic appeal to limiting them to situations akin to essential facilities, i.e., where the dominant firm has a "genuine stranglehold" on the market.[79] Otherwise, the risks of falsely imputing a margin squeeze where none exists, or where it would be inefficient to find one, are relatively high.

6.5 DIFFICULTIES WITH IDENTIFYING AN ANTICOMPETITIVE MARGIN SQUEEZE IN PRACTICE

Overview. The basic theory of margin squeeze has an obvious, intuitive appeal: a dominant firm that supplies an essential upstream input to non-integrated downstream rivals may have scope for applying an upstream price, downstream price, or combination of upstream and downstream prices that render rivals' activities uneconomic. In practice, however, margin squeeze cases can raise a number of significant difficulties. A first difficulty is that, in contrast to a number of other exclusionary abuses, a vertically integrated firm may have no incentive to exclude downstream rivals that are also upstream customers. A second difficulty is that strict application of the margin squeeze test could lead to inefficient outcomes by preventing a dominant firm from offering a rational, non-exclusionary combination of prices. The third difficulty is that the basic theory of margin squeeze assumes that all downstream firms offer similar products. Where products are differentiated, significant problems can arise in accurately identifying a margin squeeze. A fourth problem is that the basic theory of margin squeeze works best in mature, stable markets. In the case of new, dynamic markets, a margin squeeze test is not easily applied and may run the risk of hindering legitimate market growth. Finally, there are difficulties in identifying anticompetitive effects in a margin squeeze case, in particular whether the mere failure to pass a price/cost imputation test should automatically lead to an abuse or whether a more detailed factual inquiry is necessary. Each of these issues is addressed in detail below, but they all confirm a fundamental point: it should not be inferred from the mere

[77] See G Werden, "The Law and Economics of the Essential Facility Doctrine" 32 *Saint Louis University Law Journal* 462–63 (1987).

[78] Opinion of Advocate General Jacobs in Case C-7/97, *Oscar Bronner GmbH & Co. KG*v *Mediaprint Zeitungs-und Zeitschriftenverlag GmbH & Co. KG and others* [1998] ECR I-7791 (hereinafter "*Bronner*"), para. 57 ("[T]he justification in terms of competition policy for interfering with a dominant undertaking's freedom to contract often requires a careful balancing of conflicting considerations. In the long term it is generally pro-competitive and in the interest of consumers to allow a company to retain for its own use facilities which it has developed for the purpose of its business. For example, if access to a production, purchasing or distribution facility were allowed too easily there would be no incentive for a competitor to develop competing facilities. Thus while competition was increased in the short term it would be reduced in the long term. Moreover, the incentive for a dominant undertaking to invest in efficient facilities would be reduced if its competitors were, upon request, able to share the benefits. Thus the mere fact that by retaining a facility for its own use a dominant undertaking retains an advantage over a competitor cannot justify requiring access to it.").

[79] *Bronner*, *ibid.*, para. 64.

fact that a dominant firm fails a price/cost test in a margin squeeze case that an abuse has been proven.

Incentives for a vertically integrated dominant firm to exclude downstream customers. An unusual feature of a margin squeeze is that the downstream rival is at the same time a customer of the dominant firm upstream. Thus, by excluding a downstream rival, the dominant firm also reduces its upstream profits because it loses a customer. This dynamic can have substantial effects on the incentives for such conduct and may in fact amount to a disincentive to engage in a margin squeeze in the first place. While the reduced incentives for a dominant firm to engage in a margin squeeze do not mean that such abuses are necessarily irrational, a good case can be made for saying that, as in the case of predatory pricing, a plaintiff or competition authority should be required to adduce some evidence that a margin squeeze is a plausible exclusionary strategy for a dominant firm.

Whether a dominant firm has any rational incentive to engage in a margin squeeze against downstream rivals is largely an empirical question. The issue is whether the reduction in demand for the dominant firm's products upstream is off-set by additional volumes downstream that are sufficiently profitable to compensate for lost revenue upstream. The short answer is that, in general, the higher the upstream margin relative to downstream profits, the greater the disincentive to engage in a margin squeeze against downstream rivals. Much will depend, therefore, on (1) the marginal profitability of the upstream and downstream markets (if the upstream market is more profitable relative to the downstream market, the incentives to exclude downstream rivals are less); (2) the extent to which the dominant firm can capture customers lost by the exiting firm (if rivals who remain on the downstream market can also capture them, there is less incentive to exclude); (3) whether downstream rivals offer differentiated or homogenous products (if they offer differentiated products, the dominant firm's incentive to exclude them may be even less (see below)); (4) whether rivals are more efficient downstream competitors than the dominant firm (if they are, it may be more efficient for the dominant firm to close its own downstream business and sell the upstream product to such firms), etc.

The effect of a strict margin squeeze rule on efficient vertical integration. A more fundamental issue raised by a dominant firm's duty not to engage in a margin squeeze abuse against downstream rivals concerns the effect of such a duty on efficient pricing. A margin squeeze requires a vertically integrated firm to set input and final product prices at a level at which a non-integrated rival can make an adequate profit. Unless the dominant firm is actually discriminating between the prices charged to its downstream business and rivals, the duty not to margin squeeze effectively requires the dominant firm to create a single price at which non-integrated downstream rivals can survive. This duty applies even if the dominant firm is not actually losing money overall.

In many cases, the dominant firm may be required to offer third parties a combination of prices that are not efficient in the context of its own vertical integration. To see this, consider the following example: The dominant firm incurs fixed costs of €4 to produce the input needed for the production of two goods A and B. Retail costs equal €1 for each of the product. There is one consumer willing to pay €5 for good A and one consumer willing to pay €2 for good B. A vertically integrated monopolist maximises total surplus by selling good A at price of €5 and good B at a price €2, leaving a profit of €1. If the vertically integrated firm was forced to supply the input on a non-discriminatory basis, the only feasible wholesale price that would pass a margin squeeze test is €4. At this price, both the upstream unit and a downstream retail firm (selling product A at a price of €5) have a viable position and can cover their costs. However, the market for product B is not served and the total surplus is zero. The efficient outcome where both consumers are served is not attainable, as it would require a wholesale price not higher than €1. But at this price, the upstream unit cannot cover the fixed costs. Thus, the strict application of a margin test in this context leads to an inefficient outcome.

The qualitative reasons for this perverse result of a margin squeeze test may be summarised as follows:[80]

> "The presence of fixed costs in the upstream market and different consumer preferences (i.e., elasticities) over the final products can lead to different (yet efficient) prices in the retail market for products even though they have similar end to end costs. However, a requirement that competitors should be able to purchase the input at a price that allows them to compete in the retail market (i.e., a price squeeze test) in conjunction with similar retail costs does not allow the products to have different prices. This raises the price for the cheaper product and hence reduces its demand. As a result this product contributes less to the common cost, which implies that the other product has to contribute more, raising prices even further. That is, the application of a price squeeze test has had pernicious effects on the market."

That a strict margin squeeze principle may lead to questionable outcomes is illustrated by *Genzyme*.[81] Genzyme was found to have committed an abuse by supplying a package comprising its near-monopoly medicine (Cerezyme) and a service for home administration of that drug at the same price as it charged stand-alone providers of home administration services for the drug. Genzyme sold the dominant Cerezyme drug to the National Health Service (NHS) at £2.975 per unit, a price that included the provision of the separate service for the homecare administration of the drug. Genzyme's price to its own subsidiary was lower, at £2.50 per unit, giving it a margin of £0.475 on each sale. In contrast, Genzyme charged downstream rivals who needed access to Cerezyme to provide homecare services the same retail price as it charged the NHS. Because rivals had to supply the additional homecare services at their own expense, they would have made a loss on their sales to the NHS. As NHS got both the drug and the service for £2.975, and rivals would have to charge more if they supplied both, the NHS never bought from rivals. Both the OFT and Competition Appeal Tribunal (CAT) found that Genzyme's prices gave rise to a margin squeeze.

It is difficult to see, however, how forcing Genzyme to reduce the price at which it supplied Cerezyme to third parties active only in Cerezyme home delivery services would have enhanced competition. First, the extent to which there was scope for meaningful added-value competition in the relevant downstream market was limited. The key input was the Cerezyme product and this accounted for the vast proportion of the packaged price to the NHS. The value-added aspect of the home delivery service

---

[80] See P Grout, "Defining a Price Squeeze in Competition Law" in *The Pros and Cons of Low Prices* (Stockholm, Swedish Competition Authority, 2003), p. 81.

[81] *Genzyme v Office of Fair Trading* [2004] CAT 4 (hereinafter "*Genzyme*").

seemed minimal in the overall context: home delivery of Cerezyme was a "market" that was effectively created by Genzyme's discovery of Cerezyme.

Second, the upshot of the case seemed to be that Genzyme was forced to maintain the profit margins of a less efficient stand-alone provider on the downstream market. It is not even clear that the proposed remedy would have been effective in this regard. One obvious strategy for Genzyme would have been to withdraw from the downstream market altogether and continue to charge different prices to the NHS and home delivery service providers.[82]

Finally, the effect of a duty to deal on Genzyme's incentives to invest in future medicines was most likely adverse. Genzyme had developed Cerezyme at considerable expense as an "orphan drug," i.e., a medicine that treats rare, but generally fatal, diseases affecting a tiny proportion of the population. Orphan drugs benefit from a unique set of extended patent protection laws under Community legislation since, otherwise, no rational firm would invest in research and development of medicines with such a small consumer base. Requiring Genzyme to deal with non-integrated third parties on specified terms weakened Genzyme's (already weak) incentives to invest in the research and development of orphan drugs.

Applying a margin squeeze test in a manner that produces inefficient outcomes on a downstream market (i.e., higher prices, lower output, and sub-optimal common fixed-cost recovery) runs contrary to the basic tenet that competitors should only be protected to the extent that it enhances consumer welfare.[83] While subsidising inefficient entry in the short-term on the basis that the entrant would become more efficient over time may be a legitimate objective under regulatory policy, no such general mandate exists under competition law.

Margin squeezes in the case of differentiated products. Another situation in which the application of the traditional margin squeeze test based on the dominant firm's costs can lead to incorrect outcomes concerns differentiated products, i.e., where downstream rivals offer products that are differentiated in terms of quality or characteristics to the dominant firm's. In this circumstance, downstream rivals' margins may be very different to the dominant firm's, since they will face a different demand curve. Where third parties' products are differentiated, they may make adequate profits even in circumstances where the dominant firm's downstream business would make a loss if it had to pay the same input prices as it charges to third parties. Thus, the intuition behind the imputation test based on the dominant firm's costs—that they are a reasonable proxy for those of efficient rivals—may be incorrect in many cases. It only tests whether a firm supplying an identical product would be profitable or not.

---

[82] The non-discrimination clause in Article 82(c) would arguably not have applied in this instance, since the NHS and home providers were not in competition with one another.

[83] In Case C-7/97, *Oscar Bronner GmbH & Co. KG*v *Mediaprint Zeitungs-und Zeitschriftenverlag GmbH & Co. KG and others* [1998] ECR I-7791, Advocate General Jacobs confirmed the above when he stated that "the primary purpose of Article 8[2] is to prevent distortion of competition—and in particular to safeguard the interests of consumers—rather than to protect the position of particular competitors.") (para. 58).

Another reason why it may not make sense to look only at the dominant firm's cost is that the basic theory of margin squeeze relies on a simple, linear vertical chain of production, i.e., a single, clearly-identifiable upstream product and a single, clearly-defined downstream product in which the upstream product is a high, fixed proportion of total costs. In many instances, there may not be a simple linear pass through of this kind. For example, downstream rivals may have the option of using a range of different wholesale or intermediate inputs in combination in order to give them a lower overall cost than the dominant firm (who may suffer from technical, regulatory, or legacy constraints that prevent it from using some or all of the same inputs). This applies for example in the telecommunications sector where options such as local-loop unbundling, cable, mobile technologies (e.g., WiFi and WiMax), and voice over Internet Protocol may offer new entrants lower-cost technical solutions. In markets where there is no simple linear chain of production, a margin squeeze test based only on the cost structure of the dominant firm may therefore give a misleading picture of rivals' actual costs and their competitive constraints.

Applying a margin squeeze test based only on the dominant firm's costs may, therefore, result in wrongly imputing a margin squeeze in certain instances. This applies, in particular, where rivals face less elastic demand for differentiated products, have different cost structures, or have additional revenue streams that the dominant firm does not. In such cases, a margin squeeze could be wrongly found in circumstances where the dominant firm's conduct had no exclusionary effect. A good case can therefore be made for saying that a competition authority or court should, in order to find a margin squeeze, look at *both* the dominant firm's costs and those of rivals. In other words, a margin squeeze could only be shown if both tests were satisfied.[84] This is not a general endorsement of a test based on rivals' costs, but a recognition of the fact that a margin squeeze can only be said to occur with any reasonable certainty if the dominant firm's prices are not only below its own costs (treating the upstream price to third parties as a "given" for its downstream business), but also below third parties' actual costs.

Another reason for insisting on the identification of a plausible margin squeeze theory in a specific market setting is that downstream rivals lack of profitability may have nothing to do with the dominant firm's pricing. This was the case in *National Carbonising*.[85] There, the Commission ultimately concluded that there was no margin squeeze, since for both companies, industrial coke was profitable and domestic coke was not (due to competition from gas and electricity). In periods of reduced industrial activity, neither company could shut down their coke plants (a coke plant cannot be shut

[84] See P Grout, "Defining a Price Squeeze in Competition Law" in *The Pros and Cons of Low Prices* (Stockholm, Swedish Competition Authority, 2003), p. 85. The two-fold test outlined above is more likely to be effective in the context of administrative action than litigation, since details of rivals' costs may be treated as "business secrets" that should not be disclosed to the dominant firm. In the context of litigation, the same safeguards do not generally apply. Disclosing detailed cost information to a dominant upstream input supplier will usually be unattractive for a plaintiff, although it could be argued that a similar problem arises for a dominant defendant accused of a margin squeeze. Certain jurisdictions do, however, provide for the deletion of business secrets in public versions of judgments (e.g., the Competition Appeal Tribunal in the United Kingdom).

[85] See *National Coal Board, National Smokeless Fuels Limited and the National Carbonising Company Limited,* OJ 1976 L 35/6.

down), but the dominant company sold a higher proportion of industrial coke than the complainant, because it had more long-term industrial-coke supply contracts. It was true that the dominant company, because of its position, was better placed than the complainant to make long term industrial contracts with bulk buyers, but this was not an advantage which could be complained of under competition law. The fact that this was a marketing advantage and not a cost advantage did not alter this conclusion. It was not suggested that the dominant company had a duty to compensate rivals for this advantage. In short, the apparent squeeze was not *caused* by the dominant firm: it was simply a function of the inherent characteristics of the downstream market.

Margin squeeze abuses and new products and emerging markets. Several recent margin squeeze cases have arisen in the context of new products and markets (e.g., broadband Internet access). Identifying abusive conduct in such markets presents significant difficulties in practice. Competition authorities face a significant policy issue in deciding whether to intervene at an early stage—and risk hampering the development of important new markets—or waiting until the market develops, by which time intervention, if required, may be ineffective. Other specific difficulties also arise. In the first place, the practical complexities raised by margin squeeze abuses in mature markets (e.g., incentives, product differentiation, efficient vertical integration etc.) are more pronounced in markets that are not in a steady state.[86] It is notable that, until *Deutsche Telekom*, all margin squeeze cases under Article 82 EC concerned simple raw materials in mature markets.

Second, start-up losses are common in the case of markets in which dynamic efficiencies can be achieved over time. Markets with these characteristics usually require large, up-front risky investments and involve start-up losses in order to increase consumer uptake and thereby acquire the scale or experience needed to reduce costs over time. These markets are not only more likely than other markets to exhibit below-cost pricing for a period, but are also more likely to exhibit non-exclusionary reasons for doing so.[87] Efficiencies can lead to the recovery of initial losses by creating cost savings over time, as a company achieves more efficient scale, greater learning experience, or some other efficiency capable of reducing costs. Examples of legitimate means of reducing costs over time include economies of scale, market education, and learning by doing.[88]

Finally, assessing whether, in fact, the dominant firm is pricing below cost in the case of inevitable start-up losses requires certain adjustments for cost amortisation over the lifetime of the relevant business plan and asset and use depreciation. If costs were only assessed at the initial stage, they could suggest loss-making whereas, over time, the

---

[86] The OFT noted this problem in CA98/20/2002, *BSkyB*, OFT Decision of December 17, 2002, para. 344 ("The practical application of a test for margin squeeze may be complex. Precedents have not related to multi-product, high technology, expanding distribution businesses with different revenues and costs that are not in a steady state.").

[87] See Case COMP/38.233, *Wanadoo Interactive*, Commission Decision of July 16, 2003, not yet published, paras. 260–61 (Commission made allowance for features of launching a new product) and para. 264 (recognition that a more "nuanced" approach to prices below average variable cost is needed in growing markets).

[88] See Ch. 5 (Predatory Pricing).

product may in fact be profitable, or less loss-making than originally thought. Amortisation decisions also raise complexities in practice. These issues are discussed in detail in Chapter Five (Predatory Pricing).

a. Difficulties in formulating a legal test to distinguish legitimate losses in new markets from margin squeeze. Even if the dominant firm could be said to be selling at a loss for a certain period, or pricing at a level at which equally-efficient rivals would not be profitable, NCAs, NRAs, and courts must still devise useful legal tests for distinguishing legitimate start-up losses from those based on exclusionary considerations. This raises some of the most complex issues in margin squeeze cases. The Commission, NCAs, and NRAs accept in principle that there may be a legitimate (i.e., non-exclusionary) justification for setting initial low prices, including by a dominant firm.[89] At the same time, they have struggled to devise useful legal rules that distinguish situations of legitimate pricing from those involving unlawful pricing. This stems in part from evidential problems in that, often, the only evidence of the rationale for start-up losses is the company's business plan. Unless the business plan contains express evidence of anticompetitive purpose, there are practical problems in inferring such purpose from an assessment of the reasonableness or plausibility of the plan. The more important reason, however, is that, in growing dynamic markets, it is very difficult to say with confidence whether assumptions about the level of competition reflect exclusionary behaviour or merely depend on reasonable assumptions about the evolution of the market.[90]

Another problem is that theories of anticompetitive harm (or lack thereof) based on future market conditions are by nature speculative. There is significant scope for divergence between business plans and actual market outcomes. Businesses may fail or may apply overly-conservative or optimistic assessments or may simply get it wrong. The more risky the investment, the greater the scope for failure and, therefore, for assumptions in business plans that, *ex post*, turn out to be wrong. The decision to enter a particular market or to introduce a new pricing strategy is itself based on *ex ante* forecasts and takes place in a world of uncertainty. A business plan therefore represents, at best, a reasonable assessment by the company concerned of its options at a given time based on the available information. In any given scenario, companies may choose a range of different options *ex ante*, without any one of these options being unreasonable or implausible. Companies would often have chosen a different option *ex post*.

b. Possible solutions. A number of different approaches have been applied to attempt to resolve the difficulties of applying a margin squeeze test in new markets.

[89] See, e.g., Case COMP/38.233, *Wanadoo Interactive*, Commission Decision of July 16, 2003, not yet published; and *Investigation by the Director General of Telecommunications into alleged anticompetitive practices by British Telecommunications plc in relation to BTOpenworld's consumer broadband products*, November 20, 2003.

[90] As Professor Baumol notes, there is "no generally effective way" of determining whether a pricing decision is a legitimate business practice or an unlawful one. This is effectively impossible if the issue is said to turn on the probabilities of forecasts of future profits in a developing market. See W Baumol, "Principles Relevant to Predatory Pricing" in *The Pros and Cons of Low Prices* (Stockholm, Swedish Competition Authority, 2003), p. 25.

The first approach, applied in a case involving British Telecom (BT),[91] involves an assessment of the reasonableness of the dominant firm's forecasts of future profits. BT was active in the supply of retail broadband Internet access at a wholesale level and in the supply of services in the downstream retail market. Because of high start-up costs (e.g., advertising and other customer acquisition costs), BT's business plan forecast losses at the retail level for a certain period, followed by future profits as customer volumes increased and customer acquisition costs reduced. BT's rivals adopted similar strategies, but they also complained that the combination of BT's wholesale input and retail prices prevented them from earning a positive margin, i.e., a margin squeeze.

In rejecting the complaint,[92] Oftel applied a two-stage test to assess whether BT had committed a margin squeeze. First, it assessed whether BT's business case was net present value (NPV) positive—a standard technique used for measuring the profitability of investment decisions—over a core period of five years. Following certain adjustments made by Oftel to BT's business plan, Oftel found that BT's downstream business would have been profitable over this period. As a second stage, Oftel tried to correct an inherent defect in the NPV test—that it does not distinguish situations in which positive NPVs result from anticompetitive behaviour from those in which they result from legitimate competition. In an attempt to distinguish between the two situations, Oftel tested the robustness of the positive NPV results against assumptions about that which would have been "reasonable" for BT to expect in a competitive market.[93] Although Oftel disagreed to some extent with the assumptions in BT's business plan about future margins, its analysis showed a majority of positive NPVs overall. In this circumstance, and given that BT's retail prices were in any event higher than its competitors, Oftel found that the margin squeeze allegation was not sufficiently proven.

A test based on the "reasonableness" of the dominant firm's business plan raises difficulties. When a dominant firm formulates a business plan *ex ante* that forecasts profits at some future stage based on legitimate considerations (e.g., cost reductions), it cannot be right that a competition authority or court can later apply different, "reasonable" assumptions to invalidate the assumptions originally made by the dominant firm. The situation is no different if the assumptions made by the dominant firm later turn out to be wrong. If not, an abuse could be found based on a mere difference of opinion between a defendant and a competition authority, since any evaluation of future market trends may give rise to a range of different, but equally valid, opinions in any given case, without implying that any one of those opinions is necessarily invalid. No dominant firm could therefore take a pricing decision with any

---

[91] See *Investigation by the Director General of Telecommunications into alleged anticompetitive practices by British Telecommunications plc in relation to BTOpenworld's consumer broadband products*, November 20, 2003.

[92] *Ibid.* Following the adoption of a new BT business plan for broadband in 2004, Oftel's successor, Ofcom, continued to pursue certain aspects of the case, which culminated in the issuance of a statement of objections against BT in August 2004. The case is still on-going.

[93] *Ibid.*, para. 6.82. Ofcom labelled its assessment of the reasonableness of BT's assumptions as to future profits "contestability scenarios."

certainty if inevitable start-up losses are involved, which would be contrary to the principle of legal certainty.[94]

The second approach to assessing margin squeeze allegations in new markets recognises that assumptions as to future market conditions are inherently speculative and that, accordingly, there needs to be convincing evidence that those assumptions are expressly or impliedly based on exclusionary motives rather than legitimate considerations.[95] Express exclusionary evidence would require documentary or other evidence showing that the dominant firm had formulated a plan of using a margin squeeze as a means of harming competition from downstream rivals. Although not formally analysed as a margin squeeze, this was the interpretation applied by the Commission in *Wanadoo*, where there were not merely start-up losses necessary to enter the market, but an express plan of incurring whatever losses were necessary as part of a richly-documented "plan to pre-empt the market."[96] The Commission's strong reliance in *Wanadoo* on extensive documentary evidence of exclusionary intent, probable recoupment, and actual or likely exclusionary effects suggests that a high evidentiary threshold applies before start-up losses can be found predatory.

Implied exclusion would require evidence that "a business case is based on unjustified and implausible assumptions or where there has been a failure by the undertaking to take remedial action once it became apparent that it would not meet the targets."[97] Evidence of anticompetitive object could be inferred from a number of "convergent factors" that, taken together, clearly demonstrate anticompetitive purpose rather than legitimate start-up losses.[98] Thus, there must be convincing evidence that no reasonable

---

94 See H Tridimas, *The General Principles of EC Law* (Oxford, Oxford University Press, 1999) ch. 5, pp. 165–66; J Temple Lang, "Legal Certainty and Legitimate Expectations as General Principles of Law" in U Bernitz & J Nergelius (eds.), *General Principles of European Community Law* (London, Kluwer Law International, 2000), 163–84; Case C-313/99, *Gerard Mulligan and Others v Minister of Agriculture and Food, Ireland and Attorney General* [2002] ECR I-5719; and Case C-63/93, *Duff and others v Minister for Agriculture and Attorney General* [1996] ECR I-569, paras. 19–20.

95 See Case CW/00496/01/02, *British Telecom UK-SPN,* Oftel Decision of May 23, 2003. Oftel rejected margin squeeze allegations despite evidence of losses by BT for a new service on the basis that: (1) on BT's original forecast volumes, the UK-SPN service would have been a profitable service in aggregate and those call-types forecast to be below cost would be insignificantly so relative to price; (2) on actual and revised forecast volumes carried by the UK-SPN network, prices were unlikely to cover the relevant cost floor for any call-type; (3) however, BT's original business case was not implausible and, after several months, BT took the decision to close the business; (4) there was no evidence to demonstrate that the UK-SPN service had a material adverse effect on competition; and (5) there was also insufficient evidence that BT intended to pursue an anticompetitive strategy: the available evidence suggested a new business that was unsuccessful in meeting forecast demand rather than a deliberate or negligent anticompetitive strategy.

96 See Case COMP/38.233, *Wanadoo Interactive*, Commission Decision of July 16, 2003, not yet published, para. 256. See also *Deutsche Telekom AG*, OJ 2003 L 263/9, para. 179, where the Commission interpreted the application of the *AKZO* rules to a price squeeze test in a new market (broadband internet access) as requiring both below-cost selling and evidence that prices "are set as part of a plan aimed at eliminating a competitor."

97 See Guidelines on the application of the Competition Act 1998 in the telecommunications sector, OFT 417, para. 7.23.

98 See Case C-62/86, *AKZO Chemie BV v Commission* [1991] ECR I-3359, para. 80. See also Case COMP/38.233, *Wanadoo Interactive*, Commission Decision of July 16, 2003, not yet published, para.

company in possession of the information available to the dominant firm at the time it formulated its business plan would have adopted the same course of action. This evidence would need to be similar in quality to express evidence of anticompetitive intent, since, otherwise, the latter would be treated comparatively more leniently than the former, which would not make sense. In other words, there must be evidence that the business plan or projections are "unjustified or implausible;"[99] in effect, a sham. In such cases, any future recovery of losses envisaged in the business plan is premised on the additional market power that the low exclusionary prices would confer rather than legitimate efficiencies.

A test based on clear evidence of express or implied exclusionary intent is more appropriate as a competition-law test. The inherent uncertainty of future market predictions in dynamic markets, and the obvious difficulties in distinguishing legitimate and anticompetitive prices, mean that pricing abuses cases involving new products should only be pursued where there is strong evidence of anticompetitive purpose or strategy. A strict standard of evidence is an essential part of sound competition policy in the case of new products in dynamic markets. Condemning start-up losses in the case of new products in growing dynamic markets should be approached with reserve, since the welfare cost of preventing or hampering successful product launches and market development could be very high. Thus, a firm should therefore be afforded some margin of appreciation in making such assessments, in much the same way as competition authorities have discretion in making complex future economic assessments in mergers and other cases.[100]

The need for anticompetitive effects in a margin squeeze case. Chapter Four discussed whether an analysis of actual or likely effects on competition is necessary or desirable under Article 82 EC. Despite some contradictory statements in decisions and cases, it is now accepted that proof of actual or likely harm to competition is required under Article 82 EC. The contradictions in the case law have also spilled over into the area of margin squeeze. In *Deutsche Telekom*, the Commission stated that, once a margin squeeze was shown, it was not necessary to assess any effects on competition: such effects were presumed from the mere existence of a margin squeeze.[101] However, the Commission nonetheless undertook an analysis of likely exclusionary effects.[102] The Commission noted Deutsche Telekom's 90% share of the affected market and

271; and P Lowe, "EU Competition Practice on Predatory Pricing," at the seminar Pros and Cons of Low Prices, Stockholm, December 5, 2003.

[99] See Guidelines on the application of the Competition Act 1998 in the telecommunications sector, OFT 417, para. 7.23 ("It will not always be possible for an undertaking to meet all the targets set out in its business plan. Evidence of an abuse of dominance may be provided, however, where a business case is based on unjustified and implausible assumptions or where there has been a failure by the undertaking to take remedial action once it became apparent that it would not meet the targets.").

[100] See, e.g., Case C-12/03, *Commission v Tetra Laval BV* [2005] ECR I-987, para. 42 ("A prospective analysis of the kind necessary for merger control must be carried out with great care since it does not entail the examination of past events—for which often many items of evidence are available which make it possible to understand the causes—or of current events, but rather a prediction of events which are more or less likely to occur in future if a decision prohibiting the planned concentration or laying down the conditions for it is not adopted.").

[101] *Deutsche Telekom AG*, OJ 2003 L 263/9, paras. 179–80.

[102] *Ibid.*, paras. 181–83.

competitors' falling share of analogue connections.[103] The same approach was adopted in *France Télécom/SFR Cegetel/Bouygues Télécom.* The Conseil de la Concurrence, citing *Deutsche Telekom*, stated that once margin squeeze is established, it is not necessary to evaluate its actual impact on competition.[104] However, it still examined the actual scope of the margin squeeze's anticompetitive effects, particularly with respect to Cegetel. Finally, a number of national decisions have rejected margin squeeze allegations based, *inter alia*, on the lack of actual or probable anticompetitive effects.[105]

Analysis of actual or likely anticompetitive effects is particularly important in a margin squeeze. As noted above, the legal test for a margin squeeze is based on stylised assumptions that are often inapplicable, or require significant modification, in practice. In particular, the legal test only works well where downstream rivals supply homogenous goods or services, the upstream input represents a high, fixed proportion of downstream rivals' costs, and there is a simple, linear pass through of costs from the upstream level to the downstream market. Testing for actual or likely anticompetitive effects therefore helps minimise the welfare costs of wrongly finding an abuse due to the mere failure of a price to pass an imputation test.

An effects analysis in a margin squeeze case is also consistent with the Commission's recent approach to similar pricing abuses. In *Wanadoo*, the Commission undertook a detailed recoupment and effects analysis,[106] despite the fact that Wanadoo's prices were found to be below average variable cost—which had been considered as presumptively unlawful under the *AKZO* case law—and there was a range of evidence of an express exclusionary plan. The Commission relied on the fact that: (1) Wanadoo's market share rose by nearly 30% during the period of the infringement; (2) Wanadoo's main competitor at the time had seen its market share tumble; and (3) one competitor (Mangoosta) even went out of business. If this type of analysis is undertaken for the practice under Article 82 EC that is generally considered to be closest to a *per se* abuse (pricing below average variable cost), the same *a fortiori* applies for a less serious and less clear form of pricing abuse such as a margin squeeze. It would be anomalous if an effects analysis was necessary under pure predatory pricing, but not for a margin squeeze.

That actual or likely anticompetitive effects is the relevant test for exclusionary conduct under Article 82 EC is now confirmed by the Discussion Paper. It states that Article 82 EC prohibits "exclusionary conduct which produces actual or likely anticompetitive effects in the market and which can harm consumers in a direct or indirect way."[107] It adds that, the longer the conduct has already been going on, the

[103] *Ibid.*

[104] *France Télécom/SFR Cegetel/Bouygues Télécom*, Conseil de la Concurrence, Décision No. 04-D48 of October 14, 2004, para. 242.

[105] See, e.g., Case CW/00615/05/03, *Suspected margin squeeze by Vodafone, O2, Orange and T-Mobile*, Ofcom Decision of May 21, 2004; and *Investigation by the Director General of Telecommunications into alleged anticompetitive practices by British Telecommunications plc in relation to BTOpenworld's consumer broadband products*, Oftel Decision of November 20, 2003.

[106] See Case COMP/38.233, *Wanadoo Interactive*, Commission Decision of July 16, 2003, not yet published, paras. 332 et seq. (recoupment) and paras. 369 et seq. (effects on competition).

[107] Discussion Paper, para. 55.

more weight will in general be given to actual effects. Not only short-term harm, but also medium- and long-term harm arising from foreclosure will be taken into account.

The need for downstream dominance in margin squeeze cases. A final controversial issue in margin squeeze cases is whether downstream dominance is a requirement for an abuse. Certainly, a number of compelling arguments suggest that it is, or should be. First, a margin squeeze abuse is in effect a form of predatory pricing that arises in the context of vertical integration. Given that dominance in the market in which foreclosure effects are alleged is generally a requirement in a pure predatory pricing case, proof of a margin squeeze abuse would also logically require downstream dominance. Indeed, it would be curious if a margin squeeze abuse was, in practice, much easier to prove than pure predation. Second, downstream dominance seems inherent in the basic notion of a margin squeeze—that a firm controls the prices on two vertically-related markets and can therefore squeeze the margin between those two prices. If a firm only has market power in relation to prices on one of the markets concerned, it is difficult to see how a margin squeeze could arise. At the very least, it would need to be shown that the dominant firm has more power over price in the downstream market than any of its rivals. Finally, it is notable that cases in which a margin squeeze abuse has been found have generally involved dominance on both the upstream and downstream markets.[108] Cases in which margin squeeze allegations have been rejected have generally involved dominance on the upstream market only.[109]

On the other hand, it is well established under Article 82 EC that dominance and abuse may occur on different markets, in particular where there are "associative links" between the two markets that allow a firm to extend its power unlawfully from one market to the other, i.e., by leveraging.[110] Case law has also reasoned that a dominant supplier of an essential input for rivals on a downstream market has a credible threat to exclude such competitors on the downstream market, without it being necessary to show that the firm is already dominant on the downstream market.[111] In other words, a margin squeeze abuse does not involve the use of power on the downstream market to exclude rivals, but implies the use of control over an essential upstream input to *gain* market power on the downstream market by excluding competitors.

Even if downstream dominance is not a formal requirement in a margin squeeze case, it is important that a plaintiff or competition authority should substantiate a credible case of foreclosure in circumstances where the defendant is not dominant on the downstream market. Foreclosure concerns can only arise on the downstream market and these concerns are necessarily less pronounced where the market is competitive and no single firm, or group of firms, is dominant. This foreclosure analysis should therefore be similar in scope to the recoupment inquiry under predatory pricing. Relevant questions

[108] See e.g., *National Coal Board, National Smokeless Fuels Limited and the National Carbonising Company Limited,* OJ 1976 L 35/6. See also *Deutsche Telekom AG*, OJ 2003 L 263/9.

[109] See, e.g., *Investigation by the Director General of Telecommunications into alleged anticompetitive practices by British Telecommunications plc in relation to BTOpenworld's consumer broadband products*, Oftel Decision of November 20, 2003.

[110] See Case T-83/91, *Tetra Pak International SA v Commission* [1994] ECR II-755, confirmed on appeal in Case C-333/94 P, *Tetra Pak International SA v Commission* [1996] ECR I-5951.

[111] See *Genzyme* [2004] CAT 4 para. 364.

to consider might include whether: (1) there are technological changes at the upstream or downstream level that would allow rivals to base their offerings on alternative inputs; (2) rivals are likely to exit the market if a margin squeeze persists; (3) there will entry by more competitive or more determined rivals in future, and that when the dominant company increases its price, it will not attract new entry; and (4) absent new entry, the price elasticity of the product is such that, although buyers are accustomed to low prices today, they would be willing to pay significantly higher ones in the future. There must be some credible basis for saying that foreclosure concerns are likely to arise on a market in which no firm is dominant. This applies not least because of the significant uncertainty surrounding the conditions for a margin squeeze abuse and the potential adverse effect of a strict margin squeeze principle on efficient market outcomes.

6.6 DISCRIMINATORY MARGIN SQUEEZES AND RELATED STRATEGIES

6.6.1 Problem Stated

Actual discrimination by a vertically integrated dominant firm. The essential point in a margin squeeze case is that a dominant firm's activities on two levels of trade offer scope for concealing what is in effect discrimination against downstream rivals that depend on it for essential inputs. The dominant firm can extract the profit at the upstream level or the downstream level or can adjust its prices either upstream or downstream to squeeze rivals' margins. But it is also possible that the discrimination is not implied but *actual*. Actual discrimination by a vertically integrated dominant firm against non-integrated downstream rivals is also a form of exclusionary abuse. By charging non-integrated rivals a higher price than its own downstream business, offering them less favourable terms, or degrading the quality or speed of delivery of the input supplied, a dominant firm can artificially raise its rivals' costs, which may, if the harm is serious enough and the rivals are important to consumers, also harm consumer welfare. This is also a form of raising rivals' costs,[112] although this is not an especially precise label to distinguish between lawful and anticompetitive conduct.

Cases of actual discrimination arise most frequently in practice in the area of liberalised utilities where the relevant markets are not yet fully competitive. Incumbents typically retain market power following liberalisation, as well as control over essential inputs (e.g., bottleneck infrastructures). This common fact pattern can create strong incentives for incumbents to discriminate against downstream competitors.[113] The discrimination may be absolute, such as in the case of a refusal to deal, but can also take the form of price and non-price discrimination. Indeed, because incumbents are generally required under regulation to grant access to rivals, discrimination is likely to be a much more important (and insidious) issue in practice than access. The incumbent will often grant access, but make it subject to delays or onerous technical and other limitations that discriminate against rival firms.

[112] See TG Krattenmaker and SC Salop, "Anticompetitive Exclusion: Raising Rivals—Costs to Achieve Power over Price" (1986) 2 *Yale Law Journal* 209.

[113] See N Economides, "The Incentive For Non-Price Discrimination by an Input Monopolist" (1998) 16 *International Journal of Industrial Organisation* 271.

The legal characterisation of discrimination against rivals under Article 82 EC. Discrimination against rival firms under Article 82 EC has generally been assessed as an exclusionary abuse. In other words, discrimination is necessary but not sufficient: the real question is whether there has been unlawful foreclosure. For example, selective pricing by a dominant firm to rivals' customers is assessed under the principles developed in the *AKZO* case law on predatory pricing. The effects of discriminatory loyalty rebate schemes on rivals are also assessed under the principles for exclusionary conduct developed under Article 82 EC, and not as an issue of discrimination under Article 82(c). Similarly, margin squeeze cases, which involve implicit discrimination between the dominant firm's own vertically integrated business and downstream rivals, are unlawful because they are exclusionary, and not merely because they involve implied discrimination. Finally, tying and bundling cases—which are often explained by the dominant firm's desire to price discriminate in favour of users who attach more value to the tied/bundled products than to each separately—are also assessed under foreclosure principles. The same analysis should be applied to actual discrimination by a vertically integrated dominant firm: discrimination is merely a vehicle for excluding downstream rivals.

6.6.2 Examples of Discrimination By A Vertically Integrated Dominant Firm

Generally. Discrimination by a dominant firm against downstream rivals has featured in a number of cases under Article 82 EC, as well as analogous provisions of national law. In *HOV SVZ/MCN*, the dominant rail operator firm discriminated in favour of its own downstream transport subsidiary by agreeing a system of unlawful preferential tariffs with other rail operators, as well as by charging transport operators who routed shipments via non-German ports higher tariffs for rail travel within Germany, even in circumstances where the total distance covered was shorter. The tariff differences in favour of the dominant firm's subsidiary were found to be attributable to the dominant firm and the subsidiary was fully aware of the discrimination practised against operators from other Member States by its parent company. In these circumstances, the Commission found that the dominant firm was promoting its own downstream business by discriminating against rivals who depended upon it for access to rail infrastructure within Germany.[114]

A similar conclusion was reached in *GT Link*,[115] where a State undertaking acting as port operator exempted its own downstream ferry services from the payment of port duties. The Court of Justice held that the dominant firm's internal accounts should make provision for the payment of a sum equivalent to the portion of its activity in ferry services.[116] In the absence of transparent accounts, evidence that the dominant firm's

[114] See *HOV SVZ/MCN*, OJ 1994 L 104/34, paras. 87, 187, 247, and 248. Although not formally analysed as a case involving discrimination by a vertically integrated dominant firm, the Clearstream decision also seemed to have strong vertical elements, since Clearstream and Euroclear competed on various markets. In other words, Euroclear was not merely a customer of Clearstream's. See Case COMP/38/096, *Clearstream (Clearing and settlement)*, Decision of June 4, 2004, not yet published.

[115] Case C-242/95, *GT-Link A/S v De Danske Statsbaner (DSB)* [1997] ECR I-4449.

[116] See also Paris Court of Appeals, *France Télécom*, Decision of June 29, 1999 (dominant undertaking on a market for a product or service used on another market commits an abuse by offering

ferry service prices were unusually low could constitute evidence that there was no such allocation.[117]

Irish Sugar[118] also concerned discrimination against downstream rivals. Irish Sugar supplied sugar to undertakings engaged in industrial supply (e.g., to food processors). In addition, Irish Sugar was active on the retail market. Because the products sold at industrial and retail levels were essentially the same, a number of industrial sugar packers forward integrated into the supply of sugar at the retail level by launching their own brands. Irish Sugar then refused to continue to offer discounts that it had granted to purchasers of industrial sugar to those purchasers who were also active on the downstream retail market.

The Community institutions found that this was abusive discrimination, since the services offered to its sugar packer customers and its other customers are otherwise perfectly comparable at the commercial level, all conditions being taken into account. The fact that some of them decided to forward integrate to the retail level was found not to be a valid reason for refusing to grant the discount offered to other industrial sugar packers. In particular, the Court of First Instance rejected the argument that the dominant firm could distinguish otherwise equivalent transactions on the grounds that certain undertakings were also competitors on a downstream market. The Court held that Irish Sugar's argument "effectively implies that services which are identical at the commercial level, all conditions being taken into account, are not equivalent within the meaning of Article 8[2](c), depending on whether or not, for whatever reason, they share in the economic objectives which the undertaking which holds a dominant position has determined for itself."[119]

Discrimination and liberalised markets. Issues of discrimination against rivals are most likely to arise in practice in the case of liberalised utilities where the relevant markets are not yet fully competitive. Controlling abuses of market power is of critical importance in liberalised industries, such as telecommunications, as, in the years following liberalisation, incumbents will generally retain large market shares.[120] In addition, they will also control essential inputs (e.g., bottleneck infrastructures) and generally be reluctant to share them with new entrants that need them to compete with

goods or services on the secondary market at a higher price than the one they internally charge themselves for their use).

[117] *Ibid.*, para. 41.

[118] *Irish Sugar plc*, OJ 1997 L 258/1, affirmed on appeal in Case T-228/97, *Irish Sugar plc v Commission* [1999] ECR II-2969 and Order of the Court of Justice in Case C-497/99 P, *Irish Sugar plc v Commission* [2001] ECR I-5333.

[119] Case T-228/97, *Irish Sugar plc v Commission* [1999] ECR II-2969, para. 164. See also *Napier Brown/British Sugar*, OJ 1988 L 284/41, where British Sugar's refusal to supply beet-origin sugar to Napier-Brown was found to constitute discrimination against downstream rivals. Only beet-origin sugar was granted a rebate under Community price support mechanisms for sugar. The refusal to supply Napier-Brown with beet origin sugar therefore effectively raised its costs, which gave an unfair advantage to British Sugar's own downstream sugar business.

[120] See D Geradin, "The Opening of State Monopolies to Competition: Main Issues of the Liberalisation Process" in D Geradin (ed.), *The Liberalisation of State Monopolies in the European Union and Beyond* (London, Kluwer Law International, 2000), p. 182.

the incumbent in downstream markets.[121] A core problem with vertical integration when downstream markets have been opened to competition is that it creates incentives for incumbents to discriminate against downstream competitors. Such discrimination can take the form of refusal to give access to essential inputs, excessive prices charged for such inputs, discriminatory margin squeezes, or non-price discrimination such as degradation of the quality of the service offered by the dominant firm to downstream rivals or unjustified delays.[122]

The primary tool to ensure equality of opportunity for downstream rivals in liberalised industries is sector-specific rules, which are used to prevent, among other things, abuses of market power on the part of the incumbent. For example, sector-specific rules may impose rules mandating incumbents to give non-discriminatory access to their infrastructure,[123] establish price control regimes on wholesale and/or retail services in order to ensure that downstream operators' costs are not unfairly raised by discriminatory pricing by the incumbent in favour of its own downstream business,[124] or mandate transparent accounting between the incumbent's wholesale and retail arms.[125] Unless, however, there is a full separation of the wholesale and retail activities (i.e., through the creation of two distinct companies with separate ownership and a duty to trade on arms-length terms), the incumbent will always have some possibility to discriminate against downstream rivals.[126] In these circumstances, Article 82 EC has an important role to play in ensuring that downstream rivals are not unfairly discriminated against.

A number of official Community documents on the application of EC competition law in liberalised sectors confirm that non-discrimination principles lie at the core of the dominant firm's duties. For example, the Telecommunications Access Notice puts forward a general principle that "the dominant company's duty is to provide access in such a way that the goods and services offered to downstream companies are available on terms no less favourable than those given to other parties, including its own corresponding downstream operations."[127] A similar obligation is contained in the Notice on the postal sector, which provides that "operators should provide the universal postal service by affording non-discriminatory access to customers or intermediaries at appropriate public points of access, in accordance with the needs of those users" and that "access conditions including contracts (when offered) should be transparent, published in an appropriate manner and offered on a non-discriminatory basis."[128] The

[121] *Ibid.*

[122] See, e.g., Decision No. 05-D-59, *France Télécom*, Conseil de la Concurrence Decision of November 7, 2005, where the incumbent telecommunications operator was fined €80 million for delaying access to its local loop to a downstream rival from November 9, 1999, to September 15, 2002.

[123] See Directive 2002/19 on access to, and interconnection of, electronic communications networks and associated facilities, OJ 2002 L 108/7, Article 12.

[124] *Ibid.*, Article 13.

[125] *Ibid.*, Article 11.

[126] See D Geradin and M Kerf, *Controlling Market Power in Telecommunications: Antitrust Sector-specific Regulation* (Oxford, Oxford University Press, 2000) p. 59.

[127] Notice on the application of the competition rules to access agreements in the telecommunications sector, OJ 1998 C 265/2, para. 86.

[128] Notice from the Commission on the application of the competition rules to the postal sector and on the assessment of certain State measures relating to postal services, OJ 1998 C 39/02.

Notice also goes further and insists that "Member States should ensure that their postal legislation does not encourage postal operators to differentiate unjustifiably as regards the conditions applied or to exclude certain companies."[129] Thus, a strict rule applies to discrimination by a former State monopoly against new entrants in liberalised markets.

These principles were applied in the *Deutsche Post* remail case.[130] Because of different rates of tariff between Member States, it is sometimes cheaper for a sender based in Member State A to route mail destined for Member State A via Member State B (so-called ABA remail). This applies in particular where charges for domestic mail are significantly higher than the fees charged by the incumbent national operator for incoming international mail. The incumbent is allowed to reserve the right to apply the full domestic tariff where remail is used to circumvent domestic charges, but not if the sender is based outside the national territory. A dispute arose between the British Post Office (BPO) and Deutsche Post on how to identify the sender of international mailings. Deutsche Post argued that any incoming international mail containing a reference to Germany, usually in the form of a German reply address, should be considered as having a German sender, regardless of where the mail was produced or posted. It therefore intercepted large quantities of mail destined for Germany on the grounds that mere reference to a German entity in the mail allowed it to be classified as domestic mail and surcharged accordingly. The BPO argued that all outgoing mail produced and posted in the UK should be processed like international mail, regardless of its contents. This dispute caused serious delays to remail sent by the BPO.

The Commission found that Deutsche Post's practice of intercepting, surcharging, and delaying incoming remail was abusive, in particular because it unlawfully discriminated between incoming international mail, which it considered "genuine", and international mail, which it incorrectly considered to be circumvented domestic mail. In both cases Deutsche Post performed exactly the same delivery service but charged customers differently. But the Commission also noted that the discrimination in effect raised the costs of the BPO, which was a direct rival to Deutsche Post for international mail. The Commission noted as follows:[131]

> "[Deutsche Post] is in direct competition with the BPO, not in the relevant market but in the UK market for outgoing cross-border letter mail. The additional costs incurred by the BPO as a consequence of the surcharges claimed by [Deutsche Post] in combination with the frequent disruptions of the mail traffic routed by the BPO from the UK to Germany puts the BPO at a competitive disadvantage in relation to [Deutsche Post]. Since [Deutsche Post] is active on the UK market for outgoing cross-border letter mail, UK customers who have experienced problems when contracting with the BPO will be induced to use the services of [Deutsche Post] in the UK directly for the entire distribution chain in order to ensure a speedy and uninterrupted conveyance of their mail bound for Germany."

National case law has also frequently dealt with discrimination issues in the area of liberalised markets. In *Consorzio Risposta/Ente Poste Italiane*,[132] Poste Italiane Spa

[129] *Ibid.*, point 2.8.
[130] *Deutsche Post AG—Interception of cross-border mail,* OJ 2001 L 331/40.
[131] *Ibid.*, para. 132.
[132] *Consorzio Risposta/Ente Poste Italiane*, Provvedimento n. 6698 of December 17, 1998, in Bollettino 51/1998.

(PI) was found to have discriminated in favour its downstream subsidiary. PI was entrusted by law with the exclusive right to provide postal services in Italy and also occupied a dominant position on the market for electronic postal services such as telex. The Italian Antitrust Authority found that PI charged lower prices for the transmission of the electronic post through its postal network to its subsidiary than competitors. As a result, PI's subsidiary had a significant and unfair cost advantage over rivals. Much the same conclusion was reached in *Associazione Italiana Internet Providers/Telecom*,[133] where Telecom Italia SpA (TI) was found to have abused its dominant position on the market for the provision of backbone internet connectivity by charging different prices for similar services to Internet Service Providers (ISP) on the one hand and its business customers on the other, without objective justification. By reducing their profit margin, TI put the ISPs at a competitive disadvantage compared to TI in the downstream market for the provision of Internet services, where they competed with TI.

Discrimination necessary but not sufficient. The decisional practice and case law have generally applied a relatively strict rule in cases involving actual discrimination by a vertically integrated dominant firm against rivals: if the dominant firm is actually discriminating against downstream rivals, there does not appear to be any special requirement to show a serious competitive disadvantage as a result. In the case of a margin squeeze, the rival firm must show that an equally efficient firm would lose money on the basis of the prices charged by the dominant firm. Yet in cases of actual discrimination, it has generally been enough for rivals to show that they would suffer some non-trivial disadvantage by being forced to bear higher costs than the dominant firm.

This certainly makes sense: unless discrimination is checked, a dominant firm can impose an indefinite additional cost on rivals that its own downstream business does not bear. But it is also important that, as in other discrimination cases, competition authorities and courts should also undertake a meaningful analysis of the actual or likely effects of discrimination by a vertically integrated dominant firm. All of the points made in respect of margin squeeze also apply to actual discrimination. Thus, it should be assessed whether the dominant firm has any incentive to discriminate against downstream rivals. If the rivals sell differentiated products, or are more efficient producers than the dominant firm's downstream business, the incentives to discriminate are likely to be weak (or, correspondingly, the effects of discrimination are likely to be small). It should also be recalled that vertical discrimination cases are in essence constructive refusals to supply an essential input. It should therefore be assessed whether downstream rivals have access to effective alternative inputs and whether paying higher prices for the dominant firm's input has a material effect on rivals' total costs. Finally, and perhaps most importantly, the dominant firm may well have a valid reason for discriminating between its own downstream business and rivals. All the

[133] *Associazione Italiana Internet Providers/Telecom*, Provvedimento n. 7978 of January 28, 2000, in Bollettino 4/2000. See also *Ente Ferrovie Dello Stato*, Provvedimento n. 1312 of July 23, 1993, in Bollettino 18-19/1993 (Italian rail operator incumbent found to have discriminated against competitors in favour of its subsidiary on the market for the provision of container transport services by granting more favourable access conditions to the railway infrastructure) and *Cesare Fremura-Assologistica/Ferrovie Dello Stato*, Provvedimento n. 8065 of February 24, 2000, in Bollettino 8/2000 (same).

usual defences in a discrimination therefore apply, such as lower costs of serving its own business, the fact, that it downstream business serves customers with a different willingness to pay (fixed-cost recovery), favourable prices for entering new markets etc.[134]

6.7 CONFLICTS BETWEEN REGULATION AND COMPETITION LAW IN MARGIN SQUEEZE CASES

Scope for conflict between regulation and competition. Margin squeezes and cases of actual discrimination by vertically integrated dominant firms have arisen most frequently in the case of liberalised utility sectors where former monopolists continue to have control over essential inputs supplied to downstream rivals. In these sectors, two separate sets of rules can in principle be used to prevent or sanction margin squeezes and similar conduct by incumbents.[135] Margin squeezes can be controlled under Article 82 EC (and equivalent national laws). Alternatively, sector-specific rules can be used to prevent prices squeezes by mandating wholesale access on certain terms[136] or regulating prices at the retail level.[137] Both sets of rules can also be applied in parallel (e.g., *ex ante* regulation of wholesale access only; *ex post* control of retail prices under competition law). The parallel application of regulation and competition can give rise to scope for conflict, including: (1) policy decisions over whether to apply *ex ante* regulation and/or *ex post* control to margin squeeze; (2) regulatory decisions that lead to Article 82 EC violations; and (3) substantive conflicts.[138]

Policy issues. On a policy level, legislators face difficult choices in deciding whether *ex ante* regulation is better than *ex post* intervention under competition law or whether some combination of regulation and competition works better (e.g., regulation of wholesale prices or retail prices). These choices may also vary from practice to practice. For example, regulated retail prices may work best where the objective is to prevent consumer exploitation whereas regulated wholesale access may work best to prevent margin squeezes. The merits of the various forms of regulation over

[134] See Ch. 11 (Abusive Discrimination) for detailed treatment of objective justification in discrimination cases.

[135] See D Geradin and M Kerf, *Controlling Market Power in Telecommunications: Antitrust Sector-specific Regulation* (Oxford, Oxford University Press, 2000).

[136] See Article 12 of Council Directive 2002/19 on access to, and interconnection of, electronic communications networks and associated facilities, OJ 2002 L 108/7.

[137] *Ibid.*, Article 13.

[138] Regulation and competition law differ in important respects, as discussed in detail in Ch. 1 (Introduction, Scope of Application, and Basic Framework). Briefly, the relevant differences are: (1) regulatory powers in respect of a margin squeeze are in principle more extensive than those applicable under competition law (e.g., regulators can actively promote downstream competition by new entrants at the expense of the incumbent's upstream margins); (2) regulation can create *new* obligations, such as a duty to create competition on downstream markets even in the absence of any abuse of dominance; competition law can only apply existing principles to new situations; and (3) intervention under competition law should lead to more competition than it discourages; regulation sometimes impose a duty on a dominant incumbent to give access on more favourable terms to competitors which are investing in their own networks (e.g., if the regulatory framework favours network competition over service competition in the long-run), which may affect the ability and incentives of the incumbent to invest in its own infrastructure.

competition law raises complex issues beyond the scope of this work.[139] In essence, however, there is no unambiguous evidence that any single approach has significant net advantages over the other.[140]

Jurisdictional issues. Disputes can also result where the effect of regulatory action is to create competition-law violations or jurisdictional conflicts.[141] As discussed in detail in Chapter One, the general principle is that Article 82 EC does not apply where sector-specific regulation precludes the regulated firm from engaging in autonomous conduct. How "autonomous conduct" is to be defined where prices are regulated at the national level is a major issue in the *Deutsche Telekom* case, which is currently on appeal. The case concerned the prices Deutsche Telekom (DT) charged its competitors for unbundled access to local loops in Germany. The Commission received complaints from DT's competitors, who claimed that DT's access charges were incompatible with Article 82 EC.

In its defence, DT argued that its local access tariffs had been approved by the NRA, the RegTP. DT contended that if there was an infringement of Article 82 EC, the Commission should not be acting against the addressee of the regulatory framework, but against the Member State under Article 226 EC.[142] The Commission, however, rejected this argument on the ground that "competition rules may apply where the sector-specific legislation does not preclude the undertakings it governs from engaging in autonomous conduct that prevents, restricts or distorts competition."[143] The Commission argued that, despite the intervention of the RegTP, DT retained a commercial discretion, which would have allowed it to restructure its tariffs further so as to reduce or indeed to put an end to the margin squeeze.[144] On the merits, the Commission found that DT's prices, although regulated, gave rise to a margin squeeze.[145]

Substantive conflicts. The most important source of potential conflict between regulatory and competition powers in respect of margin squeeze is substantive in nature. Recent precedents have shown that the existence of regulation at the upstream level may lead to conflicts with the objectives of competition law downstream. Different situations might be envisaged. The first situation of potential conflict is where the dominant firm's *actual* costs are lower than the regulated access charges set for competitors. In this circumstance, all things equal, the dominant firm could offer lower prices to consumers without pricing below its own costs, whereas rivals, unless they were more efficient, would have comparatively higher prices, since the regulated wholesale price would represent an unavoidable cost to them.

[139] See generally D Geradin and R O'Donoghue, "The Concurrent Application of Competition Law and Regulation: The Case of Margin Squeeze Abuses in the Telecommunications Sector" (2005) 1 *Journal of Competition Law and Economics* 355–425.

[140] *Ibid.*

[141] See N Petit, "The Proliferation of National Regulatory Authorities alongside Competition Authorities: A Source of Jurisdictional Confusion," *Global Competition Law Centre Working Papers Series*, February 2004.

[142] *Deutsche Telekom AG*, OJ 2003 L 263/9, para. 53.

[143] *Ibid.*, para. 54.

[144] *Ibid.*, para. 57.

[145] *France Télécom/SFR Cegetel/Bouygues Télécom*, Conseil de la Concurrence, Décision No. 04-D48 of October 14, 2004.

This issue arose to some extent in the recent *Telecom Italia* case.[146] The NCA concluded that bundled prices offered by Telecom Italia (TI) on a tender contract gave rise to a margin squeeze. This was said to result, *inter alia*, from the fact that TI's allocation of costs for a portion of the services covered by the tender offer was below the regulated cost at which TI's rivals purchased the same essential inputs from TI. The NRA assessed rivals' ability to match TI's offer on an item-by-item basis, and not on the basis of the aggregate bundle of services included in the bid. It required TI to allocate the full regulated cost of access for each item to its bid. But it seemed that TI's *actual* cost of providing the input in question was lower than the regulated price at which the input was made available to rivals. The NRA said, however, that, under competition law, TI could not price below the regulated cost that rivals paid for the inputs concerned even if its actual costs were lower. (The case is complicated by the fact that other abuses were also found (e.g., exclusivity clauses, English clauses).)

This conclusion is questionable under competition law principles. The most widely-used imputation test for a margin squeeze is based on the dominant firm's costs. To the extent that these are lower than rivals' costs, the dominant firm's prices represent competition on the merits. The issue, then, is whether a different rule should apply under competition law when the incumbent has a comparative cost advantage over rivals due to the fact that the pricing methodology chosen by the NRA results in access charges that are higher than the dominant firm's actual costs. It is difficult to see a reason under competition law for doing this. Article 82(b) permits competition on the merits unless rivals' opportunities are "limited" *and* there is "prejudice of consumers." Requiring a dominant firm to refrain from lowering its prices to consumers in line with its actual costs on the basis that, in so doing, the dominant firm would price below a benchmark set for access by a NRA pursuant to powers under secondary Community legislation, seems to protect competitors at the expense of consumers.[147] Indeed, the case seemed more concerned with using competition law to correct for the problem of

---

[146] Case A 351, *Telecom Italia*, Decision of November 19, 2004 (hereinafter "*Telecom Italia*"). On appeal, a Lazio court annulled the TI "margin squeeze" fine (as well as the fine issued for TI's other alleged abuse (abusive contractual conditions and discounts)), but found that TI had indeed committed a margin squeeze in certain instances and left open the possibility for the Italian Antitrust Authority to issue a reduced fine. However, the Council of State partially annulled the Lazio court's judgment and reinstated the fine, reducing it to € 115 million. Its reasons are not yet publicly available.

[147] Of course, in this case, the NCA might, as occurred in *Telecom Italia*, conclude that the dominant firm was discriminating, contrary to Article 82(c), against third parties by charging them a higher price than that which it charged to its own retail business. Although the decision does not discuss this specific legal issue in detail, the NCA seems to have concluded, in line with the principle established in *Deutsche Telekom*, that the dominant firm had a duty under competition law to off-set any disadvantages caused by regulation if inaction on its part would lead to a competition-law violation. It could certainly be argued that transactions between the dominant firm and third parties and the dominant firm and its integrated business would be "equivalent transactions" subject to a non-discrimination duty under Article 82(c). This should not, however, be the end of the enquiry. Although Article 82(c) does not include the same phrase "prejudice to consumers" contained in Article 82(b), consumer welfare cannot be ignored where, as in a margin squeeze case, Articles 82(b) (foreclosure) and 82(c) (discrimination) are applied in parallel. Thus, Article 82(c) should not be applied in a manner that would cause "prejudice to consumers." This would arguably be the case where a dominant firm was prevented from pricing at a level above its own actual costs, but below the costs of rivals (even if some of those costs are the result of regulatory decisions).

regulatory delay, i.e., that TI's actual costs were lower than the regulated access charges.

A second situation is where the incumbent has to make available a certain technical means of access on non-discriminatory terms under regulation, but the incumbent still retains a cost advantage over rivals due to the fact that it has *different*, more efficient technical means of routing. For example, in the telecommunications sector, the functional and technical specifications decided by NRAs for carrier pre-selection operators (CPSOs) sometimes have inherent cost disadvantages for CPSOs, as compared to the incumbent. Frequently, CPSOs interconnect with the incumbent at the highest level in the network hierarchy, whereas the incumbent's own downstream business interconnects at the lower hierarchy levels of the network. In effect, therefore, rivals have to purchase an additional network element that the incumbent does not need for its service. The same issue arises in any situation in which an incumbent can transport voice or data by a more direct, cheaper means, while rivals use different, less direct and more expensive routing. These differences necessarily have an impact on the wholesale end-to-end costs of rivals and, in certain instances, on their ability to compete downstream with the incumbent.

Certain national decisions have touched on cost disadvantages suffered by rivals as a consequence of regulatory choices.[148] These cases are inconclusive, however, on the principles to be applied, since no margin squeeze has been found based *only* on rivals' cost disadvantages as a result of regulatory choices. It is difficult to see, however, why, as a matter of competition law, a margin squeeze abuse could be found in these circumstances. There is no duty on the dominant firm to compensate rivals for higher relative costs as a result of their choice of certain technical means of access not used by the dominant firm itself. A rival cannot claim under competition law to be entitled to the same efficiencies and cost basis as a dominant firm. There is no case law under Article 82 EC to the effect that a dominant firm must, in order to avoid an exclusionary conduct, compensate rivals for higher costs that are the result of a technical means of access under regulatory principles that is less efficient that a different means of access used by the dominant firm. And such a rule of law would be irrational.

This is indirectly confirmed by *Industrie des Poudres Sphériques*[149] and *Bronner.*[150] One of the reasons for Industries des Poudres Sphériques' apparent lack of downstream profitability was that it had higher processing costs than the dominant firm. The Court of First Instance held that, unless rivals' higher processing costs were caused by an exclusionary margin squeeze, the way in which a dominant vertically integrated undertaking decides its profit margin "is of no relevance to its effects on its competitors." Similarly, the fact that the dominant firm has lower costs than a rival is of no incidence unless the prices it charges competitors give rise to a margin squeeze.

---

[148] See, e.g., Case CW/00760/03/04, *Investigation against BT about potential anticompetitive exclusionary behaviour*, Ofcom Decision of July 12, 2004.

[149] Case T-5/97, *Industrie des Poudres Sphériques SA v Commission* [2000] ECR II-3755.

[150] Case C-7/97, *Oscar Bronner GmbH & Co KG v Mediaprint Zeitungs- und Zeitschriftenverlag GmbH & Co KG, Mediaprint Zeitungsvertriebsgesellschaft mbH & Co KG and Mediaprint Anzeigengesellschaft mbH & Co KG* [1998] ECR I-7791.

In *Bronner*, Advocate General Jacobs concluded that, unless there is an abuse, "the mere fact that by retaining a facility for its own use a dominant undertaking retains an advantage over a competitor cannot justify requiring access to it." The mere fact that a dominant firm has cost advantages over a rival cannot require the dominant firm to compensate rivals for them. If the dominant company has cost advantages in comparison with its competitor, they are legitimate, and the dominant company need do nothing to lessen the impact of the cost advantage. It is only if the dominant company charges its competitor more for some essential input which both the downstream operations must use (i.e., discrimination), or if the dominant company's downstream operations are below its costs on the basis of that price (i.e., a margin squeeze), that an abuse occurs.[151] A dominant company has no obligation to subsidise a competitor or to compensate it for any cost disadvantages. In sum, a rival cannot claim under competition law to be entitled to the same efficiencies and cost basis as a dominant firm.[152]

A final case is where the effect of regulation is that the dominant firm's own costs are *higher* than some or all of its downstream rivals. This situation can arise where an incumbent has a duty to make available a range of different technical access solutions that third parties can use alone or in combination. Suppose that, over time, rivals limit themselves to using a range of intermediate inputs whereas, for legacy or regulatory reasons, the dominant firm's own business is required to continue to use more expensive inputs. In effect, therefore, regulation creates a situation in which some or all of the dominant firm's rivals have lower costs relative to the dominant firm.

In this circumstance the question arises whether the dominant firm can lawfully price below the regulated price for the more expensive inputs. Arguably, yes. The matter could be looked at in one of two ways. A first solution is that the dominant firm would have a defence of "meeting competition" under competition law in this situation,[153] at least to the extent that it remained profitable on an end-to-end basis. This approach was rejected, however, in *France Télécom/SFR Cegetel/Bouygues Télécom*. A second solution would be to accept the argument outlined in Section 6.5 above, i.e., that a margin squeeze cannot be found unless the dominant firm is pricing not only below its

[151] The non-discrimination obligation in Article 82(c) is not relevant in this situation because the dominant firm's technical means of access and rival's are not "equivalent transactions."

[152] An example may be useful. Suppose a vertically integrated dominant firm supplies two different inputs that can both be used in similar quantities to make a final product, but the first input reduces overall production costs by 50% more than the second input. Now suppose that a competitor can only use the higher cost input to produce its products because it has an older plant that is not tooled to use the other input and it would be uneconomic for that competitor to build a new plant capable of using the lower-cost input. In contrast, the dominant firm has a newer plant that allows it to use the lower cost input, which would give it a cost advantage over the rival in the downstream market. Provided that the dominant firm has done nothing to make it more difficult for the competitor to use the cheaper input, it could not be suggested that the cost advantage created by using the cheaper input is something that the dominant firm should compensate the rival for, or that it would be abusive for the dominant firm to take advantage of it. The fact that the dominant firm also supplies the rival with the higher cost input and the rival has no effective opportunities to switch to the lower cost input for technical or other reasons does not change the analysis. Using the cheaper input is simply a legitimate advantage available to the dominant firm, but not the rival.

[153] See Ch. 5 (Predatory Pricing) for detailed treatment of the defence of meeting competition.

own costs, but also below those of its rivals. In this circumstance, the dominant firm would not commit an abuse, since its prices would remain above the (lower) costs of rivals.

Chapter 7

EXCLUSIVE DEALING, LOYALTY DISCOUNTS, AND RELATED PRACTICES

7.1 INTRODUCTION

The basic approach to exclusive dealing under Article 82 EC. Although Articles 81 EC and 82 EC share common objectives,[1] and can apply in parallel to the same matter,[2] exclusive dealing has historically been subject to much stricter treatment under Article 82 EC. Under Article 81 EC, exclusive dealing is subject to an effects analysis that requires proof of material anticompetitive effects and, if such effects are shown, an assessment of countervailing efficiencies. Given the ubiquity of vertical restraints, and the need for legal certainty, Article 81 EC has also introduced various block exemptions setting out certain "safe harbours," whereby arrangements between parties that do not possess market power (e.g., less than a 30% market share) are presumed legal, absent hardcore restraints (e.g., vertical price-fixing).[3] No presumption of illegality applies outside these safe harbours: each case must be analysed on its merits.

In contrast, Article 82 EC has historically taken a very strict approach to exclusive dealing by dominant firms, suggesting that "in principle" such arrangements are not permitted.[4] Essentially the same principles have been applied to clauses whereby a customer agrees to source "most" of its requirements from a dominant firm.[5] And the situation is the same where a dominant firm makes payment of a discount conditional on the customer dealing exclusively, or mainly, with the dominant firm. This approach has been relaxed somewhat in *Van den Bergh Foods*, although the Court of First Instance mainly analysed the case from the perspective of Article 81 EC.[6] The Discussion Paper[7] now proposes to make express a point that was implicit in *Van den Bergh Foods*: that exclusive dealing arrangements under Article 82 EC should be analysed under the same broad rubric as Article 81 EC.

---

[1] See Case 6/72, *Europemballage Corporation and Continental Can Company Inc v Commission* [1973] ECR 215.

[2] See Ch. 1 (Introduction, Scope of Application, and Basic Framework), s. 1.4.2, above.

[3] See Commission Regulation (EC) 2790/1999 of December 22, 1999, on the application of Article 81(3) of the Treaty to categories of vertical agreements and concerted practices, OJ 1999 L 336/21; Commission Notice—Guidelines on Vertical Restraints, OJ 2000 C 291/1; Commission Regulation (EC) No 772/2004 of 27 April 2004 on the application of Article 81(3) of the Treaty to categories of technology transfer agreements, OJ 2004 L 123/11; Commission Notice—Guidelines on the application of Article 81 of the EC Treaty to technology transfer agreements, OJ 2004 C 101/2.

[4] See Case 85/76, *Hoffmann-La Roche and Co AG v Commission* [1979] ECR 461, para. 121.

[5] *Ibid.*

[6] *Van den Bergh Foods Ltd*, OJ 1998 L 246/1, on appeal Case T-65/98, *Van den Bergh Foods Ltd v Commission* [2003] ECR II-4653 (hereinafter "*Van den Bergh Foods*").

[7] DG Competition discussion paper on the application of Article 82 of the Treaty to exclusionary abuses, Brussels, December 2005, (hereinafter the "Discussion Paper").

Loyalty discounts, target rebates, and related practices under Article 82 EC. A second broad category of vertical restraint that has received extensive scrutiny under Article 82 EC is so-called "loyalty," (or "fidelity," or "target") discounts. The term "loyalty discount" has no specific meaning in law or economics and may, unless further defined, encompass anything from generally innocuous practices such as quantity (or volume) discounts to potentially troublesome schemes requiring a customer to purchase all, or most, of its requirements from a dominant firm. In general, however, loyalty discounts can be defined as "pricing structures offering lower prices in return for a buyer's agreed or *de facto* commitment to source a large and/or increasing share of his requirements with the discounter."[8] Loyalty discounts can be analysed under a similar framework to exclusive dealing, since they create conditional pricing structures that may lead to *de facto* exclusive dealing. But they are clearly a weaker form of incentive than exclusive dealing and so merit less strict treatment.

As with exclusive dealing, Article 82 EC has historically adopted a strict and formalistic approach to loyalty discounts, akin to *per se* illegality for certain instances.[9] This has been criticised, since loyalty discounts can have procompetitive or anticompetitive features, or a mixture of the two. The Discussion Paper proposes a potentially important shift in the treatment of loyalty discounts under Article 82 EC. There is broad recognition that the historic policy of *per se* illegality for certain forms of loyalty discounts can no longer be justified. Instead, the Discussion Paper proposes a structured rule-of-reason inquiry based on the proportion of the market affected by the loyalty discount scheme, the terms and criteria of the discount, whether the dominant firm's prices under the scheme would lead it to price below average total cost for the portion of customers' requirements open to competition, and whether the scheme is necessary for the dominant firm to achieve efficiencies. The practical ease of application of this test remains to be seen, but, coupled with the Discussion Paper's insistence on the need to show actual or likely anticompetitive effects, it clearly illustrates a more balanced approach to loyalty discounts than previously applied under Article 82 EC.

7.2 EXCLUSIVE DEALING

7.2.1 Economics of Exclusive Dealing

Overview.[10] Competition authorities and courts have long been wary of exclusive dealing. The basic fear is that they may allow firms to exclude rivals and prevent the development of competition. The "Chicago school" formulated a simple rebuttal of the idea that exclusive dealing arrangements usually threaten competition. This view held sway under US antitrust law for some time and is partly reflected in the approach to exclusive dealing under Article 81 EC. Post-Chicago commentators have, however,

[8] See Loyalty and Fidelity Discounts and Rebates, OECD Report of February 4, 2003, (DAFFE/COMP (2002) 21), p. 7.

[9] See, e.g., Case T-219/99, *British Airways plc v Commission* [2003] ECR II-5917; Case T-203/01, *Manufacture française des pneumatiques Michelin v Commission* [2003] ECR II-4071.

[10] This section is based on a contribution by Professor David Spector (Paris Science Economiques), which we gratefully acknowledge.

questioned certain aspects of the Chicago school's critique and identified circumstances in which exclusive dealing is not efficient, or is, on balance, more harmful than good. These developments are explained in detail below.[11]

The "Chicago school" view of exclusive dealing. The "Chicago school" rebuttal of the notion that exclusive dealing is anticompetitive is two-fold. The first category of arguments is a variant of the "single monopoly critique." The idea is simply that if a supplier wants to impose exclusivity on a retailer who does not want it, it will have to "purchase" the retailer's acquiescence by charging less than the price it would have been able to charge otherwise. The supplier's price is limited by its customer's willingness to pay, which falls if exclusive dealing is imposed against the customer's best interests. This means that exclusivity is never imposed but rather purchased by the supplier (in the form of a price cut). A supplier thus has no incentive to offer an exclusive contract unless exclusivity is efficient.[12] Put differently, unless properly compensated, a customer would never agree to sign a contract which stifles competition and gives the exclusive supplier the power to raise future prices at its detriment. But the need to pay this compensation makes exclusive dealing unprofitable for a supplier, unless it also has efficiency justifications.[13]

The second aspect of the Chicago critique has to do with efficiency justifications. If exclusive dealing is not a monopolisation tool, they argued that it must have other, procompetitive motives. Exclusive dealing may be needed in order to solve a free-riding problem when the provision of a good also involves the provision of a complementary service to the buyer (who could be a retailer or a final user) which allows it to make better use of the good (e.g., supplying marketing material to a retailer, or training a buyer to use complex machinery). If these complementary services are not completely specific to the product, there is a possibility that the buyer will use them in

---

[11] See Ch. 4 (The General Concept of an Abuse), s. 4.2.1, above for a detailed treatment of the influence of Chicago and post-Chicago thinking on antitrust law.

[12] A Director and E Levi, "Law and the Future: Trade Regulation" (1956) 51(2) *Northwestern University Law Review* 281–296; R Bork, *The Antitrust Paradox: A Policy At War With Itself* (New York, Basic Books, 1978) ch. 15.

[13] Interestingly enough, more recent formal models have confirmed these basic insights: in a static market in which competing suppliers make offers to a single customer (or to a set of identical customers, with a ban on discrimination), exclusive dealing arises only if it is jointly efficient for suppliers and customers as a whole. See BD Bernheim and MD Whinston, "Exclusive Dealing," *Journal of Political Economy* 106(1), 64-103 (1998). Indeed, the possibility to offer exclusive contracts may intensify competition, as each supplier is ready to offer low prices in order to gain exclusivity. This means that even though exclusive dealing by definition reduces *ex post* competition, it may increase *ex ante* competition. See DP O'Brien and G Shaffer, "Nonlinear Supply Contracts, Exclusive Dealing, and Equilibrium Market Foreclosure," *Journal of Economics & Management Strategy* 6(4), 755-785 (1997). Far from being a theoretical oddity, the idea that competition for the exclusive supply of a retailer may lower prices is backed by some evidence. In the words of Judge Easterbrook, "competition-for-the-contract is a form of competition that antitrust laws protect rather than proscribe, and it is common. Every year or two, General Motors, Ford, and Chrysler invite tyre manufacturers to bid for exclusive rights to have their tyres used in the manufacturers' cars. Exclusive contracts make the market hard to enter in mid-year but cannot stifle competition over the longer run, and competition of this kind drives down the price of tyres, to the ultimate benefit of consumers." See *Paddock Publications Inc v Chicago Tribune Co.*, 103 F 3rd. 42, 45 (7th Circ. 1996).

future in conjunction with products purchased from the supplier's rivals. This possibility reduces the supplier's incentives to provide these services.

In principle, this problem could be solved through a market mechanism, by putting a price tag on these complementary services. However, transaction costs often prevent this: for example, it may be impossible to describe in writing the quality of the training which a supplier is offering to provide. An exclusive dealing clause helps the supplier and its customer to get around this problem. It removes the risk that the customer will free-ride on the supplier's complementary services and thus increases the supplier's incentive to provide them in adequate amount and quality.[14]

Other motives, less subtle but no less important in practice, may explain exclusive contracts. When they last long enough, they reduce a supplier's uncertainty regarding the future volume of sales, which may increase the supplier's incentives to invest in order to achieve economies of scale, or simply to reduce variable costs or increase quality. Exclusive dealing may also be necessary in order to protect the supplier's brand if there is the risk that, absent an exclusivity clause, retailers would try to free-ride on the brand's reputation by passing off an inferior product as the supplier's own.[15]

Post-Chicago theories of exclusive dealing. In the last two decades, various "post-Chicago" models have challenged the abovementioned arguments by showing that they rely crucially on a number of assumptions, in particular the following: (1) firms are assumed to be able to use nonlinear pricing; (2) all affected economic agents are assumed to be present when the exclusive contracts are negotiated; and (3) a firm entering into exclusive contracts has to compensate customers for the harm possibly caused by these contracts.

If nonlinear pricing is feasible, a firm can use it in order to extract what its product is worth to a customer simply by offering each customer the possibility of purchasing the optimal quantity against a fixed fee, equal to the entire surplus brought about by the transaction. It thus has an incentive to maximise total surplus, and will offer exclusivity only if it is efficient. But if firms are restricted to use linear pricing, exclusive dealing can work as a partial substitute to nonlinear pricing: agreeing to purchase exclusively from a given supplier is tantamount to committing to purchase a given volume from it (the entirety of its needs).[16] If this is the motive for exclusive dealing, the impact on consumer or aggregate welfare, just like the impact of "real" nonlinear pricing, is ambiguous. This is simply because two opposing factors are at play: the decline in

---

[14] H Marvel, "Exclusive Dealing" (1982) 25 *Journal of Law and Economics* 1–25; O Williamson, "Credible Commitments: Using Hostages to Support Exchange" (1983) 73 *American Economic Review* 519–40; and I Segal and M Whinston, "Exclusive Contracts and the Protection of Investments" (2000) 31(4) *RAND Journal of Economics* 603–33.

[15] On the treatment of such procompetitive motives by US courts, see J Jacobson, "Exclusive Dealing, Foreclosure, and Consumer Harm" (2002) 70(2) *Antitrust Law Journal* 311–69.

[16] This argument carries over to situations in which nonlinear pricing is legal but is insufficient to allow firms to appropriate the entire surplus of their relationships with their customers because of uncertainty about demand.

product variety harms welfare, but firms offering exclusive dealing are also induced to lower prices.[17] This rebuttal of the Chicago argument is thus not very potent.

Another theory of anticompetitive exclusive dealing challenges the assumption that the "targeted" firm is present when the exclusive contract is offered. The key idea is that an incumbent and its customers have a joint interest in lowering as much as possible the prices that future entrants will charge, if they happen to be more efficient than the incumbent—simply in order to appropriate part of the entrants' "efficiency rents." This can be done by signing an exclusive contract together with a breach penalty clause, because in order to induce the buyer to purchase from it despite the penalty, a future entrant will have to cut price.[18]

According to this theory, exclusion is not the goal, but rather an unintended side-effect of the exclusivity clause, resulting from uncertainty about future entrants' costs: while exclusive contracts coupled with a breach penalty clause induce very efficient entrants to cut prices (which is the desired outcome), they also inefficiently exclude moderately efficient entrants. Again, the real-world relevance of this theory can be disputed for at least two reasons. First, it is far from clear that a large number of the exclusive dealing contracts which have aroused antitrust scrutiny contained breach penalty clauses that were likely to be used. Indeed, many such clauses would be illegal under contract laws. Second, even if this theory were correct, its welfare impact would be ambiguous, because the inefficient exclusion of some entrants may be offset by the lowering of the prices offered by those who end up entering.[19]

The third set of theories constitutes the most convincing rebuttal of the Chicago critique. These theories again assume that the adversely affected firms are absent when exclusive contracts are offered, but they add the assumption that the incumbent firm does not need to compensate buyers for the harm caused by exclusivity because it can exploit the externalities existing between buyer decisions. The idea is that if a potential entrant faces fixed costs, an incumbent can deter entry simply by offering exclusive contracts to some, but not all, customers—just the number that is needed in order to prevent the potential entrant from achieving the minimum viable scale.

Suppose there are 100 potential buyers and an entrant cannot operate profitably unless it sells to at least 50 of them, then the incumbent can deter entry by luring 51 customers into signing an exclusive contract. This allows it to unleash its monopoly power at the expense of 100 customers, but it only has to compensate 51 of them: the core of the Chicago argument breaks down. On top of this discriminating, "divide-and-rule" strategy, the incumbent may even succeed in compensating no customer at all, simply by exploiting the lack of coordination across buyers. If every buyer is convinced that the other 99 will sign the exclusive contract anyway, it loses nothing by signing it as well, since it expects entry to be deterred irrespective of its decision. The incumbent

[17] F Mathewson and R Winter, "The Competitive Effect of Vertical Agreements: Comment" (1987) 77(5) *American Economic Review* 1057–62.

[18] P Aghion and P Bolton, "Contracts as a Barrier to Entry" (1987) 77(3) *American Economic Review* 388–401.

[19] This procompetitive effect is absent in Aghion and Bolton's simple model because it assumes a completely inelastic demand, implying that welfare is price-independent at least over some interval.

thus does not need to compensate any buyer for signing an exclusive contract, even though they are all harmed by the resulting entry deterrence.[20] In a variant of this theory, the targeted firm is assumed to be present when contracts are offered, but some future consumers are not, and depriving the targeted firm from access to the current customers is enough to induce it to leave the market because sales to future consumers alone cannot cover the fixed costs of staying.

Evaluating the competing theories on exclusive dealing. The competing theories show that exclusive dealing can be used in order to decrease competition, but only under a set of stringent conditions. Some of these conditions are common to all exclusionary strategies. For exclusive dealing to harm competition, the decrease in the alleged victims' residual demand must be is large enough to deter them from entering into or remaining in the market. This depends on their costs and on the share of the market that is foreclosed as a consequence of the disputed contracts. Another necessary condition is that the exclusion of the victims should be sufficient to increase the incumbent's market power.

But, in addition, the anticompetitive use of exclusive contracts requires some adversely affected parties to be absent when these contracts are offered—otherwise, the parties would come up with a non-exclusive, mutually beneficial alternative, according to the logic of the Coase theorem.[21] In particular, competitive harm is more likely if the alleged victim is a potential entrant rather than an already present firm, or if intertemporal economies of scale are important and future buyers are not yet able to enter into contracts. If all alleged victims were present when the disputed contracts were signed, it is relevant to ask why they were unable to respond to these contracts—coordination failures or contract complexity being possible answers.

Last but not least, an exclusionary strategy based on exclusive contracts may lack credibility. This is because once the allegedly targeted firm has decided to enter or to stay in the market in spite of the exclusive contracts designed to evict it, the allegedly excluding firm has no more incentive to keep the exclusive contracts in place. But anticipating this should cause the targeted firms to call the excluding firm's bluff. Among the possible answers to this objection are: (1) the possibility that the excluding firm will stick to exclusive dealing in order to build a reputation for toughness; and (2) the possibility that the alleged victim is uncertain as to the real motives for exclusive dealing and thus as to whether it will endure—it may not know whether it is there for exclusionary purposes only or also from procompetitive motives.

---

[20] The seminal papers are E Rasmusen, J Ramseyer, and J Wiley, "Naked Exclusion" (1991) 81(5) *American Economic Review* 1137–45; and I Segal and M Whinston, "Naked Exclusion: Comment" (2000) 90(1) *American Economic Review* 296–309. See also R Innes and R Sexton, "Strategic Buyers and Exclusionary Contracts" (1994) 84(3) *American Economic Review* 566–84. The analysis is more complex when buyers are retailers rather than final users. See J Simpson and A Wickelgren, "The Use of Exclusive Contracts to Deter Entry" *Federal Trade Commission Working Paper No. 241* (2001).

[21] However, these non-exclusive alternatives may be so complex that socially harmful exclusive dealing may arise in spite of all affected parties being present if there are limits to contract complexity. See D Spector, "Exclusive Contracts and Demand Foreclosure" *Paris Sciences Economiques Working Paper* (2006).

Whatever rule is used to handle exclusive dealing, it should make room for an efficiency defence and require that the necessary conditions for an anticompetitive impact be checked before a contract is considered unlawful. This means in particular checking whether the share of the foreclosed market is large enough to induce exclusion and whether exclusion will increase market power, explaining why the adversely affected parties could not come up with alternative, non-exclusive contracts, and addressing the credibility issue. One possible filter could be the share of the total relevant market which is foreclosed. If it is small, an anticompetitive effect is unlikely. Also, contract duration could be considered, because an anticompetitive impact is unlikely if customers are frequently released from their contractual obligations and can thus be offered contracts by entrants.[22]

7.2.2 Exclusive Dealing Under Article 82 EC

Overview. The approach to exclusive dealing under Article 82 EC can broadly be characterised by three distinct phases. The first phase—which predominated—involved treating exclusive dealing by a dominant firm as a *per se* violation. This approach persisted until very recently. The second phase reflects the approach applied by the Commission and Court of First Instance in *Van den Bergh Foods*,[23] where tentative steps were made towards adopting a rule-of-reason approach to exclusive dealing, similar to that applied under Article 81 EC. The final phase concerns explicit recognition in the Discussion Paper that exclusive dealing arrangements under Article 82 EC should be analysed under the same broad rubric as Article 81 EC. This makes sense: if an agreement could be analysed under either Article 81 EC or Article 82 EC, it would be perverse if the outcome differed materially depending on which provision happened to apply.[24] The fact of dominance clearly affects the assessment,

---

[22] This remark should not be construed as implying that competition authorities should be biased against long term exclusive contracts. In fact, both procompetitive and anticompetitive effects are more likely under long term contracts.

[23] *Van den Bergh Foods Ltd*, OJ 1998 L 246/1, on appeal Case T-65/98, *Van den Bergh Foods Ltd v Commission* [2003] ECR II-4653.

[24] An interesting question is why the Community institutions sometimes prefer to apply Article 82 EC to agreements or practices also covered by Article 81 EC. Several reasons may be offered. First, it is sometimes argued that a dominant firm can impose an "agreement" that in reality only benefits the dominant firm, so the action is more unilateral than consensual in nature. But this is not generally correct: as noted in section 7.2.1, even if exclusive dealing would harm the customer, he/she may accept it because of the dominant firm's implicit promise to share some of the (anticompetitively obtained) profits with the customer. Moreover, even if this argument is wrong, the Commission has usually reserved the right in Article 81 EC cases (e.g., parallel trade restrictions) to fine only the "beneficiary" of an agreement. Second, where a firm is dominant, the *lex specialis* of Article 82 EC should arguably be applied in preference to the *lex generalis* of Article 81 EC. Third, in many cases, complaints may be brought only on the basis of Article 82 EC. This may be because the complainant alleges a mixture of acts, some of which fall under Article 81 EC and some of which do not. It may be more convenient for the Commission to apply Article 82 EC to all the practices than to separately analyse unilateral conduct and agreements. The same might be said of a network of similar agreements. Although Article 81 EC can apply to a series of agreements, it may be more convenient for the Commission to assess the cumulative effect of the agreements under Article 82 EC. See, e.g., Case 85/76, *Hoffmann-La Roche and Co AG v Commission* [1979] ECR 461. Finally, and more pragmatically, the assessment of exclusive agreements under Article 82 EC has historically been much less rigorous than the analysis under Article 81 EC. The interventionist approach sometimes adopted by

but it cannot justify an *a priori* assumption that exclusive dealing by dominant firms is always anticompetitive.

7.2.2.1 Evolution of the decisional practice and case law

The historic approach: *per se* illegality. The strict approach to exclusive dealing under Article 82 EC is reflected in a number of leading cases in the last several decades. As early as *Suiker Unie*, the Commission and Court of Justice confirmed that discounts conditional upon customers obtaining their annual requirements from the dominant sugar cartel were abusive.[25] The clauses in question were intended to prevent customers from sourcing even a small proportion of their requirements from foreign sugar producers. The Court of Justice found that "[t]he grant of such a rebate placed customers who also buy sugar from other sources at an unjustifiable disadvantage and enabled [the dominant supplier] to 'control' the volume of supplies to its customers by foreign producers."[26]

A similar approach was applied in *Hoffmann-La Roche*, where the leading global producer of multiple vitamins, Roche, expressly or impliedly required customers to purchase all or most of their vitamins requirements from it.[27] Roche offered different costumers different prices for identical quantities of the same product, depending on whether or not they agreed to limit purchases from its competitors. Most contracts were expressly conditional upon the customer buying "all" or "most" of their annual requirements from Roche. For those contracts that did not have express clauses requiring customers to source "all" or "most" of their requirements from Roche, the Court examined their factual context and concluded that they too were conditional on the customer sourcing a "major part" of its requirements from Roche.[28] The Court of Justice concluded that "the special price offered by Roche is the consideration for the abandonment by its purchasers of their opportunities to obtain substantial proportions of their requirements from competitors."[29]

The Court applied this broad rule to any express or implied exclusive dealing obligation, as well as to commitments to source "most" (*in casu* 75–80%) or a "large proportion" of requirements from the dominant firm. It added that exclusivity would be illegal notwithstanding the fact that the contracts were concluded upon the request of the

---

the Commission in past cases may therefore explain a greater willingness to apply Article 82 EC to agreements. Of course, none of this matters unless the outcome would differ depending on which provision happened to apply. Historically, this was the case, but, as indicated by *Van den Bergh Foods*, and the Discussion Paper, the Commission will now adopt essentially the same analysis under both provisions. Accordingly, it should not now matter in principle which provision applies. See generally E Rousseva, "Modernising by Eradicating: How the Commission's New Approach to Article 81 EC Dispenses with the Need to Apply Article 82 EC to Vertical Restraints" (2005) 42 *Common Market Law Review* 587.

[25] Joined Cases 40 to 48, 50, 54 to 56, 111, 113 and 114-73, *Coöperatieve Vereniging "Suiker Unie" UA and others v Commission* [1975] ECR 1663.

[26] *Ibid.*, para. 502.

[27] *Vitamins*, OJ 1976 L 223/27, on appeal Case 85/76, *Hoffmann-La Roche and Co AG v Commission* [1979] ECR 461 (hereinafter "*Hoffmann-La Roche*").

[28] *Hoffmann-La Roche*, *ibid.*, paras. 83 et seq.

[29] *Vitamins*, above, para. 24.

purchaser.[30] The Court's reasoning was that, in the presence of dominance competition is already weakened and therefore any further interference with the market structure is likely to eliminate all competition.[31] Thus, "the concept of an abuse...*in principle* includes any obligation to obtain supplies exclusively from an undertaking in a dominant position which benefits that undertaking."[32]

Finally, in *British Plasterboard*, the Court of First Instance persisted in a strict approach to exclusive dealing under Article 82 EC. British Plasterboard and British Gypsum Ltd., the dominant plasterboard sellers in the United Kingdom, gave special payment schemes to builders' merchants who concluded exclusive purchase agreements for plasterboard. Further, they favoured customers who did not trade in imported plasterboard and pressured a consortium of importers to agree not to sell any imported plasterboard.[33] Although the Court stated that rebates granted in return for an exclusive purchasing commitment "cannot, as a matter of principle, be prohibited," but rather must be assessed in the light of "the effects of such commitments on the functioning of the market concerned...and in their specific context," it added that these considerations "cannot be unreservedly accepted in the case of a market where, precisely because of the dominant position of one of the economic operators, competition is already restricted."[34] The Court concluded that a dominant undertaking which "ties purchasers—even if it does so at their request—by an obligation or promise on their part to obtain all or most of their requirements exclusively from the said undertaking abuses its dominant position."[35] Essentially the same conclusions were reached by the Court of Justice on appeal.[36]

Towards a rule-of-reason: *Van den Bergh Foods*. *Van den Bergh Foods* is the first case evincing a greater willingness on the part of the Community institutions to apply a consistent approach to exclusive dealing under Articles 81 and 82 EC. The case concerned HB, the dominant supplier of impulse ice cream in Ireland. HB supplied retailers with freezer cabinets free of charge on condition that the cabinets would not be used to stock competing products. Around 40% of available outlets were tied up in such arrangements. HB was found dominant on the impulse ice cream market in Ireland, given its large market share, brand loyalty, and the presence of only few competitors. The Commission found that the exclusivity commitment violated both Articles 81 and 82 EC.

The chief interest of the case lies in the Court of First Instance's analysis of exclusivity requirement on appeal. The Court mainly looked at the clause from the perspective of

[30] Case 85/76, *Hoffmann-La Roche and Co AG v Commission* [1979] ECR 461, paras. 117–20.

[31] *Ibid*., para. 83.

[32] *Ibid*., para. 121 (emphasis added).

[33] Case T-65/89, *BPB Industries plc and British Gypsum Ltd v Commission* [1993] ECR II-389.

[34] *Ibid*., paras. 65–67.

[35] *Ibid*., para. 3. See also Case T-83/91, *Tetra Pak International SA v Commission* [1994] ECR II-755, on appeal Case C-333/94 P, *Tetra Pak International SA v Commission* [1996] ECR I-5951 (Court of First Instance held that where an undertaking in a dominant position directly or indirectly ties its customers by an exclusive supply obligation, that constitutes an abuse since it deprives the customers of their ability to choose the source of supply and denies other manufacturers access to the market).

[36] See, e.g., Opinion of Advocate General Léger in Case C-310/93 P, *BPB Industries plc and British Gypsum Ltd v Commission* [1995] ECR I-865, paras. 43–46.

Article 81 EC, applying its usual rule-of-reason analysis. Thus, the Court noted that the agreements tied a large part of the customer base (c. 40%) and that the exclusivity clause was an insurmountable barrier to entry. It added that there was obvious demand for other brands, but that the exclusivity clause prevented retailers from switching to other suppliers. Further the Court conceded that the agreement created certain efficiencies, but pointed out that the exclusivity clause was not indispensable to the realisation of those efficiencies.[37]

When analysing the same clause under Article 82 EC, the Court essentially summarised its reasoning under Article 81 EC. This echoes the Commission's finding that, "for the purpose of applying Article [82 EC], the circumstances surrounding the agreements and particularly their effect on the structure of competition in the relevant market must be taken into account in establishing the existence of an abuse."[38] The Court then confirmed the Commission's view that the exclusivity requirement was abusive, holding that:[39]

> "The fact that an undertaking in a dominant position on a market ties de facto...40% of outlets in the relevant market by an exclusivity clause which in reality creates outlet exclusivity constitutes an abuse of a dominant position...The exclusivity clause has the effect of preventing the retailers concerned from selling other brands of ice cream (or of reducing the opportunity for them to do so), even though there is a demand for such brands, and of preventing competing manufacturers from gaining access to the relevant market."

These statements suggest that, when assessing exclusive dealing arrangements under Article 82 EC, the Community institutions will now look closely at the actual or likely effects of a particular arrangement in the relevant market and its impact on consumers.

The Discussion Paper's proposals: full rule-of-reason. The Discussion Paper now confirms that the Commission intends to apply a full rule-of-reason approach to exclusive dealing under Article 82 EC. A number of general principles are set out in the Discussion Paper. First, exclusive dealing is considered, by nature, to have "the capability to foreclose," since such contracts require the buyer to purchase all or a significant part of its requirements from the dominant supplier.[40] Second, in order to assess whether the basic "capability" of exclusive dealing to foreclosure in fact leads to foreclosure in an individual case, the Commission will require evidence of likely or actual foreclosure effects on the market.[41] Third, the Commission will also consider whether existing and possible future competitors can counteract the dominant firm's conduct.[42] Finally, the dominant firm may put forward evidence showing why the exclusive dealing requirements did not materially harm competition or, if they did, that they were necessary to achieve certain efficiencies.[43]

---

[37] Case T-65/98, *Van den Bergh Foods Ltd v Commission* [2003] ECR II-4653.

[38] *Van den Bergh Foods Ltd*, OJ 1998 L 246/1, para. 268.

[39] Case T-65/98, *Van den Bergh Foods Ltd v Commission* [2003] ECR II-4653, para. 160.

[40] Discussion Paper, para. 149. See also Commission Notice—Guidelines on the application of Article 81(3) of the Treaty, OJ 2004 C 101/97, paras. 140, 141.

[41] *Ibid.*, para. 144.

[42] *Ibid.*

[43] *Ibid.*, para. 138.

7.2.2.2 Assessing exclusive dealing under Article 82 EC

Overview. This section outlines the analytical steps that should be taken under the rule-of-reason approach now advocated in the Discussion Paper. Describing the Community institutions' past approach is straightforward: exclusive dealing and substantial requirements contracts were treated as essentially *per se* violations of Article 82 EC. But it bears emphasis that, until final guidelines are adopted, this strict approach prevails. Were the proposals in the Discussion Paper to be adopted, a number of steps would apply in a rule-of-reason type analysis of exclusive dealing:

1. The first—and most critical—step is to assess whether exclusive dealing materially forecloses rivals' access to the relevant downstream market. This involves an assessment of, first, how pervasive the exclusive dealing requirement is in terms of market coverage and, second, if it is pervasive enough, whether rivals have other ways of accessing the downstream market.

2. Second, although materially limiting rivals' access to a relevant downstream market can result in consumer harm, this is not axiomatic. Consumer harm thus needs to be independently verified.

3. Finally, exclusive dealing usually produces efficiencies and these need to be counterbalanced against any harm they also cause to consumers. Such balancing exercises are difficult for courts and competition authorities and therefore prone to error. This suggests that great care should be taken with the first two conditions—foreclosure and harm to competition—which are generally easier to measure.

Proving material foreclosure from the relevant downstream market. It is analytically useful to distinguish two different types of exclusive dealing. The first, and most common in practice, concerns exclusive dealing that limits rivals' access to a downstream selling market by binding intermediaries and/or final retailers to the dominant firm. A second scenario is where a dominant firm denies rivals access to key inputs by making exclusive deals with the sellers. The analytical framework is essentially the same in both cases, but the costs invested in distribution (and the ability to seek out additional distribution) generally would be less than retooling (often-specialised) manufacturing assets to use different upstream inputs.

a. Exclusive dealing foreclosing downstream markets. Exclusive dealing is only objectionable if it forecloses access to a *relevant market*: the lack of access to a particular distributor or retailer is insufficient. Thus, in analysing actual or likely exclusionary effects, an important first question is the incidence of the exclusivity requirement in the relevant market, i.e., the share of the market "tied" up by exclusive dealing.[44] In many cases, the tied share will correspond to the dominant firm's market share, in which case a presumption of foreclosure arises unless rivals have other effective ways of reaching customers. The degree of dominance is therefore likely to have a substantial impact on the capability of an exclusive dealing obligation to unlawfully exclude rivals. In *Van den Bergh Foods*, the Court of First Instance even

[44] *Ibid.*, para. 145.

suggested that a 40% tied market share would constitute an abuse of a dominant position.[45] But no hard and fast market share rule should apply: much will depend on the portion of the distribution market (if any) that rivals need to achieve basic scale, which will vary from case to case. Small tied shares, however, should be presumed to have no material foreclosure effect.

Where the dominant company applies an exclusive dealing obligation to a good part of its buyers and this obligation therefore affects, if not most, at least a substantial part of market demand, the Discussion Paper states that the Commission is likely to conclude that the obligation has a market distorting foreclosure effect, and thus constitutes an abuse of the dominant position.[46] This statement seems, however, to go too far. Dominance may be found at relatively low market share levels (e.g., 40%), in which case the untied portion of the market may well be sufficient for rivals to access distributors and retailers. The key question is *how much* access to distribution rivals need and whether exclusive dealing requirements by the dominant firm limit their possibilities of accessing that necessary portion.

Merely because a material proportion of dealers are affected by the dominant firm's exclusive dealing does not, however, mean that rivals are foreclosed. A very important second factor—not mentioned in the Discussion Paper—in assessing the scope for foreclosure is whether rivals can avail themselves of *alternative distribution strategies* to avoid the effects of the dominant firm's exclusive deals. Rivals may be able to use alternative forms of distribution, persuade existing distributors to add new product lines, encourage new distribution entry, or self-distribute. A good example is the sale of airline tickets where distribution has shifted strongly away from travel agents towards distribution through dedicated airline websites and/or resellers that deal in multiple airlines. If alternative, viable distribution or sales strategies are open to rivals, the fact that the dominant firm has tied certain distributors with an exclusive deal should be irrelevant.

For example, in *Omega v Gilbarco*,[47] a US Court of Appeals concluded that exclusive dealing commitments affecting 38% of the relevant market—which the court considered to be "significant"—did not give rise to foreclosure, since alternative means of distribution through direct sales and service contractors existed and were sufficient to eliminate the scope for foreclosure. In contrast, in *Dentsply*,[48] another US Court of Appeals found that direct sales of artificial teeth products were not an effective substitute for sales through distributors. The court distinguished the mere possibility to make direct sales from the need to show that direct sales were comparable in effectiveness to sales through dealers. In other words, direct sales must be practicable

[45] Case T-65/98, *Van den Bergh Foods Ltd v Commission* [2003] ECR II-4653, para. 160.

[46] *Ibid*., para. 149. It adds that foreclosure may be assumed at low tied market share levels where the dominant firm selectively targets important customers or targets customers of specific competitors. In such cases the Commission states that it "may find that a market distorting foreclosure effect results even though the tied market share is very modest" (para. 145).

[47] *Omega Environmental Inc v Gilbarco Inc*, 127 F.3d 1157 (9th Cir. 1997) (hereinafter "*Omega v Gilbarco*").

[48] *United States of America v Dentsply International Inc*, 399 F.3d 181 (3rd Cir. 2005) (hereinafter "*Dentsply*").

and feasible in the actual market context. The court found that dealers had a controlling degree of access to the laboratories who ultimately sold the artificial teeth to consumers. The long-entrenched Dentsply dealer network with its ties to the laboratories made it impracticable for a manufacturer to rely on direct distribution to the laboratories in any significant amount. The court considered the fact that some manufacturers resorted to direct sales and were even able to stay in business by selling directly as insufficient proof that direct selling was an effective means of competition. It held that the proper inquiry is not whether direct sales enable a competitor to survive, but rather whether direct selling poses a real threat to the defendant's dominance.

Even where the market share "tied" by exclusive dealing is high, and other forms of distribution are not an effective alternative, it may be that material foreclosure does not occur because distributors' influence on sales in the relevant market is small or unimportant. For example, in *CDC v IDEXX*,[49] a US Court of Appeals held that exclusive dealing by a firm with an 80% market share and which affected around 50% of available distributors did not give rise to material foreclosure because distributors were not critical to sales on the relevant downstream market. The products concerned were haematology analysers used by vets. Distributors did not sell these products: they were in the business of giving manufacturers the names of vets who had expressed an interest in the products. For this reason and others, the court concluded that distributors were not critical to the plaintiff's sales strategy.[50]

A final, important situation in which foreclosure is unlikely to be present is when a customer conducts an open tender arrangement in which all firms meeting certain criteria are allowed to participate. In this situation firms are competing for an exclusive supply contract and the fact that the winner obtain an exclusive deal is simply the logical, procompetititive outcome. Thus, in the *Coca-Cola Undertaking*, Coca-Cola was allowed to compete for exclusive public/private tender agreements—defined as based on an open and competitive tendering process with objective, transparent, and non-discriminatory criteria.[51] In that case, the duration of any such arrangements was limited to a maximum of five years and had to allow the customer an annual option to terminate the agreement without penalty following an initial term not exceeding three years. A similar rationale was applied to event sponsorship (e.g., sporting events, festivals). Exclusive supply rights for soft drinks were permitted for events that did not exceed sixty days per year (which need not be consecutive).[52]

b. Exclusive dealing foreclosing upstream input markets. Foreclosure may also occur in regard to the supply of upstream inputs when rivals cannot purchase key inputs because of exclusive or near-exclusive deals between the seller and one or more buyers.

[49] *CDC Technologies Inc v IDEXX Laboratories Inc*, 186 F.3d 74 (2nd Cir. 1999) (hereinafter "*CDC v IDEXX*").

[50] The court also attached importance to the fact that, notwithstanding IDEXX'S very high market share, there were no material barriers to entry on the market. This finding would not be open in an Article 82 EC case, since dominance—which is an essential pre-requisite for an abuse—pre-supposes that material barriers to entry exist. But the main point—that distributors may not in fact have much impact on sales—is valid.

[51] See *Coca-Cola*, OJ 2005 L 253/21, S. II.D.2.

[52] *Ibid*., s. II.D.1.

One recent example in which potential concerns in this regard have been expressed is *De Beers/Alrosa*.[53] In 2002, De Beers, the largest diamond producer in the world, and Alrosa, the leading Russian supplier of rough diamonds, made an agreement whereby Alrosa would supply rough diamonds to the value of $800 million per annum to De Beers for a duration of five years. This was about half of Alrosa's total output and corresponded in practice to the quantities of rough diamonds Alrosa had been exporting in the previous years outside the former Soviet Union through similar past agreements with De Beers.

Although the supply agreement was not exclusive, the Commission's preliminary assessment was that De Beers held a dominant position in the world-wide rough diamonds market and that, by entering into the agreement with Alrosa, its largest competitor, De Beers would gain control over a significant source of supply on the rough diamonds market, enabling it to acquire additional market share on that market and to obtain access to an extended range of diamonds otherwise not accessible to it. The Commission considered that the agreement would thus eliminate Alrosa as a source of supply on the market outside Russia and would enhance the already existing market power of De Beers with the effect of hindering the growth or maintenance of competition in the rough diamond market. De Beers would in effect distribute about half the production of its largest competitor. The case was settled by means of commitment decision pursuant to Article 9 of Regulation 1/2003,[54] under which De Beers agreed to reduce the quantities purchased from Alrosa to a level that the Commission considers would be non-exclusionary.[55]

In general, the principles governing exclusive dealing at wholesale/retail levels can also be applied to exclusive dealing covering upstream inputs. Thus, unless a material proportion of inputs sold on the relevant market is covered by exclusive deals, foreclosure concerns cannot arise. Likewise, the ability of rivals to seek out other input sources, or to by-pass the use of an input altogether, is clearly relevant. This requires an assessment of the barriers to entry into the relevant upstream market for the input and whether other input sellers are likely to emerge. An extreme example concerns key non-replicable assets that characterise "essential facility" cases under Article 82 EC.[56] In such situations, whether the dominant firm owns the supply of the essential input, or simply controls its supply through exclusive deals, seems a distinction without substance.

---

[53] See Notice published pursuant to Article 27(4) of Council Regulation (EC) No 1/2003 in Case COMP/E-2/38.381—*De Beers/Alrosa*, OJ 2005 C 136/32.

[54] See *De Beers' commitment to phase out rough diamond purchases from Alrosa made legally binding by Commission decision*, Commission Press Release IP/06/204 of February 22, 2006.

[55] The commitments offered by De Beers relate to its purchases of rough diamonds from Alrosa and provide for the termination of purchases from Alrosa as of 2009 after a phasing out period from 2006 to 2008. During this period, De Beers' purchases of rough diamonds from Alrosa will decrease from US$ 600m in 2006 to US$ 500m in 2007 and US$ 400m in 2008. A monitoring Trustee will supervise compliance with these commitments. The text of the commitments has not yet been published, however.

[56] See Ch. 8 (Refusal to Deal).

Proving consumer harm. Article 82 EC is primarily concerned with harm to consumer welfare, which means that it is competition and not competitors that is to be protected.[57] The test in this regard is said to be "actual or likely anticompetitive effects in the market and which can harm consumers in a direct or indirect manner."[58] The Discussion Paper states, however, that "harm to intermediate buyers is generally presumed to create harm to consumers;"[59] in other words, where a firm is dominant, harm to the structure of competition at the wholesale level creates a presumption of harm to downstream consumers. This statement is reasonable, but requires certain qualifications.

First, exclusive dealing with ultimate purchasers is by nature more likely to limit rivals' ability to compete than exclusive dealing with intermediaries. Exclusive dealing with intermediate buyers/sellers is only likely to harm competition where the firms concerned are particularly important as gatekeepers to effective competition on the relevant downstream market for the final product. But it may be that sellers do not need to use intermediaries, or certain types of intermediaries, much or at all. For example, in one case,[60] distributors were only in the business of giving manufacturers the names of vets who has expressed an interest in the products and not engaged in the sale of products. Because distributors were not a critical channel in making final sales, no abuse was made out.

Second, harm to rival firms at a wholesale level does not prove consumer harm: it is, at most, a presumption. The key point is that exclusive dealing must *increase* the dominant firm's market power. Evidence of an increase in the dominant firm's market share, and a corresponding decrease in rivals' market shares, is neither necessary nor sufficient, since a market in which there is no consumer harm may exhibit the same characteristics. But such evidence, when coupled with evidence of actual or likely price increases, may provide a good basis for saying there is consumer harm. There should be no requirement, however, to show that rivals would exit the market: it may be enough if they remain in the market as marginalised firms due to the increased distribution costs they bear as a result of exclusive dealing commitments. Another reason for not insisting on total foreclosure is that exclusive dealing is often motivated by the desire to *maintain* dominance rather than to strengthen it.

Third, while harm to rivals and harm to competition have no necessary connection, there are obvious instances where harm to rivals also causes harm to consumer welfare. Exclusive dealing by a dominant firm may cause consumer injury through the delay that it imposes on the smaller rival's growth. Similarly, when a dominant firm's exclusionary conduct prevents one or more new or potential competitors from viable entry into the market, that usually not only harms the excluded firm(s), but also competition in general. Thus, the focus on consumer harm should not lead to the conclusion that harm to rivals is irrelevant. Indeed, limiting rivals' possibilities to compete is the most obvious mechanism by which consumer harm is caused in exclusive dealing cases. Access to distribution may be particularly important in markets characterised by network effects—where the value of a product/service increases with

[57] Discussion Paper, para. 54.

[58] *Ibid.*, para. 55.

[59] *Ibid.*

[60] *CDC Technologies Inc v IDEXX Laboratories Inc*, 186 F.3d 74 (2nd Cir. 1999).

each extra user (e.g., a telephone network)—since access to distribution may be needed to prevent the market "tipping" in favour of the dominant firm's technology.

Finally, the anticompetitive effects of exclusive dealing on competition are often non-price related, such as a reduction in product choice or innovation. Limitations on rivals' distribution possibilities can limit the scope and availability of products on the market and, in the long run, innovation. For example, in *Dentsply*, an important additional anticompetitive effect was that the exclusive dealing limited the choices of products open to dental laboratories, the ultimate users. A dealer locked into the Dentsply line was unable to heed a request for a different manufacturer's product and, from the standpoint of convenience, that inability to some extent impaired the laboratory's choice in the marketplace.[61]

The relevance of early termination or short duration. The short duration of an exclusive dealing arrangement, or a customer's ability to terminate it at short notice without incurring a penalty, normally mitigate its competition effects. The reason is obvious: rivals will have opportunities for frequent rebidding. Thus, for example, where the product concerned is relatively homogeneous and competitors are not capacity constrained, early termination should allow rivals to compete to supply customers' requirements on an equal footing with the dominant firm. At the same time, it is important to emphasise that long duration can, at most, only be an aggravating factor. It cannot, in itself, render unlawful a contract that does not have the anticompetitive features outlined above.

But the case law is ambiguous on whether short duration or early termination without incurring a penalty make a material difference to the analysis. Early termination has been mentioned as a positive factor in several non-EU cases, and was considered dispositive in certain of them.[62] In past Article 82 EC cases, however, early termination has usually been ignored as a factor reducing the scope for foreclosure.[63] This goes too far. The real question is the economic practicability of distributors terminating an

[61] *United States of America v Dentsply International Inc*, 399 F.3d 181 (3rd Cir. 2005).

[62] See, e.g., *Omega Environmental Inc v Gilbarco Inc, 127 F.3d 1157 (9th Cir. 1997); CDC Technologies Inc v IDEXX Laboratories Inc*, 186 F.3d 74 (2nd Cir. 1999).

[63] See Case T-65/89, *BPB Industries plc and British Gypsum Ltd v Commission* [1993] ECR II-389, para. 73. See also Case T-65/98, *Van den Bergh Foods Ltd v Commission* [2003] ECR II-4653, para. 105 (option of terminating on two months' notice considered irrelevant in light of fact that agreements were only terminated on average every eight years). Ignoring the possibility for early termination or the short duration of an exclusive dealing requirement has some basis in economics. Certain economists argue that buyers may agree to practices that are harmful to themselves and downstream consumers. The reason is based on so-called "collective action" problems among buyers. Suppose a seller offers buyers a discount for agreeing to something anticompetitive (e.g., exclusive dealing). Where many buyers face a unitary (dominant) seller, their individual action will, in itself, matter very little to the overall success or failure of the exclusionary strategy. Thus, regardless of how an individual buyer thinks other buyers will react, it has individual incentives to take the discount and agree to an anticompetitive condition. The fact that buyers actively sought an exclusive dealing commitment is also generally thought by economists to be irrelevant for the same reason (unless, perhaps, the customer is conducting an auction or asking the seller to make a specific investment). For a summary of the economic arguments, see E Elhauge, "Defining Better Monopolisation Standards" (2003) 56(2) *Stanford Law Review* 253, 284–85.

exclusive arrangement without incurring significant switching costs.[64] If they can, early termination should allow other firms to continue to compete for distributors' support. Perhaps recognising this argument, the Discussion Paper now proposes a more nuanced approach. It states that a short duration or a right to terminate does not generally limit the likely foreclosure effect of an exclusive dealing requirement, but adds that, under particular circumstances, a short duration or right to terminate at short notice may make a market distorting foreclosure effect unlikely.[65] The relevant question presumably is how much of the relevant market is unencumbered by long-term exclusive deals at the time of assessment.

Countervailing efficiencies. Even if exclusive dealing causes harm to competition, it may be that it also creates sufficient benefits for consumers to off-set that harm. Indeed, exclusive dealing nearly always generates some efficiencies at the retail or wholesale level. The Discussion Paper now makes clear that efficiencies of this kind, if present, must also be evaluated in order to demonstrate abusive conduct.[66] This makes sense, since efficiencies are routinely considered in the analysis of exclusive dealing under Article 81 EC.

The burden of proving the basic conditions for an efficiency defence rests with the dominant firm. The following cumulative conditions apply (which mirror those applied under Article 81 EC): (1) that efficiencies are realised, or likely to be realised, as a result of the conduct concerned; (2) that the conduct concerned is indispensable to realise these efficiencies; (3) that the efficiencies benefit consumers; and (4) that competition in respect of a substantial part of the products concerned is not eliminated. The practical application of these conditions is explained in detail in Chapter Four (The General Concept of an Abuse). Guidance may also be obtained from the Commission's Notice on the application of Article 81(3),[67] as well as the Commission's Guidelines on Vertical Restraints.[68] Although these documents do not, as such, apply to dominant firms, the analytical framework they outline is relevant, since the Discussion Paper confirms that the Commission intends to also apply a rule-of-reason analysis to exclusive dealing under Article 82 EC.

Exclusive dealing can generate a number of well-documented efficiencies.[69] It may, for example:[70] (1) encourage more dedicated and loyal sales efforts by wholesalers and retailers; (2) prevent "free riding" by rival firms on another manufacturer's promotional efforts and so encourage the manufacturer to make relationship-specific investments; (3) provide quality assurance; (4) ensure reliable sources of supply; (5) guarantee the seller economies of scale; (6) reduce transaction and other costs in vertical relationships;

---

[64] See *Minnesota Mining and Manufacturing Co v Appleton Papers Inc*, 35 F. Supp. 2d 1138, 1144 (D. Minn. 1999) (early termination insufficient given that practical effect of Appleton's exclusive dealing arrangements was to tie up distributors for several years).

[65] Discussion Paper, para. 149.

[66] *Ibid.*, paras. 84 et seq.

[67] Commission Notice—Guidelines on the application of Article 81(3) of the Treaty, OJ 2004 C 101/97.

[68] Commission Notice—Guidelines on Vertical Restraints, OJ 2000 C 291/1.

[69] See s. 7.2.1, above.

[70] See generally JM Jacobson, "Exclusive Dealing, Foreclosure, and Consumer Harm" (2002) 70 *Antitrust Law Journal* 311, part V.D (justification).

(7) provide a more efficient alternative to vertical integration by the dominant firm; and (8) prevent the flow of confidential information to rival firms.

An important defence for exclusive dealing in practice is that the dominant firm is making a relationship-specific investment that requires a commitment from the buyer in order to make a return on the investment. Absent some purchasing commitment from the customer, the investment may not take place. The Discussion Paper clarifies a number of points in this connection:[71]

1. An investment is considered relationship-specific if, after termination of the supply contract with that particular customer, the investment cannot be used by the supplier to supply other customers and can only be sold at a loss. Thus, the Discussion Paper states that general or market-specific investments in (extra) capacity are normally not relationship-specific investments.

2. In order to be considered "indispensable" within the meaning of the conditions for an efficiency defence, the Discussion Paper states it must be shown that the relationship-specific investment is a significant long-term investment that is not recouped in the short term and that the investment is asymmetric, i.e., that the supplier invests more than the buyer.

3. In assessing proportionality, it should be recalled that future demand may be uncertain, in which case it would be impractical to require absolute minimum amounts to be purchased. The alternative is to impose an exclusive dealing obligation until the investment is depreciated.

7.2.3 Practices Falling Short Of Outright Exclusivity

Market share discounts/requirements contracts. Market share discounts (or requirements contracts) have generally been treated more harshly than discounts linked to volume targets. This is presumably on the grounds that market share discounts require the customer to commit not to source a fixed proportion of supplies from rival firms. But market share discounts have a number of procompetitive explanations.[72] The most common reason for market share discounts is the justification for exclusive dealing generally: they encourage retailers to focus efforts on promoting a supplier's products and limit the possibility for free riding by other suppliers.[73] Further, in some markets, total demand may fluctuate for reasons outside the customer's control, such as in the case of air travel in times of political or economic instability. Rewarding retailers based on whether they increased their market share of a supplier's products may therefore be a better form of incentive than a discount linked to absolute volumes.

---

[71] Discussion Paper, paras. 84 et seq.

[72] See D Spector, "Loyalty Rebates and Related Pricing Practices: When Should Competition Authorities Worry?" in DS Evans and J Padilla (eds.), *Global Competition Policy: Economic Issues And Impacts* (LECG, 2004); DE Mills, "Market Share Discounts" *University of Virginia Working Paper*, October 7, 2004.

[73] These reasons explain why non-compete obligations, or requirements contracts covering up to 80% of the buyer's total purchases are exempted for up to five years under Article 1(b) of Commission Regulation (EC) 2790/1999 on the application of Article 81(3) of the Treaty to categories of vertical agreements and concerted practices, OJ 1999 L 336/21.

Market share discounts have been objected to in a couple of Article 82 EC cases, although the facts were somewhat extreme. In *Hoffmann-La Roche*, in addition to outright exclusivity for many customers, the dominant firm insisted on other customers' sourcing "most" (*in casu* 75–80%) or a "large proportion" of their requirements from Roche. This made sense, since outright exclusivity and contracts insisting on near-total requirements should broadly have the same effect. In *Michelin II*, Michelin's "friends club" for dealers—which granted preferential terms to selected dealers meeting certain criteria—was objected to on the grounds that: (1) a dealer could not join the club unless he achieved a certain high market share in Michelin products; (2) the dealer could not divert spontaneous demand for Michelin products; and (3) a dealer was required to carry sufficient stocks to meet that spontaneous demand immediately. These factors were considered *cumulatively* to treat the "friends club" arrangement as abusive.[74] In other words, neither the Court nor the Commission considered that a market share discount would have been abusive in its own right.

A number of comments can be made in regard to the treatment of market share discounts under Article 82 EC. First, a market share discount can be no worse than an outright exclusive deal and is, by definition, at least marginally better. A simple rule is therefore to say that if an exclusive deal would be legal, so too is a market share discount. But the converse does not apply and further analysis is needed. Second, although some commentators argue that certain market share thresholds should apply in determining the legality of market share discounts,[75] this misses the point. As with exclusive dealing, the key question is how much of total demand is foreclosed to rivals and whether the tied share prevents them from achieving access to necessary distribution or scale economies, i.e., whether access to enough of the *relevant market* is foreclosed to materially harm rivals. Clearly, however, an absence of foreclosure can be presumed at low requirements levels. At the other extreme, requirements that come close to exclusivity (e.g., 70-80%) are likely to require justification, assuming a material proportion of the relevant dealers/customers are affected by such clauses.[76]

Finally, an interesting, but unresolved, question concerns the notion developed in the Discussion Paper that dominant firms will typically have an "assured" base of sales for a certain proportion of customers' requirements, i.e., that customers will in any event source a certain percentage of their requirements from the dominant firm.[77] Although there are considerable doubts in practice as to whether such shares can accurately be identified, the logic of the Discussion Paper's position is that the dominant firm ought to be able lawfully to agree a market share discount for the portion of the customer's requirements that is "assured" (assuming the overall price remains above cost).

English clauses. Exclusive dealing may also be achieved though the use of English clauses. Such clauses can be expected to have the same effect as a single branding obligation as the dominant firm will only have to lower its price where there is a risk

[74] Case T-203/01, *Manufacture française des pneumatiques Michelin v Commission* [2003] ECR II-4071, paras. 175, 210.

[75] R Whish, *Competition Law* (2nd edn., London, Butterworths LexisNexis, 2001) pp. 642–43 (arguing for an 80% threshold).

[76] Case 85/76, *Hoffmann-La Roche and Co AG v Commission* [1979] ECR 461.

[77] Discussion Paper, para. 143.

that customers switch.[78] English clauses are generally made worse by the fact that they require the buyer to reveal the identity of the rival making the better offer as this may discourage rivals from offering better terms to the dominant firm's customers. The Discussion Paper thus states that the Commission will apply the same analysis to English clauses as it does to exclusive dealing.[79] Past case law has generally found English clauses to be anticompetitive in these circumstances. In *Hoffmann-La Roche*, such clauses were condemned under Article 82 EC, together with a variety of other "fidelity" clauses which were found to tie Roche's customers and exclude other vitamin manufacturers.[80]

However, English clauses cannot be presumed to be abusive under Article 82 EC. In the *Industrial Gases* settlement, the Commission permitted English clauses to be retained if they were included at the request of the customer and did not require the customer to supply extensive, confidential information regarding the competing offer.[81] The Commission has also stated that, at least with respect to non-dominant suppliers, English clauses may be exempted under Article 81(3) EC.[82] Thus, as with exclusive dealing requirements, the incidence of the exclusive dealing commitment on the market should be assessed, together with an analysis of its actual or likely effects.

English clauses should also be more acceptable in markets where there are a sufficient number of producers in the market so that a producer who has agreed to the English clause will not be able to identify the source of the competing offer. It may also be that information on prices does not confer a significant competitive advantage on the dominant firm, such as where products are differentiated. Indeed, there is a good argument that, unless an English clause requires the customer to identify the source of the competing offer, they should be regarded as a legitimate tool for customers to extract price concessions. In any event, the applicable rules cannot be more strict than for exclusive dealing itself so a rule of reason assessment should be conducted in each case.

Slotting allowances. Slotting allowances refer to a payment from a manufacturer to a retailer in consideration of the retailer stocking the manufacturer's product. This may be described as rent or a simply a fixed fee. The precise characterisation is unimportant: the key point is that the retailer receives some payment for shelf space. Generally, retailers soliciting rents in the form of fees or allowances is of no concern under competition law: retailers should be allowed to charge for marketing services. However, in certain cases, it may be that such schemes could be used by dominant firms to acquire exclusivity or to tie up enough of the available shelf space to preclude other competitors from entering or expanding into the market. Slotting allowances may therefore increase rivals' costs, which could in turn result in higher prices to consumers.

---

[78] *Ibid.*, para. 175.

[79] *Ibid.*

[80] Case 85/76, *Hoffmann-La Roche and Co AG v Commission* [1979] ECR 461, para. 104–05. See also *IRI/AC Nielsen Company*, XXVIth Report on Competition Policy (1996), para. 64. In the context of Article 81 EC, see *BP Kemi-DDSF*, OJ 1979 L 286/32 (English clauses considered anticompetitive on the basis that such clauses give a supplier critical information regarding competitors).

[81] See *Industrial Gases*, XIXth Report on Competition Policy (1989), para. 62.

[82] See Commission Notice—Guidelines on Vertical Restraints, OJ 2000 C 291/1, paras. 152–55.

Slotting allowances should generally be analysed under similar principles to exclusive dealing. Clearly, however, they merit less strict treatment in the absence of any express exclusivity commitment. A key condition for treating slotting allowances as potentially abusive is that they contain some objectionable clause or feature beyond mere payment for shelf space. Problems should only arise when the slotting allowance: (1) requires exclusive shelf space;[83] (2) ties up an exclusionary percentage share of shelf space devoted to a specific product category;[84] (3) limits competitors to a specific number of units; (4) exclude specific competitor units; (5) requires some form of price parity with competitors; (6) specify when and how competitors can advertise; and (7) includes an English clause. Even then, all of the principles for the analysis of exclusive dealing requirements—in particular the need to show a material actual or likely exclusionary effect—also apply to slotting allowances.

Equipment placement. Suppliers often provide storage (e.g., freezer cabinets) and other equipment (e.g., dispensers) to retailers at reduced or subsidised rates in return for exclusive stocking commitments. Such arrangement are generally innocuous and benefit suppliers, retailers, and consumers by providing better quality products, increased promotion, and providing a means of obtaining equipment that retailers would be unwilling or unable to provide themselves. When the supplier is dominant, however, Article 82 EC has placed certain restrictions on the extent to which it can insist on the exclusive use of its own products in the equipment provided. But, again, equipment placement contracts can be no worse than outright exclusivity.

Van den Bergh Foods is illustrative in this regard.[85] HB, the dominant seller of impulse single wrap ice cream in Ireland, provided freezer cabinets free of charge or at nominal rent to retailers, and also undertook to maintain those cabinets. Either party could terminate the agreement on two months' notice. HB required outlets to use the freezer for stocking only HB ice cream. There were no restrictions on customers using other freezer cabinets for rivals' products, i.e., no formal outlet exclusivity. The Commission found that, in some 40% of all outlets in Ireland, the only freezer cabinets for the storage of impulse ice cream were provided by HB.[86] Although there was nothing preventing outlets from having another cabinet, in practice they did not if they already had an exclusive cabinet supplied by HB,[87] with the result that 40% of Irish outlets were *de facto* tied to HB.[88] The Commission also found that cabinet exclusivity was not essential to achieve the efficiencies sought by HB in imposing the clause. For essentially the same reasons, the freezer exclusivity clause was regarded as abusive

[83] See *Coca-Cola,* OJ 2005 L 253/21, S. II.B1, first indent. The Undertaking also required shelf-space commitments to be unbundled (i.e., specified per brand only), but this was a voluntary commitment from the defendant rather than reflecting a strict rule.

[84] In *Coca-Cola, ibid*., the defendant agreed not to condition shelf space commitments for its cola brands on a customer's providing a proportion of its permanent ambient-temperature carbonated soft drink (CSD) sales space in excess of the national share of CSD sales accounted for by the defendant's total cola sales in the previous year, less 5% of that share, as measured by AC Nielsen.

[85] See *Van den Bergh Foods Ltd*, OJ 1998 L 246/1, on appeal Case T-65/98, *Van den Bergh Foods Ltd v Commission* [2003] ECR II-4653.

[86] *Ibid*., para. 156.

[87] Survey evidence showed that 87% of retailers did not consider it economically viable to have a second freezer cabinet. *Ibid*., para. 97.

[88] *Ibid*., para. 156.

under Article 82 EC.[89] On appeal, the Court of First Instance upheld the Commission's findings.[90]

Category management. "Category management" encompasses a range of programs involving a retailer and a supplier working together to increase the sales performance of a particular product category. Working together, the supplier and retailer treat such product categories as separate business units, developing and monitoring strategies aimed at increasing category profitability. In most programs, a leading supplier with extensive experience and marketing knowledge will assist the retailer in devising strategies intended to optimise the retail performance of the category. The supplier collects data on the category, which may include prices, unit sales, promotional plans, and other operating information for all items in the category (and not only its own brands). Such information comes from market research firms, the retailer, and its own sales data. The supplier works with the retail manager, who brings to the partnership such information as the retailer's operating statistics and information on consumer behaviour, and together, they develop a category plan for the retail establishment, setting out parameters such as which items (i.e., stock-keeping-units or "SKUs") the retailer should carry, how best to allocate shelf space for each SKU, promotional programs, and retail prices. The object of a category plan is to maximise the retailer's sales of all items in the category by identifying the products that best satisfy customer demand.

Category management can increase retail sales, lower product prices through cost savings, and result in the display of products that better serve customer requirements.[91] These benefits for consumers, retailers, and manufacturers[92] are well-documented.[93]

---

[89] See also *Coca-Cola*, OJ 2005 L 253/21, S. II.E1. Coca-Cola was allowed to insist that customer use rent-free equipment (a beverage cooler) on Coca-Cola brands provided the customer has other installed chilled beverage capacity in the outlet to which the consumer has direct access. However, where a beverage cooler is provided on a rent-free basis, and the customer does not have other installed chilled beverage capacity in the outlet to which the consumer has direct access, the customer must be free to use at least 20% of that beverage cooler's capacity for any products of its choosing. This obligation goes further than *Van den Bergh Foods*, which reflects the status of the undertaking as a voluntary commitment rather than a legal precedent.

[90] The case does not satisfactorily resolve a number of issues. If, which the Commission and Court of First Instance found, the vast majority of retailers (almost 90%) would not install an additional freezer, insisting on non-exclusivity would have resulted in other suppliers free-riding on HB's investment in the cabinet, and, most likely, HB's promotional efforts. Where different suppliers' brands were all stocked in a HB-branded freezer, there was a material risk that customers would confuse rival brands with HB brands. This would disproportionately benefit non-HB brands, since the Commission found that HB brands were strongly preferred by consumers. In these circumstances, HB was probably justified in keeping its freezers for its own use. It was also not clear how freezer capacity was to be allocated between HB and other brands at times of high demand. Thus, at a minimum, there should have been some effort by the Commission to specify how much space HB was required to dedicate to rival products and what compensatory payment rivals should have made for this service and for benefiting from association with a HB-branded cabinet.

[91] See, e.g., Europe Category Management Best Practices Report, E.C.R. (Efficient Consumer Response) 1997. See generally, RL Steiner, Category Management-A Pervasive, New Vertical/Horizontal Format (Spring 2001) 15 *Antitrust* 77.

[92] The principal beneficiaries of category management are leading brands (the suppliers of which are typically retained as management consultants) and private labels (used by the incumbent retailers). The

Retailers are helped to identify the products that are most desirable to their customers and to plan shelf space to enhance customers' shopping experiences, thereby improving the category's sales performance. Consumers benefit from improved product choice and a more attractive product layout in which it is easier to locate the desired products. Additionally, category management often translates into lower slotting allowance fees, and ultimately into lower consumer prices.[94] Suppliers can also benefit from increased product sales, even in cases where category management results in fewer SKUs or less shelf space being devoted to the category manager's product line. Finally, category management can lead to more efficient product innovation. The best product mix does not always mean the broadest possible product range.

Given the consumer benefits of category management, the appropriate legal analysis should begin from the premise that such programs are procompetitive and should not be discouraged. As the US Federal Trade Commission noted, "category management and the use of category captains can produce important efficiencies, and...FTC actions should not call these practices into question in any general way."[95] Similarly, a Commission-sponsored study on, *inter alia*, category management, supports the notion that category management practices can be found abusive only where anticompetitive effects are shown to result.[96]

A supplier might gain an anticompetitive advantage over its rivals if, as part of its role in a category management program, it is able to direct retailers' decisions about commercial terms such as pricing, product placement, and promotions in a way that would benefit its own products over those of competitors or even completely exclude competitors' products. For example, a supplier might recommend that the retailer not stock rival products, place those products in disadvantageous locations, or price them

---

losers, if any, are the suppliers of other competing brands. See Case COMP/M.3732, *Procter and Gamble/Gillette*.

[93] See Report on the Federal Trade Commission Workshop on Slotting Allowances and Other Marketing Practices in the Grocery Industry, A Report by Federal Trade Commission Staff, February 2001, pp.47–48 (hereinafter "the FTC Report"). A study into category management programs for "yellow and white fats" initiated by ECR Ireland showed that, following implementation of a category management program in a number of "test stores:" (1) category sales growth in the test stores was 100% higher than in the control stores (3.6% compared with 1.8%); (2) category profit increased by 7.05% in the test stores compared to 4.36% in the control stores; (3) category stock turns (i.e., number of occasions that stock was replenished) increased from 1.61 to 1.71 turns per week during the test; (4) off sales (i.e., potential sales of products requested by customers but not carried by the store) were reduced by 44% in the test stores compared to the pre-test figures; (5) average category promotional uplifts (i.e., sales increases in connection with product promotions) improved from 10% to 26%; and (6) 90% of shoppers interviewed stated that they found the category easier to shop. See F Smythe, "Category Management Best Practices In Ireland," *Retail News*, November 2000.

[94] See Case COMP/M.3732, *Procter and Gamble/Gillette*, para. 150.

[95] See Report on the Federal Trade Commission Workshop on Slotting Allowances and Other Marketing Practices in the Grocery Industry, *A Report by Federal Trade Commission Staff*, February 2001, p. 71.

[96] See Buyer Power and its Impact on Competition in the Food Retail Distribution Sector of the European Union, *Report for the European Commission by Dobson Consulting*, October 13, 1999, Appendix 3, p. 191, ("Clearly *per se* illegality is not an appropriate response [to category management] given the benefits involved, and the difficulty in establishing that any anticompetitive results were the *ex ante* intent.").

higher than demand will support. Such recommendations could have clear exclusionary effects if the supplier is in a position to exercise decisive influence over the retailer's decision-making on such issues (e.g., through contractual requirements or by providing strong incentives for the retailer to implement the supplier's recommendations).

In practice, however, instances where the supplier acts as the final decision-maker regarding the retailer's product presentation and promotion decisions are probably rare. In most instances, category management programs are voluntary cooperative efforts between supplier and retailer, under which the retailer remains free to disregard the supplier's recommendations,[97] to seek advice from multiple suppliers and/or independent consultants, and to end the category management relationship at any time. Moreover, the category management system is to a large extent self-policing: whenever a supplier behaves in a way that places its own interests above the aim of maximising the retailer's returns from the category, it undercuts the very rationale for the retailer of having a category management program at all.[98] Category management programs should therefore raise competitive concerns only in exceptional circumstances.[99]

7.3 LOYALTY DISCOUNTS

Overview. A weaker form of incentive that may lead to exclusive dealing is a loyalty discount (sometimes called fidelity rebate). The details of these schemes vary, but they usually have the feature that the discount is conditional upon the customer achieving a certain share or quantity of sales with the dominant firm over a period that exceeds the normal purchase frequencies in the industry concerned. For example, the customer may have to increase annual sales of the dominant firm's products by a quantity or

---

[97] In cases of significant information asymmetry between supplier and retailer, the retailer might follow the supplier's recommendations not realising that these are based on false market data and only favour the supplier's own goods to the detriment of the retailer's interest of raising the total volume of his sales.

[98] Transcript of the Federal Trade Commission Workshop on Slotting Allowances and Other Marketing Practices in the Grocery Industry (June 1, 2000), Appendix to the FTC Report, p. 332.

[99] See, e.g., *Conwood Co, LP v United States Tobacco Co*, 2002 Fed App. 0171P (6th Cir.). United States Tobacco Company (USTC), the dominant manufacturer of chewing tobacco (with a share of 77%–87%) was found guilty of exclusionary behaviour in connection with a variety of marketing practices, including category management activities. The evidence showed that, as part of its category management strategy, USTC engaged in a determined effort to reduce the presence of competitors' products in retail outlets. For example USTC routinely provided retailers with recommendations to increase the number of USTC products stocked, and to place them in the most favourable display spaces. These recommendations were supported by falsified market data (showing, *inter alia*, inflated shares for USTC products). As a result of the information asymmetry between USTC and the retailers (many of whom did not, for example, have access to Nielsen market share data), retailers were induced to follow USTC's recommendations, giving USTC substantial influence over many customers' category management decisions. USTC sales representatives also routinely rearranged retailers' product displays, leaving competitors' products in unfavourable locations or removing them altogether. Finally, USTC representatives routinely destroyed competitors' product display racks, instead "burying" small numbers of competitors' products in USTC's racks. In *Irish Sugar*, the dominant firm also engaged in similar tactics, most notably by engaging in a "product swap," i.e., replacing competitors' products on retailers' shelves with Irish Sugar's own brands. See *Irish Sugar plc*, OJ 1997 L 258/1, affirmed on appeal in Case T-228/97, *Irish Sugar plc v Commission* [1999] ECR II-2969 and Order of the Court of Justice in Case C-497/99 P, *Irish Sugar plc v Commission* [2001] ECR I-5333.

percentage that is higher than the customer achieved in the previous year with the dominant firm.

The Community institutions' treatment of such practices under Article 82 EC has attracted more criticism than perhaps any other practice. The reason is that they have generally applied a formalistic approach to loyalty discounts, treating certain forms of loyalty practices as *per se* illegal. Ambiguous language has also been used and could wrongly be read as suggesting that any discount which encourages customers to purchase more from a dominant firm is "loyalty-inducing," and therefore abusive. Virtually no economic analysis has been applied in any case. This approach ignores a number of the procompetitive reasons why firms might adopt loyalty discount practices and is out of kilter with the need to show actual or likely anticompetitive effects in competition law.

The Discussion Paper now proposes a number of important modifications to the Commission's treatment of such practices (and, for practical purposes, that of national competition authorities and courts). These proposals are developed in more detail below. In essence, however, the Discussion Paper recognises that loyalty discounts may have procompetitive motivations, makes clear that many types of loyalty discount schemes are unproblematic, even for dominant firms, proposes an effects-based analysis for assessing the legality of discount practices, and attempts to sets out a "bright-line" test for assessing the legality of potentially problematic loyalty discounts. These proposals are, on the whole, positive developments relative to the law as it stands.

7.3.1 Economics of Loyalty Discounts

Procompetitive reasons for using loyalty discounts. A common theme in the decisional practice and case law under Article 82 EC is the presumption that a dominant firm would only offer a loyalty discount in order to unlawfully exclude rival firms. For example, in *BA/Virgin*, the Court of First Instance held that "BA can have had no interest in applying its reward schemes other than ousting rival airlines and thereby hindering maintenance of the existing level of competition or the development of that competition on the United Kingdom market for air travel agency services."[100] Loyalty discounts are thus *presumed* to be motivated only by exclusionary considerations. A related point concerns the narrow interpretation given to possible "economic justification" for loyalty discounts; in essence, this is limited to cost savings. For example, in *Michelin II*, the Commission stated that "a rebate can only correspond to the economies of scale achieved by a firm as a result of the additional purchases which consumers are induced to make."[101]

Economic thinking offers no support for either of these propositions. Regarding the first, many procompetitive explanations exist for loyalty discounts, which explains why

---

[100] See Case T-219/99 *British Airways plc v Commission* [2003] ECR II-5917 (hereinafter "*BA/Virgin*"), para. 288. See also *Virgin/British Airways*, OJ 2000 L 30/1,

[101] *Michelin*, OJ 2002 L 143/1, para. 216, and Case T-203/01, *Manufacture française des pneumatiques Michelin v Commission* [2003] ECR II-4071 (hereinafter "*Michelin II*"). See also Case C-163/99 *Portugal v Commission* [2001] ECR I-2613, para. 49, where the Commission stated that discounts offered by a dominant firm "must, however, be justified on objective grounds, that is to say, they should enable the undertaking in question to make economies of scale."

they are relatively commonplace for both dominant and non-dominant firms. The second proposition set out in the case law—that loyalty discounts can only be justified by cost-savings—also lacks credibility in economic terms. Most loyalty discounts have no precise relationship between the size of the discount and the cost savings made as a result of the extra sales to the dominant firm. And any such relationship would be speculative and very hard to prove in practice in all but the simplest of cases. Instead, economists have put forward a number of other procompetitive explanations why firms, including dominant firms, offer loyalty incentives to customers, distributors, and agents to increase sales efforts.[102]

a, More efficient recovery of fixed costs. When production involves significant fixed costs, prices will be set above marginal costs. The price-cost margin must be sufficiently high to recover fixed costs; otherwise production will not be sustainable in the long run. The problem is that higher prices mean lower volume, which implies that, in order to recover fixed costs, prices may have to be set at levels significantly in excess of costs for all consumers, which can have adverse implications for consumer welfare. One way to avoid this dilemma is to charge a relatively high price for those units where the elasticity of demand is low (the assured base of sales) while at the same time charging a small price for those units for which demand elasticity is high. In this way, the manufacturer can simultaneously profit from a higher margin on the infra-marginal units without losing volume at the margin, i.e., efficient price discrimination.[103]

For example, if marginal costs are, say, 10% of the list price and there is a customer which is unwilling or unable to pay more than 50% of the list price for the product, it is in the interests of both the customer and the seller to grant the 50% discount. The seller gets a significant positive contribution to its revenues from the sale; the customer gets a product which it could not otherwise afford. The non-linear pricing typically associated with loyalty discounts is uniquely suited to enhancing output in this way by allowing buyers willing to pay less to nevertheless make a purchase at the discounted product, i.e., allow the seller to charge prices inversely related to different buyers' elasticities of demand.[104]

---

[102] See generally D Spector, "Loyalty Rebates: An Assessment Of Competition Concerns And A Proposed Structured Rule Of Reason" (2005) 1(2) *Competition Policy International* 89; D Ridyard, "Exclusionary Pricing and Price Discrimination Abuses Under Article 82—An Economic Analysis" (2003) 23(6) *European Competition Law Review* 286-303; D Spector, "Loyalty Rebates and Related Pricing Practices: When Should Competition Authorities Worry?" in DS Evans and J Padilla (eds.), *Global Competition Policy: Economic Issues And Impacts* (LECG, 2004); A Heimler, "Below-Cost Pricing And Loyalty-Inducing Discounts: Are They Restrictive And, If So, When?" (2005) 1(2) *Competition Policy International* 149; P Greenlee and D Reitman, "Competing With Loyalty Discounts," *United States Department of Justice Economic Analysis Group Working Paper 04–2* (Antitrust Division) (2004); *Selective Price Cuts And Fidelity Rebates*, Economic Discussion Paper prepared by RBB Economics for the Office of Fair Trading, July 2005; and S Kolay, SG Shaffer, and J Ordover, "All-Unit Discounts In Retail Contracts" (2004) 13(3) *Journal of Economics and Management Strategy* 429–59.

[103] See discussion in J Tirole, *The Theory of Industrial Organisation* (Cambridge, MIT Press, 1988) Ch. 3.

[104] In some cases, the welfare gains of differential pricing based on fixed-cost recovery can be enormous. See E Miravete and LH Röller, "Competitive Nonlinear Pricing in Duopoly Equilibrium: The Early Cellular Telephone Industry," *CEPR Discussion Paper No. 4069* (2003). Their analysis of

b. ***Providing better incentives to retailers.*** Loyalty rebate schemes between manufacturers and retailers can have beneficial effects for consumers by improving the incentives faced by retailers. This may solve various "moral hazard" problems in a vertical relationship, i.e., conflicts of interest between manufacturers and retailers as regards promotions, advertising, investment in more professional sale forces, etc. For example, if retailers face a low marginal input cost for a product, they will have good incentives to promote that product, or to expand sales of that product by competing on price. These incentives may be weak when the additional profit to the retailer is small. It will typically be difficult for a supplier to write an efficient contract that specifies the required effort from the retailer. This would also involve substantial monitoring and transaction costs in verifying whether the required effort had been made, as well as enforcement costs in the event of a dispute between the supplier and the retailer. The simpler solution is for the supplier to establish an incentive scheme that closely aligns their respective interests.

Take *BA/Virgin.* British Airways (BA) paid travel agents a bonus commission of 1–2% for increases in their sales relative to past sales by each individual agent. All agents received a standard commission of 7–9% in any event for each ticket sold. This scheme was objected to on the grounds that it was exclusionary. But this ignored a number of basic procompetitive features of the incentive scheme at issue. BA was looking at ways in which it could incentivise agents to sell more tickets and had to devise some useful way of rewarding agents who did so. Rewarding all agents based on absolute sales would have been inefficient, since it would have produced a significant bias in favour of larger agents or agents active in heavily-populated areas. An agent who was small but had made enormous efforts to increase its sales of BA tickets would have been penalised merely because of its size relative to a larger agent who sold more tickets, but increased its sales by a much small percentage. Standard principal/agent theory in economics indicates that BA's scheme was a reasonable and efficient way of providing incentives and rewards. And yet this scheme was considered abusive without any serious consideration of its actual or likely effects and whether alternative schemes would have fared better.

c. ***Double marginalisation.*** Another procompetitive effect of loyalty discounts is that they reduce the adverse welfare effects of so-called "double marginalisation," a problem that arises in the context of supplier/retailer relationships.[105] When a supplier has market power, its wholesale price to the retailer will be at the monopoly level. If the retailer also has a degree of market power, it will take the wholesale price as its cost and add its own monopoly mark-up to that cost. This is double marginalisation, which leads to higher consumer prices than if distribution was a competitive activity and so reduces output.

the mobile telephone industry in the United States found that if cellular operators had been restricted to using linear pricing as opposed to nonlinear pricing, consumer welfare would have been divided by three, while industry profits would have been halved: linear pricing would have resulted into a much greater per-minute rate which would have driven out low valuation customers.

[105] For an overview, see D Spector, "Loyalty Rebates and Related Pricing Practices: When Should Competition Authorities Worry?" in DS Evans and J Padilla (eds.), *Global Competition Policy: Economic Issues And Impacts* (LECG, 2004).

Both the supplier and the retailer could jointly increase their profits if retail prices were lowered. But the only way for a supplier to achieve this result under linear pricing would be to earn a zero margin. However, by charging non-linear prices, the supplier can cover its fixed costs and earn a profit while mitigating or eliminating the double marginalisation problem. This also raises consumer welfare by causing retail prices to fall more than they would under a linear pricing scheme. All-unit discounts can be a particularly effective way to reduce double marginalisation, since they reduce the retailer's wholesale price on *every* unit sold once a particular quantity or other threshold is met. Economic models show that all-unit discounts are much more effective at eliminating double marginalisation than, say, discounts that only apply to each additional unit.[106]

d. Resolving "hold-up" problems. Loyalty rebates may also contribute to resolve so-called *hold-up problems*. For example, a manufacturer may be reluctant to invest in training the sales force of its retailers because part of the knowledge transferred to them may be used to promote the sales of competitors rather than its own. This under-investment problem may be resolved if retailers could commit to concentrate their purchases from the manufacturer who trains their staff. Such commitment is however difficult and may not be credible: *ex post*, when the staff have been trained, retailers will have an incentive to purchase from the lowest-priced manufacturer. One option open to the manufacturer is to offer a market share discount, or other loyalty-inducing discount, so as to ensure that the retailer has an incentive to concentrate its purchases on its products. This solves the hold-up problem, provides incentives for complementary investments by supplier and retailers, and so increases efficiency.

Possible anticompetitive effects of loyalty discounts. In recent years there has been growing recognition within the antitrust community in the EU and elsewhere that, under certain conditions, loyalty discounts can have material anticompetitive effects.[107] In particular, it has been suggested that the incentives offered under loyalty and discount schemes may produce effects that are similar to total or partial exclusive dealing requirements. Most of these theories apply, however, under relatively narrow assumptions. Typically, they assume that the dominant firm's rivals are not yet active in the market. Where they are, they will have incurred the sunk costs of entry and so will have strong incentives to remain in the market. Also, the main theories assume that rivals do not offer differentiated products. If they do, exclusion is also less likely, since price will not be the only, or main, parameter of competition. Finally, most theories of competitive harm are based on firms with a high degree of market power. Where a firm is at the limit of what might reasonably be regarded as dominance, these theories

[106] See S Kolay, SG Shaffer, and J Ordover, "All-Unit Discounts In Retail Contracts" (2004) 13(3) *Journal of Economics and Management Strategy* 429–59.

[107] See *Loyalty and Fidelity Discounts and Rebates*, OECD Report of February 4, 2003, (DAFFE/COMP (2002) 21), p. 7; W Tom, D Balto, and N Averrit, "Anticompetitive Aspects Of Market-Share Discounts and Other Incentives To Exclusive Dealing" (2000) 67 *Antitrust Law Jo*urnal 615; and G Bulkley, "The Role of Loyalty Discounts When Consumers Are Uncertain of the Value of Repeat Purchases" (1992) 10 *International Journal of Industrial Organisation* 91–101. Somewhat related concerns have been expressed in the context of frequent-flyer programs operated by airlines: see RD Cairns and JW Galbraith, "Artificial Compatibility, Barriers to Entry, and Frequent-Flyer Programs" (1990) 23(4) *Canadian Journal of Economics* 807–16.

necessarily apply with much less force. That said, the theories at least allow identification of when and how anticompetitive harm is likely to result.

Proponents of these theories of competitive harm resulting from loyalty discount practices suggest that anticompetitive effects can arise if, by dealing with a competitor of the dominant firm for even one or a few transactions (sometimes called "marginal" purchases), a customer would face substantial price penalties or the loss of a discount from the dominant firm on other purchases that the customer has made or will make. These effects are generally considered most likely to arise where a firm has market power and faces relatively inelastic demand from customers for a high proportion of their business (the so-called assured base).

In these circumstances, it is argued that a dominant firm can use loyalty discounts to create strong disincentives for buyers to purchase from more than one seller by requiring rival sellers not only to compete on the price of the "elastic" units purchased, but also to compensate the customer for the discounts on sales for which the dominant firm faces more or less inelastic demand. Under certain conditions, this would require rivals to offer negative or near negative prices to compensate the buyer for the loss of the discount from the dominant firm. If so, there is a risk that new entrants will exit the market or become marginalised as niche players. Entry may also be deterred, since lower anticipated profits reduce the incentives to enter and may allow the dominant firm to maintain high prices. In short, it has been suggested that loyalty discounts can create significant switching cost problems for rivals of a dominant firm. They may also be a cheaper form of exclusion than strategies such as predatory pricing, since the dominant firm does not need to invest in loss-making activities in the case of loyalty discounts.[108]

An example illustrates the strong incentives that loyalty discounts can create to buy exclusively or near exclusively. Consider a situation where a customer has annual requirements of 100 units for a product and the dominant firm's list price is €10 per unit. Suppose that, for reasons of brand strength, capacity, or distribution coverage, the customer has, for the last several years, sourced 80–90% of its annual requirements from the same dominant firm. The dominant firm then proposes a discount to the customer whereby any purchases in excess of 90 units will attract a discount of 10% not only on the additional sales but also on all units purchased by the customer from the dominant firm during the year. Suppose that, towards the end of the year, the customer has purchased 90 units from the dominant firm and must decide whether to buy the 10 additional units it requires from the dominant firm or a rival. If it decides to buy from the dominant company, the incremental cost of the additional units will be zero. Thus, all other things being equal, a rival would have to give away 10 units in order to secure the business. This example illustrates how loyalty discounts can give rise to high-powered incentives, even when the rate of discount is apparently small and innocuous.

The above example is stylised and, therefore, unrealistic. In real-world markets, it has been suggested that the use of loyalty discounts is likely to have anticompetitive effects

[108] D Spector, "Loyalty Rebates: An Assessment Of Competition Concerns And A Proposed Structured Rule Of Reason" (2005) 1(2) *Competition Policy International* 89, 96–97.

only where several cumulative features are present.[109] The first condition is that the loyalty discounter can be reasonably certain that buyers have a strong preference for buying their core requirements from it, i.e., an "assured" base of sales. These are sales that the customer would be reluctant to shift to a rival, without substantial price incentives to do so. Absent an assured base of sales with a particular customer, the pricing structure offered by a dominant firm to that customer would be irrelevant. The reason is that a rival could simply contest the entirety of the dominant firm's business with the customer. The existence of an assured base of sales may be the result of customer switching costs (learning costs, transaction costs, etc.), "must stock" brands, or long-term contractual commitments. In practice, this means that loyalty and target discounts will only work well for companies with strong brands or who are essential trading partners for some other reason.

The second feature is that, as a result of a strong preference for its goods among a large number of buyers, the seller can rely on the near certainty of sales of the assured base to offer unbeatable prices for the incremental units that customers might wish to buy from rivals. Typically this will mean that prices for the assured base will be higher than the prices for the incremental units above the relevant threshold. In other words, the seller can price discriminate infra-customer depending on whether the customer will agree to buy all or nearly all of its requirements from the seller or not. This also means that the thresholds at which the discount is given are very important. Unless the thresholds are set at levels close to customers' maximum requirements—whatever they may prove to be—it is unlikely that a loyalty or target discount will offer the customer enough financial incentive to even reach the target.

The third feature is that there is no possibility for equally efficient rivals to off-set the effects of the loyalty discount scheme. In most industries, a minimum efficient scale of entry is required for viability. If loyalty discounts effectively limit rivals' ability to persuade enough non-loyal buyers to purchase their products, anticompetitive effects are more likely to occur. Loyalty discounts that allow rivals only to deal with a small proportion of the market may have other anticompetitive effects. For example, such a limitation may operate effectively as a capacity constraint and allow the dominant firm to raise prices. It may also result in the dominant firm's rivals having higher costs if serving a smaller portion of the market is more expensive. In contrast, if, notwithstanding the existence of loyalty and target rebate schemes, rivals can reach enough non-loyal buyers to achieve minimum efficient entry scale, anticompetitive effects are unlikely to arise.

Another important factor in connection with assessing the ability of rivals to negate the effects of loyalty discounts operated by dominant firms is demand growth. If demand is more or less finite, a rival seller will be more dependent on the existing customer base. In contrast, if demand is growing, the existence of new potential buyers will create opportunities for rival suppliers to achieve scale and minimise the effect of loyalty or target discount schemes in the market. In other words, if demand is growing, loyalty

[109] See *Loyalty and Fidelity Discounts and Rebates*, OECD Report of February 4, 2003, (DAFFE/COMP (2002) 21), United Kingdom contribution, pp. 169–84.

discounts will tend to have market-growing rather than "share stealing" effect and hence less impact on rivals' opportunities to sell.

7.3.2 Assessment of Loyalty Discounts Under Article 82 EC

Overview. Although the Community institutions have always stated that "quantity rebates" are legal,[110] it is nonetheless clear that Article 82 EC, as currently interpreted, places a number of restrictions on volume-related discount schemes. The precise ambit of these restrictions is, to put it mildly, not clear, for a series of related reasons. The Community institutions were initially cautious about restricting volume-related discounts, for reasons that are obvious. But, in the intervening period, statements taken from earlier, egregious cases have been applied very literally by the Commission to condemn a range of volume-related discount practices. Although the Community institutions accept that discounts may have "economic justification," virtually no economic analysis has been applied in the leading cases, either to seriously test for harm to competition or to assess whether there were benign explanations for particular practices. The cases are also contradictory: for example, in most cases, standardised volume rebates have been treated as legal and yet in one recent case, *Michelin II*, they were condemned. And now, the Discussion Paper proposes that actual or likely competitive effects should be assessed in the case of loyalty discounts and elaborates a test that has never previously been applied in any Article 82 EC case. Finally, to complicate matters further, the Court of Justice has yet to rule in *British Airways/Virgin* and it is not clear whether it will endorse the past formal practice or embrace a more economics-based approach.

This unsatisfactory state of affairs does not make the law easily amenable to clear or concise description, which is regrettable for business practices as fundamental and ubiquitous as discounts. This section therefore does a number of different things. First, although a formal analysis of loyalty discounts is generally unhelpful, it is worthwhile to at least identify the main categories of practices that have been objected to and why. The main precedents are therefore described in Section 7.3.2.1. Second, although virtually no effects analysis has been applied in loyalty discount cases to date, the Discussion Paper's general endorsement of such an analysis requires identification of the positive and negative factors that should guide an effects-based approach. Section 7.3.2.2 does this. Finally, in Section 7.3.2.3, we identify the main criticisms of the law and outline, briefly, the Discussion Paper's proposals to address them and our assessment of them.

7.3.2.1 Treatment of loyalty discounts under the case law

Definitional issues. Three main types of loyalty discount practices are discussed in this section. First, we discuss individualised "all-unit" or "retroactive" discounts. Under such schemes, a dominant firm offers customers meeting a quantity or other threshold (e.g., percentage growth in the dominant firm's sales relative to a past period) a discount that applies not only on the additional units above the particular threshold, but also to all

---

110 See, e.g., Case 322/81, *NV Nederlandsche Banden Industrie Michelin v Commission* [1983] ECR 3461, para. 71; Case C-163/99, *Portugal v Commission* [2001] ECR I-2613, para. 50; and Case T-203/01, *Manufacture française des pneumatiques Michelin v Commission* [2003] ECR II-4071, para. 58.

past sales below the threshold. Usually, there will be a series of thresholds, with each threshold containing an all-unit discount. And typically the period in which the all-unit discount applies is much longer than normal purchase frequencies in the market concerned. Second, we discuss standardised all-unit discounts. These are the same as the first scheme, but, crucially, are not tailored to individual customer's needs or growth, but apply generally to all customers. Finally, we discuss "incremental discounts." An incremental discount applies only to the additional units purchased *above* a given threshold (expenditure or quantity). In contrast to an all-unit discount, the discount is applied "per tranche," e.g., a 1% discount for units 1–10; 1.1% for units 11–20; 1.2.% for units 21–30 and so on.

7.3.2.1.1 Individualised all-unit discounts

Cautious approach in earlier case law. Earlier case law indicated a relatively cautious approach by the Court of Justice to the circumstances in which individualised all-unit discounts could be unlawful. In *Michelin I*,[111] Michelin granted discounts to tyre dealers based on annual sales targets that were established individually for each dealer on the basis of several criteria, including the dealer's estimated sales potential and Michelin's share of the dealer's total tyre sales. The dealer was not certain of the criteria that Michelin used in calculating the target, since they were not confirmed in writing but orally communicated by Michelin's representatives. Moreover, it was very difficult for the dealer to ascertain how much it was earning on sales of Michelin tyres, since dealers would often not discover what their final discounts were until they opened the envelopes that Michelin's representative gave them at the end of each year.[112]

The Court of Justice found that this system had the effect of binding tyre dealers to Michelin, restricting their effective choice of supplier. Crucial to this conclusion was the fact that: (1) the growth thresholds for each dealer were individualised and selectively applied;[113] (2) Michelin's dealers might have run the risk of losing money overall if they did not get the highest discounts;[114] (3) the discounts applied to total sales over a "relatively long reference period" (*in casu* one year) and put pressure on the buyer to reach the purchase figure needed to obtain the discount;[115] (4) the sales thresholds and discounts changed several times and were never confirmed in writing to dealers, i.e., a lack of transparency;[116] and (5) Michelin's representatives had close contacts with the dealers and applied pressure on them to reach the targets.[117]

Another element cited by the Court was the fact that Michelin was much larger than its main competitors (around 65% market share, compared to 8% for the next-largest supplier). In the Court's view, Michelin's sheer size in the relevant market made it

[111] Case 322/81, *NV Nederlandsche Banden Industrie Michelin v Commission* [1983] ECR 3461 (hereinafter "*Michelin* I").

[112] *Ibid.*, para. 28.

[113] *Ibid.*, para. 64.

[114] *Ibid.*, para. 81.

[115] *Ibid.*, para. 81.

[116] *Ibid.*, para. 83.

[117] *Ibid.*, para. 84. This included a suggestion that Michelin's representatives in practice insisted that dealers source all or most of their requirements from Michelin—the so-called "température Michelin." This allegation, made by the Commission, was not pursued on appeal before the Court of Justice.

effectively an essential trading partner for tyre dealers, who were forced to do business with Michelin. Moreover, the level of the targets on the basis of which Michelin granted the discounts represented a significant proportion of each dealer's total annual requirements for tyres. Dealers were reluctant to deal with Michelin's competitors because Michelin's target discounts represented an important proportion of their total annual income, they were uncertain (dealers could not be sure of meeting them, even toward the end of the year),[118] and the risk of not achieving a Michelin target outweighed any possible benefit that a smaller supplier might have offered by selling a comparatively small amount of product even at lower prices than Michelin offered. The system thus significantly restricted dealers' ability to choose among suppliers, particularly near the end of each annual reference period. In sum, the Court concluded that Michelin's target discounts were "calculated to prevent dealers from being able to select freely at any time in the light of the market situation the most favourable of the offers made by the various competitors."[119]

Stricter approach in recent case law. More recent case law indicates a stricter approach, at least by the Commission and Court of First Instance, to the treatment of individualised all-unit discounts. In essence, developments since *Michelin I* suggest that individualised all-unit discounts that apply over a relatively long reference period (e.g., one year) are presumed to be abusive absent valid economic justification (which is interpreted very narrowly).[120] This is evidenced most vividly by *British Airways/Virgin*.[121] BA offered agents a standard basic commission ranging from 7–9% depending on the type of flight (e.g., long haul, short haul). In addition, agents could receive a bonus commission if they increased their sales of BA tickets over a certain reference period. These included "marketing agreements" which granted a progressively higher commission to agents who increased their annual sales of BA tickets as compared to the previous year and "performance reward schemes" for agents who increased their monthly sales of BA tickets when compared to the same month in the previous year. In all cases the additional commission was low—typically 0.1%–3%—and was payable not only on the ticket sales above the sales target but also on tickets sold below the threshold once it was reached by an agent.

[118] *Ibid.*, para. 83.

[119] *Ibid.*, para. 85.

[120] See *Irish Sugar plc*, OJ 1997 L 258/1, affirmed on appeal in Case T-228/97, *Irish Sugar plc v Commission* [1999] ECR II-2969 and Order of the Court of Justice in Case C-497/99 P, *Irish Sugar plc v Commission* [2001] ECR I-5333. Irish Sugar also concerned rebates granted on the basis of individual weekly, monthly, and annual targets. While, at first sight, this seems similar to *Michelin I* and *BA/Virgin*, it is submitted that the case is more analogous to the type of exclusive-dealing commitments present in *Suiker Unie* and *Hoffmann-La Roche*. This is due to the fact that the targets were based on sales during past periods in which Irish Sugar was a *de facto* monopolist on the relevant market; in other words, the rebates were only in fact available for customers who dealt on an exclusive or near-exclusive basis with Irish Sugar See Case T-228/97, *Irish Sugar plc v Commission* [1999] ECR II-2969, para. 213 ("the choice of such a reference period implied that the 'volume-related discounts that [the applicant] granted...must have been closely related to the customer's total requirements for retail sugar'" (citing the Commission's decision, para. 152)).

[121] *Virgin/British Airways*, OJ 2000 L 30/1, on appeal Case T-219/99, *British Airways plc v Commission* [2003] ECR II-5917.

The Commission focused on BA's leading market position on the various U.K. airline markets and found that, as a result of its much larger sales base, BA could offer travel agents large monetary rebates by giving relatively small percentage discounts on their total annual BA ticket sales. By contrast, BA's competitors would have had to offer very large percentage rebates on their lower sales volumes in order to equal the rebate payments from BA.[122] Because BA's target rebates represented an important proportion of their total annual income, the Commission found that travel agents were reluctant to deal with BA's competitors, since the risk of not achieving a BA target outweighed any possible incentive that a smaller airline might have created by making an attractive offer to sell additional flights. As in *Michelin I*, travel agents were, according to the Commission, left with no realistic option as to the airline with which they dealt. The Commission also focused on BA's intent in implementing the system, concluding that BA had designed the rebates with the aim of foreclosing competitors "[BA's rebates were] intended to eliminate or at least prevent the growth of competition to BA in the UK markets for air transport."[123]

These findings were substantially confirmed on appeal by the Court of First Instance. In a rather cursory analysis on the issue of abuse, the Court found that, by reason of their progressive nature with a very noticeable effect at the margin, the increased commission rates were capable of rising exponentially from one reference period to another, as the number of BA tickets sold by agents during successive reference periods progressed.[124] Conversely, the higher revenues from BA ticket sales were, the stronger was the penalty suffered by the persons concerned in the form of a disproportionate reduction in the rates of performance rewards, even in the case of a slight decrease in sales of BA tickets compared with the previous reference period.[125] The Court added that BA's rivals were not in a position to attain a sufficient level of revenue to match the commissions offered by BA, which was an "obligatory business partner" of agents.[126] Because of these factors, the Court of First Instance concluded that BA's bonus commissions were "fidelity-building" and, therefore, unlawful. The case is currently on appeal to the Court of Justice.[127]

7.3.2.1.2 Standardised all-unit discounts

General presumption of legality. It is generally accepted that a key component of the objection to all-unit loyalty discounts is that they are based on individualised thresholds that approximate to all or most of the customer's requirements.[128] In this circumstance,

---

[122] *Virgin/British Airways*, OJ 2000 L 30/1, para. 30.

[123] *Ibid.*, para. 118.

[124] *Ibid.*, OJ 2000 L 30/1, para. 272.

[125] *Ibid.*, para. 273.

[126] *Ibid.*, paras. 217, 278.

[127] See Opinion of Advocate General Kokott in Case T-219/99 *British Airways plc v Commission* [2006] ECR I-nyr.

[128] See Case 85/76, *Hoffmann-La Roche and Co AG v Commission* [1979] ECR 461, para. 100; Case 322/81, *NV Nederlandsche Banden Industrie Michelin v Commission* [1983] ECR 3461, para. 64; and Case T-228/97, *Irish Sugar plc v Commission* [1999] ECR II-2969, para. 152. A leading former Commission official commenting on this area of law has also acknowledged the importance of the fact that the rebates in earlier case law were based on individualised targets. See L Gyselen, "Rebates: Competition on the Merits or Exclusionary Practice?" Speech at 8th EU Competition Law and Policy

it has been suggested that, by setting individualised volumes thresholds at or above the customer's purchases in a past reference period, the dominant firm can create strong incentives for the customer to match or exceed the volumes it obtains from the dominant firm.[129] This objection does not apply, to the same extent or at all, to rebates based on generally applicable (i.e., non-individualised) sales targets—whether expressed in volume or value—over a certain reference period, since they do not, except by coincidence, correspond precisely with the total requirements of any particular customer. Put differently, generally applicable sales thresholds are by definition less targeted than individualised thresholds and, therefore, less susceptible to induce anticompetitive exclusive or near-exclusive purchasing from the dominant firm. This distinction is generally reflected in the decisional practice and case law,[130] but has recently been cast in doubt by the *Michelin II* case.[131]

In *British Gypsum*,[132] a dominant plasterboard manufacturer offered standardised rebates based on the customer's projected turnover for the year. The rebates were based on generally-applicable bands of projected turnover and there was no scope for individual negotiation within the bands. Rebates were paid quarterly on the basis of projected annual turnover and applied to total purchases of plasterboard. The dominant firm did not claw back any payment from a customer whose purchases fell below the projected levels, but it did take such change in sales into account when setting rebate levels in future years. The Commission indicated that, in these circumstances, it would take a favourable view of the discount scheme, although the decision does not contain detailed reasoning as it only concerned negative clearance. Nonetheless, the Commission was very familiar with British Gypsum's discount policies, having adopted an infringement decision concerning these policies only a few years previously,[133] and the decision represented the result of negotiations with British Gypsum.[134]

More recently, in *Interbrew*,[135] the Commission approved a series of standardised rebates that applied to sales of beer at a wholesale level, subject to certain undertakings in relation to transparency. Interbrew offered standardised volume rebates, with discounts calculated on the basis of the total volume of each type of beer purchased by a

Workshop, European University Institute, June 2003, para. 3 ("The common denominator of most 'fidelity' rebate schemes condemned by the EC Commission was that the dominant company granted the rebates to its customers provided that they would achieve certain individualised volume targets during a certain reference period.").

[129] L Gyselen, *ibid.*, para. 122 ("[Individualised] rebates indeed encourage dealers to maintain—and, if possible—to increase whatever degree of loyalty they have shown towards the dominant company in the past. This is so because the targets are based on estimates of the dealers' future purchase requirements which are in turn based on their past track record during a period of equal length.").

[130] For example, in the undertaking agreed between the Commission and Coca-Cola, in *Coca Cola/San Pellegrino*, XIXth Report on Competition Policy (1989), target rebates were expressly defined as applying only to individualised discounts.

[131] *Michelin*, OJ 2002 L 143/1, para. 216, and Case T-203/01, *Manufacture française des pneumatiques Michelin v Commission* [2003] ECR II-4071.

[132] *British Gypsum*, OJ 1992 C 321/9 (hereinafter "*British Gypsum*").

[133] *BPB Industries plc*, OJ 1989 L 10/50.

[134] See XXth Report on Competition Policy (1992), p. 422 (Annex III).

[135] *Commission closes probe concerning Interbrew's practices towards Belgian beer wholesalers*, Commission Press Release IP/04/574 of April 30, 2004.

wholesaler in the course of a reference period spanning one year. Interbrew paid the rebate on invoice for the volumes of each category of beer purchased by that wholesaler in the course of the calendar year following the reference period. The Commission objected to a certain lack of transparency in this system in that wholesalers only knew the discount rate corresponding to the volume range in which their own purchases for the various types of beer happened to fall and the rates corresponding to the volume ranges situated just above and just below that range. As a condition for closing its investigation, the Commission required Interbrew to make known to wholesalers in advance all rates for all possible volume ranges.

Confusion following *Michelin II*. In *Michelin II*, discounts based on standardised sales targets over a relatively long reference period were found, for the first time, to be abusive by the Commission and Court of First Instance. Michelin offered rebates based on increases in total annual turnover achieved with Michelin France. To be eligible, a dealer had to achieve pre-determined turnover targets that applied to all dealers. While Michelin's rebate schemes varied from year to year, they had the common feature that each included a large number of different targets thresholds, ranging from 18 to 54 steps. The rebates were not paid until February in the year following that in which the tyre purchases were made.

Given the intensity of competition and the low level of margins in the sector, the Commission found that dealers were obliged to resell at a loss pending the payment of the rebates.[136] Since the rebates applied to the entire turnover achieved with Michelin and were calculated one year after the start of the first purchase, it was not possible for the dealers to determine the actual unit purchase price of the tyres before placing their last orders. This said the Commission placed them in a situation of uncertainty, prompting them to minimise their risks by purchasing wholly or mainly from Michelin. The annual reference period and the low profit margins increased the pressure on dealers to purchase from Michelin and to earn an additional rebate. Moreover, dealers were forced to agree on new quantitative commitments with Michelin before they had even received the quantity rebates for the previous year.

The Court of First Instance confirmed that the Commission had correctly characterised the rebates as "loyalty-inducing" and, therefore, abusive.[137] In reaching this conclusion, the Court of First Instance focused on the annual reference period of Michelin's rebate,[138] the fact that the rebate was calculated by reference to a customer's total turnover with Michelin during this reference period (and not only on its incremental purchases above a target figure),[139] and the circumstance that, due to the mixture of different rebates applied, it was extremely difficult for a customer to calculate the exact price of Michelin's tyres at the moment of purchase, resulting in uncertainty and dependence on Michelin.[140] The Court rejected arguments advanced by Michelin that the discounts were justified for economic reasons, as Michelin had put forward no

[136] *Michelin*, OJ 2002 L 143/1, para. 218.
[137] Case T-203/01, *Manufacture française des pneumatiques Michelin v Commission* [2003] ECR II-4071, paras. 64–66.
[138] *Ibid.*, para. 85.
[139] *Ibid.*, para. 88.
[140] *Ibid.*, para. 111.

evidence in this regard.[141] Thus, according to the Court, the Commission had correctly concluded that Michelin's rebates foreclosed competitors from the market without economic justification.[142]

The Court also distinguished the Commission's approval of a standardised rebate scheme based on annual sales in *British Gypsum* on the grounds that: (1) the rebates granted by British Gypsum were determined on the basis of the anticipated annual turnover and not on the basis of actual turnover; (2) there was no readjustment of the discount for a customer whose annual turnover was lower than that initially anticipated, which significantly reduced the pressure on the customer to make additional purchases from British Gypsum at the end of the reference period; (3) the rebates were paid quarterly; and (4) the quantity rebates applied by British Gypsum were based on actual cost savings for that undertaking.[143]

Reconciling the different approaches. *Michelin II* is not, on its face, consistent with other decisions that treated standardised volume discounts as legal. But, arguably, a number of exceptional circumstances in *Michelin II* tipped the balance. In the first place, Michelin was a recidivist, having been found guilty of similar practices in *Michelin I*. Indeed, it is questionable whether the scheme operated in *Michelin II* was in substance that different from *Michelin I*. Although the scheme in *Michelin II* was at first sight non-individualised, it comprised so many different threshold levels—in some cases almost 60 steps—that it was in practice likely to have corresponded with most customers' maximum requirements. The Community institutions may have felt a strong suspicion that it was designed as such.

Second, and perhaps decisively, the Commission found that the structure of Michelin's pricing was such that dealers risked making a loss overall for the year unless they obtained the highest discount.[144] This meant that Michelin's competitors did not merely have to offer a price on a customer's marginal requirements which matched Michelin's effective price for that quantity, but had to offer a price which was so low as to offset the loss which the dealer would make on all its purchases from Michelin if it bought from the competitor. In other words, customers risked suffering negative margins if they dealt with a competitor of Michelin. Finally, Michelin was found guilty of a number of other related abuses on the relevant market, including the imposition of tying arrangements and onerous reporting obligations on dealers. The Court indicated that the

[141] *Ibid.*, para. 108.
[142] *Ibid.*, para. 110.
[143] *Ibid.*, para. 84. These reasons do not seem particularly persuasive as a basis for distinguishing *British Gypsum*. The discount in *British Gypsum* was in practice subject to some readjustment, since British Gypsum would use actual sales as a basis for setting the thresholds in the following year. The fact that the rebate was paid quarterly seems incidental in circumstances where it was based on annual sales. In addition, the Commission noted that the rebate could also be paid annually. Finally, there is no indication in the Commission's decision that cost-savings were relevant to the issue of justification; in fact, the Commission expressly stated that the rebate was in response to the customer buyer power of larger merchants. See *British Gypsum*, OJ 1992 C 321/9, para. 6.
[144] *Michelin*, OJ 2002 L 143/1, para. 218.

cumulative effect of a dominant company's rebates and other practices may be taken into account when assessing their potential impact on competition.[145]

Thus, a number of special features were present in *Michelin II* and may have justified, exceptionally, the treatment of standardised volume rebates as unlawful. Absent these features, or analogous features, there are good reasons why standardised volume rebates should generally be lawful, even if they apply to all units purchased. This conclusion is largely confirmed by the Discussion Paper. It states that, in general, standardised volume rebates are less likely to have a loyalty enhancing effect.[146] The reasons given are essentially the same as outlined above: because the thresholds are the same for all buyers, they may be too high for smaller buyers and/or too low for large buyers to have a loyalty enhancing effect. Smaller buyers may never reach the threshold, while the larger buyers may purchase considerably more than the threshold. This implies that the burden will rest on a plaintiff or a competition authority to show that a standardised volume rebate scheme is unlawful.[147]

7.3.2.1.3 Incremental discounts

Generally lawful absent predatory pricing. Incremental discounts should be capable of being matched by equally-efficient rivals. This is because the rate of discount will only relate to the *additional* (fixed) quantities and, unlike in the case of an all-unit discount, there is no element of uncertainty as to the effective price. If the discount only applies to the quantities that exceed the relevant threshold, rivals can, and should be encouraged to, compete on the merits for those units by offering lower prices. Unlike certain all-unit discounts, the customer does not risk incurring a potential "penalty" or "tax" in dealing with a rival. The price is the same regardless of how many units it has already bought from its incumbent supplier. The economic effect of an incremental discount is therefore no greater than any other lower price for a given quantity. There is accordingly no reason to object to it unless it gives rise to predatory pricing.

The Discussion Paper now confirms that incremental discounts should be lawful absent predatory pricing.[148] It accepts that the level of the rebate percentage can create strong incentives to purchase: the higher this percentage, the lower the price for these additional purchases.[149] But, unless the dominant firm is pricing below ATC, this constitutes competition on the merits.[150] And this is true regardless of whether the threshold is set in terms of a percentage of total requirements of the buyer or an individualised volume target. Also, when the dominant company grants conditional

[145] Case T-203/01, *Manufacture française des pneumatiques Michelin v Commission* [2003] ECR II-4071, para. 111.

[146] Discussion Paper, para. 159.

[147] *Ibid*. The Discussion Paper states that, if it is established that the standard volume thresholds are well targeted (e.g., because buyers purchase more or less the same amount close to the threshold or can be classified in a limited number of size groups while combined with a linked grid of thresholds), the Commission will presume that they are set at such levels as to hinder customers to switch and to purchase substantial additional amounts from other suppliers and thus enhance loyalty. This seems to refer to the situation in *Michelin II*. In these circumstances, it is necessary to apply the proposals set out in the Discussion Paper for the assessment of all-unit discounts (see s 7.3.2.3 below).

[148] Discussion Paper, para. 168.

[149] *Ibid*.

[150] *Ibid*.

rebates on incremental purchases, but that the threshold is set in terms of a standardised volume target, the Commission will apply the rules on predatory pricing.[151]

7.3.2.2 Factors that affect the economic effects of loyalty discounts

Overview. It is clear from the previous section that the main area of concern under the case law is all-unit or "retroactive" discounts, in particular where they are individualised and apply over a relatively long reference period (e.g., one year). It is also clear, however, that such practices have been condemned without any real analysis of their effects or an indication of the analytical framework that the Community institutions have in mind—at least beyond identifying certain formal features, such as the retroactivity of the discount or the reference period.[152]

The reasons for this essentially formal approach are not entirely clear, since nothing in the case law precludes a proper effects analysis of all-unit discounts under Article 82 EC. Although the case law presumes that all-unit discounts have a "tendency" to exclude,[153] it also requires an investigation of whether the discount has a "foreclosure *effect* on the market."[154] And yet, no real effort has been made by the Commission to assess exclusionary effects in loyalty discount cases. For example, in *BA/Virgin*, the Commission calculated that an rival airline seeking to shift 1% of a travel agent's business from BA would have to offer a commission of 17.4% in order to match BA's all-unit discount.[155] But no attempt was made to assess whether rivals could profitably do this. BA's commission was already 7–10% so the additional amount that rivals needed to offer does not seem excessive in comparison.[156] Indeed, the Commission stated that effects were irrelevant: BA's schemes were abusive "*regardless* of any possibility for the travel agents or competing airlines to minimise or avoid their effects."[157]

Whatever the precise rules that will be applied by the Commission (and, by implication, national authorities and courts) to loyalty discounts in future, it is clear that the formal analysis essentially applied in past cases will be replaced with a more meaningful effects inquiry. In the first place, the most striking aspect of the Discussion Paper is its insistence on the need to show actual or likely harm to competition in abuse cases. Whether guidelines are ultimately adopted or not on Article 82 EC, this statement will almost certainly form a cornerstone of future practice. A second, obviously related,

---

[151] *Ibid.*, para. 169.

[152] The recent opinion by Advocate General Kokott essentially adopts the same formal approach, confining herself to identifying certain formal features of the scheme without any meaningful analysis of its economic effects. See Opinion of Advocate General Kokott in Case T-219/99 *British Airways plc v Commission* [2006] ECR I-nyr.

[153] See Case 322/81, *NV Nederlandsche Banden Industrie Michelin v Commission* [1983] ECR 3461, para. 71.

[154] See Case T-203/01, *Manufacture française des pneumatiques Michelin v Commission* [2003] ECR II-4071, para. 57 (emphasis added).

[155] See *Virgin/British Airways*, OJ 2000 L 30/1, para. 30.

[156] See also Case T-219/99 *British Airways v Commission* [2003] ECR II-5917. Although the Court of First Instance held that evidence of actual exclusionary effects was not required (para. 293), it concluded that the Commission had demonstrated such effects (para. 294). However, no evidence was cited in support of this conclusion beyond some general observations that related to BA's dominance.

[157] *See Virgin/British Airways*, OJ 2000 L 30/1, para. 102 (emphasis added).

reason is that, both privately and in practice, the Commission has already started to distance itself from *British Airways/Virgin* and *Michelin II.* Statements in those cases to the effect that "potential" effects are sufficient, and that a decline in the dominant firm's market share can be ignored in favour of a (circular) presumption that it would have fallen more but for the abuse, will presumably not be repeated in future. Indeed, we are involved in a number of cases at present in which the Commission and national authorities are considering the terms and conditions of the discount schemes and their effects on competition in some detail. Finally, it is also true that certain national competition authorities never shared the Commission's historic approach to loyalty discounts.

Elements of an effects-based inquiry. Assuming that an effects-type inquiry is needed, the overriding goal is to assess whether the loyalty discount impedes effective competition from equally efficient rivals—which is largely a function of the switching costs faced by customers under the scheme—and is likely to cause harm to consumers in the form of higher prices or reduced quality. Each case will of course be highly attuned to its particular facts and buyer/seller dynamics in the relevant market. But the main factors of relevance are set out below. In making this assessment, we also assume that the discount does not result in prices falling below the dominant firm's average avoidable cost for all products supplied:[158]

1. *Market coverage.* Since loyalty discounts have been most closely analogised with exclusive dealing, it should be relevant in a loyalty discount case to ask how much of the market is affected by such practices and, if the discounts concern the wholesale level, whether there are other effective routes to market. A loyalty discount can be no worse than outright exclusivity so the issue of market coverage is an important screen. If coverage is low, material anticompetitive effects can be excluded.

2. *Standardised versus individualised discounts.* Whether the discount scheme is standardised or individualised can have a decisive bearing on its assessment. Standardised schemes are generally legal, since they do not, except by coincidence, correspond with any individual customer's total requirements. They are by definition less "targeted" and more blunt. This does not mean, however, that any presumption of illegality attaches to individualised schemes. The other factors mentioned below come into play.

3. *Incremental versus all-unit discounts.* A key component of the objection to loyalty rebates is that the discount is all-unit, or "rolls back" to unit one. This retroactivity, coupled with the length of the reference period (see below), can have an important impact on the size of the switching costs that rivals need to overcome. In contrast, when the discount only applies to the units in excess of the threshold, and does not apply to purchases already made, equally efficient rivals can compete, since there is no issue of "compensation" for discounts on past purchases.

[158] For an example of how these factors might be applied in practice, see *Commissioner of Competition v Canada Pipe*, 2005 Comp. Trib. 3 (dominant firm's loyalty rebates found not to have appreciable anticompetitive effect) (currently on appeal).

4. *The level at which the threshold is set.* Whether the threshold at which the discounts applies is close to the customer's realised demand is critical. If realised demand is significantly below the level at which the threshold is set, it cannot, by definition, have any "loyalty-inducing" effect. Concerns therefore should only arise when the discount threshold is set just below, at, or above the customer's realised demand. Even then, whether the discount increases in a linear manner, or in steps, and if so, what the quantity is for each step is relevant. In particular, if realised demand is between two thresholds that have a large disparity, exclusion of rivals seems unlikely. The same analysis can be applied for a growth rebate: a rebate granting a discount for a customer purchasing, say, 10% as much as it did last year cannot be compared to one granting a discount for a 110% increase in sales.

5. *The size of the discount.* Although the effect of even a small discount that applies to all units can be significant, it is obviously relevant to assess the size of the discount. Surprisingly, this factor has received little attention in the case law, but it is obviously relevant. If the hypothetical maximum discount that a rival firm needs to offer to compete under the contract is relatively small, exclusion is unlikely. Suppose the volume margin above the threshold is 33%, and the rebate under the contract if the threshold is reached is 3%, then the maximum discount that a rival firm needs to offer in order to be competitive is of 9% (i.e., 3% divided by 33%). It should also be noted that in practice the competitor is likely to have its own discount scheme and the customer may be able to bring demand forward (e.g., by storing product) in order to avail of *both* sets of discounts. In other words, the actual discount needed by the rival to match the dominant firm's discount is in practice almost certainly less than the hypothetical maximum discount.

6. *Duration.* The reference period for which the all-unit discount applies can have an important bearing on the switching costs faced by rival firms. A longer reference period generally creates higher switching costs, particularly towards the end of the reference period. Case law has therefore mainly intervened in the case of relatively long duration reference periods—typically one year. In contrast, reference periods of short duration (e.g., three-six months) have been accepted in several cases.[159] This is because the switching costs faced by rivals are usually lower in the case of a short reference period and, as importantly, rivals have more frequent opportunities to rebid. It may also be that customers purchase most of their requirements at an early stage in the relevant period, in which case the switching costs are likely to be much smaller (or even zero) than if purchases are evenly staggered throughout the

[159] See, e.g., *Coca Cola/San Pellegrino*, XIXth Report on Competition Policy (1989) (three months); Commission Press Release IP/99/504 of July 14, 1999 (six months); and Kammergericht—Kart 32/79 *Fertigfutter*, Betriebs-Berater 1981, 1110, *Deutsche Zündholzfabriken*, FCO Report 1983/84, 86, *Dachentwässerungsartikel*, FCO Report 1984/85, 65 (all indicating that rebates based on sales over a three-month period would be acceptable). See also Opinion of Advocate General Kokott in Case T-219/99 *British Airways plc v Commission* [2006] ECR I-nyr, para. 94.

period. (Curiously, however, the Discussion Paper now proposes to generally ignore the issue of duration, which is a departure from past practice.[160])

7. *Transparency.* A key factor in *Michelin I* was that the discount scheme was unwritten and varied between customers and even from period to period for the same customer, i.e., an *ad hoc* arrangement by Michelin. An essential element of a procompetitive loyalty discount scheme is therefore transparency. While the customer may be unsure as to its total requirements for the period, it should at least be clear as to what discount applies at each sales level.

8. *Bundled versus unbundled discounts.* Case law has traditionally treated discounts that apply across multiple product lines more seriously than single-product discounts, at least where rivals do not have the same range of products as the dominant firm. Indeed, certain settlement decisions suggest that unbundling of discounts is an essential requirement. In both the *Coca-Cola Italia Undertaking*[161] and the recent *Coca-Cola Undertaking*,[162] the Commission required the defendant not to condition the supply of cola products, or the availability or extent of discounts on cola products, on the purchase of one or more non-cola products. Full unbundling goes too far, but, rightly or wrongly, the Community institutions appear to regard bundling as an exacerbating factor.

9. *Capacity, costs structures and demand growth.* Firms' capacities and costs structures and demand growth can have a decisive impact on the assessment of loyalty discounts. For example, if products are homogenous and firms are not capacity constrained, all firms should be able to compete on an equal footing, with the result that a rebate scheme cannot distort competition.[163] Indeed, it should arguably be the case that the market-leading firm is not even dominant in this situation. Industry cost structure also matters. For example, if fixed costs are high and variable costs are low, a rival firm should be willing to offer a deep discount to compensate a customer for any potential switching costs, since this would make a contribution to overheads. Finally, the evolution of overall demand on the market is relevant. If demand is growing significantly,

---

[160] See Discussion Paper, para. 161. It adds, however, as follows: "The exception is where the dominant company is no longer an unavoidable trading partner. This could be the case where the reference period is very short and therefore the customer's requirements in that period so low that the different competitors can compete for all requirements of the customer in that period, in which case the rebate system will normally not have a loyalty enhancing effect. This could also be the case where the product is homogeneous, in which case a long reference period and a high threshold may work as a disincentive to switch supplier after having started to purchase from the dominant supplier."

[161] See XIXth Report on Competition Policy 1989, para 50.

[162] See *Coca-Cola*, OJ 2005 L 253/21, Clause 6, second indent ("The Companies will not condition any payment or other advantage on a customer's agreeing that a Company's CSDs (or any subset of a Company's CSDs) comprise a specified percentage of the total number of CSD SKUs (or of that subset of CSD SKUs) listed by the customer in the previous year."). See also *Tetra Pak II*, OJ 1992 L 72/1, Article 3(3) "Discounts on cartons should be granted solely according to the quantity of each order, and orders for different types of carton may not be aggregated for that purpose.").

[163] The Discussion Paper accepts this point. See Discussion Paper, para. 146.

loyalty discounts are likely to have mainly market-expanding effects rather than simply stealing existing market shares from rivals.

10. *Business justification.* Various procompetitive reasons explain the use of loyalty discounts. To what extent these are accepted as business justification is discussed in Section 7.3.3. But overall market context can have a decisive bearing on the assessment of loyalty discounts. For example, when customers are sophisticated in procurement and/or relatively concentrated, they can protect themselves. They will usually have the ability and incentive to play various suppliers against each other to obtain the best terms.[164]

An effects analysis of the actual or likely impact of the discount scheme is clearly preferable to the largely formal approach historically applied by the Commission. But it has the major drawback that, in general, it cannot be applied *ex ante* by a firm when it is deciding its pricing strategy. Its results depend on a number of *ex post* factors and would require access to a good deal of information that the dominant firm either does not have or should not have (e.g., information on rivals' costs and discount schemes, the proportion of products sourced by a customer from rivals etc.). As such, an effects analysis is mainly of use to the dominant firm to defend complaints or litigation. It will generally not be useful when deciding upon its pricing strategy—at least with any degree of certainty—which is a major drawback.

7.3.2.3 Alternative proposals for the assessment of loyalty discounts

Criticisms of the historic approach to all-unit discounts. This section summarises the criticisms of the approach to loyalty discounts under Article 82 EC. These comments mainly apply to individualised all-unit schemes, but would apply with equal or greater force should the Commission persist with the view in *Michelin II* that standardised volume discount schemes may be abusive. The evolution of the treatment of individualised all-unit discounts under Article 82 EC has been significant. Earlier decisions and case law adopted a cautious approach that prohibited loyalty discounts only where they were conditional on exclusive or near-exclusive dealing commitments (*Suiker Unie*, *Hoffmann-La Roche*) or based on a combination of factors that effectively tied the customer to the dominant firm (*Michelin I*).

In the intervening period, the Commission and Court of First Instance have applied an expansive interpretation to these principles. More recent cases suggest that individualised all-unit discounts will be presumed abusive absent valid economic justification; in other words, a *per se* or formalistic approach.[165] This approach is

[164] Another important factor in practice is that loyalty discounts may be a method of devising optimal incentives where the customer has in any event committed to a single supplier. Suppose a customer conducts an open bid for its total requirements for a given period in circumstances where it does not know in advance what its precise total requirements will be. The winning supplier will capture all of the business, but it may be that it would nonetheless use a loyalty scheme in order to incentivise the customer to purchase more during the period of exclusivity. Such a scheme has an obvious procompetitive rationale and has neither the object nor the effect of foreclosing rival firms.

[165] This was largely accepted by the Commission. L Gyselen acknowledged that "the EC Commission has... followed pretty much of a per se approach" in the area of loyalty discounts. See L Gyselen, "Rebates: Competition on the Merits or Exclusionary Practice?" Speech at 8th EU Competition Law and Policy Workshop, European University Institute, June 2003. See also *Michelin*,

exacerbated by findings that a potential foreclosure effect is sufficient for a finding of illegality, that harm to competitors also proves harm to competition and consumers,[166] and that an abuse is established even if competitors can adopt counterstrategies to avoid the adverse effects of such a practice.[167] In these circumstances, a dominant firm might reasonably conclude that the use of loyalty discount schemes is *per se* abusive under Article 82 EC, and that only discounts granted on an individual sales transaction are immune from challenge.[168] This approach to all-unit discounts has a number of well-documented flaws.[169]

a. Lack of clear economic basis. A first criticism is that the decisional practice and case law lack a clear basis in economic principle. As outlined in section 7.3.1 above, economists accept that all-unit discounts can have a number of procompetitive explanations, including allowing more efficient fixed-cost recovery, providing better retailer incentives, and eliminating or reducing hold-up problems and double marginalisation in vertical relationships. The implicit assumption in the case law is that

---

OJ 2002 L 143/1, paras. 216, 263 ("An undertaking in a dominant position cannot require dealers to exceed, each year, their figures for the previous years and thus automatically increase its market share."). See also *Soda-Ash/Solvay*, OJ 1991 L 152/21, para. 51 ("What is important is that the terms of sale of the dominant supplier make it financially attractive for the customer to take its supplies exclusively or mainly from it. The precise means by which this result is achieved are immaterial."). Similarly there are troubling statements in *British Gypsum*, XXII Report on Competition Policy (1992), p. 422, which suggest that any discount aimed at increasing a dominant company's market share is, or is likely to be, unlawful.

[166] See *Virgin/British Airways*, OJ 2000 L 30/1, para. 105 ("The exclusionary effect of the commission schemes affects all of BA's competitors and any potential new entrants. They therefore harm competition in general and so consumers.").

[167] *Ibid.*, para. 102 ("BA is using its commission scheme to directly reward loyalty. Travel agents are encouraged to remain loyal to BA rather than to sell their services to competitors of BA by being given incentives to maintain or increase their sales of BA tickets which do not depend on the absolute size of those sales. Such commission schemes carried out by a firm enjoying a dominant position... are illegal, regardless of any possibility for the travel agents or competing airlines to minimise or avoid their effects"(emphasis added.)).

[168] L Gyselen states that "the only way to undo a rebate scheme entirely of its fidelity enhancing effect is to unbundle the sales transactions during the given reference period and to require that rebates be solely linked to volumes which the customer has firmly committed to purchase in separate sales transactions." See L Gyselen, "Rebates: Competition on the Merits or Exclusionary Practice?" Speech at 8th EU Competition Law and Policy Workshop, European University Institute, June 2003, para. 130.

[169] See, e.g., J Temple Lang and R O'Donoghue, "Defining Legitimate Competition: How to Clarify Pricing Abuses under Article 82" (2002) 26 *Fordham International Law Journal* 83; J Kallaugher and B Sher, "Rebates Revisited: Anticompetitive Effects and Exclusionary Abuse Under Article 82" (2004) 25(5) *European Competition Law Journal* 263; D Spector, "Loyalty Rebates and Related Pricing Practices: When Should Competition Authorities Worry?" in DS Evans and J Padilla (eds.), *Global Competition Policy: Economic Issues And Impacts* (LECG, 2004); D Ridyard, "Exclusionary Pricing and Price Discrimination Abuses Under Article 82—An Economic Analysis" (2002) 23(6) *European Competition Law Review* 286–303; D Spector, "Loyalty Rebates: An Assessment Of Competition Concerns And A Proposed Structured Rule Of Reason" (2005) 1(2) *Competition Policy International* 89; A Heimler, "Below-Cost Pricing And Loyalty-Inducing Discounts: Are They Restrictive And, If So, When?" (2005) 1(2) *Competition Policy International* 149; D Waelbroeck, "*Michelin II*: A *Per Se* Rule Against Rebates By Dominant Companies?" (2005) 1(1) *Journal Of Competition Law And Economics* 149; and A Winckler, "Entre Chien Et Loup, Ou La Loyauté Mal Recompensée: un commentaire critique de la décision *Royal Canin* du Conseil de la Concurrence," *Revue Lamy de la Concurrence*, November-December 2005, No. 5, p.113.

a dominant firm would only offer all-unit discounts to exclude rivals, which has no basis in economics. A *per se* approach to all-unit discounts therefore risks deterring legitimate price competition and efficient practices, or, at a minimum, practices with ambiguous effects on consumers.

b. ***Ambiguous legal test.*** The legal tests used by the Commission and Court of First Instance—that loyalty discounts are unlawful if they have a "fidelity-building" or "loyalty-inducing" effect[170]—are ambiguous. A low price, if it is low enough, will always create "fidelity" or "loyalty" in the obvious, lawful sense that it encourages buyers to purchase from the supplier offering the best terms. The term "fidelity-building" does not distinguish this form of legitimate lower price from a lower price based on anticompetitive or exclusionary conditions, which foreclose competitors by creating other difficulties or handicaps for them. Even if, which has been suggested,[171] the term "fidelity-building" were interpreted to mean ultimately "leading to exclusivity," the same ambiguities remain. The lowest price will always tend to lead to exclusivity, in the sense that it will encourage buyers to deal only with the supplier offering it. Again, this is entirely consistent with legitimate competition on the merits.

c. ***Excessively narrow appreciation of competitive effects.*** The principal objection to all-unit discounts—that the absolute amount of the discount on all products purchased from the dominant firm upon reaching a threshold could exceed rivals' minimum profitable price for the additional units that the customer would need to buy in order to reach the threshold[172]—is also problematic. The fact, if it is a fact, that rivals cannot match the dominant firm's effective price for the units at the margin should not be decisive.

[170] See, e.g., Case T-203/01, *Manufacture française des pneumatiques Michelin v Commission* [2003] ECR II-4071, paras. 60–96; and Case T-219/99, *British Airways plc v Commission* [2003] ECR II-5917, paras. 272–75.

[171] See L Gyselen, "Rebates: Competition on the Merits or Exclusionary Practice?," Speech at 8th EU Competition Law and Policy Workshop, European University Institute, June 2003, para. 122 ("In fact, the explicit exclusive dealing condition in one system does not seem to matter since the calculation method in the other type of situation is bound to *encourage* exclusive dealing.") (emphasis in original).

[172] See, e.g., Case 322/81, *NV Nederlandsche Banden Industrie Michelin v Commission* [1983] ECR 3461, para. 81 ("Any system under which discounts are granted according to the quantities sold during a relatively long reference period has the inherent effect, at the end of that period, of increasing pressure on the buyer to reach the purchase figure needed to obtain the discount or to avoid suffering the expected loss for the entire period."); *Virgin/British Airways*, OJ 2000 L 30/1, para. 30; and Case T-219/99, *British Airways plc v Commission* [2003] ECR II-5917, para 272 ("Concerning, first, the fidelity-building character of the schemes in question, the Court finds that, by reason of their progressive nature with a very noticeable effect at the margin, the increased commission rates were capable of rising exponentially from one reference period to another, as the number of BA tickets sold by agents during successive reference periods progressed."). See also L Gyselen, "Rebates: Competition on the Merits or Exclusionary Practice?" Speech at 8th EU Competition Law and Policy Workshop, European University Institute, June 2003, para. 129 ("[A] dominant company in fact bundles his customers' sales transactions for a period of time with a view to comparing—at the end of that period—the volumes purchased with those purchased in a series of sales transactions during a corresponding past period. Due to this bundling, the customer will not know the average purchase price for each unit bought in the course of the reference period until at the end of this period... The problem with this uncertainty is not only that it may put increased pressure upon the customer towards *the end* of the reference period to purchase more from the dominant company... The problem—and the main problem—is that the uncertainty is there *throughout* the reference period.") (emphasis in original).

The attractiveness of the discounts offered by a company depend primarily on the overall price: it does not depend on whether a discount is offered in the form of an all-unit discount. The customer will look at the discount package as a whole, comparing all its features with those of rival firms. It will not be only, or even primarily, be concerned with the benefit "at the margin" of a retrospective increase, if the rates of discount offered are, on the whole, less attractive than those offered by competitors, who are always free to offer their own discount packages, including loyalty discounts. The customer will calculate, as precisely as it can at the start of the trading period, the average overall rate of discount which it can reasonably expect to obtain from multiple firms. That is the end result, and the benefit at the "margin," if there is one, is only part of the calculation. In these circumstances, an approach which focuses on marginal incentives at a given moment is static and ignores the fact that, *ex ante*, multiple firms will have been engaged in a dynamic process of competition to sell as many units as possible.

d. Circular presumption of anticompetitive effect. The final criticism concerns the legal presumptions applied in the case law to assess foreclosure. The case law seems equate the (adverse) effect of a practice on the dominant firm's rivals with harm to competition. The effect of a practice on competition cannot be judged in terms of whether it causes relative changes in the position of competitors, since these effects are consistent with legitimate price competition. A low price always represents a competitive challenge for competitors: they may need to offer more generous discounts. This effect is not, however, anticompetitive or exclusionary and it does not result in foreclosure, if foreclosure is understood to mean improper exclusion from the market. The relevant question is not whether competitors were affected by a practice but whether it was exclusionary and adversely affected consumers through higher prices or lower quality and choice.

The other assumption applied by the Commission and Court of First Instance—that, notwithstanding increases in their market share, competitors would have fared better but for the abuse[173]—is even more objectionable. If a practice would be illegal because it caused foreclosure and so had anticompetitive effects, it cannot be shown to have those effects by merely stating that it is illegal.[174] This presumption might also be difficult to rebut, since it could *always* be assumed that competitors would have done better absent the behaviour in question. The situation is exacerbated by the Court of First Instance's decision to ignore evidence pointing to a lack of material effect.[175] Even in a case

[173] See, e.g., *Michelin*, OJ 2002 L 143/1, para. 241, and Case T-219/99, *British Airways plc v Commission* [2003] ECR II-5917, para. 298.

[174] The reliance by the Court of First Instance on the *AKZO* as support for the view that an examination of concrete effects on the market is unnecessary for loyalty rebate practices seems misplaced. Strict rules for predatory pricing are based on the economic insight that, in general, an anticompetitive purpose is the only rational explanation for knowingly losing money on each sale. This does not support the view that the market effects of loyalty rebates—which raise a different type of competition concern—can be disregarded for the same reason.

[175] In *Michelin II*, the Court may have been influenced by the fact that, at least in the Commission's view, the evidence submitted by Michelin was "extremely disputable." See *Michelin*, OJ 2002 L 143/1, paras. 336–37. Michelin suggested that prices in general, rather than its own prices, had decreased and that, over a 20-year period, its market share had declined.

where the practices in question had no material adverse effect on competition, an abuse could be found by relying on the assumption made by the Court. Reductions in the dominant firm's market share, and increases in rivals' shares, do not always imply that no abusive conduct has occurred. But it is equally wrong to apply a legal presumption that rivals would have gained even more market share but for the dominant firm's conduct. Such a presumption is for practical purposes impossible to rebut.

The Discussion Paper's proposals. The Discussion Paper proposes a new framework for the competitive assessment of loyalty discounts under Article 82 EC. It distinguishes between *conditional* discounts (i.e., schemes where the price charged is linked to a customer condition (e.g., meeting a sales threshold)) and *unconditional* discounts (i.e., a straightforward price reduction with no conditions attached).[176] The Discussion Paper recognises that both types of discounts may be used for efficiency reasons or for anticompetitive motives and both may have procompetitive and anticompetitive effects.

Thereafter, however, the Discussion Paper's treatment of these two types of discounts diverges. Regarding unconditional discounts, the Discussion Paper proposes to apply the usual rules on predatory pricing.[177] Concerning the treatment of conditional rebates, the Discussion Paper crucially distinguishes between conditional rebates that are granted on *all purchases* in the reference period (one year or more) and conditional rebates on *incremental purchases* above a given threshold.[178] While both types of conditional rebates may cause exclusionary effects, the Discussion Paper takes the view that the former are less likely to be objectively justified.[179]

When the discount only applies to the incremental purchases, the Commission will find an abuse only of the price for those incremental purchases is below the dominant firm's average total cost (ATC) and the part of demand covered by the rebate is sufficiently large to foreclose the market.[180] This is consistent with the existing law as outlined in Section 7.3.2.1.3 above, i.e., the general predatory pricing framework. There is a non-trivial difference, however: the cost threshold proposed for the assessment of predatory pricing is the average avoidable cost (AAC), whereas the cost threshold to be applied in the assessment of these rebates is the ATC.[181] The Discussion Paper justifies the departure from the AAC benchmark in that the use of conditional rebates for exclusionary practices entails no financial or business sacrifice, unlike in normal predation cases. This argument does not seem persuasive. Since it is perfectly rational for a company to adopt a discount policy that implies net prices above AAC and ATC, the Commission should not infer that the dominant firm intends to eliminate competitors when it observes discounts that results in net prices situated within this range. The Commission should adopt the same benchmarks it applies to predatory pricing, i.e., AAC only.

---

176 Discussion Paper, para. 137.
177 *Ibid.*, para. 171. See generally Ch. 5 (Predatory Pricing).
178 *Ibid.*, para. 151.
179 *Ibid.*, para. 174.
180 *Ibid.*, para. 168.
181 See Ch. 5 (Predatory Pricing), s. 5.3 above.

The methodology proposed by the Discussion Paper for the assessment of discounts conditional on all purchases made within a reference period is much more complex, and, in our view, unworkable in practice. To understand its logic, consider the following example. Suppose a dominant firm sells its product at €100 per unit and offers the only customer in the market a 5% discount on all of its units provided that it exceeds a target volume: 100 units. Under that discount scheme, the marginal discount at the target volume equals €500 (€5 for the marginal unit and €495 for the remaining 100 units). The net price of the marginal unit at the target volume is therefore negative and equal to –€400. If the last transaction involves more than one unit, the retroactive rebate of €495 will have to be spread over all incremental units in order to calculate the net price of those units. Thus, for instance, if the last transaction involves 10 units, the net price of each of those units will be equal to 100 – 5 – 495/10, or €45.5.

According to the Discussion Paper's new proposed framework, this discount scheme will have exclusionary effects under the following circumstances. First, the first 100 units demanded by this customer are "non contestable." That is, there is no real alternative to the dominant firm for the supply of those units, e.g., because the dominant firm is a "must have" brand or rivals lack capacity to clear the market. Second, suppose that the customer demands 10 additional units and that those extra units can be supplied either by the dominant firm or its competitors (these additional 10 units are known as the "contestable" part of the market). Suppose further that these 10 additional units can be supplied at an average unit cost of €50. Alternatively, suppose that the cost of supplying the 10 extra units is €45, but that no entrant has capacity to serve more than 5 units. To match the conditional rebate scheme of the dominant firm, those entrants will have to offer a price per unit equal to 100 – 5 – 495/5 = –€4. Under these circumstances, the discount scheme employed by the dominant firm will succeed in foreclosing this customer to potential entrants. According to the Discussion Paper, the dominant firm uses "the inelastic or 'non-contestable' portion of demand of each buyer…as leverage to decrease the price of the elastic or 'contestable' portion of demand."[182]

To generalise this example, the Discussion paper suggests the following five-step methodology:

1. For each customer, determine the relative sizes of the "non-contestable" and "contestable" portions of demand. If entrants can contest all of the demand of a given customer, then there is no risk of foreclosure.

2. For each customer, given the discount scheme employed by the dominant firm, calculate the minimum size of the contestable amount for which the net price of the additional units equals the cost of production. This is denoted in the Discussion Paper as the "required share." In the example above, if the unit cost of production is €45, the required share is 10 units.[183]

3. Compare the required share with the production capacity that each of the competitors of the dominant firm can deploy to compete for that customer. If

[182] *Ibid.*, para. 153.
[183] *Ibid.*, para. 155.

the latter (denoted as the "commercially viable share") exceeds the required share, then there is no risk of foreclosure, and *vice versa*.[184]

4. Investigate whether the dominant company applies the rebate scheme to a substantial part of the market. If not, then there is no market foreclosure even if a few customers may be captured.[185]

5. Consider whether any of the following aggravating factors are present in the case at hand: (a) the conditional rebate is *de facto* individualised (as opposed to standardised), i.e., tailored to each customer;[186] (b) customers are uncertain about the target threshold or the level of the rebate;[187] (c) the reference period is not short;[188] and (d) there is evidence of material foreclosure.[189]

On the basis of this analysis, the Commission may conclude that the rebate system is likely to result in market foreclosure and thus an abuse of dominance. This presumption may be rebutted by showing either that foreclosure is unlikely or that entry has occurred. The dominant firm may also try to objectively justify the rebate scheme.

Although this methodology has some support in economic theory, it is extremely complex to implement in practice. Indeed, our practical experience in counselling firms leads us to believe that it is impossible for a firm to apply at the time when it is formulating its pricing practices, and, as such, fails the basic requirements of legal certainty. Several difficulties arise. First, it is usually very difficult to assess the contestable and non-contestable portions of demand for each and every customer. Second, the calculation of the required share on a customer by customer basis is laborious. Third, it is unclear whether and how the required shares of each of the customers of the dominant firm should be aggregated to compare the commercially viable share of the competitors of the dominant firm. Finally, the calculation of the so-called commercially viable share is not fully specified in the Discussion Paper. Given all these difficulties, and the consequent lack of legal certainty, dominant firms wishing to comply with Article 82 EC may decide to not to make use of conditional rebate schemes, even where they enhance consumer welfare. This is obviously a highly undesirable result given the potential benefits of such schemes as outlined in section 7.3.1 above.

7.3.3 Objective Justification

Available defences. It is well-established under Article 82 EC that loyalty discounts with a "foreclosure effect" are legal when they are based on an "economically justified consideration."[190] Historically, the Community institutions have applied a narrow

[184] *Ibid.*, paras. 156 and 157.
[185] *Ibid.*, para. 162.
[186] *Ibid.*, paras. 158 and 159.
[187] *Ibid.*, para. 160.
[188] *Ibid.*, para. 161.
[189] *Ibid.*, para. 162.
[190] See, e.g., Case T-219/99, *British Airways plc v Commission* [2003] ECR II-5917, para. 293. See also Case T-203/01, *Manufacture française des pneumatiques Michelin v Commission* [2003] ECR II-4071, para. 59 ("economically justified countervailing advantage").

interpretation to objective justification for loyalty discounts, in practice limiting it to cost savings/economies of scale. As noted in previous sections, this restrictive approach ignores many procompetitive reasons why firms offer loyalty discounts. The Discussion Paper now accepts that, in principle, other categories of objective justification may be available. In order for a defence to apply, the four general conditions described in Chapter Four (The General Concept of an Abuse) must be satisfied.[191] These conditions are strict and are structured in such a way that defences are unlikely to succeed very often in practice.

a. Cost savings/economies of scale. Cost savings are an absolute defence in the case of discounts.[192] They may relate to the size of the individual transaction or delivery and to the size of total purchases by a customer in a particular period.[193] Cost savings need to be substantiated: general remarks about cost savings or better production planning are insufficient.[194] The Discussion Paper states that, in general, cost savings are likely to be present in the case of standardised volume targets, but are unlikely to require (and are unlikely to be efficiently achieved with) a rebate system where the threshold is set in terms of a percentage of total requirements of the buyer or an individualised volume target. In practice, the defence of cost savings is likely to be of limited use in loyalty discount cases, since the most problematic discounts (all-unit discounts) are unlikely to exhibit the kind of cost functions that the Commission has in mind.

b. Price reductions in return for services rendered. Price reductions may also be given in return for services provided by the buyer which are associated in some way with the sale (e.g., payment on delivery, cash payment). In *Michelin I*, the Commission

---

[191] The basic conditions are that: (1) efficiencies are realised or likely to be realised as a result of the conduct concerned; (2) the conduct concerned is indispensable to realise these efficiencies; (3) the efficiencies benefit consumers; and (4) competition in respect of a substantial part of the products concerned is not eliminated. See also Discussion Paper, s. 5.5.3.

[192] See, e.g., *HOV SVZ/MCN,* OJ 1994 L 104/34, paras. 212–13; Case T-228/97, *Irish Sugar plc v Commission* [1999] ECR II-2969, para. 173; *British Airways/Virgin,* OJ 2000 L 30/1, para. 101; and Case C-163/99, *Portugal v Commission* [2001] ECR I-2613, para 49.

[193] It is not necessary, however, that there should be a precise cost relationship between various discount thresholds within the same system: it is inherent in such systems that larger customers obtain proportionately higher discounts. See Case C-163/99, *Portugal v Commission* [2001] ECR I-2613, para. 51 ("The mere fact that the result of quantity discounts is that some customers enjoy in respect of specific quantities a proportionally higher average reduction than others in relation to the difference in their respective volumes of purchase is inherent in this type of system, but it cannot be inferred from that alone that the system is discriminatory."). There is also presumably no rule that price reductions based on cost savings are lawful only if comparable cost savings could be made in all other similar sales. Article 82 EC does not oblige the dominant company to make similar cost savings if possible in other cases, and to pass them on to other customers. It may be implicit in the cost reduction defence that the price reduction corresponds to the amount of the cost saving. But in many cases the price reduction is agreed before the precise extent of the cost reduction obtainable can be known, so the price reduction must be based on the seller's estimate of what the cost reduction will prove to be: it cannot be criticised if that estimate turns out to have been wrong.

[194] Discussion Paper, para. 173.

stated that discounts or rebates were justified if provided in exchange for valuable services performed by the customer:[195]

> "[I]t is of course permissible, in the light of the competition rules laid down in the EEC Treaty, for an undertaking granting discounts, bonuses, etc. to take account of the services which the retailer performs for the undertaking in selling its products. A particular example might be the customer service which the retailer may provide for final consumers and which the manufacturer himself would otherwise have to provide."

Similarly, in *The Coca-Cola Export Corporation–Filiale Italiana*, the Commission considered rebates "conditional on the purchase of a series of sizes of the same product" and rebates "conditional on the carrying out by the distributor of a particular activity (rearrangement and resupply of the shelves, use of advertising materials, etc.)" to be justified.[196] Finally, in *Irish Sugar*, both the Court of First Instance and the Commission confirmed that the rebates in that case would have been objectively justified if they had been based on marketing and transport costs paid by the customer, or any promotional, warehousing, servicing or other functions that the customer might have performed.[197]

An agreement that rewards customers for services rendered should be transparent in the sense that the service and the associated payment (or method of payment) are clearly specified in the relevant agreement.[198] However, it should be recalled that a number of services typically rendered by buyers are not easily quantifiable (e.g., promotional efforts). Provided the dominant firm has made some reasonable, good faith attempt to devise criteria for the objective assessment of retailer efforts, it should not be criticised on the basis that it could have chosen different, but equally reasonable, criteria.

c. ***Providing optimal incentives and preventing double marginalisation.*** The Discussion Paper now recognises that a loyalty discount scheme may be "indispensable to incite the customers to purchase and resell a higher volume and avoid double marginalisation."[199] The reasoning underlying the need for optimal incentives and avoiding double marginalisation is essentially the same, but these are somewhat different types of justification. Briefly, double marginalisation occurs when the upstream and downstream markets are not fully competitive. If the product concerned is sold by a dominant firm at uniform wholesale prices and supplied to a retailer not subject to effective competition who also charges a price above the competitive level, the result is a "double margin." This leads to higher consumer prices. An efficient way of eliminating this problem is to allow the dominant firm to apply loyalty discounts, which result in lower prices for the marginal units.

---

[195] *Bandengroothandel Frieschebrug BV/NV Nederlandsche Banden-Industrie Michelin*, OJ 1981 L 353/33, para. 45.

[196] See Commission Press Release IP/88/615 of October 13, 1988. See *BPB Industries plc*, OJ [1989] L 10/50, para. 127 (similar reasoning applied but inapplicable on the facts).

[197] Case T-228/97, *Irish Sugar plc v Commission* [1999] ECR II-2969, para. 173. See also *Irish Sugar plc*, OJ 1997 L 258/1 and Order of the Court of Justice in Case C-497/99 P, *Irish Sugar plc v Commission* [2001] ECR I-5333. However, on the facts, they found that the dominant supplier's offer of rebates based solely on the customer's place of business as a means of targeting border customers was not objectively justified.

[198] See *Coca-Cola*, OJ 2005 L 253/21, s. II.3, first indent.

[199] Discussion Paper, para. 174.

The Discussion Paper states that, for a double marginalisation defence to succeed, it must be shown that the customer has considerable market power and that without the rebate system the resulting resale price applied by the customer would be higher than the price a vertically integrated monopolist would ask, i.e., without the rebate system total output would be lower.[200] It adds, however, that avoiding double marginalisation may require the use of incremental discounts, but is unlikely to be efficiently achieved with all-unit discounts. This statement seems to go too far. In the first place, all-unit discounts have been shown to be particularly effective at eliminating double marginalisation when demand is known.[201] Further, it seems odd that lowering the price for all units—which should ordinarily lead to lower average consumer prices—should be regarded as less beneficial for consumers than lowering the price only for the marginal units (which occurs in the case of incremental discounts). The real question is whether consumer prices are lower following the loyalty discount than before and, if so, whether a less harmful form of discount would have achieved the same end, without also substantially lowering the dominant firm's profits.

Much the same analysis can be applied in assessing whether a loyalty discount is necessary to provide optimal retailer incentives. Lower prices for retailers for marginal units will usually encourage greater promotional effort, which in turn may increase output and lower prices.[202] Again, a practical difficulty for dominant firms will be to show why other, less harmful forms of loyalty discount (or other measures) would not have equally sufficed. However, it cannot be assumed *a priori* that all-unit discounts or even market share discounts are not efficient and proportionate in certain circumstances. For example, one recent study shows that, by inducing retailers to provide brand-specific merchandising services, market share discounts can improve the performance of a vertical distribution chain as a whole.[203]

d. Fixed-cost recovery. Fixed-cost recovery—allowing users with a lower valuation than the uniform price to pay less while charging those with a higher valuation more—is also an efficiency justification for loyalty discounts. This justification explains many loyalty discount practices, since the dominant firm is usually discriminating between the infra-marginal (units that customers would have purchased anyway) and marginal units (units that they could be induced to purchase with lower prices/greater retailer effort).[204] Proving efficient fixed-cost recovery may be difficult

[200] *Ibid.*

[201] See S Kolay, SG Shaffer, and J Ordover, "All-Unit Discounts In Retail Contracts" (2004) 13(3) *Journal of Economics and Management Strategy* 429–59.

[202] See *Commissioner of Competition v Canada Pipe*, 2005 Comp. Trib. 3, para. 212 (Tribunal accepted that high volumes would allow a distributor to maintain in inventory smaller, less profitable but nevertheless important products, ensuring availability of a wider range of products) (currently on appeal).

[203] See DE Mills, "Market Share Discounts," *University of Virginia Working Paper*, October 7, 2004.

[204] For these and other reasons, the United Kingdom competition authority, the OFT, recognises that "price discrimination between different customer groups can be a means of [recovering common costs]; it can increase output and lead to customers who might otherwise be priced out of the market being served. In particular, in industries with high fixed or common costs and low marginal costs…it may be more efficient to set higher prices to customers with a higher willingness to pay." See OFT 414, Assessment of Individual Agreements and Conduct, 1999, para. 3.8.

in practice. The basic idea is straightforward—that consumers are better off when the dominant firm can price discriminate using loyalty discounts—but, in the absence of good data capable of distinguishing the situation with and without the discounts, it may be difficult to draw clear conclusions.[205]

e. ***Meeting competition.*** Meeting competition is typically less relevant as a defence in the case of loyalty discounts, even if discounts obviously respond in some sense to competitive threats. Such discounts are normally calculated in advance by the dominant firm and largely without reference to competing offers. But even when loyalty discounts are introduced in response to competitive action by rivals, the Discussion Paper is sceptical that the meeting competition defence would apply.[206]

7.4 SUMMARY AND CONCLUSION

A practical synthesis of the applicable rules. The treatment of exclusive dealing, loyalty discounts, and related practices under Article 82 EC is unsatisfactory in its present state. The case law has historically applied *per se* rules to many such practices, an approach that is indefensible. The Discussion Paper recognises that the historic approach to exclusive dealing and loyalty discounts under Article 82 EC requires significant modification. We commend these efforts, but have serious doubts as to whether the complex rules it proposes in place of the existing law are capable of being applied by firms *ex ante*. Although economists accept that loyalty rebate practices can have mixed welfare effects, they have thus far failed to formulate a test that can be easily applied to disentangle the two. A strong pragmatic case can therefore be made in the case of loyalty discounts for simply applying the usual rules on predatory pricing. This may allow some harmful practices to escape censure, but this cost is almost certainly much less than the cost of over-prescriptive or unusable rules. It is therefore hoped that the pending judgment in *British Airways/Virgin* will provide more useful guidance. In this connection, is important not to lose sight of the fact that the practices discussed in this chapter involve vertical restraints and price reductions, both of which are usually viewed positively under competition law.

Although it is unclear how future policy in this area will be applied, set forth below are certain rules. These reflect a synthesis of past case law, the specific comments in the Discussion Paper on exclusive dealing and loyalty discounts, and the Discussion Paper's overriding principle that evidence of actual or likely harm to consumer welfare should guide the assessment of abusive conduct:

1. In the light of the Discussion Paper, the Commission no longer considers exclusive dealing as akin to a *per se* violation of Article 82 EC. Instead, a rule of reason analysis applies. An essential first condition in such an analysis is

[205] But see, e.g., E Miravete and LH Röller, "Competitive Nonlinear Pricing in Duopoly Equilibrium: The Early Cellular Telephone Industry," *CEPR Discussion Paper No. 4069* (2003) (finding that if US cellular operators had been restricted to using linear pricing rather than nonlinear pricing, consumer welfare would have been divided by three, while industry profits would have been halved).

[206] Discussion Paper, para. 176. This comment is made in the context of exclusive dealing arrangements, but seems to equally apply to loyalty discounts.

that a material proportion of the relevant market is "tied" by the dominant firm's exclusive arrangements. How much of the market needs to be available to rivals is a function of the scale economies needed on the relevant market at issue. Concerns are, however, extremely unlikely to arise at low tied share levels (e.g., 10%), and can arguably arise in practice only at levels of 30% or more. If access to existing distribution or inputs is materially limited, a second question is to assess whether rivals have alternative routes to market, e.g., self-distribution, direct selling etc. If they have, exclusion is unlikely. Finally, exclusive dealing usually produces efficiencies, and these need to be counterbalanced against evidence of harm. The overall question in exclusive dealing cases is whether it would increase the dominant firm's market power in the relevant downstream market. Effects on downstream product prices and quality are therefore relevant.

2. Short duration, or the ability to terminate exclusive dealing at short notice without incurring a penalty, should in most cases mitigate foreclosure concerns resulting from exclusive dealing.

3. Requirements contracts are subject to a similar analysis as exclusive dealing, but clearly merit less strict treatment as a weaker form of incentive. Indeed, no concerns should arise at relatively low market share commitment levels (e.g., 10%). Issues should only arise at levels approaching *de facto* exclusive dealing. Even then, all of the same steps are outlined above for exclusive dealing are necessary to find an abuse.

4. The fact that the customer conducts an open tender among various suppliers for its total requirements, or a proportion of them, should be an absolute defence.

5. The term "loyalty discount" does not have a clear meaning in law or economics, but it generally refers to schemes that are *conditional* upon the customer sourcing an increasing volume or share of its requirements from the dominant firm. The following types of discounts should, however, be regarded as legal, even if they enhance customer loyalty in some sense:

   – It is legal for a customer to say to a dominant firm that it intends to purchase X units or spend €Y for a business cycle and to seek the dominant firm's best price for those requirements. The fact (assuming it could even be verified) that the volume/spend equates to the customer's total requirements for that period is irrelevant. This is simply a customer-led auction and other firms can offer their best prices too.

   – Standardised discounts linked to a series of increasing volume targets over a period that exceeds normal purchase cycles in the relevant market (e.g., annual purchases) are presumptively legal. This is true even if, in meeting a threshold, the discount applies not only to the additional units, but applies retroactively to all units below the threshold. And there is no requirement to show that the discounts correspond to precise cost savings for the additional units needed to meet the relevant threshold. Standardised discounts are presumed to reflect such savings. The fact that the discount scheme relates to spend rather than volume should make no difference, since these are interchangeable in nearly all cases.

- Discounts that only apply to amounts in excess of a particular threshold (so-called incremental discounts) are legal unless the price of the additional units is below their cost of supply (usually average avoidable cost). In this situation, the discount is applied "per tranche," e.g., a 1% discount for units 1–10; 1.1% for units 11–20; 1.2.% for units 21–30, etc.

6. Firms mainly need be cautious in relation to *individualised* discount schemes that grant discounts which apply *retroactively* to units below the threshold (so-called individualised all-unit discounts). Such discounts have historically been presumed unlawful under Article 82 EC without any meaningful examination of their actual or likely effects. But the Commission and national authorities and courts are in future likely to apply an effects-based analysis to such schemes. Although each case will be highly fact-specific, the following general factors are relevant:

- The dominant firm's overall prices exceed its total product costs.
- Market context (e.g., sophisticated buyers can usually protect themselves).
- How much of the relevant market is affected by the dominant firm's schemes (only if a material proportion is affected should issues arise).
- For discounts affecting the wholesale level, whether there are other routes to market, i.e., the importance of the affected distributors for rivals.
- The level at which the threshold is set, i.e., whether the threshold at which the discount applies is close to the customer's realised demand (if realised demand is significantly below the threshold, the scheme will have no effect).
- The size of the discount.
- The length of the reference period (short reference periods may reduce switching costs and allow rivals to rebid frequently).
- Whether the scheme is transparent (the customer must know the terms of the scheme, even if it does not know how much it will ultimately sell).
- Rivals' capacities (if products are homogenous and rivals have enough spare capacity to meet market demand, a rebate scheme cannot have a foreclosure effect).
- Whether the industry has high fixed costs and low variable costs (if it has, rivals can offer deep discounts, while still paying for overheads).
- The evolution of overall demand (if demand is growing significantly, rivals may not lose market share).

- Business justification (many conditional discount schemes have a legitimate purpose, e.g., to provide optimal incentives for selling agents).

Chapter 8

REFUSAL TO DEAL

8.1 INTRODUCTION

Basic scope of the duty to deal under Article 82 EC. All firms, including dominant firms, are generally free to deal with whom they wish. But it is well established under Article 82 EC that undertakings in a dominant position may, in limited circumstances, be required to deal with third parties with whom they do not wish to enter into or continue contractual relations. This duty is highly controversial, since it interferes with freedom of contract and basic property rights, which are indispensable to a free market economy. It is therefore only applied in extraordinary circumstances. An obvious, but rare, example is where a facility cannot be duplicated due to physical constraints (e.g., a port or tunnel). A more common example concerns inputs that have traditionally been regarded as "natural monopolies"—a facility for which total production costs would rise if two or more firms produced—such as utility networks (e.g., telecommunications, gas, electricity, and water).[1] Intellectual property (IP) rights may also be subject to compulsory sharing in exceptional circumstances. In each case, however, the *sine qua non* for sharing is the same: the facility cannot be duplicated for physical, legal, or economic reasons and the refusal to share it would substantially eliminate competition.

The duty to deal under Article 82 EC has strong parallels with the "essential facilities" line of case law recognised by certain courts in the United States.[2] It bears emphasis, however, that the US Supreme Court has recently cast serious doubt on future reliance on the "essential facilities" doctrine under US antitrust law in *Trinko*.[3] The Community Courts have thus considered it "helpful" to refer to the doctrine when elaborating the scope of the various duties to deal under Article 82 EC.[4] Under this doctrine, a single

---

[1] For a detailed treatment of the concept of a natural monopoly in industrial organisation, see D Carlton and J Perloff, *Modern Industrial Organisation* (4th edn., Boston, Pearson Addison Wesley, 2005), p.104.

[2] The origin of the essential facilities doctrine is commonly traced to the United States Supreme Court Decision in *United States v Terminal Railroad Ass'n*, 224 US 383 (1912). Although the Supreme Court did not use the term "essential facility," the case has been invoked by many lower courts interpreting and applying the legal principles enumerated in the case. See, e.g., *MCI Communications Corp v AT&T*, 708 F.2d 1081, 1132 (7th Cir. 1983) ("A monopolist's refusal to deal under these circumstances is governed by the so-called essential facilities doctrine. Such a refusal may be unlawful because a monopolist's control of an essential facility (sometimes called a 'bottleneck') can extend the monopoly power from one stage of production to another, and from one market to another.").

[3] The Supreme Court held that the "essential facility" doctrine had only been applied by lower courts and not the Supreme Court itself. See *Verizon Communications Inc v Law Offices of Curtis V. Trinko LLP*, 540 US 398 (2004).

[4] See, e.g., Opinion of Advocate General Jacobs in Case C-7/97, *Oscar Bronner GmbH & Co KG v Mediaprint Zeitungs- und Zeitschriftenverlag GmbH & Co KG, Mediaprint Zeitungsvertriebsgesellschaft mbH & Co KG and Mediaprint Anzeigengesellschaft mbH & Co KG* [1998] ECR I-7791 (hereinafter "*Bronner*"), para. 45. See also Joined Cases T-374/94, T-375/94, T-384/94 and T-388/94, *European Night Services Ltd and others v Commission* [1998] ECR II-3141,

firm, or group of firms, controlling an input at an upstream level of production that is essential for competitors on a downstream market may be obliged to deal with third parties where a refusal to do so would eliminate competition on the relevant downstream market. The "essential facility principle" is not, however, a new or distinct rule under Article 82 EC: it is primarily a convenient label for cases which have in common the fact that they raise the question of when an enterprise in a dominant position can be forced to contract with another company.

The duty to deal under Article 82 EC is not a general duty to assist competitors: it can only be invoked where the refusal to deal would cause some serious harm to competition in the relevant downstream market for the final product in which the input is an essential component. As Advocate General Jacobs stated in his opinion in *Bronner*, it is important not to lose sight of the fact that "the primary purpose of Article 8[2] is to prevent distortions of competition—and in particular to safeguard the interests of consumers—rather than to protect the position of particular competitors."[5] An abusive refusal to deal under Article 82 EC is therefore an example of limiting competitors' production "to the prejudice of consumers" within the meaning of Article 82(b).[6]

The requirement for harm to competition has a number of important implications for the scope of the duty to deal. In the first place, a duty to deal is only appropriate and necessary where the downstream market is not competitive: if it is already competitive, no useful purpose would be served by imposing a duty to deal. A second important corollary of the need to focus on consumer interests is that a duty to grant access should lead to more competition than it discourages. A duty to deal involves interference with basic property rights and inevitably, to some extent, affects the incentives of the owner (and potentially others, including the requesting party) to make valuable investments in future. There must therefore be some exceptional harm to competition,[7] and,

para. 191; and Case T-52/00, *Coe Clerici Logistics SpA v Commission* [2003] ECR II-2123, para. 62, where the Court of First Instance specifically used the term "essential facilities." The Advocates General of the Court of Justice have used the term "essential facilities" in several opinions, but the Court of Justice itself has not.

[5] Opinion of Advocate General Jacobs in Case C-7/97, *Oscar Bronner GmbH & Co KG v Mediaprint Zeitungs- und Zeitschriftenverlag GmbH & Co KG, Mediaprint Zeitungsvertriebsgesellschaft mbH & Co KG and Mediaprint Anzeigengesellschaft mbH & Co KG* [1998] ECR I-7791, para. 58. See also DG Competition discussion paper on the application of Article 82 of the Treaty to exclusionary abuses, Brussels, December 2005 (hereinafter the "Discussion Paper"), para. 210 ("For a refusal to supply to be abusive, it must, however, have a likely anticompetitive effect on the market which is detrimental to consumer welfare.").

[6] See, e.g, Joined Cases C-241/91 P and C-242/91 P, *Radio Telefís Éireann and Independent Television Publications Ltd (RTE and ITP) v Commission* [1995] ECR I-743, para. 54. See also Case COMP/C-3/37.792, *Microsoft*, Commission Decision of March 24, 2004, not yet published (hereinafter "*Microsoft*"), para. 551 ("As such, the refusal was inconsistent in particular with Article 82(b) of the Treaty, which provides that abuse as prohibited by Article 82 of the Treaty may consist in '*limiting production, markets or technical development to the prejudice of consumers.*'") (emphasis added). See also Discussion Paper, para. 210 ("A refusal to supply may be classified as an exclusionary abuse.").

[7] Case C-7/97, *Oscar Bronner GmbH & Co KG v Mediaprint Zeitungs- und Zeitschriftenverlag GmbH & Co KG, Mediaprint Zeitungsvertriebsgesellschaft mbH & Co KG and Mediaprint Anzeigengesellschaft mbH & Co KG* [1998] ECR I-7791.

correspondingly, a clear benefit to competition that outweighs the harm to the property owner, for a duty to deal to arise.

The Community institutions' statements on the duty to deal. The Community institutions have made a number of general statements on their understanding of the duty to deal under Article 82 EC, including most recently in the Discussion Paper.[8] The earliest and clearest statement was set out in the Commission's interim decision in *Sea Containers-Stena Sealink*:[9]

> "An undertaking which occupies a dominant position in the provision of an essential facility and itself uses that facility (i.e. a facility or infrastructure, without access to which competitors cannot provide services to their customers), and which refuses other companies access to that facility without objective justification or grants access to competitors only on terms less favourable than those which it gives its own services, infringes Article 8[2] if the other conditions of that Article are met. An undertaking in a dominant position may not discriminate in favour of its own activities in a related market. The owner of an essential facility which uses its power in one market in order to protect or strengthen its position in another related market, in particular, by refusing to grant access to a competitor, or by granting access on less favourable terms than those of its own services, and thus imposing a competitive disadvantage on its competitor, infringes Article 8[2]."

Basic rationale for a duty to deal. The basic rationale for a duty to deal is straightforward. If an input is essential for the provisions of a product or service in a downstream market—in the sense that it is either impossible or prohibitively expensive to duplicate—it would, if denied to an undertaking operating in the downstream market, effectively remove that undertaking as a competitor. Early cases thus referred to essential transport infrastructure for which there was no effective alternative (e.g., a railroad bridge over a significant natural barrier)[10] or a strategically-located port.[11] Recently, the doctrine has become important with the liberalisation of public utilities, where access to the network is essential if downstream services are to be provided by rivals. This is particularly the case with telecom networks, where the network owner is almost invariably a network service provider, and hence competing in the downstream market with others who need access to the network.[12] But access obligations have been imposed on undertakings in a wide range of situations under secondary Community legislation.[13]

---

[8] Discussion Paper, paras. 207–42.

[9] *Sea Containers v Stena Sealink—Interim measures,* OJ 1994 L 15/8 (hereinafter *"Sea Containers/Stena Sealink*"), para. 66.

[10] *United States v Terminal Railroad Association*, 224 US 383 (1912).

[11] See, e.g., *Port of Rødby*, OJ 1994 L 55/52.

[12] See Notice on the application of the competition rules to access agreements in the telecommunications sector, OJ 1998 C 265/2, para. 88 ("If there were no commercially feasible alternatives to the access being requested, then unless access is granted, the party requesting access would not be able to operate on the service market. Refusal in this case would therefore limit the development of new markets, or new products on those markets, contrary to Article 8[2](b), or impede the development of competition on existing markets. A refusal having these effects is likely to have abusive effects."). See also Article 12 of Directive 2002/19 on access to, and interconnection of, electronic communications networks and associated facilities, OJ 2002 L 108/7.

[13] See, e.g., Article 6(1) of Council Directive 91/250 on the legal protection of computer programs, OJ 1991 L 122/42; Articles 6 and 9 of Directive 96/9 of the European Parliament and of the Council on

Where the owner of an essential facility also operates in the downstream market (e.g., an operator of a port facility and downstream shipping services operator), there may be a temptation to deny access to competitors, thus reserving the downstream market to the owner. If a facility supplied on one market is a truly essential input for the production of goods or services in a downstream market, then a competitor with control of that facility would not be competing "on the merits"—that is, by offering better goods or lower prices—on the downstream market if it restricts access to the facility, or cuts off supplies to competitors in that market. The owner of the facility is allowed to extract profits from the market on which the facility is sold—otherwise there would be no incentive to create it—but has no right to use it to monopolise a vertically related market. Essential facility cases therefore have a strong vertical element, i.e., an upstream market for the input and a downstream market in which that input is essential for competition.[14] Such conduct can harm competition and ultimately consumers.

It is also argued that it is appropriate public policy for Article 82 EC to effectively truncate some of the excesses of property rights. Property rights are general legal artefacts that seek to achieve a trade-off between free competition and the right to exclude. Anomalies and aberrations may occur in specific cases where the nature, scope, or duration of a property right is excessive. For example, a number of the leading refusal to deal cases under Article 82 EC have involved functional copyrights. It seems anomalous that a copyright—which, unlike a patent, does not protect the underlying subject-matter, but only an original expression of the subject-matter by the author—should allow the owner to monopolise a relevant market. Another important issue in the so-called new economy is the proliferation of new types of IP rights, many of which represent the outcome of vigorous (and sometimes dubious) lobbying by

the legal protection of databases, OJ 1996 L 77/20; Article 1(6) of Commission Directive 96/19 with regard to the implementation of full competition in telecommunications markets, OJ 1996 L 74/13; Article 10 of Council Directive 91/440 on the development of the Community's railways, OJ 1991 L 237/25; Article 11 of Directive 97/67 of the European Parliament and of the Council on common rules for the development of the internal market of Community postal services and the improvement of quality of service, OJ 1998 L 15/14; Article 10 of Council Regulation 95/93 on common rules for the allocation of slots at Community airports, OJ 1993 L 14/1; Article 6 of Council Directive 96/67 on access to the ground handling market at Community airports, OJ 1996 L 272/36; Article 3 of Commission Regulation 3652/93 on the application of Article 85 (3) of the Treaty to certain categories of agreements between undertakings relating to computerised reservation systems for air transport services, OJ 1993 L 333/37; Articles 16–18 of Directive 96/92/ of the European Parliament and of the Council concerning common rules for the internal market in electricity, OJ 1997 L 27/20; and Articles 14–16 of Directive 98/30 of the European Parliament and of the Council concerning common rules for the internal market in natural gas, OJ 1998 L 204/1.

[14] See Discussion Paper, para. 212. A leading treatise on US antitrust law describes the essential facilities doctrine in the following terms: "It should be clear from the outset that the essential facility doctrine concerns vertical integration—in particular, the duty of a vertically integrated monopolist to share some input in a vertically related market, which we call market #1, with someone operating in an upstream or downstream market, which we shall call market #2. If the facility is truly 'essential,' then the #1 monopoly facility also establishes a #2 monopoly....Understanding the 'vertical' nature of essential facility claims helps to focus the analysis: The essential facility claim is about the duty to deal of a monopolist who is able to supply an input for itself in a fashion that is so superior over anything else available that others cannot succeed unless they can access this firm's input as well." See PE Areeda & H Hovenkamp, *Antitrust Law*, Vol. III A (Boston, Little, Brown and Company, 1996), para. 771a.

vested interests. Many leading IP commentators argue that the increasingly broad number and scope of IP rights make it important that competition law should retain a residual role in egregious cases.[15] This does not mean that competition law should be used to reshape the existence of property rights, but it is well-established that the *exercise* of a property right may be reviewed under EC competition rules.[16] The role of Article 82 EC as a means of effectively truncating property rights is, however, highly controversial, a topic to which we return in Section 8.3.

Basic objections to a duty to deal. Despite the relatively small number of cases in which a duty to deal has been upheld, the issue has raised enormous controversy, in particular for IP rights. This has prompted some leading commentators to suggest that all unilateral refusals to deal should be treated as legal.[17] This is not, however, the case under Article 82 EC. The controversy stems from the fact that a duty to deal conflicts with a number of basic principles of competition law and industrial organisation. In the first place, freedom of contract is a fundamental principle enshrined in EC competition law and the laws of the Member States.[18] As Advocate General Jacobs stated in *Bronner*, "the right to choose one's trading partners and freely to dispose of one's property are generally recognised principles in the laws of the Member States, in some cases with constitutional status."[19] A contrary rule, which would effectively require a dominant firm to sell to any and all available buyers, would be an onerous and unjustified interference with a company's freedom to organise its commercial activities

[15] See W Cornish and D Llewellyn, *Intellectual Property: Patents, Copyright, Trade Marks and Allied Rights* (5th edn., London, Sweet & Maxwell, 2003), 755.

[16] Article 295 of the EC Treaty provides that the *existence* of property rights under national law, including intellectual property, is not affected by the provisions of the EC Treaty. The Community Courts have therefore consistently held that the determination of the conditions and procedures under which IP is protected is a matter for national law, but the exercise of an IP right may be reviewed under EU law. See, e.g., Case 262/81, *Coditel SA, Compagnie générale pour la diffusion de la télévision, and others v Ciné-Vog Films SA and others* [1982] ECR 3381, para. 13 ("the existence of a right conferred by the legislation of a Member State in regard to the protection of artistic and intellectual property… cannot be affected by the provisions of the Treaty."). See also Case 144/81, *Keurkoop BV v Nancy Kean Gifts BV* [1982] ECR 2853, para. 18.

[17] See, e.g., R Posner, *Antitrust Law* (2nd edn., Chicago, Chicago University Press, 2001) pp. 242–44. Another leading antitrust scholar argued that unilateral refusals to deal should be treated as *per se* legal except, perhaps, in the case of natural monopolies. See PE Areeda, "Essential Facilities: An Epithet In Need Of Limiting Principles" (1989) 58 *Antitrust Law Journal* 841. Both commentators agree, however, that collective refusals to deal (or unlawful boycotts) are a proper cause for concern, at least where they are used to facilitate a practice that is itself exclusionary.

[18] See Discussion Paper, para. 207 ("Undertakings are generally entitled to determine whom to supply and to decide not to continue to supply certain trading partners. This is also true for dominant companies.").

[19] Opinion of Advocate General Jacobs in Case C-7/97, *Oscar Bronner GmbH & Co KG v Mediaprint Zeitungs- und Zeitschriftenverlag GmbH & Co KG, Mediaprint Zeitungsvertriebsgesellschaft mbH & Co KG and Mediaprint Anzeigengesellschaft mbH & Co KG* [1998] ECR I-7791, para. 56. See also Opinion of Advocate General Rozes in Case 210/81, *Oswald Schmidt, trading as Demo-Studio Schmidt, v Commission* [1983] ECR 3045, at 3072 ("the applicant cannot...claim a right...to be supplied by the intervener" and that "the applicant fails to appreciate that the prohibition of agreements which restrict competition provides, as such, no legal basis for intervening in the contractual freedom of traders."). See also Case T-41/96, *Bayer AG v Commission* [2000] ECR II-3383, para. 180, confirmed on appeal in Joined Cases C-2/01 P and C-3/01 P, *Bundesverband der Arzneimittel-Importeure eV and Commission v Bayer AG* [2004] ECR I-23.

in the manner it best sees fit. The right to property is also protected under Article 295 EC and many Member States' laws.

With regard to IP rights, the Community and its Member States have also accepted a number of bilateral and multilateral obligations ensuring a common minimum level of protection. The most notable agreement is the World Trade Organisation's Agreement on Trade-Related Aspects of Intellectual Property Rights (TRIPS), which, *inter alia*, incorporates the provisions of the Berne Convention into Community law.[20] Article 13 of TRIPS requires that limitations and exceptions to the use of exclusive rights in intellectual property must: (1) be confined to certain "special cases;" (2) not conflict with a normal exploitation of the work; and (3) not unreasonably prejudice the legitimate interests of the right holder. These conditions apply cumulatively. "Special cases" under the TRIPS must be clearly defined and narrow in scope and reach in respect to the category of persons to whom the exception potentially applies.[21] Any *general* policy on forced sharing of IP rights would therefore be contrary to the Community's international obligations.

A second problem is that a duty to deal may adversely affect the incentives of innovators to develop tangible and intangible assets that enhance consumer welfare.[22] If innovators knew in advance that valuable property would be subject to mandatory sharing, they may decide not to innovate or to do so at a sub-optimal rate or scope.[23] In other words, there is a dynamic benefit at the core of IP rights, i.e., the notion that the prospect of ownership and the right to exclude in future creates an incentive *ex ante* to engage in (often costly) investment in innovation. While forced sharing of valuable property may have some short-term benefit in the form of lower prices (although even this is not necessarily true), the long-term adverse effects of reduced innovation on consumer welfare could be substantial. As Advocate General Jacobs stated in *Bronner*, incursions on the fundamental right to choose one's own trading partners requires a "careful balancing of conflicting considerations."[24]

---

[20] See Council Decision 94/800/EC of December 22, 1994, concerning the conclusion on behalf of the European Community, as regards matters within its competence, of the agreements reached in the Uruguay round (1986–1994), OJ 1994 L 336/1.

[21] See WTO Panel Report in *United States–Section 110(5) of the US Copyright Act*, WTO Document WT/DS160/R of June 15, 2000.

[22] See Discussion Paper, para. 213.

[23] The dominant policy justifying the grants of intellectual property protection to creators and innovators is utilitarianism. Under this approach, lawmakers must "strike an optimal balance between, on the one hand, the power of exclusive rights to stimulate the creation of inventions and works of art and, on the other, the partially offsetting tendency of such rights to curtail widespread public enjoyment of such creations." See W Fisher, "Theories of Intellectual Property" in *Essays in the Legal and Political Theory of Property* (Cambridge, Cambridge University Press, 2001) pp. 168–69.

[24] Opinion of Advocate General Jacobs in Case C-7/97, *Oscar Bronner GmbH & Co KG v Mediaprint Zeitungs- und Zeitschriftenverlag GmbH & Co KG, Mediaprint Zeitungsvertriebsgesellschaft mbH & Co KG and Mediaprint Anzeigengesellschaft mbH & Co KG* [1998] ECR I-7791, para. 57. See also R Posner, "Antitrust in the New Economy" (2001) 68 *Antitrust Law Journal* 929 ("The first to come up with an essential component of a new-economy product or service will have a lucrative monopoly, and this prospect should accelerate the rate of innovation, in just the same way that, other things being equal, the more valuable a horde of buried treasure is, the more rapidly it will be recovered.").

A third issue is that competition based on several undertakings using the same inputs may actually preserve monopolies by removing the requesting party's incentive to develop its own inputs. Not only is it generally procompetitive to allow companies to keep assets for their own exclusive use, but it is also procompetitive to expect other companies to develop their own assets.[25] Consumer welfare is not merely enhanced by price competition, but it may also be significantly improved by new products for which there is unsatisfied demand. Competition based on different facilities and product offerings is preferable to competition based on sharing the same facility. More generally, cooperation among competitors is subject to a strict rule under competition law, since it will always, to some extent, remove each undertaking's scope for independent action.

The fourth criticism is that property rights themselves already incorporate a trade-off between the need to promote competition by granting control to the owner on the one hand and protecting against any excesses resulting from such control by limiting the scope and duration of such rights on the other. In other words, property rights are a form of regulation. As Advocate General Jacobs noted in *Bronner*, a property right "in itself involves a balancing of the interest in free competition with that of providing an incentive for research and development and for creativity."[26] In economic terms, the protection afforded to property rights already incorporates a balance between *ex ante* incentives for innovation (so-called dynamic effects) and *ex post* inefficiencies from the exercise of market power (so-called static effects). In simple terms, the "exclusion" caused by property rights is central to the reason why such rights are granted in the first place. This balance is resolved under property laws and attempts at second-guessing it under competition law should, in general, be avoided.

A fifth criticism is that the Community institutions' elaboration of various duties to deal is curious in circumstances where they have not actively pursued excessive pricing cases. If a facility is truly essential for competition, and so allows a firm to monopolise a relevant market, the ultimate harm to consumers is monopoly pricing (and in some cases reduced innovation). But tools already exist under Article 82(a) to control excessive prices and, in general, these are easier to apply and less controversial than a mandatory obligation on a dominant firm to share assets developed or acquired by legitimate means. And yet the Commission has not routinely pursued excessive pricing claims in recent years, while it has adopted a number of decisions on refusal to deal.

A sixth criticism is that the sharing of a monopoly among several competitors does not in itself increase competition unless it leads to improvements in price and output. Where a monopoly is merely shared among two or more undertakings, nothing has been

[25] *Ibid.*, para. 58.

[26] *Ibid.*, para. 62. See also Opinion of Advocate General Poiares Maduro in Case C-109/03, *KPN Telecom BV v Onafhanklijke Post en Telecommunicatie Autoriteit (OPTA)* [2004] ECR I-1273, para. 39 ("A balance should be kept between the interest in preserving or creating free competition in a particular market and the interest in not deterring investment and innovation by demanding that the fruits of commercial success be shared with competitors."). See too Opinion of General Gulmann in Joined Cases C-241/91 P and C-242/91 P, *Radio Telefís Éireann and Independent Television Publications Ltd (RTE & ITP) v Commission* [1995] ECR I-743, footnote 10 ("It must not be forgotten copyright law—like other intellectual property rights—also serves to promote competition.").

achieved in terms of enhancing consumer welfare. Competition would only be improved if the terms on which access is offered allow the requesting parties to effectively compete with the dominant firm on the relevant downstream market. This raises the issue of whether the dominant firm is entitled to charge the requesting parties a monopoly rate or whether, in addition to granting access, there is a duty to offer terms that allow efficient rivals to make a profit. The price of access raises complex issues, discussed in Chapter Fifteen (Remedies), but it is sufficient to note here that: (1) the Community institutions have not elaborated any clear criteria for the determination of the price of access; (2) a price that would lead to the continuation of the previous monopoly price does nothing to help consumers; (3) a price that expropriates some of the property owner's reward may produce long-term inefficiencies; and (4) all prices require on-going monitoring, which the Commission has said that it does not wish to do.[27]

The final criticism is pragmatic in nature and concerns the limited abilities of competition authorities and courts to decide whether a facility is truly non-replicable or merely a competitive advantage. Deciding whether a facility can be duplicated is by nature a difficult and uncertain exercise that involves bold predictions as to future market evolution. Competition authorities and courts have no particular skills in this regard and the information available to them is often limited and may be skewed by the opposing submissions of complainants and defendants. Further, there are no reliable economic or evidential techniques for testing whether a facility can be duplicated. For example, it is often difficult to distinguish situations in which customers simply have a strong preference for one facility from situations from those in which objective considerations render their choice unavoidable. Thus, a more practical reason why duties to deal should be generally avoided is that the rate and cost of error is likely to be high.

Structure of this chapter. The following structure is adopted: Section 8.2 discusses the economics of property protection and how the exclusive control granted to property owners is, in general, procompetitive. The remainder of the chapter deals with the circumstances in which a refusal to deal constitutes a violation of Article 82 EC. The approach adopted is to distinguish between situations in which the dominant firm: (1) refuses to deal with firms who are in competition with its own downstream business, i.e., competitors; and (2) refuses to supply downstream trading parties with whom it does not compete, i.e., customers.

In the former scenario, the dominant firm is vertically integrated in the sense that it owns or controls an input and is active as a seller of a product or service incorporating that input. It may also actually sell the input separately, although this is not a pre-requisite according to the case law. These cases raise similar issues to the so-called "essential facility" doctrine recognised by some US courts; in other words cases involving foreclosure of actual or potential rivals, or examples of "limiting production" to the "prejudice of consumers" under Article 82(b).[28] The scope of the duty to deal

---

[27] See, e.g., Vth Report on Competition Policy (1975), para. 76.

[28] The Community Courts have expressly confirmed that Article 82(b) is the legal basis of the refusal to grant a first licence or contract in a number of cases. See, e.g., Case 311/84, *Centre belge d'études de marché—Télémarketing (CBEM) v SA Compagnie luxembourgeoise de télédiffusion (CLT)*

with competitors is detailed in Section 8.3.

In the second situation, the dominant firm is *not* active on the same level of trade as the requesting party, which may affect its ability and incentive to exclude. These cases raise the issue of whether the duty to deal with actual or potential downstream customers is subject to essentially the same strict conditions as a duty to deal with rivals, or whether it is simply enough to show that the dominant firm has granted one contract and that it would be unlawfully discriminating in refusing to grant further contracts to other similarly-situated customers, contrary to Article 82(c). The former approach is advocated in this chapter. The scope of the duty to deal with customers is explained in Section 8.4. Finally, the specific situation of parallel trade is also detailed in Section 8.4.

8.2 THE ECONOMICS OF REFUSAL TO DEAL

8.2.1 IP Rights

Basic rationale for IP rights. The rationale for granting and protecting IP rights is well understood in economics.[29] An IP right, like any other property right, gives its holder the ability to exclude others from using that property and thereby enables the holder to appropriate the value of the property for himself. That seldom matters much because the majority of IP rights are not valuable.[30] But some IP rights are immensely valuable: the right to exclude results in monopoly prices. In these circumstances, IP rights offer the prospect of monopoly profits and thereby stimulate socially valuable innovation and creation.

The right to exclude has a direct positive impact on the incentives for innovation. Innovators must receive a reward for risky and costly investments. This is why society generally allows, and at times even enables, firms to have market power.[31] The reward

and Information publicité Benelux (IPB) [1985] ECR 3261, para. 26; Case 53/87, *Consorzio italiano della componentistica di ricambio per autoveicoli and Maxicar v Régie nationale des usines Renault* [1988] ECR 6039; Case 238/87, *AB Volvo v Eric Veng (UK) Ltd* [1988] ECR 6211; Joined Cases C-241/91 P and C-242/91 P, *Radio Telefis Éireann and Independent Television Publications Ltd (RTE & ITP) v Commission* [1995] ECR I-743, para. 54; and Case COMP/38/096, *Clearstream (Clearing and Settlement)*, Commission Decision of June 4, 2004, not yet published, para. 222.

[29] See, e.g., D Carlton and J Perloff, *Modern Industrial Organisation* (4th edn., Boston, Pearson Addison Wesley, 2005) ch. 16 and references therein.

[30] See M Lemley, "Rational Ignorance at the Patent Office" (2000) 2 *The Berkeley Law and Economics Working Papers*. In addition, according to USPTO data, from 1999–2003 more than one sixth of the patents up for renewal were left to expire. In that period, over 260,000 patents expired because of non-renewal. Roughly 40% of all US patents are maintained though the entire 20-year period. Similarly, most new books published by a traditional publisher do not sell more than 5,000 copies. Furthermore, only 10% of New York published books sell enough copies to pay royalties beyond the author's advance—nine out of ten books return no royalties to the author. From Union Hill Press, *Industry Facts*.

[31] Note that an IP right creates a legal monopoly over a period of time, but does not necessarily give rise to a dominant position because its scope may not span the entire relevant product market. To equate intellectual property grants with monopoly power therefore confuses the distinct concepts of property, which is a legally enforceable power to exclude others from the object of ownership, and monopoly, which is power over price. See e.g., WM Landes and RA Posner, *The Economic Structure of*

must be high for innovations that require great investments. Getting a new drug to market, for example, costs an average of $800 million in capitalised costs for pre-regulatory approval research and development and $95 million for post-approval research and development.[32] A Hollywood film now costs an average of $80 million to make and market.[33] Investors can only recover the sunk costs incurred at the R&D stage if they can charge prices that exceed the incremental costs of production when the innovation is ready to be marketed.

The more important reason rewards loom large is that most efforts that could be subject to IP protection do not succeed. Most inventive efforts fail. Many of these failures are invisible: inventors who do not make something that could get a patent, much less a valuable one; songwriters whose tunes are never played; and artists whose works are never seen. But the failures show how fleeting success can be. Of all the Hollywood movies released into the theatres, only 10% ever turn a profit.[34] Only one in approximately every 435 drugs that are considered ever makes it to the market.[35] Inventors and investors will thus enter into such efforts only if they expect that the rewards for the few successes will compensate for the many failures.

The right to exclude has another important effect on the incentives for innovation. Without it, people would tend to wait for others to incur the costs and risks of innovation and then free ride on the resulting creations. In the extreme case, everyone waits for others to invest and, as a result, investment and innovation cease, and the economy stagnates.[36] An economy cannot function indefinitely on imitation: in the end, there would be nothing left to imitate.

The costs and benefits of IP protection. Economics, law, and policy have long recognised the relevance of two important and related distinctions in evaluating the role of IP rights.[37] The first distinction is *ex ante* versus *ex post*. After IP has been created, it is often most efficient to make it widely available—*ex post*, full dissemination and disclosure is optimal. But if that approach is adopted as a general policy, the IP will not be created in the first place—*ex ante*, the ability to exclude and control dissemination and disclosure is optimal for the creation of IP. The second, related distinction is *short*

Intellectual Property (Cambridge, Harvard University Press, 2003). The Court of Justice reached the same conclusion in Case 24/67, *Parke, Davis and Co v Probe, Reese, Beintema-Interpharm and Centrafarm* [1968] ECR 81, para. 72.

32 JA Dimasi, RW Hansen, and HG Grabowski, "The Price of Innovation: New Estimates of Drug Development Costs" (2003) 22 *The Journal of Health Economics* 151–85.

33 "Mutating," *The Economist*, April 24, 2003. The success rate for European movies is apparently even lower.

34 "A Fine Romance," *The Economist*, March 29, 2001.

35 Based on figures from H Grabowski, "Patents, Innovation and Access to New Pharmaceuticals," mimeo, Duke University, July 2002; and JA Dimasi, "Research and Development Costs For New Drugs by Therapeutic Category" (1995) 7 *Pharmacoeconomics* 152–169.

36 This is a variant of the well-known tragedy of the commons. See G Hardin, "The Tragedy of the Commons" (1968) 168 *Science* 1243–48. See also P Aghion and P Howitt, *Endogenous Growth Theory* (Cambridge, MIT Press, 1997).

37 See W Nordhaus, *Invention, Growth, and Welfare—A Theoretical Treatment of Technological Change* (Cambridge, MIT Press, 1969); and C Shapiro, "Navigating the Patent Thicket: Cross Licences, Patent Pools, and Standard-Setting" in A Jaffe et al. (eds.), *Innovation Policy and the Economy* (Cambridge, MIT Press, 2001) Vol. 1.

run versus *long run*. In the short run, it is possible to make consumers better off by making IP freely available, because there are benefits and no costs. In the long run, making IP freely available will likely make consumers worse off because innovation will decline.

Successful innovations can and do benefit society substantially. The traditional demand and supply diagram helps to show why (see Figure 1 below). When a new product is introduced, the value created is the area between the demand curve (D) and the cost curve (S). That is, each unit of output has a social value that is the difference between the value shown by the demand curve and the cost of producing it. The overall social value of a product innovation is the sum of those differences: the area CS + II.

Figure 1: Social Value of New Product

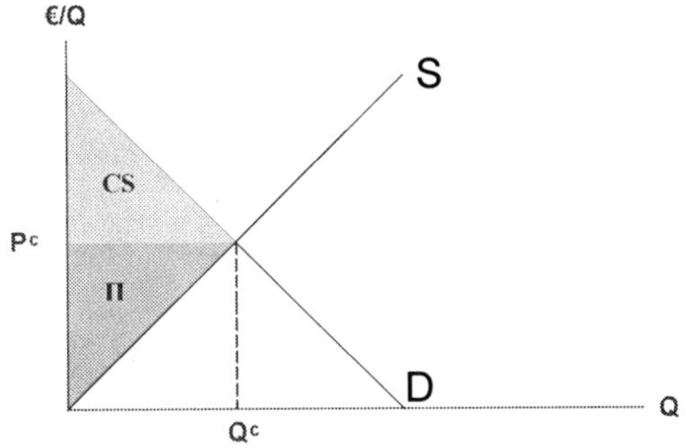

The competitive equilibrium is at (Pc,Qc) and it is located at the intersection of the supply curve, S, which is given by the incremental costs of production, and the demand curve D. Social value equals the sun of consumer surplus, CS, and producer surplus, II.

Modern economic research has documented that new products result in remarkable increases in social welfare.[38] The potential gains in consumer surplus through innovation can be enormous. A study in 1997 found that a new cereal—one made by adding apple and cinnamon to an existing cereal—created value of $78.1 million per year in the United States.[39] Innovative drugs can lead to more dramatic results: empirical data show that the value of saving or improving lives greatly exceeds the seemingly exorbitant prices of some drugs.[40] Likewise, technical change (due to

[38] See, e.g., J Hausman and G Leonard, "The Competitive Effects of a New Product Introduction: A Case Study" (2002) 50(3) *Journal of Industrial Economics* 237–63; and A Petrin, "Quantifying the Benefits of New Products: The Case of the Minivan" (2002) 110 *Journal of Political Economy* 705.

[39] JA Hausman, "Valuation of New Goods Under Perfect and Imperfect Competition" in TF Bresnahan and RJ Gordon (eds.), *The Economics of New Products* (Chicago, University of Chicago Press, 1996).

[40] The social value of increases in life expectancy due to advances in medical research from 1970 to 1990, was estimated to amount to $2.8 trillion per year. See KM Murphy and RH Topel, "The Economic Value of Medical Research" in KM Murphy and RH Topel (eds.), *Measuring the Gains from Medical Research: An Economic Approach* (Chicago, University of Chicago Press, 2003).

product and process innovations) has resulted in rapid increases in productivity and improved standards of living around the world.[41]

These social rewards come at an obvious cost. Successful IP rights may allow the holder to raise the price above the competitive level by restricting output below the competitive level. The result is the well known "monopoly-loss triangle," given by the value that consumers do not get from the output the monopolist does not produce (see area L Figure 2 below). In a concrete example, one can imagine the value that society loses when pharmaceutical companies charge prices for pills that far exceed of the cost of manufacturing those pills.

Figure 2: Monopoly-loss Triangle

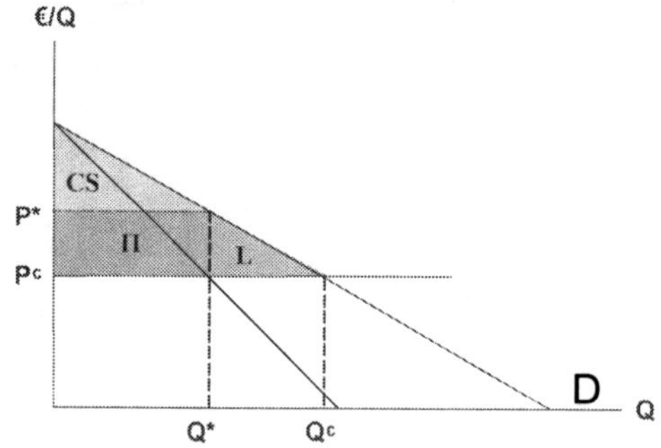

The competitive equilibrium is at (Pc,Qc). The monopoly outcome results in a higher price and lower quantity given by (P*,Q*). The result is a deadweight loss of welfare to society given by L, commonly known as the monopoly-loss triangle. Π is the monopoly profit and CS is consumer surplus. The negative impact of monopoly power on consumers' welfare is equal to the sum of the supra-competitive profits Π and the deadweight loss L.

Balancing the costs and benefits of IP protection. Policymakers must decide whether or not the gains from stimulating investment in innovation outweigh the losses from allowing a monopoly to persist. Industrial societies have long balanced these considerations and reached a general consensus that the benefits of IP protection greatly exceed the costs. What differences remain lie mainly at the margin. The current consensus may be summarised as follows.

First, societies rely on a number of "social" or "policy" instruments to stimulate intellectual creations. These include prizes, honours, social prestige, and government funding. Copyrights, patents, and trade secrets fill out the arsenal in promoting creations where exclusive control over the subject-matter is necessary to stimulate innovation and investment.

Second, governments have made complex economic policy judgments regarding IP rights, which they have chosen to enforce through laws and institutions. The logic

[41] R Fare, B Grossgopf, M Norris, and Z Zhang, "Productivity Growth, Technical Progress and Efficiency Change in Industrialised Countries" (1994) 84 *American Economic Review* 66–83; S Globerman, "Linkages Between Technological Change and Productivity Growth" in S Rao and A Sharpe (eds.), *Productivity Issues in Canada* (Calgary, University of Calgary Press, 2002) pp. 281–311.

behind this choice is that innovations—and the new and improved products and processes they entail—are valuable. While some may bemoan the high cost of pharmaceuticals, the fact is that, absent patent protection, few of these drugs would have been produced, put through clinical trials, and brought to market.[42] Yet, as observed above, these drugs have brought enormous benefits in extending and improving the quality of life.[43] The same conclusion may be drawn for many modern industries—IP protection has brought tremendous value to consumers.

Finally, governments have defined certain limits to the protection afforded by the law: IP protection comes with conditions attached. This is most obvious in the case of a patent, which allows the invention to be used by third parties 15–20 years after the patent filing. Similarly, copyrighted material can eventually be reproduced and distributed at no cost (although the duration for which exclusive rights should be granted is debated). Copyright is also limited in scope: it only grants exclusive control over the *expression* of an original idea rather than the subject-matter of the idea itself. There are also categories of intellectual matter for which it is not possible to obtain property rights.[44]

Identifying situations in which compulsory licensing can enhance welfare. From the foregoing, it should be clear that compulsory licensing has two main and opposing effects on welfare.[45] First, it reduces the incentives to innovate in the long run.[46] The

---

[42] H Grabowski, "Patents and New Product Development in the Pharmaceutical and Biotechnology Industries," mimeo Duke University, 2002; E Mansfield, "Patents and Innovation: an Empirical Study" (1986) 32 *Management Science* 173.

[43] See KM Murphy and RH Topel, "The Economic Value of Medical Research" in KM Murphy and RH Topel (eds.), *Measuring the Gains from Medical Research: An Economic Approach* (Chicago, University of Chicago Press, 2003).

[44] Some creations of the mind may be so valuable from a social standpoint that we do not want to restrict their use. For example, it is not possible to obtain protection for theorems or discoveries of general laws of nature. That is why Einstein could obtain patent protection for his many refrigerator innovations, but not for the general theory of relativity. And one must be careful not to assign property rights unnecessarily or to obvious ideas. For example, McDonald's could not protect the fast-food franchise idea, nor Wal-Mart the idea of having large superstores.

[45] "Welfare" in this context refers to social welfare (the sum of consumer and producer surpluses)—the measure economists mainly advocate for evaluating competition policy. See M Motta, *Competition Policy: Theory and Practice* (Cambridge, Cambridge University Press, 2004); OE Williamson, "Economies as an Antitrust Defence: The Welfare Tradeoffs" (1968) 58 *American Economic Review* 34; and R Schmalensee, "Sunk Costs and Antitrust Barriers to Entry" (2004) 94(2) *American Economic Review* 471. Most of what follows, however, does not depend on whether we use social welfare or the more narrow measure of consumer welfare that the EU courts and competition authorities typically use for evaluating antitrust issues.

[46] See, e.g., R Gilbert and C Shapiro, "An Economic Analysis of Unilateral Refusals to License Intellectual Property," *Proceedings of the National Academy of Sciences USA*, 1995, page 12754 ("An obligation to deal does not necessarily increase economic welfare even in the short run. In the long run, obligations to deal can have profound adverse incentives for investment and for the creation of intellectual property. Although there is no obvious economic reason why intellectual property should be immune from an obligation to deal, the crucial role of incentives for the creation of intellectual property is reason enough to justify scepticism toward policies that call for compulsory licensing."). See also See M Motta, *Competition Policy: Theory and Practice* (Cambridge, Cambridge University Press, 2004) p. 64 ("If antitrust agencies tried to eliminate or reduce market power whenever it appeared, this would have the detrimental effect of eliminating firms' incentives to innovate.").

impact on social welfare of a fall in the incentives for innovation is potentially very large and equal to the reduction in total surplus (area II + CS in Figure or 2) that results from a lower number of product and process innovations. A lower rate of innovation means less profits (area II) and lower consumer satisfaction (area CS). This negative effect will be largest when the products that competitors manufacture as a result of having access to the requested IP are close substitutes for those of the IP holder.

The second, beneficial effect is that compulsory licensing may increase competition in the short run, thus contributing to eliminate the deadweight loss of market power (area L in Figure 2) and to increase consumer welfare in the short term (area II). This effect will be largest when the degree of market power derived from the exercise of the IP right is greatest,[47] such as when access to the IP is indispensable to carry on business on that market. Compulsory licensing may also have a positive effect on consumer welfare in the long run if it facilitates the development of new products for which there is potential demand.

Determining which of the two effects is quantitatively most important is extremely difficult, since the welfare-increasing and welfare-decreasing effects of a compulsory licence cannot be accurately balanced, either *ex ante* or *ex post*.[48] Approximations are therefore necessary. A first approximation involves comparing areas CS + II (the welfare cost of compulsory licensing) and II + L (the welfare benefit of compulsory licensing), or simplifying areas CS and L, which is no doubt a complex exercise. However, in general, compulsory licensing is likely to have an overall negative impact on welfare (i.e., area CS is likely to be large than area L). This is true for two reasons. First, the available evidence indicates that innovators do not generally appropriate the entire social value of their innovations, and that most of the value of the new products and processes are sooner or later passed on to consumers.[49] Second, area L may also be small because compulsory licensing may not only reduce welfare in the long run, but also in the short run, e.g., by facilitating entry of inefficient producers, reduced product variety, and collusion.

Balancing these competing economic considerations leads to the conclusion that forced disclosure of IP is only likely to increase long-run consumer welfare when the following cumulative conditions are met: (1) the requested IP is indispensable to compete; (2) the refusal to license causes the exclusion of all competition from the downstream market;

[47] When that is the case, the difference between the price that would prevail under compulsory licensing (P^c in Figure 2) and the price without compulsory licensing (P^* in Figure 2) is largest, and hence consumer surplus (CS) is smallest.

[48] D Evans, "How Can Economists Help Courts Design Competition Rules? An EU and US Perspective" (2005) 28(1) *World Competition* 95.

[49] Professor Nordhaus of Yale University, one of the classical authors on the economics of innovation, finds using data from the US non-farm business sector that innovators are able to capture about 2.2% of the total surplus from innovation. These findings imply, first, that the private incentives to innovate are likely to be lower than the socially optimal. But also that the degree of market power *de facto* enjoyed by innovators is rather limited. Consequently, compulsory licensing is likely to depress innovation from levels that are inefficiently low, without any significant procompetitive effect in the short term. In terms of Figure 2 above, this suggests that area CS is likely to be large and area L small. See W Nordhaus, "Schumpeterian Profits in the American Economy: Theory and Measurement," (2004) *Cowles Foundation Discussion Paper No. 1457*, p. 4.

(3) the refusal prevents the emergence of markets for new products for which there is substantial demand; and (4) the products to be developed by the licensees are sufficiently differentiated from those of the IP right holder, e.g., because they satisfy needs that the existing products failed to address. Conditions (1) and (2) ensure that the short-run welfare loss resulting from a refusal to license is maximal (area L is large). Condition (4) implies that the refusal has a long-run cost as well as a short-run cost. And condition (4) says that the long-run cost of compulsory licensing—the reduction in the incentives to innovate—is low.

The last two conditions are, arguably, the most important. When (1) and (2) fail to hold, the obligation to deal is bound to have a significant adverse effect on the incentives for innovation and the creation of IP, and no social benefit, or at least a questionable one, in the short run. However, one would expect no unilateral refusal to license when (3) and (4) hold. In those circumstances, the IP holder is likely to be better off by licensing its IP by reaping some of the rents generated by the new products at no cost for its own existing business. In other words, when (3) and (4) hold, there is likely to be a mutually acceptable licence since total industry profits when there is a licence exceed total industry profits when the IP holder refuses to license.

8.2.2 Physical Property

Basic rationale for protecting physical property. The basic rationale for protecting investments in physical property is essentially the same as for IP rights. Property rights grant the owner the prospect of returns above marginal cost in the long run, which is necessary to stimulate socially beneficial investment decisions *ex ante*. Again, there is an established consensus in industrialised societies that the positive effects of investments in physical property outweigh the negative effects of prices above marginal cost for the period in which the property right benefits from protection. Similarly, while the sharing of physical property through a duty to deal will always look attractive *ex post* once a valuable asset has been created, any such general policy risks undermining the important social benefits of investment and innovation *ex ante*. As with IP, physical property rights thus create a generally desirable right to exclude.[50] What differences remain lie at the margin and are therefore the exception, not the rule.

The general equivalence of physical property and IP rights under the duty to deal. It is frequently argued that unilateral refusals to license IP rights merit a higher form of deference under competition law than refusals to supply physical assets.[51] Several reasons are typically advanced, but they are not particularly compelling, whether taken

---

[50] See, e.g., H Demsetz, "Barriers To Entry" (1982) 72(1) *American Economic Review* 47. For an overview of the literature discussing the economic justification for the protection of protection of property rights, see E Elhauge, "Defining Better Monopolisation Standards" (2003) 56(2) *Stanford Law Review* 253, 294–305.

[51] See, e.g., AB Lipsky and GJ Sidak, "Essential Facilities" (1999) 51 *Stanford Law Review* 1187; J Gleklen, "*Per Se* Legality for Unilateral Refusals to License IP Is Correct as a Matter of Law and Policy," *The Antitrust Source*, (July 2002); and H Hovenkamp, M Janis and M Lemley, *IP and Antitrust: An Analysis of Antitrust Principles Applied to Intellectual Property Law* (New York, Aspen Publishers, 2002) pp. 13–16.

alone or in combination.[52] First, it is said that the very purpose of IP rights is to grant a reward to the owner by restricting competition, in return for the benefits that valuable innovations bring to society.[53] But the same general justification can be advanced for physical property: the nature, scope, and duration of protection is the result of a legislative consensus that property rights confer net benefits to society in the form of desirable investment activity.

Second, it is said that the basic purpose of IP rights is to exclude competition and that competition law should therefore recognise that a legal monopoly is central to the reason why IP rights are granted. This reason confuses, however, the legal monopoly granted by the IP laws and the economic monopoly that competition law is concerned with. IP rights do not grant an economic monopoly: this is only the case where other products on the relevant market are not effective substitutes. Moreover, there is no intrinsic reason why IP rights should lead to a higher incidence of economic monopolies than physical property rights. The question in each case is whether consumers are willing to pay a sufficient premium for one product over other actual or potential substitutes. The acquisition of market power by IP owners is thus not automatic but is an empirical matter,[54] depending on market conditions faced by the output embodying the creation or innovation, and the existence of substitutes.[55] The same analysis applies to physical property.[56] It should also be emphasised that Article 82 EC is generally agnostic towards economic monopolies: only the abuse of a dominant position is illegal and the mere fact of holding an economic monopoly is not, in itself, unlawful. Additional elements are needed.

A third reason advanced is that IP merits a higher level of protection because it can generally be copied easily and inexpensively and cannot be exhausted. Physical facilities are generally more difficult and expensive to copy and are usually subject to capacity constraints that limit the scope for misappropriation. These differences are no doubt true, as a general matter, but they are simply a reason why IP rights grant their owner the *exclusive* right to reproduce the protected matter. Such exclusivity is not required for physical property, since the problems of misappropriation and non-exhaustion do not arise, to the same extent or at all. The fact that exclusivity may be necessary to protect an IP right from reproduction does not therefore offer a convincing

[52] See M Katz, "Intellectual Property Rights and Antitrust Policy: Four Principles for a Complex World" (2002) 1 *Journal on Telecommunications & High Technology Law* 325, 349 ("[T]he arguments for special treatment of intellectual property are incomplete. Indeed, the arguments for imposing less of a duty to deal on intellectual property than on other forms of property have been disappointingly superficial to date....[M]ore rigorous analysis is needed if one is to take seriously arguments that intellectual property is deserving of unique treatment.").

[53] See L Kaplow, "The Patent-Antitrust Intersection: A Reappraisal" (1984) 97 *Harvard Law Review* 1813, 1817.

[54] See EW Kitch, "Elementary and Persistent Errors in the Economic Analysis of Intellectual Property" (2000) 53 *Vanderbilt Law Review* 1727.

[55] See, e.g., WM Landes and RA Posner, *The Economic Structure of Intellectual Property* (Cambridge, Harvard University Press, 2003).

[56] See Department of Justice & Federal Trade Commission, *Antitrust Guidelines for the Licensing of Intellectual Property*, 1995, section 2.1 (The United States enforcement agencies attempt to "apply the same general antitrust principles to conduct involving intellectual property rights that they apply to conduct involving any other form of tangible or intangible property.").

basis for saying that Article 82 EC should treat unilateral refusals to deal in IP rights more leniently than physical property.

The same comment can be made with respect to the suggestion that IP rights merit different treatment because they are limited in time.[57] The duration of protection of property rights—whether physical or intellectual—simply represents the *outcome* of the balance made by the legislature between the need to provide incentives for beneficial social activity and the adverse welfare effects of granting owners exclusive rights or other forms of control over property. It does not in itself offer a basis for immunising certain types of rights from competition law scrutiny or applying more lenient standards. Moreover, there is no hard and fast distinction between IP rights and physical property in this regard: many leases or other rights over physical property are shorter in duration than IP rights (e.g., copyrights, which last for the life of the author plus 50–70 years thereinafter depending on the applicable legal term).

The final reason put forward is that IP rights involve more risky and costly *ex ante* investment decisions than physical property. However, there is no clear empirical basis for this assertion and a good deal of real world evidence to suggest that it is not true, or at least not universally true. For example, one of the largest investments in industrial societies in recent years has been the infrastructure and government permits required for broadband Internet access and third-generation mobile telephony. These investments compare favourably with research and development costs for valuable IP rights such as pharmaceuticals.

In sum, while the legal definition of IP rights necessarily differs in certain respects from physical property, there is no clear basis in economics for saying that IP rights merit different (i.e., more lenient) treatment in respect of unilateral refusals to deal. What matters in each case is the impact of forcing access on the incentives to invest, and not the nature of the property rights at stake. Economics therefore provides a sound basis for saying that IP rights and physical property should be treated essentially the same in analysing unilateral refusals to deal under Article 82 EC.

8.3 THE DUTY TO DEAL WITH COMPETITORS

8.3.1 Evolution Of The Decisional Practice And Case Law

Physical property. The duty of a dominant firm to grant access to essential physical property was first developed by the Commission in a series of cases in the late 1980s and early 1990s concerning physical infrastructure and networks. A number of earlier cases arose concerning essential infrastructure and services in the airline sector. Interestingly, most of the access obligations contained in the early Commission decisions have resulted in legislation creating general duties to share the facilities in

[57] See E Derclaye, "Abuses of Dominant Position and Intellectual Property Rights: A Suggestion to Reconcile the Community Courts' Case Law" (2003) 26 *World Competition* 685, 701 ("[T]here are reasons to be more prudent when imposing compulsory licences on copyright holders rather than on owners of other types of property. A difference in treatment, most probably in the direction of a lower incursion of competition law into copyright's scope than into the scope of other forms of property, is therefore justified.").

question. A series of cases involving ports and related facilities then elaborated on the duty to deal, including by specifically mentioning for the first time the term "essential facility." Finally, the Court of Justice in *Bronner* cut back the scope of the duty to deal by laying down strict conditions for such a duty to arise.

a. Commercial Solvents.[58] *Commercial Solvents* is generally regarded as the precursor to the modern case law on refusal to deal. The Court of Justice held that Commercial Solvents abused its dominant position by refusing to continue to supply aminobutanol and nitropropane, raw materials for the production of ethambutol (and for which Commercial Solvents held unique know-how in Europe), to Zoja. The basis for the refusal to supply was that Commercial Solvents was planning to vertically integrate into competition with Zoja in the downstream market for the supply of the derived product, ethambutol. Commercial Solvents' actions were thus intended to exclude Zoja from the downstream market by cutting off essential raw materials. The Court noted that Commercial Solvents had supplied Zoja with aminobutanol for some years and only terminated supplies when Zoja started competing directly with it. In these circumstances, the Court held that there was an abuse.[59]

b. Cases on airport and airline infrastructure. The earliest case creating a duty to supply infrastructure access to competitors involve airline computer reservation systems. In *London European/Sabena*,[60] Sabena refused to grant its competitor airline, London European, access to the Saphir computer reservation system (which was managed by Sabena). London European claimed that Sabena refused to grant it access to the Saphir system on the grounds that: (1) London European's fares were too low; and (2) London European had entrusted the handling of its aircraft to a company other than Sabena (i.e., tying). The Commission found that this amounted to an abuse, since it would result in the risk of the elimination of London European as a competitor on the relevant routes.

A similar conclusion was reached in *British Midland/Aer Lingus*,[61] which concerned

---

[58] Joined Cases 6/73 and 7/73, *Istituto Chemioterapico Italiano SpA and Commercial Solvents Corporation v Commission* [1974] ECR 223n (hereinafter "*Commercial Solvents*").

[59] A similar conclusion was reached in *Télémarketing*, where RTL, a dominant broadcaster, committed an abuse by refusing to sell advertising space to CBEM, a telemarketing operator. CBEM had concluded a one-year agreement with RTL allowing it to conduct telemarketing operations on RTL's broadcasts through CBEM's own telephone number. After this agreement had expired, RTL indicated that it would no longer accept advertising spots unless the telephone number used was that of its own advertising subsidiary. The Court of Justice found that this amounted to an abuse, since RTL was using its statutory broadcasting monopoly to reserve the activity of telemarketing services to its own subsidiary, thereby eliminating competition from CBEM. See Case 311/84, *Centre belge d'études de marché—Télémarketing (CBEM) v SA Compagnie luxembourgeoise de télédiffusion (CLT) and Information publicité Benelux (IPB)* [1985] ECR 3261. See also *Hugin/Liptons*, OJ 1978 L 22/23, where the Commission found that the refusal to continue to supply a customer with spare parts on the ground that the customer had established a business in servicing and the supply of spare parts in competition with the dominant supplier was abusive.

[60] *London European/Sabena*, OJ 1988 L 317/47 (hereinafter "*London European/Sabena*"). See also XXIst Competition Policy Report (1991), pp. 73–74 (similar non-discrimination duty imposed on the second other large European computer reservation system owners).

[61] *British Midland v Aer Lingus*, OJ 1992 L 96/34. See also *FAG-Flughafen Frankfurt/Main AG*, OJ 1998 L 72/30 (access to airport ground handling services).

access to interlining facilities, i.e., where airlines are authorised to sell each other's services. Aer Lingus had long cooperated with British Midland within the framework of an international multilateral agreement on interlining services. However, once British Midland commenced a competing route from London-Dublin, Aer Lingus terminated its past cooperation and refused to accept the interchangeability of British Midland's tickets on the London-Dublin route. This contrasted with the conduct of British Airways—the other competitor on the route—which continued to interline with British Midland. Aer Lingus also continued its interlining agreement with British Airways, while refusing to deal with British Midland. The Commission found that Aer Lingus' refusal to interline constituted an abuse. This was based, *inter alia*, on the importance of interlining services for a viable operation and the risk that British Midland would be eliminated as a competitor absent access. The Commission reasoned as follows:[62]

> "Both a refusal to grant new interline facilities and the withdrawal of existing interline facilities may, depending on the circumstances, hinder the maintenance or development of competition. Whether a duty to interline arises depends on the effects on competition of the refusal to interline; it would exist in particular when the refusal or withdrawal of interline facilities by a dominant airline is objectively likely to have a significant impact on the other airline's ability to start a new service or sustain an existing service on account of its effects on the other airline's costs and revenue in respect of the service in question, and when the dominant airline cannot give any objective commercial reason for its refusal (such as concerns about creditworthiness) other than its wish to avoid helping this particular competitor. It is unlikely that there is such justification when the dominant airline singles out an airline with which it previously interlined, after that airline starts competing on an important route, but continues to interline with other competitors."

c. ***Expansion of the duty to share in the port cases***. The first case specifically mentioning the term "essential facilities" was the Commission's interim decision in *Sea Containers*.[63] Sea Containers wished to introduce a new fast ferry service to the Holyhead-Dun Laoghaire route, using a wave-piercing catamaran technology. To do this, it had to rely on upstream port facilities provided by Sealink, which was also vertically integrated in the supply of passenger ferry services. Port services available at the port of Holyhead were found by the Commission to be an essential facility for the provision of such services: facilities available at other ports in the same catchment area were not effective substitutes. The Commission found that, in contrast to the establishment of its own fast ferry service, Sealink consistently delayed and raised difficulties concerning Sea Containers' possible use of existing facilities in the port, thereby discriminating against Sea Containers. In the interim, however, Sealink had offered Sea Containers access on non-discriminatory terms, which made the interim relief sought by Sea Containers unnecessary. The Commission followed this precedent in a series of subsequent decisions regarding ports and related infrastructure in other Member States.[64]

[62] *Ibid.*, para. 26.

[63] *Sea Containers v Stena Sealink—Interim measures*, OJ 1994 L 15/8.

[64] See, e.g., *Port of Rødby*, OJ 1994 L 55/52 (refusal by Danish Government to allow EuroPort A/S to build a new port in the immediate vicinity of the port of Rødby or to operate from the existing port facilities at Rødby found abusive); *Elsinore Port opened for access to a new competing ferry service,*

d. Narrowing of the scope of the duty to deal in Bronner. Despite various Commission decisions granting of access to physical infrastructure, the legal conditions under which access could be ordered were not clarified in any judgment of the Community Courts. This opportunity arose in *Bronner*, a preliminary reference from an Austrian court. The Court of Justice was asked to establish the circumstances under which a newspaper group, Mediaprint, with a substantial share of the market for daily newspaper refusing access to its home delivery network would engage in abusive conduct. Mediaprint, the owner of the delivery scheme, provided a series of services to an independent publisher, including home delivery of one of its daily newspapers. The home delivery scheme did not appear to have been sold independently, but formed part of a package including the printing and sale in kiosks of the daily newspaper in question.

The Court of Justice strongly suggested that Mediaprint had no duty to grant Bronner access to its home-delivery service. In so doing, it clarified a number of important points in respect of the duty to deal. First, the Court confirmed that the indispensability of the requested product for competitors is a critical element of any duty to deal. It held that "it would still be necessary...in order to plead the existence of an abuse within the meaning of Article 8[2]...not only that the refusal of the service comprised in home delivery be likely to eliminate all competition in the daily newspaper market on the part of the person requesting the service and that such refusal be incapable of being objectively justified, but also that the service in itself be indispensable to carrying on that person's business, inasmuch as there is no actual or potential substitute in existence for that home-delivery scheme."[65] Second, in assessing "indispensability," the question was whether there were "technical, legal or even economic obstacles" to making an alternative facility, indicating that a strict test applied.[66]

Finally, when assessing the ability of competitors to develop their own facilities, the standard was not whether the requesting party could develop another facility, but whether a company operating on the same scale as the dominant firm could do so, i.e., an objective standard based on an equally efficient entrant.[67] Taken together, the Court's judgment and the opinion of the Advocate General advocate a less interventionist approach to refusals to deal under Article 82 EC and display a greater recognition of the underlying policy and welfare considerations.[68]

Commission Press Release IP/96/456 of May 30, 1996 (refusal by Danish government to grant access to Elsinore port to the shipping line Mercandia for routes between Elsinore and Helsingborg found abusive); and *Irish Continental Group CCI Morlaix-Port of Roscoff*, XXVth Competition Policy Report (1995), para. 43 (refusal by CCI Morlaix to grant access to Irish Continental to Roscoff port for services between Ireland and France found abusive).

[65] Case C-7/97, *Oscar Bronner GmbH & Co KG v Mediaprint Zeitungs- und Zeitschriftenverlag GmbH & Co KG, Mediaprint Zeitungsvertriebsgesellschaft mbH & Co KG and Mediaprint Anzeigengesellschaft mbH & Co KG* [1998] ECR I-7791, para. 41.

[66] *Ibid.*, para. 4.

[67] *Ibid.*, paras. 44–45.

[68] For commentary on *Bronner*, see P Treacy, "Essential Facilities: Is The Tide Turning?" (1998) 19 *European Competition Law Review* 501–05; L Hancher, "A Review of *Bronner*" (1999) *Common Market Law Review* 1289–1307; and J Temple Lang, "The Principles of Essential Facilities in European

IP rights. The evolution of the law on compulsory licensing of IP rights under Article 82 EC has tracked a similar path to that of physical property. At the outset, the judgments of the Court of Justice in *Volvo/Renault* signalled a cautious approach to the duty to grant a licence under Article 82 EC.[69] Shortly thereinafter, however, an extreme case arose in *Magill* where the Community institutions treated the duty to license IP rights as a sub-set of the essential facility paradigm developed for physical property.[70] This culminated in the expansion of the duty to share in a controversial Commission interim decision in *IMS Health*,[71] followed later by *Microsoft*.[72] The most recent development—the judgment of the Court of Justice in *IMS/NDC*[73]—signals a return to a more orthodox position.

a. ***Volvo/Renault.*** The first Court of Justice judgments concerning compulsory licensing under Article 82 EC were *Volvo* and *Renault*. The cases concerned the ability of an after-sales service provider to obtain registered design rights for particular car models from the manufacturer. The Court ruled that the freedom to refuse to license an IP right was at the core of the subject matter of the exclusive right and concluded that the refusal to license a protected design, even in return for a reasonable royalty, was not in itself abusive. However, the Court did not adopt a *per se* legality standard. It made clear that the exercise of an exclusive IP right could be in breach of competition law if it involved "additional abusive conduct,"[74] such as the arbitrary refusal to supply spare parts to independent repairers, the fixing of prices at an unfair level, or the decision to cease producing spare parts for a particular car model, even though many cars of that model were still in circulation.

b. ***Magill.*** The only case in which the Community Courts have upheld a duty to license an IP right is *Magill*. Broadcasters in the United Kingdom and Ireland—the BBC, RTE and ITP—each published weekly television guides containing details of their

Community Competition Law—The Position Since *Bronner*" (2000) 1 *Journal of Network Industries* 375.

[69] See Case 238/87, *AB Volvo v Erik Veng (UK) Ltd* [1988] ECR 6211. See also Case 53/87, *Consorzio italiano della componentistica di ricambio per autoveicoli and Maxicar v Regie nationale des usines Renault* [1988] ECR 6039, which was decided on the same day as *Volvo* on substantially the same grounds.

[70] *Magill TV Guide/ITP, BBC and RTE*, OJ 1989 L 78/43 (hereinafter "*Magill*"), confirmed on appeal in Case T-69/89, *Radio Telefis Éireann (RTE) v Commission* [1991] ECR II-485, Case T-70/89, *British Broadcasting Corporation and BBC Enterprises Ltd (BBC) v Commission* [1991] ECR II-535, and Case T-76/89, *Independent Television Publications Ltd (ITP) v Commission* [1991] ECR II-575, and further confirmed in Joined Cases C-241/91 P and C-242/91 P, *Radio Radio Telefis Éireann and Independent Television Publications Ltd (RTE & ITP) v Commission* [1995] ECR I-743.

[71] *IMS Health/NDC—Interim Measures*, OJ 2002 L 59/18 (hereinafter "*IMS Health*"), withdrawn by *NDC Health/IMS Health: Interim measures*, OJ 2003 L 268/69.

[72] Case COMP/C-3/37.792, *Microsoft*, Commission Decision of March 24, 2004, not yet published.

[73] Case C-418/01, *IMS Health GmbH & Co OHG v NDC Health GmbH & Co KG* [2004] ECR I-5039.

[74] Case 53/87, *Consorzio italiano della componentistica di ricambio per autoveicoli and Maxicar v Regie nationale des usines Renault* [1988] ECR 6039, paras. 15–16 ("[T]he mere fact of securing the benefit of an exclusive right granted by law, the effect of which is to enable the manufacture and sale of protected products by unauthorised third parties to be prevented, cannot be regarded as an abusive method of eliminating competition. Exercise of the exclusive right may be prohibited by Article 8[2] if it gives rise to certain abusive conduct on the part of an undertaking occupying a dominant position.").

own TV programmes. These listings were a by-product of their main activity as broadcasters and did not require any specific investment or embody any literary or artistic value. Magill wanted to publish a comprehensive weekly TV guide with all broadcasters' listings—a product for which there was unsatisfied consumer demand—and requested the TV listing information from the three broadcasters. The broadcasters claimed their TV listings were protected by copyright and refused to make the information available. The Commission ordered the three broadcasters to provide Magill with the information it had requested. The Court of First Instance upheld the Commission's decision that the three broadcasters had abused the dominant position which they held on the markets for their television programme schedules, which was further upheld by the Court of Justice.

The Court of Justice established that the refusal to license an IP right was not in itself an abuse by a dominant firm, but could be regarded as such in "exceptional circumstances."[75] The Court regarded three circumstances in *Magill* as exceptional. First, the broadcasters' televisions listings information was an "indispensable raw material for compiling a weekly television guide" covering all the TV channels."[76] Their conduct "thus prevented the appearance of a new product, a comprehensive weekly guide to television programmes, which the appellants did not offer and for which there was a potential consumer demand."[77] Second, the TV companies, by refusing to provide essential information, "reserved to themselves the secondary market of weekly television guides by excluding all competition on that market."[78] And third, "there was no objective justification for such refusal."[79]

c. ***Ladbroke.***[80] Ladbroke, an operator of betting shops in Belgium, complained to the Commission that its French competitor, Paris Mutuel International (PMI), should be required to grant a licence of its copyright for televised pictures and sound commentaries on French horse races. On appeal following the rejection of Ladbroke's complaint by the Commission, the Court held that the *Magill* principles did not apply to a refusal by certain French race course operators to allow Ladbroke's betting shops in Belgium access to the live broadcasts of French horse races to which the French operators held the IP rights. This was because Ladbroke was not only already present on the Belgian market in question, but was in fact the leading betting operator. In other words, access to French race broadcasts could not, in fact, have been essential for Ladbroke's activities in Belgium.

d. The IMS Health proceedings. One of the most controversial applications of the duty to license under Article 82 EC is the various *IMS Health* proceedings. The matter concerned a copyright-protected data analysis structure in Germany, referred to as the "1860 brick structure," which divides the German territory into 1,860 geographic units

[75] Joined Cases C-241/91 P and C-242/91 P, *Radio Telefís Éireann and Independent Television Publications Ltd (RTE & ITP) v Commission* [1995] ECR I-743, para. 50.
[76] *Ibid.*, para. 53.
[77] *Ibid.*, para. 54.
[78] *Ibid.*, para. 56.
[79] *Ibid.*, para. 55.
[80] Case T-504/93, *Tiercé Ladbroke SA v Commission* [1997] ECR II-923. For a commentary on the judgment, see V Korah, "The *Ladbroke* Saga" (1998) 19(3) *European Competition Law Review* 169-76.

or "bricks." These bricks are designed to group doctors, patients, and pharmacies so as to allow the reporting of pharmaceutical sales data in a way that is useful for calculating the compensation of pharmaceutical company sales representatives. This aggregation of territories is also necessary for reasons of German data protection law, which prevents disaggregation of data to a level lower than three pharmacies. The bricks—which were designed by IMS with certain input from pharmaceutical company users—were mainly comprised of groupings of postcode areas. Crucially, however, these groupings were not predetermined, but required some segmentation by IMS.[81]

On July 3, 2001, the Commission adopted an interim decision, which found that the 1860 brick structure had become a *de facto* industry standard for wholesaler pharmaceutical data presentation in Germany. These factors made the 1860 brick structure an "essential facility" that had to be made available, on "reasonable terms," for incorporation in competing services. Following an appeal by IMS, the President of the Court of First Instance granted a stay of the Commission's interim decision.[82] Shortly after the Commission's interim decision, a German court hearing the copyright infringement dispute between IMS and its competitors also sought a preliminary reference from the Court of Justice on the legal conditions for a compulsory licence under Article 82 EC. The preliminary reference in essence sought to clarify a number of the Commission's more controversial findings in the interim decision.

The Court of Justice made a number of important findings regarding the scope of the duty to license under Article 82 EC. It first confirmed the long-established principle that the mere refusal to license an IP is not in itself an abuse, but that, in exceptional circumstances, the exercise of an exclusive right by the IP owner may be linked to abusive conduct. Second, the Court held that, for the refusal by a dominant IP owner to give access to a product or service indispensable for carrying on a business to be

---

[81] The following emerged from litigation in the German courts concerning the copyright. In the first place, one third of bricks in the 1860 Brick Structure do not correspond to postcode areas at all. Further, the vast majority of bricks contain two or more postcode areas (and, in some cases, up to 28 postcode areas). As there are approximately 8,200 postcode areas in Germany, there was a very large number of permutations and combinations for each brick in terms of the postcode area configuration that it ultimately contained. The design of the brick structure was not therefore objectively predetermined or unavoidable. See judgment of the *Landgericht Frankfurt* of November 16, 2000, in *IMS/Pharma Intranet* ("Objective criteria do not require dividing the area of the Federal Republic into 1,860...market segments. It is much rather the case that choosing the size of the individual segments is the result of a subjective process of weighing and balancing. The underlying basis for the market segmentation is only partially such generally accessible data as the municipality directory of the German Federal Post Office and cartographic materials. It is undisputed that a multitude of additional criteria are involved in segmenting.") (translation from German original).

[82] Case T-184/01 R, *IMS Health Inc v Commission* [2001] ECR II-3193, para. 102. The President's Order was confirmed on appeal by the President of the Court of Justice in Case C-481/01P(R), *NDC Health GmbH & Co KG and NDC Health Corporation v Commission and IMS Health Inc* [2002] ECR I-3401. IMS's appeal was discontinued following the withdrawal of the interim decision by the Commission in 2003 on the grounds that the appeal had no further object. See *NDC Health/IMS Health—Interim measures*, OJ 2003 L 268/69 and Order of the Court of First Instance in Case T-184/01, *IMS Health Inc v Commission* [2005] ECR II-nyr. The national case that led to the preliminary ruling of the Court of Justice in principle continues in Germany, although it is not clear what practical impact it could have in circumstances where, as the Court of First Instance has now confirmed, none of the Commission's findings has continuing legal effect.

abusive, three cumulative conditions must be satisfied: (1) the refusal prevents the emergence of a new product for which there is a potential and unsatisfied consumer demand; (2) the refusal is unjustified; and (3) the refusal excludes competition on the secondary market.

The Court then elaborated on these conditions in several respects. First, with respect to the issue of whether the existence of two markets—that is an upstream market for the supply of the IP and a downstream market where the IP is used for the production of another product or service—is a necessary condition for a compulsory licence of an IP, it noted that it is enough in this regard to identify a "potential" or "hypothetical" upstream market.[83] Thus, "it is determinative that two different stages of production may be identified and that they are interconnected, the upstream product is indispensable in as much as for supply of the downstream product."[84] As regards the emergence of a new product, the Court concluded that for a refusal to license to be abusive:[85]

> "[T]he undertaking which requested the licence does not intend to limit itself essentially to duplicating the goods or services already offered on the secondary market by the owner of the copyright, but intends to produce new goods or services not offered by the owner of the right and for which there is a potential consumer demand."

Finally, on objective justification, the Court noted that the assessment of potential justifications must be conducted on a case-by-case basis.

e. ***Microsoft.*** In March 2004, the Commission issued an infringement decision against Microsoft, following a lengthy investigation. It found that Microsoft had a virtual monopoly in personal computer (PC) operating system software through its various Windows products. PC operating systems are frequently connected to a more powerful multi-user computer or "server," which allows several PC users to share multiple file, print, and group and user administration services. Microsoft is also active in supplying workgroup server operating systems, where it faces competition from a range of other vendors with their own proprietary technologies. Microsoft's PC operating system near-monopoly gives it control over the proprietary protocol specifications that allow a PC to interoperate effectively with a server operating system.

The Commission's case is that Microsoft has refused to supply the protocol specifications contained in its PC operating systems to competing stand-alone vendors of server operating systems or has done so on discriminatory terms, thereby reducing the interoperability of competitors' products with its dominant Windows PC operating system product. It considers that Microsoft's advantages over competitors in this regard are not due to the inherent superiority of its server operating system products over rival products, but because of the unfair handicap faced by rivals who lack full interoperability with the Windows PC operating system product. Over time, the Commission considers that, if this situation persisted, there is a risk that competing vendors would be eliminated from the market. The Commission therefore required, as a

---

[83] Case C-418/01, *IMS Health GmbH & Co OHG v NDC Health GmbH & Co KG* [2004] ECR I-5039, *ibid.*, para. 44.

[84] *Ibid.*, para. 45.

[85] *Ibid.*, para. 49.

remedy, that Microsoft should draw up detailed lists of protocol specifications to enable third parties to interconnect with Microsoft Windows client and server operating systems so that a non-Microsoft operating system could replace a Windows server without loss of functionality. The Commission's objective is to allow competing workgroup server operating system vendors to have the same level of interoperability as Microsoft achieves between its PC and server operating system products.[86]

The Commission's legal analysis is something of a hybrid. On the one hand, it recalls the traditional criteria for a duty to license as established in *Volvo*, *Magill*, *Ladbroke* and other cases.[87] On the other hand, the Commission also indicated that the criteria for a duty to license established in these cases were not necessarily exhaustive and that a duty may also be appropriate in other circumstances.[88] In the case at hand, the Commission relied on a series of factors to justify a duty to license: (1) Microsoft's conduct was part of a general pattern of conduct, including another abuse (tying);[89] (2) Microsoft discriminated by supplying certain vendors but not others;[90] (3) Microsoft terminated past voluntary disclosures of interoperability information;[91] (4) there was a risk of elimination of competition on the server operating system because interoperability information was of "significant competitive importance"[92] and there are no substitutes for Microsoft's providing this information;[93] (5) Microsoft's refusal had an adverse impact on technical development and consumer welfare;[94] (6) a duty to disclose the specifications did not affect Microsoft's incentives to innovate: source code information—which might allow competitors to develop clone products—would not be disclosed;[95] (7) interoperability information disclosure was common in the software industry;[96] and (8) disclosure was consistent with EU legislation on the protection of software programs.[97]

f. Making sense of the case law. Due in part to limited case law, the duty to license IP under Article 82 EC lacks a clear and consistent rationale in terms of why

[86] On June 7, 2004, Microsoft appealed the decision before the Court of First Instance. Suspension of the decision was refused by the Order of the President of the Court of First Instance in Case T-201/04 R, *Microsoft Corporation v Commission* [2005] ECR II-nyr. The Order does not enter into detail on the merits of the Commission's substantive analysis, since the parties agreed in advance, for purposes of the interim measures stage, that Microsoft had a *prima facie* case on the merits, i.e., an arguable case.

[87] Case COMP/C-3/37.792, *Microsoft*, Commission Decision of March 24, 2004, not yet published, paras. 548–54.

[88] *Ibid.*, para. 555; See also para. 557, where the Commission also refers to the judgment in Case T-198/98, *Micro Leader Business v Commission* [1999] ECR II-3989 to conclude that "the factual situations where the exercise of an exclusive right by an intellectual property right holder may constitute an abuse cannot be restricted to *one* particular set of circumstances." (emphasis in original).

[89] *Ibid.*, Section 5.3.1.1.3.1.

[90] Case COMP/C-3/37.792, *Microsoft*, Commission Decision of March 24, 2004, not yet published, paras. 574 et seq.

[91] *Ibid.*, paras. 578 et seq.

[92] *Ibid.*, para. 586.

[93] *Ibid.*, paras. 666 et seq.

[94] *Ibid.*, Section 5.3.1.3.

[95] *Ibid.*, para. 714.

[96] *Ibid.*, paras. 730 et seq.

[97] *Ibid.*, paras. 743 et seq.

some cases are considered sufficiently exceptional to warrant a compulsory licence or supply contract. First, it is not clear how earlier case law such as *Volvo* relates to the "exceptional circumstances" test first mentioned in *Magill*. In particular, *Volvo* did not mention any of the "exceptional circumstances" cited in later case law, but gave other examples of abusive conduct that may be committed in connection with IP rights. Second, it is not clear whether "exceptional circumstances" simply refers to the economic consequences that logically follow from the refusal to license or also require other (abusive) acts. Finally, it is not clear whether "exceptional circumstances" are defined exhaustively in the case law or may be further developed in future cases.

The following comments are offered by way of clarification. First, there is no necessary contradiction between *Volvo* and subsequent case law on "exceptional circumstances." The Court of Justice was clear that the examples listed in that case were non-exhaustive.[98] Subsequent case law also cites *Volvo* with approval. Indeed, in *Magill*, the Court of First Instance likened the broadcasters' refusal to supply indispensable listings information to the refusal to supply spare parts in *Volvo*.[99] This analogy is not entirely apposite, but it confirms that the Community Courts did not seek to overrule *Volvo* in adopting the "exceptional circumstances" test. Most of the confusion arising from *Volvo* concerns the Court's statement that a duty to license may be an appropriate remedy for excessive prices. But this statement stands for a different principle—that a duty to deal may be an appropriate *remedy* for conduct other than a refusal to deal.[100] In most cases, reducing the price to a non-exploitative level will be the correct remedy, but, exceptionally, this may not work and a compulsory licence is required.

Second, it remains genuinely unclear whether the "exceptional circumstances" test requires other (abusive) conduct or simply refers to the adverse economic consequences of the refusal. On the one hand, the Community Courts have always said that the refusal to license cannot be abusive in itself, since this is a core moral right of the owner. This clearly makes sense, since, without more, the economic effects of a refusal to license are simply the result of the legitimate exercise of property rights granted under national laws. The mere fact that an IP right would create dominance (or even a monopoly) is not an abuse: dominance is not illegal. For these reasons, cases imposing a duty to deal have always cited other elements to justify a duty to deal. In *Magill*, the refusal prevented a new product that consumers wanted from coming onto the market. Such conduct is an example of "limiting production," which is an abuse under Article 82(b). In *IMS*, the IP right had been created in consultation with consumers and had become a *de facto* industry standard. And in *Microsoft* there were various elements other than the refusal, including a "general pattern" of abusive conduct, discrimination, and termination of past voluntary disclosures of interoperability information.

At the same time, it is not obvious that the additional circumstances cited in the case law were additional conduct autonomous from the refusal to license itself (as opposed to

[98] Case 238/87, *AB Volvo v Erik Veng (UK) Ltd* [1988] ECR 6211, para. 9 ("if it involves, on the part of an undertaking holding a dominant position, certain abusive conduct such as…").

[99] See Case T-70/89, *The British Broadcasting Corporation and BBC Enterprises Ltd (BBC) v Commission* [1991] ECR II-535, para. 60.

[100] See Ch. 15 (Remedies) for more detail on when a duty to deal may be appropriate as a remedy for another abuse.

the effects of the refusal in the particular factual circumstances in which it took place). The additional abusive conduct in *Magill* was, if anything, a failure to act, i.e., a failure by the broadcasters to meet potential demand for the new product. In *IMS*, the fact that IMS engaged customers in developing the presentation format simply had the consequence of making the product particularly suitable for their needs and so contributed to IMS's dominance. No other (abusive) conduct was cited. Finally, in *Microsoft*, the additional factors cited by the Commission were of secondary importance: for example, past dealing was simply considered to be "of interest."[101] Accordingly, one reading of the case law is that the "exceptional circumstances" test is an exception to the general rule that a refusal to license cannot in itself be abusive, i.e., a duty to deal may be imposed where the effect of the refusal on consumer welfare is serious enough.

Finally, there is some support for the view that "exceptional circumstances" are not defined exhaustively in the case law, but require assessment on a case-by-case basis. The Commission strongly advocated this approach in *Microsoft*, stating that "there is no persuasiveness to an approach that would advocate the existence of an exhaustive checklist of exceptional circumstances and would have the Commission disregard *a limine* other circumstances of exceptional character that may deserve to be taken into account when assessing a refusal to supply."[102] In *IMS Health*, the Court of Justice also indicated that the criteria laid down in the *Magill* line of case law are merely "sufficient," suggesting that they are not necessary and that other criteria could be identified.[103]

But there are problems with such a broad interpretation of "exceptional circumstances." It would be precarious, and contrary to legal certainty, if the criteria justifying a refusal to deal were open-ended and dependent on the factual peculiarities of each case. A dominant firm should not be expected to make large investments in valuable assets on the basis of unknown and unknowable criteria. Some comfort is provided by the fact that the Community institutions still consider "indispensability" and "elimination of competition" as essential elements in the "exceptional circumstances" test—at least for first-time duties to deal.

8.3.2 The Legal Conditions For A Duty To Deal With Rivals Under Article 82 EC

Overview. This section considers a number of related issues concerning the duty to deal with rivals under Article 82 EC. First, it considers when a dominant firm may be obliged to deal with rivals where it has never done so previously, i.e., where the dominant firm is fully vertically integrated and does not sell to outsiders. These are first

[101] Case COMP/C-3/37.792, *Microsoft*, Commission Decision of March 24, 2004, not yet published, para. 556.

[102] *Microsoft, ibid.*, para. 555. See also Opinion of Advocate General Jacobs in Case C-53/03, *Synetairismos Farmakopoion Aitolias & Akarnanias (Syfait) and Others v GlaxoSmithKline plc and GlaxoSmithKline AEVE* [2005] ECR I-4609, para. 68 ("the factors which go to demonstrate that an undertaking's conduct in refusing to supply is either abusive or otherwise are highly dependent on the specific economic and regulatory context in which the case arises.").

[103] Case C-418/01, *IMS Health GmbH & Co OHG v NDC Health GmbH & Co KG* [2004] ECR I-5039, para. 38.

contracts or licences. Second, it analyses how many contracts or licences a dominant firm can be obliged to make where it has been required to make a (compulsory) first contract or licence. Third, situations where a dominant firm terminates an existing supply arrangement are analysed separately. It is sometimes argued that such cases justify a duty to deal more readily than cases in which the dominant firm has never dealt with anyone. Finally, the relevance of the source or perceived strength of the property right for a duty to deal is considered.

8.3.2.1 First contracts or licences

The minimum legal conditions. Although there is some on-going dispute regarding the exhaustive scope of the conditions for compulsory dealing under Article 82 EC, the following *minimum* conditions apply: (1) there is a refusal to deal; (2) the requested party is dominant on an upstream "market" for the supply of the input and the anticompetitive effects of the refusal arise on a second downstream "market;" (3) the input in question is essential for competition on the second market, in the sense that it cannot be duplicated or can only be duplicated at an uneconomic cost; (4) the refusal to deal would eliminate competition on the second market; (5) at least in the case of IP rights, the refusal to deal prevents the emergence of a new product for which there is consumer demand; and (6) no objective considerations justify the refusal to deal. Each of these conditions is examined in detail below.

Condition #1: a refusal to deal. The Community institutions have applied an expansive interpretation to the concept of a refusal to deal. In *Deutsche Post*, the Commission stated that "the concept of refusal to supply covers not only outright refusal but also situations where dominant firms make supply subject to objectively unreasonable terms."[104] The Commission has not explained in detail what amounts to "objectively unreasonable terms."[105] One approach is to say that there is a constructive refusal to deal where the dominant firm insists on a price that is "excessive." "Excessive" in this context does not mean exploitative within the meaning of Article 82(a), but implies a price at which an equally efficient downstream operator would not be profitable. This raises similar issues to the margin squeeze principle, discussed in Chapter Six. In simple terms, a margin squeeze arises where the terms upon which the dominant firm sells an upstream input would cause the dominant firm's own downstream operation to lose money if it had to pay the same upstream input price as rivals. Thus, if the input price offered by the dominant firm would render its own downstream operations unprofitable if they had to pay it, this is a constructive refusal to deal.[106]

---

[104] *Deutsche Post AG—Interception of cross-border mail*, OJ 2001 L 331/40, para. 103. See also Discussion Paper, para. 225.

[105] See Discussion Paper, para. 225 ("[A refusal] can involve evaluating practices such as, for instance, delaying tactics in supplying, imposing unfair trading conditions, or charging excessive prices for the input.").

[106] This is not necessarily decisive in all cases, however. As discussed in Ch. 6 (Margin Squeeze), there may be circumstances in which the dominant firm's downstream operations can support lower returns on one product where other, differentiated products yield higher returns. The main reason for this is the presence of common costs for the dominant firm and different consumer preferences over the final products. In these circumstances, a stand-alone provider of one product might not be able to

The Commission has also considered dilatory tactics by a dominant firm as tantamount to a refusal to deal. For example, in the *Holyhead* case, the Commission made extensive reference to what it categorised as a dilatory or bad faith attitude by the dominant harbour operator, Sealink, towards the requesting party, Sea Containers. The Commission noted that Sealink:[107] (1) consistently delayed and raised difficulties concerning Sea Containers' possible use of existing facilities on the west side of the port; (2) delayed in making known its willingness to permit Sea Containers to operate from temporary facilities, at its own expense, on the eastern side on the port, until such time as the redevelopment works required them to be moved; (3) did not conduct its negotiations with Sea Containers by proposing or seeking solutions to the problems it was raising and that its rejection of all of Sea Containers' proposals without making any counter offer or attempting to negotiate; and (4) gave itself rapid approval for its own fast ferry service. The Commission concluded that this attitude was "entirely negative and consisted of raising difficulties" and was not consistent with the obligations on an undertaking which enjoys a dominant position in relation to an essential facility. A similar approach was taken in *Clearstream*, where the Commission contrasted a cooperative attitude towards one customer with a dilatory attitude towards another, Euroclear.[108]

Condition #2: two "markets." It has always been understood that the duty to deal under the "essential facility" principle and Article 82 EC only applied in vertical situations, that is an upstream market for the input in question and a downstream market in which that input is essential. As the leading treatise on US antitrust law—where the duty to deal was first developed—states, "it should be clear from the outset that the essential facility doctrine concerns vertical integration."[109] The same view has been taken in a wide range of articles, commentaries, and other sources of reference on the duty to deal.[110]

---

compete on the basis of the dominant firm's prices in one market, without implying that the dominant firm's prices are anticompetitive. But the point made in the text is valid as a general matter.

[107] See *Sea Containers v Stena Sealink—Interim measures*, OJ 1994 L 15/8, paras. 70–74.

[108] Case COMP/38/096, *Clearstream (Clearing and settlement)*, Commission Decision of June 4, 2004, not yet published (hereinafter "*Clearstream*"), paras. 293 et seq. See also *IMS Health/NDC—Interim Measures*, OJ 2002 L 59/18, para. 174. IMS had obtained preliminary injunctions against two competitors, NDC and Azyx, to stop suspected copyright infringements. After these injunctions had been obtained, NDC and Azyx requested a licence from IMS, offering sums of 10,000 DM and 100,000 DM, respectively. IMS refused these requests on the grounds, *inter alia*, that the proposed licence fees were insufficient. The Commission rejected this argument and suggested that, even if the initial offers were considered too low by IMS, it should have made a counter offer or indicated what a reasonable fee would have been.

[109] See PE Areeda and H Hovenkamp, *Antitrust Law*, Vol. III A (Boston, Little, Brown and Company, 1996) para. 771a. See also J Faull and A Nikpay, *The EC Law of Competition* (Oxford, Oxford University Press, 1999) pp. 625–626.

[110] See, e.g., J Temple Lang, "Defining Legitimate Competition: Companies' Duties to Supply Competitors and Access to Essential Facilities" (1994) 18 *Fordham International Law Journal* 437, 488 ("A vertically integrated company is not necessarily obliged to provide access to a facility that other companies wish to use if it is not providing them to any independent users. The key test seems to be whether its upstream and downstream operations are merely part of the same business, or separate in nature."); J Temple Lang, "The Principle of Essential Facilities in European Community Competition Law—The Position Since *Bronner*" (2000) 1 *Journal of Network Industries* 375–405; BM Owen,

a. Basic rationale. The rationale for the two market requirement has not been clearly articulated in any decision or case under Article 82 EC. But it seems to reflect the principle that monopoly power which results from a legitimately acquired property right cannot be objected to in a single market context (except, perhaps, where there is excessive pricing). It is generally procompetitive to allow a firm to keep these advantages for itself in one market and to expect rivals to develop their own products.[111]

The same does not necessarily hold good where a dominant firm seeks to use its control over an input in one market to restrict competition in a secondary market in which an input is essential for competition. This might loosely be described as leveraging, which is sometimes regarded as unlawful under competition law. Competition law tolerates a monopoly in one market—the incentives that drive innovation are generally beneficial to consumer welfare in the long run in a single market context—but does not allow a firm to use its control over an input that is essential for competition to create a monopoly in the second market. Put differently, an input that allows a firm to enjoy a monopoly in one market is considered a legitimate competitive advantage, whereas using control over that input to monopolise other markets is not always regarded as competition on the merits.

The need for two markets also has a strong rationale in IP cases because the owner has certain core moral rights in the protected matter. These core rights are sometimes referred to by the Community Courts as the "essential function."[112] For purposes of

"Determining Optimal Access to Regulated Essential Facilities" (1989) 58 *Antitrust Law Journal* 888 ("Access problems arise generally when the bottleneck monopolist is partially vertically integrated"); B Bishop and A Overd, "Essential Facilities: The Rising Tide" (1998) 4 *European Competition Law Review* 183 ("The argument for such a requirement is that it might increase competition in a downstream market to the benefit of consumers."); and M Bergman, "The *Bronner* Case—A Turning Point for the Essential Facilities Doctrine?" (2000) 21(2) *European Competition Law Review* 59 ("The most important of these are that the facility must be necessary for a firm to compete in a related market and that the competing firm must lack the ability to duplicate the facility."). See also Opinion of Advocate General Jacobs in Case C-7/97, *Oscar Bronner GmbH & Co KG v Mediaprint Zeitungs- und Zeitschriftenverlag GmbH & Co KG and others* [1998] ECR I-7791, para. 61 ("[W]here access to a facility is a precondition for competition on a related market for goods or services for which there is a limited degree of interchangeability."). For US case law, see *Alaska Airlines v United Airlines*, 948 F.2d 536, 546 (9th Cir. 1991), cert. denied, 503 US 977 (1992) ("When a firm's power to exclude rivals from a facility gives the firm the power to eliminate competition in a market downstream from the facility, and the firm excludes at least some of its competitors.").

[111] See Opinion of Advocate General Jacobs in Case C-7/97, *Oscar Bronner GmbH & Co KG v Mediaprint Zeitungs- und Zeitschriftenverlag GmbH & Co KG and others* [1998] ECR I-7791, para. 57 ("In the long term it is generally procompetitive and in the interest of consumers to allow a company to retain for its own use facilities which it has developed for the purpose of its business. For example, if access to a production, purchasing or distribution facility were allowed too easily there would be no incentive for a competitor to develop competing facilities. Thus while competition was increased in the short term it would be reduced in the long term. Moreover, the incentive for a dominant undertaking to invest in efficient facilities would be reduced if its competitors were, upon request, able to share the benefits. Thus the mere fact that by retaining a facility for its own use a dominant undertaking retains an advantage over a competitor cannot justify requiring access to it.").

[112] Joined Cases C-241/91 P and C-242/91 P, *Radio Telefís Éireann and Independent Television Publications Ltd (RTE & ITP) v Commission* [1995] ECR I-743; Case T-69/89, *Radio Telefís Éireann (RTE) v Commission* [1991] ECR II-485, para. 70. For national cases, see, e.g., *Philips Electronics NV*

Community law, the "essential function" of an IP right protects the moral rights of the author in the work and ensures incentives and rewards for creative efforts by granting the owner the exclusive rights of reproduction and commercial exploitation of the protected work.[113] It is only when the intellectual property right holder uses the rights for a purpose which goes beyond their essential function, and seeks exclusivity in a market separate from that to which the intellectual property relates, that anticompetitive conduct can be alleged, and the essential facility doctrine can apply.[114] In other words, the "exclusion" caused by IP in the market to which it relates is the key component of the owner's core moral rights.[115]

b. Treatment of the two markets requirement in the decisional practice and case law. A clear vertical separation between the upstream market in which the dominant firm controls an input and the downstream market in which that input is essential for competition is present in refusal to deal cases under Article 82 EC.[116] For example, in

v Ingman Ltd [1998] 2 CMLR 839, 853; *Sandvik AB v KR Pfiffner (UK) Ltd* [1999] EuLR 755, 787; and *HMSO v Automobile Association* [2001] ECC 272, 278.

113 See Cases 55/80 and 57/80, *Musik-Vertrieb membran GmbH et K-tel International v GEMA - Gesellschaft für musikalische Aufführungs- und mechanische Vervielfältigungsrechte* [1981] ECR 147, paras. 12–13; and Case 158/86, *Warner Brothers Inc and Metronome Video ApS v Erik Viuff Christiansen* [1988] ECR 2605, para. 13 ("The two essential rights of the author, namely the exclusive right of performance and the exclusive right of reproduction, are not called in question by the rules of the Treaty.").

114 See, e.g., Case 53/87, *Consorzio italiano della componentistica di ricambio per autoveicoli and Maxicar v Régie nationale des usines Renault* [1988] ECR 6039, paras. 15–16 ("the mere fact of securing the benefit of an exclusive right granted by law, the effect of which is to enable the manufacture and sale of protected products by unauthorised third parties to be prevented, cannot be regarded as an abusive method of eliminating competition. Exercise of the exclusive right may be prohibited by Article 8[2] if it gives rise to certain abusive conduct on the part of an undertaking occupying a dominant position.").

115 These principles have been consistently reflected in the case law on IP rights. In *Renault*, the Court of Justice held that it was not abusive in itself for car manufacturers to refuse to license third parties that wished to compete in the manufacture and sale of the protected body panels. The reason for this conclusion was that a contrary interpretation would deprive the IP owner of the exclusive rights granted by national IP laws and recognised under Community law. *Ibid.*, para. 15. The Community Courts adopted a similar approach in *Magill*. In that case, various TV companies were found to have abused their dominant position on the separate markets for TV programs and the magazines in which they were published by relying on national copyright in their program schedules to prevent the publication by a third party of a new comprehensive guide to their weekly program listings. The Court of First Instance held that the broadcasters' conduct "clearly [went] beyond what is necessary to fulfil the essential function of the copyright as permitted in Community law." Case T-69/89, *Radio Telefís Éireann (RTE) v Commission* [1991] ECR II-485, para. 73. See also *DSD*, OJ 2001 L 166/1, para. 144 ("[A]ccording to the case law of the Court of Justice and Court of First Instance, exercise of an exclusive [intellectual property] right may be prohibited by Article 82... if it gives rise to certain abusive conduct on the part of the undertaking occupying the dominant position. The crucial point is whether the conduct in question goes beyond what is necessary to fulfil the essential function of the exclusive right as permitted in Community law.").

116 See, e.g., Joined Cases 6-7/73, *Istituto Chemioterapico Italiano SpA and Commercial Solvents Corporation v Commission* [1974] ECR 223 ((1) raw material; (2) derivative products of the raw material); *FAG—Flughafen Frankfurt/Main AG*, OJ 1998 L 173/32 ((1) provision of airport facilities for the landing and take-off of aircraft; (2) ramp-handling services); *Magill TV Guide/ITP, BBC and RTE*, OJ 1989 L 78/43 ((1) broadcasting; (2) television program guides); *Sea Containers v Stena Sealink—Interim measures*, OJ 1994 L 15/8 ((1) port services; (2) passenger ferry services); Case T-

the various cases in which access to port facilities has been required by the Commission, third parties would not have been entitled to set themselves up as co-providers of port facilities: the duty to give access was strictly limited to the right to use the port for activities on the downstream passenger ferry market. In *Magill*, there would have been no suggestion that a requesting party could insist on the right to use the television companies' broadcasting equipment: the duty was limited to the downstream market for television magazines. Other situations could also be envisaged. Suppose that a manufacturer developed a production process that gave it an unbeatable cost advantage over rivals. That process could render rivals' activities uneconomic and eliminate all competition on the relevant market, but it could never be suggested that the firm with the unbeatable advantage should share its factory with rivals.

While the element of vertical integration has been clearly acknowledged in the decisional practice and case law, the precise definition of the upstream and downstream markets was not articulated until the Court of Justice's judgment in *IMS*. It will be recalled that, in the *IMS Interim Decision*, the Commission considered that two markets were not necessary for a duty to deal to arise. In that case, there was only one market—regional wholesaler data—and the IP right was specifically developed for that market and had no other independent use or existence. However, no reasons were advanced for the conclusion that two markets were not necessary: the Commission simply made the elliptic statement that the fact that the Community Courts' case law on refusal to deal involved two markets "does not preclude the possibility that a refusal to license an intellectual property right can be contrary to Article 82."[117]

In the preliminary ruling in *IMS*, the Court of Justice confirmed that two markets are a necessary condition for a compulsory licence of an IP, but that it is enough in this regard to identify a "potential" or "hypothetical" upstream market.[118] The Court expanded on this by adding that "it is determinative that two different stages of production may be identified and that they are interconnected, the upstream product is indispensable in as much as for supply of the downstream product."[119] The Court therefore suggested that it does not matter that the upstream input was never independently marketed before and is only used as a key component in the production

504/93, *Tiercé Ladbroke SA v Commission* [1997] ECR II-923 ((1) broadcast coverage of horse races; (2) operation of betting shops); Case C-7/97, *Oscar Bronner GmbH & Co KG v Mediaprint Zeitungs- und Zeitschriftenverlag GmbH & Co KG, Mediaprint Zeitungsvertriebsgesellschaft mbH & Co KG and Mediaprint Anzeigengesellschaft mbH & Co KG* [1998] ECR I-7791 ((1) distribution of newspapers; (2) publication and sale of newspapers); and Case COMP/C-3/37.792, *Microsoft*, Commission Decision of March 24, 2004, not yet published, ((1) PC operating systems; (2) work group server operating systems). See also Case C-18/88, *Régie des télégraphes et des téléphones (RTT) v GB-Inno-BM SA* [1991] ECR I-5941, para. 18 ("an abuse…is committed where, without any objective necessity, an undertaking holding a dominant position on a particular market reserves to itself an ancillary activity which might be carried out by another undertaking as part of its activities on a neighbouring but separate market, with the possibility of eliminating all competition from such undertaking.").

[117] *IMS Health/NDC—Interim Measures*, OJ 2002 L 59/18, para. 184.

[118] Case C-418/01, *IMS Health GmbH & Co OHG v NDC Health GmbH & Co KG* [2004] ECR I-5039, para. 44.

[119] *Ibid.*, para. 45.

of a final product. It is sufficient that there is "the possibility of identifying a separate market" even if none yet exists.[120]

c. ***The meaning of a "potential market."*** The Court of Justice's interpretation of the two market requirement raises a number of issues. Left unqualified, the view that a "potential market" is enough could lead to the definition of separate product markets for many IP rights that are just used as inputs —often critical ones—in products or services that are commercialised successfully. As one commentator notes, under this standard "any intellectual property right could 'hypothetically' be marketed as a stand-alone item," and hence potentially subject to an obligation to license, which would "create a huge disincentive for dominant firms to invest in new production processes that would allow them to gain a competitive advantage *vis-à-vis* competitors."[121] For example, in *IMS*, copyright in the 1860 brick structure was a key competitive advantage of IMS's downstream data service. It was developed specifically for that service and had no other commercial or independent use.

The Court's qualification that the potential market must correspond to a "stage of production" does not necessarily clarify matters either. It is not clear whether the Court regards the mere existence of a request from a third party as sufficient to create a "potential" or "hypothetical" upstream market or whether each "stage of production" must mean something identifiably distinct, either in the literal sense of there being an intermediate product (even one which has never been sold separately), or in the sense of a separate input such as a catalyst. The issue is of some practical importance, since a broad construction of the term "potential" market is likely to lead to a greater number of compulsory licensing cases.

The latter interpretation is preferable. A "stage of production" that does not correspond to a market— in the sense that it gives rise to a product or service which is sold or licensed—should not be enough in itself to entitle a competitor to demand it. A production chain cannot be divided into a series of severable stages at the request of any competitor who wishes to have access to key competitive advantages. A "stage of production" must mean something more akin to an actual market in the sense that it is something that is inherently capable of being sold or licensed to third parties (and even if the dominant firm has not yet done so). A stage of production that nobody had ever sold or licensed, or that it would never be rational to sell or license, can only be a competitive advantage. It cannot be assumed that the Court had in mind that all competitive advantages, if valuable enough, should be shared.

An example might be useful. Retail broadband internet services are provided by new entrants by accessing the incumbent operator's network at different levels. At the highest level is wholesale access, where the incumbent effectively manages rivals' wholesale services for them. At the other end, there is local loop unbundling, which allows rivals to connect at the network point closest to the customer. In between lie a range of intermediate connection solutions, such as access at the Asynchronous Transfer

---

[120] *Ibid*. See also Discussion Paper, para. 237.

[121] See D Geradin, "Limiting the Scope of Article 82 EC: What Can The EU Learn From the US Supreme Court's Judgment in *Trinko*, in the Wake of *Microsoft*, *IMS*, and *Deutsche Telekom*?" (2004) 41 *Common Market Law Review* 1519, 1530.

Mode (ATM) level or, even closer to the customer's premises, at digital subscriber line access multiplexer (DSLAM) level (a centrally-located mechanism can link customer DSL connections to the ATM line).

For intermediate connection points, different rivals might request a range of different configurations, including configurations that are not offered by the dominant firm to its own downstream business, configurations that are not even technically available, and configurations that would require the dominant firm to make significant additional investments in order to serve a particular rival. It is very questionable whether such configurations should be considered "markets" within the meaning of the case law, even if, hypothetically, they could be offered as inputs. Certainly, there would be no question of compelling a dominant firm to make specific investments in order to offer such an input. This presumably is one reason why regulation has been used to compel intermediate access and not competition law.

Condition #3: indispensability of the input for competition. The Community institutions have clearly explained the type of economic evidence that is required for establishing indispensability.[122] First, the product or service to which access is requested must be essential for the exercise of the activity in question.[123] Second, "it must be determined whether there are products or services which constitute alternative solutions, even if they are less advantageous."[124] Furthermore, "it must be established, at the very least, that the creation of those products or services is not economically viable for production on a scale comparable to that of the undertaking which controls the existing product or service,"[125] including the time reasonably required to produce them.[126] Thus, it must be shown that the cost of duplicating the allegedly essential facility constitutes a barrier to entry such that it "deters any prudent undertaking from entering the market."[127] In short, there must be no actual or potential "viable alternatives" to the dominant firm's input[128] or the cost of such alternatives is "prohibitively expensive and would not make any commercial sense."[129] In the case of IP rights, there are additional barriers in that the law prevents copying. The key question therefore is whether rivals can invent around the dominant firm's IP.

[122] For a summary, see Discussion Paper, paras. 228–30.

[123] See Case T-504/93, *Tiercé Ladbroke SA v Commission* [1997] ECR II-923 (live pictures of French races not indispensable to compete in the relevant Belgian market).

[124] Case C-418/01, *IMS Health GmbH & Co OHG v NDC Health GmbH & Co KG* [2004] ECR I-5039, para. 28 (citing Case C-7/97, *Oscar Bronner GmbH & Co KG v Mediaprint Zeitungs- und Zeitschriftenverlag GmbH & Co KG, Mediaprint Zeitungsvertriebsgesellschaft mbH & Co KG and Mediaprint Anzeigengesellschaft mbH & Co KG* [1998] ECR I-7791, at paras. 43 and 44).

[125] *Ibid.*, para. 28.

[126] See Joined Cases T-374/94, T-375/94, T-384/94 and T-388/94, *European Night Services Ltd and others v Commission* [1998] ECR II-3141, para. 209, footnote 34.

[127] Opinion of Advocate General Jacobs in Case C-7/97, *Oscar Bronner GmbH & Co KG v Mediaprint Zeitungs- und Zeitschriftenverlag GmbH & Co KG, Mediaprint Zeitungsvertriebsgesellschaft mbH & Co KG and Mediaprint Anzeigengesellschaft mbH & Co KG* [1998] ECR I-7791, paras. 66 and 68.

[128] *Ibid.*, para. 209; See also Case COMP/38/096, *Clearstream (Clearing and settlement)*, Commission Decision of June 4, 2004, not yet published, para. 227 (Clearstream a *de facto* monopolist and unavoidable trading party for primary clearing and settlement services in Germany).

[129] See *GVG/FS*, OJ 2004 L 11/17, paras. 109, 120, 148.

The key economic question is, therefore, whether the investments required for duplicating the facility to which access is requested would render entry by a reasonably efficient competitor, or a group of competitors making a joint investment, uneconomic. Of course, the impact on entry depends on the entrant's expectations about its sales and prices post-entry.[130] Bronner, for example, argued that it could not afford replicating the home-delivery system of Mediaprint because of its small distribution. However, Bronner's calculation was incorrect because it relied on an unreasonable assumption regarding its distribution after the introduction of the new home-delivery system. In this respect, the Court clarified that:[131]

> "For such access to be capable of being regarded as indispensable, it would be necessary at the very least to establish...that it is not economically viable to create a second home-delivery scheme for the distribution of daily newspapers with a circulation comparable to that of the daily newspapers distributed by the existing scheme."

Similarly, in *European Night Services*, the Court of First Instance refused to consider railway infrastructure supplied by the parents of a joint venture to the joint venture as an essential facility. There was no evidence that third parties could not obtain locomotives either directly from manufacturers or indirectly by renting them from other undertakings. Nor were there any exclusivity restrictions in the supply contracts for the joint venture, which meant that suppliers to the joint venture were free to sell to other willing buyers. The Court indicated that a high standard of proof applied to the party seeking to assert a duty to deal: it was not enough to merely assert that the joint venture was the first to acquire the locomotives in question on the market; there had to be evidence that they were alone in being able to do so.[132] The fact that the requesting party has continued to carry out its operations for a material period of time despite the refusal, in particular where it uses alternative solutions, this creates a strong inference that access is not essential.[133]

The analysis should focus on whether it is possible for a second, substitute facility to be created, and not on whether competitors will in fact make the investment.[134] There may be no competition even when competitors have access to the inputs required to compete if: (1) their products are regarded as less desirable by consumers; or (2) they are less efficient in production. A duty to deal cannot be imposed to overcome competitors' lack of efficiency relative to the dominant firm or to compensate them for the fact that consumers prefer the dominant firm's products.

[130] See M Bergman, "The Role of the Essential Facilities Doctrine," *Antitrust Bulletin*, 2001.

[131] Case C-7/97, *Oscar Bronner GmbH & Co KG v Mediaprint Zeitungs- und Zeitschriftenverlag GmbH & Co KG, Mediaprint Zeitungsvertriebsgesellschaft mbH & Co KG and Mediaprint Anzeigengesellschaft mbH & Co KG* [1998] ECR I-7791, para. 46.

[132] Joined Cases T-374/94, T-375/94, T-384/94 and T-388/94, *European Night Services Ltd (ENS), Eurostar (UK) Ltd, formerly European Passenger Services Ltd (EPS), Union internationale des chemins de fer (UIC), NV Nederlandse Spoorwegen (NS) and Société nationale des chemins de fer français (SNCF) v Commission* [1998] ECR II-3141, paras. 215–16.

[133] See Case T-52/00, *Coe Clerici Logistics SpA v Commission* [2003] ECR II-2123, para. 25.

[134] See J Temple Lang, "The Principle of Essential Facilities in European Community Competition Law—The Position Since *Bronner*" (2000) 1 *Journal of Network Industries* 375, 382.

In principle, all relevant evidence pointing to indispensability should be considered. For example, in *IMS*, one issue was whether input given by certain users into the development of the facility was a relevant barrier to entry for the production of alternative facilities. The Court of Justice suggested that a high level of participation by users in the development of the facility, on the supposition that it was proven, could create a dependency by users, particularly at a technical level. In such circumstances, the Court considered it unlikely that users would make exceptional organisational and financial efforts in order to acquire products based on other inputs. Rivals might therefore be obliged to offer terms which rule out any economic viability of business on a scale comparable to that of the undertaking which controls the protected structure.[135]

Consumer preferences for a facility cannot, however, by themselves make it essential. If rivals can economically offer alternative facilities, the fact that some or all consumers prefer the dominant firm's facility is irrelevant. In the absence of any agreement between the dominant company and its customers that they will buy exclusively from it, the way that customers exercise their right to choose which products to buy is simply the result of the legitimate interplay of competition. Users of a product may be influenced by many reasons, none of which require the seller of the product to share its advantages. Users might be influenced by the fact that they have become accustomed to the dominant company's product, or that they have trained all their employees to use it, or that the cost or inconvenience of changing is greater than the possible benefits to be obtained. The fact that users are primarily influenced by their own business reasons rather than by the relative merits of the competing products does not make a good product or a competitive advantage into an essential facility. In addition, since customer preferences are subjective, can change, may be ill-considered or even ill-informed, they could not be the basis for the test of an essential facility. The test for an essential facility is whether competitors are *objectively* able to develop and offer their own products or services for sale, not whether buyers are willing to buy them.[136]

Condition #4: elimination of competition. The key legal condition for a duty to deal is that the refusal to share the indispensable input entails the "elimination or substantial reduction of competition to the detriment of consumers in both the short and the long term."[137] This condition is the corollary of the condition that the dominant firm's input is indispensable for competition: if the input is not indispensable, it is difficult to see how the refusal to share it could have substantial effects on competition. Conversely, if an input is truly essential for competition, it would, ultimately, allow the firm or firms that own or control it to exclude all competition on the relevant downstream market in

---

[135] Case C-418/01, *IMS Health GmbH & Co OHG v NDC Health GmbH & Co KG* [2004] ECR I-5039, para. 29.

[136] Opinion of Advocate General Jacobs in Case C-7/97, *Oscar Bronner GmbH & Co KG v Mediaprint Zeitungs- und Zeitschriftenverlag GmbH & Co KG, Mediaprint Zeitungsvertriebsgesellschaft mbH & Co KG and Mediaprint Anzeigengesellschaft mbH & Co KG* [1998] ECR I-7791, para. 51.

[137] *Ibid.*, para. 61.

which the input is used. The Commission has explained this underlying policy rationale for imposing a duty to deal in the following terms:[138]

> "The duty to provide access to a facility arises if the effect of the refusal to supply on competition is objectively serious enough: if without access there is, in practice, an insuperable barrier to entry for competitors of the dominant company, or if without access competitors would be subject to a serious, permanent and inescapable competitive handicap which would make their activities uneconomic. Hence, access to a facility is 'essential' when refusal to supply would exclude all or most competitors from the market."

A strict interpretation of the criterion that the refusal to deal should have a significant, adverse effect on competition is important if the duty to deal under Article 82 EC is to retain any sensible rationale. If the downstream market is already competitive, or would become so in the near future through competitors' introducing their own products, no useful purpose would be served in imposing a duty to deal, even if the dominant firm's input is essential for competition from certain (presumably less efficient) undertakings. In economic terms, the only plausible justification for a duty to deal is that the welfare loss to consumers is very large due to the dominant firm's "genuine stranglehold" over the market.[139] Absent this condition, the usefulness of a duty to deal evaporates and the negative effects on *ex ante* investment decision making become even greater.

Surprisingly, the standard of foreclosure required for a duty to deal to arise is not entirely clear from the decisional practice and case law. In *Bronner*, the Court of Justice seemed to suggest a range of different standards. It first cited *Magill* as support for the view that a duty to deal was appropriate because it was likely to "exclude *all competition* in the secondary market of television guides,"[140] thereby suggesting a total foreclosure standard. But it later added that, in the case at hand, it would be necessary to show that the refusal was "likely to eliminate all competition in the daily newspaper market *on the part of the person requesting the service*," thereby suggesting a much lower standard. In *IMS*, the Court of Justice again repeated its formulation in *Magill* and *Bronner*, that the refusal is "such as to exclude *any competition* on a secondary market."[141]

In *Microsoft*, the Commission appeared to advocate a different standard of foreclosure again,[142] namely one where licensing is mandated if: (1) the requested IP is "necessary"

[138] See Commission submission in *The Essential Facility Concept*, Organisation for Economic Cooperation and Development (1996), p. 94.

[139] *Ibid.*, para. 65.

[140] Case C-7/97, *Oscar Bronner GmbH & Co KG v Mediaprint Zeitungs- und Zeitschriftenverlag GmbH & Co KG, Mediaprint Zeitungsvertriebsgesellschaft mbH & Co KG and Mediaprint Anzeigengesellschaft mbH & Co KG* [1998] ECR I-7791, para. 40 (emphasis added).

[141] Case C-418/01, *IMS Health GmbH & Co OHG v NDC Health GmbH & Co KG* [2004] ECR I-5039, para. 38 (emphasis added).

[142] See, e.g., D Ridyard, "Compulsory Access Under EC Competition Law—A New Doctrine of 'Convenient Facilities' and the Case for Price Regulation" (2004) 25(11) *European Competition Law Review* 670; D Geradin, "Limiting the Scope of Article 82 EC: What Can The EU Learn From the US Supreme Court's Judgment in *Trinko*, in the Wake of *Microsoft, IMS*, and *Deutsche Telekom*?" (2004) 41 *Common Market Law Review* 1519; and C Ahlborn, D Evans, and J Padilla, "The Logic And Limits Of Exceptional Circumstances Test in *Magill* and *IMS Health*" (2005) 28 *Fordham International Law Journal* 1062–1090.

for a competitor to "viably stay in the market;" (2) the refusal represents a reduction in "the level of disclosures;" (3) "there is a risk of elimination of competition" in the secondary market; (4) the refusal to supply "has the consequence of stifling innovation in the impacted market;" and (5) the refusal is not objectively justified because "on balance" the possible negative impact of an order to supply on the dominant firm's incentives to innovate is outweighed by its positive impact on the level of innovation of the whole industry.[143] This is said to represent "an altogether more open-ended approach in which [the Commission] reserves the right to consider the costs and benefits of mandating access, given the facts surrounding the case."[144]

A number of comments can be made by way of clarification. First, the test cannot be based on whether the requesting party would be eliminated from the relevant market.[145] The legal test is not harm to a competitor, but harm to competition. A test based on competitor exit would also be open to abuse, since a particularly small or inefficient competitor could insist on a contract or licence, with no net gain to competition. Thus, as the Advocate General stated in *Bronner*, "a particular competitor cannot plead that it is particularly vulnerable."[146] Foreclosure must therefore concern competitors in general and, presumably, competitors who are at least as efficient as the dominant firm.

Second, it should not be necessary to show that the refusal to deal would result in a 100% market share in every case.[147] This would be too strict and would be impossible to show in most cases. A duopoly is often uncompetitive, in particular where two companies share the same facility. The wording of Article 82(b) also requires "limiting production" to the "prejudice of consumers" and not merely to situations of total monopoly. A requirement of total monopolisation would also be open to abuse. A dominant firm could always decide to deal with, or tolerate, a particularly small, inefficient, or friendly competitor and argue that not all competition had been eliminated. This is sometimes colourfully referred to as a "bonsai competitor"—one that is kept deliberately small.

The final principle is that the standard of foreclosure should be one based on the substantial elimination of competition.[148] What qualifies as a "substantial" effect on competition may vary from case to case, but it should *at least* mean the absence of "effective competition" on the market, i.e., dominance on the relevant downstream market,[149] and arguably more. As a practical matter, duties to deal have generally been imposed in situations where the market was either a monopoly or a duopoly. In *Magill*, there were no undertakings present

[143] Case COMP/C-3/37.792, *Microsoft*, Commission Decision of March 24, 2004, not yet published, paras. 779–84.

[144] See D Ridyard, "Compulsory Access Under EC Competition Law—A New Doctrine of 'Convenient Facilities' and the Case for Price Regulation" (2004) 25(11) *European Competition Law Review* 670.

[145] See Discussion Paper, para. 231.

[146] Opinion of Advocate General Jacobs in Case C-7/97, *Oscar Bronner GmbH & Co KG v Mediaprint Zeitungs- und Zeitschriftenverlag GmbH & Co KG, Mediaprint Zeitungsvertriebsgesellschaft mbH & Co KG and Mediaprint Anzeigengesellschaft mbH & Co KG* [1998] ECR I-7791, para. 51.

[147] See Discussion Paper, para. 231.

[148] *Ibid.*, paras. 231–33.

[149] See Opinion of Advocate General Poiares Maduro in Case C-109/03, *KPN Telecom BV v Onafhankelijke Post en Telecommunicatie Autoriteit (OPTA)* [2004] ECR I-1273, para. 38.

on the relevant downstream market other than the broadcasters themselves. In *IMS*, there was a monopoly until the two new entrants became active on the market. All of the port cases involved situations in which there was either a monopoly or a duopoly. Admittedly, in *Microsoft*, several competitors were active on the relevant market at the time of the infringement. The Commission's case is that the effects on competition in this case were more subtle: absent full interoperability information, rivals were ineffective, or would quickly become so. This is a major point of factual dispute in the pending appeal.

A standard based on the substantial elimination of competition is not as permissive as it would seem. If a facility is truly essential for downstream competition, the dominant firm will either already have, or could quickly create, a virtual monopoly on the downstream market by denying rivals that input. Thus, the logic of a duty to deal is that the upstream monopoly could *ultimately* lead to a downstream monopoly, even if this has not already occurred. This means that the debate about the standard or foreclosure might more aptly be characterised as concerning the stage at which intervention occurs. If intervention occurs at an early stage, competition may not yet be eliminated, without implying that the market would remain competitive in the future. In contrast, if intervention occurs at a late stage, the dominant firm is likely to have excluded all or most competition through its control over the essential input and may even have a monopoly.

Condition #5: new product. A corollary of the Community Courts' consistent holding that, in the case of IP rights, a refusal to deal is not in itself unlawful is that there must be some "additional element" which justifies treating a refusal to deal as abusive. That "additional element" cannot be the fact that the IP would lead to an economic monopoly in the market where the IP applies if it is not shared with rivals. Such effects are inherent in the scope of the grant of the IP right in the first place. Some additional impropriety or abuse that adversely affects consumer welfare is therefore required. In *Magill*, the additional element was that the refusal prevented the emergence of a "new product" for which there was consumer demand.

The rationale for the new product condition is two-fold. First, there is no general justification for ordering a licence that would allow the production of copies of the dominant firm's products, since this would deprive the IP owner of the reward for his creative efforts.[150] The second reason is that a duty to deal is only appropriate where there is a clear benefit to competition in ordering access, or, put differently, "prejudice to consumers" under Article 82(b) if a licence is not granted. If consumers receive a market option that did not exist previously and for which there is demand, there is a clear benefit to consumer welfare. Where the requesting party wishes to supply essentially the same product or service, the benefits to competition are far from guaranteed. In that case, the principal benefit of ordering access would be increased price competition, but this will be a direct function of the royalty charges that the

[150] Advocate General Gulmann put the matter as follows in *Magill*: "Where the product is one that largely meets the same needs of consumers as the protected product, the interests of the copyright owner carry great weight. Even if the market is limited to the prejudice of consumers, the right to refuse licences in that situation must be regarded as necessary in order to guarantee the copyright owner the reward for his creative effort." See Opinion of Advocate General Gulmann in Joined Cases C-241/91 P and C-242/91 P, *Radio Telefis Éireann and Independent Television Publications Ltd (RTE & ITP) v Commission* [1995] ECR I-743, para. 97.

requesting party pays the dominant firm. Depending on what those terms are, the scope for increased price competition may in fact be quite limited.[151] The new product requirement therefore serves the important function that access should only be ordered where there is some clear, identifiable benefit to competition.

It bears emphasis, however, that the Commission does not apparently consider the new product requirement to be essential to the "exceptional circumstances" test. As discussed in Section 8.3, the Commission considers that other "exceptional circumstances" may be present, which thus far have been limited to the interoperability issues identified in *Microsoft*. It appears to be common ground, however, that the indispensability and the elimination of competition are necessary criteria. Nonetheless, this open-ended interpretation of Article 82 EC raises significant concern, not least because the Commission has not elaborated on what alternative "exceptional circumstances" might be.[152]

a. The meaning of a "new product." The practical application of the new product criterion has not raised difficulties in the limited case law to date. In *Magill*, it seemed obvious that a single, composite television guide was a new *kind* of product when compared to the existing guides based on each broadcaster's own listings. It was also clear that there was demand for the new kind of product and that consumer welfare would be enhanced by a duty to deal. A consumer planning a week's viewing could rely on a single, convenient guide rather than having to purchase multiple guides and cross reference them for viewing purposes.

In *IMS*, it also seemed clear that the requesting parties' services were not new when compared to IMS's existing services. They argued in the interim proceedings before the Court of First Instance that their data services were different to IMS's because they included certain data not contained in IMS's offering (e.g., products returned by wholesalers) and allowed for more frequent data delivery. In his Order, the President rejected this argument, noting that their services were "differing only as to detail from the services offered by [IMS]" and that they were "at most, new variations of the same

[151] For the terms on which access should be ordered, see Ch. 15 (Remedies).

[152] A highly questionable conclusion, however, is the statement in the Discussion Paper that a refusal to license an IP right "which is indispensable as a basis for follow-on innovation by competitors may be abusive even if the licence is not sought to directly incorporate the technology in clearly identifiable new goods and services" (Discussion Paper, para. 240). This merits several comments. First, IP rights are not held on trust for any competitor willing to assess their utility for possible follow-on innovation. A licence can only be ordered where there is an abuse and the refusal to license in itself is not an abuse. Second, this comment is contrary to the Community Courts' interpretation of the "new product" requirement. As discussed above, a "new product" requires evidence of unsatisfied consumer demand and not merely evidence of speculative future research into innovation that may or may not lead to identifiable new products for which there is demand. Third, the fact that an IP right is "indispensable" for follow-on innovation is not an abuse. The statement ignores the most important legal condition: that the refusal would substantially eliminate competition. This requires an assessment of the relevant market in which the alleged follow-on innovation would compete and whether competing technologies exist or could be developed without relying on the IP right in question. Fourth, as explained in the next section, a dominant firm always has a valid defence if it has a plan to bring the innovation for which access to the IP is requested to market itself. Finally, the statement seems circular: access to an IP right will almost always be "indispensable" if a firm intends to make a follow-on innovation based only or mainly on the IP right in question.

services and on the same market as [IMS]."[153] There was limited scope for added-value competition in circumstances where IMS and its competitors would be reporting the same underlying raw data in the same presentation format.

The new product criterion has been criticised by certain commentators as "problematic,"[154] leading to "undesirable consequences,"[155] or "lacking solid economic foundation."[156] This is only true, however, if the assessment of this criterion is reduced to a fruitless debate about degrees of novelty. For example, the law would descend into nonsense if the debate in *Magill* turned on whether presenting listings in a new colour or format was sufficiently "new." Although these "improvements" in the television listings would result in product variants that did not exist before, a test based on trivial changes would be meaningless and would lack any useful limiting principle. In any given case, there will always be a large number of changes that could be made to a product to improve it in minor ways and it will usually to be possible to find a consumer somewhere who attaches nominal value to such improvements.

An intelligent application of the new product criterion should be based on a number of considerations. In the first place, it should be for the party asserting a duty to deal to put forward evidence of its plans to produce a new product, since that information will not be in the possession of the dominant firm. Second, the product should not merely be new in the sense that it represents some incremental or minor improvement on existing products. Rather, the product should be a *new kind of product* in the sense that it creates a new type of market option that did not previously exist, i.e., no firm—dominant or otherwise—offers a comparable product. This implies that a "new product" materially increases product quality and/or levels of innovation. For example, in *Magill*, a composite magazine was clearly a new kind of product, whereas simply changing the format of the existing products, while adding some novelty, would not be. Similarly, the high speed ferry service that the requesting party wished to launch in *Sea Containers-Stena Sealink* represented a vast improvement on existing services, cutting journey times by less than half. A final principle, grounded in economics, is that a new product is one which satisfies potential demand by meeting the needs of consumers in ways that existing products do not. That is, a new product *expands* the market by bringing in consumers who were not satisfied before. It is in this sense that the new product creates a new option, not just variations of the same product as supplied by the IP holder.

Suppose there is a market in which products *A*, *B*, *C*, *D* and *E* are sold. Product *F* is a "new product" if it expands the market, so that the total demand for *A-F* exceeds the demand for *A-E*. Where total demand remains unchanged, Product *F* is not a new product. The new product should therefore be market-expanding rather than simply

---

[153] See Case T-184/01 R, *IMS Health Inc v Commission* [2001] ECR II-3193, para. 101.

[154] See, D Geradin, "Limiting the Scope of Article 82 EC: What Can The EU Learn From the US Supreme Court's Judgment in *Trinko*, in the Wake of *Microsoft*, *IMS*, and *Deutsche Telekom*?" (2004) 41 *Common Market Law Review* 1519, 1531.

[155] *Ibid.*

[156] See D Ridyard, "Compulsory Access Under EC Competition Law—A New Doctrine of 'Convenient Facilities' and the Case for Price Regulation" (2004) 25(11) *European Competition Law Review* 670.

steal share from existing products. In *Magill*, a guide that combined all television listings together was likely to have attracted new consumers into the market. In contrast, a guide that is merely a variant of an existing guide is unlikely to expand demand significantly: it will more likely only shift demand from the existing guide.

The degree of expansion should also be considered. Whenever a firm introduces a product, it expands the market somewhat. A product should only be regarded as "new," however, if it expands the market by a "significant" amount. This statement can be illustrated with the help of the following diagram, which is based in what economists denote as Hotelling's linear city. In Figure 3 below, the new product *B* expands the market by bringing in consumers that were not interested in product *A*. The new product condition is satisfied below, but it would not be if products *A* and *B* competed head-to-head for the same set of consumers.

Figure 3

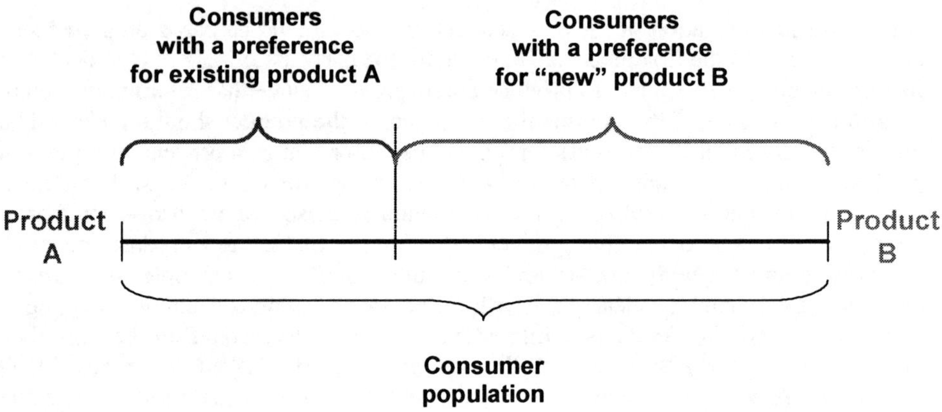

The following assumptions apply: Consumers are located in the linear city. They have heterogeneous preferences with respect to products *A* and *B*. Consumer preferences with respect to a product are more intense when it is located closer to that product. In the diagram, products *A* and *B* compete in the same relevant product market. A price reduction in product *A* is likely to cause a reduction in the sales of product *B*. Yet, at current prices, the addition of product *B* to the market increases consumer welfare by adding an entire class of consumers whose preferences were such that they preferred not to buy product *A*.

b. The relevant market in which the new product should arise. Another issue is whether the new product should be in the same relevant market as the dominant firm's product, a separate market, or whether it can relate to either market. Statements in a number of cases suggest that the new product should compete with the dominant firm's own products, i.e., in the same market. First, in *Bronner*, Advocate General Jacobs defined the duty to deal as arising when the refusal "prevents a new product from coming on a neighbouring market in competition with the dominant undertaking's own product on that market."[157] Second, in the *IMS* preliminary ruling, Advocate General Tizzano defined a *new* product as one "in competition with" the dominant firm's own products.[158] Finally, the Court of Justice in IMS emphasised that the new product(s) are to be offered on the same (secondary) market where the IP owner is active.[159] This interpretation certainly has some logic. The basic rationale for a duty to deal is that the dominant firm is effectively discriminating against downstream rivals by refusing to make available an essential input that the dominant firm supplies to its own downstream business. Where the dominant firm is not present on the market, it cannot be accused of favouring its own business.

However, limiting a duty to deal only to products that compete directly in the same relevant market with the dominant firm's is arguably too prescriptive. First, the key legal test under Article 82(b) is whether competitors' production is "limited" and there is "prejudice to consumers." Where a refusal to deal with competitors prevents rivals from offering consumers new products on other markets, there are two types of consumer harm: (1) consumers are deprived of something for which they have unsatisfied demand; and (2) the dominant firm's stranglehold on the market for the existing product is maintained. Either ought to be sufficient.

A second practical point is that is will in most cases be extremely difficult, if not impossible, to determine from the outset how demand for the requesting party's (new) product will evolve and how this will affect market definition. The extent to which product differentiation will result in the emergence of products attracting new customer categories can only be determined by the market in the longer term. Indeed, a compulsory licence may itself precipitate changes in demand. For example, following *Magill*, the broadcasters themselves subsequently switched to the production of composite television listing guides.

Finally, there is something of a logical contradiction between the notion that a new product should cater for demand not satisfied by existing products and yet should be confined to the same relevant market as the dominant firm's products. In many cases, the fact that a new product meets demand that is presently unsatisfied will imply that it constitutes a separate relevant market. It would be odd if new products that are most innovative, and therefore most likely to create new markets, were least likely to justify a duty to deal.

c. ***The new product condition and physical property***. A curious feature of the decisional practice and case law is that the new product criterion does not seem to apply in the case of access to physical property. It is not entirely clear whether this is a deliberate policy decision on the part of the Community Courts or is the inadvertent result of the narrowly framed questions to come before them. On the one hand, physical

[157] Opinion of Advocate General Jacobs in Case C-7/97, *Oscar Bronner GmbH & Co KG v Mediaprint Zeitungs- und Zeitschriftenverlag GmbH & Co KG, Mediaprint Zeitungsvertriebsgesellschaft mbH & Co KG and Mediaprint Anzeigengesellschaft mbH & Co KG* [1998] ECR I-7791, para. 43 (emphasis added).

[158] Opinion of Advocate General Tizzano in Case C-418/01, *IMS Health GmbH & Co OHG v NDC Health GmbH & Co KG* [2004] ECR I-5039, para. 62.

[159] *Ibid.*, para. 52.

property does not restrict the right to produce an identical product as IP does. On the other, the general economic equivalence of physical and intellectual property might suggest that the new product criterion is equally appropriate in the case of physical property. If consumers obtain a new market option that did not exist previously, there is a clear benefit to competition. If they do not, the benefits of forced sharing are far from obvious. This applies equally to IP and physical property. It is also notable that, in a number of cases in which mandatory sharing of physical assets was ordered, the requesting party in fact wished to offer a new product. For example, in *Sealink/Sea Containers*, Sea Containers wished to offer a new high speed ferry service that the dominant firm did not offer at the time.

Condition #6: objective justification. The final condition for a duty to deal is that there are no objective reasons that would justify the dominant firm's refusal to deal. While this requirement has been consistently mentioned in the decisional practice and case law, the precise scope of the defence has not been clearly articulated. Indeed, case law to date appears to have taken a strict approach to objective justification.[160] The range of acceptable justifications for a refusal to deal will vary from case to case depending on the facts. In principle, however, a number of defences should be valid. For example, the Access Notice on telecommunications mentions the following categories of objective justification:[161]

> "Relevant justifications in this context could include an overriding difficulty of providing access to the requesting company, or the need for a facility owner which has undertaken investment aimed at the introduction of a new product or service to have sufficient time and opportunity to use the facility in order to place that new product or service on the market."

In the case of physical facilities, the absence of available capacity must also be a relevant defence.[162] Creditworthiness is also a legitimate reason for refusing to deal, or, more generally, that the requesting party would be unsuitable, unreliable, or

[160] For example, in the *IMS Interim Decision*, IMS argued that it was entitled to refuse to deal with one of the requesting parties, NDC, since senior managers within that undertaking had been subject to a criminal complaint relating to the theft of business secrets from IMS on the relevant market. The Commission rejected this defence on the grounds that, first, the complaint was at a preliminary stage and, second, that the complaint was against individuals and not the company itself. It also stated that, even if none of the above factors were present "it is incumbent on IMS to address any perceived harm it has suffered through alleged criminal behaviour through appropriate lawful means, and not by attempting to eliminate competition in the relevant market." See *IMS Health/NDC—Interim Measures*, OJ 2002 L 59/18, para. 173. The Commission was also unreceptive to the argument that the requesting parties did not offer sufficient royalties and, as noted above, appeared to suggest that there were affirmative good faith duties on the dominant firm to indicate an acceptable figure.

[161] See Notice on the application of the competition rules to access agreements in the telecommunications sector—framework, relevant markets and principles, OJ 1998 C 265/2, para. 91. See also P Lugard, "ECJ Upholds *Magill*: It Sounds Nice In Theory, But How Does It Work In Practice?" (1995) *European Business Law Review* 233. On objective justification generally, see J Temple Lang, "The Principle of Essential Facilities And Its Consequences In European Community Competition Law" in A Peacock (ed.), *The Political Economy of Broadcasting* (Oxford, Regulatory Policy Institute Essays in Regulation, 1996) no. 7, p. 28.

[162] See Discussion Paper, para. 234.

unsatisfactory as a trading party.[163] There may also be issues concerning quality degradation or security that would justify the refusal to admit new users.[164] Thus, in *DuPont Holographic System*, a refusal to supply a protected hologram system for graphic art purposes was held justified because DuPont wanted to reserve its technology for security purposes and feared a loss of security if it was licensed for graphics.[165] The fact that, prior to the request for access, the dominant firm intended to phase out the product in question for use in certain applications is also a defence,[166] as is the requesting party's technical inability to use the facility.[167] Finally, where products are in short supply, it may be reasonable for a dominant firm to prioritise long-standing over occasional customers.[168]

Defences based on capacity limitations, quality degradation, and safety will, however, be scrutinised carefully. In *Frankfurt Airport*,[169] the airport operator argued that its refusal to allow self-handling or additional ramp handling suppliers was justified by a lack of capacity and concerns over safety and quality degradation. An expert's report was also submitted by the airport operator to bolster these concerns. The Commission did not accept this report at face value, but set up a group of technical experts consisting of representatives of the airport operator and the complainant and chaired by an independent expert. When the technical group could not reach an unanimous conclusion, the Commission appointed a leading industry expert to compile a detailed independent report. The Commission evaluated the various reports in reaching its conclusion that the airport operator's defences were, for the most part, unjustified.[170]

In the case of IP rights, the dominant firm should also have a defence if it intends to bring to market itself the "new product" that the requesting party wishes to offer. This

---

[163] See Notice on the application of the competition rules to access agreements in the telecommunications sector—framework, relevant markets and principles, OJ 1998 C 265/2, para. 85; *British Midland v Aer Lingus*, OJ 1992 L 96/34, para. 25.

[164] See, e.g., *Sea Containers v Stena Sealink—Interim measures*, OJ 1994 L 15/8, para. 74.

[165] See Case CP/1761/02, *E.I. du Pont de Nemours & Company and Op. Graphics (Holography) Limited*, Decision of the Office of Fair Trading on September 9, 2003, para. 34 ("DuPont has informed the OFT that it has adopted an overall strategy of promoting the security and authentication applications of HPF. Part of this strategy is the large scale supply of unprocessed HPF only to undertakings with experience of and premises already suited to highly secure production. DuPont considers that in order to obtain large scale contracts with these customers it must be able to guarantee complete supply chain security. DuPont has concerns about its ability to provide this guarantee if it continues to supply HPF to customers for use in graphic arts applications.").

[166] *Ibid.*, para. 33 ("DuPont has subsequently confirmed that it has now ceased using HPF to produce standard holograms for use in graphic arts applications and that the process of ceasing production of all HPF holograms will be completed by 2004. It therefore appears unlikely that DuPont's refusal to supply unprocessed HPF to OPG is aimed at eliminating competition in any downstream or associated market in which OPG is currently active.").

[167] See Discussion Paper, para. 234.

[168] See *ABG/Oil Companies operating in the Netherlands*, OJ 1977 L 117/1.

[169] See *FAG-Flughafen Frankfurt/Main AG*, OJ 1998 L 72/30 (hereinafter "*Frankfurt Airport*").

[170] A more controversial aspect of the decision was the Commission's suggestion that the dominant airport operator had a duty to carry out certain adjustments to the existing infrastructure in order to make capacity available (*ibid.*, paras. 86–87). The Commission reasoned that the airport operator could have: (1) added capacity; (2) closed a limited number of stands in order to free up capacity; and (3) relocated certain cargo services. Presumably, the Commission had in mind a number of existing options open to the airport operator at little or no cost, rather than suggesting that it should incur additional costs that would ultimately be passed on to the airport users.

is important in practice, since many inventions involve improvements or upgrades on existing products. If the dominant firm was not entitled to refuse to license in these circumstances, competitors would effectively have a right to share in new inventions. This would be unwarranted, since the justification for a compulsory licence—that consumers will benefit from a new product that did not exist previously—is lacking if the dominant firm intends to bring that product to market itself. One important limitation in this regard is that the dominant firm must have some reasonable plan in place to develop the "new product" itself at the time when the licence request is made. If not, a dominant firm could always argue *ex post* that it intended to make the same innovation as the requesting party.[171]

A final important issue is whether a refusal to deal can be objectively justified by the fact that the requested input is the result of significant research and development or is extremely valuable for some other reason. In other words, the issue arises whether satisfaction of the basic criteria for a duty to deal is sufficient justification for access to be ordered or whether the dominant firm is still entitled to refuse to deal because its property represents the result of significant investment or original work. A defence along these lines has been referred to in certain decisions at national and Community level and is now explicitly recognised in the Discussion Paper.[172] At the interim measures stage in *Microsoft*, the President of the Court of First Instance considered that this ground of objective justification was at least arguable in principle. He noted that, unlike the IP rights in *Magill* and *IMS*, Microsoft's IP "relates to secret and valuable technology."[173] In *DuPont Holographic System*, the Office of Fair Trading went further. It noted that DuPont's holographic film product was the result of original research and development and that the mere fact that it had certain unique advantages over rival products at the time was not a reason in itself to compel a duty to deal:[174]

> "Unprocessed HPF is the product of research and development by DuPont. The effect of treating every new product which, at the time of its discovery, had unique properties as an essential facility (if this product was a necessary input into a downstream market), would be to permit an excessive degree of interference with the freedom of undertakings to choose their own trading partners. As stated above, competition law should have this effect only in exceptional circumstances."

The availability and scope of such a defence raises difficult issues. It seems circular to some extent to argue that a duty to deal is appropriate because an input is indispensable for competition and then to allow a defence based on the fact that the dominant firm has

---

[171] This also highlights a practical difficulty with the "new product" requirement: it may require the party requesting a licence to disclose its plans for a new product to the IP owner to prove the justification of its request. This difficulty seems unavoidable given the test as formulated by the Community Courts, but it could lead to conflict over which party first adopted the idea for a new product. On the plus side, it is likely to discourage unmeritorious compulsory licence applications, since only undertakings that genuinely require access to the dominant firm's inputs to develop new kinds of product would have a strong incentive to disclose their plans.

[172] Discussion Paper, para. 235.

[173] See the Order of the President of the Court of First Instance on December 22, 2004, in Case T-201/04 R, *Microsoft Corporation v Commission* [2005] ECR II-nyr.

[174] Case CP/1761/02, *E.I. du Pont de Nemours & Company and Op. Graphics (Holography) Limited*, Decision of the Office of Fair Trading on September 9, 2003, para. 29.

developed a valuable asset through investment. The defence could be invoked precisely in those circumstances in which the adverse effects of a refusal to deal on competition were most likely to be serious.

But there is undoubtedly a problem with the current legal conditions for a duty to deal in that they place undue emphasis on the static, or short-term, effects of the refusal to deal on competition. There is no meaningful analysis of the long-term effects of a duty to deal on innovation and investment, i.e., dynamic competition. Many valuable IP rights for example will, if they are valuable enough, attract large rewards for their owners and exclude competition by rival firms. This is central to the reason why such rights are granted in the first place. Once an extremely valuable asset has been created, and so allows a firm to achieve a near-monopoly position, the benefits of sharing it will always look attractive *ex post*. However, it is precisely this prospect of large future profits that spurs risky decision-making *ex ante*. Thus, Article 82 EC should give greater recognition to the fact that much of the "foreclosure" created by property rights is vital to a market economy, even if such property is "essential" to rivals.[175]

A significant problem arises, however, since there is no reliable way in which a competition authority or court can balance *ex post* the benefits of a duty to deal against its adverse effects on *ex ante* incentives for innovation and investment. The Commission tried to undertake such an analysis in *Microsoft*, but its approach looked mainly at *ex post* considerations.[176] In the absence of useful quantitative techniques, second-best solutions may be employed. For example, there are industries in which empirical evidence shows that the principal parameter of competition is research and development. An obvious case concerns the pharmaceutical industry where valuable patents may allow firms to achieve large net profits. Large profits are necessary, however, to fund research efforts on other potential products—most of which never lead to commercial products.[177] In these circumstances, it may be questioned whether a general duty to share essential IP—even when limited to the development of new kinds of products—would be appropriate as a matter of public policy. These considerations are by no means unique to the pharmaceutical sector, but would equally apply to any other industry or product where empirical evidence, experience, or logic suggest that general duties to share valuable assets would discourage more competition than they created.

At the other extreme, there may be circumstances that allow a competition authority or court to conclude that a duty to deal would not cause much harm to investment incentives. The Discussion Paper mentions a few examples,[178] commenting that, in general, a defence is unavailable when the investments in question would likely have been made even if the investor had known that it would have a duty to supply. This may be the case where the input in question is indispensable only because the owner enjoys or has enjoyed until recently special or exclusive rights. Another example cited is where the original investment was made by a public authority using investment

[175] Discussion Paper, para. 235.

[176] See Case COMP/C-3/37.792, *Microsoft*, Commission Decision of March 24, 2004, not yet published, paras. 704 et seq.

[177] *Ibid.*, Section 8.2.

[178] Discussion Paper, para. 236.

criteria that likely would have led to the investment being made even if there would have been a duty to supply. Finally, the Discussion Paper states that some IP rights do not involve much investment. In practice, however, there are likely to be enormous problems in trying to disentangle the sources of funding for a facility. Passing value judgments on IP rights based on the level of monetary investment is also problematic, since this is often a matter of perspective. Moreover, valuable inventions result from creativity, which is not merely or mainly a function of financial investment. These issues are discussed in more detail in Section 8.3.2.4 below.

8.3.2.2 How many contracts must be concluded by the dominant firm

Overview. The previous section dealt with the circumstances in which a dominant firm active on a downstream market can be compelled to deal with rivals when it has not done so previously, i.e., the duty to make a *first* compulsory contract or licence with rivals. If the dominant firm has already made one contract with a rival, the issue arises whether it can be obliged to offer a second or subsequent contracts to other rivals under Article 82 EC and, if so, how many. As a practical matter, this issue is likely to be of limited importance, for several reasons:

1. Where a duty to deal is appropriate, the Commission's practice has been to apply a duty to deal to all undertakings present on the relevant market. In *IMS* for example the Commission required a duty to license to "all undertakings currently present on the market for German regional sales data services." Similarly, in *Microsoft*, the interoperability remedy applied to any undertaking active in the workgroup server area. These extensive duties most likely reflect the Commission's desire to act in a non-discriminatory manner with respect to the range of potential requesting parties.[179] The same approach is likely to be taken in civil litigation at national level, at least where the relevant procedural rules allow cases raising the same issue to be joined.

2. Assuming capacity is available—and in IP cases it nearly always will be—it may be rational for the dominant firm to grant subsequent contracts in circumstances where one contract has already been granted. This applies in particular if the licensees wish to offer differentiated products that do not compete head-to-head with the dominant firm's own products.

3. Depending the lapse of time between the first contract and subsequent requests, the basic legal conditions that justified a first contract may not be met for subsequent contracts. The firm in question may no longer be dominant or, even if it is, the input in question may no longer be indispensable if technology has moved on. Thus, each request for a contract would need to be assessed on the basis of the relevant facts at the time the request is made.

[179] Thus, in *Magill* the Commission ordered ITP, BBC and RTE "to supply each other and third parties on request and on a non-discriminatory basis with their individual advance weekly programme listings and by permitting reproduction of those listings by such parties." See *Magill TV Guide/ITP, BBC and RTE*, OJ 1989 L 78/43, Article 2. See also para. 27, where the Commission stated that "to confine an order for the supply of these listings to ITP, BBC and RTE, inter se, would discriminate against third parties wishing to produce a comprehensive weekly guide in a manner which would not be compatible with Article 8[2]."

The issue may nonetheless arise where a dominant firm has made a first contract or licence with a rival and another rival seeks a subsequent contract or licence. How many contracts the dominant firm can be *obliged* to grant rivals may therefore be relevant. The issue involves the simultaneous application of the principles of foreclosure under Article 82(b) and non-discrimination under Article 82(c). Three different approaches could be taken: (a) a strict duty of non-discrimination; (b) no duty to grant any subsequent contracts; or (c) a duty to contract only to the extent that the refusal would harm competition. The last approach seems the correct one.

a. A strict duty of non-discrimination. A first approach is to say that, once a first contract or licence is granted—whether voluntary or compulsory—the dominant firm has a duty to deal with any other undertaking that meets the conditions of Article 82(c), i.e., it is similarly situated to the undertaking receiving the first contract or licence, it would suffer a competitive disadvantage through the refusal to license, and no justification exists for the refusal to grant a subsequent licence.[180] In other words, the only issue is whether the dominant firm is discriminating against subsequent requesting parties.

This approach is highly questionable. It would be curious, and perverse, if the conditions for the award of a first contract were much more onerous than the conditions for the award of subsequent contracts. Under this approach, subsequent contracting parties would simply need to show that they were in a similar position to the first contracting party and that they would suffer a competitive disadvantage unless they received access to the essential input. Given the broad interpretation applied to Article 82(c), these conditions would likely be satisfied in the case of the vast majority of refusals to deal and would mean that, once a dominant firm has offered one contract or licence, it would be obliged, under a non-discrimination principle, to offer contracts to all comers. The dominant firm would then have a serious disincentive to offer a voluntary first contract. Rivals that did not meet the strict conditions for a first compulsory contract would also be encouraged to simply wait until a duty to deal had been imposed and then insist on another contract on non-discrimination grounds. Another anomaly would be that, in the absence of an express requirement of "consumer prejudice" under Article 82(c), the first licence to a rival under Article 82(b) would be subject to the need to show consumer harm, whereas any subsequent licence under Article 82(c) may not be.[181]

b. No duty not to grant any further contracts. A second approach to the question of how many contracts the dominant firm should be obliged to make is that, once the dominant firm has granted one contract or licence, it can refuse to grant any further contracts or licences on the grounds that not "all competition" would be eliminated by a subsequent refusal to deal. This approach is ingenious, but wrong, since it would be open to serious abuse in practice. A dominant firm could always avoid effective competition by granting a licence to a small, inefficient, or friendly rival that makes no

[180] For detailed treatment of the conditions under Article 82(c) see Ch. 11 (Abusive Discrimination).

[181] Ch. 11 (Abusive Discrimination) argues that this interpretation of Article 82(c) would be wrong and that consumer welfare is implicit in Article 82(c). Otherwise, discrimination that enhances consumer welfare overall would be unlawful. This cannot have been intended under Article 82(c), but the issue remains unresolved under the case law.

meaningful contribution to competition on the downstream market. Competition does not merely mean the presence of one rival firm: it involves a process of rivalry. If this were accepted, the entire premise of the duty to deal—that it would bring to an end a serious handicap to effective competition on the downstream market—would be called into question.

c. ***A duty to contract only to the extent that the refusal would harm competition.*** The final, correct approach is that the dominant firm need only grant a subsequent contract where *all* of the conditions for a first compulsory contract are met.[182] Of course, the fact that one or more contracts have already been granted ought to make it inherently less likely that further contracts are needed. Indeed, if a first contract is granted, and a subsequent refusal to deal would still eliminate competition, the first contract was arguably not an effective remedy. But the Commission or a national authority can only award a contract to a firm willing to take it. There may well be situations where, at the time a first contract is made, there *happens* to be only one requesting party and that party turns out not to be an effective competitor. The key issue therefore is whether a subsequent contract or licence is necessary to prevent substantial anticompetitive effects on the downstream market (assuming all of the other conditions for a duty to deal are met). No additional contracts would be required if the market was already reasonably competitive:[183] another contract would only be justified where the refusal would result in the market remaining uncompetitive. How many contracts or licences are needed will vary from case to case, depending on how scattered the competitive fringe is, their available capacity, and barriers to entry and exit. But, in most cases, one or two efficient competitors ought to be enough to generate reasonable competition in most markets, with the result that the decision to refuse to admit further rivals would not harm consumers.

Situations in which non-discrimination duties towards rivals may exceptionally be appropriate. There are potential exceptions to the principle that the dominant firm can only be obliged to make a subsequent contract with a rival if the conditions for award of a first contract are satisfied. Non-discrimination duties towards rivals may be appropriate in at least two situations under Article 82 EC. The first concerns collective refusals to deal. Although the duty to deal under Article 82 EC is usually thought of in connection with single dominant firms, similar issues arise where two or more companies make arrangements to establish joint or reciprocal operations. In these circumstances, third parties may find that they cannot do business with the companies involved, or that they can do so only on less favourable terms than those given by the parties to one another or to the joint venture. The question therefore arises whether the

---

[182] See J Temple Lang, "Anticompetitive Non-Pricing Abuses Under European and National Antitrust Law" in B Hawk (ed.), 2003 *Fordham Corporate Law Institute* (New York, Juris Publishing, Inc., 2004) 245.

[183] This appears to have been the conclusion reached in *Intel Corporation v Via Technologies Inc. and Elitegroup Computer Systems (UK) Ltd*, [2002] EWHC 1159 (Chancery Division), para. 178 ("[O]ne of the essential elements in the exceptional circumstances requirement is the elimination of all competition in the relevant market. Here the allegedly dominant undertaking has granted licences and is not the only player in the market. It is not sufficient for VIA to say that Intel and its licensees are less innovative than VIA for it to overcome this hurdle."). The judgment was overturned on appeal, but the correctness of Mr. Justice Collins' conclusion on this issue was not cast in doubt.

parties should be entitled to refuse to do business with third parties, or entitled to give third parties less favourable terms than they give to one another.

This area of law is primarily the province of Article 81 EC, since there will typically be agreements between the joint venture or consortia members. Thus, in granting an individual exemption under Article 81 EC for such arrangements, the Commission has routinely considered whether the joint venture parties should grant competitors non-discriminatory terms when, if they were not so required, the parties would be in a position to eliminate competition in respect of a "substantial" part of the products concerned either by refusing to supply competitors or by supplying them only on substantially less favourable terms.[184] The same general principles applies in respect of standard setting organisations, where the Commission has routinely insisted on equal access to the standardised technology for non-members.[185]

Substantially the same principles apply under Article 82 EC, since the decisions and cases under Article 81 EC are most analogous to situations in which the joint venture owning the essential facility is in a dominant position. The fact that the users are also shareholders does not significantly alter the legal or economic position. Accordingly, the duty of a group of collectively dominant companies that own or control essential infrastructure or assets not to discriminate against non-member rivals is arguably higher than in the case of a single firm owning such a facility.[186] This distinction reflects the fact that a group of competitors acting in concert in such circumstances can achieve a monopoly not by developing better quality products, but through the joint acquisition or amalgamation of assets, which is in principle treated more strictly under competition law. Imposing a duty to deal on a multi-firm combination is also much easier to administer, since the combination will already be admitting several independent undertakings and their terms of access provide a benchmark for additional undertakings. Multi-firm combinations controlling essential facilities are therefore likely to have a non-discrimination duty towards rivals, assuming of course that all other conditions for a duty to deal are satisfied.

The above principles have generally been applied by the Community institutions in the case of jointly-owned facilities. This was in essence the rationale behind the *European Night Services* case, although, on the facts, the Court of First Instance overturned the Commission's conclusion that a non-discrimination duty should apply,[187] since the

[184] See, e.g., *IGR Stereo Television-Salora*, XIth Competition Policy Report (1981) para. 63; *DHL International*, XXIst Report on Competition Policy (1991), para. 88; *Eirpage*, OJ 1993 L 306/22, para. 20; *Infonet*, XXIInd Report on Competition Policy (1993), p. 416; *EBU-Eurovision*, OJ 1993 L 179/23, Art. 2; *BT-MCI*, OJ 1994 L 223/36, para. 57; *ACI (Channel Tunnel)*, OJ 1994 L 224/28, Art. 2; *Night Services*, OJ 1994 L 259/20, Art. 2; *Gas Interconnector*, XXVth Competition Policy Report (1996), para. 82; *Atlas*, OJ 1996 L 239/23; *Unisource*, OJ 1997 L 318/1; and *British Interactive Broadcasting/Open*, OJ 1999 L 312/1.

[185] See M Dolmans, "Standards For Standards" (2002) 26 *Fordham International Law Journal* 163, 171–174 (Commission generally insists on open and non-discriminatory access for non-members as a condition for exemption under Article 81(3) EC).

[186] See PE Areeda, "Essential Facilities: An Epithet In Need Of Limiting Principles" 58(3) *Antitrust Law Journal* 841, 843.

[187] See *Night Services*, OJ 1994 L 259/20, Article 2.

infrastructure in question was not an essential facility.[188] Similarly, in the cases involving airline computer reservation systems, the two major systems were jointly owned by several European airlines.[189] The airlines were also users of both facilities and some of them were dominant in their national markets. In these circumstances, they each had duties not to discriminate in favour of the system in which they were shareholders.

A second possible exception concerns the abusive refusal to supply essential interoperability information or other abuses that rest on a similar non-discrimination theory. In *Microsoft*, the duty to deal with all comers appears to have been motivated by the Commission's conclusion that the refusal to share interoperability information discriminated against rivals and denied work group server operators the ability to compete on an equal playing field. In this circumstance, the basis for the remedy was itself a discriminatory refusal to deal and the Commission may have felt that consumer welfare was best served by ending the discrimination and allowing the market to decide which products they prefer on the basis of quality and price rather than arbitrarily selecting *ex-ante* which licensees would likely contribute most to the competitive process. This implies that a duty to deal with all comers is only justified where the constituent element of the refusal to deal involves discrimination against rivals and unfairly impairing the quality of their products.

8.3.2.3 Terminating a course of dealing

Overview. Earlier precedents such as *Commercial Solvents* and *Télémarketing*[190] concerned situations in which the dominant firm terminated past cooperation with a third party, whereas more recent cases such as *Bronner*, *Magill*, and *IMS Health* concerned the duty to grant first-time access to new customers. These precedents have generated a great deal of discussion on whether a dominant firm's duty to deal with new trading parties under Article 82 EC is different from its duty in respect of existing trading parties. This distinction has been picked up on in the Discussion Paper, which suggests that the applicable principles are different.[191] But there is no real discussion of *why* this is, or should be, the case, other than to note that past dealing shows that dealing was efficient at one stage or may have induced specific customer investments.[192] It is also important to appreciate that termination of supplies is mainly relevant where the dominant firm deals with an actual or potential rival. Terminating supplies in circumstances where the dominant firm is not active in the same downstream market as the customer is generally of no concern under competition law, as discussed in Section 8.4 below.

---

[188] Joined Cases T-374/94, T-375/94, T-384/94 and T-388/94, *European Night Services Ltd (ENS), Eurostar (UK) Ltd, formerly European Passenger Services Ltd (EPS), Union internationale des chemins de fer (UIC), NV Nederlandse Spoorwegen (NS) and Société nationale des chemins de fer français (SNCF) v Commission* [1998] ECR II-3141, para. 207.

[189] See *London European/Sabena*, OJ 1988 L 317/47; and XXIst Competition Policy Report (1991), pp. 73–74.

[190] See Case 311/84, *Centre belge d'études de marché—Télémarketing (CBEM) v SA Compagnie luxembourgeoise de télédiffusion (CLT) and Information publicité Benelux (IPB)* [1985] ECR 3261.

[191] Discussion Paper, Section 9.2.1.

[192] Discussion Paper, para. 226.

Arguments for applying different standards to termination of dealings. A number of commentators argue that the case law on new customers is distinct from that concerning existing customers.[193] The principal argument is that prior dealing may have led a rival to make specific investments, leading to a legitimate expectation of future dealings. Indeed, the Commission has recently suggested that a past course of dealing may give rise to a "legitimate expectation" of future dealings.[194] Another argument is that there must always be a reason why a dominant firm terminates past, and presumably efficient, cooperation with a rival and that an anticompetitive inference may be appropriate in certain circumstances. Past terms may also offer a useful starting point for determining the terms of a new contract, a problem that is apt to be acute in refusal to deal cases where there was no prior dealing. There is some support for this view in the case law,[195] including in *Microsoft*, where the Commission considered a prior course of dealing between Microsoft and its rivals to be "of interest" in determining whether a duty to deal was appropriate.[196] The Discussion Paper also suggests that terminating supplies puts the dominant firm in a worse position than if it never dealt at all. Indeed, it goes as far as to suggest that "if the input owner is itself active in the downstream market and terminates supplies to one of its few competitors, it will normally be *presumed* that there is a negative effect on competition on the downstream market."[197]

Arguments against applying different standards to termination of dealings. Other commentators have rejected the relevance of a prior course of dealing and argue that the case law represents a unified set of principles.[198] Several reasons are said to justify this

[193] See, e.g., V Hatzopoulos, "Case Notes on *IMS*" (2004) 41 *Common Market Law Review* 1613 (suggesting that *IMS* confirms that there is a refusal to supply doctrine distinct from the *Commercial Solvents* line of case law); and B Sher, "The Last of the Steam-Powered Trains: Modernising Article 82" (2004) 25(5) *European Competition Law Review* 243 (one rule for existing customers, another for new customers).

[194] See Case COMP/38.096, *Clearstream* (Clearing and Settlement), Commission Decision of June 2, 2004, not yet published, paras. 242–43.

[195] See Opinion of Advocate General Jacobs in Case C-53/03, *Synetairismos Farmakopoion Aitolias & Akarnanias (Syfait) and Others v GlaxoSmithKline plc and GlaxoSmithKline AEVE* [2005] ECR I-4609, para. 66 (two different rules: one for existing customers and one for new customers under the essential facilities analogue); and *Genzyme Ltd v The Office of Fair Trading* [2004] CAT 4, para. 571 (UK Competition Appeal Tribunal distinguished between *Bronner* on the one hand and the *Commercial Solvents* and *Télémarketing* judgments on the other).

[196] Case COMP/C-3/37.792, *Microsoft*, Commission Decision of March 24, 2004, not yet published, para. 556.

[197] Discussion Paper, para. 222 (emphasis added).

[198] See, e.g., R Subiotto and R O'Donoghue, "Defining the Scope of the Duty of Dominant Firms to Deal with Existing Customers under Article 82 EC" (2003) 12 *European Competition Law Review* 683 (distinction between dominant firms' duties towards new and existing customers "arbitrary;" both new customers and existing customers are subject to the requirement that the requested input or facility be "essential"); and D Geradin, "Limiting the Scope of Article 82 EC: What Can The EU Learn From the US Supreme Court's Judgment in *Trinko*, in the Wake of *Microsoft*, *IMS*, and *Deutsche Telekom*?" (2004) 41 *Common Market Law Review* 1526 (implying that *Commercial Solvents* and the essential facility doctrine constitute a single line of case law). A number of US commentators make a similar point. See, e.g., E Elhauge, "Defining Better Monopolisation Standards" (2003) 56(2) *Stanford Law Review* 253, 313; and GO Robinson, "On Refusing To Deal With Rivals" (2002) 87 *Cornell Law Review* 1203.

conclusion. First, arguments based on "legitimate expectations" as a result of past dealings go too far. A legitimate expectation under Community law is only capable of creating a legally-enforceable obligation against a Community institution, not a private undertaking. The argument that the rival may have made specific investments based on past supply also seems weak. Either those investments were reasonable in the circumstances—in which case there should be a contractual remedy—or they are not, in which case Article 82 EC should not be used to remedy investments that were not justified by any legitimate contractual reliance.

Second, the facts in *Commercial Solvents* and *Télémarketing* and the language used by the Court of Justice are consistent with its later statements in cases such as *Bronner*, suggesting that the case law represents a single, unified set of principles. In *Commercial Solvents*, the dominant company was the only source of the raw material in question: the Court specifically rejected claims that other nascent technologies in the trial stage were a substitute for Commercial Solvents' raw materials.[199] The need for an essential input in the case of existing customers was made more express by the Court in *Télémarketing*, where it interpreted *Commercial Solvents* as limited to situations in which an undertaking holds a dominant position on the market in respect of an input that is "indispensable for the activities of another undertaking on another market."[200]

Third, later decisions and judgments on the duties to deal with new customers expressly cite the *Commercial Solvents* line of case law as the basis for the duty to deal with new customers, thereby suggesting that the underlying principles are the same as in the case of existing customers. For example, in *Sea Containers-Stena Sealink*—the first decision expressly mentioning the term "essential facility"—the Commission cited *Commercial Solvents* and *Télémarketing* for the proposition that "an undertaking which occupies a dominant position in the provision of an essential facility and itself uses that facility (i.e., a facility or infrastructure, without access to which competitors cannot provide services to their customers), and which refuses other companies access to that facility without objective justification or grants access to competitors only on terms less favourable than those which it gives its own services, infringes Article 8[2]."[201] Similarly, for IP rights, the Court of Justice has also cited the *Commercial Solvents* line of case law as the legal basis for a duty to deal.[202] Indeed, it is not even clear that a hard and fast distinction can be made between case law involving "new" and "existing" customers: a number of cases associated with the duty to deal with "new" customers in fact involved the termination of past cooperation or discriminatory refusals to deal.[203]

[199] Joined Cases 6/73 and 7/73, *Istituto Chemioterapico Italiano SpA and Commercial Solvents Corporation v Commission* [1974] ECR 223, para. 13.

[200] Case 311/84, *Centre belge d'études de marché—Télémarketing (CBEM) v SA Compagnie luxembourgeoise de télédiffusion (CLT) and Information publicité Benelux (IPB)* [1985] ECR 3261, para. 26.

[201] *Sea Containers v Stena Sealink—Interim measures*, OJ 1994 L 15/8, para. 66, footnote 6.

[202] Joined Cases C-241/91 P and C-242/91 P, *Radio Telefís Éireann and Independent Television Publications Ltd (RTE & ITP) v Commission* [1995] ECR I-743, para. 56.

[203] See, e.g., *British Midland v Aer Lingus*, OJ 1992 L 96/34 (Aer Lingus refused to continue with British Midland on interlining facilities, while continuing to deal with British Airways); *Magill TV Guide/ITP, BBC and RTE*, OJ 1989 L 78/43 (broadcasters provided listings free of charge to overseas publications and newspapers); Case COMP/C-3/37.792, *Microsoft*, Commission Decision of March 24,

Finally, a legal principle to the effect that the substantive test for a duty to deal would vary depending on whether the trading party was new or an existing customer would be precarious. It would imply that a dominant owner of an input would be able to exploit the property exclusively if it operates in a vertically integrated fashion at all times, but would be compelled to deal it if, at any point in time in the past, it considered it more efficient to deal with an independent operator. The law might then be reduced to happenstance and would become less predictable. At the extreme, such a duty might lead to the dominant firm not dealing with any rival, even when it was efficient to do so. A dominant firm is in principle entitled to chose its trading parties and to cease or vary the terms of any past cooperation. What was efficient in the past may not be so today.

Evaluating the competing views. On balance, the argument that the duty to deal with an existing trading party is subject to different legal conditions than the duty to deal with a new competitor seems overstated. That is not, however, to say that a prior course of dealing is of no relevance. Clearly, it is, but the real question is what has changed? Where a dominant firm has been supplying a downstream trading party, and then terminates the relationship, the reason for that termination should be looked at where it has a sufficiently serious effect on competition. (If the termination has no effect on competition (e.g., where there are sufficient other downstream competitors), there would be no reason to enquire into the reason.) There should be no presumption that termination of existing dealings is either immune from criticism or suspect. A fact-based inquiry into the reasons for the termination is necessary in each case.

The dominant firm should therefore be required to explain a decision to terminate an existing relationship. There are many procompetitive reasons why a dominant firm would stop dealing with a past trading party. One is that the dominant firm is forward-integrating itself and customers are better-served by a vertically integrated operator than a non-integrated firm (which will generally be true given lower transaction and other benefits of vertical integration).[204] Another is that the dominant firm is exiting the particular application served by the trading party. The dominant firm's costs may also have changed or it may have introduced an improved product commanding a higher price.

It may be that an inference of anticompetitive intent would be appropriate in certain circumstances. For example, the termination may be used as a way to discipline a customer for dealing with a rival. A common fact-pattern in many network industries is that a firm initially adopts an "open" policy on interoperable products, but then later refuses to interoperate or does so on less favourable terms. If an anticompetitive bent is revealed, and the other conditions for a refusal to deal are met, the fact that the dominant firm dealt with rivals in the past may offer a useful indication that a duty to deal can work and what the future terms might be. Of course, what was acceptable in the past may not be in future, but it is much easier to adjust past terms for changes in circumstances than to create new terms for something that was never sold to anyone.

2004, not yet published (less information provided to Sun Microsystems than other rivals); and Case COMP/38/096, *Clearstream (Clearing and settlement)*, Commission Decision of June 4, 2004, not yet published, para. 216 (refusal to deal and discriminatory refusal to deal "two manifestations of the same behaviour").

[204] See Discussion Paper, para. 224.

8.3.2.4 Relevance of the source and perceived value of the property right

Situations where the value of the property right is perceived to be weak. It is sometimes argued that the duty to deal under Article 82 EC is mainly justified where a competition authority or court perceives the value of the IP right in question to be weak.[205] But even if competition authorities and courts were well-equipped to distinguish "good" and "bad" IP rights—which is doubtful—this argument is unpersuasive. In the first place, while it may be true to say that there was some doubt surrounding the justification for the IP rights at issue in *Magill* and, to a lesser extent, *IMS*, the same could not be said about other cases in which a duty to deal has been considered appropriate. The most notable examples are *Microsoft* and the *Intel/Via* case before the United Kingdom courts,[206] each of which concerned valuable IP and related rights.

Furthermore, it is *ultra vires* for the Community institutions to question the existence or validity of property rights granted under national law: only their exercise is subject to Community law. It would be highly unsatisfactory if the Community institutions did not formally question the existence or validity of property rights, but informally decided cases by passing unpublished value judgments on the perceived strength of the property rights at issue. Decisions would then be rendered for reasons other than those stated in the text itself and that would be unlawful if they were made express. Finally, if certain property rights are aberrant, the correct remedy is to amend the legislation that creates such aberrant rights. This does not mean that competition law has no role to play, but it means that competition law should not, in the first instance, be a means of correcting defects in property laws.

Situations where property results from public funding. Another argument is that a duty to deal is appropriate where the property in question results from the use of public funds (e.g., a former state monopoly) or is a natural monopoly.[207] It is true that EU Member States spend a greater proportion of GDP on public investments in physical facilities than, say, the United States, which may explain why there is a greater

---

[205] See, e.g., I Forrester, "Compulsory Licensing in Europe: A Rare Cure to Aberrant National Intellectual Property Rights?," testimony to the Department of Justice/Federal Trade Commission Intellectual Property hearings (2002) (suggesting that it would be "unimaginable…that a truly innovative piece of technology (a pharmaceutical patent or novel software code, for example) would be treated in such a manner."); and M Delrahim, "Forcing Firms to Share the Sandbox: Compulsory Licensing of Intellectual Property Rights and Antitrust," paper presented at the British Institute of International and Comparative Law, London, May 10, 2004 ("United States commentators had another problem with *Magill* and *IMS*: each case involved a weak copyright in what might well have been considered uncopyrightable facts in the U.S. A major part of both decisions seems to have been the concern that the underlying intellectual property was questionable….I believe that the *Magill* and *IMS Health* cases may provide little precedent for a future case that features undisputed software rights, for example, or strong patent rights.").

[206] *Intel Corporation v Via Technologies Inc and Elitegroup Computer Systems (UK) Ltd*, [2002] EWCA Civ. 1905, December 22, 2002 (Court of Appeal) (Via's claims that it was entitled to manufacture and sell chipsets compatible with Intel's Pentium 4 product considered arguable, for purposes of summary judgment, under Article 82 EC). The case has since resulted in a settlement agreement between the parties.

[207] See PE Areeda and H Hovenkamp, *Antitrust Law*, Vol. III A (Boston, Little, Brown and Company, 1996) para. 771.

incidence of forced sharing in the EU.[208] But it is hard to see why the public source of the funding for the property should lead to a stricter legal standard. First, the wording of Article 82 EC does not allow a distinction to be made between property that results from public and private funding.[209] The wording of Article 295 EC would also preclude discrimination between property rights along these lines.

Second, it will not always be easy to say that the source of the funds is unambiguously public in nature. Much of the infrastructure offered to former state monopolies has been the subject of significant improvements following privatisation, with the result that the sources of the funding are now mixed. Third, if certain assets cannot be economically duplicated by private funding, the proper course is to regulate the natural monopoly created by public funds, which the Commission has done in the case of virtually all utility networks. Competition law should not generally be used to plug gaps in regulation.

Finally, the Commission itself has rejected this argument. In *Frankfurt Airport*, the airport operator argued that its historical legal monopoly on the provision of ramp-handling services justified a refusal to deal. The Commission concluded that the historical character of the monopoly was irrelevant: what mattered was the airport operator's conduct on the market.[210] This suggests that the Commission is indifferent to the historical source or reason for a monopoly once the substantive conditions for a duty to deal are satisfied.

Conclusion. The perceived weakness of certain property rights, or the public source of their funding, may explain why certain refusal to deal cases are pursued, but it does not offer a useful legal test for determining the legal conditions under which a duty to deal is appropriate. At most, the fact that a facility is a natural monopoly, the result of a former statutory monopoly, or publicly-owned helps explain the type of cases that, as a matter of policy, are thought most likely to confer the greatest benefit to competition in ordering access and the least harm to the property owner. Limiting the use of the doctrine of forced sharing to these situations is therefore a convenient policy argument to place general restrictions on the duty to share in order to limit its harmful effects rather than a substantive principle.

8.4 DUTY TO DEAL WITH CUSTOMERS UNDER ARTICLE 82 EC

Overview. The preceding sections dealt with the circumstances in which a dominant firm competes with actual or potential downstream rivals and refuses to make first or subsequent contracts with those rivals. In exceptional circumstances, such conduct may violate Article 82(b), the clause dealing with exclusionary abuses under Article 82 EC. Different considerations apply where the dominant firm is not active as a seller on the

[208] See D Geradin, "The Opening of State Monopolies to Competition: Main Issues of the Liberalisation Process" in D Geradin (ed.), *The Liberalisation Of State Monopolies In The European Union And Beyond* (The Hague, Kluwer Law International, 2000) p. 183.

[209] Other provisions of the EC Treaty grant the Commission extensive powers to deal with anti-competitive actions by the State and public authorities. For a brief overview, see Ch. 1 (Introduction, Scope Of Application, and Basic Framework).

[210] See *FAG-Flughafen Frankfurt/Main AG*, OJ 1998 L 72/30, paras. 97–98.

downstream market, but is simply active as an upstream supplier of inputs or final products to customers, i.e., the dominant firm is not vertically integrated, but only acts at an upstream market level.

A number of issues arise. The first is whether and in what circumstances a dominant firm can be obliged to deal with a customer and in particular whether the conditions for a duty to deal are the same or different as in the case of duties in respect of rivals. The second concerns situations in which the product supplied by the dominant firm is not an input used for transformation, but concerns a final product for distribution or resale. Case law indicates that it may be an abuse to terminate dealings with distributors or resellers, but the precise rationale for this conclusion has not been clearly articulated. The final situation concerns the special case of parallel trade and whether unilateral output restrictions by a dominant firm of the quantities supplied to parallel traders constitute an abuse. Each of these situations is considered below.

8.4.1 The Duty To Supply Inputs To Customers

Duty to supply inputs to customers analogous to the duty to deal with rivals. An important threshold question is whether a dominant firm can be compelled to deal *at all* with a customer if it is not vertically integrated, i.e., if it is not active on the same level of trade as its customers. The basic reasons are two-fold. First, if the dominant firm is not present on the downstream market, it is not foreclosing rivals or restricting competition in favour of its own business. In particular, it is not sacrificing any profit in the hope of recouping this sacrifice later. Abuse must imply some degree of impropriety or benefit to the dominant firm. Second, terminating one supply relationship has no necessary connection with harm to consumer welfare. As the Discussion Paper notes, "if there are several competitors in the downstream market and the supplier of the input is not itself active in that market, the impact on competition of the termination may be small unless the exclusion is likely to lead to collusion."[211]

Obiter statements in Article 82 EC case law suggest that no duty can arise where the dominant firm is not itself present on the market for which access to the input is sought. In *Ladbroke*, one of the factors cited by the Court of First Instance in denying a duty to deal was that the dominant firm was not active at all on the relevant downstream market where access to its inputs was sought.[212] The leading treatise on US antitrust law makes a similar point:[213]

---

[211] Discussion Paper, para. 222.

[212] Case T-504/93, *Tiercé Ladbroke SA v Commission* [1997] ECR II-923, para. 130 ("in the absence of direct or indirect exploitation by the sociétés de courses of their intellectual property rights on the Belgian market, their refusal to supply cannot be regarded as involving any restriction of competition on the Belgian market."). See also Discussion Paper, para. 72 (Whereas the aim in the situations described above is to exclude B, a rival in the upstream market, in the typical refusal to supply case the aim is to exclude an already active or a potential participant in the downstream market, for instance Z (vertical foreclosure). From a competition policy point of view, *this is mostly only a worry if the dominant company A is itself active downstream.*") (emphasis added).

[213] See PE Areeda and H Hovenkamp, *Antitrust Law*, Vol. III A (Boston, Little, Brown and Company, 1996) para. 771a (emphasis in original).

"[P]erhaps the monopoly gas pipeline owner sells no gas of its own but only operates the pipeline. It then sells space to some firms but not others, and the latter claim essential facility. But in such a case it is hard to conceive of an *antitrust* rationale for enforcing a duty to deal that does not involve some kind of integration between the pipeline and the gas shippers with whom it is dealing. If the pipeline owner refuses the plaintiff for lack of space there is no antitrust problem at all. If it refuses the plaintiff merely for personal or other non-economic reasons, the refusal may be governed by tort law but antitrust is not apt. If it refuses the plaintiff because it has exclusive contracts with existing customers, then antitrust may be apt, but then we have moved into the realm of vertical integration as well....[A]ctionable essential facility claims always (or virtually always) involve vertical integration."

The issue remains unresolved under Article 82 EC. However, unlike US law, Article 82 EC also contains a broad non-discrimination clause: Article 82(c). Thus, at the very least, it is arguable that, if the dominant firm is not vertically integrated, but has made one contract—whether compulsory or voluntary—similarly-situated customers may be able to claim further contracts by relying on the non-discrimination clause in Article 82(c). Some commentators state, correctly, that Article 82(c) cannot apply unless the dominant firm has already made at least one contract: if there is no first contract, the dominant firm cannot be discriminating.[214] But this is largely academic: the dominant firm must always be supplying *someone*, whether its own downstream business—in which case the rules on the duty to deal with actual or potential rivals apply—or at least one customer—in which case discrimination issues may arise.

The number of contracts that a dominant firm may be required to grant to customers under Article 82(c) has not formally arisen in the decisional practice and case law. A number of principles nonetheless seem reasonably clear.[215] First, the conditions of Article 82(c) must obviously be satisfied. These are discussed in detail in Chapter Eleven (Abusive Discrimination), but may be briefly summarised as follows. The situation of the first and subsequent customers must be "equivalent" from the perspective of the dominant firm and the customers. There must also be discrimination, either in the sense that the dominant firm refuses to deal outright with further customers or deals on discriminatory terms that in effect amount to a refusal to deal. Finally, and crucially, the second or subsequent customers must suffer a competitive disadvantage in relation to the first customer, which requires that the customers compete with each other. Unless all of these cumulative conditions are present, Article 82(c) cannot apply.

Second, the fact that the dominant firm has concluded one contract with a customer should not lead to a duty to deal with every subsequent party that makes a request. Otherwise, the dominant firm would be seriously discouraged from making a first contract. The value of any first contract might also need to be renegotiated if the decision to grant one contract would oblige the dominant firm to make others, which would increase transaction costs. These considerations apply *a fortiori* in the case of IP rights, since the value of a first licence would be directly affected by any subsequent

[214] See J Temple Lang, "Anticompetitive Non-Pricing Abuses Under European and National Antitrust Law" in B Hawk (ed.), 2003 *Fordham Corporate Law Institute* (New York, Juris Publishing, Inc., 2004) 235–340.

[215] See generally J Temple Lang, "Anticompetitive Abuses Under Article 82 EC Involving Intellectual Property Rights" in CD Ehlermann and I Atanasiu (eds.), *European Competition Law Annual 2003: What Is an Abuse of Dominant Position?* (Oxford, Hart Publishing, 2006), p. 589.

licences. The dominant firm remains entitled, as a general matter, to exercise the prerogatives of any property owner and to organise its dealings with downstream trading parties in the manner that it considers most useful. It is true that the objections to a duty to deal with additional downstream customers in circumstances where the dominant firm already deals with at least one customer are less strong than in the case in which a dominant firm is obliged to deal with a direct rival. But this should not at the same time mean that the dominant firm's property rights cease to have any meaningful content.

Finally, the key issue in refusal to deal involving customers concerns the objective justification for the refusal to deal with further customers. A dominant firm must always have some reason to refuse to make a profitable deal. In the case of refusal to deal with customers, the self-interest of the dominant firm to avoid direct competition is not present to the same extent or at all as it is in the case of refusals to deal with rivals. At a minimum, the categories of objective justification available in the case of refusal to deal with rivals should also be open to the dominant firm in the case of refusal to deal with additional customers. In addition, there will be specific defences available to the dominant firm in the case of refusal to deal with customers. The most obvious additional defence is that the dominant firm has made an exclusive contract with the first customer and does not wish to undermine the value of that contract, and any efficiencies that justified it, by making further contracts. In other words, if the dominant firm could lawfully make the contract with the first customer exclusive, the refusal to deal with further customers must be lawful too.

Does the input supplied to customers also need to be an "essential facility"? One unresolved issue concerning the duty to deal with customers is whether a duty to contract is also subject to the condition that the product in question is essential for competition or whether the mere fact of discrimination suffices. The former interpretation is preferable. After all, the only real difference between the situations involving a duty to deal with rivals and a duty to deal with customers is that, in the latter case, the dominant firm considers it more efficient to operate through independent undertakings than to partially integrate. If the inputs that the dominant firm owns or controls are essential for downstream competition, and the other additional elements for an abusive refusal to deal are present, the effect of a refusal on the downstream market is likely to be similar in each case. This implies that the legal principles for ordering access should be similar too.

A second or subsequent customer would therefore need to show an abuse capable of justifying the grant of a compulsory contract; in other words, that the conditions for a compulsory first contract are met and that a further contract is still needed to prevent serious anticompetitive effects on the downstream market in which the dominant firm's input is essential for competition. The fact that one contract had already been concluded by the dominant firm would also mean that subsequent contracting parties face a higher hurdle: they would need to show that the downstream market remains uncompetitive following the grant of a first contract, as well as satisfying all the other conditions for the award of a first contract. The mere fact of discrimination would not suffice.

There is some support for the above interpretation in the recent *Clearstream* decision.[216] Clearstream, a dominant supplier of so-called primary clearing and settlement services for securities issued under German law, was found to have unlawfully refused to supply such services to Euroclear, an intermediary for so-called secondary clearing and settlement services. The primary and secondary clearing and settlement services at issue in the decision were different activities, with the result that, for the specific service at issue, Euroclear was a customer of Clearstream's, not a direct competitor.

The Commission found that the primary clearing and settlement services offered by Clearstream were an essential facility, since they could not be practically or economically replicated by Euroclear, and that Clearstream, as a *de facto* monopoly provider of the relevant services, had a duty to make them available to Euroclear. The Commission also found that Clearstream had discriminated against Euroclear, contrary to Article 82(c), by supplying access to the relevant services to other customers immediately upon request. Importantly, however, the Commission did not treat the issue of discrimination as a stand-alone infringement, but concluded that it was part of the overall refusal to supply the essential facility clearing services.[217] This suggests that the legal duty to deal with subsequent customers has been assimilated with the principles regarding first contracts, i.e., essential facilities. This interpretation makes sense, since the law on refusal to deal would then be subject to a single, unified set of principles.

8.4.2 Refusals To Deal Arising At The Level Of Distribution Or Resale

Essential facility principles generally inapplicable. The previous sections concerned the duty of a dominant firm controlling an essential upstream input to deal with undertakings that transform the input into a final product sold on a downstream market. Different principles apply where the refusal to deal does not concern an upstream input that is transformed by rivals or customers, but where the product in question is used only for distribution or resale. The essential facilities analogue outlined in the preceding sections does not generally apply in the case of refusals to deal arising at the level of distribution or resale.[218] This is because the essential facility principles only apply where there is scope for value-added competition,[219] which is usually only possible in the case of inputs used for transformation into a final product. In the case of

[216] See also *ATTHERACES Ltd & Anr v The British Horse Racing Board & Anr*, [2005] EWHC 3015 (Ch., December 21, 2005), paras. 258 et seq. (essential facility-type analysis applied to refusal to deal with a customer).

[217] See Case COMP/38/096, *Clearstream (Clearing and Settlement)*, Decision of June 4, 2004, not yet published, para. 222.

[218] See, e.g., Commission submission in "*The Essential Facility Concept*," Organisation for Economic Cooperation and Development (1996), p. 98 ("[T]he rules about the duty to supply downstream competitors do not apply to distributors since a refusal to supply a particular distributor does not have a significant effect on competition.").

[219] See J Temple Lang, "The Principle of Essential Facilities in European Community Competition Law—The Position Since *Bronner*" (2000) 1 *Journal of Network Industries* 395, 397 ("[A] condition of the essential facilities principle is that the downstream activities must constitute a real market involving added value services: if it is merely distribution or resale of products produced upstream, there is not enough competition to protect.").

physical property, the requesting party uses the essential input to offer a final product or service downstream. In the case of IP, the input is essential to offer a new kind of product. The essential facility principle therefore assumes that firms can increase competition by adding value to the input or by offering differentiated products.

The same rationale does not apply in the context of a distribution or resale, since downstream trading parties are merely reselling the dominant firm's product. There is no scope for meaningful competition between a dominant supplier and its distributors/retailers where the latter merely engage in resale or distribution. If companies, all of which are using the same facility, can do little more than sell the result to consumers with substantially the same format and price (which will be governed by the access charges that competitors pay to the owner of the facility). Put differently, if there is no meaningful competition worth protecting between a dominant firm and its distributors and/or resellers, there is no harm under competition law resulting from a refusal to deal.

Another reason why the essential facility principles do not apply in the context of distribution and resale is that the injury to competition through a refusal to deal can be no greater than if the dominant firm forward integrates. The only "harm" therefore is one integrated firm supplies the same quantity of products that were previously supplied by two independent firms. Such "harm" has no necessary connection with harm to competition. This principle was confirmed by *Filtrona/Tabacalera*.[220] Filtrona argued that Tabacalera had abused its dominant position as a purchaser of cigarette filters in the Spanish cigarette market by increasing its own production of ordinary cigarette filters from 44% to 100% of its own requirements, thereby discontinuing its purchases from Filtrona. The Commission held that: (1) a company's production of its own requirements is not in itself an abnormal act of competition (production by cigarette manufacturers of their own filters is common practice in the industry); (2) Tabacalera's decision was justified on economic grounds, in particular because it enabled it to achieve economies of scale and generally to reduce production costs; and (3) no special circumstances suggested that Tabacalera's decision was part of an abusive behaviour or strategy. The case thus confirms that vertical integration without anticompetitive purpose is not abusive even if the effect is that a dominant firm ends a previous course of dealings with an existing customer.

The rationale for case law requiring a duty to deal in the context of distribution or resale. A small number of decisions and cases under Article 82 EC have found that it may be an abuse for a dominant firm to refuse to deal with downstream distributors or resellers. The first case is *United Brands*.[221] The Court of Justice held that it was abusive for the dominant supplier to terminate supplies to its distributor, Oelsen, on the grounds that the distributor had participated in an advertising campaign for a competitor of the supplier. The Court seemed to elaborate a more general principle to the effect that a dominant firm "cannot stop supplying a long-standing customer who abides by regular commercial practice, if the orders placed by that customer are in no way out of

[220] *Filtrona/Tabacalera,* XVIVth Report on Competition Policy (1989), para. 61 (hereinafter "*Filtrona/Tabacalera*").

[221] Case 27/76, *United Brands Company and United Brands Continentaal BV v Commission* [1978] ECR 207 (hereinafter "*United Brands*").

the ordinary."[222] However, it later tempered that statement by stating that the refusal should have a possible consequence that "it might in the end eliminate a trading party from the relevant market" and that the dominant firm can always take reasonable steps to protect its commercial interests.[223]

Later, in *Boosey & Hawkes*,[224] the Commission clarified further the circumstances in which a dominant firm is entitled to refuse to continue to deal with existing customers. Boosey & Hawkes refused all further supplies to a customer who had transferred its central activity to the promotion of a competing brand of musical instruments. An important evidentiary point in this connection was that Boosey & Hawkes had embarked on a plan to exclude the competitive threat from that rival and that the refusal to supply the customer was part of that plan.[225] While the Commission found that the sudden and complete termination of supplies was, on the facts, disproportionate, it confirmed that a dominant firm can lawfully terminate relations with reasonable notice and that there is no obligation on a dominant firm to subsidise competition to itself:[226]

> "There is no obligation placed on a dominant producer to subsidise competition to itself. In the case where a customer transfers its central activity to the promotion of a competing brand it may be that even a dominant producer is entitled to review its commercial relations with that customer and on giving adequate notice terminate any special relationship."

Although it seems reasonably clear that the essential facility analogue under Article 82 EC does not apply in the case of mere distribution or resale, the rationale for the above decisions and case law is obscure. A number of different approaches might be considered. The first approach is to argue that the dominant firm has a duty to deal where the refusal to do so would eliminate the trading party from the market. This is not, however, a useful legal principle. The mere fact that a trading party exits the market has no necessary connection with effects on competition. If this were accepted, a dominant firm would commit an abuse each time that it forward integrated, which the Commission has rejected in *Filtrona/Tabacalera*. The law would also be reduced to happenstance in this circumstance, since abuses could be found if the distributor or retailer was particularly small or inefficient. This approach also ignores the many situations under EC competition law in which a firm is entitled to limit the number of its trading parties though exclusive or selective distribution arrangements.

A second approach is to argue that the dominant firm must behave in a proportionate manner and should not suddenly terminate a trading party that has established a long-standing relationship or some other form of dependence on it. But this principle fares no better than the first. It would have the perverse consequence that a dominant firm could never safely terminate an exclusive distribution arrangement. Issues of dependence are better dealt with under contract law or national laws that protect situations of "economic dependence" in distribution arrangements. The fact that Council Regulation 1/2003 expressly permits national laws to adopt stricter or different

---

[222] *Ibid.*, para. 6.
[223] *Ibid.*, para. 6.
[224] *BBI/Boosey & Hawkes—Interim measures*, OJ 1987 L 286/36 (hereinafter "*Boosey & Hawkes*").
[225] *Ibid.*, para. 19.
[226] *Ibid.*

standards to Article 82 EC further bolsters this argument. If a particular category of trading party is considered to be vulnerable by the Community institutions, the proper course would be to adopt legislation requiring certain minimum obligations upon termination, as occurred in the case of commercial agents.[227] The use of general competition laws to protect categories of distributors or retailers considered to be dependent on large manufacturers should be avoided.

The final (and correct) approach is to treat decisions such as *United Brands* and *Boosey & Hawkes* as situations in which the dominant firm is trying to impair rivals' competitiveness by denying them access to distribution: the refusal to supply *indirectly* had the object or effect of foreclosing a rival of the dominant firm by engaging in acts of reprisal against its actual or potential customers.[228] In both *United Brands* and *Boosey & Hawkes*, the dominant firm only refused to deal because the customer had either started selling a competing brand (*Boosey & Hawkes*) or was engaged in promotional activities for a competitor (*United Brands*). Although the contract between the dominant firm and the customer was not exclusive in nature, the dominant firm could, in effect, insist on exclusivity by threatening the withdrawal of supplies in the event that the customer dealt with a competitor. Thus, by insisting that customers should only deal with the dominant firm, this "might in the end eliminate a [competitor] from the relevant market."[229]

Whether an abuse arises would involve consideration of a number of factors. As a preliminary matter, it should be determined whether there is dominance at the level of distribution in the sense that the dominant firm controls the majority of actual or potential distribution outlets. The range of distribution options available to rivals would need to be assessed, including self-distribution. Second, it would need to be determined whether the denial of distribution outlets to rivals was likely to have a material effect on competition in the relevant final product market.[230] If the downstream market is reasonably competitive, there is usually no reason to order the dominant firm to allow its distributors to deal with rival products. Finally, the issue of objective justification should be considered. In particular, the Commission has confirmed in *Boosey & Hawkes*, that it may, with reasonable notice, be legitimate for the dominant firm to terminate relations with a customer who transfers its main activity to dealing in competing products. A genuine conflict of interest should always be a defence.

---

[227] See Council Directive of 18 December 1986 on the coordination of the laws of the Member State relating to self-employed commercial agents, OJ 1986 L 382/17.

[228] See R Subiotto and R O'Donoghue, "Defining the Scope of the Duty of Dominant Firms to Deal with Existing Customers under Article 82 EC" (2003) 12 *European Competition Law Review* 683, 688.

[229] Case 27/76, *United Brands Company and United Brands Continentaal BV v Commission* [1978] ECR 207, para. 183.

[230] See, e.g., Case T-65/98, *Van den Bergh Foods Ltd v Commission* [2003] ECR II-4653 (control over approximately 40% of available distribution outlets was considered, on the facts, to have a material adverse effect on the downstream market). For a discussion of the treatment of exclusivity requirements under Article 82 EC, see Ch. 7 (Exclusive Dealing, Loyalty Rebates, and Related Practices).

8.4.3 Refusal To Deal And Parallel Trade

No presumption of abuse. Although no general duty to deal arises in the context of distribution and resale, the overriding importance of the integration of the single market under the EC Treaty raises the legal issue whether a refusal to deal by a dominant firm with undertakings engaged in arbitrage (or parallel trade) within the EU can be considered an abuse. It is well established that an agreement between two or more undertakings with the object or effect of limiting parallel trade within the EU constitutes a restriction of competition.[231] Agreements that limit parallel trade from non-Member States to the EU may also, in certain circumstances, violate Article 81 EC.[232]

No such general principle applies, however, in respect of unilateral action under Article 82 EC, even if such action results in a reduction of the volume of products sold for parallel trade. In the first place, an agreement between two independent undertakings to act in concert in respect of limiting parallel trade is different in nature from the unilateral decision by a firm, including a dominant firm, to decide with whom it will deal and for which quantities. The fact that, in some general sense, the practical effect of the refusal to supply *resembles* a violation of Article 81 EC does not automatically mean that there has been a violation of Article 82 EC.[233] Similarly, the fact that a dominant firm's unilateral decisions produce effects that it could not bring about by agreements, and which might be contrary to Article 81 EC if they were agreed between two undertakings, should not render its conduct abusive.

Second, a dominant firm's freedom of contract, its right to dispose of its property in the manner it sees fit, and the right to optimise its commercial interests carry great weight.[234] In the most extreme case, a dominant firm could withdraw its products entirely from a market where its profits were eroded by parallel trade, which the Community Courts have held would be lawful, even if it would obviously eliminate any scope for parallel trade.[235] A dominant firm is *a fortiori* entitled to take other

---

[231] See, e.g., Case C-279/87, *Tipp-Ex GmbH & Co KG v Commission* [1990] ECR I-261, para. 22; and Case 19/77, *Miller International Schallplatten GmbH v Commission* [1978] ECR 131, para. 7.

[232] See, e.g., Case C-306/96, *Javico International and Javico AG v Yves Saint Laurent Parfums SA* [1998] ECR-I-1983.

[233] See Opinion of Advocate General Jacobs in Case C-53/03, *Synetairismos Farmakopoion Aitolias & Akarnanias (Syfait) and Others v GlaxoSmithKline plc and GlaxoSmithKline AEVE* [2005] ECR I-4609, para. 53. See also Joined Cases C-2/01 P and C-3/01 P, *Bundesverband der Arzneimittel-Importeure eV and Commission v Bayer AG* [2004] ECR I-23, para. 87 ("[T]he mere fact that the unilateral policy of quotas implemented by Bayer, combined with the national requirements on the wholesalers to offer a full product range, produces the same effect as an export ban does not mean that the manufacturer imposed such a ban or that there was an agreement prohibited by Article 8[1](1) of the EC Treaty."). *A contrario*, the mere fact that unilateral conduct has effects similar to an Article 81 EC violation does not prove an abuse.

[234] See Opinion of Advocate General Jacobs in Case C-53/03, *Synetairismos Farmakopoion Aitolias & Akarnanias (Syfait) and Others v GlaxoSmithKline plc and GlaxoSmithKline AEVE* [2005] ECR I-4609, para. 67.

[235] See Case C-249/88, *Commission v Belgium* [1991] ECR I-1275, para. 20 ("As the Belgian Government rightly observes, differences in the price of the same product, from one Member State to another, may be accounted for by the commercial strategy of the manufacturing undertaking, and a hindrance to imports may not be inferred from the mere fact that an undertaking abandons the marketing of a given product on the market of a Member State on the ground that the maximum price

reasonable measures to protect its profitability and that of its distributors in the importing Member State. Finally, there is no general duty under Article 82 EC to deal. As with any duty of forced dealing, it can only be imposed "only after a close scrutiny of the factual and economic context, and even then only within somewhat narrow limits."[236]

A refusal to deal in the context of parallel trade may, however, be abusive in certain circumstances. In particular, an intention to limit parallel trade may render abusive a refusal of supply by a dominant undertaking, since it is normally aimed at removing a source of competition from the dominant undertaking on the market in the Member State of import, i.e., competition from arbitrage. For example, a refusal to deal with parallel traders that was discriminatory and resulted in the imposition of excessive prices by the dominant firm in the Member State of destination of the imported products may be an abuse.[237] Even assuming that a sufficient effect on competition could not in all cases be shown, an additional argument can be made in support of such a conclusion on the basis of the market-partitioning object of the conduct at issue.[238] The Commission has relied in the past on clear evidence of threats to terminate distributors as punishment for export activity and, in some cases, on actual implementation of threats.[239] Contractual restrictions that seek to limit or prevent the scope for arbitrage may also be abusive. In *United Brands*, a key feature of the abuse was that the dominant firm prevented trade in bananas by prohibiting the sale of green bananas (yellow bananas would deteriorate too quickly to allow transportation to other Member States). It is one thing for a dominant firm to unilaterally decide that it will not sell to undertakings engaged in parallel trade, but quite another to agree a contractual restriction with another party specifically intended to prevent all parallel trade.

The special case of pharmaceuticals. Refusal to deal in the context of parallel trade has arisen most frequently in the pharmaceutical sector. Several characteristics of this industry create scope for parallel trade.[240] First, most Member States control prices of prescription medicines through extensive national regulation. Different mechanisms are used to set and control prices, including direct price controls, profit caps, negotiated prices, agreed reimbursement rates, and reference pricing, (i.e., when prices are set by reference to prices in other Member States), and internal reference pricing where the price would be based on groupings of supposedly similar products in that Member State. Large disparities in the prices of medicinal products in the Member States are

imposed on it is inadequate. It may be observed, for example, that, in order to avoid parallel exports, an undertaking may have an interest in not marketing its products in a Member State at a price which it considers to be insufficient.").

[236] *Syfait*, above, para. 67.

[237] See Case T-198/98, *Micro Leader Business v Commission* [1999] ECR II-3989.

[238] *Syfait*, above, para. 70.

[239] See, e.g., *Tipp-Ex*, OJ 1987 L 222/1 (evidence and implementation of threats); *John Deere,* OJ 1985 L 35/38 (evidence of threats); *Sperry New Holland*, OJ 1985 L 376/21 (reduction and termination of supplies); *Konica,* OJ 1988 L 78/34 (evidence of threats); and *Johnson and Johnson*, OJ 1980 L 377/16 (evidence of threats).

[240] See OECD Report on *Competition and Regulation Issues in the Pharmaceutical Sector* (2000).

engendered by the differences existing between the State mechanisms for fixing prices and the rules for reimbursement.[241]

Second, even where pharmaceutical manufacturers retain some residual discretion in setting launch prices, differences in national wealth and health budgets between Member States may require manufacturers to engage in price discrimination.[242] As a result, price differentials for the same product between Member States may be high in many cases.[243] Price discrimination is generally efficient when it leads to higher output than would occur if the seller charged a uniform price to all buyers.[244] Efficiencies result primarily from the fact that buyers willing to pay less than the uniform price would still receive the product, whereas, in the case of a uniform price, they would not.

Finally, pharmaceutical wholesalers must hold an adequate range of products to meet the requirements of a specific area. They must also be able to deliver requested supplies within a short time.[245] Member States may specify certain minimum obligations in this connection on holders of distribution licences. This creates certain obligations on manufacturers to supply wholesalers with minimum stocks of medicines for the domestic market.

The above factors create an environment that offers scope for profitable arbitrage between Member States. Large disparities in price caused by national price legislation and price discrimination are relied upon wholesaler arbitragers who export pharmaceutical products from lower-price countries to higher price countries, leading to a considerable growth in parallel trade in pharmaceutical products.[246] The impact of parallel trade on consumer welfare varies between the short and long term. In the short term, there is some net gain to consumers in the form of lower prices from increased intra-brand and inter-brand competition. For this reason, a number of Member States stipulate the use of a certain minimum percentage of parallel trade products by prescribing doctors where available. Because of reimbursement schemes for most medicines, however, the parallel trader has little incentive to pass the full benefit of the

---

[241] See Opinion of Advocate General Jacobs in Case C-53/03, *Synetairismos Farmakopoion Aitolias & Akarnanias (Syfait) and Others v GlaxoSmithKline plc and GlaxoSmithKline AEVE* [2005] ECR I-4609, paras. 77–79.

[242] Economic conditions between the former 15 EC Member States and recently-acceded Member States vary significantly. The acceding countries account for approximately 8.5% of the GDP generated by the EU 15, with a GDP per capita ranging between 69% (Slovenia) and 42% (Estonia) of the EU-15 average. See *Eurostat Yearbook 2002* (Chs. 3 and 6); and the Commission's Strategy Paper, *Towards the Enlarged Union*, COM (2002) 700 (final).

[243] See A Towse, "What are the Short and Long Run Implications for the UK of Parallel Trade in Pharmaceuticals?," Working Paper, 1997, London, Office of Health Economics, pp. 1–20.

[244] See Ch. 11 (Abusive Discrimination) for a review of the economics of price discrimination.

[245] See Council Directive 2001/83 on the Community code relating to medicinal products for human use, OJ 2001 L 311/67 (as amended by Directive 2004/27 of the European Parliament and of the Council, OJ 2004 L 136/34), Article 1(18).

[246] By 2004, before any possible impact from EU accession, parallel imports accounted for 5% or more of total EU sales of pharmaceuticals (20% in the UK) and, for some products, parallel trade represented more than half of sales in major markets. See P Kanavos, J Costa-i-Font, S Merkur, and M Gemmill, "The Economic Impact of Pharmaceutical Parallel Trade in European Union Member States: A Stakeholder Analysis," Special Research Paper (2004), *London School of Economics Health & Social Care*.

lower-priced product onto the final consumer. The most likely outcome therefore is that parallel traders, not consumers, benefit most from parallel trade.[247]

In the long term, pharmaceutical manufacturers argue that consumers suffer a significant net loss through parallel trade.[248] They say that parallel trade from low-priced to high-priced countries forces average prices down towards marginal cost and that pricing at or near marginal cost in a handful of countries can suffice to make average prices worldwide inadequate to cover the fixed cost of research and development. In the long run, a manufacturer faced with such a scenario might decide to reduce certain research and development on future products. This is exacerbated by the existence of national price controls, since one effect of parallel trade is to export the price regulation of the low-priced country to the high-priced country, which, again, may confiscate research and development expenditure from the manufacturer.[249]

Decisions at national and EU level have sought to grapple with these competing considerations, with mixed results.[250] The issue has now been partly determined in *SYFAIT*, which concerned the reduction by a pharmaceutical manufacturer operating in Greece of quantities supplied for parallel trade by Greek wholesalers. The Advocate General was sympathetic to the view that the pharmaceutical industry's specific characteristics justified the refusal by a dominant manufacturer to supply products for parallel trade.[251] Among the factors mentioned by the Advocate General were:[252] (1) that parallel trade is mainly the result of disparities in national price regulation; (2) that consumers may not always benefit from parallel trade; and (3) the need for manufacturers to recover their high fixed costs for research and development. These special features offered were considered by the Advocate General to constitute objective justification for a refusal to deal with parallel traders but he considered it "highly unlikely" that the same features would be present in any other industry.[253]

It is not clear, however, why the considerations relied upon by the Advocate General render the pharmaceutical industry unique in comparison to other industries. The first reason—the existence of national price regulation—has generally been found to be

---

[247] In 1998, the Commission stated that "parallel trade creates inefficiencies because most, if not all, of the financial benefit accrues to the parallel trader rather than to the health care system or patient." See Commission Communication on the *Single Market in Pharmaceuticals*, COM (1998) 588.

[248] See, e.g., PM Danzon & A Towse, "Differential Pricing for Pharmaceuticals: Reconciling Access, R&D and Patents," *AEI-Brookings Joint Centre Working Paper No. 03–7* (July 2003), pp. 13–14.

[249] See JS Venit and P Rey, "Parallel Trade and Pharmaceuticals: A Policy in Search of Itself" (2004) *European Law Review* 153.

[250] For a detailed review of national decisions and judgments on refusal to deal and parallel trade in pharmaceuticals, see European Federation of Pharmaceutical Industries and Associations (EFPIA), *Article 82 EC: Can It Be Applied To Control Sales By Pharmaceutical Manufacturers To Wholesalers?*, Research Paper, November 2004.

[251] See Opinion of Advocate General Jacobs in Case C-53/03, *Synetairismos Farmakopoion Aitolias & Akarnanias (Syfait) and Others v GlaxoSmithKline plc and GlaxoSmithKline AEVE* [2005] ECR I-4609, paras. 77–99.

[252] *Ibid.*

[253] *Ibid.*, para. 102.

irrelevant by the Community Courts.[254] A number of other government measures may have a similar determinative influence on the scope for arbitrage. For example, the majority of the cost to consumers for motor fuel and motor vehicles is comprised of government taxes, none of which are standardised. Variations in these taxes may have a decisive influence on whether arbitrage is possible.

The second reason—that consumers in the importing State do not necessarily receive the benefit of the lower price—also seems inconclusive. A violation of Article 82 EC cannot depend on estimates of how much money the dominant firm would lose if it had to supply a given extra quantity, or even by comparing that amount with the benefit to consumers in the importing Member State. The concept of an abuse is objective: it does not depend on an assessment of whether a particular seller would make more or less money in its unilateral decisions to sell to third parties. Furthermore, it would be unsatisfactory if intervention under competition law depended on whether conduct would increase consumer welfare more than it reduces the seller's profits. Such a rule could not easily be applied by the dominant firm at the time it formulates its supply decisions, since much of the information that affects the net benefit to consumers will depend on supervening events (e.g., government decisions on prices and reimbursement rates, exchange rates etc.).

Finally, the cost structure of the pharmaceutical industry is far from unique in comparison to other industries that involve large, risky capital costs (e.g., telecommunications). In other words, while the Advocate General's conclusion in respect of the pharmaceutical industry was clearly correct, his opinion should not preclude *a priori* a similar analysis in other industries that have some or all of the features relied upon by the Advocate General.

Problems with administering a duty to deal in the case of all parallel trade. One factor not mentioned by the Advocate General, but which arguably justifies treating virtually all straightforward refusals to deal in the context of parallel trade as lawful, concerns the difficulties of administering a rule that treats a unilateral refusal to deal as unlawful in certain circumstances.[255] Any principle of law which says that it would be abusive for a dominant firm to refuse to supply customers with additional quantities, or to reduce existing quantities supplied, on the basis that the customer intended to export them would raise significant implementation difficulties and produce surprising results. The effect may be that the legality of the same act would depend on whether the customer intended to export or not. A rule of law based on such a statement of intention would likely be precarious. All customers could declare an intention to export, regardless of their true intention, so as to have a claim to all quantities ordered. The fulfilment of their declaration could not be guaranteed. Customers who failed to express such an intention would open themselves to the possibility of not receiving all

[254] See, e.g., Joined Cases C-267/95 and C-268/95, *Merck & Co Inc, and others v Primecrown Ltd, and others* [1996] ECR I-6285, para. 47. See also Joined Cases C-427/93, C-429/93 and C-436/93, *Bristol Myers Squibb v Paranova A/S and others* [1996] ECR I-3457, para. 46; and Case 16/74, *Centrafarm BV et Adriaan de Peijper v Winthrop BV* [1974] ECR 1183, paras. 15–17.

[255] R Subiotto and R O'Donoghue, "Defining the Scope of the Duty of Dominant Firms to Deal with Existing Customers under Article 82 EC" (2003) 12 *European Competition Law Review* 683, 692.

the quantities ordered. In short, it is questionable whether such a rule would be compatible with principles of legal certainty.

Chapter 9

TYING AND BUNDLING

9.1. INTRODUCTION

Overview. Tying and bundling are ubiquitous business practices. Shoes are sold in pairs; hotels sometimes offer breakfast, lunch, or dinner bundled with the room; there is no such a thing as an unbundled car; no self-respecting French restaurant would allow its patrons to drink a bottle of wine not coming from its own cellar; McDonalds is known for its Happy Meals and leading football clubs for their season tickets; book stores increasingly offer three books for the price of two, etc.

Tying and bundling typically involve both costs and benefits from an efficiency standpoint. They may result in lower production costs, reduce transaction and information costs for consumers, and provide consumers with increased convenience and variety. The pervasiveness of tying and bundling in the economy shows that they are generally beneficial: they could not survive in competitive markets if they were not. Of course, these practices may also cause consumer harm. This could happen when the firm making use of them enjoys monopoly power and causes the exclusion of competitors. But it could not happen when the tying/bundling firm lacks significant market power.

Definitional issues. Tying and bundling generally refer to the combined sale of more than one product. Various types of tying and bundling can be distinguished, depending on how many components of a bundle/tie are also sold individually. We focus here on three variants: pure bundling, tying, and mixed bundling:

1. *Pure bundling* is observed when none of the package components are offered individually; each of them can only be acquired as part of the bundle. That is, given two products, A and B, only the package A-B is available. Moreover, they are offered in fixed proportions: e.g., a bottle of shampoo with a bottle of hair conditioner. Examples of pure bundling are fixed price lunch menus, bed with breakfast accommodation, and mandatory warranties. In *Napier Brown-British Sugar*,[1] for instance, the Commission condemned British Sugar's practice of denying its customers the possibility to collect their orders directly from the factory and forcing them instead to use the producer's delivery service.

2. *Tying* refers to situations where some of the goods contained in a package are offered on their own (the so-called tied products), whereas others are not available individually (the tying products). Thus, consumers of the latter (the tying products) are forced to acquire the former (the tied products). For example, given two products, A and B, if product A is tied to product B a

---

[1] *Napier Brown/British Sugar*, OJ 1988 L 284/41.

customer who wants to buy A must also buy B, whereas it is possible to buy product B without buying product A. In *Microsoft*, the Commission accused the software company of attempting to monopolise the market for media players by requiring OEMs to ship their PCs with Windows Media Player pre-installed.[2]

3. *Mixed bundling* describes the practice of selling each product as part of a package, as well as individually. Furthermore, to be interesting for consumers, the bundle price must be lower than the sum of individual prices.[3] For two products, A and B, mixed bundling means that both A and B are sold individually as well as in a bundle A-B. Examples of mixed bundling include season tickets, round-trip airline tickets, and value meals at McDonald's. In the case of airline tickets, customers can buy two single tickets separately at a price that is normally higher than the round-trip ticket. The same applies to Happy Meals at McDonalds. Buying each part of one of the meals on offer separately is more costly than buying the entire meal as a package. Firms often offer multi-product rebates, i.e., percentage discounts on every purchase of each of their products. The effects of these bundled rebates are similar to those of mixed bundling: customers can purchase the products concerned individually, each from a different supplier, or as a package from a single supplier. The second alternative involves a discount.[4]

Two or more products can either be tied together physically (i.e., a technological tie) or through contractual obligations that prescribe joint sale (i.e., a contractual tie). The authorities in both the EU and the US draw a distinction between contractual and technological tying. The Commission seems to take a tougher stance towards contractual tying than technological tying. Although both types of tying may have similar anticompetitive effects, technological tying may give rise to significant efficiencies, which are likely to benefit consumers and which could not be obtained by other means.

[2] Case COMP/C-3/37.792, *Microsoft*, Commission Decision of March 24, 2004, not yet published.

[3] See B Nalebuff, "Bundling, Tying, and Portfolio Effects," *DTI Economics Paper No. 1*, Part 1 (2003).

[4] In a mixed bundling scenario, the implicit price of product A as part of the A-B bundle is cheaper that its price as a stand-alone product. That is, the customer enjoys a discount in the price of A conditional on the joint purchase of some quantity of B. This quantity tends to be fixed at a small number (often equal to one) of units. Other bundled rebate schemes may involve more pricing flexibility. For example, the implicit price of A may be a function not only of the quantity of B bought from the same provider (as in the mixed bundling case), but also of the quantity purchased from another supplier (such as, for example, when discounts are conditional on certain market share or portfolio commitments). These commercial instruments may have similar efficiency effects. For example, the OECD states that "[t]he effect of requiring the customer to purchase a bundle of products and services may be the same as requiring a market share commitment. The customer may find in either case that attempting to purchase from rival suppliers causes it to lose the savings associated with bundling or discounting and thus make the effective price of supplies from a rival supplier unacceptably high." See OECD, "Loyalty and Fidelity Discounts and Rebates," DAFFE/COMP(2002)21, (2003), p.191.

The basic legal approach to tying and bundling. Under EC competition law, tying may be regarded as a restrictive agreement under Article 81 EC,[5] or as abusive behaviour under Article 82 EC, and in particular Articles 82(b) and 82(d). In this chapter we consider when tying and bundling constitute an abuse of a dominant position. In principle, tying and bundling can produce the following anticompetitive effects: foreclosure, price discrimination, and high prices.[6] But tying and bundling can also generate significant efficiencies (e.g., lowering production, information, and transaction costs), including in situations in which they have anticompetitive effects.

The Commission has issued four negative decisions concerning tying.[7] The first three involved contractual tying. Although the Community institutions have dealt with tying and bundling in a relatively small number of cases only, the issue of tying and bundling has received considerable recent attention as a result of the Commission's *Microsoft* decision,[8] which remains pending on appeal before the Community Courts. In *Microsoft*, the Commission acknowledged that Microsoft's bundling of its media player with Windows involved a degree of technological integration.[9]

In the US, initial hostility to tying was largely directed against contractual tying, while technological integration was frequently dismissed on the basis that courts were not well placed to decide on product design decisions.[10] In *ILC Peripherals Leasing*,[11] for example, IBM's integration of magnetic discs and a head/disc assembly was held not to amount to an unlawful tying arrangement. The hostile approach towards contractual tying was revised in *Jefferson Parish*,[12] where the Supreme Court accepted that tying could have some merit, but struggled to devise a test that distinguished good tying from bad tying. Technological integration continued to be treated more favourably, however. For example, in *Microsoft*, the plaintiffs alleged that Microsoft had violated US antitrust law by contractually and technologically bundling Internet Explorer with its Windows operating system.[13] The Appeals Court rejected the *Jefferson Parish* test and concluded

[5] See, e.g., Commission Notice—Guidelines on Vertical Restraints, OJ 2000 C 291/1.

[6] See DG Competition discussion paper on the application of Article 82 of the Treaty to exclusionary abuses, Brussels, December 2005 (hereinafter, the "Discussion Paper"), para. 179.

[7] *Napier Brown/British Sugar*, OJ 1988 L 284/41; *Eurofix-Bauco/Hilti*, OJ 1988 L 65/19; *Tetra Pak II*, OJ 1992 L 72/1; and Case COMP/C-3/37.792, *Microsoft*, Commission Decision of March 24, 2004, not yet published.

[8] *Ibid.*

[9] *Ibid.*, para. 1015 ("Given the way Microsoft has structured technically, contractually and commercially its offering of the bundled operating system and media player, an effective un-tying can only take place once Microsoft has unravelled the various links that tie these two products.").

[10] See *Telex Corp v International Business Machines Corp.*, 367 F. Supp. 258, 268 (N.D. Okla. 1973), rev'd, 510 F.2d 894 (10th Cir. 1975).

[11] See *ILC Peripherals Leasing Corp v International Business Machines Corp.*, 448 F. Supp. 228, 233 (N.D. Cal. 1978).

[12] *Jefferson Parish Hospital Dist. No. 2 et al. v Hyde*, 466 US 2 (1984). A similar rule has very recently been reiterated by the Supreme Court. See *Illinois Tool Works Inc. v Independent Ink, Inc.*, R-38, Docket 04-1329, March 6, 2006 ("Many tying arrangements, even those involving patents and requirements ties, are fully consistent with a free, competitive market.").

[13] See *United States v Microsoft Corp.*, Civil Action Nos. 98-1232 and 98-1233 (TPJ), Direct Testimony of Franklin M. Fisher, January 5, 1999, at paras. 79–81.

that software platforms, such as Windows, should be subject to a rule of reason balancing anticompetitive effects and efficiencies.[14]

Structure of this chapter. This chapter is organised as follows. Section 9.2 describes the main contribution of economics to the understanding of tying and bundling practices. This section is important, since recent economic contributions help clarify when tying is problematic. Section 9.3 then describes the treatment of the main types of tying and bundling practices under Article 82 EC, including contractual tying, technological tying, mixed bundling, and the specific case of "aftermarkets." The *Microsoft* case is also discussed separately because of its obvious importance.[15] Section 9.4 is a more advanced section that discusses suggested alternative ways of looking at tying under competition law. Finally, Section 9.5 contains a short conclusion.

9.2 THE ECONOMICS OF TYING AND BUNDLING

Overview. The economics literature shows that tying and bundling often improves economic efficiency,[16] that it may be used for anticompetitive purposes,[17] and that its motivation is sometimes price discrimination with generally ambiguous implications for economic welfare.[18] Economic theory by itself only says that tying and bundling practices might have both anticompetitive and procompetitive effects. The consensus among economists is that one must conduct a detailed factual investigation before concluding that tying is harmful.[19] As one commentator notes, "while the analysis vindicates the leverage hypothesis on a positive level, its normative implications are less clear. Even in the simple models considered here, which ignore a number of other possible motivations for the [tying] practice, the impact of this exclusion on welfare is uncertain."[20]

[14] *United States v Microsoft Corp.*, 253 F.3d 34 (D.C. Cir. 2001).

[15] Case COMP/C-3/37.792, *Microsoft*, Commission Decision of March 24, 2004, not yet published.

[16] See, e.g., A Director and EH Levi, "Law and the Future: Trade Regulation" (1956) 51 *Northwestern University Law Review* 281–96; RA Posner, *Antitrust Law: An Economic Perspective* (Chicago, University of Chicago Press, 1976); RH Bork, *The Antitrust Paradox* (New York, Basic Books, 1978) pp. 378–79. See also DS Evans and M Salinger, "Quantifying the Benefits of Bundling and Tying", Working Paper (2002); and P Seabright, "Tying and Bundling: From Economics to Competition Policy," Edited Transcript of a CNE Market Insights Event, September 19, 2002.

[17] See, e.g., MD Whinston, "Tying, Foreclosure and Exclusion" (1990) 80 *American Economic Review* 837; and DW Carlton and M Waldman, "The Strategic Use of Tying to Preserve and Create Market Power in Evolving Industries" (2002) 33 *RAND Journal of Economics* 194.

[18] See DW Carlton and JM Perloff, *Modern Industrial Organisation* (3rd edn., Boston, Addison Wesley Longman, 2000) pp. 289–91.

[19] See DW Carlton and M Waldman, "The Strategic Use of Tying to Preserve and Create Market Power in Evolving Industries" (2002) 33 *RAND Journal of Economics* 194; and KN Hylton and M Salinger, "Tying Law and Policy: A Decision-Theoretic Approach" (2001) 69 *Antitrust Law Journal* 469, at 470–71.

[20] See, e.g., MD Whinston, "Tying, Foreclosure and Exclusion" (1990) 80 *American Economic Review* 837.

9.2.1. Efficiency Motivations

Overview. Tying and bundling can lower production and distribution costs and provide convenience. These practices may, among other things: (1) create economies of scale and scope in production and distribution;[21] (2) reduce the costs of searching for the most appropriate combination of products that satisfy a complex need;[22] (3) give rise to new or improved products and services;[23] (4) help manufacturers ensure quality;[24] and (5) avoid double marginalisation problems.[25]

Economies of scale in production and distribution. Tying may give rise to both economies of scale and scope in production and distribution. For example, machines may be utilised to manufacture two or more products allowing the producer to reduce the size or complexity of its factories. Marketing and distribution costs may also be reduced when various products or services are combined. In media markets, for example, economies of scope between delivery infrastructures and content allow cable operators and ADSL providers to bundle Internet access, pay TV, and telephony in what is known as a "triple play."

Some authors deny that tying could give rise to savings in production costs.[26] They argue that there is no reason *a priori* why products that are jointly produced should necessarily be sold together. This is true, but misses the fact that there may be significant diseconomies of scope in producing multiple separate products. Multiple offerings can increase the fixed and variable costs of production in several ways.[27] Evans (2005) refers to studies of automobile manufacturers showing that increasing the number of options available to customers increases what are called "complexity costs."[28] Evans and Salinger (2004) have documented how the cost of producing an additional pill that contains both headache and pain reliever medicine is lower than to produce two.[29]

---

[21] See, e.g., SJ Davis, KM Murphy and J MacCrisken, "Economic Perspectives on Software Design: PC Operating Systems and Platforms" in DS Evans (ed.), *Microsoft, Antitrust and the New Economy* (Massachusetts, Kluwer Academic Press, 2002) p. 361.

[22] See DS Evans, AJ Padilla and M Polo, "Tying in Platform Software: Reasons for a Rule of Reason Standard in European Competition Law" (2002) 2 *World Competition* 509.

[23] See, e.g., A Petrin, "Quantifying the Benefits of New Products: The Case of the Minivan" (2002) 110 *Journal of Political Economy* 705–29.

[24] See RA Posner, *Antitrust Law: An Economic Perspective* (Chicago, University of Chicago Press, 1976).

[25] See A Cournot, *Recherches sur les Principes Mathématiques de la Théorie des Richesses* (Paris, Hachette, 1838); and J Tirole, *The Theory of Industrial Organisation* (Cambridge, MIT Press, 1988) pp. 333–35.

[26] K-U Kühn, R Stillman and C Caffarra, "Economic Theories of Bundling and their Policy Implication in Abuse Cases: An Assessment in Light of the Microsoft Case," CEPR Discussion Paper No. 4756, (2005).

[27] JG Sidak, "An Antitrust Rule for Software Integration" (2001) 18(1) *Yale Journal on Regulation* 29–30.

[28] DS Evans, "Tying: the Poster Child for Antitrust Modernisation", Working Paper November 2005.

[29] DS Evans and M Salinger, "The Role of Cost in Determining When Offer Bundles and Ties," Working Paper, May 2004.

Reduction in search costs. Tying reduces the costs of searching for the most appropriate combinations of products that satisfy a complex need, and it greatly simplifies use. At one time, software technologies such as toolbars, modem support, power management, and sound were all formally offered as stand-alone products. Today, they are universally offered as an integrated, "bundled" part of the operating system. The widespread use of bundled software is itself a function of better technology—faster speed and expanded memory. But, perhaps most importantly, it is a response to consumers who value the ease of use of bundled software.[30]

Product improvement. When products are tied or bundled, the whole may be worth more than the sum of its parts; the resulting combined product offers benefits to consumers above and beyond the individual components added together. To take a simple example, today consumers enjoy breakfast cereals featuring a dizzying array of combinations of ingredients (fruits, nuts, grains), shapes (flakes, squares, doughnuts), textures, and tastes.

Quality assurance. Because firms bring skill, knowledge, experience, and other resources to tying or product integration, allowing consumers to assemble the individual components themselves may affect the quality of the final product, to the detriment of both producers and consumers. For example, in earlier decades of the electronics industry, hobbyists and other interested consumers could find the component parts of radios and other simple electronic equipment, and with some effort, assemble them by themselves. However, with the increasing sophistication—miniaturisation, digitisation, and other complexities of electronics equipment—it is nowadays more difficult to ensure that the final product will meet with consumer satisfaction. When the consumer assembles the product, it may not be clear if any malfunctions are the fault of the consumer or the component suppliers. Equipment manufacturers may suffer from an undeserved reputation for poor quality, and it may be more difficult for consumers to identify substandard manufacturers. Bundling components together gives both the consumer and the producer more certainty regarding product quality.

Avoidance of "double marginalisation." Augustin Cournot showed in work published in 1838 that a firm monopolising the markets for two complementary products A and B would charge lower prices than two separate monopolists, each selling a different product would do.[31] This is because the integrated monopolist takes into account the positive effect on the demand of product B of a reduction in the price of product A, and *vice versa*. This positive externality is instead disregarded by each of the two single-product monopolists. This is similar to the well-known "double marginalisation" problem in the analysis of vertical integration, where a monopoly provider of two goods at different levels of supply will maximise its profits across the two goods, while separate providers will price each good at the individual profit-maximising price.[32]

[30] See DS Evans, AJ Padilla and M Polo, "Tying in Platform Software: Reasons for a Rule of Reason Standard in European Competition Law" (2002) 2 *World Competition* 509.

[31] A Cournot, *Recherches sur les Principes Mathématiques de la Théorie des Richesses* (Paris, Hachette, 1838).

[32] J Tirole, *The Theory of Industrial Organisation* (Cambridge, MIT Press, 1988) pp. 333–35.

The same logic implies that complements may be priced lower if offered by the same firm in a bundle. Kuhn, Stillman, and Caffarra (2004) have argued that this effect has nothing to do with bundling: when a monopolist sells complementary goods, it sets lower prices for them than independent producers do because it internalises the positive pricing externality between the complements, and not because of bundling.[33] This is only partly correct, however. As shown by Whinston (1990),[34] a firm selling A and B together is likely to charge lower prices than a firm selling the two products separately. When a monopolist in market A ties A with B, it is effectively linking its sales of product A to the sale of product B. Any reduction in the volume of B caused by a high price for B would also cause a reduction in the sales of product A. As a result, its incentive to price B aggressively would be greatly increased.[35]

While it is often recognised that these efficiencies effects are likely to explain why tying and bundling are so widely observed in practice, their importance tends to be neglected or obscured in antitrust cases. For example, its is often argued that while there are no doubt advantages to tying for consumers who want all components of the tie, there is no reason why those components could not be sold separately as well for those who do not. Such an argument misses a fundamental point about the basic economics of tying and bundling: the savings that result from the joint manufacturing and joint distribution of products and services. In the absence of economies of scale and scope, competition would result in firms offering products that meet each customer's ideal specifications. When scale and scope economies are present, however, the production and distribution of a number of distinct product offerings becomes disproportionately costly. In those circumstances, tying or pure bundling can arise in competitive markets even though some customers feel forced to accept components they do not want.[36]

9.2.2 Possible Anticompetitive Motivations

Overview. A few decades ago, economists associated with the "Chicago school"[37] showed that, as a matter of theory, there are many circumstances in which businesses cannot use tying to leverage a monopoly position in one market in order to secure extra profits elsewhere—a result known as "the single monopoly profit theorem."[38] In the 1990s, however, the so-called post-Chicago economic literature showed that the "single profit monopoly theorem" is not as robust as the Chicagoans suggested. The theorem depends, at least in its most extreme form, on the assumption that the tied market is "perfectly" competitive. When this fails to hold, the theorem *may* fail.

[33] K-U Kühn, R Stillman and C Caffarra, "Economic Theories of Bundling and their Policy Implication in Abuse Cases: An Assessment in Light of the Microsoft Case" CEPR Discussion Paper No. 4756, (2005).

[34] MD Whinston, "Tying, Foreclosure and Exclusion" (1990) 80 *American Economic Review* 837.

[35] Bundling and tying may, however, result in greater prices if they become a way for competing firms to differentiate their products and thus relax price competition. See J Carbajo, D De Meza and D Seidman, "A Strategic Motivation for Commodity Bundling" (1990) 38 *Journal of Industrial Economics* 283–98.

[36] DS Evans and M Salinger, "The Role of Cost in Determining When Offer Bundles and Ties," Working Paper, May 2004.

[37] See generally Ch. 4 (The General Concept of an Abuse), Section 4.2, above.

[38] This section borrows extensively from C Ahlborn, DS Evans and AJ Padilla, "The Antitrust Economics of Tying: A Farewell to *Per Se* Illegality" Spring 2004, *Antitrust Bulletin*.

Economists have developed a series of highly stylised models to try to understand the competitive implications of tying and bundling when the structure of the tied market is oligopolistic, rather than perfectly competitive. They showed that a firm enjoying monopoly power in the tying good might have an anticompetitive incentive to tie when the tied good market is imperfectly competitive if, *in addition*, tying keeps potential rivals out of the market for the tied product or, alternatively, helps the monopolist to preserve its market power in the tying product. The basic mechanism that leads to the exclusion of actual and potential competitors from the tied good is "foreclosure;" by tying, the monopolist deprives its competitors in the tied good market of adequate scale, thereby lowering their profits below the level that would justify remaining active in (or, alternatively, entering) that market.

Single monopoly theorem. A central insight of the Chicago school is that a firm enjoying monopoly power in one market (the market for the tying good) could not increase its profits, and instead might reduce them, by monopolising the market for another good (the market for the tied good). This notion is commonly referred as the "single monopoly profit theorem." This theorem does not say that monopolists will not engage in tying and bundling. Nor does it say that monopolists cannot make greater profit by tying and bundling. Rather, what is says is that monopolists cannot secure greater profit merely by leveraging their monopoly from one market to another and that they must be engaging in tying and bundling to improve quality or lower cost.

The intuition behind this result is simple. Consider first the case where the demands for the two goods are independent, so that the quantity demanded by consumers of one of the goods is independent of the price of the other. Assume that there is unit demand for both goods, A and B, and that they are produced at constant marginal and average costs c_A and c_B, respectively. The monopolist in A may offer a bundle containing A and B at a price p_{AB}. Absent bundling the monopolist would charge the full valuation v_A (assumed to be common to all consumers) for product A, so that the implied price for B as part of the bundle is given by $p_{AB} - v_A$. Let us denote the implied price by q_B. For the bundle to sell at all, q_B needs to be set at or below c_B, the competitive price in the market for B. The reason is that consumers derive zero net utility from A, as the price equals their valuation, so that the only way the bundle could increase their net utility is by giving them access to good B more cheaply than an purchasing B individually would. Setting $q_B = c_B$ would not increase the monopolist's profit, whereas setting $q_B < c_B$ would actually decrease it. There is thus no incentive for the monopolist to bundle.

If the demands for the two goods were, instead, complementary and the two products consumed with fixed ratios,[39] a monopolist could only benefit from the tied good being competitively supplied, since all of the monopoly rents available in the two markets

[39] The single-monopoly profit theorem fails to hold when the two goods are consumed in variable proportions. Trying to extract the rents generated in the tied market through the pricing of the monopoly product is not a valid strategy in that case, since consumers would substitute away from the monopoly product. However, that does not imply that tying is necessarily anticompetitive when goods are consumed in variable proportions. On the contrary, it is precisely under such kind of consumer preferences that the monopolist has an interest in tying to price discriminate efficiently. See DW Carlton and JM Perloff, *Modern Industrial Organisation* (3rd edn., Boston, Addison Wesley Longman, 2000).

could be captured by a monopoly in one of them.[40] Richard Posner illustrated this result with a simple example: let a purchaser of data processing be willing to pay up to $1 per unit of computation, requiring the use of one second of machine time and ten punch cards, each of which costs 1 cent to produce. The computer monopolist can rent the computer for 90 cents a second and allow the user to buy cards in the open market for one cent a card or, if tying is permitted, he can require the user to buy cards from him at 10 cents a card—but in that case he must reduce his machine rental charge to nothing, so what has he gained?[41] Most strikingly, perhaps, under those same circumstances, if the monopolist faced competition from a more efficient firm in the tied market, it could do no better than abandoning the market for the tied good while, at the same time, raising the price of the monopoly good.

Implications for tying and foreclosure. The key condition for the "single monopoly profit theorem" to hold is that the tied product is supplied competitively. To the extent that tying can be a profitable strategy for a tying-good monopolist, it derives its value from its potential to alter the structure of the market for the tied good. If the latter is perfectly competitive, affecting the market structure is not feasible. If, on the other hand, the market for the tied product is oligopolistic as a result of, e.g., economies of scale, tying can be a means to 'foreclose' sales in the tied-good market, which may render the rival's operations unprofitable.

Whinston's (1990) seminal article formally analyses the conditions under which the "single-monopoly-profit theorem" fails to hold.[42] This paper shows that leveraging a monopoly position in the tying market onto an adjacent (tied) market may be profitable when the tied market is subject to economies of scale and therefore imperfectly competitive. Leveraging successfully induces the exit (or deters the entry) of competitors in the tied market.

Suppose, for example, that a firm selling two goods, A and B, enjoys a monopoly position in the market for product A but faces competition (actual or potential) in the market for product B. Suppose also that the demands for products A and B are independent, so that the quantity sold of each of them is independent of the price of the other. Given the monopoly rent it earns on A, the firm wants to ensure that it all consumers purchase that product, be it alone or as part of a bundle. By tying the two products, it has to make sales of good B in order to make sales of A. As a result, its incentive to price B aggressively would be greatly increased, taking sales away from its rival.[43] This is achieved by sacrificing part of the monopoly rent in A to make the prices for product B lower through cross-subsidisation. Both the monopolist's and its competitors' profits from the sale of product B would fall, but the impact on the latter would be far greater. The monopolist's capture of sales from its rivals makes the latter less effective competitors, especially in the presence of economies of scale in production. The reduction in (gross) profits may induce the monopolist's competitors to

[40] RH Bork, *The Antitrust Paradox* (New York, Basic Books, 1978) p. 378–79.

[41] RA Posner, *Antitrust Law: An Economic Perspective* (Chicago, University of Chicago Press, 1976).

[42] MD Whinston, "Tying, Foreclosure and Exclusion" (1990) 80 *American Economic Review* 837.

[43] This is referred to by Whinston as "strategic foreclosure" and can occur even when the rival is more efficient, i.e., has lower marginal cost of production, in product B. *Ibid*., p. 844.

exit the market for product B, or not to enter into it if they were potential competitors, especially when the (fixed) set-up cost for the latter are substantial. In such cases, tying could both increase the monopolist's profits and harm consumers, but it does not have to. The welfare effects are unclear both for consumers and, even more so, in terms of aggregate efficiency.[44]

Like any other game-theoretic analysis, Whinston's model is fragile; minor changes in assumptions can lead to dramatic differences in results. Most importantly, Whinston's leveraging result requires that: (1) the monopolist of product A be able to commit to tying;[45] and (2) tying leads to market foreclosure. Otherwise, the monopolist's strategy would be self-defeating. Tying would just serve to increase the intensity of price competition in the market. The leveraging result also depends on the interrelationship between the demands for the two goods. Monopolising the tied market might lead to lower sales and lower prices in the monopoly market when the two goods are perfect complements and tying causes the exit (or prevents the entry) of more efficient producers of good B.[46] In that case, the incentives to tie would be reduced.

Tying and entry deterrence. In the wake of Whinston's contribution, various authors have developed models aimed at relaxing the conditions under which tying may be anticompetitive. Nalebuff, for example, constructs a model where a firm producing goods A and B has a credible incentive to tie them together in order to deter entry.[47] In contrast to Whinston's model, tying makes entry more difficult not because the monopolist is committed to a price war, but because it deprives the entrant of adequate scale. Credibility is not an issue here because even when entry is not foreclosed, the price for good B and the monopolist's profits are higher with a tie than without. The intuition is as follows. In Nalebuff's model, tying becomes a way for the competing firms to differentiate their products and thus relax price competition. The monopolist sells both A and B tied together, whereas the entrant sells only product B. The monopolist attracts those customers with a high valuation for both A and B and charges them a high price, while the entrant sells to those consumers of good B who have a low valuation for good A and charges them a low price. Essentially, the monopolistic good provides a shield against (potential or existing) competitors on the other market. The value of this "protection from competition" increases with the degree of complementarity between the goods.[48]

A similar outcome is obtained in a model developed by Chen,[49] although he considers a situation in which the market for tying good A is duopolistic and that for the tied good B is perfectly competitive. Pure bundling emerges as an equilibrium strategy for one of

[44] MD Whinston, "Tying, Foreclosure and Exclusion" (1990) 80 *American Economic Review* 837.

[45] Once the monopoly position in market B has been established, the firm would actually prefer to unbundle the goods, instead of continuing to cross-subsidise.

[46] Or, in the context of product differentiation, of higher quality versions of product B.

[47] B Nalebuff, "Bundling as an Entry Barrier" (2004) 119 *Quarterly Journal of Economics* 159. See also B Nalebuff, "Bundling," *Yale ICF Working Paper n. 99–14* (1999).

[48] If, in contrast, valuations of goods are negatively correlated, it is more likely that bundling is used as a price-discrimination surrogate than in a bid to leverage market power. Moreover, observing a single price in a market may indicate that explicit price discrimination is prohibited in that market. Bundling with this purpose could then become a particularly valuable strategy.

[49] Y Chen, "Equilibrium Product Bundling" (1997) 70 *Journal of Business* 85.

the duopolists, whereas the other confines itself to offering A only. This once again enables firms to differentiate their products and to reduce competition. It should be noted, however, that if there is an antitrust concern when bundling is used as a method of product differentiation in the tying market, it is one of (tacit) coordination, and not of exclusionary behaviour.[50]

In contrast to Chen's model, in which bundling is used to divide up an oligopolistic market through product differentiation, Carlton and Waldman argue that leveraging a monopoly position onto another market through tying may not be as much about increasing profits in that market as it is about deterring future entry into the monopoly (tying) market.[51] In that sense, their contribution also differs from the models by Whinston and Nalebuff, respectively, where the focus is on strengthening the position in the tied market. In the Carlton-Waldman model, there are two goods: the primary good (the tying good or monopoly product) and a complementary good (the tied good). The primary good can be used by itself. The complementary good can be used only in conjunction with the primary good.[52] Their theory is built on the assumption that potential competitors may refrain from entering the monopoly market if they face the incumbent as their sole complementary good producer. The monopolist, therefore, has an incentive to monopolise the tied good in order to protect its rents. Entry into the tying market obviously would dissipate some of the rents made in that market. But it would also make it impossible to extract rents from the market for the complementary good, as the incumbent would find it costly to raise its price in the tying market because of the competition from the newly established entrant.

The incentives of the incumbent to monopolise the complementary good market may exist even when entry is costless provided there are network externalities in that market, i.e., consumers' valuations for the complementary good were an increasing function of the number of other users. Carlton and Waldman show that tying the complementary good to the monopoly product gives the monopolist a head start in the race to become the standard in the market for the complementary good. This incentive exists because the incumbent sees its monopoly position in the primary good market subject to the threat of entry. Otherwise, it would prefer to have competition in the complementary good market, so as to ensure the adoption of the best standard and to appropriate the rents generated by that standard via a higher price in the primary product market.

Notwithstanding its conceptual simplicity, the validity of the theory developed by Carlton and Waldman relies on a number of strong assumptions that do not always fit well with the facts of the markets under scrutiny. First, Carlton and Waldman's theory requires that entry into the tied market be very costly. Otherwise, the strategy of foreclosure could be defeated by the simultaneous entry into the two complementary markets. Second, their theory does not fare well when the product sold in the monopoly market has a life of its own, i.e., when some consumers have a demand for the

[50] See B Nalebuff, "Bundling, Tying, and Portfolio Effects" *DTI Economics Paper No. 1*, Part 1 (2003) p. 46.

[51] DW Carlton and M Waldman, "The Strategic Use of Tying to Preserve and Create Market Power in Evolving Industries" (2002) 33 *RAND Journal of Economics* 194.

[52] The authors cite as an example a computer (primary good) and a printer (complementary good).

monopoly good only. In this case, the profitability of entry in the monopoly market is much less affected by the monopolisation of its complementary market.

Tying and the incentives to innovate. A variant of the previous effect has been suggested by Choi and Stefanidis.[53] They note that entry into both the tying and the tied market may be risky, e.g., where this requires an investment in R&D projects with uncertain outcomes. Competing against a bundle may require that a competitor enters both markets. That is, entry in one market is profitable only if the rival also manages to enter into the other market. However, the joint probability of being successful on both fronts is smaller than that of being able to enter a single market only. The expected return from R&D investments is lower as a consequence, which in turn impacts negatively on the willingness to exert such efforts in the first place.

Price discrimination. Tying and bundling can also serve as surrogates for price discrimination, especially in situations where price discrimination is prohibited explicitly. Most of the earlier economic literature on tying and bundling focused on price discrimination as the main motivation for such strategies.[54]

Economists have shown that a multi-product monopolist maximises its profits by offering a pure bundle when consumers' valuations for the component goods are not perfectly correlated. That is, a monopolist producing A and B will maximise profits by selling the bundle A-B only, if its customers do not have the same valuations for A and B (i.e., their valuations are not perfectly and positively correlated).[55] Economists have also shown that this may increase consumer welfare. However, this last result is not robust.[56] This is because bundling and tying may force some consumers to purchase more than they wish to consume, and this can create distortions in resource allocation.

---

[53] JP Choi and C Stefanidis, "Tying, Investment, and the Dynamic Leverage Theory" (2001) 32 *RAND Journal of Economics* 52. See also JP Choi, "Antitrust Analysis of Tying Arrangements," *CESifo Working Paper No. 1336* (2004), pp. 11–20.

[54] See, e.g., LM Burnstein, "The Economics of Tie-in Sales" (1960) 42(1) *Review of Economic Studies* 68–73; GJ Stigler, *The Organisation of Industry* (Homewood, Richard D Irwin, Inc., 1968); RA Posner, *Antitrust Law: An Economic Perspective* (Chicago, University of Chicago Press, 1976); WJ Adams and WL Yellen, "Commodity Bundling and the Burden of Monopoly" (1976) 90(3) *The Quarterly Journal of Economics* 475–98; R Schmalensee, "Commodity Bundling by Single-product Monopolies" (1982) 25(2) *Journal of Law and Economics* 183–99; R Schmalensee, "Gaussian Demand on Commodity Bundling" (1984) 57 *Journal of Business* 211–30; and J Sidak, "An Antitrust Rule for Software Integration" (2001) 18(1) *Yale Journal on Regulation* 1–83.

[55] See RP McAfee, J McMillan and MD Whinston, "Multiproduct Monopoly, Commodity Bundling, and Correlation of Values" (1989) 114 *Quarterly Journal of Economics* 371–83.

[56] Salinger (1995) points out that the net effect of bundling can be positive or negative depending on the precise distribution of reservation values, while Bakos and Brynjolfsson (1996), using a model with bundling of many goods, show that the effects of bundling on social welfare depend crucially on marginal costs. In particular, when marginal costs are zero and consumers have non-negative valuations, bundling increases efficiency when it increases the fraction of consumers purchasing the bundle. This is due to the fact that each purchase creates some benefits at no additional costs, thus, the increase in the total volume of sales by the multi-product monopolist reduces the deadweight loss associated with a single price monopoly strategy. However, if there are positive marginal costs associated with the provision of each good, even if there is increase in the fraction of consumers served, bundling can be socially inefficient. See MA Salinger, "A Graphical Analysis of Bundling" (1995) 68

The intuition behind this result is clearer when the valuations for A and B are negatively correlated. Suppose there are 100 potential consumers of these two products. Suppose further that 50 customers are willing to pay €100 for product A and €20 for product B, whereas the other 50 are willing to pay €100 for product B and €20 for product A. If the monopolist were to sell A and B separately, its optimal pricing strategy would be to charge €100 for each of them. As a result, the first 50 consumer would purchase A but no B and the remaining 50 would purchase B but no A. In that case, the monopolist profits would equal €100 × €100 = €10,000, whereas the consumers surplus would be equal to zero. Alternatively, the monopolist could have bundled A and B together, offering a pure bundle at €119. Every consumer would find it optimal to purchase the bundle. The monopolist's profits would equal €119 × €100 = €11,900 and consumer surplus would be equal to 10.

9.2.3 Empirical Evidence

Evans and Salinger. While most of the contributions to the literature on tying and bundling stress the importance of various efficiencies associated with such practices, there is almost no empirical evidence on the sources and magnitude of these efficiencies. There is also no evidence attempting to discriminate between the various motivations that may explain tying and bundling: efficiencies, price discrimination, and anticompetitive leveraging.

A notable exception is a series of articles by Evans and Salinger,[57] which take an important step towards filling this gap in the literature. They have investigated the conditions under which a firm manufacturing products A and B would choose to offer: (1) individual components only; (2) a mixed bundle; (3) a pure bundle; (4) a bundle and component A individually; and (5) a bundle and component B individually. The following conclusions were offered:

1. *Mixed bundling* may arise in a competitive environment when bundling gives rise to moderate cost savings: there are marginal cost savings from bundling, but the marginal costs of the bundle are still higher than the marginal costs of single components. The fixed costs associated to each new product offering are not too high, so that the firm is able to offer profitably the individual components as well as the bundle. Demand is substantial for each of the three offerings.

2. *Pure bundling* may result in equilibrium if: (a) economies of scale are very large (even if no consumers strictly prefer the bundle); or (b) economies of scale are moderate, but while the demand for the bundle is high the demand for at least one of the components is low. In these cases, the firm finds it optimal

Journal of Business 85–98; Y Bakos and E Brynjolfsson, "Bundling Information Goods: Pricing, Profits and Efficiency," *Working Paper Series MIT Sloan School of Management* (1996).

[57] DS Evans and M Salinger, "Why Do Firms Bundle and Tie? Evidence from Competitive Markets and Implications for Tying Law" (2005) 22 *Yale Journal on Regulation* 37–89; DS Evans and M Salinger, "An Empirical Analysis of Bundling and Tying: Over-the-Counter Pain Relief and Cold Medicines," Prepared for CESifo Summer Institute 2004 Meeting on "Recent Trends In Antitrust," Venice, Italy, July 21–22, 2004; and DS Evans and M Salinger, "The Role of Cost in Determining When Firms Offer Bundles and Ties," Working Paper, May 2004.

> to offer only the bundle. There is no exclusionary intent; the reason for not offering some customers their desired components alone is an efficient reaction to survive in a competitive market.

Evans and Salinger support these findings with evidence from three types of products: decongestants/pain relievers, foreign electrical adaptors, and optional equipment for automobiles. The authors discuss the rationale for the tying and bundling practices observed in these markets and find strong evidence for a cost savings motive. Leveraging can be ruled out as the motivation behind these bundles, since all the markets are relatively competitive; price discrimination is a possible motive only in one case.

a. Cold medicines. The first product group studied was cold medicines. Someone with a cold would typically need a decongestant and a pain reliever. In contrast, a person with a headache needs only a pain reliever, and someone who has congestion needs only a decongestant. In practice, mixed bundling is prevalent: there are products that serve people who suffer from both a cold and a headache, as well as products that cure only one ailment. The bundle is typically offered at a discount compared to the components. Although price discrimination cannot be ruled out as a potential rationale, the authors provide several arguments why the explanation is most likely related to the existence of marginal costs savings, as well as economies of scale in the market for pain relievers/decongestants.

b. Foreign electrical adapters. Tying is a common practice in the market for foreign electrical adapters, as sold by RadioShack, a major US retailer of electrical products. The market for this product is certainly competitive, with many suppliers and low entry barriers. RadioShack offers in its retail shops the adapters for different world regions in a bundle, depriving customers from the possibility to buy single adaptors for their preferred region. However, RadioShack also sells separate adaptors for the different regions on its website. The most plausible explanation for this observed practice is to save on the fixed costs of offering additional products. Leveraging theories can be ruled out as possible explanations, since the markets are competitive.

c. Optional automobile equipment. In their third case study, Evans and Salinger track the optional equipment available for three mid-size sedan cars (Ford Taurus, Toyota Camry, and Honda Accord) from the mid-eighties to the present. Their main finding is that car manufacturers have moved from mixed bundling to tying. Additional equipment, such as AM/FM radios or air-conditioning systems were typically available as an option during some time, only to become tied to the car after a while. This trend was accompanied by increasing competition during the period under analysis. This trend cannot be explained as an attempt to better price discriminate, since tying is less effective for this purpose than mixed bundling. Leveraging motives can also be excluded since new entrants initiated tying before the incumbents. Moreover, it seems highly implausible that automobile companies such as Toyota and Ford tried to monopolise the car radio market. Instead, cost-savings may again be the driving force of the tying practice. Marginal cost savings are likely to be negligible, but economies of scale seem to be present. Although difficult to verify, the evidence suggests that the fixed costs of producing and distributing a car increase with product complexity. It is thus plausible that car manufacturers engage in tying so as to reduce the degree of complexity in production and especially distribution.

9.2.4 Conclusions

General consensus. Most economists now would agree on three fundamentals in regard to tying and bundling. First, tying is a pervasive practice that, in many instances, gives rise to substantial efficiencies. Both economies of scale and marginal cost savings usually play an important role in a firm's decision to provide a bundle instead of components. Mixed bundling and tying often arise in the presence of such cost savings. Second, the circumstances in which tying would lead to anticompetitive effects are restricted and hard to verify. The models that have been put forward for the purpose of identifying such effects rely on highly specific market structures, and the results are very sensitive to changes in the underlying assumptions. Finally, any attempt to balance efficiency gains against possible anticompetitive effects is complex.

9.3 THE APPROACH TO TYING AND BUNDLING UNDER ARTICLE 82 EC

Overview. The Commission has issued only a handful of negative decisions concerning tying and bundling. Most of those decisions involved contractual tying: Article 82(d) prohibits "making the conclusion of contracts subject to acceptances by the other parties of supplementary obligations which, by their nature or according to commercial usage, have no connection with the subject of such contracts."

The Commission's policy regarding tying and bundling has not been constrained by the precise wording of Article 82(d), however. On the contrary, it is now clear that tying abuses might arise even where the products concerned are linked by nature or normal commercial usage.[58] Furthermore, they have not been limited to the textbook example of coercing consumers of a dominant tying product into buying the tied product by contractual agreement, but have been identified in a variety of business practices. Mixed bundling and rebate systems, for example, have both been found to have similar effects on competition as tie-in agreements.[59] Contractual tying and the integration of products have been assessed in the same way without taking into account the different underlying effects on competition and efficiency considerations.[60] Finally, although the Commission stated in *Hilti* that objective justification for tying would be considered as a defence, this required evidence more convincing than any of the cases reviewed could provide.[61]

The limited number of precedents, and the lack of consistency between them, make the law on tying and bundling difficult to describe. The following approach is adopted. Section 9.3.1 describes contractual tying, a practice that has characterised most of the limited Article 82 EC precedents on tying. Section 9.3.2 discusses technological tying.

---

[58] *Tetra Pak II*, OJ 1992 L 72/1.
[59] See Section 9.3.4 below.
[60] Case COMP/C-3/37.792, *Microsoft*, Commission Decision of March 24, 2004, not yet published.
[61] *Eurofix-Bauco/Hilti*, OJ 1988 L 65/19.

Section 9.3.3 discusses *Microsoft*. This case is separated from contractual tying and technological tying, both because it is important enough to merit separate discussion and because certain commentators (and obviously Microsoft) do not regard it as a "classical" case of tying. Section 9.3.4 describes the law on mixed bundling. The rules in this regard are now clearer than for other forms of tying following publication of the Discussion Paper on Article 82 EC. Section 9.3.5 discusses the specific case of "aftermarkets" where tying allegations are often raised against producers of primary equipment and aftermarket consumables. Finally, Section 9.3.6 attempts to summarise the Community institutions' basic approach to tying and bundling.

9.3.1 Contractual Tying

Case law. In the case of contractual tying, the theory is that customers would have bought the tied good from an alternative source if that had been possible. It was impossible for them to do so because the supplier of the dominant tying good offered customers no choice but to buy that firm's tied good. In other words, in these cases, the tying practice involved an *actual* restriction of customer choice that resulted in market foreclosure.[62]

a. Eurofix-Bauco/Hilti.[63] This case concerned the behaviour of Hilti in the sale of certain power-actuated fastening (PAF) systems, used in the construction industry. At the time of the investigation, Hilti was the largest manufacturer of nail guns in the EU (with a share just over 50%). Nail guns use nails and cartridge strips, which are specifically adapted to a particular brand of nail gun. Hilti had patent protection for its guns, cartridge strips, and nails.[64] However, this patent protection had not prevented several manufacturers from producing a range of nails with similar characteristics for specific use in Hilti nail guns.

---

[62] Other cases under Article 82 EC have raised analogous issues to tying. In *Napier Brown v British Sugar*, Napier Brown, a sugar merchant in the United Kingdom, alleged that British Sugar, the largest producer and seller of sugar in the United Kingdom, was abusing its dominant position in an attempt to drive Napier Brown out of the UK sugar retail market. In the subsequent proceedings, the Commission objected to British Sugar's practice of offering sugar only at delivered prices so that the supply of sugar was, in effect, tied to the services of delivering the sugar. Having concluded that British Sugar was dominant in the market for white granulated sugar for both retail and industrial sale in Great Britain, the Commission took the view that "reserving for itself the separate activity of delivering the sugar which could, under normal circumstances be undertaken by an individual contractor acting alone" amounted to an abuse. According to the Commission, tying deprived customers of the choice between purchasing sugar on an ex factory and delivered price basis, eliminating all competition in relation to the delivery of the products. See *Napier Brown v British Sugar*, OJ 1988 L 284/41. Refusal to deal cases might also be characterised as "tying" in the sense that the dominant firm reserves unto itself the relevant downstream market. See Ch. 8 (Refusal to Deal). Finally, certain exclusive dealing cases have raised issues analogous to tying. See, e.g., *Van den Bergh Foods Ltd,* OJ 1998 L 246/1, on appeal Case T-65/98, *Van den Bergh Foods Ltd v Commission* [2003] ECR II-4653 (tying of freezer cabinet supply to use of dominant firm's ice-cream products). These cases raise somewhat different issues to tying *per se* and are accordingly discussed in various other chapters.

[63] *Eurofix-Bauco/Hilti*, OJ 1988 L 65/19.

[64] *Ibid.* Hilti's patent protection for nail guns was due to expire between 1986 and 1996, depending on the country and patent feature involved. Hilti also obtained patents for certain nails in all Member States except Denmark. At the time of the investigation, these patents had expired in some Member States and were due to expire in all Member States by 1988.

Competing nail producers complained to the Commission that Hilti was engaging in abusive actions that, they claimed, had severely limited their penetration into the market for Hilti-compatible nails. These practices included, among other things, the tying of the sale of nails to the sale of cartridge strips, the refusal to honour guarantees where customers used third party nails in their Hilti guns, the refusal to supply cartridge strips to customers who might resell them, and "frustrating or delaying legitimately available licences available under Hilti's patents."[65] Rivals claimed that the sale of nails was tied to the sale of cartridge strips in two ways. First, Hilti refused to sell cartridges to a number of customers unless they also purchased a sufficient number of Hilti nails: this is a classic example of contractual tying. Second, Hilti reduced the discount on cartridges for other customers when they did not also purchase Hilti nails. The Commission reasoned that whilst the latter example was not an absolute tie, it was tantamount to one because of the impact on customer behaviour.

In its analysis, the Commission identified three different product markets, namely: (1) nail guns; (2) Hilti-compatible cartridge strips; and (3) Hilti-compatible nails.[66] It took the view that Hilti was dominant in all three markets.[67] The Commission then concluded that tying the sale of cartridge strips to the sale of nails constituted an abuse of the dominant position. The Commission ruled that Hilti's policies left consumers with no choice over the source of their nails and as such abusively exploited them. In addition, the policies all had as object or effect the exclusion of independent nail makers who may have threatened Hilti's dominant position[68] The Commission also came to a conclusion of abuse regarding Hilti's restriction of its guarantee:[69]

> "Whilst it may be legitimate not to honour a guarantee if a faulty or sub-standard non-Hilti nail causes malfunctioning, premature wear or breakdown in a particular case, such a general policy in the circumstances of this case amounts to an abuse of a dominant position in that it is yet another indirect means used to hinder customers from having access to different sources of supply."

Hilti argued that its business practices were motivated by safety and reliability concerns. The Commission rejected these arguments in the circumstances of the case and, furthermore, questioned whether safety and reliability could be regarded as an objective justification for an otherwise abusive behaviour.[70] Whilst the Commission recognised that tying could be beneficial for consumers, it stated that the defendant would need to produce convincing evidence.

Hilti appealed to the Court of First Instance, which upheld the Commission's decision.[71] The Court of First Instance rejected Hilti's view that PAF systems, encompassing nails, nail guns and cartridge strips, were a single product, observing as follows:[72]

---

[65] *Ibid.*, para. 98.
[66] *Ibid.*
[67] *Ibid.*
[68] *Ibid.*, para. 75.
[69] *Ibid.*, para. 79.
[70] *Ibid.*
[71] Case T-30/89, *Hilti AG v Commission* [1991] ECR II-1439. A further appeal by Hilti to the Court of Justice was also unsuccessful. See Case C-53/92P, *Hilti AG v Commission* [1994] ECR I-667.

> "It is common ground that since the 1960s there have been independent producers, including the interveners, making nails intended for use in nail guns. Some of those producers are specialised and produce only nails, and indeed some make only nails specifically designed for Hilti tools. That fact in itself is sound evidence that there is a specific market for Hilti-compatible nails."

The presence of third-party suppliers active in the market for the tied good, but not for the tying good, was taken to be sufficient evidence that the two are separate products. This is clearly incorrect, however. To see why suppose that A is the tying product and B is the tied product. Under *Hilti*, A and B are separate products if there is a market for B alone—as evidenced perhaps by firms supplying only B. This rule leads to absurd conclusions: shoes with laces are not single products, nor are cars with air conditioners, cold medicine with pain relievers included, planes with engines, the *Financial Times* with its crossword puzzle, computers with hard drives, phones with SIM cards, or an MBA at INSEAD with accounting classes required.

The *Hilti* single-product test also does not capture those product configurations that are the source of the competitive distortion they believe tying law should remedy. A firm has engaged in tying under the *Hilti* analysis if it offers customers AB without also offering customers A. If there is no material demand for A, then the failure to offer A cannot have any competitive consequences. Material demand for A *and* B is required for the decision to offer only AB to restrict consumer choice in a way that is meaningful. Indeed, lack of material demand for A is the test that is needed to eliminate cases such as shoes with shoelaces and cars with tyres that people view as integrated products.[73]

b. Tetra Pak II.[74] This case also concerned the tying of consumables to the sale of the primary product. Tetra Pak is the major supplier of carton packaging machines and materials required for the packaging of liquid and semi-liquid food. The company is active both in the non-aseptic packaging of liquid food (such as fresh milk) and in the aseptic packaging of liquid food to be stored in a non-refrigerated environment. At the time of the investigation, Tetra Pak had a market share of 45–50% in the former and 90–95% in the latter.[75]

As in *Hilti*, the Commission identified the market for the primary product (packaging machines) and the consumables as separate markets (cartons). Because packaging machines and cartons for the aseptic and non-aseptic process are not interchangeable, the Commission identified four relevant markets. Tetra Pak's market share in the aseptic packaging market allowed the company to impose a number of contractual obligations on its customers. Among others, Tetra Pak obliged purchasers of its packaging machines to use only Tetra Pak cartons. Also, the company required a

---

[72] *Ibid.*, para. 68.

[73] PE Areeda, E Elhauge, and H Hovenkamp, *Antitrust Law* (Boston, Little, Brown and Company, 1996) vol. X, at para. 1745d2.

[74] *Tetra Pak II*, OJ 1992 L 72/1, on appeal Case T-83/91, *Tetra Pak International SA v Commission* [1994] ECR II-755, confirmed in Case C-333/94 P, *Tetra Pak International SA v Commission* [1996] ECR I-5951.

[75] B Nalebuff, "Bundling, Tying and Portfolio Effects," *DTI Economics Paper No. 1*, Part 2—Case Studies (February 2003), p. 9.

monthly report on carton use be submitted and retained the right to inspect the packaging machines without notice.

While Tetra Pak argued that the tying practices were justified on technical grounds, liability reasons and public health considerations,[76] the Commission,[77] upheld by the Community Courts,[78] condemned the tying as abuse of a dominant position. The Commission argued that the tying practice was targeted at eliminating competition in the market for the consumables (cartons). Additionally, the tying practices together with the control of carton use were a perfect metering device that allowed Tetra Pak to price discriminate between customers.

The Court recognised the complexities surrounding the technical grounds and liability reasons proposed as defences by Tetra Pak, but held that these could be resolved through less restrictive means than contractual ties. In response to Tetra Pak's argument that Article 82(d) could not apply to ties between its packaging machines and cartons because of the natural links between the two, the Court stated:[79]

> "It must moreover be stressed that the list of abusive practices set out in the second paragraph of Article 8[2] of the Treaty is not exhaustive. Consequently, even where tied sales of two products are in accordance with commercial usage, or there is a natural tie between the two products in question, such sales may still constitute abuse within the meaning of Article 8[2] unless they are objectively justified."

Tetra Pak also defended its tying practices by asserting that tying is a common industry practice in the market for non-aseptic packaging. The Court did not find this to be the case, and noted that even if such practices were common in the competitive market for non-aseptic packaging, this would not justify their use in the market for aseptic packaging given Tetra Pak's dominant position. Among other remedies, the Commission obliged Tetra Pak not to require purchasers of its packaging machines only use its cartons. This was aimed at facilitating entry into the market for cartons, as well as preventing Tetra Pak from practicing price discrimination.

9.3.2 Technological Tying

IBM Undertaking.[80] Although no formal decision was taken, the *IBM Undertaking* is of special interest because it raised the issue of technological tying. In 1980, the Commission opened proceedings into IBM's business practices with regard to its mainframe computers, the System/370. It alleged that IBM held a dominant position for the supply of the two key products for the computers, namely the central processing unit (CPU) and the operating system. The Commission challenged, among other things,[81]

---

[76] B Nalebuff, "Bundling, Tying and Portfolio Effects" *DTI Economics Paper No. 1*, Part 2—Case Studies (February 2003) p. 10.

[77] *Tetra Pak II*, OJ 1992 L 72/1.

[78] Case T-83/91, *Tetra Pak International SA v Commission* [1994] ECR II-755, on appeal Case C-333/94 P, *Tetra Pak International SA v Commission* [1996] ECR I-5951.

[79] *Ibid.*, para. 37.

[80] *IBM*, 1984 OJ L 118/24.

[81] IBM was also accused of: (1) failing to supply manufacturers in sufficient time with the technical information needed to permit competitive products to be used with the System/370; (2) not offering System/370 CPUs without the basic software included in the price (software tying); and

IBM's integration of memory devices with the CPU and the bundling with the basic software applications. Both practices coerced IBM's customers to purchase products (memory devices and software applications) which they could have acquired elsewhere. Informal discussions between the Commission and IBM ultimately led to a settlement of the case. IBM undertook to offer its mainframe computer CPUs in the EU either without memory devices or with the minimum capacity required for testing.[82]

9.3.3 *Microsoft*

Overview. There are not many competition cases that receive global coverage and are known outside of the small world of competition economists and lawyers. The *Microsoft* case is one of those, being perhaps one of the most interesting and controversial current antitrust cases on both sides of the Atlantic. This is so for a number of reasons. First, it concerns Microsoft, a company that has long incited strong opinions and passions. Second, it involves markets and products which are new and technologically complex. Third, it gives rise to interesting and difficult legal and economic questions. And, finally, it is forcing antitrust commentators to think long and hard about the appropriate legal standards for the assessment of tying and bundling.[83]

The various Community proceedings. In March 2004, the Commission found that Microsoft had infringed Article 82 EC by not offering computer manufacturers and end users the choice of obtaining Windows without certain media player technologies.[84] The Commission objected to the tying practice, arguing that competition in the media player market would be eliminated. The Commission argued that Microsoft's practice to bundle its Windows Media Player (WMP) into Windows "is an example of a more general business model which deters innovation and reduces consumer choice in any technologies which Microsoft could conceivably take interest in and tie with Windows in the future."[85] It also found that tying of WMP with Windows was motivated by a desire to maintain a monopoly in the operating system market, i.e., by gaining ubiquity and not licensing others to use its Windows media format for rival media players, Microsoft can foreclose new operating system entrants.[86]

The Commission provided a concise summary of why it believed that Microsoft's failure to offer an alternative version distorted competition: "Tying WMP with the

(3) discriminating between users of IBM software, i.e., refusing to supply certain software installation services to users of non-IBM CPUs.

[82] IBM also undertook to disclose, in a timely manner, sufficient interface information to enable competitors to produce IBM-compatible hardware and software.

[83] See, e.g., DS Evans, AJ Padilla and M Polo, "Tying in Platform Software: Reasons for a Rule of Reason Standard in European Competition Law" (2002) 2 *World Competition* 509; C Ahlborn, DS Evans and AJ Padilla, "The Antitrust Economics of Tying: A Farewell to *Per Se* Illegality" Spring 2004, *Antitrust Bulletin*; and DS Evans and AJ Padilla, "Tying Under 82 EC and the Microsoft Decision: A Comment on Dolmans and Graf" (2004) 4 *World Competition* 503–12. For a different perspective, see B. Nalebuff, "Bundling, Tying and Portfolio Effects", *Report for the UK Department of Trade and Industry*, 2003; and M Dolmans and T Graf, "Analysis of Tying Under Article 82 EC: The European Commission's Microsoft Decision in Perspective" (2004) 27(2) *World Competition* 225–44.

[84] Case COMP/C-3/37.792, *Microsoft*, Commission Decision of March 24, 2004, not yet published.

[85] "Quote via Windows à la carte," *The Economist*, March 25, 2004.

[86] Case COMP/C-3/37.792, *Microsoft*, Commission Decision of March 24, 2004, not yet published,, paras. 972-974.

dominant Windows makes WMP the platform of choice for complementary content and applications which in turn risks foreclosing competition in the market for media players."[87] As the Commission noted in its press release, "the investigation concluded that the ubiquity which was immediately afforded to WMP as a result of it being tied with the Windows PC OS artificially reduces the incentives of music, film and other media companies, as well as software developers and content providers to develop their offerings to competing media players."[88] Economists refer to the feedback effects the Commission identifies as "indirect network effects."[89]

Although the Commission observed the efficiencies in using WMP as a platform for software content and applications in its ruling, it found that tying was not indispensable to achieving these efficiencies, and that efficiency motivations were therefore no defence. The Commission ordered that Microsoft must offer a version of Windows with the media player removed. The Commission seems to favour a Windows *à la carte*,[90] where PC makers are free to choose which components Windows they wish to use and which they do not. Microsoft has appealed the Commission's decision to the Court of First Instance and a final judgment is still pending.

On June 7, 2004, Microsoft appealed the Commission's decision before the Court of First Instance. Microsoft seeks the annulment of the decision or, in the alternative, annulment of or a substantial reduction in the fine. Microsoft also applied for suspension of the Commission's remedies. This application was dismissed by Order of the President of the Court of First Instance, Judge Vesterdorf.[91] In his opinion, the evidence adduced by Microsoft was not sufficient to show that the remedies imposed by the Commission would cause serious and irreparable harm to Microsoft in the event that the Court rules in its favour in the main action.

Implementation of the Commission's remedies is proving difficult, however. These difficulties are discussed in more detail in Chapter Fifteen (Remedies). Briefly, a major issue with the unbundling of WMP is that Microsoft has decided to charge the same price for the unbundled Windows and a Windows/WMP bundle, which, not surprisingly, makes it hard to see why vendors and consumers would choose an unbundled version. A monitoring trustee has been appointed by the Commission to play a "proactive" role in monitoring Microsoft's compliance with the remedies imposed by the Commission.[92] The monitoring trustee was tasked with issuing opinions, upon application by a third party or the Commission or on its own initiative, on whether Microsoft had failed to comply with the decision in a particular instance or on any other

[87] Case COMP/C-3/37.792, *Microsoft*, Commission Decision of March 24, 2004, not yet published, para. 842.

[88] Commission Press Release IP/04/382 of March 24, 2004.

[89] See M Katz and C Shapiro, "Systems Competition and Network Effects" (1994) 8(2) *Journal of Economics Perspectives* 93–115; SJ Liebowitz and S Margolis, "Network Externality: An Uncommon Tragedy?" (1994) 8(2) *Journal of Economic Perspectives* 133–50; and SJ Liebowitz and SE Margolis, "The Fable of the Keys" (1990) 33(1) *Journal of Law and Economics* 1–25. See also Case COMP/C-3/37.792, *Microsoft*, Commission Decision of March 24, 2004, not yet published, para. 842.

[90] "Quote via Windows à la carte," *The Economist*, March 25, 2004.

[91] See Case T-201/04R, *Microsoft Corp v Commission*, Order of December 22, 2004.

[92] Case COMP/C-3/37.792, *Microsoft*, Commission Decision of March 24, 2004, not yet published, paras. 1043–48.

issue that might be "of interest with respect to the effective enforcement" of the decision. Proceedings in this regard remain on-going,[93] and the Court of First Instance has not yet ruled on the merits of the appeal.

Reasons for the *Microsoft* controversy. The *Microsoft* case has provoked widely-differing views on whether the outcome of the Commission's decision is correct. The effects of the decision are largely unknown, since the remedy has not yet been implemented and would take a significant period of time to assess its effects even when implemented. Moreover, the effects of the decision that have been posited are often skewed, since they emanate from entities or individuals with a strong vested interest in the outcome. With these caveats in mind, we set out below some of the reasons why the Commission's decision is considered controversial. These are not *necessarily* the views of Microsoft (though some may be) and we take no position either way on their merits: they are simply set out since they are of interest to anyone thinking about the implications of the decision.

A first criticism is that the Commission's decision misinterprets the role of network effects. The Commission's theory rests on a number of testable assumptions: (1) that there are strong indirect network effects; (2) that these network effects are likely to cause the streaming media player market to tip; and (3) that the market is about to tip. Microsoft does not dispute that the media player business is characterised by indirect network effects. Content providers are likely to encode in formats that are popular, and end users are attracted to formats for which there is significant content. However, the existence of network effects does not necessarily imply market tipping. Firm-specific network externalities may cause a market to tip in favour of the leading player, but not always, e.g., if the products are sufficiently differentiated and if multi-homing is possible and attractive. Multi-homing is when a user joins several networks simultaneously—in the context of this case, when a content provider encodes in several formats and/or when users employ several different media players. The literature on tipping has recognised the importance of multi-homing and product differentiation for the possibilities of tipping.[94]

Microsoft argues that end-users multi-home because: (1) media players are available for free and take up little hard disk space, so that there are limited impediments to having multiple players on the machine; and (2) media players are differentiated products. Consumers use the one that is best for a particular purpose. The cost savings from standardising on one player may be small relative to the benefits of using several. Microsoft also argues that content providers and application developers multi-home.

---

[93] It appears that the monitoring trustee has fulfilled the role intended by the Commission, as it was widely reported that in December 2005 the Commission issued a Statement of Objections alleging that Microsoft had failed to comply with certain of the remedies ordered in the 2004 decision, based in large part on reports from the monitoring trustee finding that Microsoft's compliance efforts were ineffective in bringing about the desired results. See "Commission warns Microsoft of daily penalty for failure to comply with 2004 decision," Commission Press Release IP/05/1695 of December 22, 2005. At the date of publication, Microsoft is still considered not to be in full compliance. See "Commission sends new letter to Microsoft on compliance with decision," IP/06/298 of March 10, 2006.

[94] See J Tirole, "The Analysis of Tying Cases: A Primer," *Competition Policy International*, vol. 1, n.1, Spring 2005.

This is because the cost of writing for multiple media players is said to be small and consumer demand is said to be sufficiently strong that the extra revenues associated with encoding in multiple formats exceed the incremental costs.

Microsoft argues that product differentiation and multi-homing make it unlikely that the streaming media player market defined by the Commission will tip in favour of WMP. This is based on several arguments, all of which are strongly disputed as a matter of fact by the opposing parties. First, it says that content providers have incentives to use competing formats, since they want their content to be as widely playable as possible. They will encode in an additional format provided that the cost of doing so is less than the extra revenue associated to distribution through that new format. The precise extent to which content providers do actually encode in additional formats is, however, an issue of dispute between the parties.

Second, Microsoft argues that end users have strong incentives to use more than one media player. Media players are freely downloadable and offer many differentiated and competing functions and styles. The same occurs for other types of content: there is content available in multiple formats and content available in just one. To access all types of content, one needs to install multiple media players. The extent to which, in fact, computer OEMs pre-install more than one media player, or consumers are willing to install more than one media player, is another area of dispute between the parties.

Finally, Microsoft argues that the main websites increasingly provide content in more and more formats rather than specialising in any single format. Microsoft argues that this is not the characteristic of a market which is about to tip. It further argues that consumers have not seen their choice restricted by the inclusion of streaming media capabilities in Windows. Again, the extent to which this is true as a factual matter is a major issue on appeal.

A final reason for possible controversy is a legal point. Prior to its decision in *Microsoft*, the Commission's formal approach to tying and bundling could be characterised as a modified *per se* illegality standard. It involved four stages: (1) to establish *market power* (dominance) of the seller in relation to the tying product; (2) to identify *tying*, which required proof that customers are forced to purchase two separate products (the tying and the tied product); (3) to assess the *effects of tying on competition*; and (4) to consider whether any objective justification for tying exists.

A key requisite in the Commission's "classical" tying cases was, therefore, the finding that consumers had been coerced. However, in *Microsoft*, the Commission acknowledged that Microsoft's practices could not be characterised as "classical tying" in which foreclosure results from the fact that consumers would take a competing product if given the choice to do so. It noted as follows:[95]

---

[95] Case COMP/C-3/37.792, *Microsoft*, Commission Decision of March 24, 2004, not yet published, para. 833. Interestingly, the test proposed for the analysis of tying and bundling in the Discussion Paper also does not require establishing that consumers have been coerced or, in other words, showing that there would be positive demand for the two products if there were to be sold separately. According to the Discussion Paper it is enough to show that there is demand for the tied good. See Discussion

> "It will be shown that inasmuch as tying risks foreclosing competitors, it is immaterial that consumers are not forced to 'purchase' or 'use' WMP [Windows Media Player—the tied good]. As long as consumers 'automatically' obtain WMP—even if for free—alternative suppliers are at a competitive disadvantage. This is because no other media player vendor can guarantee content and software developers similar platform ubiquity."

Thus, Microsoft argues that the distorting effects of its bundling practices result not from the direct observable coercion of consumers, but from indirect future effects that the Commission considered would result from actions taken by other economic actors. On the other hand, the Commission and the complainants argue that, in practice, there is no effective choice on the part of computer OEMs and consumers. Again, these issues of fact will be decided in the pending appeal.

9.3.4 Mixed Bundling

9.3.4.1 Overview

Definition. "Mixed bundling" or "financial tying" refers to situations in which a firm offers a lower price to customers purchasing two or more products together than to customers purchasing them separately. Unlike contractual tying, mixed bundling does not involve the imposition of direct "obligations" to buy product A as a condition for the right to buy product B. The customer has a *choice* to buy either the package or the separate pieces. There is, in other words, no contractual or direct coercion. Whether there is economic coercion (i.e., whether the choice is commercially possible) and an exclusionary effect will depend on the prices and costs of the package and the individual components and their impact on purchasing behaviour.

There is some debate among antitrust commentators whether mixed bundling should be analysed under the principles of tying, exclusive dealing, predatory pricing, or refusal to deal. The particular categorisation seems unimportant, however, and potentially misleading if assigning mixed bundling to one category or another would lead to a materially different assessment. The essential points to understand are that mixed bundling is a vertical practice and, as such, may have a range of procompetitive explanations, but may also in certain cases materially harm competition. In particular, mixed bundling can create strong incentives for customers to buy two products from one supplier and, by implication, make life difficult for rival suppliers who only sell one of the products in question. Whether this harms competition cannot be inferred from the categorisation applied to mixed bundling but must follow from an analysis of its effects in specific cases.

Ubiquity of mixed bundling. It is important to appreciate that mixed bundling is pervasive in developed economies. The most obvious example is restaurants where a two- or three-course meal from a restricted set of courses is usually offered at a reduced price compared to the price of each course separately. But there are also countless other examples, such as packages of television channels, season tickets for sporting and other events, selling film with camera, package holidays, round-trip airline tickets etc. Mixed

---

Paper, para. 186. This issue is discussed in section 9.3.1 above in the context of the separate product test in *Hilti*.

bundling is pervasive for obvious reasons.[96] First, there will usually be cost savings associated with supplying two products together, including economies of scope, reduced transaction costs for firms, and lower information costs for consumers. In the example of the restaurant menu, there will be certain cost-savings associated with offering a reduced menu choice (economies of scale and scope), and possibly less waste.

A second reason is that it is well-established in economics that bundling can be an effective pricing mechanism by which firms capture economic surplus from consumers (see section 9.2 above). In the case of packages of television channels, the consumer typically has a lower valuation for some of the additional channels, but is still willing to pay a price that exceeds the marginal cost of supplying the extra channel(s) (which is likely to be very low). This is essentially a form of price discrimination: the firm can increase profits by discriminating in favour of customers who attach additional value to a lower-priced package.[97] The widespread use of mixed bundling in competitive markets should lead to the conclusion that it is presumptively efficient. While the same conclusion cannot be unreservedly accepted in the case of markets in which firms exercise market power, there is no case either for saying that the efficiencies that drive bundling in competitive markets can be ignored in the case of dominant firms.[98]

9.3.4.2 The legal treatment of mixed bundling

Overview. Mixed bundling has received widely divergent treatment under antitrust law. A spectrum of different approaches have been applied. The strictest, and least defensible, approach has been that applied by the Commission in Article 82 EC cases settled by way of undertakings, where the Commission has either prohibited mixed bundling outright or allowed it only where there were specific cost-savings referable to

---

[96] See WJ Adams and WL Yellen, "Commodity Bundling and the Burden of Monopoly" (1976) 90(3) *The Quarterly Journal of Economics* 475–98; Y Bakos and E Brynjolfsson, "Bundling Information Goods: Pricing, Profits, and Efficiency" (1999) 4(12) *Management Science* 1613–30; DS Evans and M Salinger, "Why Do Firms Bundle and Tie? Evidence from Competitive Markets and Implications for Tying Law" (2005) 22 *Yale Journal on Regulation* 37; BH Kobayashi, "Not Ready for Prime Time? A Survey of the Economic Literature on Bundling," *Law and Economics Working Paper Series 5-35*, October 25, 2005, George Mason University Law School. For a non-technical summary, see DL Rubinfeld, "3M's Bundled Rebates: An Economic Perspective" (2005) 72 *University of Chicago Law Review* 243; and "Selective Price Cuts And Fidelity Rebates," *Economic Discussion Paper prepared by RBB for the Office of Fair Trading*, July 2005.

[97] See G Crawford, "The Discriminatory Incentives to Bundle in the Cable Television Industry," *University of Arizona Department of Economics Working Paper* (finding a 5.5% decrease in consumers surplus, 6.0% increase in firm's profits, and 2.5% increase in total surplus as a result of television channel bundling).

[98] See BH Kobayashi, "Not Ready for Prime Time? A Survey of the Economic Literature on Bundling," *Law and Economics Working Paper Series* 5-35, October 25, 2005, George Mason University Law School, p. 1 ("[W]hile the literature has demonstrated that use of bundling can generate anticompetitive harm, it does not provide a reliable way to gauge whether the potential for harm would outweigh any demonstrable benefits from the practice. Thus, this review of the economic literature generally confirms the... position... regarding the underdeveloped state of the economics literature and the wisdom of delaying the promulgation of antitrust standards for bundling. In the future, economists should seek to expand their understanding of both the anticompetitive and procompetitive reasons firms engage in bundling. This will entail studying the reasons bundling is adopted by firms without market power, relaxing the assumption of monopoly in theoretical models, and generating testable hypotheses and the data to test them.").

the bundle. A second approach is to apply a full rule of reason analysis based on material evidence of harm to competition and an absence of countervailing benefits. This is the approach recently applied in the US case, *LePage v 3M.*[99] A third approach is to apply an implied predatory pricing test to the *tied product*. This is the approach currently advocated by the Commission in the Discussion Paper and was the approach applied by the Office of Fair Trading in *BSkyB.*[100] A final approach is to treat mixed bundling as *per se* legal unless the *total* price of the bundle is below the *total* cost of supplying it. This is a pure predatory pricing test. *LePage v 3M* aside, this is the prevailing approach under US antitrust law. Each of these approaches is described in more detail below.

a. Per se illegality absent cost savings. A surprising number of Commission settlements and decisions treat mixed bundling as *per se* illegal absent clearly identifiable cost-savings. This approach was first set out in the *Coca-Cola Italia Undertaking.*[101] In 1987, the Commission initiated a proceeding with respect to certain of Coca-Cola's business practices in Italy, following a complaint by an Italian beverage producer, San Pellegrino. The complaint concerned certain practices of the Italian branch of Coca-Cola within Italy almost entirely in the "take-home" distribution channel, and alleged violations of Articles 81 and 82 EC. The Commission issued a Statement of Objections alleging that Coca-Cola held a dominant position in an Italian "cola market" and that by entering into the arrangements Coca-Cola had violated Article 82 EC. The Commission challenged, *inter alia*, the fact that Coca-Cola offered discounts to retailers based on a package offering of cola and non-cola products, i.e., mixed bundling. To bring the proceedings to an end, Coca-Cola agreed not to condition the supply of cola products, or the availability or extent of discounts on cola products, on the purchase of one or more non-cola products. A similar prohibition was contained in Article 3(3) of the *Tetra Pak II* decision which provided that "discounts on cartons should be granted solely according to the quantity of each order, and orders for different types of carton may not be aggregated for that purpose."[102] And the most recent *Coca*

[99] *LePage's Inc v 3M (Minnesota Mining and Manufacturing Co),* 324 F.3d 141 (3d Cir 2003) (en banc), cert. denied, 124 S. Ct. 2932 (2004).

[100] CA98/20/2002, *BSkyB*, OFT Decision of December 17, 2002.

[101] See XIXth Report on Competition Policy (1989), para 50. The Undertaking was signed by Coca-Cola in December 1989, and on that basis the Commission terminated the Italian proceeding. See Commission Press Release IP/90/7 of January 9, 1990.

[102] *Tetra Pak II*, OJ 1992 L 72/1. In several cases, the French Conseil de la Concurrence (Competition Council) has examined bundled rebates and treated them as unlawful without detailed effects analysis. See, e.g., Decision *France Telecom/Office d'annonces,* No 96-D-10, February 20, 1996, affirmed on appeal in Cour d'appel de Paris, February 18, 1997 (bundled rebate granted to advertisers that bought advertising space simultaneously both in the departmental telephone directory and the local telephone directory found to artificially deter advertisers from buying space from rivals); *Lilly France*, Decision No 96-D-12, March 5, 1996 (Lilly France fined for bundling rebates across a monopoly product, Dobutrex, and a competitive product, Vancomycine, creating an artificial barrier to entry for competitors on the Vancomycine market. See also *Canal+/TPS,* No 03-MC-01, Decision of January 23, 2003 (interim measures). But see Decision n° 05-D-13 of March 13, 2005, *Canal Plus*.

Cola Undertaking in 2005 also effectively requires the unbundling of discounts on the company's core brands.[103]

A somewhat more lenient approach was applied in *The Digital Undertaking* in 1997. The Commission accepted an Undertaking from Digital Equipment Corporation (Digital) concerning the marketing and pricing of services for Digital computers in Europe.[104] The Commission's investigation followed complaints received from two third-party-maintenance companies (TPMs). The Digital services under investigation consisted of hardware support for Digital systems (HWS), operational and remedial software support for Digital operating systems software and related layered products (SWS), and update licence subscriptions for such software (LS). These services were offered separately as well as in the form of a package, called "Digital Systems Support" (DSS). The TPMs argued that the pricing and packaging of Digital's computer services prevented effective competition in the supply of hardware maintenance and software support services for Digital systems.

Following Digital's response to the Statement of Objections, contesting all of the Commission assertions, the Commission accepted an undertaking from Digital, which closed the case without further action. In respect of the tying and price discrimination allegations outlined above, the undertaking reflects the principle that a supplier may pass on cost savings and countervailing benefits derived, *inter alia*, from efficient packaging to its customers. As a "bright-line test" in the specific case of Digital, the undertaking fixes the package price reduction at no more than 10% of the sum-of-the-pieces price for DSS.[105]

An approach that treats mixed bundling as *per se* illegal, or illegal absent specific cost-savings, is unjustifiable. Mixed bundling is ubiquitous and generally has a strong, non-exclusionary rationale. These legitimate explanations for mixed bundling also apply in the case of dominant firms, even if they cannot be unreservedly accepted. Allowing mixed bundling in the presence of cost savings is useful but by no means sufficient. Many forms of mixed bundling do not reflect specific cost savings, but concern pricing structures that allow efficient price discrimination in favour of customers that have a higher willingness to pay for a package of goods or services than stand-alone products. A rule preventing mixed bundling may therefore have the perverse effect of preventing consumers from purchasing products that might otherwise have purchased. In fairness to the Commission, however, the cases in which this approach has been applied concerned undertakings offered by firms as a pragmatic way of resolving lengthy

---

[103] See *Coca-Cola*, OJ 2005 L 253/21, clause 6, third indent ("The Companies will not condition any payment or other advantage on a customer's agreeing that a Company's CSDs (or any subset of a Company's CSDs) comprise a specified percentage of the total number of CSD SKUs (or of that subset of CSD SKUs) listed by the customer in the previous year.").

[104] Commission Press Release IP/97/868 of October 10, 1997.

[105] To allow calculation of the DSS fee at 90% of the sum-of-the-pieces price, Digital offers stand-alone HWS on a subscription basis (whereas before the new portfolio was introduced, it had been available only on a "time and materials" basis). In addition, it charges a flat SWS per computer system (as opposed to groups of computers on any one site, as it did in the past). These changes are secondary, and designed to allow transparent package pricing.

investigations and providing legal certainty for the future. The same conclusions would almost certainly not have been reached in a reasoned final decision.

b. ***Rule of reason.*** A number of cases in the EU and elsewhere have applied a full-scale rule of reason analysis to mixed bundling. A good example is the *GE/Amersham*,[106] a decision under the EC Merger Regulation. The Commission's analysis of the potential for the merged entity to engage in mixed bundling practices to create foreclosure comprised several distinct stages. First, the Commission established its theory of possible competitive harm—namely that the merged entity would engage in various types of anticompetitive bundling. Second, having identified a relevant theory of possible harm, the Commission assessed whether, in the case at hand, the merged entity would be able to engage in it, in particular through its ability to "leverage its pre-merger dominance in one product to another complementary product." Third, the Commission assessed whether, even if such a strategy was possible, there was a "reasonable expectation that rivals will not be able to propose a competitive response." Fourth, if rivals were not able to respond, the Commission assessed whether "their resulting marginalisation will force them to exit the market." Finally, even if rivals would exit the market, the Commission assessed whether the merged firm could "implement unilateral price increases and such increases need to be sustainable in the long term, without being challenged by the likelihood of new rivals entering the market or previously marginalised ones re-entering the market."[107]

A similar analysis was applied in the US case *LePage v 3M*. In that case, 3M, the dominant producer of transparent tape, bundled rebates relating to the purchase of its private label tape—a product in which it faced significant competition from LePage's—with a requirement that customers purchase other products from 3M's range that LePage's did not offer. There was no suggestion that any of 3M's prices were below cost. Notwithstanding this, the majority opinion found evidence of significant exclusionary effects based on the following circumstances: (1) prior to the 3M program, LePage's sales had been "skyrocketing" (440% increase over three years); (2) 3M's sales increased 478% during the period of the discount program; (3) LePage's in turn lost a proportional amount of sales; (4) during the period of 3M's bundled discounts LePage's earnings as a percentage of sales plummeted to below zero; and (5) internal 3M documents showed that the purpose of the discount program was to exclude competitors and raise prices to consumers once they had exited. The case is highly controversial under US law. This is mainly because it deviates from the bright-line predatory pricing test for pricing behaviour established by the Supreme Court in *Brooke Group*,[108] thereby running a significant risk of chilling price competition.[109]

---

[106] Case COMP/M.3304 *GE/Amersham*.

[107] *Ibid*., para. 37. See also Decision n° 05-D-13 of March 13, 2005, *Canal Plus* (mixed bundling considered lawful based, *inter alia*, on the offer's short duration, lack of adverse effect on the complainant, and its procompetitive effects (e.g., greater economies of scale, reduced billing costs)).

[108] *Brooke Group Ltd v Brown & Williamson Tobacco Corp*, 509 US 209, 227 (1993).

[109] Most US commentators have been critical of the judgment. For an overview of the main criticisms, see DA Crane, "Multiproduct Discounting: A Myth of Nonprice Predation" (2005) 72 *University of Chicago Law Review* 27–48; TA Lambert, "Evaluating Bundled Discounts" (2005) 89 *Minnesota Law Review* 1688; and RA Posner, "Vertical Restraints and Antitrust Policy" (2005) 72

A rule of reason approach to mixed bundling is clearly preferable to presumed illegality, since it at least allows some assessment of the obvious benefits of mixed bundling. But it also has significant drawbacks. First, it is not reasonable to subject every-day pricing decisions by firms to a complex *ex post* balancing act of competition harm and benefits. Firms must be able to know, within reason, whether their conduct is lawful at the time they decide to engage in such conduct. It is not reasonable to condition the legality of their conduct on supervening events and on information that they will not have access to at the time when they formulate their pricing policy. A second, more fundamental objection is that a test that compares harm to competitors and the effect of conduct on prices over time lacks any clear rational principle. A dominant firm is allowed to harm its rivals by legitimate competition. Observing harm to rivals during a period in which a dominant firm used mixed bundling, even if causally-related to the mixed bundling, proves nothing about harm to competition. Finally, the Commission's use of a rule of reason-type analysis in merger cases is grounded in very different considerations to Article 82 EC. A merger assessment simply asks whether the merger would create or increase market power in future: whether the conduct that would cause this is abusive or not is beside the point (even if the Commission may have to consider the effect of behavioural commitments offered by the parties not to engage in abusive acts[110]).

c ***The Discussion Paper's approach: implied predatory price test.*** The Discussion Paper proposes a clearer and economically more appropriate test to assess mixed bundling. The test is based on the assumption that economic coercion could be proven by analysing the implied price charged for the allegedly *tied* component.[111] The question is then whether the price charged for the tied product supplied as part of the package is so low as to prevent equally or more efficient suppliers from offering a competitive alternative. If the implied price is below that level or even negative, competitors may be forced to decline invitations to bid, thereby leaving customers no choice but to obtain the package from the dominant firm. If, on the other hand, the implied price for the tied component is above that level, competitors can meet demand for the "tied" product from customers who buy the "tying" product on a stand-alone basis. This means that consumers have an economically viable choice of taking the different components from different suppliers. If there is choice, there can be no coercion, and the tying claim must fail.

The Discussion Paper proposes a five-stage test in this regard: (1) dominance of the seller in at least the tying product market; (2) the existence of two separate products; (3)

University of Chicago Law Review 229. *Le Page v 3M* is by no means unique, however, in condemning bundled rebates as exclusionary under Section 2 of the Sherman Act. See, e.g., *SmithKline Corp v Eli Lilly & Co,* 575 F.2d 1056 (3d Cir. 1978). That said, the *Brooke Group* standard is generally applied, with *Le Page* largely being ignored in practice.

[110] Cases T-310/01, *Schneider Electric SA v Commission* [2002] ECR II-4071, Case T-77/02, *Schneider Electric SA v Commission* [2002] ECR II-4201; Case T-5/02, *Tetra Laval BV v Commission* [2002] ECR II-4381; Case T-80/02, *Tetra Laval BV v Commission* [2002] ECR II-4519; and Case C-12/03, *Commission v Tetra Laval BV* [2005] ECR I-987.

[111] Under US antitrust law, this approach was apparently taken only in one extreme case where the allegedly tied product was initially included into the package without increasing the package price at all. See *Multistate Legal Studies v. Harcourt Brace Jovanovich*, 63 F.3d 1540, 1549 (10th Cir. 1995), cert. denied, 116 S. Ct. 702 (1996).

evidence of "coercion" of customers; (4) a restrictive effect on competition; and (5) the absence of an efficiency defence or an objective justification. Step (3) merits further discussion.[112] The Discussion Paper recognises that, in mixed bundling cases, whether consumers are foreclosed to competitors (i.e., coerced) depends on the size of the bundled discount. If, for each of the products within the bundle, the price charged by the dominant firm covers its long-run incremental costs (LRIC), then such price cannot, except in exceptional circumstances, be regarded as exclusionary.[113] LRIC measures all product-specific costs, i.e., fixed costs and variable costs, but excluding common costs.[114] In a very simple example, if the tying product alone costs €60 and the package of the two products costs €70, the implied price of tied product is €10. The question is thus whether the LRIC of the tied product are less than €10.

These principles have already been applied in at least one previous case: *BSkyB*, a decision by the Office of Fair Trading (OFT).[115] BSkyB was accused of abusing its dominant position on the United Kingdom markets for the wholesale supply of TV channels carrying sports content to appear only on pay-TV sports channels and premium pay TV film channels. Among the abuses alleged was that "mixed bundling" by BSkyB foreclosed entry to the wholesale premium channel markets. As the number of channels in any package increased, the price of subscribing to an additional premium channel (i.e., the implied price) progressively decreased relative to their stand-alone price.

In a detailed and forensic decision, the OFT concluded that the mixed bundling practiced by BSkyB was not abusive within the meaning of the Chapter II prohibition of the Competition Act 1998—which is identical in substance to Article 82 EC. The principal findings were as follows:

1. Mixed bundling, as a form of second degree price discrimination, may result in increased efficiency by allowing higher levels of output (i.e., more sales of premium channels), and improved allocative efficiency resulting from customers facing prices closer to marginal costs.

2. Mixed bundling can, however, pose a dilemma for competition authorities: balanced against the anticompetitive concern that rivals can be foreclosed through such discounts is the consideration that a degree of mixed bundling is to be expected, and can well be desirable, in conditions such as those found in pay TV broadcasting. In particular, fixed costs (e.g., of acquiring content rights) are high in relation to the incremental costs of supplying additional subscribers. When the fixed/incremental cost ratio is high, it is neither unnatural nor undesirable for suppliers to offer discounts to consumers taking additional products as the incremental cost of supplying those extra products to consumers is relatively low.

3. In assessing allegations of anticompetitive mixed bundling, the OFT attached significance to whether the incremental price of an additional product (e.g., a

[112] Discussion Paper, para. 183.
[113] Discussion Paper, para. 190.
[114] See Ch. 5 (Predatory Pricing) for a detailed discussion.
[115] CA98/20/2002, *BSkyB*, OFT Decision of December 17, 2002.

channel) in a bundle of products is more or less than the incremental cost of supplying that product. The test proposed by the OFT was whether the implied price for incremental channels was less than the incremental avoidable cost per additional subscriber of supplying such channels. The rationale is that if, in each case, such incremental price does not exceed such incremental cost, BSkyB would have been forgoing profit (i.e., before any foreclosure effects are taken into account). Thus where: (a) incremental price exceeds incremental cost, the OFT believes that there would need to be strong independent evidence of anticompetitive foreclosure to reach a finding of abuse; (b) where incremental price is below incremental cost, this pricing would often be considered anticompetitive. It could be an abuse of a dominant position, especially in the presence of evidence of foreclosure of competitors.

4. There was limited evidence of foreclosure of rival channels resulting from mixed bundling. The implied incremental price of BSkyB's premium sports channels always exceeded their incremental cost. Consequently, the OFT did not consider further whether BSkyB's mixed bundling had foreclosed entry to potential suppliers of premium sports channels, given the absence of additional evidence showing anticompetitive intent or effects. In contrast, BSkyB did not demonstrate that its incremental implied price for premium film channels exceeded the incremental avoidable cost per additional subscriber of supplying such channels. Accordingly, to assess whether this constituted an infringement of the Chapter II prohibition, the OFT considered whether there was evidence of foreclosure of competitors who would otherwise supply premium film channels as a result of such below-cost incremental pricing. The OFT concluded that there was no foreclosure, since, among other things, BSkyB in any event held the majority of the rights to the relevant premium content films.

The structured rule of reason approach to mixed bundling set out in the Discussion Paper, and applied in *BSkyB*, is obviously better than either *per se* illegality or an unstructured rule of reason. It captures the economic insight that mixed bundling produces many economic benefits for consumers, while also recognising that mixed bundling can harm equally efficient rivals and, separately, competition. More importantly, it corrects the significant problem with the full-scale rule of reason approach by providing a bright-line test of legality (i.e., whether the implied price of the tied product exceeds its LRIC) that a dominant firm can apply at the stage when it embarks upon a pricing practice. Finally, the structured rule of reason approach also has the benefit that failing a modified price/cost test does not result in an automatic finding of illegality, but that evidence of actual or likely foreclosure and harm to competition is also required.

d. Per se legality absent predatory pricing for the overall package. Certain commentators argue that mixed bundling should be presumed legal unless the *total price* of the bundle is below the *total cost* of supplying it and there is evidence of recoupment.[116] This implies that the only relevant legal rule is the general predatory pricing test. This view reflects several considerations. First, the LRIC price-cost test proposed in the Discussion Paper may prove difficult to implement in practice, especially in emerging markets or in multi-product industries.[117] Second, identifying when mixed bundling harms social welfare and when the purpose is efficiency or price discrimination is extremely complex. In other words, given that the impact of mixed bundling on social welfare is *a priori* ambiguous, and the ability of courts and competition authorities to distinguish whether it leads to an increase or a fall in welfare is necessarily limited, a bright-line test based on a pure predatory pricing analysis is considered to be the optimal rule. This approach has not, however, gained widespread acceptance under Article 82 EC.

9.3.5 Tying In Aftermarkets

The Discussion Paper's comments on abuse. Consumers of a product, typically a durable good (e.g., a jet engine), often need to subsequently purchase a complementary follow-on product (e.g., spare parts or maintenance and repair services). The market for the durable good is denoted as the "primary market" or the foremarket, while the markets for the follow-on products are known as "secondary markets" or "aftermarkets." Examples of foremarkets and aftermarkets include inkjet printers and replacement cartridges, game consoles and game cartridges, electric toothbrushes and replacement heads, and photo cameras and their repair parts. Indeed, in both *Hilti* and *Tetra Pak II*, the tied products were consumables of the tying product, i.e., they were sold in aftermarkets.[118]

This fact-pattern raises two principal issues under Article 82 EC. The first, discussed in detail in Chapters Two (Market Definition) and Three (Dominance), is whether a supplier of primary equipment can be considered dominant in aftermarket consumables for its own products. The issue is complex in practice, but the following basic conclusions apply:

1. If the secondary products are compatible, then there are separate product markets for the primary good and the secondary good.

2. If the secondary products are incompatible and an increase in aftermarket prices affects consumers' choices in the foremarket, then there is a single system market. The increase in aftermarket price will impact foremarket competition when: (a) consumers take into account the prices for the secondary product when purchasing the primary good; and (b) there are no, or limited, switching costs in the primary market.

3. If secondary products are incompatible and an increase in aftermarket prices does not affect consumers' choices in the foremarket, then there is a single market for the primary good and a series of brand specific aftermarkets.

[116] See, e.g., TJ Muris, "Antitrust Law, Economics, and Bundled Discounts," submitted on behalf of the United States Telecom Association In Response To The Antitrust Modernisation Commission's Request For Public Comments, July 15, 2005.

[117] This issue is discussed in detail in Ch 5 (Predatory Pricing).

[118] See *Eurofix-Bauco/Hilti*, OJ 1988 L 65/19 and *Tetra Pak II*, OJ 1992 L 72/1.

If dominance exists, the second issue is whether there is an abuse, in particular whether a dominant supplier can be found liable for abusive tying. In this regard, the Discussion Paper states as follows:[119]

> "If a dominant position on an aftermarket has been established..., the Commission presumes that it is abusive for the dominant company to reserve the aftermarket for itself by excluding competitors from that market. Such exclusion is mostly done through either tying or a refusal to deal. The tying can come about in the various ways described in the section on tying. The refusal to deal may, for instance, involve a refusal to supply information needed to provide products or services in the aftermarket; a refusal to license intellectual property rights; or a refusal to supply spare parts needed in order to provide aftermarket services."

These comments are surprising and would, if implemented, lead to a standard for intervention against tying in aftermarkets that is more strict than that applied in both *Hilti* and *Tetra Pak II*, not to mention much more hostile to tying than the standard recently applied in *Microsoft*. Holding a dominant position is not illegal: there must in addition be evidence of abusive conduct.[120] The fact that dominance arises in a relevant market for the consumables of a durable good does not lead to a different conclusion. Moreover, given the typically procompetitive nature of tying, no abuse can be established without a rigorous analysis and a careful balancing of the procompetitive and anticompetitive effects of the tying (or bundling) practice. For example, it may be that the dominant firm's consumables are vastly superior to rivals' products or not priced at an excessive level. In this regard, the Discussion Paper's comments on aftermarkets are not even consistent with its comments on tying generally. Its comments on aftermarkets sound like a *per se* prohibition, which was precisely what the Discussion Paper was intended to move away from.[121]

9.3.6 Classifying The Overall Approach To Tying Under Article 82 EC

***Per se* illegality or rule of reason?** Prior to the Commission's decision in *Microsoft*, the Community institutions were largely perceived to have applied a modified *per se* prohibition, which could be satisfied by a finding of: (1) market power; (2) separate products; and (3) coercion. According to *Napier Brown/British Sugar*, tying did not

[119] Discussion Paper, para. 264.

[120] Case 322/81, *NV Nederlandsche Baden-Industrie Michelin v Commission* [1983] ECR 3461, para. 10 ("[A] finding that an undertaking has a dominant position is not in itself a recrimination."). See generally Ch. 3 (Dominance).

[121] It is also worth noting that US courts have retreated significantly from the findings of the Supreme Court in *Kodak* concerning aftermarkets (*Eastman Kodak v. Image Technical Servs.* (90-1029), 504 U.S. 451 (1992)). See, e.g., *PSI Repair Servs., Inc. v. Honeywell, Inc.*, 104 F.3d 811 (6th Cir. 1997) (limiting *Kodak* to situations where the firm with market power in the putative tying product altered its policy after the consumers were locked-in, i.e., after they had purchased the durable good); *United Farmers Agents Ass'n v. Farmers Ins.* Exch., 89 F.3d 233 (5th Cir. 1996) (same); *Digital Equip. Corp. v. Uniq Digital Techs.*, 73 F.3d 756 (7th Cir. 1996) (same); *Lee v. Life Ins. Co. of North America*, 23 F.3d 14 (1st Cir.), *cert denied* 513 U.S. 964 (1994) (same); *SMS Sys. Maint. Servs., Inc. v. Digital Equip. Corp.*, 11 F. Supp. 2d 166 (D. Mass. 1998) (same). See also *Campos v. Ticketmaster Corp.*, 140 F.3d 1166 (8th Cir. 1998) (requiring an antitrust plaintiff invoking *Kodak* to prove that the consumer faces real information costs); and *Queen City Pizza, Inc. v. Domino's Pizza, Inc.*, 124 F.3d 430 (3d Cir. 1997) (construing *Kodak* narrowly, to apply only to situations where all of *Kodak's* factual eccentricities are present: the consumer must encounter switching and information costs and the allegedly tied product must be unique and therefore not interchangeable).

need to have any significant effect on the tied market. In *Microsoft*, the Commission appears to have recognised that, at least in certain cases, it is necessary to consider, in addition, whether: (4) there is a restrictive effect on competition for the tied product; and (5) there is objective and proportionate justification for the coercion.[122] The Discussion Paper adopts a similar line.

In *Microsoft* the Commission claimed to have "followed a 'rule of reason' approach to establish whether the anticompetitive effects of tying outweigh any possible procompetitive benefits" and that this "is precisely the framework for tying cases that US Court of Appeals laid down."[123] As the former Commissioner for Competition, Mario Monti, emphasised, "the Commission has not ruled that tying is illegal *per se*, but rather developed a detailed analysis of the actual impact of Microsoft's behaviour, and of the efficiencies that Microsoft alleges. In other words we did what the US Court of Appeals suggested should be done: we used the rule of reason although we don't call it like that in Europe."[124]

A recent article by Dolmans and Graf (2004)[125] has analysed the case law described in the previous section (including *Microsoft*) to establish the conditions under which tying and bundling can be found abusive under Article 82 EC. The authors conclude the Commission and the Community Courts follow a five-pronged test, which requires: (1) dominance of the seller in the market for the tying product; (2) the existence of a tied product distinct from the tying product; (3) evidence of coercion of customers; (4) a restrictive effect on competition for the tied product; and (5) the absence of objective and proportionate justification for the coercion.

According to Dolmans and Graf, Article 82 EC requires the defendant to substantiate efficiencies, to show that they cannot be achieved by less restrictive means, and to demonstrate that the efficiencies outweigh the anticompetitive effects. The five-pronged test described by Dolmans and Graf, and which they regard as reflecting a rule

[122] See M Dolmans and T Graf, "Analysis of Tying Under Article 82 EC: The European Commission's Microsoft Decision in Perspective" (2004) 27(2) *World Competition* 225–44. This is also the view adopted in the Discussion Paper, which proposes to: (1) identify which customers are tied as a result of the commercial practices of the dominant firm; and (2) assess which part of the market is foreclosed as a result of the tying and/or bundling practice. Thus, if the Commission concludes that "the dominant company ties a sufficient part of the market, the Commission is likely to reach the rebuttable presumption that the tying practice has a market distorting effect and thus constitutes an abuse of dominant position." See Discussion Paper, para. 188. According to the Discussion Paper the Commission will take into consideration the following factors in its assessment of likely effects: (1) the tied percentage of sales; (2) the strength of the dominant company; (3) the identity of the tied customers; (4) the number of consumers that buy both products (multi-home); (5) the existence of economies of scale, learning by doing economies, or network effects; (6) the degree of product differentiation; (7) the market performance of the dominant company and its competitors; and (8) the countervailing strategies available to competitors and customers. See Discussion Paper, paras. 196–203.

[123] Commission Press Release of March 24, 2004, MEMO/04/70.

[124] Statement by M Monti of March 24, 2004, No. 47/04.

[125] See M Dolmans and T Graf, "Analysis of Tying Under Article 82 EC: The European Commission's Microsoft Decision in Perspective" (2004) 27(2) *World Competition* 225–44.

of reason approach to tying and bundling, fits well with the framework proposed in the Discussion Paper.[126]

Others disagree. For Evans and Padilla (2004), neither the Commission's treatment of tying and bundling nor the Dolmans and Graf test embody a rule of reason approach.[127] According to Evans and Padilla, a rule of reason approach generally consists of four steps:[128]

> "First, to be condemned as exclusionary, a monopolist's act must have an 'anticompetitive effect.' That is, it must harm the competitive *process* and thereby harm consumers. In contrast, harm to one or more *competitors* will not suffice. Second, the plaintiff, on whom the burden of proof of course rests, must demonstrate that the monopolist's conduct indeed has the requisite anticompetitive effect. Third, if a plaintiff successfully establishes a prima facie case ... by demonstrating anticompetitive effect, then the monopolist may proffer a 'pro-competitive justification' for its conduct. If the monopolist asserts a pro-competitive justification—a non-pretextual claim that its conduct is indeed a form of competition on the merits because it involves, for example, greater efficiency or enhanced consumer appeal—then the burden shifts back to the plaintiff to rebut that claim. Fourth, if the monopolist's pro-competitive justification stands unrebutted, then the plaintiff must demonstrate that the anticompetitive harm of the conduct outweighs the procompetitive benefit."

According to Evans and Padilla (2004), there is a fundamental distinction between a rule of reason test and the Dolmans-Graf/Commission tests. Under a rule of reason standard, defendants have to demonstrate efficiencies, but it is the plaintiff who must demonstrate that the anticompetitive effects outweigh the procompetitive ones. Which of the two approaches is correct will likely be determined in the pending *Microsoft* appeal.

9.4 SUGGESTED ALTERNATIVE APPROACHES TO TYING

Overview. Uncertainty over what is, or should be, the legal standard for tying and bundling practices has led to the suggestion of various alternative legal rules. The best legal standard is, of course, one that perfectly ferrets out anticompetitive ties from procompetitive ones, and does so at low costs. Unfortunately, courts and competition authorities are only human and make errors. The possibility of errors in assessing tying arrangements is magnified when we confront fragile theories of tying with imperfect information concerning marketplace realities. For example, despite vindicating the

[126] See Discussion Paper, Section 8. The Discussion Paper not only requires that the dominant company demonstrate that the procompetitive effects of tying (or bundling) more than offset its potentially adverse effects. It must also show that those efficiencies cannot be achieved in a less restrictive manner. Furthermore, the Commission may find a tying (bundling) practice abusive even if its net effect on consumer welfare is *positive*. This will be the case if: (1) the practice forecloses a significant part of the tied market; and/or (2) the dominant company's market share is 75% or more. See Discussion Paper, paras. 91-92.

[127] DS Evans and AJ Padilla, "Tying Under 82 EC and the Microsoft Decision: A Comment on Dolmans and Graf" (2004) 4 *World Competition* 503–12.

[128] *United States v Microsoft*, 253 F.3d 34 (D.C. Cir. 2001), para. 95–97.

leverage hypothesis under certain circumstances, Whinston (1990) notes that the specification of a practical legal standard is extremely difficult.[129]

No matter what legal standard is chosen, the errors will go both ways: some ties that are harmful will be blessed and some ties that are beneficial will be condemned. Determining the right legal standard depends on prior beliefs concerning: (1) the relevance of harmful tying; and (2) the ability of the courts to separate harmful from beneficial tying.[130] A *per se* illegality rule is most appropriate if one believes that tying is frequently harmful and that the courts cannot accurately separate harmful from beneficial ties. In this case, it is better to condemn all ties than to risk approving many harmful ties only to save a few beneficial ties.

A *per se* legality rule is most appropriate in the reverse case. Letting a few harmful ties through is a small price to pay for allowing businesses to engage in beneficial ties without the risk of erroneous condemnation. Between these two extremes, one could progress from modified *per se* illegality (tying bundling are illegal if certain conditions are found to hold), to rule of reason, to modified *per se* legal (i.e., tying and bundling are legal except in exceptional circumstances).[131] With this in mind, the various alternative approaches to tying are set out below.

First alternative—unstructured rule of reason. The principal implication of several decades of economic investigation into the competitive effects of tying is that there should be *no* presumption on the part of competition authorities that tying and bundling are anticompetitive, even when undertaken by firms with monopoly power. Although recent developments in economic thinking, such as the post-Chicago models of anticompetitive tying, have provided several examples of situations where these activities may be anticompetitive, they do not disturb the consensus view that tying and bundling are a constant feature of economic life, and that the primary motivations for this form of strategic behaviour are the realisation of substantial efficiencies that lead to both higher profits and increased consumer welfare. Economic theory supports a rule of reason approach to tying in which the potential anticompetitive effects and efficiency benefits of tying are carefully balanced given the facts of the case.

The rule of reason approach to tying has found new support in a recent report prepared for the UK Department of Trade and Industry by Professor Nalebuff and his co-author David Majerus.[132] This report will do much to refine thinking about tying and bundling. Nalebuff and Majerus evaluate eleven antitrust and merger cases from various jurisdictions where the legality of bundling and tying practices was thoroughly examined. They find that in three of those cases the competition authorities incorrectly

---

[129] MD Whinston, "Tying, Foreclosure and Exclusion" (1990) 80 *American Economic Review* 837, at 856.

[130] For a formal approach to this issue, see KN Hylton and M Salinger, "Tying Law and Policy: A Decision-Theoretic Approach" (2001) 69 *Antitrust Law Journal* 469.

[131] *Ibid.*

[132] B Nalebuff and D Majerus, "Bundling, Tying and Portfolio Effects" *DTI Economics Paper No. 1*, Part 2–Case Studies (February 2003).

concluded that tying was illegal when, in fact, it was not harmful to consumers.[133] In none of those cases, however, did the authorities conclude incorrectly that tying was socially beneficial when it was not. That is, while there is evidence of "false convictions," there is no evidence of "false acquittals." Moreover, in seven of the eleven cases—that is, in 64% of the sample—tying was not harmful to consumers.[134]

From this report, one can draw the following policy implications: (1) the observed hostility towards tying is unjustified, since even tying that has been challenged is often welfare increasing; (2) a *per se* illegality approach to tying, whether in its strict or modified versions, makes no economic sense, as it often leads to the prohibition of beneficial tying practices; and (3) the analysis of the competitive impact of tying and bundling requires balancing of efficiencies and possible anticompetitive effects—that is, it demands a rule of reason approach.

Rule of reason analyses are typically conducted through the so-called method of the competitive balance, where the potential procompetitive and anticompetitive effects of tying are balanced in light of the available evidence. Yet in the case of tying, a simple balancing test faces some considerable difficulties. First, comparing the efficiency effects and the anticompetitive effects of tying is necessarily an extremely complex exercise. On the one hand, measuring the benefits of tying in terms of transaction costs and convenience may prove difficult. In addition, the game-theoretic models developed in recent years to show the possibility of anticompetitive tying do not provide a universally applicable checklist that competition authorities can safely use in their rule of reason analyses. While it is possible to construct more or less formal stories in which tying can prove anticompetitive, the difficulty is that the facts never match up exactly with the assumptions of the economic models, and multiple explanations are plausible. As Carlton and Waldman note:[135]

> "[T]rying to turn the theoretical possibility for harm…into a prescriptive theory of antitrust enforcement is a difficult task. For example, the courts would have to weigh any potential efficiencies from the tie with possible losses due to foreclosure, which by itself is challenging due to the difficulty of measuring *both* the relevant efficiencies and the relevant losses."

---

[133] See *Eurofix-Banco v Hilti,* OJ 1988 L 65/19; Case COMP/M.2220, *GeneralElectric/Honeywell*; and United Kingdom Competition Commission on the Interbrew SA and Bass PLC transaction, "A Report on the Acquisition by Interbrew SA of the Brewing Interests of Bass PLC," January 2001.

[134] See *Eurofix-Banco v Hilti,* OJ 1988 L 65/19; Case COMP/M.2220, *General Electric/Honeywell*, Commission decision of 3 July 2001; United Kingdom Competition Commission on the Interbrew SA and Bass PLC transaction, "A report on the acquisition by Interbrew SA of the brewing interests of Bass PLC", January 2001; "Completed acquisition by SMG plc of 29.5% shareholding of Scottish Radio Holdings plc," Report under section 125(4) of the Fair Trading Act 1973 of the Director General's advice, 21 June 2001, to the Secretary of State for Trade and Industry under section 76 of the Act; "Foreign Package Holidays: a report on the supply in the UK of tour operators' services and travel agents' services in relation to foreign package holidays," United Kingdom Monopolies and Mergers Commission, Cm 3813, 19 December 1998; "Investigation by the Director General of Telecommunications into the BT Surf Together and BT Talk and Surf Together pricing packages", Oftel, 4 May 2001; and *Jefferson Parish Hospital Dist. No. 2 et al. v Hyde*, 466 US 2 (1984).

[135] See DW Carlton and M Waldman, "The Strategic Use of Tying to Preserve and Create Market Power in Evolving Industries" (2002) 33 *RAND Journal of Economics* 194, 215 (emphasis added).

Most importantly, a simple balancing test approaches individual cases treating each candidate explanation as equally likely. However, the evidence from Nalebuff and Majerus (2003) implies that there should be no presumption that tying is anticompetitive, even when undertaken by firms in a dominant position. If anything, the presumption should be that tying often has beneficial effects.

Second alternative—structured rule of reason. Under this approach, any claim of anticompetitive tying would have to pass through three stages. The first two stages screen out ties that could not be anticompetitive given the facts of the case. The last stage balances anticompetitive and procompetitive effects for those ties that survive the first two screens. In the first two stages, the burden of proof is placed on the prosecution; in the last stage, the burden of proof is shared by both sides: the defendant must prove the existence and magnitude of the alleged efficiencies, while the prosecution must establish that the anticompetitive effects of tying more than offset its efficiency effects.

The game-theoretic models developed by post-Chicago economists do not provide a universally valid set of conditions that could be used by competition authorities as a safe checklist in their rule of reason analyses of tying and bundling. What these models do suggest is a series of screens for determining whether antitrust authorities should investigate and ultimately condemn a tying arrangement. This section draws mainly on a three-screen implementation suggested by Ahlborn *et al.* (2004) to identifying cases of illegal tying or bundling.[136] However, other authors have also put forward a similarly structured approach,[137] and we briefly discuss how their assessment criteria differ from those of Ahlborn *et al.* (2004) at each of the three screens.

a. First screen: is an anticompetitive effect possible? The first screen is whether it is possible that the tying practice in question could have anticompetitive effects. The models described in Section 9.2 provide a set of conditions that are necessary (but not sufficient) for tying to have anticompetitive effects:

1. *Market power for the tying firm.*[138] Without substantive market power, the tying firm either has no anticompetitive incentive to bundle, or its aim to exclude competitors by means of tying and bundling will be thwarted by its competitors.

2. *Imperfect competition in the tied market (e.g., due to fixed costs).* In a perfectly competitive market (with no fixed costs), a tying monopolist's attempts at stealing the business from its competitors in the tied good market would be inconsequential.

---

[136] C Ahlborn, DS Evans and AJ Padilla, "The Antitrust Economics of Tying: A Farewell to *Per Se* Illegality" *Antitrust Bulletin*, Spring 2004.

[137] K-U Kühn, R Stillman and C Caffarra, "Economic Theories of Bundling and their Policy Implication in Abuse Cases: An Assessment in Light of the Microsoft Case," *CEPR Discussion Paper No. 4756*, (2005).

[138] See, e.g, P Seabright, "Tying and Bundling: From Economics to Competition Policy," Edited Transcript of a CNE Market Insights Event, September 19, 2002 (visited Feb. 13, 2003).

3. *Commitment to tie.* Whinston (1990) has shown that without commitment to bundling, tying may not be credible and may fail to generate anticompetitive effects. Note, however, that credibility need not be an issue when consumers have heterogeneous valuations for the tying good.[139]

4. *Competitors' inability to match the tie.* Tying may not allow the near-monopolist to profitably leverage its market power in the tying good onto the tied good market if its competitors were able to respond with bundles of their own.[140]

5. *Likelihood of competitor exit.* Anticompetitive tying may be profitable if it leads to market foreclosure. However, exit may be difficult to predict, as its likelihood depends on numerous market parameters.[141]

6. *Entry barriers.* Even if some competitors exit the tied good market, without entry barriers it is unlikely that the tying firm would be able to raise price, as new competitors would quickly enter and erode any anticompetitive rents.

7. *Absence of buyer power.* Even if some competitors exited the tied good market, and entry barriers were sufficient to preclude new entry, a tying firm facing a concentrated demand side may not be able to raise the price of its bundle.[142]

These criteria are not empirically demanding. They entail investigations into market structure in which economists routinely engage. Ties that do not pass through this screen would need to be subjected to a second screen—a further analysis to determine whether they are likely to have anticompetitive effects.

Kühn et al. (2005) suggest that certain screens should be applied to preclude further investigation. These are: (1) does the firm under scrutiny enjoy market power in at least one of the bundled products?; (2) are the bundled products complements?; and (3) are there significant asymmetries between the product lines of competing firms? If the answer to any of these three questions is no, then the bundling arrangement at issue should not be challenged.

The first rule essentially corresponds to Criteria 1 and 2 above. The second rule is not explicitly considered in the above list, although it could be argued that complementarity enhances the credibility of a commitment to tie (Criterion 3). As for the third rule, Kühn et al. content themselves with the mere observation that product lines are asymmetric, whereas Criterion 4 above requires that rivals are unable to overcome the

[139] See B Nalebuff, "Bundling," *Yale ICF Working Paper Series No. 99-14* (1999).

[140] See B Nalebuff, "Competing Against Bundles," *Yale School of Management Working Paper No ES-02* (2000). Nalebuff shows that, under certain conditions, competitors may not match the bundle of the incumbent even when they have the ability to do so. And in some other cases, matching tying may turn out to be inefficient even if it prevents market foreclosure.

[141] See DW Carlton and M Waldman, "The Strategic Use of Tying to Preserve and Create Market Power in Evolving Industries" (2002) 33 *RAND Journal of Economics* 194 (profitable tying may give rise to anticompetitive effects even if competitors do not exit the market provided that they become sufficiently marginalised).

[142] See B Nalebuff, "Bundling and the GE-Honeywell Merger," *Yale School of Management Working Paper No ES-22*, (2002).

asymmetry and offer the same bundle as the dominant firm. Interestingly, there is no equivalent to Criteria 5 through 7. The comparison implies that it is more likely for a bundling arrangement to pass the first screen than it is under the test put forward by Ahlborn *et al.*

b. Second screen: is an anticompetitive effect plausible? Suppose market circumstances make it possible that tying might have an anticompetitive effect. The next question is then whether the tying arrangement under consideration is likely to have an anticompetitive effect. Answering this question requires: (1) positing some "theory" that describes how the tying arrangement will lead to anticompetitive effects; and (2) determining whether that "theory" applies to the factual circumstances at hand. This is empirically more demanding than those applied for the first screen. Ties that do not pass through this second screen would need to be subjected to a third screen to determine whether there are offsetting efficiencies. Kühn *et al.* (2005) agree that "in each individual case it will be necessary to show that there exists a coherent theory, broadly fitting the easily observable characteristics of the industry, which demonstrates that foreclosure effect—not limited to exit—are plausible."[143]

c. Third screen: are there offsetting efficiency benefits? Assuming the case survived the first two screens, the defendant would then be allowed to argue that the practice is motivated entirely by efficiencies. These efficiencies should be only achievable through the tie. If the tie is shown to have beneficial effects, the prosecution should then demonstrate that the efficiencies are insufficient to offset any anticompetitive effects.

This final screen requires a determination of whether the tie generates efficiencies (as most ties do) that can only be achieved through a tie, and whether these efficiencies are greater than the anticompetitive effects of the tie. In conducting this analysis one would need to consider dynamics and uncertainty. The anticompetitive effects demonstrated in the existing theoretical models take place over time—market foreclosure leads to exit, which leads to higher prices. One therefore needs to discount these effects to reflect the fact that they occur in the future and are uncertain.[144] Once again, this is an empirically demanding task, as Carlton and Waldman have recently explained:[145]

> "We would like to caution that trying to turn the theoretical possibility for harm [...] into a prescriptive theory of antitrust enforcement is a difficult task. For example, the courts would have to weigh any potential efficiencies from the tie with possible losses due to foreclosure, which by itself is challenging due to the difficulty of measuring both the relevant efficiencies and the relevant losses."

---

[143] See K-U Kühn, R Stillman and C Caffarra, "Economic Theories of Bundling and their Policy Implication in Abuse Cases: An Assessment in Light of the Microsoft Case" *CEPR Discussion Paper No. 4756*, (2005), p. 26.

[144] AJ Padilla, "The Efficiency Offence Doctrine in European Merger Control" M Reynolds and W Rowley (eds.), *International Merger Control: Prescriptions for Convergence* (International Bar Association, 2002) 117–23.

[145] DW Carlton and M Waldman, "The Strategic Use of Tying to Preserve and Create Market Power in Evolving Industries"(2002) 33 *RAND Journal of Economics* 194, 215.

Kühn *et al.* (2005) also recognise that bundling can generate efficiency benefits and that they should be taken into consideration even when the conditions for justified intervention set out in the first two stages are fulfilled. However, they differ from Ahlborn *et al.* (2004) as to how the burden of proof should be allocated. Kühn *et al.* (2005) argue that the burden of proof should be placed on the defendant because the company has private information about how it achieves these efficiencies.

Third alternative—modified *per se* legality. The structured rule of reason test, while better than the unstructured rule of reason test, is likely to be too difficult to implement in practice. The second and third screens in the test involve highly demanding empirical analysis. The structured rule of reason test may often prove inconclusive. As a result, the competition authorities and the courts may decide in favour of a simpler *per se* standard. But if that is the case, given that there is no support for treating tying practices under either a *per se* illegality or modified *per se* illegality rule, the only realistic option opened to antitrust authorities is a (modified) *per se* legality standard.

This standard would presume that tying is procompetitive unless a plaintiff could present strong evidence that tying did not result in efficiencies but was used mainly to obtain or maintain a monopoly, or that there are significant anticompetitive effects that outweigh procompetitive effects.[146] Such evidence would require a significant demonstration that there was a causal link between the practice and a likely reduction in consumer welfare. Tying could still be found illegal but probably only in 'exceptional' circumstances.[147] As such, one can view the modified *per se* legal approach as a version of rule of reason in which the burden of proof for establishing anticompetitive effects is high.[148] Of course, a modified *per se* legality rule will result in more false acquittals than a rule of reason standard. The cost of incremental false acquittals must be therefore compared to the cost of the additional administrative costs of having to proceed through a series of complex screens as well as the costs of false convictions from applying that structured analysis.

9.5 CONCLUSIONS

Significant progress but controversy persists. The approach to tying and bundling under Article 82 EC has moved from *per se* illegality to what some regard as a correct rule of reason analysis and others consider an excessively interventionist modified *per se* illegality rule. The Commission's decision in *Microsoft* and the Discussion Paper published by DG Competition both recognise that these business practices have procompetitive and anticompetitive effects and advocate a move away from a *per se* illegality standard. These developments are clearly welcome.

The controversy now concerns the balancing of those effects and, in particular, the issue of who should be required to conduct such a complex exercise. The Discussion Paper

[146] KN Hylton & M Salinger, "Tying Law and Policy: A Decision-Theoretic Approach" (2001) 69 *Antitrust Law Journal* 469, 470–71.

[147] DS Evans and AJ Padilla, "Designing Antitrust Rules for Assessing Unilateral Practices: A Neo-Chicago Approach" (2005) 72(1) *University of Chicago Law Review* 73–98.

[148] C Ahlborn, DS Evans and AJ Padilla, "The Antitrust Economics of Tying: A Farewell to *Per Se* Illegality" *Antitrust Bulletin*, Spring 2004, at 66.

states that the burden of proof falls on the dominant company, which is arguably not in line with current economic thinking. Whereas tying and bundling are ubiquitous in competitive markets, and thus presumptively efficient,[149] the efficiency benefits are commonly difficult to prove. As noted by Evans and Salinger (2005), "even in competitive industries where we are confident that efficiencies are the only plausible explanation for the practice, solid empirical evidence is not easy to produce."[150] Given that most real-world tying and bundling is driven by efficiency and the anticompetitive effects of these practices are so hard to identify in practice, several economists have advocated that the burden of proof concerning the competitive balance of procompetitive and anticompetitive effects should be placed on the plaintiff: "the benefit of doubt should go to defendants, not to plaintiffs."[151]

Some authors go even further and state that "to intervene in a tying case it should not be enough that there exists an anticompetitive rationale for tying that fits the broad outlines of the case." Instead, they would argue that "because of the frequency with which ties serve an efficiency rationale, there should optimally be no plausible efficiency rationale for the tie and the facts of the case should clearly support the anticompetitive rationale."[152]

[149] See RA Posner, *Antitrust Law* (2nd edn., Chicago, University of Chicago Press, 2001), 253. See also R Epstein, "Monopoly Dominance or Level Playing Field? The New Antitrust Paradox" *University of Chicago Law Review*, 72(1), 49-60 (2005); DS Evans and AJ Padilla, "Designing Antitrust Rules for Assessing Unilateral Practices: A Neo-Chicago Approach," *University of Chicago Law Review*, 72(1), 73-98 (2005), 81; and P Areeda and H. Hovenkamp, *Antitrust Law*, (2nd ed., Boston, Little, Brown and Company, 2004), 220.

[150] DS Evans and M Salinger, "Why Do Firms Bundle and Tie? Evidence from Competitive Markets and Implications for Tying Law," 22 *Yale Journal of Regulation* (2005), 85-86.

[151] DW Carlton, "A General Analysis of Exclusionary Conduct and Refusals to Deal–Why *Aspen* and *Kodak* are misguided," (2001) *Antitrust Law Journal* 675.

[152] DW Carlton and M Waldman, "Theories of Tying and Implications for Antitrust," *NBER Working Paper*, July 2005, 26.

Chapter 10

EXCLUSIONARY NON-PRICE ABUSES

10.1 INTRODUCTION

Definition. Exclusionary strategies by a dominant firm are not limited to non-remunerative price cuts designed to cause rivals' market exit, i.e., predatory pricing.[1] A range of other, more subtle non-price strategies aimed at raising rivals' costs, to the detriment of consumers, may also be available to dominant firms. An oft-quoted, but extreme, example is blowing up a rival's factory. This would not only be criminal, but may also be anticompetitive if it causes an increase in the rival's costs that appreciably affects competition. More orthodox examples might include vexatious litigation, use and abuse of regulatory processes to delay or prevent the launch of rivals' products, predatory design changes, and abuses in connection with standard-setting organisations. Although these practices are disparate, they have the unifying feature that they all involve limiting rivals' production by methods other than offering better products, service, or lower prices. Such practices are therefore contrary to Article 82(b), which prohibits a dominant firm from "limiting production" where this also causes "prejudice of consumers."

Practices of this kind have sometimes been referred to as "non-price predation,"[2] "raising rivals' costs strategies,"[3] and "cheap exclusion."[4] But these terms lack precision, or are apt to mislead, in certain respects. Non-price predation is an under-inclusive term, since most of the objectionable practices do not involve the element of profit sacrifice that is inherent in predation claims. Raising rivals' costs is also problematic as a label, since one obvious, but procompetitive, way of raising rivals costs would be to increase output and lower prices to non-predatory levels that prevent rivals from achieving the necessary returns to scale. Cheap exclusion is a useful catch-all phrase, but it ignores the fact that a number of exclusionary non-price abuses may involve substantial costs to the dominant firm, e.g., vexatious litigation. Some of the practices discussed in this chapter are undoubtedly "cheap" in the sense that they have little efficiency-enhancing justification (e.g., concealment or false statements in relation to patents), but most of them involve activities that are generally procompetitive (e.g., product innovation). The remainder of this chapter therefore uses the term

---

[1] See Ch. 5 (Predatory Pricing).

[2] See "Non-Price Predation" (1986) 16(2) *Journal Of Reprints For Antitrust Law And Economics*.

[3] See TG Krattenmaker and SC Salop, "Anticompetitive Exclusion: Raising Rivals' Costs To Achieve Power over Price" (1986) 96 *Yale Law Journal* 209; and SC Salop and DT Scheffman, "Cost-Raising Strategies" (1987) 6 *Journal of Industrial Economics* 19.

[4] See SA Creighton, Director, Bureau of Competition, Federal Trade Commission, "Cheap Exclusion," Charles River Associates 9th Annual Conference, *Current Topics in Antitrust Economics and Competition Policy*, Washington D.C., February 8, 2005, available at http://www.ftc.gov/speeches/creighton/050425cheapexclusion.pdf. See also S Creighton, BD Hoffman, T Krattenmaker and E Nagata, "Cheap Exclusion" (2005) 72 *Antitrust Law Journal* 975.

"exclusionary non-price abuses," on the basis that this phrase more accurately captures the core concern under Article 82 EC.

Reasons why exclusionary non-price abuses may be common. A number of considerations suggest that exclusionary non-price strategies may be more common than pure price predation, although there is little or no empirical data to back up this up.[5] First, unlike predatory pricing, exclusionary non-price abuses are likely to be much less costly to the perpetrator. In a predatory pricing case, the dominant firm must increase output and lower prices, in the hope that this will exclude rival firms. This will generally be costly for the dominant firm, since it will typically have to incur losses over a much larger output than rivals. Moreover, the dominant firm would also need to have a reasonable prospect of recovering its losses through increased prices in future, i.e., a speculative investment. In contrast, many forms of non-price exclusion may be more or less costless and the adverse effects on rivals are generally less speculative. For example, filing a false patent claim is no more costly than telling the truth and may even be cheaper. Improperly using regulatory procedures to stymie rivals may also be relatively costless, in particular where a group of firms act in concert.

Second, exclusionary non-price strategies are usually less risky for a dominant firm. Most of them involve behaviour that is, in general, entirely rational and lawful. Litigation to defend key commercial assets is usually a core obligation of a company towards it shareholders. Moreover, even unsuccessful litigation by a dominant firm cannot be presumed to reflect anticompetitive motives: the fact that the litigation was unsuccessful *ex post* does not mean that it was ill-founded *ex ante*. Likewise, it is entirely legitimate for a firm with valuable assets to take full advantage of any regulatory or government procedure that would allow it to extend their scope of protection or insulate them in other legitimate ways from rivalry. Indeed, the power to petition the government and to defend commercial interests in civil courts is constitutionally-guaranteed in many Member States. Identifying situations in which there is no objective basis for availing of an otherwise lawful right to petition courts or government is therefore extremely difficult. Detection is also likely to be difficult because many anticompetitive raising rivals' costs strategies do not result in market exit. Instead, the dominant firm's strategy may raise rivals' costs by enough to render them ineffective as a competitive threat, even if this does not force the rivals to quit the market.

Finally, the ways in which a dominant firm can unlawfully exclude rivals through non-price strategies are myriad. Whatever the specificities, predatory pricing always involves setting prices below an appropriate measure of cost in the hope that rivals' exit allows the dominant firm to increase prices in future. In contrast, the anticompetitive means of non-price exclusion are potentially limitless. For example, a number of different problems can arise in the context of standard setting organisations where

---

[5] In the United States, there are very few reported cases of successful predatory pricing claims, but quite a few regarding non-price strategies. See S Creighton, BD Hoffman, T Krattenmaker and E Nagata, "Cheap Exclusion" (2005) 72 *Antitrust Law Journal* 975. In contrast, in Europe, there are a relatively large number of cases in which price predation has been made out, but only a handful concerning non-price strategies. But it is clear that non-price strategies are also becoming a greater enforcement priority in Europe.

patent holders "hold up" licensees by waiting until participants are locked into the standard and then charge an "excessive" royalty for undisclosed patents covered by the standard.[6] Other practices might include removing a competitors' products from retail outlets,[7] destroying competitors' sales displays,[8] anticompetitive collective boycotts,[9] deliberately changing a product design to render it incompatible with interoperable rival products,[10] false claims that the dominant firm's product works across multiple platforms,[11] bringing baseless litigation,[12] and petitioning for the imposition of anti-dumping duties on rivals.[13] A multitude of different factual settings could also be envisaged.

Role of Article 82 EC in exclusionary non-price abuse cases. Most examples of exclusionary non-price abuses involve activities that may be contrary to criminal, contract, or tort laws. In addition, standard-setting organisations and regulatory procedures will in many cases have internal rules and remedies to deal with abuses of procedure or misrepresentations, including mandatory arbitration. In these circumstances, the residual role for competition law enforcement has been questioned. This is mainly on the grounds that, although such practices do not involve "competition on the merits" and may impair rivals' opportunities, they do not necessarily result in harm to competition and the rare cases in which they do are extremely difficult to detect.[14] Proponents of this view therefore consider the risk of deterring legitimate activity more important than the small number of cases in which they may harm competition.

But if, which seems clear, there are circumstances in which such actions *can* harm competition, the case for intervention under competition law is well-founded. It is also important to emphasise that remedies under systems of law other than competition law pursue different objectives. For example, most contract and tort laws are limited to ensuring compensation for loss or damage *inter partes*. Under competition law, the harm resulting from such practices is not necessarily, or even primarily, limited to injury to one or more parties: it concerns injury to competition and consumers. Private suits will also be motivated by considerations of business cost and benefit rather than the public imperative of enforcing competition laws. Remedies in a private context may

---

[6] See, e.g., *In re Union Oil Company of California,* Dkt. No. 9305 (March 4, 2003) (Complaint), available at http://www.ftc.gov/os/2003/03/unocalcmp.htm (hereinafter "Unocal"). On June 13, 2005, the defendants agreed in a consent decree with the Federal Trade Commission not to enforce the patents that were, alleged to be causing the "hold up" problem. See also *In re Rambus Inc.,* Dkt. No. 9302 (F.T.C. Feb. 23, 2004) (Initial decision dismissing complaint), available at http://www.ftc.gov/os/adjpro/d9302/040223initialdecision.pdf, appeal docketed before Commission (hereinafter "Rambus").

[7] See *Irish Sugar*, OJ 1997 L 258/1, affirmed on appeal in Case T-228/97, *Irish Sugar v Commission* [1999] ECR II-2969 and by Order of the Court of Justice in Case C-497/99 P, *Irish Sugar plc v Commission* [2001] ECR I-5333 (hereinafter "*Irish Sugar*").

[8] See, e.g., *Conwood Co. v US Tobacco Co.,* 290 F.3d 768 (6th Cir. 2002).

[9] See, e.g., *Allied Tube & Conduit Corp. v Indian Head, Inc.,* 486 US 492 (1988).

[10] See, e.g., *Decca Navigator System,* OJ 1989, L 43/27.

[11] See, e.g., *United States v Microsoft Corp.*, 253 F.3d 34, 76-77 (D.C. Cir. 2001).

[12] Case T-111/96, *ITT Promedia NV v Commission* [1998] ECR II-2937.

[13] Case T-5/97, *Industrie des Poudres Sphériques SA v Commission* [2000] ECR II-3755.

[14] See, e.g., PE Areeda & H Hovenkamp, *Antitrust Law* (New York, Aspen Publishers, 1996).

also not be attuned to the consumer welfare concerns that mainly underpin Article 82 EC. In sum, there is clearly an important, if sometimes residual, role for Article 82 EC to play in cases involving allegations of exclusionary non-price abuses.

Limited decisional practice and case law under Article 82 EC. Cases involving exclusionary non-price abuses have thus far been an extreme rarity under Article 82 EC. There are only a handful of precedents that are directly on point,[15] as well as an equally small number that indirectly concern anticompetitive raising rivals' costs strategies.[16] But it is clear that this area of law is an increasing enforcement priority for competition authorities and courts in the EU and elsewhere. There has recently been one major case at EU level concerning allegations of anticompetitive impediments to generic drug entry,[17] as well as a number of similar cases at national level in Italy.[18] These cases have been prompted by widespread attempts by public authorities to reduce expenditure on healthcare by promoting generic entry, as well as by increased recognition among competition authorities that exclusionary non-price abuses can be harmful. Enforcement outside the EU has also drawn attention to this particular issue. In particular, enforcement action by the US government agencies in two recent high-profile matters—*Unocal* and *Rambus*—has heightened awareness of the scope for using anticompetitive tactics within private standards setting organisations. For these and other reasons, it seems certain that enforcement in this area is likely to increase in the coming years.

10.2 EXAMPLES OF EXCLUSIONARY NON-PRICE ABUSES

Overview. The ways in which firms can unlawfully raise their rivals costs or exclude them through non-price strategies are numerous. Certain established practices have nonetheless gained a reasonable degree of acceptance in the decisional practice and case law. First, product design changes may be abusive in circumstances where they are purely made to render rivals' products incompatible and involve no technical improvement on the replaced product. Second, litigation or other proceedings brought purely to harass rivals may be abusive. Third, government or regulatory procedures may be used and abused for unlawful ends, in particular in the case of generic drug products. Fourth, standard setting organisations may present scope for one or more participants asserting ownership over essential proprietary technology underlying a standard after the standard is adopted. Fifth, it may in exceptional cases be an abuse to acquire intellectual property rights from a third party or to internally develop a series of

[15] See *Decca Navigator System*, OJ 1989, L 43/27.

[16] See *Irish Sugar*, OJ 1997 L 258/1, affirmed on appeal in Case T-228/97, *Irish Sugar v Commission* [1999] ECR II-2969 and by Order of the Court of Justice in Case C-497/99 P, *Irish Sugar plc v Commission* [2001] ECR I-5333. See also Case T-5/97, *Industrie des Poudres Sphériques SA v Commission* [2000] ECR II-3755.

[17] See Commission fines AstraZeneca €60 million for misusing patent system to delay market entry of competing generic drugs, Commission Press Release IP/05/737, June 15, 2005. The Commission also carried out "dawn raids" at the premises of Lundbeck and others in relating to conduct impeding generic drug competition: see http://www.eubusiness.com/Pharma/051025163459.2am0hgxi.

[18] See *Merck Italia s.p.a.* (Case A 364, interim measures, June 17, 2005) and *GlaxoSmithKline* (Case A.363, investigation opened on February 25, 2005) (decision pending).

complementary rights to block or impede rivals' access to a market. Finally, there are a range of miscellaneous practices that have been said to raise concerns of abuse in certain circumstances, e.g., false advertising or disparagement of rivals' products. The various scenarios and applicable principles are considered in detail below.

10.2.1 Predatory Design Changes/Product Introduction

Product introduction or changes generally presumptively lawful. Competition authorities and courts have generally avoided evaluating whether new product introductions, or changes to existing designs, that adversely affect the compatibility of rival products are abusive. One exception concerns the bundling of two separate products and whether this can be abusive in certain circumstances. This issue is discussed in detail in Chapter Nine (Tying and Bundling). For expositional simplicity, this section focuses on the circumstances in which changes to a *single product* can be abusive, i.e., absent actual or implicit tying.

In general, there are good reasons to be cautious about treating product introductions or changes as abusive. A first reason is that innovation is probably the most valuable form of procompetitive activity and an enforcement policy that runs even a remote risk of chilling such activity can cause enormous harm to consumer welfare. Second, there is no *general* principle of law that a firm, even a dominant firm, has a duty to make its products compatible with rivals' products (although limited exceptions have been recognised, *inter alia*, in Community legislation[19]). Third, in many cases—particularly those involving network effects—consumer welfare may in fact be enhanced by allowing a single facility that consumers prefer to prevail, rather that promoting compatibility between a range of competing facilities.[20] Finally, even if interoperability was legally required in all cases, and was unambiguously good for consumers, there is no clear legal or economic test that would allow a court or competition authority to distinguish between legitimate product improvements and improvements that were designed purely to limit rivals' marketing. The analytical process most likely to be applied in such cases—second-guessing disputes between experts as to a product's

[19] For example, Article 6 of the Software Directive requires owners of copyright in computer programs to allow reproduction of the program code and translation of its form where this is indispensable to obtain the information necessary to achieve the interoperability of an independently created computer program with other programs, provided that: (1) these acts are performed by the licensee or by another person having a right to use a copy of a program, or on their behalf by a person authorised to do so; (2) the information necessary to achieve interoperability has not previously been readily available to the person seeking interoperability; and (3) these acts are confined to the parts of the original program which are necessary to achieve interoperability. Moreover, this exception does not allow: (1) the code and translation to be used for goals other than to achieve the interoperability of the independently created computer program; (2) to be given to others, except when necessary for the interoperability of the independently created computer program; or (3) to be used for the development, production or marketing of a computer program substantially similar in its expression, or for any other act which infringes copyright. Finally, nothing in Article 6 can unreasonably prejudice the copyright holder's legitimate interests or conflicts with a normal exploitation of the computer program. See Council Directive of May 14, 1991, on the legal protection of computer programs, OJ 1991 L 122/42.

[20] For an outline of the economic reasons why competition to produce a single facility may be preferable to competition to create or maintain different compatible facilities, see A ten Kate and G Niels, "Below cost pricing in the presence of network externalities" in *The Pros And Cons Of Low Prices* (Stockholm, Swedish Competition Authority, 2003), p. 97.

relative strengths and weaknesses—is highly likely to lead to haphazard, inconclusive, and incorrect outcomes. Taken together, these considerations strongly imply that the introduction of a new product, or altering existing products, is presumptively lawful under Article 82 EC, even if it affects the compatibility of rival products.

Possible findings of abuse in exceptional cases. In exceptional cases, however, there may be evidence that a product was introduced or altered solely to render rivals' products incompatible and exclude them from the market, to the detriment of consumers. For the policy reasons outlined above, such cases must be rare indeed and pursued only in circumstances where the totality of the evidence clearly corroborates an anticompetitive strategy. The best example is *Decca Navigator*.[21] The Decca Navigator System (DNS) is an international radio navigation system used for shipping and other purposes worldwide. It consisted of: (1) transmission of signals by land-based stations operating in groups; and (2) devices placed on board the means of transport which receive these signals (receivers). Racal Decca was the only provider of transmission signals in certain Member States and was also active as a manufacturer of receivers for those signals. Although Racal Decca at one time controlled patents that prevented third parties from manufacturing receivers for DNS signals, those patents expired in the 1960s.

During the 1980s a number of undertakings began manufacturing receivers in competition with Racal Decca's system. Racal Decca concluded internally that its prospects of preventing such entry by claiming copyright in the transmission signals, or alleging breaches of unfair competition laws, were slim. Racal Decca therefore deliberately sought to alter the transmission signals in a way that rendered competing receivers essentially unusable, but allowed its own products to continue to work effectively. Internal documents from the company left no doubt as to the intention behind these changes. They noted that "it was decided that alterations to the transmissions would be by far the best method of preventing [rivals'] sales."[22] Indeed, Racal Decca refused to answer requests from the Danish authorities as to the reasons behind the signal changes, since this would reveal "that the improvements are shams and intended to do no more than frustrate competitive products."[23] The policy of changing signals was referred to as its "strongest weapon" against rivals' new offerings.[24] In one case, Racal Decca even wrote to a competitor and used the alteration of signals as a means of discouraging them from entering the market and, when the alteration was actually carried out, warned users about the consequent inaccuracy of the rival's receivers. Racal Decca also used the alteration of the signals as a means of procuring anticompetitive market-sharing agreements with the new entrants as a settlement of the dispute.

The Commission concluded that the changes made by Racal Decca were "deliberate" and solely intended to cause the malfunctioning of competing devices.[25] Complaints

---

[21] *Decca Navigator System*, OJ 1989 L 43/27.
[22] *Ibid.*, para. 25.
[23] *Ibid.*, para. 27.
[24] *Ibid.*
[25] *Ibid.*, para. 108.

were also made by customers (including users of Racal Decca's own devices), governments, and the International Association of Lighthouse Authorities, most of whom pointed out what the real purpose of the signal changes was, i.e., exclusionary conduct. The signal changes caused great disturbance to the shipping community, as well as loss and damage. There was no evidence that the signal changes made any improvement over existing products and all evidence pointed to the fact that the alterations were made solely to exclude competitors, which also caused loss to users. In these circumstances, an abuse contrary to Article 82 EC was found.

Although it was not a case arising under Article 82 EC, the findings made by the US Court of Appeals in *Microsoft* also show the high standard required for abusive product designs or changes.[26] One aspect of the case concerned Java, a set of technologies developed by Sun Microsystems, that posed a potential threat to Microsoft's Windows product a software development platform. Netscape, Microsoft's internet browser rival, agreed with Sun to distribute a copy of the Java runtime environment—the programming tools for developing Java applications—with every copy of its Netscape Navigator product. Microsoft, too, agreed to promote the Java technologies, but at the same time took steps to maximise the difficulty with which applications written in Java could be ported from Windows to other platforms, and *vice versa*.

Microsoft designed a Java Virtual Machine (JVM)—which translates byte code into instructions to the operating system—incompatible with the one developed by Sun. Sun had already developed a JVM for the Windows operating system when Microsoft began work on its version. The JVM developed by Microsoft allows Java applications to run faster on Windows than does Sun's JVM, but a Java application designed to work with Microsoft's JVM did not work with Sun's JVM and *vice versa*. This was unobjectionable in itself. Microsoft's Java implementation included, in addition to a JVM, a set of software development tools it created to assist independent software vendors in designing Java applications. These tools were incompatible with Sun's cross-platform aspirations for Java, but, again, this was unobjectionable in itself.

The gravamen of the case, however, was that Microsoft deceived Java developers regarding the Windows-specific nature of the tools. Microsoft's tools included certain keywords and directives that could only be executed properly by Microsoft's version of the Java runtime environment for Windows. Java developers who relied upon Microsoft's public commitment to cooperate with Sun, and who used Microsoft's tools to develop what Microsoft led them to believe were cross-platform applications, ended up producing applications that would run only on the Windows operating system. There was a good deal of internal Microsoft evidence (e.g., emails and other documents) which confirmed that Microsoft deliberately intended to deceive Java developers, and predicted that the effect of its actions would be to generate Windows-dependent Java applications that their developers believed would be cross-platform, with the ultimate objective of thwarting Java's threat to Microsoft's monopoly in the market for operating systems. One Microsoft document, for example, stated that a strategic goal was to "kill cross-platform Java by grow[ing] the polluted Java market." In these circumstances, and because Microsoft offered no procompetitive explanation for its campaign to

[26] See *United States v Microsoft Corp.*, 253 F.3d 34, 76–77 (D.C. Cir. 2001).

deceive developers, the Court of Appeals concluded that the Windows alterations in respect of Java were exclusionary, in violation of Section 2 of the Sherman Act 1890.

10.2.2 Vexatious Litigation

The fundamental right to bring litigation. The right to bring civil litigation and other claims to assert or defend key interests is a key component of the rule of law, enshrined in the constitutional laws of the Member States, as well as general principles of Community law. As the Court of First Instance has held, "access to the Court is a fundamental right and a general principle ensuring the rule of law, it is only in wholly exceptional circumstances that the fact that legal proceedings are brought is capable of constituting an abuse of a dominant position within the meaning of Article 8[2] of the Treaty."[27] The fact that litigation was ill-advised, imprudent, or ultimately unsuccessful does not make the basic right to bring it any less valid. In exceptional cases, however, litigation may be pursued by a dominant firm as a tactic to exhaust smaller rivals' resources and delay or prevent entry. Where anticompetitive litigation of this kind by a dominant firm can be identified, it is an abuse contrary to Article 82 EC.

Criteria for anticompetitive litigation under Article 82 EC. The leading Article 82 EC precedent to date on anticompetitive litigation is *ITT/Promedia*.[28] The case concerned litigation between the incumbent telecommunications operator in Belgium, Belgacom, and Promedia, an undertaking active in the publication of business directories. Promedia and Belgacom brought a series of claims and counterclaims in the Belgian courts. In parallel, Promedia pursued many of the same claims before the Commission. Following the rejection of its complaint, Promedia appealed to the Court of First Instance.

The main interest in the judgment lies in the Court's elaboration of the conditions for anticompetitive litigation. The Court accepted the Commission's conclusion that two cumulative conditions must be established in order to identify situations in which bringing legal proceedings amounts to an abuse. It is necessary that the action: (1) cannot reasonably be considered as an attempt to establish the rights of the undertaking concerned and can therefore only serve to harass the opposite party; and (2) is conceived in the framework of a plan whose goal is to eliminate competition. The first criterion implies that the action is, on an objective view, manifestly unfounded. The second criterion requires evidence that the aim of the action is to eliminate competition.

Both criteria must be fulfilled in order to establish an abuse: the fact that unmeritorious litigation is instituted does not in itself constitute an infringement of Article 82 EC unless it has an anticompetitive object. Equally, litigation that may reasonably be

[27] See Case T-111/96, *ITT Promedia NV v Commission* [1998] ECR II-2937, para. 60 (citing Case 222/84, *Johnston v Chief Constable of the Royal Ulster Constabulary* [1986] ECR 1651, paras. 17–18). Under Article 6 EC, the EU is founded on the principles of liberty, democracy, respect for human rights and fundamental freedoms, and the rule of law, principles which are common to all Member States. The second paragraph provides that the EU shall respect fundamental rights, as guaranteed by the European Convention for the Protection of Human Rights and Fundamental Freedoms and as they result from the constitutional traditions common to the Member States, as general principles of Community law.

[28] *Ibid.*

regarded as an attempt to assert rights *vis-à-vis* competitors is not abusive, irrespective of the fact that it may be part of a plan to eliminate competition.[29] The conditions thus embody a clear element of objective unreasonableness in bringing the action, as well as subjective awareness of the anticompetitive motive of such litigation. It is not enough that an action turns out to be unfounded in law. By the same token, the fact that the dominant firm prevailed in litigation should be an absolute defence, unless, perhaps, there was some subsequent authority for saying that no reasonable court could have reached the conclusion that it reached.

Distinguishing anticompetitive and legitimate litigation. Distinguishing legitimate litigation from the anticompetitive kind is not easy in the abstract, not least because each case will be highly fact-specific. But a useful contrast can be made between the allegations made in the *ITT/Promedia* and *Decca Navigator* cases, both discussed above. The former might be characterised as a case in which there was bitter, but not obviously unfounded, litigation between the parties, whereas the latter involved a situation in which the litigation contemplated was considered objectively baseless by the firm itself.

The background in *ITT/Promedia* was as follows. Promedia had, for some years, an agreement with the former Belgian state telecommunications and postal monopoly to publish a business listings directory. When the agreement came up for renewal, the incumbent telecoms operator, Belgacom, broke off negotiations and issued an invitation to tender for third party publishers. Undeterred, Promedia then announced in a press release that it had decided to continue to publish its business directory and intensified efforts to canvass the sale of advertising space in preparation for the new edition. Belgacom warned its customers that any canvassing or sales activities by Promedia were undertaken without its authorisation and fell outside the scope of any contractual relationship. Belgacom also informed its customers that it had decided to publish its own official telephone directory, in cooperation with a partner specialising in that field, and would contact customers to inform them of the possibilities of advertising in the next edition of the official annual telephone directory.

Promedia brought an action against Belgacom alleging that Belgacom had infringed Belgian legislation on commercial practices, as well as Belgian competition law and Article 82 EC. It also sought an order requiring Belgacom to cease spreading false, misleading and disparaging information concerning its telephone directory activities. Belgacom counterclaimed that, in the absence of an authorisation from the national regulator, any canvassing or sale of advertising space by Promedia was contrary to Belgian law and Article 82 EC. It also applied for an order requiring the applicant to cease all canvassing and/or sales activities until such time as it had obtained the authorisation in question. Both of Promedia's claims were upheld, including on appeal.

Belgacom then commenced a third action, requiring Promedia to comply with certain obligations under the earlier agreements with Promedia. In essence, these sought to require Promedia to disclose to Belgacom certain data and other items in its possession that Belgacom wished to use to publish its own directory, as well as seeking damages

---

[29] Case T-111/96, *ITT Promedia NV v Commission* [1998] ECR II-2937, paras. 55–57.

for non-disclosure. Belgacom's application was dismissed at summary judgment and in full proceedings, on the grounds that the original agreement was anticompetitive and unenforceable. Promedia's counterclaim for frivolous and vexatious litigation was also dismissed.

When Belgacom refused to provide Promedia with the necessary subscriber data, Promedia sought a declaration from the Belgian courts that Belgacom's refusal to supply it with subscriber data on fair, reasonable, and non-discriminatory terms constituted an unfair commercial practice under Belgian law and an abuse under Article 82 EC. Belgacom again counterclaimed, arguing that Promedia's application for access to the subscriber data was contrary to Belgian law and Article 82 EC. A Belgian court granted Promedia's application and commissioned an expert to determine a royalty. Belgacom's counterclaim was dismissed, but Promedia's secondary claim that Belgacom's counterclaim was frivolous and vexatious was also dismissed.

On appeal from a Commission decision rejecting Promedia's complaint, the Court of First Instance concluded that, as the Belgian courts had ruled, Belgacom's claims and counterclaims were not manifestly baseless. The issue was not whether Belgacom's claims were wrong in law, but whether there was, at the time they were made, a reasonable basis for bringing them. Regarding Belgacom's claim that Promedia was not authorised under national law to publish telephone directories, the Court concluded that the relevant Belgian provisions were reasonably clear that prior authorisation was required. The effect of the legislation was therefore that Belgacom was the only undertaking entitled to publish such directories. The Court held that the purpose of Belgacom's first two actions—which sought to establish that Promedia had no right under Belgian law to publish a directory without authorisation from the competent authorities—involved "the assertion of what Belgacom, at the moment when it brought those two actions, could reasonably consider, on the basis of [Belgian law]."[30] Of course, the Belgian courts ultimately concluded that the legislation in question was contrary to EC competition law, but the Court held that Belgacom's reliance on that legislation in litigation was not, at the time when that litigation was commenced, baseless. The actions could not have been said to be brought only for the purpose of harassing Promedia.

Although it was not pursued as a vexatious litigation case, *Decca Navigator* concerned a situation in which there was widespread awareness within the company that litigation to prevent rivals from using receivers in competition with Racal Decca's own receivers would be objectively baseless and was thus brought only for the purpose of excluding competitors. It will be recalled that Racal Decca's patents, which prevented third parties from manufacturing receivers for the standardised transmission signals, expired in the 1960s. Racal Decca then investigated whether it could claim copyright on transmission. Internal documents from the legal department said that "the position on copyright was not very hopeful" and that "there was no basis for claiming copyright," except, perhaps, on lists of information regarding masts etc. But even the latter was considered "no more than arguable" by Racal Decca.[31] Regarding unfair competition

[30] *Ibid.*, para. 93.

[31] See *Decca Navigator System*, OJ 1989 L 43/27, paras. 22–23.

claims, the legal department concluded that "to commence a legal action without any real chance of success, without any real legal basis, would cause, sooner or later, embarrassment."[32] Thus, there was a reasonable basis for saying that litigation by Racal Decca to enforce copyright or unfair competition laws would have been objectively baseless.

There was also ample evidence of anticompetitive object or intent—the second criterion in *IIT/Promedia.* It will be recalled that Racal Decca's policy of altering transmission signals brought no discernible improvement and was expressly introduced for the sole purpose of frustrating rivals' entry. There was also evidence, reported on the basis of Racal Decca information, that "Racal Decca's tactics towards [rivals] [wa]s to exhaust them by cases in eight countries at a time" and that "Racal Decca pursue the consistent policy of asking a long series of questions in each single case, questions which demand an answer from [rivals], and Racal Decca reckon to fatigue [rivals] on legal questions rather than beat them on legal ground."[33] In other words, had the copyright claims been pursued, the case looked like a candidate for anticompetitive litigation, contrary to Article 82 EC.

10.2.3 Use And Abuse Of Regulatory Or Government Procedures

The scope for using regulatory or government procedures for abusive ends. Administrative regulation of multiple aspects of market entry, product approval, and marketing is pervasive in modern economies. When regulatory or government approval is required for the marketing of a product or service, it can create potentially limitless scope for the use and abuse of such procedures for anticompetitive ends. Even known sceptics of antitrust enforcement recognised from the outset that the use of government and regulatory procedures provides potentially fertile ground for exclusionary conduct.[34] Outright exclusionary tactics might include bribery, but, in practice, are more likely to involve subtle attempts to use and abuse government and regulatory procedures to stymie the launch of competing products or artificially their costs of production. Such tactics are a valid concern under Article 82 EC where they seek to petition approval procedures without legitimate business justification and there is actual or likely harm to competition as a result.

Examples. A number of possible tactics for using legal and regulatory procedures for anticompetitive ends have been directly and indirectly identified in the case law as abusive means of limiting rivals' production, to the detriment of consumers. An early case, *Osram/Airam*,[35] concerned abusive registration of trademarks. Airam, a small Finnish lamp producer, complained that Osram, one of the largest European producers of lamps at the time, had opposed, for purely anticompetitive reasons, its registration of the trademark "Airam" in Finland and Germany. Osram's supposed basis for doing this was that "Airam" risked confusion with its own trademark "Osram." Following intervention by the Commission, the parties agreed that Airam could use the trademark

[32] *Ibid.*, para. 25.

[33] *Ibid.*, para. 50.

[34] See, e.g., R Bork, *The Antitrust Paradox: A Policy at War with Itself* (New York, Free Press, 1978), Ch. 18 (Predation Through Governmental Process).

[35] See XIth Report On Competition Policy (1981), para. 97.

anywhere within the EU provided certain measures were taken to distinguish the products and avoid the (very minimal) scope for confusion. The Commission stated that a dominant firm that registers a trademark which it knows or ought to know is already used by a competitor infringes Article 82 EC where such action limits the scope for the rival penetrating the dominant firm's market.

Another allegation that has featured in the case law concerns the invocation of EU anti-dumping laws—which allow for the imposition of duties on foreign products that are considered to have been "dumped" on the EU market—for exclusionary ends. For example, in *Industrie des Poudres Sphériques*, the applicant, Industries des Poudres Sphériques (IPS) alleged that a rival firm, Pechiney Électrométallurgie (PEM), had made improper use of EU anti-dumping procedures in an effort to exclude it from the market. PEM was the sole Community producer of primary calcium metal and also marketed broken calcium metal (a derivative of primary calcium metal). IPS competed with PEM in the derivative market for broken calcium metal. The Court of First Instance rejected this argument in rather cursory fashion, noting that "recourse to a remedy in law and, in particular, participation by an undertaking in an investigation conducted by the Community institutions, cannot be deemed, of itself, to be contrary to Article 8[2] of the Treaty." It added that anti-dumping procedures aim to re-establish undistorted competition in the market in the interest of the Community, reflected in a thorough investigation conducted by the Community institutions during which the interested parties are heard, possibly leading to the adoption of a binding Community measure. In these circumstances, "to assert that mere recourse to such a procedure is, of itself, contrary to Article 8[2] of the Treaty amounts to denying undertakings the right to avail themselves of legal instruments established in the interest of the Community."[36]

The principles applicable to abusive invocation of anti-dumping procedures are almost certainly the same as for vexatious litigation generally, discussed above. Thus, it would need to be shown that petitioning for the imposition of such duties was objectively baseless, i.e., there was no reasonable basis for seeking duties, and, in addition, that the petitioning party intended to invoke the proceedings for anticompetitive purposes. Of course, there are wider issues as to whether anti-dumping laws can *in themselves* be anticompetitive because of the price protection they afford to EU-based producers and the different standards of predatory pricing that are applied to such producers. This raises complex issues that fall outside the scope of this work. But there is undoubtedly some tension between anti-dumping laws designed to protect EU-based producers from foreign price competition and competition laws intended to ensure a system of undistorted competition. The basic, but not very satisfactory, solution is to say that both protectionist and competition objectives form part of EU law and, to the extent possible, should not undermine each other.

[36] Case T-5/97, *Industrie des Poudres Sphériques SA v Commission* [2000] ECR II-3755, para. 213. See also *Soda-Ash/Solvay*, OJ 1991 L 152/21, para. 10, where the Commission noted, without drawing any legal conclusions, that "[a] major plank of Solvay's commercial policy in the soda-ash sector is to ensure the maintenance of the anti-dumping measures in place against the United States producers of heavy ash as well as the east European light ash suppliers." The anti-dumping duties on United States imports were under review at the time of the decision and Solvay pressed hard for their renewal, as well as the extension of anti-dumping duties to other imported material.

The specific case of impeding generic drug entry. The only cases to date in which the use and abuse of regulatory approval procedures have been found to raise abusive concern impediments to generic drug entry by patent holders. The availability of generic drugs is a major public policy issue for the EU Member States, principally due to the rapid increase in health care costs. Under generic substitution legislation in the EU, less expensive generic drugs can (and, in some cases, must) automatically be substituted for branded equivalents. This rule, however, does not necessarily apply to generics of different dosages, different formulations (e.g., instant for continuous release), or different delivery systems (e.g., capsules for tablets). Observers have noted that by withdrawing a particular version of a branded drug, for which there are approved generic substitutes, in favour of another version, for which there are not, the extent of generic substitution can be decreased (or eliminated), thereby extending the life cycle of the branded monopoly drug. The withdrawal of a branded drug to which a generic applicant has referred and relied in its own application for approval would potentially extend the life cycle further (i.e., in the absence of data on which to refer, the generic manufacturer would need to conduct its own clinical trials albeit with a decreased incentive to do so).

A second set of tactics concerns misrepresentations or other efforts to mislead regulatory approval agencies into granting unwarranted initial or extended patent protection to a drug. For example, in *Biovail*,[37] the US Federal Trade Commission objected to certain declarations made by Biovail in connection with a patent listing. Biovail acquired an exclusive licence to a patent from DOV. The licence included plans for the companies to jointly develop diltiazem products using this patent, a type of drug that Biovail already produced and held patents in under the name "tiazac." Andrx, a generic entrant, after learning that DOV was unable to give it a licence to the acquired patent due to its exclusive agreement with Biovail, petitioned the Food and Drug Administration (FDA) to require Biovail to delist the patent on the grounds, *inter alia*, that Biovail's acquiring the patent was anticompetitive. The FDA sought confirmation from Biovail that the acquired patent was properly listed for tiazac. Biovail submitted a declaration stating that the acquired patent was eligible for listing in connection with its tiazac product, which led the FDA not to delist it. The Federal Trade Commission alleged that Biovail's declaration to the FDA was misleading because it did not clarify whether the term "tiazac" meant its original, approved tiazac or the revised, and unapproved, form of the product using the acquired patent. The effect of Biovail's conduct was to trigger a second 30-month stay on Andrx's generic entry under the applicable legislation. Andrx contended that these actions deprived consumers of the benefits of lower-priced generic competition that might have been possible had Andrx been able to enter the market sooner. A consent decree agreed with Biovail essentially allowed Andrx to market its generic product long before the stay had expired.[38]

a. Competition policy issues. Generic drug competition raises two issues that are of significant interest to the Commission and competition authorities and courts from a

[37] See *In re Biovail Corp.*, Dkt. No. C-4060, 2002 WL 31233020 (Oct. 2, 2002) (consent order), available at http://www.ftc.gov/os/2002/06/biovailelanagreement.pdf.

[38] See also *In re Bristol-Myers Squibb Co.*, Dkt. No. C-4076, 2003 WL 21008622 (F.T.C. Apr. 14, 2003) (consent order), available at http://www.ftc.gov/os/2003/03/bristolmyersconsent.pdf.

competition policy perspective: (1) the use (and abuse) of intellectual property to preclude or impede competition; and (2) the use (and abuse) of national and EU-wide drug approval processes to preclude or impede competition. The Commission has indicated its willingness to challenge the exercise by branded pharmaceutical companies of intellectual property rights to prevent or impede generic competition, to pursue aggressively narrow interpretations of intellectual property laws, and to threaten challenges under the antitrust laws to the enforcement by branded pharmaceutical companies of intellectual property rights that are outside these narrow limits. It can no longer be assumed therefore that strategies with support in intellectual property laws necessarily absolve a firm of liability under Article 82 EC. Indeed, the former Commissioner responsible for Competition Policy, Professor Mario Monti, specifically cited the example of a patent holder withdrawing a product to delay generic entry as a core policy concern:[39]

> "Another allegation is that patent holding companies sometimes withdraw and deregister one particular formulation of their drug and have it replaced by another formulation in order to delay market entry of equivalent generic drugs. Here another piece of Community legislation is highly relevant: the 1965 Directive on market authorisations for branded drugs. Manufacturers of generic drugs can obtain a market authorisation under an abridged procedure if there is a "reference product" on the market. To put it simply: if the reference product is withdrawn from the market, market entry of generics is delayed....[C]onsumers are entitled to cheaper equivalent generic drugs or upgraded versions of patented drugs *if* the companies which try to bring these drugs to the market do so without infringing the existing patents....We are determined to do it. It is actually our duty to do it."

b. Decisional practice and case law under Article 82 EC. Decisions and cases on unlawful impediments to generic entry under Article 82 EC are limited in number.[40] The most notable case concerns allegations against AstraZeneca that it misused the patent system and other regulatory procedures for the marketing of pharmaceutical products.[41] In 2003, the Commission sent a Statement of Objections to AstraZeneca

[39] M Monti, "EC Antitrust Policy In The Pharmaceutical Sector," speech at the Alliance Unichem conference, Brussels, March 26, 2001.

[40] Two further Italian cases concern allegations of unlawful impediments to generic entry (*Merck Italia s.p.a.* (Case A.364, interim measures, June 17, 2005) and *GlaxoSmithKline* (Case A.363, investigation opened on February 25, 2005, still pending)). However, the cases do not concern the use and abuse of regulatory procedures, as alleged in *AstraZeneca*, but the use of valid intellectual property and related rights to refuse a licence for the production of the relevant active ingredients for use in other countries, i.e., compulsory licensing. The cases essentially result from Italian laws intended to compensate for the fact that supplementary protection certificates (SPC) in Italy last much longer than in other Member States. A combination of two laws introduced in 2002 allow for the following procedure in respect of products that are subject to extended SPC protection in Italy: (1) third parties may request a voluntary licence of the active ingredient protected by the SPC granted under Italian law, but only for use in exports to countries where no patent protection or SPC exists for the same ingredient; (2) where no agreement is reached between the parties, the matter is referred to mediation; and (3) where no licence is agreed under the mediation procedure, the matter may be referred to the Italian antitrust authority. Compulsory licensing is discussed in Ch. 8 (Refusal to Deal).

[41] See Commission Press Release IP/05/737 of June 15, 2005, currently on appeal in Case T-321/05 *AstraZeneca v Commission*, OJ 2005 C 271/24. The Commission also carried out "dawn raids" at the premises of Lundbeck and others in relation to conduct impeding generic drug competition: see http://www.eubusiness.com/Pharma/051025163459.2am0hgxi.

outlining its preliminary conclusion that these tactics were abusive and pursued for the purpose of blocking or delaying market entry for generic products. Two principal allegations were made.

The first is that AstraZeneca misrepresented to a number of national patent offices the dates on which it first received marketing authorisation for its Losec product, a stomach ulcer treatment. Under Community law, supplementary protection certificates (SPCs) may be available for certain medicines. SPCs extend the basic patent protection for medicinal products by a maximum of five years to take into account the period of time that may have elapsed between the filing of a patent application and authorisation to market the patented product. The key point is that, under the relevant legislation, products that were already on the market when the legislation entered into force are only entitled to extra protection if the first market authorisation in the EU was granted after certain cut off dates. The date on which Losec first received market authorisation was therefore crucial. The Commission alleged that AstraZeneca concealed certain information from the national patent offices regarding the date of the first marketing authorisation for Losec, thereby enabling AstraZeneca to obtain extra protection for Losec in certain countries. The Commission considers that the company would not have obtained the extra protection in the absence of its misrepresentations.

The second practice alleged concerns the misuse of rules and procedures applied by the national drug approval agencies that issue market authorisations for medicinal products. AstraZeneca is alleged to have switched its Losec capsules (the original formulation) for a tablet formulation of Losec combined with requests by AstraZeneca to certain national drug approval agencies to de-register the market authorisations for the capsules. De-registration is relevant for generic producers because generic products, can, in principle, only obtain a marketing authorisation if there is an existing reference authorisation. The same applies to parallel importers and import licences. Taken together, the Commission believes that both practices were intended to block or delay access to the market for generic versions of Losec and parallel imports.

On June 15, 2005, the Commission adopted a decision fining AstraZeneca €60 million for these practices. Announcing the decision, the Commissioner responsible for competition policy, Neelie Kroes, stated as follows:[42]

> "I fully support the need for innovative products to enjoy strong intellectual property protection so that companies can recoup their R & D expenditure and be rewarded for their innovative efforts. However, it is not for a dominant company but for the legislator to decide which period of protection is adequate. Misleading regulators to gain longer protection acts as a disincentive to innovate and is a serious infringement of EU competition rules. Health care systems throughout Europe rely on generic drugs to keep costs down. Patients benefit from lower prices. By preventing generic competition AstraZeneca kept Losec prices artificially high. Moreover, competition from generic products after a patent has expired itself encourages innovation in pharmaceuticals."

c. ***Legal principles.*** Although the decisional practice and case law on the use and abuse of intellectual property rights and regulatory procedures to impede generic competition is sparse and inconclusive, a number of principles seem reasonably clear.

[42] See Commission Press Release IP/05/737 of June 15, 2005.

The overriding principle is that when a dominant firm takes steps with no legitimate business justification to discourage or eliminate generic competition, it can be found guilty of a violation of Article 82 EC. The withdrawal of a product and its replacement with another that is functionally equivalent (whether or not it has marked improvements) in order to preclude or obstruct generic competition can be characterised as such conduct. The following general principles are suggested:

1. The first step in analysing the conduct is to assess its impact on generic competition. If the impact of the conduct is to seriously restrict the scope of generic competition, then the focus turns to the evaluation of the procompetitive justifications for the conduct. A number of procompetitive justifications can be imagined (e.g., safety/quality concerns).

2. Where the issue concerns the replacement of an existing product with a new dosage or method of administration, the second step is to consider whether the new replacement product is advantageous relative to the replaced product. If it is not, it might be presumed that the only reason for the introduction of the new version and the discontinuation of the old version is to limit generic competition. Such conduct is likely to be found to be anticompetitive.

3. Third, assuming the new formulation has advantages relative to the original product, the focus then shifts to whether there are legitimate reasons why the branded company would not offer both the new and the old product, thereby allowing the new product to compete on the merits with generic versions of the original product. Among these might be diseconomies of scope in producing the two products, including manufacturing diseconomies, additional inventory costs, etc. Arguments may be raised that the limited withdrawal of the old product (i.e., from only certain markets) suggests that anticompetitive motives rather than diseconomies are driving the decision.

4. Fourth, in assessing whether such reasons are sufficient to justify eliminating the original product, a useful starting point is to ask whether the same decision would have been taken in the absence of generic competition. If the answer is yes, then it can be presumed that the costs of supporting two products are not outweighed by the consumer benefits measured as the revenue from the continued sale of the original product, thereby providing a legitimate business justification for its discontinuance. If the answer is no, then the question becomes whether the volume of the original product sold in the face of generic competition and competition from the new formulation is so low as to make its continued offering uneconomical. That is, whether standing alone it can be demonstrated that the original product's revenue does not justify its continued production and sale. (It is certainly a legitimate business justification to discontinue a product if the product is losing money.) If, on the other hand, but for the effect on generic competition, it would have been profitable for the branded company to continue offering for sale the original product alongside the new formulation, discontinuance of that product will likely be found on balance to be anticompetitive. Evidence that both products are sold profitably in other countries would tend to contradict an assertion that it is unprofitable to continue to sell both products.

5. Finally, in addition to objective economic evidence, courts and the antitrust enforcement agencies will also consider evidence of the subjective intent of the branded company in pulling the version of the product subject to generic competition. Thus, if there are internal memoranda, correspondence, emails etc. which suggest that the motivation for the decision to pull the original product is to reduce generic competition, these documents will be considered good evidence that the conduct is on balance anticompetitive notwithstanding any proffered legitimate business justifications.

d. Conclusion. While there is no rule under Article 82 EC that requires a firm to continue to offer a product in order to aid competitors, there is growing precedent for the proposition that a change in business behaviour motivated by a desire to disadvantage competitors, and which otherwise has no legitimate justification (or whose business justification is small compared to the impact on competition), violates Article 82 EC. This risk applies in particular given the heightened antitrust scrutiny under which the pharmaceutical industry operates. The risk associated with a strategy of pulling a product in favour of a new formulation with no generic competition is high. In this regard, internal documents suggesting that the strategy is in whole or in part motivated by its impact on generics may render the risk unacceptable.

10.2.4 Abuses In Standard-Setting Organisations

Definition of standards. Standards are technical specifications that provide common designs for products or processes. Several different kinds of standards may be distinguished. First, there are legislative standards where the government, or some other lawmaking body, adopts technical specifications for the common design of products. For example, in the area of telecommunications, the Community institutions have adopted a number of technical specifications on equipment that are designed, *inter alia*, to prevent incumbent operators from excluding foreign rivals by maintaining non-compatible specifications for essential equipment.[43] Second, there are quasi-legislative standards developed for specific industries by regulatory authorities, such as the European Telecommunications Standards Institute (ETSI). These are formal commercial standards adopted by officially-recognised standard-setting bodies and may be used for example in invitations to tender for public contracts. Third, there are standards that arise from commercial agreements between industry participants. For example, companies in the banking sector have adopted a number of common methods of clearing cheques electronically between banks. Finally, the specifications used by a single firm's product may in exceptional cases become a *de facto* standard where the firm's specifications are very widely demanded and used by consumers. Microsoft's Windows operating system is sometimes said to be a *de facto* standard of this kind.

Benefits and drawbacks of standards. Standards have clear and well-documented benefits to society and competition. Most obviously, they reduce the cost of products by allowing products from different manufacturers to interoperate. For example, consumers can choose from a range of different vendors and proprietary software and hardware in deciding on a home computer set-up, e.g., an Intel semi-conductor chip,

---

[43] See, e.g., Commission Directive 88/301/EEC of May 16, 1988 on competition in the markets in telecommunications terminal equipment, OJ 1988 L 131/73.

IBM computer processor, Microsoft software, Lexmark printer, and AOL broadband connection, due to the multiplicity of interoperable and common specifications. In a business environment, the advent of network computing would have been impossible, or at least much more expensive, but for common specifications between the various network elements. In some cases, the benefits of standardisation are not merely economic. For example, one reason for the large number of deaths in a blaze that destroyed the city of Baltimore in 1904 was the incompatibility of out-of-State fire hoses with the city's water hydrants.[44] In sum, standardisation, in all its forms, can produce significant benefits for society and consumer welfare.

Standardisation may, however, also reduce consumer welfare in certain respects. A first problem is that standards can reduce inter-technology competition by specifying a single standard where several different standards could co-exist and compete. Although, in some cases, competition between different technologies can increase costs for consumers—such as in the case of purchasers of Betamax video cassette recorders and tapes who had to later invest in VHS technology—inter-technology competition is likely to produce benefits in most cases. A second, and more common, problem is that a standard may embody proprietary technology that allows the owner(s) to block rivals, extract excessive royalties, and leverage their ownership of the essential technology underlying the standard into related markets. A key consideration therefore for standard setting organisations (SSOs) is to be clear whether a standard is covered by essential proprietary patents, who owns them, whether there is an obligation to disclose the rights in advance, and what the royalty terms should be.

"Submarine" intellectual property rights and other hold up problems in SSOs. One widespread allegation that has emerged in the context of SSOs concerns situations in which the owner of essential proprietary intellectual property rights (IPR) underpinning a standard deliberately conceals (or otherwise fails to disclose) the existence of such rights until after the standard incorporating the essential rights is adopted. The SSO may be falsely encouraged into adopting a standard that relies on (undisclosed) IPRs, which may allow the IPR owner to "hold up" the standard process by demanding excessive royalties for the essential patents from rivals and other users. This practice is sometimes referred to as "submarine" or "ambush" IPRs.

Allegations of this kind have been made in a number of cases in the United States. Surprisingly, the issue has not yet formally arisen in the EU. For example, in *Rambus*, the Federal Trade Commission alleged that Rambus, a computer chip manufacturer, engaged in anticompetitive acts to encourage JEDEC, a private SSO, to adopt a standard that JEDEC had no reason to believe was subject to Rambus patents. JEDEC's rules require advance disclosure of patented technologies incorporated in a standard and to be licensed royalty-free or otherwise on reasonable and non-discriminatory (RAND) terms. Rambus is alleged to have failed to make advance disclosure of its ownership of patents in the standard, thereby creating a materially false and misleading impression that the standardised technology would not infringe its patents. These actions are alleged to

---

[44] Example cited in A Abbott, "The Right Balance Of Competition Policy And Intellectual Property Law: A Federal Trade Commission Perspective," Fifth Annual Trans-Atlantic Antitrust Dialogue, *British Institute Of International And Comparative Law*, London, May 9, 2005.

have harmed other participants in the SSO and consumers through demands for substantial royalties. Similar allegations have been made in the *Dell*[45] and *Unocal* cases—both of which were concluded with consent decrees requiring the firms concerned not to enforce the essential patents underlying the standard—although the latter concerned hold-up problems in government standards setting, not the private sphere.

The treatment of submarine, ambush, and other hold up problems in SSO IPR policies. The IPR policies of SSOs have long sought to identify ways in which participating firms can be prevented from holding up the standards process by relying on undisclosed essential patents. Several different techniques have been employed, with mixed results. A first solution, implemented by ETSI in 1993, is to impose, as a condition for membership, a requirement to licence all essential IPRs unless a particular right was withheld within 180 days from the *start* of the standards work, i.e., licence by default. This requirement applied even if IPRs were unknown or unpublished and even if the standard was not yet known. Following a complaint, the Commission objected to this condition under Article 81 EC,[46] since licensing by default discouraged competition through innovation. Exclusion from ETSI membership also impacted on the excluded party's competitive position through the loss of the right to influence standards (e.g., right to propose/block technologies).

A second solution, proposed by the World-Wide Web Consortium (W3C), is that, as a condition of participating in a working group, each participant (i.e., W3C Members, W3C team members, invited experts, and members of the public) agrees to make available on a royalty-free basis any essential claims related to the work of that particular working group. There is also an escape clause which allows a patent to be withheld within 150 days from the first public working draft and the IPR owner may also leave within 90 days from the first public working draft. If a patent has been disclosed that may be essential to the standard, but is not available royalty-free, an *ad hoc* group may recommend designing around it or cancelling the working group, i.e., an agreement to boycott the essential proprietary technology. This policy presents many of the same concerns as the 1993 ETSI IPR policy in that exclusion from membership may impact on the refused party's competitive position and mandatory royalty-free licensing educes the incentive to innovate. The escape clause clearly mitigates these concerns and suggests that an analysis would need to be made of the procompetitive and anticompetitive concerns in each case.

A third, intermediate solution is that implemented under the revised ETSI IPR policy and the Digital Video Broadcasting (DVB) consortium. This requires timely disclosure of "essential patents" and advance declarations of any intent to license or withhold

---

[45] See *Dell Computer Corp.*, 121 FTC 616 (1996) FTC Lexis 291, (May 20, 1996). The Federal Trade Commission found that Dell had encouraged adoption of the Video Electronics Standards Association local bus standard, while concealing the existence of a blocking patent and actually stating positively that it had no such IPRs. Dell eventually agreed to a consent decree not to assert its patents. The precedential value of the case is not clear, since it was pursued under unfair competition laws, not antitrust laws, and there was a strong dissent.

[46] See Open Letter from the EC Commission to ETSI and CBEMA (February 1994) (not published) (on file with authors) (outlining Commission preliminary views on a complaint brought against ETSI).

them. If the patents are licensed, they should be irrevocable and on RAND terms. For example, Article 4.1 of the ETSI IPR Policy provides that "...each Member shall use its reasonable endeavours, in particular during the development of a [Standard...in which it participates] to...inform ETSI of [Essential] IPRs in a timely fashion" and that "a [member] submitting a technical proposal for a [standard]...shall, on a *bona fide* basis, draw the attention of ETSI to any of that [member's] IPR which might be [essential] if that proposal is adopted."

The obligations do not, however, imply any obligation on ETSI members to conduct IPR searches. The DVB project adopted a somewhat similar approach. Unless expressly withheld, a DVB member has the right up until the time of final adoption as a standard by a recognised standards body of an approved specification to declare that it will not make available licences under an IPR that was subject to the undertaking for licensing. But, crucially, this right can only be asserted in the "exceptional circumstances" that the Member can demonstrate that a "major business interest" will be "seriously jeopardised."[47]

A final solution is to allow the SSO participants to collectively agree technology licensing terms in parallel with, or prior to, the adoption of the standard.[48] This approach obviously seeks to avoid the problem of conducting the negotiation of licensing terms *ex post* when essential, but undisclosed, patents have been asserted and the owner is therefore in a much stronger position to extract potentially onerous terms from other SSO participants. One obvious difficulty with this approach is that collective setting of licence terms among the SSO members may be contrary to Article 81 EC. But it is strongly argued by enforcement officials and commentators that parallel or advance negotiation of licence terms in this context is not a *per se* violation of the laws on anticompetitive agreements and, indeed, should in most cases be treated as lawful under an analysis of the procompetitive effects of *ex ante* negotiations.[49] Proponents of this view argue that the collective setting of terms in this context should be viewed as an output-enhancing joint venture where the participants seek to bring beneficial output—a standard—to the market, with the usual benefits that this entails. Agreements on licence terms in this context are not akin to cartels that have no redeeming features: indeed, they will typically have mainly procompetitive features and help avoid the anticompetitive features of *ex post* licensing negotiations with an SSO member that owns previously undisclosed essential patents.

The treatment of submarine, ambush, and other hold up problems in SSOs under Article 82 EC. The various policies and instruments used to resolve the hold-up problems that can arise in a standards context are limited in certain respects. IPR policies that allow licensing by default of essential patents or collective decisions to boycott non-disclosed technology may in themselves raise concerns under competition

[47] See DBV IPR Policy, Article 14.3, available at http://www.dvb.org/index.php?id=26.

[48] See G Ohana, M Hansen, and O Shah, "Disclosure and Negotiation of Licensing Terms Prior to the Adoption of Industry Standards: Preventing Another Patent Ambush?" (2003) 24(12) *European Competition Law Review* 644. See also A Abbott, "The Right Balance Of Competition Policy And Intellectual Property Law: A Federal Trade Commission Perspective," Fifth Annual Trans-Atlantic Antitrust Dialogue, *British Institute Of International And Comparative Law*, London, May 9, 2005.

[49] *Ibid.*

laws. The intermediate solution—whereby SSO members are obliged to make advance disclosure and indicate an intention to license or disclose them—is also subject to the right to withdraw at any time prior to the adoption of the standard in the case of major business interests. While this may help avoid problems of *ex post* demands for excessive royalties, it has the practical downside that it is likely to delay, and in some cases prevent, adoption of the agreed (and presumably optimal) standard. Finally, there is no formal decision under Article 81 EC indicating that the competition authorities and courts would take a favourable view of *ex ante* collective negotiations on licensing terms. It is also likely that each case would need to be assessed on the merits, which would deprive SSO members of the legal certainty that they would need in entering into such negotiations.

A further problem is that it is far from clear that Article 81 EC could apply to the types of hold-up problems commonly founds in SSOs. While hold-up problems can create anticompetitive concerns, Article 81 EC has certain limitations as an instrument designed to remedy such concerns. First, Article 81 EC requires an anticompetitive "object or effect," whereas the objectives of SSOs and their IPR policies are generally procompetitive. Second, and more importantly, unless the SSO IPR policy contains very detailed contractual rules on advance disclosure and withdrawal, many of the actions in the context of hold-ups are purely unilateral, e.g., non-disclosure or concealment. This applies not least because the Community Courts have recently applied a strict interpretation of the concept of an agreement under Article 81 EC.[50] While, previously, the Commission had treated largely unilateral conduct that arose in the context of a framework of contractual arrangements as falling within Article 81 EC, recent case law applies a higher standard requiring express or tacit acquiescence to the specific conduct at issue between two or more parties.[51] Article 81 EC will not therefore generally apply in the context of hold-up problems in SSOs. Finally, the usual remedy for a violation of Article 81(1) is the nullity of the agreement under Article 81(2). In these circumstances, the remedy would be the nullity of the standard, which would punish the victims of the violation and probably reduce competition overall.[52]

---

[50] See Joint Cases C-2/01 P and C-3/01 P, *Bundesverband der Arzneimittel-Importeure eV and Commission v Bayer* [2004] ECR I-23.

[51] *Ibid.*

[52] The recent US litigation in *Rambus* has cast doubt on the scope for applying laws on anticompetitive agreements to hold-up problems in SSOs, although the reasoning is very specific to the facts of the case. It will be recalled that Rambus is alleged to have failed to disclose in advance its ownership of patents in the standard, thereby creating a materially false and misleading impression that the standardised technology would not infringe its patents. A Virginia court initially upheld the claim against Rambus, but this was reversed on appeal. Essentially, the Court of Appeals applied a very narrow interpretation of the applicable IPR policy in concluding that Rambus had not breached its duty to disclose. It concluded that Rambus' patents (before adjustment) did not read on the standard, even though Rambus believed they did and that the IPR policy was not clear enough—although members believed it required disclosure. Rambus still faces the antitrust complaint filed by the Federal Trade Commission alleging an anticompetitive scheme of patent misuse. See *Rambus, Inc. v Infineon Technologies AG*, No. Civ. A. 3:00CV524, 2001 WL 913972 (E.D. Va. August 9, 2001), on appeal *Rambus Inc. v Infineon Technologies AG*, No. 01-1449 (Fed. Cir. January 29, 2003). The US Supreme Court refused to hear a further appeal from Infineon in the matter.

Problems with applying IPR policies and Article 81 EC to hold-up problems in SSOs have led competition authorities and courts to consider the use of laws on unilateral conduct, such as Article 82 EC, to remedy non-disclosure or late disclosure of essential patents. The legal principles applied in this regard are not entirely clear, since the cases in which a duty to make the patents available—*Dell* and *Unocal*—were settled with consent decrees in which the defendants agreed not to enforce, *vis-à-vis* other SSO members, the essential patents incorporated in the standard. The following sections consider the likely assessment of hold-up problems under Article 82 EC.

a. Dominance. Article 82 EC only applies to firms that are dominant at the time the alleged abuse is committed. There is no scope for applying Article 82 EC to conduct that would tend to create a dominant position where none exists at the time the conduct was carried out, which is, in theory, possible under other laws on unilateral conduct, such as Section 2 of the US Sherman Act 1890. The formal requirement of dominance imposes significant limitations on the application of Article 82 EC to the conduct of SSO participants, since it would preclude an argument that the owner of essential non-disclosed patents would, by virtue of this fact, be able to exercise future market power over rival firms and consumers. Competition authorities and courts would thus be prevented from conducting the type of analysis that sometimes undertaken in technology markets under merger control rules, where account is taken of pipeline products in assessing the extent to which nascent technologies would create dominance in the near future.[53]

The mere fact that a firm owns patents or other proprietary rights that are essential for a standard does not mean that it is dominant. As in any other case, dominance should be assessed on the basis of whether there are competing technologies outside the relevant SSO for application in the standardised product market. This is an empirical matter and no *a priori* assumptions can be made regarding the ownership of essential patents and dominance. Thus, it would need to be investigated whether all inter-technology competition is excluded, whether the owner of the essential patents is an indispensable trading partner, whether compliance with the standard is essential to enter the market, and whether the standard is a barrier to new technology entry. Market shares are likely to be of less importance in the context of essential patents over technology: the issue is more concerned with the barriers to entry created by the legal ownership of essential patents and whether competition from other technologies is possible. But it is unlikely at the same time that dominance could be found in the absence of market shares of the order of 30–40% or more. There may also be factors constraining dominance, such as mutual dependence in case of blocking patents.

b. Non/late disclosure to SSO participants as an abuse. The basic theory of abuse in non-disclosure cases is that a company, which is already dominant in a relevant market, and which allows or encourages others to develop a standard, knowing that the standard being developed will lead users to infringe its IPRs, and which does not

[53] See, e.g., *Glaxo Wellcome/SmithKline Beecham,* OJ 2000 C 170/6, para. 70 ("In the pharmaceuticals industry, a full assessment of the competitive situation requires examination of the products which are not yet on the market but which are at an advanced stage of development."). See also *AstraZeneca/Novartis,* OJ 2004 L 110/1; and *Pfizer/Warner Lambert*, OJ 2000 C 210/9.

disclose the existence and relevance of the IPRs until after the standard has been developed, and then insists on payment of royalties or insists on imposing restrictions in its licensing agreements, commits an abuse. Such conduct may in principle violate a number of clauses of Article 82 EC. The obvious concern is that the dominant owner of the essential IPRs would violate Article 82(a) by demanding unfair and/or excessive royalties. There is also a concern under Article 82(b) that such conduct could limit rivals' production and cause prejudice to consumers in the form of increased costs that are passed on by the SSO participants.

A number of comments can be made regarding proof of an abuse in this scenario. First, the fact that ETSI and other SSOs have rules requiring disclosure at an early stage shows that disclosure is normal practice and that a failure to do so might not be regarded as "normal competition" within the meaning of the general definition of abuse in *Hoffmann-La Roche*.[54] A second, related point is that there is probably a good faith expectation among SSO participants that essential patents will be disclosed in advance. In a recent decision, the Commission has suggested that a past course of dealing may give rise to a "legitimate expectation" of future dealings.[55] Although, formally, a legitimate expectation under general principles of Community law is only capable of creating a legally enforceable obligation against a Community institution, and not a private undertaking, it might be argued by analogy that there are good faith disclosure obligations among SSO participants. It also seems implicit in the favourable treatment of joint venture arrangements among competitors under EC competition law that the participants should not engage in any acts that are unnecessary to achieve the objectives of the SSO and result in anticompetitive effects beyond those inherent in collaboration among competitors. Bad faith non-disclosure probably fits this category, since it has no obvious procompetitive features and several potential anticompetitive ones.

Third, there are obviously a range of possibilities in terms of non-disclosure. Cases in which a firm knows it owns essential IPRs and deliberately conceals their existence (e.g., by failing to respond to specific questions) should be treated more severely than situations in which a firm inadvertently fails to disclose essential IPRs, or where it discloses them late but in good faith. Indeed, a striking feature of cases to date in which non-disclosure claims have been pursued by the enforcement agencies is that they have all concerned allegations of deliberate attempts to provide misleading and false information. Inadvertent non-disclosure or late but good faith disclosure arguably therefore does not even constitute an abuse.[56] A commitment to licence any non-disclosed but essential patents on RAND terms should also preclude a finding of abuse,

[54] See Case 85/76, *Hoffmann-La Roche v Commission* [1979] ECR 461, para. 91 (Abuse defined as "behaviour...which, through recourse to methods different from those which condition normal competition in products or services on the basis of transactions of commercial operators, has the effect of hindering the maintenance of the degree of competition still existing in the market or the growth of that competition.").

[55] See Case COMP/38/096, *Clearstream (Clearing and settlement)*, Commission Decision of June 4, 2004, not yet published, paras. 242–243.

[56] See M Dolmans, "Standards For Standards" (2003) 26 *Fordham International Law Journal* 163, 189.

since this already provides for the most likely remedy under competition law,[57] unless the licensee knew that the patent was invalid or non-essential.

Fourth, an abuse can only be found where the standard increases the market power of the dominant firm in some way. A dominant company is not otherwise obliged to warn everyone who it knows might be working on something which might need a licence of its IPRs. This implies that there is a causal connection between non-disclosure and the alleged anticompetitive effects. The basic theory of the abuse assumes that if the existence of the essential IPRs had been disclosed, the standard either would not have been written at all—in other words no increase in market power would have occurred—or could have been written differently, so as to avoid or make optional the use of the IPRs asserted post-adoption (i.e., invented around). In other words, hold up theories under Article 82 EC imply that it was not inevitable that the standard would have ended up written in the same way had all essential IPRs been disclosed in advance. The extent of the culpability would therefore depend, among other things, on the extent to which the company had encouraged or urged the development of the standard or directed it in a direction that made infringement of the IPR more likely.

Finally, the non-disclosure must lack objective justification. In practice, it would be hard to think of a justification for non-disclosure, except, perhaps, to argue that if a good enough patent search had been done, the patents would have been found (which would not apply if the IPRs were not published somewhere).

c. ***Compulsory licensing to third parties under Article 82 EC.*** The preceding analysis dealt with the circumstances in which non-disclosure of essential IPRs to other SSO participants might constitute an abuse, i.e., dealings within the SSO between insiders. Another issue concerns the duty of the SSO and/or the IPR owner to grant licences to *third parties*, i.e., outsiders. In practice, this issue is likely to be of limited concern. First, it will in nearly all cases be rational for the SSO participants to make the standard as widely available as possible. Concerns that they might charge excessive royalties should be tempered by the risk that such action could lead to the withdrawal of the standard or regulation of its terms. Second, where a SSO imposes restrictions on competition that are not *de minimis* in nature under Article 81 EC, companies that participate in the drawing up of a standard are usually required to license any IPRs included in the standard on RAND terms to any company wishing to use the standard.[58] Finally, even where the SSO does not impose any obvious restrictions on competition, the Commission's guidelines on agreements among competitors indicate that jointly dominant firms may be required to make *de facto* standards available to third parties:[59]

> "There will be clearly a point at which the specification of a private standard by a group of firms that are jointly dominant is likely to lead to the creation of a de facto industry standard. The main concern will then be to ensure that these standards are as open as possible and

[57] *Ibid.*, 191.

[58] See *XIth Report on Competition Policy* (1981), points 63–64; *XIVth Report on Competition Policy* (1984), point 92. See also Commission Communication on Intellectual Property Rights and Standardisation, COM 92/445, October 22, 1992, paras. 6.2.1.1 and 6.2.1.2.

[59] See Commission Notice—Guidelines on the applicability of Article 81 of the EC Treaty to horizontal cooperation agreements, OJ 2001 C 3/2, paras. 174–75.

> applied in a clear and non-discriminatory manner. To avoid elimination of competition in the relevant market(s), access to the standard must be possible for third parties on fair, reasonable and non-discriminatory terms. To the extent that private organisations or groups of companies set a standard or their proprietary technology becomes a de facto standard, then competition will be eliminated if third parties are foreclosed from access to this standard."

Nonetheless the issue may arise whether a dominant firm, or group of firms, may be obliged to license standardised technology to rival firms. This possibility clearly exists under Article 82 EC and the refusal to deal doctrine is treated in detail in Chapter Eight. No new substantive test is needed in the case of standards, since these are simply a bundle of IPRs, which have been subject to mandatory dealing obligations in other contexts under Article 82 EC. Briefly, the conditions for a compulsory licence under Article 82 EC are: (1) there is a refusal to deal; (2) the requested party is dominant on an upstream market for the supply of the input and the anticompetitive effects of the refusal arise on a second downstream market; (3) the input in question is essential for competition on the second market, in the sense that it cannot be duplicated or can only be duplicated at an uneconomic cost; (4) the refusal to deal would eliminate competition on the second market; (5) the refusal to deal prevents the emergence of a new product for which there is consumer demand; and (6) no objective considerations justify the refusal to deal.

It is noteworthy that two of the three cases in which the Commission has imposed a compulsory licence of an IPR concerned *de facto* standards developed by a single firm where issues of interoperability were found to play an important role. In *IMS*, a copyright-protected presentation format for pharmaceutical sales data, developed in consultation with users, was found to be a *de facto* industry standard that needed to be made available on RAND terms to competing data service vendors.[60] In *Microsoft*,[61] the Commission required the defendant to make the protocol specifications for its computer operating system available to competing vendors of server operating systems in order to ensure interoperability. One important consideration in this connection is the Commission's conclusion that there is a duty to license essential interoperability information underpinning a standard to rival firms where the refusal to do so would substantially eliminate competition. This is based, *inter alia*, on the fact that secondary Community legislation provides for a degree of interoperability in the case of computer programs. In other words, the Commission considers that the conditions for a refusal to deal outlined above are not necessarily exhaustive and that interoperability may be another reason to compel sharing. Whether the Commission is right in this regard is a major plank of Microsoft's appeal and is discussed in detail in Chapter Eight.

10.2.5 Abusive Acquisition Or Accumulation Of IPRs

Distinction between acquiring IPRs and own development of IPRs. In exceptional cases, acquiring or accumulating IPRs may constitute an abuse under Article 82 EC. A distinction should be made between a dominant firm's acquiring IPRs from third parties and internal development by the dominant firm of new IPRs. The former is in principle subject to a stricter rule, since a firm cannot, in general, agree to acquire essential inputs

[60] *IMS Health/NDC*, OJ 2002 L 59/18 (interim measures).

[61] Case COMP C-3/37.792, *Microsoft*, Commission Decision of March 24, 2004, not yet published.

that would confer or increase market power. Agreements of this kind are reviewable under Article 81 EC.[62] In contrast, a firm is generally entitled (and positively encouraged) under competition laws to internally develop valuable IPRs, even if they lead to market power. Or, put differently, competition law is more suspicious of contractual relations between two or more competing firms than unilateral action by a single firm. Most of the problematic cases concern patents, since copyright protects the original expression of an idea, and not, as in the case of patents, the underlying process. Trademarks by nature also have inherently less scope for unfairly excluding rival firms.

Abusive acquisition of patents from third parties. Agreements concerning the acquisition of IPRs primarily fall under Article 81 EC. In *Tetra Pak I*,[63] however, the Commission found that, in exceptional circumstances, it could also be an abuse for a dominant firm to acquire key technology from third parties where the effect of doing so would be to limit market entry and production. Tetra was found to have committed an abuse when, through the purchase of the Liquipak Group, it acquired the exclusive licence from the British Technology Group (BTG), a publicly-funded body that engaged in research for commercial uses, for a sterilisation technology for cartons.

The reasons for the Commission's conclusion were as follows: (1) Tetra was already a virtual monopolist on the relevant market (sterilised milk cartons); (2) sterilisation technology was the key competitive driver in the relevant market; (3) Tetra owned the principal proprietary technology for carton sterilisation; (4) the BTG technology was the only other commercially viable technology on the relevant market at the time; (5) while there were several other undertakings that were competitors of Tetra, the entity acquired by Tetra had an exclusive licence for BTG sterilisation technology; and (6) acquiring an exclusive licence to the other main competing technology prevented, or at least considerably delayed, the entry of new competitors in a market where very little if any competition existed.

Cases of this kind under Article 82 EC are in practice likely to be rare. In *Tetra Pak I*, the Commission was forced to apply the doctrine developed in *Continental Can*,[64] where the Court of Justice held that mergers and acquisitions could, in certain circumstances, also fall under the prohibition in Article 82 EC. The Commission held that Tetra's acquisition of an exclusive licence to the BTG technology was "as equivalent in effect on this market to a take-over."[65] *Continental Can* is generally regarded as a striking example of judicial legislation intended to compensate for the fact that there were no Community rules on merger control at the time. It is unlikely that the Commission would seek to rely on this doctrine today, not least because Article 81 EC or merger control laws are the main instruments for dealing with licence agreements or take-overs. Moreover, the scope for applying Article 82 EC in this scenario is limited. It can only be applied when the acquiror is *already* dominant on the relevant market(s)

---

[62] The better view is that rights contained in licensing arrangements do not in themselves confer control for purposes of merger control laws. See generally, N Levy, *European Merger Control Law: A Guide to the Merger Regulation* (LexisNexis, 2003), Chapter 6.

[63] *Tetra Pak I (BTG licence)*, OJ 1988 L 272/27.

[64] Case 6/72, *Continental Can v Commission* [1973] ECR 215.

[65] *Tetra Pak I (BTG licence)*, OJ 1988 L 272/27, para. 47.

at the date of the licence acquisition and cannot therefore challenge transactions that create dominance.

Abusive registration and proliferation of internally-developed patents. More complex issues arise when a firm does not acquire patents from third parties, but implements a defensive policy of developing a series of patents around a product that have the object or effect of building a patent barricade. This practice, which is sometimes referred to as a "patent thicket," can create situations in which rival firms cannot avoid infringing another firm's patents or incur substantially increased costs in inventing around them, which can lead to increased costs being passed on to consumers. Such problems are most likely to occur in industries where innovation primarily takes place in increments, such as software, and, to a lesser extent, pharmaceuticals and biotechnology.

A number of general comments can be made by way of introduction. First, the problem of patent thickets is real in practice and there is good reason to also believe that it is significant. There is ample testimony in the context of the US agencies on-going review of the interface between IPR and antitrust laws that patent thickets can stifle innovation and increase costs.[66] There is also evidence that such strategies are pursued deliberately for the sole purpose of excluding rivals, that a much larger number of patents have been granted in recent years, that the scope of such patents is broader than in the past, and that a greater number of patents receive unmeritorious protection.[67]

Second, to the extent there is a problem with patent thickets, it is not confined to issues under Article 82 EC, or, indeed, EC competition law generally, but concerns wider and more fundamental issues concerning patents and patent enforcement. Concern has been expressed that an excessive number of overbroad patents are granted in certain industries and that courts may also be too willing to uphold them and that a greater role should be played by competition law in truncating the anticompetitive effects of such rights. This is a complex issue on which no clear consensus has emerged beyond agreement on the obvious principle that both IPR and competition laws should seek to

[66] See, e.g., US Federal Trade Commission, "To Promote Innovation: The Proper Balance of Competition and Patent Law and Policy," published in October 2003, p. 165 ("Many panellists and participants expressed the view that software and Internet patents are impeding innovation."), document available at http://www.ftc.gov/os/2003/10/innovationrpt.pdf. See also C Shapiro, "Navigating the Patent Thicket: Cross Licences, Patent Pools, and Standard-Setting," University of California at Berkeley, March 2001, available at http://faculty.haas.berkeley.edu/shapiro/thicket.pdf ("In short, our patent system, while surely a spur to innovation overall, is in danger of imposing an unnecessary drag on innovation by enabling multiple rights owners to tax new products, processes and even business methods. The vast number of patents currently being issued creates a very real danger that a single product or service will infringe on many patents. Worse yet, many patents cover products or processes already being widely used when the patent issued, making it harder for the companies actually building businesses and manufacturing products to invent around these patents. Add in the fact that a patent holder can seek injunctive relief, i.e., can threaten to shut down the operations of the infringing company, and the possibility for hold up becomes all too real.").

[67] Evidence submitted to the Federal Trade Commission suggested that companies sometimes reallocate significant portions of developers' resources to increase their patent portfolio for purely defensive reasons and that the engineers' time dedicated to assisting in the filing of defensive patents, which "have no...innovative value in and of themselves," could have been spent on developing new technologies. *Ibid.*, p. 9.

encourage innovation. But, clearly, if too many, or excessively broad, patents are being granted and enforced, the primary solution is to amend the IPR laws. Competition laws should play a secondary role and should not *generally* be expected to correct defects in the patent systems (although it may be appropriate to apply competition law solutions at the margins where abusive conduct is made out). Some industry participants recommend more radical steps, such as only allowing copyright protection in certain industries—which would in principle be less restrictive than patents—and/or favouring open source rights (i.e., developed without reliance on IPRs). Less radical steps would include greater possibilities for post-grant challenge and review for a limited period, a possibility that exists to some extent in certain Member States (e.g., United Kingdom).

Finally, businesses have themselves developed a number of methods to mitigate the potential harm to innovation caused by patent thickets. These include cross-licensing, patent pools, advance disclosure and/or RAND terms in the context the licensing policies of SSOs (see above), and patent settlement disputes.[68] Patent pools, cross-licences, and settlements may be reviewable under Article 81 EC. The basic rules are that: (1) cross-licences should reflect legitimate cooperation and should not be used as a means of agreeing royalty rates that disguise a cartel;[69] (2) patent pools should be limited to essential, complementary patents, and not direct substitute technologies, i.e., the companies must genuinely have rival blocking patents;[70] (3) cross licences are generally to be preferred to patent pools, since they are a less restrictive alternative of dealing with hold-up issues; and (4) a patent settlement dispute should not allocate markets (e.g., where the patent holder pays the entrant to refrain from marketing its product for a period of time) in a way that unreasonably eliminates competition.[71]

Whether and in what circumstances defensive accumulation of patents to block or delay entry by rivals constitutes an abuse under Article 82 EC remains unclear.[72] A first

[68] See generally C Shapiro, "Navigating the Patent Thicket: Cross Licences, Patent Pools, and Standard-Setting," University of California at Berkeley, March 2001, available at http://faculty.haas.berkeley.edu/shapiro/thicket.pdf.

[69] See Commission Notice—Guidelines on the application of Article 81 of the EC Treaty to technology transfer agreements, OJ 2004 C 101/2.

[70] *Ibid.*

[71] See A Abbott, "The Right Balance Of Competition Policy And Intellectual Property Law: A Federal Trade Commission Perspective," Fifth Annual Trans-Atlantic Antitrust Dialogue, *British Institute Of International And Comparative Law*, London, May 9, 2005.

[72] Litigation between Valeo SA and LuK Lamellen und Kupplungsbau Beteiligungs KG (LuK) in France raised this legal issue, but the case was ultimately settled. The proceeding concerned a patent infringement action filed by LuK against Valeo following the public confiscation of Valeo's radial dual-mass flywheel (DMF) by LuK at the Paris Auto Show. Valeo alleged that LuK had abused its dominant position on the market for DMF by systematically and unlawfully extending divisional patent applications to cover competitors' inventions, including vexatious patent infringement proceedings against competitors, even though LuK was aware of the fact that the proceedings had no real chance of success because the underlying patents had been unlawfully extended. The Paris *Tribunal de Grande Instance* dismissed LuK's action in particular on the ground that the underlying patents were unlawfully extended and hence void. The Tribunal also ruled in response to a counter-claim submitted by Valeo that "this proceeding was lodged [by LuK] vexatiously." It therefore awarded LuK damages in the amount of €750,000 and a compensation for attorney's and court fees in the amount of €200,000. The Tribunal also considered whether the litigation amounted to an abuse of dominance under Article 82 EC and the corresponding provision of French law, but stayed this aspect of the proceeding while it sought

comment is that there must be a very strong presumption that the internal development of patents, and reliance on the exclusionary rights that they entail, is legal in all but extreme cases. The right to develop and enforce patents is positively encouraged under competition law and this right is not, in general, considered less valid simply because a firm has a large number of patents or those patents make it more difficult for rivals to enter markets. Any contrary rule that favoured more general inquiry into the reasons for developing and asserting patents would run a real risk of chilling innovation.

Second, a strong case for enforcement action can be made in situations in which a patent is procured by fraudulent representations or knowledge on the part of the person seeking it that the patent is invalid, assuming there is some non-trivial impact on competition.[73] Litigation or other action to enforce such rights should be regarded as abusive in the circumstances outlined in the preceding sections. Indeed, the problem of fraudulently procuring patents, or asserting patents that are known to be invalid, is not confined to patent thickets, but concerns a more general question of when it is abusive to assert baseless claims in litigation, discussed in Section 10.2.2.

Finally, the most difficult cases concern situations in which the dominant firm's patents are legitimately procured and valid, but their sheer number and/or scope raise rivals' research and development costs or prevent entry. The most appropriate analysis is probably that conducted in the case of impeding generic drug entry, discussed in Section 10.2.3 above. A first step is to assess the impact of the dominant firm's defensive patent policy on rivals. If the impact of the conduct is to seriously restrict rivals' entry possibilities, or substantially increase their costs, then the focus turns to the evaluation of the procompetitive justifications for the conduct.

The second step is to consider whether the incrementally added patents had any technological advantages over prior patents. This will often be complex, but is a key question that cannot be avoided if any meaningful conclusions are to be drawn. If later patents have no material advantage over earlier patents, there might be a rebuttable presumption that later patents were added only to stymie rivals. The dominant firm might be able to rebut this presumption by showing for example that it took the action in order not to be blocked itself from using certain inventions in future.

Third, it might be useful to ask whether the dominant firm would have pursued the same strategy in the absence of competitive entry. As in the *AstraZeneca* case, evidence that the dominant firm selectively pursued a defensive policy of accumulating patents only in countries in which it was exposed to direct competition might support an inference that the policy had objectives other than protecting the value of its inventions.

---

the opinion of the national competition authority on whether LuK was dominant on the relevant market. On November 9, 2005, the competition authority concluded that LuK was dominant. The case was ultimately settled between the parties. See *Société LuK Lamellen und Kupplungsbau Beteiligungs GmBh v SA Valeo*, judgment of January 27, 2005 (Third Chamber).

[73] See, e.g., *In re Biovail Corp.*, Dkt. No. C-4060, 2002 WL 31233020 (Oct. 2, 2002) (consent order), available at http://www.ftc.gov/os/2002/06/biovailelanagreement.pdf (discussed above) and *Bristol-Myers Squibb Co.*, FTC Docket No. C-4076 (Apr. 14, 2003) (consent order), available at http://www.ftc.gov/os/2003/03/bristolmyersconsent.pdf (alleged false listings and false statements to the US patent and drug approval authorities, leading to anticompetitive effects in anti-cancer and anti-anxiety drugs).

Finally, it may be useful to consider evidence of the subjective intent of the dominant firm in formulating its patent policy (e.g., internal memoranda, correspondence, emails etc.). The evidence would need to be clear, since any valid patent is intended to exclude rivals. There would need to be evidence pointing to a shift in the dominant firm's policy, i.e., that the strategy was only implemented to increase rivals' entry costs and not to protect new, valuable inventions.

10.2.6 Miscellaneous Practices

Other possible example of exclusionary non-price abuses. Although the range of exclusionary non-price abuses is myriad, a number of other categories of potential abuse merit discussion. A recurring theme with these miscellaneous categories is that, in theory, conditions may be identified in which the practice could result in anticompetitive harm. But, in practice, it is difficult to transform many of these "possibility theorems" into operational rules that clearly distinguish lawful and unlawful conduct. A sound practical case can therefore be made for doing nothing, except, perhaps, in egregious cases (e.g., cumulative behaviour). An example of the latter situation might include the product swap arrangements in *Irish Sugar*.[74] When a competing sugar brand, Eurolux, was launched in Ireland, the dominant supplier, and its integrated distribution arm, agreed with one wholesaler and one retailer that they would exchange their own sugar for Eurolux sugar. Both the Commission and the Community Courts agreed that product swapping is an abuse. This is hardly surprising: the dominant firm's actions had the same effect as sabotaging the rival's production plant, the only difference being the cost to the dominant firm. But the other situations in which miscellaneous abuse concerns have been raised are far less clear. These are considered below.

a. Hiring key rival personnel. Whether a dominant firm's acquiring key personnel from a rival firm can constitute an abuse raises difficult issues. On the one hand, if, under certain circumstances, it is objectionable to acquire a competitor or purchase key intellectual property or other assets, much the same logic can be applied to hiring key rival personnel, if they are important enough. On the other hand, the freedom of individuals in an open market economy to pursue alternative employment should be more or less unfettered outside of contract law. Moreover, other laws—such as tort law, unfair competition, and restraint of trade laws—elaborate a number of principles regarding the circumstances in which it may be unlawful for an employer to hinder employees from seeking out alternative possibilities, as well as offering protection to firms from inducements to commit breaches of contract by dominant and non-dominant firms.

In these circumstances, the only situation in which a dominant firm's hiring could be considered abusive is probably where the dominant firm hires key personnel from one or more rivals and either pays them to do nothing or requires them to do something

[74] See *Irish Sugar*, OJ 1997 L 258/1, affirmed on appeal in Case T-228/97, *Irish Sugar v Commission* [1999] ECR II-2969 and by Order of the Court of Justice in Case C-497/99 P, *Irish Sugar plc v Commission* [2001] ECR I-5333.

unrelated to their expertise.[75] The analogy might be acquiring a key patent to suppress its use. These situations are most likely rare, since a dominant firm ought rationally to prefer to put valuable acquired talent to good use than to do nothing with it. There would also need to be good evidence that the personnel concerned were a key competitive advantage and, correspondingly, that the loss of such personnel materially affected the rival's ability to compete, and, separately, that there was harm to competition.

b. Excessive promotional spending. Another question is whether "excessive" advertising spending can constitute an abuse in itself. Again, the case for a stand-alone violation along these lines seems weak. Firms compete in various ways—most obviously by lowering their price and increasing output—and advertising is simply another way of doing this. Of course, in some industries, high advertising spend may well create a barrier to entry for smaller firms. But advertising is simply another cost of doing business and any increased expenditure on advertising is therefore governed by the same principles as are any other cost items: total revenues should be greater than total cost. This means that claims involving excessive advertising can be treated in the same way as predatory pricing claims generally, discussed in Chapter Five. There is some dispute about whether advertising should be treated as a fixed or variable cost, but this concerns the technical aspects of the rules on predatory pricing rather than implicating an entirely new set of principles. Even if advertising expenditure is very high, the same rule applies: revenues should exceed costs. There should be no rule that the total net increase in revenue as a result of additional advertising should exceed the additional costs of advertising. As with any other cost, the issue is overall revenue and costs, not individual items.

The dominant firm should also not be criticised if expenditure in advertising turns out to generate less revenue than anticipated and results in net losses. Like any other speculative investment in promotion, the dominant firm's *ex ante* assumptions may turn out to be wrong and all that can be required is that the dominant firm has some reasonable basis for expecting profits, e.g., based on the results of similar campaigns in the past.

c. False advertising and disparagement of competitors. False advertising or false disparagement of rivals' products is clearly unethical and unfair in some sense. It will also in many cases constitute a violation of unfair competition laws or other tort laws relating to business activity. Under Article 82 EC the main issue concerns identifying a causal link between false or misleading statements and the maintenance or increase in the dominant firm's market power. For example, the falsehood may have little or no market impact, either because the statement is a one-off, the rival firm immediately corrects it, the dominant firm is legally prevented from repeating it, or consumers know that it is untrue. The legal test would presumably be similar to tort law, i.e., existence of a falsehood, material reliance, and causally-related harm, with the additional requirement that the action produced actual or likely competitive harm.

[75] One US court seemed to think that this principle was arguable under the antitrust laws. See *Universal Analytics v MacNeal Schwendelr Corp*, 707 f. Supp. 1170 (C.D. Cal 1989).

A stronger case can be made for treating false advertising as abusive where it is part of cumulative evidence of anticompetitive conduct. A number of cases under Article 82 EC have made clear that the cumulative effect of practices may be abusive, even if none individually would be.[76] For example, most national laws on unfair competition can only give remedies for each instance of false advertising and, perhaps, increase sanctions for repeat infringements in the same territory. But suppose a dominant firm made a series of false declarations regarding a rival's product in several Member States. The cumulative effect of these statements on the rival's sales is likely to be much greater than the effect of any individual statement. In such circumstances, it may be appropriate to assess the totality of the conduct under Article 82 EC, since, otherwise, the dominant firm may find it more profitable to keep repeating the statements.

d. Advance disclosure of new products. Firms, dominant and non-dominant, often preannounce new products in order to inform consumers and generate advance demand. This is a common phenomenon in the software industry, where the term "vapourware" is sometimes used to refer to announced software that may never materialise or that misses its announced release date, i.e., statements, before the product is available for purchase, regarding the features or expected release date of the product. One possible effect of such conduct is that it may eliminate demand for competing products in the interim. In most cases, such action is legitimate and procompetitive. It is obviously desirable that consumers should be well-informed and pre-announcements of new products will usually provide valuable information to consumers who are in the process of making a choice between competing products. For this reason, unless they are knowingly false—in the sense that the product is not in fact introduced or a materially different product is introduced—preannouncements have been treated as presumptively legal under laws governing unilateral conduct.[77] The fact that the dominant firm's pre-announcement was intended to, or in fact did, divert sales from rivals in the interim does not affect this conclusion. But even false statements would presumably require evidence that the impact of the advance disclosure on rivals' sales was more than merely *de minimis* and that the pre-announcement was a causal factor in this connection.

e. Excessive research and development and product variation. A final possibility theorem identified by some commentators is that excessive research and development or product variation can create a barrier to entry for rival firms, leading to anticompetitive effects. For example, some commentators have produced models which show that: (1) a

[76] Case T-203/01, *Manufacture française des pneumatiques Michelin v Commission* [2003] ECR II-4071, para. 111 ("Furthermore, *the quantity rebates formed part of a complex system of discounts*, some of which on the applicant's own admission constituted an abuse....") (emphasis added). See also *ECS/AKZO,* OJ 1985 L 374/1, para. 82 ("The behaviour of AKZO has to be considered as a whole"); and *Napier Brown/British Sugar*, OJ 1988 L 284/41, para. 66 ("taken in the context of the other abuses as outlined above").

[77] See, e.g., *MCI Communications v American Tel. & Tel. Co.*, 708 F.2d 1081, 1129 (7th Cir.); and *ILC Peripherals Leasing Corp. v IBM Corp.*, 458 F. Supp. 423, 442 (N.D. Cal. 1978) (both refusing to find liability for pre-disclosure in the absence of knowingly false information). For a good summary of the principles under US law on preannouncements, see "*Memorandum Of The United States Of America In Response To The Court's Inquiries Concerning "Vapourware*" in *United States v Microsoft*, Civil Action No. 94-1564 (SS), available at http://www.usdoj.gov/atr/cases/f0000/0050.htm.

firm that offers an additional product can capture business from rival firms for other products when consumers prefer to concentrate their purchases at a single supplier; (2) this may lead firms to offer excessive product variety from a social standpoint; (3) a firm may even completely foreclose competing firms from the market by introducing a new product; and (4) forbidding new product introductions may sometimes be appropriate public policy.[78]

While these possibilities may be theoretically sound, it is hard to see the case for a general rule under Article 82 EC to the effect that such activities should be curtailed and, more importantly, whether any rule could accurately distinguish the rare cases in which net harm results from desirable market activities without also chilling investment and product innovation. A good practical case can therefore be made for saying that the only administrable rule in such scenarios is that that the revenues generated by any product-specific investment—be it research and development or adding new product lines—should exceed the costs, i.e., the rules on predatory pricing, discussed in Chapter Five.

[78] See P Klemperer and AJ Padilla, "Do firms' product lines include too many varieties?" (1997) 28(3) *RAND Journal of Economics* 472–88.

Chapter 11

ABUSIVE DISCRIMINATION

11.1 INTRODUCTION

Discrimination and EC competition law generally. Determining the welfare effects of discrimination lies at the core of much of competition-law enforcement. A number of quantitative techniques in merger control for example attempt to measure whether the merged entity would be able to profitably engage in price discrimination between marginal and non-marginal customers. In the area of cartels, price discrimination may be used by one of the members as a means of disguising deviation from the agreed course of action.

Issues of discrimination also traverse many abuses under Article 82 EC. Loyalty discounts and other forms of volume reductions may involve commitments by a seller to price discriminate in favour of large volume buyers or buyers meeting other conditions. Margin squeeze cases also involve actual or concealed price discrimination by a vertically integrated dominant firm in favour of its own downstream business. Essential facility cases also involve discrimination in the sense that the dominant firm discriminates in favour of its own vertically integrated business by denying downstream rivals access to essential inputs. Finally, one explanation for tying and bundling practices is the dominant firm's desire to extract greater consumer surplus from undertakings that value the tied/bundled products more than they value each product separately, i.e., price discrimination. Thus, in broad terms, the analysis of the effects of discrimination, and in particular price discrimination, underpins much of EC competition law.

The different categories of discrimination under Article 82 EC. As discussed in detail in Chapter Four (The General Concept of an Abuse), two broad categories of discrimination should be distinguished under Article 82 EC.[1] The first concerns discrimination by a dominant firm which produces effects *vis-à-vis* its rivals. Such conduct can give rise to "primary-line" injury in antitrust economics. The principal issue is whether the practice in question is exclusionary, not merely (or mainly) whether

---

[1] For more detailed treatment of the different types of discrimination, see, e.g., J Temple Lang and R O'Donoghue, "Defining Legitimate Competition: How to Clarify Pricing Abuses under Article 82 EC" (2002) 26 *Fordham International Law Journal* 83, 115; J Temple Lang, "Anticompetitive Non-Pricing Abuses Under European And National Antitrust Law" in B Hawk (ed.), *Fordham Corporate Law Institute* (New York, Juris Publishing Co, 2004) vol. 26, pp. 235-340; D Géradin and N Petit, "Price discrimination under EC Competition Law: The Need for a Case-By-Case approach," *Global Competition Law Centre Working Papers Series, GCLC Working Paper 07/05*, p. 7, available at http://gclc.coleurop.be/documents/GCLC%20WP%2007-05.pdf; and *The Pros and Cons of Price Discrimination*, Swedish Competition Authority, November 2005, available at http://www.kkv.se/bestall/pdf/rap_pros_and_cons_pricediscrimination.pdf.

it involves discrimination. For example, in a predatory pricing case, the allegation is often that a dominant firm has selectively offered discounts to rivals' customers, while maintaining higher prices for its own customers. In this situation, the legal issue is not whether the dominant firm's prices discriminate between its own customers and those of rivals—clearly they do—but whether the dominant firm's prices can be regarded as predatory and exclusionary, contrary to Article 82(b). Discrimination is neither necessary nor sufficient in this context.[2] Exclusionary abuses that involve elements of discrimination by a dominant firm against its rivals—whether on horizontally-related or vertically-related markets—are dealt with in other chapters.[3]

A second category concerns discrimination by a dominant supplier between its customers. In this scenario, the dominant firm is *not* present on the relevant market in which the discrimination is said to produce adverse effects. Thus, the dominant firm gains no competitive advantage over a rival firm in discriminating. This type of discrimination can give rise to "secondary-line" injury in antitrust economics. This category of discrimination is treated in detail in this chapter. The concern in this scenario is that the dominant firm is "applying dissimilar conditions to equivalent transactions with other trading parties, thereby placing them at a competitive disadvantage," contrary to Article 82(c). The use of the phrase "transactions with other trading parties" confirms that the non-discrimination clause in Article 82(c) is not primarily concerned with discrimination against rivals with whom the dominant firm does not have a direct transactional relationship, but with distortions of competition between the dominant firm's customers (or "trading parties").[4]

---

[2] This was essentially the conclusion reached by the US Supreme Court in *Brooke Group v Brown & Williamson Tobacco* (92-466), 509 US 209 (1993). The Court held, *inter alia*, that cases involving primary-line injury should, even if they involve discrimination, be assessed under Section 2 of the Sherman Act 1890 rather than the non-discrimination principles contained in the Robinson-Patman Act 1936. Thus, the issue was not whether the prices were discriminatory, but whether exclusionary in the sense that: (1) they were below an appropriate measure of cost; and (2) there was a case of probable recoupment.

[3] For example, Ch. 5 (Predatory Pricing) deals with the circumstances in which selective pricing by a dominant firm to rivals' customers may be an abuse. Ch. 6 (Margin Squeeze) addresses a specific form of discrimination by a dominant vertically integrated firm against downstream rivals: reducing the margin between the wholesale and retail price to a level that renders rivals' operations uneconomic. Ch. 7 (Exclusive Dealing, Loyalty Discounts, and Related Practices) deals, *inter alia*, with the circumstances in which rebates that discriminate in favour of marginal customers constitute an abuse. Ch. 8 (Refusal to Deal) treats situations in which a dominant firm discriminates in favour of its own downstream business by denying downstream rivals access to essential inputs, including whether, and in what circumstances, a dominant firm can be forced to make further contracts or licences where it has already granted one or more contracts or licences. Finally, Ch. 9 (Tying and Bundling) explains the circumstances in which tying and bundling practices—which are often motivated by the dominant firm's desire to price discriminate between users—may be abusive.

[4] The different types of discrimination may of course result from the same conduct. A discriminatory rebate scheme could, for example, foreclose competitors of the dominant firm, as well as distort competition between downstream customers with whom the dominant firm does not compete. This was essentially the conclusion of the Community institutions in *British Airways/Virgin*. The Commission objected to the exclusionary effects of British Airways' travel agency commission scheme *vis-à-vis* rival airlines and, separately, to the discriminatory effects between travel agents of the payment of different levels of commission. See *Virgin/British Airways*, OJ 2000 L 30/1, on appeal Case T-219/99 *British Airways plc v Commission* [2003] ECR II-5917. Discrimination may also occur

Reasons to distinguish anti-rival discrimination and discrimination between customers. The distinction between discrimination against rivals and discrimination between customers is not merely semantic or a matter of legal neatness. In each case, the factual setting, the dominant firm's incentives, and the likely effects of the dominant firm's conduct are different. The dominant firm's incentives to exclude direct (or horizontal) rivals are likely to be greatest, since it will always, to some extent, benefit from the exit of a rival firm. Where the dominant firm is vertically integrated and supplies non-integrated rivals with inputs, it may also have strong incentives to exclude them by raising their costs. The precise incentives are an empirical matter and essentially turn on the relative profitability of the upstream and downstream markets. If the upstream market is much less profitable than the downstream market, it may be rational for the dominant firm to exclude rival downstream firms, in particular where it expects to win most sales from exiting or marginalised rivals.

In contrast, in the case of discrimination between customers with whom the dominant firm does not compete—pure secondary-line injury—the dominant firm has no obvious interest in taking action that would affect the competitiveness of one customer when compared to another. It would gain no advantage in doing so and might even suffer a disadvantage through a reduction in its sales. This also strongly suggests that when discrimination of this kind occurs, the dominant firm is likely to have a valid reason for distinguishing between the two sets of customers. Indeed, as developed in more detail in Section 11.5, it is hard to see any convincing competition-law rationale for intervention in cases of secondary-line injury in itself.[5]

The Community institutions' general approach to Article 82(c). At first sight, Article 82(c) looks a broad and potentially anticompetitive provision in so far as it would seem to restrict buyers' ability to negotiate different prices or terms with a dominant firm. In practice, however, Article 82(c) has been used very sparingly by the Community institutions to condemn different prices or terms offered to customers or other trading parties. (Evidence of discrimination against rivals has featured prominently in exclusionary abuse cases, but these raise different issues, discussed in other chapters.) In essence, Article 82(c) has been applied in two principal scenarios. The first—and predominant—use of Article 82(c) has been to condemn practices that directly or indirectly discriminate based on the nationality or residence of the customer.

against undertakings that are simultaneously both customers and competitors of the dominant firm, such as in a margin squeeze case, discussed in Ch. 6 (Margin Squeeze), above. In such situations, the dominant firm is discriminating between associated and non-associated downstream companies.

[5] Another important reason why it may be necessary to decide which category conduct with discriminatory aspects falls is that, unlike Article 82(b), Article 82(c) makes no explicit reference to "prejudice to consumers" (or any other analogous phrase that clearly incorporates the interests of consumers in the legal analysis). Instead, the issue seems to turn on whether the discriminated party suffers a "competitive disadvantage;" in other words, whether the party paying the higher price or receiving worse terms suffers a non-trivial disadvantage relative to its rivals on the same level of trade. Harm to competition—that is direct or indirect harm to consumers—does not necessarily feature in the analysis under Article 82(c). Ch. 4 (The General Concept of an Abuse) explains why there are compelling legal and economic arguments that consumer welfare should be the basis for all abuses under Article 82 EC. The basic argument is that a non-discrimination principle that protects a particular trading party, without more, only protects competitors, not competition.

Such conduct offends a core tenet of the EC Treaty and has, perhaps understandably, been subject to a strict rule under Article 82 EC.

A second application of Article 82(c) is where the primary objection is that the dominant firm's conduct unlawfully excludes rivals, but also has the ancillary effect of discriminating between the dominant firm's customers. A good example is loyalty rebate practices, discussed in Chapter Seven. The principal objection to such practices is that they can, in certain circumstances, have the effect of unlawfully excluding rival firms. But an incidental effect of loyalty schemes that grant discounts to customers who increase their individual sales in comparison to a past reference period is that two customers selling the same quantities can receive different discounts depending on whether and to what extent they increased their sales relative to the past or not. Thus, in a small number of cases involving exclusionary loyalty discounts, the Commission has also concluded that the discount scheme resulted in unlawful discrimination between customers.[6] It seems unlikely, however, that the discrimination allegations would have been pursued but for the primary findings relating to exclusionary conduct.

Outside these two principal scenarios, the application of Article 82(c) to condemn different prices or terms has been an extreme rarity. This makes sense. The main reasons are as follows and are developed in detail in this chapter. First, as explained in Section 11.2, economists do not consider discrimination to be *a priori* good or bad for consumer welfare. Many forms of discrimination enhance consumer welfare—mainly by allowing consumers with lower willingness/ability to pay to purchase something that they could not if different (lower) prices were not permitted. Condemning discrimination therefore requires clear evidence of actual or likely harm to consumer welfare. Second, different prices and terms are ubiquitous in real-world markets, which means that the practical scope of a strict non-discrimination rule would be enormous. This phenomenon is likely to increase further in an era of increasing digitalisation where producers' marginal costs of supply are typically low and so allow greater scope for differential pricing. Third, the impracticality of rules that would insist on uniform prices and terms is obvious. Significant uncertainty and complications would arise in commercial dealings were Article 82 EC to require uniform prices and terms. Finally, experience with strict non-discrimination laws in other jurisdictions—most notably the United States Robinson-Patman Act 1936—has been uniformly negative from a consumer welfare perspective.[7] The result has been the protection of less efficient producers and higher average uniform prices for consumers. This legislation is expected to be repealed in 2007 and, for practical purposes, has been essentially ignored in an important recent Supreme Court ruling.[8]

---

[6] See *Virgin/British Airways*, OJ 2000 L 30/1; and *Soda Ash/Solvay* OJ 2003 L 10/10. See also Case 85/76, *Hoffman-La Roche v Commission* [1979] ECR 461, para. 90.

[7] See US Department of Justice Report on the Robinson-Patman Act, (2000) 24(1) *The Journal of Reprints for Antitrust Law and Economics* 257-258. This issue is discussed in more detail in Section 11.5 below.

[8] See *Volvo Trucks N. Am., Inc. v Reeder-Simco GMC, Inc.*, No. 04-905, 2006 WL 43971, (January 10, 2006).

11.2 THE ECONOMICS OF PRICE DISCRIMINATION

Overview. People generally disagree about how much something is worth. Some would pay a lot for it; others only a little. Price discrimination arises when companies seek to profit from differences in valuation by charging different prices for different units and/or to different customers.[9] A more precise definition of price discrimination that considers the cost involved in the supply of the good holds that "a firm price discriminates when the ratio of prices is different from the ratio of marginal costs for two goods offered by a firm."[10] While these definitions leave open the question of when two goods are "different" or the "same," they show the vertical character of price discrimination. Price discrimination describes the practice of firms treating their (downstream) customers (either final consumers or buyers of an intermediate good) differently. (Similar analogies can be made with different non-price terms, but only price is dealt with here for reasons of simplicity.)

Very often firms can and do price discriminate, often in astoundingly multifarious ways.[11] For example, airlines generally operate complex yield-management systems whereby they try to differentiate ticket prices between customers based on time of purchase, ticket flexibility etc. Price discrimination is an ubiquitous business practice,[12] which, on its own, does not evidence market power.[13] Even where there is market power, price discrimination is a type of behaviour that almost invariably enhances market efficiency, although not necessarily consumer welfare.[14] No unambiguous *a priori* conclusions can, however, be drawn in respect of the effects of price discrimination on consumer welfare: an effects analysis is necessary in each case.

11.2.1 Conditions For Price Discrimination

Overview. Price discrimination is very common, but not universal. It is only possible under certain conditions. These are the ability to: (1) sort customers according to their valuation; and (2) prevent arbitrage between customers. There is no general agreement,

---

[9] See TP Gehrig and R Stenbacka, "Price discrimination, competition and antitrust", in *The Pros and Cons of Price Discrimination* (Swedish Competition authority, 2005).

[10] G Stigler, *A Theory of Price* (4th edn., New York, MacMillan, 1987). A similar definition equates price discrimination to the practice of selling two "similar" products that have the same marginal costs at different prices. See M Armstrong, "Economic Models of Price Discrimination" (2005), unpublished manuscript.

[11] See, e.g., the amount of price discrimination on display in just one Broadway theatre (in what is a highly competitive industry) in P Leslie, "Price Discrimination in Broadway Theatre" (2004) 35(3) *RAND Journal of Economics* 520–41.

[12] See e.g., the extensive, unanimous discussion (involving a round-table discussion of six leading US academic economists) in the *Empirical Industrial Organisation Roundtable*, Federal Trade Commission, 2001, at p. 104ff.

[13] S Carbonneau, P McAfee, H Mialon and S Mialon, *Price Discrimination and Market Power*, Emory Economics 0413, 2004, mimeo.

[14] See R Schmalensee, "Output and Welfare Implications of Monopolistic Third-Degree Price Discrimination" (1981) *American Economic Review* 239–4. See also AS Edlin, M Epelbaum and WP Heller, "Is Perfect Price Discrimination Really Efficient: Welfare and Existence in General Equilibrium" (1998) 66 *Econometrica* 897–922.

however, on whether market power is necessary for price discrimination: many studies suggest that it is not and that it occurs in competitive markets too.[15]

Condition # 1: customers can be sorted. The most obvious pre-requisite for price discrimination is that suppliers are able to sort customers so that those with a higher valuation for the good are charged a higher price. Suppliers can sort customers in a number of ways—a fact recognised almost a century ago by Pigou:[16]

- *First-degree price discrimination.* It is relatively straightforward for suppliers to sort their customers when the terms of sales are settled through individual negotiation. In this case, sellers can tailor the price to fit the preferences and outside options of each individual customer. This is known as first-degree price discrimination. First-degree price discrimination is common when selling intermediate and industrial goods, for example in the sale of commercial aircraft.[17]

- *Second-degree price discrimination.* Not all products are sold through individual negotiation; many are sold at list prices instead. Sorting, and hence price discrimination, is still possible, but now suppliers must offer a range of different "deals" and let consumers sort themselves by picking the one they prefer.[18] This is known as second-degree price discrimination. There are many ways to offer a range of deals and induce self-sorting. One method is to create different versions of the product.[19] For example airlines target business travellers with a high willingness to pay by offering a ticket which is more expensive, but which has features that they consider important.[20] Another way to charge more to customers with a higher willingness to pay is to bundle the product with a complementary "metering" input. For examples suppliers of photocopy machines often require customers to buy toner cartridges. Customers that do a lot of photocopying, and

---

[15] See, e.g., ME Levine, "Price Discrimination Without Market Power" (2002) 19 *Yale Journal of Regulation* 1-36 (suggesting that: (1) price discrimination is common in an economy which is generally competitive; (2) there is no necessary link between price discrimination and dominance and its preservation; and (3) price discrimination is a normal response to the existence of common costs and does not in and of itself suggest market power.). See also B Klein & JS Wiley, "Competitive Price Discrimination as an Antitrust Justification for Intellectual Property Refusals to Deal" (2003) 70 *Antitrust Law Journal* 610 (competitive price discrimination "normal and pervasive"); and JB Baker, "Competitive Price Discrimination: The Exercise of Market Power Without Anticompetitive Effects (Comment on Klein and Wiley)" (2003) 70 *Antitrust Law Journal* 643 (arguing that there is no necessary connection between price discrimination and anticompetitive effect, but that there is such a connection between price discrimination and market power).

[16] See AC Pigou, *The Economics of Welfare* (1st ed, London, McMillan, 1920).

[17] See H Varian, "Price Discrimination" in R Schmalensee and R Willig (eds.), *Handbook of Industrial Organisation Volume I* (Amsterdam, North Holland, 1989), ch. 10, p. 604.

[18] M Motta, *Competition Policy: Theory and Practice* (Cambridge, Cambridge University Press, 2004), p. 492.

[19] In some cases companies will incur additional costs creating an inferior version of their product, in order to facilitate price discrimination. This practice is termed "versioning." See H Varian, "Price Discrimination," in R Schmalensee and R Willig (eds.), *Handbook of Industrial Organisation Volume I* (Amsterdam, North Holland, 1989), ch. 10, p. 599.

[20] These features include the ability to change or cancel the journey at short notice, access to a lounge where the traveller can work, faster check-ins so that less time is wasted in queues, and more comfortable seats, so the traveller arrives better able to do business.

presumably are willing to pay more, will use more toner, and indeed pay more. Companies can also implement second-degree price discrimination by charging different unit prices depending on the amount bought (non-linear pricing).[21]

- *Third-degree price discrimination.* The final type of sorting is to charge different prices to customers on the basis of some easily observable and enforceable criterion, such as time of day, or age of customer, which is correlated with willingness to pay.[22] For example, cinemas offer reduced ticket prices for students and people below a certain age, or bars offer consumers a reduced price within a well-defined span of time (happy hour).

Condition # 2: there is no arbitrage. In order to engage successfully in price discrimination a firm must be able to prevent resale or arbitrage. This is certainly fulfilled in the case of services—which cannot be resold in general—but can also be effected by instruments such as warranties, adulteration, or contractual remedies that reduce the scope for arbitrage. But it is also a feature of appropriate sorting mechanism that customers have no *incentives* to resell. In some instances of price discrimination (discrimination by geographic location, for instance), the firm must have the possibility to prevent arbitrage (e.g., by contract clauses). The debate over parallel imports of a variety of goods highlights the important role that arbitrage can play in preventing price discrimination. For example car manufacturers have, in the past, sought to prevent dealers in one country from selling in another, in order to sustain different prices in different countries,[23] although such efforts are generally unlawful if concluded by agreement.

11.2.2 Welfare Effects of Price Discrimination

Effects generally ambiguous or positive. Price discrimination is an ubiquitous and multi-faceted phenomenon. It is therefore not surprising that it is difficult to provide a clear-cut appraisal of its effect on economic welfare. Price discrimination may occur both in monopolistic and in (relatively) competitive markets, and might be targeted at final consumers (price discrimination of final good) or intermediate suppliers. Pigou's tripartite classification of price discrimination is mainly useful to identify *when and how* price discrimination can occur: it does not help explain its welfare implications. Some generalisations are, however, set out below.

We do not deal with one important potential effect of price discrimination: its ability to undermine stability in a cartel or an interdependent oligopoly. This mainly raises issues under Article 81 EC, although it may also have implications for the definition of collective dominance under Article 82 EC—in particular where the market has parallel most-favoured customer (MFC) clauses—a topic that we discuss in detail in Chapter Three (Dominance). The potential *abusive* effects of MFC clauses are, however, discussed in Section 11.4 below.

---

[21] See H Varian, "Price Discrimination" in R Schmalensee and R Willig (eds.), *Handbook of Industrial Organisation Volume I* (Amsterdam, North Holland, 1989), ch. 10, p 611.

[22] *Ibid.*, p. 617.

[23] M Motta, *Competition Policy: Theory and Practice* (Cambridge University Press, 2004), pp.493, 495-496.

a. Price discrimination generally leads to higher profits for suppliers. Price discrimination leads to higher profits for suppliers, at least in the absence of some of the strategic effects discussed below. The reason is very simple: suppliers set prices to maximise profits. If charging different prices to different customers leads to higher profits they will do so; if not, they will not. The effect of price discrimination on profits has a knock-on effect on investment. If price discrimination is possible, it is more likely that companies will be able to cover investment costs and pay for overheads, which will encourage entry and, in some cases, innovation.

Price discrimination allows fixed costs to be recovered more efficiently if different buyers have variations in willingness or ability to pay. As a basic premise, economists consider that marginal cost pricing—pricing at the level of the extra cost of producing the last unit of production—maximises consumer welfare. This runs into problems for industries (of which there are many) that have high fixed costs and need to recover as much of those costs as possible in order to survive in the long term. There is also an additional problem in many "new economy" industries where marginal costs are very low, but research and development and innovation costs are high. In these situations, it makes sense that a company may wish to price above marginal cost in order to recover some fixed costs for those who are willing to pay more and at or near marginal cost for those who can only afford to pay less, but might not otherwise be able to afford the product or service in question. So if marginal costs are, say, 10% of the list price and there is a customer which is unwilling or unable to pay more than 50% of the list price for the product, it is in the interests of the dominant firm (and, in this case, the consumer) to grant the 50% discount. The dominant company gets a significant positive contribution to its revenues from the sale.

b. Price discrimination can lead to higher or lower output, depending on the circumstances. Price discrimination can affect the level of output in a market, and therefore the overall level of welfare.[24] There are two countervailing effects. First, a company that can price discriminate may increase output because it is willing to sell to niche markets that would otherwise not be supplied at all. A company that must charge the same price to everyone will be reluctant to supply customers who are not willing to pay very much. If the company offered a low price to these customers it would have to offer the same low price to all its other customers, lowering profits overall. On the other hand if the company can charge different prices to different customers, it faces no such problem. In this case it can supply the low value customers without undermining the profitability of the rest of its business.[25] Thus, in the example cited above, the customer gets a product that it could not otherwise afford. The transaction is economically rational and procompetitive from a consumer welfare point of view.[26]

[24] *Ibid.*, pp. 495-496.

[25] See H Varian, "Price Discrimination" in R Schmalensee and R Willig (eds.), *Handbook of Industrial Organisation Volume I* (Amsterdam, North Holland, 1989), ch. 10, p. 622; M Motta, *Competition Policy: Theory and Practice* (Cambridge University Press, 2004), p. 496.

[26] See Office of Fair Trading, Guideline Assessment of Individual Agreements and Conduct, OFT 414, para. 3.8 ("Price discrimination between different customer groups can be a means of [recovering common costs]; it can increase output and lead to customers who might otherwise be priced out of the

Second, a company that can price discriminate may restrict output because it is able to raise prices to customers with a high valuation. A company that can price discriminate can set very high prices to those groups with a high valuation of the product, without prejudicing their ability to supply other groups. These high prices will lead the targeted groups to buy less than they would otherwise do, so that output to this group is lowered.

The overall effect on output and on total welfare is thus ambiguous.[27] The exception is when customers are sorted through individual negotiation (first-degree price discrimination). In this case, price discrimination always leads to higher output because the company has no incentive to limit supply to any customer: as long as the customer will pay more for an additional unit than the marginal cost, the supplier will be willing to add the unit to the contract.

c. Price discrimination in inputs can put some firms at a competitive disadvantage. Article 82(c) sets out one way in which price discrimination can be harmful. If one company pays more for its inputs than its competitors do, it may be at a competitive disadvantage. If the two buyers of the relevant input compete with each other and arbitrage is not possible, a difference in treatment can distort competition between the buyers if it has a material impact on the total costs of the buyer paying the higher price. The higher input costs may mean the company sells less than rivals, or is even forced to exit the market, even if it has better products or is otherwise more efficient. However, whether there is an effect on *competition overall* (as opposed to competition between the two buyers) requires much more rigorous assessment: the exit or marginalisation of one firm on a downstream market is irrelevant if there are a sufficient number of other sellers. Treating secondary-line discrimination as an abuse should therefore be approached with considerable caution.

d. Price discrimination in inputs can lead to lower input prices overall. Price discrimination can also be procompetitive in exactly those circumstances where Article 82(c) is concerned about possible harm—when a company with market power upstream is supplying downstream customers who compete against each other. In these circumstances, the upstream company may find that it cannot exploit its market power, and can only sell at low prices, unless it can credibly commit not to price discriminate.[28]

The upstream company would like to sell at a high price to a downstream customer. This customer may be willing to pay a high price, but not if it believes it will have to compete against rivals who purchased the input at a lower price. If the upstream company is able to price discriminate the customer will, rightly, fear that as soon as it has signed an agreement the supplier will have an incentive to solicit its rivals, offering them lower prices to induce them to buy more. Knowing this, the customer will refuse to pay a high price.

market being served. In particular, in industries with high fixed or common costs and low marginal costs it may be more efficient to set higher prices to customers with a higher willingness to pay.").

[27] See M Motta, *Competition Policy: Theory and Practice* (Cambridge University Press, 2004), p. 496.

[28] P Rey and J Tirole, "A Primer on Foreclosure," in *Handbook of Industrial Organisation*, M Armstrong and R Porter (eds.), vol. III (Amsterdam, North Holland, 2003).

If the upstream company is now forced, by competition law, to set the same price to all its customers then it can credibly commit to the first customer that it will not find itself undercut by rivals who were supplied at a lower price. As a result the customer will be willing to pay more than before.[29] Price discrimination in this case leads to a "commitment problem" for the monopolist that makes it more difficult to exert market power.

11.2.3 Conclusion

The complexity of the consumer welfare effects of price discrimination in practice. Price discrimination, if successful, increases firms' profits. What effect this has on consumer welfare, however, can only be decided in individual cases, since it is generally ambiguous. In thinking about effects arising from changes to producer welfare on consumer welfare, it is important to remember that the pattern of price discrimination paid by final customers may be very different from that faced by the intermediate supplier. For example, retailers may face complex non-linear tariffs (second degree price discrimination) when buying wholesale goods, but will often sell these goods on to final consumers at a constant unit price.

Turning to the effects themselves, it is possible that consumers do benefit from price discrimination. Customers may buy more of an intermediate good if they are charged a different unit price depending on how many units they buy, according to a scheme that is tailored to them, as discussed in detail in Chapter Seven (Exclusive Dealing, Loyalty Discounts, and Related Practices). These customers may face a lower marginal cost than they would if they paid the same price for all units, and they may pass on this lower marginal cost to their final customers in the form of lower unit retail price. If so, the practice is good for both economic efficiency and consumers.

However, even in this relatively clear-cut case, there is another factor to take into account which could mean that consumers pay higher prices even though marginal costs have fallen. The problem arises from the different role played by marginal and average input costs. Non-linear tariffs for inputs mean that suppliers can have a high average input cost even though their marginal input cost is low. Low marginal costs encourage low prices, but if the resulting profits are too small to cover the average cost of inputs, some companies may be forced to exit the market, weakening the intensity of competition, and allowing the remaining companies to set higher prices and so earn higher margins.

In practice, the outcome for consumers will be even more complex. If there are only limited differences in the non-linear tariff faced by different suppliers (i.e., the extent of third degree price discrimination is limited), then different suppliers will face different input costs for their marginal units. Whether this is good or bad for consumers depends on whether consumers can choose freely between the supplier with high costs and the supplier with low costs. If not, for example because consumers without a car have no

[29] For an application of this analysis to the media sector, see G Abbamonte and V Rabassa, "Foreclosure and vertical mergers: The Commission's Review of Vertical Effects in The Last Wave Of Media and Internet mergers: *AOL/Time Warner, Vivendi/Seagram, MCI/Worldcom/Sprint*," (2001) 22 *European Competition Law Review* 6.

option but to use the local shop, then those consumers that are "captive" to the high cost supplier will be disadvantaged, while those that can choose the low cost supplier will benefit. The balance could go either way.

11.3 LEGAL CONDITIONS FOR ABUSIVE DISCRIMINATION

Overview. The following sections detail the interpretation of the constituent elements of Article 82(c) in the decisional practice and case law, namely the concepts of "equivalent transactions," "dissimilar conditions," and "competitive disadvantage." (Objective justification is treated separately in Section 11.5.) Two important considerations should be appreciated, however, from the outset. First, there is a high degree of overlap between the conditions for the application of Article 82(c). For example, the reasons why two transactions are not "equivalent" are often the same as why it would be objectively justified for a dominant firm to differentiate between the two customers.

Suppose a dominant firm charges two sets of buyers different prices on the basis that one set of buyers has greater utility for the input in question (e.g., the first set of buyers only use the input in one downstream activity whereas the second set use it in two or more activities). Assuming that this was a legitimate explanation for the difference in treatment, it could either be said that it constituted "objective justification," or that the transactions with the two sets of buyers were not "equivalent." The same argument could be made in relation to different treatment based on lower costs of serving one customer over another. It could be argued that the two transactions are not "equivalent" for purposes of Article 82(c) or, if they are, that any discrimination is justified by the lower costs of serving one customer. In other words, the boundaries between the different conditions of Article 82(c) are not rigid in many cases.

A second important consideration is that case law offers limited guidance on the interpretation of the legal conditions in Article 82(c). This is in part because the interpretation of the conditions for the application of Article 82(c) is very fact-specific to each case. Another possible reason is that most cases of abusive discrimination concerned a series of cumulative abuses. In this circumstance, the Community institutions may have felt less compelled to engage in an exhaustive analysis of secondary-line effects that may have logically followed from a proven primary-line abuse.

For example, in *Irish Sugar*,[30] the dominant manufacturer was found to have offered rebates to customers located at border areas in order to prevent foreign imports. The Community institutions found that this was an abuse because, first, it had exclusionary effects *vis-à-vis* competitors and, second, it distorted competition among the dominant firm's customers. They may have felt that, in circumstances where the dominant firm had been found to have unlawfully excluded its competitors, it had greater freedom to discriminate between customers, to the detriment of customers paying the higher prices.

---

[30] Case T-228/97, *Irish Sugar v Commission* [1999] ECR II-2969.

11.3.1 Equivalent Transactions

Basic definition. Whether transactions are "equivalent" must be looked at in the light of all the circumstances and cannot be assessed solely from the perspective of either the dominant firm or its trading parties. In principle, all relevant evidence should be looked at in determining whether transactions are "equivalent," including the physical or chemical composition of the products, their functional or performance characteristics, physical appearance, and the extent to which they are fungible (e.g., command similar retail prices). Article 82(c) is not, however, concerned only with comparisons between two products or services: the key point is that the "transactions" are equivalent.

Detailed application. A useful definition of "equivalent transactions" is provided by a decision of the authority responsible for the interpretation of Article 60 of the now-defunct European Coal and Steel Community Treaty, which held that "transactions are comparable if they are concluded with competing purchasers, involve the same or similar products and their other relevant commercial features do not essentially differ."[31] A number of issues are raised by this basic definition.

a. Basic similarity between the compared products/services. A first, basic requirement is that the compared products or services are similar in some physical or functional sense. An obvious case arose in *United Brands* where the bananas marketed by the dominant firm had the same origin, belonged to the same variety, and were almost the same quality.[32] The compared products do not, however, need to be identical in all respects as long as the essence of what is provided to one customer is similar to that provided to others. Thus, in *Aéroports de Paris*, the Commission considered that groundhandling services (e.g., freight and mail handling, aircraft cleaning and servicing, and catering) provided by the airport operator were equivalent to the services provided by those air carriers who were licensed to provide some of their own groundhandling services. The self-handing services provided by a carrier for its own operations benefited from the services of the airport managing body in the same way as groundhandling services for third parties. The principal difference between the two categories of groundhandling services was whether the airline in question had sufficient volume to justify self-provision, but this did not change the essence of the service provided.

Evidence that two products offered by the dominant firm are substitutable offers a good indication that the transactions are equivalent. In *Deutsche Bahn*,[33] the complaint concerned an allegation that rail tariffs applied by the German rail operator to the carriage by rail of sea-borne containers between Germany on the one hand, and the Belgian and Dutch ports on the other, were much higher than those applied to the same containers over the same distance via the German ports. The Commission concluded that transport services via the German ports were substitutable for transport services via the Belgian and Dutch ports, at least where the total distances covered were similar.

---

[31] See Decision 30-53 of the High Authority, OJ 1953 L 6/111 (as amended by Decision 72/440/ECSC, OJ 1972 L 297/39).

[32] Case 27/76, *United Brands Company v Commission* [1978] ECR 207, para. 204.

[33] *HOV SVZ/MCN*, OJ 1994 L 104/34 (upheld on appeal in Case T-229/94, *Deutsche Bahn v Commission* [1997] ECR II-1689).

This was based on evidence that liner shipping conferences charged the same price regardless of whether the port of origin was German, Belgian, or Dutch. Later, in treating these two categories of transport contracts as equivalent transactions for purposes of Article 82(c), the Commission referred to its earlier discussion regarding the full substitutability of transport routed via German ports and transport routed via Belgian and Dutch ports, adjusting, where appropriate, for differences in distances between the routes compared.

In *Clearstream*,[34] the Commission concluded that two different types of intermediaries for security clearing and settlement services formed part of the same customer group and that discrimination by a dominant supplier between these two types of customers concerned the application of dissimilar conditions to "equivalent transactions." The case concerned clearing and settlement services for securities. Clearing and settlement are necessary steps for a securities trade to be completed. Clearing refers to the process which ensures that the buyer and the seller have agreed on an identical transaction and that the seller is selling securities which it is entitled to sell. Settlement is the transfer of securities from the seller to the buyer and the transfer of funds from the buyer to the seller, as well as the relevant annotations in securities accounts. So-called secondary clearing and settlement services are provided through intermediaries, such as central securities depositories (CSDs), international central securities depositories (ICSDs), and banks. In addition to the intermediary services required to complete a securities transaction, securities also need to be "safekept" in the sense that they must be actually deposited with the entity that holds a security in physical or electronic form, which is sometimes referred to as primary clearing. In contrast to final custodians, intermediaries perform services in relation to securities but do not hold securities in final custody.

Clearstream, the only provider of final custody for clearing and settlement services under German law, was found guilty of unlawful discrimination in its service fees for cross-border transactions with intermediary CSDs on the one hand and ICSDs on the other. In its defence, Clearstream argued that CSDs and ICSDs were not comparable customer groups, since their functions differed. The Commission rejected this argument. It noted first that the nature of the services supplied by Clearstream to these intermediaries were comparable, i.e., primary clearing and settlement services. The Commission also rejected the argument that CSDs' and ICSDs' functions differed. In particular, Clearstream argued that, unlike CSDs, ICSDs do not act as final custodians of securities, which Clearstream said increased the level of risk. The Commission agreed that, in other contexts, CSDs' and ICSDs' services may differ, but that, for purposes of the case at hand, both CSDs and ICSDs offered comparable services, i.e., secondary clearing and settlement of securities issued in accordance with German law. The Commission also dismissed the argument that ICSDs differed from CSDs because ICSDs' historical origin lay in the trade of securities outside exchanges. The Commission concluded that only the present-day nature of the services mattered, not their historical origin.

[34] Case COMP/38/096, *Clearstream*, Commission Decision of June 2, 2004 (hereinafter, "Clearstream") (not yet published).

One interesting situation where transactions were not considered "equivalent" concerned a complaint against the imposition of sequential use coupons on airline tickets.[35] As with other airlines, British Airways (BA) offers lower-priced tickets for indirect flights via its hub airport on condition that the customer uses the indirect portion of the ticket in the proper sequence. For example, in the case at hand, the complainant purchased a ticket from Milan–London and onward from London–Dar es Salaam, but sought to board the flight in London without having used the Milan–London coupon of the ticket. BA refused on the grounds that the ticket had not been used in its proper sequence, which was a condition of the lower price. (The direct flight from London–Dar es Salaam was more expensive.) The passenger complained to the Commission that BA's insistence on sequential use of ticket coupons for Milan/London/Dar es Salaam discriminated between customers purchasing tickets in different EU Member States. The Commission rejected this argument on the grounds that an indirect ticket for Milan/London/Dar es Salaam was a different product to a direct ticket for London/Dar es Salaam. Because different product markets were implicated, the transactions were not "equivalent" according to the Commission.

b. Similar commercial context of the compared transactions. Unlike other non-discrimination laws (e.g., the United States Robinson-Patman Act), Article 82(c) does not require that the products concerned should be of "like grade and quality." Rather, the key issue is whether the "transactions" are "equivalent," which suggests that the commercial context of the compared transactions plays a paramount role. Although the precise meaning of equivalent commercial transactions has not been formally articulated in any decision or judgment, a number of potential differences between transactions could be envisaged.

One of the most important issues in practice is whether deliberate product differentiation by a manufacturer means that two transactions involving similar but differentiated (e.g., branded goods versus private label) products are "equivalent" under Article 82(c). A good case can be made for saying that goods subject to a valid trademark are not "equivalent transactions" to similar, but non-branded, goods. Usually, such differentiation leads consumers or users to attach different values to the two products. If the differences in relative valuation are significant enough, the goods cannot be considered "similar" for purposes of Article 82(c). For example, a manufacturer offers both a branded product and a brand of the retailer's choice, and engages in heavy advertising of the former. Such differentiation, if it leads to consumers paying a price premium for the branded product should lead to the terms of the two transactions not being considered "equivalent." In contrast, suppose that a manufacturer sells a variety of differentiated products to well-informed buyers who use them for their own consumption. In this case, the buyers would presumably know that the goods in question were functionally equivalent and would be unlikely to exhibit a purchasing preference based on label differentiation. In this situation, the products in question would most likely be similar.

[35] See Case COMP/A.38763/D2, *Sequential Use Of Coupons*, Commission communication pursuant to Article 7(1) of Commission Regulation (EC) 773/2004, July 14, 2005 (on file with authors).

More generally, transactions are not likely to be equivalent if the value of a first contract would be substantially affected by the dominant firm's decision to grant second or subsequent contracts. For example, the value of a first intellectual property licence may be substantially affected if the dominant firm offers a second licence to a licensee in a territory where the first licensee also operates. It would usually be impractical to require a dominant firm to renegotiate first contracts each time it concluded a second or subsequent contract. The better view therefore is that, if the terms of a later contract would be substantially different from the terms of a first contract negotiated (both negotiated on arm's-length terms), the two transactions are not "equivalent." This also means that a dominant firm could lawfully refuse to make a second contract, on the same terms or at all, if it could lawfully have granted a first exclusive contract.

c. ***Proximity in time.*** An essential component of any meaningful definition of equivalent transactions is that the transactions must be reasonably proximate in time. If not, a dominant firm would be indefinitely exposed to discrimination claims based on past transactions. Issues may arise concerning timing and in particular whether and to what extent transactions with a first customer can be compared to subsequent transactions and for how long. While the dominant firm cannot escape liability by arguing that, at the time it offered a first contract, no other customer existed,[36] subsequent contracts may differ in material respects and, therefore, not be "equivalent." For example, supplying an input to a direct competitor is obviously different from supplying an input to a customer with whom the dominant firm does not compete. A licence for a new, untried technology may be offered on more favourable terms than a licence for a proven technology. A dominant firm may also distinguish transactions based on the circumstances of the contracting party. A dominant firm should be allowed to offer different terms to undertakings that have a proven record of successful exploitation of its technology than to undertakings entering an application for the first time. There may also be procompetitive reasons why the dominant firm would wish to offer more favourable terms to new entrants than to existing customers. In other words, there may be a variety of legitimate reasons why contracts by the same grantor do not need to contain similar terms.

Although the factual circumstances will vary from case to case, the essential point seems clear: (1) if a dominant company sells quantities of a standard product at the same price for a period, there is no discrimination; (2) if, after a while, it lowers its price, and sells steadily at that price, there is no discrimination: the former higher prices were lawful when they were charged. More difficult issues arise if the higher price (or royalty) was included in long-term supply contracts or long-term licences. Then, if the dominant company begins to charge lower rates in new contracts, it must (if the other conditions of Article 82(c) are met) lower the price in the older contracts insofar as they are still in force. In other words, discrimination is illegal if it is simultaneous, but not if it is consecutive. Contracts thus need revision under Article 82(c) only if they are continuing and *coincide in time* with more favourable contracts.

---

[36] See Case T-128/98, *Aéroports de Paris v Commission* [2000] ECR II-3929, para. 169.

11.3.2 Dissimilar Conditions

Treating like situations differently. Article 82(c) states that in order for discrimination to constitute an abuse of a dominant position, the dominant company must apply "dissimilar conditions, thereby placing [other trading parties] at a competitive disadvantage." Whether conditions are "dissimilar" is a question of fact based on a comparison of the terms of the "equivalent" transactions: they are either different or they are not. The key test therefore is whether two equivalent transactions produce differential rates of return for the dominant firm. The reasons for such differences are generally irrelevant at this stage of the analysis. These reasons are assessed below under "objective justification."

Treating dissimilar situations the same. From the very outset, the Court of Justice made clear that discrimination under EC competition law not only covers treating like situations differently, but also treating different situations the same.[37] This makes sense, since the essence of discrimination is two differential rates of return. Whether such returns arise as a result of the dominant firm having the same cost for two sales but different prices, different costs but the same prices, or different costs and different prices is immaterial provided the transactions are equivalent. In practice, however, it is not easy to envisage many situations in which a dominant firm would wish to treat different situations the same. The most likely scenario concerns a State undertaking who wishes to impose a handicap on foreign undertakings by refusing to extend more favourable terms to the latter by artificially assimilating them with domestic undertakings. This might for example arise in the area of health and social welfare (assuming of course that the entity in question is an "undertaking" for purposes of Article 82 EC).

Need for the dominant firm's knowledge of the fact of discrimination. Unlike other non-discrimination laws (e.g., Section 50(1)(a) of the Canadian Competition Act), there is no requirement that the dominant firm should be aware that it is applying dissimilar conditions to equivalent transactions. This omission is problematic, since, in many cases, the dominant firm will be unaware that it is discriminating. Suppose that a dominant seller supplies a product to two undertakings with retail outlets in two geographic locations that are not proximate to each other, i.e., the customers do not compete with each other. Suppose then that one customer, unknown to the seller, opens a new outlet in proximity to the other seller. The retailers would then be competing purchasers but the dominant seller would not know that it was discriminating between them. This is obviously unsatisfactory: a dominant firm should be in a position to judge in advance whether its conduct is likely to be lawful or not. This means that there is a good case for saying that discrimination implies that the dominant firm knew, or should have known, that it was discriminating. The latter might include situations in which the customer informed the dominant firm that it was entering into competition with another buyer or the dominant firm cannot have been unaware of this fact (e.g., if it made deliveries to the customer's new outlet).

---

[37] Case 13/63, *Italy v Commission* [1963] ECR 165, para. 6 ("Discrimination in substance may consist not only in treating similar situations differently, but also in treating different situations identically.").

11.3.3 Competitive Disadvantage

The lack of clarity on the meaning of "competitive disadvantage." To what extent, if any, there is a need to show that the party paying the higher price or receiving worse terms suffers a *material* competitive disadvantage, or whether a competitive disadvantage is presumed from the mere fact of discrimination, remains unclear. The issue has not been directly addressed in the case law and what case law does exist is inconsistent. A number of different interpretations could be advanced: (1) that there must be evidence of actual or likely material competitive disadvantage suffered by the party discriminated against; (2) that competitive disadvantage may be logically inferred from an examination of the relevant circumstances; or (3) that the mere fact of discrimination creates a presumption of competitive disadvantage.

a. Evidence of actual or likely material competitive disadvantage. The first interpretation of competitive disadvantage is that, in order to establish abusive discrimination, a competition authority or plaintiff needs to establish not only the fact of differential treatment, but, in addition, that the party paying the higher price or receiving the less favourable term suffers a material competitive disadvantage relative to the other party. This strongly implies that, at least in the situation where the dominant firm discriminates between undertakings with whom it does not compete, the trading parties must be in competition with one another for Article 82(c) to apply.

A number of leading commentators have suggested that this is, or ought to be, the approach under Article 82(c). One commentator stated that "the obligation of equal treatment between customers mentioned in Article 8[2](c) is only a qualified one" and that a "price differential (or other discriminatory treatment) is unlawful only if it imposes a competitive disadvantage upon certain customers."[38] More recently, another commentator argued that a difference in treatment is contrary to Article 82(c) "only if it gives rise to a *significant* competitive disadvantage."[39] Since the dominant enterprise will not necessarily know enough about non-associated companies' affairs to be able to judge this, the question is "whether a reasonable company in the position of the dominant enterprise should have known that a significant competitive disadvantage was likely to arise."[40] This interpretation is also consistent with the non-discrimination clause in Article 60 of the now-defunct European Coal and Steel Community Treaty, which has been interpreted to mean that conditions are dissimilar only if the price differs *appreciably* from the price published.[41]

Several cases have found abusive discrimination in situations where the differences in treatment between trading parties were more than isolated and *de minimis*. For example, in *Soda-ash-Solvay*,[42] Solvay operated a policy of granting customers

[38] R Joliet, "Monopolisation and Abuse of Dominant Position," (1970) 31 *Collection Scientifique de la Faculté de Droit de l'Université de Liége*, p. 244.

[39] J Temple Lang, "Anticompetitive Non-Pricing Abuses Under European And National Antitrust Law" in B Hawk (ed.), *Fordham Corporate Law Institute* (New York, Juris Publishing Co, 2004) vol. 26, 235-340, 248 (emphasis in original).

[40] *Ibid.*

[41] See Decision 30/53 of the High Authority, OJ 1954 L 217/1 (as amended by Decision 72/440/ECSC, OJ 1972 L 297/39).

[42] *Soda-ash–Solvay*, OJ 1991 L 152/21.

substantial financial inducements to obtain from Solvay all or the major part of the marginal tonnage that might otherwise have been obtained from a competitor. In addition to giving rise to primary-line discrimination against competing suppliers of Solvay, the rebate system was also found to be contrary to Article 82(c). The Commission found that the discrimination had a considerable effect upon the costs of the affected undertakings, since, after fuel costs, the input supplied by Solvay was the most expensive item in the manufacturing process (up to 70% of the raw material batch cost). The increased cost of soda-ash thus affected the profitability and competitive position of glass manufacturers, clearly placing them at a competitive disadvantage.[43] Several other Commission decisions and judgments of the Community Courts have also discussed the criterion of "competitive disadvantage" separately and did not assume that it automatically followed from a mere showing of discrimination.[44]

The recent opinion in *British Airways/Virgin* tends to support the need for at least likely evidence of a distortion of competition between the trading parties. First the Advocate General stated that a relationship of competition must exist between the relevant trading partners of the dominant undertaking. Only then can a "competitive disadvantage" arise. She added that, secondly, the conduct of the dominant undertaking must be

[43] Non-discrimination laws in the Member States and other jurisdictions generally treat the fact of discrimination and a "competitive disadvantage" as separate criteria. In the United Kingdom, the Office of Fair Trading has rejected several complaints on the grounds that any discrimination was either inherently procompetitive or had no material effect. See, e.g., *BSkyB*, (Decision of December 17, 2002) (structure of discount scheme unlikely in practice to have affected competition); and *BT/BSkyB* (Decision of May 15, 2003) (low take-up of the promotion meant that it did not have, and was unlikely to have, a material effect on competition). See also the Decision by the United Kingdom energy regulator, Ofgem, in *London Electricity* (Decision of September 12, 2003), para. 41 ("The fact that there was a severely limited take up of the offer meant that the price discrimination between former [London Electricity] customers who had switched and [London Electricity] customers who had not switched did not have an anticompetitive effect. Because there was no anticompetitive effect it followed that there was no evidence of abuse and therefore the Authority concluded that there was no material effect on competition."). In France, Article L. 442-6-1 of the Code de commerce contains similar wording to Article 82(c). French courts have held that competitive advantage is a separate criterion. See, e.g., *Ciba-Geigy*, Cour d'appel de Versailles, October 24, 1996. See also *Société Office d'Annonces (O.D.A.) c/ Becheret*, Cour de cassation, Chambre Commerciale, April 6, 1999. US courts have held that only price discrimination that creates a probability of substantial competitive injury is actionable. See, e.g., *Falls City Indus. v Vanco Beverage Inc.* 460 U.S. 428, 435 (1983). The Supreme Court has also held that an inference of discrimination is justified only where: (1) there are substantial price differences; (2) they exist over a lengthy period; (3) they involve a product for resale; and (4) competition among resellers is keen and typified by low margins. See, e.g., *FTC v Morton Salt*, 334 U.S. 37 (1948) and *Volvo Trucks N. Am., Inc. v Reeder-Simco GMC, Inc.*, No. 04-905, 2006 WL 43971, (January 10, 2006). Moreover, this inference may be rebutted where there is no causal link between the price differences and lost profits or share, or where the disfavoured firm has nonetheless prospered. Conversely, no inference of injury to competition is permitted where the discrimination is not considered substantial. See, e.g., *Chrysler Credit Corporation v J. Truett Payne Co.*, 670 F. 2d. 575, 581.

[44] See *Tetra Pak II*, OJ 1992 L 72/1, para. 154. See also Opinion of Advocate General Mischo in Case C-82/01 P, *Aéroports de Paris v Commission*, [2002] ECR I-9297, paras. 210 and 211; Opinion of Advocate General Cosmas in Case C-344/98, *Masterfoods*, [2000] ECR I-1369, para. 63; Case T-228/97, *Irish Sugar v Commission* [1999] ECR II-2969, paras. 125, 138, 140 and 145; Joined Cases 40-48, 50, 54 to 56, 111, 113 and 114-73 *Suiker Unie v Commission* [1975] ECR 1663, paras. 524-28; *Chiquita*, OJ 1976 L 95/1, II.A.3.(b); *Irish Sugar plc*, OJ 1997 L 258/1, paras. 140-42, 146-48; *Ilmailulaitos/Luftfartsverket*, OJ 1999 L 69/24, paras. 42–43.

"likely in the particular case to distort that competition, i.e. to prejudice the competitive position of some of the dominant undertaking's trading partners in relation to the others." However, proof of quantifiable damage or an actual, quantifiable worsening of the competitive position of individual trading partners of the dominant undertaking actually took place cannot, according to the Advocate General, be demanded.[45]

b. Logical inference of competitive disadvantage from the totality of circumstances. A second interpretation is that a competitive disadvantage can be logically inferred from an examination of the market circumstances in which the abuse arises. There is some support for this interpretation in the decisional practice and case law. One such decision is *Chiquita*,[46] where the Commission held that United Brands' price differentials of 30–50% to distributors and ripeners of Chiquita bananas in different Member States, coupled with a contractual clause preventing the resale of green bananas, constituted unlawful discrimination. The Commission stated that the distributors were placed on "an unequal competitive footing" if they wanted to sell Chiquita bananas in Member States other than those in which they were established. The Commission found that it would have been relatively easy for distributors to enter into competition with each other, since distributors purchased the same bananas free of rail from Rotterdam or Bremerhaven and used their own means of transport. The Commission concluded, however, that, as a result of the imposition by United Brands of price differentials depending on the destination of the bananas and, more importantly, a clause preventing the resale of green bananas, "[c]ertain distributor/ripeners are accordingly placed at a competitive disadvantage." Absent the discriminatory conduct, wholesalers could easily have competed away the significant price differences that resulted from the discriminatory conduct. The inability of certain distributors to do so thus created an obvious competitive disadvantage.

c. Mere discrimination enough to raise a presumption of competitive disadvantage. A final interpretation is that a finding of discrimination also establishes that a competitive disadvantage would result; in other words, the mere fact of differential treatment is sufficient to create a "competitive disadvantage." In *Corsica Ferries I*,[47] the Port of Genoa was accused of applying discriminatory tariffs for piloting services offered to non-Italian flag carrying ships. In its defence, the Italian government argued that the differences were justified on the ground that intra-Community shipping transport is not in competition with the domestic shipping transport activity of cabotage. The Advocate General rejected this argument and held that "[i]t appears implicitly from Community case-law...that the Court does not interpret that phrase restrictively, with the result that is not necessary, in order to apply it, that the trading partners of the undertaking responsible for the abuse should suffer a competitive disadvantage against each other or against the undertaking in the dominant position."[48] The Court of Justice

[45] See Opinion of Advocate General Kokott in Case T-219/99 *British Airways plc v Commission* [2006] ECR I-nyr, paras. 124-125.

[46] *Chiquita, ibid.*

[47] See Opinion of Advocate General Van Gerven in Case C-18/93, *Corsica Ferries Italia* [1994] ECR I-1783, para. 32. See also Case C-179/90 *Merci convenzionali porto di Genova SpA v Siderurgica Gabrielli SpA* [1991] ECR I-5889, paras. 18-19.

[48] See Opinion of Advocate General Van Gerven in Case C-18/93, *Corsica Ferries Italia* [1994] ECR I-1783, para. 34.

did not address the issue in its judgment, but merely noted that, under Article 86 EC, the Member State had an obligation not to create price approval structures that could induce a State undertaking to apply discriminatory tariffs. The element of discrimination based on nationality or residence arguably explains the strict approach adopted by the Court in this case.

In *Irish Sugar*, the dominant undertaking operated several different rebate practices designed to respond to the threat of competitive sugar imports into Ireland. These included selective rebates to customers located on the Northern Ireland border who were exposed to imports of sugar from the United Kingdom and other Member States. Customers located outside the affected border areas did not receive a comparable rebate. The Court of First Instance held that these discounts were discriminatory, since customers in border and non-border areas were treated differently based on purchases of the same amounts. The Court did not explain, however, to what extent retailers in border and non-border locations competed with each other or how competition between them would have been harmed by the size of the discount. It merely noted that customers "were not able to benefit, outside the region along the border with Northern Ireland, from the price reductions caused by the imports of sugar from Northern Ireland."[49]

More recently, in *British Airways/Virgin*, the Court of First Instance upheld the Commission's finding that the payment of bonus commissions by British Airways to travel agents, depending on the extent to which they increased sales of British Airways' tickets in comparison with a previous reference period, gave rise to unlawful discrimination. The bonus schemes at issue could in theory have resulted in different rates of commission being applied to the same amount of revenue, since they depended not on absolute increases in sales, but on the extent to which an agent had increased its sales compared to its sales in the previous reference period.

The Court did not analyse in detail, however, whether this was in fact the case and, if so, precisely how the payment of a small percentage bonus commission to certain agents placed agents receiving a lower commission at a competitive disadvantage and to what extent. The differences in commission seemed insignificant on the face of it: all agents received the standard commission in any event; the maximum additional commission was only 1–2%. And yet, there was no analysis of the relative sizes of travel agents and whether the absolute value of the bonus paid to one agent was material in relation to the turnover of the competing agents in the same catchment area etc. Instead, the Court simply noted that travel agents depended on airlines for their income and that competition between agents "was naturally affected by the discriminatory conditions of remuneration."[50]

[49] Case T-228/97, *Irish Sugar v Commission* [1999] ECR II-2969, para. 188. Similarly, in *Deutsche Bahn*, the Court of First Instance concluded that price differences as low as 5% gave rise to a competitive disadvantage. See Case T-229/94, *Deutsche Bahn v Commission* [1997] ECR II-1689, para. 86. The Court of First Instance did not analyse in detail how such small differences in treatment were material, in particular in the presence of much larger differences. But, again, this case is best explained on the basis that the German rail operator was, in effect, discriminating against undertakings who routed traffic via non-German ports, i.e., indirect nationality discrimination.

[50] See Case T-219/99 *British Airways plc v Commission* [2003] ECR II-5917, para. 238.

Reconciling the different approaches. A number of comments can be made regarding the above approaches. A first comment is that there is no convincing basis for saying that a competitive disadvantage can be automatically inferred from any difference in treatment, i.e., without any inquiry into the actual, likely, or logical effects of the difference in treatment. This approach would mean that minor differences in treatment that had no competitive impact, or *de minimis* impact, would be deemed abusive. It may be that in many cases the dominant firm would have objective justification for such differences in treatment, but it makes no sense to require the dominant firm to offer an elaborate explanation for conduct that has little or no competitive effect.

A second comment is that any sensible policy on discrimination under competition law should require a logical connection between the fact of differential treatment and a meaningful "competitive disadvantage" suffered by the party paying the higher price or receiving worse terms. A meaningful competitive disadvantage can only begin to arise if the customers are in competition with one another at the same level of trade and the disadvantage suffered by one customer has a material impact on its total costs or some other important aspect of its business.[51] For example, significant differences in the price of a raw material that forms a large proportion of the customer's total input costs could have a material impact on the customer's ability to compete with downstream rivals. In contrast, where the raw material is only used in small or variable proportions, it is difficult to see how price differences can have more than a trivial impact on the customer's overall competitiveness. What kind of evidence is needed to substantiate a meaningful competitive disadvantage will vary from case to case, but there should in most cases be evidence of actual harm or, absent such evidence, a case of likely harm based on a logical inference from the relevant circumstances.

A final comment is that inferring a competitive disadvantage from the mere fact of differential treatment would be less problematic if the objective justification criterion

---

[51] See Opinion of Advocate General Kokott in Case T-219/99 *British Airways plc v Commission* [2006] ECR I-nyr, paras. 124-125. A number of cases seem at first sight inconsistent with the notion that the customers should in some sense compete with each other, but it is submitted that, on closer analysis, no inconsistency arises. In Case 226/84, *British Leyland Plc v Commission* [1986] ECR 3262, the price differences primarily affected consumers, who were not generally in competition with one another, rather than the dealers selling the cars. However, the differences also affected competition between dealers in different States, insofar as they were supplying to buyers resident in other Member States. See also Case T-228/97, *Irish Sugar v Commission* [1999] ECR II-2969, paras. 138-139, where the dominant firm granted a rebate on sugar purchases to customers who exported to other Member States, while refusing to grant a rebate to customers purchasing the same amounts for domestic sale. The Court of First Instance found that this amounted to discrimination on several levels. First, it distorted competition between the exporters and suppliers of sugar in the Member State of import (who did not receive a rebate from Irish Sugar). Second, there was discrimination among exporters, since the rebate was not linked to actual volumes exported. Finally, there was discrimination between undertakings who engaged in both export and domestic supply and undertakings who were only engaged in domestic supply. In all of these cases, the trading parties were active on the same level of trade. Moreover, it could also be argued that the underlying rationale was a series of cumulative abuses carried out by Irish Sugar in order to insulate the Irish market from competition. Granting incentives for export was one obvious way of limiting domestic competition. See also Case 27/76, *United Brands Company v Commission* [1978] ECR 207, where there was limited competition between wholesalers in different Member States, but this was precisely because United Brands contractually restricted such competition by insisting on a clause that effectively prohibited resale.

took the welfare-enhancing effects of discrimination into consideration. For example, in *British Airways/Virgin*, the Community institutions' failure to examine in detail whether and to what extent agents receiving lower bonus commissions suffered a competitive disadvantage would not have mattered much had they undertaken a proper analysis of the objective justification for British Airways' efforts to incentivise its agents. In general, efforts to reward agents on the basis of increases in their sales relative to past sales have a strong procompetitive rationale. Unfortunately, however, the Community institutions gave no serious consideration to this issue under the heading of objective justification. Thus, another reason why the competitive disadvantage criterion requires a meaningful showing of adverse effect is because the Community institutions' analysis of objective justification is minimal and ignores basic economic thinking. It should be emphasised, however, that a meaningful analysis of the competitive disadvantage criterion is *not* a substitute for a proper analysis of objective justification. Competitive disadvantage only measures the disadvantage suffered by the party paying the higher price or receiving worse terms: it does not measure whether the disadvantage restricts competition, i.e., consumer interests. Only the objective justification criterion performs this function.

11.4 SPECIFIC EXAMPLES OF ABUSIVE DISCRIMINATION UNDER ARTICLE 82(C)

Overview. The enforcement of Article 82(c) at Community level has been limited to date and has generally been confined to two principal situations. The first is where an undertaking—usually State-owned or controlled—is granted a legal monopoly over the provision of a service or product and directly or indirectly discriminates between domestic and foreign transactions. The prohibition of discrimination on grounds of nationality or residence underpins the core objectives of the EC Treaty, as set forth in Article 12 EC.[52] But, at the outset, the authors of the EC Treaty considered that the chapter dealing with competition law required a specific provision to deal with discrimination on nationality or residence grounds.[53] This was based on the widespread existence of State monopolies and other exclusive rights and the expectation at the time that these may have encouraged favouritism towards national interests and a corresponding bias against trade from other Member States. As the Community Courts have held, a system of undistorted competition, as laid down in the EC Treaty, can be

[52] See also Article 20, 21 and 23 of the EU Charter of Fundamental Rights (and chapter II of the Draft Constitution for Europe) under the heading "Equality." Equal treatment, which requires that comparable situations not be treated differently and different situations not be treated alike, unless such treatment is objectively justified, is a general principle of Community law. See, e.g., Case 203/86, *Spain v Council* [1988] ECR 4563, para. 25; Case C-15/95, *EARL de Kerlast v Union régionale de coopératives agricoles (Unicopa) and Coopérative du Trieux* [1997] ECR I-1961, para. 35; Case C-292/97, *Kjell Karlsson and Others* [2000] ECR I-2737, para. 39; Case C-14/01, *Molkerei Wagenfeld Karl Niemann GmbH & Co. KG v Bezirksregierung Hannover* [2003] ECR I-2279, para. 49.

[53] See J Temple Lang, "Anticompetitive Non-Pricing Abuses Under European And National Antitrust Law" in B Hawk (ed.), (2003) *Fordham Corporate Law Institute* (New York, Juris Publishing Co, 2004) pp. 235-340.

guaranteed "only if equality of opportunity is secured as between the various economic operators."[54]

The second situation in which Article 82(c) has primarily been applied concerns cumulative abusive conduct by a dominant firm. Findings of discrimination have been made in many cases where the primary allegation was that the dominant firm unlawfully excluded competitors through stand-alone violations of Article 82 EC. For example, in *Irish Sugar*,[55] the primary finding was that the dominant sugar supplier had unlawfully excluded new entrants by offering selective discounts to their actual and potential customers, while maintaining higher prices in geographic areas where new entrants had limited activities. The corollary of this was that customers in areas not exposed to competition paid higher prices than those in areas where competition between the new entrant and the dominant firm was more pronounced, which the Commission characterised as abusive discrimination. In circumstances where the dominant firm directed selective discounts at rivals' customers, the Community institutions may have felt more confident that the resulting disparity in treatment among downstream trading parties gave rise to a separate abuse. Indeed, a striking feature of the decisional practice and case law is that discrimination is very rarely pursued as a violation in its own right. Outside the area of discrimination on the grounds of nationality, most cases involving abusive discrimination have primarily concerned unlawful exclusion of rivals.

Identifying all possible categories of abusive discrimination in a market economy is virtually impossible given the potentially limitless number of transactions in which buyers receive different prices and terms and conditions. That said, a number of reasonably well-established situations in which discrimination raises potential concerns under Article 82 EC may be discerned from the case-law and decisional practice. These include: (1) "pure" secondary-line discrimination; (2) direct and indirect discrimination on nationality grounds; (3) discrimination aimed at partitioning national markets; (4) most-favoured nation clauses; and (5) discriminatory supplies in times of shortage. Each of these categories of abusive discrimination is analysed in detail below. But it is important to recall that, in each case, the potential objective justification for a difference in treatment also needs to be assessed.

11.4.1 Pure Secondary-Line Discrimination

Anticompetitive effects of a strict non-discrimination rule. Different prices and terms are ubiquitous in real-world markets, including many markets in which no single firm or group of firms is dominant. For example, most modes of transport distinguish between peak and off-peak travel, offering lower rates for buyers who are prepared to travel at times when demand is lower. Similarly, seats in an airplane are sold at different prices based on variables such as the type of travel desired, (e.g., business travel as distinct from leisure), ticket flexibility, time of purchase, and routing (indirect flights are usually cheaper since they take longer). Many services also distinguish between buyers based on their objective characteristics, ability to pay, or time sensitivity. Cinemas and theatres routinely offer discounts to students or pensioners, in particular when demand is low (e.g., afternoon shows). These forms of price

[54] See Case C-202/88, *France v Commission* [1991] ECR I-1223, para. 51.
[55] Case T-228/97, *Irish Sugar v Commission* [1999] ECR II-2969, para. 188.

discrimination are generally procompetitive, since they are designed to maximise the use of the relevant assets and therefore output. There is also a net consumer benefit in many cases, since certain users may be able to purchase a product or service that they could not afford at (higher) uniform prices.

A requirement that a dominant firm should treat all trading parties equally would be onerous and could lead to perverse outcomes. For example, it would mean that, if a dominant firm wanted to lower its price in a negotiation with one party, it would also have to lower its price in every comparable transaction to avoid allegations of discrimination. Rules would also be needed to determine whether a dominant company which lowered its price in one case would have to apply the reduction retroactively with respect to existing contracts, or only in subsequent contracts. A rule would also be needed to determine how long the enterprise would have to continue to charge the same price before it could raise its price again. It is obvious that companies do not do this and that their commercial dealings would become cumbersome if they were forced to do so.

A strict non-discrimination rule would also remove an important parameter of competition: the ability of trading parties to use their negotiating skill to obtain better terms and reduce procurement costs. If a dominant firm could not offer better terms without extending the same terms to all buyers, it might mean that, once a higher price is agreed with one buyer, that price would become a floor that the dominant company could use to resist any further attempts by other trading parties to get a better price, even in circumstances where it might otherwise have been willing to offer one. The law could then be used by dominant firms as a basis for refusing to lower prices or offer better terms, which could lead to higher prices overall for consumers and trading parties. Non-discrimination rules could also encourage parallel pricing in oligopolistic markets, since the collectively dominant firms would have legitimate reasons for not deviating from uniform prices. Indeed, recognising these potential anticompetitive effects, the Commission has suggested that a non-discrimination (or "most-favoured-customer") clause could itself cause competition problems if it prevented other trading parties from negotiating better prices or terms.[56]

Examples of abusive secondary-line discrimination. At Community level, findings of discrimination based only on differences in the prices or terms offered to two or more similarly-situated customers have been an extreme rarity under Article 82 EC. Instead, discrimination claims have generally been linked to some other form of egregious conduct, such as nationality discrimination or anticompetitive measures intended to partition markets along national lines. The Community institutions' reluctance to apply Article 82(c) in cases where the only conduct alleged is a difference in price or terms to similarly-situated customers most likely reflects the fact that price discrimination is ubiquitous (including by non-dominant firms) and probably efficient in most cases, as well as the concern that a strict non-discrimination rule would likely have the perverse effect of raising prices overall, increasing scope for collusion, and preventing firms from negotiating better prices and terms. For this reason, the Community institutions

[56] See *Kabel-metal-Luchaire*, OJ 1975 L 222/34. The treatment of most-favoured-customer clauses under Article 82 EC is discussed in detail in Section 11.4.4 below.

have never suggested that a dominant firm is under a strict obligation to offer similar prices and terms to all trading parties active at the same market level.

There are, however, a handful of cases in which offering different terms to two or more similarly-situated customers has, in itself, been found to constitute unlawful discrimination. This possibility was first mentioned in early cases such as *Suiker Unie* and *Hoffmann-La Roche* where a further objection to the dominant firm's exclusive contracts and requirements contracts was that they resulted in buyers that purchased the same absolute amounts receiving different prices.[57] But no serious effort was made by the Court of Justice to analyse why the mere fact of receiving different prices affected competition between the customers. Instead, it merely noted that customers competed with each other and must therefore have been affected by different prices.

In *Soda-Ash/Solvay*, the dominant firm was found guilty of a number of exclusionary practices directed at rivals, including exclusive contracts, payments in return for exclusivity or near-exclusivity, and rebates on customers' marginal requirements that rivals could not economically match. In addition to its exclusionary object and effect, the Commission found that the rebate system applied by Solvay also fell under the express prohibition in Article 82(c) against the application of dissimilar conditions to equivalent transactions. This conclusion appears to have been motivated by a number of cumulative considerations:

1. Solvay was found to have discriminated in order to secure the whole or the largest possible percentage of the customer's requirements.[58] This was arguably the key concern, since it would probably have been unlawful for the dominant firm to insist that a favourable price was conditional upon the customer sourcing all or most of its requirements from it. Price discrimination with a similar object therefore merited the same treatment.

2. The rebate conditions were applied in an arbitrary fashion by Solvay. Even within a particular Member State there were considerable differences both as to the size of the rebate and other inducements and the triggering tonnage at which it was activated. The effect was that a large customer could pay substantially more per tonne than a smaller producer even though both were buying their total requirement from Solvay. The implication was that a transparent system of rebates based on objective thresholds would not have been open to the same objection.

Crucially, the Commission attached importance to the fact that the price discrimination "had a considerable effect upon the costs of the undertakings affected," since the relevant input accounted for up to 70% of the customer's total costs.[59] In these circumstances, price discrimination could have a direct and material impact on the disadvantaged customer's profitability and competitive position.

[57] See Joined Cases 40-48, 50, 54 to 56, 111, 113 and 114-73, *Coöperatieve Vereniging "Suiker Unie" UA v Commission* [1978] ECR 1663, paras. 524-28. See also Case 85/76, *Hoffmann-La Roche v Commission* [1979] ECR 461, para. 90.

[58] *Soda-Ash/Solvay*, OJ 1991 L 152/21, para. 61.

[59] *Ibid.*, para. 64.

Two other cases involving discrimination by a dominant firm between intermediaries also treated mere differences in prices as capable of amounting to unlawful discrimination. In *British Airways/Virgin*, the dominant firm paid a bonus commission to travel agents who had increased their sales relative to sales in a past period. The Commission found that this gave rise to unlawful discrimination, since two agents selling the same absolute number of tickets would receive different commissions if one agent had increased its sales by a greater proportion of its past sales relative to the other agent. The basis for this finding is not entirely clear, since a system based on absolute sales levels would have produced much larger distortions in favour of agents with a larger catchment area.

On appeal, the Court of First Instance attached importance to the finding that British Airways was at the time an "obligatory business partner" for agents in the sense that, for many ex-United Kingdom routes, agents had no choice but to deal with British Airways.[60] In these circumstances, the Court concluded that differences in commission for the same absolute amount of ticket sales "naturally" affected competition between agents.[61] The Court made no serious effort to quantify the extent of the difference in treatment, to see whether it affected competition between agents in the same geographic area, to assess whether the difference in commission affected the agent's total costs and profits, and to assess whether a material affect on total costs or profits could have been off-set by revenues from other airlines and other sources. A statement that competition was "naturally" affected is insufficient. The Court's findings on this issue are currently on appeal.

Similarly, the price discrimination finding in *Clearstream* was also expressly based on the notion that, for primary clearing and settlement services for securities issued under German law, Clearstream had a *de facto* monopoly, with no realistic prospect for new entry.[62] Euroclear, the disadvantaged party, therefore had no choice but to deal with the dominant primary clearing and settlement provider for German securities and any discrimination would have had an unavoidable impact on its secondary clearing and settlement activities. The discrimination between Euroclear and other categories of intermediary was also significant. While data on the precise charges are treated as confidential in the public version of the decision, it is noteworthy that a 50% reduction in Clearstream's charges to Euroclear in 2002 was considered necessary to terminate the infringement.[63] A final, important comment is that the discrimination was persistent, lasting over five years, which meant that the price differences per transaction were likely to have had a significant cumulative impact on Euroclear.

Conclusion. The Community institutions have, rightly, only treated pure secondary-line discrimination as unlawful in limited circumstances. The cases are characterised by the presence of some or all of the following features. First, the dominant firm is an unavoidable trading party, either in the sense that it has a *de facto* monopoly or that customers have no choice but to do deal with the dominant firm for a high portion of

[60] Case T-219/99 *British Airways plc v Commission* [2003] ECR II-5917, para. 217.
[61] *Ibid.*, para. 238.
[62] Case COMP/38/096, *Clearstream*, Commission Decision of June 2, 2004, not yet published, para. 208.
[63] *Ibid.*, para. 341.

their requirements. While dominance always implies some barriers to entry, situations in which a trading party has no choice but to deal with the dominant firm for all or most of its requirements clearly offer more scope for material adverse effects. Second, the discrimination must be significant, i.e., the disfavoured party must be paying significantly in excess of what the favoured party pays.

Third, the discrimination should be persistent in that it lasts for a period long enough to have some non-trivial impact on the disfavoured customers' activities. Fourth, the product or service supplied by the dominant firm should represent a large proportion of the customer's total costs. If not, it is hard to see how price differences could have a material impact on the customer's downstream activity. The totality of the trading party's revenues should be looked at in this connection, since it may be diversified or not particularly reliant on the dominant firm for some other reason.

Finally, it is also notable that, in each case in which secondary-line discrimination was considered an abuse in itself, the dominant firm was also found guilty of a series of other abuses. In many cases, the other abuse was the primary conduct complained of and the secondary-line discrimination merely a logical consequence of that conduct. This suggests that the Community institutions are generally unlikely to take action where the *only* allegation is that the dominant firm has charged different prices to non-associated companies.

11.4.2 Nationality Discrimination

Direct discrimination on nationality grounds. Article 12 of the EC Treaty prohibits discrimination on the grounds of nationality. Although primarily directed at the activities of Member States rather than private actors, the Community institutions have also prohibited discrimination on the grounds of nationality under Article 82 EC. The enforcement of Article 82(c) against nationality discrimination has presumably been influenced by Article 60(1) of the now-defunct ECSC Treaty, which provides that "pricing practices...shall be prohibited, in particular: [...] discriminatory practices involving, within the common market, the application by a seller of dissimilar conditions to comparable transactions, especially on grounds of the nationality of the buyer." Significantly, and unlike other forms of discrimination, discrimination on the grounds of nationality is apparently *not* subject to a need to show any effect on competition: such effects are presumed from the mere fact of discrimination. Thus, in its decision in *1998 Football World Cup*, the Commission held that discrimination on the basis of nationality by a dominant firm fell within Article 82(c) "notwithstanding the absence of any effect on the structure of competition."[64]

An obvious case of discrimination was *GVL*,[65] where a copyright management society with a monopoly in Germany refused to conclude management contracts with non-national or non-resident performing artists and refused to protect the rights of such artists in Germany in any other way. The Commission found that GVL's failure to conclude management agreements with foreign artists where the latter were not resident in Germany, or otherwise to manage performers' rights vested in such artists in

[64] *1998 Football World Cup*, OJ 2000 L 5/55, para. 100.
[65] *GVL*, OJ 1981 L 370/49.

Germany, constituted, in so far as such artists possessed the nationality of another Member State or were resident in a Member State, an abuse of a dominant position.

On appeal, the Court of Justice held that GVL conducted its activities in such a way that any foreign artist who was not resident in Germany was not in a position to benefit from rights of secondary exploitation, even if he/she could show that he/she held such rights (either because German law was applicable or because the law of some other State recognised the same rights).[66] It added that such a refusal by an undertaking having a *de facto* monopoly to provide its services for all those who may be in need of them, but who do not come within a certain category of persons defined by the undertaking on the basis of nationality or residence, must be regarded as an abuse of a dominant position.[67]

The prohibition on nationality discrimination covers not only a refusal to deal with undertakings in other Member States, but also covers charges for the same service that vary depending on whether the recipient is a domestic or foreign undertaking. In *Corsica Ferries II*,[68] the Italian authorities induced the beneficiary of an exclusive right to provide compulsory piloting services in the port of Genoa to apply different tariffs to maritime transport undertakings, depending on whether they operated transport services between Member States or between ports situated within the national territory. The Court of Justice held that this constituted a violation of Article 82(c) (read in conjunction with Article 86 EC), since there were no objective reasons for charging different fees for a service that was identical in nature for domestic shipping companies and those operating in other Member States.

Indirect discrimination on nationality grounds. Discrimination on nationality grounds is not limited to direct refusals to deal with some parties based on nationality or residence, but may also include indirect discrimination, such as offering discounts that, in practice, only domestic undertakings can benefit from. In *Deutsche Bahn*,[69] the Court of Justice found that Deutsche Bahn's conduct had contributed directly to the differing rail transport rates within Germany. Rail transport to and from German ports, such as Hamburg, was charged at considerably lower rates per kilometre than rail transport that originated from non-German ports, such as Antwerp and Rotterdam, even in circumstances where the distances from the non-German ports were shorter. Thus, there was a protective system of tariffs for carriage by rail passing through German ports, which created a disadvantage for companies operating on the non-German transport operators.

---

[66] See Case 7/82, *Gesellschaft zur Verwertung von Leistungsschutzrechten mbH (GVL) v Commission* [1983] ECR 483. See also *SACEM & SABAM*, IVth Report On Competition Policy, paras. 112 et seq, and *Boat Equipment*, X[th] Report On Competition Policy, paras. 119-20.

[67] *GVL*, OJ 1981 L 370/49, para. 57. See also Case 155/73, *Giuseppe Sacchi* [1974] ECR 409 (abusive for an undertaking possessing a monopoly on television advertising to discriminate in its charges or conditions between commercial operators or national products on the one hand, and those of other Member States on the other, as regards access to television advertising).

[68] Case C-18/93, *Corsica Ferries Italia Srl v Corpo dei Piloti del Porto di Genova* [1994] ECR I-1783.

[69] Case T-229/94, *Deutsche Bahn AG v Commission* [1997] ECR II-1689.

Portuguese Airports concerned a series of volume discounts that were granted on the basis of the number of landings made in the major Portuguese airports.[70] The Court of First Instance did not infer discrimination from the mere fact that, under a system of quantity rebates, larger customers obtain higher average reductions than smaller customers.[71] Instead, the Court seemed to focus on the fact that the discounts created a situation of *de facto* discrimination against non-Portuguese airlines. Although the system of discounts was open to all airlines, the highest discounts were, in practice, only by the two leading Portuguese airlines, TAP and Portugalia. The Court held that the discounts conferred "an advantage on carriers who operate more than others on domestic rather than international routes and so leads to dissimilar treatment being applied to equivalent transactions, thereby affecting free competition."[72]

In *1998 Football World Cup*, the Commission also objected to a number of requirements in respect of ticket distribution that indirectly discriminated against nationals from Member States other than France (the-then host country). The general public were free to purchase entry tickets direct from the organising authorities on condition that they provided a postal address in France to which the tickets could be delivered. Thus, only by entering into wholly arbitrary, impractical, and exceptional arrangements could most of the general public resident outside France have obtained tickets direct from the organisers. The Commission concluded that the effect of the requirement to provide a postal address in France was to discriminate specifically against the general public resident outside France, given that those resident in France were significantly better placed to meet that requirement. The Commission also concluded that there was discrimination in circumstances where non-French nationals could only apply for tickets in writing, whereas French residents could reserve by telephone, through French banks, or though electronic means only available in France.

11.4.3 Discrimination Intended To Partition National Markets

Possible anticompetitive effects of a strict rule on geographic price discrimination. In a number of cases the Community institutions have found abusive discrimination where a dominant firm's prices or terms and conditions created artificial barriers to trade between Member States, thereby contributing to market segmentation. The competition-law rationale of these cases is not entirely clear; in many ways, the case law seems more bound up in the single market objectives of the EC Treaty than pure competition concerns. This doubtless reflects the fact that Article 82 EC is not stand-

[70] Case C-163/99, *Portugal v Commission* [2001] ECR I-2613.

[71] See also *Ilmailulaitos/Luftfartsverket,* OJ 1999 L 69/24. In two cases concerning royalty rates set by a dominant copyright-management society that were considerably higher than those applied in other Member States, the Court suggested that a discriminatory pricing analysis could be applied. In the event, the Court opted for an analysis under Article 82(a) and excessive pricing. See Case 395/87, *Ministère Public v Tournier* [1989] ECR 2521. See also Joined Cases 110/88, 241/88 and 242/88, *Lucazeau v SACEM* [1989] ECR 2811.

[72] Case C-163/99, *Portugal v Commission* [2001] ECR I-2613, para. 66. See also *Portuguese Airports*, OJ 1999 L 69/31, para. 35 ("It is obvious that such a system has the direct effect of placing airlines operating intra-Community services at a disadvantage by artificially altering the cost to the undertakings, depending on whether they operate domestic or intra-Community services.") See also *Brussels National Airport*, OJ 1995 L 216/8, para. 17 (system of landing fees favoured the national airline, Sabena, in which the Belgian State was a shareholder).

alone legislation, but forms part of the EC Treaty, which includes market integration as an overarching objective.

While the political economy of enforcement activity against geographic price discrimination is understandable given the overall context of the EC Treaty, limiting different rates of returns between geographic markets is likely to lead to competitive harm in many instances.[73] Many forms of price discrimination between Member States are beneficial, in particular where they allow consumers in Member States with lower GDP to avail of products at lower prices than pertain in Member States with higher GDP. This is particularly relevant for many new accession states.[74] Insisting that prices should reduce to the lowest level applicable in one Member State could result in higher average prices for all consumers in the long run. Alternatively, such rules could lead to dominant firms withdrawing entirely from lower-priced markets for fear that prices there would become a benchmark for discrimination claims in other Member States, which would be legal.[75] In short, a prohibition of geographic price discrimination could result in higher average prices or in certain (lower-priced) markets not being served at all.

These considerations apply in particular in the pharmaceutical sector, where large disparities in price caused by national price controls and price discrimination by manufacturers create significant opportunities for wholesaler arbitragers who export pharmaceutical products from lower price countries to higher price countries.[76] In the long term, pharmaceutical manufacturers argue that consumers suffer a significant net loss through parallel trade.[77] They say that parallel trade from low-priced to high-priced countries forces average prices down towards marginal cost, and that pricing at, or near, marginal cost in a handful of countries can suffice to make average prices worldwide inadequate to cover the fixed cost of research and development. A manufacturer faced with such a scenario might ultimately decide to reduce certain research and development on future products.

The potential negative effects of parallel trade on manufacturers' research and development are said to be exacerbated by the existence of national price controls.[78]

---

[73] See W Bishop, "Price Discrimination under Article 86: Political Economy in the European Court" (1981) 44 *Modern Law Review* 288-89.

[74] Economic conditions between the former 15 EC Member States and recently-acceded Member States vary significantly. The acceding countries account for approximately 8.5% of the GDP generated by the EU 15, with a GDP per capita ranging between 69% (Slovenia) and 42% (Estonia). See *Eurostat Yearbook 2002* (Chs. 3 and 6) and the Commission's Strategy Paper *Towards the Enlarged Union*, COM (2002) 700 final.

[75] See, e.g., Case C-249/88, *Commission v Belgium* [1991] ECR I-1275, para. 20.

[76] By 2004, before any possible impact from EU accession, parallel imports accounted for 5% or more of total EU sales of pharmaceuticals (20% in the United Kingdom) and, for some products, parallel trade represented more than half of sales in major markets. See P Kanavos, J Costa-i-Font, S Merkur, & M Gemmill, "The Economic Impact of Pharmaceutical Parallel Trade in European Union Member States: A Stakeholder Analysis," *Special Research Paper* (January, 2004), London School of Economics Health & Social Care.

[77] See, e.g., P Danzon & A Towse, *Differential Pricing for Pharmaceuticals: Reconciling Access, R&D and Patents*, AEI-Brookings Joint Centre Working Paper No. 03-7 (July 2003).

[78] See J Venit & P Rey, "Parallel Trade and Pharmaceuticals: A Policy in Search of Itself" (2004) *European Law Review* 153.

Member States have widely diverging approaches to price regulation of pharmaceuticals. Some Member States are willing to pay higher prices to ensure wider availability of key medicines on the national territory; others pay less, either because they have lower (or simply different) national healthcare priorities or cannot afford to pay more. One consequence of promoting parallel trade from low- to high-priced countries is that the high-priced Member State is effectively asked to accept the national policy considerations that underpin the system of price regulation in the low-priced country. Exporting price regulation from one country to another in this way may confiscate manufacturers' research and development expenditure: prices in the low-priced country would likely have been different (i.e., higher) had they known that they would need to be extended to other countries because of parallel trade.

Limited decisional practice and case law. In view of the significant welfare concerns that are likely to arise from a strict prohibition on geographic price discrimination, the decisional practice and case law do not generally treat price discrimination that leads to market partitioning as unlawful in itself. Rather, such discrimination is considered abusive where used as a *means* to facilitate another independent violation of Article 82 EC. In *United Brands*, the Court of Justice found that the dominant company had discriminated between wholesaler banana ripeners. It had sold the same bananas at the same Community ports at different prices to different wholesaler ripeners operating in different Member States, on the basis of the retail prices charged in each State. It was able to do this because it effectively prevented arbitrage and re-exports by contractually prohibiting the wholesalers from selling unripened bananas. Once ripe, bananas are so fragile and perishable that no trade is possible, except immediate delivery to nearby retailers. The key aspect of United Brands' behaviour therefore was not merely the fact that it had different prices, but that it used contractual terms that, in effect, amounted to an export ban.

Although the Court found geographic price discrimination to be an abuse in itself, implicit in its reasoning was that price differences could have been competed away by wholesalers but for the contractual restrictions on arbitrage.[79] The Court confirmed that Article 82 EC does not prevent a dominant enterprise from setting different prices in different Member States, in particular where the price differences are justified by differences in market conditions and in the intensity of competition.[80] However, it may not go further and apply "artificial" price differences by insisting on contractual clauses that limit exports.[81]

---

[79] See also *Chiquita*, OJ 1976 L 95/1, s. II.A(b) ("Accordingly, the distributor/ripeners which are charged such differing prices by UBC are also placed on an unequal competitive footing if they wish to sell UBC bananas in Member States other than those where they are established and for which UBC had supplied such bananas. This would be relatively easy for them to do, provided that they were allowed to sell green UBC bananas, since most of them buy the bananas f.o.r. Rotterdam or Bremerhaven and use their own means of transport. Certain distributor/ripeners are accordingly placed at a competitive disadvantage. Competition is thereby distorted.").

[80] Case 27/76, *United Brands Company v Commission* [1978] ECR 207, para. 228.

[81] *Ibid.*, para. 232. As noted, the Court did not object to retail price differences between Member States where these were the result of the normal interplay of supply and demand on the relevant market. Instead, the objection appeared to be that United Brands was in effect short-circuiting the interplay of supply and demand at the wholesale and retail level by insisting that wholesalers pay according to

The link between discrimination with market-partitioning effects and the need for an independent abuse was made more explicit in *British Leyland*.[82] The dominant firm charged a higher fee for certificates of conformity with national technical requirements for left-hand drive cars than for certificates for (otherwise identical) right-hand drive cars, to discourage imports of left-hand drive vehicles into the United Kingdom. This was discriminatory according to the Commission, which was not seriously contested in the Court of Justice.[83] The core of the case, however, was not discrimination *per se*, but the fact that the dominant firm imposed an excessive fee for essential conformity certificates required by individuals importing a left-hand-drive car into the United Kingdom. For right-hand-drive vehicles the certificate cost £25. The Court of Justice concluded that this represented the economic value of the service so a price of £150 or £100 for a certificate of conformity for a left-hand-drive car was excessive.

In *Tetra Pak II*, the Commission found that Tetra Pak's selling prices for its cartons were abusive because they varied considerably from one Member State to another. On closer examination, however, geographic price discrimination was simply the logical *result* of other abusive practices. In particular, Tetra Pak was found to have committed an abuse by imposing a range of unfair contractual clauses that, taken together, limited possibilities for equipment resale and for customers to switch to other suppliers. These included: (1) contractual clauses preventing a customer from adding (or removing) accessory parts to a machine purchased from a dominant supplier; (2) the need to obtain prior permission from the dominant supplier for the resale or transfer of the equipment; (3) exclusive rights to repair and maintain a machine for the lifetime of that machine; (4) equipment leases of excessive duration; and (5) long-term maintenance contracts that allowed a dominant firm to unilaterally set the price of maintenance.

Tetra Pak also engaged in a series of exclusionary abuses against rival firms, including predatory pricing. These cumulative measures made it possible for Tetra Pak to apply a "market compartmentalisation policy," thereby preserving or strengthening its dominant position.[84] In other words, the issue was not so much that Tetra Pak charged different prices within the same geographic market, but that it applied a series of measures intended to tie customers to its products and limit rivals' marketing possibilities. Geographic price discrimination was proof that these measures had a significant cumulative effect.

Finally, in *Micro Leader*,[85] Microsoft prohibited the importation of certain French-language software from Canada (where prices were said to be low) to Europe (where prices were said to be higher). A number of European wholesalers complained to the Commission, which found that Microsoft's actions fell within the lawful enforcement of its copyright and that there was no evidence of the wrongful exercise of that right. The Commission added, however, that an abuse might arise in circumstances where

United Brands' determination of what the relevant local market would bear. By "artificial," the Court of Justice thus seemed to have in mind that United Brands segregated the market from the outset, without allowing prices to be determined as a result of normal competition at the retail and wholesale levels.

[82] *British Leyland*, OJ 1984 L 207/11.

[83] Case 226/84, *British Leyland Plc. v Commission* [1986] ECR 3263, paras. 26, 30, 36.

[84] See *Tetra Pak II*, OJ 1992 L 72/1, para. 154.

[85] Case T-198/98, *Micro Leader Business v Commission* [1999] ECR II-3989.

Microsoft charged lower prices on the Canadian market than on the European market for equivalent transactions if European prices were, in addition, excessive within the meaning of Article 82(a). In other words, the Commission did not seem concerned with the fact of geographic price discrimination as such, but whether it was used as a *means* to exploit consumers into paying the higher prices.[86]

Towards a more nuanced approach to geographic price discrimination. There are a number of indications that the Community institutions and national authorities now adopt a more economic approach to geographic price discrimination. In particular, in the area of pharmaceuticals, there is growing recognition that geographic price discrimination may, on balance, be a good thing. In *SYFAIT*, Advocate General Jacobs was sympathetic to the view that the pharmaceutical industry's specific characteristics justified geographic price discrimination and created no general duty to supply parallel traders.[87] Among the factors mentioned by the Advocate General were:[88] (1) that parallel trade is mainly the result of disparities in national price regulation; (2) that consumers may not always benefit from parallel trade; and (3) the need for manufacturers to recover their high fixed costs for research and development. Much the same point was made in a recent French case concerning parallel trade by wholesalers.[89] The *Conseil de la Concurrence* reasoned that national price regulation removed producers' ability to freely set their prices and that, in this circumstance, insisting on price uniformity was tantamount to exporting the price regulation of one Member State to another.[90]

Although Advocate General Jacobs stated in *SYFAIT* that the features justifying geographic price discrimination in the pharmaceutical sector were "highly unlikely" to be present in other industries, recent case law suggests otherwise.[91] In *Sequential Use Coupons*,[92] the Commission upheld a condition of travel on an indirect flight that the passenger had to board the plane on the first leg (*in casu* Milan–London) in order to benefit from a lower fare as compared to direct travel (*in casu* London–Dar es Salaam). The passenger complained that this condition effectively precluded a British traveller from purchasing a less expensive ticket abroad, thereby segmenting markets

[86] Similar allegations were made in a complaint regarding Apple's iTunes on-line music download service. Which?, a consumers' association in the United Kingdom, complained to the Office of Fair Trading (OFT) that Apple's iTunes service discriminated on price according to the user's country of residence and that UK users were unable to benefit from cheaper prices charged on other European iTunes sites, as access to sites serving other countries was barred to non-residents. The OFT decided that the Commission is better placed to consider this matter. See OFT Press Release of December 3, 2004, *OFT Refers iTunes complaint to Commission*.

[87] See Opinion of Advocate General Jacobs in Case C-53/03, *Synetairismos Farmakopoion Aitolias & Akarnanias (Syfait) and Others v GlaxoSmithKline plc and GlaxoSmithKline AEVE* [2005] ECR I-4609, paras 77-99.

[88] *Ibid.*

[89] See Decision No 05-D-72 of December 20, 2005 concerning practices carried out by certain manufacturers in respect of parallel trade in medicines.

[90] *Ibid.*, paras. 267, 269, 270.

[91] See Opinion of Advocate General Jacobs in Case C-53/03, *Synetairismos Farmakopoion Aitolias & Akarnanias (Syfait) and Others v GlaxoSmithKline plc and GlaxoSmithKline AEVE* [2005] ECR I-4609, para. 102.

[92] Case COMP/A.38763/D2, *Sequential Use Of Coupons*, communication pursuant to Article 7(1) of Commission Regulation (EC) 773/2004, July 14, 2005 (on file with authors).

geographically. The Commission rejected this argument, since an indirect flight from Italy to Dar es Salaam via London was simply a different product to a direct flight from London to Dar es Salaam, i.e., there was no market segmentation because the products were different to begin with.

The Commission's conclusion shows a more nuanced and circumspect approach to geographic price discrimination than some earlier decisions. The clause at issue was necessary to allow airlines to efficiently price discriminate between users who wished to avail of a cheaper, indirect flight, and those who were willing to pay more for a direct flight. Such price discrimination increased competition between airlines, since it allowed airlines operating from different hubs to compete with direct flights from other hubs by offering a lower-priced indirect flight option. Sequential use rules were a means to prevent arbitrage between the discriminated customers, which was essential if low prices and greater choice to customers using an indirect flight were to be maintained. In the absence of sequential use rules, airlines would probably be forced to increase fares, or discontinue or reduce services on indirect routes. Airlines adopt different price strategies to maximise overall revenue, and in doing so, are able to make capacity on less convenient routings available at a cheaper price. To remove sequential use rules would probably have had negative effects on consumer choice, prices, and competition.

11.4.4 Most-Favoured Company Clauses

Definition. Most-favoured company (MFC) clauses (also known as most-favoured nation clauses (MFN)) comprise a range of contractual devices used by buyers and sellers to obtain more favourable terms from a counterparty. In essence, these clauses provide that the beneficiary will receive the best available terms on the market, i.e., that the buyer or seller will not discriminate against it by offering better terms to any other trading party. In general, MFC clauses should be regarded as legal under Article 82(c), since they are consistent with the objectives of that clause, i.e., to prevent discrimination. In certain circumstances, however, MFC clauses have been found to create competition concerns by creating a barrier to entry for other buyers or by limiting the scope for price reductions. For example, where a MFC clause benefits a dominant purchaser, it may act as a barrier to entry for the seller to deal with other buyers. The potential competitive effects of MFC clauses are outlined below, followed by a description of their treatment in the decisional practice and case law. Some suggested principles are included in a final section.

Procompetitive effects of MFC clauses. MFC clauses can generate important efficiencies,[93] which explains in part why they are relatively commonplace. First, MFC clauses can reduce transaction and information costs by eliminating the need to seek out information and negotiate a series of price reductions/increases over the lifetime of the contract. This can be an efficient way for the buyer or seller to receive better terms

[93] See J Baker, "Vertical Restraints With Horizontal Consequences: The Competitive Effects Of 'Most-Favoured Customer' Clauses" (1996) 64 *Antitrust Law Journal* 517; M Denger, et al., "Vulnerability of Most Favoured Nation Clauses Under Federal Antitrust Law" (Nov. 1995) *Antitrust Report* 4; and A Dennis, "Most Favoured Nation Contract Clauses Under the Antitrust Laws" (1995) 20 *University of Dayton Law Review* 821.

without engaging in lengthy or complicated negotiations. Second, MFC clauses can facilitate future price adjustments in long-term contracts in response to changes in market conditions. Third, MFC clauses may eliminate opportunism that would otherwise occur in a series of short-term contracts, thereby encouraging more efficient long-term contracts, and promoting investment and market development. This may be important where there are investments in relationship-specific assets by the seller or buyer. Finally, MFC clauses may facilitate risk-sharing by providing for more efficient risk allocation than would occur under fixed price contracts or cost-plus contracts.

Potential anticompetitive effects of MFC clauses. MFC clauses may also have anticompetitive effects under certain conditions.[94] First, although the intuition is that MFC clauses generally lower prices, they may also have the opposite effect. If a seller gives a discount to one buyer, it will know that it is contractually bound to give the same discount to all MFC beneficiaries. This can operate as a "penalty" on price cuts by a seller to other buyers, since the seller will not only have to factor in the immediate cost of the discount to the first buyer, but also the cost of extending the same discount to other MFC beneficiaries. The net effect may be a reduced incentive for a seller to offer a lower price to any buyer, leading to higher prices overall. These effects are likely to be most pronounced where there are buyers who, absent the MFC, would have had power to negotiate a lower price, or where there are certain buyers with lesser ability to pay.

Concerns in this regard should, however, be placed in context. In any market where prices are transparent, or easily obtainable through market intelligence, sellers will in practice face similar pressure to extend more favourable terms granted to one buyer to another buyer. Even a dominant seller faces finite demand and some degree of customer pressure. A MFC clause admittedly makes the problem more acute, since the seller has a contractual obligation to make the more favourable terms known to the MFC beneficiary and to compensate the buyer to the same extent. But it should not be assumed that MFC clauses create unique concerns in this regard: they simply bring into sharper focus concerns that are inherent in many buyer and seller relationships, including relationships involving dominant buyers and sellers.

The second competition concern under MFC clauses is that they might facilitate seller coordination. If a seller offers a discount to one buyer, and the contract requires the seller to reduce the price to other buyers, actual price levels in the market are more likely to be detected. As noted, MFC clauses in favour of sellers may also act as a penalty for selective discounting, which might stabilise prices and lead to coordination among suppliers. The presence of MFC clauses among rival sellers may also facilitate monitoring of pricing behaviour: if other sellers have similar clauses, they can learn about discounts from their customers when the MFC clause is triggered. Thus, the effect of MFC clauses may be the stabilisation of prices at oligopoly levels. Indeed, recognising these concerns, contractual clauses requiring a trading party to disclose

---

[94] *Ibid.*

rivals' prices to the dominant firm have generally been treated as unlawful under Article 82 EC and, on occasion, under Article 81 EC.[95]

Whether this second possible anticompetitive consequence of MFC clauses itself give rises to an abuse under Article 82 EC is very questionable, although a case could be made under Article 81 EC.[96] If MFC clauses lead to coordination among sellers, it may be that this would offer evidence of links capable of giving rise to an inference of collective dominance between those sellers. However, for Article 82 EC to apply, there must also be an abuse and the mere existence of parallel interests among oligopolists has not in itself been found to be an abuse to date.[97] Accordingly, for Article 82 EC to apply, it would be necessary not only to show a risk of coordinated behaviour as a result of the MFC clause, but also some other anticompetitive effect consistent with an abuse (e.g., excessive pricing).

The final possible anticompetitive feature of MFC clauses is that they can act as a barrier to entry for other buyers. As noted above, MFC clauses can deter sellers from offering a lower price to new buyers in order to avoid a contractual obligation to extend the same terms to the MFC beneficiary, which can dampen price competition. A further consequence is that MFC clauses in favour of incumbent buyers may deter sellers from

[95] "English clauses"—clauses that require the buyer to report any better offer and allowing him only to accept such an offer when the supplier does not match it—have on occasion been held to be restrictive of competition. In Case 85/76, *Hoffmann-La Roche v Commission*, [1979] ECR 461, English clauses were condemned under Article 82 EC, together with a variety of other "fidelity" clauses which were found to tie Roche's customers and exclude other vitamin manufacturers. In *BP Kemi-DDSF*, OJ 1979 L 286/32, English clauses were considered to violate Article 81 EC on the basis that such clauses give a supplier critical information regarding competitors. However, in the *Industrial Gases* settlement, the Commission was willing to allow English clauses to be retained if they were included at the request of the customer and only to the extent that they did not require the customer to supply extensive, confidential information regarding the competing offer. See *XIXth Report on Competition Policy* (1989), para. 62. Furthermore, the Commission has stated that, at least with respect to non-dominant suppliers, English clauses may be exempted under Article 81(3) EC. See Commission Notice, Guidelines on Vertical Restraints, OJ 2000 C 291/1, paras. 152-55. In sum, it would appear that English clauses are more likely to be tolerated in markets where the producer is not in a dominant position, where there are a sufficient number of producers in the market so that producer who has agreed to the English clause will not be able to identify the source of the competing offer, and when that producer would not be able to obtain a significant competitive advantage from information obtained throughout the operation of the English clause. See Ch. 7 (Exclusive Dealing, Loyalty Discounts, and Related Practices), s 7.2, above.

[96] See Commission Press Release IP/04/1314 of October 26, 2004. Without prejudice to any admission of liability by the defendants, the Commission closed its investigation into MFC clauses found in the contracts of the Hollywood film studios with a number of European pay television companies after the studios decided to withdraw the clauses. The Commission believed that these clauses had the effect of aligning the prices of the broadcasting rights bought by the television companies. The MFC clause gave the studios the right to enjoy the most favourable terms agreed between a pay-TV company and any one of them. The Commission's preliminary assessment found that the cumulative effect of the clauses was an alignment of the prices paid to the major studios, in particular because any increase agreed with a major studio triggered a right to parallel increases in the prices of the other studios. The Commission considered that these clauses were at odds with the basic principles of price competition. Central to the Commission's case was the proliferation of these clauses, with many similarities, in the contracts of the distribution arms of the eight major Hollywood studios. Price alignment would not appear to have been likely absent the network of clauses.

[97] See Ch. 3 (Dominance).

dealing with new buyers altogether where the cost of extending to the incumbent buyer the terms offered by the new buyer exceeds the price offered by the new buyer. This problem is likely to be more acute where the new buyer's product is lower in quality than the incumbent buyers, or where the industry is characterised by high fixed costs and the incumbent buyer has a large share of a market with static demand.

Suppose Buyer A has a monopoly share of a relevant market, with total annual revenues of €150. In that market, Seller X provides Buyer A with access to a non-substitutable input at a total annual cost of €100. Assume further that access to this input is the only fixed cost incurred by buyers in the relevant market and that Seller X has zero marginal costs in providing the input to each buyer. Assume Buyer B is willing to enter the market, but can only afford to pay €10 per annum for the input sold by Seller X based on the expectation that it will capture a 10% share of the relevant market. If Buyer A has a MFC clause, Seller X would incur a net "loss" of €80 overall (-€100 + €10 + €10) in selling to Buyer B. In contrast, if there was no MFC clause, it would be incrementally profitable for Seller X to sell to both Buyers A and B. This example is of course highly stylised, since, in the absence of the MFC clause, Seller X would probably have an incentive to reduce the input price to Buyer A on the basis that Buyer A's total revenues would decrease following new entry. Moreover, there will usually be scope for a seller to offer more favourable terms to other buyers in less direct ways, such as revenue-sharing arrangements.

Treatment of MFC clauses in the case law. There are no formal decisions under Article 82 EC concerning the treatment of MFC clauses: in *Hoffmann-La Roche,* neither the Court of Justice nor the Commission took issue with the MFC clause operated by Roche. Further, case law under Article 81 EC offers limited guidance on the position under EC competition law. In *Kabelmetal/Luchaire*,[98] the Commission found that an obligation upon Kabelmetal (the licensor) to apply to Luchaire (the licensee) any more favourable licence terms that it granted to any other licensee did not violate Article 81(1). Nonetheless, the Commission did not rule out that similar provisions could restrict competition in other markets, stating that "[i]n specific cases, however, particularly where the market situation was such that the only way to find other licensees was to grant them more favourable terms than those granted to the first licensee, this obligation could be an obstacle to the granting of further licences and therefore constitute an appreciable restriction of competition."[99] These statements do no more than confirm that MFC clauses may have procompetitive and/or anticompetitive features, without elaborating on the principles relied upon by the Commission to distinguish these features.[100]

[98] *Kabel-metal-Luchaire*, OJ 1975 L 222/34.

[99] *Ibid.*, para 8(i).

[100] Similarly, the Commission Notice, Guidelines on Vertical Restraints, OJ 2000 C 291/1, para. 47, makes passing reference to MFC clauses in noting that they may indirectly contribute to resale price maintenance, without, however, explaining when precisely these alleged anticompetitive features would materialise. In any event, the Guidelines have no necessary implications for the treatment of MFC clauses where dominant buyers and sellers are concerned.

An informal decision in *ACNielsen* case is more instructive, at least with regard to the circumstances in which MFC clauses might act as a barrier to entry.[101] The Commission objected to an MFC clause in a standard contract between Nielsen and retail stores for the supply of sales data under which retailers were obliged to extend the same terms offered to other buyers of data to ACNielsen. The Commission found Nielsen, the beneficiary of the MFC clause, to be dominant in the downstream-market for retail tracking services for certain goods. The Commission argued that through exclusive data supply agreements in certain countries and MFC clauses elsewhere, Nielsen created barriers to entry and thus abused its dominant position.

Several elements appear to have triggered the Commission's intervention and the settlement of the case via an undertaking. First, Nielsen was responsible for a significant part–and in many cases all–of the retailers' revenues derived from the supply of sales data. The retailers were therefore reluctant to supply data to third parties at a lower price, since that would entail a significant loss of revenue to them. Second, competitors or new entrants had no realistic alternative to dealing with the retailers, because there were no other satisfactory sources of supply. An incomplete data set was commercially worthless. Finally, in addition to being essential for market entry, data acquisition was a high fixed cost for competitors and new entrants. As a virtual monopolist on the relevant market, Nielsen could afford to spread these fixed costs over a much larger revenue base than competitors and new entrants and thus pay a relatively high price for data. In contrast, it may have been uneconomic for competitors operating on a small scale to pay a similar data fee. The Commission found that this created a barrier to entry for new entrants, given high start-up costs and lack of economies of scale.[102]

---

[101] See XXVIth Report on Competition Policy (1996), para. 64.

[102] See also *Online Travel Portal*, OJ 2001 C 323/6, where the Commission objected to MFC treatment by an on-line travel joint venture (Opodo) established by competing airlines. The joint venture business plan originally envisaged that airlines wishing to enter into marketing agreements with Opodo would have to undertake as a minimum requirement to provide Opodo with access to published and unpublished fares available through online channels and with the lowest fares made available to other online travel agents (i.e., MFC treatment). The Commission was concerned that these provisions would restrict competition in the travel agency services market. As a condition for exempting the joint venture, the Commission therefore required the joint venture shareholders not to discriminate against non-members in the provision of information and services to the joint venture. Again, however, the case reveals very little about the Commission's thinking in regard to MFCs, since it simply applies the general principle that a joint venture between competing undertakings should grant non-member competitors non-discriminatory terms when, if they were not so required, the parties would be in a position to eliminate competition in respect of a substantial part of the products concerned (either by refusing to supply competitors or by supplying them only on substantially less favourable terms). Similar obligations have been imposed in several previous cases. See, e.g., *IGR Stereo Television/Salora*, XIth Competition Policy Report (1981) p. 63; *DHL International*, XXIst Report on Competition Policy (1991), para. 88; *Eirpage*, OJ 1991 L 306/22, para. 20; *Infonet*, XXIInd Report on Competition Policy (1993), p. 416; *EBU/Eurovision*, OJ 1993 L 179/23, Art. 2; *BT/MCI*, OJ 1994 L 223/36, para. 57; *ACI*, OJ 1994 L 224/28, Art. 2; *Night Services*, OJ 1994 L 259/20, Art. 2; *Gas Interconnector*, XXVth Competition Policy Report (1996), para. 82; *Atlas/Phoenix/Global One*, OJ 1996 L 239/23; *Unisource*, OJ 1997 L 318/1; and *British Interactive Broadcasting/Open*, OJ 1999 L 312/1.

Suggested principles. In the absence of any formal decisions concerning the treatment of MFC clauses under Article 82 EC, considerable uncertainty remains as to the stance that would be taken by courts and competition authorities. The following principles are suggested by way of guidance:

1. MFC clauses should raise a strong inference of legality, since they are standard devices whereby buyers seek to obtain more favourable prices, which is the type of conduct that competition law seeks to encourage.[103] MFC clauses should thus only be regarded as unlawful where there is clear evidence of material harm to competition.

2. MFC clauses are less likely to raise concern where they are offered by a *dominant seller* to downstream customers. This is consistent with the fact that MFC clauses in this scenario seek to avoid the very concern expressed in Article 82(c), namely that a dominant firm would discriminate between its trading parties. Nonetheless, MFC clauses may be objectionable when: (a) the customer has significant bargaining power; (b) market prices tend to fluctuate but the existence of an MFC clause impairs a producer's ability to adjust his prices; and (c) the only way for the supplier to attract new customers is to sell at a lower price. No presumption of law can be derived, however, from these statements; in each case, the procompetitive features of the MFC clause must be balanced against any evidence that it causes material competitive harm to other buyers.

3. MFC clauses are more likely to cause concern where they benefit a *dominant purchaser* who controls a significant percentage of the relevant downstream market and there is evidence of anticompetitive effect. Although there is no case law to this effect under Article 82 EC, case law in the United States suggests that MFC clauses in favour of a dominant buyer can raise concerns where they raise rivals' costs and discourage new entry. In *Vision Service Plan (VSP),*[104] the Federal Trade Commission challenged a MFC clause where optometrists would agree to offer VSP their lowest fee offered to any other patient or patient group. VSP had a dominant position in many markets and a substantial position in others. In addition, VSP controlled a substantial share of the relevant insurance market.[105] The anticompetitive effect of the MFC enforcement appears to have been substantial; the Federal Trade Commission's

---

[103] This was in essence the opinion of Chief Judge Posner in *Blue Cross & Blue Shield United v Marshfield Clinic*, 65 F.3d 1406, 1415 (7th Cir. 1995) (amended opinion).

[104] *United States v Vision Service Plan*, 60 Fed. Reg. 5210, 1995 WL 27332 (D.D.C. Jan. 26, 1995).

[105] No precise market share threshold has been indicated before MFC clauses raise concerns, although, in practice, intervention under U.S. law has only occurred where the dominant firm controlled a very high proportion of the relevant market. See *RxCare of Tennessee, Inc.*, No. 951-0059, 1996 FTC LEXIS 284 (F.T.C. June 10, 1996) (complaint and final order) (MFC imposed by a pharmacy network that included 95% of all pharmacies in Tennessee and accounted for more than half of all Tennessee residents with third-party pharmacy coverage); *United States v Delta Dental Plan of AZ*, 59 F.R. 47349 (Sept. 15, 1994) (85% of dentists in the State of Arizona received a significant part of their income from Delta Dental); and *United States v Oregon Dental Service*, 1995 WL 481363, No. C95-1211 (N.D. Cal. 1995) (90% of Oregon's dentists were Oregon Dental Service providers and most received a significant part of their income from Oregon Dental Service).

case was that claims were on average $25–$30 higher in areas in which VSP had a substantial presence when compared to areas in which it was a minor player. These factors persuaded VSP to enter into a consent decree.

4. Even where there is a dominant purchaser, it is important to distinguish between MFC clauses that involve buyer protection (see above) and those that involve seller protection (i.e., where the dominant buyer agrees to pay the same price to a seller as it pays to the highest-price seller). In the latter case, the effect of the MFC clause will generally be neutral or even benign. The buyer is forced to disclose only higher prices paid to other sellers, not lower prices. The buyer will also have less of an incentive to pay a high price to any seller, which ought to increase the buyer's ability to bargain for lower prices. The overall effect is likely to be lower, not higher, prices by sellers. Coordination concerns are also likely to be less pronounced in this scenario, since any uniformity of prices will tend to be at a lower level.

11.4.5 Discriminatory Supplies In Times Of Shortage

Lawful to prioritise long-standing customers. A dominant firm may, in times of shortage, discriminate in terms of supplies between customers, in particular by favouring long-standing customers over occasional customers. In *ABG/Oil Companies*,[106] the Commission seemed to indicate that dominant firms were subject to a strict non-discrimination principle when deciding which customers they could deal with. The Commission stated that an "abuse within the meaning of Article 8[2] of the Treaty may be defined as any action of an undertaking in a dominant position which reduces supplies to comparable purchasers in different ways without objective justification, and thereby puts certain of them at a competitive disadvantage to others," and that "a dominant undertaking must allocate any available quantities to its several buyers on an equitable basis."[107]

The Court of Justice substantially limited the broad principles enunciated by the Commission on appeal.[108] First, abusive discrimination implies that there is "an obvious, immediate and substantial competitive disadvantage" and that the customer's continued existence is jeopardised.[109] Second, the Court made it clear that it may be objectively justified for a dominant firm to terminate supplies where this is the consequence of internal reorganisation of the company.[110] Finally, a dominant firm can prioritise long-standing customers over occasional customers in times of shortage.[111] The Community institutions will verify, however, that there is a genuine shortage and that the reduction in quantities supplied is not merely a pretext for a refusal to supply.[112]

[106] *ABG/Oil Companies*, OJ 1977 L 117/1.
[107] *Ibid.*, Part. II.B.
[108] Case 77/77, *Benzine Petroleum Handelmaatschappij BV (BP)v Commission* [1978] ECR 1513.
[109] *Ibid.*, para. 20 (citing the Commission's findings).
[110] *Ibid.*, para. 28.
[111] *Ibid.*, para. 32.
[112] See *Napier Brown/British Sugar*, OJ 1988 L 284/41, para. 23 (Commission concluded that British Sugar's refusal to supply industrial sugar to Napier Brown was not as a result of shortages that necessitated a quota system, but was an *ex post* attempt to justify British Sugar's refusal to supply).

11.5 OBJECTIVE JUSTIFICATION

The central role of objective justification in discrimination cases. The objective justification criterion is of paramount importance in discrimination cases under Article 82(c). In the first place, the conditions concerning equivalent transactions, dissimilar conditions, and competitive disadvantage are mainly jurisdictional rather than substantive and, in essence, only seek to measure whether one party in a comparable situation to another party suffers a competitive disadvantage as a result of different treatment by a dominant firm. In other words, these conditions measure, at most, harm to a particular company. Such harm has no necessary connection with the type of harm to consumers that Article 82 EC is concerned with.

A second reason why there needs to be a proper evaluation of objective justification in discrimination cases is that, as shown in Section 11.2 above, discrimination has ambiguous welfare effects; indeed, many forms of discrimination enhance consumer welfare overall. Thus, even discrimination with clear procompetitive effects would give rise to a "competitive disadvantage" once the mere fact of discrimination was shown. The objective justification criterion therefore performs the vital function of ensuring that Article 82(c) does not lead to perverse, anticompetitive outcomes, i.e., treating conduct that enhances competition as unlawful.

A final reason why the objective justification criterion requires detailed consideration is that experience in other jurisdictions with a long history of anti-discrimination laws has shown that strict rules lead to anticompetitive outcomes, including collusion among sellers and higher prices. The United States has had non-discrimination antirust laws for almost seventy years in the guise of the Robinson-Patman Act 1936. In an extensive review, the Department of Justice concluded that the legislation has had clear anticompetitive effects and very little procompetitive effect, with the result that, today, there is no enforcement at federal level (although private plaintiff lawyers continue to bring actions).[113] Further, in the context of an on-going review to modernise U.S.

[113] See US Department of Justice Report on the Robinson-Patman Act, (2000) 24(1) *The Journal of Reprints for Antitrust Law and Economics* 257-258 ("The perversity of the Robinson-Patman Act is that it achieves for many sectors of the American economy precisely those ill effects of concentration about which the American public is rightly concerned...Robinson-Patman really serves as 'fair trade' at the manufacturer level. By promoting 'price caution,' Robinson-Patman encourages the maintenance of uniform list prices in oligopolistic manufacturing industries. At the same time, by discouraging bargaining on the part of buyers, Robinson-Patman decreases the possibility that a retailer will receive a lower price, pass it on to the consumer, and thus initiate a competitive struggle in the retailer sector which will ultimately result in more efficient operation and lower prices for the consumer."). The report also concluded that the legislation also failed in its basic objectives, i.e., protecting smaller businesses. It stated that "the narrow protectionist purpose of Robinson-Patman and its anticompetitive effect far outweigh the Act's perceived benefits for the existence of small businessmen" and that "Robinson-Patman provides relatively ineffective assistance to small business" (*ibid.*, 259). For similar criticisms, see H Hovenkamp, "The Robinson-Patman Act and Competition: Unfinished Business" (2000) 68 *Antitrust Law Journal* 130; and ABA Antitrust Section, Monograph No. 4, *The Robinson-Patman Act: Policy And Law, Volume I* (1980).

antitrust law, the Department of Justice has recommended that consideration should be given to the repeal of the Act, since it has harmed consumer welfare:[114]

> "Virtually every antitrust commentator who has examined this Act has concluded that it is inconsistent with effective competition policy and is anti-consumer. For decades, neither the Antitrust Division nor the Federal Trade Commission has devoted resources to enforcing the Act, because enforcement is harmful to consumers. Nonetheless, the Act continues to be the basis for private lawsuits seeking treble damages and attorney's fees. Burdensome and expensive litigation cannot be justified absent a strong showing of benefit to consumers. The Commission should study whether to recommend repeal of the Act."

The need for a more detailed review of the objective justification criterion under Article 82(c). Case law to date has undertaken a limited review of the economic reasons why it may be rational and procompetitive for a dominant firm to engage in discrimination. *British Airways/Virgin* is illustrative in this regard. It will be recalled that the dominant firm paid travel agents a bonus commission of 1–2% for increases in their sales relative to past sales by each individual agent. All agents received a standard commission of 7–9% in any event for each ticket sold and British Airways' rivals were free to offer whatever commissions they wished to incentivise sales of their tickets. The Commission objected to this scheme on the grounds that agents who sold the same absolute amount of tickets could receive different levels of bonus commissions depending on whether they had increased their sales relative to sales in a past reference period. The Court of First Instance essentially agreed with the Commission's findings, noting that, by remunerating at different levels services that were nevertheless identical and supplied during the same reference period, the bonus commission scheme distorted the level of remuneration that the agents received from British Airways. The Court added that discriminatory levels of remuneration "naturally" distorted competition between agents.[115]

The Community institutions' conclusion that agents selling the same absolute amount of tickets could receive different commissions was perhaps true, but this ignores a number of basic procompetitive features of the incentive schemes at issue. British Airways was looking at ways in which it could incentivise agents to sell more tickets and had to devise some useful way of rewarding agents who did so. Measuring agents' performance in the airline industry is not easy, since demand is a function of the agent's combined efforts (e.g., promotional services, customer support, etc.) and external factors affecting aggregate demand (e.g., the economy, and geopolitical considerations). In these circumstances, it seemed reasonable to base the bonus commission on those variables that are most closely connected to the agent's decisions, i.e., individual promotional and marketing efforts. The agent's sales relative to a past period were a reasonable proxy for these efforts.

In markets where aggregate demand can fluctuate materially, and independently of any retailer actions, a rebate scheme defined with reference to absolute volumes of sales could end up rewarding size or luck rather than effort. For example, high street agents

[114] See letter by Assistant Attorney-General R. Hewitt Pate to the Antitrust Modernisation Commission dated January 5, 2005.

[115] Case T-219/99 *British Airways plc v Commission* [2003] ECR II-5917, paras. 236, 238.

in a city would typically have a much larger catchment area than agents serving a local town, without implying that the latter had made any less effort to increase sales. Rewarding agents on the basis of total absolute sales levels could therefore also have a distortive effect by creating a bias in favour of larger agents.

In circumstances where any incentive scheme would produce distortions at some level, British Airways' decision to link the bonus commission to each agent's individual efforts seemed a reasonable and efficient way of giving incentives to agents. Standard principal/agent theory in economics indicates that British Airways' scheme was an efficient way of providing incentives and rewards. And yet the scheme was considered to give rise to abusive discrimination without any serious consideration of its actual or likely competitive effects and whether alternative schemes would have fared better.

Irrespective of the merits of British Airways' arguments, it is important that issues of objective justification should receive serious consideration by competition authorities and courts. The scope of the current jurisprudence is limited and this cannot be attributed to poor arguments by defendants to justify different treatment among customers. Instead, there appears to be an implicit assumption that discrimination is necessarily anticompetitive, without any evidential or economic analysis of whether this is actually the case or likely to be so. Unless Article 82(c) is to make the same mistakes that have discredited anti-discrimination legislation in other jurisdictions, it is important that the Community institutions should adopt a concept of "objective justification" which, consistent with economic thinking, recognises the output enhancement that can result from many forms of discrimination.

Examples of objective justification. While the Community institutions have not been receptive in practice to defences based on objective justification, a number of categories have been recognised, at least in principle, in the case law. As early as *United Brands*, the Court of Justice made clear that a dominant company is entitled to charge differential prices based on a number of factors, including, but not limited to, transport costs, taxation, customs duties, wages, currency fluctuations, and the intensity of competition. The Commission has also accepted price reductions for "special customer status (e.g. [company] employees, affiliated companies, global and multinational accounts, educational and non-profit institutions, or government institutions)."[116] The list is not exhaustive: in the same way as price discrimination is commonplace, a wide range of procompetitive reasons may explain such behaviour. The most obvious defences are set out below.

a. Cost reductions and volume discounts. Differences in the cost of serving one customer over another (e.g., transport costs, taxes) provide an absolute defence to any discrimination charge.[117] Indeed, if the costs of serving two customers are different, the transactions are arguably not even "equivalent" for purposes of Article 82(c). In a similar vein, the Community institutions have invariably found that standard volume rebates (e.g., offering a 10% discount to all customers whose purchases exceed a certain

[116] M Dolmans and V Pickering, "The 1997 Digital Undertaking" (1998) 2 *European Competition Law Review* 113, para. 2.1. See also para. 4.1 (customised or non-standard product offerings).

[117] See, e.g., *HOV SVZ/MCN*, OJ 1994 L 104/34, paras. 212-13 (defence based on cost differences accepted in principle but rejected on the facts).

threshold level) unobjectionable. This likely reflects the fact that, in most cases, some cost savings result from serving larger customers, as well as the commercial reality that large buyers expect to receive better commercial terms.

In *Hoffmann-La Roche,* the Court of Justice held that quantity discounts linked to customers' purchasing volume were permissible.[118] It found, however, that, on the facts, the price advantages granted were not based on the differences in volumes bought from Roche, but were expressly conditioned on the supply of all, or a very large proportion, of a customer's total requirements by Roche.[119] Similarly, in *Irish Sugar,* the Court accepted that Irish Sugar's border rebates in the retail sugar market would have been justified if they had been related to the purchasing volume of Irish Sugar's customers.[120] In that case, however, the rebates had been based solely on the customer's place of business (i.e., the rebate was granted only in cases where Irish Sugar considered that the price difference between Northern Ireland and Ireland might have induced cross-border trade), which was not an objective economic justification.

Likewise, discounts or rebates that reasonably reflect anticipated cost savings or economies of scale have generally been regarded as objectively justified and hence not abusive. In *Digital/Granada,* for example, the Commission accepted an undertaking from Digital concerning the marketing and pricing of services for Digital computers that allowed Digital to offer owners of Digital systems reductions from list prices if they reflected reasonable estimates of average cost savings or countervailing benefits.[121] In *Brussels National Airport (Zaventem),* the Commission accepted that the airport authority's discount system on landing fees charged to airlines could be justified by economies of scale, i.e., if the authority showed that it cost less, in terms of administration and staff, to supply services to a carrier with a large volume of traffic at the airport.[122] More recently, the Commission recognised the same principle in its *Virgin/British Airways* decision: "a dominant supplier can give discounts that relate to efficiencies, for example discounts for large orders that allow the supplier to produce large batches of product."[123] Most recently, in *Clearstream,* the Commission clearly accepted that a difference in the costs of serving two customer groups is a valid defence,[124] but, after a detailed enquiry into the relevant costs of serving each customer, rejected this defence on the facts.

It is not clear, however, whether the Commission considers that quantity rebates are legal only when they are based on identifiable cost savings clearly referable to the additional increase in volume. It is hard to see a good reason for such a rule, since there is rarely an exact relationship between the discounts offered under a volume rebate

---

[118] Case 85/76, *Hoffmann-La Roche v Commission* [1979] ECR 461, para. 89.

[119] *Ibid.*

[120] Case T-228/97, *Irish Sugar v Commission* [1999] ECR II-2969, para. 173.

[121] See Commission Press Release IP/97/868 of October 10, 1997. See also Case C-163/99, *Portugal v Commission* [2001] ECR I-2613, para 49 (discounts offered by a dominant firm "must, however, be justified on objective grounds, that is to say, they should enable the undertaking in question to make economies of scale.").

[122] *Brussels National Airport (Zaventem),* OJ 1995 L 216/8.

[123] *Virgin/British Airways,* OJ 2000 L 30/1, para. 101.

[124] Case COMP/38/096, *Clearstream,* Decision of June 2, 2004, not yet publsihed, paras. 313 et seq.

system and cost savings generated by supplying the additional volumes.[125] The procompetitive importance (and the universal use) of volume rebates is obvious and should not depend on whether the dominant firm can precisely identify corresponding cost savings. A dominant company may also decide that a large order is so important for stabilising and planning its long-term production that it should give a price reduction to obtain it, even if it does not give rise to corresponding cost reductions.[126] For these reasons, the Community Courts have made clear that a defence based on volume discounts does not need to show a precise relationship between the various discounts: it is inherent in such systems that larger customers obtain proportionately higher discounts.[127]

b. Price reductions in return for services rendered. Price reductions may also be given in return for services provided by the buyer which are associated in some way with the sale. In *Michelin I*, the Commission stated that discounts or rebates were justified if provided in exchange for valuable services performed by the customer:[128]

> "[I]t is of course permissible, in the light of the competition rules laid down in the EEC Treaty, for an undertaking granting discounts, bonuses, etc. to take account of the services which the retailer performs for the undertaking in selling its products. A particular example might be the customer service which the retailer may provide for final consumers and which the manufacturer himself would otherwise have to provide."

[125] This consideration cannot, however, be the sole justification for the positive treatment of volume discounts. As Ridyard explains, "there is almost no plausible cost function that would make this kind of discount scheme "cost-related" in the sense that the differences in price were explained by differences in the costs of supply." See D Ridyard, "Exclusionary Pricing and Price Discrimination Abuses under Article 82—An Economic Analysis" (2002) 6 *European Competition Law Review* 289.

[126] This view was accepted under German law in *Mehrpreis von 11%,* Bundesgerichtshof, judgment of October 30, 1975, Wirtschaft und Wettbewerb/E BGH 1413. The applicant, a regional electricity supply company, charged the defendant, a small electricity utility, 11% more for the supplied electricity than a public utility company. The defendant argued that the 11% surcharge constituted an abuse of market power by the applicant. The German Supreme Court held that there was an objective justification for the applicant's inconsistent pricing policy. First, the lower price conceded to the public utility company constituted a legitimate discount based on the fact that the expected quantity of electricity to be purchased by the public company was to be almost ten times more than that to be purchased by the defendant. Second, the public utility company—in contrast to the defendant—contractually renounced its right to expand its own production of electricity, thereby guaranteeing that a certain volume of electricity would be purchased.

[127] See Case C-163/99, *Portugal v Commission* [2001] ECR I-2613, para. 51 ("The mere fact that the result of quantity discounts is that some customers enjoy in respect of specific quantities a proportionally higher average reduction than others in relation to the difference in their respective volumes of purchase is inherent in this type of system, but it cannot be inferred from that alone that the system is discriminatory."). There is also presumably no rule that price reductions based on cost savings are lawful only if comparable cost savings could be made in all other similar sales. Article 82 EC does not oblige the dominant company to make similar cost savings if possible in other cases, and to pass them on to other customers. It may be implicit in the cost reduction defence that the price reduction corresponds to the amount of the cost saving. But in many cases the price reduction is agreed before the precise extent of the cost reduction obtainable can be known, so the price reduction must be based on the seller's estimate of what the cost reduction will prove to be: it cannot be criticised if that estimate turns out to have been wrong.

[128] *Bandengroothandel Frieschebrug BV/NV Nederlandsche Banden-Industrie Michelin*, OJ 1981 L 353/33, para. 45.

Similarly, in *The Coca-Cola Export Corporation–Filiale Italiana*, the Commission considered rebates "conditional on the purchase of a series of sizes of the same product" and rebates "conditional on the carrying out by the distributor of a particular activity (rearrangement and resupply of the shelves, use of advertising materials, etc.)" to be justified by legitimate business reasons.[129] Finally, in *Irish Sugar*, the Court of First Instance confirmed that the rebates in that case would have been objectively justified if they had been based on marketing and transport costs paid by the customer, or any promotional, warehousing, servicing or other functions that the customer might have performed.[130] However, on the facts, it found that the dominant supplier's offer of rebates based solely on the customer's place of business as a means of targeting border customers was not objectively justified.

In terms of avoiding discrimination, an agreement that rewards customers for services rendered should respect two principal criteria. First, the obligation to be performed by the customer should be transparent in the sense that the service and the associated payment are clearly specified in the relevant agreement.[131] Second, the conditions for the payment of the fee for the service rendered should, to the extent possible, be based on objective criteria applicable to all customers. In this regard, it should be recalled that a number of services typically rendered by buyers are not easily quantifiable (e.g., promotional efforts). Accordingly, provided the dominant firm has made some reasonable, good faith attempt to devise criteria for the objective assessment of retailer efforts, it should not be criticised on the basis that it could have chosen different, but equally reasonable, criteria.

c. ***New products and new markets***. As noted in Chapter Five (Predatory Pricing), price reductions given by a dominant firm when launching a new product or entering a new market are generally lawful.[132] These practices are not generally designed to exclude competitors or to differentiate between customers, but represent a short-term effort to increase demand for a new product by allowing users to try the product at favourable rates for a limited period. One apparent difficulty with this is that if a price reduction is lawful when entering a new market, should it not be lawful when selling to a new customer of the dominant enterprise? The answer seems to be that selling to a new customer in the same market, although procompetitive, might create the kind of competitive disadvantage between customers that Article 82(c) was, wisely or unwisely, intended to prevent. Selling in a new market, whether a new geographical market or a new product market, will not create a disadvantage as between competing customers of the dominant company, as long as the markets are genuinely separate.

d. ***Fixed cost recovery.*** Fixed-cost recovery—allowing users with a lower valuation to pay less while charging those with a higher valuation more—should also be

[129] See Commission Press Release IP/88/615 of October 13, 1988. See *BPB Industries*, OJ [1989] L 10/50, para. 127 (similar reasoning applied but inapplicable on the facts).

[130] Case T-228/97, *Irish Sugar v Commission* [1999] ECR II-2969, para. 173.

[131] See *Coca-Cola*, OJ 2005 L 253/21, Section II.3, first indent.

[132] See, e.g., the 1997 Digital Undertaking, (1998) 2 *European Competition Law Review*, 108 ff, para. 2.1. See also para. 4.1 (customised or non-standard product offerings), allowing Digital to grant price reductions for "short-term promotional programs" provided that these are published, available on a non-discriminatory basis, and do not result in below-cost pricing.

a justification for different prices or terms. Dominant companies with high fixed costs should be free to charge different prices to different customers if it benefits both parties to the lower-price transaction. In circumstances where a firm has high fixed costs and low marginal costs, any price that makes a positive net contribution to revenues should normally be regarded as lawful. For these and other reasons, the UK competition authority, the OFT, recognises that "price discrimination between different customer groups can be a means of [recovering common costs]; it can increase output and lead to customers who might otherwise be priced out of the market being served. In particular, in industries with high fixed or common costs and low marginal costs...it may be more efficient to set higher prices to customers with a higher willingness to pay."[133] In other words, fixed-cost recovery should be a defence in cases involving price discrimination.

e. ***Charges according to intensity of use or value in use.*** A dominant firm may also engage in more complicated forms of price discrimination in order to extract more surplus from consumers when their total expenditure does not rise in a linear (or proportionate) manner to the amount purchased. One example is a two-part tariff, which is increasingly used in services in order to extract more of the surplus from consumers who make greater use of the good. The basic scheme is that the consumer pays a lump sum to access the good or service and thereafter pays a fee per unit based on usage. For example, companies that offer printing and photocopying management services often charge clients according to intensity of usage (e.g., per page). Similar principles apply to other forms of non-linear pricing, including quantity discounts, pricing schedules, and other situations in which certain consumers are prepared to pay a premium for priority access (e.g., last-minute business travel). In each case, the basic point is the same: the dominant firm price discriminates according to the intensity or nature of use.[134]

How non-linear pricing along the lines outlined above should be treated under Article 82 EC has not formally arisen in any case at Community level. In 2004, however, the German Federal Supreme Court adopted a broadly favourable approach to such schemes under the national law equivalent of Article 82 EC.[135] The case concerned different royalties charged by German horse racing societies to betting franchises and individual price-making bookmakers. The dominant race societies charged betting offices that belonged to franchised systems a lower price for a licence to transmit live television broadcasts of horse races than they charged independent bookmakers for the same broadcasts. This was based on the difference between pool (or tote) betting operated by the franchises, whereby all of the sports bets for a given horse are pooled and the total divided among the winning bettors (with the franchise taking a portion for running the sports pool). In contrast, the bookmakers were engaged in individual price making. The dominant firm justified the different royalties on the

[133] OFT 414, *Assessment of Individual Agreements and Conduct*, 1999, para. 3.8.

[134] For a detailed treatment of the economics of nonlinear pricing schemes, see DW Carlton & JM Perloff, *Modern Industrial Organisation*, (4th edn., Boston, Pearson Addison Wesley, 2005), Ch. 10 (Advanced Topics In Pricing).

[135] See *Galopprennübertragung*, Bundesgerichtshof, judgment of February 10, 2004, Wirtschaft und Wettbewerb/E DE-R 1251. For commentary, see Anmerkung zum BGH-Urteil "Galopprennübertragung" vom 10. Februar 2004, in: Entscheidungen zum Wirtschaftsrecht (EWiR) 16/2004, p.807-808.

basis that the racing societies benefited to a greater extent from the betting offices' activities than from the bookmakers' activities. This was because the franchised betting offices only acted as agents for betting contracts concluded between the betters and the racing societies, whereas the bookmakers also entered into betting contracts on their own account, which did not benefit the racing societies.

On appeal from the Higher Regional Court, the Federal Supreme Court concluded that the racing societies two-part royalty scheme was objectively justified as a legitimate business practice. The Higher Regional Court found that the usage that the buyer can make of the product may justify discriminatory pricing. Since the betting offices used the live pictures for only one type of activity (tote betting), whereas the bookmakers used it for two types of activities (tote betting and own bets), and the bookmakers made approximately the same turnover with tote betting and own bets, the Higher Regional Court held that the racing societies' decision to charge the bookmakers double the price they charged the betting offices was objectively justified. In remitting the case to the Higher Regional Court for further fact-finding, the Federal Supreme Court found that the issue was not the usage that the buyer made of the product, but that the racing societies benefited from the betting offices' activities to a greater extent than from the bookmakers' activities. The Supreme Court thus accepted that price discrimination could be objectively justified according to the greater benefit that the *seller* obtains from selling to certain customers.

The Court did not seem concerned with the argument that, in so doing, the dominant racing societies were in effect discriminating against downstream rivals, i.e., the bookmakers. Instead, the Court considered that the price differences were a normal commercial practice because they granted more favourable terms to undertakings that promoted the dominant firm's business by bringing in new customers. Were this view accepted under Article 82 EC, it would mean that dominant firms have a broad discretion to charge different prices based on the relative profitability of transactions.[136]

f. ***Meeting competition and non-discrimination***. Chapter Five (Predatory Pricing) discussed in detail the circumstances in which a dominant firm can defend prices that would otherwise be regarded as exclusionary under Article 82(b) on the grounds that they were intended to meet competition from a rival. In essence, the chapter concluded that: (1) such a defence should be permissible in limited circumstances; (2) the strength of such claims is greater in circumstances where the dominant firm prices at a level above its average variable cost, but below average total cost, than in cases in which it prices below its average variable cost; and (3) meeting competition in the case of prices above average total cost should be conclusively presumed lawful except, perhaps, where exclusionary selective pricing is carried out as a part of a cumulative set of abuses. A more difficult question is whether undercutting a competitor's price is a defence where Article 82(c) would otherwise be infringed. In other words, when the defence of meeting competition is valid under Article 82(b) (foreclosure), does this also immunise

[136] But contrast *ATTHERACES Ltd & Anr v The British Horse Racing Board & Anr*, [2005] EWHC 3015 (Ch. December 21, 2005) (British Horse Racing Board's charges to one race broadcaster based on a percentage of net revenue found to be discriminatory and anticompetitive on the facts).

the dominant firm from claims of discrimination under Article 82(c) by the customers who continue to pay the higher price?

A number of general comments can be made by way of introduction. How far Article 82 EC is intended to protect competitors, and how far it should be interpreted to limit the extent to which dominant companies can compete, is obviously fundamental. It is also clear that even dominant companies may compete, and should be encouraged to do so. If one customer can get a competitor to offer a low price, other similarly situated customers should be able to do so too, and matching that price is not likely to create a competitive disadvantage. Any interpretation which discourages a dominant company from lowering its price, even in one individual transaction, should be looked at very critically. Low prices for some sales are better than no low prices at all.

A potential conflict between the principles of foreclosure under Article 82(b) and discrimination under Article 82(c) would arise, for example, if two rivals were bidding for a long-term contract for a substantial quantity, so that if the dominant company offered a specially low price to meet or undercut its rival's, it would create a disadvantage for its other customers, unless it reduced its price to them also (assuming that the transactions were similar). However, were a dominant company prevented from undercutting a competitor's price in that situation, not only would the dominant company be discouraged from competing, but its rival would have the benefit of a "price umbrella." The rival would know (if prices were transparent or the customer was reliable) that the dominant company could not undercut its price without extending the same reduction to all its other customers, at least in "similar" transactions. The rival would therefore know that it need not undercut the dominant company's standard price by very much or at all. The customer will also have an interest in claiming that a rival is offering a lower price, with the result that the lawfulness of a dominant company's price would depend to some extent on the customer's truthfulness. It is also likely that a dominant company will find itself competing against two rivals whose prices are unlikely to be identical. In these circumstances it may match the lower price, but this means that it undercuts the higher of the two rivals' prices. It would be odd, to say the least, to say that it was acting lawfully if the buyer was planning to take the lower price offer, but acting unlawfully if it planned to take the higher of the two offers. In other words, a rule that limited a dominant company from meeting competitive offers could itself lead to anticompetitive and perverse results. It could also lead to companies' verifying each other's prices, which could give rise to serious issues under Article 81 EC.

There are also likely to be wider benefits to a rule that allowed a dominant firm to meet and undercut rivals' prices. If the dominant company was free to meet or undercut its rival's price in one transaction, it presumably would have to do the same thing again when its rival offered the same low price to other buyers, with the result that the general price levels should come down. The better view therefore is that a dominant company may either meet or undercut a rival's price even when that would be likely to create a competitive disadvantage for its other customers, since (if the rival remains in the market) the disadvantage is not likely to be a lasting one.

The above conclusion is consistent with the Commission's increasing insistence that EC competition law is to protect consumers and competition (and not competitors), as well as the conclusion that Article 82(c) should, in common with the other clause of Article 82 EC, be interpreted in a manner consistent with consumer welfare. It would be questionable if consumers were denied the benefit of a non-exclusionary low price on the grounds that, in not offering the same price to all similarly-situated customers, the dominant firm would be creating a disadvantage for the party paying the higher price. Such disadvantage has no necessary connection with harm to competition. At the extreme, the dominant firm may be tempted not to offer a discount to any customer for fear of having to extend the same discount to all customers. This interpretation of the law should be resisted under Article 82(c).

g. ***Other possible defences.*** Although the issues do not seem to have arisen formally in any case, a number of other defences could be envisaged in discrimination cases. First, it should be a defence to show that the lower price to one category of customers was due to the dominant company's goods being obsolete or perishable. Second, it should also be a defence to show that the dominant company's price reduction was needed to help the buyer to respond to competition or to enter a new market, or for some other procompetitive reason. Third, it may be a defence for the dominant firm to refuse to allow additional parties to access its infrastructure where there was little or no commercial benefit for the dominant firm in doing so.[137] Finally, if the dominant firm could show that the product specification in the transaction, although similar to that in other sales, is unique, or that the transaction is one in which the buyer will be reselling under the seller's label rather than under its own, defences should be available. In many cases, several of the above defences will be available simultaneously.

11.6 SUMMARY AND CONCLUSION

The need for great caution in respect of discrimination. A lengthy chapter on discrimination runs the risk of being interpreted as overstating the importance of discrimination cases in practice. Such an inference would be mistaken. Discrimination itself, as a potential abuse concern, should have a limited role under Article 82 EC. All discrimination against rivals—or primary-line injury—should be assessed under the principles concerning exclusionary abuse, and not discrimination as such. If this were accepted, then discrimination would simply be a factor that may be relevant to assessing

[137] See, e.g., *Pay-TV-Durchleitung*, Bundesgerichtshof, judgment of March 19, 1996, Wirtschaft und Wettbewerb /E BGH 3058. The defendant, an operator of installations for the transmission of radio and TV programs, refused to transmit pay-TV programs offered by the applicant through its distribution grid free of charge, whereas it granted access free of charge to other suppliers. The German Supreme Court held that the differential treatment was justified. The Court found that the applicant's program, due to the encrypted transmission, was only accessible to a small and exclusive circle of viewers. Offering the applicant's pay-TV program would not therefore significantly add to the attractiveness of the defendant's services. As the defendant could expect to receive only minimal additional benefit for the transmission of the applicant's pay-TV programs by attracting new viewers, it was legitimate for the defendant to gain compensation for his service from the applicant. German courts have typically been receptive to defences based on objective justification and have clarified that German law "contains no general most favourite-nation clause intended to force the dominant company to grant everyone the same, most favourable-conditions, in particular, prices." *Ibid.*, at 3063 (translation from original).

exclusion, without any presumption being attached either way to the fact of discrimination. A possible exception, discussed in Chapter Six, concerns actual discrimination by a vertically integrated dominant firm against downstream rivals, which is subject to a strict rule.

If the foregoing were accepted, then the role of Article 82(c) would mainly concern discrimination by a dominant firm between downstream customers with whom it does not compete (secondary-line injury). In this regard, it is very difficult to see a strong case for competition-law intervention. First, discrimination has ambiguous effects on consumer welfare and many positive effects in several scenarios. Second, competition law, and abuse of dominance, is, or should be, mainly concerned with conduct that affects inter-brand competition. The case for preventing intra-brand discrimination by a single supplier is far from obvious under Article 82 EC. Third, in most situations involving discrimination, the dominant firm should have a valid reason for differentiating between customers, since a supplier has no general interest in weakening the position of one of its customers relative to another. Its interests plainly are that all customers sell as much as possible, since it would generally suffer harm from distortions of competition on the downstream market. Finally, and most importantly, experience with strict non-discrimination rules in other jurisdictions—in particular the Robinson-Patman Act 1936—has been uniformly negative: consumers pay more, since only competitors benefit from the legislation. In short, general restrictions on different prices and terms almost certainly lead to higher uniform prices and worse terms.

The foregoing are essentially policy reasons for limited enforcement action against discrimination between customers. But the wording of Article 82(c) leads to a similar conclusion. The requirement that the transactions are "similar" should mean that the commercial context and situation of the compared customers is similar. "Competitive disadvantage" means that the customers are in competition with one another and that any discrimination has a material effect on competition between them. Finally, "objective justification" means that the dominant firm can put forward legitimate reasons for any difference in treatment, including that the discrimination tended to enhance consumer welfare. Were Article 82(c) to be interpreted as not including an assessment of consumer welfare, perverse and anticompetitive outcomes would follow. We accept, however, that, for reasons of political economy and otherwise, discrimination based on nationality or residence may be subject to a strict rule under Article 82(c). Taken together, the above comments would ensure that Article 82(c) plays an appropriate but limited role as an instrument to counteract discrimination that operates to consumer detriment.

Chapter 12

EXCESSIVE PRICES

12.1 INTRODUCTION

Excessive prices and EC competition law. Issues of "unfair" or excessive pricing traverse a number of potential abuses under Article 82 EC. Many refusal to deal cases, for example, do not involve outright refusals, but situations in which a dominant firm insists on access terms that are uneconomic for the requesting party. Margin squeeze cases can also involve a wholesale price that is excessive in relation to the retail price: a margin squeeze arises when the price charged by the dominant firm for an input is so high that its own downstream business would be unprofitable if it had to pay the same wholesale price as it charges rivals. Tying and bundling allegations may also involve issues of excessive pricing. In deciding whether two products are *de facto* tied, it may be relevant to ask whether the stand-alone price for each product is so high that the dominant firm is for practical purposes refusing to supply them independently. Price discrimination abuses, by which a dominant firm applies dissimilar conditions to equivalent transactions, may also raise excessive pricing concerns for the party paying the higher price.

The concern regarding excessive prices under Article 82(a) is, however, narrower in scope. Article 82(a) does not concern excessively high prices that exclude competitors or place trading partners at a competitive disadvantage. Instead, a firm with market power violates Article 82(a) if it "directly or indirectly" imposes "unfair purchase or selling prices or other unfair trading conditions." Article 82(a) thus applies to situations where the prices or terms offered to a customer are unfair or excessive. Such practices are regarded as an "exploitative" abuse, since they result in a direct loss of consumer welfare.[1] In economic terms, the dominant firm takes advantage of its market power to "extract" rents from customers that could not have been obtained by a non-dominant firm.[2] Similar prohibitions on excessive prices exist under the competition laws of the Member States.[3]

In theory, a dominant firm can violate Article 82 EC not only by charging excessively high prices as a seller, but also by imposing excessively low prices through the exercise of monopsony purchasing power. There are no reported cases in which a violation of Article 82 EC has been found on the basis of a dominant buyer applying excessively low prices. The few precedents that do exist have all rejected such claims. Whether

---

[1] As opposed to exclusionary abuses, where consumer welfare is harmed indirectly, i.e., as a result of the loss of competition resulting from the elimination or marginalisation of competitors.

[2] Case 27/76, *United Brands Company v Commission* [1978] ECR 207, para. 249 (The dominant firm uses its position to "reap trading benefits that it would not have reaped if there had been normal and sufficient effective competition.").

[3] There is no comparable cause of action against "excessive prices" in the United States. See generally PE Areeda & H Hovenkamp, *Antitrust Law* (Boston, Little, Brown and Company, 1996).

and in what circumstances excessively low prices might constitute an abuse is discussed in Chapter Thirteen, where other exploitative abuses involving unfair contract terms are also considered.

The economic and legal definition of an "excessive" price. There is no generally accepted definition in economics of what an unfair or excessive price is. For Marxist economists, the "fair" price of a product would be equal to the value of labour involved in its production.[4] Classical economists would also endorse a cost-based theory of value.[5] For neo-classical economists, the "fair" value of a good or service would be given by its "competitive" market price, which is the equilibrium price that would result from the free interaction of demand and supply in a competitive market.[6] This was also the interpretation given to the notion of "fair" prices by scholastic economic thought,[7] and is also the interpretation used by the ordoliberal school of economic thought, which had a major impact on the development of EC competition policy.[8] For the ordoliberals, a price is "fair" when it is the result of "free and honest" competition; in other words, dominant firms should set "competitive" prices, i.e., they should act "as if" they operated in competitive markets.[9] Modern industrial organisation theorists would define excessive prices as those which are set *significantly* and *persistently* above the competitive level as a result of the exercise of market power.[10] All these definitions, including the last, are however ambiguous and somewhat circular.

The Community Courts have adopted a definition of excessive prices that appears to follow the ordoliberal tradition, but their definition too is imprecise and difficult to administer in practice. According to the Court of Justice, a price is excessive when it bears no relationship to the "economic value" of the product supplied.[11] From a pragmatic point of view, the challenge is how to determine the "economic value" of a product, and in particular how competition authorities and courts can distinguish between a price that corresponds to the "economic value" of the product and one that does not; in other words, how to distinguish prices that are high, but nonetheless competitive, and "unfairly" high prices. The resolution of this issue is of great importance, since the effect of price interventions on consumer welfare is wholly dependent upon the ability of competition authorities and courts to establish whether or not prices are excessive in practice. As one commentator notes, Article 82 EC "assumes that high pricing is unfair...that unfairly high pricing can be identified by courts, and it implies that courts are better mechanisms than markets to correct unfairly high pricing."[12]

---

[4] See K Marx and F Engels (ed.), *Das Capital* (New York, Humboldt Publishing Co., edn. 1887).

[5] See, e.g., JA Schumpeter, *History of Economic Analysis* (Oxford, Oxford University Press, 1954) pt. III, ch. 4.

[6] See, e.g., A Marshall, *Principles of Economics* (London, Macmillan, edn. 1890).

[7] See, e.g., JA Schumpeter, above, pt II, ch 2.

[8] See Ch. 1 (Introduction, Scope of Application, and Basic Framework) above.

[9] This is the formula for unfair prices adopted by the German Act against Restraints of Competition GWB, para. 19, s 4, No 2.

[10] See J Tirole, *The Theory of Industrial Organisation* (Cambridge, MIT Press, 1988).

[11] See Case 27/76, *United Brands Company v Commission* [1978] ECR 250.

[12] See E Fox, "Monopolisation and Dominance in the United States and the European Community: Efficiency, Opportunity, and Fairness" (1986) *Notre Dame Law Review* 992.

In practice, the problem of identifying unlawful excessive prices is apt to be acute. The basic assumptions underlying excessive pricing are not necessarily justified: it is hard to distinguish fair and unfair prices; high prices may be welfare-enhancing where they promote investment and innovation; and many excessive pricing problems are resolved by the market itself, i.e., without outside interference. This does not imply, however, that enforcement under Article 82(a) is unwarranted: Article 82(a) addresses an obvious, legitimate, and core concern of EC competition law—that a firm, or group of firms, with market power would seek to exercise that power to charge prices above the competitive level, with the attendant welfare loss that such behaviour can cause to consumers. The enforcement of Article 82(a) must, however, take into account a number of conceptual and practical difficulties discussed in this chapter.

12.2 THE ECONOMICS OF EXCESSIVE PRICES

Overview. As noted above, economists define excessive prices as those which are set significantly and persistently above the competitive level. In some industries, that competitive benchmark is naturally given by the price that would apply in a perfectly competitive market—one where all firms act as price-takers and set prices at the marginal (or incremental) cost of production. This is because at the perfectly competitive price the market outcome is: (1) allocatively efficient—no consumer with a valuation for the good or service in excess of its (marginal) cost of production is left without it; and (2) productively efficient—production costs are minimised. In many other industries, the perfectly competitive ideal is unrealistic. In those industries, pricing at perfectly competitive levels would yield overall losses in the short term and under-investment in the long term.

Pricing in a perfectly competitive market. In a perfectly competitive market, there are many firms supplying the goods and services that consumers wish to acquire, and production is subject to constant, or decreasing, returns to scale.[13] Each firm faces a perfectly elastic demand and, consequently, has no power to sustain prices above cost; or more precisely, above the incremental cost of production. If a firm tried to raise prices above that level, its customers would switch to competitors and it would incur losses. Therefore, the "perfectly competitive" price is given by the incremental cost of production, which corresponds to the level of output at which the market clears (i.e., where supply meets demand). The competitive equilibrium is shown in Figure 1 below.

The competitive price, p^c is given by the intersection between the demand curve *D* and the supply curve *S*, which in a perfectly competitive market corresponds to the curve that maps for each production level (*Q*) the incremental cost of production (*MC*). No firm would charge a price above the competitive level because its market share would drop to zero instantaneously. And no firm would charge a price below its incremental cost of production, because then it would lose money on the marginal customers, and, under certain conditions, (e.g., constant returns to scale), it may even prefer to close the business and forego the sunk costs invested to start up the business.

[13] That is, an increase in the use of inputs of X per cent (the scale of production) leads to an increase in output of X per cent (constant returns to scale) or less (decreasing returns to scale).

Figure 1: The competitive price

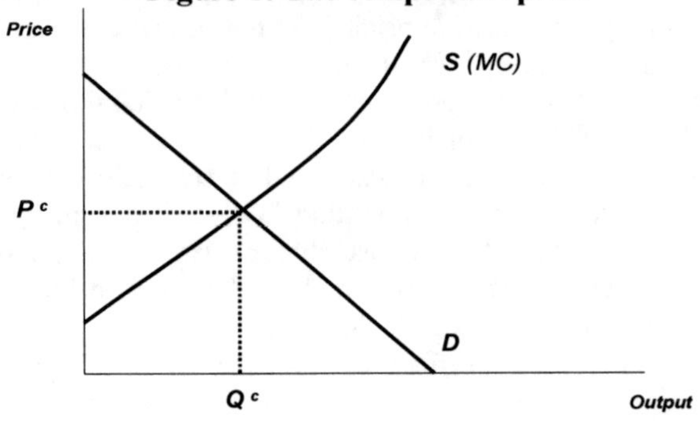

Allocative efficiency. At the perfectly competitive price, all consumers with a willingness to pay in excess of the incremental cost of production get to buy the goods or services traded in the market. At higher prices, there would be consumers who valued the goods or services more than their costs of production but could no longer afford them. An increase in prices above the competitive level therefore has two negative effects on consumer welfare: first, it transfers rents from consumers to firms, as every consumer who purchases the goods and services on offer pays more for them than in a competitive market; second, it destroys rents by forcing out of the market some consumers with relatively modest valuations.

These two effects are illustrated in Figure 2 below. The first effect is given by area *A*, while the second effect is given by area *B*. The sum of areas *A* and *B* measures the reduction in consumer welfare resulting from supra-competitive prices. In economic theory, area *B* is known as the "deadweight loss of monopoly," since it measures the loss in overall welfare (consumer welfare plus firms' profits) resulting from a market price above the competitive benchmark.[14] In economic terminology, at perfectly competitive prices, the allocation of resources is allocatively efficient and all gains from trade are exhausted. There is no deadweight loss.

Figure 2: Allocative efficiency

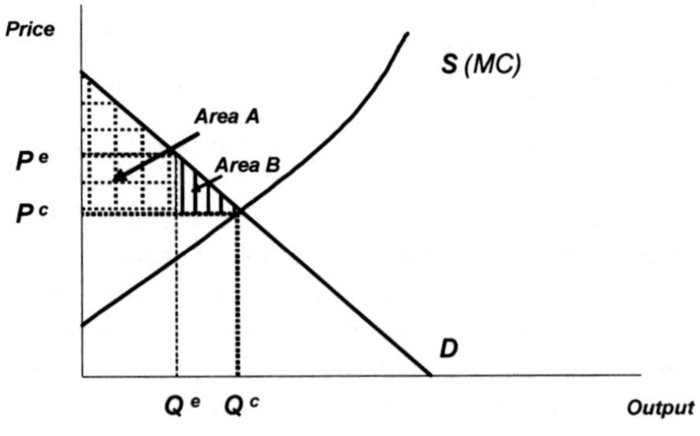

[14] The "deadweight loss of monopoly" does not include area *A*, because this area corresponds to the increase in profits associated with the supra-competitive price. Hence, area *A* captures a pure transfer of rents from consumers to firms.

Productive efficiency. When prices are set at the perfectly competitive level, the market equilibrium is also productively efficient: production is undertaken by the most efficient firms, i.e., those with the smallest marginal costs of production. Firms with marginal costs of production above the competitive price remain inactive as, otherwise, they would incur losses. The same outcome is not guaranteed when the equilibrium price exceeds the competitive price due to market power. In those circumstances, it is possible that production is undertaken by both efficient and less efficient firms.

Dynamic efficiency. The perfectly competitive ideal is, however, not applicable to many, or even most, actual markets. Competition is rarely static and industries often exhibit significant economies of scale and/or scope (i.e., increasing returns to scale).[15] In dynamic industries, where typically fixed costs are high and incremental costs are low, the "competitive" price is not given by marginal costs. Rather, it is efficient to charge prices according to customers' willingness to pay, so as to cover fixed costs in the least output-restricting way.[16] If firms operating in such industries were forced to charge prices equal to marginal cost, they would not be able to recover the cost of past investments and, consequently, their incentives to invest and innovate would vanish. Instead, the equilibrium prices will be above the marginal cost of production so as to cover the fixed costs of production. The price-cost margin will be higher for those goods and services for which the elasticity of demand is lower, so as to minimise the quantity distortion that is associated with high prices.[17]

As illustrated in Figure 3 below, a strict policy regarding excessive prices is equivalent to the introduction of an upper limit on profits.[18] And, as such, it may have a detrimental effect on firms' incentives to innovate. Given that profits are uncertain *ex ante*, a firm would be willing to invest only if the expected return on its investment exceeds the cost of capital. A price cap imposes a limit on the firm's expected revenue, which may render the investment unprofitable. In Figure 3, investment is profitable *ex ante* when the firm's pricing policy is unrestricted (where profits are given by the dotted-line distribution), but not when there is an upper bound on profits (as illustrated by the continuous-line distribution).[19] In the latter case, the expected rate of return is insufficient to cover the company's cost of capital. A rational firm would not make such an investment if it knew *ex ante* that prices and profits would be capped *ex post*. A strict policy on excessive prices could therefore chill beneficial investment activity.

---

[15] That is, an increase in the use of inputs of X per cent (the scale of production) leads to an increase in output of more than X per cent.

[16] See C Ahlborn, DS Evans and AJ Padilla, "Competition Policy in the New Economy: Is European Competition Law Up to the Challenge?" (2001) 5 *European Competition Law Review* 164.

[17] This is because consumers with a lower elasticity of demand respond less to changes in prices. The negative impact on their satisfaction (or utility) of a price increase is smaller than for individuals with a higher elasticity of demand.

[18] The problem illustrated in Figure 3 is well established in economic literature. See, e.g., J Hausman and JG Sidak, "A Consumer Welfare Approach to the Mandatory Unbundling of Telecommunications Networks" (1999) 109 *Yale Law Journal* 417-88. See also G Sidak and D Spulber "The Tragedy of the Telecommons: Government Pricing of Unbundled Network Elements Under the Telecommunications Act of 1996" (1997) 97 *Columbia Law Review* 1081-150. The discussion in this chapter extends a widely-recognised line of analysis to the regulation of prices implicit in the application of Article 82(a).

[19] This figure is taken from J Hausman, "Valuing the Effects of Regulation on New Services in Telecommunications" (1997) *Brookings Papers on Economic Activity: Microeconomics*, pp. 1-38.

Figure 3: The effect of a strict policy on excessive pricing on investment

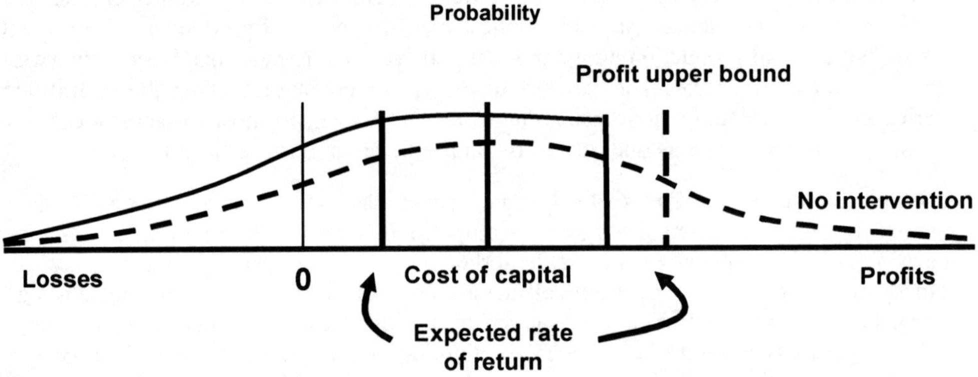

Conclusion. In a perfectly competitive market: (1) the equilibrium price is given by the marginal cost of production; and (2) the allocation of resources is both allocatively and productively optimal. Yet, in reality, virtually no market qualifies as perfectly competitive. In most markets production is subject to economies of scale and scope, and firms do not face a perfectly elastic demand curve. Instead, firms typically produce and sell differentiated products and operate technologies subject to increasing returns to scale. In most actual markets, firms have the *incentive* and the *ability* to set prices higher than the cost of production. They have the ability to do so because they enjoy some degree of market power, which in turn is the result of product differentiation and economies of scale. They have the incentive to price above cost, because otherwise they would incur losses, which would be greater the higher their fixed costs. Price-cost margins will be typically larger in dynamic industries where innovation constitutes a key competitive variable. In such industries, prices will need to be set significantly above marginal cost to fund initial capital outlays and compensate for associated risk.

12.3 THE LEGAL TEST(S) FOR EXCESSIVE PRICES

Overview. Excessive pricing precedents at Community level have been limited in number to date. The most prominent cases are *United Brands*, *General Motors,*[20] *British Leyland,*[21] and, most recently, the *Port Of Helsingborg.*[22] In *United Brands* the Court of Justice stated that "[c]harging a price which is excessive because it has no reasonable relation to the economic value of the product supplied [is]…an abuse."[23] The Court also introduced a two-stage test for determining whether a price is reasonably

[20] Case 26/75, *General Motors Continental NV v Commission* [1975] ECR 1367.

[21] Case 226/84, *British Leyland Plc. v Commission* [1986] ECR 3263.

[22] Case COMP/A.36.568/D3, *Scandlines Sverige AB v Port of Helsingborg*, Commission Decision of July 23, 2004 ("*Port of Helsingborg*"), not yet published, para. 102. See also Case COMP/A.36.568/D3, *Sundbusserne v Port of Helsingborg*, Commission Decision of July 23, 2004, not yet published, para. 85.

[23] Case 27/76, *United Brands Company v Commission* [1978] ECR 207, para. 250.

related to the "economic value" of the product supplied.[24] The Court held that "the questions therefore to be determined are whether the difference between the costs actually incurred and the price actually charged is excessive, and, if the answer to this question is in the affirmative, whether a price has been imposed which is either unfair in itself or when compared to competing products."[25]

Building on the approach in *United Brands*, the Court of Justice in *General Motors* and *British Leyland* considered the pricing behaviour of two firms enjoying a legal monopoly. In both cases, the Court related the price charged by the dominant company to some indicator of the "economic value" of the service in question: the prices charged by competitors or the prices charged by the dominant firm at different points in time. In *General Motors* the Court found the explanations provided by the dominant firm convincing; in *British Leyland* it did not.

The most recent decision in *Port of Helsingborg*—in which excessive pricing complaints were rejected—indicates that the Commission applies a high standard of proof before concluding that a price bears no relation to the "economic value" of a product. In particular, it will consider a wide range of tangible and intangible factors that may affect the value of a product from the perspective of both consumers and the dominant seller.

The two-stage test for excessive prices in *United Brands*. The leading case at Community level on excessive pricing is *United Brands*. United Brands Company (UBC) was the largest banana company in the world through its Chiquita brand of bananas. UBC shipped bananas to the EU through two main ports, Bremerhaven and Rotterdam. The fruit then needed to be ripened by specialist ripeners. UBC accounted for 45% of bananas sold in Belgium, Luxembourg, Denmark, Germany, Ireland, and the Netherlands, which were considered as a single relevant geographic market.

In its decision,[26] the Commission considered that UBC had a dominant position in bananas on the relevant markets, and had abused that position by: (1) contractually preventing its distributors/ripeners from reselling bananas while still green; (2) price discriminating between the Scipio group (with whom UBC had a particularly close business relationship) and other distributors/ripeners; (3) imposing unfair (i.e. excessive) prices for the sale of Chiquita bananas for customers (other than the Scipio group) in Belgium, Luxembourg, Denmark, and Germany; and (4) refusing to supply to a particular Danish customer, Oelsen, who dealt in rivals' products. Only the excessive pricing issue is described here.

The Commission placed great emphasis on price differentials between Member States in the context of its discussion of excessive pricing. Various comparators were used to establish that UBC's prices to customers in Belgium, Luxembourg, Denmark, and Germany were excessive. The Commission looked at price discrepancies between branded and unbranded bananas, finding that Chiquita bananas were sold at a premium

---

[24] C Esteva-Mosso and S Ryan, "Article 82—Abuse of a Dominant Position" in J Faull and A Nikpay (eds.), *The EC Law of Competition* (Oxford, Oxford University Press, 1999) ch. 3, p. 190.

[25] *United Brands*, above, para. 252.

[26] *Chiquita*, OJ 1976 L 95/1.

of 30–40% when compared to UBC's unbranded bananas. The Commission also compared the prices charged by UBC for its Chiquita bananas with those of competitors, finding that Chiquita bananas were slightly more expensive than bananas sold by competitors.

But the key exercise was the comparison of UBC's prices across Member States. UBC's lowest prices were charged for products destined for Ireland. In an internal document, UBC appeared to acknowledge that a profit was still made on these sales, which the Commission claimed set an upper bound on UBC's costs (UBC later denied the Irish profitability claim.) The Commission reasoned that prices for Dublin must have included the costs of delivery to Rotterdam and the additional cost of delivery from there to Dublin. Prices to Denmark, the Netherlands, Belgium, Luxembourg, and Germany were almost twice as high. Based on this evidence, the Commission decided that UBC's prices outside Ireland were excessive. The Commission did not attempt to establish UBC's production costs in determining a "fair" price. Its sole determination of cost was dependent on the supposed profitability of banana sales in Ireland. Yet, in its appeal, UBC claimed it had made losses in Ireland during the period under analysis. It also claimed that it had failed to earn any profits on the relevant market in the period from 1973 to 1978 (save in 1975).

The Court of Justice then applied a two-stage test to assess the Commission's findings on excessive prices. This test requires, first, comparing actual costs and prices (the price-cost limb of the test), and, second, determining whether a price is excessive in itself or by comparison to competitors' products (the price comparison limb of the test). The Court held, among other things, that the fair price "could, *inter alia*, be determined objectively if it were possible for it to be calculated by making a comparison between the selling price of the product in question and its cost of production, which would disclose the amount of the profit margin."[27] The Court noted that the Commission had failed to analyse UBC's production costs—a task that was regarded as manageable in that particular case. The Court considered that the use of the prices charged in Ireland as a cost benchmark was questionable, noting that "there is doubt which must benefit the applicant, especially as for nearly 20 years banana prices, in real terms, have not risen on the relevant market."[28] The Court thus concluded that the Commission had failed to satisfy the first part of the test. The Court made clear that the burden of proof is on the Commission to demonstrate, based on cogent evidence, the existence of unfair prices: "however unreliable the particulars supplied by [the dominant company]..., the fact remains that it is for the Commission to prove that [the dominant company] charged [excessive] prices."[29] Furthermore, the Court considered that the price differential with UBC's competitors was only 7%, which "cannot automatically be regarded as excessive and consequently unfair,"[30] and so concluded that the Commission had also failed to satisfy the second part of the test. In sum, the Court found that the Commission had failed to establish that the prices charged by United Brands were not related to the

[27] Case 27/76, *United Brands Company v Commission* [1978] ECR 207, para. 251.
[28] *Ibid.*, para. 251, para. 265.
[29] *Ibid.*, para. 264.
[30] *Ibid.*, para. 266.

economic value of its product. The Court annulled the portion of the Commission's decision dealing with excessive prices. The other three abuses were upheld.

One issue that remained unclear following *United Brands* was whether the Court of Justice's two-stage test is cumulative or alternative. Some commentators argued that:[31] (1) the two steps of the test "should not necessarily be used cumulatively;" and (2) the direct cost calculation should enjoy priority. They refer to the various decisions of the Court of Justice concerning the royalties charged by SACEM, a copyright royalty collector.[32] In those decisions, "it was recognised that a price-cost comparison would be impossible, given the nature of the product—the creation and protection of a musical piece."[33] The judgment in *Bodson* is also interpreted in a similar light,[34] since the Court appeared to rely on the comparative market test in isolation as a possible method to determine whether a price was excessive.[35]

Other commentators argue, more persuasively, that the test is two-fold.[36] This approach is preferable, for several reasons. Calculating a price-cost margin is a meaningless exercise for the purposes of Article 82(a), unless: (1) it is assumed that any price exceeding cost be abusive; or, (2) there is a workable "competitive benchmark" with which to compare the price-cost margin derived in the first stage. But the first option would imply condemning the pricing policies of most firms operating in oligopolistic markets and cannot therefore constitute a suitable basis for public policy. The second option implies a cumulative interpretation of the Court of Justice's test, where the comparison limb of the test enjoys similar prominence to the price-cost limb of the test.

Any doubt in this regard must now be considered as having been comprehensively resolved by the Commission's decision in *Port of Helsingborg*, where the Commission made clear that the test for excessive pricing is two-fold:[37]

> "The questions to be determined are as follows: (i) 'whether the difference between the costs actually incurred and the price actually charged is excessive and, if the answer to this question is in the affirmative,'...(ii) 'whether a price has been imposed which is either unfair in itself

[31] See M Motta and A de Streel, 'Exploitative and Exclusionary Excessive Prices in EU Law' in CD Ehlermann and I Atanasiu (eds.), *European Competition Law Annual 2003: What Is an Abuse of Dominant Position?* (Oxford, Hart Publishing, 2006), p. 91. See also N Green, "Problems in the Identification of Excessive Prices: The United Kingdom Experience in the Light of *Napp*" in CD Ehlermann and I Atanasiu (eds.), *European Competition Law Annual 2003: What Is an Abuse of Dominant Position?* (Oxford, Hart Publishing, 2006), p. 79.

[32] Case 395/87, *Ministère Public v Tournier* [1989] ECR 2521. See also Joined Cases 110/88, 241/88, 242/88 *Lucazeau v SACEM* [1989] ECR 2811.

[33] M Gal, "Monopoly Pricing as an Antitrust Offence in the U.S. and the EC: Two Systems of Belief About Monopoly?" (2004) *Antitrust Bulletin* 33-36.

[34] Case 30/87, *Corinne Bodson v SA Pompes funèbres des régions libérées* [1988] ECR 2507 (hereinafter "*Bodson*").

[35] See E Pijnacker Hordijk, "Excessive Pricing Under EC Competition Law: An Update in the Light of 'Dutch Developments'" in B Hawk (ed.), *Fordham International Antitrust Law and Policy* (New York, Juris Publishing, Inc., 2002) pp. 469-72.

[36] See C Esteva-Mosso and S Ryan, "Article 82—Abuse of a Dominant Position" in J Faull and A Nikpay (eds.), *The EC Law of Competition* (Oxford, Oxford University Press, 1999) p. 192.

[37] Case COMP/A.36.568/D3, *Scandlines Sverige AB v Port of Helsingborg*, Commission Decision of July 23, 2004, not yet published, paras. 147, 149. See also Case COMP/A.36.568/D3, *Sundbusserne v Port of Helsingborg*, not yet published, para. 85.

> or when compared to the price of competing products'....In paragraph 252 of the United Brands judgment, the Court made a clear distinction between, on the one hand, the question whether the difference between the price and the production costs—the profit margin—is 'excessive' and, on the other hand, the question whether the price is unfair. Had it been otherwise, there would have been no reason for the Court, once the first question has been answered in the affirmative, to proceed to the question whether the price is unfair in itself or when compared to the price of competing products."

The concept of "economic value" in *United Brands*. The meaning of the term "economic value" first used in *United Brands* is far from clear. In subsequent cases, the Commission has interpreted the principle that competitive prices should reflect the "economic value" of the product or service in question as implying that a seller should not charge identical prices for products that serve the same purpose but have grossly different cost components, or charge radically different prices for services with the same cost structure. In *General Motors*, the Commission found that General Motors' pricing for vehicle conformity inspections was unfair. General Motors charged the same fee for its European models (manufactured by its subsidiary Opel) as its own American models, although inspecting the former was much less costly. In *British Leyland*, the company charged significantly different prices to issue certificates for left-hand-drive and right-hand-drive cars, although the costs of inspection were largely identical. *General Motors* and *British Leyland* seem to relate the "economic value" of a product to its costs. Yet, according to standard economic theory, the economic value of a product or service is determined jointly by consumers' willingness to pay and the costs of supply.

In *Port of Helsingborg*, the Commission relied on an interpretation of "economic value" that is more compatible with economic theory. First, the Commission stated that "the economic value of the product/service cannot simply be determined by adding to the approximate costs incurred in the provision of this product/service...a profit margin which would be a pre-determined percentage of the product costs. [Rather, the] economic value must be determined with regards to the particular circumstances of the case and take into account also non-cost factors such as the demand for the product/service."[38]

Second, the Commission explained why demand-side considerations are also relevant in the calculation of the economic value of a product or service: "customers are notably willing to pay more for something specific attached to the product/service that they consider more valuable. This specific feature does not necessarily imply higher production costs for the provider."[39] Thus, the costs of supply are not the only, or even the main, determinant: demand-side considerations are also important.

Third, the Commission noted that it may be necessary in some cases to charge high prices in order to recover large initial investments. It noted that the port of Helsingborg has very high sunk costs, which were not accounted for in the port operator's audited financial accounts. If the port would have to rebuild the existing installations used by the ferry-operators from scratch, or construction of a new ferry port at the same location

[38] Case COMP/A.36.568/D3, *Scandlines Sverige AB v Port of Helsingborg*, Commission Decision of July 23, 2004, not yet published, para. 232. See also Case COMP/A.36.568/D3, *Sundbusserne v Port of Helsingborg*, Commission Decision of July 23, 2004, not yet reported, para. 207.

[39] *Port of Helsingborg, ibid.*, para. 227. See also *Sundbusserne, ibid.*, para. 205.

were envisaged, the costs incurred by such a port to provide the same level of services and facilities to the ferry operators would be far higher than the costs accounted for by existing.[40]

Fourth, the Commission found that the intangible value of the port should be included in an assessment of its "economic value." It stated that the ferry operators benefited from the fact that the location of the port of Helsingborg met their needs perfectly. This intangible value could be taken into account as part of the economic value of the services provided by the dominant port operator, even though it was not reflected in its annual accounts.[41]

Finally, the Commission indicated that it might be relevant to include any opportunity cost—other uses to which the assets in question could be put—in the calculation of "economic value." The Commission stated that the land used by the port for the ferry operations is very valuable in itself and that keeping the ferry operations there instead of using the land for other purposes is likely to represent an opportunity cost to the port owner.[42]

Implementation of the *United Brands* test in subsequent cases. In broad terms, the Community institutions have applied four principal benchmarks to implement the Court of Justice's two-stage test in *United Brands*: (1) price-cost comparisons; (2) price comparisons across markets or competitors; (3) geographic price comparisons; and (4) comparisons over time. This is consistent with the Court's statement in *United Brands* that many "ways may be devised—and economic theorists have not failed to think up several—of selecting the rules for determining whether the price of a product is unfair."[43]

Most of the above benchmarks were first mentioned in *United Brands*, *General Motors*, and *British Leyland*, but they have been elaborated upon in subsequent decisions by the Community institutions, national competition authorities, and courts. No hard and fast rules can be discerned, however, regarding the circumstances in which any one benchmark, or combination of benchmarks, should apply: much will depend on the nature of the available evidence in each case. Thus, "it appears that in each and every case a pragmatic approach has been found with the actual facts of the case and the availability of evidence of suitable comparables ultimately dictating which comparables are actually chosen."[44]

***a. Price-cost comparisons*.** The first limb of the *United Brands* test requires comparing the price charged for the product or service under scrutiny with an appropriate measure of the costs of producing the good or delivering the service. If the difference between price and cost is "excessive"—i.e., higher than a given benchmark—then the first limb of the test is satisfied. Note however that, "[t]he fact that the

---

[40] *Port of Helsingborg, ibid.*, para. 209.

[41] *Ibid.*

[42] *Port of Helsingborg, ibid.*, para. 209.

[43] Case 27/76, *United Brands Company v Commission* [1978] ECR 207, para. 253.

[44] N Green, "Problems in the Identification of Excessive Prices: The United Kingdom Experience in the Light of *Napp*" in CD Ehlermann and I Atanasiu (eds.), *European Competition Law Annual 2003: What Is an Abuse of Dominant Position?* (Oxford, Hart Publishing, 2006), p. 79.

[dominant firm's] charges would be non-cost based or the pricing non-transparent do not constitute as such abuses under Article 82 of the EC Treaty."[45] Also, "the mere fact that revenues may exceed costs actually incurred is not sufficient to conclude that the difference is 'excessive' in the meaning...of the *United Brands* judgment."[46]

Although price-cost comparisons have been performed in several cases,[47] there is no well-specified standard of application. A number of issues arise in connection with price-cost comparisons, including the choice of an appropriate cost measure, the definition of a reasonable profit margin, the treatment of problems in relation to multi-product firms, and the provision of incentives for cost reductions.

First, a price-cost comparison requires identification of an appropriate measure of costs.[48] Economic theory suggests that, in a competitive equilibrium, the price or a good or service should equal its incremental cost of production. The problem lies in calculating the "incremental" cost of production where there are common costs, since there are various methods for the allocation of indirect costs, general expenditures, and common costs, none of which is entirely satisfactory. Sector-specific regulations may sometimes provide useful guidance in this respect. In *Ahmed Saeed*, for example, the Court of Justice relied on Article 3 of Directive 87/601/EEC to use long-term fully-allocated costs to construct an appropriate cost measure for the purposes of determining whether prices were excessive in the airline sector.[49] However, the economic literature has criticised the use of fully-allocated costs in exercises of this nature, as they lead to measures of cost that are not incremental and may incorrectly justify high prices. Further, allocating costs to an individual operation is more a matter of judgment than precision, since there is no uniquely correct way to allocate common or joint costs between different product lines.[50]

Economists have advocated the use of alternative cost concepts that differ in the way they deal with the allocation of common costs. The most popular of these concepts is the long-run average incremental cost (LRAIC): the total value of the costs that are needed to enter a market and begin supplying a product, as an average over total output.

---

[45] Case COMP/A.36.568/D3, *Scandlines Sverige AB v Port of Helsingborg*, Commission Decision of July 23, 2004, not yet published, para. 97.

[46] *Ibid.*, para. 142.

[47] See, e.g., *United Brands*, above; Case 298/83, *CICCE v Commission* [1985] ECR 1105; Joined Cases 110/88, 241/88, 242/88, *Lucazeau v SACEM* [1989] ECR 2811. See also Case 66/86, *Ahmed Saeed Flugreisen and Silver Line Reisebüro GmbH v Zentrale zur Bekämpfung unlauteren Wettbewerbs e.V.* [1989] ECR 803 ("*Ahmed Saeed*"). National competition authorities have also undertaken price-cost comparisons in excessive pricing cases. See, e.g., *Veraldi/Alitalia*, Decision of November 15, 2001, where the Italian Competition Authority (ICA) applied an extensive cost analysis based both on the cost-prices test and on the comparison test. The ICA, after comparing the revenues to the cost, found that Alitalia was earning a operating margin of 30%, which was not considered to be conclusive evidence of abusive pricing.

[48] In *United Brands*, the Court held that the total cost of production is the appropriate measure of cost in excessive pricing cases, at least when the dominant firm produces a single product. See Case 27/76, *United Brands Company v Commission* [1978] ECR 207.

[49] Case 66/86, *Ahmed Saeed Flugreisen and Silver Line Reisebüro GmbH v Zentrale zur Bekämpfung unlauteren Wettbewerbs e.V.* [1989] ECR 803, para. 43.

[50] See Ch. 5 (Predatory Pricing), Section 5.4 for a detailed discussion.

Common costs are excluded: only the costs that are causally related to the activity at issue are included in LRAIC. The LRAIC is thus equal to the long-run average avoidable cost of production (LRAAC),[51] plus the sunk costs incurred upon entry. Unfortunately, there is no consensus about which of these concepts is best, and all of them pose significant difficulties in implementation.[52] The Court of Justice recognised these difficulties in *United Brands* when it noted that there may at times be "very great difficulties in working out production costs which may sometimes include a discretionary apportionment of indirect costs and general expenditure and which may vary significantly according to the size of the undertaking, its object, the complex nature of its set up, its territorial area of operations, whether it manufactures one or several products, the number of its subsidiaries and their relationship with each other."[53]

Second, any definition of what constitutes a reasonable profit margin must take into account a whole range of factors, including, e.g., economies of scale, sunk costs, and risk. Profit margins differ across industries, and high profit margins may reflect the required compensation for the risk associated with large upfront investment costs or research and development expenditure. Too low a profit margin may reduce *ex ante* investment and harm consumers in the long run. In *Ahmed Saeed*, the Court of Justice held that prices may legitimately reflect "the needs of consumers, the need for a satisfactory return on capital, the competitive market situation…and the need to prevent dumping."[54] But in many industries, there will simply be no reliable way of approximating a "reasonable" profit, in particular if this involves an analysis of items such as the intangible value of assets and any relevant opportunity cost.

Third, a comparison of costs and prices is particularly problematic in the case of multi-product firms. In a competitive market, the optimal strategy for such firms is to set prices so that the overall costs of production, including all common costs, are covered. This implies different price-cost margins for products facing demands with different price elasticities: more elastic demand will be associated with lower profit margins and *vice versa*. The pricing policy of a multi-product firm should therefore be analysed in its entirety and not in a piecemeal fashion, product by product. In general, no meaningful policy implication can be derived from the analysis of the price-cost margins of individual products manufactured and commercialised by a multi-product firm. A number of possible solutions were discussed in Chapter Five (Predatory Pricing), but, as noted, each solution is arbitrary to some extent. Put simply, there is no single, correct way to allocate common costs across multiple products.

---

[51] The LRAAC is the total value of costs that are avoided in the long run if a company *stops* supplying a particular product, as an average over total company output. If LRAAC exceeds current market prices, it would be cheaper and more rational for a firm to shut down the relevant product line than to continue in business.

[52] See e.g., *Flugpreisspaltung,* Bundesgerichtshof, judgment of July 22, 1999, NVZ 2000, p. 326, where the Federal Supreme Court upheld the decision by the Kammergericht that quashed the Bundeskartellamt's Decision on the grounds that the airline's fixed operating costs must be taken into account. The Federal Supreme Court, at the same time, required that the costs must be properly allocated. See also Ch. 5 (Predatory Pricing) above, for a review of the treatment of the different cost concepts under Article 82 EC.

[53] Case 27/76, *United Brands Company v Commission* [1978] ECR 207, para. 254.

[54] Case 66/86, *Ahmed Saeed Flugreisen and Silver Line Reisebüro GmbH v Zentrale zur Bekämpfung unlauteren Wettbewerbs e.V.* [1989] ECR 803, para. 43.

One possibility would be to consider simultaneously the legitimacy of all the pricing decisions of the multi-product firm, ignoring the fact that its different activities constitute separate product markets. This approach is akin to the "portfolio pricing" argument rejected by the United Kingdom Competition Appeals Tribunal (CAT) in *Napp*.[55] The CAT concluded that "it is not appropriate, when deciding whether an undertaking has abused a dominant position by charging excessive prices in a particular market, to take into account the reasonableness or otherwise of its profits on other, unspecified, markets comprised in some wider but undefined 'portfolio' unrelated to the market in which dominance exists."[56]

Finally, the dominant firm's average total cost may be lower than that of its rivals, for example due to cost-saving innovations or other efficiency-enhancing reasons. Forcing a dominant firm to reduce its prices so as to match the margin of its (inefficient) competitors could diminish its incentives to cut costs in the future, which would harm consumers in the long run. On the other hand, an inefficient dominant firm should not be relieved from scrutiny if the true reason for its high prices is high costs due to its own inefficiency. The Court of Justice held in *Lucazeau* that the relevant costs for the purposes of the assessment of Article 82(a) are those of an efficient firm.[57] However, no clear guidance was provided on how to assess what an efficient firm's costs would be.

b. Comparisons across competitors. An approach commonly employed by the Community Courts in Article 82(a) cases to implement the second limb of the *United Brands* test is to compare the price charged by the dominant firm with the prices charged by competitors.[58] In *General Motors*, the evidence suggested that other manufacturers charged approximately half the certification fee charged by General Motors. General Motors charged a high price for the production of documentation based on conformity inspections, without which car owners could not bring their cars into Belgium. Purchasers having chosen a General Motors vehicle were locked-in when it came to purchasing inspection services. In *United Brands*, the price of Chiquita bananas was 7% higher than the price of bananas sold by rivals, the Court of Justice concluded that this difference could not be regarded as excessive, but did not state what an excessive difference would have been. In any event, comparing the prices charged by different competitors is also fraught with difficulty, since differences in price may simply reflect differences in quality, with higher quality products commanding a premium.

c. Geographic comparisons. A method commonly relied upon by the Community institutions to test whether the second limb of the *United Brands* test is satisfied is a

[55] Case CA98/2/2001, *Napp Pharmaceuticals Holdings Ltd and Subsidiaries*, Decision of Director General of Fair Trading on March 30, 2001 ("*Napp*"), on appeal *Napp Pharmaceutical Holdings Limited and Subsidiaries v Director General of Fair Trading* [2002] CompAR 13.

[56] *Napp Pharmaceutical Holdings Limited and Subsidiaries v Director General of Fair Trading* [2002] CompAR 13, para. 413.

[57] Joined Cases 110/88, 241/88, 242/88, *Lucazeau v SACEM* [1989] ECR 2811, para. 29.

[58] See Case 78/70, *Deutsche Grammophon v Metro* [1971] ECR 487, where the Court of Justice stated that a finding of excessive prices could be based on a price comparison between two competitors. See also Joined Cases 110/88, 241/88, 242/88, *Lucazeau v SACEM* [1989] ECR 2811, para. 25.

comparison of the prices prevailing in different Member States.[59] The Court of Justice has held that price differentials between Member States may be excessive if unjustified and particularly significant in size. In some cases, the exercise was to compare the prices of a given product charged by the same firm at different locations. For example, in *United Brands*, the prices of Chiquita bananas in Denmark were 138% higher than in Ireland.

In other cases, the comparison involved the prices of similar products or services offered by different companies in different Member States. For example, in *Lucazeau*, the Court of Justice found that the royalty rate charged by a French musical copyright management society to French discotheques was significantly higher than the European average and held that this was an indication of excessive prices.[60] Likewise, in *Tournier*, the Court held that "when an undertaking holding a dominant position imposes scales of fees for its services which are appreciably higher than those charged in other Member States and where a comparison of the fee levels has been made on a consistent basis, that difference must be regarded as indicative of an abuse of a dominant position."[61] National cases have also applied a similar approach. For example, in *Vitamin B 12*,[62] the appeals court (*Kammergericht*) concluded that a price on the German market that exceeded the price on the Swiss market by more than 50% must be considered as significantly exceeding the competitive price level.

Comparing prices across Member States also has significant limitations. Any price comparison must be carried out on a consistent basis to ensure that products of the same quality are compared and that similar volumes are also considered. There may be differences in direct costs caused by local taxes or the particular characteristics of the local labour market, which may justify different prices. Differences in prices may also legitimately respond to different market conditions. The levels of income of consumers and the elasticities of demand for a particular product may vary widely from one Member State to another, and a firm's appropriate response is to set prices accordingly. Moreover, whereas a product may be well established in one Member State, it may still need to gain acceptance in another, which would explain a much lower price in the second country. Finally, prices may not be comparable because of different charging systems (e.g., different types of fees), which render a comparison meaningless.[63]

For these reasons, the Court of Justice expressly recognised in *United Brands* that prices may differ across regions for objective reasons and that a dominant firm is not obliged to adopt uniform pricing in each Member State.[64] Indeed, the Court did not object to the fact that prices were different across Member States due to local marketing conditions:

---

[59] See e.g., Case 27/76, *United Brands Company v Commission* [1978] ECR 207; *Deutsche Post AG/Interception of cross-border mail*, OJ 2001 L 331/40; Case 395/87, *Ministère Public v Tournier* [1989] ECR 2521; *Lucazeau, ibid.*; *Deutsche Grammophon, ibid.* See also Case 40/70, *Sirena S.r.l. v Eda S.r.l. and others* [1971] ECR 69.

[60] *Ibid.*, para. 25.

[61] Case 395/87, *Ministère Public v Tournier* [1989] ECR 2521, para. 38.

[62] *Vitamin B 12*, Kammergericht, judgment of March 19, 1975, WuW/E 1975, 649.

[63] Case COMP/A.36.568/D3, *Scandlines Sverige AB v Port of Helsingborg*, Commission Decision of July 23, 2004, not yet published, para. 175. See also Case COMP/A.36.568/D3, *Sundbusserne v Port of Helsingborg*, Commission Decision of July 23, 2004, not yet published, para. 149.

[64] Case 27/76, *United Brands Company v Commission* [1978] ECR 207, para. 228.

the objection was that United Brands' policy led to "artificial" price differences.[65] Similarly, in *Port of Helsingborg*, the Commission rejected the argument that it should compare profit levels between different ports in order to ascertain whether charges imposed by Helsingborg were excessive. Several reasons were cited.[66] First, the Commission noted that a detailed analysis revealed that each port differs substantially from the others in terms of its mix of activities, the volume of its assets and investments, the level of its revenues, and the costs of each activity. It reasoned that a port should not be regarded as a single business in terms of its profitability: if some activities are run at a loss, these will mask profits derived by other operations when considering the overall profits of the port.

Second, the comparison would need to be consistent and undertaken at a level of detail similar to that undertaken by the Commission for the port of Helsingborg, with similar uncertainties as regards the precise level of the costs, profits, and equity attributable to the ferry operations. Third, the Commission found that there would be insuperable difficulties in establishing valid benchmarks which would imply that, for the port taken as reference, the profits (and the equity) related to the ferry operations are segregated from those of the other activities. Finally, a comparison between the profits of the ferry operations in different ports would be too dependent on the markets on which they operate, the individual cost structure of the companies (e.g., possible economies of scope and scale, existence of cost efficiencies), the level of their investments, how these are financed, as well as internal decisions regarding the remuneration of the share holders.

A final flaw in the geographic comparison approach is that it implicitly assumes that the price in the low-price country is a benchmark for the competitive price in the country where the alleged abuse took place.[67] This assumption is problematic, since the price in the reference country may itself be too high (which would lead to the incorrect conclusion that the price under analysis is not excessive when it is), or too low (which would lead to a finding of excessive prices when in reality the price charged was legitimate). This was the problem uncovered by the Court of Justice in *United Brands*, where the Commission had relied on Irish prices as a benchmark, but there were reasons to believe that those were below cost and, hence, below the competitive level.

d. Comparisons over time. The Community institutions have sometimes assessed the movement of prices over time in order to determine whether excessive increases have been made. In *British Leyland*, the Court of Justice upheld the Commission's finding that British Leyland had set unfair prices. British Leyland held a legal monopoly to issue national certificates of conformity for vehicles in Great Britain. British Leyland demanded a high price for type-approval certificates. To determine whether the fees charged for the certificates were excessive, the Court looked at the

[65] *Ibid*, para. 233.

[66] Case COMP/A.36.568/D3, *Scandlines Sverige AB v Port of Helsingborg*, Commission Decision of July 23, 2004, not yet published, paras. 155-56.

[67] See Case 30/87, *Corinne Bodson v SA Pompes funèbres des régions libérées* [1988] ECR 2507. In this case, which concerned funeral services in areas of France where there were monopoly concessions granted by local authorities, the Court relied on a comparison with prices in areas where there were no such concessions.

evolution of prices over time. The Court noted that fees had increased 600% during the period under examination and concluded that the differential was unjustified and the higher prices were excessive.

The need to show that prices are significantly above the "competitive" benchmark. Although it is not clear which benchmarks should be applied in excessive pricing cases, and doubtful whether any single benchmark is capable of yielding unambiguous results in practice, an important common feature of cases in which excessive prices have been found is that the price was not merely above the relevant benchmark, but was *significantly* above it. By ensuring that the price should be "significantly" above the competitive level, and not merely above it, this criterion helps avoid the costly errors of falsely finding an excessive price where there is none. Two Commission officials note as follows:[68]

> "It is clear that a market comparison can only provide an indication of an abuse, if the difference between the prices charged on the various markets is significant. On the contrary, in cases were the prices charged deviate only slightly from the price level on comparative markets, this disparity could not be considered as giving a prima facie indication for abuse. Depending on the merits of each individual case, the benchmark for Commission intervention may vary considerably. In [one case], a difference of more then 100% between the price examined and the price levels in comparative markets was found to be unacceptable. In other cases, however, the Commission might have to intervene even if this difference is significantly smaller. In any event, even where a significant difference exists, the undertaking concerned always has the possibility of demonstrating that higher prices are objectively justified."

For example, in *British Leyland*, the Court of Justice noted that the certificate fees had increased by 600% during the period under examination, which was excessive. In a case involving Deutsche Telekom, a comparative market study ordered by the Commission assumed that, in the absence of special circumstances, a price is highly likely to be abusive if it is considered more than 100% higher than prices in comparable competitive markets.[69] A similar margin was considered excessive in the circumstances of the *ITT/Promedia* case.[70]

Many national authorities have reached similar conclusions. In *Napp*,[71] it was suggested that the price difference between two segments of the same overall market was as high as 1400% in some cases. More generally, the OFT's *Draft Guidelines On The Assessment Of Conduct* state that, "[i]n assessing questions about excessive pricing, the OFT would usually look for evidence that prices are substantially higher than would be expected in a competitive market."[72] German law has also adopted a "significant excess" approach to unfair pricing in a number of cases.[73] Under this approach, a

---

[68] See M Haag and R Klotz, "Commission Practice Concerning Excessive Pricing In Telecommunications" (1998) 2 *Competition Policy Newsletter*.

[69] See Commission Press Release IP/96/975 of November 11, 1996.

[70] See Commission Press Release IP/97/292 of April 11, 1997.

[71] *Napp Pharmaceutical Holdings Limited and Subsidiaries v Director General of Fair Trading* [2002] CompAR 13.

[72] *Assessment of Conduct*, Office of Fair Trading Draft Competition Law Guideline For Consultation, April 2004, para. 2.6.

[73] See *Flugpreisspaltung*, Bundesgerichtshof, judgement of July 22, 1999, NVZ 2000, 326.

company's pricing policy is abusive, within the meaning of section 19(4) of the German Act against Restraints of Competition, if its prices *significantly exceed* the competitive comparison price. This high threshold is imposed: (1) to correct for possible errors when comparing the prices of the dominant firm with those of similar products/services that have developed or would have developed under effective competition (the so called "competitive comparison prices"); and (2) to increase the likelihood that the allegedly excessive price results from the market dominance of the company in question, i.e., a causal link exists.[74] What is considered "significant" is determined with respect to how closely the market structure on the reference market resembles the structure of the market under scrutiny and to what extent reliable evidence is available that allows a proper comparison of both markets.[75] In cases where the structure of the market in question and the reference market are very similar and sufficient market information is available, the prices available in the reference market are taken as representative of the competitive price level. In cases where the two markets are dissimilar or where there is little meaningful market data, a "margin" between the prices of the company under scrutiny and those in the reference market is accepted as legitimate.[76]

The above precedents confirm an important point: a price difference in excess of that in a competitive market is not necessarily, or *ipso facto*, unlawful under Article 82 EC. And this is true *regardless* of the benchmark chosen to determine the excess. There are many markets which are not perfectly competitive. In such markets, price levels are often slightly above, and sometimes well above, perfectly competitive levels. But that does not mean that the prices in question are unlawful. If that were the law, there would have been a great numbers of instances in which unlawful prices would have been found, which is not the case.

A number of cautionary comments should, however, be added. A first comment is that, while excessive prices have generally been found only where the excess was significant, it cannot be assumed that lower margins are necessarily immune from scrutiny. A second comment is that, while high margins may indicate an excessive price, they are also a necessary feature of many industries with long-term capital costs, as well as intellectual property. In other words, while the need for a significant excess is a useful limiting principle to avoid costly errors, no upper or lower boundary can be rigorously specified. Finally, if the chosen benchmark is inherently poor at predicting a competitive benchmark—which is true of several of the benchmarks indicated above—

[74] Following the amendment of the GWB in 1980, there has been some discussion as to whether a "significant" excess of the competitive price level is still required. While the proviso in the GWB that expressly required a "significant" excess of the competitive price has been dropped, German courts continued to require such a significant excess.

[75] *Valium I*, Bundesgerichtshof, judgment of December 16, 1976, BGHZ 68, 23, 33, 37.

[76] See *BAB-Tankstelle Bottrup Süd*, OLG Düsseldorf, judgment of June 26, 1979, WuW/E OLG 2135, 2137. See also *Valium I*, Bundesgerichtshof, judgment of December 16, 1976, BGHZ 68, 23, 33, 37, where the *Kammergericht* compared certain pharmaceuticals produced by Roche to the same medication produced by the Dutch company, Centrafarm. Following a number of adjustments to Centrafarm's prices, the *Kammergericht* found that Roche's price exceeded the competitive comparison price by 28%, which, in the circumstances, it considered excessive. The Federal Supreme Court quashed the judgment of the *Kammergericht*, *inter alia*, because the *Kammergericht* had not established that Roche's price significantly exceeded the competitive comparison price given the existing differences between the market of reference and the market under analysis.

choosing some arbitrary figure above this benchmark to determine a significant excess may not yield meaningful results either. The significant excess is only significant in relation to whatever benchmark itself is chosen and this, too, may be suspect. The need for a significant excess might therefore be an attempt to place a gloss or limiting principle on an otherwise unclear set of principles.

12.4 DIFFICULTIES WITH THE CURRENT APPROACH TO EXCESSIVE PRICES UNDER ARTICLE 82 EC

Overview. Enforcement policy under Article 82 EC in regard to excessive prices has been criticised on several different levels. A first basic objection is that no generally accepted criterion exists in the decisional practice and case law to determine when prices are "excessive." Further, even if a criterion, or series of criteria, could be agreed upon as a benchmark, determining an excessive price in practice is extremely complex and subject to a number of difficulties. A second criticism is that prices above marginal cost are common and necessary in many industries where high profits are necessary to recover large up-front capital and other fixed costs. Third, any policy on excessive prices is likely to yield incorrect predictions in many instances and the cost of such errors is likely to be higher than the cost of allowing certain excessive prices to escape censure. Fourth, little or no guidance is offered in the decisional practice and case law on what might constitute objective justification for a price that exceeds the relevant criterion for determining an excessive price. Finally, devising effective remedies in excessive pricing cases raises difficult issues.

Legal test for identifying excessive prices fundamentally imprecise. The basic benchmarks identified in Section 12.3 for the assessment of excessive prices under Article 82(a) suffer from a high degree of imprecision and present significant implementation difficulties in practice. The basic two-stage test laid down in *United Brands* provides little, if any, guidance for competition authorities, courts, and, more importantly, for any firm that is, or may be, dominant. The first limb of the test—the price-cost comparison—is difficult to implement in practice, since it will typically involve complex evaluations of the dominant firm's costs across multiple products and time periods. Significant conceptual difficulties also arise (e.g., what the appropriate measure of cost is or should be) and the decisional practice and case law offer little or no guidance on these issues. Moreover, courts and competition authorities generally lack the resources to conduct detailed price-cost comparisons. Even regulators with sector-specific knowledge, staff accountants, and detailed information often struggle to undertake exercises of this kind.

The second limb of the *United Brands* test—whether the price is unfair in itself or when compared to competing products—is even more problematic, since there is no reliable standard for determining a "competitive" profit margin in most industries. This applies in particular for industries based on intellectual property, significant fixed costs, and dynamic competition. The second limb of the test is also subjective: there is no objective way in which it could be specified at what point a price is excessive "in itself."[77] None of the other suggested benchmarks clarifies the analysis either. For example, regarding the comparison with rivals' products, it is unclear what competing products should be taken in consideration in the analysis of excessive prices, how one can make sure that one is comparing like with like, and what adjustments should be made if prices charged by competitors are also excessively high or, conversely, predatory. The answers to these questions necessarily involve value judgments and no guidance is offered in the decisional practice and case law as to what criteria should guide the assessment. Thus, even Commission officials accept that "[t]he *United Brands* case highlights the major difficulties of proof associated with finding an abuse of excessive pricing, and probably explains the relative dearth of instances in which the Commission has intervened in those cases."[78]

The test(s) for excessive pricing can also be criticised on grounds of legal certainty. Any legal rule that seeks to prohibit excessive pricing must be reasonably capable of *ex ante* application by a dominant firm at the time it formulates its pricing policy.[79] It is not clear which benchmarks should be applied by a dominant firm in order to assess whether its prices could be regarded as excessive and what adjustments, if any, should be applied to those benchmarks in a particular case. Moreover, even if a clear benchmark, or series of benchmarks, could be identified, the dominant firm may have to undertake an onerous enquiry in order to assess whether a pricing policy is lawful or not. For example, in determining excessive prices in the telecommunications sector, the Commission has assessed comparative prices across several Member States and services, often relying on external experts. Such information may be available to the Commission through the exercise of its legal powers to compel the production of information and documents, but it is not clear how a dominant firm could undertake a similar inquiry, or whether it would be reasonable to expect it to do so.

Importance of prices above marginal cost for dynamic efficiency. The decisional practice and case law suggests that the EU competition authorities and courts place a greater value on short-run allocative and productive efficiency than on long-run dynamic efficiency. In particular, the basic legal test in *United Brands* suggests that a dominant firm should ensure that, at any given point in time, the margin between cost and price is not too great. This test places undue emphasis on short-run considerations, whereas many industries operate under a longer run horizon. Many industries require large, up-front risky investments and involve start-up losses in order to increase consumer uptake and thereby acquire the scale or experience needed to reduce costs over time. This dynamic pricing facilitates the recovery of initial losses by creating cost savings over time as a company achieves more efficient scale, greater learning experience, or some other efficiency capable of reducing costs. In the long run of

---

[77] See C Esteva-Mosso and S Ryan, "Article 82—Abuse of a Dominant Position" in J Faull and A Nikpay (eds.), *The EC Law of Competition* (Oxford, Oxford University Press, 1999) p. 189 ("The determination of an exploitative effect necessarily involves, therefore, the need to make a subjective judgment as to the appropriate level of prices and output in a particular market.").

[78] *Ibid.*, p. 192.

[79] See R Whish, *Competition Law* (4th edn., London, Butterworths, 2001) pp. 634-35 ("[E]ven if it is accepted...that exploitative pricing should be controlled, there is the difficulty of translating this policy into a sufficiently realistic legal test. A legal rule condemning exploitative pricing needs to be cast in sufficiently precise terms to enable a firm to know on which side of legality it stands.").

course, successful companies in dynamic industries may generate returns far in excess of the cost of supplying the product in question. But these apparently "excessive" returns are generally procompetitive, since they reward beneficial investment and innovation and compensate the firm for failed projects. Examples might include the pharmaceutical industry and network industries, such as telecommunications, software, credit cards, etc.

It is not clear how markets with the above features are or should be treated under Article 82(a). For example, it is unclear which costs should be taken into account in order to benchmark prices, in particular whether it is legitimate to incorporate past investment costs when calculating the relevant cost benchmark. Nor is it clear whether it would be acceptable to incorporate into the cost benchmark compensation for risk. There is no definitive indication in the case law of which costs must be taken into account and how they should be calculated. This is important because in dynamic industries, prices must be sufficiently high to compensate for past investment and risk. If this compensation is not incorporated as part of the cost benchmark, prices may be regarded as excessive when they are not. And if firms are not allowed to charge high prices to reward their investments and the associated risks, then their incentives to invest and innovate may reduce or even disappear.

The relevance of dynamic efficiencies was considered in the *Napp* case, although the reasoning of the authorities in that case is not entirely satisfactory. Napp, a pharmaceutical company, was the first to launch a sustained release morphine product (MST) in the United Kingdom, where it held a patent on the drug until 1992. In the market for MST, there are two customer segments: the community (or general practitioner) segment and the hospital segment. Approximately 85–90% of the market was supplied by wholesalers to community pharmacies to be used by patients as prescribed by their primary care physicians, while the remainder was purchased directly by hospitals from manufacturers to be used for in-patient care, as prescribed by hospital doctors or specialists. However, the community segment was to some extent "captive," since the brand of MST prescribed in the hospital segment was almost invariably prescribed in the community segment due to patient familiarity, etc. Napp had market share in excess of 90% in both segments. The Office of Fair Trading (OFT) decided that Napp enjoyed market dominance because of those high market shares and the existence of considerable barriers to entry. The OFT also found Napp's pricing policies for MST to be both predatory and excessive. Napp's practice of pricing the drug at a very low level in the hospital segment was ruled predatory and its pricing at a high level in the community segment was ruled excessive. On appeal, the Competition Appeal Tribunal (CAT) upheld these findings.

Napp sought to justify its high prices for MST in the community segment by reference to the importance of *ex ante* uncertainty in the pharmaceutical industry and dynamic competition. It argued that prices in a dynamically competitive market would allow recovery of past investments in R&D and promotion over the life cycle of the product as a whole. This dynamic provides pharmaceutical firms "with the appropriate incentive to invest in such R&D, education, training, and promotion to the extent that consumers collectively are willing to fund such investment. Any such competitive price will take account of the *ex ante* uncertainty as to whether a particular product will succeed."[80] Napp reasoned that any assessment of whether prices are excessive must take into account *ex ante* uncertainty, noting specifically that the pharmaceutical industry "is a research-based, innovative industry, in which a few successful 'winners' must not only repay their own development and promotion costs, but must also fund the research and development of a large number of other products which do not cover their own costs, as well as ongoing research into new products, very many of which ultimately turn out to be unsuccessful."[81] Napp went on to argue that *ex ante* uncertainty meant that Napp's pricing should be assessed according to a "portfolio-based approach," where prices and profitability for a range of different products are jointly assessed.[82]

The OFT and the CAT addressed a number of the points made by Napp. Although the OFT accepted that there must be some cost recoupment during the patent period, it reasoned that, after expiration, such recoupment should decline. With regard to Napp's arguments about the need to apply a dynamic concept of competition, the OFT claimed that "such arguments cannot serve as a justification for a product to earn a limitless stream of monopoly profits through keeping out competitors" and that "[w]hen a monopoly comes to an end, whether due to the expiry of a patent or otherwise, and competitive entry occurs, this will normally have some impact on prices....most branded pharmaceutical products suffer very extensive falls in market share when they come off patent."[83]

The CAT agreed, noting that "Napp's original investment in MST was made in the early 1980s in launching and promoting a product which, at the time, represented an important innovation. [However,] Napp has provided no figures as to what that initial investment was. In the absence of any indication to the contrary, we would expect that initial investment to have been recouped long ago."[84] The OFT and CAT added that while brand value may involve a price premium, such a premium could not be as high as 40% (Napp's prices were 33–67% higher than those of its competitors). Finally, the CAT rejected the argument that *ex ante* uncertainty justified high *ex post* prices. In particular, regarding the "portfolio pricing" version of the argument, the CAT stated, "it is not appropriate...to take into account the reasonableness or otherwise of its profits on other, unspecified, markets comprised in some wider but undefined 'portfolio' unrelated to the market in which dominance exists."[85]

While the UK authorities' findings may have been strongly influenced by the facts of the case—in particular that Napp's prices for the same product differed dramatically between the hospital "gateway" segment and the "captive" community segment—a

[80] *Napp Pharmaceutical Holdings Limited and Subsidiaries v Director General of Fair Trading* [2002] CompAR 13, para. 354.

[81] *Ibid.*, para. 356.

[82] *Ibid.*, paras. 357, 361.

[83] *Napp Pharmaceutical Holdings Limited and Subsidiaries v Director General of Fair Trading* [2002] CompAR 13, paras. 367, 369.

[84] *Ibid.*, para. 407.

[85] *Ibid.*, para. 413. See also para. 417, where the CAT went on to stress that "in the case of many pharmaceutical products, the expiry of a patent leads to competitive (often generic) market entry... In the present case, however, Napp has maintained *both* the price of MST *and* an exceptionally high market share for many years."

number of their findings show a narrow appreciation of the concept of dynamic competition. For example, there is no reason why recoupment of investment on a particular pharmaceutical product should be limited to the period of patent protection or, indeed, to any specific period following patent expiration. The concept of dynamic pricing in the pharmaceutical industry implies that high profits on successful products are necessary due to the high costs and failure rate of most products.[86] This does not mean that all pharmaceutical prices should escape censure, but nor is there any basis for saying that profits should be limited to the recovery of the costs of the product at issue or capped at some point in time.

The bias towards short-run efficiency is, to some extent, the natural implication of a policy that attacks "high" prices *per se*, without specifying limiting principles that restrict intervention to industries where market power is not the result of investment and innovation, but legal monopolies or other insuperable barriers to entry. As one commentator notes, a firm that has acquired "its market power through investment, innovations, and advertising (and maybe even a good share of business luck)" should not be punished for it. That firm generally "has the right to set high prices since these are the reward[s] for its investments" and "[i]ntervening by imposing lower prices would be tantamount to depriving it of its risky investments, and discourage it and other firms from investing in the future."[87] Competition law is intended to encourage competition and, perhaps most importantly, dynamic competition. But competition will be encouraged only if, sometimes, companies that develop successful products are allowed to keep whatever profits they make from them. It may have been that this particular argument did not apply to Napp's activities but there is no reason *a priori* to exclude it.

The EU approach to excessive prices appears to be very different from the position adopted in the United States, where greater emphasis is placed on fostering investment and innovation. The U.S. Supreme Court, in a recent seminal case, stated as follows.[88]

> "The mere possession of monopoly power, and the concomitant charging of monopoly prices, is not only not unlawful; it is an important element of the free-market system. The opportunity to charge monopoly prices—at least for a short period—is what attracts 'business acumen' in the first place; it induces risk taking that produces innovation and economic growth."

Scope for high error costs. Optimal competition policy should avoid that a violation is found when there is none (so-called false negatives) and that genuine violations do not go unpunished (so-called false positives). In practice, no workable set of principles can avoid some of these errors, so the issue is which type of error is more costly on balance. Regarding excessive prices, the imprecision of the legal test simply reflects the

---

[86] See GJ Glover, "Competition in the Pharmaceutical Marketplace," presentation to the *United States Department Of Justice/Federal Trade Commission Hearings On Intellectual Property And Antitrust Law*, available at http://www.ftc.gov/opp/intellect/020319gregoryjglover.pdf (March 19, 2002) p. 4 (finding that most drugs do not cover their research and development costs and that firms increasingly rely on a small number of "blockbuster" drugs to sustain on-going activities).

[87] M Motta, *Competition Policy: Theory and Practice* (Cambridge, Cambridge University Press, 2004), p. 69.

[88] See *Verizon Communications, Inc v Law Offices of Curtis V. Trinko LLP* 157 L. Ed. 2d 823, 836 (2004).

fundamental problem that there is no workable definition of a competitive price. For this reason, any policy that seeks to detect excessive prices is likely to yield incorrect decisions in practice. In some instances the authorities may conclude that prevailing market prices are competitive when they are not. In others they may conclude that prices are excessive when in reality they are competitive.

All the above errors are costly. In the first set of cases output is lower than optimal—some consumers are forced out of the market when they should not have been. In the second case, profits are kept artificially low, which reduces the incentives to invest and innovate to the ultimate detriment of consumers. But, in the absence of significant barriers to entry, the first type of error—the false condemnation of legitimate prices—is both more likely and more costly. This is because when entry is possible, any supra-competitive rents resulting from excessively high prices will be competed away by new entrants undercutting the incumbent. That is, excessive pricing will often be corrected by market forces and, therefore, will be short-lived and relatively harmless. In contrast, the cost of falsely condemning certain prices as excessive is likely to be long-term and harmful.

Lack of guidance on possible objective justifications for high prices. One fundamental question that remains largely unanswered concerns the factors that could be invoked as objective justification in excessive pricing cases. There are many reasons why prices may exceed costs or some other measure of the competitive benchmark, including, most notably, industries that need to fund innovation and investment. It is clear that the Community Courts are in principle willing to consider objective justification in excessive pricing cases. For example, the Court of Justice annulled the Commission's decision in *General Motors* because the company had provided an "an adequate explanation" for its prices.[89] It is also clear that the burden of proof regarding objective justification will fall on the dominant firm. In *Tournier* for example, the Court of Justice noted that if the prices charged by the dominant firm are appreciably higher than in other Member States, "it is for the undertaking in question to justify the difference by reference to objective dissimilarities between the situation in the Member State concerned and the situation prevailing in all the other Member States."[90]

Yet, it is not entirely clear what will be regarded as a valid objective justification. In *General Motors*, the Court of Justice based its ruling against the Commission on the fact that the instances of alleged excessive pricing were limited and therefore of "minute importance"—it referred to five cases over a five-month period.[91] It also considered positively the fact that the applicant had "very quickly reduced the charge for the

---

[89] Case 26/75, *General Motors Continental NV v Commission* [1975] ECR 1367, para. 21.

[90] Case 395/87, *Ministère Public v Tournier* [1989] ECR 2521, para. 38.

[91] Case 26/75, *General Motors Continental NV v Commission* [1975] ECR 1367, paras. 16-18. See too OFT *Guidelines in relation to Chapter II prohibition under the UK Competition Act 1998*, OFT 402, 1999, para. 4.7, where the Office of Fair Trading recognised that there may be "many objective justifications for prices that are apparently excessively high. First, in competitive markets prices and costs vary over time and there are likely to be periods when high profits can be earned.... Secondly, undertakings in competitive markets might be able to sustain high profits for a period of time if they are more efficient than their competitors."

inspection of imported vehicles" following the complaints of the affected parties.[92] In contrast, in *British Leyland*, the Court did not accept the applicant's arguments that the excessive fee was charged for only four months, and that it quickly reduced the fee when the infringement was pointed out to it.[93] The Court also rejected British Leyland's argument that the abuse had produced no effect.[94] The Court appeared convinced that British Leyland's conduct had deliberately "[made] the re-importation of left-hand-drive vehicles less attractive,"[95] and that such conduct was necessarily regarded abusive.

Difficulties with devising appropriate remedies. A final problem with the application of Article 82(a) to excessive prices lies in the design of appropriate remedies. An obvious option is to impose some form of price regulation—possibly a price cap—on the dominant firm. However, this is unlikely to work well in practice. The problem is two-fold. First, determining what is the appropriate level for the price cap is a non-trivial exercise for the very same reason that it is difficult to characterise the value of the "competitive" price. As one commentator notes, "[u]ltimately to determine, with pin-point accuracy, the precise margin which may be said to be reasonable and non-abusive, is an exercise fraught with difficulty."[96] Second, courts and many competition authorities are not well equipped to act as price regulators, with the on-going monitoring and compliance issues that this implies.[97] Experience with price regulation in sectors in which detailed information is available to specialist regulators has been mixed, and there are suggestions that price controls may, on balance, lead to more harm than good.[98] These problems are *a fortiori* more acute in the case of competition authorities and courts charged with general powers over a wide range of industries, such as the

[92] *General Motors*, above, para. 19.

[93] Case 226/84, *British Leyland Plc. v Commission* [1986] ECR 3263, paras. 31-32.

[94] *Ibid.*, para. 33.

[95] *Ibid.*, para. 29.

[96] See N Green, "Problems in the Identification of Excessive Prices: The United Kingdom Experience in the Light of *Napp*" in CD Ehlermann and I Atanasiu (eds.), *European Competition Law Annual 2003: What Is an Abuse of Dominant Position?* (Oxford, Hart Publishing, 2006), p. 80.

[97] See Report by the Economic Advisory Group on Competition Policy, "*An Economic Approach to Article 82*," July 2005, p. 11 ("If it was just a question of short-run versus long-run effects, one might be tempted to put the immediate gain of today's consumers above everything else. However, a policy intervention on such grounds requires the competition authority to actually determine what price it considers appropriate, as well as how it should evolve over time; for this it is not really qualified. Moreover, such a policy intervention drastically reduces, and may even forego the chance to protect consumers in the future by competition rather than policy intervention. A regime in which consumer protection from monopoly abuses is based on competition is greatly to be preferred to one in which consumer protection is due to political or administrative control of prices. In most circumstances therefore, the competition authority ought to refrain from intervening against monopolistic pricing and instead see to it that there is room for competition to open up.").

[98] See, e.g., D Carlton & J Perloff, *Modern Industrial Organisation* (4th edn., Boston, Pearson Addison Wesley, 2005) p. 682 ("Government regulation of firms may increase welfare in markets that are not perfectly competitive. Unfortunately, actual regulation often deviates considerably from optimal regulation and exacerbates market efficiencies....Optimal regulation can force a monopoly to set the competitive price. However, if the monopoly is badly regulated, shortages occur or the monopoly is encouraged to produce inefficiently. Even where regulations are properly applied, the cost of administering them may exceed the benefits.") and p. 705 ("[T]here is considerable doubt that regulatory bodies do lower prices.").

Commission and national authorities and courts. As the U.S. courts have noted, "judicial oversight of pricing policies would place the courts in a role akin to that of a public regulatory commission."[99] It is perhaps not surprising, therefore, that, outside the regulatory context, it is only rarely that the Commission has made findings of excessive pricing.[100]

Another option is to rely on structural remedies. These could take two forms: (1) forced divestitures; or (2) structural changes aimed at lowering the barriers to entry in the market under scrutiny. The scope for structural remedies is discussed in detail in Chapter Fifteen (Remedies), but, in general, the second option above is to be preferred, in particular when barriers to entry are the result of an unregulated legal monopoly, other forms of exclusive rights, or inefficient regulation. Where entry is possible, excessive pricing problems will generally be short-lived and relatively harmless. Forced divestiture is extremely difficult to implement in practice, since, in many industries, there is no precise relationship between market share and prices and, hence, it is not clear what level of assets should be transferred to competitors to achieve the desired downward effect on prices.

12.5 ALTERNATIVE APPROACHES TO EXCESSIVE PRICING UNDER ARTICLE 82 EC

Overview. There is general, but hardly surprising, agreement that the Commission, national competition authorities and courts should apply Article 82(a) rarely,[101] and that a high level of proof should be adopted.[102] The Commission too seems to share this conservative approach towards the application of Article 82(a). It has stated that, even if it does not renounce the right to pursue excessive pricing cases, "its decision-making practice does not normally control or condemn the high level of prices as such," but "examines the behaviour of the dominant company designed to preserve its dominance, usually directed against competitors or new entrants who would normally bring about effective competition and the price level associated with it."[103] The Commission thus appears to suggest that it is unlikely to go after excessive prices *per se*, but will focus on exclusionary practices that could lead to exploitation.

[99] *Berkey Photo, Inc v Eastman Kodak Co* 603 F.2d 263, 294 (2nd Cir. 1979).

[100] See Vth Report on Competition Policy (1975), para. 76 (Commission expressed reluctance to act as price control authority). See also M Haag and R Klotz, "Commission Practice Concerning Excessive Pricing In Telecommunications" (1998) 2 *Competition Policy Newsletter* ("The Commission itself never aspired to use Article 8[2] EC Treaty in order to act as a price setting authority...Recent Commission practice in cases concerning the telecommunications sector is fully in line with this general policy.").

[101] See R Whish, *Competition Law* (4th edn., London, Butterworths, 2001) p. 635 ("Given these problems, it is not surprising that competition authorities prefer to deploy their resources by proceeding against anticompetitive abuses that exclude competitors from the market rather than establishing themselves as price regulators.").

[102] See M Motta and A de Streel, "Exploitative and Exclusionary Excessive Prices in EU Law" in CD Ehlermann and I Atanasiu (eds.), *European Competition Law Annual 2003: What Is an Abuse of Dominant Position?* (Oxford, Hart Publishing, 2006), p. 124 ("[W]e suggest that the Commission uses its power with great parsimony and that the Court sets high level of proof.").

[103] XXIVth Report on Competition Policy (1994), point 77.

The above "conservative" approach to Article 82(a) makes sense, but it leaves firms that are (or may be) dominant in somewhat of a quandary. Even if there is general agreement that excessive pricing cases should be rare, and that they should be pursued only where the evidence is strong, the fact remains that, first, the Commission has not renounced its powers to apply Article 82(a) (and could not in any event) and, second, it remains unclear when Article 82(a) will be applied and what the relevant legal test is. The Commission's most recent decision in *Port of Helsingborg* shows a greater appreciation on its part of the need to develop a more coherent economic framework for the analysis of excessive prices. Thus, the Commission accepts that: (1) price/cost comparisons are generally not a meaningful comparator; (2) "economic value" is the key consideration; (3) "economic value" should include compensation for large risky initial investments and any intangible value attributable to the assets in question; and (4) excessive prices are not necessarily unlawful in industries in which competition is dynamic in nature.

While these comments are clearly to be welcomed—and go some way to addressing some of the general criticisms made of excessive pricing analysis under Article 82(a)—the fact remains that the Commission has not formulated a clear, predictable test that would allow a firm to determine at the time it decides a pricing policy whether its prices are, or might be, excessive. Another important consideration is that national competition authorities have clearly been very active in the area of excessive pricing and are likely to remain so while many national markets continue to be subject to barriers to entry. They may not feel compelled to share the Commission's reticence to pursue excessive pricing cases.

The above considerations have led a number of competition authorities and commentators to propose refinements to the analysis of excessive prices. Broadly speaking, four proposals have gained prominence. The first is based on a comparison of the dominant firm's rate of return with its cost of capital, i.e., accounting profits. The second alternative does not represent a major departure from existing practice, but emphasises the importance of robustness by finding excessive prices only where a series of different, but corroborative, tests point to the same conclusion. Similarly, the third and fourth proposals do not specify new benchmarking tests, but seek to identify administrable limiting principles to ensure that intervention on the freedom of firms to set their prices occurs only when it is likely to improve market outcomes.

The "excess profits" approach. As explained in Section 12.2 above, in dynamic industries, where investment and innovation are the key drivers of competitive success, it is by and large impossible to define "competitive" prices on the basis of a simple price-cost test. To avoid this difficulty, certain national competition authorities have advocated reliance on profit benchmarks rather than prices to assess excessive prices. For example, the Dutch Competition Authority has adopted decisions concluding that a price was excessive because it exceeded the total economic costs that an (efficient) undertaking may attribute to the provision of its services, which include a reasonable rate of return, given by a base rate plus a risk mark-up.[104]

[104] See, e.g., Case 273 and 906, *Vereniging Vrije Vogel v KLM* and *Stewart v KLM* (2000) Dutch Competition Authority, and *Report on Schipol's Tariffs* (2001).

This approach relies on standard accounting measures of returns on capital invested, a technique that is often used by firms in determining whether to make investments.[105] More specifically, this approach would treat the dominant firm's prices as excessive if the firm's return on capital is greater than its weighted average cost of capital (WACC), i.e., the weighted average of the cost of equity and the cost of debt, where the weights are given by the debt-equity ratio of the dominant firm (also known as the gearing ratio). The measure used to assess the profitability of the particular product or service is its internal rate of return (IRR). The IRR equates the sum of all negative discounted cash flows to that of all positive discounted cash flows over the entire lifetime of the product, so that the product's net present value (NPV) is zero. If the IRR is greater than the WACC, the prices charged for that product are deemed excessive.

In competition cases, the authorities are normally interested in profits over a shorter time period than the entire lifecycle of the product, so the rate of return calculation is often truncated to form a "truncated IRR." The truncated IRR is defined as the discount rate for which the value of the assets at the start of the assessed period (rather than the initial value of the assets) is equal to the discounted cash flows over the period plus the value of the assets at the end of the period.[106] This approach requires an accurate estimate of asset values at the beginning and end of the period over which prices were allegedly anticompetitive.

Compared to a simple price-cost comparison, the truncated IRR approach has the advantage of taking a more dynamic perspective. However, even its advocates note that the truncated IRR approach raises a number of problems for the assessment of excessive pricing.[107] First, reliable estimates are unlikely to be obtained if the company's sector is characterised by rapid technological change. Second, it requires reliable data on cash flows and asset values, which may not always be available.[108] Third, there are significant difficulties in measuring the truncated-IRR of a single business line for a multi-product firm. As a report prepared for a national competition authority notes:[109]

> "There may be no single method of allocation that is obvious or correct. For competition policy purposes, value-based cost drivers should be used with caution, as a circularity problem may arise. For example, if revenue is used as a cost driver, excessively high profits tend to be overlooked, since higher prices lead to higher levels of cost allocated to that line of business and, consequently, lower estimates of profitability."

In any event, and irrespective of the precise implementation, the excessive profits approach is vulnerable to accounting complications, giving rise to considerable conceptual and measurement problems. For example, accounting complications result when considering pricing strategies designed to maximise the sales of a group of related

[105] For background, see OXERA, *Assessing profitability in competition policy analysis*, Office of Fair Trading, Economic Discussion Paper No. 6 (July 2003).

[106] See, e.g., Case 273 and 906, *Vereniging Vrije Vogel v KLM* and *Stewart v KLM* (2000) Dutch Competition Authority. See also *Report on Schipol's Tariffs* (2001).

[107] See, e.g., *Vereniging Vrije Vogel v KLM* and *Stewart v KLM, ibid.* See also *Report on Schipol's Tariffs, ibid.*

[108] OXERA, *Assessing profitability in competition policy analysis*, Office of Fair Trading, Economic Discussion Paper No. 6 (July 2003) table 4.2.

[109] *Ibid.*, para. 1.37.

goods and services rather than a single product. Further complications arise when the manufacturing of the product under analysis is undertaken in different stages by multiple company divisions, across multiple countries, over multiple years, etc. Accounting procedures do not, for example, provide for capitalisation of R&D and advertising, do not address inflation, and do not properly adjust rates of return for risk.[110]

The fundamental problem, however, is that accounting profits do not reflect economic profits except under the most unrealistic assumptions.[111] The relationship between accounting and economic rates of return hinges on the time shape of net revenues, something that varies across industries, across firms within an industry, and even across time for a given firm. Nor can the divergence between the two rates be assumed away as small. As the most trenchant critics of this approach illustrate with their calculations, "there is no way in which one can look at accounting rates of return and infer anything about relative economic profitability or, *a fortiori*, about the presence or absence of monopoly profits."[112] In sum, the "excess profits" approach to the identification of excessive pricing is no less controversial than the direct price-cost approach.

The limitations on accounting rates of return as a benchmark for excessive prices have been well-understood by certain national competition authorities and courts. In 2000 the Finnish Competition Authority (FCA) proposed that the Competition Council declare that the Port of Helsinki had abused its dominant position by charging excessive prices (passenger fees) between 1997–99.[113] To justify the excessive pricing claim, the FCA mentioned, *inter alia*, that taking into account the prevailing rate of interest and the average cost of capital, the return on invested capital of the Port of Helsinki had, at least during 1997–99, clearly exceeded a reasonable return required for an investment with a comparable level of risk. The FCA calculated the return on invested capital on the basis of the WACC and CAP models. Moreover, the rate of interest (9%) on a loan paid to the City of Helsinki exceeded the rate of interest in loans granted on market conditions.

On appeal, the Market Court considered that the determination of an acceptable rate of return of an undertaking by using the WACC or CAP models is inherently uncertain because the results depend crucially on the data used, such as the amount of tied capital, return on the tied capital, risk-free rate of interest, general risk premium, and company-specific risk premium. Even small changes in the input data lead to considerable differences in the results obtained. The Market Court held that profitability calculations can serve as an indication, but only if there is *also* other evidence supporting the claim of excessive pricing. In light of the fact that the passenger fee had remained unchanged from 1993, and that the claim of excessive pricing only considered the period from 1997

[110] See GL Salamon, "Accounting Rates of Return" (1985) 75 *American Economic Review* 495. Salamon also finds that the accounting rate of return contains systematic measurement error. Firm size, control type (management versus ownership, for example), and accounting methods were all found to influence the calculated accounting return.

[111] See FM Fisher and JJ McGowan, "On the Misuse of Accounting Rates of Return to Infer Monopoly Profits" (1983) 73 *American Economic Review* 82.

[112] *Ibid.*, 90.

[113] Decision of the Finnish Market Court of October 11, 2002 (117/690/2000).

to 1999, the Market Court found insufficient evidence to show that the passenger fee was excessive.

A possible alternative would be to compare the profit rates of the dominant firm to the profits obtained by similar companies in other geographic markets. This possibility was considered by the Commission in *Port of Helsingborg*. The Commission concluded that "[t]here would be insuperable difficulties in this case in establishing valid benchmarks"[114] for this comparison. For example, the comparison between the profits of the ferry operations in different ports "would be too dependent on the markets in which they operate, the individual cost structure of the companies (possible economies of scope and scale, existence of cost efficiencies), the level of their investments, how these are financed, as well as internal decisions as regards the remuneration of the shareholders." [115]

An even more objectionable approach to excessive pricing cases is the use of regulated returns on capital, or other price or profit caps under regulatory powers, as the basis for claims that prices violate competition law. Whatever the merits of relying on the return on capital as a measurement of the reasonableness of a dominant firm's prices, the comparison of prices with a *regulated* return on capital (or any other financial cap) is unsound. Utility regulators are responsible for regulating a wide range of industries: gas, electricity, water, telecom, rail, airports and postal services. One of their functions in this connection is to set price limits for those parts of those industries where firms have significant monopoly power. In setting these price limits, regulators need to decide what would constitute a "fair" rate of profit, but this is only set in the light of whatever relevant policy objective is being pursued by the government at the particular time. Such policies have *no* necessary connection with the objectives of excessive pricing policy under competition law.[116] Thus, even if, for policy reasons, the rate of return is regulated for one area of a company's activity, this has no bearing on whether its prices in an unregulated area of activity are excessive for competition law purposes. In particular, a regulated return on capital does not provide any indication of fair pricing in an unregulated area.

The "predominance of evidence" approach applied in *Napp*. The predominance of evidence approach was applied in *Napp*, the leading United Kingdom case on excessive pricing. This approach consists of using several cost, price, and profitability benchmarks simultaneously in order to verify the legitimacy of a given pricing policy. Implicit in this approach is the notion that no single benchmark is capable of yielding reliable results as the sole test for an excessive price. Under the predominance of evidence approach, a price is then regarded as excessive if all benchmarking exercises

[114] Case COMP/A.36.568/D3, *Scandlines Sverige AB v Port of Helsingborg*, Commission Decision of July 23, 2004, not yet published, para. 156. See also Case COMP/A.36.568/D3, *Sundbusserne v Port of Helsingborg*, Commission Decision of July 23, 2004, not yet published, para. 178.

[115] *Port of Helsingborg, ibid.*, para. 157. See also *Sundbusserne, ibid.*, para. 135.

[116] A regulated rate of return is a maximum rate of return on capital based on specifically defined concepts and imposed for reasons of industrial policy or consumer protection. These policy reasons are typically irrelevant to the question whether a given price was or was not excessive and contrary to Article 82(a). That is a question of law, and not a question of policy. In general, changes in policy should not have a bearing on the implementation of Article 82(a).

point in the same direction. This approach also has implications for the interpretation of Article 82 EC, since Section 60 of the Competition Act 1998 requires the United Kingdom competition authorities to interpret domestic law consistently with EC competition law.

The detailed application of this approach was as follows. The OFT first stated that a price is considered excessive "if it is above that which would exist in a competitive market and where it is clear that high profits will not stimulate successful new entry within a reasonable period."[117] According to the OFT, the method for ascertaining whether a price is above what would otherwise exist in a competitive market can be approached in two ways: (1) by benchmarking price-cost margins; and (2) by benchmarking prices. In fact, the OFT did both.[118] In benchmarking price-cost margins, the OFT compared Napp's profit margins across the two consumer segments and also compared its profit margins to those of its competitors. Napp earned 40–60% margins for the hospital segment and in excess of 80% profit margins for the community segment.[119] Napp's next most profitable competitor earned "less than 70%" in the community segment.[120] The OFT also compared Napp's prices to those of competitors. The OFT found that, in the community segment, Napp's prices were 33–67% higher than those of its competitors.[121] Napp's prices were also compared to its own prices over time: Napp's prices for the community segment did not change for 10 years after patent expiration.[122] In comparing Napp's prices to its own prices within and outside the United Kingdom, the OFT found that Napp's community segment charges were over 10 times more than hospital prices,[123] and between four and seven times higher than export prices.[124] The CAT also seemed to approve the OFT's "preponderance of evidence" standard: "in our view those [price and margin] comparisons, taken together, amply support the Director's conclusions that Napp's prices...were...well above what would have been expected in competitive conditions."[125]

While the ultimate conclusion in *Napp* may have been correct, it is unclear why the answers to several imprecise tests—even if producing mutually consistent results—should be more credible than the answer to one imprecise test. Indeed, the comparisons performed by the OFT in *Napp* were no less controversial than those performed by the Commission in *United Brands*. For example, the OFT used Napp's prices while enjoying patent protection as a proxy for supra-competitive prices. The OFT reasoned that, since a monopolist can be expected to charge excessive prices, the prices charged

[117] Case CA98/2/2001, *Napp Pharmaceuticals Holdings Ltd and Subsidiaries*, Decision of Director General of Fair Trading on March 30, 2001, para. 203.

[118] *Ibid.*

[119] *Ibid.*, para. 224.

[120] *Ibid.*, para. 226.

[121] Case CA98/2/2001, *Napp Pharmaceuticals Holdings Ltd and Subsidiaries*, Decision of Director General of Fair Trading on March 30, 2001, para. 207.

[122] *Ibid.*, para. 213.

[123] *Ibid.*, para. 217.

[124] *Ibid.*, para. 221.

[125] *Napp Pharmaceutical Holdings Limited and Subsidiaries v Director General of Fair Trading* [2002] CompAR 13, para. 397.

before the patent expired must have been excessive. Consequently, the prices charged by Napp after the patent expired should be well below those charged while the patent was valid to be regarded as legitimate. Whilst it is true that patent law grants firms a certain period of time in which to recoup up-front costs, there is no reason in law or practice why profits should be expected to dramatically reduce in the period following patent expiration. Indeed, it is common that off-patent drugs maintain a significant premium over rival products due to the manufacturer's on-going brand recognition or advertising.

The other price comparisons performed in *Napp* fare no better. The OFT noted that Napp charged more to the community segment than it did to the hospital segment, but this comparison, by itself, did not prove excessive prices. Napp's hospital prices were found to be predatory, which should in itself invalidate the hospital segment prices as a comparison standard. Napp's competitors also offered substitute products that were above Napp's hospital segment prices. The hospital segment price therefore seemed incorrect as a comparator for what a "competitive" price would be in the community market. The prices charged by Napp's competitors to the consumer segment were lower than Napp's consumer segment price, but this also seems inconclusive as proof of excessive prices. Napp's product had been the market standard for two decades and probably commanded both brand recognition and consumer trust. Yet the OFT decided that brand recognition did not merit a 40% premium. Although any hard-and-fast number as a standard for "excessive" brand name value would be arbitrary, a number of off-patent medicines routinely command premiums of 40% or more over non-branded rival products.

The "sector-specific" approach. Certain commentators argue that Article 82(a) should *only* be enforced on newly liberalised sectors, such as the telecommunications and energy industries, as a complement to the liberalisation process.[126] The argument used to defend the introduction of this industry-specific standard in the application of Article 82(a) is based on the notion that, first, market power in liberalised sectors is usually the result of State intervention and legal privilege rather than the consequence of superior efficiency, and, second, that those sectors are characterised by high barriers to entry which prevent new entrants from competing away supra-competitive profits.

A number of comments can be made regarding this approach. First, Article 82(a) does not distinguish between newly-liberalised and other sectors and there may be issues of discrimination if enforcement policy was expressly directed only at the former. Second, it would need to be defined when this approach would be applied. For example, many excessive pricing cases do not concern utility sectors as such, but instances in which Member States have granted exclusive rights to an undertaking without any corresponding regulation of prices. Third, this approach in essence amounts to advocating abstinence in most cases. Although the Commission and national authorities and courts pursue excessive pricing cases relatively infrequently, advocating abstinence would not be accepted for policy and other reasons. Fourth, while it may, sometimes,

[126] See, e.g., M Motta and A de Streel, "Exploitative and Exclusionary Excessive Prices in EU Law" in CD Ehlermann and I Atanasiu (eds.), *European Competition Law Annual 2003: What Is an Abuse of Dominant Position?* (Oxford, Hart Publishing, 2006), p. 91.

be relevant to inquire into the provenance of market power,[127] there is no case for treating all firms with market power in newly-liberalised sectors *a priori* as "idle monopolists." Indeed, evidence suggests that many incumbents in the telecom and energy sectors throughout Europe invest significant sums on innovation and other forms of competition.[128] Fifth, this approach seems largely superfluous, since most liberalised sectors are already subject to price or profit control measures. Finally, and most importantly, this approach ultimately lacks precision. Its proponents would need to clarify: (1) what industries would be covered and why; (2) the conditions under which a former State monopoly would be cleared of any taint of suspicion about its past privileges; (3) how to deal with the practical reality that most former incumbents have a mixture of products in which they have a privileged position and products where they do not (e.g., issues of common costs, different rates of return etc.); and (4) the benchmarks that should be applied.

The "exceptional circumstances" test. Certain commentators have argued that the choice of policy towards excessive prices should be directed at minimising the cost of decisional errors: i.e., concluding that prevailing market prices are competitive when they are not (false positives) or, alternatively, that prices are excessive when in reality they are competitive (false negatives).[129] They argue that all of these errors are costly: in the first set of cases, as indicated in Section 12.2, the allocation of resources is allocatively and productively inefficient; in the second set of cases, the incentives to invest and innovate are diminished. But, on balance, they claim that economic theory and evidence suggest that the second type of error (false negatives) is at least as likely as the first and is more costly when it occurs.

Several reasons are advanced for this conclusion. First, the cost of false negatives is necessarily small in industries where barriers to entry are not significant, since market forces can be relied upon to eliminate excess profits within a reasonable period of time, thus increasing the cost of intervention relative to its benefits. Furthermore, false convictions are more likely to occur, particularly in those cases where they are most costly, namely in dynamic industries and in industries where investment drives competition and welfare. In those industries the welfare value of innovation is great, but the price-cost margins that firms require to compete are also large. Hence, the authors conclude that the policy which maximises long-run welfare in industries with low or modest barriers to entry is one that leaves firms, including dominant firms, free to charge prices above cost and earn positive, and possibly high, profits.

The key consideration is to limit intervention to cases in which entry barriers are very high and, therefore, where there is a reasonable prospect that consumers could be

---

[127] See J Vickers, "How Does the Prohibition of Abuse of Dominance Fit with the Rest of Competition Policy?" in CD Ehlermann and I Atanasiu (eds.), *European Competition Law Annual 2003: What Is an Abuse of Dominant Position?* (Oxford, Hart Publishing, 2006), p. 155 ("Appropriate public policy towards firms with actual or potential market power depends on the cause of the market power.").

[128] See, e.g., R Le Maistre, "Europe Doubles Down on DSL" document available at http://www.lightreading.com/document.asp?doc_id=45593&site=lightreading (January 7, 2004).

[129] See DS Evans and AJ Padilla, "Excessive Prices: Using Economics to Define Administrable Legal Rules" (2005) 1 *Journal of Competition Law and Economics* 97-122.

exploited. The need for a strict enforcement policy is less obvious in circumstances where the market is contestable, since high prices would ordinarily attract new entrants that would compete away the excessive margins. The market is also generally quicker and more effective at correcting excessive prices than administrative action or litigation, which takes time and tends to be haphazard.

Intervention should thus be limited to "exceptional circumstances": (1) the firm enjoys a near-monopoly position in the market, which is not the result of past investments or innovation; (2) that position is protected by insurmountable barriers to entry; (3) the prices charged by the firm greatly exceed its average *total* costs; and (4) there is a risk that those prices may prevent the emergence of competition in adjacent markets. These conditions, which should be applied on a case-by-case basis, are cumulative: it is enough that one of them does not hold to conclude that prices are not "unfairly" high. Conditions (1), (2) and (3) taken together indicate that the expected cost of a false conviction is relatively small, while the expected cost of a false acquittal is large. However, these conditions are not sufficient to justify intervention, since a firm could still be dissuaded from undertaking costly investment projects if it knew that prices or profits would be capped *ex post*. Condition (4) is therefore a way to ensure that the cost of a false acquittal is orders of magnitude much larger than the cost of a false conviction.[130] This condition is consistent with the case law. As noted by one commentator, many excessive pricing cases brought by the Commission "were essentially of exclusionary rather than of exploitative nature and involved a second legal objection that centred on barriers to entry or to market integration."[131] For example, in *British Leyland*, the high fees charged by British Leyland were regarded by the Court of Justice as part of a plan to discourage the re-importation of left-hand-drive vehicles.

Although some of the criticisms levied against the "sector specific" approach to excessive pricing also apply here, the exceptional circumstances approach clearly has a number of commendable features. In particular, the emphasis on whether significant barriers to entry exist and would allow the dominant firm to maintain its near-monopoly position is an important clarification. In an excessive pricing case, it should always be relevant to ask why the customers that are said to be exploited cannot switch to rivals' substitute products. One obvious reason is because the relevant market has very high entry barriers that limit the prospects for entry. Of course, a finding of dominance, if made correctly, means that some non-trivial barriers to entry exist. But there are clearly different degrees of impediments on entry: some will inevitably decline in the medium to long-term; others will not due to legal restrictions or serious structural problems on the relevant market. One example of a very high barrier to entry would be where a

---

[130] Condition (4) is in line with Sir John Vickers' explanation that the OFT's position in *Napp* would have been different if Napp's pricing to the hospital segment had not been judged to be exclusionary. See J Vickers, "How Does the Prohibition of Abuse of Dominance Fit with the Rest of Competition Policy?" in CD Ehlermann and I Atanasiu (eds.), *European Competition Law Annual 2003: What Is an Abuse of Dominant Position?* (Oxford, Hart Publishing, 2006), p. 147. The CAT also suggested in *Napp* that Napp's maintaining high prices in the community segment for MST was made possible because of its exclusionary practice in the hospital segment, although it was also clear that both the excessive pricing and exclusionary pricing practices were stand-alone violations.

[131] See M Gal, "Monopoly Pricing as an Antitrust Offence in the U.S. and the EC: Two Systems of Belief About Monopoly?" (2004) *Antitrust Bulletin* 40.

Member State grants exclusive rights or other privileges to an undertaking without any accompanying limitation on the prices that the beneficiary can charge. For example, in *British Leyland*, the principal reason that the dominant firm could exploit consumers was because a registration document was a prerequisite for export and the dominant firm was, at the time, the only source of that document, i.e., a *de facto* monopoly.

A dominant firm could also employ contractual devices that limit switching possibilities. For example, a monopoly provider of telecommunications equipment could contractually tie customers to long-term rental contracts that prevent them from avoiding the possibility of paying excessive rental charges by purchasing the equipment outright. (In that case, the contract itself may also be unlawful.) In contrast, if customers were free to terminate the rental contract at reasonable notice without incurring any penalty, and purchase the equipment from another source at a reasonable price, there would be no anticompetitive reason why the consumer should pay an excessive price. If the customer could terminate the contract without a penalty, the contract would not be a barrier to switching, whereas, if it could not, the dominant firm could exploit the customers' inability to switch. An excessive price is one that is significantly and persistently above that which could have been obtained in conditions of effective competition. It can arise only if there are not, in the relevant market, conditions of effective competition, of which the buyer or lessee could have taken advantage. A price cannot be excessive if the alleged victim at all times had a choice as to whether to pay the price or, in the case of rental payments, whether to go on making the payments.

12.6 CONCLUSION

Towards a clearer definition of excessive prices. A dominant firm imposing unfair selling prices violates Article 82(a). The objectives of this provision lie at the core of EC competition law: to prevent the exploitation of consumers by firms with significant market power. However, the enforcement of Article 82(a) faces numerous conceptual and practical problems. A first problem is that it is difficult to define, let alone measure, with precision what an excessive price is. Economic theory has defined the notion of a perfectly competitive price—the price that prevails in a perfectly competitive market where there are many, relatively small, competing firms, all of them acting as price takers and setting prices at marginal cost. But most actual markets differ from the perfectly competitive ideal: production is subject to significant economies of scale and scope and companies, large or small, are able to influence the market price through their actions. An enforcement policy that treated as excessive any price above the perfectly competitive benchmark would produce a paradoxical result: dominant companies could only be economically viable if they violated the law.

A second issue is that a policy which attacks high prices *per se* may hurt, rather than encourage, the competitive process. Companies operating in industries where competition takes place via investment and innovation need to be able to appropriate the returns of their investments when successful. Otherwise, they would not invest in the first place, to the ultimate detriment of consumers who will end up with less variety and lower quality. Finally, the design of optimal remedies for excessive pricing is far from obvious. Competition authorities and courts are not well-equipped to regulate prices.

Structural remedies will often be difficult to articulate and very costly. In short, there are a number of conceptual and practical difficulties surrounding excessive prices and, hence, the likelihood of error is high.

There is growing consensus on the need to identify administrable limiting principles to ensure that Article 82(a) is enforced only when strictly necessary, i.e., minimising the likelihood of costly false convictions. The emerging consensus is that intervention should be restricted to industries: (1) protected by high barriers to entry;[132] (2) where one firm enjoys considerable market power; and (3) where investment and innovation play a relatively minor role.[133] There is much less consensus, however, on how to distinguish excessively high prices from competitive prices, since all possible benchmarks are subject to criticism.

The answer seems to be to use *all* possible benchmarks, and to restrict intervention to those cases where, first, all benchmarking exercises produce a consistent result, and, second, the difference between the prices charged by the dominant firm and the benchmarks used is substantial. This requires, however, the existence of meaningful benchmarks, i.e., benchmarks which contain valuable, though limited and imperfect, information on the fairness of the prices under analysis. In *Port of Helsingborg*, for example, the Commission concluded that this was not possible: there was "insufficient evidence to conclude that the port fees charged by [the Port of Helsingborg] to the ferry operators would be unfair when compared to the port fees charged in other ports."[134] This conclusion was reached due to the "difficulties in making meaningful comparisons with other ports, as regards the level of their respective fees." [135] But it is perfectly possible that good data are available in other cases (e.g., where rivals offer similar products or the dominant firm sells a similar product in other relevant markets) and allow consistent conclusions to be drawn.

All of this suggests that a multi-stage approach to the assessment of excessive pricing by dominant firms is appropriate. As a first stage, the structure of the market under scrutiny would be analysed. The investigation of the pricing policy of the dominant firm should continue only when it is found that: (1) the market is protected by high barriers to entry; (2) consumers have no credible alternatives to the products of the dominant firm; and (3) firms compete in a mature environment, where investment and innovation play little or no role. As a second stage, the prices and price-cost margins of the dominant firm are compared to a battery of "competitive" benchmarks. Those prices are considered abusive when: (4) most or all benchmarking exercises point in the same direction; and (5) the differences between the dominant firm's prices and the various competitive benchmarks are "substantial."

[132] See *Assessment of Conduct*, OFT Draft Competition Law Guideline For Consultation, April 2004, para. 2.6.

[133] *Ibid.*, para. 2.20.

[134] Case COMP/A.36.568/D3, *Scandlines Sverige AB v Port of Helsingborg*, Commission Decision of July 23, 2004, not yet published, para. 207. See also Case COMP/A.36.568/D3, *Sundbusserne v Port of Helsingborg*, Commission Decision of July 23, 2004, not yet published, para. 183.

[135] *Port of Helsingborg, ibid.*, para. 202. See also *Sundbusserne, ibid.*, para. 178.

Chapter 13

OTHER EXPLOITATIVE ABUSES

13.1 INTRODUCTION

The extension of Article 82(a) to exploitative abuses other than excessive pricing. Unfair terms and conditions within the meaning of Article 82(a) are not limited to excessive prices, discussed in the previous chapter. In a small number of cases, the Community institutions and national authorities have considered that other unilateral practices by a dominant firm may take unfair advantage of its market power and so exploit trading parties. This possibility was first mentioned in earlier cases concerning obligations imposed by national copyright collection societies on holders of copyright to assign their worldwide rights (and not merely to license the rights that the societies in question were able to manage, directly or indirectly, for them).[1] Another example concerns the ability of a dominant purchaser of goods or services to impose unfairly low prices on trading parties or other examples of the exercise of monopsony power.[2]

The unifying rationale of these cases is not easily stated, but it seems to reflect the consideration that a firm without dominance would not be able to impose such terms on consumers and trading parties, or at least not to the same extent. This view of Article 82 EC has almost certainly been conditioned by the historical influence of ordoliberal thinking, which had a material impact on the initial development of Article 82 EC. Ordoliberal thinking objected not only to exclusionary acts by a dominant firm, but also required that firms with market power should behave "as if" there was effective competition.[3] This was based on broad notions of "fairness", i.e., that a dominant firm should not exploit consumers with onerous prices or terms.

Scope of this chapter. Given the dearth of case law on exploitative abuses other than excessive pricing, this chapter is modest in its objectives. It essentially discusses two main categories of abuse that have acquired a reasonably clear meaning in the decisional practice and case law. The first is abuse of seller power, or abusive monopsony purchasing behaviour, whereby a dominant purchaser of goods or services

---

[1] See Case 127/73, *Belgische Radio en Televisie v SV SABAM and NV Fonior* [1974] ECR 51. See also Joined Cases 110/88 and others, *Lucazeau v Société des Auteurs, Compositeurs et Editeurs de Musique* [1989] ECR 2811; Case 395/87, *Ministère public v Jean-Louis Tournier* [1989] ECR 2521; *GEMA*, OJ 1971 L 134/15; *GEMA II*, OJ 1972 L 166/22; Joined Cases 55/80 and 57/80, *Musik-Vertrieb membran GmbH et K-tel International v GEMA—Gesellschaft für musikalische Aufführungs- und mechanische Vervielfältigungsrechte* [1981] ECR 147; Case 7/82, *Gesellschaft zur Verwertung von Leistungsschutzrechten mbH (GVL) v Commission* [1983] ECR 483; Case 155/73, *Giuseppe Sacchi* [1974] ECR 409; and Case 402/85, *G Basset v Société des auteurs, compositeurs et éditeurs de musique (SACEM)* [1987] ECR 1747.

[2] See Case 298/83, *Comité des industries cinématographiques des Communautés européennes (CICCE) v Commission* [1985] ECR 1105.

[3] See Ch. 1 (Introduction, Scope of Application, and Basic Framework).

pays excessively low prices to its suppliers or agents. The second category concerns practices that have been suggested in the case law as amounting to abusive or "unfair" contract terms. A workable definition of such terms is not easy, but essentially asks whether the clause is one that would be imposed and accepted in competitive conditions, and whether the gains in efficiency, if they are shared or passed on, are sufficient to outweigh the onerous effect for the other parties bound by the clause. The case law envisages a number of situations in which contract terms may be onerous and abusive, in particular in respect of technology licensing.

13.2 ABUSE OF MONOPSONY PURCHASING POWER

Overview. Buyer power is simply market power on the buying side of the market. It is relevant in two principal situations under Article 82 EC, both of which have led to a lively recent debate among economists and lawyers.[4] First, buyer power may limit the exercise of seller power and thus constitutes a factor of potential relevance to the assessment of dominance. This is discussed in detail in Chapter Three (Dominance). If buyer power can act as a countervailing force to the effects of seller power, it follows that buyer power can *itself* rise to the level of dominance. This gives rise to the second principal aspect of buyer power under Article 82 EC: the circumstances in which a dominant buyer can exploit its position (e.g., by paying abusively low prices). This aspect of buyer power forms the main focus of the present chapter.

13.2.1 Basic Economics Of Monopsony Power

No fundamental distinction from seller power. Buyer power—which is sometimes referred to as monopsony power—typically arises in vertically-structured industries where the downstream market is more concentrated than the upstream market.[5] For example, large supermarket chains are often said to possess market power *vis-à-vis* their suppliers, which may allow them to engage in anticompetitive conduct.[6] For this reason, excessive concentration on the buying side has sometimes been objected to under EC merger control rules.[7] Buyer power can also manifest itself where inputs have limited uses (e.g., custom-made equipment). But, even then, buyers' ability to depress prices in the long run is likely to be limited, since input sellers will not have incentives to invest in assets that produce very low (or negative) returns.[8]

---

[4] See, e.g., AA Foer, "Introduction to Symposium on Buyer Power and Antitrust" (2005) 72 *Antitrust Law Journal* 505–08.

[5] See R Inderst, "Buyer Power: A Theorist's Perspective," presentation given at UK Competition Commission (2005), available at http://faculty.insead.edu/inderst/personalwebpage/bp_inderst.pdf

[6] Buyer power has also been an issue in industries such as health care services, farming, and natural resource extraction. See AA Foer, "Introduction to Symposium on Buyer Power and Antitrust" (2005) 72 *Antitrust Law Journal* 505.

[7] See, e.g., *Crown Cork & Seal/CarnaudMetalbox*, OJ 1996 L 75/38; *Kesko/Tuko*, OJ 1997 L 174/47; *Blokker/Toys "R" Us*, OJ 1998 L 316/1; *Rewe/Meinl*, OJ 1999 L 274/1; and *Carrefour/Promodes*, OJ 2000 C 164/5.

[8] See DW Carlton & JM Perloff, *Modern Industrial Organisation* (4th edn., Boston, Pearson Addison Wesley, 2005) ch. 4, pp.107–110.

Cases involving dominant buyers are essentially the same as seller dominance. In the same way as a dominant seller can increase prices above the level that would prevail in a competitive market, a dominant seller, or group of sellers, can depress the price of inputs below the level that would prevail in a competitive buying market, which in turn can lead to reduced capacity and market participation at the upstream level. Resources are allocated inefficiently in this instance. In addition, when the dominant buyer also has power as a seller in the output market in which the input is transformed, it may be able to increase sale prices. Cases involving a dominant buyer should thus be assessed by relying on the standard methods used for accessing seller power.[9]

Potential adverse welfare effects. Although the basic analysis of buyer and seller power is essentially the same in economics, the adverse welfare effects for consumers of monopsony purchasing behaviour are generally less obvious than in the case of seller power.[10] Two situations should be contrasted. The first is where a dominant buyer exercises power to pay too *low* a price for inputs purchased. Such conduct can "exploit" sellers in the same way as a dominant seller can exploit buyers. The welfare effects of paying too little for inputs are generally neutral, or perhaps even benign, for consumers. Where reductions in the cost of input purchases are passed on to consumer in the form of lower prices in the output market, consumers benefit.[11] Where they are not, the principal effect of monopsony purchasing behaviour is to transfer wealth from sellers of inputs to buyers. Wealth transfers cannot be objectionable in themselves under Article 82 EC, since, otherwise, competition law would protect individual competitors, not competition. Thus, a key component of the anticompetitive exercise of buyer power to pay too low a price for inputs is that it should also involve a *reduction in output*.[12]

A second practice that dominant buyers may commit is paying too *high* a price for inputs, or "overbuying." A dominant buyer could pay prices for inputs that lead it to make a loss in the output market ("predatory overbuying") or a dominant buyer may remain profitable, but use overpaying as a means of raising rivals' costs. Such conduct raises different issues to paying too low prices for inputs. The main concern is that such conduct can exclude rival firms, not that it exploits sellers (quite the contrary). There is

---

[9] See M Schwartz, *Should Antitrust Assess Buyer Market Power Differently than Seller Market Power?*, comments presented at DOJ/FTC Workshop on Merger Enforcement Washington DC, February 17, 2004, available at http://www.usdoj.gov/atr/public/workshops/docs/202607.htm.

[10] See PW Dobson, M Waterson and A Chu, "The Welfare Consequences of the Exercise of Buyer Power," *Office of Fair Trading Research Paper*, 16, September 1998.

[11] See Guidelines on the assessment of horizontal mergers under the Council Regulation on the control of concentrations between undertakings, OJ 2004 C 31/5, para. 62 ("If increased buyer power lowers input costs without restricting downstream competition or total output, then a proportion of these cost reductions are likely to be passed onto consumers in the form of lower prices.").

[12] See *Rewe/Meinl*, OJ 1999 L 274/1, para. 71 ("The exercise of buyer power which leads to the securing of a more favourable purchase deal is not to be considered *per se* detrimental to the economy as a whole. Especially where the supplier side is itself highly concentrated and powerful, buyers are faced with effective competition in their own selling market and hence are compelled to pass on any savings to their own customers, buyer power can prevent monopoly or oligopoly profits from being earned on the supply side. However, if the powerful buyer himself occupies in his selling market a strong position which is no longer kept sufficiently in check by the competition, any savings can no longer be expected to be passed on to customers.").

a case in economic theory for treating such conduct as abusive.[13] But implementing a clear test for identifying abusively high purchase prices, without at the same time reducing competition in procurement, is very difficult. Unless there is a bright-line benchmark, like a predatory pricing rule, the problems of determining a "fair" buying price are similar to trying to determine a "fair" selling price. As discussed in detail in Chapter Twelve (Excessive Pricing), there is no objective method to determine when a selling price is "fair." This applies *a fortiori* to determining a "fair" buying price. Unless the dominant firm is making a loss in the relevant output market—which can be assessed under traditional predatory pricing rules—economics does not allow easy identification of when input prices are "too high."[14]

13.2.2 Conditions For A Possible Abuse

No general case for treating dominant firm's efforts to lower costs as abusive. Buyer power concerns have featured more prominently in recent merger decisions and discussion of merger control policy, particularly in relation to the retail sector (e.g., supermarkets). Similar issues have been raised under Article 81 EC by the increased use of buying cooperatives. Potential concerns in this regard are well-founded, since monopsony purchasing can lead to many of the same anticompetitive outcomes that result from monopoly power. But the operational basis for defining rules circumscribing unilateral conduct by buyers is much less clear. The decisional practice and case law under Article 82 EC have overwhelmingly focused on abuses of seller power, not buyer power. What limited precedent does exist indicates that competition authorities are generally not receptive to claims involving excessively low purchasing prices and certainly much less so than claims of excessively high prices. In other words, there appears to be a strong aversion to legal paternalism when it comes to negotiations between independent market participants.[15]

In *CICCE*, the Court of Justice considered a preliminary reference that arose from an undertaking claiming that undertakings with exclusive broadcasting rights in France had paid unfairly low licence fees for the purchase of movies. The Court dismissed the appeal, but made a number of passing observations on the abuse of excessively low prices. First, it did not appear to dispute the Commission's assertion that unfairly low purchase prices can in principle constitute an abuse. Second, the Court indicated that,

---

[13] See SC Salop, "Anticompetitive Overbuying by Power Buyers" (2005) 72 *Antitrust Law Journal* 669–715.

[14] One recent US case treated dominant buyer behaviour as abusive even when the buyer made a profit overall in the selling market. See *Confederated Tribes of Siletz Indians of Oregon v Weyerhaeuser Co.*, 411 F.3d 1030 (9th Cir. 2005). The rationale of the case is vague, since the court specified no objective standard for determining when a buying price is too high. Instead, it asked whether the dominant firm "purchased more [inputs] than it needed or paid a higher price for [inputs] than necessary," and so prevented competitors "from obtaining the [inputs] they needed at a fair price." *Ibid.*, 411 F.3d at 1037 n.8. The judgment is currently before the US Supreme Court in a petition for writ of certiorari. The case has been strongly criticised as departing from clear case law on predatory pricing, thereby adding uncertainty in buying markets. See JL McDavid and JL Ellsworth, "Predatory Purchasing?" *The National Law Journal*, November 14, 2005. On predatory pricing generally, see Ch. 5 above.

[15] See AT Kronman, "Paternalism and the Law of Contracts" (1983) 92 *Yale Law Journal* 763.

as in the case of excessively high prices, the relationship between the cost and the "economic value" of the input might be relevant to determine whether the dominant firm's prices were abusive. Third, the Court accepted that it was impossible, in view of the variety of potential criteria for assessing the value of films, to determine a yardstick that was valid for all films. Average prices were therefore meaningless and the specific "economic value" of each film had to be evaluated. Finally, it is notable that the Court essentially ignored findings by the national competition authority in France that the dominant firms' purchase prices were abusive.

Much the same conclusion was reached in *The Association of British Travel Agents and British Airways plc*, where the Office of Fair Trading (OFT) also rejected monopsony purchasing claims.[16] British Airways (BA) was accused of abusing its dominant position as a buyer of travel agents' services by reducing booking payments from £6 to £2.50 for economy tickets and from £11 to £5 for premium tickets. This coincided with greater availability of electronic tickets on BA's website, which were more efficient for BA to process. The travel agents alleged that the reduced booking payments did not cover their costs for each booking.

The OFT rejected these allegations. First, there was no discrimination between on-line and telephone booking methods, since BA's own telephone booking service and shops also charged additional fees, reflecting the higher cost of non-electronic transactions. Second, the other major airlines had adopted a similar approach to BA. Third, the OFT considered it unlikely that BA could exercise anti-competitive buyer power over travel agents, since they could switch their services to other airlines, as well as package holidays and charter operators. Finally, while agents were historically paid on the basis of commission from airlines, there was no reason, given the service they provided, why they could not charge consumers directly for value-added services. In this regard, the OFT noted that the key issue for the consumer was the total ticket price and not the individual elements of it. For these reasons, the OFT concluded that BA was not obliged, simply by virtue of any market power that it may have as a buyer of travel agency services, to make booking payments to travel agents that covered the full cost they incurred in issuing tickets, since travel agents could have supplemented their income by charging service fees (which many now do).[17]

Possible abuse in exceptional circumstances. Possible abuses of buyer power have been mentioned in certain circumstances. A number of examples could be envisaged under the practices of standard-setting organisations (SSOs). SSO members may be dominant with respect to a particular technology market. They may for example use their collective power to compel the licensing of patents or to specify royalty rates from licensors that are below a competitive level. For example, when SSOs do not adopt rules on how royalties from essential patents incorporated in the standardised

[16] See CA98/19/2002, *The Association of British Travel Agents and British Airways plc*, December 11, 2002.

[17] See also Case COM/118/02, *The Increase in the Wholesale Price of Electronic Top-Up by Vodafone Ireland Limited*, October 25, 2002 (Irish Competition Authority) (reduction in payments to mobile phone pay-as-you-go resellers not found abusive).

technology should be calculated, owners of essential patents may later insist on royalty rates that are too high and so hold up the technology roll-out. One solution to this problem is to allow the SSO members to discuss royalties in advance, either by making unilateral announcements or by allowing joint discussions. In the latter case, concern has been expressed that the SSO members could use joint *ex ante* royalty discussions to force patent holders to offer royalty rates below the competitive level. Some argue that joint negotiations of licensing terms "would essentially allow an industry to impose licence terms on a patent owner" and that "[r]equiring specific terms...will be equivalent to a compulsory licensing approach."[18] But such conduct would primarily be an issue under Article 81 EC. SSOs are also less likely, in general, to be found dominant on relevant antitrust markets, either because the market is nascent or competing technologies exist.

Another situation in which paying excessively low prices to suppliers or agents might be abusive is where the dominant purchaser also exercises dominance on the selling market. The economics of monopsony are ultimately the same as the economics of monopoly,[19] except that whereas a monopolist directly reduces supply for the purpose of raising price (which may reduce consumer welfare), a monopsonist achieves the same ultimate effect indirectly by refusing to buy more inputs or buying them at an excessively low price. But if a firm is simultaneously a monopsonist (towards input suppliers) and monopolist (towards final customers), then there may be a double reduction in final supply, in which case the welfare effect is, unsurprisingly, worse than if only one of either monopoly or monopsony existed.

This possibility has been alluded to in a couple of decisions under national abuse of dominance laws. In *Reduction In Travel Agent Commissions By Aer Lingus plc*,[20] the Irish Competition Authority investigated whether a reduction by the national flag carrier in travel agency commissions from 9% to 5% was an abusive exercise of monopsony power. The complaint was rejected. The Competition Authority reasoned that, even if the reduction in travel agent commissions led to a reduction in the number of viable travel agents, this did not mean that competition between travel agents was also distorted. While the reduction in commissions may have affected the welfare of travel agents, it did not follow that there was corresponding damage to the consumer or the competitive process. Further, there was also a good deal of evidence to suggest that, prior to the reduction in commissions, travel agent numbers were declining anyway, while demand for travel had increased. This suggested that other, more efficient forms of ticket distribution had evolved. Finally, the Competition Authority noted that travel agents could in any event charge additional service fees for the expertise they provide to consumers (which many in fact now do). In these circumstances, the Competition

[18] See RJ Holleman, *A Response: Government Guidelines Should Not Be Issued In Connection With Standards Setting*, comments to the Federal Trade Commission Competition and Intellectual Property Law and Policy in the Knowledge-Based Economy, available at http://www.ftc.gov/os/comments/intelpropertycomments.

[19] See G Noll, "'Buyer Power' and Economic Policy" (2005) 72 *Antitrust Law Journal* 589–624, 591 ("Asymmetric treatment of monopoly and monopsony has no basis in economic analysis.").

[20] Case COM/15/02, *Reduction In Travel Agent Commissions By Aer Lingus plc*, June 10, 2003.

Authority found no basis in law or fact for treating the commission reductions as abusive.

The Competition Authority went on, however, to allude to the potential for abusive conduct. It stated that the exercise of monopsony power requires "that it [is] correlated with market power on the seller side."[21] It added that "a firm with market power on both sides can reduce the price it pays for inputs—the services of travel agents—in order to reduce overall supply of airline tickets sold so that prices to the consumer can be raised."[22]

The comment that excessively low prices may be an abuse if linked to other conduct was also made in the OFT's decision in *Bettercare II*,[23] which concerned the alleged payment of excessively low fees for suppliers of residential home services. The OFT rejected the abusive pricing allegation, adding that, "[i]n the absence of barriers to exit by suppliers from the relevant market, a purchaser which paid excessively low prices would be unable to obtain supply beyond the short term even if it was a monopsonist."[24] This was on the basis that excessively low purchase prices will normally be self-correcting. But the OFT added that excessively low prices might constitute an abuse in "exceptional circumstances,"[25] such as where the dominant buyer price discriminated between sellers.

Statements that monopsony purchasing may be abusive in exceptional circumstances are perhaps valid as an overall comment. But, if such behaviour is abusive only when carried out in conjunction with other seller-side conduct, such as excessive pricing or discrimination, it is difficult to see what buyer power abuses add to the existing law. Price discrimination may be an abuse contrary to Article 82(c) (though there are a large number of valid reasons why a buyer or seller would apply different terms among similarly-situated trading parties). Output limitation and price rises may also, if they are significant enough, constitute excessive pricing, contrary to Article 82(a).[26]

Although the definition of what constitutes an excessive price is far from clear, a rule of law which said that it would be an abuse for a dominant buyer to reduce payments to sellers in an effort to limit output and reduce prices would be even more precarious. It would need to be specified at what point output reductions/price increases that do not give rise to excessive pricing nevertheless constitute an abusive exercise of monopsony purchasing power. This would be even more uncertain, and open to divergent interpretations, than determining whether final selling prices are in themselves excessive. In other words, if monopsony purchasing could be an abuse even in circumstances where prices on the selling market do not rise to the level of excessive prices, the law would be even more complicated and unclear. At the same time, if

---

[21] *Ibid.*, para. 2.13.
[22] *Ibid.*
[23] Case No. CE/1836–02, *BetterCare Group Ltd/North & West Belfast Health & Social Services Trust*, December 18, 2003.
[24] *Ibid.*, para. 56.
[25] *Ibid.*
[26] See Ch. 12 (Excessive Prices).

monopsony purchasing is only contrary to Article 82 EC if it results in excessive pricing on the selling market, this adds nothing of substance to the existing law.

13.3 UNFAIR AND EXPLOITATIVE CONTRACT TERMS

13.3.1 Reasons For A Limited Case Law

Differences between competition law and consumer protection. Unfair and exploitative contract terms can be broadly described as unfair trading conditions. However, the precise definition of such terms is ambiguous, since, outside the area of excessive pricing, cases that raise issues of exploitative abuse have been an extreme rarity under Article 82 EC. The lack of non-price cases on exploitative abuses probably reflects a number of considerations. First, most Member States have long had their own rules of contract and tort law against "unfair" terms.[27] While the individual details vary, many of these laws seek to protect consumers from what might be regarded as unconscionable terms.

Second, a number of specific rules have been enacted at EU level to prevent unfair terms for consumers. These include EU legislation governing unfair terms,[28] as well as specific examples of such terms in the areas of doorstep selling, consumer credit, package travel, timeshare contracts, distance selling, sale of goods and guarantees, electronic commerce, and injunctions.[29]

Third, specific of competition law legislation prohibits certain unfair terms. The best example concerns the types of restrictions that are permissible for a licensor to impose on a licensee under the Technology Transfer Block Exemption Regulation (e.g., mandatory assignment or grant-back clauses).[30] Indeed, it is notable that many of the

---

[27] For example, the German Act Against Unfair Practices Act Against Unfair Practices (*Gesetz gegen den unlauteren Wettbewerb* (UWG)) sets forth a number of "ethical" standards for the conduct of a trade or business. Firms are obliged for example to advertise their products and services truthfully to consumers and to refrain from certain forms of comparative advertising or terms (e.g., "the best" or "the largest") that cannot be clearly verified. Measures also exist to protect competitors, such as unfairly disparaging rivals' offerings. Similar laws exist in other Member States (e.g., France). For a detailed review, see *Unfair Commercial Practices: An Analysis of the Existing National Laws on Unfair Commercial Practices Between Business and Consumers in the New Member States*, and *An Analysis of the Existing National Laws on Unfair Commercial Practices Between Business and Consumers in the New Member States with regard to the Directive on Unfair Commercial Practices*, both coordinated by C van Dam, British Institute of International and Comparative Law, London, available at www.europa.eu.int/comm/consumers/cons_int/safe_shop/fair_bus_pract/ucp_general_report_enpdf and www.europa.eu.int/comm/consumers/cons_int/safe_shop/fair_bus_pract/ucp_national_report_enpdf.

[28] See Council Directive 93/13/EEC of April 5, 1993, on unfair terms in consumer contracts, OJ 1993 L 95/29.

[29] See generally C Quigley, *European Community Contract Law* (London, Kluwer Law International, 1997).

[30] See Commission Regulation (EC) No 772/2004 of 27 April 2004 on the application of Article 81(3) of the Treaty to categories of technology transfer agreements, OJ 2004 L 123/11 (hereinafter "Technology Transfer Block Exemption"); Commission Notice—Guidelines on the application of Article 81 of the EC Treaty to technology transfer agreements, OJ 2004 C 101/2. Article 5, provides that the block exemption shall not apply to "(a) any direct or indirect obligation on the licensee to grant

clauses in licensing agreements condemned in past case law are now expressly mentioned under Technology Transfer Block Exemption. For example, the contractual terms in *Tetra Pak II*, whereby Tetra Pak reserved for itself the intellectual property rights in any modifications to its equipment undertaken by the user, do not benefit from the Technology Transfer Block Exemption (though individual exemption might still be possible).[31] The same applies to clauses preventing the licensee from challenging the validity of the licensed technology (subject to the licensor's right to reserve the right to terminate the agreement in this instance) and clauses between non-competing undertakings preventing the licensee from exploiting its own technology or carrying out independent research and development.[32] Hardcore restrictions in vertical and horizontal licences may also be abusive, at least where the issue is that a dominant licensor is exploiting a licensee.

Fourth, Regulation 1/2003 expressly permits Member States to apply national laws that "predominantly pursue an objective different from that pursued by Articles 81 and 82 of the Treaty."[33] There is no obligation that such laws should be interpreted consistently with Article 82 EC (although there may be issues if the application of such laws cause harm to consumer welfare). And it is almost certainly easier for Member States to apply these laws than to treat unfair terms under the constraints imposed by Article 82 EC (e.g., proving the existence of a dominant position, abuse, absence of proportionate business justification, and effect on intra-Community trade).

A final important point is that unfair terms have no *necessary* connection with harm to competition, even if, in a broad sense, they both concern aspects of consumer welfare. The commonly-understood objectives of competition law are much narrower in scope

an exclusive licence to the licensor or to a third party designated by the licensor in respect of its own severable improvements to or its own new applications of the licensed technology; (b) any direct or indirect obligation on the licensee to assign, in whole or in part, to the licensor or to a third party designated by the licensor, rights to its own severable improvements to or its own new applications of the licensed technology." Article 4(1) of the Technology Transfer Block Exemption provides that the following clauses cannot benefit from exemption in agreements between non-competitors: (a) minimum resale price maintenance; (b) certain passive sales restrictions on licensees; (c) restrictions on intra-channel sales in selective distribution; (d) bans on spare parts sales by OEM licensees; and (e) restrictions of active and passive sales to end users by selective distributors operating at the retail level. Article 4(1) of the Technology Transfer Block Exemption provides that the following clauses cannot benefit from exemption in agreements between competitors: (a) restrictions in agreements between competitors include resale price maintenance (maximum and minimum); (b) reciprocal output limitations (unilateral limitations on licensees are, however, allowed); (c) certain market or customer allocations; and (d) restrictions on licensees' ability to exploit their own technology or on the parties' ability to carry out research and development.

[31] Technology Transfer Block Exemption, Article 5, provides that the block exemption shall not apply to "(a) any direct or indirect obligation on the licensee to grant an exclusive licence to the licensor or to a third party designated by the licensor in respect of its own severable improvements to or its own new applications of the licensed technology; (b) any direct or indirect obligation on the licensee to assign, in whole or in part, to the licensor or to a third party designated by the licensor, rights to its own severable improvements to or its own new applications of the licensed technology."

[32] *Ibid.*

[33] See Council Regulation 1/2003 on the implementation of the rules on competition laid down in Articles 81 and 82 of the Treaty, OJ 2003 L 1/1, Article 3(3).

than the wider consumer protection goals that are sometimes pursued by the EU legislature and national governments. Article 82 EC is primarily concerned with the need to "protect competition in the market as a means of enhancing consumer welfare and ensuring an efficient allocation of resources."[34] The primary means by which that objective is pursued is to prohibit, and, if necessary, remedy, exclusionary conduct that gives rise to scope for consumer harm. In limited cases, Article 82(a) may also challenge the direct exercise of market power through excessive prices or unfair contract terms. But the essential legitimacy of this intervention is limited to conduct that can be shown to lead to an actual or likely reduction in consumer welfare.

In contrast, most consumer protection laws pursue a wider agenda that has no necessary connection with a reduction in consumer welfare (but nor is there any necessary contradiction between the two regimes either).[35] For example, EU legislation on timeshare contracts was primarily enacted to prevent opportunism by individuals willing to exploit linguistic difficulties and differences in national property laws.[36] It has nothing to do with the exercise of market power. Similarly, rules on consumer credit and distance-selling are more concerned with ensuring that contractual terms are clear, transparent, and uniform rather than preventing conduct that resides in market power. Of course, competition law should have consumer welfare at heart, and consumer laws should have the need to maintain effective competition at heart. Both sets of rules must also be mindful that excessive regulation, whatever its form, is also likely to harm consumer welfare. Markets should not only be free of abusive behaviour, and unfair trading terms, but they should also be free of undue regulation.[37]

13.3.2 Legal Test For Abusive And Unfair Contract Terms

Earlier decisions somewhat vague. The dearth of case law on abusive and unfair trading terms has rendered it difficult to define a precise test for unfair contract terms. In particular, older case law dealing with the issue does not establish a principled test for determining when specific contract terms violate Article 82 EC. A broad and unsophisticated test based on the concept of the "necessity" of the relevant contract term

---

[34] See Commissioner N Kroes, "*European Competition Policy—Delivering Better Markets and Better Choices*," European Consumer and Competition Day, London, September 15, 2005, available at http://www.europa.eu.int/comm/competition/speeches/index_speeches_by_the_commissioner.html.

[35] Some US commentators argue that the consumer protection and antitrust policies pursued by the US Federal Trade Commission share common ground. See, e.g., TB Leary, "Competition Law and Consumer Protection Law: Two Wings of the Same House" (2005) 72(3) *Antitrust Law Journal* 1147 (arguing that competition law focuses on supply side distortions and consumer protection law focuses on demand side distortions, with the result that both legal regimes have common philosophical roots and both can be analysed in economic terms). See also CO Hobbs, "Antitrust and Consumer Protection: Exploring the Common Ground" (2005) 72(3) *Antitrust Law Journal* 1153.

[36] See Directive 94/47/EC of the European Parliament and the Council of 26 October 1994 on the protection of purchasers in respect of certain aspects of contracts relating to the purchase of the right to use immovable properties on a timeshare basis, OJ 1994 L 280/83.

[37] See J Vickers, "The future of UK consumer regulation: a practical proposal," speech to the Trading Standards Institute conference, Brighton, June 21, 2005, available at http://www.oft.gov uk/News/Speeches+and+articles/2005/sp0405.htm.

was advanced in *BRT/SABAM*.[38] The case concerned the application of Article 82 EC to contracts concluded between SABAM (the Belgian Association of Authors, Composers, and Publishers) and two authors. The unfair conditions alleged by the applicants were that SABAM required the global assignment of all copyrights, both present and future, and that the rights assigned would continue to be exercised exclusively by SABAM for five years following the withdrawal of a member. The Court of Justice suggested, without expressing a final view, that the post-term reservation of copyrights would probably be abusive because it was not "absolutely necessary for the attainment of the object of the contract"[39] and "thus encroach[ed] unfairly upon a member's freedom to exercise his copyright."[40]

A subsequent Commission decision in *GEMA II* elaborated in more detail on the concept of abusive contractual terms.[41] GEMA, a German copyright collection society, added a clause to its statutes providing that the assignment of rights to GEMA precluded the beneficiary from making grants either directly or indirectly of a share of his/her revenue to parties who had entered into collective agreements with GEMA, or with other collecting societies, where said parties, when using the GEMA repertoire, would "favour unjustifiably" certain works of the beneficiary. The reason for this clause was to prevent discrimination if the user directly or indirectly (i.e., via an intermediary (e.g. a subsidiary)) shared in the GEMA member's royalties for the work used.

The Commission raised no objection this amendment, but made a number of observations on abusive contractual terms. First, the Commission stated that, following *BRT/SABAM*, the decisive factors in a copyright collection case was whether the clause in question exceeded the limits absolutely necessary for effective protection (the "indispensability test") and whether they limit the individual copyright holder's freedom to dispose of his work no more than need be (the "equity test"). Second, regarding indispensability, the Commission concluded that it was indispensable that GEMA should have joint, uniform control of the rights assigned it and that non-discrimination was essential, since GEMA's membership also included users of music in the guise of publishers, whose interests often coincide with those of manufacturers and broadcasting companies, but not with those of authors. Third, despite GEMA's acknowledged interest in the uniform determination of charges, the clause in question would constitute an abuse if it was not indispensable, or excessive, i.e., inequitable. Finally, regarding the equity test, the Commission concluded that GEMA acted proportionately, since it restricted itself to prohibiting the beneficiaries from granting shares of royalty revenue

---

[38] Case 127/73, *Belgische Radio en Televisie v SV SABAM and NV Fonior* [1974] ECR 313.

[39] *Ibid.*, para. 1.

[40] *Ibid.*, para. 15. Regarding "encroachment," the Court proposed a general balancing test of the various competing interests in copyright collection cases ("[A]ccount must be taken of all the relevant interests, for the purpose of ensuring a balance between the requirement of maximum freedom for authors, composers, and publishers to dispose of their works and that of the effective management of their rights by an undertaking which in practice they avoid joining....[A]ccount must however be taken of the fact that an undertaking of the type envisaged is an association whose object it is to protect the rights and interests of its individual members against...major exploiters of musical material.") (paras 8–9).

[41] *GEMA II*, OJ 1982 L 94/12. See also *GEMA I*, OJ 1971 L 134/15.

to users only where the purpose was to favour certain works of the beneficiaries. The mere fact that a user directly or indirectly shared in GEMA members' royalties for the work used was not sufficient to activate the clause: evidence of unjustified discrimination was required. The Commission considered that the clause therefore struck an appropriate balance between the overall collective interests of the members and the freedom of users to enter into cooperative arrangements with GEMA members.

Although the two-stage test based on "indispensability" and "equity" offered some useful indicators of what might constitute an abusive contractual term, significant uncertainty remained regarding the detailed application of these concepts. In particular, it was not clear what the "necessity" of a term to a contract meant, what considerations were relevant to the assessment of "equity," and whether further balancing based on the principle of proportionality was required where a clause was necessary but raised equitable concerns. Moreover, the Community institutions' comments were mainly made in the context of the very specific arrangements that govern copyright collecting societies, where the interests of the society and its members have closer alignment than in the case of most other commercial contracts. Guidance on the treatment of different clauses in other industries was therefore limited.

Further elaboration in subsequent cases. *Tetra Pak II* represents the most comprehensive review by the Community institutions of a series of onerous contractual conditions governing the lease, purchase, and use of machines and consumables offered by a dominant carton manufacturer.[42] The case concerned a cumulative series of abuses, including measures directed at excluding rival firms (e.g., predatory pricing). In terms of exploitative contractual terms, the following terms contained in contracts for the sale or lease of Tetra Pak equipment were found to be abusive by the Commission (and confirmed by the Community Courts on appeal):

1. An absolute right of control over the equipment configuration which prohibited the buyer from adding accessories to the machine, making modifications to the machine, and adding or removing anything to or from it, and from moving the machine. The Commission concluded that these obligations had "no connection with the purpose of the contract," "deprived the purchaser of certain aspects of his property rights," and had the "effect of making the customer totally dependent on Tetra Pak's equipment and services;"[43]

2. Clauses concerning the operation and maintenance of equipment, which gave Tetra Pak the exclusive right to maintain and repair equipment, the exclusive right to supply spare parts, and an obligation on the user to inform Tetra Pak of any improvements or modifications to the equipment and to grant Tetra Pak ownership of any resulting intellectual property rights. The Commission found that these clauses effectively bound the customer completely to Tetra Pak and

[42] *Tetra Pak II*, OJ 1992 L 72/1, on appeal Case T-83/91, *Tetra Pak v Commission* [1994] ECR II-755.

[43] *Ibid.*, paras. 105–7.

precluded, except in limited instances, any possibility of having maintenance and repair services provided by the user's own technical staff;[44]

3. Clauses requiring the transfer of ownership or use of equipment, including the need for the customer to obtain Tetra Pak's agreement before selling or transferring the use of the equipment, reserving to Tetra Pak the right to repurchase the equipment at a pre-arranged fixed price, and the need to ensure that any subsequent vendor also assumed the same obligations. The Commission found that these clauses limited the purchaser's potential use of goods for which Tetra Pak had supposedly granted it full ownership. Not only did they have no connection with the purpose of the purchase contract, but they were also distortive by their very nature by granting Tetra Pak sole ownership of the rights to any improvements made by the user;[45]

4. Long leases ranging from three years to nine years. The Commission found that this duration was excessive and therefore constituted a further abuse. In particular, the nine-year term equalled or exceeded the technological (if not physical) life of the machines in question. But the Commission added that the minimum term of three years should also be considered to constitute an abuse in so far as, in a sector in which there is rapid technological development, it unduly bound the leaseholder to Tetra Pak;[46] and

5. Over and above the usual damages and interest clauses, Tetra Pak reserved the right to impose a penalty on any leaseholder who infringed any of its obligations under the contract, the amount of such penalty being fixed at Tetra Pak's discretion, up to a maximum threshold, according to the gravity of the case (*in casu* US$ 100,000, which represented between 20–80% of the cost of a new machine). Not surprisingly, the Commission found that this clause made the system intended to prevent Tetra Pak equipment from being transferred without its knowledge "completely airtight" and was therefore abusive.[47]

---

[44] *Ibid.*, para. 108.

[45] *Ibid.*, para. 115.

[46] *Ibid.*, paras 140–41. See also Case 247/86, *Société alsacienne et lorraine de telecommunications et d'electronique (Alsatel) v SA Novasam* [1988] ECR 5987. Alsatel, a telecommunications equipment vendor with a leading share in a region of France, imposed clauses in its standard form contracts requiring, *inter alia*, lengthy rental terms and penalties in the event of early termination. Novasam, a customer, terminated before expiry three contracts for the rental and maintenance of Alsatel phone equipment. Alsatel sought to recover a penalty, and in its defence Novasam argued that some of the clauses in the contracts were unlawful. Alsatel required contracts to be signed for the rental and maintenance of equipment for 15 years, but the contract was automatically extended for a period equivalent to its initial duration if, due to any modifications to the installation, the initial rent was increased by 25% or more. In addition, for changes, moves, extensions and any other modifications to the service, Alsatel customers were not permitted to turn to another supplier, and thus Alsatel could fix the price of any modifications unilaterally. The case did not, however, elaborate on whether these clauses were abusive, since Alsatel was not considered to be dominant in the relevant equipment installation and rental market in France.

[47] *Tetra Pak II*, OJ 1992 L 72/1, on appeal Case T-83/91, *Tetra Pak v Commission* [1994] ECR II-755, para. 127.

Another example of particularly onerous terms is *AAMS*.[48] AAMS, a body forming part of the financial administration of the Italian State, engaged in the production, import, export and wholesale distribution of manufactured tobaccos. It held the exclusive right to produce manufactured tobacco in Italy, which it did both on its own account and on behalf of rivals. In addition, AAMS engaged in the import, introduction into the country by way of intra-Community acquisition, distribution, and sale of manufactured tobacco. The Commission found that various clauses in AAMS's distribution contracts were unfair and abusive. Clauses included: (1) a time limit for the introduction of new cigarette brands onto the Italian market (i.e., a bi-annual limitation); (2) a limit on the number of new brands allowed on the Italian market; (3) maximum monthly limits of cigarettes allowed on the Italian market; (4) very restrictive terms for the increase in monthly limits; (5) an unnecessary obligation to affix the Italian State monopoly abbreviation on each package; and (6) quality controls that were wholly unnecessary. These clauses were reinforced by unilateral action by AAMS to limit the possibilities for additional distribution in Italy.

The decisions in *Tetra Pak II* and *AAMS* are useful in that they added a new dimension to the test for abusive contractual terms. The basic principle applied is that the term had to be reasonably necessary in view of the object of the contract. But, as a second stage, the Community institutions asked whether the term was "reasonable," bearing in mind the legitimate interests of the dominant firm, its trading parties, and ultimately consumers. The usefulness of these precedents is, however, also limited. In the first place, the vast majority of the terms used by Tetra Pak and AAMS were onerous in the extreme: it is notable for example that the defendants made little effort to defend them on appeal. It was not therefore clear how less onerous, but nonetheless potentially unreasonable, terms would be treated. Second, many of the terms were objectionable not only because they exploited the customers, but also because they had the effect of denying rival firms sufficient customers to gain economies of scale and scope in order to mount a more effective challenge to Tetra Pak's near-monopoly and AAMS' actual monopoly. The exploitative abuses thus reinforced the exclusionary abuses found by the Community institutions. Finally, and perhaps more importantly, because the facts of the case were egregious, the Community institutions did not feel the need to elaborate on how the "reasonableness" criterion was to be judged in other cases. It was not clear for example what competing interests were relevant, how these should be weighed, and whether otherwise legitimate reasons for a clause could be subject to an additional requirement of proportionality (i.e., that a less restrictive clause would have been equally effective).

Towards a more objective test. In *DSD*,[49] the Commission articulated a more comprehensive definition of unfair terms outside the egregious facts of *Tetra Pak II*. It found that Der Gruene Punkt-Duales System Deutschland AG (DSD), the creator the "Green Dot" recycling trademark, had abused its dominant position in the market for the organisation, collection, and recycling of sales packaging in Germany, essentially

[48] *Amministrazione Autonoma dei Monopoli di Stato*, OJ 1998 L 252/47, upheld on appeal in Case T-139/98 *Amministrazione Autonoma dei Monopoli di Stato v Commission*, [2001] ECR II-3413.

[49] *DSD*, OJ 2001 L 166/1.

because it charged licence fees in circumstances where the trade mark was not actually used. DSD operates a nationwide system for the collection and recovery of sales packaging designed to meet the requirements of the German Packaging Ordinance. DSD is the only undertaking in Germany operating such an extensive system. Its system is termed a "dual" system as the collection and recovery of packaging is effected outside the public waste disposal system and is operated by a private undertaking under a service agreement with DSD.

DSD is financed by fees from undertakings who become members of the system by signing a trade mark agreement, permitting them to use the Green Dot trade mark on their sales packaging, and exempting them from the obligation to take back such packaging, once used, to the actual point of sale. The principal clauses of relevance in this agreement are: (1) DSD is the owner of the Green Dot trade mark and grants manufacturers and distributors the right to use this on their packaging; (2) DSD undertakes to effect the collection, sorting and recovery of used packaging so as to exempt users from their take-back and recovery obligations under the German packaging Ordinance; (3) the user is obliged to use the trade mark on all registered packaging for domestic consumption, although DSD may release it from this obligation; (4) the user has to pay DSD a licence fee for all packaging bearing the Green Dot mark, with exceptions requiring a separate written agreement; and (5) the licence fee may be unilaterally adjusted by DSD.

The Commission primarily focused on the clauses of the trade mark agreement that required the licensee to pay DSD a fee in respect of all of the packaging distributed by it in Germany bearing the Green Dot mark. The Commission noted that DSD links the fee payable under the agreement not to use of the service exempting the other party from its take-back and recovery obligations (which is the service DSD actually provides), but solely to the use of the Green Dot mark on sales packaging (which did not necessarily relate to a service provided by DSD). The Commission found that an abuse occurs where an undertaking is obliged to pay a dominant firm a fee for the entire quantity of its packaging activities regardless of whether they use the dominant firm's waste collection system. To use a rival system, users would have to pay an extra fee, creating an additional financial burden, whereas, if they used the DSD system solely, there would be no double payment.

In terms of its legal reasoning, the Commission classified DSD's clauses as imposing unreasonable prices and commercial terms contrary to Article 82(a). According to the Commission, unfair commercial terms exist "where an undertaking in a dominant position fails to comply with the principle of proportionality."[50] In particular, an abuse arises where the price charged for a service is clearly disproportionate to the cost of supplying it. DSD incurs only minimal costs authorising sales packaging to be marketed with the Green Dot mark. Its costs are incurred in operating a system for collecting, sorting, and recycling sales packaging. In these circumstances, the Commission considered that DSD imposed unreasonable prices whenever the quantity of packaging bearing the Green Dot mark was greater than the quantity of packaging

[50] *Ibid.*, para. 112.

making use of the exemption clause. Although DSD does allow for the possibility of exceptions, the Commission concluded that the contract was formulated in such a way that the decision to grant the exception need not be linked to any predetermined criteria, thus had unlimited discretion. Thus, as long as DSD "makes the licence fee dependent solely on the use of the mark, it is imposing unfair prices and commercial terms on undertakings which do not use the exemption service or which use it for only some of their sales packaging."[51]

DSD argued that the clause governing the payment of fees was justified by the need to protect its trade mark. It argued that the trade mark necessarily loses its identifying power where it is carried on packaging that is to be collected by a competing system. The more packaging carries the trade mark without belonging to the system, the greater the loss of identifying power, which could lead to the trade mark's identifying power being weakened to such an extent that large sections of the public no longer understood it as indicating exemption from the take-back obligation and the possibility that it could be collected by the DSD system.

The Commission rejected this argument, reasoning that: (1) the Green Dot trade mark does not imply that collection by means of the DSD system constitutes the only collection possibility; (2) consumers' decisions to convey any particular item of packaging for recycling by a competitor of the DSD system is influenced by a number of factors (e.g. acquired disposal habits, attitudes, type of packaging, product use, accessibility of the point of sale, take-back incentives): the essential function of the Green Dot trade mark is therefore fulfilled when it signals to consumers that they have the *option* of having the packaging collected by DSD; and (3) it was not practicable to establish a system whereby only a partial quantity of the packaging should carry the trade mark, since the consumer may not decide on the form of collection until after purchasing the goods in question. But this issue is strongly contested on appeal by DSD who argues that sales packaging carrying the Green Dot trade mark is, in the mind of the final customer, firmly linked to the packaging waste disposal service established by DSD.

The Commission's detailed treatment of abusive contract terms in *DSD* usefully clarifies the scope of Article 82(a) in such cases. The Commission maintains the view set out in earlier cases: is the clause central to the object of the contract? But, as a second stage, it considers whether it is proportionate, bearing in mind the parties' respective interests. Although proportionality is more art than science, its meaning is reasonably well-established in EC competition law. In basic terms, it requires a balancing between the object of the contract, the terms of the contract, and the contractor's justification for those terms. Thus, the clause should: (1) have a legitimate objective other than consumer exploitation; (2) be "effective," that is to say, capable of achieving the legitimate goal; (3) be "necessary" in the sense that there is no alternative that is equally effective in achieving the legitimate goal but less with a restrictive or less exploitative effect; and (4) be "proportionate," in the sense that the legitimate objective

[51] *Ibid.*, para. 113.

pursued by the dominant firm should not be outweighed by its exploitative effect on the trading party in question.

A more circumspect view of unfair terms? Recent Commission decisions post-modernisation illustrate perhaps a more circumspect view of the role of Article 82(a) in assessing the fairness of contractual terms. In *Sequential Use of Coupons*, the Commission considered whether a standard airline ticket contract term which requires the sequential use of coupons in flight travel constituted an unfair contract term contrary to Article 82(a).[52] Sequential use restrictions stipulate that a passenger purchasing an indirect flight at a lower price than a direct flight must, in order to avail of the lower price, use the successive flight coupons fully and in sequence. The complainant purchased a British Airways airline ticket from Venice to Dar Es Salaam, via London. However, she travelled by private jet from Italy to London, thus not using the first portion of her flight coupon. On arrival in London, she attempted to board the second leg of her purchased ticket—the flight from London to Dar Es Salaam—but was refused because she had not used her ticket coupons in sequence as she had not availed of the first leg of the ticket. She complained, *inter alia,* that the sequential use of coupons term was unfair and unreasonable and constituted an abuse of British Airway's alleged dominant position.

The Commission dismissed the complaint on the basis that British Airways was not in a dominant position in the relevant product market. However, even if British Airways had been found to be in a dominant position, the Commission felt that the sequential use of coupons clause did not constitute an abusive contract term. It referred to the findings of the Office of Fair Trading (OFT), which had already considered the clause from the perspective of Community legislation on unfair contract terms.[53] The OFT considered that so long as customers were made aware of the need to use the flight coupons in sequence, the sequential use of coupons did not amount to an unfair term. In addition, it noted that "different ticket configurations may constitute different products, each with its own price."[54] Reference was also made to the opinion of the Commission Directorates-General for Health and Consumer Protection, and Energy and Transport, in the context of their Consultation Paper on Airlines' Contracts with Passengers (2002). This document also concluded that sequential use restrictions are acceptable so long as the customer is made aware of the strict conditions.[55] The Commission also noted that consumers could protect themselves by purchasing flexible tickets or tickets that allow for refunds. For these reasons, the Commission felt that the sequential use of coupons in airline tickets did not constitute an unfair term.[56]

---

[52] See Case COMP/A.38763/D2, *Sequential Use Of Coupons*, communication pursuant to Article 7(1) of Commission Regulation (EC) 773/2004, July 14, 2005 (on file with authors) ("*Sequential Use of Coupons*").

[53] See Council Directive 93/13/EEC of April 5, 1993, on unfair terms in consumer contracts, OJ 1993 L 95/29.

[54] See UK action under Council Directive 93/13/EEC of April 5, 1993 (explanatory note), Airline Flight Contracts RP 1724 September 2000, p.2.

[55] *Sequential Use of Coupons*, above, para. 21.

[56] *Sequential Use of Coupons*, above, para. 37.

The Commission's conclusion illustrates a more nuanced and circumspect approach to the issue of abusive contractual terms than the legal paternalism that sometimes characterised earlier decisions. The clause at issue was necessary to allow airlines to efficiently price discriminate between users who wanted a cheaper, indirect flight, and those who were willing to pay more for a direct flight. Such price discrimination increased competition between airlines, since it allowed airlines operating from different hubs to compete with direct flights from other hubs by offering a lower-priced indirect flight option. Sequential use rules were a means to prevent arbitrage between the discriminated customers, which was essential if low prices and greater choice to customers using an indirect flight were to be maintained. In the absence of sequential use rules, airlines would probably be forced to increase fares or discontinue or reduce services on indirect routes. Airlines adopt different price strategies to maximise overall revenue, and in doing so, are able to make capacity on less convenient routings available at a cheaper price. To remove sequential use rules would have had negative effects on consumer choice, prices, and competition.

The Commission also considered that consumers' interests were adequately protected. Airlines did not have an unqualified right to refuse passengers from boarding where coupons have not been used sequentially. Multi-lateral agreements on international air travel provide that if a passenger wishes to change any part of his or her transportation, he or she should contact the airline in advance. The fare would then be recalculated on the basis of the changed itinerary and the passenger would be given the choice of accepting the new price or maintaining the original transportation ticketed. In addition, if a passenger advises the airline in advance that he or she will not be using a flight, the airline will not cancel the return or onward flight reservations. Again, the fare would have to be recalculated. If a change is required due to *force majeure*, the airline must use reasonable efforts to transport the passenger to his or her next stopover or final destination, without recalculation of the fare.

Summary. The legal test for exploitative non-price terms, in so far as one can be verbalised, involves several stages. First, the clause in question must be connected with the purpose of the contract and necessary for some efficiency generated by the contract. For example, in the copyright collecting society cases, it was obviously necessary and efficient for the copyright owners to assign certain rights to the society to allow for exploitation of the package of rights and the collection of fees. In contrast, if a clause has no benefit at all for consumers (e.g., where it gives a public utility power to enter premises without permission or to cut off essential services without notice, or grants immunity from liability for negligence), an abuse might be presumed. Second, if it is to be treated as objectionable, the clause in question must harm the other trading party, usually by requiring it to forego a right that it would otherwise have under competitive conditions. An example might include a non-reciprocal obligation to cross-licence intellectual property rights royalty-free to the dominant company. Finally, assuming that the clause is necessary to achieve some efficiency related to the contract, but also harms the trading party in question, issues of reasonableness and proportionality may be decisive. Such issues necessarily involve questions of judgment and policy rather than precision, but the use of proportionality in EC competition law is well established.

13.3.3 Conclusion

The limited role of Article 82 EC in respect of unfair terms. Article 82(a) is neither a piece of consumer protection legislation nor a code of conduct for trading standards. Such objectives are best pursued by specific legislation with a broader remit than the relatively narrow consumer welfare concerns that underpin Article 82 EC. Article 82(a) is not, however, redundant as a basis for assessing abusive contractual clauses. In certain circumstances, the existence of market power, and the degree of independence of action that dominance confers, may lead to the imposition of contractual terms that could not be imposed by a non-dominant firm. In other words, if a clause could not be imposed under competitive conditions, it may well be abusive. It bears emphasis, however, that such cases have been an extreme rarity under Article 82 EC.

One area where Article 82 EC is likely to continue to play a role in practice concerns abusive clauses in technology licensing agreements. Although the Technology Transfer Block Exemption sets out the most important rules in this regard, a small number of clauses may be problematic because they allow a dominant licensor to take advantage of its position to extract onerous terms from a licensee. The principles applicable in this regard are essentially the same as for abusive contractual clauses generally. Thus, it would need to be shown that the clause bears no reasonable relationship to the object of the contract, that it requires the licensee to forego a right that it would otherwise have under competitive conditions, and that the clause is neither reasonable nor proportionate bearing in mind the respective interests of the licensee and licensor. In essence, objectionable clauses are onerous, one-sided, and unfair.[57]

Beyond the above examples, it remains to be seen what role Article 82(a) will continue to play in respect of unfair contractual terms. In the first place, the Commission has stated that its review of Article 82 EC is intended to shift the focus away from nebulous concepts such as "fairness" and towards a narrower appreciation of Article 82 EC that is firmly rooted in consumer welfare objectives and coherent theories of competitive harm.[58] Second, the fact the Member States are expressly permitted under the modernisation reforms to apply laws that pursue a predominantly different purpose to Article 82 EC makes even clearer the distinction between consumer protection and

[57] Owners of patents that are essential for a standard may of course agree with any other owner of patents that are essential for the same standard that they will reciprocally license one another, royalty-free, or with one party paying the other only a net sum resulting from off-setting one royalty against the other. That however is merely a book-keeping arrangement, which does not entitle either party to pass on or sub-license the rights which it is receiving to any other company. Similarly, cross-licensing agreements are generally useful and efficiency-enhancing—in particular where they are non-exclusive and contain no obvious restriction—and are not objectionable as such. Both of these situations raise different issues to a dominant licensor's insisting on receiving a licence royalty-free from a licensee.

[58] See Commissioner N Kroes, "Preliminary Thoughts on Policy Review of Article 82," speech at the Fordham Corporate Law Institute, New York, September 23, 2005 ("I am aware that it is often suggested that—unlike Section 2 of the Sherman Act—Article 82 is intrinsically concerned with 'fairness' and therefore not focused primarily on consumer welfare. As far as I am concerned, I think that competition policy evolves as our understanding of economics evolves. In days gone by, 'fairness' played a prominent role in Section 2 enforcement in a way that is no longer the case. I don't see why a similar development could not take place in Europe.").

trading standards laws on the one hand, and competition law on the other. Finally, the EU and national legislatures have themselves been increasingly active in adopting specific legislation aimed at setting out common minimum standards for clauses that most affect consumers in practice. The proliferation of such legislation creates an even stronger case for saying that competition law, and in particular Article 82 EC, should play a residual role in respect of unfair contractual terms.

Chapter 14

EFFECT ON TRADE

14.1 INTRODUCTION

Basic role of the effect on trade concept. The effect on trade criterion plays purely a jurisdictional function: it determines whether EC competition law or national competition law is applicable to a particular case. Whereas Article 82 EC applies only to practices that are capable of appreciably affecting trade between Member States, national abuse of dominance laws apply to practices that are not capable of having such effects. In other words, Article 82 EC is confined to practices that are capable of having a minimum level of cross-border effects within the Community: national law deals with everything falling short of this.

The effect on trade criterion has assumed greater importance following the Commission's modernisation reforms in 2004, since the enforcement of EC competition law by national courts or competition authorities is triggered by the presence of an effect on intra-Community trade. However, it is arguable that the practical significance of failing this jurisdictional test is limited, in particular in respect of Article 82 EC. In the first place, each Member State now has national competition law provisions which are modelled on Article 82 EC. Thus, a national court or competition authority would be able to review an agreement or practice even if it did not affect intra-Community trade, subject to a sufficient nexus existing with domestic trade.

Further, Article 3(2) of Regulation 1/2003 allows Member States to adopt and apply, within their territory, stricter national abuse of dominance laws than Article 82 EC. This is an important difference from the corresponding provision of Regulation 1/2003 dealing with the parallel application of Article 81 EC, which prevents Member States from applying stricter standards than Article 81 EC under national law. The practical result of this difference in approach is that the effect on trade concept assumes greater importance in the context of Article 81 EC, since the presence of an effect on trade precludes the application of stricter of different standards under national law. In contrast, under Article 82 EC, there is currently scope for the application of stricter national laws even if intra-Community trade is affected.

Broad interpretation of the effect on trade concept under Article 82 EC. Cases analysing in detail the effect on trade concept are rare, but a number of general principles have gained acceptance in the decisional practice and case law of the Community institutions. First, the term "effect" is neutral: the conduct in question merely has to alter the normal flow of trade or cause the market to develop differently from the way it would have developed absent the abuse. The conduct does not necessarily need to have a harmful effect on the market. The effect on trade test is thus distinct from the substantive assessment of whether the purported abuse has a negative effect on consumer welfare.

Second, the concept not only encompasses conduct that is likely to interfere with the pattern of trade between Member States, but also includes conduct that affects the structure of competition inside the Community. This is significant for Article 82 EC cases. Since *ex hypothesi* Article 82 EC cases involve the presence of one or more firms with a position of such economic strength that they have a degree of immunity from the normal disciplining effects that a competitive market entails, their conduct is more often than not likely to affect the competitive structure.

Finally, the concept of effect on trade must be interpreted and applied in light of the EC Treaty objective of the creation of a single market. Thus, the jurisdictional requirement is easily met in cases which involve conduct that tends to foreclose a national market or is capable of partitioning a market between Member States. As such, even if an abuse covers only a single or part of a Member State, it may be capable of appreciably affecting trade between Member States if it generally makes it more difficult for competitors from other Member States to penetrate that market.

Notice on the effect on trade. In 2004, the Commission issued a Notice providing guidance on the effect on trade concept contained in Articles 81 and 82 of the EC Treaty.[1] Although the Notice is not formally binding on Member States, it is intended to give guidance to national courts and competition authorities in their application of the effect on trade concept contained in Articles 81 and 82 EC.[2] Moreover, as a practical matter, the Notice was agreed in consultation with the Member States, which gives it further binding force. The Notice summarises the decisional practice and case law of the Community institutions in relation to the interpretation of the effect on trade concept of Articles 81 and 82 EC, sets out the methodology for the application of the effect on trade concept and provides guidance on the application of this methodology within four contexts: (1) agreements or practices covering several Member States; (2) agreements or practices covering a single Member State; (3) agreements or practices covering only a part of a Member State; and (4) agreements or practices involving undertakings located in third countries.

14.2 BASIC LEGAL CONDITIONS FOR EFFECT ON TRADE

Summary of the relevant conditions. Under the decisional practice and case law of the Community institutions, the following conditions apply to the criterion of effect on trade under Article 82 EC: (1) trade between at least two Member States must be affected; (2) there must be an influence on trade patterns; (3) the influence may be direct, indirect, actual or potential; and (4) the influence must be appreciable. Each of these concepts is examined in detail below.

[1] Commission Notice—Guidelines on the effect on trade concept contained in Articles 81 and 82 of the Treaty, OJ 2004 C101/81 (hereinafter, the "Notice on Effect on Trade").

[2] See Notice on Effect on Trade, para. 3.

Condition #1: trade between Member States. The Community institutions have applied an expansive interpretation to the criterion that a dominant firm must have engaged in conduct which has an effect on "trade" between Member States. The Community Courts have made clear that the definition of trade covers not only the supply of goods, but also of services such as financial services, professional services, employment services, postal services, utility services, health services, the management of artistic copyrights, the performance of individual artists, television broadcasts, and economic aspects of sports.[3] Thus, in simple terms, the term "trade" includes all forms of economic activity.[4] Conceivably, the only excluded activities would be those that are non-economic or non-commercial in ,n surveillance or air space supervision).[5]

The requirement that there must be an effect on trade "between Member States" implies that there must be an impact on cross-border economic activity. This condition is capable of covering a number of situations. The most obvious involves abuses that cover or are implemented in *several* Member States. An abuse that covers a single Member State is also presumed capable of affecting trade between Member States where the abuse makes it more difficult for competitors from other Member States to penetrate that market.[6] Situations which require individual analysis involve abuses that cover only part of a Member State, or involve extra-Community imports and exports. Broadly speaking, such cases are capable of affecting trade between Member States, but may fail on the grounds that the effect on trade between Member States is not appreciable.

Condition #2: an influence on trade patterns. There are two ways of establishing that the abusive conduct of a dominant firm may affect trade between Member States. The

[3] See, e.g., Case 172/80, *Gerhard Züchner v Bayerische Vereinsbank AG* [1981] ECR 2021 (banking and money transmission); Case 45/85, *Verband der Sachversicherer e.V. v Commission* [1987] ECR 405 (insurance); Joined Cases C-215/96 and C-216/96, *Carlo Bagnasco and Others v Banca Popolare di Novara soc. coop. arl.* [1999] ECR 135 (retail banking services); *CNSD*, OJ 1993 L 203/27 (customs agents); Case C-309/99, *J.C.J. Wouters, J.W. Savelbergh and Price Waterhouse Belastingadviseurs BV v Algemene Raad van de Nederlandse Orde van Advocaten* [2002] ECR I-1577 (legal services); Case C-41/90, *Klaus Höfner and Fritz Elser v Macrotron GmbH* [1991] ECR I-1979 (public employment agency); *REIMS II*, OJ 1999 L 275/17 (postal services); *Ijsselcentrale*, OJ 1991 L 28/32 (electricity); Case C-475/99, *Firma Ambulanz Glöckner v Landkreis Südwestpfalz* [2001] ECR I-08089 (ambulance services); Case 127/73, *Belgische Radio en Televisie v SV SABAM and NV Fonior* [1974] ECR 313 (management of artistic copyrights); *RAI/Unitel*, OJ 1978 L 157/39 (opera singers); *Eurovision*, OJ 2000 L 151/18 (TV sports broadcasts); and *Deutsche Telekom AG*, OJ 2003 L 263/9 (telecommunication services).

[4] See Notice on Effect on Trade, para. 19. See also Case 172/80, *Züchner v Bayerische Vereinsbank* [1981] ECR 2021.

[5] In this respect, some commentators suggest that guidance may be derived from the concept of an "undertaking" under Article 82 EC. See, e.g., J Faull, "Effect on Trade Between Member State and Community: Member State Jurisdiction" (1989) *Fordham Corporate Law Institute* 488, where he argues that "[t]he economic activity which must be engaged in for there to be an 'undertaking' within the meaning of Articles 8[1] and 8[2] is almost constitutive of 'trade' for the purposes of those provisions." The definition of an "undertaking" is detailed in Ch. 1 (Introduction, Scope of Application, and Basic Framework).

[6] See Notice on Effect on Trade, para. 93. See also Case 322/81, *NV Nederlandsche Banden Industrie Michelin v Commission* [1983] ECR 3461, para. 51.

first relates to the pattern of trade and the second to the competitive structure. In both cases there is an underlying commitment to the fundamental objective of creating a single market from the territories of the Member States.[7] These principles are reflected in the Commission's Notice on Effect on Trade.

a. ***Alteration to the pattern of inter-State trade.*** The first test developed by the Court of Justice establishes that the condition is satisfied where it is "possible to foresee with a sufficient degree of probability on the basis of a set of objective factors of law or fact that the agreement or practice may have an influence, direct or indirect, actual or potential, on the pattern of trade between Member States in such a way that it might hinder the attainment of the objectives of a single market."[8] This is a neutral test. It is not a condition that trade be restricted or reduced.[9] Nor is it relevant for purposes of jurisdiction that the abuse has in fact caused an increase in trade.[10] In other words, it is sufficient for jurisdiction purposes that the conduct is capable of having a positive or negative effect on the pattern of trade between Member States. Community law jurisdiction is established where the abuse causes trade to develop *differently* from the way it would have developed in the absence of such abuse.[11] This is consistent with the Community Courts' teleological interpretation of the EC Treaty, which aims to create a system of undistorted competition rather than to increase trade as an end in itself.

In practice, a finding of an alteration to the pattern of inter-State trade depends on a number of considerations that, taken individually, may not be decisive. These include, in Article 82 EC cases, the nature of the agreement or practice, the nature of the products covered by the agreement and the existence of regulatory trade barriers.[12] For instance, abuses that partition a market between Member States are regarded, by their nature, as capable of affecting cross-border trade.[13] Similarly, when, by their nature, products are easily traded across borders or are important for undertakings that want to expand their activities geographically, Community law jurisdiction is more readily

[7] J Faull, "Effect on Trade Between Member State and Community: Member State Jurisdiction" (1989) *Fordham Corporate Law Institute* 489.

[8] Case 56/65, *Société Technique Minière (L.T.M.) v Maschinenbau Ulm GmbH (M.B.U.)* [1966] ECR 235, 249.

[9] See, e.g., Case T-141/89, *Tréfileurope Sales SARL v Commission* [1995] ECR II-791, para. 57; *Volkswagen*, OJ 2001 L 262/14, para. 88. See also Case T-208/01, *Volkswagen AG v Commission* [2003] ECR II-5141. As far as exports are concerned, see, e.g., Case T-29/92, *Vereniging van Samenwerkende Prijsregelende Organisaties in de Bouwnijverheid and others v Commission* [1995] ECR II-289, paras. 226–40.

[10] See Joined Cases 56 and 58/64, *Établissements Consten S.à.R.L. and Grundig-Verkaufs-GmbH v Commission* [1966] ECR 299, 341. See also *Napier Brown/British Sugar,* OJ 1988 L 284/14, para. 80.

[11] See, e.g., Case 71/74, *Frubo v Commission* [1975] ECR 563, para. 38. See also Joined Cases 209 to 215 and 218/78 *Heintz van Landewyck SARL and others v Commission* [1980] ECR 3125, para. 172; Case T-61/89 *Dansk Pelsdyravlerforening v Commission* [1992] ECR II-1931, para. 143; and Case T-65/89 *BPB Industries Plc and British Gypsum Ltd v Commission* [1993] ECR II-389, para. 135.

[12] See Notice on Effect on Trade, para. 28.

[13] Case T-70/89, *British Broadcasting Corporation and BBC Enterprises Ltd v Commission* [1991] II-535, para. 65.

established.[14] Conversely, when there is limited demand for products offered by suppliers from other Member States or when the products are of limited interest from the point of view of cross-border establishment (or the expansion of the economic activity carried out from such place of establishment), Community law jurisdiction is less likely to be established.[15] Finally, if there are absolute barriers to cross-border trade between Member States, which are external to the agreement or practice, trade is likely to be regarded as incapable of being affected unless those barriers are likely to disappear in the foreseeable future.[16] Such barriers are distinguishable from those that are not absolute, but merely render cross-border activities more difficult, such as consumers' preference for a particular technical standard.[17] Similarly arguments that inter-State trade is not affected because the undertakings concerned were not interested in trading between Member States due to fiscal barriers will generally be rejected, not least because it is even more important in situations where the scope of competition is limited by legislation that firms should not make agreements or engage in practices which eliminate the scope of competition that remains.[18]

---

[14] See Notice on Effect on Trade, para. 30. See also Case C-309/99, *JCJ Wouters, JW Savelbergh and Price Waterhouse Belastingadviseurs BV v Algemene Raad van de Nederlandse Orde van Advocaten* [2002] ECR I-1577, para. 95. In this case, members of the Dutch Bar adopted a regulation whereby multi-disciplinary partnerships between members of the Bar and accountants were prohibited. In determining that intra-Community trade was affected by the regulation, the Court of Justice emphasised that the regulation applied to lawyers of other Member States, that, increasingly, commercial law regulated trans-national transactions and that firms of accountants looking for lawyers as partners were generally international groups present in several Member States.

[15] See, e.g., Joined Cases C-215/96 and 216/96, *Carlo Bagnasco and Others v Banca Popolare di Novara soc. coop. arl. and Cassa di Risparmio di Genova e Imperia SpA* [1999] ECR I-135, para. 51.

[16] See Notice on Effect on Trade, para. 41.

[17] *Ibid.*, para. 32. See also Case 107/82, *Allgemeine Elektrizitäts-Gesellschaft AEG-Telefunken AG v Commission* [1983] ECR 3151, paras. 61–65, where AEG claimed that, as regards colour television sets, the application of its distribution system could not have affected parallel imports into France because standards used in Germany (PAL) were different to that used in France (SECAM) and there was considerable cost in converting sets. The Commission had contended that, whilst differences of a technical nature were liable to make trade between Member States more difficult, they nevertheless did not have the effect of making such trade impossible between Germany and France. The Court agreed with the Commission and further noted that AEG also manufactured, under review, sets that could operate with both systems and which were in special demand in the frontier regions of Germany and France. That fact was sufficient for the conclusion to be drawn that AEG's policy was capable of affecting the export of colour television sets from Germany to France.

[18] See, e.g., Joined Cases 240 to 242, 261, 262, 268 and 269/82, *Stichting Sigarettenindustrie and others v Commission* [1985] 3331, paras. 18–29, where the applicants argued that the Netherlands' excise duty legislation and price orders deprived undertakings of any flexibility in their pricing policy and made it impossible for competitors to establish price differences thereby excluding competition between Member States through parallel imports. The Commission had determined that, whilst the Netherlands' legal framework limited to some extent the scope for competition in the industry, it could not be argued that there is no scope at all for competition or that the scope was so limited that there would no longer be any scope for active competition. The Court of First Instance agreed. It held "[the legislation] may indeed cause practical difficulties for a manufacturer who desires to change his retail prices. But those difficulties are merely temporary. Furthermore [the legislation] expressly makes derogations possible. Finally [it] does not prevent a manufacturer introducing a new product from applying to it a price different from those of his competitors at the outset, and thus creating a price

b. Alteration to the competitive structure. An alternative test was formulated in *Commercial Solvents*. In that case, the Court of Justice held that "[w]hen an undertaking in a dominant position with the common market abuses its position in such a way that a competitor in the common market is likely to be eliminated, it does not matter whether the conduct relates to the latter's exports or its trade within the common market, once it has been established that this elimination will have repercussions on the competitive structure within the common market."[19] In subsequent cases, this principle has been interpreted and applied to mean that the effect on trade test is satisfied where a dominant firm's conduct impacts or changes the structure of competition in the EU.[20]

The Community institutions have in practice found that structural changes are capable of altering inter-State trade in three ways. First, the very fact of eliminating a competitor may be sufficient for trade between Member States to be capable of being affected.[21] This would be the case, for example, where a dominant firm sought to remove a competitor whose activities include imports (whether for transformation or resale) and/or exports within the EU.[22] This may even be the case where a competitor that risks being eliminated mainly engages in exports to third countries.[23] Second, the elimination of one competitor may have an impact on other competitors' behaviour. In particular, through its abusive conduct, a dominant firm can signal to its competitors that it will discipline attempts to engage in real competition.[24] Third, competitors' foreclosure from a dominant firm's trading parties or customers may hamper the attainment of a single market between Member States. This would typically occur in cases involving the use of fidelity rebates, tying, or other devices aimed at inducing exclusivity.[25]

Condition #3: direct, indirect, actual or potential influence. In order for Article 82 EC jurisdiction to be established, it is not necessary to demonstrate that the conduct complained of actually affects trade between Member States in a discernible way. It is

difference which would enable him to increase his market share." It was therefore concluded that, although the legislation gave the tobacco manufacturer less scope for price competition, it left the manufacturer scope for creating a price difference between its products and those of its competitors, by reducing his prices or by holding them at the same level while other manufacturers increase theirs.

19 Joined Cases 6 and 7/73, *Istituto Chemioterapico Italiano S.p.A. and Commercial Solvents Corporation v Commission* [1974] ECR 223, para. 33.

20 See, e.g., Case 27/76, *United Brands Company v Commission* [1978] ECR 207, para. 201. See also Case 322/81, *NV Nederlandsche Banden Industrie Michelin v Commission* [1983] ECR 3461, para. 51.

21 See Notice on Effect on Trade, para. 75.

22 See, e.g., *Napier Brown/British Sugar,* OJ 1988 L 284/41. See also Joined Cases C-241/91 P and C-242/91 P, *Radio Telefis Eireann (RTE) and Independent Television Publications Ltd (ITP) v Commission* [1995] ECR I-743.

23 See, e.g., Joined Cases 6 and 7/73, *Istituto Chemioterapico Italiano S.p.A. and Commercial Solvents Corporation v Commission* [1974] ECR 223, para. 33.

24 *De Post/La Poste*, OJ 2002 L 61/32, paras. 74–79. See also Notice on Effect on Trade, para. 75.

25 See, e.g., *Soda-ash/Solvay,* OJ 2003 L 10/10, para. 65; Case 322/81, *NV Nederlandsche Banden Industrie Michelin v Commission* [1983] ECR 3461, para. 51; Case 61/80, *Coöperatieve Stremsel- en Kleurselfabriek v Commission* [1981] ECR 851, paras. 22–23.

sufficient that the agreement or practice is "capable" of having such an effect.[26] In determining whether the agreement or practice has the potential effect of altering trade patterns, foreseeable market developments must be taken into account. Thus, even if trade is not capable of being affected at the time the agreement is concluded or the practice is implemented, Article 82 EC remains applicable if the factors which led to that conclusion are likely to change in the foreseeable future such as the adoption of liberalisation measures.[27] Moreover, even if at a given point in time market conditions are unfavourable to cross-border trade, for example because prices are similar in the Member States in question, trade may still be capable of being affected if the situation may alter as a result of changing market conditions. What matters is the ability of the agreement or practice to affect trade between Member States and not whether at any given point in time it actually does so.[28] Arguments that inter-State trade is not affected because the undertakings concerned are not interested in trading in another Member State or are not in a position to do so is treated with scepticism, not least because the situation may change in the immediate future.[29]

The Community institutions have also made clear that the condition covers both direct and indirect effects on trade patterns.[30] An example of direct effects being produced is when a supplier limits distributor rebates to products sold within the Member State in which the distributors are established. Such discounting practices would increase the relative price of products destined for exports thereby rendering export sales less attractive and less competitive.[31] An example of indirect effects being produced is when the agreement or practice relates to an intermediate product which is not traded, but which is used in the supply of a final product, which is traded.[32] Indirect effects on trade between Member States may also occur when a manufacturer limits warranties to products sold by distributors within their Member State of establishment. Because they would not be able to invoke the warranty, such provision could create disincentives for consumers from other Member States to buy the products.[33]

Finally, it should be noted that where a dominant firm adopts various practices in the pursuit of the same aim, for instance, practices that aim at foreclosing competitors, Article 82 EC will apply to all practices forming part of this overall strategy provided that at least one of these practices is capable of appreciably affecting inter-State trade.

[26] See, e.g., Case T-228/97, *Irish Sugar plc v Commission* [1999] ECR II-2969, para. 170; Case 19/77, *Miller International Schallplatten GmbH v Commission* [1978] ECR 131, para. 15.

[27] See Notice on Effect on Trade, para. 41.

[28] *Ibid.*, para. 42.

[29] Case 19/77, *Miller International Schallplatten GmbH v Commission* [1978] ECR 131, paras. 14–15.

[30] See, e.g., Case T-86/95, *Compagnie Générale Maritime and others v Commission* [2002] ECR II-1011, para. 148. See also Joined Cases C-395/96 P and C-396/96 P, *Compagnie Maritime Belge Transports SA and others v Commission* [1996] ECR II-1201, para. 202.

[31] See Notice on Effect on Trade, para. 37.

[32] *Ibid.*, para. 38. See, e.g., Case 123/83, *Bureau national interprofessionnel du cognac v Guy Clair* [1985] ECR 391, para. 29. See also Joined Cases C-89/85, C-104/85, C-114/85, C-116/85, C-117/85 and C-125/85 to C-129/85, *A. Ahlström Osakeyhtiö and others v Commission* [1993] ECR I-1307, paras. 139–44.

[33] See *Zanussi*, OJ 1978 L 322/36, para. 11. See also Notice on Effect on Trade, para. 38.

In other words, it is sufficient that at least one of the practices that form part of the strategy of exclusionary or exploitative behaviour is capable of affecting trade between Member States.[34]

Condition #4: appreciability. The effect on trade criterion includes a quantitative element, limiting Community law jurisdiction to abuses that are capable of having effects of a certain magnitude.[35] The assessment of appreciability depends on the circumstances of each individual case, in particular the nature of the agreement and practice, the nature of the products covered and the market position of the undertakings concerned. When, by its very nature, the agreement or practice is capable of affecting trade between Member States (e.g., because its concerns imports and exports), the appreciability threshold is lower than in the case of agreements and practices that are not by their very nature capable of affecting trade between Member States. In addition, the stronger the market position of the undertakings concerned, the more likely it is that an agreement or practice capable of affecting trade between Member States can be held to do so appreciably.[36]

Given that in Article 82 EC cases *ex hypothesi* a firm is in a dominant position, the circumstances in which its abusive behaviour would not be regarded as being capable of appreciably affecting inter-State trade are, unsurprisingly, extremely limited.[37] One such situation is if the excluded competition is confined to a national or local market and the abuse has little application to cross-border transactions. In that scenario, it would probably not have an appreciable effect on trade between Member States unless it has the consequence of deterring foreign penetration of the national market.[38] Similarly, inter-State trade would not be capable of being appreciably affected if the excluded competition is confined to a geographic territory outside the Community and the abuse has little impact on intra-Community trade.[39]

14.3 SPECIFIC APPLICATIONS OF THE EFFECT ON TRADE CONCEPT

Overview. The following section details how the broad preceding principles are applied in practice. Four types of situations are distinguished: (1) abuses covering several Member States; (2) abuses covering a single Member State; (3) abuses covering

[34] See Notice on Effect on Trade, para. 17. See also Joined Cases C-395/96 P and C-396/96 P, *Compagnie Maritime Belge Transports SA and others v Commission* [1996] ECR II-1201, para. 204.

[35] See Notice on Effect on Trade, para. 44.

[36] *Ibid.*

[37] See Notice on Effect on Trade, para. 53. The Commission considers that where an agreement by its very nature is capable of affecting trade between Member States, for example, because it concerns imports and exports or covers several Member States, there is a rebuttable positive presumption that such effects on trade are appreciable when the market share of the parties exceeds the 5% threshold.

[38] See, e.g., Case 22/78, *Hugin Kassaregister AB and Hugin Cash Registers Ltd v Commission* [1979] ECR 1869.

[39] See, e.g., Case T-198/98, *Micro Leader Business v Commission* [1999] ECR II-3989.

only a part of a Member State; and (4) abuses involving undertakings located in third countries.

14.3.1 Abuses Covering Several Member States

Presumption of effect on trade. Where a dominant undertaking engages in exploitative or exclusionary abuses in more than one Member State, whether carried out through agreements or through unilateral conduct, such conduct is presumed, by its very nature, to be capable of affecting trade between Member States.[40] These include: abuses which involve international transactions,[41] abuses directed at customers that are active in several Member States,[42] and abusive conduct directed at competitors situated in other Member States.[43] In addition, trade between Member States is capable of being affected even if the competitor that risks being eliminated mainly or solely engages in exports to third countries, if it is situated within the EU. For example, in *Commercial Solvents*,[44] CSC and Instituto, its subsidiary, were found to have infringed Article 82 EC by discontinuing supplies to their Italian-based competitor, Zoja. On appeal, CSC argued *inter alia* that Article 82 EC was not applicable since such refusal did not effect trade between Member States. It argued that third countries were the most affected since Zoja sold 90% of its production outside the EU. The Court effectively held although the abuse related to exports to third countries, given that the competitor was established in a Member State, its elimination as a competitor would have had repercussions on the competitive structure within the EU.[45]

The capacity of the abuse to affect trade between Member States is presumed to be appreciable where abuses cover several Member States. Given the market position of the dominant undertaking concerned and the fact that the abuse is implemented in several Member States, the scale of the abuse and its likely impact on patterns of trade is normally such that trade between Member States is capable of being appreciably affected. The very existence of a dominant position in several Member States implies that competition in a substantial part of the EU is already weakened. When a dominant undertaking further weakens competition through recourse to abusive conduct, for

---

[40] See Notice on Effect on Trade, paras. 61–76.

[41] See, e.g., *Deutsche Post AG,* OJ 2001 L 331/40; Case COMP/38.096, *PO/Clearstream,* Commission Decision of June 2, 2004 (not yet reported); *Visa International,* OJ 2002 L 318/17.

[42] See Notice on Effect on Trade, para. 95. Where a dominant firm engages in abusive discrimination between domestic customers, trade between Member States may be appreciably affected if those customers are engaged in export activities and are disadvantaged *vis-à-vis* buyers from other Member States.

[43] See, e.g., Joined Cases C-241/91 P and C-242/91 P, *Radio Telefis Éireann (RTE) and Independent Television Publications Ltd (ITP) v Commission* [1995] ECR I-743, para. 70, where the Court of First Instance found that the RTE had excluded all potential competitors on the geographical market consisting of one Member State (Ireland) and part of another Member State (Northern Ireland) and had thus modified the structure of competition on that market, thereby affecting potential commercial exchanges between Ireland and the United Kingdom.

[44] Joined Cases 6 and 7-73, *ICI and CSC v Commission* [1974] ECR 223, paras. 30–35.

[45] See, e.g., Case 22/79, *Greenwich Film Production v Société des auteurs, compositeurs et éditeurs de musique (SACEM)* [1979] ECR 3275, para 11.

example by eliminating a competitor, the ability of the abuse to affect trade between Member States is thus normally appreciable.

14.3.2 Abuses Covering A Single Member State

Effect on trade not precluded. The fact an abuse is confined to a single Member State does not mean that trade is incapable of being affected within the meaning of Article 82 EC. As the Court held in *United Brands,* "if the occupier of a dominant position, established in the common market, aims at eliminating a competitor who is also established in the common market, it is immaterial whether this behaviour relates to trade between Member States once it has been shown that such elimination will have repercussions on the patterns of competition in the common market."[46] Indeed, the Community Courts have ruled in that abusive behaviour extending over the whole of the territory of a Member State has the effect of reinforcing the compartmentalisation of markets on a national basis, thereby holding up the economic integration which the EC Treaty is designed to bring about.[47]

In *Michelin I*,[48] for example, Michelin argued that since the rebate system was confined to the territory of one Member State, it was not capable of affecting trade between Member States. In that case, Michelin, which had a share of 57–65% of the relevant tyre market, granted discounts to tyre dealers in the Netherlands based on annual sales targets that were established individually for each dealer. Having noted that 25–28% of tyres competing with Michelin tyres on the Netherlands market came from other Member States and the discount system prevented competing foreign manufacturers from penetrating the Netherlands market, the Court agreed with the Commission's findings that the rebate system harmed the establishment of a single market between the Member States.[49] This decision demonstrates that it is precisely because a dominant firm has the economic strength to obstruct importers' access to its national market that its abusive conduct, although limited to a national market, is normally regarded as capable of appreciably affecting inter-State trade.[50] This is especially true when the

[46] Case 27/76, *United Brands Company v Commission* [1978] ECR 207, para. 201.

[47] See, e.g., *Deutsche Telekom AG*, OJ 2003 L 263/9, para. 184. See also *DSD*, OJ 2001 L 166/1, paras. 155–60. See too Notice on Effect on Trade, para. 94 ("An effect on [inter-State] trade may arise from the dissuasive impact of the abuse on other competitors. If through repeated conduct the dominant undertaking has acquired a reputation for adopting exclusionary practices towards competitors that attempt to engage in direct competition, competitors from other Member States are likely to compete less aggressively, in which case trade may be affected, even if the victim in the case at hand is not from another Member State.").

[48] Case 322/81, *NV Nederlandsche Banden Industrie Michelin v. Commission* [1983] ECR 3461.

[49] See Case 322/81, *NV Nederlandsche Banden Industrie Michelin v. Commission* [1983] ECR 3461, paras. 101–4. See also *Bandengroothandel Frieschebrug BV/NV Nederlandsche Banden-Industrie Michelin*, OJ 1981 L 353/33, para. 51. See also *Deutsche Post AG*, OJ 2001 L 331/40, para. 134.

[50] See Notice on Effect on Trade, para. 96 ("In the assessment of [abuses of dominant positions covering a single Member State] it must also be taken into account that the very presence of the dominant undertaking covering the whole Member State is likely to make market penetration more difficult. Any abuse which makes it more difficult to enter the national market should therefore be considered to appreciably affect trade. The combination of the market position of the dominant

elimination of such trade would lead to the reinforcement of a near-monopoly in a Member State.[51]

Need to assess the importance of affected customers to rivals. Furthermore, it is immaterial that the exclusionary abuse engaged in by the dominant undertaking only affects certain buyers within the national territory if those buyers are the most likely to be targeted by competitors from other Member States. A dominant undertaking can significantly impede trade by engaging in abusive conduct *vis-à-vis* "strategic" customers.[52] Practices consisting of offering lower prices to customers that are the most likely to import products from other Member States make it more difficult for competitors from other Member States to enter the market. For example, it may be that a particular channel of distribution constitutes a particularly important means of gaining access to broad categories of consumers. Hindering access to such channels would likely have a substantial impact on trade between Member States.[53]

Irish Sugar provides a good example.[54] It concerned a series of cumulative measures by the dominant sugar producer in Ireland designed to keep out competitive imports of sugar produced in other Member States. Among the measures employed by Irish Sugar were selective pricing, export rebates, price discrimination, granting rebates to customers located in border areas, product swaps and fidelity rebates, and target rebates. The border rebates were a scheme entered into by Irish Sugar and its distribution arm, SDL, under which rebates were offered only to retail customers located close to the border with Northern Ireland, where Irish Sugar had lost sales to competing sugar imports from the United Kingdom. In upholding the Commission's finding that the border rebates were abusive and capable of affecting trade between Member States, the Court of First Instance focused on the market-partitioning effect of the rebates, specifically, the fact that the rebate formed "part of a strategy of the applicant to protect its domestic market and its position on that market from competition from imported sugar."[55]

No effect on trade in purely local demand scenarios. Nevertheless, in cases involving products or services that have purely local demand, i.e., non-tradable across

undertaking and the anticompetitive nature of its conduct implies that such abuses have normally by their very nature an appreciable effect on trade.").

[51] See, e.g., Case T-65/89, *BPB Industries plc and British Gypsum Ltd v Commission* [1993] ECR II-389, paras. 153–59, where British Gypsum, the dominant and only producer of plasterboards in Great Britain, tied customers into, *inter alia,* exclusive purchase obligations to induce them not to trade in imported plasterboards. The Commission held that since British Gypsum's only competitors were importers, such measures were liable to substantially affect inter-State trade.

[52] See Notice on Effect on Trade, para. 96. If the exclusionary abuse engaged in by the dominant undertaking only affects "non-strategic" buyers, inter-State trade is unlikely to be capable of being appreciably affected unless they constitute a substantial share of the purchase market within the Member State.

[53] *Ibid.*, para. 95.

[54] *Irish Sugar plc*, OJ 1997 L 258/1, affirmed on appeal in Case T-228/97, *Irish Sugar plc v Commission* [1999] ECR II-2969. See also Order of the Court of Justice in Case C-497/99 P *Irish Sugar plc v Commission* [2001] ECR I-5333.

[55] Case T-228/97, *Irish Sugar plc v Commission* [1999] ECR II-2969, para. 201.

Member States, or where the affected competitor operates on a purely domestic basis, or where the affected customer operates only within a single Member State and does not make up a significant share of the purchase market nor is strategically important for market penetration purposes, an appreciable affect on trade between Member States may not be readily established. The most notable Article 82 EC example is *Hugin*.[56] This case concerned the prohibition by Hugin of sales of spare parts of cash registers to companies outside its distribution network. Hugin refused to supply Liptons, an independent repair services provider, with spare parts to its cash registers. The supply of spare parts formed an integral part of the maintenance and repair services. The Commission found that this resale policy affected trade within the meaning of Article 82 EC because Hugin's subsidiaries and distributors, and in particular those situated in other Member States, were prohibited from supplying Liptons with spare parts. This finding, however, was rejected by the Court of Justice. The Court found that there was no inter-State trade for repair services: Liptons' business was largely confined to the London area and had never extended beyond the United Kingdom. Such limitation was due to the nature of the services in question, which were essentially local since repair services could not be operated profitably beyond a certain distance from the commercial base of a company. The competitive structure was thought to be the same in other Member States.

Further, the Court held that there could not have been inter-State trade for the supply of spare parts to independent operators. The Court was influenced by the fact that the value of the spare parts was "in itself relatively insignificant" and were therefore "not such as to constitute a commodity of commercial interest in trade between Member States." In addition, sales prices for spare parts were the same in different Member

[56] See, e.g., Case 22/78, *Hugin Kassaregister AB and Hugin Cash Registers Ltd v Commission* [1979] ECR 1869. See also, for similar principles that apply in the context of Article 81 EC, Case 246/86, *Carlo Bagnasco* [1989] ECR 2117, paras. 48–52. See also *Nederlandse Vereniging van Banken ("Dutch Banks")*, OJ 1999 L 271/28, paras. 58–65. In *Carlo Bagnasco*, the Court of Justice held that, although the great majority of Italian banks were members of the Association of Italian Banks (ABI), the ABI standard conditions that governed the contracts for current accounts, and in particular the provisions that governed the provision of general guarantee for the opening of a credit facility, did not appreciably affect inter-State trade. Its analysis was based on the following three elements. First, the economic activities concerned (acceptance giro) were largely limited to Netherlands territory. Second, the overwhelming majority of acceptance giro contracts (about 91%) were conducted on behalf of the major banks (ABN AMRO, Rabo, ING Bank and Postbank). Foreign banks accounted for less than 1% of the acceptance giro contracts concluded. They also accounted for a very modest share of the acceptance giro transactions processed: less than 1% for debits and less than 5% for credits. Third, about one-third of the foreign banks active in the Netherlands did not offer the acceptance giro product. As regards the twenty seven foreign banks which did offer the product, the opportunity to offer the product was not an important factor in their Decision to enter the Netherlands market, given its relatively limited importance to their customers. The same reasoning was applied in *Dutch Banks*, where the Commission concluded that the acceptance giro system was not capable of appreciably affecting inter-State trade because of the low level of cross border acceptance of giros and the fact that non-participation in the agreement would not preclude non-Dutch banks from entering the Netherlands market.

States.[57] The Court's finding of the unfeasibility of cross-border trade based on the value of the product and the fact that there was no price differential between Member States is somewhat perplexing. First, if, as accepted by the Court, the supply of spare parts formed an integral part of the maintenance and repair services, then the business of selling spare parts to independent operators would have been potentially lucrative, since it was not possible for an independent provider of repair and maintenance services to remain in business without access to spare parts. A cost-based valuation of the spare part would not have necessarily reflected its "value" from the perspective of customers. Second, according to previous decisions, even if current market conditions are unfavourable to cross-border trade because prices are similar across Member States, trade may still be capable of being affected if market conditions are likely to change in the foreseeable future.[58] It seems circular to argue that trade for spare parts could not have existed between Member States because there were no price arbitrage between Member States when Hugin's resale policy precluded any opportunity of price arbitrage from occurring. It is conceivable that intra-Community competition in the supply of spare parts would have resulted had Hugin's authorised distributors been permitted to sell spare parts to independent operators and, by implication, compete on price. But while the Court's finding on this issue may be peculiar on the facts, the decision does not call into question the principle that trade between Member States is probably not capable of being appreciably affected where an analysis of demand and supply indicates that trade in the product or service in question is purely or largely domestic.

14.3.3 Abuses Covering Only A Part Of A Member State

Need to assess relative economic importance of affected territory. The capacity of a dominant firm to affect inter-State trade where its dominance covers part of Member States depends on whether that part of a Member State constitutes a substantial part of the EU. In the application of this criterion, the Community institutions have consistently taken into account the size of the market, the importance of the market, and nature of the product.[59] Thus, regions of a Member State have, depending on the share of overall production or consumption in the EU it represents, been held to constitute a substantial part of the EU. For example, in *Suiker Unie*,[60] the Court of Justice held the Belgo-Luxembourg sugar market was a substantial part of the common market in sugar based on the following elements. First, there was substantial market "opportunity" for competitive sugar imports. Second, the ratio of the volume of a region's production of sugar to total Community sugar production was significant (approx. 8–9.5%). Third,

---

[57] Case 22/78, *Hugin Kassaregister AB and Hugin Cash Registers Ltd v Commission* [1979] ECR 1869, para. 23.

[58] See Notice on Effect on Trade, para. 41. See, e.g., Case 107/82, *Allgemeine Elektrizitäts-Gesellschaft AEG-Telefunken AG v Commission* [1983] ECR 3151, paras. 61–65.

[59] See Notice on Effect on Trade, para. 98. See also Joined Cases 40 to 48, 50, 54 to 56, 111, 113 and 114–73, *Coöperatieve Vereniging "Suiker Unie" UA and others v Commission* [1975] ECR 1663, para. 371, where the Court of Justice held that "the pattern and volume of the production and consumption of the said product as well as the habits and economic opportunities of vendors and purchasers must be considered."

[60] *Ibid.*

the ratio of volume of a region's consumption of sugar to total Community sugar consumption was also significant (approx. 5%).[61]

Inter-Member State travel facilities presumed to have an effect. Where an undertaking has dominance over a facility such as an airport or a port, whether its abuse is capable of appreciably affecting trade between Member States depends on whether the infrastructure in question is used to provide cross-border services and, if so, to what extent.[62] Generally this will require an assessment of the volume of traffic in the facility and its importance in relation to overall volume of traffic to and from that particular facility.[63] For example, in *Paris Airports*,[64] the Commission concluded that inter-State trade was appreciably affected by Aéroports de Paris' abuse of airport management services with respect to Orly and Charles De Gaulle (CDG) airports on the ground that there was a substantial flow of passenger and cargo traffic on domestic and intra-Community flights to and from these Paris airports. Specifically, Orly and CDG were the largest French airports in terms of domestic and international traffic: the distribution of passenger traffic at the two airports was approximately 32 million for CDG and approximately 27 million for Orly. Passengers and goods leaving or arriving in the Paris region (one of the largest economic areas in the EU) used air transport services to and from Orly and CDG which served all the main domestic and EU airports. Orly and CDG were hubs for the transfer of many passengers wishing to go from one French region to a region in another Member State and *vice versa*. The major international airports outside the EU were served by air transport services from the two Paris airports. Lastly, as regards intra-Community traffic, 63% of total passengers using the two Paris airports were domestic or EU commuters. In the same year, domestic and EU cargo traffic, accounted for some 19% of goods traffic in the two airports.

Furthermore, even where an airport predominantly supports domestic traffic an appreciable effect on inter-State trade may nevertheless be demonstrated where there is

[61] It should be noted that while the importance of a region may be reflected by the percentage of the EU's total volume of production or consumption of a product that it represents, even an extremely small percentage would not necessarily preclude it from being a "substantial part." See, e.g., Case 77/77, *Benzine en Petroleum Handelsmaatschappij BV and others v Commission* [1978] ECR 1513, where Advocate General Warner expressed the fact that Luxembourg, which, at the time, had a population equal to only 0.23% of the Community would not preclude it being a substantial part of the common market. The Court of Justice did not address this issue, since it annulled the Commission's finding on abuse of dominance on other grounds.

[62] See Notice on Effect on Trade, para. 98.

[63] For cases concerning port services see, e.g., Case 179/90, *Merci Convenzionali Porto di Genova v Siderurgica Gabrielli* [1991] ECR I-5889, para. 15; Case C-18/93, *Corsica Ferries Italia Srl v Corpo dei Piloti del Porto di Genova* [1994] ECR I-1783, para. 41; Case C-163/96, *Silvano Raso and others* [1998] ECR I-533, para. 26; *Sea Containers v Stena Sealink/Interim measures*, OJ 1994 L 15/8, para. 77. For airport services, see, e.g., *Alpha Flight Services/Aéroports de Paris*, OJ 1998 L 230/10, paras. 77–82, 133; *Flughafen Frankfurt/Main AG*, OJ 1998 L 72/30, para. 58; *Portuguese airports*, OJ 1999 L 69/31, paras. 20–22; and *Ilmailulaitos/Luftfartsverket*, OJ 1999 L 69/42, paras. 57–61.

[64] *Alpha Flight Services/Aéroports de Paris*, OJ 1998 L 230/10, paras. 77–82, 133.

close connection with an international hub.[65] For example, in *Ilmailulaitos/Luftfartsverket*,[66] the Commission found an effect on trade between Member States despite the fact that four of the five Finnish airports concerned predominantly offered domestic flights. Instead, noting that these airports operated between two and six flights each day to Stockholm, and from Stockholm passengers could connect with flights to Amsterdam, Billund, Brussels, Copenhagen, Düsseldorf, Frankfurt, Gothenburg, Hamburg, London, Manchester, Milan, Munich, Paris and Vienna, on either Lufthansa/SAS or Finnair (on a code-sharing basis with its partners), the Commission held that inter-State trade was affected from these airports. As regards the international airport, Helsinki, which handled 7.7 million passengers, the Commission held that the question of effect on trade between Member States was beyond doubt because it was Finland's international airport.

14.3.4 Abuses Concerning Trade Outside The EU

Generally. Article 82 EC does not apply to agreements or practices that relate exclusively to trade outside the EU. On the other hand, Article 82 EC is not excluded simply because one or more of the parties is located outside the EU if the agreement or practice produces effects inside the EU. Moreover, where the agreement/practice relates to imports into or exports out of the EU to or from third countries, the requisite effect on trade between Member States is readily established.

Conduct affecting imports into the EU. Imports can affect the conditions of competition in the importing Member State, which in turn may have an impact on exports and imports of competing products to and from other Member States. In addition, it may bring about an isolation of the internal market. This is the case, for instance, if, in the absence of the agreement or practice, imports to the EU would be possible and likely. Restricting imports could reduce the supply of products and competition within the EU, thereby affecting patterns of trade inside the EU. Accordingly, agreements whereby competitors in the EU and in third countries share markets, e.g., by collectively agreeing not to sell in each other's home markets or by concluding reciprocal (exclusive) distribution agreements are likely to capable of appreciably affecting trade within the EU.[67]

Conduct affecting exports outside the EU. In the case of exports, the effect on trade criterion may be satisfied where the object of the agreement is to prevent re-export to home markets or to divert surpluses from within the EU to third countries with a view to coordinating their market conduct inside the EU. Such export agreements serve to reduce price competition by limiting output inside the EU, thereby affecting trade between Member States. Without the export agreement, these quantities might have

---

[65] Compare *Portuguese Airports*, OJ 1999 L 69/31, paras. 20–22, where, as regards four airports on the Azores archipelago, the Commission found no effect on trade between Member States because traffic was either entirely domestic or from third countries.

[66] *Ilmailulaitos/Luftfartsverket*, OJ 1999 L 69/42, paras. 57–61.

[67] See Notice on Effect on Trade, para. 104. See, e.g., Case 51-75, *EMI Records Limited v CBS United Kingdom Limited* [1976] ECR 811, para. 28.

been sold inside the EU.[68] For example, in *Tretorn*, the Commission found that a ban on exports from the EU and into Switzerland had an effect on Member State trade since it prevented Swiss dealers from buying in one Member State and re-exporting to a second Member State.[69]

Conduct affecting re-importation possibilities into the EU. Trade may also be capable of being affected when the agreement prevents re-imports into the EU. This may, for example, be the case with vertical agreements between EU suppliers and third country distributors, imposing restrictions on resale outside an allocated territory, including the EU. If, in the absence of the agreement, resale to the EU would be possible and likely, such imports may be capable of affecting patterns of trade inside the EU. The leading case on re-imports is *Javico v Yves Saint Laurent Parfums* ("YSLP").[70] The case concerned a distribution agreement whereby Javico was given exclusivity to sell YSLP products into Russia, Ukraine, and Slovenia. Under the contract Javico was obliged to ensure that the final destination of those products would be in the above territories. Shortly after concluding the contract, YSLP discovered that Javico was selling into the UK, Belgium and the Netherlands, and sued Javico for breach of contract.

The Court of Justice ruled that, while the agreement did not have the object of restricting competition with the EU, it had such effect. In this regard, the Court suggested that an appreciable effect on trade between Member States could be demonstrated where: (1) the EU market for the relevant products is oligopolistic, such that competition between suppliers is limited; (2) there is an appreciable price difference between product sold in the EU and third countries that would not be eroded by costs of re-importation (e.g., customs duties and transport costs); and (3) the products intended for markets outside the EU account for more than "a very small percentage" of the total market for those products in the EU.[71] These principles are reflected in the Commission's Notice on Effect on Trade.[72] A notable omission, however, is the requirement that the EU market is oligopolistic, which implies that the Commission will seek to facilitate the conditions for entry by importers from third countries even where the EU market is largely competitive.

For other types of arrangements, the Commission considers that it is normally necessary to proceed with a more detailed analysis of whether or not cross-border economic activity inside the EU, in particular, "to examine the effects of the agreement or practice on customers and other operators inside the EU that rely on the products of the

[68] See Notice on Effect on Trade, para. 105.

[69] *Tretorn and others*, OJ 1994 L 378/45, paras. 64–65.

[70] Case C-306/96, *Javico International and Javico AG v Yves Saint Laurent Parfums SA* [1998] ECR I-1983.

[71] *Ibid.*, paras. 22–27. See also Notice on Effect on Trade, para. 109, where the Commission has elaborated that in assessing whether product volumes are significant, "regard must be had not only to the individual agreement concluded between the parties, but also to any cumulative effect of similar agreements concluded by the same and competing suppliers."

[72] Notice on Effect on Trade, para. 109.

undertakings that are parties to the agreement or practice."[73] This category, for example, includes agreements or practices relating to the provision of services or products to customers in third countries. In *French-West African Shipowners' Committees*, which concerned cargo-sharing arrangements between shipping companies operating on French ports and ports serving West and Central African countries, the Commission held trade between Member States was capable of being appreciably affected because: (1) French shipping lines would acquire privileged access to the routes and therefore gain a material competitive advantage in world trade over the lines of other Member States; (2) competition between French exporters and importers and exporters and importers of other Member States would be distorted as a consequence; and (3) trade could be deflected away from ports in France to those elsewhere in the EU because of the discriminatory terms.[74]

[73] *Ibid.*, para. 107.
[74] *French-West African Shipowners' Committees*, OJ 1992 L 134/1, para. 43.

Chapter 15

REMEDIES

15.1 INTRODUCTION

Legal basis for remedies. Regulation 1/2003 provides the legal basis for the imposition of remedies for infringements of Article 82 EC, which provides that "where the Commission...finds that there is an infringement of...Article 82 [EC] of the Treaty, it may by decision require the undertaking...concerned to bring such infringement to an end."[1] This basic power has been spelled out in the implementing regulations for over 40 years, as the original Council Regulation 17 of 1962 contained an identical provision.[2] Regulation 1/2003 adds precision to the legal basis, however, providing further that the Commission, "may impose...any behavioural or structural remedies which are proportionate to the infringement committed and necessary to bring the infringement effectively to an end."[3]

Main types of remedies under Article 82 EC. As the above statement from Regulation 1/2003 indicates, the main remedies available for infringements of Article 82 EC fall broadly into two types: behavioural remedies and structural remedies. Behavioural remedies require that the dominant undertaking act or refrain from acting in a specified way (e.g., a prohibition on below-cost pricing). Structural remedies, by contrast, do not involve commitments as to the undertaking's future conduct but permanent changes to the structure of the dominant undertaking (e.g., an obligation to divest, a requirement to split up a dominant firm into independent units). Since abuses of dominance tend by their nature to be based on conduct (or refusal to act) by the dominant firm, it is not surprising that behavioural remedies are by far the most common. Indeed, as explained below, structural remedies have been an extreme rarity under Article 82 EC. Thus, Regulation 1/2003 sets forth an express preference for behavioural remedies, providing that "[s]tructural remedies can only be imposed either where there is no equally effective behavioural remedy or where any equally effective

---

[1] Council Regulation (EC) No 1/2003 of December 16, 2002 on the implementation of the rules on competition laid down in Articles 81 and 82 of the Treaty, OJ 2003 L 1/1 (hereinafter "Regulation 1/2003"), Article 7(1). The powers of national competition authorities and courts to impose remedies under Article 82 EC are in principle co-terminous with those of the Commission (although they cannot impose fines for abuses with effects outside their national territories). Throughout this chapter, unless stated otherwise, references to powers held by the Commission refer also to powers held by national authorities.

[2] Council Regulation 17 of February 6, 1962, First Regulation implementing Articles 8[1] and 8[2] of the EC Treaty, Article 3(1), OJ 1962 L 13/204. The legal powers conferred by Regulation 1/2003 are either identical to or broader than those conferred by Regulation 17. References below to cases decided under Regulation 17 should thus be interpreted as applying equally to Regulation 1/2003 unless otherwise noted.

[3] Regulation 1/2003, Article 7(1).

behavioural remedy would be more burdensome for an undertaking concerned than the structural remedy."[4]

Structure of this chapter. This chapter is organised as follows. Section 15.2 describes the general principles governing the imposition of remedies, discussing in particular the objectives of remedies and the principles of effectiveness and proportionality. Section 15.3 explains the principal types of administrative decisions that may be taken in respect of infringements of Article 82 EC. Specifically discussed are: (1) interim measures; (2) commitment decisions; (3) undertakings; and (4) final infringement decisions. Section 15.4 describes the main types of remedies that may be imposed, including (1) fines; (2) the various types of behavioural remedies; and (3) structural remedies. Finally, Section 15.5 summarises the current status of private enforcement of EC competition law.

15.2 GENERAL PRINCIPLES GOVERNING REMEDIES

15.2.1 Objectives Of Remedies

Terminating the infringement. Article 7(1) of Regulation 1/2003 grants the Commission the power to impose remedies for Article 82 EC infringements, subject to two conditions: (1) a remedy may only be imposed "where the Commission...finds that there is an infringement of...Article [82];" and (2) the remedy must aim "to bring such infringement to an end." It is clear, then, that the central objective of any remedy for abusive conduct under Article 82 EC is to terminate the infringement. In many cases, a straightforward 'cease and desist' order may be sufficient to achieve this. Where affirmative conduct by the defendant is found to be abusive, Commission infringement decisions will expressly or at least implicitly require that the conduct in question be brought to a halt. For example, in *Microsoft*, the Commission concluded that Microsoft had violated the Article 82 EC prohibition on tying by bundling its Windows Media Player (WMP) with its dominant Windows operating system. The Commission's remedy for this infringement was to bring an end to the tying by requiring Microsoft to offer a version of the Windows operating system that does not include WMP.[5]

Where the abuse consists in a refusal to act, an affirmative order requiring the defendant to behave in a certain way may serve the same purpose as a prohibition on conduct, i.e., bringing the infringement to an end. The Commission's power to order affirmative conduct to remedy abusive behaviour has been established in several judgments. For example, in Commercial Solvents the Court of Justice explained that Article 3 of Regulation No 17 (the precursor to Article 7(1) of Regulation 1/2003) "must be applied in relation to the infringement which has been established and may include an order to do certain acts or provide certain advantages which have been wrongfully withheld as

---

[4] *Ibid.*

[5] Case COMP/C-3/37.792, *Microsoft*, Commission Decision of March 24, 2004, not yet published (hereinafter "*Microsoft*"), para. 1011.

well as prohibiting the continuation of certain action[s], practices or situations which are contrary to the Treaty."[6]

An example of an affirmative order to remedy an abuse is the *Magill* case, where the identified abuse consisted in the refusal by television networks to supply programming information necessary for the production of television listing guides. The Commission found that the television programming information was indispensable for a publisher of television guides and that refusal to provide such information to listing guide publishers was an abuse. The Commission ordered the networks to put an end to the breach by ordering them to supply third parties with their advanced weekly program list on a non-discriminatory basis. The Court observed that remedies should be fashioned "according to the nature of the infringement found and may include an order to do certain acts or things which, unlawfully, have not been done as well as an order to bring an end to certain acts, practices or situations which are contrary to the Treaty."[7]

Eliminating past abusive effects. Sometimes, however, simply bringing a halt to the objectionable conduct, whether through prohibitions on conduct or affirmative requirements to act, would allow the dominant firm to continue to enjoy the fruits of its past abusive behaviour. Abusive behaviour may have irreversible consequences that are not addressed by simple prohibitions on the unlawful conduct in the future.[8] In recognition of this, a series of Commission decisions and Community Court judgments have established the principle that, upon discovery of an Article 82 EC infringement, it is appropriate to adopt a remedy aimed not only at terminating the abuse, but also at restoring and preserving effective competition.

A good illustration is the *AKZO* case.[9] The Commission found that AKZO had abused its dominant position through several measures intended to harm or exclude its competitor ECS. In addition to prohibiting six specific types of behaviour in which AKZO had engaged, the Commission imposed a rule effectively requiring AKZO to pass on any discounts that it would offer to customers in respect of whose business it was in competition with ECS also to its other customers (for whom AKZO was not

[6] Joined Cases 6-7/73, *Istituto Chemioterapico Italiano SpA and Commercial Solvents Corporation v Commission* [1974] ECR 223 (hereinafter "*Commercial Solvents*"), para. 45.

[7] *Magill TV Guide/ITP, BBC and RTE*, OJ 1989 L 78/43, confirmed on appeal in Case T-69/89, *Radio Telefis Éireann (RTE) v Commission* [1991] ECR II-485, Case T-70/89, *British Broadcasting Corporation and BBC Enterprises Ltd (BBC) v Commission* [1991] ECR II-535, and Case T-76/89, *Independent Television Publications Ltd (ITP) v Commission* [1991] ECR II-575, and further confirmed in Joined Cases C-241/91 P and C-242/91 P, *Radio Telefis Éireann and Independent Television Publications Ltd (RTE & ITP) v Commission* [1995] ECR I-743, para. 90 (hereinafter "*Magill*"). See, e.g., *BBC v Commission, ibid.*, para. 71 ("The power conferred on the Commission by Article 3 to require the undertakings concerned to bring an infringement to an end implies, according to established case-law, a right to order such undertakings to take or refrain from taking certain action with a view to bringing the infringement to an end.").

[8] See SC Salop and RC Romaine, "Preserving Monopoly: Economic Analysis, Legal Standards, and Microsoft" (1999) 7(1) *George Mason Law Review* 617–71 (arguing that the goal of remedies in monopolisation cases—the US counterpart to abuse of a dominant position—is not merely to prohibit the unlawful conduct but to achieve the competitive trajectory that was disrupted by the anticompetitive conduct).

[9] *ECS/AKZO*, OJ 1985 L 374/1, upheld on appeal in Case C-62/86, *AKZO Chemie BV v Commission* [1991] ECR I-3359 (hereinafter "*AKZO*").

competing).[10] AKZO appealed this measure as unfair, arguing that it would effectively prevent AKZO from retaining customers approached by ECS. The Court of Justice disagreed, holding that the remedy was legitimate since it was intended "to prevent the repetition of the infringement and to eliminate its consequences." The judgment makes clear that the Court was conscious that the measure would make it difficult for AKZO to counter any attempt by ECS "to win back from [AKZO] the customers whom [AKZO] has taken from ECS unlawfully;" this was legitimate as a means of "enabling ECS to re-establish the situation that existed before the dispute."[11]

Finally, the Community Courts have established that the Commission is entitled to take decisions declaring conduct that had already been terminated by the undertaking concerned to be an infringement.[12] The Commission may find that there is a danger that the unlawful practice would be resumed if the company's obligation to terminate it were not expressly confirmed. In addition, in a few instances the Commission has indicated expressly that an objective in issuing an infringement decision is to set a precedent for third parties even if this is not strictly necessary with respect to the firm under investigation. For example, in the *Deutsche Post* case,[13] the Commission found that Deutsche Post had terminated the infringement in question and stated that it had no reason to believe that Deutsche Post continued to apply the identified abusive pricing and rebate policies. Nevertheless, the Commission proceeded to issue a decision, not only to "ensure with certainty" that Deutsche Post had terminated the infringement, but also to clarify the Commission's position and "deter…any other undertakings that might be implementing or contemplating" practices similar to those that the Commission had found abusive.[14]

Summary. From the above cases it may be extrapolated that remedies under Article 82 EC may be imposed in furtherance of the following objectives:

---

[10] *Ibid.*, Articles 1, 3.

[11] Case C-62/86, *AKZO Chemie BV v Commission* [1991] ECR I-3359, paras. 155, 157. A similar line of reasoning in the context of Article 81 EC is reflected in *TACA*, where the Commission determined that, in order to bring the effects of an Article 81 EC infringement to an end, third parties should be allowed to renegotiate or terminate agreements that were entered into in the context of the infringement, since "the effects of the infringements identified in the contested decision might continue to exist if the addressees of that decision were able to continue to enjoy the economic advantages secured by ongoing contracts entered into on the basis of [the infringement]." The Commission explained that allowing third parties to renegotiate or terminate agreements was "necessary and valid, since its purpose is to ensure that competition on [the relevant market]…is returned as soon as possible to the conditions which would have prevailed in the absence of the unlawful coordination….Furthermore, it prevents the applicants from continuing to enjoy the fruits of their unlawful arrangement." The Court of First instance ultimately held that the Commission had not provided adequate reasons to establish that such measures were necessary, but accepted that the Commission is in principle entitled to impose remedies designed to restore the conditions of competition that would have prevailed in the absence of the unlawful conduct. See *Trans-Atlantic Conference Agreement*, OJ 1999 L 95/1, annulled on appeal in Joined Cases T-191/98 and T-212/98 to T-214/98, *Atlantic Container Line AB and Others v Commission* [2003] ECR II-3275 (hereinafter "*TACA*"). See also *Astra*, OJ 1993 L 20/23.

[12] Case 7/82, *Gesellschaft zur Verwertung von Leistungsschutzrechten mbH (GVL) v Commission* [1983] ECR 483, paras. 16–28.

[13] *Deutsche Post AG*, OJ 2001 L 125/27.

[14] *Ibid.*, para. 48.

(1) terminating the identified infringement (whether by prohibiting abusive conduct or, where the abuse is a refusal to act, ordering certain behaviour); (2) preventing repetition of the abuse (whether in the form of repeated infringements or engaging in similar conduct that has the same effect); (3) eliminating the consequences of the abuse (i.e., re-establishing or maintaining effective competition); and (4) establishing a legal precedent to provide guidelines for third parties (although it is doubtful that this could be an independent ground to justify the imposition of remedies that were otherwise unwarranted).[15]

15.2.2 Remedies Must Be Effective

Prohibiting conduct with equivalent effect to the abuse. The requirement that a remedy must be effective empowers the Commission to prohibit conduct that may have an equivalent effect to the identified abuse. A simple cease and desist order will not bring about the end of an abuse if the undertakings concerned can continue other practices that have the same effect. Accordingly, several Commission infringement decisions require the defendant to refrain from the prohibited conduct, as well as any other conduct that may have a similar or equivalent object or effect.[16]

For example, in relation to the identified tying infringement in *Microsoft*, in addition to ordering Microsoft to offer a version of the Windows operating system without WMP, the Commission required that Microsoft "refrain from using any technological, commercial, contractual or any other means which would have the equivalent effect of tying WMP to Windows."[17] The Commission listed several examples of activities that could be considered as having an effect equivalent to tying but stated that the listed examples were "without prejudice as to what other conduct would amount to a measure equivalent in its harmful effects to tying."[18] In case Microsoft were to cause the performance of the "unbundled" version of Windows to suffer, the Commission

---

[15] Some commentators have argued that, in recent years, Commission remedies in Article 82 EC cases have sought a different objective as they have increasingly been "looking forward at the desired conduct rather than looking backward and ensuring the discontinuation of the abuse." Thus, it is argued, by starting with the desired remedy rather than the theory of the abuse, the Commission has used Article 82 EC as an adjunct to industrial policy rather than as a pure competition law tool, to the detriment of business generally. See IS Forrester, "Article 82: Remedies in Search of Theories?" in B Hawk (ed.), *International Antitrust Law & Policy, 2004 Fordham Corporate Law Institute* (New York, Juris Publishers, Inc., 2005) p 167.

[16] See, e.g., *Cewal, Cowac and Ukwal*, OJ 1993 L 34/20, Article 4 ("The undertakings concerned by this Decision are hereby required to refrain in future from any agreement or concerted practice which may have the same or similar object or effect as the [prohibited] agreements and practices."); *Eurofix-Banco v Hilti*, OJ 1988 L 65/19, Article 3 ("Hilti AG shall forthwith bring to an end the infringements referred to in Article 1 to the extent that it has not already done so. To this end Hilti AG shall refrain from repeating or continuing any of the [specified] acts or behaviour...and shall refrain from adopting any measures having an equivalent effect."); and *Tetra Pak II*, OJ 1992 L 72/1, Article 3 ("Tetra Pak shall refrain from repeating or maintaining any act or conduct described [above] and from adopting any measure having equivalent effect.").

[17] Case COMP/C-3/37.792, *Microsoft*, Commission Decision of March 24, 2004, not yet published, para. 1012.

[18] *Ibid.*, paras. 1013 and 1014.

reserved the possibility to review its decision and impose an effective alternate remedy.[19]

The Commission has discretion to tailor remedies to the specific circumstances of the case so that they are effective in achieving the desired objective. As noted above, under Article 7(1) of Regulation 1/2003, the Commission is empowered to impose "any behavioural or structural remedies" necessary. The Commission's discretion to fashion effective remedies was, however, clear even under Regulation 17/62. In *Commercial Solvents*, the Commission found that the refusal by the dominant supplier of a chemical raw material (CSC) to supply a manufacturer of a downstream product (Zoja) was abusive. The Commission's decision included not only an order to bring the infringement to an end, but also a requirement that CSC supply specified quantities of the material to Zoja immediately and provide a proposal to the Commission as regards its intentions for the subsequent supply to Zoja.[20] On appeal, the Court of Justice confirmed that, having established the infringement, "[i]n order to ensure that its Decision was effective" the Commission was entitled to go beyond a simple prohibition and could determine and order the supply of Zoja's minimum requirements "to ensure that the infringement was made good and that Zoja was protected from the consequences of it."[21]

Duty to inform victim of abusive conduct of new practices. In some cases the Commission has ordered additional measures beyond prohibitions of conduct where such measures were necessary to ensure that the remedy has its intended effect. One such device is the requirement for a dominant firm to notify its customers about new rights created as a result of the prohibition of certain contractual terms imposed by the dominant supplier. In *AKZO*, for example, where the identified abuse was linked to exclusivity agreements, the Commission required AKZO not only to end the agreements, but to notify the relevant customers.[22] The recent commitment decision in *Coca-Cola* includes a similar condition.[23]

Third-party implementation. In cases where the Commission has determined that a reporting mechanism would be insufficient as a means of overseeing compliance and effective implementation of remedies, the Commission has sometimes insisted on the appointment of a monitoring trustee. In *Microsoft*, for example, a monitoring trustee was appointed to play a "proactive" role in monitoring Microsoft's compliance with the

---

[19] *Ibid.*, para. 1012.

[20] *ZOJA/CSC ICI*, OJ 1972 L 299/51, Articles 1, 2.

[21] Joined Cases 6-7/73, *Istituto Chemioterapico Italiano SpA and Commercial Solvents Corporation v Commission* [1974] ECR 223, para. 46.

[22] *ECS/AKZO*, OJ 1985 L 374/1, Article 4 ("AKZO Chemie BV shall inform those of its customers for flour additives in the United Kingdom and Ireland which have accepted a stipulation whether oral or in writing, express or implied, requiring them to obtain the whole or effectively the whole of their requirements from AKZO Chemie BV that such a stipulation is not binding on them.").

[23] Section F of the Undertaking requires the relevant companies to publish the Undertaking and a list of countries to which it is applicable on their websites, as well as to include in the general conditions of sale on the back of their invoices a statement that the customer is free to list, buy, and sell any carbonated soft drink of any third party (reflecting the substantive commitment in Section II.A.1 of the Undertaking). See *Coca-Cola*, OJ 2005 L 253/21 (hereinafter "*Coca-Cola*").

various behavioural commitments imposed by the Commission.[24] The monitoring trustee was tasked with issuing opinions, upon application by a third party or the Commission or on its own initiative, on whether Microsoft had failed to comply with the decision in a particular instance or on any other issue that might be "of interest with respect to the effective enforcement" of the decision.[25]

15.2.3 Remedies Must Be Proportionate

Basic definition. While the principle of effectiveness acts to extend the Commission's discretionary power in setting remedies, the principle of proportionality enshrined in Article 5(3) of the EC Treaty serves as a limitation on the Commission's authority: "any action by the Community shall not go beyond what is necessary to achieve the objectives of this Treaty." This principle is formalised in Article 7(1) of Regulation 1/2003, which provides that when acting on a complaint or infringement of Articles 81 and/or 82 EC, the Commission may only impose remedies that are "proportionate to the infringement committed." The Court of Justice has interpreted the principle of proportionality to mean that remedies adopted pursuant to EC law "must not exceed what is appropriate and necessary to attain the objective pursued."[26] This means, first, that where there is a choice between several equally appropriate and necessary measures, recourse must be had to the least onerous, and second, that the disadvantage caused by the remedy must not be disproportionate to the objectives pursued.[27]

Proportionality largely a function of the objectives pursued in setting the remedy. The remedy must also not be disproportionate to the objectives pursued in setting the remedy. This aspect of the test appears to be largely a matter of balancing the intrusiveness of the remedy on the defendant against the importance of addressing the infringement. In upholding the Commission's decision against an argument that the remedy (compulsory licensing) violated the principle of proportionality, the Court of Justice clarified that "the principle of proportionality means that the burdens imposed on undertakings in order to bring an infringement of competition law to an end must not exceed what is appropriate and necessary to attain the objective sought, namely re-

---

[24] Case COMP/C-3/37.792, *Microsoft*, Commission Decision of March 24, 2004, not yet published, paras. 1043–48.

[25] It appears that the monitoring trustee has fulfilled the role intended by the Commission, as it was widely reported that in December 2005 the Commission issued a Statement of Objections alleging that Microsoft had failed to comply with certain of the remedies ordered in the 2004 decision, based in large part on reports from the monitoring trustee finding that Microsoft's compliance efforts were ineffective in bringing about the desired results. See "Commission warns Microsoft of daily penalty for failure to comply with 2004 decision," Commission Press Release IP/05/1695 of December 22, 2005. At the date of publication, Microsoft is still considered not to be in full compliance. See "Commission sends new letter to Microsoft on compliance with decision," IP/06/298 of March 10, 2006.

[26] See, e.g., Case C-426/93, *Germany v Council* [1995] ECR I-3723, para. 42; Case 15/83, *Denkavit Nederland BV v Hoofdproduktschap voor Akkerbouwprodukten* [1984] ECR 2171, para. 25; Case 122/78, *SA Buitoni v Fonds d'orientation et de régularisation des marchés agricoles* [1979] ECR 677, para. 16; and Case 66/82, *Fromançais SA v Fonds d'orientation et de régularisation des marchés agricoles (FORMA)* [1983] ECR 395, para. 8.

[27] See, e.g., Case C-426/93, *Germany v Council* [1995] ECR I-3723, para. 42; Joined Cases 279/84, 280/84, 285/84 and 286/84, *Walter Rau Lebensmittelwerke and Others v Commission* [1987] ECR 1069, para. 34.

establishment of compliance with the rules infringed."[28] Because the Commission's remedy was "the only way of bringing the infringement to an end,"[29] it was not disproportionate.

In *Microsoft*, in defence of its requirement that Microsoft offer an "unbundled" version of the Windows operating system without WMP in order to address the identified tying infringement, the Commission emphasised that the remedy would "not hinder Microsoft's ability to market its media player nor will it restrain its behaviour other than prohibiting tying or measures having equivalent effect. In particular, Microsoft will be able to continue to offer a bundle of Windows and WMP."[30] The Commission held effects of the remedy on Microsoft were therefore not disproportionate to the objective sought (i.e., addressing the foreclosure effect of the identified tying infringement).

Strong presumption that structural remedies are disproportionate. Regulation 1/2003 expressly acknowledges that behavioural remedies are, in general, the proportionate remedy in an abuse case. Article 7(1) of Regulation 1/2003 provides that "structural remedies can only be imposed either where there is no equally effective behavioural remedy or where any equally effective behavioural remedy would be burdensome for the undertaking concerned than the structural remedy." The implication is that the more burdensome structural remedies will violate the principle of proportionality unless there is no suitable behavioural alternative. As Recital 12 of Regulation 1/2003 confirms: "changes to the structure of an undertaking as it existed before the infringement was committed would only be proportionate where there is a substantial risk of a lasting or repeated infringement that derives from the very structure of the undertaking."

15.3 PRINCIPAL TYPES OF ADMINISTRATIVE DECISIONS

15.3.1 Interim Measures

Legal basis for interim measures. Regulation 1/2003 provides a new legislative basis enabling the Commission to adopt decisions imposing interim measures. Article 8(1) of Regulation 1/2003 provides that "in cases of urgency due to the risk of serious and irreparable damage to competition, the Commission, acting on its own initiative, may by decision, on the basis of a prima facie finding of infringement, order interim measures." Interim measures must be for a limited period of time and may be renewed in so far as is necessary and appropriate.[31]

The remedies that may be applied on an interim basis will normally be behavioural rules and are in principle the same as those that could be applied following an infringement decision (see section 15.4.2 below). A complainant may never obtain by interim measures a remedy that goes further than what would be appropriate if the complainant

[28] Joined Cases C-241/91 P and C-242/91 P, *Radio Telefís Éireann and Independent Television Publications Ltd (RTE & ITP) v Commission* [1995] ECR I-743, para. 93.

[29] *Ibid.*, para. 91.

[30] Case COMP/C-3/37.792, *Microsoft*, Commission Decision of March 24, 2004, not yet published, para. 1023.

[31] Regulation 1/2003, Article 8(2).

ultimately won on the merits.[32] In particular, a complainant cannot obtain interim measures preventing any conduct which could not be found to be an abuse in a final decision. The Commission usually reserves the right, however, to require incidental procedural steps in interim measures cases. For example, in *National Carbonising*, the Commission made an order for disclosure of facts and figures on a professional advisers only basis, to speed up the resolution of the issues.[33] Interim reporting of sales invoices was also imposed in *AKZO* in order to allow the Commission to monitor every sale made by the dominant firm in the affected markets.[34]

Prior to the enactment of Regulation 1/2003, there had been no express legislative basis for the Commission to order interim remedies. In *Camera Care*, however, the Court of Justice held that Article 3 of Regulation 17/62 empowered the Commission to adopt interim measures where these were indispensable for the effective exercise of its function.[35] The case law developed by the Community Courts forms the basis of the interim measures test now embodied in Regulation 1/2003[36] (although as explained below the two are not identical).

Two points should be noted at the outset regarding the Commission's practice on interim measures. First, despite having the authority to adopt interim measures since the *Camera Care* judgment in 1980, the Commission has rarely used this power under Article 82 EC.[37] Given this lack of experience, many aspects of the test for interim measures remain relatively undeveloped in the Commission's practice. Second, the differences between the test previously applied by the Commission and the Community Courts under Regulation 17/62 and the test in Article 8 of Regulation 1/2003 raise

---

[32] See, e.g., Cases 228 and 229/82, *Ford of Europe Incorporated and Ford-Werke Aktiengesellschaft v Commission* [1984] ECR 1129; Case C-149/95 P-R, *Commission v Atlantic Container Line AB and Others* [1995] ECR I-2165; and Case T-23/90, *Automobiles Peugeot SA and Peugeot SA v Commission* [1991] ECR II-653.

[33] *National Coal Board, National Smokeless Fuels Limited and the National Carbonising Company Limited*, OJ 1976 L 35/6.

[34] *ECS/AKZO*, OJ 1983 L 252/13, Article 4.

[35] "[T]he Commission must…be able…to take protective measures to the extent to which they might appear indispensable in order to avoid the exercise of the power to make decisions given by Article 3 from becoming ineffectual or even illusory because of the action of certain undertakings. The powers which the Commission holds under Article 3(1) of Regulation No 17 therefore include the power to take interim measures which are indispensable for the effective exercise of its functions, and, in particular, for ensuring the effectiveness of any decisions requiring undertakings to bring to an end infringements which it has found to exist." Case C-792/79 R, *Camera Care Ltd v Commission* [1980] ECR 119 (hereinafter "*Camera Care*"), para. 18.

[36] Recital 11 of Regulation 1/2003 refers specifically to the acknowledgement of the Court of Justice of the Commission's power to adopt decisions ordering interim remedies.

[37] See, e.g., *NDC Health/IMS Health: Interim Measures,* OJ 2002 L 59/18; *BBI/Boosey & Hawkes: Interim Measures,* OJ 1987 L 286/36; *ECS/AKZO: Interim Measures*, OJ 1983 L 252/13; *Irish Continental Group v CCI Morlaix: Interim Measures*, (1995) 5 *Common Market Law Reports* 177; *Sealink/B&I Holyhead: Interim Measures*, (1992) 5 *Common Market Law Reports* 255; and *National Coal Board, National Smokeless Fuels Limited and the National Carbonising Company Limited: Interim Measures*, OJ 1976 L 35/6. The Commission's interim measures practice has also developed in cases where the Commission has rejected an application for interim measures, but these cases typically do not result in published decisions. See, however, *Sea Containers v Stena Sealink: Interim measures* OJ 1994 L 15/8. See also *Phoenix/IBM*, XXIInd Report on Competition Policy, p. 426 and *TESN*, XXIInd Report on Competition Policy, p. 426.

questions as to the continued validity of the limited precedents that do exist. As a result, notwithstanding the recent legislative clarification of the Commission's power to order interim measures, there is uncertainty surrounding the Commission's interim measures powers today. These issues will be developed further below with reference to the test as formulated in Regulation 1/2003.

The requirements for adoption of interim measures. Article 8(1) of Regulation 1/2003 (quoted above) indicates that three elements must be present for the Commission to order interim measures.

a. Prima facie finding of infringement. The imposition of interim measures inevitably affects the rights of the company concerned, limiting its freedom of action or requiring it to forgo a competitive advantage in the absence of a formal finding that it has acted unlawfully. To justify this, there must be a sufficient level of probability that the company has violated Article 82 EC. The Commission and Community Courts have offered different interpretations of the requisite standard of assurance that an infringement has occurred to justify the granting of an interim remedy. In *La Cinq*,[38] the Commission rejected an application for an interim injunction since, *inter alia*, an initial summary examination of the facts did not show that there had been "clear and flagrant infringement (*prima facie* infringement)" of EC competition law. On appeal, however, the Court of First Instance held that the Commission's formulation contravened the previously established rule that the level of probability of infringement required to support an interim measures order cannot be the same as the level of probability required for a final infringement decision. The Commission's "clear and flagrant" condition for interim remedies would effectively require the existence of the infringement to be established at the stage of *prima facie* appraisal. This places too high a burden on the applicant and would very likely prejudice the outcome of the final determination—both undesirable consequences given the fact that time constraints and the abbreviated interim hearing make the interim measures stage an inadequate substitute for a full hearing. The Court therefore rejected the Commission's identification of the requirement of a *prima facie* infringement with the requirement of finding a "clear and flagrant" infringement.[39]

The Community Courts have articulated a number of different formulations of the test, all of which set a relatively low threshold. In *Peugeot*, the Court of First Instance upheld the Commission's order of interim measures since "at first sight, there were serious doubts as to the legality" of the defendant's conduct.[40] Other relevant cases have involved applications for interim measures against the implementation of Commission decisions, employing a variety of formulations of the test such as: "the challenge...is based on serious considerations such as to make the legality of those measures doubtful to say the least"[41] and "the grounds...appear, on first examination, not to be manifestly without foundation."[42] Although they are not identical, each of these formulations presents a relatively low evidentiary threshold for showing a *prima*

---

[38] Case T-44/90, *La Cinq SA v Commission* [1992] ECR II-1 (hereinafter "*La Cinq*").
[39] *Ibid.*, paras. 61–62.
[40] Case T-23/90, *Peugeot v Commission* [1991] ECR II-653 (hereinafter "*Peugeot*"), paras. 62–63.
[41] Case 232/81 R, *Agricola commerciale olio Srl and others v Commission* [1981] ECR-2193.
[42] Case 3/75 R, *Johnson & Firth Brown v Commission* [1975] ECR 7.

facie infringement, effectively shifting the determination whether to implement interim measures substantially onto the second limb of the test.

b. Urgency due to the risk of serious and irreparable damage to competition. The second condition for interim measures under Article 8(1) of Regulation 1/2003 is a showing of "urgency due to the risk of serious and irreparable damage to competition." In *IMS Health*, the President of the Court of First Instance explained that "urgency" and "serious and irreparable harm" are not separate limbs of the test for interim remedies, since "if a risk of serious and irreparable harm exists, urgency is inevitably simultaneously established."[43] The two apparent conditions are therefore effectively merged into one: the requirement that adoption of an interim measure is urgent has, since *Camera Care*, simply meant that action is needed to prevent serious and irreparable harm.[44]

In contrast to the case-law developed by the Community Courts under Regulation 17, which referred to "a risk of serious and irreparable damage to the *applicant*,"[45] Regulation 1/2003 refers to damage to *competition*. This echoes the 'other limb'[46] of the Community Courts' urgency test, according to which an applicant must show a risk of "intolerable damage to the public interest."[47] "Public interest" is not clearly defined in the case law. In *Camera Care*, considerations such as protection of Member States' interests and those of their citizens, and objectives of competition policy, were given as examples of the public interest.[48] This is not an exhaustive list, and there no doubt remains scope for development by the Commission of what "damage to competition" means.

A key question is the extent to which damage to competition will be inferred upon a showing of likely damage to *competitors*. Certain authors argue that damage to individual private undertakings will still be relevant, even where this cannot be construed as damage to competition policy: "Article 8(1) refers simply to 'damage to competition', which, it is submitted is to be understood as embracing either damage to undertakings, or to competition, or both."[49]

This view is not clearly correct. There is evidence that the Council's reference to "damage to competition" in Regulation 1/2003 was deliberately intended to exclude the "damage to the applicant" that had been used in the Community Courts' jurisprudence under Regulation 17/62. The Explanatory Memorandum to the proposal for Regulation 1/2003 expressly advocates a shift from a focus on the interests of the complainant to a focus on the interests of competition in general in evaluating whether interim measures

---

[43] *Ibid.*, para. 54.

[44] Case C-792/79 R, *Camera Care Ltd v Commission* [1980] ECR 119, para. 19.

[45] Case T-44/90, *La Cinq SA v Commission* [1992] ECR II-1, para. 94.

[46] L Ortiz Blanco, *EC Competition Procedure* (Oxford, Oxford University Press, 2006), 14.06 ("Such measures are to be taken only in cases of proven urgency, in order to prevent the occurrence of a situation likely to cause serious and irreparable damage to the party applying for their adoption or intolerable damage to the public interest.").

[47] Case T-184/01 R, *IMS Health Inc v Commission* [2001] ECR II-3193, para. 53.

[48] Case C-792/79 R, *Camera Care Ltd v Commission* [1980] ECR 119, para. 19.

[49] CS Kerse & N Kahn, *EC Antitrust Procedure* (5th edn., London, Sweet & Maxwell, 2005) para. 6-035.

are appropriate.[50] In light of this, the better interpretation of "damage to competition" is that harm to individual competitors will only be relevant to the extent that it represents damage to competition as a whole.

As regards what it means for harm to be "irreparable", the Court of First Instance in *La Cinq* overturned the Commission's standard whereby damage would be irreparable when "[it] cannot be remedied by any subsequent decision." The Court found that this test would be almost impossible to meet, thus depriving the Commission in substance of its power to adopt interim measures. The Court held that damage would be irreparable where [it] could no longer be remedied by the decision to be adopted by the Commission upon the conclusion of the administrative procedure.[51] Thus, harm may be "irreparable" even if it could in principle be remedied by a judgment from a national or Community Court.

In cases under Regulation 17/62, "serious and irreparable" damage has been identified in situations where there is a risk that a competitor will be driven out of business,[52] or where applicants for relief may suffer considerable competitive disadvantage with a lasting effect on their position.[53] However, in light of the new Regulation 1/2003 "damage to competition" requirement, such evidence may no longer be sufficient to warrant interim measures.

As noted above, under the "public interest" limb of the test in the case law, interim measures were appropriate when "intolerable damage" was likely to be caused to the public interest. There is little Community Court or Commission guidance on the meaning of "intolerable" here, although the concept seems to imply a degree of seriousness requiring exceptional measures.[54]

The *IMS Health* case may provide the best indication as to future interpretation of "serious and irreparable harm." In its decision ordering interim measures against IMS Health (compulsory licensing of intellectual property), the Commission found that, in the absence of a licence, both of IMS's competitors faced having to withdraw from the relevant market, leaving IMS as the only supplier, and characterised this as "intolerable damage to the public interest."[55] The President of the Court of First Instance suspended this decision, finding that the risk of IMS's competitors going out of business was not

---

[50] *Proposal for a Council Regulation on the implementation of the rules on competition laid down in Articles 81 and 82 of the Treaty*, COM (2000) 582 final, Explanatory Memorandum, Article 8 ("The Commission acts in the public interest and not in the interest of individual operators. It is therefore appropriate to ensure that the Commission has an obligation to adopt interim measures only in cases where there is a risk of serious and irreparable harm to competition. Companies can always have recourse to national courts, the very function of which is to protect the rights of individuals.").

[51] Case T-44/90, *La Cinq SA v Commission* [1992] ECR II-1, para. 80 (referring to *Camera Care*).

[52] *BBI/Boosey & Hawkes—Interim Measures*, OJ 1987 L 286/36. In *NDC Health/IMS Health: Interim measures*, OJ 2002 L 59/18, the Commission cited its determination that IMS Health's competitors were faced with the risk of going out of business in support of its finding of serious and irreparable damage (paras. 189–90).

[53] *Langnese-Iglo GmbH*, OJ 1993 L 183/19.

[54] CS Kerse & N Kahn, *EC Antitrust Procedure* (5th edn., London, Sweet & Maxwell, 2005) para. 6-035.

[55] *NDC Health/IMS Health: Interim measures*, OJ 2002 L 59/18, para. 195.

so high. In so holding, the President emphasised the "inherently exceptional nature of the power to adopt interim measures" and called for a balancing exercise to be carried out, in particular "where the public interest invoked by the Commission...relates, in substance, primarily to the interests of the applicant's competitors."[56]

This order highlights an issue that had been undeveloped in the Commission's decisional practice: the need to consider the possibility that both the applicant (as a result of the challenged conduct) and the respondent (as a result of ordered interim measures) may face irreparable harm. In its decision, the Commission did not adequately consider the nature of the harm facing IMS Health, i.e., the loss of its intellectual property rights.[57]

The President's balancing approach clarifies the need to consider possible irreparable harm to *both* parties. In fact, the President found that IMS's competitors would not be faced with going out of business in the absence of interim measures, and therefore did not need to consider where the balance of interests would lie if both the competitors and IMS had been faced with irreparable harm. However, the emphasis placed on the continuing viability of IMS's competitors implies that, if a failure to grant interim measures would have resulted in the exit of all IMS's competitors from the market, this would have represented irreparable harm to competition that might have outweighed the irreparable harm to IMS's market position and to its intellectual property rights.

While it is important to bear in mind that the Commission's interim measures powers under Regulation 1/2003 are somewhat different to its previous powers, the President's interpretation would seem a reasonable approach in reconciling the notions of "harm to competitors" and "harm to competition." The threatened exit of all competitors from a market in the absence of interim measures should in most cases represent harm to competition that is likely to outweigh the harm caused to the respondent by an interim measures order.

c. ***The Commission, acting on its own initiative.*** The most significant difference between interim measures under Regulation 17 and the new requirements of Article 8 of Regulation 1/2003 is that on its face the latter does not allow complainants to request the Commission to issue interim measures. Article 3 of Regulation 17/62 (the legislative basis for interim measures under the previous regulatory regime) referred to the Commission "acting on a complaint," which under the Community Courts' interpretation allowed complainants to request the Commission to adopt interim measures and to challenge the Commission's response to such a complaint. Article 7 of Regulation 1/2003 includes the same "acting on a complaint" language in the context of an application for a final infringement decision. By contrast, Article 8 of Regulation 1/2003 only allows for interim measures to be issued by the Commission "acting on its own initiative." Thus, all procedures for the adoption of interim remedies must now be

[56] Case T-184/01 R, *IMS Health Inc v Commission* [2001] ECR II-3193, para. 145.

[57] The Commission found that these rights could be adequately protected by royalty payments in *NDC Health/IMS Health: Interim measures*, OJ 2002 L 59/18, para. 200, a conclusion rejected by the President of the Court of First Instance in Case T-184/01 R, *IMS Health Inc v Commission* [2001] ECR II-3193, paras. 125–29.

initiated by the Commission, apparently in its discretion.[58] This change in approach may have several significant consequences.

First, the potential for judicial review of refusals to adopt interim measures under Article 232 EC will be curtailed.[59] Complainants will apparently be unable to challenge a refusal by the Commission to adopt interim measures, since interim measures decisions are no longer contingent upon "the institution concerned...[first being] called upon to act."[60] There is some question whether the Community Courts will accept this limitation, since the analysis in *Camera Care* was predicated on the view that the Commission's power to adopt interim measures was inherent in the power to adopt decisions against infringements, now granted by Article 7 of Regulation 1/2003. There may therefore be scope for third parties to force a review of the Commission's failure to adopt interim measures based on this provision.[61] Clarification from the Community Courts will likely be needed.

Second, preventing applicants from requesting interim measures will probably decrease still further the frequency with which the Commission seeks to apply interim remedies. It was often in the interests of complainants to request interim measures from the Commission in order to protect themselves from the infringements they alleged. Under Regulation 1/2003, applicants will no longer be able to raise such arguments. This change will be exacerbated by the fact, as outlined above, that interim remedies will no longer be granted in the interests of competitors or complainants where these do not correspond to the interests of competition more generally. Therefore, ironically, the effect of granting the Commission express power to order interim measures may well be to reduce the frequency with which the process is used.

A third significant consequence of allowing the Commission alone to initiate interim remedies relates to the balancing exercise that must take place in any action for interim remedies. Under Regulation 17 and the case law, where complainants requested an interim injunction, the balance was largely between the competing interests of the parties.[62] As explained above, the Commission's Explanatory Memorandum indicates

---

[58] Although there is nothing to prevent a complainant from urging the Commission to adopt interim measures, the complaint will need to allege serious and irreparable damage to competition (i.e., a public interest criterion) rather than harm to the applicant.

[59] See CS Kerse & N Kahn, *EC Antitrust Procedure* (5th edn., London, Sweet & Maxwell, 2005) para. 6-032. See also L Ortiz Blanco, *EC Competition Procedure* (Oxford, Oxford University Press, forthcoming (2006), Chapter 14, section A.

[60] Article 232(2) EC.

[61] See CS Kerse & N Kahn, above, para. 6-032, who argue that the Community Courts may continue to apply the *Automec* jurisprudence to enable complainants to challenge the Commission for failing to act. See Case T-64/89, *Automec Srl v Commission* [1990] ECR II-367. However, the Commission has stressed that Article 8 of Regulation 1/2003 should be construed as preventing complainants from applying for interim measures under Article 7(2), noting that "[r]equests for interim measures by undertakings can be brought before Member States' courts which are well placed to decide on such measures." Notice on the handling of complaints by the Commission under Articles 81 and 82 of the EC Treaty, OJ 2004 C 101/65, para. 80.

[62] For an example of the intricate balancing this can involve, see *NDC Health/IMS Health: Interim measures*, OJ 2002 L 59/18, withdrawn by *NDC Health/IMS Health: Interim measures*, OJ 2003 L 268/69, and Case T-184/01 R, *IMS Health Inc v Commission* [2001] ECR II-3193, para. 134–50,

that under Article 8 of Regulation 1/2003 the emphasis will shift from the interests of the complainant to those of competition generally. The new regime therefore poses challenges for respondents facing a potential interim remedy, since defending an argument put by the Commission that competition in general will suffer serious and irreparable harm may be more difficult to rebut than arguments seeking a balance between the interests of rival firms. However, as noted above, this risk for respondents may be mitigated by the withdrawal of the rights of complainants to insist on interim measures, which may mean that interim measures cases become even more infrequent.

Conclusion. In keeping with the general theme of Regulation 1/2003, the effect of Article 8 may be to further decentralise the application of interim measures for apparent violations of EC competition law. Despite endowing the Commission for the first time with an express power to order interim remedies, the scope of this power seems to be limited in comparison to that created by the *Camera Care* jurisprudence. The fact that applicants will apparently no longer be able to request interim measures; the fact that the Commission must consider the interests of "competition" as opposed to those of individual competitors; the reference by the President of the Court of First Instance in *IMS* to the "exceptional nature" of interim measures; and the comparative speed and ease with which applicants can obtain interim relief before national courts all suggest that the already limited involvement by the Commission in interim measures cases will in future become even less frequent. Indeed, this is an outcome that the Commission itself encourages.[63]

15.3.2 Commitment Decisions

15.3.2.1 Overview

Legal basis for commitment decisions. Regulation 1/2003 introduced a new kind of settlement decision, by which companies' commitments to the Commission are made legally binding. Article 9 of Regulation 1/2003 states as follows

> "Where the Commission intends to adopt a decision requiring that an infringement be brought to an end and the undertakings concerned offer commitments to meet the concerns expressed to them by the Commission in its preliminary assessment, the Commission may by decision make those commitments binding on the undertakings. Such a decision may be adopted for a specific period and shall conclude that there are no longer grounds for action by the Commission."

Recital 13 of Regulation 1/2003 provides some additional guidance as to the

confirmed on appeal by the President of the Court of Justice in Case C-481/01P(R), *NDC Health GmbH & Co KG and NDC Health Corporation v Commission and IMS Health Inc* [2002] ECR I-3401.

[63] Commission Notice on the handling of complaints by the Commission under Articles 81 and 82 of the EC Treaty OJ 2004 C 101/65, para. 80. In fact, two recent Spanish judgments appear to represent the first interim measures decisions adopted by any national court for a violation of Article 82 EC. See "DLA Piper Strikes Twice Obtaining the Granting of Interim Measures in Two Different Cases Regarding an Infringement of Article 82 of the EC Treaty," DLA Piper Rudnick Gray Cary Press Release of January 13, 2006. The United Kingdom has also adopted a similar recent decision. See *Statement on London Metal Exchange interim measures direction*, OFT Press Release of March 2, 2006.

Commission's intentions regarding the new procedure:[64]

> "Commitment decisions should find that there are no longer grounds for action by the Commission without concluding whether there has been or still is an infringement. Commitment decisions are without prejudice to the powers of competition authorities and courts of the Member States to make such a finding and decide upon the case. Commitment decisions are not appropriate where the Commission intends to impose a fine."

The new commitment decision is analogous to the commonly-used US "consent decree"[65] in that both are negotiated resolutions of civil investigations, which were previously without express legal basis under EC competition law.[66] There are, however, several important differences between the two procedures. First, commitment decisions involve no finding that the undertaking in question has broken EC competition law in the past (whereas US consent decrees typically include an express admission by the settling party of having violated the law). Second, commitment decisions will not be used in cases where the Commission is imposing fines (whereas US consent decrees commonly include negotiated fines). Finally, commitment decisions do not require court approval in the public interest (whereas US consent decrees must be approved by a Federal Court, representing an additional procedural safeguard).

Reasons why commitment decisions may be appealing. The commitment decision is a welcome addition to the range of possible resolutions of Article 82 EC investigations: in principle, settlement represents a cheaper and faster way of addressing harmful effects of anticompetitive conduct, which is the primary goal of enforcement policy. Both companies and competition authorities may see significant advantages in pursuing settlement instead of a formal procedure leading to an infringement decision under Article 7 of Regulation 1/2003. From the perspective of a company under investigation in an Article 82 EC case, the possibility of negotiating a settlement may be attractive for several reasons, including:

1. *No formal finding of a violation.* The commitment decision will not include a finding that the company's past conduct violated Article 82 EC. As noted above, Recital 13 of Regulation 1/2003 makes clear that commitment decisions will conclude only that there are "no longer grounds for action by the Commission without concluding whether there has been or still is an infringement." A finding of past Article 82 EC infringement—which would include express conclusions on market definition, dominance, and abuse—could have adverse consequences such as facilitating private claims for damages. The precedential value of commitment decisions for private damage actions is considered below, but the fact that commitment decisions will

[64] Regulation 1/2003, Recital 13. The last sentence of Recital 13 means that commitments are not cases for plea bargaining to agree on the amount of a fine which the company would not challenge. Imposing a fine necessarily involves a finding that there has been an infringement, which is inconsistent with the fact that in commitment decisions the Commission does not make any finding whether there was an infringement.

[65] See M Furse, "The Decision to Commit: Some Pointers from the US" (2004) 35(1) *European Competition Law Review* 5.

[66] See Section 15.3.3 below.

include no finding of past infringement will be an important attraction of the process for many companies.

2. *More efficient process.* Because commitment decisions make no finding as to whether there has been an abuse, the settlement process is more efficient. Issues of market definition and dominance, which may be at the centre of dispute in a procedure leading to an infringement decision, are largely set aside, allowing discussion to focus on the specific conduct at issue. While the settlement process may still be lengthy and complex, it is likely to save management time and legal and economist fees as compared to a contested proceeding leading to a final decision, which will include more formal steps (potentially including appeals to the Community Courts) and touch on a broader range of disputed issues.

3. *Greater insight into a competition authority's views.* The likely outcome of an Article 9 procedure will be more transparent to the company. If the company is able to engage the competition authority in settlement discussions, then the process of drafting a commitment, discussing it with the competition authority, and responding as appropriate will give the company important insight into the competition authority's perspective and intentions, which the competition authority may have no reason to explain fully during a contested proceeding. At the same time, the negotiation process allows the company to offer and defend behavioural rules that have been shaped in such a way as to be applicable in practice, which would not necessarily be the case with a remedy imposed unilaterally by the competition authority. Negotiating rules of conduct bilaterally may also give the company more influence over the final outcome, as there should be greater opportunity to advocate particular rules and oppose others.

4. *Clarification on key practices.* The commitment decision procedure facilitates the design of specific rules of conduct, which can provide important clarification on acceptable practices in unclear areas of law (e.g., pricing and rebate practices). In some situations, the fact that the agreed rules of conduct are clear may be almost as important to companies as what the actual rules are. A commitment decision creates an opportunity for a company to develop an acceptable set of conduct guidelines, approved by the competition authority, under which the company can run its business in the future.

5. *No publicity.* By entering into a negotiated settlement with the competition authority, the company may minimise the adverse publicity and attendant reputational damage that almost invariably accompany contested formal proceedings.

6. *No fine.* Commitment decisions carry no fine.

The Article 9 process may also have significant attractions for competition authorities:

1. *Quick resolution.* Commitment decisions should represent the quickest means of bringing anticompetitive behaviour to an end and restoring effective

competition to the market. Although there are no fixed deadlines for completion of either process, given Article 9's more streamlined procedure it should ordinarily take a competition authority substantially less time to reach a commitment decision than a final infringement decision. This difference is even greater when one considers that the Court of First Instance has often suspended Commission infringement decisions pending appeal, which normally takes an additional two or more years.[67] The prospect of having new behavioural rules implemented up to several years sooner as a result of a commitment decision creates a strong incentive for competition authorities to negotiate settlements. This may be a particularly important consideration in new or rapidly developing markets.

2. *Better use of limited resources.* Commitment decisions make more efficient use of limited enforcement resources. As described below, the process under Article 9 is relatively streamlined and informal, reducing or eliminating several of the steps competition authorities must take before reaching a prohibition decision (e.g., the need to gather evidence, draft and defend one or more Statements of Objections, and conduct an Oral Hearing). Because it better allows the competition authority and company to focus discussion on the specific conduct at issue, the efficiency of the Article 9 process should be as attractive to resource-constrained competition authorities as it is to companies.

3. *Scope for more creative and effective remedies.* The competition authority may be able to obtain a more wide-reaching remedy through commitments than it could impose in an infringement decision.[68] For example, as an inducement to settlement discussions or for reasons of convenience, a company may offer to apply a commitment in geographic or product markets that did not form part of the competition authority's investigation or in which it is not (or may not be) dominant. With such a commitment, the competition authority is obtaining something that it would not have been able to impose on its own.[69]

4. *Easier resolution of complex cases.* Commitment decisions may be a convenient means of closing particularly difficult cases. On occasion, a competition authority may decide that the burden or risk of continuing with an ongoing case outweighs its likely benefit. This might be so, for example, in a

---

[67] The Court of First Instance's refusal to suspend the Commission's decision in the *Microsoft* case was the exception rather than the rule. See Case T-201/04R, *Microsoft Corp v Commission*, Order of December 22, 2004.

[68] In respect of US consent decrees, which in this regard are analogous to commitment decisions, it has been noted that some consent decree remedies appear to go beyond what the government could realistically anticipate as a remedy in a contested case. See AD Melamed, "Antitrust: The New Regulation" (1995) 10(1) *Antitrust* 14.

[69] The clearest example of this to date is the *Coca-Cola* decision under Article 9. Notwithstanding the fact that the Commission's investigation covered only four Member States, the negotiated commitments potentially apply in all EU Member States in which The Coca-Cola Company's carbonated soft drinks account for more than 40% of sales and more than twice the share of the nearest competitor. In addition, The Coca-Cola Company is required to use its best efforts to ensure that all of its EU bottlers—including those that were not part of the Commission's investigation—commit to abide by the commitments. See *Coca-Cola*, OJ 2005 L 253/21.

case involving a specialised or unusual set of facts, where proving an abuse would require detailed and time-consuming analysis and where a final decision would be of limited precedential value. Similarly (if less desirably), a competition authority might decide to settle for a commitment in a case in which it had already expended substantial resources if it began to doubt its ability to prevail through a contested proceeding (e.g., because it realised that the factual evidence, the economic assessment, or the legal principles involved were weak, unconvincing, or controversial).

Notwithstanding these attractions for all interested parties, commitment decisions will not be appropriate in all cases. The most straightforward reason is related to the fact that commitment decisions cannot include fines. In cases where there is substantial evidence that a company has violated a well-established, uncontroversial legal rule, the competition authority may decide that punishing the past misconduct through fines is an important element of its enforcement action. Commitment decisions are also unlikely to be attractive to the competition authority in situations where it perceives the need to set a clear and unequivocal precedent. Because they are negotiated settlements, where both sides may need to make concessions, commitment decisions do not necessarily define the boundaries between lawful and unlawful conduct. Only in a formal infringement decision can the competition authority make a clear, binding statement that particular conduct violates Article 82 EC. Commitment decisions thus cannot establish decisive precedents in the same way as infringement decisions, which may make them unsuitable for some cases.

Use of the commitment decision procedure to date. Since Regulation 1/2003 has been in force, the Commission has issued only three final decisions under Article 9: *Bundesliga*,[70] *Coca-Cola*,[71] and *De Beers/Alrosa*,[72] with the latter two cases concerning unilateral conduct under Article 82 EC. However, a number of additional cases are in advanced stages of the process under Article 9, with commitment decisions pending.[73] Thus, while the Article 9 process has been attractive and is anticipated to be used with some regularity in future, as of early 2006 it remains novel and neither the Commission nor national competition authorities have yet developed fully a policy on commitment decisions.[74]

---

[70] *Joint selling of the media rights to the German Bundesliga*, OJ 2005 L 134/46 (hereinafter "*Bundesliga*") (joint selling of television and radio broadcasting rights for football matches in Germany).

[71] *Coca-Cola*, OJ 2005 L 253/21 (highly specific commitments on a range of commercial practices relating to sale of carbonated soft drinks, including exclusivity, target rebates, tying, assortment rebates, shelf space payments, financing agreements, availability agreements, sponsorship, tender agreements, and technical equipment placement).

[72] See De Beers' commitment to phase out rough diamond purchases from ALROSA made legally binding by Commission decision, Commission Press Release IP/06/204 of February 22, 2006.

[73] *Repsol CPP SA*, OJ 2004 C 258/7 (non-compete clauses in distribution agreements between oil company and petrol stations); *BUMA* and *SABAM*, OJ 2005 C 200/11 (collective licensing of music copyrights for online use); and *Premier League Football*, Commission Press Release IP/05/1441 of November 17, 2005 (joint selling of television football broadcasting rights).

[74] Commitment decisions by national competition authorities are likely to be based on national laws. However, some Member States have adopted commitment decisions under EC competition law, in the

15.3.2.2 Commitment decision procedure

Formal steps for adopting commitment decisions. As noted in the preceding section, one of the chief attractions of Article 9 for both companies and competition authorities is its comparatively streamlined procedure, which allows the parties to focus more on the substantive issues and minimises burdensome formal requirements. The principal formal steps leading to a Commission decision under Article 9 are the following.[75]

a. ***Initiation of proceedings.*** Recital 13 of Regulation 1/2003 establishes that commitment decisions may only be taken in "proceedings." In the traditional parlance, the Commission initiates "proceedings" in an Article 82 EC investigation by issuing a Statement of Objections, which frames the Commission's concerns and formalises the Commission's intention to take a final decision in the case. Under Article 9, proceedings may be opened through issuance of a Statement of Objections, but this is not required. Merely making public the fact that the Commission has initiated proceedings, by so stating on the Commission's website, suffices.[76] In addition to formally enabling the Commission to adopt a decision under Article 9, the initiation of proceedings relieves Member State competition authorities of their competence to apply Article 82 EC against the relevant company in respect of matters within the scope of the Commission's investigation.[77] The only time restriction is that proceedings must be initiated, at latest, by the time the Commission issues a Statement of Objections, a preliminary assessment under Article 9(1) of Regulation 1/2003, or a public Notice under Article 27(4) of Regulation 1/2003 (see below).

b. ***Preliminary assessment.*** Article 9(1) provides that the commitments on which an Article 9 decision is based must "meet the concerns expressed to [the relevant companies] by the Commission in its preliminary assessment." The required content of the preliminary assessment is not specified, but it appears to be intended to serve the same formal purpose as a Statement of Objections in a proceeding leading to an infringement decision, i.e., to inform the companies of the Commission's initial concerns and give them an opportunity to respond. Like a Statement of Objections, the preliminary assessment is sent only to the relevant companies and is not made public

---

absence of any parallel national provision. For example, on November 30, 2005, the Belgian Competition Council closed proceedings against Coca-Cola Beverages Belgium (CCBB) on the basis of a range of commitments (mostly related to discriminatory pricing issues). This is the first time commitments have been accepted in Belgium to formally close an abuse of dominance proceeding. The Belgian Competition Act does not empower the Competition Council to adopt commitment decisions. However, the Council found that it was empowered to accept commitments and close proceedings in this way based on the directly applicable nature of Regulation 1/2003, Article 5 of which enables national competition authorities to accept commitments when applying Article 82 EC in national proceedings. See Decision 2005-I/O-52.

[75] Because the Commission's final and pending Article 9 decisions to date have all involved investigations that were initiated before the entry into force of Regulation 1/2003, the cases so far have often included procedural steps (e.g., Statements of Objections) that will not necessarily be taken in future Article 9 proceedings.

[76] Commission Regulation (EEC) No. 773/2004 relating to the conduct of proceedings by the Commission pursuant to Articles 81 and 82 of the EC Treaty, OJ 2004 L 123/18, Article 2. See also *Coca-Cola*, OJ 2005 L 253/21.

[77] Regulation 1/2003, Article 11(6).

(although a summary of the preliminary assessment is provided in the Commission's final decision under Article 9).

In practice, however, it appears that, at least in some cases, the preliminary assessment will be a short formal document that is not a central element of the Article 9 process. In the *Coca-Cola* case, the Commission delivered its preliminary assessment on October 15, 2004. The companies submitted commitments formally on October 19, 2004. It was reported that discussions between the Commission and the addressees of the *Coca-Cola* decision over draft commitments had already been ongoing for several months, and in fact the Commission had already consulted with interested third parties on draft commitments. Thus, it seems very likely that the proposed commitments had, in fact, already been agreed before the Commission issued the preliminary assessment. The preliminary assessment was probably drafted to correspond to the commitments, rather than the commitments being designed to address the Commission's concerns as stated in the preliminary assessment. From the parties' perspective, the preliminary assessment would therefore have been largely a formality. Importantly, therefore, unlike a Statement of Objections—which is scrutinised and subject to endorsement at various levels within DG Competition before being issued—the preliminary assessment does not appear to serve as a significant check on the administrative process.

c. ***Notice for public comment***. Article 27(4) of Regulation 1/2003 provides that "where the Commission intends to adopt a decision pursuant to Article 9…, it shall publish a concise summary of the case and the main content of the commitments or of the proposed course of action." It adds that "[i]nterested third parties may submit their observations [by a specified date]." This summary is published in the Official Journal, in all the EU official languages (and thus represents a potential source of delay). The summary should be sufficient to make the Commission's concerns and the proposed commitments clear, such that third parties have a meaningful opportunity to comment. In addition to the Commission's summary, the full non-confidential text of the draft commitments is published on the Commission's website in the original language.[78] Interested third parties normally have one month in which to make comments.

The opportunity for all interested third parties to comment on a draft decision is an unusual element of the Article 9 process, which is not guaranteed under the general Regulation 1/2003 framework leading to final infringement decisions (or, for that matter, in merger proceedings). This difference perhaps reflects the novelty of the Article 9 process and its relative lack of other procedural safeguards. The Commission has stated that if the feedback from third parties on the draft commitments reveals weakness in the proposed course of action, it may seek to renegotiate or abandon the draft commitments or even "revert to the prohibition scenario."[79] The limited experience to date indicates that the Commission has received numerous third-party comments in at least some Article 9 cases, and that these comments have been taken into account in the Commission's final decisions.[80]

[78] Commission MEMO/04/217 of September 17, 2004.

[79] Commission MEMO/04/217 of September 17, 2004.

[80] In the *Coca-Cola* case, for example, the Commission published the full text of draft commitments on its website on October 19, 2004 and its Article 27(4) Notice on November 26, 2004. The Hearing

d. ***Reviews by Member State Advisory Committee and Hearing Officer.*** Both the Member State Advisory Committee and the Hearing Officer review the record and issue reports on the Commission's draft decision, which are published in the Official Journal. The Opinion of the Advisory Committee is issued following discussion of the Commission's draft decision in a meeting. This Opinion states whether the Advisory Committee agrees with the Commission on issues such as: whether the proceedings can be concluded by means of a decision under Article 9; whether, in light of the commitments offered, there are no longer grounds for action by the Commission; and whether the Commission should make the commitments binding on the undertakings concerned. The Opinion also summarises the voting by Advisory Committee members (i.e., unanimous, majority/minority, abstentions). The Advisory Committee Opinions in Article 9 cases to date have been brief and have signalled unanimous or majority agreement with all relevant Commission actions.[81]

The Final Report of the Hearing Officer summarises the procedural steps in the case, focusing in particular on the steps taken by the Commission to "market test" the draft commitments. Consistent with the Hearing Officer's defined role, the report concludes only whether the case calls for any particular comments as regards the right to be heard. The reports issued to date have not identified any such concerns.[82]

e. ***Publication of decision.*** Shortly after publication of the Advisory Committee and the Hearing Officer reports,[83] the Commission issues its final decision along with the final and legally binding commitments covered by the decision. The Commission's emerging practice seems to be to publish on its website the full decision and commitments, edited to remove any business secrets, in three languages: the *Bundesliga*[84] and *Coca-Cola*[85] decisions were published in English, French, and German. At the same time, a one-page summary of the decision is published in the Official Journal in all official EU languages. The final decision is substantially more detailed than the Article 27(4) Notice. The *Bundesliga* and *Coca-Cola* decisions follow a similar format. One notable element of the decisions is a detailed description of the preliminary assessment, including (in the *Coca-Cola* case, which is the only one

---

Officer's Final Report on the case states that the Commission received 33 observations from interested third parties. The commitments published in connection with the Commission's final decision on June 22, 2005, differ in several respects from the October 19, 2004, version, indicating that the commitments originally agreed between the companies and the Commission were modified in order to address the third-party comments received in response to the Article 27(4) Notice.

[81] Opinion of the Advisory Committee on restrictive practices and dominant positions given at its 390th meeting on May 20, 2005, concerning a draft decision in Case COMP/A.39.116/B2—*Coca-Cola*, OJ 2005 C 239/20; Opinion of the Advisory Committee on restrictive practices and dominant positions given at its 386th meeting on December 6, 2004 concerning a preliminary draft decision in Case COMP/A.37.214–*DFB*, OJ 2005 C 130/04.

[82] Final report of the Hearing Officer in Case COMP/39.116, *Coca-Cola*, OJ 2005 C 239/19; Final report of the Hearing Officer in Case COMP/37.214, *DFB Joint Selling of Media Rights*, OJ 2005 C 130/2.

[83] In the *Bundesliga* and *Coca*-Cola cases, the final decision has been published about one month after the Advisory Committee and the Hearing Officer reports.

[84] *Joint selling of media rights to the German Bundesliga*, OJ 2005 L 134/46.

[85] *Coca-Cola*, OJ 2005 L 253/21.

pursuant to Article 82 EC) summaries of the Commission's preliminary findings on market definition and dominance, as well as the practices raising concerns.

Need to avoid impression that violations have been found. As indicated above, a primary attraction of the Article 9 process for companies is the fact that commitment decisions do not include any finding that the company's past conduct violated Article 82 EC. Offering commitments under Article 9 is not an admission of having broken the law, and companies will not enter the process if it is likely to be regarded as such. If Article 9 is to be successful, it is imperative that final commitment decisions not create the impression—which could influence third parties such as potential private plaintiffs, national competition authorities, and national courts—that the Commission has concluded that the conduct underlying the commitments violated Article 82 EC. This will require careful drafting, as the Commission will probably feel compelled to set forth its concerns in sufficient detail to justify imposing the commitments, but it must do so without stating that it had identified legal violations.

The *Coca-Cola* decision tries to strike this balance in the conclusion section, which refers expressly to Recital 13, states that the concerns in the preliminary assessment represent "the *preliminary* view of the Commission" and formally concludes that "[i]n light of the commitments offered, the Commission considers that there are no longer grounds for action on its part."[86] It is to be hoped that third parties heed this language and do not seek to use commitment decisions as evidence of past legal violations that the Commission did not identify.

Procedural safeguards. The relatively streamlined Article 9 process should facilitate the efficient resolution of appropriate Article 82 EC cases. This efficiency, however, comes to some extent at the expense of procedural safeguards to protect the rights of defence. Companies are not required to offer commitments, and probably will in most cases have entered the settlement process voluntarily. The Commission has stated that commitment decisions will be "solicited by a company under investigation and agreed by the Commission where its enforcement priorities justify this choice."[87] Nevertheless, the Article 9 process offers companies little protection against the possibility that the Commission may (against the threat of fines and extended investigation) seek to impose commitments that are more restrictive than what Article 82 EC requires.[88]

At least four key safeguards that form part of the general process leading up to an infringement decision under Article 7 of Regulation 1/2003 are absent from the Article 9 process. First, under Article 9 no Statement of Objections is required. The Statement of Objections is a vital safeguard in the general process, as it must clearly articulate the Commission's theory of harm and the evidence that substantiates it, giving the parties an opportunity to respond. As explained above, while the Article 9 preliminary assessment appears to serve largely the same formal purpose as a Statement of Objections, in practice it appears to be a substantially less important element of the process (at least in some cases drafted after the commitments have already been agreed).

[86] *Ibid.*, paras. 57, 60 (emphasis in original).

[87] Commission MEMO/04/217 of September 17, 2004.

[88] See J Temple Lang, *Commitments Decisions and Settlements with Antitrust Authorities and Private Parties Under European Antitrust Law*, Fordham Antitrust Conference, September 2005.

Second, the parties to an Article 9 proceeding have no express right of access to the Commission's case file. As the Commission has recognised, access to the file is one of the procedural guarantees intended to protect the rights of the defence. This right, however, extends only to recipients of a Statement of Objections, and does not apply in the context of an Article 9 proceeding.[89]

Third, the Article 9 process does not include an oral hearing. Under the general procedure, the oral hearing represents what may be the parties' only opportunity to advocate their position before Member State representatives and to confront third-party complainants directly.[90] There is no such opportunity under Article 9. Fourth, commitment decisions are largely unconstrained by the supervisory authority of the Community Courts, as the threat of appeal is limited. This issue is addressed in more detail in the next section below.

The relative lack of procedural safeguards in the Article 9 process is not an unambiguous shortcoming. Dispensing with some of the general process's formal steps (particularly the Statement of Objections and oral hearing) contributes substantially to the Article 9 process's efficiency, which as noted above is one of its key attractions. One improvement that would not be procedurally burdensome would be for the Commission to give companies in settlement discussions timely opportunity to review and comment on any "key documents" in the Commission's file, analogous to the process now followed under the EC Merger Regulation.[91] This would allow the parties better to understand the source and nature of the Commission's concerns, informing discussion as to whether commitments in a particular area are justified and, if so, facilitating the drafting of suitably tailored provisions.

15.3.2.3 Legal effect of commitment decisions

General legal effect on addressees. Under Article 9(1), the commitments forming part of a commitment decision are made "binding" on the companies that offered them (which will be the addressees of the Commission's decision).[92] This means that, if a commitment is violated, the Commission (or a national competition authority or court) may enforce the commitment directly, without having to prove that the conduct in question was otherwise unlawful (i.e., that the company in question abused a dominant position). Violation of the commitment is itself the legal offence. Under Articles 23

[89] See Commission Notice of December 13, 2005 on the rules for access to the Commission file in cases pursuant to Articles 81 and 82 of the EC Treaty.

[90] Although, as noted above, the Member State Advisory Committee offers an Opinion on Article 9 commitment decisions, its review is based only on materials provided to it by the Commission.

[91] See DG Competition best practices on the conduct of EC merger control proceedings, paras. 45–46.

[92] The *Coca-Cola* decision includes an interesting device intended to extend the effect of the commitments to companies other than the decision's addressees. The commitments require The Coca-Cola Company (TCCC) to use its best efforts to ensure that all EU bottlers of Coca-Cola carbonated soft drinks sign the commitments and agree to an amendment of their bottler's agreements with TCCC stating that the bottler will abide by the terms of the commitment decision. These measures will not make the commitments binding on non-addressee bottlers, but as a practical matter should make it more likely that the commitments will be followed across the EU. This would presumably have been a significant attraction for the Commission in settling the case, since the Commission's investigation was limited to just four countries. See *Coca-Cola*, OJ 2005 L 253/21

and 24 of Regulation 1/2003, the Commission can also impose fines and periodic payments on companies that fail to comply with a binding commitment, in exactly the same way as these sanctions apply to violations of Article 82 EC. (Enforcement of commitment decisions by national competition authorities and courts is addressed below.)

Addressee's ability to appeal a commitment decision. In light of the lack of procedural safeguards, as outlined above, to ensure that the Commission does not impose unduly broad or burdensome commitments in an Article 9 process, an interesting question arises as to whether the addressee of a commitment decision is entitled to appeal the decision to the Community Courts. One can imagine a situation in which the Commission—upon threat of an infringement decision including large fines and/or onerous behavioural rules—effectively coerces a company into agreeing to commitments that go beyond what Article 82 EC could require. Should such a company be entitled to appeal the Article 9 decision that makes the commitments binding?

In support of such a right of appeal, advocates would point to the Court of Justice's *Wood Pulp* judgment, where the Court rejected the Commission's argument that because an undertaking constituted a unilateral act, the companies who had offered the undertaking were not entitled to appeal. The Court stated as follows:[93]

> "The obligations imposed on the applicants by the undertaking must be regarded in the same way as orders requiring an infringement to be brought to an end, as provided for by Article 3 of Regulation No 17... In giving that undertaking, the applicants thus merely assented, for their own reasons, to a decision which the Commission was empowered to adopt unilaterally."

This, so the argument would run, establishes that a commitment equals an order requiring a company to bring an infringement to an end and that the company giving the commitment is therefore entitled to appeal a commitment—including one made binding in a commitment decision—in the same way as it could appeal an infringement decision.

In interpreting this passage, however, the context in which the Court made its statement is critical. The undertakings in question were attached to a Commission infringement decision—which the parties clearly were entitled to appeal—and were offered in exchange for reduced fines. The Court's rationale for analogising the undertakings in this case to a cease and desist order is that the Commission could unilaterally have adopted a decision ordering the companies to abide by the same rules.[94] That is not true

[93] Joined Cases C-89, 104, 114, 116, 117 and 125 to 129/85, *A. Ahlström Osakeyhtiö and Others v Commission* [1993] ECR II-1307 (hereinafter "*Wood Pulp*"), para. 181.

[94] Some commentators interpret this passage as meaning that "an action will lie against commitments entered into by undertakings in the context of a Commission investigation into infringements of competition law," reiterating the Court's language that "[s]uch commitments are to be equated to orders requiring an infringement to be brought to an end [...]." This suggests a broad interpretation that would make all undertakings appealable. However, the authors immediately make clear that the rationale for this is that the undertakings in question are not voluntary. In making the undertakings, the companies in question "acquiesce in fact to a decision which the Commission itself could have taken. Entry into such commitments is therefore not an act ascribable to the undertakings, but the corollary of an act of the Commission against which an action will lie." K Lenaerts and D Arts,

of all undertakings, and it is in particular not true of commitments made binding pursuant to an Article 9 decision. Commitment decisions expressly do not involve any finding that there has been an infringement, so the Commission is not "unilaterally empowered" to impose any rules at all against the company that offered the commitments.[95]

The better view is that commitment decisions should not be appealable by the addressees. As a practical matter, a company might find itself forced to choose between agreeing to commitments and extended litigation to prove that the commitments are unwarranted. However, there is no legal requirement for companies (or the Commission) to enter into settlement discussions or to offer commitments that would be intended to form the basis of an Article 9 decision—the process is voluntary and can only proceed if both sides agree. Even if the Commission were to seek to impose unwarranted commitments on a company, the company could always decline and force the Commission to prove its case by issuing an infringement decision, which could then be appealed. This is what would have happened under Regulation 17/62, when commitment decisions did not exist; thus, a determination that addressees may not appeal commitment decisions does not deny companies any right that they held previously.

Even more importantly, a contrary conclusion would have clear adverse consequences. The prospect of appeals would compromise what is perhaps the central attraction of the Article 9 process for both companies and the Commission: bringing investigations to an acceptable conclusion quickly and efficiently. If the Commission believed that a commitment decision was likely to be appealed by the parties (with implementation potentially suspended during the appeal), its incentive to enter into settlement discussions would be substantially diminished. This would reduce the likelihood that Article 9 would be used at all, undermining a potentially useful mechanism for resolving Article 82 EC investigations, to the detriment of all concerned.

Effect on third parties. Commitment decisions are silent on whether there has been or still is an infringement of Article 82 EC, and therefore cannot be cited as proof of infringement in a private action for damages (e.g., by a customer or competitor) against the company that made the commitment. The fact that the Commission has expressed preliminary concerns and imposed rules to address those concerns may create an impression that there had been unlawful activity, which could influence national courts,

Procedural Law of the European Union (London, Sweet & Maxwell, 1999) p. 149, 7-021. Other commentators emphasise the same point, concluding that an agreement between the Commission and an individual is only subject to appeal by the individual if it is the result of a unilateral decision of the Commission. See HG Schermers and DF Waelbroeck, *Judicial Protection in the European Union* (6th edn., The Hague, Kluwer Law International, 2001) p. 355, para. 712.

[95] It is also worth noting that in the context of the *Wood Pulp* case, the undertakings that were voided related to the Commission's effort to address what it viewed as unlawful price signalling and artificially created market transparency. The Court held that the Commission had failed to establish that the measures in question were unlawful and annulled that part of the decision. It would have been anomalous for the Court to overturn part of the infringement decision while at the same time keeping in force behavioural restrictions that were intended to address that infringement. See Joined Cases C-89, 104, 114, 116, 117 and 125 to 129/85, *A. Ahlström Osakeyhtiö and Others v Commission* [1993] ECR II-1307.

and private plaintiffs will undoubtedly try to use commitment decisions in this way. However, by offering a commitment, the company is not admitting that its conduct was unlawful. As explained above, there is no assurance that the commitment does not go further than what Article 82 EC requires; it follows that past conduct inconsistent with the commitment was not necessarily unlawful.

In recognition of this, the Commission has made clear that a third party seeking damages through private enforcement will still have to prove that the past behaviour of the company was illegal[96]—i.e., defining a relevant market, establishing dominance, and proving an abuse—as well as that the behaviour caused loss, and the amount of that loss. In this respect, commitment decisions will be substantially less valuable than a Commission decision finding that an infringement has been committed, which leaves a plaintiff only with the task of proving causation and quantum of damage.[97]

As regards the possibility of appealing a commitment decision, the position of third parties differs from that of addressees. It is likely that interested third parties could appeal the Commission's acceptance of a settlement as a "negative" decision refusing to establish an infringement of competition law by adopting a formal infringement decision. The Court of Justice's *Metro* judgment established that persons entitled to raise complaints regarding violations of Articles 81 and 82 EC are also entitled to appeal refusals by the Commission to act on such complaints.[98] In *Metro II*, the Court of Justice specified that the class of persons entitled to appeal a refusal to adopt an infringement decision was not limited to formal complainants.[99] These judgments predate the commitment decision process, and none of the commitment decisions issued to date has been appealed. However, given the fact that a commitment decision includes no finding of infringement and will impliedly, if not expressly, state that conduct in accordance with the commitments is legal, it will amount to at least a partial rejection of the complaint that this conduct is illegal.[100] It is likely that under this line of precedent all third parties that have established an interest in the proceeding (e.g., by complaining and submitting observations to the Commission) would be entitled to appeal the commitment decision to the Community Courts.

---

[96] Commission MEMO/04/217 of September 17, 2004.

[97] See J Temple Lang, *Commitments Decisions and Settlements with Antitrust Authorities and Private Parties Under European Antitrust Law*, Fordham Antitrust Conference, September 2005.

[98] "It is in the interest of a satisfactory administration of justice and a proper application of Articles 8[1] and 8[2] that natural or legal persons who are entitled…to request the Commission to find an infringement of Article 8[1] and 8[2] should be able, if their request is dismissed either wholly or in part, to institute proceedings in order to protect their legitimate interests. In those circumstances, the applicant must be considered to be directly and individually concerned…by the contested decision." Case 26/76, *Metro SB-Großmärkte GmbH & Co KG v Commission* [1977] ECR 1875 (hereinafter "*Metro*"), para. 13. See also Case T-193/02, *Laurent Piau v Commission* [2005] ECR II-nyr, para. 38; Case T-37/92, *Bureau Européen des Unions des Consommateurs and National Consumer Council v Commission* [1994] ECR II-285, para. 36; and Case T-186/94, *Guérin Automobiles v Commission* [1995] ECR II-1753, para. 39.

[99] Case 75/84, *Metro SB-Großmärkte GmbH & Co KG v Commission* [1986] ECR 3021 (hereinafter "*Metro II*"), paras. 21–23.

[100] J Temple Lang, *Commitments Decisions and Settlements with Antitrust Authorities and Private Parties Under European Antitrust Law*, Fordham Antitrust Conference, September 2005.

Effect on national competition authorities and courts. Article 10 EC obliges national competition authorities and courts to cooperate with the EC institutions and not to jeopardise the achievement of the Community's objectives. This includes in particular a duty to enforce Commission decisions[101] and a duty not to adopt decisions or judgments inconsistent with competition decisions of the Commission.[102] It follows that national competition authorities and courts must enforce Commission commitment decisions, which will generally make clear that they are intended to create rights for third parties.[103] This means that national competition authorities may investigate and, if appropriate, act on complaints that companies have violated an EC commitment decision, enforcing the decisions through whatever powers are available under their national laws.[104] Similarly, national courts must enforce commitments by any means provided for by national law, including interim measures and damages. Even without express national legislation, Article 10 EC requires national courts to provide remedies to enforce rights given by EC Community law.[105] The Commission's Notice on cooperation between the Commission and the courts confirms the Commission's view that "national law must provide for sanctions which are effective, proportionate and dissuasive."[106] Since the commitments are binding on the companies that offered them, national authorities and courts may enforce the commitment without having to prove that the conduct was otherwise unlawful.

Potentially a more important question for companies is the extent to which a Commission commitment decision will provide protection against future challenge of the same or related practices before national competition authorities or courts. On one hand, it is clear that a Commission commitment decision does not eliminate the possibility of any future enforcement action at a national level. Recital 22 of Regulation

[101] See HG Schermers and DF Waelbroeck, *Judicial Protection in the European Union* (6th edn., The Hague, Kluwer Law International, 2001) pp. 112–15. For a detailed discussion see J Temple Lang, "The Principle of Effective Protection of Community Law Rights" in D O'Keefe and A Bavasso (eds.), *Judicial Review in European Union Law* (The Hague, Kluwer Law International, 2000) Vol. 1, pp. 235–74.

[102] Regulation 1/2003, Articles 3, 11, 15, and 16; Case C-344/98, *Masterfoods Ltd v HB Ice Cream Ltd* [2000] ECR I-11369; Case C-234/89, *Stergios Delimitis v Henninger Bräu AG* [1991] ECR I-935 and Case 14/68, *Walt Wilhelm and others v Bundeskartellamt* [1969] ECR 1.

[103] See Case 9-70, *Franz Grad v Finanzamt Traunstein* [1970] ECR 825, para. 5; Case T-24/90, *Automec Srl v Commission (Automec II)* [1992] ECR II-2223 and Case C-253/00, *Antonio Muñoz y Cia SA and Superior Fruiticola SA v Frumar Ltd and Redbridge Produce Marketing Ltd* [2002] ECR I-7289.

[104] See J Temple Lang, *Commitments Decisions and Settlements with Antitrust Authorities and Private Parties Under European Antitrust Law*, Fordham Antitrust Conference, September 2005. M Sousa Ferro, "Committing to Commitment Decisions—Unanswered Questions on Article 9 Decisions" (2005) 26(8) *European Competition Law Review* 451–59 suggests that national competition authorities may not be free to enforce Commission commitment decisions, but only on the grounds that the possibility has not been mentioned expressly.

[105] See Case C-213/89, *The Queen v Secretary of State for Transport, ex parte: Factortame Ltd and others* [1990] ECR I-2433. See also J Temple Lang, "The Principle of Effective Protection of Community Law Rights" in D O'Keefe and A Bavasso (eds.), *Judicial Review in European Union Law* (The Hague, Kluwer Law International, 2000) Vol. 1, pp. 235–74.

[106] Commission Notice on the cooperation between the Commission and the courts of the EU Member States in the application of Article 81 and 82 EC, OJ 2004 C 101/54, para. 10, citing Case 68/88, *Commission v Greece* [1989] ECR 2965, paras. 23–25.

1/2003 states that "commitment decisions adopted by the Commission do not affect the power of the courts and the competition authorities of the Member States to apply Article 81 and 82." Similarly, Recital 13 states that although commitment decisions conclude merely that there are no longer grounds for action by the Commission and not whether there has been or still is an infringement of EC Community law, they are "without prejudice to the powers of competition authorities and courts of the Member States to make such a finding and decide upon the case."[107]

In its clarifying remarks, the Commission states that the addressees of Article 9 decisions "may still face enforcement action before Member States' authorities and courts, provided that the uniform application of the competition rules throughout the EU is not jeopardised."[108] This qualification in the Commission's statement is critical as it highlights that national authorities' and courts' power to proceed against companies that have entered Commission commitment decisions is not unlimited. With respect to future violations of an existing Commission commitment, as explained above it is clear that national authorities and courts may—indeed must—enforce the Commission's decision. Several other scenarios are possible, however, which be summarised as follows.

First, a national court or competition authority could find that conduct inconsistent with a Commission commitment decision, but that took place before the commitment was given, was illegal under EC community or national competition laws. The commitment decision could not, however, create a presumption that past conduct inconsistent with the commitment was unlawful. Such a presumption would, first, be contrary to Article 9, which expressly provides that commitment decisions make no finding as to whether or not there has been any past infringement. It would also seriously discourage companies from offering commitments, since it would make doing so tantamount to admitting past violations. Such a presumption would therefore also be contrary to EC competition policy and thus in violation of the Article 10 EC duty of cooperation.[109]

Second, since Member States are allowed to adopt national laws in relation to unilateral conduct that are stricter than Article 82 EC,[110] national courts and competition authorities will remain free to find that a company's past or future conduct infringes such a stricter national law even if it is entirely in accordance with its EC competition law commitments.

Third, and more difficult, is the question whether national authorities or courts may find that past or future conduct consistent with commitments embodied in an Article 9 decision violates Article 82 EC. As noted, Article 9 decisions do not conclude whether or not there has been or still is an infringement, but only that there are no longer grounds for action "*by the Commission.*" The possibility of further related action by a Member State authority is not precluded, and in fact Recitals 13 and 22 of Regulation 1/2003 quoted above seem expressly to contemplate the possibility of such action.

[107] Regulation 1/2003, Recitals 13, 22.

[108] Commission MEMO/04/217 of September 17, 2004.

[109] See J Temple Lang, *Commitments Decisions and Settlements with Antitrust Authorities and Private Parties Under European Antitrust Law*, Fordham Antitrust Conference, September 2005.

[110] Regulation 1/2003, Article 3(2).

However, the fundamental goal of ensuring uniform application of EC competition rules throughout the EU—which the Commission cites as the primary qualifier on the power of national authorities to take enforcement action against companies that have entered commitment decisions—mitigates against the ability of Member State authorities and courts to condemn behaviour consistent with Article 9 commitments under Article 82 EC. By agreeing to commitments that constitute affirmative obligations (i.e., rules that require a company to behave in a certain way or that clearly imply what the company will do[111]), the Commission is effectively determining that such conduct is consistent with EC competition law. It would contradict the Commission's decision, and thereby undermine the uniform application of EC competition rules, if a national court or authority were to conclude that conduct that is clearly envisaged and permitted by a commitment decision is contrary to EC competition law. Therefore, to the extent that a company's past or future conduct is in accordance with its affirmative obligations under a commitment decision, national authorities and courts may not find that the company has infringed Article 82 EC.

In practice, Member State competition authorities and courts seem likely to be strongly influenced by the Commission's decision that, in light of commitments offered, further action against the relevant companies for conduct consistent with the commitments is unwarranted under EC competition law. Notwithstanding the decentralisation initiative brought about by Regulation 1/2003, for the foreseeable future some Member State authorities and courts will lack the experience and expertise of the Commission in applying EC competition law and will probably hesitate to take action that could be viewed as inconsistent with the Commission's. Unless circumstances in a particular country differ materially from those considered by the Commission in settling its own investigation, it seems unlikely that a Member State authority or court would adopt a more aggressive decision that would implicitly question either the Commission's interpretation of EC competition law or its enforcement priorities.[112] Notwithstanding the lack of clear legal assurance, companies should be reasonably confident that their future conduct consistent with EU commitments will not be found unlawful.

Need for caution in respect of precedential value of commitment decisions. It is important to bear in mind that commitment decisions, unlike infringement decisions, cannot establish legal rules or standards that apply directly to third parties. Companies

[111] For example, the commitments in the *Coca-Cola* decision include detailed rules governing how various commercial arrangements must be structured, including e.g., the offering of assortment rebates based on a specified unbundling of brands, term limits for various types of contracts, and certain allowances for exclusive supply arrangements in connection with sponsorship agreements, etc. See *Coca-Cola*, OJ 2005 L 253/21.

[112] The strong influence of commitment decisions on national authorities may be illustrated by the circumstances of the *Coca-Cola* case. In addition to the Commission's investigation into certain commercial practices of The Coca-Cola Company and its bottlers, related (but not identical) investigations by national competition authorities were actively ongoing in countries such as Spain and Belgium. Shortly after finalisation of the Commission's Article 9 decision, both the Spanish and Belgian cases were settled, in large part on the basis of the companies' EU commitments. See Decision of the Service for the Defence of Competition of July 15, 2005 in Case no. 2146/00 ("*Acuerdo de sobreseimiento*"); Belgian Competition Council decision n°2005-I/O-52 of November 30, 2005, *Distri-One S.A. / Coca-Cola Enterprises Belgium S.P.R.L., Belgian Official Gazette* of December 22, 2005, 55.371.

and lawyers will no doubt scrutinise commitment decisions closely, as they may represent among the best available indications as to the Commission's thinking on important issues (e.g., fidelity rebates, as treated in detail in the *Coca-Cola* decision). However, decisions under Article 9 are negotiated settlements; they lack the adversarial element that is needed to establish legitimate legal rules. Companies may agree to restrictions on their conduct that could not be compelled by Article 82 EC simply on grounds of pragmatism: if a particular restriction is commercially acceptable, there may be little cost in committing to abide by it, and potentially some gain. Simple cost-benefit analysis may thus lead firms to agree to more restrictive conditions than the law requires. Or a rule of conduct may be a practical compromise, negotiated so as to be easily applied in practice rather than to be legally correct.[113] Within the context of the particular case, this may not be problematic, since no one is harmed. But the same restriction might be highly costly or burdensome if applied to other firms. There can therefore be no legitimate presumption that the behavioural rules drawn up in commitment decisions define the boundary between lawful and abusive conduct or that the same restrictions should be applied directly to other, even similarly situated firms.

15.3.3 Undertakings

Informal but effective procedure. Under Regulation 17/62, the Commission resolved a number of cases through informal settlements embodied in undertakings through which companies made promises to the Commission to behave, or not to behave, in particular ways. There was no express legal basis for these undertakings, and their legal effects—particularly whether they were binding in the sense of Article 9 commitments—were never conclusively determined. Some of the most important Article 82 EC cases settled through undertakings were the following:[114]

1. *IBM* (1984).[115] The Commission had sent IBM, then the world's largest computer manufacturer, a Statement of Objections alleging that IBM's failure to disclose interface information for its dominant products to other manufacturers, as well as various bundling practices, violated Article 82 EC. IBM offered undertakings to address the concerns, on the basis of which the Commission "suspended" its proceeding.

2. *Coca-Cola* (1989).[116] The Commission terminated an investigation under Article 82 EC into certain commercial practices of the Coca-Cola system in Italy on the basis of undertakings offered by The Coca-Cola Export Corporation. The undertaking covers fidelity rebates associated with the sale of Coca-Cola, and includes specific rules relating to exclusivity, target rebates, and tying.[117]

[113] See J Temple Lang, *Commitments Decisions and Settlements with Antitrust Authorities and Private Parties Under European Antitrust Law*, Fordham Antitrust Conference, September 2005.

[114] See also *La Poste/SWIFT*, OJ 1997 C 335/3.

[115] Commission XIV Competition Policy Report (1985) para. 94, pp. 77–79.

[116] Commission XIX Competition Policy Report (1990) para. 50, pp. 65–66.

[117] As described above, The Coca-Cola Company was involved in one of the first commitment decisions issued under Article 9 of Regulation 1/2003, which covers similar issues as the 1989 undertaking in greater detail. See *Coca-Cola*, OJ 2005 L 253/21.

3. *Microsoft* (1994).[118] Microsoft offered undertakings to the Commission that paralleled a settlement agreed with the US Department of Justice at the same time in relation to Microsoft's licensing practices for the Windows operating system. The Commission had been prepared to send a Statement of Objections alleging that these practices were exclusionary and unlawful. On the basis of the undertaking, the Commission closed its ongoing interim measures case.

4. *ACNielsen* (1996).[119] The Commission, following receipt of a complaint, had issued a Statement of Objections alleging that ACNielsen had abused its dominant position in the market for retail tracking services by, *inter alia*, concluding exclusive supply contracts and offering discounts to customers who purchased ACNielsen's services on a multinational basis. ACNielsen offered an undertaking to address these concerns, including an agreement to "unbundle" pricing for all its multinational contracts. On this basis, the Commission was satisfied that ACNielsen "would not be in breach" of Article 82 EC in the future.

5. *Digital Equipment* (1997).[120] The Commission had sent a Statement of Objections arguing that Digital had infringed Articles 81 and 82 EC through tying and discriminatory practices. Digital gave a series of undertakings providing for separate marketing of hardware maintenance services, publication of price lists, and separate quotations for each component service. Digital also undertook to operate a transparent and non-discriminatory discount policy, and, if it offered a discount on a package, to offer the same discount on each service separately. The Commission found that these undertakings would meet the concerns that had been expressed by complainants and closed the investigation on this basis.

As these summaries indicate, notwithstanding their lack of clear legal basis, the Commission employed undertakings as a means of resolving several important and high-profile Article 82 EC cases. Given the availability of commitment decisions under Regulation 1/2003, however, such informal settlements through undertakings may now be obsolete.[121] Informal undertakings are no doubt an efficient way to dispose of cases, but the Article 9 procedure is also relatively streamlined, and it is difficult to see what other advantages informal undertakings might offer from the Commission's perspective. On the other hand, the fact that formal Article 9 commitments are binding on the parties, as well as the greater transparency of the Article 9 process, will no doubt be attractive to the Commission. The Article 9 process seems more likely to be employed in cases where settlement is appropriate.

---

[118] Commission XXIV Competition Policy Report (1994) para. 212, pp. 121, 364–65.

[119] Commission XXVI Report on Competition Policy (1996) pp. 144–148.

[120] See M Dolmans & V Pickering, "1997 Digital Undertaking" (1998) 19(2) *European Competition Law Review* 108–15.

[121] See J Temple Lang, *Commitments Decisions and Settlements with Antitrust Authorities and Private Parties Under European Antitrust Law*, Fordham Antitrust Conference, September 2005.

15.3.4 Final Infringement Decisions

Essential elements. As explained above, Article 7(1) of Regulation 1/2003 provides that where the Commission finds an infringement of Article 82 EC it may by decision require the infringement to be brought to an end. There is no required format for infringement decisions, but they must meet the requirements of Article 253 EC, principally that they must "state the reasons on which they are based." The main elements of Commission Article 82 EC infringement decisions are: (1) a preamble that provides a narrative of the decision; (2) a description of the facts; (3) a legal assessment; and (4) the articles of the decision, which are the operative parts of the decision and set out the finding of an infringement and its duration, identify the undertaking(s) concerned, and describe the remedy required by the Commission (including fines, cease and desist orders, compulsory dealing obligations, etc.).

The most common type of infringement decision in an Article 82 EC case includes both a declaration that there has been an infringement and a "cease and desist" order requiring the infringement to be terminated. Where the infringement consists of a failure to act, the Commission may order the undertaking concerned to take specific affirmative action.[122] In order to ensure that the decision is effective, the Commission may also include a "like effects" order whereby the defendant is prohibited from engaging in conduct that may have the same effect or object as that found to infringe Article 82 EC.[123] In order to clarify its legal position and reduce the likelihood of future breaches, the Commission may also issue decisions declaring specific conduct unlawful even if the undertaking concerned has already terminated the infringement.[124] Final decisions also typically include additional remedies. These may involve fines and/or behavioural remedies. Exceptionally, structural remedies may be imposed. The principal types of remedies are discussed below.

15.4 PRINICIPAL TYPES OF REMEDIES

15.4.1 Fines

Legal basis. Article 23(2) of Regulation 1/2003 sets out the Commission's basic legal power to impose fines. Fines of up to 10% of an undertaking's total worldwide annual turnover in the preceding business year[125] may be imposed where, either intentionally or negligently, the undertaking: (1) infringes Article 82 EC; (2) contravenes a Commission interim measures decision under Article 8 of Regulation 1/2003; or (3) fails to comply

---

[122] Joined Cases 6-7/73, *Istituto Chemioterapico Italiano SpA and Commercial Solvents Corporation v Commission* [1974] ECR 223.

[123] See, e.g., Case COMP/C-3/37.792, *Microsoft*, Commission Decision of March 24, 2004, not yet published; Article 4; *Cewal, Cowac and Ukwal*, OJ 1993 L 34/20, Article 4; *Eurofix-Banco v Hilti*, OJ 1988 L 65/19, Article 3; and *Tetra Pak II*, OJ 1992 L 72/1, Article 3.

[124] Case 7/82, *Gesellschaft zur Verwertung von Leistungsschutzrechten mbH (GVL) v Commission* [1983] ECR 483, paras. 16–28.

[125] See *Pioneer Hi-Fi Equipment,* OJ 1980 L 60/21 (confirming that the 10% ceiling for fines refers to the total worldwide sales of all products, not only those affected by the infringement). Although the case arose under Council Regulation 17/62, and not Regulation 1/2003, it is submitted that the principle remains unchanged.

with a commitment decision under Article 9 of Regulation 1/2003. Article 23(3) of Regulation 1/2003 adds that, in fixing the amount of the fine, the Commission shall have regard to both the gravity and duration of the infringement. These basic legal powers to impose fines essentially mirror the Commission's previous powers under Council Regulation 17/62,[126] with the obvious exception that commitment decisions are a new innovation under Regulation 1/2003.[127] Article 23(5) also makes clear that fining decisions are not of a criminal law nature: they are intended to "suppress illegal activities and to prevent any recurrence."[128]

The Fining Guidelines. In 1998 the Commission published a Notice setting out guidelines on the method by which it calculates fines for violations of Articles 81 and 82 EC.[129] The Fining Guidelines create "legitimate expectations" for undertakings *vis-à-vis* the Commission; in other words, "the Commission may not depart from rules it has imposed on itself."[130] The principle of legitimate expectations does not prevent the Commission from changing its policies, but it requires the Commission to exercise its powers in the way in which it has said that it would exercise them. If the Commission publishes guidelines that it plans to apply *pro future*, it creates the expectation that its discretion will be exercised in compliance with those guidelines.[131] The fact that the Commission has the power to alter its fining policy does not prevent it from being bound by the principle of legitimate expectations after it has published its Fining Guidelines. An extensive body of case law has built up around the meaning of specific terms in the Fining Guidelines, but this invariably concerns the application of Article 81 EC in cartel cases, and not Article 82 EC.

Intention and negligence. The imposition of fines requires evidence that the infringement was committed intentionally or negligently. "Intention" does not require actual knowledge that the conduct would violate EC competition law: it refers to an intention to restrict competition and not to an intention to infringe specific provisions of the EC Treaty.[132] Thus, it is sufficient if the undertaking "could not have been

---

[126] Council Regulation 17 of February 6, 1962, First Regulation implementing Articles 8[1] and 8[2] of the EC Treaty, Article 3(1), OJ 1962 L 13/204.

[127] Although the power to adopt interim measures was not expressly mentioned in Regulation 17/62, the Commission typically accompanied such decisions with clauses providing for fines in the event of non-compliance. See, e.g., *IMS Health/NDC—Interim Measures*, OJ 2002 L 59/18, Article 3.

[128] Case 45/69, *Boehringer Mannheim GmbH v Commission* [1970] ECR 769, para. 53.

[129] Guidelines on the method of setting fines imposed pursuant to Article 15(2) of Regulation No 17 and Article 65(5) of the ECSC Treaty, OJ 1998 C 9/3 (hereinafter the "Fining Guidelines").

[130] See, e.g., Case T-224/00, *Archer Daniels Midland Company and Archer Daniels Midland Ingredients Ltd v Commission* [2003] ECR II-2597, paras. 182 and 267.

[131] The Community Courts have held that the Commission creates legitimate expectations, e.g., when it has adopted general policy statements. See Case C-152/88, *Sofrimport SARL v Commission* [1990] ECR I-2477; Case C-81/72, *Commission v Council* [1973] ECR 575. This view finds support also in legal scholarship. See B Vesterdorf, *Neueste Entwicklungen in der Rechtsprechung der Europäischen Gerichtshöfe*, 9. St. Galler Internationales Kartellrechtsforum, April 25, 2002.

[132] See, e.g., Case T-29/92, *Vereniging van Samenwerkende Prijsregelende Organisaties in de Bouwnijverheid and others v Commission* [1995] ECR II-289, paras. 356–58; Case T-61/89, *Dansk Pelsdyravlerforing v Commission* [1992] ECR II-1931, para. 157; and Case C-279/87, *Tipp-Ex GmbH & Co KG v Commission* [1990] ECR I-261.

unaware" that its conduct would restrict competition.[133] The fact that previous case law found an abuse in similar circumstances is usually decisive proof of intent.[134] Negligence has a similarly broad meaning. The concept of negligence "must be applied where the author of the infringement, although acting without any intention to perform an unlawful act, has not foreseen the consequences of his action in circumstances where a person who is normally informed and sufficiently attentive could not have failed to foresee them."[135]

Although "intention" and "negligence" have a broad meaning, the Commission has, perhaps surprisingly, refused to impose fines in a number of Article 82 EC cases. In *Decca Navigator*, the Commission imposed no fine on the grounds, *inter alia*, that the abuse was novel and complex.[136] In *Clearstream*, the Commission justified a decision to impose no fines for an abusive refusal to deal on the grounds that: (1) clearing and settlement had not been subject to prior decisions under Article 82 EC; (2) complex issues also arose around market definition and sector-specific issues such as internalisation, both of which had a decisive bearing on the case; and (3) cross-border trade in securities was evolving. In the light of these elements, the Commission concluded that it could reasonably be argued that it was not sufficiently clear to the defendants that their conduct was abusive.[137] By contrast, in *Wanadoo*, the Commission refused Wanadoo's request that no fines should be imposed on the grounds that the Commission had departed from previous cost standards mentioned in the decisional practice and case law. The Commission declined on the basis that all it had done was apply a modification to past standards rather than propose an entirely new method of cost calculation.[138]

The fact that the dominant firm was unsure of the status of the conduct may also be evidence of a lack of intent or negligence. In *United Brands*, the Commission did not impose a fine on United Brands for having prohibited its ripener/distributors from reselling its bananas while still green, as that prohibition appeared in the general conditions of sale notified by United Brands with a view to obtaining an exemption.[139] Similarly, in *Van den Bergh Foods*, the agreements were notified by the dominant undertaking with a view to obtaining individual exemption. Although the agreements were regarded as being both a restriction of competition and an abuse, they were not

[133] See Case 19/77, *Miller International Schallplatten GmbH v Commission* [1978] ECR 131. For a detailed discussion, see Joined Cases T-191/98 and T-212/98 to T-214/98, *Atlantic Container Line AB and Others v Commission* [2003] ECR II-3275, paras. 1597–634.

[134] See, e.g., *Virgin/British Airways*, OJ 2000 L 30/1, para. 118; *Michelin*, OJ 2002 L 143/1, para. 354.

[135] See Opinion of Advocate General Mayras in Case C-26/75, *General Motors Continental NV v Commission* [1975] ECR 1367, at 1389.

[136] *Decca Navigator System*, OJ 1989 L 43/27 (hereinafter "*Decca Navigator*"), para. 133.

[137] Case COMP/38/096, *Clearstream (Clearing and settlement)*, Commission Decision of June 4, 2004, not yet published (hereinafter "*Clearstream*"), para. 344.

[138] Case COMP/38.233, *Wanadoo Interactive*, Commission Decision of July 16, 2003, not yet published (hereinafter "*Wanadoo*"), para. 410.

[139] *Chiquita*, OJ 1976 L 95/1, confirmed by the Court in Case 27/76, *United Brands Company and United Brands Continentaal BV v Commission* [1978] ECR 207.

penalised with fines.[140] In *TACA*, the Commission refused to discount the fine due to the fact of notification, but the Court of First Instance held on appeal that the Commission should have taken this factor into account.[141] These precedents are likely to be of limited relevance today following the abolition of the system of notification under Article 81 EC and the proposed repeal of the legislation at issue in *TACA*.[142]

The Commission's on-going review of Article 82 EC is likely to have mixed effects on whether infringements can be characterised as intentional or negligent. On the one hand, it will be much harder for firms to argue that conduct mentioned in the Discussion Paper as a possible abuse should not attract fines. There is also greater insistence on the need to show anticompetitive effects, which, if shown, will presumably justify higher fines than in previous cases in which no such requirement existed. On the other hand, the Discussion Paper proposes a number of modifications and exceptions to past case law and it may be appropriate not to impose fines in cases in which the practical application of these changes is articulated for the first time. For example, for pricing abuses, the Discussion Paper reserves the right to depart from cost tests based on the dominant firm's own costs (the equally efficient competitor test) and to use the costs of "apparently efficient" competitors.[143] Given that the dominant firm cannot be expected to assess the legality of its conduct in the light of actual or hypothetical competitors' cost structures, it may be difficult to show intent or negligence in such cases.

The steps involved in calculating fines. Although the Commission retains a certain discretion in respect of fines, and is not required to follow an exact mechanical formula, the Fining Guidelines at least require the Commission to follow a consistent rubric in calculating fines. The methodology has been described in the following terms by the Court of First Instance:[144]

> "The first paragraph of Section 1 of the guidelines provides that, in setting fines, the basic amount is to be determined according to the gravity and duration of the infringement, which are the only criteria referred to in Article 15(2) of Regulation No 17.
>
> According to the guidelines, the Commission is to take as the starting point in calculating the amount of the fines an amount determined according to the gravity of the infringement (the general starting point). In assessing the gravity of the infringement, account must be taken of its nature, its actual impact on the market, where this can be measured, and the size of the relevant geographic market (first paragraph of Section 1.A). Within that framework, infringements are to be put into one of three categories: minor infringements, for which the likely fines are between ECU 1 000 and ECU 1 000 000, serious infringements, for which the likely fines are between ECU 1 million and ECU 20 million, and very serious infringements,

---

[140] *Van den Bergh Foods Ltd*, OJ 1998 L 246/1, on appeal Case T-65/98, *Van den Bergh Foods Ltd v Commission* [2003] ECR II-4653 (hereinafter "*Van den Bergh Foods*").

[141] *Trans-Atlantic Conference Agreement*, OJ 1999 L 95/1, annulled on appeal in Joined Cases T-191/98 and T-212/98 to T-214/98, *Atlantic Container Line AB and Others v Commission* [2003] ECR II-3275.

[142] See Proposed Council Regulation COM 2005/651 of December 14, 2005; and Commission Press Release IP/05/1586, of December 14, 2005; See also Frequently Asked Questions MEMO/05/480.

[143] See DG Competition discussion paper on the application of Article 82 of the Treaty to exclusionary abuses, Brussels, December 2005, para. 67.

[144] See Case T-23/99, *LR AF 1998 A/S, formerly Løgstør Rør A/S v Commission (Pre-insulated Pipes)* [2002] ECR II-1705, paras. 224–31.

for which the likely fines are above ECU 20 million (first to third indents of the second paragraph of Section 1.A). Within each of these categories, and in particular as far as serious and very serious infringements are concerned, the proposed scale of fines is to make it possible to apply differential treatment to undertakings according to the nature of the infringement committed (third paragraph of Section 1.A). It is also necessary to take account of the effective economic capacity of offenders to cause significant damage to other operators, in particular consumers, and to set the fine at a level which ensures that it has a sufficiently deterrent effect (fourth paragraph of Section 1.A).

Account may also be taken of the fact that large undertakings usually have legal and economic knowledge and infrastructures which enable them more easily to recognise that their conduct constitutes an infringement and be aware of the consequences stemming from it under competition law (fifth paragraph of Section 1.A).

It may be necessary in some cases to apply weightings to the amounts determined within each of the three categories in order to take account of the specific weight and, therefore, the real impact of the offending conduct of each undertaking on competition, particularly where there is considerable disparity between the sizes of the undertakings committing infringements of the same type. Consequently, it may be necessary to adapt the general starting point according to the specific nature of each undertaking (the specific starting point) (sixth paragraph of Section 1.A).

As regards the factor relating to the duration of the infringement, the guidelines draw a distinction between infringements of short duration (in general, less than one year), for which the amount determined for gravity should not be increased, infringements of medium duration (in general, one to five years), for which the amount determined for gravity may be increased by up to 50%, and infringements of long duration (in general, more than five years), for which the amount determined for gravity may be increased by 10% per year (first to third indents of the first paragraph of Section 1.B).

The guidelines then set out, by way of example, a list of aggravating and attenuating circumstances which may be taken into consideration in order to increase or reduce the basic amount….

By way of general comment, it is stated that the final amount calculated according to this method (basic amount increased or reduced on a percentage basis) may not in any case exceed 10% of the worldwide turnover of the undertakings, as laid down by Article 15(2) of Regulation No 17 (Section 5(a)). The guidelines further provide that, depending on the circumstances, account should be taken, once the above calculations have been made, of certain objective factors such as a specific economic context, any economic or financial benefit derived by the offenders, the specific characteristics of the undertakings in question and their real ability to pay in a specific social context, and that the fines should be adjusted accordingly (Section 5(b))."

Accordingly, the assessment of fines comprises the following four key stages: (1) determining a "starting point" based on the gravity of the infringement; (2) if appropriate, applying a multiplier for deterrence; (3) increasing for each year of duration of the infringement; and (4) adjusting upwards or downwards for aggravating/mitigating factors. However, in light of the Commission's discretion, any fines imposed necessarily fall within a relatively broad range, depending on the starting point established by the Commission. Moreover, at each step in the calculation, the Commission may increase the fines within a similarly broad range. The cumulative effect of these steps is, however, subject to the 10% worldwide turnover upper limit set out in Article 23 of Regulation 1/2003.

a. Gravity. Regarding "gravity," the Fining Guidelines distinguish three categories of infringement: (1) minor; (2) serious; and (3) very serious. Minor infringements are described as "trade restrictions, usually of a vertical nature, with a limited market impact and substantially affecting a limited part of the Community market."[145] Infringements of this kind justify the use of a range between €1,000 and €1 million as a starting point for gravity. For example, in the *1998 World Cup* case, the Commission imposed a symbolic fine of €1,000 for a discriminatory ticket selling policy.[146] This was based on the fact that, although such conduct represents a breach of fundamental Community principles, the ticketing arrangements were similar to those adopted for previous World Cup finals tournaments. The Commission therefore concluded that the organiser was not, at the time, aware that its sales arrangements were in breach of Community law.

Serious infringements will typically be found in cases of abuse of dominant position, as well as of horizontal restrictions with a wider market impact and affecting extensive areas of the common market. The likely range for gravity in such cases is between €1 million and €20 million. For example, in *British Airways/Virgin*, the Commission classified British Airways' rebate practices as a serious infringement based, *inter alia*, on the fact that they had been consistently condemned in past decisions and case law.[147] Similar reasoning was applied in *Michelin II* to classify abusive loyalty rebates as a serious infringement.[148] The same infringement may also be classified as minor or serious for different periods. In *Deutsche Telekom*, the Commission classified a margin squeeze infringement as serious for an earlier period, but minor for a later period in which Deutsche Telekom had reduced the unlawful changes substantially.[149]

Finally, very serious infringements involve, *inter alia*, cases of "clear-cut abuse of dominant position by undertakings holding a virtual monopoly."[150] In *Microsoft*, the Commission relied on a series of factors to characterise Microsoft's abuses as "very serious," including: (1) refusal to supply and tying by undertakings in a dominant position had already been ruled against on several occasions by the Community Courts; (2) Microsoft's near-monopoly share in the client PC operating system market; (3) the significant value of the affected markets; and (4) the effects of the tying conduct on the competitive landscape for the delivery of content over the Internet and on multimedia software.[151]

b. Deterrence. The Fining Guidelines state that deterrence may also be used to increase the basic amount for gravity. No indication is, however, provided of when increases for deterrence might be justified and, if so, what level of increase will be

---

[145] Guidelines on the method of setting fines imposed pursuant to Article 15(2) of Regulation No 17 and Article 65(5) of the ECSC Treaty, OJ 1998 C 9/3, Section 1.A.

[146] *1998 Football World Cup*, OJ 2000 L 5/55, paras. 121–25.

[147] *Virgin/British Airways*, OJ 2000 L 30/1, para. 118.

[148] *PO-Michelin*, OJ 2002 L 143/1, para. 354.

[149] *Deutsche Telekom AG*, OJ 2003 L 263/9, paras. 206–07, currently on appeal in Case T-271/03, *Deutsch Telekom AG v Commission*, OJ 2003 C 264/29.

[150] Guidelines on the method of setting fines imposed pursuant to Article 15(2) of Regulation No 17 and Article 65(5) of the ECSC Treaty, OJ 1998 C 9/3, Section 1.A.

[151] Case COMP/C-3/37.792, *Microsoft*, Commission Decision of March 24, 2004, not yet published, paras. 1061–68.

applied: there is simply a general reference to the fact that account should be taken of the necessity of setting the fine at a level which ensures that it has a "sufficient deterrent effect." For example, in *Microsoft*, the Commission relied on Microsoft's significant economic capacity to cause harm to justify an increase of 200% for deterrence.[152]

c. ***Duration.*** The amount determined for gravity is then increased according to the duration of the infringement found. Unlike gravity and deterrence, this is a mechanical calculation. The Fining Guidelines indicate that the Commission will not increase the amount in case of infringements of short duration, defined as less than one year. For infringements of medium duration (i.e., one to five years), the amount determined for gravity can be increased up to 50%. Finally, infringements of long duration (i.e., more than five years) justify increases of up to 10% per year.

d. ***Aggravating/mitigating factors.*** Once the basic amount has been calculated, it can be increased in presence of aggravating circumstances such as, *inter alia*, recidivism ("repeated infringement of the same type by the same undertaking(s)"), obstruction ("refusal to cooperate with or attempts to obstruct the Commission in carrying out its investigations"), leadership or instigation as to the infringement ("role of leader in, or instigator of the infringement"), or the "need to increase the penalty in order to exceed the amount of gains improperly made as a result of the infringement when it is objectively possible to estimate that amount."[153]

Conversely, the basic amount is subject to reduction where there are attenuating circumstances such as "exclusively passive or 'follow-my-leader' role," "non-implementation in practice of the offending agreements or practices," "termination of the infringement as soon as the Commission intervenes," "existence of reasonable doubt on the part of the undertaking as to whether the restrictive conduct does indeed constitute an infringement," or "infringements committed as a result of negligence."[154] Reductions for mitigating factors should be applied to the basic amount determined for gravity and duration, and not to the amount arrived at following any increases for aggravating factors.[155]

Aggravating and mitigating factors have generally be more relevant in cartel cases—in particular, on the issue of whether a firm was a cartel leader or merely played a passive role. But aggravating and mitigating circumstances have been mentioned in certain Article 82 EC decisions. In *Michelin II*, Michelin received a 50% increase based on the fact that the Commission regarded this as a similar type of offence to *Michelin I*.[156]

Obvious grounds for reduction is the fact that the practice in question has not previously been regarded as abusive. This was mentioned as a relevant mitigating factor in *Napier*

[152] *Ibid.*, para. 1076.

[153] Guidelines on the method of setting fines imposed pursuant to Article 15(2) of Regulation No 17 and Article 65(5) of the ECSC Treaty, OJ 1998 C 9/3, Section 2.

[154] *Ibid.*, Section 3.

[155] See *Deutsche Telekom AG*, OJ 2003 L 263/9, para. 212. See also Case T-220/00, *Cheil Jedang Corp v Commission* [2003] ECR II-2473, para. 226.

[156] *Michelin*, OJ 2002 L 143/1, para. 363. See *Bandengroothandel Frieschebrug BV/NV Nederlandsche Banden-Industrie Michelin*, OJ 1981 L 353/33.

Brown/British Sugar.[157] In *Deutsche Telekom*, the fact that the retail and wholesale charges under review were subject to sector specific regulation since 1988 at national level until the date of the decision justified a 10% reduction from the basic amount.[158] At the extreme, novelty may lead to a zero fine, as occurred in *Decca Navigator*.[159]

The Commission may also reduce the fine if the defendant adopts a cooperative attitude, e.g., by not substantially contesting the facts on which the Commission bases its allegations. In *Decca Navigator*,[160] the Commission imposed no fines based, *inter alia*, on the defendant brought the practices to the Commission's attention. However, in *Deutsche Post*, the Commission refused to apply this rule, since the relevant contracts were the entire factual basis upon which the Commission concluded that Deutsche Post committed an abuse, i.e., Deutsche Post could not very well challenge the very existence of the contracts.[161]

Evolution of Commission policy on fines under Article 82 EC. As with other areas of Commission fining policy, fines under Article 82 EC have evolved significantly over time. In the early years, fines were rare and, even when adjusted today for inflation, tended to be small. For example, in *Hoffmann-La Roche*, a fine of €300,000 was considered sufficient for a series of abusive exclusive dealing practices.[162] A €1 million fine imposed for price discrimination and refusal to supply in *United Brands* was the highest until the 1980s.[163]

Beginning in the 1980s, fines increased significantly. In *AKZO*, a fine of €10 million—reduced to €7.5 million on appeal—was imposed for predatory pricing.[164] In *Hilti*, unlawful loyalty rebate practices attracted a fine of €6 million.[165] Similar practices in *Soda Ash* attracted a fine of €20 million in 1990, although this was reduced on appeal

---

[157] *Napier Brown/British Sugar*, OJ 1988 L 284/41.

[158] *Deutsche Telekom AG*, OJ 2003 L 263/9, para. 212. See also *Deutsche Post AG—Interception of cross-border mail*, OJ 2001 L 331/40 and *GVG/FS*, OJ 2004 L 11/17, para. 164.

[159] *Decca Navigator System*, OJ 1989 L 43/27.

[160] *Ibid.*, para. 133.

[161] *Deutsche Post AG*, OJ 2001 L 125/27, para. 52.

[162] *Vitamins*, OJ 1976 L 223/27, on appeal Case 85/76, *Hoffmann-La Roche & Co AG v Commission* [1979] ECR 461. See also *ZOJA/CSC ICI*, OJ 1972 L 299/51 (€200,000, reduced to €100,000 on appeal); *General Motors Continental*, OJ 1975 L 29/14 (€100,000, annulled on appeal); and *Hugin Kassaregister*, OJ 1978 L 22/23 (€50,000, annulled on appeal). Originally, fines were expressed in European Currency Units (ecus), but Council Regulation 1103/97 provided that references to ecus should be replaced by a reference to the euro at a rate of one euro to one ecu. See Council Regulation (EC) No 1103/97 on certain provisions relating to the introduction of the euro, OJ 1997 L 162/1.

[163] *Chiquita*, OJ 1976 L 95/1. In *European Sugar Industry*, OJ 1973 L 140/17, fines of €1,500,000 and €1,000,000 were imposed on Raffinerie Tirlemontoise and Sucres & Denrées, respectively, but this concerned a series of infringements of both Articles 81 and 82 EC.

[164] *ECS/AKZO*, OJ 1985 L 374/1, on appeal Case C-62/86, *AKZO Chemie BV v Commission* [1991] ECR I-3359.

[165] *Eurofix-Bauco v Hilti*, OJ 1988 L 65/19. See also *Bandengroothandel Frieschebrug BV/NV Nederlandsche Banden-Industrie Michelin*, OJ 1981 L 353/33 (€680,000 reduced to €300,000 on appeal); *BL (British Leyland)*, OJ 1984 L 207/11 (€350,000); *Napier Brown/British Sugar*, OJ 1988 L 284/41 (€3,000,000); *London European/Sabena*, OJ 1988 L 317/47 (€100,000); *BPB Industries plc (Gypsum)*, OJ 1989 L 10/50 (€150,000 fine imposed on BPB; €3,000,000 on Gypsum).

for largely procedural reasons.[166] In *CEWAL*, individual fines as high as €9.6 million were imposed for exclusionary pricing practices.[167] In *Deutsche Bahn*, the Commission imposed a fine of €11 million for geographic price discrimination of the kind at issue in *United Brands*.[168] But the most dramatic increase in fines was *Tetra Pak II*, where Tetra Pak received a fine of €75 million for a series of exclusionary practices affecting the packaging sector, where it held a virtual monopoly.[169]

Current practice. The entry into force of the Fining Guidelines led to a significant increase in fines under Article 82 EC (and even more so under Article 81 EC for serious horizontal infringements). Major abuse cases began to routinely attract fines in excess of €20 million or more. In *Deutsche Post*,[170] exclusionary pricing practices attracted a fine of €24 million. Similar practices in *Michelin II* were fined €19.76 million.[171] In *TACA*, individual fines as high as €41 million were imposed, but the decision was annulled on appeal for procedural reasons.[172] There are also recent indications of a policy of even higher fines in abuse cases. A wholly unprecedented fine of €497 million was imposed in *Microsoft*.[173] Although the case was extremely high profile and important, the Commission followed this fine shortly thereafter with a €60 million fine in *AstraZeneca* for abuses in connection with patent approvals.[174] Serious abuses in important sectors of the economy can therefore be expected to attract very high fines in future.

National competition authorities applying Article 82 EC have also adopted very high fines in certain cases.[175] In 2001, the Italian Antitrust Authority (IAA) fined *Assoviaggi*

---

[166] *Soda-Ash/Solvay*, OJ 1991 L 152/21.

[167] *Cewal, Cowac and Ukwal*, OJ 1993 L 34/20, upheld on appeal in Joined Cases T-24/93, T-25/93, T-26/93, and T-28/93, *Compagnie Maritime Belge Transports SA and Others v Commission* [1996] ECR II-1201; and in Joined Cases C-395/96 P and C-396/96 P, *Compagnie Maritime Belge Transports SA and Others v Commission* [2000] ECR I-1365

[168] *HOV SVZ/MCN*, OJ 1994 L 104/34. See also *Irish Sugar plc*, OJ 1997 L 258/1, affirmed on appeal in Case T-228/97, *Irish Sugar plc v Commission* [1999] ECR II-2969 and Order of the Court of Justice in Case C-497/99 P, *Irish Sugar plc v Commission* [2001] ECR I-5333 (€8,800,000, reduced to €7,883,326 on appeal); *Amministrazione Autonoma dei Monopoli di Stato*, OJ 1998 L 252/47 (€6,000,000); and *Virgin/British Airways*, OJ 2000 L 30/1 (€6,800,000).

[169] *Tetra Pak II*, OJ 1992 L 72/1.

[170] *Deutsche Post AG*, OJ 2001 L 125/27.

[171] *PO-Michelin*, OJ 2002 L 143/1. See also Case COMP/38.233, *Wanadoo Interactive*, Commission Decision of July 16, 2003, not yet published (€10.35 million).

[172] *Trans-Atlantic Conference Agreement*, OJ 1999 L 95/1, annulled on appeal in Joined Cases T-191/98 and T-212/98 to T-214/98, *Atlantic Container Line AB and Others v Commission* [2003] ECR II-3275.

[173] Case COMP/C-3/37.792, *Microsoft*, Commission Decision of March 24, 2004, not yet published. This fine was higher than the largest individual fine imposed by the Commission in any cartel case to date. The highest previous fine in a cartel case was the €462 million fine (after leniency) imposed on Hoffmann-La Roche in the vitamins cartel. See *Vitamins*, OJ 2003 L 6/1.

[174] See Commission Press Release IP/05/737 of June 15, 2005, currently on appeal in Case T-321/05, *AstraZeneca v Commission*, OJ 2005 C 271/24.

[175] A member of the Commission's Legal Service has argued that Regulation 1/2003 grants national competition authorities the power to impose fines for the effects of violations of Articles 81 and 82 EC extending beyond their national territory, i.e., extra-territorial jurisdiction. This is based on the argument that: (1) as from May 1, 2003, the power of national competition authorities to impose fines has as its legal basis Article 5 of Regulation 1/2003; (2) in the absence of any wording restricting this

approximately €26.8 million for fidelity-enhancing and exclusive practices.[176] In 2004, the IAA fined Telecom Italia €152 million for various pricing abuses.[177] High recent fines have also been a feature in France, such as the €20 million fine imposed on France Telecom and SFR for predatory pricing.[178] Other Member States, such as the United Kingdom, continue, however, to impose relatively modest fines for abuse of dominance, which most likely reflects the fact that their competition laws are still relatively new in terms of application.[179]

Low level of predictability. Predictability in relation to fines under Article 82 EC remains low (and certainly lower than in the area of cartels where the Commission now follows a reasonably well-established rubric). This is not only a function of the fact that

competence to the national territory, this power covers the whole Community territory; (3) the principle of *ne bis in idem* prohibits double prosecution for the same infringement, not merely for the same effects of an infringement: once certain conduct has been punished, it cannot be prosecuted again on the basis of different effects; and (4) given (3), and the resulting risk of either *bis in idem* or under-punishment, national competition authorities have not only the power, but are also obliged when imposing fines to take into account the effect in the whole Community territory. He argues that national competition authorities' extra-territorial power to impose fines "would also have the desirable effect of encouraging the harmonisation of national laws with regard to penalties imposed by national competition authorities, so as to ensure that penalties are sufficiently high in all Member States and that all competition authorities, when setting the amount of penalties, take into account the full effect of violations of Articles 81 and 82 EC throughout the territory of the Community." See WPJ Wils, "The Principle of 'Ne bis in Idem' in EC Antitrust Enforcement: a Legal and Economic Analysis" (2003) 26(2) *World Competition* 147. This argument is surprising and wrong, for several reasons. First, nothing in Regulation 1/2003 confers additional extra-territorial competence on national competition authorities or national courts. That means that each national authority can fine only for conduct and effects in its Member State. If that means that conduct or effects in one or more other Member States would go unpunished, either the other national authorities must be free to fine for the effects in their States, or (if they are not free to do so) the Commission should take (or should have initially taken) the case. It seems unthinkable that a change as profound as a new extra-territorial power would be mentioned nowhere in Regulation 1/2003. Second, Article 5 of Regulation 1/2003 provides that fines can only be imposed where provided for under the national law of the Member State concerned. No Member State has adopted laws allowing for fines in the case of extraterritorial effects. Finally, if each Member State could fine for all Community-wide effects, it is difficult to see the rationale for the extensive case allocation and cooperation procedures set out in Regulation 1/2003. Case allocation is expressly based on the principle that only the best placed authority or authorities should act. If there are effects in multiple Member States, the Commission should normally act and can fine for all Community-wide effects. If two or more national authorities act in parallel in the same matter, they can and should cooperate, but each is limited to imposing fines for the effects of the conduct on their national territory. In sum, although it is obviously desirable to avoid multiple procedures in different Member States, Regulation 1/2003 did not confer any extra-territorial jurisdiction on national competition authorities that they did not have previously.

[176] Case A291, *Assoviaggi/Alitalia*, Decision of June 27, 2001.

[177] Case A 351, *Telecom Italia*, Decision of November 19, 2004.

[178] *France Télécom/SFR Cegetel/Bouygues Télécom*, Conseil de la Concurrence, Décision No. 04-D48 of October 14, 2004.

[179] See, e.g., *Napp Pharmaceutical Holdings Limited and Subsidiaries v Director General of Fair Trading* [2002] CompAR 13 (£2.2 million for excessive and predatory pricing); *Aberdeen Journals Limited v Office of Fair Trading* [2003] CAT 11 (£1 million for predatory pricing); and *Genzyme Ltd v The Office of Fair Trading* [2004] CAT 4, judgment of March 11, 2004 (£3 million for margin squeeze). Individual fines for abuse cases are not published in Germany. Certain jurisdictions (e.g., Ireland) do not grant national competition authorities the power to impose fines: cases must instead be brought before national courts.

there are comparatively few decisions imposing fines under Article 82 EC. The main reason is that, notwithstanding the Fining Guidelines, the Commission enjoys significant discretion in setting fines under Article 82 EC. With the exception of duration, the various steps set out in the Fining Guidelines vest a significant amount of discretion in the Commission (e.g., deciding the amount for gravity and applying additional multipliers for deterrence and aggravating factors).

The most significant source of discretion is when an infringement is classified as "very serious"—which many abuse cases have been. In this circumstance, the Commission considers that it enjoys a large discretion in setting a starting point beyond the €20 million lower limit. For example, in *Microsoft*, there was no indication from the €20 million lower limit mentioned in the Fining Guidelines that a starting point for gravity of almost €166 million would be justified, still less the possibility that this figure would then be doubled for deterrence. Moreover, no detailed reasons are given in the decision to explain the weight attached to particular factors: they are essentially listed and a total figure is arrived at for gravity without explaining the contributory role of each element. It is also worth noting that the Community Courts have been much less willing to reduce fines in Article 82 EC cases than they have in cartel cases. The reductions that have been made typically resulted from procedural violations.[180]

15.4.2 Behavioural Remedies

Overview. Most violations of Article 82 EC stem from behaviour by a dominant firm, in which case the principal remedy consists in an order to bring the abusive conduct to a halt. This section describes the kinds of behavioural remedies that are applied in order to address the principal Article 82 EC violations.[181] It is worth recalling, however, that the distinction between structural and behavioural remedies is not always clear-cut. For example, compulsory dealing under Article 82 EC has structural elements in that it involves a partial transfer of tangible or intangible assets to one or more third parties.

[180] See most notably Joined Cases T-191/98 and T-212/98 to T-214/98, *Atlantic Container Line AB and Others v Commission* [2003] ECR II-3275.

[181] It is also possible for an abuse to reside in contract and most abuses in fact do in some sense. Under Article 81(2), agreements contrary to Article 81(1) are automatically void. There is no parallel sanction in Article 82 EC, although it is clear at least that the abusive clause would be unenforceable. The effects of the non-enforceability of that clause on the remainder of the contract is a question for the law governing the contract, subject to the overriding public policy consideration that the effects of Article 82 EC cannot be derogated from by contract. A question arises, however, as to what effect an abusive clause in one contract has on downstream contracts concluded on the basis of the unlawful agreement. Under Article 81 EC, the nullity of a restrictive upstream agreement does not automatically extend to downstream agreements linked to the upstream agreement. See *Astra*, OJ 1993 L 20/23, paras. 32–33; *Trans-Atlantic Conference Agreement,* OJ 1999 L 95/1, paras. 577–82. However, the effect of the nullity of the upstream agreements implies the termination of their own restrictive effects, as well as the elimination of restrictive effects residing in contracts concluded with third parties under the terms of the unlawful upstream agreement. Where the downstream contracts were determined under conditions of distorted competition, contract partners may be given the right to terminate or renegotiate these contracts to eliminate their restrictive effects. The intention is to allow the contract partner to renegotiate the contract on the terms that would likely have been obtained but for the prejudice suffered through the upstream infringement, on the basis that firms should not be entitled to derive advantage from an unlawful agreement. Although there is no precedent on this issue, the same rationale would probably apply to a parallel situation under Article 82 EC.

Similarly, in *Microsoft*,[182] requiring Microsoft to offer a version of its Windows operating system without WMP would require potentially significant changes in Microsoft's product offering. But the distinction between behavioural and structural remedies is nonetheless useful and valid as a general matter: it distinguishes continuing behaviour (behavioural remedies) and one-off acts (structural remedies).

15.4.2.1 Exclusionary pricing abuses

Practice. The Community institutions have typically remedied exclusionary low prices (e.g., predatory pricing) with fines and by requiring the price to be raised to a non-exclusionary level.[183] (There could be no case for regulating the dominant firm's costs and trying to get it to reduce them in an effort to make a profit: the only thing the dominant firm can control is its price.) In *ECS/AKZO*[184] the Commission imposed a more stringent set of remedies, but these were purely intended as interim measures to preserve the *status quo ante*. Thus, AKZO was prohibited from deviating from a specified price schedule annexed to the interim decision and from granting any terms of credit or conditions of supply that directly or indirectly caused the effective delivered price of the relevant products to be below the price set out in the annex. AKZO was, however, permitted to offer or supply the products at prices below those set out in the annex if this was necessary in good faith to meet (but not to undercut) a lower price shown to be offered by another supplier ready and able to supply the same product to that undertaking.

The Commission has also extracted less orthodox remedies in certain predatory pricing cases. For example, in return for clearing a partnership between Austrian Airlines and Lufthansa, the Commission required, *inter alia*, that, each time the airlines reduced a published fare on a route where they face the presence of a new entrant, they should apply the same fare reduction, in percentage terms, on three other routes on which they did not face competition.[185] This remedy is ingenious, but it is doubtful whether it could be lawfully imposed in a final decision. Firms could not lawfully be compelled to reduce their prices in markets in which no abusive conduct is alleged or found. Moreover, care would need to be taken with such remedies. They might have the perverse effect of making life even tougher for rivals in the other markets.

Much the same principles can be applied to remedies in a margin squeeze case: the margin between the two prices should be increased to whatever is deemed to be a non-exclusionary margin.[186] Whether the wholesale price should be decreased, or the retail price increased, or some combination of the two, depends on the facts of the particular case and what the dominant firm is willing to do. As noted in Chapter Six (Margin Squeeze), a margin squeeze may arise because the dominant firm increases the wholesale price to an exclusionary level—a constructive refusal to supply—or reduces the retail price to a predatory level. Which type of margin squeeze is being practised

---

[182] Case COMP/C-3/37.792, *Microsoft*, Commission Decision of March 24, 2004, not yet published.

[183] See, e.g., *Tetra Pak II*, OJ 1992 L 72/1, Article 3(3); Case COMP/38.233, *Wanadoo Interactive*, Commission Decision of July 16, 2003 (not yet published), Article 2.

[184] *ECS/AKZO—Interim Measures*, OJ 1983 L 252/13.

[185] See "Commission announces intention to clear partnership between Austrian Airlines and Lufthansa," Commission Press Release IP/01/1832 of December 14, 2001.

[186] See, e.g., *Deutsche Telekom AG*, OJ 2003 L 263/9.

may affect the appropriate remedy. But care should also be taken in devising remedies in a margin squeeze case. Reducing the wholesale price may be ineffective if the reductions in wholesale charges are simply competed away in the retail market. Similarly, increasing the dominant firm's retail price is likely to be pointless if it is already higher than rivals' retail prices.[187]

15.4.2.2 Remedies for excessive pricing

Practice. Excessive pricing cases raise additional complications for competition authorities and courts, since they may force them into acting as price regulators, e.g., to monitor the evolution of future prices in the light of market developments. The Commission has frequently expressed a general reluctance to do this.[188] The usual remedies in excessive pricing cases have been fines and directions to reduce the price to a non-exploitative level. Proving excessive pricing requires a court or competition authority to identify the excess relative to the benchmark that would apply in a competitive market. Thus, the remedy will generally be to reduce the excess. But excessive prices may also be linked to exclusionary conduct, in which case it will first be necessary to stop the exclusionary conduct.[189] Finally, it should be recalled that the Court of Justice has held that a compulsory licence may be an appropriate remedy in the case of excessive prices in connection with intellectual property rights.[190] This is presumably subject to the requirement that the usual remedy—reducing the price by the excessive amount—would not be effective.

But competition authorities may also be more willing to consider structural remedies in the case of excessive pricing. In general, persistently excessive prices imply structural market failure, with the result that remedying that failure may be more effective than on-going price regulation. As discussed elsewhere in this chapter, structural remedies raise significant complexities and may in fact lead to a reduction in consumer welfare overall. Accordingly, they should only be used as a remedy of last resort. Excessive pricing cases, however, might be a good candidate for considering structural remedies, but only where there is strong evidence that the market will not correct itself over time.[191]

---

[187] For an interesting discussion of the practical aspects of the remedy in a margin squeeze case, see *Genzyme Limited v Office of Fair Trading* [2005] CAT 32.

[188] See Vth Report on Competition Policy (1975), para. 76 (Commission expressed reluctance to act as price control authority). See also M Haag and R Klotz, "Commission Practice Concerning Excessive Pricing In Telecommunications" (1998) 2 *Competition Policy Newsletter* ("The Commission itself never aspired to use Article 8[2] EC-Treaty in order to act as a price setting authority…Recent Commission practice in cases concerning the telecommunications sector is fully in line with this general policy.").

[189] See, e.g., *Napp Pharmaceutical Holdings Limited and Subsidiaries v Director General of Fair Trading* [2002] CompAR 13 (excessive pricing for an outpatient product made possible because of predatory pricing in "gateway" hospital market).

[190] See Case 238/87, *AB Volvo v Erik Veng (UK) Ltd* [1988] ECR 6211. See also Case 53/87, *Consorzio italiano della componentistica di ricambio per autoveicoli and Maxicar v Regie nationale des usines Renault* [1988] ECR 6039, which was decided on the same day as *Volvo* on substantially the same grounds.

[191] See Report by the Economic Advisory Group on Competition Policy, "*An Economic Approach to Article 82*," July 2005, p. 11 ("If it was just a question of short-run versus long-run effects, one might

In *Greenstar*, a decision of the Irish Competition Authority, structural remedies were discussed as a solution for excessive pricing in the refuse collection sector.[192] Although no evidence of excessive pricing was found, the Competition Authority considered the possibility of structural remedies on the grounds that "the market for household waste collection is not working well for consumers."[193] The Competition Authority discussed two options: (1) the creation of a waste regulator; and (2) the introduction of competitive tendering for the provision of household waste collection in defined geographic areas. Regulation was ruled out, for essentially the same reasons as why price regulation by competition authorities is generally ineffective (e.g., need for ongoing monitoring and price regulation). But the Competition Authority concluded that consumers' interests could be addressed through competitive tendering of exclusive contracts. It reasoned that competition *for* the market (as opposed to *in* the market) could yield significant cost savings, increase efficiency levels, and ensure value for money. The Competition Authority therefore recommended a "radical overhaul of the current regulatory framework for household waste collection services."[194] Although the Competition Authority's recommendations are not binding, the decision shows a willingness of competition authorities to look at more innovative solutions in excessive pricing cases.

15.4.2.3 Remedies in discrimination cases

Effectively enforcing non-discrimination obligations. Non-discrimination obligations feature prominently in Article 82 EC decisions. The most common situation is where a dominant supplier of an essential input supplies rivals on a downstream market and engages in actual or implied discrimination against downstream rivals. Examples include refusal to deal, margin squeeze, and other raising rivals' costs strategies.[195] Non-discrimination obligations are particularly important in recently-liberalised markets where incumbents retain control over essential inputs.[196] Non-

---

be tempted to put the immediate gain of today's consumers above everything else. However, a policy intervention on such grounds requires the competition authority to actually determine what price it considers appropriate, as well as how it should evolve over time; for this it is not really qualified. Moreover, such a policy intervention drastically reduces, and may even forego the chance to protect consumers in the future by competition rather than policy intervention. A regime in which consumer protection from monopoly abuses is based on competition is greatly to be preferred to one in which consumer protection is due to political or administrative control of prices. In most circumstances therefore, the competition authority ought to refrain from intervening against monopolistic pricing and instead see to it that there is room for competition to open up.").

[192] Case COM/108/02, Alleged excessive pricing by Greenstar Recycling Holdings Limited in the provision of household waste collection services in northeast Wicklow, August 30, 2005, Enforcement Decision Series, No. E/05/002.

[193] *Ibid.*, p. 41.

[194] *Ibid.*, p. 47.

[195] See Ch. 8 (Refusal to Deal) and Ch. 6 (Margin Squeeze).

[196] See, e.g., *IGR Stereo Television-Salora*, XIth Report on Competition Policy (1981), para. 63; *DHL International*, XXIst Report on Competition Policy (1991), para. 88; *Eirpage*, OJ 1993 L 306/22, para. 20; *Infonet*, XXIInd Report on Competition Policy (1993), p. 416; *EBU-Eurovision*, OJ 1993 L 179/23, Art. 2; *BT-MCI*, OJ 1994 L 223/36, para. 57; *ACI (Channel Tunnel)*, OJ 1994 L 224/28, Art. 2; *Night Services*, OJ 1994 L 259/20, Art. 2; *Gas Interconnector*, XXVth Competition Policy Report (1996), para. 82; *Atlas*, OJ 1996 L 239/23; *Unisource*, OJ 1997 L 318/1; and *British Interactive Broadcasting/Open*, OJ 1999 L 312/1.

discrimination obligations can also arise where the dominant firm is not active on the downstream market, but engages in discrimination that materially limits the ability of non-associated companies to compete with each other.

The main issue in discrimination cases is making the non-discrimination obligation effective in practice. Such obligations require on-going monitoring. Moreover, because of information and other asymmetries, a company which is being discriminated against does not always know what treatment other companies are getting, and therefore does not know that it could complain. The existence of a transfer price between the dominant firm's two operations may be useful, but has obvious limitations. In the first place, transfer prices are often set for reasons that have nothing to do with ensuring that the downstream operation pays a price that would be non-exclusionary if charged to third parties. It may therefore be over-inclusive or under-inclusive. Further, a transfer price is useless if the discrimination concerns non-price factors, such as quality degradation, or if there are concealed financial transfers.

The Commission has attempted to address this problem in one of two ways. The first is to delegate to a national authority the supervisory task.[197] But this simply transfers the problem rather than solves it. A second, more effective solution is to require the companies concerned to get their auditors, as part of their annual audit, to certify that the company has treated equally all those companies that it was obliged to treat equally. Auditors should certify that all relationships have been conducted on a non-discriminatory basis, and if necessary that the relationships between a parent company and its subsidiary have been on an arms'-length basis. Certain methodologies exist in this connection, such as the OECD Transfer Pricing Guidelines.[198] This task is obviously easier if the two parts of the operation are clearly separated and if relations between them are formalised and recorded, which the Commission could also require.[199]

Another key element is what constitutes a breach of the non-discrimination obligation and what legal consequences follow from that. In practice, a dominant firm might commit numerous small instances of discrimination that have no material impact on the discriminated party. It might seem excessive to invalidate a commitment decision or commence protracted infringement proceedings for small breaches of this kind. Thus, in merger and joint venture cases, the Commission has sometimes stated that breaches would not be considered to infringe the conditions unless the breaches have a "substantial" impact on the market, or are otherwise serious. Of course, such provisions have the effect of making the non-discrimination obligation no longer automatic and controversial to apply, thereby decreasing its deterrent effect. A stronger general case can be made for an automatic violation resulting from any discrimination. It would make sense, however, for such a decision to include a review clause, in particular where the non-discrimination duty concerns access to facilities that rivals may be able to self-provide in future.

---

[197] See, e.g., in the context of monitoring excessive pricing, Commission Press Release IP/02/1852 of 11 December 2002; and Commission Press Release IP/98/707 of 27 July 1998.

[198] See "Transfer Pricing Guidelines for Multinational Enterprises and Tax Administrations," OECD Publishing (2001).

[199] See *Deutsche Post AG*, OJ 2001 L 125/27.

15.4.2.4 Compulsory dealing remedies

Introduction. A surprising feature of decisions in which a duty to deal has been imposed or considered under Article 82 EC is the absence of any detailed or principled discussion of the terms on which access should be mandated. In *Magill*, the Commission left the parties to agree the terms of the licence, failing which some of the cases were determined by specialist tribunals such as the Copyright Tribunal in the United Kingdom. In *IMS Health*, the parties were granted a short period to agree licence terms, failing which an expert was to be appointed to determine the appropriate royalty. This never actually happened, since the decision ordering access was suspended immediately by the President of the Court of First Instance. A similar arrangement has been used in *Microsoft*, where the conditions of the licence and the appropriate royalty remain under discussion. All of these cases specify the use of "fair, reasonable, and non-discriminatory" (FRAND) terms without giving content to this obligation.

Clearly, the terms of a duty to deal are of the utmost importance. At the one extreme, it would make little sense to order a duty to deal if the terms of the licence or contract were so onerous as to make the party advocating a duty to deal unable or unwilling to make a profitable contract. Indeed, it would be ironic, to say the least, if the terms of a duty to deal were so onerous as to amount to a constructive refusal to deal: the whole process would then become circular and pointless. At the other extreme, it would be unjustifiable if, in addition to ordering access, some of the value of the dominant firm's property was confiscated by access terms intended to stimulate new entrants. It would also be contrary to the aims of Article 82 EC if a duty to deal resulted in terms that promoted inefficient entry.

The lack of clarity or guidance on the terms of a duty to deal is not merely an administrative inconvenience that can be dealt with in the rare cases in which a duty to deal is imposed. It also has a decisive impact on the extent to which firms are likely to refuse to deal. For example, suppose that the terms of a duty to deal allowed the dominant firm to charge any profit-maximising price it wished. Absent some irrational animosity towards potential trading parties, the dominant firm should ordinarily be willing to deal on such a basis. The dominant firm should be indifferent as to whether it makes the monopoly profit at the level of the input or the product in which that input is included. Indeed, it may well prefer to become a rent collector than to compete downstream.

Vagueness regarding the appropriate terms of a duty to deal is also likely to impact on the effect on investment decisions of a duty to deal. *Ex ante* decisions on investments are governed by a forward-looking assessment of expected costs, risk, and returns. The risk that a firm might be subject to a duty to deal in future may be relevant in this connection, since it could impact on expected future profits. But if the terms of access could vary from zero to any profit-maximising price that it wishes, it would be very difficult to come up with reliable estimates as to project viability. At the extreme, this might scupper certain valuable investments.

Courts and competition authorities not generally suited to act as price regulators. Whatever the particular policy objectives or objections, any terms of a duty to deal that require determination by a court or competition authority place the authority concerned in the role of a price regulator. For the same reasons why courts and competition authorities have generally avoided trying to establish a "competitive price" in excessive pricing cases,[200] so too they face difficulties in setting terms of a duty to deal that are consistent with the divergent interests of the parties concerned, as well as the overriding need to ensure effective remedies in their capacity as enforcers of Article 82 EC. Even specialist regulators with detailed knowledge of industries and extensive information powers have had mixed results in determining "competitive" or "efficient" prices. There is no reason to suppose that generalist courts and competition authorities would fare better and, indeed, many reasons to believe that they would do worse.

Issues raised by the interoperability remedy in *Microsoft*. The *Microsoft* decision illustrates many of the problems that bedevil compulsory dealing cases.[201] As a remedy for the abuse found in the workgroup server market, the Commission required Microsoft to disclose all information that third party developers need to achieve interoperability with Microsoft's PC and workgroup server operating systems. And yet, almost two years later, the remedy has still not yet been implemented. Some of the delays reflect the inherent complexity and controversy of the case, but most of them are likely to arise to a greater or lesser extent in other compulsory dealing cases, in particular for intellectual property.

Following the rejection of Microsoft's request for suspension of the Commission's decision, Microsoft adopted a Workgroup Server Protocol Program ("WSPP") intended to comply with the Commission's disclosure obligation. In a decision rendered on November 15, 2005, pursuant to Article 24(1) of Regulation 1/2003, the Commission identified a number of shortcomings in Microsoft's WSPP and required compliance by December 15, 2005. On December 15, 2005, Microsoft issued a revised set of WSPP documentation. Acting on a recommendation from the trustee appointed to oversee the remedy, the Commission issued a Statement of Objections. This preliminary document states that Microsoft is in default, and threatens a fine of €2 million per day for each day of continued non-compliance. At the date of publication it was not clear what action, if any, would follow Microsoft's response. A number of implementation problems are said to arise—all of which are strongly contested by Microsoft.[202]

First, it was suggested by the Commission that Microsoft has based itself on a excessively narrow and formalistic interpretation of computer protocols to limit the scope of information disclosed under its WSPP. This is said by the Commission to conflict with the Commission's decision, which is not based on a particular notion of computer protocols. Rather, the decision is goal-oriented in that it requires Microsoft to

[200] See Ch. 12 (Excessive Prices).

[201] This section describes the controversy over the implementation of the interoperability remedy in Microsoft relying on publicly available documents only. The comments below should not be seen as supporting or otherwise the positions of Microsoft or the Commission in the appeal before the Court of First Instance. The reader should be advised that the authors and their respective firms have acted, and still act, on opposite sides of this case and maintain different views as regards the merits of the positions taken by the Commission and Microsoft.

[202] See "Competition: Commission warns Microsoft of daily penalty for failure to comply with 2004 decision," Commission Press Release IP/05/1695 of December 22, 2005.

disclose all information necessary to achieve interoperability with its dominant operating systems.

Second, on royalties, the decision requires Microsoft to make available its interoperability information on reasonable and non-discriminatory terms. The Commission has suggested that Microsoft's proposed royalty structure would force third party developers to pay royalty fees that exceed Microsoft's downstream price for its own work group server operating system. The Commission has taken the position that, to be reasonable, any royalty charged by Microsoft cannot exceed what a non-dominant company would charge for similar information. Moreover, Microsoft can only charge a royalty for information that embodies innovative elements of a genuine commercial value. It cannot charge for the "strategic value" that Microsoft derives from the dependency of third party developers on its interoperability information (though in practice separating these two value components may not be easy). The Commission also suggests that, to date, Microsoft has failed to demonstrate that its protocol information effectively contains any genuine value. Review of the information disclosed by Microsoft has shown that this information essentially consists in commonplace protocol sequences and private extensions to public industry standards. The implication, according to the Commission, is that the only value in keeping such information secret lies in the fact that this allows Microsoft to hamper competition and preserve its operating system monopoly, i.e., not to protect innovation.

Third, the Commission suggests that Microsoft's terms and conditions prevent the implementation of the interoperability information in software products distributed under open source licences. In a letter of June 1, 2005, the Commission expressed its initial view that there is no justification for excluding open source implementation of interoperability information that does not embody innovative elements of a genuine value. Microsoft has brought a separate appeal against this letter that remains pending.

Finally, as part of its disclosure obligation, Microsoft must give interested third parties the opportunity to evaluate the interoperability information offered by Microsoft, before entering into a binding licensing agreement. The Commission has suggested that Microsoft has designed the evaluation process in an obstructive way that prevents any meaningful evaluation. In particular, it is said that representatives of interested parties have only had three days to review the information on offer at Microsoft's locations; they may not bring computers or other technical equipment with them; and the information is presented to them without any meaningful structure or explanation.[203]

[203] The Trustee appointed by the Commission to oversee implementation of the remedies stated as follows: "Any programmer or programming team seeking to use the Technical Documentation for a real development exercise would be wholly and completely unable to proceed on the basis of the documentation. The Technical Documentation is therefore totally unfit at this stage for its intended purpose." The report also states that, "the documentation appears to be fundamentally flawed in its conception, and in its level of explanation and detail... Overall, the process of using the documentation is an absolutely frustrating, time-consuming and ultimately fruitless task. The documentation needs quite drastic overhaul before it could be considered workable." See "Commission warns Microsoft of daily penalty for failure to comply with 2004 decision," Commission Press Release IP/05/1695 of December 22, 2005.

The basic options for determining access terms. Given the difficulties of courts and competition authorities acting as price regulators, it should always be incumbent upon the parties concerned to try and agree terms on a voluntary basis. If agreement cannot be reached, a range of options might be considered. It is important to emphasise, however, that the terms of access may vary from case to case, such that there is no single, correct methodology. Each methodology has certain drawbacks and the precise nature of these disadvantages will vary depending on whether the interests of the requesting party, the dominant firm, or the process of competition (or some combination of all three) take priority. For example, it might be argued in intellectual property cases that it is particularly important not to appropriate the dominant firm's return on its invention and to allow licence terms that reflect the dominant firm's loss of profits through licensing.

The basic options for access terms are: (1) royalty-free or costless access; (2) cost-based access; (3) terms that compensate the dominant firm for lost profits or "opportunity cost;" and (4) *ex ante* construction of a "competitive" access price. However, whichever option happens to be appropriate, there is no compelling reason why the principles should differ depending on whether the input in question is intellectual or tangible property. As explained in detail in Chapter Eight (Refusal to Deal), both types of property should generally be regarded as equivalent for purposes of a duty to deal under Article 82 EC (even if there may be features of either type of property that plead in favour of the use of one option over another in individual cases).

a. Royalty-free or costless access. Where a duty to deal concerns information that is not protected by intellectual property (e.g., trade secrets), a number of cases have suggested that royalty-free access may be appropriate. In *Tetra Pak II*, the Court of First Instance held that a royalty-free licence was appropriate where disclosing the relevant specifications that customers and competitors needed to make packing cartons compatible with Tetra Pak's packaging machines did not touch upon Tetra Pak's intellectual property rights. A number of decisions under the EC Merger Regulation reached a similar conclusion regarding technology interface information, although these cases are arguably different, since the commitments were intended to promote inter-technology competition.[204] The same argument was made in *Microsoft*. The licensees argued that a rational operating system developer such as Microsoft should welcome the development of software products that interoperate with its system platform, since this would increase the attractiveness of the platform. Thus, rather than hurting it, royalty-free disclosure of interface information would reward the operating system developer. This solution was not accepted by the Commission, since it seemed that the interoperability information to be disclosed is protected, in part, by intellectual property rights or trade secrets. A final situation in which royalty-free or costless access may be appropriate concerns situations in which the dominant firm has voluntarily licensed other undertakings for free. Although a dominant firm is always entitled to change its

[204] See Case COMP/M.2861, *Siemens/Dräger* (obligation to disclose interface information without fee); *Atlas*, OJ 1996 L 239/23 (obligation to disclose interface information—royalties not mentioned); and Case COMP/M.1601, *AlliedSignal/Honeywell* (obligation to provide interface information—royalties not mentioned).

licensing policy, past or presents terms of dealing may offer some basis for calculating the terms of new licensees' contracts.

b. Cost-based access. Assuming the dominant firm's property is protected by intellectual property or has clear value for some other reason, cost-based access will generally be inappropriate in duty to deal cases. Cost-based access is of course the predominant benchmark under regulated access to utility networks. But the principles used for access pricing in the context of regulation will more often than not be inapplicable for access terms determined under competition law. While the specifics of regulation vary, access pricing in the utility sector is generally intended to positively encourage new entry by creating cost-based access. This may require incumbents to subsidise less efficient entrants, in particular where the relevant regulatory framework favours service-based competition over network competition. There would be no basis for doing this under competition law. Much of the detailed learning on regulated access pricing either cannot therefore be applied under competition law or requires modification in an unregulated environment.

Of course, cost-based access need not mean the actual cost incurred in the development of the asset in question. More appropriate measures would include: (1) replacement cost; or (2) reproduction cost. Replacement cost is the cost that would be incurred by a potential buyer to create a replica of the asset. This would include not only the basic cost of development, but also other adjustments to determine a cost that is indicative of the present-day market value of the asset. Reproduction cost is the cost of constructing, at current prices, an exact replica of the asset in question, using the same materials, labour, standards and design employed in its original creation, including any inefficiencies and obsolescence associated with the original development of the asset.

One important problem with using replacement/reproduction cost (or other measures of cost-based value) in compulsory dealing cases, however, is that it is inherent in the decision to grant access that the asset in question has a high degree of *uniqueness*. If not, no duty to deal would presumably have arisen in the first place. Particularly for intellectual property rights, many commentators argue that replacement cost is inappropriate and that value can be captured only on the basis of cash flow.[205] Where the property concerned is the result of intellectual endeavour or substantial investment cost-based access does not take properly into account the dynamic incentives of investment decisions and would not therefore correctly reward the dominant firm for the investments made. The investment may have been extremely risky *ex ante* and rewarding a dominant firm with a return equal to the discount rate, or the cost of capital, would severely reduce its incentives to invest in the development of new products. Moreover, the value associated with an asset is often unrelated to the cost of replacement or reproduction.

The incentive for a competition authority or court setting contract terms according to this methodology would be to set a low access price in order to encourage entry, thus leading to lower prices, higher output, and an increase in static efficiency. However, this would lead to significant negative consequences for dynamic efficiency, as *ex ante*

[205] See T Copeland, T Koller, and J Murrin, *Valuation: Measuring and Managing the Value of Companies* (3rd edn., New York, John Wiley & Sons, 1990) p. 216.

the dominant firm would be discouraged from investing in new products due to the risk that it is forced to license them in the future at prices no greater than the cost of the investment. This could reduce the basic incentives that motivate socially-beneficial investment. Cost-based access is also generally inappropriate for another reason: many inventions result from clever ideas rather than labour- or capital-intensive activity. Limiting the return on brilliant inventions to the value of the labour or capital employed is likely to lead to significant consumer harm in the long run.

c. ***Terms that compensate the dominant firm for lost profits.*** The access terms most favourable to the dominant firm are those which would keep it "whole" in the sense that they would compensate for any profits lost in dealing with other trading parties as a result of a duty to deal. One methodology used to calculate the dominant firm's opportunity cost in supplying new trading parties is the efficient component pricing rule (ECPR).[206] This principle has been used in a number of regulatory decisions and it is sometimes argued that it should also be applied to compulsory dealing under Article 82 EC. This assumes that the objective of a remedy under Article 82 EC is to send a strong signal in terms of the protection of intellectual property and other valuable property rights and to minimise the damage to dynamic economic incentives that compulsory dealing might bring.

The ECPR prescribes that, in a competitive market, a firm selling to a competitor the facilities necessary to provide a final service or product that the seller could also provide should demand a price equal to the profits the original firm would have received it had provided the service itself, i.e., all the pertinent opportunity costs. A price equal to the opportunity cost prevents the subsidisation of competitors through too low a price. Its proponents therefore argue that it only promotes equally or more efficient entry. Effectively, the ECPR price is set equal to the opportunity cost to the dominant firm of making a contract with a rival. Therefore, if one firm makes a contract, that firm should compensate the dominant firm for all its expected lost profits; if two firms make a contract, they should each pay half of the dominant firm's expected loss in profits when two firms enter the market etc. The expected loss in profits involves two interrelated

[206] The ECPR was first introduced in WJ Baumol and JG Sidak, *Toward Competition in Local Telephony* (Cambridge, MIT Press, 1994). See also WJ Baumol and JG Sidak, "The Pricing of Inputs Sold to Competitors" (1994) 11 *Yale Journal of Regulation* 171–202; and R Willig, "The Theory of Network Access Pricing" in HM Trebing (ed.), *Issues in Public Utility Regulation* (East Lansing, Michigan State University Public Utilities Papers, 1979). A number of jurisdictions have adopted ECPR or its variants. The concept was applied in the 1990s in New Zealand and New Zealand's highest legal body, the Privy Council, was criticised for its endorsement of the ECPR in the interconnection dispute between TCNZ and Clear, respectively the network operator and the entrant in New Zealand. See *Clear Communications, Ltd v Telecom Corp of New Zealand, Ltd*, slip op. (H.C. Dec. 22, 1992), rev'd, slip op. (C.A. Dec. 28, 1993), rev'd, [1995] 1 N.Z.L.R. 385 (Oct. 19, 1994, Judgment of the Lords of the Judicial Committee of the Privy Council). In the United States railway industry, the Interstate Commerce Commission applied the rule in several railroad rate cases involving trackage rights. See *St Louis SW Ry—Trackage Rights over Missouri Pac RR—Kansas City to St Louis*, 1 I.C.C.2d 776 (1984), 4 I.C.C.2d 668 (1987), 5 I.C.C.2d 525 (1989), 8 I.C.C.2d 80 (1991). In telecommunications, the California Public Utilities Commission implicitly adopted ECPR in 1989 (but called it imputation) as part of its reform of regulation of local exchange carriers, reaffirming its decision in 1994. See *Alternative Regulatory Framework for Local Exchange Carriers*, Invest. No. 87-11-033, 33 C.P.U.C.-2d 43, 107 P.U.R.4th 1 (1989), and Decision 94-09-065 at 204–24 (September 15, 1994).

aspects: the loss in volume of sales due to entry into (or growth in) the market by the new entrants and the loss in margins due to lower prices.[207] The final terms are the sum of the expected loss in profits from the products no longer sold (because customers are buying the competitors' products) *plus* the lower margin on the products that are sold (lower margins because customers threaten to buy the competitors' products) *minus* any cost savings to the dominant firm.

There are a number of potential difficulties with ECPR as a remedy in duty to deal cases under Article 82 EC.[208] The first problem is that it would result in the dominant firm retaining supra-normal profits if it was making such profits at the time a duty to deal was imposed. Although refusal to deal cases do not formally contain findings of excessive pricing, they sometimes implicitly assume that the dominant firm is charging, or could charge, excessive prices and earn supra-normal profits, precisely because it controls an input that is indispensable for competition. This is a less serious concern in the context of regulation—where ECPR has mainly been applied—since the regulator can usually regulate the wholesale and/or retail prices in order to eliminate excess profits. As one economist notes:[209]

> "ECP[R] provides a rational basis for competition in the competitive activity, but it does nothing to alleviate the monopoly problem which must exist if the asset in question is a true essential facility. If a necessary condition for identifying an essential facility is that the asset is not subject to effective competition, a solution that leaves the asset owner free to set price levels for use of the asset, and indifferent as to whether it shares the asset with its competitors, cannot be satisfactory."

This criticism has been addressed by modifying ECPR to take account of the post-entry price reduction due to competition.[210] This involves consideration of: (1) the volume of the dominant firm's retail sales displaced by the new entrant(s); (2) the dominant firm's profit margin on selling the input to third parties (the mark-up over incremental cost whose role is to recover the opportunity cost of providing access); and (3) the change in the dominant firm's retail profit margin as a result of entry.

Second, ECPR only takes account of the interests of the seller. It does not consider the willingness to pay of the buyer, which is relevant in duty to deal cases. The absolute

---

[207] See RT Rapp and PA Beutel, "Patent Damages: Updated Rules on the Road to Economic Rationality," NERA Report (1999); and S Addanki, "Economics and Patent Damages: A Practical Guide" NERA Paper (1993).

[208] See *Albion Water Limited v Director General Of Water Services* [2005] CAT 40, paras. 337 et seq.

[209] See D Ridyard, "Essential Facilities and the Obligation to Supply Competitors under UK and EC Competition Law" (1996) 8 *European Competition Law Review* 450. See also AE Kahn and WE Taylor, "The Pricing of Inputs Sold to Competitors: A Comment" (1994) 11(1) *Yale Journal on Regulation* 231 ("Unsurprisingly...opponents of interconnection charges proposed by [incumbent] telephone companies...protest that the entitlement claimed by the LECs to recover the 'opportunity costs' of business lost to competitors is merely a rationalisation for the continued collection of monopoly profits. They are right, it could well be."). See also N Economides and LJ White, "Access and Interconnection Pricing: How Efficient is the 'Efficient Component Pricing Rule'?" (1995) 40(3) *Antitrust Bulletin* 557.

[210] See JG Sidak and DF Spulber, "Network Access Pricing and Deregulation" in *Industrial and Corporate Change* (Oxford, Oxford University Press, 1997) Vol. 6, No. 4, pp. 757–82.

maximum price that an entrant would be willing to pay would be the total expected additional profits it expected to make from obtaining access to the dominant firm's inputs. At the extreme, when the reservation price of the dominant seller is higher than the price the buyer is willing to pay, the parties will be unable to reach a mutually acceptable deal, and therefore the input in question will not be sold.[211] Thus, ECPR could be counterproductive when it results in no contracts for the supply of the input.

A final problem is that ECPR is uncertain because it concerns expected values of prices and costs, which may be different from the actual figures. There is inherent uncertainty in the valuations, and the actual realised loss in profits will almost certainly differ from the *ex ante* expected value. This is especially true when there is the possibility of more than one firm entering the market.

d. Constructive a "competitive" access fee ex ante. Problems with cost-based access and the ECPR lead to an intermediate solution in the determination of access terms: a market-based price. Under this approach, a competition authority or court attempts to construct an access price based on rates that are observed for assets that are reasonably comparable to the dominant firm's asset. Such market rates are presumed to be the result of arm's-length negotiations between willing parties and, as such, reflect the economic benefits that the parties expect to realise from the requesting party's use of the asset in question. This is a similar exercise to what the parties themselves go through in trying to voluntarily agree an access charge in compulsory dealing cases. The only difference is that a court or competition authority is the final arbiter.

A number of potential benchmarks could be used and there is much to be said for using a series of benchmarks in parallel. The most accurate benchmark is the terms on which the dominant firm makes the asset available in analogous competitive markets. If no present market exists, past terms are a good starting point, adjusted, where appropriate, for developments in the intervening period. A second broad benchmark is rivals' terms of access for similar assets in comparable markets. As noted in Chapter Twelve (Excessive Prices), competitors' prices are sometimes used to determine whether a price is excessive or not. A similar approach could be used to determine a "competitive" access rate. Finally, excessive pricing cases have also relied on the "economic value" of the asset in question.[212] These approaches most likely require adjustments between different firms for quality and product differences, overhead differences, and commercial policy differences, as well as the difficulties of comparing different markets. In addition, there is a practical problem in compulsory dealing cases that the asset in question is, by definition, unique and cannot therefore be easily compared to other assets or markets. But these difficulties are often confronted by courts and specialist authorities (e.g., patent tribunals and courts) in practice. The solutions found may not be optimal or very scientific, but they are designed to at least achieve a workable outcome.

Conclusion. Surprisingly, there is almost no precedent or discussion of the terms of a duty to deal under Article 82 EC. Clearly, given the well-known problems of price

[211] See T Valletti and A Estache, "The Theory of Access Pricing: an Overview for Infrastructure Regulators," CEPR Discussion Paper Series #2133.

[212] See Ch. 12 (Excessive Prices).

regulation by courts and competition authorities, there is much to be said for trying to get the parties concerned to agree terms. If courts and competition authorities are required to set terms, it is important to understand that there is no single, correct solution. Some commentators argue that the correct solution is to permit a fee that compensates the dominant firm for the opportunity cost of licensing (ECPR). This is said to strike an adequate balance between the dominant firm's need to recover investments and maintain incentives to innovate, while allowing the requesting party to earn a revenue from incremental efficiencies that the dominant firm does not provide. This theory is said by some to be controversial—mainly because it could perpetuate excessive prices on the downstream market—and has not been applied under Article 82 EC to date. In these circumstances, courts and competition authorities are likely to make do with the same techniques they rely upon in other cases in which they have to set prices or margins, in particular excessive pricing and margin squeeze cases. The overriding objective of a competition authority will be to set an access price at which a reasonably efficient firm could make a material contribution to competition on the downstream market.

15.4.2.5 Remedies in tying cases

Contractual tying. In cases when the purchase of a dominant product is conditioned upon purchase of a second product from the dominant firm, the Commission's practice has been to end the tie (as well as imposing fines). Thus, in *Hilti*, Hilti was required to end an abusive practice of tying the sale of nail guns to nail cartridges, to refrain from repeating or continuing any similar acts or behaviour, and to refrain from adopting any measures having an equivalent effect.[213] Similar measures were imposed in *Tetra Pak II*.[214] In addition, Tetra Pak was required to amend or delete the offending contractual clauses from its machine purchase/lease contracts and carton supply contracts and to submit copies of the new contracts to the Commission. Annual reporting obligations were also imposed.

"Technological tying." In some cases a tie is not effected by contract, but by the technical integration of two separate products.[215] Where such conduct amounts to an abuse, complex technical and pricing issues may arise in devising effective remedies. In *Microsoft*, the Commission found the Microsoft had abusively tied its WMP to the Windows PC operating system. By way of remedy, it required Microsoft to offer Windows without WMP in Europe. This was clearly the obvious solution, but its implementation raises a number of important practical issues, which have thus far not been resolved.[216]

A first issue concerns the geographic scope of the remedy. The Commission's untying remedy is limited to the EU. In contrast, the Commission's substantive findings were

---

[213] *Eurofix-Bauco v Hilti*, OJ 1988 L 65/19, Articles 1 and 3.

[214] *Tetra Pak II*, OJ 1992 L 72/1.

[215] See Ch. 9 (Tying and Bundling).

[216] This section describes some of the objections raised to the bundling remedy imposed by the Commission in *Microsoft*. The comments below should not be seen as endorsing or otherwise the positions of the complainants in this case. The reader should be advised that the authors and their respective companies have acted, and still act, on opposite sides of this case and maintain different views as regards the merits of the positions taken by the Commission and Microsoft.

based on a relevant market for streaming media players that is worldwide in scope. Complainants have argued that, given the worldwide nature of the media player market, Microsoft's continued tying practice outside the EU would also impact competition in the EU. They argue that, in line with the doctrine of effects set out in *Gencor* and other cases,[217] the Commission would have had the power to extend its remedy also to sales outside the EU. It seems that the Commission considered itself competent to impose a worldwide remedy but limited its scope out of deference to the US authorities who had imposed their own remedies in the various proceedings against Microsoft.

A second issue is the pricing of the bundled and unbundled versions of unbundled Windows and the Windows/WMP bundle. Microsoft has decided to charge the same price for the unbundled Windows and a Windows/WMP bundle, which, not surprisingly, makes it hard to see why vendors and consumers would choose an unbundled version. However, the Commission's decision does not explicitly deal with the pricing of unbundled Windows. In particular, it does not state whether Microsoft may price unbundled Windows at the same price as a Windows/WMP bundle. The decision does state that Microsoft may not adopt measures that have an equivalent effect to the tie. Complainants argue that charging the same price for the unbundled Windows and the Windows/WMP bundle perpetuates the tie, since it leaves customers with no commercial realistic reason not to take the bundle.

Finally, the remedy is prospective only in nature and does not deal with distortions of competition that the complainants say have already resulted from the tying of Windows and WMP. While the Commission's unbundling remedy stops future abuses, complainants say that it does not address the effects of Microsoft's past conduct. Microsoft's abusive practice was found to have lasted for five years, which the Commission found had allowed it to establish WMP as the dominant media player. Because of the "network effects" that characterise competition in media players, the complainants argue that Microsoft's past conduct will continue to distort consumer decisions even though it is stopped for the future. Some of them have therefore suggested that the particular facts of the case would have warranted specific remedies to undo the effects of Microsoft's past conduct. It is not clear whether the Commission would be minded to do this, but there is precedent for such a remedy.[218]

"Mixed bundling." Abusive tying may also be effected by a package price for two products that is lower than the stand-alone price of each product, which is sometimes referred to as "mixed bundling" or financial tying. Remedies for mixed bundling are directly related to the substantive rules applied to such practices. For example, in the *Digital Undertaking*,[219] the Commission applied a strict standard that mixed bundling was only permitted to the extent that it resulted in cost savings in supplying the products as a bundle. The Commission thus accepted that a supplier may pass on cost savings derived from efficient packaging to its customers. As a "bright-line test" in the specific

[217] Case T-102/96, *Gencor Ltd v Commission* [1999] ECR II-753.

[218] See Section 15.2.1 above for a full discussion.

[219] See M Dolmans & V Pickering, "1997 Digital Undertaking" (1998) 19(2) *European Competition Law Review* 108–15.

case of Digital, the Undertaking fixes the package price reduction at no more than 10% of the sum-of-the-pieces price for the package.

As discussed in Chapter Nine (Tying and Bundling), the Discussion Paper now proposes to apply an implied predatory pricing test to mixed bundling, i.e., whether the price of the tied product is below its average long-run incremental cost (LRIC). The price of the tied product should thus be higher than the price of the package less the standalone cost of the tied product. So if the tying product alone costs €60 and the package costs €70, the implied price of the tied product is €10 and the question is whether this exceeds its LRIC. Where it does not, the price should be increased to cover the LRIC of the tied product.

15.4.3 Structural Remedies

15.4.3.1 Introduction and overview

Legal basis. Antitrust law itself was founded on a case involving the ordered break-up of a dominant firm: Standard Oil.[220] Yet only in 2004 did the Commission expressly acquire the power to apply such structural measures. In addition to the behavioural remedies described above, Regulation 1/2003 provides the Commission with the power to impose structural remedies in appropriate cases. Article 7(1) states that the Commission "may impose...any behavioural or structural remedies which are proportionate to the infringement committed and necessary to bring the infringement effectively to an end."

Recital 12 of Regulation 1/2003 describes structural remedies as "changes to the structure of the undertaking as it existed before the infringement was committed." Changes to the structure of a company may range from a complete break-up or dissolution to the divestiture of a particular unit or holding or less intrusive measures such as accounting separation. But it is critical to realise that structural remedies are not mechanisms to alter an otherwise lawful market structure: they are only appropriate as a remedy for abusive conduct, and, even then, only where behavioural remedies would be ineffective. This point was well-put by the Report by the Economic Advisory Group on Competition Policy on Article 82 EC:[221]

> "In focusing on consumer welfare, one must not fall into the trap of seeing competition policy as a tool of active policy intervention designed to correct the inefficiencies associated with monopolies and oligopolies so as to maximise some measure of welfare. Competition policy is based on the principle that competition itself is the best mechanism for avoiding inefficiencies, so the competition authority should not try to let its own intervention replace the role of competition in the market place. The powers given to the competition authority are, with very few exceptions, powers to prohibit certain behaviours and certain developments, not powers to actively determine where the market participants should be going. The authority can ban certain agreements, certain practices and certain mergers, but it should not tell the markets participants what they should do instead."

[220] *Standard Oil Co v United States*, 221 U.S. 1, 37–40 (1911). For subsequent similar cases, see, e.g., *United States* v *Paramount Pictures, Inc*, 85 F. Supp. 881 (S.D.N.Y. 1949); *United States v AT&T Co.*, 552 F. Supp. 131 (D.D.C. 1982).

[221] See Report by the Economic Advisory Group on Competition Policy, "*An Economic Approach to Article 82*," July 2005, p.10.

A new power? Until recently, the extent of the Commission's power to apply structural remedies for abusive conduct under Regulation 17/62 was unclear. Arguably, however, the power to impose structural remedies was implicit in Regulation 17/62, which gave the Commission the power "to order an undertaking to bring the infringement to an end." If structural remedies were necessary to prevent the infringement from continuing, so the thinking went, then the Commission implicitly had the power to apply them.

The notion of an implied power to impose structural remedies can be traced back to *Continental Can* in 1973, where the Court of Justice held that "abuse may...occur if an undertaking in a dominant position strengthens such position in such a way that the degree of dominance reached substantially fetters competition."[222] In this case—importantly, decided before the introduction of the EC Merger Regulation—the Commission had found that Continental Can had abused its dominant position by acquiring a competitor, and ordered divestiture of the acquired business. The Court of Justice overturned the Commission's decision on factual grounds, but endorsed the Commission's right to apply structural remedies under Article 82 EC in appropriate cases.[223]

The rule established in *Continental Can*—that where the identified abuse is a structural transaction, Article 82 EC allows the imposition of structural remedies—seems uncontroversial today. A more recent Commission decision, however, took the principle further. In *Deutsche Post*,[224] the Commission found that Deutsche Post had used profits from its letter mailing business (where it held a reserved monopoly) to fund predatory pricing by its parcel delivery business (where it faced competition) through unlawful cross-subsidisation. Given the long history of abusive conduct and the extreme difficulty of preventing such conduct on an ongoing basis, the Commission concluded that a separation of the two businesses was the only remedy that could guarantee that the infringement would be put to an end. As part of the resolution of the case, Deutsche Post undertook to legally separate the two divisions, placing its parcel delivery business in a new, independent subsidiary.[225] This would, among other things, facilitate accounting of the transfer prices paid by the parcel business to the letter business as a means of monitoring for cross-subsidisation. The Commission did not mandate a divestiture of the parcel delivery business; whether it would have had the legal authority to do so under Regulation 17/62 remains an open question.

Attraction of structural remedies for competition authorities. Structural remedies have significant attractions from the competition authority's perspective. Although

[222] Case 6/72, *Europemballage Corporation and Continental Can Company Inc v Commission* [1973] ECR 215, para. 26.

[223] Similarly, in the *Gillette* case, twenty years later, the Commission found that Gillette's indirect acquisition of a minority stake and other associated rights in a competitor (not captured by the EC Merger Regulation) violated Article 82 EC. The Commission ordered Gillette to divest its equity stake. See *Warner-Lambert/Gillette and Others*, OJ 1993 L 116/21.

[224] *Deutsche Post AG*, OJ 2001 L 125/27.

[225] See Commission Press Release IP/01/419 of March 20, 2001.

structural remedies can involve substantial transaction costs,[226] and take time to implement (given the likelihood of appeals), once in place they take effect more or less immediately and are difficult to circumvent. Structural remedies are intended to permanently diminish or remove the dominant firm's incentive to violate Article 82 EC by modifying its market position. As a consequence, they should reduce the likelihood of repeat infringements. Moreover, since abusive conduct may have irreversible market consequences, behavioural remedies may be insufficient to restore the market to the competitive structure that existed before the anticompetitive conduct occurred.[227] Finally, since they are usually one-time actions (e.g., breaking up of a company), structural remedies also generally require little ongoing supervision or monitoring by public authorities. Structural remedies might therefore be more effective and less costly and burdensome to implement than behavioural remedies in certain cases.

15.4.3.2 Conditions for ordering a structural remedy

Overview. Notwithstanding the advantages of structural remedies outlined above, in implicit recognition of their highly intrusive nature, Article 7(1) of Regulation 1/2003 makes clear that structural remedies are only to be employed in exceptional circumstances, that is where "there is no equally effective behavioural remedy or where any equally effective behavioural remedy would be more burdensome for the undertaking concerned than the structural remedy." Recital 12 explains that this rule derives from the principle of proportionality: "changes to the structure of an undertaking as it existed before the infringement was committed would only be proportionate where there is a substantial risk of a lasting or repeated infringement that derives from the very structure of the undertaking." From this, it follows that three cumulative conditions must be satisfied before structural remedies may be imposed in an Article 82 EC case: (1) structural remedies are a remedy of last resort, i.e., behavioural remedies would be insufficient; (2) structural remedies must be effective; and (3) structural remedies must be proportionate.

Condition #1: a remedy of last resort. Structural remedies may only be imposed if there is no equally effective behavioural remedy for the abuse (and not merely for the underlying uncompetitive nature of the market, unless that is due to the abuse). If a behavioural remedy is sufficient to bring the identified infringement to an end, and to restore the market to its competitive state before the infringement took place, it would have to be regarded as effective, in which case no structural remedy could be imposed. In making this assessment, particularly in rapidly developing industries, it will be critical for the competition authority to consider the extent to which, prompted by behavioural remedies, competition might be expected to re-emerge naturally given the market circumstances, making structural intervention unnecessary.

Condition #2: structural remedies must be effective. Even if there is no suitable behavioural remedy, for a structural remedy to be imposed it must be effective in bringing the infringement to an end. An obvious case is where there is a causal link

---

[226] See Report for the Commission by the Economic Advisory Group for Competition Policy, *An Economic Approach to Article 82 EC*, July 2005, p. 46.

[227] See SC Salop and RC Romaine, "Preserving Monopoly: Economic Analysis, Legal Standards, and Microsoft" (1999) 7(1) *George Mason Law Review* 666.

between the structure of the dominant firm and the infringement (though this is not necessary in all cases). For example, in the *Deutsche Post* case, according to the Commission's analysis, by controlling both a monopoly business (letter mailing) and a competitive business (parcel delivery), Deutsche Post had an economic incentive to use profits from the monopoly business to unlawfully subsidise the competitive business. The agreed structural remedy of transferring the parcel division to a wholly-owned subsidiary would not remove this incentive, since the profits of both entities would still flow to the same parent. However, legal separation, coupled with an obligation for Deutsche Post to submit annual itemised statements of the transfer prices paid by the parcel business for all goods and services acquired from the letter carrying monopoly, was effective since it increased financial transparency, enabling the Commission to monitor and identify possible future cross-subsidisation.[228]

Condition #3: structural remedies must be proportionate. If there is no equally effective behavioural remedy, and a structural remedy would be effective in bringing the identified infringement to an end, it must still be determined that the structural remedy is proportionate to the infringement. According to Recital 12 of Regulation 1/2003, if a structural remedy is to be considered proportionate, there must be a substantial risk of a lasting or repeated infringement that derives from the very structure of the undertaking. As with any remedy under Article 82 EC, the proportionality element appears to be largely a matter of balancing the intrusiveness of the remedy (which will be high in the case of structural remedies) against the importance of addressing the infringement. The Commission will likely retain substantial discretion in making this determination, which will be closely related to the question of whether there are any suitable behavioural remedies. Factors that should be relevant include whether behavioural remedies regarding any similar infringements have been effective in the past and whether behavioural remedies could be efficiently monitored to ensure compliance.

An additional question in assessing proportionality is the extent to which the impact of structural remedies on third parties should be taken into account. This may be particularly relevant when the break-up of a firm is being considered, as such a measure could affect the interests of shareholders in the dominant firm more directly than would behavioural remedies. Arguably, the threat of competition-law sanctions is a foreseeable risk that shareholders should have taken into account when investing in a "dominant" company. However, this strict approach has not generally been followed. In *DuPont*,[229] the United States Supreme Court affirmed the lower court's refusal of the government's request to order the divestiture by DuPont of its shareholding in General Motors, on grounds that other remedies were equally effective and that a divestiture would have seriously harmed shareholders (who would have faced heavy dividend taxes and seen the value of their shares depressed). Similarly, one of the considerations in the US *Microsoft* case that led to the reversal of the lower court's proposed break-up of Microsoft was a structural remedy's potential effect on Microsoft's shareholders.[230]

---

[228] See Commission Press Release IP/01/419 of March 20, 2001.

[229] *United States v E.I. DuPont de Nemours & Co.*, 366 U. S. 316 (1961).

[230] *United States v Microsoft Corp.*, 97 F. Supp. 2d 59, 64 (D.D.C. 2000) (final judgment), vacated, 253 F.3d 34 (D.C. Cir. 2001).

These judgments reflect the sensible view that, if anything, the effects of structural remedies on third parties uninvolved in the infringement—such as shareholders—should play a greater role in the proportionality assessment than the effects on the company itself (which might be considered the architect of its own problems).

Finally, in assessing proportionality it should be borne in mind that structural remedies may cause the loss of substantial efficiencies realised by the firm, which could in turn have negative effects for consumers. The objective of a remedy is to end an infringement and restore effective competition, not to punish the offender. The restoration of effective competition serves the ultimate goal of benefiting consumer welfare, which in turn is affected by the efficiency of the market. This means that economic analysis of the efficiency of a structural remedy—that is, how well the remedy will restore competition and, ultimately, benefit consumers—is an important element in determining whether the benefits of the remedy will exceed its costs.[231]

As the power to impose structural remedies under Article 82 EC is essentially new, there is no empirical evidence on the costs and benefits of such remedies.[232] Some evidence exists under US antitrust law, however. Around twenty three monopolisation cases resulted in divestiture remedies, with information on the consequences only being available in around half of those cases.[233] Overall, the picture that emerges is quite negative in terms of the benefits of structural remedies. Only the AT&T break-up in 1984 is considered to have been a success and, even then, the reasons for its success appear to have been as influenced by industry deregulation and technology developments as the break-up itself. Reasons suggested for the "poor overall record" of divestitures under US abuse of dominance laws include:[234] (1) the industry had already changed because of the significant delay in implementing the remedy (typically five years or more); (2) enforcement officials tend to lose interest at the relief stage; and, most importantly, (3) the intractable problems in industrial organisation economics of formulating a clear link between industry structure and optimal performance.

[231] Economists have proposed different ways of measuring the efficiency of structural remedies. For example, Sidak and Shelanski propose a welfare test requiring that: (1) the remedy produces a net gain in static economic efficiency; (2) net gains in static economic efficiency overcome potential losses in dynamic efficiency; and (3) enforcement costs are taken into account. See HA Shelanski and JG Sidak, "Antitrust Divestiture in Network Industries" (2001) 68 *University of Chicago Law Review* 1.

[232] Divestitures under the EC Merger Regulation are not generally in point, since they are voluntary arrangements submitted by the notifying parties to *reduce market power* created by a particular transaction. Structural remedies under Article 82 EC are designed to *efficiently remedy abusive conduct*, which is altogether different and more complex. That said, it is interesting to note that many problems have limited the effectiveness of merger divestiture remedies too. A recent Commission study on the effectiveness of transfers of businesses as remedies under the EC Merger Regulation found that only 56% of cases resulted in "effective" remedies, i.e., "clearly achieved their competition objective." See European Commission *Merger Remedies Study* (October 2005), chart 27, available at http://www.europa.eu.int/comm/competition/mergers/others/remedies_study.pdf.

[233] Figures taken from RA Posner, *Antitrust Law* (2nd edn., Chicago, University of Chicago Press, 2001), p.107. See also K O'Connor "The Divestiture Remedy in Sherman Act Section 2 Cases" (1976) 13 *Harvard Journal of Legislation* 687.

[234] Posner, *ibid.*, pp-111-112.

15.4.3.3 Case study: *Microsoft*

Structural remedy considered but rejected. The highest-profile examination of structural remedies in a unilateral conduct case was in *US v Microsoft*, when an injunction by a US District Court ordering that Microsoft's operating systems and applications businesses be broken up into independent entities was reversed on appeal by the Court of Appeals for the District of Columbia.[235] Although the case was obviously decided under a different legal system and different laws, it has interesting parallels for the application of structural remedies under Article 82 EC.

The District Court's structural remedy was rejected on several grounds. First, the District Court had not held an evidentiary hearing to consider factual disputes that were relevant at the remedy phase of proceedings.[236] Microsoft had identified 23 witnesses who, had they been permitted to testify, would have challenged a wide range of the plaintiffs' (i.e., the US Department of Justice, supported by a number of industry participants) factual representations in support of structural remedies. The feasibility of dividing Microsoft was contested by the testimony of Microsoft's President and CEO, who maintained that Microsoft is organised as a unified company and that "there are no natural lines along which Microsoft could be broken up without causing serious problems."[237] The likely impact of a structural remedy on consumers was also disputed. Whilst the plaintiffs' economists testified that splitting Microsoft in two would be socially beneficial, the company offered to prove that the proposed remedy would "cause substantial social harm by raising software prices, lowering rates of innovation, and disrupting the evolution of Windows as a software development platform."[238] In addition, the possible adverse affect of a break-up on shareholder value was highlighted.[239] The Court of Appeals held that Microsoft's evidence should have been considered before a structural separation of the company was ordered. Moreover, the District Court failed to provide an adequate explanation as to how structural relief would remedy the anticompetitive conduct found.[240]

Second, the legal basis for the structural separation was undercut by the failure of the plaintiffs' attempted monopolisation and tying claims, along with their failure to sustain the claims that had challenged Microsoft's right to compete outside its operating system monopoly by integrating new functions into Windows. The failure of these claims substantially undermined the justification for a structural remedy, as the findings of unlawful conduct endorsed by the Court of Appeals were less serious than those upheld by the District Court.

---

[235] Cases No. 00-5212 consolidated with No. 00-5213, *USA v Microsoft Corp,* 253 F.3d 34 (DC Cir. 2001).

[236] *Ibid.,* p. 96.

[237] Testimony from S Ballmer, *ibid.*, reprinted in Defendant's Offer of Proof at 23–26, reprinted in 4 JA at 2764–67.

[238] Defendant's Offer of Proof at 6, reprinted in 4 JA at 2747.

[239] Microsoft proffered testimony from Goldman, Sachs & Co. and Morgan Stanley Dean Witter that dissolution would adversely affect shareholder value, contrary to the plaintiffs' investment bankers, which had claimed that a break-up could actually create shareholder value. *Ibid.* at 17, 19, reprinted in 4 J.A. at 2758, 2760.

[240] Cases No. 00-5212 consolidated with No. 00-5213, *USA v Microsoft Corp,* 253 F.3d 34, 99 (DC Cir. 2001).

In light of the Court of Appeals' judgment, the plaintiffs decided it would be best to settle the case.[241] The Department of Justice took the view that the dubious possibility of eventually securing the break-up of Microsoft was not worth the time and effort it would have taken to continue litigating the case. The plaintiffs therefore abandoned their claim for structural relief in an effort to ensure that proceedings moved quickly, and a resolution based on behavioural commitments was struck.[242]

The *Microsoft* proceeding indicates the exceptional nature of structural remedies and the many practical issues that may limit their effectiveness.[243] The shortcomings that the Court of Appeals identified in the District Court's break-up order are closely related to the Regulation 1/2003 requirements that there be no less burdensome alternative and that structural remedies must be proportionate to the infringement, neither of which had been adequately proven. It is important to note that the parallel investigation of Microsoft by the Commission, which also ended with a behavioural remedy,[244] was undertaken under Regulation 17/62 where, as explained above, the Commission's power to order structural remedies for non-structural infringements was unclear. If the same facts had been assessed under Regulation 1/2003, the legal basis for structural remedies would obviously have been stronger. But similar questions as to the need for and proportionality of structural remedies would have dominated the debate, and it seems likely that the Commission would still have had a preference for behavioural remedies. If nothing else, the various Microsoft proceedings show just how exceptional structural remedies are likely to be in practice.

15.5 PRIVATE LITIGATION AND REMEDIES

15.5.1 Introduction

Desire for greater private enforcement. The EC Treaty places individuals at the heart of EC competition policy, since it includes competition law amongst the tools to be used in order to achieve purposes such as economic development and an improved standard of living. In practice, however, private actions have not played a prominent role in the enforcement of EC competition law. In the United States, enforcement of the antitrust laws is dominated by private actions, which represent over 90% of all federal antitrust cases filed.[245] By contrast, EC competition enforcement has been almost exclusively

[241] CA James, Assistant Attorney General, Antitrust Division, US Department of Justice, *The Microsoft Settlement: A Look to the Future*, before the Committee on the Judiciary, US Senate, 12 December 2001. The change in tactic by the Department of Justice also corresponded with a change in the US political administration.

[242] See *United States v Microsoft*, CA No. 98-1232 (CKK) (November 6, 2001).

[243] Some commentators have argued that the practical difficulties and radical nature of structural remedies have been overstated. Thus, they argue that structural remedies should not be a remedy of last resort, but a viable option to be assessed on its legal, administrative, and economic merits. RH Lande "Why are We So Reluctant to 'Execute' Microsoft?" (2001) 1 *Antitrust Source* 1. Contrast JE Lopatka, "Devising a Microsoft Remedy that Serves Customers" (2001) 9 *George Mason Law Review* 691 (arguing that a structural remedy against Microsoft would destroy efficiencies and harm consumer welfare, and advocating behavioural remedies as an alternative).

[244] Case COMP/C-3/37.792, *Microsoft*, Commission Decision of March 24, 2004, not yet published.

[245] For example, in the year to March 31, 2004, private plaintiffs filed 693 of the 715 total antitrust case filed in US federal courts. See Administrative Office of the US Courts, Federal Judicial Caseload

driven by public authorities. Civil litigation for damages under EC competition law is rare, and even rarer in cases based on Article 82 EC infringements. A 2004 study for the Commission identified only 28 cases from 1958 to 2004 in which antitrust damages were awarded, leading to the conclusion that damages actions for breach of EC competition law are in a state of "total underdevelopment."[246] This figure almost certainly understates the effects of private litigation, not least because a relatively high proportion of cases have settled after litigation was commenced. But it is true to say that private litigation is not a remedy of first resort as it is in the United States.

This seems likely to change. Successive Commissioners for Competition have advocated the development of private enforcement as an important prong of EC competition policy.[247] As part of this effort, at the end of 2005 the Commission released a Green Paper for public comment on various policy options that would facilitate private damages actions for breach of EC competition rules.[248] However, while the Green Paper is the Commission's most concrete step toward developing private enforcement, it is limited to identifying some obstacles and presenting options for discussion—no immediate action is contemplated. This section describes the current state of the law and the existing obstacles to private enforcement of EC competition law.

15.5.2 Goals Of Private Enforcement

Public and private interests partly complementary. Civil litigation is the primary means by which private parties may enforce the rights afforded them by competition law directly, through injunctive relief or damages against another private party or the State. Private litigation is not aimed at protecting the public interest but at protecting individuals' "subjective rights under Community law."[249] Such subjective rights include victims' right to compensation for losses sustained as a result of competition law violations. The Commission regards improving citizens' awareness of and ability to enforce directly their rights under EC competition law as important, in part because

---

Statistics, Table C-2. For a detailed discussion of the ratio of private to public antitrust actions in the United States, see DH Ginsburg and L Brannon, "Determinants of Private Antitrust Enforcement in the United States" (2005) 1(2) *Competition Policy International* 29–43.

[246] Ashurst, "Study on the Conditions of Claims for Damages in Case of Infringement of EC Competition Rules," August 31, 2004, (D Waelbroeck, D Slater, and G Even-Shoshan prepared the "Comparative Report," while E Clark, M Hughes, and D Wirth prepared the "Analysis of Economic Models for the Calculation of Damages") (hereinafter "Ashurst Study").

[247] See, e.g., M Monti, "Private Litigation as a Key Complement to Public Enforcement of Competition Rules and the First Conclusions on the Implementation of the New Merger Regulation," speech n°04/403, September 17, 2004, IBA–8th Annual Competition Conference, Fiesole (Italy); N Kroes, "Enhancing Actions for Damages for Breach of Competition Rules in Europe," speech n°05/533, Speech at the Harvard Club, September 22, 2005, New York (USA); and N Kroes, "Damages Actions for Breaches of EU Competition Rules: Realities and Potentials," speech n°05/613, October 17, 2005, Opening speech at the conference "La Reparation du Prejudice Cause par une Pratique Anti-Concurrentielle en France et à l'Etranger: Bilan et Perspectives," Cour de Cassation, Paris (France).

[248] Commission, Green Paper of December 19, 2005, on damages actions for breach of the EC antitrust rules, COM(2005) 672 final, SEC(2005) 1732 (hereinafter the "Green Paper").

[249] Regulation 1/2003, Recital 7.

the possibility to be awarded damages "makes the competition rules instantly relevant for citizens."[250]

From the Commission's perspective, an important indirect benefit of private litigation is that it adds to the total amount of competition law enforcement, contributing to deterrence and consequently to compliance with competition rules. Private litigants may supplement public enforcement, for example, by taking action against infringements that the competition authorities are unwilling or unable to pursue (e.g., due to lack of resources).[251] Increased private action may also improve the detection rate of competition infringements, as private parties who are victims of anticompetitive conduct may be better placed than public enforcers to identify violations.[252] The Commission thus regards private enforcement as a complement to public enforcement and has made facilitation of private enforcement a clear policy goal.

This initiative has not been without its critics, even from within the Commission. For example, one Commission official argues that public enforcement is inherently superior to private enforcement, partly since it benefits from more effective investigative and sanctioning powers than private actions, which are driven purely by private profit motives and are globally more costly for society. He also points out that the goal of obtaining compensation for victims of anticompetitive conduct is substantially undermined by the practical difficulties plaintiffs face to actually obtain damages. Finally, he argues that deterrence should be achieved through tougher public sanctions (including jail sentences) and increased resources for competition authorities, rather than the threat of private damages actions.[253] In response to such concerns, the Commission's recent statements underline the need to "strike the right balance" between effective private enforcement and excessive litigation[254] and the desire to "foster a competition culture, not a litigation culture."[255] The current view of Commissioner Kroes, which is likely to set policy at DG Competition for the next several years, is that increased vigilance by individuals in the enforcement of EC competition law is likely to benefit the global economy and should therefore be encouraged.[256]

---

[250] N Kroes, "Enhancing Actions for Damages for Breach of Competition Rules in Europe," speech n°05/533, Speech at the Harvard Club, September 22, 2005, New York (USA). See also Commission Staff Working Paper of December 19, 2005, Annex to the Green Paper on damages actions for breach of the EC antitrust rules, COM(2005) 672 final, SEC(2005) 1732 (hereinafter "Staff Paper"), para. 7.

[251] M Monti, "Private Litigation as a Key Complement to Public Enforcement of Competition Rules and the First Conclusions on the Implementation of the New Merger Regulation," speech n°04/403, September 17, 2004, IBA–8th Annual Competition Conference, Fiesole (Italy), p. 2.

[252] See D Woods, A Sinclair, and D Ashton, "Private Enforcement of Community Competition Law: Modernisation and the Road Ahead" (2004) 2 *Competition Policy Newsletter* 33.

[253] WPJ Wils, "Should Private Enforcement Be Encouraged in Europe?" (2003) 26 *World Competition* 473.

[254] N Kroes, speech n°05/533, above.

[255] N Kroes, speech n°05/533, above; Staff Paper, above, para. 12.

[256] A similar argument was used over forty years ago in favour of the direct effect of Community law in Case 26/62, *NV Algemene Transport en Expeditie Onderneming van Gend & Loos v Netherlands Inland Revenue Administration* [1963] ECR 95, at s. II B ("The vigilance of individuals concerned to protect their rights amounts to an effective supervision in addition to the supervision entrusted by Articles 169 and 170 to the diligence of the commission and of the Member States.").

15.5.3 Legal Basis For Private Enforcement

National courts' duties and role. Because there is no Community Court competent to hear damages actions brought by private plaintiffs for breach of EC competition law, private enforcement is built on the possibility for individuals to invoke EC competition law before national courts, which must apply it directly.[257] The direct applicability of Articles 81 and 82 EC has been long recognised in the case law,[258] and the ability of national courts to apply EC competition law is now formalised in Article 6 of Regulation 1/2003.[259]

Although litigation in national courts is based on national procedural rules, the principle of the primacy of Community law and the duty of loyal cooperation under Article 10 EC impose constraints on national courts in the handling of private damage actions based on alleged EC competition law violations. The first consequence of these principles is that national courts are obliged to construe national law in light of Community law[260] and even to disapply any provision of national law that would be contrary to Community law.[261] National courts will thus not be able to apply national laws that frustrate damage actions under EC competition law.

Some additional constraints on national courts posed by the Community law primacy principle are now embodied in Regulation 1/2003. Article 3 of Regulation 1/2003 compels national courts to apply EC competition law if the conduct in question may affect trade between Member States. The courts may apply national competition law alongside the Community provisions, but only if the outcome under the national law does not differ from that under Community law. The only exception being that national laws on unilateral conduct may be more strict than Article 82 EC.[262] In addition, Article 16 of Regulation 1/2003 promotes the uniform application of Community law by prohibiting national courts from issuing judgments running counter to a previous Commission decision relating to the same agreement or practice.[263]

---

[257] The UK *Promivi* case is a prominent example of successful private action, where direct purchasers of vitamins claimed damages in the aftermath of the Commission's decision in the *Vitamins* cartel. An important feature of the case is that the plaintiffs succeeded in consolidating all their European claims before the English courts, despite the fact that they had purchased only from the defendant's German subsidiary. Consequently, the plaintiffs were able to take advantage of English laws, which are advantageous for private enforcement, particularly in reducing the costs of bringing the action. See *Provimi Ltd v Aventis*, [2003] EWHC 961 (Comm).

[258] Case 127/73, *Belgische Radio en Televisie v SV SABAM and NV Fonior* [1974] ECR 313, para. 16 ("as the prohibitions of Articles [81] (1) and [82] tend by their very nature to produce direct effects in relations between individuals, these articles create direct rights in respect of the individuals concerned which the national courts must safeguard.").

[259] See Regulation 1/2003, Article 6 ("National courts shall have the power to apply Articles 81 and 82 of the Treaty.").

[260] Case C-106/89, *Marleasing SA v La Comercial Internacional de Alimentacion SA* [1990] ECR I-4135.

[261] Case 106/77, *Finanze dello Stato v Simmenthal SpA* [1978] ECR 629.

[262] Regulation 1/2003, Article 3(2). Pursuant to Article 3(3), the application of national legislation the primary objective of which is different from Articles 81 and 82 may lead to a different outcome.

[263] This provision formalises the *Masterfoods* doctrine from Case C-344/98, *Masterfoods Ltd v HB Ice Cream Ltd* [2000] ECR I-11369, paras. 49–52.

The procedural autonomy enjoyed by Member States in the absence of harmonisation[264] is also limited by the two cornerstone Community law principles of equivalence and effectiveness, derived from Article 10 EC. The equivalence principle requires national courts not to treat claims founded on Community law less favourably than claims under national law. Consequently, all the mechanisms available to individuals to enforce their rights under national competition law are extended to EC competition law. The effectiveness principle goes further, providing that Member States may not render enforcement of Community law impossible or extremely difficult. National courts may even be forced to invent remedies that do not exist in national law if their absence puts at risk the effectiveness ("effet utile") of EC competition law.[265]

This principle has been central in the development of EC competition law on private enforcement. In the *Banks* case in the early 1990s, Advocate General Van Gerven argued that the effectiveness principle supports allowing damages actions for loss sustained by EC competition law violations, and invited the Court of Justice to develop a case law to this effect.[266] The Court declined to set such a precedent in that case, but moved in this direction several years later in the landmark *Crehan* judgment, holding that:[267]

> "The full effectiveness of Article [81 EC]...would be put at risk if it were not open to any individual to claim damages for loss caused to him by a contract or by conduct liable to restrict or distort competition....[T]he existence of such a right strengthens the working of the Community competition rules and discourages agreements or practices, which are frequently covert, which are liable to restrict or distort competition. From that point of view, actions for damages before the national courts can make a significant contribution to the maintenance of effective competition in the Community."

Crehan opened the way to greater private enforcement of EC competition law. Although the judgment concerned Article 81 EC, the Court's holdings clearly go beyond the facts of the case to apply also to non-contractual relationships, including breaches of Article 82 EC. Nevertheless, *Crehan* did not create a new remedy as such: it attempted to fit a remedy within existing principles of Community law. Thus, "the consequences in civil law attaching to an infringement of [Articles 81 and 82 EC]...are to be determined under national law..., subject, however, to not undermining the effectiveness of the Treaty."[268] In other words, the principle of private litigation has been recognised in Community law, but it must be implemented by national law.

A number of Member States have already introduced reforms or made legal developments of varying degrees of ambition in an effort to facilitate private damages

---

[264] Case 33/76, *Rewe-Zentralfinanz eG et Rewe-Zentral AG v Landwirtschaftskammer für das Saarland* [1976] ECR 1989, para. 5; Case 45/76, *Comet BV v Produktschap voor Siergewassen* [1976] ECR 2043, para.12.

[265] Case C-213/89, *The Queen v Secretary of State for Transport, ex parte: Factortame Ltd and others (Factortame I)* [1990] ECR I-2433.

[266] Opinion of Advocate General Van Gerven in Case C-128/92, *HJ Banks & Co Ltd v British Coal Corporation* [1994] ECR I-1209.

[267] Judgment in Case C-453/99, *Courage Ltd v Bernard Crehan and Bernard Crehan v Courage Ltd and Others* [2001] ECR I-6297, paras. 26–27.

[268] Case T-395/94, *Atlantic Container Line AB and Others v Commission* [2002] ECR II-875, para. 414.

actions.[269] The most ambitious is Germany, where a 7th Amendment to the Act Against Restraints of Competition (ARC) was introduced with effect from July 1, 2005, to apply a consistent set of procedural and substantive rules for private damages actions under EC and German competition laws, including for abuse of dominance.[270] Several changes are envisaged:

1. On a jurisdictional level, the aim is to centralise damages actions in competition cases around a single court of first instance for each district (*Landgericht*). The federal states may also designate a single court of appeal in each federal state to hear appeals in competition cases.

2. Plaintiffs can bring damages actions for competition claims in these designated courts, either by specifying the amount of the damage (*Leistungsklage*) or seeking a declaratory judgment (*Festellungklage*), with damages to be determined later.

3. The ARC lays down rules of standing and certain substantive rules for damages recovery. In principle, any party affected by a competition-law violation, including indirect purchasers, can bring a claim. A corollary of this is that the ARC allows defendants to raise the "passing on" defence (i.e., the claim that the plaintiff passed on any price increase to its own customers) in mitigation of any damages claim. However, defendants will enjoy no presumption here and must prove that their customers passed on price increases in order to obtain a damages reduction. This may be difficult in light of the tight rules governing discovery in Germany.

4. The ARC applies the general principles on damages—that recovery should be limited to the amount of the overcharge and/or lost profits—but Section 33(3) allows the court to apply certain assumptions (e.g., increase in the defendant's profits as a result of the infringement) as a basis for *estimating* damages.

The United Kingdom has also introduced a series of potentially important legislative and common law changes designed to facilitate private damages actions:

1. Section 58A of the Competition Act 1998 provides that the national courts are bound by a decision of the Office of Fair Trading (OFT) finding an infringement under EC or national competition laws. The same applies to a judgment of the Competition Appeal Tribunal (CAT) upholding an OFT infringement decision.

2. Section 47A of the Competition Act 1998 allows the CAT to hear damages claims based on an infringement decision by the OFT under EC or national competition laws (and a CAT judgment upholding such a decision) or an infringement decision of the Commission under Articles 81 or 82 EC. The existence of such an infringement obviates the need for a plaintiff to prove that

---

[269] See generally D Woods, A Sinclair, and D Ashton, "Private Enforcement of Community Competition Law: Modernisation and the Road Ahead" (2004) 2 *Competition Policy Newsletter* 33.

[270] For an overview, see A Rinne and K Lübbe-Späth, "Private Antitrust Litigation in Germany" *The European Antitrust Review 2006*, pp.132–35.

a violation has occurred so the trial can focus on issues such as causation and quantum.

3. In *Provimi*,[271] the High Court confirmed that, where there is a domestic element to a competition law violation, a claimant can bring an action in the English courts in respect of *all* of its European losses, i.e., there is no need for separate proceedings in each Member State in which it suffered loses. The jurisdictional nexus is that one of the defendants must be domiciled in the UK or have a subsidiary located there.

4. Finally, apart from the above changes, the civil courts have awarded damages in at least one reported case. In *Crehan*,[272] the Court of Appeal awarded damages of £131,336 plus interest to an applicant who had suffered losses under an anticompetitive agreement tying his public house to a brewer. The Court of Appeal assessed damages as *actual lost profits* from the date of the agreement until the applicant gave up possession of the lease (this judgment is on appeal to the House of Lords).[273]

Recent reforms in France have also vested the sole competence to apply EC and national competition law in eight specialist courts of first instance.[274]

15.5.4 Obstacles To Effective Private Enforcement

Overview. The Ashurst Study and the Commission Green Paper, which summarises a more complete Staff Paper,[275] identify a series of obstacles to the development of private litigation, and in particular damages actions for EC competition law infringements. Although the Commission openly endorses the development of private litigation, the Green Paper is formally intended only to launch public debate and therefore merely identifies various issues and options; the Commission offers no view of its own and does not propose that any specific action be taken. The following paragraphs outline the main obstacles to effective private enforcement that have been identified.

Diversity and legal uncertainty. The diversity and sometimes legal uncertainty in regard to private enforcement of EC competition law almost certainly hinders or dissuades potential plaintiffs from bringing cases. In the absence of Community-wide rules, each Member State has its own rules governing civil litigation, and the systems differ widely. The Commission's study on private enforcement describes the situation as one of "extreme diversity." While the practical obstacles to effective private

---

[271] *Provimi v Aventis* [2003] EWHC 961 (Comm).

[272] *Crehan v Inntrepreneur* [2004] EWCA 637. This proceeding led to the reference to the Court of Justice in Case C-453/99, *Courage Ltd v Bernard Crehan and Bernard Crehan v Courage Ltd and Others* [2001] ECR I-6297

[273] But contrast *Yeheskel Arkin v Borchard Lines Limited & Ors* [2003] EWHC 687 (Comm), where the High Court rejected a damages claim in a predatory pricing case on the grounds, *inter alia*, that the applicant's response was to cut its prices to unsustainable levels, rather than exit the market. This was found to break the chain of causation, although the conclusion seems harsh in the circumstances.

[274] See Decree No 2005-1/36 of December 30, 2005, JO No 304, p. 20831.

[275] Commission Staff Working Paper of December 19, 2005, Annex to the Green Paper on damages actions for breach of the EC antitrust rules, COM(2005) 672 final, SEC(2005) 1732.

competition law enforcement in some Member States remain high, others are more receptive to private actions, either due to features of their procedural law or because they have adopted specific legislation relating to competition law claims.

To create clearer legal basis and promote uniformity, some commentators have advocated the enactment of supporting Community legislation: a regulation could lay down the main substantive criteria to be fulfilled and a directive could give guidelines regarding procedural issues, leaving some freedom to the Member States concerning their actual implementation. Commission Notices, including a restatement of the current case law of the Community Courts, could help private parties and national judges to apply European law.[276]

Issues of substance. A successful damages claim usually requires the plaintiff to prove: (1) fault by the defendant; (2) the existence of damages; and (3) a causal link between the fault and the damage. The Green Paper presents questions to be decided and identifies various policy options regarding these elements.

a. Fault requirement. The Green Paper asks: (1) whether proof of an infringement should automatically imply fault (i.e., making competition authorities' decisions binding on civil courts as regards the existence of an infringement); (2) whether such a presumption should be made only in the case of serious antitrust violations; and (3) to what extent defendants should be able to present exculpatory evidence.

b. Definition and quantification of damages. The Green Paper distinguishes between the appropriate definition of damages and the methodology for the quantification of damages. On the first issue, the Green Paper identifies two principal policy options, both currently used in some Member States, to define damages: (1) on the basis of the loss suffered by the victim or; (2) on the basis of the illegal gain made as a result of the infringement. A further question relates to the inclusion of pre-judgment interest in the plaintiff's damage award. US-style treble damages are not envisaged, but the Green Paper contemplates the possibility of doubling damages.[277] As regards quantification of damages, the Green Paper identifies questions regarding the relevance of economic quantification methods and on the need for the enactment of damages quantification guidelines. Another issue discussed is the utility of "split proceedings" that separate the liability and damages phases of a civil trial, which would provide incentive for parties to settle the amount of damages following a finding of liability.[278]

---

[276] See, e.g., Van Gerven, "Private Enforcement of EC Competition Rules," provisional background paper at the Joint EU Commission/IBA Conference on Antitrust Reform in Europe: a Year in Practice, March 10–11, 2005, Brussels. Van Gerven develops in this paper some themes that he had already raised in his opinion in *Banks*. See Opinion of Advocate General Van Gerven in Case C-128/92, *HJ Banks & Co Ltd v British Coal Corporation* [1994] ECR I-1209.

[277] In the US, mandatory trebling of damages is partly aimed to compensate for the absence of right to recover pre-judgment interest. Treble damages also increase incentives for plaintiffs to bring lawsuits and for defendants to settle cases.

[278] According to the Green Paper, similar proceedings already exist in one form or another in the Czech Republic, Spain, France, Ireland, Italy, Malta, Poland, Denmark, Germany, Estonia, the Netherlands, Portugal, and Slovenia.

c. ***Causation.*** Establishing the causal link between the loss sustained and the anticompetitive conduct may represent one of the highest hurdles for plaintiffs.[279] The Green Paper does not propose any direct solution, but presents various possibilities aimed at overcoming disadvantages faced by plaintiffs in terms of information asymmetries (since relevant documents and information will normally be held by defendants) and reducing plaintiffs' evidentiary burden of proof.

d. ***Passing-on defence and the standing of indirect purchasers.*** These two related issues raise questions of both substance and procedure. In most EU Member States, damages are strictly compensatory in nature, which precludes a victim from seeking damages to compensate a harm that it has not suffered personally. Thus, for instance, direct customers of a dominant undertaking may not be able to claim damages for the full difference between the competitive price and the excessive price charged by the dominant undertaking if they have passed the higher price through to their own customers. Allowing defendants to raise such a "passing-on" defence increases the complexity of damages actions because it creates the need to analyse the distribution of a price increase along the entire supply chain of the relevant product.[280]

On the other hand, disallowing the passing-on defence may mean that defendants are required to pay for the same damage several times if both direct purchasers and indirect (downstream) purchasers are allowed to claim compensation. This problem can, in turn, be addressed by denying standing to indirect purchasers (as is the rule in US federal courts), which simplifies litigation and avoids the difficult questions of quantification and distribution of damages amongst direct and indirect purchasers. At the same time, however, it seems paradoxical that the real victims of anticompetitive conduct (assuming the excessively high prices were passed on by direct purchasers) could not

[279] For example, in the *Arkin* case, the plaintiff alleged that it had been driven out of business by a cartel. The High Court decided, however, that the plaintiff's own irrational pricing behaviour was the cause of its losses, and held that the requisite causal link between the defendants' conduct and the loss suffered had not been established. See *Yeheskel Arkin v Borchard Lines Limited & Ors* [2003] EWHC 687 (Comm). Similarly, in the *Hendry* case, the High Court dismissed a damages claim brought by snooker professionals against a professional snooker association because the plaintiff was unable to adduce sufficient evidence of loss and of the causal link to the alleged infringement. The Court seems to have also considered that the claimant was partly liable for the anticompetitive behaviour and therefore barred from claiming damages. See *Hendry a.o. v The World Professional Billiards and Snooker Association Ltd*, [2002] ECC 8.

[280] In the United States, the *Hanover Shoe* doctrine prohibits defendants from raising the "passing on" defence in federal courts (thereby allowing direct purchasers to obtain damages even if they have passed some or most of the overcharges to their own customers), while the *Illinois Brick* doctrine holds that only direct purchasers can sue for damages in federal courts. See *Hanover Shoe v United Shoe Mach. Corp.*, 392 US 481 (1968) and *Illinois Brick Co. v Illinois*, 431 US 720 (1977). The US Supreme Court recognised in *Illinois Brick* that the only ways of avoiding unacceptable multiple liability were either: (1) to allow indirect purchasers to sue but repeal *Hanover Shoe*; or (2) to retain *Hanover Shoe* but prohibit action by indirect purchasers. The Court chose the second option. See R Posner and W Landes, "Should Indirect Purchasers Have Standing to Sue Under the Antitrust Laws? An Economic Analysis of *Illinois Brick*" (1979) 46 *University of Chicago Law Review* 602. Many states, however, have passed "*Illinois Brick* repealer" legislation granting standing to indirect purchasers to sue in state courts. See, e.g., KJ O'Connor, "Is the *Illinois Brick* Wall Crumbling?" (2000) 15 *Antitrust* 34.

seek compensation. The Green Paper merely presents the various policy options; again, the Commission expresses no preference among the possibilities.[281]

Procedural issues. Plaintiffs face a number of formidable procedural obstacles to bringing claims.

a. Access to evidence. Since the plaintiff bears the burden of proof, it needs access to evidence. The Commission is concerned, however, that evidence of complex anticompetitive practices might be difficult for private applicants to gather. The Green Paper suggests three ways to tackle this obstacle: (1) enacting specific disclosure rules tailored for antitrust damages proceedings; (2) facilitating access to documents held by competition authorities; and (3) alleviating the burden of proof borne by plaintiffs.

b. Document discovery. When evidence is held by private parties, the core problem faced by plaintiffs in many Member States is identification of the documents. In civil law countries, courts may require, *ex officio* or on a party's application, the production of certain documents only if they are specifically identified in advance.[282] The Green Paper proposes to relax this rule by requiring disclosure of reasonably identifiable documents or classes of such documents. This would allow plaintiffs to obtain access to documents held by the defendant even if the plaintiff cannot identify specific individual documents. Disclosure would be ordered by a court upon consideration of preliminary evidence submitted with the application. The disclosure rules would be complemented by rules prohibiting the destruction of relevant evidence or ensuring that documents be retained throughout the proceedings.

c. Access to competition authority documents. Plaintiffs lack access to documents held by competition authorities. The Green Paper asks whether parties in proceedings before a competition authority should be required to provide private plaintiffs with documents submitted to that authority. Such an obligation would, according to the Commission, exclude leniency applications and would be subject to confidentiality rules according to the law of the forum. The Green Paper also asks whether national courts should have the ability to request access to the Commission's own investigation files, subject to the protection of business secrets.

d. Burden of proof. The Green Paper sets forth a range of options with respect to the burden of proof, in particular on the possibility: (1) to make competition authorities' decisions binding on civil courts; (2) to create presumptions as a result of a refusal to disclose evidence; and (3) to modulate the burden of proof based on the degree of information asymmetry between plaintiffs and defendants.

e. Collective actions. Damages suffered individually by final consumers and low volume purchasers will often be too small to make litigation worthwhile even if the aggregate harm caused by anticompetitive behaviour is large. The Commission seems convinced that effective private enforcement requires some form of collective action to

[281] As explained above, recent legislation in Germany includes a rule allowing indirect purchasers to sue for damages.

[282] By contrast, in common law jurisdictions such as the United Kingdom, disclosure of all relevant information is customarily allowed. See Civil Procedure Rules (CPR) 31.6 for standard disclosure in English civil proceedings.

consolidate small claims and spread the costs of litigation. A distinction must be made between collective actions and US-style "class actions," as the second type of action may be introduced on behalf of an unidentified group of people. In the EU, for the most part only collective actions, often launched by consumer associations, exist. The Green Paper asks whether this possibility should be opened to groups of purchasers other than final consumers.

f. ***Costs of action.*** Litigation is expensive. The generally applicable rule in the EU according to which the unsuccessful party pays the other party's costs deflates legal costs for successful plaintiffs. However, it also creates risk, as due to the inherent uncertainty in bringing a lawsuit, a plaintiff will always expose itself to the risk of losing the case and having to pay not only its own legal costs, but also the defendant's. This may deter private damage claims. The Green Paper asks whether it would be appropriate to exempt unsuccessful plaintiffs from paying the defendant's legal costs, save where actions have been introduced in a "manifestly unreasonable manner."

A related issue that bears importantly on the cost of private litigation is contingent fees for attorneys. Contingent fees are arrangements whereby lawyers can be retained by allegedly injured plaintiffs, but no fees are due to counsel unless a monetary settlement or judgment for the plaintiff is obtained. Legal fees are paid from the damages recovered by the plaintiff and are typically set as a proportion of the recovery. Contingent fees have been a major driver of class-action litigation, including antitrust litigation, in the United States. In Europe, however, with some limited exceptions, contingent fees are prohibited. Perhaps as a result of a widespread perception that contingent fees contribute to a culture of litigation, the Green Paper does not address this issue and widespread change here seems unlikely.

Practical experience with private litigation in the United States. The United States has the most developed system of private antitrust enforcement globally. Although private litigation has greatly increased the deterrent effect of US antitrust laws, there is growing consensus that the system has, over time, led to over-deterrence that chills competitive behaviour, as well as being fundamentally unfair to defendants in many instances.[283] These issues are complex, but the following general issues should be noted in the context of any meaningful discussion of the potential increase in private antitrust enforcement in the EU:

1. The US treble damages remedy has been in place since passage of the Sherman Act in 1890. Many query why treble damages apply for antitrust violations, but not for other violations that are equally or more serious (e.g., environmental pollution, securities fraud, consumer product safety).

2. Since the early 1900s US courts have held that co-defendants jointly and severally liable for each other's actions under the antitrust laws. This makes

[283] See DH Ginsburg and L Brannon, "Determinants of Private Antitrust Enforcement in the United States" (2005) 1(2) *Competition Policy International* 31. See also W Breit and KG Elzinga, *The Antitrust Penalties: A Study in Law and Economics* (New Haven, Yale University Press, 1976); and W Breit and KG Elzinga, "Private Antitrust Enforcement: The New Learning" (1985) 28 *Journal of Law and Economy* 405.

defendants significantly more attractive as a class to plaintiffs, since plaintiffs can pursue the defendants with the "deepest pockets."

3. The introduction and development of the Federal Rules of Civil Procedure, first established in 1938, have liberalised pleading rules and facilitated class actions. For example: (a) plaintiffs need only file a "notice pleading" to initiate a lawsuit; (b) liberal standards allow most plaintiffs to advance past the pleading stage and obtain significant discovery from defendants; (c) discovery in US litigation, particularly in antitrust, can take years and be very costly; and (d) federal courts typically apply liberal standards to certifying class actions.

4. In 1981, the US Supreme Court held that co-defendants in antitrust cases have no right of contribution from co-defendants. Together with joint and several liability, this creates situations in which marginally culpable and relatively small defendants who are unable or unwilling to offer attractive early settlement sums are left with liability wholly disproportionate to their sales after larger and more culpable firms had settled.

5. Antitrust law suits are tried by jury, which are notoriously unpredictable.

6. Defendants face potential damages claims from multiple sources: (a) government enforcement remains active: both the federal government and multiple state governments can and do bring enforcement actions against antitrust defendants; (b) direct purchasers of a product have standing to sue for overcharges under federal antitrust law; (c) indirect purchasers of a product have standing to sue for overcharges under the laws of a number of US states; and (d) competitors have standing to sue for lost profits under either federal or state law.

Combined, these factors lead to enormous pressure on defendants in a multi-defendant case to settle even a weak case. A defendant that does not settle early faces the prospect of a jury trial in which it may be liable not only for its own actions, but also for the actions of other, more culpable defendants that have already settled with plaintiffs. At the same time, criminal penalties have increased very substantially over time. The threat of massive fines and even jail time provides the most important deterrence against anticompetitive behaviour in the US system. It is not clear that the "extra" deterrence provided by private damages actions, at least at the level provided for under the current system, is necessary or advisable. The nature of the US litigation system, including discovery costs, can lead risk-averse defendants to settle even unmeritorious claims. Cases are not decided on their merits, but settled to avoid years of costly litigation and the uncertainty of the U.S jury system.

Initiatives to mitigate the undue burden of the system on competition are being discussed within the Antitrust Modernisation Commission. In 2004, the Antitrust Criminal Penalty Enhancement and Reform Act has enacted measures aimed to limit the civil liability of corporations that participate in the DOJ's corporate leniency program to single damages attributable to its own share of commerce affected by the violation. It is also notable that, while the Canadian and Australian private enforcement systems have been inspired by the US system, they have adapted it to avoid numerous pitfalls (e.g., no treble damages but modest punitive damages and pre-judgment interests, limited discovery, no nation-wide certification of class actions, settlements to be approved by courts, etc.).

15.5.5 Conclusion

Uncertainty as to the future role of private litigation. Private competition law litigation is still in its infancy in Europe, but there is momentum behind it. There appears to be emerging consensus regarding the advantages of appropriately constrained private enforcement in terms of compensating victims of anticompetitive conduct and enhancing deterrence. But significant obstacles remain. The diversity of legal regimes in the various Member States makes the possibility that Member States will on their own adopt reasonably consistent enforcement mechanisms appear remote, yet the authority of the Community institutions to adopt and require Member States to apply a uniform and effective set of rules is unclear at best.

Nevertheless, given the Commission's evident determination to foster private actions, it may be expected to exercise its persuasive authority to try to get Member States to adopt accommodating procedural and substantive rules. The established Community law principles of equivalence and effectiveness may help private action to develop, and indeed some Member States have already implemented measures to facilitate private enforcement. So private enforcement of EC competition law will no doubt play a greater role in the coming years.

It is of course to be hoped that excesses of US litigation noted above are avoided. This may have implications for both the underlying substantive antitrust rules and the appropriate level of damages for infringements. First, private enforcement of competition laws does not necessarily generate sound rules and policy, as private complainants may be expected to press the courts to condemn business behaviour when it is in their own interest, regardless of whether the underlying conduct actually harmed competition. Second, the US system may result in defendants paying several times more than treble damages, as the legal system allows for civil and criminal government fines, treble damages actions by direct purchasers, and treble damages actions by indirect purchasers in many states (the "cluster-bomb" effect[284]). As the US Supreme Court noted recently, while there is broad international consensus about the legality of certain kinds of conduct (such as price fixing), countries "disagree dramatically about appropriate remedies."[285] A private enforcement system should allow for the fair compensation of injured customers and consumers and preserve and promote an effective competitive market structure in the interest of consumer welfare, without imposing unjustified burdens on companies and the legal system or giving rise to windfalls and inordinate legal costs.

---

[284] RA Posner, "Antitrust in the New Economy" (2001) 68 *Antitrust Law Journal* 935. See also M Denger and DJ Arp, "Does Our Multifaceted Enforcement System Promote Sound Competition Policy?" (2001) 15 *Antitrust* 43. On the other hand, some commentators have argued that current US antitrust damages do not even total treble damages and are insufficient to deter antitrust violations optimally. See, e.g., RH Lande, "Why Antitrust Damage Levels Should be Raised" (2004) 16 *Loyola Consumer Law Review* 329.

[285] *F Hoffman La Roche Ltd v Empagran SA*, 542 US 155 (2004) (03-724), 315 F.3d 338.

Given the likely resistance in many Member States to broad change on vital practical issues not specifically related to the competition laws, such as class litigation, contingent fees for attorneys, and discovery, the problems of runaway litigation that have been encountered in the United States seem unlikely to become a serious difficulty in Europe for the foreseeable future. Private damages actions under EC competition law will probably be based for the most part on cartel cases where a competition authority has already identified the infringement and where damages can reasonably be assessed based on demonstrable harm to the plaintiffs. The Green Paper also comes at a time when the US antitrust community is reconsidering critically the benefits of an enforcement system based on private damages actions.[286] It indicates that the Commission is genuinely open to receiving assistance in framing its policy on private damages actions for breach of EC competition rules. A balanced approach that takes appropriate account of the interests of all constituencies would no doubt be the best outcome of the process.

[286] See, e.g., *Antitrust Remedies in the 21st Century*, Chair's Showcase Program, ABA Section of Antitrust Law 50th Annual Spring Meeting, April 2002.

INDEX